The publisher gratefully acknowledges the generous contribution to this book provided by the Music in America Endowment Fund of the University of California Press Foundation, which is supported by a major gift from Sukey and Gil Garcetti, Michael Roth, and the Roth Family Foundation.

Brass Diva

Brass Diva

The Life and Legends of Ethel Merman

CARYL FLINN

UNIVERSITY OF CALIFORNIA PRESS
BERKELEY LOS ANGELES LONDON

University of California Press, one of the most distinguished
university presses in the United States, enriches lives around
the world by advancing scholarship in the humanities, social
sciences, and natural sciences. Its activities are supported by
the UC Press Foundation and by philanthropic contributions
from individuals and institutions. For more information, visit
www.ucpress.edu.

University of California Press
Berkeley and Los Angeles, California

University of California Press, Ltd.
London, England

Library of Congress Cataloging-in-Publication Data

Flinn, Caryl.
    Brass diva: the life and legends of Ethel Merman / Caryl
Flinn.
        p.   cm.
    Includes discography (p.), filmography (p.), and index.
    ISBN 978-0-520-22942-6 (cloth : alk. paper)
    1. Merman, Ethel.   2. Singers—United States—
Biography.   3. Motion picture actors and actresses—
United States—Biography.   I. Title.
    ML420.M39F55 2007
    782.1'4092—dc22
    [B]   2007029515

Manufactured in the United States of America

16   15   14   13   12   11   10   09   08   07
10   9   8   7   6   5   4   3   2   1

This book is printed on Cascades Enviro 100, a 100%
post-consumer waste, recycled, de-inked fiber. FSC recycled certified and processed chlorine-free. It is acid-free,
Ecologo certified, and manufactured by BioGas energy.

CONTENTS

Appearing on *The Perry Como Show* in 1957, Ethel Merman complains to her soft-spoken host, "Every TV show I'm on makes cracks about my voice. Just once, I'd like to go on a show where they considered me to be a lovely, delicate, feminine dame." "You don't need to yell," he replies. So the two decide to sing a song quietly, "When the Red, Red Robin Comes Bob, Bob Bobbin' Along." The duet is quite touching, and a twinkle dances in Merman's eye. She seems relaxed with Como, pleased to be singing this way—in her voice there is no harshness, no punched-out notes. But as they near the end of the number, Ethel decides to go back to being Ethel Merman, feigning frustration about bottling it all up. Like a kid, she pleads, "Oh, come *on,* let me belt!" Como literally stands back as Ethel lets it rip, ending the number with volume and a bang. After the audience laughs and applauds, the overhead boom mike is lowered into the TV frame. It is shattered, with wires and springs sticking out from all sides.

Ethel was correct: nearly every TV appearance she made drew cracks about her voice, and that big voice has arguably overshadowed all other facets of her persona and performing skills. Ethel Merman was the unrivaled star of a steady stream of musical comedy hits, from *Girl Crazy* in 1930, through *Anything Goes, Panama Hattie, Annie Get Your Gun, Call Me Madam,* and *Gypsy,* to *Hello, Dolly!* in 1970. Among the dozens of songs she introduced were "I Got Rhythm," "Life Is Just a Bowl of Cherries," "Anything Goes," "Blow, Gabriel, Blow," "There's No Business Like Show Business," and "Everything's Coming Up Roses." For almost half a century, Merman reigned over Broadway not just as its queen but as its queen during its period of greatest achievement, the golden age of musical theater. She worked with royal talents, including George Gershwin, Cole Porter, Irving Berlin, Jule Styne, and Stephen Sondheim, performing some of *their* best work. Porter even said, "I'd rather write for Ethel than for anybody else in the world."[1] Merman simply sits on the top of American musical theater. "You could teach a course on the history of twentieth-century musical through Ethel Merman," says singer Klea Blackhurst. "She intersects with everything and everyone, even Richard Rodgers. She never did a Rodgers and Hammerstein musical, but they were her producers in *Annie Get Your Gun*. Everything feeds back to her."[2]

What Merman could do like no one else was project her voice to the very back walls of a theater, important in the days before amplification. When most singers projected like that, their voices were diminished in other ways, but when Merman "belted," there was no distortion or loss of clarity. Irving Berlin was right when he cracked, "When you write lyrics for Ethel, they better be good, for if they're bad everybody's going to hear them anyhow."[3] Her innate sense of rhythm was extraordinary, her breath control a marvel, her diction impeccable: you could hear every letter of every word when Ethel sang, no matter how loudly or softly she delivered it. And, as Perry Como learned, she could handle light, jaunty tunes (or, on other occasions, lullabies, ballads, jazz numbers, and torch songs) as deftly as rousing anthems like Berlin's "There's No Business Like Show Business," the song from *Annie Get Your Gun* with which she is practically entwined.

For most people who heard Ethel Merman perform live, her voice was less a voice than a mesmerizing force. Said one reviewer of the 1940s *Panama Hattie*, "She blows through the script like a cyclone. . . . Broadway, not Park Avenue, finds its voice in her, and everyone listens to her enraptured."[4] People who saw Ethel in *Gypsy* (1959) recall being "frozen, spellbound" by a voice that was "bigger than the entire theatre."[5] To many, the voice seemed grander than nature itself, and over her career, critics and composers had fun comparing it to marching bands, calliopes, and sonic booms; to Arturo Toscanini, she sounded like a castrato.

For many, however, it's the full-out belt that is *the only* thing known as "Ethel Merman," especially outside Broadway circles. A young performer recalled a singing class in a drama school in the Southwest: "There were a couple times in rehearsals when my musical director would say, 'Good, now "*Mermanize it!*" ' and these people, who were very young and had hardly even *heard* of her, knew *exactly* what to do to produce the 'Merman effect' when they sang."[6] It's precisely that Merman effect that outstrips Ethel Merman in so many ways. Even during her own lifetime, people often assumed that Merman herself was articulated in the character of her voice: brash, full of vitality and resilience, and with an inflection that, however firm its homegrown Astoria accent, seemed to take its cues from some other, joyous world.

In many ways, this is not an unfair understanding. Merman's vitality was legendary, and she was a colorful figure offstage as well as on, as revered for her quick comebacks and put-downs as for her distinctive voice. In her second autobiography, for instance, she teased readers with the chapter title "My Marriage to Ernest Borgnine," suggesting an inside view of their infamously short union. Its contents? A single blank page. Or, on her famous lack of stage fright, "What's there to be scared of? I know my lines." She was hardworking and tough, performing in an era that required eight shows a week without microphones and, in the first decades, air-conditioning. So few were her sick days that her *Call Me Madam* understudy, Elaine Stritch, was able to check in, check out, and go to New Haven to work on another show. And the world-famous insurers, Lloyds of London, once labeled Ethel their best risk.

Her sense of humor was as robust as her voice. One of the most hilarious moments of Merman ever captured on film is a cameo she did in the 1980 disaster spoof *Airplane!* in which she plays Lieutenant Hurwitz, a soldier suffering from war trauma. So severe is his condition that the poor man believes he's Ethel Merman. When the camera reveals Hurwitz, there is seventy-two-year-old Merman in hospital pajamas, sitting up in her sickbed, belting out "Everything's Coming Up Roses" from *Gypsy*. It takes several attendants to sedate the lieutenant. Few stars of Merman's stature would even have considered doing such a hammy send-up of their persona, but she enjoyed the appearance (one day of work, after all) as much as audiences did.

Like Lieutenant Hurwitz, everybody believes they know who Ethel Merman was, and she remains a popular and often fun reference point today. Yet the popular conception of Merman as the irrepressible, big-voiced wonder fails to cover all that she meant to Americans over the decades. Nor does it do justice to her personal life. Given that her career spanned from Tin Pan Alley to disco and moved from costars such as Bing Crosby to Jack Klugman, Betty Boop to Batman, one would be hard-pressed to find just one "Ethel Merman" over the years. The sheer number of myths that circulate around her (Did she never actually tour? Was she in any flops? Did she really have an affair with *Valley of the Dolls* author Jacqueline Susann?) create an unsteady icon that the ardor of both fans and detractors intensifies. And people are rarely neutral about Ethel Merman.

Merman's singing career ran from the late 1920s to the early 1980s, during which time the Broadway musical was transformed several times over; entertainment forms and media came and went, along with different music, comedy, and acting styles. She began in the waning days of vaudeville and peaked in the era of light book musical comedies whose thin stories were little more than excuses for composers to show off their tunes. These shows were written with specific stars in mind rather than with sophisticated story lines or character development. Merman's shows were "hers" in a way that is no longer possible today, adding to her impact as a performer. With the exception of *Gypsy* (and to a lesser extent *Annie Get Your Gun*), Merman never did an "integrated" musical in which stories and music advanced each other or complex, well-developed characters were featured.

Early on, in the 1930s, one critic called Ethel a "coon shouter,"[7] the happily outdated expression used to describe black powerhouses such as Ma Rainey and "ethnic whites" who performed in African-American styles or in blackface, such as "Noisy Sophie Tucker." But it was rare for Anglo-Saxon whites to receive the epithet. It's almost as if Merman's voice, rhythm, and lung power were too instinctive to belong to a WASP, and a number of related assumptions—about race, ethnicity, social station—did, in fact, cling to her public image for over forty years. So, too, did the nuanced prejudices of these assumptions: Merman and her voice were ostensibly crass and primal; her voice alone, uncrafted or even coarse. In the words of one New Yorker, "She didn't sing, she honked."[8]

As for her roles, whether onstage or on-screen, Merman usually played the tough cookie with a soft heart and a crush. In her thirteen musicals, she never played a typical romantic female lead. Yes, she often got her man *(Stars in Your Eyes, Call Me Madam)*, but usually the affair was too forced to make sense, a point made even through casting. In the stage version of *Call Me Madam,* for instance, the prime minister of Lichtenburg was played by opera-trained Paul Lukas and, on film, by the even more implausible George Sanders. Hollywood had plenty of trouble with Merman's image, deeming it too brash for the film industry's more genteel notions of romance and womanly glamour. Indeed, Merman's femininity was always bedeviled: a castrato for Toscanini; the fantasy lesbian in the Jacqueline Susann rumor; the male Lieutenant Hurwitz in *Airplane!* Her gender never seemed to coincide fully with American norms, but at the same time, it didn't escape them either, especially for Ethel in real life.

Privately, Merman could be as hard as her stage image, but that hardness has assumed such legendary proportions that it's come to overshadow her other features. An entire book could be written of zingers attributed to Merman; one, for instance, is that, during a rehearsal, she told her accompanist, "Look, pal, do me a favor. Take the Vienna rolls off your fingers!"[9] But what's not clear from this remark (which she did make) is that the pianist in question, Lew Kessler, had a long working relationship with Merman and that, with these words, Ethel was merely teasing an old friend. The private Merman was, like all of us, contradictory, but the traits that sit most uneasily with her public persona are those that point to her softness—the affection that could exist in a "Vienna rolls" comment, for instance. Those closest to her knew that Ethel was often extremely diffident and vulnerable, especially when not called on to perform as "Ethel Merman." "That's what the public finds hard to believe about her," says close family friend Tony Cointreau. "And that vulnerability came out in close relationships with men."[10]

When she first hit the big time, young Ethel Merman was New York City's "girl next door." She went from being a stenographer in Queens to being the toast of Broadway when, literally overnight, on October 14, 1930, the second-string singer brought the house down with her performance of George and Ira Gershwin's "I Got Rhythm." Across the greater New York area, young working women responded to her as a Depression-era fantasy come true, and for over a decade, the press stressed Merman's natural, wholesome look, her untrained voice, and her down-to-earth personality. By 1946, she seemed ideal for Irving Berlin's song "Doin' What Comes Natur'lly," which he wrote with her in mind for *Annie Get Your Gun.* At 1,147 performances, *Annie Get Your Gun* was Merman's biggest hit to date—and her best role. As Annie Oakley, Merman personified American grit, determination, and vitality, things that she personified offstage as well, whether in her wartime benefits or at home, where she was raising two children with journalist husband Robert Levitt.

By the 1950s, a middle-aged Merman shifted gears. For nearly six years, she left Broadway to play the stay-at-home wife to third husband Bob Six, president and founder of Continental Airlines, in a suburb of Denver, Colorado. She lived there with daughter Ethel and son Robert, her children from the marriage to Levitt. Her proximity to Los Angeles, she said, would help her career in television, a new medium whose mass appeal Ethel instinctively appreciated. That career, however, like the one in the movies, never really took off, and Merman remained the perennial TV guest: here with Lucille Ball, there with Judy Garland, or in Westinghouse's abridged versions of big Broadway shows. Ethel did have her successes on the small screen, such as the legendary 1953 *Ford 50th Anniversary Show,* in which she duets with "rival" (actually, good friend) Mary Martin. But she really wanted steady work, vying twice for a sitcom of her own, one in the mid-1960s and the other in the mid-1970s. Neither made it to serialization.

When she returned to Broadway in 1959 for *Gypsy,* based on the memoirs of Gypsy Rose Lee, Ethel Merman reinvigorated her stage career and at the same time reinvented herself. In addition to carrying a solid score—including "Everything's Coming Up Roses" and "Some People"—Merman did so well portraying Mama Rose that, for many people, she *became* the overbearing "jungle mother," as Rose's actual daughter, Gypsy Rose Lee, called her. Merman's heartfelt yet ferocious depiction of Rose was an acting triumph and resecured her top place on Broadway. At the same time, it added a new dimension to her persona: there was something delightfully, madly, over the top about Mama Rose that, among other things, made her a bit camp. This was a vaudeville-era character who was a dramatic, colorful survivor.

Audiences were beginning to view Ethel Merman the same way. As Broadway's golden queen, she was also its robust veteran and, like vaudevillian stage mother Rose, an icon of tough staying power. With her career having begun in a very different era, Merman's image was now infused with an old-fashionedness that many people revered, many camped up, and many simply enjoyed. She herself was able to accommodate it all, turning her attentions to one last Broadway show (*Hello, Dolly!*—again, written with her originally in mind), TV work in specials and guest spots, and traveling across North America on concert tours.

Merman's long career was a lightning rod that reverberated with iconic historical moments and public figures of over half a century of American life. She made it to the top in the Depression-era *Girl Crazy,* performed at presidential inaugurations from FDR's to Ronald Reagan's, and played gangster molls, gun-toting pioneer women, the child-eating Mama Rose, and the cross-gendered Lieutenant Hurwitz. There was a religious Ethel, an ill-mannered Ethel, and, of course, the greatest star of Broadway Ethel. Some New Yorkers remember Ethel Merman as a woman who was dedicated to her parents or as a regular gal with whom they volunteered at Roosevelt Hospital. For some Americans, Merman was the star who answered their letters when they were serving in World War II or who did a special show for their sick children. For others, she was "too much," too brash, too tough. Baby boomers may have been introduced to her as Gopher's mom on *The Love Boat;* to young singers, Ethel Merman is the "belt" to which they aspire. For her son, Bob Levitt Jr., she was a "presence" who sang rhyming songs at bedtime before she left to do her shows.

History has downplayed these different Ethels, leaving us with only one or two: old Broadway's life force and queen or the boisterous camp icon. Of course, it's easy to have fun with either of these Ethels—camp icon Ethel has scores of new personae on the Internet alone—but with either one, too much gets left behind. Even the legendary belting Broadway Ethel fails to account for the singer who performed beautiful ballads and doesn't convey the reality of a performer whose favorite and most cherished costars were the Muppets.

How then to tell the life story that moved a woman from being the "trumpet-throated" flapper who sang with crooner Rudy Vallee to the septuagenarian behind *The Ethel Merman Disco Album?* It's difficult to trace in a single line the life of a woman who brings a smile to one's face even when singing songs that bring tears to the eyes. (Or am I alone with that response?) How to approach a legend whose fans will shun you if you trespass into "their" territory, who are mortified if you misidentify one date of an obscure radio broadcast? How to account for the others, the people who wildly misremember her: "Wasn't she the one who sang 'God Bless America'?" (No, that was Kate Smith); "She did the swimming movies, right?" (Esther Williams); or "I loved her in *I Love Lucy!*" (Ethel Mertz, played by Vivian Vance). How can an icon be simultaneously so frozen in the history of "old Broadway" and so chaotically cross-referenced?

My own Ethel quest began, without my knowing it, as a child. The home I grew up in was filled with original cast recordings and soundtracks, all from shows and films that I had never seen. I was too young and my mom too small-town to venture into the cosmopolitan streets of Manhattan. Since the contents of our collection were governed by her tastes and since her tastes leaned toward what might be called the G-rated musical comedy—Rodgers and Hammerstein, Julie Andrews vehicles, fantasies in which hope and romance could thrive, not the grittier stuff of *Applause, Gypsy,* or anything by Stephen Sondheim—Ethel's voice was not in my house. Mom never talked about her, and I can only assume that she did appreciate her talents but found them a little rough for her liking. In order to hear Ethel and the grown-up shows, I had to go over to Holly's, where we sang our hearts out. Years later, during college, Ethel reentered my life. Settling into our dorm rooms, all of the guys were jockeying to be owner of the loudest stereo set. You could hear Bruce Springstein's "Born to Run" from every point on the campus. Yet my friend David blasted out Ethel Merman in singular, defiant protest. She was back. For me, tracking Ethel these last four years has been a way to track my own past, filling in the missing parts and some of the fun that I want to put there.

My sources were official and unofficial: stage and film archives in New York and Los Angeles; interviews with surviving friends and family members, including son Bob Levitt Jr. It involved casual conversation with regular Merman fans as well as detractors. My aim has not been to uncover a singular, authentic Ethel Merman—she was too complex a phenomenon for that—but to trace the different Mermans who lived, privately and publicly, for so many Americans across the twentieth century.

ONE

Beginnings

Late in 1932, New York's hottest singing sensation appeared in *Take a Chance,* a new Buddy DeSylva musical playing on Broadway. As nightclub singer Wanda Brill, Ethel Merman sang a bluesy ballad that paid tribute to a woman of ill-repute from fin de siècle New Orleans:

> Eadie was a lady,
> Though her past was shady . . .
> She had savoir-fairy
> Eadie had class
> With a capital K

The song's affectionate bawdiness was also apparent in Merman's costuming. Accentuating the hourglass figure popular in Eadie's time, Merman wore a tight, long red satin dress edged in black lace. Accessories included a boa, a headdress, and plenty of kohl around the eyes.

This was twenty-four-year-old Ethel Merman's third show, but it wasn't the first time she'd played a sassy-but-sensible singer/working-class girl. That had begun with her debut in the Gershwin brothers' *Girl Crazy,* two years earlier. What Wanda Brill—and this song especially—did was help hone the likable streetwise image that the star was already acquiring. The archetypal unpolished, tough though good-hearted woman, Wanda/Ethel was more suited to make fun of sex than to pine at its feet.

"Eadie Was a Lady" was *Take a Chance*'s hit number, mixing languorously delivered bluesy jazz with a strong melodic line. It needed a singer who could punch out its rhythm, sustain its long notes, and project it from the chest area, not the throat, thereby avoiding lighter, more delicate sounds. So perfectly suited was the song to the young singer with the big voice that, in both articles and fan mail, people referred to her as "Eadie."

Earlier that year, Merman had spent a day at Paramount Studios in Astoria, Queens, filming a one-reeler called *Old Man Blues*. The thin story line involves a young woman pining for a lost lover. Ethel sings in the woods, where she's joined by a villainous older man in dark robes who informs us through song that he is feeding off the young woman's despair. Then, when her lover suddenly appears, Old Man Blues slinks off. The short, atmospheric picture creates a fairy-tale world filled with forlorn maidens, lost suitors, and threatening older men/moods/spirits, a fable of romantic love triumphing over despair. In her frilly dress with a wide, full skirt and a bodice trimmed with ribbons, all topped by a wide-brimmed bonnet, Ethel seems the very paragon of antebellum gentility. Her song, "He Doesn't Love Me Anymore," woefully moans love's departure. It has none of the strong beats of "Eadie," instead boasting a measured rising and falling melody. The piece is light, delicate, and airy, delivered as if Merman were Jeanette MacDonald giving us the best of a film operetta.

Today, it's easier to picture Ethel Merman as Eadie than as a singer of wispy operetta. But back in 1932, there was an easy coexistence between the two songs and their singer. American music then had more interaction between legitimate, high singing and the songs and singing styles of popular culture. Something in the early '30s enabled the Broadway belter who would soon dominate twentieth-century musical theater to span the gamut from bawdy American blues to light European operetta. How did these musical styles shape how people were responding to her, and what do they tell us about American entertainment and its audiences or about class, ethnicity, femininity, and gender at the time? How did they help transform the young singer from Queens into the bigger-than-life production that soon became "Ethel Merman"? And how did Ethel Merman find her place within the musical environment in New York of the period?

Astoria Roots

On the northwestern tip of Queens lies Astoria, a town of affordable beginnings and home to many immigrant American families. It was first settled in the seventeenth century, after Englishman William Hallet exchanged seven coats, fourteen kettles, a blanket, and beads for fifteen hundred acres. Before long, generations of German, Czech, Irish, Italian, and Greek immigrants arrived and developed the area, and, in 1870, Astoria was incorporated into

Long Island City, which was itself incorporated into New York City twenty-eight years later. By the time Ethel Merman's story begins in the early twentieth century, the social fabric and business and cultural lives of Astoria were thriving, its prosperity a direct result of the central and southern Europeans who'd made their homes and livelihoods there: "Germans built the gold standard in pianos at Steinway; Italians made violins."[1] Astoria was a vibrant, varied community, a microcosm for the ethnic diversity of immigrant New York in the nineteenth and early twentieth centuries.

It was here that Edward and Agnes Zimmermann made their home. The couple were direct descendants of German and Scottish families that had eventually settled in the New York area during the mid-nineteenth century. Agnes Gardner Zimmermann had been born there in 1884 in a Scottish-Irish household, where she was one of twelve children. Little is known about Agnes's siblings except that one of her brothers, Willie, died as a youngster from choking on a banana and that one of her sisters lived nearby her home as an adult. Her father passed away before she gave birth to her one daughter, and her mother, Mary Gardner (née Hunter), died when little Ethel was eight.

Of small to medium build, the brown-haired Agnes was not a physically imposing woman. At the same time, her stern, attractive face had a near-severity to it. "Gram was lean and wiry," recalls grandson Bob Levitt Jr. "She had a tightness to her, but she also had a simple kindness. She never got very deep, but she was reliable."[2] Not sophisticated, certainly not lighthearted or playful, she was a proper woman, a tidy, efficient homemaker, with skills that helped the Zimmermann household stay on course and prosper.

Edward Zimmermann, "Pop," was born October 20, 1880,[3] four years before his wife. He was born at home, on 36th Street in Manhattan, to a family that was among the waves of German immigrants in the nineteenth century. Levitt recalls stories that his grandfather's family had fought alongside Union soldiers in the Civil War when immigrant men were commonly asked to prove their loyalty through military service. By the time of his generation, Edward's family had been fairly Americanized, but his German roots held fast. He loved German dishes—which Agnes couldn't prepare—and he knew enough of the language to enjoy *Die New Yorker Staats-Zeitung*, the city's main German-language paper. His early scrapbooks reveal a glimpse of that heritage, as well as the active cultural life of German immigrants at the time. On Christmas Day, 1931, *Die New Yorker Staats-Zeitung* ran a photo of a young singing sensation in the city. Under the caption, Edward translated word-for-word, "Ethel Merman is one of the extraordinary songstresses in George White's 'Scandals' appearing at the Apollo Theatre."[4]

Despite the Zimmermann name, Edward's family had no traceable Jewish roots—his famous daughter would spend her life insisting that the two *n*'s were proof enough of that—but it is possible that Jewishness was something that the family had left behind on the way to America. Edward's own family was Lutheran. "As far as religions go," Ethel, who was raised as an Episcopalian, would later say, "the Zimmermanns are all mixed up."[5]

Pop worked as a bookkeeper at James H. Dunham and Company, at 345 Broadway, in lower Manhattan, a wholesale dry goods firm that remained his employer for life. Diligent and meticulous, Edward would eventually help Ethel hone her money management skills and manage her accounts when she entered show business; he was also a notary and later signed off on some of her contracts with the 20th Century–Fox film studio. Her father may also have helped her invest her earnings at the beginning of her career—Merman was a careful, savvy stock market investor—but the exact nature and extent of his involvement are unknown.

Ethel said, "My dad is a mensch. He's not as hep . . . as my mother, [who] springs quicker than my dad. But he's smart as the devil. Mom, though, is the hard head, the Scottish shrewdness, the good manager type [who] wouldn't let anybody cheat her [and had] a certain amount of steel in her soul."[6]

Edward met Agnes when she was employed as an office worker in the city. In her free time she sang in a choir. "She was a good alto," recalls Ethel. They met "on one of those hayrides boys and girls used to organize . . . or maybe it was a sleigh ride" and, according to Ethel, had a small wedding.[7] After they married, Agnes quit her job to become a full-time homemaker in Astoria.

Edward and Agnes produced one child, Ethel Agnes Zimmermann. On January 16, the heavily pregnant twenty-four-year-old Agnes was attending a friend's wedding in the neighborhood when the labor pains began. She rushed to her mother's house, where she made her home with Edward, and there gave birth to their daughter. On April 19, they baptized little Ethel Agnes Zimmermann in the Reformed Presbyterian Church of the Redeemer, on nearby Crescent Street.

And so Ethel Merman was born on January 16—in 1906, 1908, 1910, 1911, and 1912. All have been given as her actual birth year by official newspaper reports, biographies, theater archives, and marriage, death, and birth certificates of Ethel and her family. When celebrity hit, Ethel hardly discouraged the confusion, aiming at the later years whenever pressed for specifics.

Curiously, the World of Merman has not cared that much about setting the record straight. When she died in 1984, no less a source than the *New York Times* offered two different years, and today, the Museum of the City of New

York, which houses her biggest archive collection—her scrapbooks—contains three conflicting years in its records. In her second, final autobiography, written at age seventy, Merman offers a clever dodge: "I was born in my parents' bedroom on January 16. *The World Almanac* says it was 1909. I say it was 1912. But what difference does it make as long as I feel thirty-three?"[8]

Given how frequently celebrities pare down their age, perhaps the real question is: why did Ethel shave off only four years—why not ten? The answer seems simple. With ten years missing, several key Merman myths would be pulled off course. She would have been but twelve when she made her Broadway debut, fourteen when playing the world-weary Wanda Brill. She would have been nothing but a twinkle in her daddy's eye when as a young girl she sang to troops stationed on Long Island before they were shipped out for combat in World War I. Her vanity didn't make Ethel care *that* much about her age, and she seemed to know instinctively the importance of some of these stories. Why should she scuttle such colorful milestones, especially since they were an authentic part of her?

By the early to mid-1930s, after her success was established, Merman and the New York press seemed to have mutually settled on 1911 or 1912 as the official year of her birth. Before then, sources are fuzzier and more flexible, with the notable exception of the New York City municipal records. There, we learn that the Broadway icon who began her life as Ethel Agnes Zimmermann came into the world on January 16, 1908.

The birth records of early New York provide a fascinating portal into a truly lost past. Family physicians who brought babies into the world had to complete the birth forms that were deposited in the municipal files. Some physicians had the new fathers fill out certain portions, regardless of their ability to understand written English. The questions and categories are straightforward but revealing of the times: fathers' occupations are listed; no space is provided for the mothers'. Another line requests the race of the infant only if the child is "not white." (Here some of the fathers entered "German.")

In both of her autobiographies, Merman says that she was born—"it was 1912!" one can almost hear her boom—at 359 Fourth Avenue, Astoria. Several sources indicate a residence on 33rd Street; the official municipal record gives 265 Fourth Avenue, Long Island City. Whatever the precise address (more on this below), the house itself was an unexceptional three-story, wood-framed duplex where Ethel's maternal grandmother had made her home. The ground floor was rented out, and the second floor was home to some of Ethel's relatives on her mother's side: Aunt Mary and Uncle Harry Pickett and a cousin on her mother's side, Claude Pickett. Ethel and her parents occupied the top floor. Two doors down and around the corner, near a small apple orchard, was the family of Margaret Sharkey, Merman's maternal aunt.

Edward's side of the family, by contrast, was less present in the young family's life. His mother had died when he was eight, and his father had also passed away before Ethel was born. "I was never as close to that side of the family as to the Gardners," Ethel told her biographer."[9] Overall, though, the young household kept to itself, and the ties with even Agnes's relations didn't really thrive once the Zimmermanns moved into Manhattan after Ethel's career took off. Bob Levitt Jr., for instance, recalls having only minimal contact with his mother's cousins while growing up, and close friend Tony Cointreau remembers an awkward cocktail party that Ethel threw after she retired from the stage. Sometime in the early 1980s, Ethel invited a cousin over to her apartment for the first time. "No one had anything in common," Cointreau recalls. Even their drinking habits were different; the family kept requesting elaborate cocktails, and a frustrated Ethel had to tell them to keep the requests simple.

Ethel cherished Pop's largely gentle temperament. Of her parents, he was "the sweeter, easygoing type."[10] Yet even if he was an "angel," as Ethel later told her son, the Zimmermann household was "STRICT! I couldn't get away with *anything*, especially with Pop." And the man could hold a grudge. Levitt recalls that Pop and his brother had had a rift—"about what, Mom never knew. But it was absolutely permanent, and they never spoke to each other. That's what Mom grew up with."[11] Ethel inherited this obstinate side, and Levitt believes this probably contributed to his mother's ability to cut people permanently out of her life ("Some things in life aren't even worth regretting," she would say),[12] especially when she felt taken advantage of. At the same time, Ethel's upbringing ingrained in her a strong sense of sentimentality, the flip side of grudges—clinging to the past for its fond memories rather than focusing on its fallouts.

Ethel was an attractive young girl. She had very dark wavy hair that she usually wore long. Her complexion was slightly dark, and her round, deep brown eyes animated her face. Looking back, Merman described herself as "pudgy" to her biographer, saying, "My stomach stuck out a little."[13] Photographs suggest otherwise, showing an attractive girl, often adorned in the decorative bow typically worn by young girls in family portraiture of the time. "I had sort of long hair and my Mother used to roll my hair up in curls around the bottom and . . . put a big bow across here and my hair was loose and soft. . . . Never wore it braided, always soft, hanging." Agnes didn't sew, so she and Ethel would go into the city for her dresses and buy nice shoes at

Coward's. ("My mother would say 'never wear cheap shoes,' and I have never had trouble with my feet.")[14] One of her aunts made skirts for Ethel—pleated, plaid, worn with pullover sweaters or blouses. She did not like hats, and she did not wear them. And she did not like frilly, girly outfits or accessories, a fact that her first biographer changed to keep her image in line with the heavily accessorized women Merman depicted onstage.

Sources vary on whether Merman grew up in her birth home or if the family moved when she was a girl. Family caregivers and Merman researchers, such as Al F. Koenig Jr., maintain that the Zimmermanns stayed put until relocating to Manhattan in 1931 (other reports say 1933), after Ethel's career was established, and Merman contributes to the confusion on the point. In her first autobiography, she gives 2903 1st Avenue as the place where she grew up; in her second, 31st Avenue. Her biographer Bob Thomas claimed it was 359 Fourth Avenue. Saved mail to the family postmarked in November 1931 was received at both 2908 31st Avenue and 3056 30th Street.[15] Like the birth address, the record will never be set entirely straight, if for no other reason than at the time the U.S. Postal Service and addresses in general were more relaxed and less regimented than they are now. Populations were smaller, and community members were more aware of their neighbors than many are today. Mail could reach families in small towns with just a name and a town on the envelope; inscriptions could approximate a family's location with cross streets and still arrive. Changes to Astoria's street plans have also confounded the record, with buildings, addresses, and street names of the period rerouted or gone altogether. As early as 1950, Ethel went "home" to search for her childhood house and couldn't find it. "It was terrible to see. It's all built up," she said.[16] In a very real sense, the precise locations of Merman's childhood years are lost to history.

Ethel's bond with her parents was founded on mutual devotion and a strong sense of duty and affection, even if, as her son attests, it was not the most emotionally resonant of relationships. All her life, he recalls, "they would talk every day my Mom was in town, but they spoke quite superficially. That was all they needed."[17] It might not have been the deepest of relationships, but the loyalty and devotion were there in a way that few people experience. That stability may have provided the groundwork for Ethel's longing for similar levels of loyalty in her own marriages and family life, a dream that would prove more elusive.

Agnes and Edward were hard-wired with what Levitt describes as "a sense of order," propriety, and pragmatism. He recalls never spotting a speck of dust in their house, and his grandfather's ledger pencils were always sharpened and neatly arranged on top of his mahogany office desk. "Pop was very prescribed, set in his ways, formalized," he recalls, noting how much love there was in all of that order. Pop would "go to the office and do eight hours of adding and subtracting at his own desk (always in his head, without the benefit of an adding machine, much less a calculator), but when he was home he'd sit at his own desk, a very warm and radiant piece of furniture, to do his clipping work for Mom, his keeping of her personal 'books,' and whatever other tasks required a flat surface, nicely polished and always dusted by Gram, Pop's beloved Agnes."[18] In ways, Edward and Agnes were right out of central casting: the German and the Scotswoman with an impeccably neat home, the paragon of affection, discipline, and order. Merman inherited these traits many times over—in her grooming, her housecleaning, and her work habits.

They also shaped her relationship to money. "I think her father's a thrifty German," said friend and colleague Dorothy Fields in a 1950s interview. "His attitude was, 'Don't let them get you baby. You see that you get yours.'"[19] (Of her parents, though, Agnes was more suspicious about being cheated.) Ethel benefited from that no-nonsense pragmatism and acquired a matter-of-fact attitude about her career that floored many a lesser star. She also profited from her parents' cautiousness with money; every grocery bill that came in, Ethel double-checked.

To be sure, such attitudes were common among working- and lower-middle-class families and immigrants struggling to maintain their footing in the New World—and soon struggling in the Great Depression. But on this latter point, the Zimmermanns were less typical, for not only did they ride out the Depression years, they even prospered: Edward held onto his job throughout, and his daughter soon hit the big time in a way nobody ever could have anticipated.

The Young Singer

From the start, Agnes and Edward wanted their daughter to be able to stand on her own two feet, something she claimed she was doing "from the age of five." On this point too, the Zimmermanns were both of their time and station and *not* quite of it. Daughters of working-class families needed to acquire practical, employable skills, to be sure, but landing a husband was usually part of their training. Instead, Mom and Pop Zimmermann urged their daughter to focus on making a living and to be self-sufficient above all. By the time she was singing her ode to "Eadie" in *Take a Chance,* one writer would spin that protofeminist point of her life story fairly liberally: "Of the entire group [in high school], Ethel was the only one whose dreams didn't consist of a little white house with a pot of geraniums in the kitchen and a couple of fat babies in the yard. Ethel knew what she wanted. No man could dominate her life."[20]

No one knew that Ethel's autonomy would come from her voice, but music was a central part of her upbringing. At age three, she began singing around the house. (Musical show writing team Howard Lindsay and Russel Crouse later quipped, "There was terrific excitement in the Zimmermann home when they discovered that young Ethel could talk, too.")[21] Ethel and her parents averred that the boom in her voice was always there and that neighbors could tell whenever the wide-eyed Zimmermann girl was singing. This was no doubt true, but not because of Ethel's lung power, ample though it was. For it was hard *not* to hear aspiring singers or musicians practice in their homes: windows were open whenever weather permitted. Astoria was a tightly knit community, and residents of the early decades of the 1900s spent much of their time socializing and milling outdoors before radios and television sets would insulate them inside. So as true as this story is about Ethel's childhood singing—and she and her biographers repeated it often—it would have been the same for *any* singer or musician growing up at the time. In short, the tale lingers not for its historical exactitude but to showcase the lung power that was considered the hallmark of the Merman voice.

Like many middle-class American families, the Zimmermanns had a piano, which Edward played on Sundays or while unwinding from work. Agnes had sung in choirs, but it was Pop who remained musically active, playing keyboards in a small amateur combo that played locally. He was also the organist at his Masonic Lodge—"Never at church," said Ethel. Again, in this era just before radio and when phonographs were still relatively uncommon, songs were popularized through sheet music and pianos. Edward played while his daughter sang. "My father . . . taught me to read music and to play the piano—but not well."[22] Although Edward read music, he couldn't sight read or play by ear.

One of the pillars of the Merman myth is that she was an untrained singer ("I never had a lesson in my life!"), and so the question of her ability to read music comes up from time to time. Now, among the giants of American popular music, figures who didn't read music are not difficult to find; Irving Berlin, for instance, couldn't and could play only in F$\sharp$ major. (He had a "trick piano" especially made that was outfitted with a transposing keyboard.) With La Merm, however, things are not very black and white. In the early 1960s, when she appeared on Judy Garland's TV show in a now-classic episode with Barbra Streisand, the three Divas of Belt shared a giggle about their inability to read music. Yet as a guest on *The Mike Douglas Show* a decade later, Merman said, "Oh yes, I read music. My father taught me." A few years later, on *The Merv Griffin Show,* when Griffin teased her, "Still no lessons, still not able to sight read?" Ethel did not disagree.

Given her phenomenal instincts as a singer and her successes, it scarcely matters that Ethel Merman didn't read music (or, more likely, didn't read it well). Her ear was incredible, and she had a knack for nailing songs after only one or two hearings. "I'd send her a tape in the morning," recalled pianist, arranger, composer, and close friend Roger Edens, "and by the afternoon, she'd learn a new song or a new arrangement. It was amazing."[23] Merman was happy to have learned music the way she did, since most "girl singers are usually forced at the beginning to sing in a choir. They always sounded like they had a muffin in their mouth," she quipped.[24] A happy result: she was never self-conscious about technique or breath; "I sing honest," she'd say.[25]

Ethel gave her first public performance at age five. "There was a Captain Eddie who put on an annual performance called 'La Parada' to benefit the Tubercular association," she told biographer Pete Martin.[26] Pop accompanied Ethel on a song she sang for her mother, "She's Me Pal"—a distaff variation of Vincent Bryan and Gus Edwards's "He's Me Pal"—and "How Ya Gonna Keep 'Em Down on the Farm?" She also sang at picnics at the Women's Republican Club of Astoria, in which Agnes was active. "Pop accompanied me on the piano, and I must have been a hit, because I appeared there often, billed as 'Little Ethel Zimmermann.'"[27] She sang at her father's Masonic Lodge, where her mom's best friend, Marie Gardiner, a local singing star, also performed. "Sometimes there would be singing contests for five dollar coin pieces. I remember winning some." She sang at local churches. Because the Church of the Redeemer, where she'd been baptized, didn't allow girls to sing, she "ended up at the Dutch Reformed church most of the time," where "the choir was mixed."[28]

Agnes and Edward encouraged their daughter's interest in music by taking her to hear contemporary singers. Their home was only a few blocks from the subway, and it was an easy ride into Manhattan's theater district. So it became a tradition on Sundays, when Tom Mossman, a family friend who worked with Edward, joined the family for lamb or roast beef ("Mom was a great cook," recalls Ethel), that every other week "Uncle Tom" took Ethel to the matinee at the Palace, the historic vaudeville theater erected to great fanfare in 1913. Eventually, Agnes started going there with her daughter on Friday evenings, since it was not a school night, and Ethel remembered, "We sat in the first row of the second balcony, where the seats cost forty-six cents. Then later we moved down to the back of the first balcony, where seats went for eighty-three cents."[29] At the Palace, Ethel experienced singing sensations such as Grace La Rue, belter Blossom Seeley (1891–1974), and Nora Bayes (1880–1928), the popular chanteuse and musicals star to whom Ethel would soon be compared. As Ethel later told her biographer, she also liked performers Dorothy Fielding and Betty Fields. Already nursing aspirations to become a singer, the young girl memorized all of their songs.

Tin Pan Alley and Ethnic Interplay

Tin Pan Alley describes not just the reigning popular music of the 1910s and 1920s but the place that produced it, New York City's West 28th Street, headquarters to the country's largest music publishers. Earlier, Tin Pan Alley had been located farther downtown, before the theater district moved north to midtown and the area we now associate with Broadway. This was a busy, clanging, boisterous part of the city, where participants and passersby could hear tunesmiths working songs out on their pianos, singers practicing, musicians rehearsing. Everywhere song pluggers hustled singers into performing songs of their music publisher, a new practice that benefited all parties. In the '20s, spurred by the rise of radio, record labels were cropping up everywhere, catering to mass and niche markets alike. There were "race records," recording labels primarily for African Americans, labels for klezmer music, and so on.

The typical Tin Pan Alley song was composed of thirty-two bars that broke down into four eight-bar phrases and followed the standard A-A-B-A form. With language taken from colloquial speech, these songs often told small stories about topics or figures gleaned from current events or even from other songs and singers. Tin Pan Alley borrowed liberally from earlier minstrel, folk, and tavern songs in addition to contemporary jazz and ragtime, especially their rhythmic patterns and accentuation. Its songs ranged from ballads through African-American blues to send-ups of Scottish, Irish, and Yiddish airs.

Another feature of Tin Pan Alley was its mode of production. Tunes were written quickly and were just as quickly thrown into the world. For all their catchy charm and contemporary flavor, however, these Tin Pan Alley songs were driven first and foremost by profit. They were never considered a form of personal or artistic expression (in contrast to classical or art music). Rather, they were products of a bustling metropolis and modern technologies that could mass-reproduce songs and deliver them to consumers through nightclub and stage performances, sheet music, records, and radio.

Many Tin Pan Alley songwriters were Jewish immigrants, working at a historical moment before they "became white,"[30] and for some, Tin Pan Alley and ragtime offered the fantasy of leaving their ethnic and European roots behind in the process of assimilating into American culture. The music that resulted, though, can hardly be called ethnically unmarked, even if its African-American, Irish, and Jewish influences are not as mutually distinct as we might think. Music historian Mark Grant has made precisely this point, noting, for instance, that these traditions favor consonants and lyrical clarity over "legitimate" singing's rounded vowels and tonal beauty; the impact of Irish ballad singing was such, he notes, as to inform "Jewish Irish tenor" Al Jolson. A particular technique associated with Jolson, the spoken tremolo, "is not exclusively Hebraic and cantoral in origin, as some commentators have claimed, because it clearly occurred in the singing of performers of other ethnicities" (British, American, Irish).[31]

Most of the white female vocalists Ethel admired performed Tin Pan Alley songs. African-American singers, by contrast, found their greatest successes recording blues for race records aimed at African-American consumers (a few labels were even black-owned). By the end of the 1920s, however, as blues caught on with white audiences, bringing bigger profits, even greats such as Ma Rainey (1886–1939) were consigned to the sidelines as black male recording artists—and, eventually, white men—took over. The blues got smoothed out. By this time, Ma Rainey, Bessie Smith (1894–1937), and other female black singers of renown, including future Broadway and film star Ethel Waters (1896–1977), had to sing second-tier Tin Pan Alley songs to get by.

In the 1910s and '20s, white female singers, especially gentile ones, typically performed in what might be called an exaggerated "feminine" style. Upper registers, slides of pitch, and a light, fluttering, tremulous vibrato were favored by vocalists and stage stars such as Ruth Etting, Marilyn Miller, Helen Kane (on whom cartoon Betty Boop was modeled), and Helen Morgan ("Julie" in the original *Show Boat*). Recordings of Ruth Etting's "You're the Cream in My Coffee," for instance, reveal a smooth delivery, minimal chest projection, and almost no accentuation on the downbeats. For most white female singers, crisp enunciation was also de rigueur, something that was largely eschewed by blues singers working out African-American traditions. (Ethel Waters often faced accusations from the black press of being a "race traitor" precisely for her crisp diction.)

It was common for nonblack female singers to assume different ethnic identities in performing Tin Pan Alley songs, especially in pieces pitched for comic effect. Nora Bayes, for instance, sang "How Can They Tell That I'm Irish"; the Yiddish performer Fannie Brice did "I'm an Indian" using a central European–Yiddish dialect and phrasing. And Sophie Tucker was not just the "last of the red hot mamas" but began her career as a "coon shouter," when producers had the Yiddish Russian perform in blackface before they knew what to do with her. Along with that blackness came clichéd assumptions about the women's bodies and their overall decorum. Compared with the white "jazz baby" of the '20s, wrote one journalist, "your coon shouter was a lusty, rounded lady. She was all curves. Her voice was a wild, raucous yell, and perfect intonation was her least concern."[32] Earthy, sexualized, African-American attributes were assigned to women whose material or performance style seemed to fit the bill, *regardless* of race: there was the bluesy work of Libby Holman and the "sassy," overtly sexual Mae West. In the early '60s, a Los Angeles critic called Merman a coon shouter, and in the mid-'50s, after the opening of *Anything Goes,* another wrote of "her progress from coon shouter to the most subtle lyric-putter-over extant, enhancing her appeal by deft repression, making her a most engaging comedienne as well as songstress."[33] (Note that the critic measures progress in terms of leaving African-American influences behind.) For some, Merman's "belt" style clinched her link to blackness: "The belting voice is a voice of strength . . . it is a voice that evokes darkness in tone and timbre, a 'colored' voice [in contrast to] the 'whiteness' always ascribed to [Julie] Andrews's voice."[34]

Non-Anglo performers such as Tucker and Brice were among the "white ethnic" immigrants who formed a significant part of New York City's social and cultural landscape of the era. (At times, Poles, Italians, and Greeks were classified into a single group, placed a step above African Americans and a step below Anglos and established nationals such as the Germans.) What set these female singers apart from Anglo singers was not so much their voices per se as the techniques and material they borrowed from a diverse set of ethnic and racial traditions.

And so a marked ethnic mobility infiltrated the songs, singers, and audiences of Tin Pan Alley, a mobility fully appropriate to the city's demographics of the time. More than a half century later, critics such as Stanley Crouch would ascribe to this musical period a fantasy of ethnic transcendence,[35] but we might also consider the phenomenon in terms of an *expansion* of ethnic associations rather than their transcendence. Merman's public persona, for instance, which borrowed techniques of these early vocalists, would be marked by a variety of non-Anglo features, even long beyond this historical period.

Ethel's childhood fascination with popular female singers and stars was able to flourish. She had a chance to catch glimpses of some of them at the nearby Paramount Astoria Film Studios on the corner of 6th and Pierce, just around the corner from the Zimmermann home. Founded in 1920, not long before the film industry packed up for Hollywood, this East Coast production facility produced a full fourth of all U.S. films between 1921 and 1927. As a result of financial troubles, the migration west, and the costly upheaval of transitioning to sound, however, production eventually tapered off.

For young Ethel, the early location could not have been better. Whenever she and her friends caught wind that a film was being shot, they would stop playing their hopscotch game of "Hopsy" and run to the fence that surrounded the studio, where, through carved-out holes ("I wasn't responsible for gouging any," said Ethel),[36] they caught glimpses of stars such as Greta Nissen, Adolph Menjou, and Greta Garbo arriving at work in their luxurious cars. Ethel's favorite was Alice Brady, whom she said she "worshipped."[37]

Somewhere between the age of six and nine,[38] Ethel hit the small big time when she performed "How Ya Gonna Keep 'Em Down on the Farm (after They've Seen Paree)?" "He's Me Pal," "Maggie Dooley," and other numbers for U.S. troops stationed at Camp Mills and Camp Upton, on Long Island, where the doughboys were training before being shipped off to Europe. Ethel's future colleague Irving Berlin would immortalize his early experience as a soldier at Camp Upton (then Camp Yankhank) in "Oh, How I Hate to Get Up in the Morning," in which the famous night owl lodges his goodhearted complaint. Ethel loved the experience: "I remember one Christmas day when I gladly abandoned my new toys, hopped into an ambulance—since no passenger car was available—and traveled to Camp Mills to entertain the troops."[39] This started Merman's lifelong tradition of giving "something for the boys" in uniform.

Despite the tough but tender love of her parents, Ethel had some lonely times growing up. She could usually bring her problems to Pop, but sometimes, as she later told interviewers, she wished for a sister, especially when she was a little older and started to be interested in boys. Being an only child may have deprived her of some steam-venting pastimes, and as an adult Merman retained a childlike love of secrets, games, and gossip. At the same time, having the undivided attention of one's parents was not so bad and likely enhanced Merman's enormous self-confidence and sense of being in the center of all things.

If Merman's childhood was basically happy, her education was routine. She attended grade school at P.S. No. 4, a school that, while a long walk from her home, was still the closest. High school was William Cullen Bryant High School, near the Bridge Plaza in Long Island City. Ethel was reasonably active as a student, but she kept her musical activities to herself, never joining the school's drama or glee club. As a senior, she was literary editor of *The Owl,* the school's literary magazine and newsletter, and was secretary of the student union.

Agnes Sharkey was a cousin of Ethel's who was employed as a seventh-grade teacher. Pop and (especially) Mom thought this was great and wanted Ethel to follow in her footsteps. Teaching was good, practical work for a young woman. But Ethel already had her heart set on a career as a singer, and teaching was *not* in the cards. The compromise? While at Bryant High, Ethel pursued the four-year stenographer course of study to gain her the practical, bankable skills she could always fall back on. Following a course in commercial, as opposed to general, bookkeeping,[40] Ethel mastered bookkeeping, shorthand (the Pitman method), and typing—and earned great marks.[41]

According to Ethel, she was a good student. "I never fought with other kids," she told her biographer, and "I was always pretty good at math."[42] Less successful were her history classes (she failed once) and gym (physical stamina aside, Ethel was not athletically inclined). Ethel accounted for her lack of extracurricular activities to biographer George Eells: "I guess I was too involved in my studies"[43]—not a terribly convincing claim. Certainly Ethel was not one to blow off schoolwork, but neither did she give it obsessive attention. When interviewed in the 1950s, her teachers remembered the young Zimmermann girl as a sparkling character with good, but not exceptional, abilities.[44]

The teenage Merman was an attractive young woman: she had an ample chest, a long waist, shapely arms, and great legs. She was not particularly tall: just over five feet, five inches, a fact that surprises fans, who believe that Ethel Merman must have been much, much larger. Throughout most of the late 1910s and '20s, she wore her hair in a modified bob, popular among young urban women. Ethel never had an inflated sense of her looks and was always matter-of-fact with interviewers about her assets (legs, eyes) as well as her less-than-perfect features. But in 1934, columnist Louis Sobol decided to remodel the newly arrived star's self-conception, writing that Ethel had told him: "I was an ungainly child . . . and heartbroken about it, for I thought I never would have a chance to be on the stage. I thought beauty was the one and only 'open sesame' to the theatre and the screen. . . . even when I began taking part in amateur shows around Astoria . . . I felt I would never grow up beautiful enough to be an actress."[45] It was all part of creating Ethel Merman.

When Ethel, her parents, and childhood chums were interviewed in mid- to late life, all had surprisingly little recall of the star's childhood years. Merman's memory of her friends, for instance, was as vague as her knowledge of her family background. Some people stuck: she had met Alice Welch in the bookkeeping program, and the two remained friends for much of her life; she also played with a girl named Martha Neubert. But where boys were concerned, Ethel was fuzzier. In her second autobiography, she says that she tried to impress her "first big crush" by coaxing her father to go to the piano to accompany her the moment she saw the boy coming down their street on Sundays on his way to the ballpark.[46] Because of this, she said, this lad was probably her only classmate who knew that she sang, but for the life of her, she couldn't recall his name. High school boyfriends fared little better, fading behind other, more vividly recalled details. "[I don't] remember if I went to senior prom with 'Frank or Clem.' . . . That's the time I had my first evening dress. It was peach taffeta. When I graduated from P.S. No. 4, I wore a uniform of old rose and white. We had to make our own in sewing or we couldn't graduate."[47] Although Merman's memory wasn't purposefully selective, it does suggest a playful (however unconscious) reluctance to discuss entanglements with the opposite sex, a trait she would guard for life.

"Mom didn't talk much about her childhood, her parents, or their background. She wasn't trying to hide anything; her focus just wasn't there."[48] Today, Bob Levitt Jr. is one of the few people around able to give intimate accounts of the Zimmermann family. Other first- and secondhand personal accounts are few and far between; three of Ethel's four husbands, her parents, and her second child have died, and close family friends in Queens and their offspring have either passed away or scattered to places unknown. Yet even during her lifetime, when the press interviewed friends, parents, and associates, it was primarily *Merman's* version of her past (bolstered by her autobiographies and scrapbooks) that illuminated the early days. By necessity, that version is subjective and, in the first autobiography at least, heavily scripted. But when all is said and done, not much is there: Ethel's childhood years were too early to have been tracked by Pop's scrapbooks, which focus not on young Ethel Zimmermann but on the public Ethel Merman. And even Levitt admits he knows little about the background of either his mom or his grandparents. Given her lifelong adulation of her folks and the very real pride Ethel took in her roots, it's rather striking that she rarely talked about her past or showed much interest in the family tree.

The discrepancies surrounding Ethel's early residences, which spring largely from Merman's own accounts, offer another case in point. Here as well, her poor recall on the point is scarcely deliberate (unlike her birthday), but her inability to remember reveals a certain disinterest all the same. By her own admission, Ethel was not the introspective type, and dwelling on details of the past was not her style. What this suggests is that for her—and the image she would cultivate as Ethel Merman, not Zimmermann—the precise details of her family's back history mattered less than a few particulars to round out the contours, such as the Astoria location; her parents' class, religion, and ethnic backgrounds; and her exposure to early singing stars.

When she graduated from high school in 1924, Ethel signed up at an employment agency located near the school, quickly procuring a job at Boyceite, a nearby firm on Queens Boulevard in Long Island City. The company manufactured an antifreeze product and paid Ethel twenty-three dollars per week. She did well there and advanced quickly. Within six months, she'd acquired a new job, at B[ragg] K[leisrath] Vacuum Booster Brake Company, another company with a delightfully improbable name that had opened across the street on the second story of the EPCO Building (its namesake, Etched Products Corporation, occupied the first). Booster's product was a power brake for industrial use in tractors and trailers. Production facilities were near the office site where Ethel worked. Among her duties was typing material to be sent to patent attorney Louis Seigel Whittaker, and, according to Ethel, she never typed up a technical reference she didn't understand (contradictorily, she also averred never to have understood how the brake worked). Small matter. Young Ethel was now pulling in thirty-five dollars a week—very good pay for a stenographer at the time.

Her main role at the company was working as the personal secretary of co-owner Caleb Bragg, a well-to-do businessman and sportsman. Bragg liked to travel in high circles, socializing with Broadway luminaries such as Gertrude Lawrence, producers Earl Carroll and George White, and, apparently, a lot of nice-looking chorus girls. Louis Schurr (future agent of Bert Lahr and Bob Hope) recalls that Bragg owned a variety of ships, "a racking boat, one called *The Bootlegger* and *The Casey Jones* in addition to several speed boats."[49] (His houseboat, *The Masquerader,* reportedly capsized during one of the rare times Ethel was invited to join him and his society friends.) Overall, Ethel found the dapper bachelor gentlemanly but aloof, and she "rarely talked to him." Vic Kleisrath, Bragg's partner and the technician of the pair, was more approachable, "a very regular fellow,"[50] and Ethel was even able to call him by his first name. It was Kleisrath who had interviewed and hired her. Sometimes on weekends, he would invite Ethel to his family home in Port Washington, where bands would play and Ethel would sing along. Ethel also socialized with other young women from Queens who worked at the brake company, among them Edna Ackerman and Josephine (Josie) Traeger, who remained a close friend for decades.

Although she was a conscientious worker, Ethel was clearly biding her time until her singing career got off the ground. "Every night, promptly at the stroke of 5, like a princess in a fairy tale, Miss Zimmerman [sic] dropped the last of her letters in the basket of outgoing mail, and with it her business attitude";[51] then she left to perform at venues across the metropolitan area. Ethel's first radio appearance, "Ethel Merman Time," on WHN, dates from this mid-1920s period. The pace was grueling, since Ethel's night gigs involved commuting to other boroughs to perform, and she would start many a workday with little sleep. Solution? A warning system she and her coworkers devised to keep Bragg from catching Ethel when she was getting some shut-eye on the job. The phone operator had a buzzer that rang a large gong, and different numbers of rings announced different people; "Bragg had three, the head of purchasing had four." Arriving exhausted, Ethel slept on the back room cot until the boss's arrival. (Fortunately, Bragg rarely got to work before ten or ten-thirty.) When her coworkers spotted him approaching the building, they pulled levers, causing eight "gongs" to sound at the nearby production plant—the cue to warn her that Bragg was on-site. The warning gave her enough time to get up, get dressed, and be at her desk by the time he entered. As far as she knew, her boss never caught on.[52]

It was during this time at the brake company that a legendary Merman story was born. It involved a letter of introduction that Bragg wrote on Ethel's behalf to George White, the former Ziegfeld dancer who was now the celebrated Broadway producer of *George White's Scandals,* the spectacular revue that was a huge event every year that it was mounted. Hoping to procure a singing position in the upcoming edition, Merman approached Bragg for an introduction to the Broadway impresario, and he dictated a letter to her. It was, she recalls, "very short" and didn't mention anything about her singing because, she explains, he had never heard her sing.[53] The note landed Ethel a five-minute interview in the outer vestibule of Mr. White's office at the Apollo Theatre Building on 42nd Street. Sorry, White told her, but he had hired Frances Williams to sing in the show. But wait—he was looking for another showgirl. Would this interest her? Merman, hunting bigger game, declined.

By the time she hit the big time, the letter of introduction had assumed legendary proportions. In 1937, a newspaper story ran called "Ethel Once Wrote Own Reference":

> The writer ventured to predict quite confidently that, given the chance, she would quickly prove herself a performer of starring caliber, a name to conjure with in electric lights, a potential draw for the cash customers of both the Broadway sector and elsewhere. . . .
>
> Miss Merman, the records show, has made good on the predictions of the letter, but it must not be supposed that Mr. Bragg, fine gentleman that he is, had really foreseen these potentials in her. For it was none other than Ethel herself who had composed the letter, typed it, and brought it to him for signature.[54]

Once her career took off and Merman's image as a plucky broad took hold, the fiction of the stenographer-with-unbounded-ambition was easy for people to swallow. It was the Depression after all, when working people across the country were looking for lucky breaks, even if only in fantasies and tall tales. In Merman's case, the story only ripened with age. Fifteen years later, Wolcott Gibbs revised it to say that she had left White's office "in disgust" after he told her, "All I can give you is a job in the [chorus] line." "Nope," she retorted. "Not in any line."[55] By that point, Merman's fame for gutsy ripostes was well entrenched, and Gibbs updated the story to reflect it.

Merman's background as a stenographer infuses the myth of her as a practical, self-sufficient, and professional woman. She came by that image honestly, making use of her secretarial skills throughout a half-century career, taking shorthand in meetings, run-throughs, and rehearsals and then typing up script changes. Ethel always kept elaborate personal business records, a date and address book (including everyone's birthday and a list of escorts arranged under *D,* for dates), and typed up guest lists for parties she'd attended and the menus of fancier dinner engagements. When her father started the scrapbooks, Ethel dated and identified the materials she passed along to him. "She answers everything [she] gets, her bills and everything, takes care of them. If she gets a note or present or anything, she sits there and in longhand writes it out," said accompanist Lew Kessler.[56] Merman never hired a personal secretary but answered her own fan mail; well into her seventies, if an interviewer prompted her, she would scrounge up a typewriter and bang out the keyboard exercise: "One of the boys quickly threw the large javelin beyond the maximum distance and won the prize."

Ethel's sense of self-sufficiency and work ethic infiltrated her public persona as well. There was no reason to distance herself from it, and she never did. (Later in life, financial adviser Irving Katz told her she didn't need to work another day in her life. Proud as that made her, Ethel never stopped working or wanted to.) From the start, the autonomy that Ethel's business and secretarial skills gave her pleased her, and, indeed, she had an independence that few female stage stars of the time had. During the Depression, the image of honest, hardworking Ethel inspired countless young working women across the New York City area. Half a century later, that image endured as the septuagenarian Ethel awed audiences by criss-crossing North America in concert and television appearances. Merman was a workhorse, reliable, matter-of-fact, down-to-earth. Today, any devoted Ethel fan knows about her job before she entered show business; as one gypsy who worked with her in the 1950s said, "Ethel never forgot her roots."[57]

Venues for Young Singers

Along with other nascent forms of the Broadway musical, revues such as *George White's Scandals* provided important venues for popular singers of the time. These shows introduced hits to audiences, and in the 1920s, radio and electric phonographs enabled songs to reach a mass audience almost instantly. This was a period when new songs spread quickly, especially in New York. "The world was so much smaller then," says singer Klea Blackhurst today. "People forget that, or that [Lew] Brown, [Ray] Henderson, and [Buddy] DeSylva were the Beatles of their time. Their songs were *everywhere* and were enormously popular."[58] Ethel Merman's New York was the New York of Irving Berlin, Yip Harburg, Harold Arlen, Vernon Duke, Jerome Kern, the Gershwin brothers, and Cole Porter.

At this early stage in the development of what we know as the Broadway musical, popular songs were rarely tied to particular stories, characters, or settings. They could be easily dropped into club performances, radio shows, and even other stage, club, and cinematic productions. New York song and stage still enjoyed a relatively strong hold on popular culture. By the end of the '20s, motion pictures began to encroach on the national reach of the Great White Way, to be sure, but still, many of the country's new hit songs, trends, stars, and stories were getting their start there.

Nightclubs, cabarets, and vaudeville offered other venues for singers, although only the top singers had solo shows. More typically, vocalists appeared in variety acts that interspersed popular songs with magic acts, theatrical skits, operettas, arias, short films, and comedy routines. Stature was measured by one's place in the program. In these early engagements, rising stars like Merman opened before headlining acts or before a feature motion picture. "They rotated programs," recalls Marilyn Baker, a child at the time and the daughter of Eddie Cantor. "I would go down to Brooklyn and watch Ethel Merman, and then this dreadful movie would come on—something with Marlene Dietrich in it—that I didn't want to see. So I'd go out and walk around, then get back into the place when Merman was singing again. I'd do this all day long."[59] By the mid- to late '30s, when Ethel started appearing in her own films, other performers—often vaudevillians on the wane—warmed up audiences for *her*. But by then, it was a practice on its way out—too vaudevillian and too costly (though useful to entice Depression audiences in); by the early 1950s, live singers seldom opened for feature films.

Living in Astoria, Ethel was in close proximity to the bustling New York music scene. She told her first autobiographer that when a song plugger informed her that "she didn't have to do it for free," she began to be paid for her singing appearances in the area: $7.50 for weddings and parties.[60] (That Ethel or her parents could have been this naive is unlikely.) At the Ross Music Store on nearby Steinway Avenue, the aspiring singer received complimentary sheet music, a common practice then. Alan Eichler, grandson of proprietor Abraham Ross, recalls that sometimes Ethel came in just to copy the lyrics.[61]

Back at Camp Mills in the mid-1910s, Ethel was billed as "Little Ethel Zimmermann." By 1927 at least, she was singing as Ethel Merman. She changed her name soon after high school while contemplating her singing career. (She'd later crack, "If you put Zimmermann up in lights, you'd die from the heat.")[62] At first, Ethel pushed for the WASPier sounding "Alice Gardner," after a cousin from her mother's family (not the singer), but that proposition infuriated Edward. So another compromise was struck: Ethel dropped the first and last letters of the cumbersome "Zimmermann" to become Ethel *Merman*. Exactly when she did this is impossible to settle. In her first autobiography, she writes that it was 1930,[63] but sheet music and club programs reveal that this happened at least three years earlier. It is not likely that Ethel ever performed professionally as Ethel Zimmermann.

Success as Ethel Merman was swift. In 1927 her photo appeared on the sheet music covers for "Just Another Day Wasted Away" and "Side by Side" and, in 1928, "After My Laughter Came Tears," incontestable signs of a growing reputation. On September 10, 1928, the *New York Sun* ran a small photo of the performer posing with her accompanist. Other artifacts beyond the music industry hint at her growing renown, such as a 1928 tobacco trading card that fans could collect and swap. Eventually, these kinds of items, along with product endorsements, would forge specific perceptions of her and guide her evolving persona as a star, but in the late '20s, the products were too random to lend much of a sense of Ethel as a personality.

Nineteen twenty-eight was a busy year. It saw Merman earning ten dollars for her "cabaret act" at Keens English Chop House in midtown Manhattan. A cozy, dark old tavern, Keens was "the kind of place that Charles Dickens might have frequented in his day."[64] That same year, she sang at the Democratic convention that nominated Franklin Delano Roosevelt as governor of New York. By September 1929, the busy young singer, still in the employ of the brake company, was hired for two weeks at sixty dollars a week at a nightspot and restaurant just below street level on 57th Street near Carnegie Hall. The place was called The Little Russia.[65]

Her first autobiography gives The Little Russia as the place of Ethel's first professional performance. Transcripts, however, reveal that Merman told interviewer-writer Pete Martin otherwise, that her first gig was in fact at Keens. Martin excised that from the public record, presumably because "Keens Chop House" lacked the luster of the more prestigious The Little Russia. The facts are corrected in Ethel's subsequent autobiography, which not only includes Keens English Chop House but locates it at 72 West 36th Street.

It was at The Little Russia that Merman caught the eye of future agent Lou Irwin. Impressed, he sent his card over and asked to sign her up. "Since I was underage, Mom and I went over after working hours and we made a deal with Lou to represent me for nine years."[66] Irwin arranged singing jobs for her at Les Ambassadeurs, the rooftop club at Manhattan's Winter Garden Theatre, where Merman preceded headlining comic trio Lou Clayton, Eddie Jackson, and Jimmy Durante with songs like "I've Got a Feeling I'm Falling." Irwin also secured a booking at the Pavilion Royal on Long Island and at the Palace, where Ethel had seen her favorite singers as a child (by now, the Palace was one of the last active vaudeville houses in the city).[67] Ethel also had engagements at Keith's 86th Street Theatre and at the Ritz Theatre in Elizabeth, New Jersey.

During this period of the late 1920s, Ethel performed with piano man and arranger Al Siegel (1906–66). Siegel enjoyed a long if uneven career as accompanist, arranger, and coach for singing stars such as Betty Hutton, Dorothy Lamour, Martha Raye, Grace Moore, Virginia O'Brien, Shirley Temple, Benay Venuta, and Betty Grable (whom, according to Lindsay and Crouse, Siegel discovered).[68] Siegel enjoyed his biggest successes on Broadway, moving to Hollywood in the 1930s after some health problems and finally turning his hopes to television in the 1950s. "He had a good eye for talent," recalls Roger Edens. At the time Siegel met Ethel, he was coaching a number of female singers in New York, including ex-wife Bee Palmer/Bea Wayne. Some speculate that Siegel coached all of his clients to do the things that later became Merman trademarks: holding a note for as long as possible, adding grace notes. He may also have encouraged the extensive hand and arm movements that would become key to Ethel's delivery.

Exactly when Siegel and Merman paired up is not known. Edens claims Siegel found her "singing in a little cellar"—probably The Little Russia—and that Lou Irwin introduced them. Clippings show that as early as 1928, Merman and Siegel performed in a cabaret act together for a good portion of the year. Merman later insisted that she and Siegel had worked as a team for only four or five months, beginning in 1930. Their relationship would prove volatile, ending in a mysterious break in 1930 or 1931, after which Ethel refused to discuss Al Siegel for the rest of her life. Periodically, the threat of lawsuits erupted, usually launched by him at Merman. The bone of contention was how much Siegel had actually shaped Merman's performance style and was responsible for her success. Ethel said he did nothing but accompany her; Siegel claimed more. Both claims seem reasonable. Given Ethel's considerable raw talent, it is unlikely that Siegel shaped the voice itself much. "Her voice was already her own and not really his style," recalls Edens. "She has one basic thing that is strictly Merman, and that is projecting a song."[69] Lew Kessler agrees. Regarding Merman's ability to sustain long notes, for instance, he says Siegel "just happened to find something. . . . a lot of arrangers think of things, and he just arranged the number and it clicked. It just happened to work. . . . he could have thought it up for some other dame and nothing would have worked."[70] Still, it is easy to infer that Siegel exerted *some* influence on the pre-celebrity Merman, given that he arranged material for other singers to transform them into hot new "girl singers." With Ethel, as Kessler says, his techniques just "clicked" in a way that they didn't with his other clients.

One of their early documented performances together was at the Ritz in Elizabeth, New Jersey. "A new singing team has come into existence," said *Variety*'s review, "with interesting arrangements by Siegel. And the girl can sing."[71] They performed at the Brooklyn Paramount Theatre, and on Sunday nights, Siegel accompanied her at the Pavilion Royal, where each was paid $25 for their first night there. She was such a sensation that the following week they were paid $75 apiece, and the week after that, $150.

Merman's repertoire was fairly standard for the time, and in that way, she was like any number of white girl singers trying to make it big. For, although Ethel is considered unique today, Klea Blackhurst maintains that back then "she *wasn't* unique. She was singing hugely popular songs, the same repertoire as anyone else."[72] At the same time, Ethel was savvy enough not to box herself in with too limited a repertoire, telling one reporter, "A few blues are all right, but to get by you've got to give them some sweet, dreamy things, too. They're going back to the sentimental ballads of thirty years ago. And how they beat their hands together when you sing one of them!"[73] She moved with ease from ballads, torch songs, and slow sentimental tunes to numbers of great speed and lyrical complexity. But not all her shows were so varied. When she was at the Pavilion Royal, for instance, she performed the torchy "Little White Lies," "I've Got a Feeling I'm Falling," and "Moanin' Low," the last made famous that year by Libby Holman.

Even back then, Ethel's performance style seemed the theatrical equivalent of her matter-of-fact personality: she just planted her feet onstage, faced the audience, and sang. It would become a defining trait for over fifty years. But in the 1920s and '30s, it was hardly idiosyncratic. Theater and opera singers alike were trained "just to face forward and sing to the proscenium."[74] This approach, of course, was required for technical reasons: before theaters were amplified or performers miked, in order to project one's voice and be heard over the orchestra, belting was almost a physical necessity. A singer's movement was similarly constrained. In opera, physical movement had to be carefully blocked; in musical theater, it was kept to an absolute minimum, often restricted to upper-body gestures.[75] Even popular orchestrations of the period tended to highlight strings over the brass section to facilitate hearing the voices onstage.

Belting

For as much as the world associates Ethel Merman with belting, there is no public record of that term used in connection with her before 1952. This is not to say that belting didn't exist, but that it was not named as such. "The only way to fill the theater," says singing voice specialist Jeannette LoVetri, "was to shout, or to sing like an opera singer, because those resonances seemed to project all the way to the back row. Before the advent of amplification, the performers who had the strongest, the clearest, and the most dynamic sounds were the ones you could hear, and those were the people that 'worked.'"[76]

Vocal specialist Linda Carroll explains, "The cultivation of voices such as [those of] Kate Smith and Ethel Merman occurred during a time when there was no difference between concert singers, opera singers and popular singers in the elements of training," adding that the same tension between bel canto and *canto declamato* applies to the popular crooners of the 1940s and the rock-and-roll "screamers" of the 1970s.[77]

Belting is a bit like pornography: everyone recognizes it, but defining it is altogether another thing. "Most people associate belting with some kind of louder singing that's closely associated with speech," says LoVetri. Many people think of belting as a chest sound that kicks into gear at the high end of a singer's comfortable range. "One of the things that you hear in a belt voice like Merman's when they're up high is a lot of tension, and the tension sounds exciting. It reminds people of a yell, and when do human beings yell? We yell when we're excited, whether out of fear or joy."[78] Klea Blackhurst disagrees: "That just makes it a *speech* quality."[79] What she finds important is how belting involves the entire body and requires the kind of extreme effort that classical trainers teach *against,* their belief being that only a relaxed body can produce full sounds. "Belting is an incredibly physical way to sing," says Blackhurst, adding, "but you can't make it look that hard. If you do, it looks mannered."[80]

If, as Blackhurst says, belting is a highly physical form of singing, it is also connected to the body in other, more abstract, psychological ways. In contrast to belting, people tend *not* to associate physical exertion with, say, crooning or jazz scat singing. Moreover, because to belt means to lay a force or blow on something else, "the strict dictionary definition of belt requires an interaction between performer and listener,"[81] an impact that is experienced in physical and visceral ways. So it made sense for the press to write of Merman, in 1940, "When she walks, it's like a swing band in a jam session. And when she sings, she makes your ears tingle . . . her voice dances in your ears and rings down along the bloodstream."[82] Or, in 1955, "She is not just a voice, but . . . she gives the sort of all-out performance which is rarely seen. Judy Garland and Al Jolson are the only other entertainers this reviewer has seen who gave themselves, body and soul, to the audience."[83] Without that emotional force, belting techniques are just tricks; without that sense of personality, impact, and the relationship between performer and audience, belting does not exist.[84]

During the premike and preamplification era, projection was less of an issue in nightclubs and other informal musical venues than in the large theater and opera houses. Singers could move a bit more in these smaller spaces, although there, too, the style remained essentially the same: performers sang straight out to the audience. In Yiddish theater, for instance, performers made no attempt to naturalize their performance but just put the music out there, acknowledging the audience and its response with a relaxed style and interactions. There, one could find a lot more swaying shoulders, especially among female singers of the time, from whom greater bodily display was expected.

When Ethel sang, she was able to convey movement and energy through highly animated facial expressions. From the beginning, her startled, twinkling eyes relayed an energetic spirit and sense of pep. She drew attention to her hands and arms by moving them out and upward to near eye level. Ethel had jewels sewn onto the wrists of her sleeves and wore large bracelets and rings so that she could literally twinkle while staring into her audience. This historically based performance style remained with Merman for life, long after it had faded from the general scene. She rarely looked at costars when singing onstage, often infuriating them and fueling accusations of egomania. A good example can be seen on the kinescope of her historic 1953 duet with Mary Martin on television. True to her stage image, Mary Martin is interactive, affectionately putting her hands on Merman's shoulders and looking at her. Merman, on the other hand, stares straight ahead nearly the entire time, beaming her gaze at the studio audience and camera.

Again, Blackhurst puts the matter into historical context. "Ethel started singing before there were mikes. And she never altered her performance for a mike."[85] It may appear mannered today—or even to people watching her telecast with Martin in the 1950s—but Ethel came of age in an era marked by certain technological limitations, orchestration styles, and performance standards. Moreover, even the material she performed, like other songs, theatrical sketches, and comic routines of the time, acknowledged the proscenium and the audience's presence through direct gazes, knowing winks and gags, and verbal repartee with them. This was an era of show making, not one in which songs or plays would produce a self-contained, "natural" world set apart from the performance situation, but one where numbers were acknowledged as such.

This performance style also contributed to Ethel's association with a mix of ethnicities. By Ethel's time, Germans had resided in the United States long enough to be considered part of the American white mainstream, a categorization furthered by their white skin and Saxon heritage. By this time, in short, Germans weren't considered foreign in the same way that newer nationals and immigrants were; for instance, the more recent Greeks and Poles were deemed less American, less "white" than their German-American counterparts.

Nonetheless, Ethel didn't always come across in the same way that other white, gentile performers did, despite her Anglo vocal features. Her robust, direct style had more in common with Yiddish performers like Brice (someone else who rarely accommodated a mike) than with Marilyn Miller. And the "white ethnic" singers also tended to gravitate to songs that expressed bawdy humor, hardly surprising from a white-dominated culture that tied humor and sexuality to nonwhite ethnicities. Here, too, Merman fit the bill.

Preparing to Launch

Despite all the attention lavished on her voice, Merman, now in her early twenties, was not hard on the eyes. She was a very attractive young woman, if not a cookie-cutter glamour queen, and didn't look much different than she did as a teen. A photo dated from the mid- to late 1920s shows her with a twinkling, impish charm. Her dress, shoes, and pose convey the sense of crisp youth and bubbly, well-groomed vitality. A little later, in the mid-'30s, a newspaper would use the same picture with the caption "At 5′6″ and 118 lbs, Ethel's thigh reveals. . . ." Images like this, coupled with her oft-announced secretarial background and the constantly affirmed love of her folks, bathe the early Merman in an astounding wholesomeness.

It was sometime late in 1929 or early 1930 that Lou Irwin arranged for Ethel to audition at the Warner Bros.' East Coast studios. Accounts vary as to who attended the audition, whether it was Harry Warner, Archie Mayo (the director of the studios), or both. Recalls Lou Irwin, "Lewis Warner, Harry's son, thought she was terrific."[86] Ethel indeed wowed them, and Warners signed her for a six-month contract with options for another seven (or nine) years under the studio's Vitaphone banner.[87] Her contract stipulated that whether she worked or not, she would draw a salary of $125 per week. Ethel finally quit her secretarial job: "Bragg just wished me well. That was all."[88] But things didn't ignite, and Warner Bros. barely used her. Ethel played a small role in the nine-minute *The Cave Club,* which Vitaphone publicized as a "flash," a short spectacle film, as opposed to a story-driven drama or comedy. *Publix Opinion,* the official industry press sheet for Paramount subsidiary Publix's exhibitors, gave it the following write-up:

> A subject with song and dance, in two scenes—one a primitive Night Club with Amazon gals doing their stuff—then a mystic glass[—]and one gets an insight into night life of today, giving the idea that entertainment tastes have

changed but little. The hostess, Marjorie Leach, does a Texas Guinan as she presents the girls and speciality numbers, among which is a good adagio team. A fair flash which has the elements to appeal in audiences of the second choice houses . . . it is not strong enough to hold the closing spot on the program.[89]

Ethel had shot her number at the Warner Avenue J studio, in Brooklyn. "I acted as a mechanical rabbit for a posse of hard-breathing cannibals or animals,"[90] she said later of the experience. She said she sang a "weird song" in an elaborate jungle number "with a lot of tom toms." Unsurprisingly, Ethel soon soured on the arrangement with Warners. She was getting paid, but she wasn't getting anything to do. "I got tired of all that waiting around," she said, eventually asking to be released from her contract. Irwin remembers it differently: "Warners could have encouraged her option," but they "dropped her."[91]

At the end of 1929, Ethel, usually the model of health and energy, underwent a tonsillectomy. This surgery wouldn't become the Big Story that the one thirty years later was, when she broke a blood vessel in her throat during *Gypsy*. But even at this early stage, her voice was deemed important enough to be a news item. As Merman (with the help of her first biographer) later embellished, "Could be, having my tonsils chopped out had a permanent effect on my voice and made it louder. They had to go in so deep for my tonsils they severed a couple of blood vessels and I had to be sewn up."[92] Again, this seems less the real Ethel Merman talking than the voice associated with "Ethel Merman," the public production, whose iconoclastic toughness was being extended to her body itself, almost a Deep Throat *avant la lettre*. Insists Blackhurst, "She was *not* a freak of nature. But I do think all her vocal styling was her choice. And that's what people wanted."[93] (If Merman objected to this exaggeration or caricature of her physical attributes, she hardly let on. As she later told Pete Martin, "Dr. Stuart Craig would say 'I can't even see your vocal cords. They must be somewhere down in your calves.' So I get the picture that mine are different from everybody else's, at least where they're placed.")[94]

A month after the tonsillectomy, Lou Irwin secured an engagement in Miami for Ethel to "recover" at the lush Roman Pools Casino, where she was billed as "Ethel Merman, Beautiful Talkie Star." Although Agnes liked to accompany her daughter when she traveled, functioning as nurse, escort, and informal business agent, she did not accompany Ethel on her first trip out of the tri-state area, probably because of the expense. Merman made $300 a week in Miami, five times what she'd been earning at The Little Russia. During her month and a half there, she worked alongside rubber-mouthed comedian Joe E. Lewis and, as a program indicates for the night of January 31, Grace Kay White, Ralph Wonders, Irving Aaronson, and the Commanders. "Moanin' Low" was still one of her big numbers.

Back in New York, Irwin booked Merman a total of three times on the RKO Keith Palace circuit and, on September 13, 1930, she played the Palace Theatre on 47th Street for the first time. With Al Siegel at the piano, she opened the second act after an orchestral "Ain't Misbehavin'." All we know about that night is that she performed a variety of contemporary hit tunes, since program notes offer nothing more specific than "Modern Songs in Modern Style." Ethel split her pay of $500 a week with Siegel. The following summer on July 20, she appeared at the Palace for a second time and was held over the next week, practically unheard of in Palace history.[95] But before then, after the first Palace engagement, Ethel had an other gig that was bringing in cash that she didn't have to share with Siegel. She was earning $375 a week rehearsing for a new George and Ira Gershwin show. The show was called *Girl Crazy,* and it was preparing to open at the Alvin Theatre.

———

TWO

From Stenographer to Star

She zoomed to the stars in a single night—a rocket shot
skyward with ammunition supplied by Gershwin.

GUY BOLTON

"I Got Rhythm" wasn't just an opening line or even a
song title; it was a statement of purpose, a rallying cry,
a declaration of everything that the Gershwins, and for
that matter, all of American music, were about.

WILL FRIEDWALD

Girl Crazy and the Big Break

Few legends about Ethel Merman are actually corroborated by historical
record. One, however, is beyond dispute: the evening she became an overnight
sensation, October 14, 1930, after performing "I Got Rhythm" at the opening of *Girl Crazy.* Without having had a singing lesson in her life, this fifth-
billed performer brought the house down when she held the C above middle
C on the word *I*—and held it and held it. When awarding her a special Tony
forty years later, Peter Ustinov said, "She stepped out to sing and the walls
withdrew two inches." The rest, as they say, is history.

Vinton Freedley, who produced the show with partner Alex A. Aarons,
had discovered Merman during her engagement at the Brooklyn Paramount.
Jimmy Durante, who had worked with Merman at Les Ambassadeurs, had
urged Freedley to check her out, and the producer was so impressed that he
invited George Gershwin to hear her, and the composer was no less impressed
than he. Gershwin immediately arranged for Ethel to audition for *Girl Crazy,*
the show he and his brother Ira were writing at the time. As Ethel later told
Pete Martin, "It was like meeting God. . . . Not only was I meeting the

Gershwins," she said, "but I had never seen such a tall building before. I was just a kid, from Queens."[1] After taking the elevator all the way up to their rooftop floor at 31 Riverside Drive, she auditioned with "Exactly Like You" and "Little White Lies," songs that she had been performing at the Brooklyn Paramount. Then George Gershwin "auditioned" for Ethel the songs he wanted her to sing from *Girl Crazy:* "I Got Rhythm," "Embraceable You," "Bidin' My Time," "But Not for Me," "Sam and Delilah," and "Boy, What Love Has Done to Me." After this, the great composer said, "Miss Merman, if there's anything you'd like to change, I'd be happy to do so." Stunned, all she could say was, "They'll do very nicely." Later, Gershwin would give Ethel part of his original penciled score of *Girl Crazy.*

A new Gershwin show was a guaranteed event in New York. But *Girl Crazy* was anticipated for its talent in other departments as well. Gershwin regular Allen Kearns was the male romantic lead (this was Kearns's third musical with them); the dancing stars were the De Marcos (Rene and Antonio); and the female lead was a nineteen-year-old dancer named Ginger Rogers, whom the producers signed on at the salary of fifteen hundred dollars a week. Recalls Roger Edens, "That was big stuff—she was nice looking, she could act some, but she couldn't sing—and you have to have somebody to sing a Gershwin score."[2] (It was while working on *Girl Crazy* that Fred Astaire first met Rogers. Aarons called on Astaire, playing in a show down the street, to help with the choreography for "Embraceable You.") Roger Edens accompanied. The main comic part went to Yiddish veteran Willie Howard in a role originally planned for Bert Lahr, whose work in *Flying High* kept him from accepting. Ethel came onboard via the Palace, where Gershwin had booked her: "Edens says he was only rehearsing, but they went up there and signed you and found Al Siegel to play for you."[3]

John McGowan and Guy Bolton wrote the book, whose story follows Danny Churchill (Kearns), a girl-crazy New York heir whose father sends him off to the old Buzzards Ranch in Custerville, Arizona, which Dad assumes will hold no distractions in the form of wine, women, or song. Danny turns the place into a dude ranch, stuffing it with the very urban vices his father had tried to preempt: alcohol, gambling casino, and imported New York chorines. Predictably, Danny meets the love of his life, G-rated postmistress Molly Gray (Rogers). Ethel portrayed Molly's jaded, experienced counterpart, the worldly Kate Fothergill, a nightclub singer and the long-suffering wife of a hopeless gambler—a character type that would stick to her for a decade.

Thematically, *Girl Crazy,* like many musical comedies of the time, reflected a country of immigrants, with stories of Americans-in-the-making. Like a western, it opposed urban communities and values to rural ones: there is New

York and there is the frontier West; there are Jewish cab drivers and there are gentiles. Danny, for instance, travels from New York to Custerville in a taxi (fare: $742.30), driven by Yiddish-speaking Gieber Goldfarb (Howard). At one point Goldfarb speaks Yiddish to a completely comprehending Native American in an ethnic crossover that may have been less offensive to audiences then than it might seem to twenty-first-century sensibilities.[4]

Ethel was still engaged at the Palace when rehearsals began. She ran from one job to the other, just as she had done when working at Booster Brake. The press took note of her pace, reporting that Miss Ethel Merman didn't need to take vitamins, but perhaps they might consider taking her. When *Girl Crazy* went to Philadelphia for tryouts, the audience response was extremely encouraging, and the group was convinced it had a good show on its hands. Still, no one was prepared for what happened when it opened in New York's three-year-old Alvin Theatre.

Composer George Gershwin had been conducting his own work for most of 1930, and on that warm October night, he did just that with *Girl Crazy*, leading an orchestra that included Red Nichols, Benny Goodman, Gene Krupa, Glenn Miller, and Tommy and Jimmy Dorsey. At the onstage piano was Roger Edens, sitting in for Al Siegel, who had called in ill, some say with a case of stage fright. Agnes and Edward Zimmermann were in the audience to see their daughter; Siegel may or may not have actually come to watch. Producer Alex Aarons, a nervous wreck, hid out backstage in the packed house.

The first act was going well. Merman sang the second to last song as Kate, in Danny's new Arizona club. "Sam and Delilah" recounts the story of a "loose woman who falls for a married man and refuses to let him return to his wife alive" (one reviewer called it a "mixture of Wild West, Negro spirituals and Broadway 'blues'").[5] The audience loved it. Recalled Ethel, "Everybody screamed and you know, I thought something fell down or something, but it was only the audience reaction to a young girl coming out singing a song." Ira Gershwin was especially relieved, since he felt he hadn't done his best with the lyrics: "placing . . . 'hooch' and 'kootch' on long full notes of a slow-blues tune. . . . I got away with it thanks to Merman's ability to sustain any note any human or humane length of time. Few singers could give you *koo*—for seven beats . . . and come through with a terrifically—*tch* at the end."[6]

But it was when the twenty-two-year-old stenographer reemerged for the act's last number that Broadway history was made. Wearing a simple red blouse and black slit skirt, Ethel sang "I Got Rhythm." Ira's lyrics brimmed with confidence and gusto—no half-blue lament here. (His quick staccato words had not been easy to come up with, though: the dummy lyric used for a long time was "Roly-poly / Eating slowly / Ravioli / Better watch your diet or bust.")[7] Merman's voice was perfect for its energetic rhythm and almost pentatonic sound. With the song's high ratio of notes to lyrics (four notes for three words for the title refrain alone), a singer without Merman's crisp diction or unable to handle fast pacing would sink like a stone. Ethel sailed. With galelike power, she gave it her all, holding onto that *I-I-I-I* for over sixteen (some say up to thirty-two) measures.[8] One writer said it was "a feat equivalent to swimming the length of an Olympic-size pool at least twice without coming up for air." The audience went wild, leaping to its feet, and cheered for more. "By the fourth bar, the audience was going nuts," recalls Roger Edens. "She did about ten encores" before the show could go on.[9]

Dorothy Fields, who was in the audience that night, has said, "I've never seen anything like it on the stage except Mary Martin when she did *My Heart Belongs*. It . . . was an ovation like you just can't believe. And she seemed a little stunned herself, and you know, she stood there not quite believing it. And encore after encore. . . . No one had ever held a note like that . . . beyond the length of endurance."[10]

First-act closers are traditionally show-stoppers, but that night "I Got Rhythm" was less a stopper than an explosion. Shell-shocked producer Aarons practically collapsed—he thought a gunshot had gone off—and then saw that the shot was the roar of the crowd. "American audiences don't cheer. Italian audiences at the Scala in Milan yes, but American audiences at the Alvin in New York . . . ," he said later to Guy Bolton.[11] When the first-act curtain came down, he, Freedley, Bolton, McGowan, and the Gershwins knew the show was a hit. An excited George Gershwin ran to Ethel's dressing room to dispense a critical piece of counsel: never, he told her, take a singing lesson.

Later, Gershwin said that he lost three pounds that evening just from sweat. Merman, by contrast, scarcely realized what had happened. After the show, she took the subway back home to Astoria and the next day, October 15, returned to the city for a luncheon date at the Gershwins'. Entering the penthouse, she saw that newspapers were scattered everywhere, covering the piano, the floor, furniture. Had she seen the reviews? No. They read them to her: "Miss Merman's effect . . . was such that there was every reason to believe that they would make her sing it all night"; ". . . Ethel Merman, whose peculiar song style was brought from the night clubs to the stage to the vast delight last evening of the people who go places and watch things being done." The *New York Daily Mirror* reported that Merman "tied the proceedings in knots," predicting "this girl bids fair to become the toast of Broadway."[12]

Critics struggled to compare Ethel with other singers or to find the words to describe this "musical fire engine."[13] "Without losing her personal quality, she combines a number of the virtues of Libby Holman and Ruth Etting."[14] Yet Merman was "not mournful and lugubrious like Libby Holman," not "tear-stained and voice-cracked. Rather she approaches the sex in a song with something of the philosopher. She rhapsodizes, but she analyzes. She seems to aim at a point slightly above the entrails, but she knocks you out all the same."[15]

For *Time,* Ethel was simply the show's "biggest asset."[16] Of the show, Baird Leonard opined that it didn't "come within a mile of the score . . . [and] just when you have made up your mind that you are in the wrong theatre, a little girl, Ethel Merman by name, strolls casually in singing about Sam and Delilah . . . and *Girl Crazy* becomes what it is, a good show. Miss Merman's other big number, 'I Got Rhythm,' puts her at the head of the class of those girls who chant in our odd, modern manner."[17] Pop pasted the glowing reviews into his scrapbooks, albums that seemed filled with a new mission: documenting the ascent of a Broadway star.

Every Broadway historian and serious Merman fan knows the stories about *Girl Crazy*'s opening night and Gershwin's advice against singing lessons. Merman told and retold them to reporters for half a century. Both stories helped solidify her image as an untrained *natural,* her Broadway success a matter of being discovered, like prospectors digging for gold. Later, she claimed she "had it easier than Cinderella," her gifts recognized by no less a prince than George Gershwin. Equally crucial factors were the sustained note and the force and clarity of her voice while sustaining it. With such colorful descriptions as the Olympic pool remark, the press was turning the big-lunged Ethel into a force of nature, one that was nearly superhuman.

In addition to the voice, there was also Merman's commanding presence and her rather stunning self-confidence. Guy Bolton recalled in 1960, "Ethel . . . had the same confident stage presence, the same trumpet-toned voice that she has today."[18] Her son remembered in 2004, "She *always* would say how much she *loved* her work, and that she took enormous pride in what she could do, but she never wanted to be seen as 'full of herself.' . . . What *I* would call being full of an *appreciation* of herself, she'd simply call self-assurance or self-confidence."[19]

The idea of Ethel's overnight discovery resonated deeply with contemporary audiences. It made sense: during the Depression, the fantasy of leaving one's socioeconomic station and hitting the big time was utterly compelling. Of course, that myth had long been pivotal to the American success story, one in which pull-yourself-up-by-the-bootstraps determination—material conditions be damned—was all it took. In this narrative, success was a matter of individual resolve, not collective action. That ethos was reflected in the popular nineteenth-century boys' stories of Horatio Alger, in tales of upward mobility whose heroes were made of determination and hard work, assisted here and there by a big dollop of good luck.

Early Broadway shows had capitalized heavily on such myths in the late 1910s and '20s, especially in stories involving women moving from rags to riches; Marilyn Miller's fame, for instance, had been secured by one such show, 1920s *Sally*. In Ethel's case, however, it was her actual life story that fit the mold rather than any show or character she portrayed. Early program notes read like Alger stories in miniature. For *Girl Crazy:* "Ethel Merman less than a year ago was pounding a typewriter in an auto appliance plant in Long Island City. It was here, most likely, that she 'got rhythm.' . . . last spring Miss Merman met Al Siegel and they formed an alliance for vaudeville. Their act put them in top demand and, after a swing around the country, they landed in Brooklyn, where they stayed for seven weeks. This appearance preceded their present engagement." Hyperbole was already at work: Siegel and Merman never went around the country; her only trips outside the New York area were the Philadelphia tryouts of *Girl Crazy* and the engagement in Miami. Other versions emerged. The *New Movie Magazine* wrote, "Here is the story of a girl who didn't wait to be discovered, but went out and fought her way to success."[20]

Broadway had thus unearthed Ethel's talents and justly rewarded them. The real Broadway, of course, has always been a rather undemocratic, vicious beast, but small matter: its shows are there to peddle myths, not to live up to them. And the myth of an outsider talent being recognized has become such a staple as to be the mainstay of the story lines themselves—a tradition still upheld by early twenty-first-century hits such as *Wicked* and *Hairspray*. The 1930 success of *Girl Crazy* suggests that the show contained just the right kind of fairy-tale dust for all concerned: singing star, viewers, producers. The show was, after all, up against some tough odds: the stock market crash of 1929 had ended many a new Broadway opening (especially for musicals, always more costly). In addition to preempting most theater construction, the crash helped hasten the demise of the large revues that had dominated the Great White Way for over a decade.

Not quite a story of rags to riches, Ethel Merman's is one of raw talent paying off overnight in a fairy tale of promise and song and dance numbers. (Why has no one made a musical out of it? If New York mayor Fiorello LaGuardia got one, why not Ethel Merman?) When Pete Martin asked her outright,

"Ethel, would you say you had to struggle or was it a little like Cinderella?" she responded, "I think it was a little like Cinderella because *Girl Crazy* was given to me on a silver platter. . . . I mean that part made me overnight." And then she went to say how she was very fortunate, since after *Girl Crazy* there was "one thing right after the other. They kept going up up up up up up up all the time. So there's somewhat of a Cinderella story, I think, Pete." (Martin decided to put harder edges on her modesty, rendering it tougher, vernacular, and more "Merman": "I made Cinderella look like a sob story. . . . The way I figure it, Cindy's tale is a downbeat one compared to mine.")[21]

Unlike the Horatio Alger myths, Cinderella—a sort of distaff equivalent—does not participate in her fate so much as await it. Yet Merman's background as a stenographer casts her as a toiler with spunk and drive (recall the revisionist rumor of her writing her own recommendation), a woman who doesn't passively await anything. At the same time, however, and despite being a real workhorse, Ethel never had to struggle to break into the business. And she never pretended that she did.

Whatever form it took, Ethel's (quasi) rags-to-riches story fueled the hopes of everyday people across a variety of social and economic lines. Any office girl or newspaper boy could make it, just as a boy born in a log cabin could become president in this imaginary world of equal opportunity. The twenty-two-year-old woman was ideally cast, and the press played it up:

> Every office and every community has its "Ethel Merman." You all know the girl. She is around 20, maybe a stenographer, or department store clerk or school teacher. She does her daytime job well and then at night is the life of the party. But most of these "Ethel Mermans" are never heard of in Hollywood or on Broadway. And why? Because they are unwilling to work and fight for stardom. . . . It's really all a matter of courage. [That's] the kind of determination and never-say-die attitude which brought the real Ethel Merman to the peak of success.[22]

Now, it's always best to take any story of "firsts"—first nights, first inventions, first discoveries—with a grain of salt, for they too are myths, myths of beginnings and of origins. In the beginning there was Merman. And she was good. And on the seventh day, she quit her day job. And on October 14, 1930, that woman emerged into the light. Yet as much as that evening put Merman into musical theater history, it's important to stress that she was *not* an unknown quantity before then. As Edens later reminded his interviewer, "By the time of *Girl Crazy*, Ethel Merman was well known around town. Out of town tryouts had established she was gonna be a knockout."[23] Dorothy Fields remembered, "I knew her when she tried out for *International Revue,* a show that [Jimmy] McHugh and I did. . . . Mermsy . . . came to the Mills Office to try out. She was a stenographer and she had a great voice, but they wanted a Gertrude Lawrence type for this revue. . . . [Producer Lew] Leslie had this passionate crush on Gertrude Lawrence and was determined to get her. . . . it was our misfortune, because shortly after that, she did *Girl Crazy.*"[24]

Girl Crazy: Impact and Aftermath

At the time of *Girl Crazy,* the Broadway musical was a form very much under construction, still in its growing pains. The plot lines were mostly thin and undeveloped, despite exceptions like Jerome Kern's monumental *Showboat* in 1927. Plots and characters usually existed to move the proceedings from one production number to another; there was not necessarily any meaningful relationship among them. Unlike *Porgy and Bess* (1935), the Gershwin brothers' exquisite "folk opera" that melded serious story line to sophisticated score, *Girl Crazy* was not terribly ambitious or novel. People enjoyed it, and George's score was duly lauded, but as a musical, little of it was truly exceptional. In fact, it might not enjoy its rather exalted place in musical theater history if it hadn't *been* for Ethel Merman.

In the 1920s, a show run of one hundred performances was enough to make it a hit; in the early '30s, it took a run of about two hundred to see a return of the initial investment. *Girl Crazy* ran for 272 performances, longer than *Porgy and Bess* would (its innovations puzzled more than a few critics and theatergoers). *Girl Crazy*'s numbers were respectable indeed. It closed in June 1931, partly because of the summer heat, which always caused the box office to dip, especially since New York theaters were not yet air-conditioned.

Girl Crazy and especially its songs—"I Got Rhythm" in particular—have enjoyed a good afterlife. Twice, in 1932 and 1943, Hollywood released adaptations; Judy Garland and Mickey Rooney starred in the 1943 version. A third, heavily modified one came out in 1965—*When the Boys Meet the Girls,* which featured Connie Francis and a most unusual blend of musical costars: Louis Armstrong, Herman's Hermits, and Liberace.

For Merman, *Girl Crazy* exemplified the kind of musical that would characterize almost all of her work on Broadway: lighthearted stories filled with catchy, show-stopping numbers. And the songs were what mattered. Before it opened, critics may not have considered nightclub performer Ethel Merman as so completely different from other girl singers, but once *Girl Crazy* started, reviewers were tripping over themselves trying to separate her from the rest of the pack. Reviews would single out her "rock solid," physical sense of rhythm and quickly dubbed her New York's "Rhythm Girl."[25] *Girl Crazy's* fine score showed the world how Merman could punch out strong rhythmic phrasing of her material, marking the beat hard and keeping to it. She negotiated complex rhythmic patterns and high note-to-word ratios with ease ("I Got Rhythm" has both) and held down strong melodic and rhythmic lines alone and in duets. In many instances, it was Merman's delivery that has made "her" hits as memorable as they've become.

"I Got Rhythm" is a case in point. As a 1930 reviewer wrote, Ethel's best work was not in Libby Holman–styled "torch songs" but in "rhythm songs" like Gershwin's tune.[26] "Rhythm" enjoys as solid a place in the history of Broadway as it does in jazz and was recorded by artists such as Lionel Hampton, Art Tatum, Louis Armstrong, Red Nichols (the trumpeter responsible for assembling the orchestra for *Girl Crazy's* premiere), Benny Goodman, the Dorsey brothers, Ella Fitzgerald, Ethel Waters, and Lena Horne. Still, Merman's version remains quintessential; "Rhythm" belongs to her in a way that history won't change. Twenty years after introducing it to the world, she took its refrain for her first memoirs, *Who Could Ask for Anything More?* owning the piece as singers often do (Mary Martin's autobiography is *My Heart Belongs . . .*).

Other popular hits of the twentieth century have been permanently "Mermafied" through her initial performance of them. Cole Porter's "Blow, Gabriel, Blow," for instance—a piece that *describes* Merman's voice as crisply as she performed it—has been covered by singers such as Mary Martin, Carol Burnett, Patti LuPone, Klea Blackhurst, and, improbably, Jonathan Pryce[27]—yet in the public imagination, Merman's version towers over theirs.

While *Girl Crazy* was still on the boards, Ethel continued working at other singing jobs during evenings after the show or on days off, exhibiting the same energy she'd had when holding a full-time day job. She performed at Manhattan's prestigious Casino in the Park several times, sometimes sharing the bill with members from the Gershwin show. One night she played there with the De Marcos dancing team; another time, with material arranged and played by Edens.

Merman had great fondness for the enormously talented Roger Edens (1905–70), whom she and other intimates called Buster. Merman described their friendship as close as one between brother and sister, with a sweet and special closeness that would last their entire lives. Writes son Bob Levitt, "Mom would become the Queen of Broadway and Buster, Roger Edens, would become one of the most clever and kindly gentlemen in all of show business; a sweet *giant* of unpretentious creativity, a large, soft-speaking man from Texas—funny and sharp, honest and loyal and musical from head to toe. Every Queen should have a Buster! Roger was such a *good* Buster he had *two* Queens. Mom shared him with Judy Garland. Reflecting on that in her autobiography, she says, '. . . he was as close to her as he was to me.'"[28]

In her autobiography, Ethel mentioned her shows with Edens at the upscale Central Park Casino. "We got as big a thrill peeking out at the audiences as they did listening to us. Before we'd go on, Buster would say, 'Eth, look who's sitting there tonight.' And we'd be thrilled to see Mayor Jimmy Walker, Marlene Dietrich, A. C. Blumenthal and Peggy Fears, Noel Coward. . . . It was like getting paid for doing something you would gladly pay to do."[29] Edens later recalled the same thing: "It was so much fun to see her with all these people with *savoir faire* and she loved it. You know, there's a great naivety in Ethel. Completely. She and I would stay in one of the back rooms and look through to see who was out there tonight."[30] For Bob Levitt, in those moments, "Ethel and Buster were peeking out at *their own future;* their soon to come parity with the Central Park Casino's elite clientele. But knowing my mother as I do . . . I feel comfortable in my guess that Ethel and Buster were not just 'under the influence' of being in thrilling company, they were already high—on their own genius."[31]

Ethel's other off-board activities included a benefit on Sunday, December 20, 1930; earlier that year, on November 4, and later on March 31, 1931, she teamed up again with Edens, this time playing with Leo Reisman's orchestra along with the popular and widely liked piano player Eddy Duchin. Edens accompanied Ethel again at the Palace with fellow composer and pianist Johnny Green, playing on twin pianos (both Edens and Green would go on to have stellar careers in Hollywood at MGM's Music Department). And Ethel was making frequent live appearances at film theaters, opening for pictures at Manhattan's Paramount and in the Bronx at the Paradise. Later, in Jersey City, she opened for *Red Headed Woman,* whose star, Jean Harlow, would soon be announced as a big Merman fan.

New York's top nightclub performers at the time included Rudy Vallee, Guy Lombardo, Morton Downey, and Cab Calloway. Ethel performed with them all, appearing with Vallee and Downey in the spring while *Girl Crazy* was still running. Her busy schedule was not restricted to clubs, and in March she and *Girl Crazy* costar W. M. Kent were photographed "signing the petition to call the new Hudson Bridge Washington Bridge."[32] On April 23, 1931, she appeared on the NBC radio show *The Bond Bread Sunshine Program* (the same official letter inviting her also requested her autograph), and, that same month, Ethel was featured in newspaper ads for "Rhythm Clothes," specially dubbed that at Bloomingdale's for its fifty-ninth anniversary.

One of the ways that Broadway shows of the time generated publicity was through photo-comic strips that ran in newspapers. Stars were photographed, and their faces were placed in animated situations. Typically two or three actors would appear chatting, and the strip would culminate in a hokey gag. Olive Brady (Tess Parker in *Girl Crazy*) and Merman were featured in one:

BRADY: I saw you at Dave's party last night.

MERMAN: I hoped you wouldn't.

BRADY: Who's that terrible-looking man you were with?

MERMAN: My husband. [looking up a little haughtily]

BRADY: My mistake. [embarrassed]

MERMAN: No, mine![33]

As by-the-numbers as the gag is, the press was already at work on Ethel's image: a woman for whom romance was something to joke about; marriage, a goofy tough-luck story. That aspect of Merman's persona would be fed by future roles and fortified toward the end of her real life, when, after four failed marriages, she told interviewers she was better off single and was definitely *not* on the market, laughing it off with, "What, with my track record?" That casualness didn't reflect Ethel's actual feelings about marriage or her respect for it as an institution, but even the 1930s comic shows the production of the Merman public persona—ironically, at a point when Ethel was still very much an eligible bachelorette.

Ethel was actively enjoying her new social life. She enjoyed the company of successful New York businessmen, wisely eschewing men in show business. To the press Ethel was discreet and deliberately sketchy about her romantic entanglements, although some of them, such as the one with Stork Club proprietor Sherman Billingsley, soon became a well-known secret. For now, though, Ethel was playing the field, simply enjoying the new world with men newly available to her.

Merman's career began in an era when stars could, in a sense, emerge organically, free of prefabrication and hype. This is not to say, however, that the media were anything but fully involved in transforming the young woman into a certain type of woman, a certain type of star. We read over and over that Ethel wanted to be a singer from the get-go (which is true) but never dreamed of becoming a Broadway musical star (probably also true). But from the start, there was already a blurry boundary between Merman and the media. A year after her big break in *Girl Crazy,* Merman told an interviewer, in a characteristic mix of pride, modesty, and frankness:

> The more I talk to stage stars about their early beginnings the more I realize how lucky I have been. Perhaps the fight to get on top eluded me because I had no burning ambition for the stage. I did feel that I would love to loll in the spotlight of stage popularity, but I made no definite move for a stage career. As a matter of fact, I did not consider myself possessed of the necessary qualifications for success and, therefore, kept from looking for a theatrical engagement. I imagine there must be any number of girls like myself who can sing or dance or act, but somehow they haven't the courage to forsake what they're doing for a try at the stage. And, in a way, they cannot be blamed. I heard so much of the hardships of the theatre that I was honestly scared off.[34]

As Mermanesque as this might appear, the heavy hand of an editor is in evidence. What high school kid tosses out lines such as "forsake what they're doing" or "I did not consider myself possessed of the necessary qualifications for success and, therefore, kept from looking for a theatrical engagement"? The revised speech shows that the press was casting Ethel in the mold of a well-raised young lady, one with properly reined-in ambitions.

Equally appropriate to the image the media was cultivating was Ethel's enthusiasm for the leading female entertainers of the day, especially singers. Today, of course, it's hard to find an entertainer in North America who doesn't report having been starstruck as a child or having entertained fantasies of becoming one herself, whatever her origins. But when Ethel was coming into her own, the machinery of the star system was relatively unestablished, and her open admission to being both fan and prospective star was nowhere near as commonplace as it is now. Indeed, Ethel's remarks seem closer to what working-class women would admit to gossiping about around the water cooler; few successful grandes dames of theater or opera would publicly announce such enthusiasm for other entertainers and potential competitors.

George White's Scandals of 1931

During the 1920s, audiences had flocked to revues, especially those put on by leading impresarios Florenz Ziegfeld, Earl Carroll, and George White. White had been producing his huge *Scandals* revue on Broadway almost every year since 1920 (he skipped 1930). By the early '30s, the heyday of the revue had run its course, but for some reason, during the 1931–32 season, all three of the top producers released shows—and *George White's Scandals of 1931* was one of two biggest he'd ever put on.[35]

Knowing that Merman would give the show the adrenaline it needed, White paid a reported twenty-five thousand dollars to buy her out from her contract with Aarons and Freedley, and in August, she signed up and joined the *Scandals,* already in tryouts in Newark. *Scandals* opened on September 14, 1931, at the Apollo Theatre, at 219 West 42nd Street. Lew Brown and Ray Henderson wrote the songs (partner DeSylva had recently left for Hollywood). Ethel introduced the show's hit, "Life Is Just a Bowl of Cherries," a song that offered a palliative to Depression-era America. Act 1 began with "The Marvelous Empire State," a skit with Ray Bolger (the "extraordinary toe and heel clown") and "The Most Beautiful Show Girls on the Stage";[36] it closed with Everett Marshall performing "That's Why Darkies Were Born" in blackface. This was not a typical closing number or a typical blackface. Brown's lyrics showed both compassion and complacency regarding the racism that forced a people to "laugh at trouble" and "be contented with any old thing." It was a sign of a subtle shift. Though Broadway was still a largely segregated, white-dominated affair at the time, that same season saw all-black shows such as *Fast and Furious* and *Singin' the Blues* opening, and two years later, Ethel Waters would be performing as the only black headliner in Irving Berlin's revue *As Thousands Cheer,* singing the plaintive "Suppertime," a story of a woman preparing dinner knowing that her husband, a lynching victim, will not be returning home for it.

Merman's other numbers in *Scandals* included "Ladies and Gentlemen, That's Love" and "My Song" in a duet with "Vagabond Lover" Rudy Vallee, the radio and club star making his Broadway debut. (Writing in openly gay codes, critic Brooks Atkinson said that the appearance transformed Vallee "from a lavender myth to a likable reality.")[37] Lavender or not, Merman later couldn't recall even shaking hands with her big costar. Al Goodman conducted, and every night Ethel sang the show's penultimate number, and the finale, "The Wonder Bar," with the entire company.

For the *Scandals,* reviews were good, and for Merman, they were remarkable. The *New Yorker* wrote, "There is nothing startling about [the show], but, while it is going on, you get the feeling of having a good time, which is, I suppose, practically the same thing as *having* a good time. . . . [Merman is there] with a new set of gestures and a voice which excites without embarrassing."[38] "Ethel Merman has been called in to croon things in her lusty way, whereby she seems to take all Newark and Nebraska into her confidence in one fell whoop."[39]

A New Jersey man who had seen the show sent Ethel a letter: "I saw 'Scandals' last Monday night and I applauded your singing so energetically and with such enthusiasm that when I stopped I discovered that my wrist watch had also stopped. Since it was you that made me applaud so much, thereby causing my watch to go out of order, I am looking to you for a new one. Its value is $12 and I thank you in advance."[40] There's no indication how Ethel responded.

Walter Winchell reckoned that in a twenty-two-month career, the young singing star had taken in a hundred thousand dollars—an impressive figure, but then Winchell always obsessed over salaries.[41] Although Ethel's going rate was half of Ruth Etting's, the figures are nonetheless staggering, given that this was taking place in a city reeling from the Depression. (Just seven months before the *Scandals of 1931* opened, the sixty-branch Bank of the United States tanked, affecting four hundred thousand depositors. With over a third of New York's residents affected, it became the worst bank failure in American history.)

The *Scandals of 1931* ran for six months and over two hundred performances. It became legendary, not only because of its robust run, or the talents of Merman, Bolger, Vallee, and the Howards or Marshall's astonishing blackface, but also for a small public brawl that broke out between George White and Lew Brown in the lobby on opening night. Reports vary on what sparked the altercation; neither was known to be a particularly calm fellow. Brooks Atkinson wrote that it was a result of an attempt by Brown and the other composers to get an injunction against White, who had made changes to the show's music without their written consent. Brown and White never worked together again.

It was with *Scandals* that Merman could tease George White about his earlier offer to put her in the chorus after reading Caleb Bragg's letter of introduction. These jokes were not a problem, and Ethel was as at ease interacting with the show's big-time producer as she was with its gypsies. Among the latter was an aspiring young singer named Alice Faye, who at one point asked Merman for a ten-dollar loan. Ethel preserved Faye's thank-you in her scrapbook.

Playbill's "Who's Who in the Cast" wrote, "Ethel Merman is considered by George White as one of the outstanding musical comedy stars of the contemporary theatre. . . . Her appearance at the Palace Theatre won her new honors and she was signed for an important role in 'Girl Crazy,' her first

Broadway appearance, last season. Critics and public alike hailed her as one of the real 'finds' of the decade. Mr. White plans to present her as the star of a new musical comedy when the current 'Scandals' terminates its run."[42] Although White and Merman never did that next show, we do learn just how much the star-making machinery considered her secretarial background key in the making of Ethel Merman.

Early Film Work

Warner Bros. had been the first of Hollywood's major studios to take a gamble with sound. It was they who produced *Don Juan,* the first picture to use synchronized sound in 1926, and they who caused a huge sensation the following year in *The Jazz Singer,* when Al Jolson said, "You ain't seen nothin' yet!" directly, it seemed, to the audience. Other studios were sent scrambling, and Paramount made an especially energetic push into sound, particularly with musicals—a genre suddenly made possible by technology. Paramount adopted stories that had been Broadway musical successes and raided its talent, luring in proven talent such as Rouben Mamoulian, Bing Crosby, and Fred Astaire.

Despite her disappointing experience with Warners, Ethel signed on with Paramount, and in 1930, just before *Girl Crazy,* she appeared in her first feature film, *Follow the Leader.*[43] Initially, *Leader* had run on Broadway as *Manhattan Mary,* an Ed Wynn (1886–1966) vehicle in which he perfected his comic routine as the "Perfect Fool." Gertrude Purcelle and Sid Silvers adapted it from the stage, and the director was Paramount's Norman Taurog (uncle of Jackie Cooper), who went on to helm a long list of short and feature-length musicals, with stars from Ethel to Elvis Presley. *Leader* has Wynn playing a former acrobat, now a bumbling waiter at a restaurant owned by the mother of Ginger Rogers's character. There, a group of gangsters, the Hudson Dusters, force Wynn to kidnap star performer Helen King (Merman) so that Mary Brennan (Rogers) can take her part in *George White's Scandals.* (Some say that Ethel was the last-minute replacement for Ruth Etting, the more established singer to whom the young star was now being compared.) As Helen King, Merman gets to perform Sammy Fain and Irving Kahal's "Satan's Holiday."

Like comedy typical of the era, the humor in *Follow the Leader* was corny and self-conscious, not attempting to cloak its schtick in too much naturalism; Wynn's squeaky voice alone made that impossible. *Leader* incorporated references to current events, situations, and individuals (e.g., Prohibition, George White), even details of its cast members' lives. For instance, although Ethel wouldn't appear in *George White's Scandals* until a year later, it was quite plausible that she might already be its star performer. That she and Ginger Rogers both worked together in *Girl Crazy* within months of *Leader's* release enriches its story, especially since reports varied on just how well Rogers handled the lesser-billed Merman's success in the play. And the presence of Rogers's fictional mother in the movie was not far from real life, since Mother Rogers exerted very tight control over her daughter's career.

The bulk of Merman's work with Paramount, however, was in one- and two-reelers from 1930 to 1933. These short movies would be shown before feature films or in mixed programs interspersed with live acts in a revuelike structure of mixed spectacles. Most shorts ran for about ten minutes, just long enough to sketch out the slimmest of stories and contain two or three songs. The work was hardly taxing for Ethel, and she shot most of these shorts while she worked on *Girl Crazy, Scandals,* and *Take a Chance* at the old Paramount Studios around the corner from the family home in Astoria. Each movie took about a day of her time, and in all, Merman appeared in *Her Future, Devil Sea, Be Like Me, Ireno, Roaming, Old Man Blues, Let Me Call You Sweetheart, Time on My Hands, You Try Somebody Else,* and *Song Shopping.*

The most innovative ones were produced by the New York animation studio of Dave and Max Fleischer, whose films combined animation with live-action photography, something that mainstream studios rarely explored until decades later. The Fleischer Brothers routinely inserted popular performers like Cab Calloway and Rudy Vallee into their cartoons. Paramount was able to get the singers to appear at reduced rates by booking their live acts into the company's film theaters shortly after the shorts were released, enhancing visibility for everyone concerned. In their *Let Me Call You Sweetheart, Time on My Hands,* and *You Try Somebody Else,* Ethel was the featured guest star of their animated flapper heroine Betty Boop, who had also hosted Calloway and Vallee. For the most part, Ethel was rarely required to "interact" with animated portions. *You Try Somebody Else,* for instance, starts with live-action footage of Ethel on a house porch, singing the eponymous song, whose lyrics suggest that she and her lover should try new partners and, when the experiment fails, they'll "be together again." Ethel isn't giving a terribly emotional performance, resembling a schoolteacher recounting a story more than an emoting vocalist. But even though she moves little, there is a twinkle in her eye. The song "You Try Somebody Else" is equally cut adrift from the animated action, which follows a goofy prisoner, released and then "brought together again" in jail after Miss Boop frustrates his attempt to burgle her home. Merman, still on her porch, closes the film, exhorting viewers to sing along as the bouncing ball jumps atop the lyrics on the bottom of the screen. After a few verses, cartoon hieroglyphics replace words (a drawing of an eye standing in for *I*), lending a goofy, surreal air to the proceedings. *Time on My Hands* also features crazy, creative animation (fish, worms, Betty Boop as a mermaid under water) sandwiching Ethel, who sings the title song while seated on the hands of an oversized clock, poised and quietly glamorous, quite unlike Harold Lloyd, whose famous dangling-from-a-clock sequence of *Safety Last!* (1923) the setting evokes.

In *Song Shopping* (1933), Ethel was given featured billing and performs without La Boop. This short gives a wonderful sense of what Merman's performance at the time might have been like. It opens and closes with animated follies of music-making animals at a "song shop," where notes are made out of swatted flies and watermelon seeds, broken records spit out of a meat grinder, mice's curled tails become G clefs, and so forth, and we see a clever cartoon take on the mass production of popular songs. After this introduction, the live-action footage of Ethel begins, accompanied by Johnny Green, now a rehearsal pianist, arranger, and conductor at Paramount. She sings Coslow and Harling's "Sing, You Sinners" and then introduces Green's own "I'm Yours" as one that the audience can follow along with the bouncing ball. After this, Ethel playfully tells Green, "Here's one they'll sing, one you *didn't* write!" and reprises "Sing, You Sinners" in a more syncopated, animated rendition directly facing the camera. *Song Shopping* is a rarity for showing Merman not as a character but as singer Ethel Merman, enjoying banter with Green and lighting up the number with her lively style. *Song Shopping* is a rarity in another way also, having been long unavailable for viewing.[44]

Paramount also distributed Ethel's other, non-Fleischer shorts. The stories hew more or less to the same formula: a down-and-out young woman about to be sentenced for a crime or forced to cope with a philandering husband, an absent lover, or an overbearing father, but thanks to a last-minute change for the better, the situation ends on an upbeat note. This narrative movement, slim as it is, allowed each short to include different types of songs to be performed; in most, the first song was a plaintive, blues-inflected ballad and the second is a rousing cheerer-upper, the musical corollary to the thin story's happy ending (in *Be Like Me,* Ethel sings the same piece two different ways). The tales are predictable fare for Depression-era theatergoers, who might identify with the first Ethel, down-and-out, only to be cheered up by the second one.

Her Future (1930) takes place in one location: at the side of a judge's podium. A young Ethel stands with downcast eyes, awaiting a verdict for an unnamed crime. She wears a dark dress and cap and the long, knotted pearls of a flapper. In this short's rare moments of dialogue, the lawyer of Ethel's character tells the judge that this is her first crime and that his client has confessed to it. The judge looks down and instructs her, "Explain to the court, in your own way, why [you are] here." Merman responds by singing "My Future Just Passed," a tale of broken illusions that makes numerous references to God. The judge decides to release her, and when he asks her her plans, she launches into "Sing, You Sinners," recounting a trip to Dixie, where the "darkies" know how to harmonize. "Bless mah song," she sings. "If you wanna be saved, you gotta behave." Merman, who has respectfully removed her hat for the performance, maintains a persistent animated smile, raises her arms overhead and to the side, turning her hands inward at the wrists in an evangelical delivery she will perfect four years later with Cole Porter's "Blow, Gabriel, Blow."

The next short, *Devil Sea* (1931), starts off on an equally grim note: an older man reports to Ethel's character that her man has been lost in a sea storm. She responds by performing Vernon Duke's bluesy "Devil Sea." In midsong she addresses the sea directly in the spoken song popular at the time (think Al Jolson): "What's another tear to you / It's just another drop of water." Merman moves her hands slightly here, as if to mimic the undulating waves of the sea. And then, the same man returns with the good news that her lover is alive, and Merman bursts into the jazzy, upbeat "I've Got My Man" with much more animated hand movement, entering into a call-and-response with undepicted horns.

Director Casey Robinson (1903–79) had made two-reelers with Helen Kane before he directed Merman in *Roaming* (1931), a film for which young Johnny Green supplied two songs. Ethel plays Mary Rock, daughter of Colonel Rock, whose traveling medicine show she shills. It opens with Mary guiding a horse-drawn wagon through a wooded area singing "Hello, My Lover, Goodbye," in which she laments her inability to find love because of her life on the road. Her second number is an exuberant "Shake Well Before Using," in which Mary invites a grumpy audience to buy the family product, so that they can smile as she does.

When a local man flirts with Mary, he is ordered away by her father, who chides her for her romantic yearnings: "Remember, you're a show girl, and to these yokels that means you're an indecent girl." The prediction proves true when the same man pounces on Mary after the show. Yet as the Rocks leave town the next day and he stows away on their wagon, Ethel/Mary forgives him just as abruptly as Merman discovered that her partner was still living in *Devil Sea*. Sophisticated, these things are not; delightful, they are.

Old Man Blues (1932) is the least Mermanesque of the shorts. This is the one that evokes operetta, with all dialogue sung and Merman nearly trilling several lines. Once again the action occurs on a single set, a fog-shrouded woods with an eerily ethereal quality. (Max E. Hayes did set design.) Beginning with a close-up of "Helen and Paul" carved into a tree and then revealing to us that the tree no longer stands, this is Ethel's only one-reeler that shows the passage of time and, in that regard, offers a bit more complexity than the others. A tall enigmatic man in a long dark robe and hat (Hal Forde) appears beside Helen, Ethel's character, and the two duet in "Old Man Blues," in which this villainous figure tells her that now that her man is gone, *he* will always be there to laugh at her distress. She has "sent for him," he informs her, by sending her man away. No, she sings, he "wasn't sent off, he just went off—why, I'll never know."

Ethel's delivery here is about as close as she came to light opera, and a number of singers, vocal coaches, and other professionals maintain that Ethel could have had a career in that world. "Judging from the recordings she made in the thirties," says Gary Wedow, chorus master of the New York City Opera, "Merman would probably have made a good opera singer."[45] Operetta's appearance in this film is curious, for, by the late 1920s and early '30s, it seemed one of the few forms of American popular music that was a holdout of "pure" white European culture. Although its popularity was on the wane, it hadn't vanished entirely, especially in Hollywood, thanks in large part to Jeanette MacDonald and Nelson Eddy. Its overlap with Merman is restricted to this brief film.

Ethel's second song, "He Doesn't Love Me Anymore," is a somber ballad. But, surprise! Paul returns, first through a reflection in a pond into which Helen is considering throwing herself. "He Doesn't Love Me Anymore" becomes "*You*'ll Never *Leave* Me Anymore," which she sings while clutching the suddenly materialized man. Old Man Blues skulks off.

Ireno and *Be Like Me* (both 1931) feature characters that are in keeping with the persona that her stage and singing roles were swiftly establishing. In *Ireno*—not to be confused with the 1919 stage musical *Irene* or with Ethel's future role as Reno Sweeney in *Anything Goes*—Ethel plays New York singer-actress Irene, in town to divorce absentee husband Cliff. She mingles among a group of wealthy visitors, laughing and drinking as they proclaim, "Everyday is independence day" in Reno, referring to Nevada's liberal divorce laws. Like theirs, Irene's view of marriage and divorce is caustic and supremely casual: "Pretty place, Reno. The judge separates you from your husband, and the wheel separates you from your money."

Once Cliff's name comes up, however, sincerity eclipses Irene's cavalier cynicism. The lyrics of "Shadows on the Wall" recount her being haunted by his after-image. (In an interesting visual, their relationship is depicted *as* a shadow show, shot from behind a curtain with the back lighting and silhouette common to studio musicals of the period.) When Cliff literally emerges out of the shadow to Irene's table, it takes but a moment for her to change her mind and forgive him. She sings an upbeat "Wipe That Frown Right Off Your Face," not just to Cliff, but to the entire group in Reno. It's a song that redresses not only Irene's romantic woes but also the travails of contemporary audiences, with lines referring to people whose "spirits are busted . . . this must be readjusted." It is pitched to lift the mood of an entire movie theater, much as Merman—and perhaps "Irene" the stage star—was doing in live shows. Indeed, this film shows very little stretch between Irene the performer and Merman the performer, giving audiences a great look at Ethel's emerging performance style: the hanky clutched in her hand, the numerous sparkling bracelets. What's more, Ethel moves with special ease in *Ireno,* whose camerawork is more fluid than in the other films. She enunciates every letter, every syllable, of the rousing song, and its very lyrics seem to allude to her as a star: "If you can't sing good, just sing loud."

Be Like Me follows much the same formula and, like *Ireno,* nears the kinds of characters Merman was and would be playing on the boards. It also shows the extent of the "ethnic flexibility" in Ethel's persona. Here she plays Eve, a saloon girl–bartender in a southwest mining town. When the local boss announces that the State Department is no longer going to protect the thinly populated area and that he'll be taking "the Americans" (i.e., the white folks) to San Francisco, he also announces that he plans to leave behind Merman's love interest, Billy "Smitty" Smith, a small, feckless fellow who bears the same name as the man Merman will marry at the end of the decade.

Eve is the toughest—and least Anglo—of the "broads" Ethel played in the shorts. Her dark curled hair—topped with a big curl on the cheek—is short enough to show large hoop earrings; her outfit consists of a houndstooth skirt and a gathered blouse. Eve's interactions with Rita, her Chicana coworker, are relaxed, as they are with a black worker reporting trouble in the mine. The café's customers are a pair of Africans: one a white colonial caricature, replete with pith helmet, pinched British accent, and monocle; the other a black Francophone. Their presence is quite unmotivated by the story line, serving, one supposes, as comic viewers of the imminent brawl and adding to the picture's strange ethnic styling. Ethel/Eve, for her part, is an Anglo dressed like a Spanish señora who speaks in a Long Island accent.

Significantly, Ethel moves with more ease here than she mustered in the staid *Old Man Blues.* Her songs first urge her saloon audience to look for happiness ("Be Like Me"), and then, alone with the rather dull Smith, turns to the blusier "After You've Gone." After Smith implausibly vanquishes his boss in a brawl, Ethel turns "After You've Gone" into a syncopated festival of joy, scatting several phrases with lifted eyes and arms—vintage Merman.

At the time these short films were made, even big-budget Hollywood features were limited by technological restrictions. This was the beginning of the sound era, when bulky sound-recording devices were attached to the camera, often curtailing its movement. Miking actors was a challenge, so their movements, too, were restricted (something *Singin' in the Rain* sent up in 1952). In the quickly produced, cheap one-reelers, that pared-down aesthetic is even more apparent. Workmanlike and unambitious, they have no aspirations to be anything but vehicles to hang songs on, providing just enough information and visual detail to sketch out a character, a situation, and, sometimes, an identifiable location. With the exception of *Ireno*'s shadow game, Ethel's nonanimated shorts offer few stylistic flourishes. Even the actors were kept to a minimum, with only three people appearing in *Devil Sea, Her Future,* and *Old Man Blues.*

Yet two of these modest films fly in the face of that plain, to-the-point aesthetic. Both *Her Future* and *Devil Sea,* directed by Mort Blumenstock,[46] have a strikingly antinaturalist aesthetic. (Al Siegel is credited with their musical arrangements, although that seems to have no bearing on their look.) The towering podium of *Her Future,* for instance—a good fifteen feet—undoes conventional perspective, dwarfing the judge seated behind it and Merman standing in front of it. Shots are canted, perspective skewed, with walls, floors, and ceilings meeting at impossible corners and angles, and high-key lighting produces shadows in unexpected places. In a sense, the jagged look fits the broken illusions Merman sings about, with the illusion of credible surroundings so destroyed. Much the same occurs in *Devil Sea,* where the action starts atop a tall angled staircase before moving to the floor below in a basementlike interior, where Ethel performs her songs. Like that of *Her Future,* the space is physically impossible.

The visuals of both pictures seem to have popped right out of German expressionism, the movement that characterized Germany's art cinema from the late 1910s to the mid-'20s (e.g., *The Cabinet of Dr. Caligari*). Expressionism looked for ways to press "interior" psychological elements, such as character disturbances or imbalance, onto surface mise-en-scène and visuals. It's rather remarkable that such run-of-the-mill American movies can be read as text-book expressionist pieces, with the dark underside of their story lines (crime and possible incarceration in one, death in the other) conveyed visually, as they are. At the same time, though, these shorts were never intended to present complex characters struggling with madness or despair, but existed simply to showcase a few popular tunes. That incongruity is echoed by placing a working-class all-American figure, Ethel Merman, within this aesthetic of high European art. (Even at this early point in her career, Ethel had gone on record for disliking modern art or even reading books.)

Despite this odd incongruity, the two shorts are not at all campy. When Merman's characters close each of them with fun-loving jazz numbers, the camera simply zeroes in on her, and we lose sight of the improbable, night-marish sets. Perhaps what these pictures ultimately show is how readily in-fluences cross borders between countries and traditions and, in the process, cross the sense of "high" and "low" class or entertainment styles. And there Ethel Merman is, caught in the middle. And given that Merman's appear-ances were being noted by *Die New Yorker Staats-Zeitung* at the time, perhaps this imported visual style was something recent German émigrés might rec-ognize. It is hard to say.

Since little of Merman's career is preserved on film, this handful of shorts provides compelling documentation of her early singing and performing style. "They show how physical Merman was as a performer," says Klea Blackhurst.[47] They also reveal her instinctive sense of control, her comic tim-ing, and her complete lack of stage nerves; she is remarkably at ease in front of the camera. Strangely, however, she seldom talked about the films, not be-cause they were embarrassments, as *The Cave Club* was, but perhaps because they seemed inconsequential in the face of her other work. In her second au-tobiography, for instance, Merman ignores them altogether. She never ac-quired copies of the shorts, despite her penchant for saving all of her record-ings, press clippings, and the like. Tony Cointreau recalls that in the 1970s or '80s the two of them went to the home of a fan in order to view them.[48]

Like press and publicity photos of the time, the films reveal an attractive woman, full-figured but not abundantly so, neither heavy nor thin. And as unself-conscious as she is with her body, it's the face that is most expressive and striking. With her round cheeks and open mouth, Merman seems to light up when she sings, her dark eyes twinkling when performing the upbeat numbers.

That attractiveness is arguably all the greater for not resembling other al-abaster faces or cookie-cutter beauties of the time. And although the press never failed to take note of her appearance—stressing her good looks during this early to mid-1930s period—even then, Ethel's looks were never the mainstay of her image. Both the press and her fans gravitated to her voice, her energy, and her down-to-earth style: "Looks? No, Ethel's not a beauty, and shorn of her plumage and makeup, she might resemble any other nice little girl from Astoria. Her taste in clothes is nothing to shout about; her background is unexciting. But Ethel's got a quality which has made sirens of certain women since Eve was born. Ethel has a greedy, lusty, honest-to-goodness love for life."[49]

Take a Chance

The story of Merman's next hit, *Take a Chance,* can't be told without telling the story of a flop that never made it to Broadway. Back in New York from Los Angeles, Buddy DeSylva partnered with Laurence Schwab to write and produce a show about putting on a show, called *Humpty Dumpty.* Jewish comic Lou Holtz was cast as a theatrical angel who, with his family, provides seventy-five thousand dollars to finance a revue lampooning events of American history, such as the Boston Tea Party and Betsy Ross sewing the first flag. Merman's role was playing torch singer Wanda Brill.

Humpty Dumpty went into rehearsals, and its previews were set to begin at the Nixon Theatre in Pittsburgh, a city that never had the weight that New Haven had as a preview town. Perhaps this was a good thing, for when it opened there on September 26, 1932, *Humpty Dumpty* closed within a week. DeSylva and Schwab did serious surgery, shortening the show, and changing title, book, music, and cast; they briefly renamed it *We Three* and replaced Holtz with Jack Whiting, whom they deemed stronger leading-man material. They added a romantic story with a character played by June Knight; Jack Haley replaced singer Eddie Foy Jr. Vincent Youmans was hired to patch up Richard Whiting and Nacio Herb Brown's score. Ethel Merman was one of the few original featured players whom the producers retained as *Take a Chance* was born.

It got strong reviews in Philadelphia, Wilmington, and Newark. Still, bad luck dogged the show. Merman came down with the flu, causing the November 18 performance in New Jersey to be canceled and the New York opening to be delayed. And on November 24, fire damaged about a third of the entire wardrobe.

Two days later, *Take a Chance* finally opened at the Apollo Theatre, two months to the day of its disastrous Pittsburgh preview. It was an apposite title, opening in the worst year of the Depression and competing against shows such as *Of Thee I Sing, Face the Music, Dinner at Eight, Gay Divorcee,* and Noel Coward and Alfred Lunt in *Design for Living.* The chance paid off. Critics and crowds alike enjoyed it, especially Ethel's four numbers, "You're an Old Smoothie," sung with Haley; her solos, the evangelical "I Got Religion" and "Rise and Shine"; and the fourth, the runaway hit of the show, "Eadie Was a Lady," the homage to the turn-of-the-century madam. Originally the last was written for performer Walter O'Keefe, known for novelty numbers such as "The Man on the Flying Trapeze" and "When Yuba Plays the Tuba down in Cuba." But when DeSylva and Schwab couldn't secure him, they turned the piece into a bigger production number, getting Richard Whiting to modify the lyrics and Roger Edens, already working with Merman, to arrange. (DeSylva also cowrote.) It was so big a hit, its lyrics were printed in the *New York Times.*

One reviewer of the cynical, slightly bawdy torch ballad said, "Perhaps only two persons in all this world savor all the salt that lies in that song, Ethel Merman and Mae West."[50] It was not the only time the two were compared. In "Mae West Old Story, Says Ethel Merman," the *Los Angeles Times* reports, "Accused of sailing in on the Mae West vogue, Ethel chuckles naughtily. 'I began that vogue. I was singing "Eadie was a Lady" all dressed up with the wiggly hips an' everything before Mae West's first picture, "Night after Night," came out. Also, West was the sort of a hussy I was in *Girl Crazy* as the wife of the gambler . . . so I shall always claim Mae sailed to glory on my vogue.'"[51] Their images would be intertwined throughout their lives, as strong, lusty women and as widely impersonated icons among gay men, show queens, and others.[52] Papers of the time wrote that "Eadie" made an impression on no less than Hollywood's "Blond Bombshell," Jean Harlow, who played the recording, she said, to get in the mood for her roles.[53]

Critic Bernard Sobel observed that "Eadie" and *Take a Chance* sailed on a wave of 1890s nostalgia that was also showing up in other Broadway shows of the time, such as the new George White musical *Melody* and *One Sunday Afternoon.* "How nostalgic this song and setting made us for days gone when naughtiness thrived so happily," he wrote.[54] *Take a Chance* was old-fashioned in other ways as well. Some reviewers complained about the outdated physical style of vaudevillian veterans Ole Olsen and Chic Johnson (who replaced Jack Haley and Sid Silvers on June 5): "There was no place for the old-time recruits from burlesque," one opined.[55] John Mason Brown noted that Chic Johnson was "fidgeting and writhing" during one of Ethel's songs; he "should have known better than to try to outplay her . . . he did everything but reach up to the top balcony and turn a spotlight on himself during her song."[56] Whatever other nostalgia *Take a Chance* was trading in, vaudevillian humor, by contrast, had run its course.

Merman, however, could do no wrong. With "Rise and Shine," said one reviewer, she shows herself to be a "revivalist of no mean horsepower. She exhorts you, it is true, to flee not sin but the Depression and all its works. . . . the mood of Vincent Youmans' rugged tune . . . comes straight from the Negro spirituals. And Miss Merman translates its religious ecstasy into an inspirational language of arms and hands and shoulders that is all her own."[57] Ethel's now-trademark hand and arm gestures were gaining note (the *Stage* even sneaked a cameraman into the theater to capture them on film), and reports didn't lack for evangelical (and racial) undertones, especially when commenting on "Rise and Shine":

[Here are her] characteristic devotions: the fluttering hands; the doubled fist extended toward you . . . as though to seize your soul and raise it to heaven; the swing of the hips as she walks, the rolling of the shoulders and the accompanying wave of the head; the cocky stride . . . suggestive of the ancient cake-walk; the clasping of quivering hands, imploring the audience to join in glory; the outspread palms, the raised fingers, the hands flinging at you a message of joy; and, at last, the arms stretched up to Heaven, and the whole body straining to follow upward as though one ounce more of faith would give it soaring wings.[58]

Critics also lauded Merman's ability to turn risqué material into good clean fun, and in that regard she differed deeply from West, who had actually done jail time for her risqué plays in the 1920s. Merman could convey a false, knowing, playful naïveté (for as much as the press had made her the gal next door, that gal was tougher and worldlier than most). That perception attached itself to Ethel on and off the stage. Of the two main categories into which female performers were put at the time, glamour and comedy, Merman was already veering toward the latter. She was too robust and physical for conventional romantic roles and situations, yet at the same time, as a comedian, Ethel was never as over-the-top or as sexually caricatured as West.

In 1932, censorship was a less institutionalized, cautious affair than it is today. Still, some of the press complained that *Take a Chance* took *too many* chances with its potshots at religion, especially in Ethel's numbers. Significantly, no one described Ethel herself as vulgar—that would come later—but some critics found Wanda Brill too bawdy and the book too risqué. (Critic

Ashton Stevens concluded that the reason "Eadie" became such a smash was that it had not been approved or licensed for radio transmission, enhancing the song's appeal onstage and in other venues.)[59]

For a show studded with references to religion and sex, it is surprising even in pre-Code Hollywood that *Take a Chance* was adapted for the silver screen in 1933. Buzz flew about possible optioning: "Only Merman from the original cast will be used and only 'Eadie' and 'Smoothie' songs from the original will be used," wrote *Variety*.[60] Filming was to begin in July at the Eastern Studio in Astoria—the neighborhood's old Paramount Studios. June Knight was retained for the picture, but in the end it was Lillian Roth who played "Wanda Hill."

Ethel didn't take it too hard. By now, she had signed on with Victor records for a sixteen-song recording deal,[61] receiving a hefty five hundred dollars a side against a three-hundred-dollar royalty, an unusually high figure for the time, as the company told reporters. (Singers were rarely paid for both sides of a 78, typically being compensated only for the "hit" side.) Ethel, DeSylva, and company were able to capitalize on *Take a Chance* in other ways. In May 1933, she appeared in *Variety* and the *New Yorker* advertising Lux soap, which always hired glamorous stars to promote its product: "Ethel Merman, feminine star of 'Take a Chance,' says, 'I insist on Lux for my stockings, lingerie—anything washable at all."[62] She also hawked cosmetics and toiletries for Saks in June 1933 and was shown surrounded by shoes in another ad: "I don't 'Take a Chance' when I wear Ansonia Shoes. I Know They Are the Last word in Smartness"—at $5.94 a pair![63] A contest featuring her and her *Take a Chance* costars Haley, Silvers, and bit players Al Downing and John Grant invited readers to provide captions to its "short story snap shots" comics for a twenty-five-dollar prize.[64] And in March 1933, newspaper reports said DeSylva was planning a new musical for Merman, provisionally called *Eadie*.

Take a Chance had given Broadway's critics and its luminaries the chance to note Ethel's extraordinary discipline. DeSylva has said that watching her performances was like going to a movie, they were so invariable.[65] "She was completely reliable, not rote or mechanical," adds Cointreau, saying that Ethel generated the same electric energy and fresh sense of timing whether it was her first night or her hundredth.[66] Marilyn Baker agrees: "They say that Ethel would walk through her shows, especially matinees. Well, I've probably seen more Merman performances than anyone else, and I can tell you, she never walked through a performance. She always gave 100%."[67]

Perhaps a watch could be set to Merman's performances, but she was every bit as able to ad lib if the need arose, to ride with the punches and launch zippy comebacks as quickly as she did offstage. *Take a Chance* had a scene in which Jack Haley's character presents Wanda with a pin. One night, he found the box empty. Panicked, Haley "dashed off to get [it] while she ad-libbed a few lines. When he returned and whispered to her that the pin couldn't be found, the mighty Merman calmly turned to the audience and said, 'Ladies and gentlemen, this is the part where I'm supposed to get the pin. You can't see it—but it's there. Isn't it a lovely piece of junk? All right—now I have it on. Haley, take it from here.'"[68] And they carried on. Ethel kept a tight rein on professional behavior, though, as if deciding which instances could withstand spontaneity or a joke. For instance, in a live version of *Anything Goes,* which aired on NBC in 1954, costar Bert Lahr slips and calls her Annie Oakley (Merman's character from the 1946 *Annie Get Your Gun*) when she's playing Reno Sweeney, the intended of Sir Evelyn *Oakleigh.* The tight shot shows Lahr's flubbed line registering in his face, and he's quite ready to laugh, but Ethel won't bite, continuing with her dialogue without so much as twitching a muscle. But her costars knew Ethel to be a great practical joker. When Haley and Ethel did their love duet in *Take a Chance,* for instance, Sid Silvers, unseen by the audience, would look at her with eyes crossed, trying to bust her up. "Miss Merman," wrote Maurice Zolotow, "is known to other performers as a 'red-hat' . . . someone who 'breaks up' easily when another performer on the stage does something just for his benefit."[69]

Take a Chance was one of the few shows that Merman took out of town. After its Broadway run of 242 shows and some thirty-one weeks, it moved to Chicago's Erlanger Theatre, where it opened on July 10, 1933, for a one-week run. Although the response was good—reviews were positive and box office was strong—Ethel did not enjoy herself, complaining to reporters about the lack of a night life and about the more reserved Chicago audiences. "Merman was afraid of Chicago," recalled Roger Edens. "Afraid. Everybody in New York knew that Ethel was a native of New York but she wasn't a household word in Chicago and Chicago is notorious for being slightly cool to Broadway shows."[70] Ethel Merman, New Yorker, was being born.

THREE

The Early Thirties

To Ethel Merman,
On the Boston Opening of "Red, Hot and Blue":

It's a great day for Boston,
That brings a clever lady to us,
And the play going fans will
Over you make a great fuss.
You'll have boys running in circles,
And the girls raving too,
But it will be all in fun dearie,
They'll be all loving you.

God bless you fair Lady,
On your travels both near and far,
Hard work and real talent,
Made of you a brilliant magnetic star,
I would use the word tremendous,
But Durante might yell,
So Good Luck and fair sailing,
From depths of heart Ethel I wish you well.

poem from Boston fan Jack Curry

A story circulated that young Ethel Merman was so naive that she was almost convinced she needed a passport to move to Manhattan. With the success of *Take a Chance* under her belt, she used that passport for permanent residency in Manhattan when she moved to a tony 25 Central Park West address, bringing her parents, Edward and Agnes, to a neighboring apartment. Adjacent to Central Park at the northern tip of the theater district, the new location made work a short walk or a cab ride away. The Zimmermann clan stayed here for some twenty years, literally moving up as Merman's career ascended, going from the fifteenth to the twenty-first and twenty-second floors—the penthouse with rooftop pools and sunning area. As of this writing, the Century Apartments building was still standing, looking forlorn in the deep shadow of the Trump Towers across the street.

Merman would be connected to New York with a near-unrivaled intensity. Some simple historical reasons lie behind this: she was, after all, a Broadway star, not a Hollywood one, and only rarely did she tour with a shows. "Why should I care what they think about me in Poughkeepsie?" was the crack she fed to reporters. It was in Manhattan that Ethel moved from one stage hit to the next, and it was there that she caused a sensation every time she did. People were able to experience her not just as a singer but also as a performer in shows that added greater resonance to the songs than they might have had out of this kind of context. New Yorkers would soon come to see Ethel not simply as a homegrown commodity but as one of their own: "My mother had a palpable relationship with the New York public," says her son. "One of the things New Yorkers know best and deal with most naturally is *other* New Yorkers. . . . My mother was a New Yorker through and through."[1]

Others found New York embodied in Ethel Merman. After their work together in the 1950s, Mitzi Gaynor said, "Ethel Merman is New Yorkers' dream of what a woman should be: brassy, proud, with a wonderful sense of humor and survival."[2] That New Yorkification was already at work in the early 1930s when the press wrote, "More than being a vibrant person, she is the embodiment of the whole of Broadway, Show Biz, and Tin-Pan Alley. . . . Present-day America has long since taken her to its heart. She is the epitome of its sense of rhythm and the perfect expression of its high spirits and its energy. Her blood stream is a combination of plasma and mazda. Everything Miss Merman touches leaps into life. Every line she reads, every song she sings, is as illuminated as the most dazzling of Times Square's electric signs."[3] And "Ethel Merman's pronunciation of Show-Business English brands her unmistakably as a native of parts not far from Times Square."[4]

It was, in fact, usually the voice that secured the connection with the city: John Chapman wrote, "As an interpeter *[sic]* of Gershwin, Porter and the others she has been, with her physical style and her absolutely sure delivery, 'the to.' Hers is not a beautiful voice, nor a haunting one; it has no more subtlety than Bob Feller's fireball—but Miss Merman can put it right smack over every time. Her enuciation *[sic]* has not the softness of a stylish accent, but is what it always was—plain Queens County, Long Island; yet it is perfect."[5] For Wolcott Gibbs, her voice "is simply the pleasant speech of Astoria, the L. I. accent somewhat overlaid with grace notes she has picked up in the wider world."[6] (Significantly, Merman never covered her accent in speech, even when working in Hollywood, where region-neutral voices were preferred.) But it was *New York Times* critic Bosley Crowther who produced one of the most famous New Yorkifications: "She has a lusty voice which can hold onto and play around with a note as long as the Chase National Bank."[7]

Ethel in Los Angeles

Late in December 1933, Ethel and her mother took a train from Manhattan to Los Angeles, where Ethel was going to work on another picture for Paramount Studios. After finding an apartment, Ethel and Agnes spent their first Christmas apart from Pop, who was still in New York. The move had gone smoothly, although a couple of weeks after arriving, a flood damaged some of their items in storage. "Much to the disgust of Ethel Merman . . . her wardrobe trunks, valued at $300, are a total loss, she learned from the insurance company today. It seems that during the New Year flood her all-metal trunks, stored in the basement of her apartment house, 'floated' out into the basement garage and were crushed between the cars of Mae West and George Raft [neighbors in the building]. The insurance company, when asked to take care of the damage, said it was 'sorry.'"[8]

Ethel had moved to LA to shoot *Cruise to Nowhere,* a shipwreck comedy eventually retitled *We're Not Dressing.* Based on J. M. Barrie's *The Admirable Crichton,* the story starts aboard a luxury yacht owned by heiress Doris Worthington (Carole Lombard). Stephen Jones (Bing Crosby) is a sailor who has caught the heiress's eye, just as *she's* caught the eye of two faux "princes," gold diggers played by Jay Henry and a young Ray Milland. Stephen keeps his distance, tending to his duties (one is taking care of Droopy, the heiress's pet bear, who responds well to his crooning), and is soon fired for his inattentions and "impertinence." Doris's uncle Hubert (Leon Errol, in a part intended for W. C. Fields) spends most of his time drinking and is the generationally mismatched romantic partner of Doris's friend Edith (Merman). Once at sea, the charts fly out the window, and Uncle Hubert takes the helm, promptly running the ship into a reef. In various twosomes, the crew pours into lifeboats or facsimiles thereof—a bicycle mounted on two planks, for the comic relief team of Edith and Hubert. Stephen, who has given his life vest to an unconscious Doris, floats on a barrel with Droopy, who swims them to shore.

Predictably, they have landed on an isolated jungle island, and Stephen is the only group member with survival skills to cook and build shelter, so the others are forced to help him (as Doris pouts on the sidelines). Elsewhere on the island are lions and other animals, which Droopy has now joined, as well as two naturalists, played by Gracie Allen and George Burns, who are pursuing some harebrained research. They learn of the crew's fate through a radio, one of Gracie's many contraptions that she places all over the island. When Doris realizes that their rescue is assured, she befriends Gracie and George and borrows some clothes and building supplies from them, which she then arranges to float to the crew's area of the island in an attempt to catch Stephen's eye. She and Stephen talk, discussing *The Admiral Crichton,* the story on which *Dressing* is based, and its romance between a sailor and a spoiled "little prig"—and Stephen finally admits his love for Doris. When he learns of the ruse she set up with the help of the naturalists, however, he quickly retracts his admission. Feeling ridiculed and angry, he chains Doris up in Droopy's irons but tells her he will refrain from other, presumably violent punishment in a scene that is a little creepy. Finally, as the various couples are rescued from the island, Doris pleads her case to the sailor, assuring him that her love is true. Elsewhere, Edith has to reassure Hubert that she is interested in him and him only, and the picture concludes with Bing singing his love to Droopy's owner.

The comedy reunited Ethel with director Norman Taurog, whom columnist Sidney Skolsky described as "a blimp-like person who issues orders kindly."[9] Top billing went to Crosby, whom Paramount promoted as "singing more songs in one movie than ever before!" and to Carole Lombard. Ethel's second-string credit comes after Burns and Allen's but before Leon Errol's. Throughout the movie, she is set off visually from Lombard, wearing her very dark hair in a short bob in contrast to Lombard's loose, platinum hair. Ethel/Edith is clad in dark-colored clothes, whereas Carole/Doris wears pale satin. Lombard's character is an uptight, spoiled heiress, whereas Merman's, although wealthy, is "of the people," first shown playing cards with the ship's group as Lombard gazes dreamily off the deck.

The movie is Crosby's all the way. He dominates most every scene as the young, dreamy, principled sailor; he is shot with a soft, romantic look, wearing eye shadow that gives him the allure popular with leading men of the late 1920s. The real Crosby, however, was somewhat less dreamy. On more than one occasion, studio gofers had to hunt him down when he didn't show up, finding him eating out or, more often, playing at local golf courses.

Songs were written by Harry Revel and Mack Gordon, and Crosby sings more than seven of them, several, such as "May I?" and "Love Thy Neighbor," more than once. (Droopy the bear can only be tamed when he croons

"Goodnight, Lovely Little Lady.") Ethel has two numbers, "It's Just a New Spanish Custom" and "Let's Be Domestic," and a quick phrase of a third, "It's the Animal in Me." To promote her, Paramount told the press, "Special guards were placed at the doors of the 'We're not Dressing' sound stage at Paramount when Ethel Merman, singing actress, recorded her new songs in the picture" to deter rival "spies."[10] Other reports state that Merman was mobbed by visitors, and once again, "special guards were called to clear the set . . . Hollywood rarely gets excited about performers [anymore]!"

"It's Just a New Spanish Custom" is heard at the beginning of the picture. It is sung for humor, after Edith imbibes part of Uncle Hubert's potent bartending concoctions. When Hubert joins her in dance, goofy sound effects (kazoolike whistles, etc.) accompany them as one kicks the other in the derriere or when the couple makes a dramatic tangolike turn. It's hardly an "ethnic" performance like the one in *Be Like Me,* but "Custom," a song littered with references to Spanish novelties, nonetheless relies on non-Anglo cultures for its laughs.

"Let's Be Domestic" is another comic number, and its humor stems from the very *un*domestic setting of its background; Ethel/Edith sings it as she and Leon Errol/Hubert dash in and out of their new, poorly constructed island huts. In Ethel's other song, the quick refrain of "It's the Animal in Me," she/Edith tries to assure Errol/Hubert that he is the sole recipient of her passions. Crosby sings countless song pieces and refrains, but unlike his, "Animal" doesn't refer to any songs that Ethel has sung earlier. Why? Paramount cut "Animal" from the film and shelved it. Extant records don't fully indicate why. Evidence indicates that censors were concerned with its lyrics' overtones; lines such as "rabbits have habits and so have I," wrote Joseph Breen, were "vulgarly suggestive."[11] Producers may have felt the song would have added too much to the picture's seventy-four minutes or perhaps that it detracted from Crosby, their main attraction. All Ethel knew was that two weeks of recording had gone down the drain.

She may not have had been given star treatment, but Ethel's character is handled with a dignity that motion pictures would not always give her. Her wealthy-but-not-stuck-up character conveys elegance, humor, and humanity. There is nothing caricatured about Edith/Ethel, who is dressed in very attractive dark gowns and evening wear throughout. Her voice, the gags, even the pratfalls—nothing is demeaning to her. (Carole Lombard underwent just as many indignities in her role.) The only anticipation of a bawdy comic Merman occurs when Edith and Hubert, digging for clams, try to start a fire by rubbing some rocks together. He tells her to "hit it harder." "I was only trying to act like a lady," she responds. To which he says, "Why? With all *your* talents?"

We're Not Dressing was released at the end of April 1934. Once again Paramount distributed enormous amounts of promotional material and tie-ins. Given the title, most had to do with clothing: hats promoted by Burns and Allen; "the Bing Crosby Shirt"; and a clothing store promotion by George Burns, who was photographed in a barrel, urging newspaper readers, "Come Down in a barrel, for a complete head-to-toe Spring Outfit, only $49.75 at Wertheimers."[12]

Back in New York for the premiere, Ethel gave the usual round of interviews. Focusing on her singing, one of the resulting articles (titled " 'Forget Your Diaphragm!' Say Crosby and Merman, 'Just Go Ahead and Sing!' ") quotes her as saying, "I went to a music teacher, but the first thing he did was to tell me I wasn't contracting on my diaphragm, and that I probably would never get anywhere unless I watched those breathing muscles. The minute I did so I found I couldn't breathe naturally. That one interview was enough. I went ahead trying to put feeling into my songs, rather than keeping tab on my diaphragm."[13] In addition to never having had singing lessons, Ethel and Bing had another thing in common: both liked to chew gum while they sang, a game they played during production to keep things interesting.

In general, the movie was well received. But Ethel was delighted to be back in New York, even if she remained guarded about her criticism of life in Los Angeles: "Hollywood is a 9 o'clock town with a marvelous climate that affords a wider variety of outdoor diversions than any place in the world."[14] (In reality, Ethel was not a big fan of the great outdoors.) But there was little time for reflection. By fall, she would be in rehearsals for her next Broadway show, *Anything Goes.*

An American Genre

Ethel's stage career took off nearly a year to the day of the stock market crash of 1929. Although it's hard to tell from her own career trajectory, Broadway in the 1930s never recovered to reclaim the widespread cultural power it had in the '20s. By now, it was losing impact and influence to new, mass-transmitted forms, such as radio and film. Indeed, Broadway suffered more than Hollywood and lost many of its talents during the Depression to the deeper pockets of the sunny West Coast: Jimmy McHugh, Roger Edens, Rouben Mamoulian, Fred Astaire, Katharine Hepburn, Eddie Cantor, Bob Hope. The number of Broadway shows opening each season was steadily dropping, especially musicals and revues—a trend that was evident as early as *Girl Crazy.*

The 1930s saw the musical theater undergo considerable change and development. It welcomed the opening of landmark works such as *Porgy and Bess;* more generally, the decade saw a movement away from revues and toward book musicals, those musical comedies with light story lines that enabled easy, if not fully credible, transitions from one number to the next via thinly developed characters and situations—musicals like *Girl Crazy.* An even more important change—and change for the better—involved *who* was working on the Broadway musicals of the '30s. This was the period in which Rodgers and Hart, the Gershwins, Cole Porter, and Irving Berlin did some of their best work. And people like Merman were there to sing that work for audiences.

Thus, even if Hollywood was beginning to cast long shadows, Broadway was into its golden age. (This was also the golden age of popular music, doubling the impact of the musicians in these overlapping worlds.) Plenty of stars kept New York as home; along with Merman were Lunt and Fontanne, Durante, Berlin, Jerome Kern, and audiences continued to turn out for the songs, dances, jokes, costumes, and sets that dazzled the Great White Way. Shows extended promises of hope, potential, fairness, and success; in short, they offered possibilities, fantasies of alternative worlds and feelings to theatergoers (and still do). Even those with serious themes, such as *The Cradle Will Rock,* played out that social hope of how life might be different. (The show's opening night was a fantasy of disenfranchised people overcoming the odds; after composer Marc Blitzstein, producer John Houseman, and others were locked out of their theater as the result of a storm of political censorship, they walked downtown to perform the show with a skeletal cast, a crew, and no more music than Blitzstein's piano onstage.)

That Broadway could get away with more than Hollywood's heavier-coffered but more heavily regulated productions meant the musical had a bit more room to engage those fantasies of other worlds. This aspect of musical theater again helps anchor it deeply in the hearts of fans; it is small wonder that the Broadway musical has always held a special place for so many people, especially those for whom "different worlds" and social organizations have special impact (for instance, gay, lesbian, or queer-identified people).

Although the musical theater is a uniquely American form of entertainment, many of its aesthetic roots are European (French burlesque, British melodrama, operetta). Moreover, as a business—show business—musical theater is typically viewed as entertainment, not art, which gives the musical a rather middle-brow status that has made it an easy target for culture vultures to dismiss for its ostensibly uncultured status and profit orientation. And, despite sparkling exceptions like *The Cradle Will Rock, Candide, West Side Story,* and many others, musicals are not known for taking many political or aesthetic risks, golden era or no. The aim, especially during the Depression, was generally to please, to uplift, and at times to gently, very gently, edify.

As the musical continued to develop, it distanced itself from operetta (too highbrow, European), and from vaudeville and music hall (too lowbrow, working class), to become an exemplar of middle-brow American values. In the early 1930s, its audience was still primarily New Yorkers, and the city was still a city of many working-class immigrants. Broadway remained a relatively affordable form of entertainment, though somewhat less so than in the '20s and much less so than its new rival, sound cinema. Not only did Broadway entertainment embrace American values, it often defined and announced them. Audience members could easily digest its normative fictions as so many spectacular numbers, star turns, and captivating, light, enjoyable tales. The musical comedy was a good salesman. Even *Girl Crazy* dramatized the power of entrepreneurial thinking, assimilation, true love, and responsible citizenship. The Protestant work ethic and its moral equivalent (good is always recognized and rewarded) was told and told again. Reward often took the form of true love (and, in the Depression, a surprise stash of cash to boot—Romeo has an inheritance!). Half fantasy, half ideology, musicals offered a Manichaean world of easily separated good and evil, where the pretentious, corrupt, or mean-hearted would get their comeuppance in the end—and it was characters like Ethel's that would robustly (if naively) dole out their just desserts.

Merman was and would remain one of the most profoundly American figures of this relatively young American genre. Brash and down-to-earth, she moved and spoke in the vernacular of Broadway. (Even if Mary Martin was no less the quintessential American—she, too, excelled as Annie Oakley—her incarnation of that quintessence was more genteel, demure, and not at all "New York.") In other words, Ethel Merman brought bustling vitality to the musical, but the musical also brought it to her and helped with the "Americanization of Merm." Ethel was indeed the perfect star for Depression-era Broadway, with her seemingly irrepressible vitality and her chipper, but devoid of saccharine, spirits. Then there was her own life story, much like the book of a Depression-era musical itself. And she was an interesting woman who broke the rules, with her unusual voice and brassy style, and also embodied them, with her pragmatism and work ethic.

The 1934–35 season was not a bad one for Broadway. Dramas such as *The Children's Hour, The Petrified Forest, Dark Victory*, with Tallulah Bankhead (soon to be Merman's companion on the social circuit), and *Romeo and Juliet*, with Katharine Cornell, were doing well. Some of the musicals found refuge in older fare, such as the operettas *Revenge with Music* and *The Great Waltz*. The new revue *Life Begins at 8.40* sparkled with its contemporary sets, songs, and style. But the biggest musical event of the season was Cole Porter's *Anything Goes*.

Cole Porter

Cole Porter was born in Peru, Indiana, in 1891 and was raised in a well-to-do family. Encouraged by an adoring mother, he wrote songs—music and lyrics both—as a boy. He graduated from Yale University as a pre-law student to placate his father, but the experience seemed only to confirm his passion for music, and he ultimately dropped out of Harvard Law School. And while his first Broadway efforts in the mid-1910s were not well received, by the late '20s and '30s, Porter had become the toast of the town.

In 1919, during one of his many periods in Europe, the gay Porter married wealthy divorcée Linda Thomas in a more or less asexual union (Linda had just left an abusive marriage). But theirs was a fond intimacy, and Cole remained deeply devoted to Linda "in his own fashion." Both had health problems: Linda's respiratory ailments eventually killed her; Porter, for his part, endured a debilitating horse riding accident that occurred in 1937. It crushed bones in both legs and necessitated dozens of surgeries, an eventual leg amputation, and painkillers that, combined with alcohol abuse, slowly transformed the composer into a frail, withdrawn man. He kept working until the 1958 amputation and died six years later.

Whether as composer or social figure, Porter was renowned for combining the debonair wit and cosmopolitanism of his urbane lifestyle with naughty bits that shocked. His lyrics and rhymes came from a variety of high and vernacular, exotic and banal sources. He would drop phrases in French, use rhythms from North Africa, reference the Taj Mahal, Mickey Mouse, Fred Astaire's feet, Camembert cheese, and Pepsodent toothpaste. "A Porter song is a luxury item," wrote Walter Clemons, "expensively made . . . and extravagantly rhymed. In a way no other songs of the period quite did, Porter created a world. It was a between-the-wars realm of drop dead chic and careless name-dropping insouciance. And it was a sexy place to be invited."[15]

Anything Goes was Ethel's fourth Broadway show and her first with Porter. Over the following decade, Porter and Merman worked together on three other shows: *Red, Hot and Blue! Something for the Boys,* and *Panama Hattie.* None rivaled *Anything Goes,* which most Broadway historians and critics rank along with *Kiss Me Kate* as Porter's best work. In 1934, it was certainly his best to date, and Ethel was well aware of what the show and his songs did for her own career. "It gives me a chance for the first time to sing straight lyrics that aren't of the torch song order," she told the press. She loved the score. "It's the first time I haven't been expected to shout about endearing sentiments in a volume of voice calculated to shake the luster off the crystal chandelier in the lobby. . . . now . . . I don't have to sound like the Sandy Hook foghorn with such songs as 'You're the Top' and 'Anything Goes.' "[16]

How *Anything Goes* came to pass is a legendary tale for Broadway mavens and Mermaphiles alike. Vin Freedley, now working without Alex Aarons, was looking for a vehicle for William Gaxton. The other male lead, intended for Bert Lahr, went to Victor Moore. During the summer of 1934, they lined up Porter, who was abroad in France, for the songs, the majority of which he wrote quickly. For the book, Freedley secured Guy Bolton, then in England, and P. G. Wodehouse, in France. Howard Lindsay was brought on to direct. The comedy took place on a gambling ship; the hook was that the boat sank. In mid-August, Bolton and Wodehouse gave Freedley their book, which they called *Hard to Get.* Freedley, the story goes, was unsure about how funny audiences would find the tale. No sooner had he read it than fate stepped in. On September 8, a fire gutted the real-life pleasure cruise SS *Morro Castle,* just off the coast of New Jersey. One hundred thirty-four people died. A musical comedy about a sunken boat was now unthinkable.[17]

By this point Bolton and Wodehouse had other commitments, forcing Freedley to scramble for new writers. Director Howard Lindsay, who also had several shows under his belt as a writer, agreed to write on the condition that he be given a collaborator. The question was, who? According to Cole Porter, after speaking with Lindsay about the issue, he mentioned it to magazine illustrator Neysa McMein. The next day, McMein called Cole to tell him she had had a dream about Russel Crouse, and McMein's dreams, Porter maintains, were taken very seriously around town. Porter recommended Crouse, who had done a couple of shows, *Hold Your Horses* and *The Gang's All Here,* neither a resounding success. But his promise was evident, and, apparently with the blessing of McMein, he was brought onto the project. (The story is that, when Freedley went to look for him, Crouse was working in an office literally across the street.) *Anything Goes* marked the first time Crouse and

Lindsay worked together—the first show for one of Broadway's greatest playwriting teams of the century. According to colleague Nunnally Johnson, Lindsay "was a great technician, and Crouse was very good with ideas. Wonderful working team, the best of them."[18]

The pairing was as happy as it was long-lived. When asked the usual question of how they actually worked together, Crouse joked that each one wrote every other word. "Deciding who should write the first word was really the only difficulty we had with *Anything Goes*. We finally tossed a coin, borrowed from Cole, who was busy writing the music and didn't need it. Mr. Lindsay won."[19] Their revisions could scarcely keep pace with the schedule Freedley had established for the show. "By the time rehearsals started," said Ethel, "all we had was the first act—and that had large holes in it. Suddenly we'd come to an empty place in the book and Howard and Buck [Crouse's nickname] would say, 'Now this is a very funny scene which we haven't written.'"[20]

Crouse recalls:

> Mr. Porter was equal to all the emergencies we created and I think we hold the record. The show did not even have a name for days and days. . . . Billy Gaxton finally baptized it accidentally. In answer to a question as to whether he would mind making an entrance a minute after the curtain went up, Mr. Gaxton replied "In this kind of a spot, anything goes!" We all leaped on the last words and an electrician started spelling them in electric lights. Mr. Porter dashed off to write a title song. He came in with it the next day.[21]

Lindsay and Crouse finished the story the night of the first dress rehearsal. Protagonist Billy Crocker (name taken from a friend of Porter's at Yale) is bidding adieu to society girl Hope Harcourt (Bettina Hall) on the ship that's taking her to Europe, where she intends to marry a dull Englishman of means. Crocker (Gaxton) misses the debark call and finds himself stowing away in a room he shares with U.S. Public Enemy No. 13 (Victor Moore), disguised as Rev. Dr. Moon, who carries a machine gun—called "putt putt"—in a saxophone case most all of the time. Ethel plays nightclub singer and former evangelist Reno Sweeney, who is sweet on Billy Crocker. Once he discovers Moon's real identity, Crocker becomes mistaken for Public Enemy No. 1, and he and other characters have to assume various disguises—sailors, Chinese couples, priests, a Pomeranian dog—in a slapdash series of mistaken identities. For its comedy, *Anything Goes* was also banking on America's fascination with gangster culture. Just a few years earlier, Hollywood had released *Public Enemy* and *Scarface,* and in 1934, the real Public Enemy No. 1, John

Dillinger, was shot dead, as were Bonnie Parker and Clyde Barrow. But this play was among the first attempts to treat that material comically.

The show previewed on November 5 at the Colonial Theatre in Boston, where ticket prices ranged from $.83 for the second balcony to $3.30 for orchestra seats. The crew didn't know what to expect in Boston, given all the changes so late in the game. There was, moreover, a blunder that night on Bill Gaxton's part. "Billy had on white tie and tails, and the audience was supposed to think [he and Hall] had stayed . . . out until four or five in the morning, necking. Afterward, Billy was to make an entrance into his stateroom, find Victor Moore. . . . The trouble was Billy had forgotten that he was to go into the next scene without changing costume, and in making his quick run from the poop deck he'd absent-mindedly taken off his trousers. After leaving the girl on deck, he entered the stateroom with his trousers draped over his arm, and said, 'What a night, what a dawn, what a sunrise!'"[22] Surprisingly, the Boston censors didn't make anything of it. The show went off without a hitch; in fact, critics raved. "Here is the best musical play in many years, not moons," wrote George Holland, who predicted *Anything Goes* would run until "Red Day" (May Day), when Ethel would be returning to Hollywood for her contract with Goldwyn.[23]

More raves greeted the show when it came to the Alvin Theatre on Broadway. "Anything Goes . . . Everything's Right," said one.[24] The principals scored, and critics singled Ethel out for high praise. Ethel Merman sang with "magnetic authority," said Brooks Atkinson.[25] Another reviewer wrote, "Miss Merman runs away with the show. The explanation is a simple one—Miss Merman has almost an exclusive on the Porter songs. But while the songs are largely responsible for the high rating that musical attains, it is also true that the songs are the sort that require the right delivery. And Miss Merman is 100% right. She stops the show before five minutes have elapsed . . . and then proceeds to tear them apart all evening."[26] Merman's singing and Porter's writing were singled out for their accomplishments. Said one reviewer, this was not just the usual "Al Siegel arrangements. . . . the Porter lyrics are trickier than a Japanese wrestler, yet as this girl sings 'em not a syllable is lost and not an inflection misplaced."[27] Porter's "Blow, Gabriel, Blow," "You're the Top," "I Get a Kick out of You," and "Anything Goes" would remain permanently linked to Merman—and she with them. For John Mason Brown on his third viewing of the show, Merman was "still sunshine on Broadway incarnate . . . the perfect interpreter of Cole Porter."

In many ways, Porter was the utter antithesis of Merman. He led the life of an urbane, high-society gadabout, and Merman was down-to-earth, comparatively uneducated, and lowbrow. When interviewing him for her 1950s autobiography, Pete Martin tried to get Cole to dish some dirt on their differences: "You are suave, sophisticated; Merman to me is sort of bourgeoisie, she sort of stands for variety shows." Porter didn't bite: "Her ear was so perfect, she'd drop [words] better than a Frenchman. . . . she was essentially Broadway and I was not."[28] Ethel explained that their relationship worked well because Cole and Linda were enthusiastic about people "who had the courage to be themselves."[29] Ethel's colorful, down-to-earth side gave Cole a playful way to rail against the ennui of everyday life and middle-class convention. So if their relationship was a clashing of class sensibilities, Cole and Ethel nonetheless shared a common target: staid people and staid lives. Cole delighted in her brass sparkle and was not the least bit interested in condemning it. He and Linda regularly invited her to their large elaborate Christmas parties. "Other performers," Cole later told Pete Martin, "couldn't command the attention of such a drunk crowd."[30]

Moreover, Cole simply adored Ethel's talent, and she his. Both were hard-toiling perfectionists who knew how to bring out the best in the musical gifts of the other. Later, Porter said, "She can sing anything. But I really tailor-made [my songs] for her because I know her range so well. Her greatest note is A natural,"[31] so he would end phrases on this note. He was awed by how Ethel would "flat a note" for comic effect (if "sharping" is "unpleasant," flatting is "funny," something heard to great effect in the lyric "floozy" in De-Sylva's "Sam and Delilah"). Porter also admired how she could create blue notes, "clinkers," as Merman explained to Martin, that get a "wonderful reaction."

Cole also appreciated Ethel's impeccable diction, noting her especially well-enunciated *D*'s: "A difficult thing for people singing, especially in America, because our diction is so sloppy."[32] He also enjoyed her innate rhythm and ability to handle his songs' elaborate, often unorthodox rhythms; only someone like Merman could stress his half-note triplets in "I Get a Kick out of You."

Why shouldn't Cole and Ethel have adored each other? Their collaboration produced some of the biggest hits of the musical theater. "Sometimes I'd sing in one breath 'Flying too high with some guy in the sky is my idea of nothing to do'; sometimes I'd break it into two breaths if I was tired, and breathe after 'sky.' Only Cole would notice, "because that was one thing he loved, that one particular phrase without a breath." Not many vocalists can instinctively hold the "-if-" of the syllable in "terrifically" (in "I Get a Kick out of You") to such effect.

What's more, the two didn't stop with professional appreciation. The Merman scrapbooks preserve a loving cascade of Cole's calling cards, all handwritten in Porter's delightful knotty scrawl. In the autumn of 1949, for instance, when Linda Porter was hospitalized with a bronchial attack, he wrote Ethel, gently asking, "Could you send her a little message?" and Ethel obliged. On NBC radio's *Ethel Merman Show* she said, "This is for my pal Linda Porter" before singing Cole's "You're the Top."[33]

After *Anything Goes,* Ethel didn't open a single show for which Porter didn't send a card and gift. He was almost recklessly generous, something made possible by his wealth, of course, but made real only by his heart. Ethel, for her part, had such respect for him that she never treated him with patronizing kid gloves, even after the accident that left him badly injured. Porter did his utmost to keep his infirmity from guests, and when he was no longer able to walk, his assistants would tell guests to leave the room while they carried him from one spot to another. He would be placed on the couch, and Ethel would be the only guest who plunked herself down next to him; others kept a more decorous distance across the room. No other friend had—or would have been able to get away with—such casual closeness with the composer.

Two decades after *Anything Goes,* Porter did confide in Martin that he had admired Merman before they ever worked together, adding, "I don't believe she had much faith in me [nor did her agent Lou Irwin]. She had a clause she wouldn't go into the show unless she approved every number I'd written for her. To make more sure, she insisted I go over to her family flat where her Mother and Father and Lou Irwin had to pass on the songs I had." They didn't pass on "Blow, Gabriel, Blow," which he rewrote to their approval (a big coup, since Porter was known not to revise his songs). Ethel, he recalled, said she wanted a more "fluid" melody. "I remember she talked with somebody connected with the show and they told me only afterwards that she didn't think that 'You're the Top' would register. It was different from anything that had been written, you know."[34] *Anything Goes* was the first score written with Ethel's voice specifically in mind, and her role, Reno Sweeney, another brassy nightclub singer, was also the first to be expressly written for her.

If there were any tensions in the cast during the show's run, no one let on. Ethel especially enjoyed Bill Gaxton, the show's most established star, who reportedly insisted on sharing his top billing with her and Victor Moore. (Gaxton's wife, Madeline, remained one of Ethel's closest friends, long after Gaxton's death in 1963.) During the 1934 holiday season, Bill and Madeline elicited Ethel's help in selecting their customized Christmas card, settling on "The Gaxtons say 'You're the Top.'" (Pack rat Ethel saved all three mock-ups.) During the run, Ethel also enjoyed a warm relationship with Freedley, of whom Porter said in more bitter years, "He has every background to be a very nice man and is essentially not."[35] But all were riding high. Onstage and on radio, Freedley would introduce his protégée: "Nobody who has heard her could ever ask for anything more!"[36]

In December 1934, the principals of *Anything Goes* were feted in the Caprice Room of the Hotel Weylin, an event for which set designer Donald Oenslager had copied one of the show's sets. That month, Ethel also attended a postshow birthday party with Cole, hosted by über-hostess Elsa Maxwell at the Waldorf-Astoria. The theme was a Turkish ball, and the four hundred guests, including Ethel, came in costume or were supplied with one at the door. Maxwell positioned herself by the fifteen-foot birthday cake and sang Porter's "I Have a Shooting Box in Scotland," which he had written at Yale for a show called *Paranoia*.[37]

Anything Goes cost $59,000 and made about $480,000, and it gave Ethel's star power a huge boost.[38] A gossip column reported that she'd rejected work on a Fox picture with Maurice Chevalier to stay on the boards with *Anything Goes*.[39] People started speculating about who would reprise the Merman role in London—Gertrude Lawrence? A brief dance craze based on the show called *The Merman* appeared in New York, and in 1934 Ethel was named the most imitated singer in clubs.[40] By this point, the press was beginning to refer to Ethel as La Merman or The Merman, showing affection for and possessive pride in their homegrown star. Her acting and comedic skills began to get more attention, too. "The caliber of Miss Merman's performance is such that she is no longer merely a thrilling 'torch-singer' but a comedienne with few equals. She has an ease and a natural sense of comedy."[41] None other than former Broadway song-and-dance man James Cagney also took note of her, praising Merman's work in *Anything Goes*.

During the run, Ethel recorded "You're the Top" and "I Get a Kick out of You" with Johnny Green's band. (Cast recordings would not be standard practice for another ten years.) On March 4, 1935, she and Gaxton helped dedicate radio station WOR's new fifty-thousand-watt transmitter in a publicity appearance perfectly suited for the young "leather lunged diva."[42] Freedley introduced the pair; then Merman sang "I Get a Kick out of You," and Gaxton, "You're the Top," the easier song to sing. After the Valentine's Day show—its ninety-ninth performance—Merman replaced torch-singing queen Libby Holman as top-billed singer at the Central Park Casino in a fifteen-minute show at 12:30 A.M. "They eat it up," she told the *Brooklyn Eagle*. "I begin with the chorus of 'Rise and Shine' from *Girl Crazy* and 'Life's

Just a Bowl of Cherries' . . . and then there's a hot piano break and I go into 'Dahlia's a Floozie.'"[43] Two days after her Casino opening, Lux—the soap of glamour—took out a full two-page ad in the *New Yorker:* "*Anything Goes* is Top on Broadway . . . and Lux is top in its wardrobe room."[44]

With its abundance of tie-ins and promotional gimmicks, *Anything Goes* was no different from other shows. Porter later recalled the song-writing contests Freedley had set up, asking people to write a refrain to his lyrics to win a pair of tickets to the show. (Freedley and Gaxton were judges, and possibly Ethel, but not Cole.) In addition to Ethel and Lux, Gaxton endorsed Dunhill's Charbert's eau de cologne, "the Gentleman's Toiletry," sold in the shape of a flask bottle. Macy's ran a full-page ad promoting its fashions along with *Anything Goes*.[45] Ethel gave more interviews than ever and, by now, was clearly quite relaxed with the press, greeting them in loungewear and offering them highballs with an informality that U.S. celebrity no longer knows.

Critics were taking note of not only her talents and her celebrity but also her energy and busy schedule. Wrote one, "By the time the afternoon notices of 'Anything Goes' were on the newsstand it was apparent that for the moment, at least, Miss Merman was also Miss America, Miss Manhattan, Miss Lux-Lifebuoy-and-Rinso, Miss Alkaline Side and all the various other indorsement [sic] aliases which are the prerequisites of celebrity."[46] The piece went on to say that Ethel was now posing for photos and portraits just three times per day. Another wrote, "She is encored to exhaustion in several songs, which will be hits of the year. 'I Get a Kick . . . ,' 'You're the Top,' 'Anything Goes,' and 'Blow, Gabriel, Blow.'"[47] The encore tradition, which had begun so explosively for Merman with *Girl Crazy,* was picking up even more steam. When she was in Boston for previews, reviews reported, "Although it was long after 11 o'clock the audience insisted upon recalling Miss Merman more than half a dozen times after her singing of the lively ditty called 'Buddy Beware.'" During the run, Ethel was also a desired radio guest. By 1935, she had appeared three times on *The Rudy Vallee Hour* and had made frequent appearances on the popular *Rhythm at 8,* recording one session with Al Goodman's Orchestra on August 7.

The figure of Ethel Merman is so entwined with vitality that it is surprising to see just how much energy the woman actually had. Merman seemed to be utterly inexhaustible, making endless appearances at clubs and benefits during the early and mid-1930s. In some ways, the New York entertainment world was not terribly different from what it is today, with performers given daunting promotion schedules. There were the endless publicity stunts, which for rising, not fully established stars like Ethel were especially gimmicky; trade papers featured Ethel's name in crossword puzzles or in quick quizzes about current events and personalities.

Merman has always, even in death, been dogged by the question of how "into" her hard work she was, whether she walked through her shows, whether her performances were reliable to the point of being perfunctory. Did she sing full out, every show, every rehearsal, pulling back only for quieter numbers? Today, the word from casual Merman fans on the street is split, some maintaining that her performances (or at least her attitude) became dulled during long runs. It scarcely helped when Ethel, always matter-of-fact, told reporters that while she was singing, she'd often think of what to add to her grocery list, and in *Anything Goes* she took up Gaxton's challenge to keep brittle in her mouth for an entire performance, songs and all. But most people, especially those who knew Merman, believe there was nothing rote or unprofessional about her working habits. When Martin interviewed her, he told Merman what Cole Porter had said about her: "When you are singing for twenty people you give it just as much and put out just as much, as if you were singing for 2,000 people, or 20,000 people; that when you're singing, you're transfixed, as if you are in a form of Heaven."[48] Whether transfixed or reflecting about her groceries, Ethel gave it her all, and this is what people who had actually seen her always recall, ranging from close friends such as Tony Cointreau to people who never knew her offstage.

Ethel left *Anything Goes* in July 1935—past the "Red Day" that the press had predicted—and was replaced by Benay Venuta (1911–95), a Broadway performer who often played roles carved out by Ethel and who would be friends with Ethel for much of her life. Following Merman in *Anything Goes,* Venuta had some big shoes to fill but did just that starting July 22, 1935, singing the show a tone lower than her predecessor. Vivian Vance—the future Ethel Mertz on *I Love Lucy*—had been Merman's understudy, and she stayed on as Venuta's. Victor Moore stayed too, reportedly turning down a lucrative movie deal with Zeppo Marx to keep the show going. Brooks Atkinson wrote, "Perhaps [Venuta] will not object to the statement that Our Ethel can have no successors. She is unique. . . . When a singer has that much magnetic authority over a song it appears to become her property: the theatregoer forgets that someone else wrote it."[49] *Anything Goes* ran to a total of 420 performances, a strong run. Soon, it would be staged in London, filmed in Hollywood (twice), and, in the '50s, truncated for television—Ethel appeared in two of those televised versions.

As early as January 1935, Vin Freedley was in Los Angeles negotiating the show's film rights with Paramount. He received a reported eighty-five thousand dollars, plus 10 percent of gross, once rentals passed the one-million-dollar mark.[50] Lewis Milestone *(All Quiet on the Western Front)* was set to direct, and, at the time of the deal, Paramount was eager to use Bing Crosby for Billy Gaxton's role. Beyond that, however, casting wasn't settled. Rumors buzzed: Moore's "Public Enemy" would be played by W. C. Fields and then Frank Morgan and Charlie Ruggles (who got the part). Maybe Queenie Smith was going to take over the Ethel Merman role? Speculation abounded.

Ethel left for Hollywood to do the film in August 1935 with hopes and head held high. Again, Agnes went with her and "had this to say of the 24-year-old 'torch singer': My Ethel is just a home girl!"[51] New York City had been throwing itself at Ethel's feet, and her persona was becoming established there, but her fame and public persona had not been cemented in Hollywood. And Ethel just wasn't crazy about LA, still complaining about how early the city closed down at night. During the day she loved soaking up the sun, but other than that, there wasn't much of Southern California life that really appealed to her. "Don't get me wrong, I like to go to Hollywood once in a while and make pictures all right. But what a dead life it is out there. There's just nothing to do. New York's the place for me, and anybody that's got the swing of it like I have can't break out of it so easily. Yes sir, Broadway's the life and I'm going to stick by it as long as I can."[52] And, "In Hollywood, there's one big clique and no matter how big a name you have on Broadway, until you've made a hit in the movies, you don't exist. Broadway welcomes everyone."[53]

Anything Goes had the misfortune of being filmed the year after Hollywood had established the Hays Office, a self-policing censorship bureau to create and uphold guidelines for "appropriate" content. A public relations creation as much as anything else, the office was the result of the industry submitting to mounting pressure from Catholic and other groups about the cinema's purported moral excesses and indecency. It culminated in the half-absurd, half-draconian "Production Code," which would, among other things, determine how many seconds a kiss on the mouth could last, place married people in separate beds (always with one leg on the floor), and censure expressions such as "They're nuts." Broadway *never* experienced this level of institutionalized censorship—one perk of not having the extensive national reach of Hollywood's mass-produced product.

Gimmick though it may have been, the Hays Office had real teeth and masticated *Anything Goes,* particularly Porter's songs. "In view of the flavor of the lyrics, the title itself *[Anything Goes]* might be objected to."[54] "Your attention is called to the scene where a religious hymn entitled 'Blow, Gabriel, Blow' is burlesqued."⁵⁵ "Gabriel" and "All through the Night" were fully scuttled, and the lyrics of three remaining numbers, "Anything Goes," "You're the Top," and "I Get a Kick out of You," were dramatically overhauled. In "Kick," "sniffing cocaine" became "whiffing perfume from Spain." It's hardly surprising that Cole Porter, a fan of neither revisions nor censorship, handed the task of writing new song lyrics to Ted Fetter, whose final work *Variety* eventually deemed "below the standard of those set by the originals."⁵⁶

Other changes were afoot. Paramount expanded the Billy Crocker role to show off Crosby and gave him top billing over Ethel. (She was billed over Ruggles in Victor Moore's role, however.) Studio press sheets (newspaper-length artifacts that were filled with articles and tips for theater owners on how to market the movie through contests, posters, give-aways, tie-ins, etc.) maintained that Ethel had an unrequited crush on Crosby and other nonsense. They said she "still fears the long arm of the law" for peeking into the Paramount Studios as a kid in Astoria.⁵⁷ Clearly, Paramount knew how to make Crosby the enticing star, but what to do with Ethel Merman was rather less clear, trying in the end to cast her as a good little girl.

Back home in New York, the press was cheering for their woman:

> This flicker is a return engagement for Ethel Merman at Paramount. She never really got a chance in *We're Not Dressing*. Much of her work was not in the released picture, and one number [will appear in] *The Big Broadcast*. They didn't appreciate what they had. It will be different for Miss Merman in *Anything Goes*. . . . She has a better screen makeup [*sic*], and is wearing her own hair and not a wig as she did in *We're Not Dressing*. Ethel Merman will be seen as Ethel Merman in *Anything Goes*.⁵⁸

She may well have been more "Ethel Merman" in the film, but there was not much of her to see. In the final cut, her role was substantially reduced; and her performance style, curtailed. Unable to move around as she liked to do on a stage, Ethel sang "I Get a Kick out of You" perched atop a neon-lit moon suspended from a nightclub ceiling. "If Ethel Merman could get her feet on the ground for a minute, she might be able to make a fair stab at singing a song," read one review. "Ethel is growing weary of motion pictures. . . . so far, she says, the studios have done everything possible to interfere with normal vocalizing." In *We're Not Dressing* she sings one number while pitching about on a boat deck in a storm; another, in the "upper branches of some trees a la Tarzan. . . . [In *Anything Goes*] she sings the title song wearing a fifty pound metal and beaded dress, while running up and down stairs . . . and 'I Get a

Kick' . . . floating over the heads of some people in a night club. She duets 'You're the Top' with Bing Crosby and as far as Ethel can make out she's supposed to be hanging from a chandelier."[59]

The Modern All-American Girl

The image of the all-American girl was being propagated all across the country, a soothing alternative to the more contentious icon of womanhood at the time, the suffragist. Suffragists, often the butt of jokes, experienced an especially strong backlash after World War I. (Their goals were trivialized or considered unpatriotic.) Modernity, too, brought threats and anxieties to the country at large. People fretted about the undoing of traditional gender roles, the possibility of losing jobs (to women? to machines?), the loss of rural values, and the vague gloom of a society homogenized on a grand scale with the intent of stamping out individualism. Women were entering the workforce in greater numbers and were visible in areas that had previously been controlled exclusively by (white) men. How to reassure a changing American landscape, how to soften the impact of women's growing autonomy? Answer: extoll the virtues of a domesticated "all-American girl." This is precisely what Florenz Ziegfeld had been doing in his Broadway revues since the end of the nineteenth century in his *Ziegfeld Follies* from 1907 to 1928 and in his film *Glorifying the American Girl,* which also featured a pre-Tarzan beefcake named Johnny Weissmuller.

It's scarcely surprising that these anxieties were worked out iconically through female archetypes that symbolized one sexual extreme or another. Hollywood had its vamp, Theda Bara, and its virgins such as Mary Pickford and Lillian and Dorothy Gish. Broadway never played the gender extremes quite so hard, but even so, Merman was a rare breed, able to borrow from both types. Publicity photos establish that Ethel was being presented less as an all-American sweetheart than as an all-American *modern*. Young, white, self-sufficient, down-to-earth, trendy, and "hep," the modern woman was somewhat less demure than her sweetheart counterpart. Above all, she was a friend to the latest trends and advances in American business and industry. What better way to establish her than with advanced technologies that showed off American know-how? People of the time were fascinated with trains, cars, and, especially, planes—all that modernity could offer. Amelia Earhart and Charles Lindbergh were heroes, and radio, stage, print, and screen recounted aviator and aviatrix stories with abandon.

Entire studies have explored how modern technology and its products came to be gendered in particular ways. Modernity meant mass production, more leisure time, and more consumption. Whether as workers or as consumers, women were suddenly taking charge of purchases for the home. The 1920s, like the '50s after them, saw a glut of products aimed at making lives easier for female homemakers: vacuum cleaners and ice boxes in the '20s, blenders and specialty ovens in the '50s. In turn, these sorts of products would be aligned with women, either through women's actual consumption of them or through the illusion of consuming a "woman," say, with the purchase of a hot new car.

The 1920s had left behind a considerable legacy of products and of consumers used to enjoying them. Production had been robust, and goods multiplied. To make operating and owning these products seem alluring, advertisers presented scenarios in which "modern" women interacted with the new devices, a tradition that remains with us today. Female stars entering the publicity machine were hired to promote high-end luxury products such as automobiles, since there seemed to be something novel, even adventurous, about a woman operating a large, motorized vehicle.

Ethel fit into this trend in interesting ways. Publicity agents posed her in what can only be described as vehicular situations: One features a self-sufficient Ethel changing the tire on a car, advertising an auxiliary metal rim that would "enable the woman driver to drive to the nearest service station" with a flat.[60] Another has her sitting in some indescribable exercise-as-flying-machine contraption that is almost as bizarre as her bike-on-seaboards in *We're Not Dressing.* (In reality, Ethel wouldn't have had a clue about what to do with such devices; she rarely drove and her idea of exercising, she said, was sun tanning.) Still, the publicity contributed to Merm's image as a hands-on, hep working girl, and the well-publicized details of her pre–show biz career added a touch of authenticity to the quirky photos.

Because of her very long career, Merman's trek through American culture can be measured in part by different forms of transportation, literally moving as it did from buggies, trains, and steamships to cars and airplanes. Privately, the young Ethel didn't travel much, and when she gave up her private car ("too impractical") in favor of cabs and walking in New York, it made the papers. She didn't enjoy touring, and in general, up until midlife, Ethel preferred to stay close to home. In the 1950s, this changed first with a new residence in Colorado and then even more after *Gypsy,* when a footloose Ethel Merman traveled around the world.

When she was positioned as a "modern woman" in the late 1920s to mid-1930s, Merman was not too different from other young stars of the time; these were the kinds of women who, the press intimated, could change a spare just as easily as they could impart grooming tips. Ethel may have been in a league of her own as a singer and Broadway performer, but newspaper photos show that the media weren't ready to capitalize exclusively on that, focusing instead on making Ethel seem like other contemporary female entertainers.

It was, for example, utterly routine for the press to stage pictures as stars arrived or departed from New York's Penn and Grand Central stations. On July 21, 1938, Ethel posed at the back of the Twentieth Century train, holding a lantern. Someone urged her to start swinging the lantern, and when she did, the train started to lurch out of the station and a surprised Ethel had to be helped off. The incident was dutifully reported, and as a result, the Railroad Trainmen's Union gave Ethel honorary membership. Two weeks later, Bloomingdale's chimed in, promoting six-inch train lanterns for a dollar apiece.

Another photo, appearing in the Apollo Theatre program the week of May 15, 1933, shows an attractive Ethel in a low-backed gown; she was photographed from behind in a typical glamour pose, hand on hip. The design is a sleek art deco. Appearing to her right, however, is not a pitch for fashion gowns but the following "quote": "I am told that American women spend billions of dollars every year for cosmetics and facial care. Also that 45% of all motorists who are injured in automobile accidents are cut by broken, flying glass. Why in the world will a woman who spends so much time and money in caring for her beauty, expose it so thoughtlessly to such a hazard? I'll never be able to understand it . . . with Safety Glass so easily and inexpensively obtainable, and its protective value so thoroughly proven. —Ethel Merman."[61] The effect is almost humorous, having glamour girl Merman offer technical advice on car glass. But modern travel, like the modern woman, remained a cultural obsession, even in Ethel's shows: the long taxi ride to Arizona in *Girl Crazy,* the ship scenes in *Anything Goes,* in *We're Not Dressing,* and in Ethel's upcoming Eddie Cantor film, *Kid Millions.* Later, Ethel would be in a car caper, *It's a Mad, Mad, Mad, Mad World,* and, later still, in *Airplane!* This is not to suggest that Ethel was alone in being linked to travel—indeed, it makes her quite ordinary—but the range of her career and the persistence of these images offer a literal pun of a woman truly on the move. (The link was even supported in her real-life marriage to Continental Airlines CEO, Robert Six, in the 1950s.)

Ethel was able to get her name in public by doing benefit performances of her shows or songs from her shows and recordings. The appearances fortified aspects of her emerging star persona: the good-hearted girl next door, the team player supporting important national, international, and humanitarian causes, a "trouper" for organizations in the Greater New York area. The charity work gave Merman's image a wholesomeness that remained with her the rest of her life, even though some of her less wholesome social behavior would complicate it in years to come. The frequency of this work clinched Ethel's image as a vibrant, energetic modern—a young gal on the go who made time for others in her busy professional life. Beyond its impact on her image, however, Merman's charity work demonstrated her strong personal and professional commitment to Broadway. Many of the organizations she supported assisted unemployed actors during the Depression and the war.

Work included benefits for the Theatre Wing and the young Actors Equity. On December 20, 1931, she did a Sunday benefit for the New York Christmas and Relief Fund along with Everett Marshall, William Demarest, Kate Smith, and her costar from *Scandals,* Ray Bolger. She did benefits for the Milk Fund; she appeared for the Federation for the Support of Jewish Philanthropic Societies; for the Jewish Consumptives' Relief Society, where she was billed with Fannie Brice, George Jessel, and Bill Robinson;[62] and for the Israel Orphan Asylum. Whether Merman was popularly perceived as Jewish at this point is unclear. These events included prominent Jewish participants such as Fannie Brice, Sophie Tucker, Eddie Cantor, Al Jolson, and Paul Muni along with gentile performers such as Bill Robinson, a diversity that increased as Hitler's machinery intensified and U.S. policy became less isolationist.

Throughout her life, Merman and Jewishness had a conflicted, contradictory relationship; "Jewish jokes" may have been a staple in her repertoire of off-color jokes. Merman was a product of an era that used ethnic, regional, and national orientation as the butt of gags that ranged from immigrant and "country rube" jokes to blackface, with white (and occasionally Jewish and other white ethnic) entertainers performing in guises, in part to "Americanize" their diverse audiences. American culture put up few obstacles for Anglos who did this kind of humor in the 1930s and '40s, but Merman's uneasy relationship with Jewishness endured decades after the culture had changed and these jokes had become passé.

Movies with Eddie Cantor

One of Hollywood's imports from New York in the 1930s was Eddie Cantor (1892–1966), the enormously talented Jewish singer and comic personality known as Banjo Eyes. Like other future Merman costars such as the Ritz Brothers, Cantor came from New York's immigrant lower East Side, and like them he was schooled in physical humor and bad puns. But Cantor enjoyed wider crossover success in film than these other costars did (as well as on Sunday evenings, on radio's *Chase and Sanborn Hour*). His yearly films, contracted with Sam Goldwyn, were big-budget, highly anticipated affairs. Ethel starred in two of them. The first, *Kid Millions* (1934, initial title: *Treasure Hunt*), featured Cantor as an orphan who inherits twenty-seven million dollars from a fortune his father discovered in Egypt. Other parties quickly plot to contest the claim; Ethel's character, Dot, is paired with a thug who plans to "knock off" Eddie; Dot must pretend to be his long-lost mother. (Cantor was Merman's senior by more than fifteen years. In a wise comic decision, the film did nothing to make her appear old enough to pass.)

Its gags trade on the worst of puns: "Okay, toots!" he tells a girl who then pulls a chain on a boat to make it toot. "Show him you're not yellow!" he says in a roomful of people of color. The film is saturated with ethnic "color": the African-American duo the Nicholas Brothers give an amazing performance; Cantor performs Irving Berlin's "Mandy" in blackface and in Egyptian garb; "sultanlike," as he says, he rides camels, sings "Let My People Go," deals with a sheikh who's enraged with Eddie's father, who, the sheikh says, "ravaged the heritage of my ancestors." Eddie also has to get out of marrying the sheikh's daughter, and after his escape (with fortune intact), the film concludes with him and Dot, back in the West, driving through a huge, fairy-tale ice cream factory for kids in a color sequence that shows off the picture's big budget. (Ethel's future friend Lucille Ball had a small role as one of the glamorous "Goldwyn Girls.")

Kid Millions is pure Cantor, with hammy, ethnic comedy, "laughs aplenty,"[63] and spirited musical numbers. Merman's role was based on already-established character traits: an ethnically unspecified moll with chutzpah who schemes but deep down is of good heart. It was a good-natured, physical, fun image palatable for kids (it's reasonable for Ethel to ride with Cantor in the ice cream factory) yet naughty enough to be of little interest to them (affecting her impact in *Happy Landing,* her film with Sonja Henie). *Kid Millions* also knew to bank on the Merman voice; before it even shows her, we hear her singing lines from "An Earful of Music," which the *Hollywood Reporter* called "a peach of a song number."[64]

Kid Millions was written by Arthur Sheekman, Nat Perrin, and Nunnally Johnson. In the mid-'30s, Johnson was one of three Hollywood writers able to get solo credit on a picture. (Dudley Nichols and Robert Riskin were the other two.) He didn't for this film, simply because he didn't finish it. "I got a huge sum, because I was giving up a six week vacation to do it," he recalled.[65]

The film's songs were by various writers, including Burton Lane and Harold Adamson; Walter Donaldson and Gus Kahn wrote "Earful of Music," and "Mandy" was the blackface classic of Irving Berlin.

Kid Millions was shown widely around New York in arrangements that again spoke to the city's diverse population and interest in worldwide events. In Brooklyn, it shared billing with *Three Songs about Lenin,* "a fine tribute to Lenin on the 17th anniversary of the Revolution," in a curious mix of political activism and orientalist comedy.[66]

Merman was invited to be in Cantor's feature the following year, *Strike Me Pink,* his first female costar to be asked back. She was delighted; she liked working with Cantor and singled him out for praise in her mixed experiences on the West Coast: "Eddie Cantor . . . was swell to me. He's funny off the screen, too."[67] Her costars were comedian Harry Parke (also known as Harry Einstein), as the character Parkyakarkus, from Cantor's radio show; his principal female sidekick was Sally Eilers, playing Claribel, the secretary to the timid pants presser depicted by Cantor. The story follows "Eddie" when, after taking a correspondence course in courage, he opens the Dreamland Amusement Park (shades of *Kid Millions*) but runs into problems when gangsters want to install rigged gambling machines there. Merman plays Joyce, a nightclub singer whom he falls for. Directing the picture, budgeted at one million dollars, was Norman Taurog, who had done Ethel's short pictures; its cinematographer was the legendary Gregg Toland *(Citizen Kane).* Ethel performed "Shake It Off with Rhythm," "Calabash Pipe," "First You Have Me High, Then You Have Me Low."[68]

At this point, Merman was relatively untried as a movie actress, but she impressed Samuel Goldwyn with her professionalism. She also impressed Cantor. According to his daughter Marilyn, he knew she was a hard worker, and he liked her reliability and lack of pretension. Ethel showed up on time, knew her lines, and took direction well. "With Merman," says Marilyn, "Daddy knew that he'd get a scene done in just one or two takes. Daddy liked that." Another reason he enjoyed working with her, according to Marilyn, was that he simply appreciated her gifts as an entertainer, and he loved being surrounded by strong talent. For her father, Marilyn said, it "raised the bar for everyone. And Daddy knew Merman felt the same way."[69]

The two loved to kid around, and *Kid Millions* gave them their lifelong nicknames for each other: to Ethel, Cantor would always be "Junior"; and she, his "Mother." Marilyn recalls going backstage with her dad at one of Merman's later Broadway shows. Winding his way to her dressing room, he yelled, "Mother, Mother," and Ethel was screaming back, "Junior!" Merman's role as Cantor's mom was the first in a long series of mothers, and colleagues from Mitzi Gaynor to Jerome Robbins would address cards, telegrams, and letters to Miss Merman as "Mom."

Marilyn Cantor and Other Fans

Of Eddie and Ida Cantor's five daughters, Marilyn was the second youngest, born in 1924. She wasn't even a teenager when she became one of Ethel Merman's biggest fans. The first show she ever saw was *Anything Goes*. Merman wowed her. Seventy years later, she recalled, "I went *insane!*" She immediately called her dad in Los Angeles. "Daddy," she said, "I just saw the best singer. You have to work with Ethel Merman, Daddy, she's the greatest there is!" Well, Cantor said, it just so happens I'm in the room with Samuel Goldwyn. Why don't you tell him about her? So the child gets on the phone: "Mr. Goldwyn, you've got to get Ethel Merman to come work for you. She'll be a hit, and you'll be sorry if you miss out." The pitch apparently worked; Goldwyn arranged for Merman to come out for a screen test, and she would appear in his next two Eddie Cantor spectacles. Marilyn said, "As I girl I felt *completely* responsible for starting Ethel's film career."

One day, Marilyn skipped school in order to attend one of Merman's four-show performances in Brooklyn, probably at the Paramount (this is where she was too bored to sit through Marlene Dietrich), and her father found out. Furious, Cantor sent his assistant Maurice down to the theater. The moment Marilyn saw him, she knew she'd been caught. The punishment? Maurice quietly handed her a glass of milk and a sandwich so that the truant girl didn't miss lunch. And then they stayed for the rest of the show. Marilyn saw every one of Merman's shows after that. "I tried to watch *Annie Get Your Gun* once every week in 1946. I saw her in *everything* after that, including the 1966 revival."

Marilyn saved everything she could on Ethel, neatly and chronologically arranging ticket stubs, photos, and news items in her scrapbook. Small wonder that she got along well with Edward Zimmermann, since he was essentially doing the same thing. Her memories of him are warm, but of Ethel, she says their encounters were mixed. "She was kind to me when I was little and when she was working with Dad," she says. The most exciting moment was when Ethel took note that Marilyn was surrounding herself with Merman souvenirs and clippings and said, "Looks like you're the Ethel Merman fan club!" and from then on forwarded some of her fan mail to Marilyn. Marilyn then became president of the Ethel Merman Fan Club and enrolled the fans who wrote letters to Ethel. ("They were mostly girls like me, from different states.") Her most successful accomplishment as president involved a write-in radio contest, sponsored to determine the audience's favorite singer at the time. Marilyn recalls that Ethel's name was up against bigger, more established singers. Pressing the fan club into action, she persuaded everyone to vote: "We made Merman a winner! She wasn't the best known of the group, but we all voted. Oh, I was so surprised to find out that those contests were real!"

The famous daughter's fascination with the rising star made good press. One article reported that Eddie Cantor's daughter Marilyn was such an Ethel Merman fan that she refused to go to school in Los Angeles until her father, who was preparing a trip to New York, took her along so she could see *Red, Hot and Blue!*[70] (Not true, says Marilyn, although it reminded her of the day she skipped school.) Another of Pop's scrapbook clippings mentions an anniversary party that Eddie and Ida threw, where Marilyn impersonated Merman; it notes that the young girl "knew all her songs, her motions, how she breathed." Mouthing the lyrics along with a record on a hidden phonograph, the early karaoke star was a hit.

Marilyn wasn't the only dedicated girl fan. One whose enthusiasm rivaled hers was Esther Hader of Brooklyn. Esther kept a handmade Ethel Merman scrapbook that included autographed pictures of Ethel (including one in color), pictures of Ethel from magazines and newspapers, and memorabilia, from *Anything Goes* to Ethel's 1938 motion pictures with Fox. Sometimes she cut out only the pictures of Merman, sometimes just her heads. She kept tickets to shows, programs, and notes from Ethel herself. There is the Christmas telegram Ethel sent one year; Esther also saved a ticket to a CBS radio show captioned, "Ethel sent it."[71] Esther's devotion shows the obsessive, sweet passion of young fans. But Merman's responsiveness and care are just as touching; how many stars send special Christmas telegrams to ordinary fans?

Other fans sent Ethel published reviews of her shows that they hand typed for pages and pages, sometimes making corrections to typos or, better, making changes to offer their own judgment calls. And not all of the young star's fans were girls. Carl Fleming Jr. of Brookline, Massachusetts, wrote a poem with each line beginning with the letters from Ethel's vertically spelled-out name; he sent her "A scrapbook made especially for you [with 'Ethel Merman' written in a stunning imitation of her own autograph] in appreciation of the lovely photography you sent to me."

The press took note of Ethel's prodigious fan base among grown-ups. In January 1943, New York columnist Burton Rascoe approached people he didn't know to ask, "Do you like Ethel Merman, and if so why?" "My findings were positive but various. Among males between the ages of 17 and 30 . . . they are hog-wild about her; however, from 30–110 years of age the male gender is mostly nearly nuts about her." Women from seventeen to thirty, he said, were 90 percent for her and 10 percent "dead set" against her. Women between thirty and forty (Merman's own age) were 70 percent for and 30 against. When asked why they liked her, he reports, most men said, "She is the only woman I know who can sing without having a voice."

Other responses: "She is funny looking—certainly not a pretty girl—but she makes all pretty girls of the stuck-up kind look like dehydrated potatoes." "She is natural . . . nothing fazes her. . . . I bet she could spot a phony on sight and never have any hesitancy about telling him off." "She's like Eva Tanguay was in the old days. There is a natural, uninhibited lustiness about her, something healthy in her brazen sureness of herself." Rascoe speculates, "The reason men like Ethel is that she is the exact opposite of their sisters. . . . You feel that she's the sort of girl you could pal around with and she'd never get you wrong."[72]

Ethel may have had different attractions for different fans, but most appreciations can be summed up thus: Ethel Merman had a lusty, honest-to-goodness love for life. Her ability to divert and entertain endeared her to the "tired executive," that archetypal theatergoer who takes in a show after a hard day at the office. In the mid-'30s, one columnist wrote, "Ethel is the idol of the Tired Business Man in all his phases, including Park Ave. execs and Washington Senators and financial big-shots. Many a disgruntled wife, following her husband down the aisle of the Alvin Theatre, where *Red, Hot and Blue!* is the current Merman Magnet, murmurs: 'What's she got, anyway . . . ?'"[73]

It's hard to imagine Merman actually pitting men against women, but such is the work of the press. In a piece called "Why Men Adore Ethel Merman," in *Romantic Stories* (its readership pitched mainly to women and girls), we read:

> Ethel herself doesn't take her torch songs seriously. For that matter, her impish, mirth-provoking grin sets her down as one unhandicapped by too serious an outlook on life in general. "They're gag songs—all gags," she chuckles. "They haven't a thing to do with real life." But when she sings, try to convince a man in her audience that she doesn't mean it, that her passionate overflow of love isn't secretly intended for him alone! It's what they have wanted to hear all their lives, a fundamental need of the male ego unsatisfied until Ethel Merman came along. No wonder they call her the First Lady of the Torch. No one can dispute her right to the title, unless it be the Statue of Liberty.[74]

After extolling "her vitality which is evident in all her movements," a male columnist writes that, when Ethel sings, "That's sex appeal, a million men will tell you; sex appeal that makes a siren like Dietrich look anemic!" seemingly echoing young Miss Cantor's preferences.

In the early 1930s, stars often gave beauty secrets in papers and magazines devoted to women. Ethel was no different. In one piece, she goes on at length about nail care—from her fondness of painting them with the whites of the half-moons visible to her reminders that women should have manicures at least twice a week so that their nails don't dry out, and always, always, to moisturize their nails every night, as she does. Ethel advises against putting eye shadow on anywhere but the eyelid. "That was my first big mistake, before I got used to stage make-up. I brought the color right up to the line of my brow, and did I look terrible! I was a sight." Blondes in particular, she warns, can easily appear "overpainted."[75]

These newspaper and magazine articles were usually written in-house and then attributed to various guest stars. The kinds of columns and tips attributed to her, though, helped add to the Ethel Merman persona, of being a practical, well-groomed girl who, unlike her blond sisters, wasn't interested in appearing garish or going for too much. (Stories of Merman overpainting herself when left to her own devices anticipate what a few claim about Ethel in her later years, although one reviewer of the 1930s *Red, Hot and Blue!* remarked that he couldn't see how she could keep her eyes open, her eyelashes were so heavy.)

Ethel Merman entered show business when fan magazines and gossip sheets were becoming widespread and were enjoying wide popularity and influence, especially among female readers. Stars' lives were presented, held up for fascination, emulation, or envy. Trade papers like *Variety* (both East and West Coast versions), *Screen,* and *Stage* were part of this new wave of publicity and promotion of stars, as were the press sheets that accompanied films. Syndicated newspaper columns peddled the latest news and gossip from Broadway and Hollywood. It was, in short, an age of early star worship. Ethel's open appreciation of other stars was part of this culture, just as surely as it was tied to her almost childlike fascination with her own celebrity, a facet of her that mingled freely with the honest pride she had in her achievement. That fascination was lifelong, a constant theme of her autobiographies, scrapbooks, and tales for interviewers. She loved meeting stars and political figures, and the scrapbooks show her comments written on ambassadors' place cards: "he was the one who . . . ," even if only to identify them for her dad.

The Animal in Her

In 1935, Ethel appeared in a motion picture and didn't do a stitch of work for it. Paramount's *The Big Broadcast of 1936* was a compilation film, directed once more by Norman Taurog. It featured an array of stars, including Amos and Andy, George Burns and Gracie Allen, Bing Crosby, Bill Robinson, the Nicholas Brothers, Mary Bolan, Charlie Ruggles, and the Vienna Boys' Choir in a mash of a few newly done routines and (mostly) existing footage. Its plot line is threadbare: faced with financial trouble and likely closure, New York radio station WHY enters a contest with a $250,000 purse for producing the year's best broadcast. The two leads (Jack Oakie and Henry Wadsworth) travel around with their "Radio Eye" machine to transmit skits and songs in a kind of nascent televisual form. They win when, held as prisoners on the Isle of Clementi, the judges take their odd experience to be well-written intrigue. Ethel appears near the very end, "broadcast" on the Radio Eye, where she is introduced as "Ethel Merman of Broadway." It was a supremely easy way for Paramount to capitalize on a star they didn't know what to do with. The prerecorded "It's the Animal in Me" shows our city girl traipsing across the jungle (rear projection conspicuously evident), swinging on vines, sliding down poles, and finally arriving in front of a set of chorus girls and trained elephants. Filmed in low-budget Busby Berkeley style—even going into a trademark overhead shot—the sequence gives Ethel less than three minutes in a movie that is nearly two hours long.

Broadcast opened in New York on Friday, September 13, to standing-room-only crowds. (Ethel later quipped that it was a great way to get paid twice for so little work.) Photos of her with her animal costars hit the press, and although this coverage was neither new nor unique (reports of Ethel acquiring a new pet dog were run-of-the-mill, as they were for most stars), it does suggest that shooting comic (or at least nonromantic) stars like her among "low" beasts seemed somehow more appropriate than doing so in front of grand mansions or expensive cars.

Red, Hot and Blue!

Merman's next show was *Red, Hot and Blue!*—another star vehicle with a silly plot. Her character, Nails Duquesne, is a former manicurist who inherits millions from her husband. The newly minted philanthropist holds a "coming-out party" for five parolees, including "Policy" Pinkle (Jimmy Durante, perfectly cast), who actually *prefers* the jail. Nails's task is to run a lottery in order to track down "baby," the girl whom lawyer Bob Hale (Bob Hope) loved as a child and now wants to marry. She'll be easy to detect, Hale says, since a long time ago she sat down on a hot waffle iron. The lost love turns out to be a "floozy" named Peaches, who is in their own gang. Although Hale is puzzled by what he ever saw in her, no one's disappointment is greater than Nails's, who has grown sweet on Bob Hale/Hope, in the first of Ethel's improbable pairings on Broadway. ("When Bob Hope says he loves Ethel Merman, it seems only part of the kidding," wrote one reviewer. "He's a decidedly tepid hero.")[76] After some skirmishes with the government, which is watching to make sure that the lottery ends up in a genuine marriage to the winner, the Senate declares the lottery unconstitutional, and Bob and Nails marry.

Originally intended as an Eddie Cantor vehicle under the title *Chutes and Ladders, Red, Hot and Blue!* was produced by Vin Freedley. The newly formed team of Lindsay and Crouse wrote the book, and songs were by Cole Porter in his widely anticipated first show since *Anything Goes.* Songs included "Hymn to Hymen," a risqué tribute to a false god of marriage: "So Hymen, thou phony / God of matrimony, / We say baloney to thee." Merman's numbers, "Ridin' High," "Down in the Depths on the 90th Floor," "You're a Bad Influence on Me," "Red, Hot and Blue," and, especially, "It's De-Lovely" (sung in a duet with Bob Hope), had more staying power.

After previews in Boston and New Haven, *Red, Hot and Blue!* opened on October 29, 1936, at the Alvin. That evening, as with any opening night, Cole Porter was not having fun. "The morning after an opening of one of my own shows," he wrote, "is more or less the same as any other morning, except that I sleep much later. In the case of *Red, Hot and Blue!,* I broke my record by exactly ten minutes." One by one he got telephone calls from Freedley, Merman, then Durante, who all asked, "How are you feeling?" Once he told them fine, they hung up. When Ethel called, though, he had mixed feelings. "I wasn't sure what to do. I love Ethel. . . . [But u]sually, when Ethel phones me it is to suggest changes in her songs, and this was one morning when I did not feel like doing anything of the kind."[77] He took the call.

Reviews said that Merman's voice was in its best form yet, and *Red, Hot and Blue!* would run for a respectable 183 performances. No one pretended that the show was earth-shaking, and Brooks Atkinson noted that the ghost of Ethel and Porter's previous "gangster musical, *Anything Goes*" was "haunting the makers of *Red, Hot, and Blue,* to their disadvantage."[78]

Red, Hot and Blue! has gone down in the books for several behind-the-scenes stories. One is a sweet one: Bob Hope, residing at 65 Central Park West at the time, would pick up Ethel at her 25 Central Park West address while walking down to the Alvin. Another involved them in a less tranquil moment. It was starting to get around town that you didn't mess with Ethel Merman, especially onstage. Bob Hope did. One night, he delivered his scripted lines to her while he was lying down, and the audience howled. Merman was furious. Not only had Hope deviated from the script, but he had done so at her expense. Not one to be upstaged, she told him, "Do that one more time and I'll flatten that ski nose of yours even more," and had producers give him a warning. Hope stuck to his lines.

The most famous anecdote involves billing for the show. Durante and Merman were the two featured players, and neither wanted to cede top billing to the other. Durante was the established star, the beloved old-time vaudevillian, but Merman was hot, and her star was ascending. Their agents were at it for weeks, and no one budged. Finally an agreement was struck: the names of the two stars were inscribed on what resembled the crossed planks of a railroad crossing sign so that neither appeared "first," and every few weeks their names would be reversed. As the newcomer, Bob Hope was on a horizontal plank underneath.

These last two stories circulated widely and offered the press (and the producers) a calculated way to give the public some behind-the-scenes information. By now, consumers expected that kind of thing, however apocryphal or controlled the material that was parceled out. Moreover, the show's producers, agents, and stars must have approved of the leaking of these backstage escapades; they were, after all, lighthearted tensions rather than vicious dramas. Even so, their accounts dovetailed only to a limited extent: one version has Durante relinquishing top billing after he'd been told that, as the senior entertainer, it would reflect well on him to permit "ladies first"; Ethel claims it was the result of producers seeing the wisdom of awarding her top star billing; Hope, six decades after the incident, said the "crossroads" solution was his idea.

Billing skirmish aside, relations were cordial among the three, especially between Merman and Durante. The two had a genuine affection for each other, openly admiring the other's skills and wisecracks. Durante would joke that when he met his costars, he would be disappointed if they weren't in complete awe of him. And so he sniffed around Merman in rehearsals, who finally went up to her elder colleague, eyeballed his outfit, and said, "Say Jimmy, do you think that style of suit is ever coming back?"[79] He cracked up. Over the years, the two of them did dozens of benefits and TV and radio shows together. On January 24, 1954, they performed in an abbreviated version of *Red, Hot and Blue!* for NBC; twenty-five years later, when Durante was on his deathbed, Ethel visited him, staying over an hour, talking, singing, and reminiscing. She could barely keep her composure when she left her old friend, who had not recognized her for a moment.

The same day that *Red, Hot and Blue!* closed, Saturday, April 10, Ethel did a radio show and told audiences, "Well, we're closing on Broadway tonight," and then sang "I've Got My Love to Keep Me Warm."[80] Hollywood would end up adapting *Red, Hot and Blue!* for the screen, though not until 1949, when Betty Hutton was given Ethel's role.

With the New York run behind her, Ethel uncharacteristically agreed to take *Red, Hot and Blue!* to Chicago, where it proceeded to break records at the Grand Opera House. Producer Freedley was on hand to introduce it when the show opened there on April 13. Once again Ethel did not enjoy being on the road. While gracious to the Chicago press, she still complained about being in a city that shut down so early and that remained so cold.

Red, Hot and Blue! gave critics a chance to note Merman's comedic abilities more than ever; it also gave a slight spin on her image as the all-American girl. For no longer did she simply embody traits like down-to-earth fire and determination; now her characters had a relationship to the U.S. government. Although Ethel's characters had yet to become heroines on the side of public good, her shows were presenting a slightly more politicized sense of what that public good entailed. And although Ethel would never have played in overtly political shows like *Pins and Needles* or *The Cradle Will Rock,* certain politicized traits started to settle on her persona: she was on her way to becoming the girl who, intentionally or not, was happy to do good for her country, to follow the rules and support the powers that be. Her next show, *Stars in Your Eyes,* a send-up of left-leaning screenwriters in 1930s Hollywood, unionization, and FDR's cultural programs, made this unambiguously clear. But before then, Ethel returned to Hollywood for another shot at movie stardom.

FOUR

To Hollywood and Back Again

Ethel's big break in Hollywood, such as it was, came in 1938, when 20th Century–Fox released three Merman pictures: *Happy Landing, Alexander's Ragtime Band,* and *Straight, Place and Show.* A clipping she saved from January 18 predicts "Ethel Merman's Film Rise Certain."[1] She had been signed for a three-picture deal beginning October 25, 1937,[2] and by Christmas she was living in Los Angeles. Though she lacked the clout to procure special treatment—Ethel was not, after all, a "star" borrowed from another studio—she was able to amend the billing clause "to provide for featured screen credit [with] only the names of three other artists to precede Merman's name on each picture."[3] She was paid twenty-five thousand dollars for the first picture, *Happy Landing,* Fox's third vehicle for their contracted skating star, Sonja Henie (1912–69).

Sonja Henie was the young Norwegian-born star who was so popular in the 1930s and '40s that her fan mail rivaled that of Shirley Temple, Fox's trophy child star. The only times Henie's volume slipped beneath Temple's was when Temple had just released a film, such as *Little Princess* in spring 1938. Clean-cut and happy, Henie was wildly popular among children, especially girls and young teens who wrote the bulk of the fan mail. (In fact, when volume dipped, Fox attributed it "to the coming of spring and the children who write the majority of fan mail being . . . out of doors.")[4]

Ethel, by contrast, never received much mail from film fans. Children were hardly going to be responsive to Flo Kelly (her role in the Henie film) and similar characters. Nor was Ethel Merman a big national name shining with stardust for young fans, who were likely searching for role models like themselves (Henie) or for grown-up glamour icons like Alice Faye. (Of course, as an East Coast quantity, Ethel had no shortage of fan letters, poems, and the like from kids who'd seen her there.) Fox also noted in one of its seasonal assessments of letters that "comedians [or, we should add, second-string players] never receive as much mail as heroes or 'glamour boys and girls.'"[5]

Merman's fan mail count was low for other reasons as well. Like all the studios, Fox was concerned mainly with its contract players, not people who were brought in for a picture or two, like Merman, and that's where its publicity *and* record-keeping energy lay. Every month, the fan mail department released figures for correspondence received by house performers: sometimes top scorers would receive over twenty-one thousand letters per month (a very high count, but more common by the mid-'40s, perhaps because of the war), sometimes around three thousand. The count for most stars in the midrange, such as Alice Faye, fluctuated month to month, depending on appearances, publicity, and, especially, whether she'd just been in a film. The top three or four players at Fox stayed relatively constant from the late 1930s to the early '50s, when Ethel worked there. The big winner was wartime pinup girl Betty Grable, although once Marilyn Monroe entered the scene, the gap between first and second scorer closed. Occasionally, studio personnel wrote notes to explain why someone's mail count had gone up or down over the month—if there had been a radio address, the release of a rival's film, and so forth. For Merman, Fox briefly listed a post office address for her fans, but there is no indication that her letters were ever tallied or preserved.

Happy Landing

The story of *Happy Landing* was generic enough for early treatments to be called "Sonja Henie Production #2."[6] The movie opens with a big send-off of nightclub bandleader Duke Sargent (Cesar Romero), who is bringing his band by plane to Europe—he considers himself too important and in too much of a rush to go by boat—along with a hundred thousand golf balls to keep them afloat in case they hit water. The press sees the stunt for the hammy gimmick it is; so does Duke's earnest, eyeball-rolling colleague, Jimmy Hall (Don Ameche).

Duke is late to arrive, delayed while in the arms of Flo Kelly (Merman), who has been secretly taping his sweet talk for future blackmail. After a struggle, pal Jimmy crashes the recording, and Duke is free to go. The plane runs out of fuel in a fairy tale of a town in Norway, where Trudy Eriksen (Henie) is dreaming of her "storybook lover," a fantasy encouraged by what a local witch tells her: her husband will appear from "far, far away," and will be tall and dressed like a prince. Enter Duke in dashing aviator clothing.

Trudy is convinced it is fate: "A gypsy told me!" Duke flirts openly with her until he learns that, according to local custom, he has proposed to her by asking her to dance two times.

The event is the town's annual ice festival, and a lavish spectacle scene shows off Trudy/Henie's ice skating. Duke tries to make a hasty exit; dialogue more than intimates that he has had legal troubles from past womanizing. In a slightly queer moment, Jimmy tells Trudy, "Don't pay attention to my friend—he's a woman hater." (Romero was a closeted gay man. To help manage that "problem" and stir up interest for the film, Fox fabricated a romance between Romero and Merman.)

Duke's band continues to perform back in New York, where a love-struck Trudy shows up, unannounced, determined to follow her destiny. Good guy Jimmy starts to fall for her and introduces her to her first hamburger in a diner scene that delighted Henie's fans. The high-rolling Duke has moved on, using women as muses—"She had a song in her!" he will say, and now uses Trudy's line "A gypsy told me!" as part of his performance routine.

Flo has moved on as well, now on the arm of a wealthy elderly man, whom she introduces with Mermanesque flair as "Count Filmore Veryschmarty." She performs a spirited swing number, "Hot and Happy," in a long slit dress, with her signature bracelets, raised hands, and sustained notes, holding "Oh!" for a very, very long time. Near the end of the picture, she sings "You Appeal to Me" with Romero at the piano, a song whose hard-boiled lyrics are appropriate to Flo's affair with Duke: "I never believed in cupid . . . because of all the things he did to me."

By the end of the film, Jimmy and Trudy are coupled, as are the squabbling, volatile Flo and Duke. At one point, Duke pleads to Jimmy, "She beats me! She's trying to kill me for 'getting a good song out of a blonde.'" Flo confides in Jimmy, "I love him, even though he's an alley cat" (a line that raised objections from Breen's censorship office), and Jimmy produces her record— on which Duke's sweet talk has ostensibly been recorded—to force Duke into marrying her. Finale? Duke looks pained as the two newlywed couples go skating together. (Ethel—not her character—is visibly uncomfortable, small surprise given that she had hurt her ankle rehearsing the scene.) In fact, Romero, Ameche, and Merman were poor skaters, although Romero was helped by his experience as a dancer.

Studio head and producer Darryl Zanuck (1902–79) was known for his hands-on approach and typically went through nearly every script and draft of his movies. With *Landing,* there was some difficulty pulling together a plausible narrative for the skating star. (Initially, she was Swiss and going to fall for an American hockey player.) Zanuck's primary concern for the picture was that "care should be taken to keep Sonja Henie's vehicles free of [the sexual angle] . . . even though that element is introduced via Lynette [later, Flo]."[7] At first, when Ethel was considered for the part of Ameche's love interest, Zanuck wondered, "She may be too tough a type."[8]

Early drafts had "Lynette" performing scenes in negligees, doing an off-screen "strip tease" in the men's room, receiving a "copped feel" "under the robe," and "throwing herself at Bob brazenly" (Zanuck's remarks).[9] Both Zanuck and the censors objected to such details. For Breen, that was his job; Zanuck was less guided by moral concern but instinctively knew what would be expected and tolerated of a Sonja Henie movie. He proved right. On its release, some critics voiced relief at the movie's "gay, frothy success";[10] here was a kids' movie without the controversy caused by another children's film several months earlier—Disney studio's *Snow White,* whose evil witch upset critics almost as much as she did children.

For anyone who is not a Henie fan, *Happy Landing* is not terribly interesting. Its story is standard issue, and only the skating numbers show off strong production values and care. But *Happy Landing* is interesting for building on Ethel's film persona, the hard and scheming but ultimately good-hearted woman "romantically" paired with an insincere (drunk, comic—choose one) secondary man. Zanuck's concern about Ethel's being "too tough" shows just how established that persona was, even though she had not worked extensively in Hollywood by this point. It was an image that was a flattened distillation of the roles she played on Broadway, stripped of their vibrant context—not to mention their musical authority.

Whatever its limits, *Happy Landing* is a curious document of its time. It's a film that champions international tolerance when the United States watched from the sidelines as Europe was being swirled into war. Its international "flavor" is assured through endless bad jokes about accents and comparisons of American and European cultures (hamburgers and swing versus fairy tales and fortune tellers). Yet *Happy*'s script is hardly a sanctuary for international tolerance: At one point, Jimmy scolds Trudy, "That's the trouble with you foreigners. You can't get it through your heads that you're in a free country now. If you don't want to work, you don't have to. And if your boss gets tough with you, you tell him to cut it out," suggesting a workers' paradise where people are free from harassment and where working itself is strangely optional.[11]

So interchangeable is the film's depiction of "old Europe" that Fox used the same set for its Norwegian village that it had used for *Heidi,* the Shirley Temple hit set in the Swiss Alps, the year before. Clichés are also evident when

Duke approaches a bandleader to play a "European song" and is told "we don't do swing" before the band plays generic "oom pa pa" music. The idea of old-Europe-as-fairy-tale was a staple in operetta, and it inflected Ethel's work from *Old Man Blues* to *Call Me Madam* and *Happy Hunting*. In *Happy Landing,* it works to showcase America's patronizing good-neighbor policy before the fact, a point reflected even in the casting, with "Latin lover" Cesar Romero (born to Cuban parents in New York) and Norwegian Henie, who also, it was claimed, "discovered" Latina bombshell Carmen Miranda for Fox.

Merman, wrote one review, "sings with her usual lid-off verve";[12] said another, "Ethel Merman's impudent personality comes through for the first time in the movies."[13] Most reviews, though, had little to say about her, lavishing most of their attention on Henie in her third feature; some compliments were doled out to Romero for doing well in a nondancing role. Most of Pop's scrapbook clippings involved newspaper pictures of Ethel socializing with "Butch" (Romero). Ethel and Butch had gotten along well while making the film—both had a penchant for practical jokes—but after a while, as she wrote in her memoirs, she tired of her costar's enthusiasm for their fabricated affair. Gossip columnist Ed Sullivan announced: "After all the talk of Ethel Merman and Cesar Romero, it was just 'publicity hooey.'"[14]

Alexander's Ragtime Band

Less than eight weeks after the wrap of *Landing,* Ethel was scheduled to start work on her second film. Her salary was upped to $27,500 for six weeks' work. More important, *Alexander's Ragtime Band* was an altogether different picture from *Happy Landing*. It was going to be an extravagant, two-million-dollar production promoted heavily by the studio, "produced in lavish proportions!" The project was green-lighted by Zanuck himself to showcase the music of Irving Berlin. Much was made of the fact that its story line spanned three long decades, an epoch stuffed with Berlin's music. For the picture, Berlin would produce two new songs ("Now It Can Be Told," "My Walking Stick"), but most attention was given to existing classics. The picture sailed on a wave of spectacle and nostalgia.

The plot follows Alexander/Aleck/Roger (Tyrone Power, one of Fox's top male players), a classically trained violinist who prefers the lowbrow life of his swing band, with Davey the drummer and composer Charlie (Jack Haley and Don Ameche, also Fox contract players). Their success starts once they perform "Alexander's Ragtime Band," a song that was once part of Stella Kirby's act (played by Fox's Alice Faye). Stella, first a rival, joins the band and quickly transforms from a cheap saloon singer into dignified glamour gal. She begins a love affair with Aleck that capsizes when she accepts an offer to go to New York as a solo act. Aleck rebukes her angrily.

A distraught Aleck joins the army with Davey (World War I has started), where the two put on a show. Back in New York after the war, Aleck discovers that Stella and Charlie have married. Only now—over an hour into the film—does Ethel appear. She plays Jerry Allen, the singer who replaces Stella in Aleck's band. Now a smashing success, the band plays Paris, but Aleck is still carrying the torch for Stella, as Stella is for him. Charlie, who recognizes this, lets her go, and in a parallel story, Jerry sees through Aleck's attempts to persuade himself that he now loves *her*.

Stella's solo singing career starts to dive. But a happy ending is forthcoming, in Carnegie Hall, where Alexander's band has been scheduled. Aleck's snobby former music teacher is in attendance, lending his prestige and approval to the new swing-jazz sensation. Stella rides aimlessly in a cab (driven by John Carradine in a terrific cameo), listening to the radio broadcast of the performance. Unbeknownst to her, the cab driver recognizes her and coaxes her into the hall, where she reunites with Aleck and the band.

Zanuck was intensely involved in developing *Alexander*'s script, as was his wont, making literally hundreds of specific suggestions to Kathryn Scola, Lamar Trotti, and Richard Sherman to make the story more economical, to create a "boffo" impact, and to clarify character motivations. What he wanted was "a really great human interest story."[15] Aleck, he said, was stuck-up and boring. Of the first revised draft, he wrote, "I take an instant dislike to Alex, and I love Charly [*sic*]—it's ok to love Charly, but to dislike Alex is dangerous—he seems dull—self-centered." The musical numbers gave Zanuck nothing to worry about, and his enthusiasm for the project was solid from the start: "I think this picture has an opportunity of being the best picture of 1937."[16]

Irving Berlin was very involved from the beginning and in fact drafted the movie's initial story line with Richard Sherman. Zanuck wanted a biopic about Berlin, an angle that did not interest the songwriter: "I was so concerned about not having this story resemble my life in any way that I purposely made the character of Don Ameche (Charlie) a songwriter." Berlin's demurral was partly out of modesty, but he was also eager for his songs to stand on their own merits, for "the old songs [to] come through as popular songs that the band was playing rather than having them written for any character in the story."[17]

And that was how the film was received. Wrote the *Hollywood Reporter*, "While box offices may recently have been reflecting audience disfavor for musicals, this picture, with at least 25 numbers, is by no means a musical in the accepted film sense. Rather is it *[sic]* the aggrandizement of the evolution of American popular music and a monument to Irving Berlin, who made that music so distinctive that his songs alone are a record of three colorful decades of American life. So perfectly are this film story and the music interwoven that it seems that, in its construction, the songs themselves wrote the script."[18]

Despite her earlier complaints about working for the movie business, Merman was delighted to be invited back. She and Agnes had rented a house; Fox put Ethel on a diet and lightened her "naturally dark hair . . . to a more flattering auburn," a color she retained for much of her life.[19] Principal photography began on January 31, 1937, and three months later, the last retakes were finished. During production, Tyrone Power gave Ethel pointers on how to deal with watching the daily rushes, which she hated: "You have to think of the person on the screen in the third person," he told her. The shy side of Merman was at work. After filming wrapped, Ethel stayed in Los Angeles to record the picture's songs for about three weeks, finishing on May 13.

Alexander's Ragtime Band marked the first time Ethel worked with Irving Berlin. "I'd only seen her in the Follies," he told George Eells later. The movie reunited her with Jack Haley from *Take a Chance,* Ameche from *Happy Landing,* and Alice Faye, who'd borrowed ten dollars from her as a chorus girl in *George White's Scandals.* That loan was now ironic, a harbinger of Ethel's career in pictures. The studio producers had deemed Faye, the blond ingenue—and the lesser singer—as stronger box office; Ethel later called her Fox's "little girl on the lot . . . their bread and butter at the time."[20]

Ethel's Jerry Allen combines two different characters from earlier script drafts. Ruby was a tough-as-nails singer capable of defending herself physically, and Evelyn was a wealthy English widow who became Aleck's paramour and benefactress. Evelyn steps aside romantically, as Jerry does in the final film, when she realizes Aleck is still in love with Stella. Ruby and Evelyn are highly incongruous characters, but neither one of them is eligible for the romantic prize. And so Ethel portrayed Jerry, the two of them combined, in another of Hollywood's not-get-the-guy roles for her.

The androgynously named Jerry is a real pal, one who gets Aleck to "snap out of his daze" after the war. She tells him, disingenuously, that she's not the marrying kind when she sees that his heart is elsewhere. Of course, Ameche's character does the same thing with Stella, but at least he had been allowed a romantic and even marital relationship, whereas Ethel's character is kept to the sexual sidelines. Rather than be the subject of "A Pretty Girl Is Like a Melody," for instance, Jerry sings it. She performs in men's tails and top hat in "My Walking Stick," a delightful number in which she prances on top of sixteen top hats (silk-covered iron molds) lined up between chorus line members. (If it sounds familiar, it should. Berlin had originally written the piece for the Fred Astaire movie *Carefree,* but Astaire said it too closely resembled his earlier "Top Hat" number and had it removed. Merman is now doing Astaire, tails and all!) Ethel recorded two other numbers that were deleted from the final print, "Marching along with Time" and "Slumming on Park Avenue."[21] And in the film it is "cuddly" Alice Faye who sings the eponymous "Alexander's Ragtime Band."[22]

As part of the band's Parisian performance, Ethel/Jerry sings "Pack Up Your Sins (and Go to the Devil)." The four-year-old Breen office was not amused. Swing, like ragtime and the blues before it, had often been called "devil's music," and so the radar was up. (In 1937, the Daughters of the American Revolution were so outraged at bandleader Vincent Lopez for arranging patriotic American songs to swing that they issued an appeal to President Roosevelt for his censure.) A protracted dialogue between the studio and the censorship office ensued: Breen wrote to Fox's Col. Jason Joy, "The lyric to 'Pack up your sins and go to the devil' may possibly be offensive to religiously inclined people. It contains one Code violation, the phrase 'No one gives a damn.' Also the line 'H-E double-L is a wonderful spot' may be deleted by censor boards."[23] Lyrics were modified, but concerns remained:

> We have received and read the additional lyric for the song 'Pack up your sins.' . . . As we wrote you on Feb 18th, it seems to us that the general flavor of this song is unfortunate, and will give offense to religious-minded people, and others. We recommended at that time that you avoid using it in this picture. We again repeat this recommendation, inasmuch as it seems to burlesque one of the fundamental tenets of the Christian religion. This song would therefore seem to be not only questionable from the standpoint of general audience sensibilities, but also a violation of that clause of the Code covering the treatment of religion in pictures.[24]

The lyrics were tinkered with some more, and Breen signed off on it, reluctantly, but not before Fox producers assured that Ethel Merman wasn't going to do anything devilish in performance. (This was a singer who had recorded a bluesy ballad, "Satan's Li'l Lamb," in 1932.) The final product was, at best, a missed opportunity and, at worst, pathetic. Ethel/Jerry stands on a small platform surrounded by rising "smoke," made by forcing the steamlike vapor of dry ice from the large troughs containing it. She has a sequin leotard on over dark stockings, all cloaked under a large dark cape—the kind a devil might wear—along with some asbestos she and the chorines wore for protection against the dangerous vapor. In nearly four minutes, Ethel moves only once, at the very end, when she raises her arms straight overhead. That's it. What should have been a vibrant, bouncy production number isn't. But she is very fetching in her horns.

Of note is Ethel's rendition of "Heat Wave," first written for the 1933 show *As Thousands Cheer,* in which it was made famous by Ethel Waters. Based on a record-breaking heat wave New York had experienced, the song takes the perspective of an animated weather forecaster who blames the heat on "southern winds" and on a woman whose "seat waved." (The chorus agrees, "She certainly can can-can.") In the initial rendition, Berlin's lyrics gave the heat wave a Latin source, and the music (especially its rhythms) shows a Latin calypso influence. "Heat Wave" was further racialized by its own history. *As Thousands Cheer* broke a bit of a race barrier by giving Ethel Waters star billing along with whites Marilyn Miller and Clifton Webb, who sometimes refused to appear with her at events. (In addition to "Heat Wave," Waters sang "Suppertime," the showstopping number about a lynch victim.)

Like most of its other numbers, *Alexander's Ragtime Band* adapts "Heat Wave" to a swing style, though without its normally strong rhythmic patterns. But it's the song's racialization that really changes. First, it is performed in the bastion of upper-crust European-American culture, Carnegie Hall. Singing it, Ethel is clad all in white and eschews the "animated" style of Waters's meteorologist (and Merman's own usual performance style, for that matter). Moreover, the all-white male and female chorus members are wearing strangely anachronistic costumes that conjure up the antebellum South. What this has in common with a New York heat wave is left for the viewer to imagine; production notes do not explain the decision.

Lyrics were cleaned up, with the cause of the blistering temps traced back to a woman waving her *feet,* not her seat. Reasonably, Ethel found this absurd. Fox seemed intent on domesticating both the song and the Merman image, which had scarcely been WASPier before this picture. As she later told the press, people at Fox had been "ordered to 'keep (this girl Merman) down.' I don't blame them."[25] By bleaching "Heat Wave" of potential racial color and sexuality, Fox opted for a bouncy, if neutered, performance, one that was probably all the more racist for its alterations.

Perhaps it is not a surprise that no people of color appear in *Alexander*, although whites perform in blackface in the army scenes. But ethnic, class, and racial markers certainly appear as a means of gauging the band's professional success. Over the course of the film, Aleck's band goes from "playing the devil's music" at "a noisy, smoke-laden dive, the lowest of the low, on the Barbary Coast,"[26] to Carnegie Hall, bringing swing music into respectability; that's why Aleck's stuck-up music teacher needs to be present, to approve.

Audiences found *Alexander's Ragtime Band* to be a fun jaunt down memory lane. No question about it, though, as one critic wrote, it was "honoring a form of music that was already on its way out."[27] Berlin and Merman seemed to be aware that the material was dated when they talked about the film. Merman, for instance, promised it would give audiences "a new ragtime . . . forget all about swing. It is done for!"[28]

Nostalgic or not, *Alexander's Ragtime Band* had recouped its negative cost within a month of its release. It generated quite a bit of mail from fans, many believing these to be the best performances of Faye and Power, the ones against which later performances would be measured. Fans adored what they called Ameche's "Christian values" and his perfect teeth. The movie's success was such that a St. Louis woman named Mary Cooper Oehler (later Dieckhaus) filed suit against Fox, claiming it had taken her unpublished story "Love Girl" as the basis for *Alexander*. Lawsuits like that were (and remain) common, and Fox referred to her as the woman who suffered from "plagiarism complex,"[29] an unkindness that was not unwarranted: Oehler and her associates fudged dates and names on documents such as her copyright requests. Miraculously, she won the initial court decision, but Fox overturned it—two years, several lawyers, and a Pinkerton agent later. Oehler appealed the decision all the way to the U.S. Supreme Court, which refused to hear the case.

Alexander's gala premiere was in Los Angeles on May 24, 1938, at the Carthay Circle Theatre, followed by an enormous party at the Trocadero. It opened in full release a week later. Merman received telegram after telegram of congratulations, from Fox executive Sol Wurtzel's ("I think your performance in *Alexander's Ragtime Band* is the first real step toward success in motion pix which you so well deserve") to loyal fan Mary Cantor's. Louella Parsons loved it, calling it "one in a million";[30] Ruth Arell wrote, "Yes, when Ethel sings, you understand fully why they named that highspeed gasoline 'Ethyl.' She's got the same high-grade, anti-knock, long-wearing quality."[31]

Straight, Place and Show

Ethel had made it up the LA ladder, attending a bon voyage party for Darryl Zanuck and his wife, who were about to leave for Europe on the deluxe liner *La Normandie,* before she herself returned east to New York. After a week there visiting her parents, she returned to Hollywood to complete her third Fox picture, which was scheduled to begin shooting on May 23. *Straight, Place and Show* was a vehicle for the Ritz Brothers, Fox's vaudeville-schooled team whose pun-filled high jinks paved the way for later trios, such as the Three Stooges. At the time, Harry, Al, and Jimmy Ritz (tame in their private lives) were a sort of second-tier Marx Brothers, and like other specialty acts contracted with the studios, Ritz Brothers movies were spit out with regularity, with story lines so mechanical as to be almost incidental. Studio execs were more concerned with showcasing their physical antics and verbal gags.

Straight, Place and Show was a horse race caper that capitalized on the great popularity of racing at the time; Ethel's scrapbooks include a column that described and then placed odds, racetrack style, on stars. (Earlier, in 1932, an ad for B. F. Keith Palace's show used a racetrack form, listing performers as horses, among them a young "Ethel Herman.")[32] To publicize the picture, Ethel made at least one recorded appearance at the Santa Anita racetrack.

Straight, Place and Show establishes its lighthearted mood with its opening animated credits that show all three brothers riding one horse. New York writer Damon Runyon (1884–1946) provided the material on which the screenplay was based; Merman's two numbers, "With You on My Mind" and "Why Not String along with Me?" were written by Lew Brown and Lew Pollock. A young Jule Styne was among those credited for his provision of "special extra material."

Richard Arlen and Phyllis Brooks starred as Denny Paine and Barbara Drake, lovers whose engagement is broken off by Barbara's excessive devotion to her show horse, Playboy. Denny wins Playboy from her in a huffy, angry bet, and the horse serendipitously ends up at the Ritz Brothers' pony ring. With Denny's engagement off, society girl Linda (Merman) moves in on him but retreats to help Barbara regain both horse and the man whom she still loves. ("Barbara is still a favorite; I catch on," Ethel says in the betting lingo that pervades the film.) After a zany performance at a steeplechase race, with the Ritz Brothers all riding Playboy (backward), Playboy wins the team a purse of twenty-five thousand dollars, and Denny and Barbara reunite.

Straight, Place and Show has Merman depicting another clean-cut "Pal Jerry" kind of woman in Linda, a supporting character whose primary function is to step aside so that the feuding lovers can reunite. Yet it was different from Ethel's other Hollywood fare in that Linda exudes more warmth than most of her other character roles. Linda's friendship with Barbara is genuine: "He loves you. Denny is playing to win; I say this from my heart," she tells "Babs," with whom she is closer than any of the men—even the comic men, to whom she was usually relegated in studio movies. Zanuck fought for that characterization. Responding to script drafts as late as April 1938, he complained that Linda "has been made a bitch where there is no necessity for it at all. She can still be the clever, smart and sophisticated girl that she starts out to be with a great sense of humor, etc. and she should end up that way. We must avoid the feeling there is in it now that she is trying to thwart the situation."[33]

Merman performs her two numbers of the movie in splendid voice. For as much as she later professed to dislike *Straight, Place and Show,* she conveys a warmth, dignity, and classiness in song as well as in her overall performance. One thing that didn't change, however, was that in her songs, she scarcely moves an inch, something that always frustrated her about performing for cameras. But here, the stillness registers as sedateness rather than constraint, as it had in *Alexander's Ragtime Band.* It's also interesting to note that *every* character moves in and out of different classes, as well as ethnic and national groups; the film has references to a wrestler called "the Terrible Turk/the Maniac of Mesopotamia," and the Ritz Brothers' rivals are three South American jockeys. While hardly a thoughtful movie on this front, at least Ethel's character is not singled out for that kind of ethnic treatment.

While the script was under development, changes included the title *(Sarasota Chips),* characters (a Communist was removed), and cast (this, too, was first envisioned as an Eddie Cantor vehicle). To appease the censorship office, a number of references had to be removed—too much drinking, double entendres, and so forth. Zanuck's response to the project went from proclaiming, "insane hoke . . . this is Mack Sennett . . . awful," as he'd scribbled on the first revised treatment script, to a secretary's note saying, "Mr. Zanuck is greatly enthused."[34] Shooting ended the second week of July 1938, with the picture going over its $717,000 budget by about $33,000.[35]

Reviews of the "horse opera" were predictable, saying that fans of the Ritz Brothers' style of comedy would love it, and others would not. Critics tended to describe it as either vaudeville or burlesque—in other words, nothing new. Ethel's role didn't generate much ink, although one paper referred to her as "velvety voiced."[36] Overall, *Straight, Place and Show* was a big letdown after the big success of *Alexander's Ragtime Band*. Merman despised it and, in her second autobiography, refused to identify the movie by name, much less discuss it. Fox, too, kept its distance, pulling its commitment to her for the time being. "We are not optioning," Zanuck wrote in an internal memo.[37] In her memoirs, Ethel would note, "The end of my work in Hollywood also wrote *finis* [a favorite expression] to Lou Irwin as my agent. . . . It was cold down there on the face on the cutting room floor."[38] Irwin was the Ritz Brothers' agent as well. They, too, released him after *Straight, Place and Show* was released.

Ethel arrived back in New York on July 19, 1938. To the press, she was typically candid—and sometimes surprisingly indiscreet—about her experiences on the West Coast. New York fans were always eager to hear her comparisons:

> They're pretty crazy out there. I worked two extra weeks on a sequence for the Crosby picture and then they cut it out. Now they're going to use it in another picture! . . . Sam Goldwyn [is] . . . not as bad as the stories about him . . . the fuss the censors made about that picture *[Kid Millions]*! In one scene, a flock of little kids are shown eating ice cream. When they turn away from the tables, their tummies are all swollen. The censors passed the scenes showing the boys that way but they raised a kick about the girls. Imagine, eight- and nine-year-olds![39]

Two days after her return, the local papers ran a syndicated photo of her from *Ragtime*—notably, not *Happy Landing* or *Straight, Place and Show*. And for the publicity-stunt photo of her holding a lantern on a caboose of a train when the train started to pull out of the station, the caption gave a wink only to *Ragtime:* "She Started a Heat Wave."

Ethel reestablished herself quickly. On August 3, she did a radio version of *Alexander's Ragtime Band* as Stella—not Jerry—with guests Walter Winchell, Al Jolson, Eddie Cantor, and Sophie Tucker. Hugely successful, the broadcast proved a sound way not only to honor Berlin but also to promote the picture. As one reviewer put it,

> Ethel Merman is acknowledged to be one of the grandest musical comedy singers in existence. She is also an actress of no mean ability, as evidenced by

her playing of Alice Faye's role in the *Alexander's Ragtime Band* radio broadcast. Yet, did you note how obvious were the efforts to cut and play down her part in the picture? The sequence in which first Merman, and then Faye sing "Blue Skies" appeared to be a deliberate move to show Miss Merman to disadvantage. The song was perfectly suited to Miss Faye's type of singing and definitely unsuited to Miss Merman. The title song, "Alexander's Ragtime Band," was meant for the latter, but Faye got the number![40]

Back on her home turf, Ethel let it rip; she knew what the local press would eat up. "Broadway is a 'snap' compared to movieland. Out there . . . they treat you like an animal act. The directors and press agents crack the whip and you go through your paces . . . never had a chance to enjoy the so-called California climate. Why, when I got back to New York, the East River looked like nature's masterpiece."[41] Tired of bouncing back and forth with little time to settle into California, she said that "it got so the Pullman porters thought I was a traveling saleswoman."[42]

By no means was Merman consistent in her press reports of the time. Her eagerness for Hollywood success remains evident: pasted right next to a clipping stating that she wants to stay in Hollywood ("I've always had a gig back in New York that made me go back and never settle down here") is one, four days later, entitled "Merman Loyal to New York." "Despite the fact that she has a long-term contract with 20th Century–Fox," it exaggerates, "Ethel Merman maintains that her home address will be New York and that she will commute to Hollywood for the three pix yearly for which she is signed."[43] In truth, Ethel would not work again for Fox for over ten years.

Stars in Your Eyes

Hollywood may have been through with her for now, but Broadway was not. Ethel's next show was *Stars in Your Eyes*. Late in 1938, producer Dwight Deere Wiman (1895–1951) announced that he had signed Ethel Merman to star in a new musical called *Swing to the Left*. It was to go into rehearsal once he was done with his current show, *Great Lady*. *Swing* was written by J. P. McEvoy and went into preparation with heavy revisions, eventually becoming the show *Stars in Your Eyes*.

Action takes place on Sound Stage 7 of the Monotone Picture Corporation, where a movie called *Old Kentucky* is in production. There are concerns about the movie's story, and in order to make it more relevant, it is updated to the present and redubbed _New Kentucky_. A new writer, John Blake (Richard Carlson), is brought in on the basis of his work in writing a socially conscious documentary called _Plain People from the Plains_ (a reference to _The Plow That Broke the Plains,_ a film that examined harsh conditions faced by American farmers in 1936). But not everyone at Monotone is convinced that the cause-driven Blake is the right man, and he is told in regard to the director: "Wilder's afraid of this scene we're about to shoot. I hope you're not getting too significant—We'll get into trouble!"

Merman plays Jeanette Adair, the spoiled star who is used to getting her way. Diva Jeanette is dead set against changes or making the picture "relevant"—until she meets Blake. Then _New Kentucky_ briefly meets with her approval, until Blake writes a big role for ballet dancer Tata (Tamara Toumanova), with whom he has been flirting. Bill (Jimmy Durante), a pitchman (originally, the role was for a union organizer), provides comic relief with classic Durante lines. Pitching a mob scene: "I'm walking down the street today and I bumps into a guy. So I apologizes. But he ain't satisfied. He demands an autopsy." Elsewhere: "They're on the edge of a precipice!"

Dawson (Richard Barbee), the picture's producer, is getting sick of forcing political relevance into the show. Blake is urged to go back to Nebraska but refuses. By now, Dawson and Jeanette have both backed out, and Jeanette has blackballed Tata from getting a job anywhere else. It is left to Bess, the screenwriter (Mildred Natwick), to get people back onboard and to convince Jeanette to be the show's new backer. Tata quits. Jeanette gets Blake drunk in her room, reading _Alice in Wonderland_ to try to seduce him. (Audiences cracked up when she read, "Alice was beginning to get very TIRED of sitting by her sister on the bank and of having nothing to do.") A boozy fantasy number ensues in which Blake imagines he is Monotone's president before morphing into a Russian ruler . . . who is married to Jeanette. Once awake and sober, Blake leaves Hollywood, and Tata and Bill plan to make the film elsewhere.

Music was by Arthur Schwartz and lyrics by Dorothy Fields; the legendary Joshua Logan directed. It was when Logan was brought onboard that the show's political and social commentary was excised in order to enhance its entertainment value. Dancers included Dan Dailey Jr. (Ethel's future costar), a young Jerome Robbins (her future director), and Alecia Alonzo. Jo Mielziner again did stage design. Logan loved working with Ethel, calling her the best instinctive actress he had ever worked with. To show it, he gave her a small silver cup with the inscription "To Sarah Bernhardt Jr., from Josh." It thrilled her enormously.

Ethel's songs included "This Is It," "Just a Little Bit More," "I'll Pay the Check," "A Lady Needs a Change," and, with Durante, "It's All Yours." The last was the show-stopper, and every night Ethel and Durante would try to crack each other up while they did it, with audiences lapping it up.

Stars' self-conscious story of filming a musical covers the rehearsals, squabbles, love affairs, and constant revisions made during production, and Merman's Jeanette splendidly sends up the kind of star who isn't half as divine as she thinks she is. At one point, Bess, the screenwriter, trying to make a phone call during a shoot, tells the party on the line, "Just a minute, Moe, I gotta be quiet. Sarah Bernhardt Jr. is about to louse up a scene"—a reprise of Logan's much less ironic gift. Other inside gags include Jeanette using Ethel's own drink of choice (champagne) to intoxicate Blake; her character's name—not the usual "Nails" and "Flo"—is a light Euro-mash of Jeanette MacDonald and Adele Astaire; lines like "Don't say 'yes' until I've finished talking" conjure up Hollywood's iconic studio moguls, and so forth. But the biggest bull's-eye was the southern diva Merman depicted, a direct allusion to David O. Selznick's highly publicized search for Scarlett O'Hara in his upcoming adaptation of *Gone with the Wind.*

After previews in New Haven and Boston, *Stars* opened on Thursday, February 9, 1939, at the Majestic Theatre. It closed 127 performances later on May 26, Ethel's poorest run. At around the hundredth performance, producers had actually cut ticket prices in anticipation of the New York World's Fair.

The show did not do well with reviewers: "Apparently Mr. McEvoy's book was originally intended either as a satire on Hollywood Leftism or on Hollywood's fear of Leftist movements. I am not quite sure which was meant, but it certainly doesn't matter, since any attempt at social significance was carefully deposited on the stage's equivalent of the cutting-room floor during the course of the rehearsals and tryouts."[44] Though the story didn't enthrall, critics joined audiences in applauding the robust performances of Durante and Merman (and now Ethel had top billing over him!). Said John Mason Brown, "If vaudeville is ever revived, it will be by people as magnetic and courageous as Jimmy Durante and Ethel Merman."[45] One columnist spoke of "the return of vaudeville" in *Stars,* in other shows on the boards such as *Hellzapoppin',* and even in the city's nightclub acts: "Billy Rose started the new trend at the Casa Manana; Strand [is] using acts like Ethel Merman bringing it back."[46] It was the high power of Merman and Durante's performance rather than vaudeville per se that was generating so much enthusiasm.

The show was recognized in national venues as a genuine sensation. In February, *Life* magazine ran a large glossy photo of the *Stars in Your Eyes* audience enthusiastically applauding, and Merman took her copy and circled two people on it, with a long arrow going to the bottom of the page: "Mother and dad," whom she always brought to her shows.[47]

Ethel's comedic skills—her timing, delivery, and use of her face and body—were receiving more and more recognition. And the references to her voice's force, especially its brashness, were on the rise. Indeed, between her and Durante—who could spin the English language into a nutty dictionary of puns and gags—it is small wonder that one of the most printed images from the show showed him leaning over Merman with a "hush" finger over his mouth. As a reviewer put it, "A calliope is as quiet as a sylvan nook compared to Miss Merman. Mr. Durante can make the fog horn of the Normandie sound like a child's whistle."[48]

Big-Voiced Merman

Given that Ethel's voice has been the most "Mermanized" of her features—not unreasonably, for a singer—it is not altogether surprising that that voice has taken on a life of its own. Much of the effectiveness of Merman's belt derives from the impression it gives of physical accomplishment, as opposed to the lighter, more disembodied style of other singers. (Recall the comparison of her sustained note in "I Got Rhythm" to swimming laps in an Olympic-sized pool.) The same analogy can be applied to dancer Gene Kelly's style: Kelly's body seemed to celebrate the sheer strength his movements required. In contrast, Fred Astaire made his movements look effortless, as if he were dancing on air rather than earth. Kelly struck a more working-class, tough image—not that of a man in top hat and tails. Although these class distinctions didn't disadvantage either of the two dancers (in fact, Astaire's characters typically *were* working class—"hoofers" who happened to make the big time), the "airier" realms of Astaire's dancing, like nonbelt singing styles, stereotypically are linked to higher social positions or decorum. Never high art or transcendent—as the critic who said that Merman's voice aims "slightly above the entrails"[49]—her vocal style only reinforced her image as an earthy, unpretentious woman who spoke and lived in the vernacular of the street.

If it was one thing, the Merman voice was strong: her lung power was remarkable, and she sang her songs with the kind of vitality that could cut the oxygen from a room. This is why few people know of ballads like "Satan's Little Lamb" and why many would be surprised to see her doing "Red Robin" with Perry Como. Over time, descriptions of her voice's "loudness" increased as reviewers responded to that feature at the expense of its other ones. In other words, the press helped limit and ultimately make Merman's vocal strength a cliché. As early as 1943, one critic took note, writing, "The few persons—and they are remarkably few—who do not enjoy her, feel that she is too loud, too devoid of subtlety and describe her as brassy but, making all allowances for discrepancies of opinion, this is to do her less than justice. Substitute the word exuberant for loud, and I think you have the essence of her personality.... The voice and personality still have the infectious heartiness of a good brass band, but time has taught her to soften the attack just a little, to let her personality come through without too sharp an attack."[50]

By the late 1930s, the press had in fact let the tags of jazz, blues, and torch singer fall by the wayside in favor of commenting on Merman's loudness. Not all of the references were meant critically at the time ("substitute the word exuberant"), but the trend only escalated, and after the war, the loudness became increasingly brushed with negative connotations. Given changes in music, vocal styles, and recording technologies of the time, this is hardly surprising. Since the early 1930s, with the rise of crooners such as Rudy Vallee, Bing Crosby, Frank Sinatra, and, later, Nat King Cole, Perry Como, Pat Boone, and Dean Martin, *male* vocalists were certainly eschewing the physical, performative style of Al Jolson, Eddie Cantor, Cab Calloway, and others.

And if, by the '50s, rock-and-roll vocalists would be called screamers (Little Richard perhaps being king) and were also dubbed "too loud," they were not belters, and much of their volume was produced by electric amplification. Of course, it would be simplistic to equate people's grumbling over Ethel's "loud" voice with the rejection of rock and roll, for at that point, many of the anti-Merman grumblers were younger music critics. While some of them were no fans of rock and roll, others were, and Ethel's voice may have seemed too much a voice of the past. But back in the late '30s, this trend in people's response to the distinctive, energetic voice was beginning to coalesce. The difference was, calling it loud was a way of having fun with it, of loving and even worshipping the powerful spell it cast.

As Jeanette Adair, Ethel might well have derived satisfaction in sending up the Hollywood divahood that had eluded her thus far. One interview ran: "Miss Merman prefers playing on the stage to motion pix and radio work. 'For one thing,' she said,

> you've got an audience to play to. And you don't have to get up at five in the
> morning like you do in Hollywood. They, they'll rehearse and even film one
> scene over and over until it's perfect. Of course, that [sic] good because it keeps

you on your toes. But anyway, I like the people in New York City better. In Hollywood, there's one big clique and no matter how big a name you have on Broadway, until you've made a hit in the movies you don't exist. Broadway welcomes everyone, and has a grand time doing it.[51]

Madame DuBarry

Ethel's next appearance on the boards was in *DuBarry Was a Lady,* with a book by Herbert Fields and Buddy DeSylva. Ethel had worked with DeSylva before in *Take a Chance,* but *DuBarry* was his first show as solo producer, and he reportedly put a hundred thousand dollars of his own money into it. Songs were by Cole Porter, working on his first show since *Leave It to Me!* in 1938–39. The story revolves around an actual historical figure, early nineteenth-century Duchesse Marie-Caroline de Barry, who, at sixteen, married the only Bourbon family member likely to produce an heir. While pregnant, she watched as her husband was stabbed to death after an evening at the theater, and over the next decade, the widowed duchess created a big following in Parisian circles through her active social life. In the process, though, she created friction with the royal family, much as Princess Diana did a century and a half later. Eventually de Barry was imprisoned for trying to secure her son the French throne, and adding to her intrigue was the fact that she had a baby in jail and never divulged the father's identity.

An unconventional woman at the cusp of the modern age, Duchesse de Barry personified a less stiff, less remote royal figure even if she was also perceived as a sign of all that was *wrong* with monarchy. The tensions made her story ideal fare for modern audiences, and, indeed, it was not new to Broadway: an operetta loosely based on her life had appeared in 1932. The DeSylva-Fields book, however, was concerned less with her actual story than with the springboard she offered their own. We open with a nightclub washroom attendant, Louis (sometimes written as "Louie") Blore (Bert Lahr), who wins the Irish Sweepstakes. With his new wealth, he hopes to woo the club's top singer, May Daly (Merman), who herself is involved with a married newspaperman, Alex Bartin. Louis decides to slip a Mickey Finn into his rival's drink but accidentally drinks the concoction himself. In the ensuing fantasy, he becomes French king Louis XV, and May Daly, his mistress. But even in the fantasy, May/DuBarry's heart is elsewhere. The "Louis" of the fantasy suffers further indignities when his son shoots an arrow into his britches. (Prone, the poor man complains of looking like a weathervane, to which Ethel's DuBarry retorts, the king can always hang a flag out on Bastille Day.) When Louis comes to, he has a change of heart and gives Alex ten thousand dollars of his winnings so that the young man can divorce his wife and marry May. Since most of the rest goes to taxes, Louis resumes his menial job.

The role was perfect for Lahr, who had made a fine art of playing put-upon, fumbling, snarly men: his was "a face that was obviously invented for falling on."[52] Madame DuBarry, some maintain, was a part initially conceived for Mae West,[53] whose ribald persona seemed ideally suited and helped people resume connections between West, Ethel, "Eadie," and the like. Miss West, though, was more interested in her film career at the time; 1940 would be the year that *My Little Chickadee* with W. C. Fields was released. Ethel was billed second to Lahr but proved to be his comedic equal—and not bad at the Mae West stuff either. And, as an object of romantic fantasy (however wise-cracking), her character was given something of a new twist.

Unfortunately, it was not Cole Porter's best set of songs. They weren't weak, just not up to the elevated bar he'd established in *Anything Goes*. Naughtier numbers were used in the fantasy sequence when Louis tries to bed DuBarry, "But in the Morning, No!" (banned on radio) and "Give Him the Oo-La-La." The sequence also contained a sweet ballad, "Do I Love You?" which was a huge radio hit. Songs set in the nightclub scenes were more burlesque, like "Katie Went to Haiti," again a nod to "Eadie." The clear nightly favorite, though, was Merman and Lahr's duet in which, as May and Louis, they sang Cole's sprightly rhymes in "Friendship": "If you're ever in a jam / Here I am. / If you ever need a pal, / I'm your gal." Porter had to write extra verses in the Boston previews so that they didn't run out in all the encores.

Ethel had to miss the marriage of her friend and future godmother of her children, Eleanor Holm, to Billy Rose during previews, which had started November 9, 1939, at the Shubert in New Haven before moving to Boston and Philadelphia. Reviewers found the first act long, and a few complained about the number of "sentimental songs," but most enjoyed the score, the book, and the costumes. (The responses to the show's lusty humor were mixed.) On two things there was total consensus: Lahr and Merman.

On December 6, 1939, *DuBarry* opened in New York at the 46th Street Theatre and became the season's hit, one of only two shows to exceed two hundred nights. Ethel received congratulatory notes from Walter Annenberg, Louella Parsons, Buddy DeSylva ("You're the nicest girl I ever worked with and the cleverest—good luck"), Patrice and Damon Runyon, Irving Berlin ("I'll be out front rooting"), New York mayor Jimmy Walker, Ray Goetz, Katharine Hepburn, J. Edgar Hoover, and Clyde Tolson. All of the entertainment gossipers received her well: Winchell, Hopper, Parsons, Sobol, Sullivan. (Sobol thanked Ethel for a recording she had sent him; Louella Parsons, a basket of heather. Their notes, preserved in the scrapbooks, show not only Ethel's professional courtesy but also her savvy in greasing the wheels of the press.)

Reviewers loved the onstage antics between Lahr and Merman, "shows in themselves," according to John Mason Brown.[54] (At one point, when King Louis/Lahr is chasing Madame DuBarry/Merman around a bed, he suddenly reversed direction and got such a laugh from the crowd that they kept it in.)[55] Raoul Pène Du Bois's set design and costumes also drew unanimous praise. (Merman had seven costume changes.) But the book took a few knocks. Scarcely ambitious and with no pretensions of being so, "its wit is almost nil, but its wisecracks are raw as a cannibal sandwich, suggestive as a red light burning in the hall."[56] "No two entertainers other than Bert Lahr and Ethel Merman could carry [off] this plot, plus the songs they sing, without driving the audience into the street screaming for the morals squad. The subject of sex is belabored mightily throughout this opus, with no suggestion of kid gloves."[57]

Of course, charges of vulgarity were nothing new to Broadway. Ethel's own musical comedies had usually provided a nod-and-wink attitude toward sex, and during the 1930s, Broadway in general was doing what post-Code Hollywood could no longer get away with, Mae West or not. As a critic had said of *Red, Hot and Blue!* "Freedley's new musical is a riot of low comedy. It is not only very low, but is almost the bottom,"[58] not unreasonable for a story featuring a search for a woman with burn patterns on her bottom. Then there were the opening lines of *Stars in Your Eyes:* A movie set carpenter is hammering and mutters, "How do I keep these damn things in? I've nailed 'em as deep as I can." Then a chorus girl, adjusting what the script describes as "a very low necked bodice," repeats the same line.

Still, it was *DuBarry* that pulled out all the stops. One Philadelphia previewer went so far as to call the book pornographic.[59] Of its many reviews—saved, every one of them, by Edward Zimmermann—the best was offered in this: "*Dubarry* is about as lowdown as the most prolific patron of peepshows could desire. But, as the individual three seats to my right remarked tersely, 'I don't mind smut so long as it's clever.'"[60]

Reviewers may have deemed *DuBarry* a bit raw, but they were clear that Ethel Merman was not. She was the opulently dressed DuBarry, still dispensing beauty tips. "Ethel Merman—Just a Home-Loving Girl"—subtitled "You Wouldn't Think So, However, If You Saw Her DuBarry in Musical Comedy."[61] The press acknowledged Ethel's ability to handle coarse material and remain "natural," almost pure: "'I follow stage directions, of course,' she said, 'but not to the letter. . . . I do whatever comes to me naturally at each performance.' Offstage Miss Merman is completely natural. She seems to have not a single glamour girl trick or pose or gesture up her sleeve. She has great respect of her ability to put over a song, but she doesn't think her talent gives her a right to be temperamental or late for appointments. . . . Ethel Merman is known as a 'good egg.'"[62]

Of course, people knew Ethel to use language and jokes offstage that would make the proverbial sailor blush, apparently outdone only by Tallulah Bankhead. Onstage, Ethel tamed those qualities without ever apologizing for them. "It is rough and rather coarse in spots," ran a *DuBarry* review, "but the very frankness of its bawd[iness] and the blithe refusal of the stars even to admit that there is anything to be abashed about should disarm the sternest moralist."[63] What Ethel did was create a sense of both bawdiness *and* good clean fun.

What was beginning to intensify was a lifelong tension between Ethel's skills as an attractive singer and those of a boisterous comic. In the late 1930s in shows like *Stars in Your Eyes* and *DuBarry*, Ethel was allowed to be both. (A female critic even described Ethel's DuBarry as "gorgeously comic.")[64] But the balance would prove hard for her—or for any other female performer—to keep.

Throughout the 1930s, Merman's musical comedies had contained risqué elements, partly the vestiges of vaudeville and burlesque comedy, partly the influence of costars such as Lahr, Durante, Haley (vaudeville hams all), the characters she portrayed (gangster molls, brassy single women), and the lyrics of her songs ("Anything Goes," "Eadie Was a Lady"). In the early '30s, critics would blame the book or the lyricist if things bordered on racy. By now, at the end of the decade, such complaints were beginning to spill over, indirectly, onto performers. Ethel was lucky to avoid the slime.

As far as Broadway musicals were concerned, the complaints over *DuBarry*'s rough gags suggest two things. First, that the lighthearted book musical was getting tired. Broadway audiences had experienced a decade of light escapist fare in the '30s, but they had also experienced the novelty of shows like *Porgy and Bess*. The second issue involves the entertainment industry's relationship to world events at hand. By the time *DuBarry* ran, war was consuming Europe, and despite the official isolationism of U.S. policy, concern was mounting for the situation and for the refugees and orphans that fascism was already churning out. Stars like Merman were already going to rally after rally to lend their names to fund-raising and relief efforts.

In times like this, lighthearted fare can turn on itself, for it's a fine line that separates escapist, pleasurable diversion from entertainment that is out of touch, inappropriate, or insensitive. *DuBarry* ran at a time when *Life with Father, Too Many Girls, Leave It to Me!* and *Pins and Needles* were also on Broadway, and while none tackled the war or other current events, critics rightly viewed *DuBarry* as one of the more dated shows. It took no risks except that of not taking any.

As the United States grew more sensitized to the conflict, the values it wanted to uphold grew more conservative and old-fashioned. The obvious irony here is that "older fashioned" forms of comedy were becoming less acceptable, deemed in poor taste: vaudevillian double entendres were flying in the face of family-friendly fare and a nation wanting to unite through homespun humor and honorable women. Sex found expression in monogamous marriage, and jokes were of the "good, clean fun" variety. Obviously this isn't what Broadway theater (and to a reduced extent, film and radio) was going to provide in toto; after all, "adult" stars like Tallulah Bankhead, Beatrice Lillie, and Noel Coward were in their prime.

Despite Americans' reelection of the liberal FDR to a third term in 1940, a more conservative ethos ruled the day, and by the time of *DuBarry,* entertainment was a more conservative beast than it had been during the days of *Take a Chance.* In regard to Ethel, this meant several things. First, we are seeing the early signs of her spirited characters becoming more politicized; second, by contrast, that "all-American girl-next-door" persona is mutating into a tough-talking woman of experience, an image enhanced by stories of her offstage battles, such as those with Durante and Hope. Thus, while Ethel still embodied wholesome energy and verve, the good stenographer was giving way to a brassier, harder persona, a trend that intensified as years went by. But bright or tarnished, underneath was a generous, even vulnerable, woman, whether onstage or off.

Ethel Merman at lamppost, 1930s. Courtesy of Sydelle Kramer.

Ethel with the scrapbooks maintained by her father. Courtesy of the Museum of the City of New York.

Ethel, age three, with her cousin Claude Pickett (standing). Courtesy of the Museum of the City of New York.

Ethel as a young girl with an unidentified boy. Courtesy of the Museum of the City of New York.

Ethel the stenographer, mid-1920s. Courtesy of the Museum of the City of New York.

A modest flapper. Courtesy of the Museum of the City of New York.

Sheet music featuring Ethel Merman, 1927. Courtesy of the American Musical Institute.

At the radio mike, early 1930s. Courtesy of the Museum of the City of New York.

Ethel arrives in Los Angeles, 1933. Syndicated ACME photograph;
courtesy of Al F. Koenig Jr.

Ethel and Leslie Stowe in the expressionist short *Devil Sea,* 1931. Author's collection.

Hal Forde and Ethel in the fairy-tale short *Old Man Blues*, 1932.
Author's collection.

Ethel (center) sings "Eadie Was a Lady" in *Taking a Chance*, 1932.
Courtesy of the Museum of the City of New York.

Unhappy on a hoop: filming *Anything Goes*, 1936.
Courtesy of UCLA Arts Special Collection.

Ethnic disguise in the film version of *Anything Goes*.
Courtesy of UCLA Arts Special Collection.

Warhol-esque layout of scrapbook page.
Courtesy of the Museum of the City of New York.

Fan Esther Hader's scrapbook
cover. Courtesy of the Museum
of the City of New York.

Photo sent by Ethel Merman
to Esther Hader. Courtesy
of the Museum of the City
of New York.

Paramount Pictures publicity shot with "modern technology."
Courtesy of the Academy of Motion Picture Arts and Sciences.

"Heat Wave" in *Alexander's Ragtime Band*, 1938.
Courtesy of the Academy of Motion Picture Arts and Sciences.

With Jimmy Durante in *Stars in Your Eyes,* 1939. © Playbill, used by permission; courtesy of the Museum of the City of New York.

Seducing Richard Carlson in *Stars in Your Eyes.* Photograph by Lucas & Pritchard; courtesy of Sydelle Kramer.

Ethel arrives in Hollywood, 1937. Syndicated ACME photograph;
Courtesy of Al F. Koenig Jr.

With *Happy Landing* costars Don Ameche (left) and Cesar Romero, 1938.
Courtesy of Sydelle Kramer.

FIVE

Broadway's Brightest

The Early Forties

New Year's, 1939. Ethel saw in the new decade with the city's social elite, playing around as she crowned the colorful former mayor Jimmy Walker with a paper party hat. Ethel was just a month into her run as Madame DuBarry, and by now she had more than Bert Lahr pining at her feet. If the 1930s had established her as Broadway's rising star, the 1940s made her its queen. Her ascent had been as steady as a steamroller. Commanding more salary than any of her contemporaries in musical comedy, Ethel kept breaking her own records, getting extra salary through the sorts of contract stipulations that stars had rarely seen before—percentages of a show's run when touring, et cetera. Producers didn't flinch, since they knew that an Ethel Merman musical was money in the bank. They could raise ticket prices and still fill the house. (Tickets for her upcoming *Panama Hattie* would top at $4.40, compared with $3.30 for the long-running hit *Hellzapoppin'.*) It didn't matter that Ethel wouldn't tour; she brought in the dough. She was hardworking, reliable, healthy, rarely missed a performance or rehearsal, and stayed with shows for their New York run. Small wonder Lloyds of London liked her so much.

Throughout the decade, Merman's career would continue its unshakable course: she was on top, period. Her stage work prompted one critic to single out Ethels Merman and Waters as "uniquely American," high praise indeed in a country preparing to enter a war to protect American interests.[1] But the 1940s were also a period of change in the way that Broadway musicals were written, performed, and marketed, and those changes would affect La Merm.

Ethel enjoyed a gratifying personal life. To fete her thirty-second birthday, she threw a party for the *DuBarry* cast and crew, and famous fan friends, including J. Edgar Hoover and Clyde Tolson, his companion, dropped by. Agnes and Pop were still living near her in the 25 Central Park West building, they were still in good health, and the three kept one another up to date, even though Ethel saw less of them, for Ethel was now a regular in the city's posh café society scene, frequenting such clubs as the Stork Club, the Casino, and El Morocco with Tallulah Bankhead, Noel Coward, Eleanor Holm, Beatrice Lillie, and the Duke and Duchess of Windsor. Things were good.

For the first half of the new year, Merman was still dating millionaire Sherman Billingsley (1896–1966), the charismatic, married owner of the Stork Club. Billingsley had a checkered past in financial affairs, but small matter—he was as much a New York institution as the nightclub he owned. On any given night, the city's brightest stars flocked to the Fifth Avenue club, and Billingsley adored their luster. He generously showered regulars with gifts and favors, particularly the women and particularly Merman. Whenever she opened a show or celebrated the anniversary of one, Billingsley had a case of Bollinger champagne (her favorite) delivered to her dressing room. Ethel had developed the unusual habit of taking her champagne on the rocks, but professional gossip Walter Winchell countered that she preferred it warm. (It seemed all that mattered to the cattier set was that Ethel imbibed it "incorrectly.") Billingsley lavished presents on Ethel for birthdays and other special occasions; Dorothy Fields reported that he even gave her a yacht, *The Seagull,* for which she reportedly hired the captain of the yacht of her former boss Caleb Bragg.

Although the Merman-Billingsley affair was widely known, people around them were discreet, and Merman and Billingsley were careful not to flaunt it. For instance, at the Stork Club's New Year's Eve bash in 1939, patrons were seated at small round tables as a small band performed. Merman and Billingsley had the best seats, in the center of the room next to the ensemble, but they were at different tables. Ethel was escorted by *New Yorker* cartoonist Peter Arno, and Billingsley was busy hosting his guests. Newsreels show the two casting periodic glances at the other while making merry at their respective tables.

Merman had had plenty of high-profile escorts. She enjoyed the company of wealthy men, who doubtless enjoyed the sheen of her celebrity. Frequent escorts included media mogul Walter Annenberg and Alter (Al) Goetz, a well-to-do stockbroker who, like Billingsley, was married but, unlike him, didn't give the impression that he was about to leave his wife. "Al Goetz is the one guy she was mad about. She was insane about him," said Dorothy Fields.[2] They remained close for decades, and Ethel would see Goetz when she was single. (When she was married, as future husband Bob Levitt Sr. would say, "It would never enter her mind to cheat; she's really a very straight-laced woman.")[3] Trying for a scoop, columnists Louella Parsons and Hedda

Hopper at one point announced the clandestine wedding of Merman and the married Goetz. Ethel dutifully glued the reports into her scrapbooks and probably had a good laugh.

Merm was tougher onstage and as a businesswoman than she was in affairs of the heart. At the time, she truly believed that Billingsley was going to divorce his wife and marry her. Recalls Fields, "When it got to be one of those things where I knew Sherman was never going to marry her and leave Hazel and the kids, I just knew it, I told him so and that's what barred me from the Stork Club."[4] But when Ethel discovered that Hazel Billingsley had become pregnant in the summer of 1940, she terminated the relationship immediately. "Ethel was a sitting duck for men," says Cointreau, who saw these patterns repeat as she grew older. "She had a vulnerable side and she wanted to be taken care of. That was Ethel's soft side that people don't see. Maybe they don't *want* to see it."[5]

Ethel was full of contradictions when it came to romance, men, and sex. On the one hand she was open and matter-of-fact, especially in her on-screen persona, and offstage she made off-color jokes as if it were the most natural thing in the world. She also had what her son calls a genuine "inner yearning" for the love and stability that a conventional family life and an authoritative husband were supposed to provide. In many ways, Ethel was a real homebody—not at all the modern 1930s woman too busy or having too much fun for marriage. "The picture of Ethel as a [boisterous, partying] Broadway type is really not accurate . . . [it's] a superficial picture," Levitt Sr. said.[6] There was something charmingly traditional, almost anachronistic, about Ethel's expectations of love and marriage. Yet between her strong personality and the pressures of her career and celebrity, Ethel would never become that stay-at-home, subservient wife, however potent that fiction might have been for her emotionally.

In July 1940, around the time of the split from Billingsley, *DuBarry* was still going strong. DeSylva had dealt with the challenge of bringing audiences into the still un-air-conditioned theaters by giving his key stars, Merman and Lahr, raises and upping chorus members from forty to forty-five dollars per week.[7] Lahr and Merman used their weight to ensure that chorus members were still paid during their one week's vacation. Apparently, when one of the show's chorines returned from her vacation, she was sporting a sunburn the color of "the pigment used on fire engines. There was an audible buzz in the audiences when she first traipsed onstage." Quipped Ethel, "Honey, they must have had you on the slow-burner." Seeing the young woman's embarrassment, Lahr said, "Never mind, now, she's a nice kid! As you can plainly see, she kept her pants on, didn't she?" For five minutes the show stopped, the audience was laughing so hard.[8]

After a nine-month run, Ethel left *DuBarry* on August 24, in order to start rehearsals for her next show, *Panama Hattie*. *DuBarry* was moved from the large 46th Street Theatre to the smaller Royale Theatre, actually to make room for the upcoming *Hattie*. Bert Lahr stayed on there, and papers were abuzz speculating about his next costar. Mae West was again proposed, as was Lupe Velez. In the end, it was understudy Betty Allen who took over, just as she had done when Ethel left *Take a Chance*. (After Allen stepped down in nine weeks, Gypsy Rose Lee, the future *Gypsy*, became the next DuBarry.) MGM secured the movie rights to *DuBarry* in what must have been an ironic acquisition, since, according to Gerald Bordman, the script was first developed as a picture but rejected by Hollywood.[9] Once again, the studio passed over Ethel, giving her role to redhead Lucille Ball to help showcase its Technicolor technology. Red Skelton played Lahr's role in the picture, which also featured Gene Kelly.

Panama Hattie

Hattie had much of the same talent behind it as *DuBarry:* Cole Porter for songs and lyrics, Buddy DeSylva as producer, costume designer Du Bois, and choreographer Bob Alton. Edgar MacGregor was signed on to direct, and Herbert Fields and DeSylva did the book. DeSylva was well aware of Merman's earning power at this point and, for his new play, rewarded her by giving her billing over the title for the first time in her career. She was delighted, of course, but she knew that DeSylva knew that that billing helped the show as much as it did her. Over the course of the new production, Ethel and De-Sylva expressed their mutual gratitude through various gifts and affectionate notes; he even gave Ethel her costumes from *DuBarry* after the run.

The busy and multitalented DeSylva had two other shows on the boards that season, *DuBarry* and *Louisiana Purchase*. After that, he would return to Hollywood, where he was first contracted by Paramount for possible adaptation of his shows. Like Zanuck at Fox, DeSylva had a keen eye for topical themes and big stories: *DuBarry* played off the Irish sweepstakes; *Hattie,* the Panama Canal; *Louisiana Purchase* banked on the corruption scandal of Louisiana politician Huey Long. Also like Zanuck—though without his gruff personal style—DeSylva solicited input from his stars and collaborators, compensating them well for their efforts.

Panama Hattie was written with Ethel in mind, and it shows. Hattie Maloney is a wise-cracking, fashion-challenged owner of the Tropical Shore, "a gay and very garish cabaret." Nick Bullett (can a man be more virile?), a former football player, works in the control house of the U.S.-operated Canal Zone and is up soon for promotion in the military. Nick is a widower, and his eight-year-old daughter, Geraldine ("Jerry"), was raised by her grandmother until the latter's death. The play begins with Jerry's imminent arrival in Panama from Philadelphia (meaning: high society) escorted by her English butler. Hattie and Bullett are dating, to the consternation of the jealous, scheming Leila, the admiral's daughter, who views Hattie as a gauche lowlife.

Hattie is nervous about getting on the good side of the upscale Jerry, a well-founded fear. Her sartorial excesses form a substantial part of the play's laughs and are essential to the class antagonism between Hattie and Nick's high-society family. The book's description of Hattie reads like a catty cliché of Merman: "a good looking young woman who is not too well bred, having been educated mainly in the school of life. She is rowdy and jolly. . . . [Her] taste in dress is furious. She can't wear all her clothes at once, but she'd like to . . . she usually rattles from inexpensive jewelry." In a pivotal scene in the first act, young Jerry removes the gaudy excesses of Hattie's outfit bit by bit—ruffles, accessories, bows—simplicity being the hallmark of social and sartorial propriety. Once Hattie is literally dressed down, the two sing "Let's Be Buddies," a duet that secures their new bond. Leila, however, schemes to sabotage Hattie's reputation and gets Admiral Randolph to turn against her on a false charge, putting Hattie's engagement with Nick on ice along with his chances for promotion. Elsewhere in the zone, several spies are lurking, and they hide a bomb in a shack. In twists that get incrementally more outlandish, Jerry unknowingly carries the bomb to Nick, thinking it's a picnic lunch, but Hattie inadvertently averts disaster, saving Nick, Jerry, and the entire Canal. Nick's superior, the admiral, decides Hattie is okay and promotes Nick. Hattie has become acceptable marriage material for all concerned.

The show was a classic piece of lowbrow fare. Not addressing the war per se, it acknowledged the political situation by using America's interests in the Canal as narrative pretext. (Using politics as jokes and ruses would often be harder to pull off during the Cold War.) Still, like other musical comedies of the time, *Hattie* offered rumblings of darker things to come, even in casual references, such as when Woozy, the lusty, goofball sailor (Rags Ragland), who, after failing to get the admiral's daughter to go out with him and the sailors, accuses her of being on a communist list.

The role of Hattie was no stretch for Ethel; that was a done deal. But who was going to play Jerry, the daughter? Over the summer, entertainment journalists speculated: "Musical Comedy Is Written to Feature Shirley Temple."[10] Given Temple's star power of the period, it's unlikely that producers *weren't* hoping to land the curly-haired superstar. But it's equally unlikely the show would have gone forward as a Merman vehicle had Miss Temple taken the part. True, Ethel liked surrounding herself with professionals and was not the jealous monster many make her out to be. At the same time, she scarcely relished playing second fiddle to anyone on the boards, especially not an adorable child. In Hollywood, she was willing to put up with it as she tried to establish a career there, but on her home turf, where she'd worked hard for top billing, she was not going to be upstaged by Little Miss Temple. (A staged publicity photograph of the two gives a glimpse of how Ethel might really have felt about the child star.)

Temple's people were quick to squelch rumors that the motion picture princess would appear in the show; speculation then fell to the young Jane Withers, with Joan Carroll eventually landing the part. Like Miss Withers, Carroll had been in a number of second-tier films that were cashing in on the popularity of Temple, and she complained to the press how tired she was of always being compared with her. During *Hattie,* she and Ethel got along famously: Ethel gave Joan a watch and kept the childish drawing of herself that Joan sent with her thank-you note.

The show also featured Arthur Treacher, who had had a small part in the film of *Anything Goes.* Treacher was known for playing English butlers and played that role here as well; Betty Hutton, who had stayed in *DuBarry* until summer, was also featured. DeSylva cast Jimmy Dunn, a friend of his (and, as it happened, known for playing Shirley Temple's father in the pictures) as Nick Bullet, in a decision that set the pattern of many shows to come: Merman's leading man could not be too charismatic or too big a star. Dunn was selected for being able to portray a regular, pleasant, guy, which guaranteed that the audience's attention would go to Merman—as if it wouldn't to begin with. At the same time, that kind of casting made it hard for a credible relationship between real equals to form, something that would affect the way people responded to Ethel as a public icon and, privately, as a woman.

Hattie's script and staging offered a sparkling showcase for Merman's talents. As usual, her entrance was carefully crafted: sailors in the crowd yell up into Hattie's house, pleading with her to sing, so all that audiences first get of her is her distinctive voice. The show is stuffed with smart

Merman-friendly retorts: when a character announces, "Four guys here to see you!" Hattie responds, "Only four? I must be slipping!" Sexual jokes and double entendres abounded from other characters as well: a woman flirting with a reluctant Treacher plans out their married life together, and when she announces she wants "ten or twenty children," he sighs, "Oh, the fertility of it all."

DeSylva had first approached Cole Porter about doing a new Merman show in which, he said, she would play a character based on "Katie Went to Haiti," one of his songs from *DuBarry*. Porter suggested that DeSylva set the new piece in Panama or Cuba instead, since, he said, few white people lived in Haiti. (Americans were likely to be more familiar with the Panama Canal, too.) Either way, the locale gave Porter the chance to borrow from Caribbean, Latin, and North African influences, which often marked his work. Those influences are there from the start in an opening number that also showcases Porter's trademark racy lyrics:

> A stroll on the Plaza Sant' Ana
> Is better even than a promenade in Central Park
> You meet ev'ry rank, ev'ry station
> And what a combination
> Of the white meat and the dark. . . .
> So try a little stroll on the Plaza Sant' Ana
> Don't wait until mañana . . .

A New Haven preview of a Cole Porter vehicle was always a special occasion, since he was an alumnus of Yale there. But any out-of-town tryout of an Ethel Merman show was an event in itself, since it gave out-of-town theatergoers not just a sneak preview of the newest show of Broadway's reigning star but one that she would not be taking on the road after its run. And so *Hattie* opened there on October 3 to a completely sold-out house. Reviews were positive, and basically there was no stopping *Panama Hattie* from becoming a hit. This was the case even in Boston, the next preview town, and the October 7 preview at the Shubert Theatre had to be delayed twenty-four hours to give the crew time to pack and set up the heavy treadmills used in the show. (Jerry walks on them while carrying her father's lunch/bomb to give the impression of much distance being covered.) At an astronomical twelve thousand dollars to build and twenty-five hundred to install, the treadmills cost the company five hundred dollars per week to operate.[11]

At the Boston Shubert, tickets had gone on sale two days earlier than usual, and mail orders on the first day broke records, exceeding five thousand dollars.[12] To accommodate the demand, *Panama Hattie* ended up staying there a week longer than scheduled, closing on the 26th. Audiences and (most) critics loved it and truly loved the woman who led it: for the last few years, began one, Ethel Merman had been proving herself "something more than a blues singer"; now she was a "great comedienne" who "mows them down," words that would have been reserved strictly for her voice earlier.[13] Other critics in Boston complained that Ethel was being worked too hard to carry the show, that there was insufficient support from the cast, that the talents of Arthur Treacher weren't being exploited, et cetera. (This complaint could and did accompany most every Merman musical, since she did carry entire shows on her shoulders.) A few Boston critics, like their New Haven counterparts before them, were irritated by the show's *DuBarry*-esque crudeness, finding it inappropriate in a show that had the "dignity of Treacher" or Joan Carroll's "innocence."

A Broadway myth is that Boston openings bring good luck to shows. Another one is: don't open in New York with too strong an advance showing; it will draw out the vultures. *Hattie* was pushing both superstitions to the limits: it had received Boston's blessing, had good advances, but still no vultures. It received another blessing two days before the Broadway opening, when *Time* magazine put Ethel Merman on its cover.

When *Hattie* opened in New York that Wednesday, October 30, 1940, Ethel got telegrams of best wishes from Ida and Eddie Cantor ("Marilyn inherits her liking for you from us"); Al Jolson, Helen Hayes, Bob Hope, Marie DeSylva, John Ford, Joe E. Lewis, Joan Crawford ("Ethel dear—I hope it's all you dream"), William Gaxton, and Victor Moore (who sent three, signing them "Padre," referring to his *Anything Goes* role). A happy DeSylva wrote, "I'm glad I'm the first producer to star you alone. I think you deserve it. Love, Buddy."[14] New York reviews were positive, with much less griping about the show's vulgarity; some, in fact, applauded the show's ability to combine children and a sentimental streak with bawdy burlesque—*Gypsy*, anyone? Merman was the perfect "hussy without a smirk" and exuded rowdy innocence. Said Brooks Atkinson, "No one else could do it with so much forthright vigor and at the same time keep it sanitary. For Miss Merman is an honest ballad singer who plays no tricks on the customers and does not truckle for guffaws. She can make a song seem like a spontaneous expression of her personality, which may be regarded as the ultimate skill in the art of singing songs. Only Ethel Waters is Miss Merman's equal in this respect."[15]

As usual, critics enjoyed finding words to do justice to the Merman voice and her daunting presence: "She has that thing in her voice that enables her to build a fire under any song she sings."[16] "Miss Merman . . . blows through the script like a cyclone. . . . Broadway, not Park Avenue, finds its voice in her, and every one listens to her enraptured."[17]

At the time *Panama Hattie* was running, Broadway audiences could also take in *Romeo and Juliet* with Olivier and Vivien Leigh, *Lady in the Dark,* and *Pal Joey.* But Atkinson was right to note that, along with Ethel in *Hattie,* the other hot ticket in town was Ethel Waters as Petunia in *Cabin in the Sky,* the all-black musical. Between them, these two all-American Ethels had Broadway in the palm of their hands.

Hattie's songs include Porter classics such as "My Mother Would Love You," "I've Still Got My Health," and "Make It Another Old Fashioned, Please." The Moroccan influence is evident in this last, bluesy number, its beguine tempo reminiscent of "Begin the Beguine." What audiences ate up night after night was once again a duet, one that Hattie shares with young Jerry, "Let's Be Buddies," a charming, sentimental ballad that is suggestive of a lullaby.[18] It was a softer Merman voice and image at work here, something Irving Berlin would develop in his score for *Annie Get Your Gun.* Critics were unanimous in their enthusiasm for both the song and its two singers. Louis Kronenberger praised the "remarkable eight-year-old named Joan Carroll," adding, "Probably that's the only age a girl could be to make any headway in the same show as Ethel Merman."[19] "Buddies" would remain a lifelong favorite of many Merman fans, especially those who appreciate Ethel's abilities with ballads and quieter songs. Today, her granddaughter Barbara Geary counts it among her favorites.

The Hattie-Jerry relationship was pivotal to *Hattie's* appeal, and emotionally it outstripped Hattie's relationship with the leading man by a long shot. As Boston critics noted, Jerry's young character helped turn an otherwise risqué play into family-friendly fare, widening its potential appeal; it never hurt a show to lure more families into matinees. In times of war, the innocence and promise children represent become treasured symbolic goods, used as powerful ideological weapons and, if the timing is right, a way to pull in strong profits. Hollywood was reaping a fortune off Temple, Elizabeth Taylor, Mickey Rooney, and Judy Garland; even Lassie, the family dog, had her own feature film. Yet child labor laws presented production obstacles, especially in New York. Recalls Porter, "I wrote *[Hattie]* in a rhythm that can be walked to, in order to compensate for Joan having been prevented by law from dancing, and with a patter in between so that Joan could recite instead of courting jail by singing."[20] (In a few years, Equity actors would rally to have child labor laws relaxed.)

Ethel was now in her midthirties, and, while hardly unusual for a woman that age to be cast as a mother or maternal figure, her case proved curious. "Now we have the lusty and likable Ethel Merman . . . with a throat bursting with romantic and comical songs and a heart bursting with motherly love."[21] Critics note the "instinct of motherhood" Ethel had begun to exhibit in current roles over previous ones,[22] an emphasis that made Ethel's stage image more domestic, but ironically it also conspired to keep her from being fully adult, at least at this moment in her career. Ten years down the road would produce a mature "maternal" side to Merman's public persona, but for now, Ethel/Hattie was as much mothered *by* the young girl as she was mother to her. It is the socially precocious Jerry, after all, who teaches working-class Hattie how to "tone down" her appearance and adopt proper dress and social behavior.[23] (Ethel's character would undergo similar domestication in *Annie Get Your Gun.*) Not romantic, not adult, and with a frankness about sex, Ethel's image had something perennially childlike about it, something that would shape perceptions of her offstage, whether the facts were there to substantiate them or not.

Mrs. Smith

Soon after *Hattie* had gone into rehearsals, Arthur Treacher and his wife, now good friends of Ethel, introduced the star to William Smith, the film agent who represented Treacher. Smith was apparently not much more colorful than his name, but in less than three months, he and Ethel Merman were married. On November 15, 1940, after the matinee performance of *Panama Hattie,* they took the train down to Elkton, Maryland—where East Coast celebrities went for quickie marriages. Ethel's age was given as twenty-eight; Smith's, thirty-nine. Witnessing at the clerk's office were her mother, her father, and the Treachers. Once the papers were signed, the newlyweds returned to Penn Station, where Smith carried Merman off the train for awaiting photographers. Then the newly minted Mrs. Smith did her evening show.

Trying to pump up the bland union, Dorothy Kilgallen reported on November 4—over a week before the event—that Merman might have married "handsome Hollywood agent" Bill Smith.[24] Ed Sullivan was the first to report the actual union, the day after it had occurred—evidence that he and Ethel were on good terms. (Of all the gossip columns of the period, his is the most factual as far as Merman stories were concerned.) After the nuptials were announced, the *Hollywood Reporter* reported, a tad improbably, that Ethel was planning to live in Hollywood with Smith after the run of *Panama Hattie*.[25] Other Los Angeles papers chimed in, gloating, "Ethel Merman Now Mrs. W. B. Smith: Blues Singer Becomes Bride of Local Actors' Agent."[26] Every press report mentioned the bicoastal nature of the alliance, and while Los Angeles papers predicted a West Coast residence for them, New Yorkers banked that the couple would remain there. Manhattan's tony Pierre Hotel comped the newlyweds with their own apartment for a year, which Dorothy Fields had decorated while the couple was out of town.

The Smiths never moved in. Their marriage was as short as their courtship. According to Bob Levitt Sr., Ethel told him that in reality it lasted only a few weeks. In just four months, in March, papers were reporting that the marriage was on the rocks, and Smith soon instigated divorce on grounds of desertion, which Ethel did not contest. The papers duly noted the dissolution of the union, but there wasn't a whiff of scandal. Ethel was benefiting from the solid relationships she'd cultivated with writers and columnists such as Sullivan. Although she was not the only star who actively fostered good relations with them, she was able to keep her career freer from scandal longer than most. Gossipers never directly referred to her well-known affair with Billingsley, for instance, and even oblique references to her being escorted by a "famous restaurateur" were rare. So although the divorce from Smith had the potential to damage her all-American image, it did not. It was a divorce, not a scandal.

Other factors helped too. Sex and romance were not what made Ethel Merman big; her vitality was. "You'll never hear a break in her voice, indicating that life is just too, too much. Even when she sings one of those tearful bits, bewailing the loss of a man, she does it with a sly verve which suggests she'll get over it," wrote the *Philadelphia Inquirer*.[27] And so Ethel, who often played vibrant women who didn't quite need men, was being given an almost asexual veneer that made her actual romantic entanglements almost uninteresting. Serious surgery would have been bigger news than a divorce; after all, physical weakness seemed more scandalous and unlikely than a matrimonial misstep.

For her part, Ethel didn't dwell on the marriage or its failure. She and Smith simply didn't hit it off and were not a good match. She never denied that it was a rebound marriage to get back at Billingsley, who was stunned when he heard the news. Bill Smith does not figure in either of her autobiographies, and she preserved few records of their union. One, a telegram from Buddy DeSylva—who affectionately signed his notes "the Boss" or "Buddo"—advised Ethel not to go to Chicago for a romantic reconciliation: "It is extremely bad flying weather at present," he writes. "I am not speaking selfishly for *Panama Hattie* but for Mermo. When you won't let Bill fly and you want to fly yourself, I'd like to ask you when you are going to get smart."[28] According to Tony Cointreau, Ethel "always spoke well of him."[29] Bill Smith lived out the rest of his life as a publicist at Fox, passing away in 1983, just two months before Ethel.

War and Changes in American Entertainment

Despite the official isolationist policy of the United States in the years and months before the attack on Pearl Harbor, entertainment industries on both coasts were revving up their engines, eager to assist the international community (or give the appearance of wanting to assist) and to get on the right side of their own government, just in case. In New York the American Theatre Wing operated the Stage Door Canteen on 44th Street, where servicemen could go for coffee or a meal, enjoy the company of young women, and take in shows by stars of the entertainment world. Ethel and other Broadway luminaries frequented the establishment after their shows or on days off, singing hits and performing routines from their shows. The Hollywood Canteen on the West Coast functioned much the same way.

A patriotic wave was flooding the entertainment world in other ways too, namely, in the form of rallies, bond fundraisers, and other relief efforts. To be sure, almost all of American mass culture (ads, songs, radio shows) and the ideology behind it (patriotism, proper gender roles) were permeated by the imminent threat of military conflict. It was clear that American isolationism was becoming less a position that escaped the war than a fantasy made untenable by it, as an awkward remark of New York mayor LaGuardia reveals. At a rally for Finnish relief that Ethel attended in January 1940, LaGuardia called the Nazi invasion of Finland "one of the cruelest acts in history," adding, "The American people will respond as they always have responded. They will do their part. They are not taking sides."[30]

Unlike today, a time when news reports and popular American entertainment collide to the point of indistinguishability, the media in 1939 were not predisposed to blurring lowbrow forms with such serious events as the war. Yet Ethel's scrapbooks show the inevitable connections between them, even if those connections were produced by a simple casual reference. An untitled

1939 clipping, for instance, mentions Germany's repeated threats to the United Kingdom and a bombing in a Munich beer hall ("Why wasn't the bomb placed there a year ago, when all the Nazis were there?") and goes on, "It is not considered good newspaper tactics to knock down one's story, but in this war, apparently, anything goes, as Prophetess Ethel Merman sang so sweetly only yesterday, on Broadway."[31] (Read in hindsight, it seems far too casual a remark for the grim events at hand.)

Although the war has a strong presence in the Merman scrapbooks, it's only as an afterthought, one nearly as casual as the "anything goes" remark. A photo taken in May 1940 shows Ethel relaxing at a restaurant table with Noel Coward, who was "away from Paris blackouts for six months." The *Hartford Times* ran the story "Comedians Take Broadway's Mind off World Strife" with the subheading "Serious Dramas in Minority as War Grows Worse."[32] The sole reason these clippings are in Ethel's scrapbook is that they make references to her. Not a political creature by nature ("Mom didn't have a political bone in her body," says Levitt Jr.),[33] Ethel, like many Americans, was less interested in pondering the issues than in supporting political positions that felt right to her.

Part of what seemed right was doing benefits. Pop preserved pages and pages of announcements, receipts, cards, thank-yous, and press clippings documenting his daughter's work on stages and radio and at rallies, events, the Canteen, and other venues where she maintained the tradition she'd begun in the 1930s, pursuing it with even more energy now. Between January and May 1940, for instance, she appeared at a star-studded benefit on Broadway for the Finnish Relief Fund and a production of *DuBarry* benefiting the Actors' Fund, and she did work for the Associated Actors and Artists in America. On March 24, she and Bert Lahr shivered in very cold weather riding in the Easter Parade, an event aired on radio; on April 21, there was a municipal benefit for France at the Waldorf-Astoria; and, on May 10, an Allied Relief Ball was held, at which, for five dollars, attendees could get a drink and enjoy headliners such as Merman, Cantor, Beatrice Lillie, and emcee Noel Coward. The event raised nearly forty-five thousand dollars.[34]

Ethel's wartime benefits were not only good publicity but also came from the heart. Her work ethic extended to a strong sense of civic duty, of doing one's part for others and for country. It was nothing more or less than that. Yes, she was enthralled by the big brass and heads of state she now rubbed shoulders with, but even her awe of them was ingenuous, rooted in her upbringing and the attitudes of Mom and Pop. They had given their daughter an old-fashioned, if simple, respect for their station. For as self-centered and tight with the penny as Ethel could be, she always gave back in these other ways, something clear from the letters of gratitude she saved from servicemen who recalled a kind word or song sung when she visited them in the hospital or how a letter from her had cheered up a dying child. Ethel maintained her feverish pace of charity work throughout the 1930s and '40s, and, although that work tapered off somewhat after the war, she continued doing benefits for groups whose causes she supported for the rest of her life.

Irving Berlin and Merman: Broadway Superpatriots

When he was asked to describe the place of Irving Berlin in American music, Jerome Kern said, "Berlin has *no* place in American music, HE IS AMERICAN MUSIC."[35] Few composers offer the spirited celebration of Americana that Irving Berlin does in classics such as "Alexander's Ragtime Band," "White Christmas," and "God Bless America." "Irving Berlin helped write the story of this country by capturing the best of who we are and the dreams that shape our lives," Walter Cronkite said in a tribute to the composer near the end of his life.[36]

Berlin, a Russian Jewish immigrant, joined the U.S. Army in World War I. Afterward he put his experiences to song, mounting the Broadway revue *Yip Yip Yaphank* (1918). Theatergoers found it a bit too old-fashioned and sentimental, so Berlin put one of his songs, "God Bless America," on ice until the late 1930s, when he had to be encouraged to try it again. But reusing earlier material was not a problem. When Sgt. Irving Berlin (as programs list him) opened his *This Is the Army,* on July 4, 1942, he recycled *Yip Yip* songs such as "Mandy" and "Oh, How I Hate to Get Up in the Morning." Some may take this as a sign of Berlin's opportunism or his self-promotion, and, to be sure, Berlin was obsessed about his work remaining viable in the public eye. Cole Porter told of a game he would play by taking bets on how long it would be before Berlin steered a discussion to one of his songs, no matter how far from the topic at hand. The usual time? Under five minutes, Porter laughed. Porter said he'd experimented once by bringing up the Dalai Lama, and it didn't take Berlin any longer to bring the discussion back to his work.[37] Self-absorbed or not, Berlin's patriotism was as ingenuous as it was generous. After cutting short *This Is the Army*'s Broadway run, he toured with the army and the USO, handing over all proceeds—nearly ten million dollars—to the army.[38]

By no means was Berlin alone in supporting the cause or in writing nationalistic jingoes—Rodgers and Hart did "Keep 'Em Rolling"—but his were especially enjoyable. "When That Man Is Dead and Gone" tells the story of Satan, who arrives on earth in the form of a small man with a dark mustache. Bill Robinson danced to it once on top of a large Nazi coffin in a September 1941 rally at Madison Square Garden,[39] and Ethel sang it (and "Keep 'Em Rolling") on several occasions.

Berlin's celebrations of America were the ideal vehicle for Ethel, both as a vocalist and as a public figure: she presented the material with a contagious enthusiasm that could easily lift morale. (Kate Smith's "God Bless America" may have been too hymnlike for Ethel's energy.) Ethel's close connection to Berlin in fact facilitated the patriotization of her own image. Even their backgrounds were similar: Both had entertained World War I doughboys, when Berlin was a young composer-soldier and Ethel, a child, sang on Long Island. Both had grown up in the New York of central and east European immigrants and held close to their roots all their life. Like many celebrities of such humble beginnings, Ethel and Berlin were happy to make life better for others if they could. Eddie Cantor was the same way, going so far as to put his career on the line to improve labor conditions by leading the huge strike that led to the establishment of Actors Equity in 1919. Berlin, more conservative (disapproving of the formation of the "union" ASCAP, the American Society of Composers, Authors and Publishers), was into flag waving, morale building, and celebrating some of the hokier nuggets of Americana. Ethel's style was closer to Berlin's, sharing his lifelong passion for country, middle-class comforts, and opportunities without undue introspection or desire for change.

Ethel performed frequently at the Stage Door Canteen and visited naval yards (as early as 1931, she and the principals of *Girl Crazy* performed for the USS *Salt Lake City* crew when it was anchored off the Upper West Side);[40] she christened military vessels, posed with sailors, and even presented a Brooklyn crew with a mascot goat. Merman sang to soldiers as they pulled out of dock and posed with Russian gunmen from Stalingrad relaxing on leave at the Canteen. She often gave tickets to military personnel to see her shows and was especially generous to hospitalized members and their children. Although she stayed in New York—unlike performers such as Marlene Dietrich or Bob Hope, who traveled extensively—Merman's patriotic efforts were given exposure well beyond the region, thanks to newsreels, radio, and syndicated photos and stories.

Like other celebrities, Ethel knew her benefit efforts were part of her professional responsibilities, but in her case what she did deeply correlated with who she really was. For compared with other entertainers such as Betty Grable and Rita Hayworth, whose pinup work during the war transformed them into national fetish figures more than patriotic icons, Merman had the perfect energy for a nation that liked to define itself in terms of vitality and spirit.

Helping Ethel's transformation were her frequent public appearances with government officials locally and nationally, from Jimmy Walker and Fiorello LaGuardia to J. Edgar Hoover and FDR. Although she'd been appearing with politicians for over a decade, now she was not just rubbing elbows with them socially but also working alongside them quite publicly (and getting fan mail from them privately). This was no truer than with New York politicians, who appreciated the asset that Ethel was to the city. Ethel's traveling in the same social circles as politicians scarcely made her different from other stars, but it helped cast her image in a more overtly political light than before.

Ethel had a special admiration of FDR and always kept a signed autograph of him on her wall. Their mutual respect was kindled by their bonds as New Yorkers and as people whose successes coincided during the same historical moment. "Mom liked FDR, she liked his company, and, of course, she deeply respected the office of the president," says her son today.[41] Afterward, Ethel would turn to the political party more in keeping with her position as a woman of elite stature and wealth, as Levitt puts it. "Like a lot of people then, and even now, Mom believed in the political myth that Republicans are the 'hard work' party, and the Democrats are 'on the dole party.'"[42] (Agnes and Pop were lifelong Republicans as well.)

Ethel's work in lighthearted musical comedies didn't hurt her transformation into a patriotic icon. Sometimes it was the titles alone that showed off the new veneer—*Red, Hot and Blue!, Stars in Your Eyes,* and the upcoming *Something for the Boys* (1943)—but her characters resonated that way as well. In *Panama Hattie,* she was an uncouth American who proves her worth to both man and country by exposing terrorists in U.S.-controlled territory; *Something for the Boys* features an even more outrageous twist that starts with Ethel as a munitions plant worker and ends with her intercepting enemy radio signals. Merman's mildly credible depiction of a munitions worker reveals how much her background as a working-class woman didn't vanish when her image took a new direction.

Other attributes also stayed the same, even as they were being redirected. By wartime, for instance, the press was connecting the Merman voice to the factory lines: "She'll never be signed by the Metropolitan Opera," wrote one review, "but her singing . . . is ideal for musical comedy. Her voice cuts right through sheet steel, yet it's not unpleasant."[43] Ads and promotion work show just how thickly the patriotism of Rosie the Riveter was being shellacked onto Merman.

Gender roles and war always make for curious bedfellows. One piece, discussing the toned-down women's fashions necessitated by wartime scarcity, featured a photo of Ethel wearing a man's tailored pin-striped jacket along with four other women in slacks. Evidently, such a look needed explanation, which the author offers by asking a psychiatrist to respond to this trend of "mannish suits, fly front coats, tailored shirts." We learn that the trend "is probably due to the chaotic times, to our something like wartime preparations for national defense in which women are competing." In short, it's just a fad, we're assured, since women want to remain "women at all times."[44] And thus Ethel and other women were kept soft and "feminine," whether they were working in factories or "cutting sheet steel" in musical comedies. One of the most amusing ways that Ethel was made patriotic (and femme) comes from Dorothy Kilgallen, writing then in "Voice of Broadway": "Ethel Merman has one freckle shaped like a star on an American flag, but you can only see it when she wears an evening dress."[45]

Though Ethel was at the top of her game in the early 1940s, Broadway was not. This circumstance was due not to the war, which was actually lifting the American economy and consumer leisure spending, but to the toll taken by the dual threats of the Depression and motion pictures. Broadway had not been able to rebound from the Depression as quickly or as thoroughly as Hollywood, which had lured patrons back with air-conditioned theaters, double features, and popcorn. On Broadway, a year after the stock market crash in 1929, seventeen legitimate theaters had been converted to movie houses. Stage musicals in particular, with their big budgets, suffered—recall the downturn in revues—and by 1940, the Big Stem was producing less than half the number it had in the '20s.

Broadway's national influence, moreover, was waning, particularly in introducing trends in music, fashion, stars, stories, and gossip. This shift had less do with the Depression than with the changing popularity of entertainment forms and the ascent of mass media. Broadway simply did not enjoy the wide reach of film; show tours, no matter how numerous, were not going to change that. Motion pictures had become an established, eminently affordable form of entertainment for Americans of all means; in 1940 New York, you could see a movie for only a quarter. Radio was even cheaper—free after the purchase of the set.

Still, ticket prices for musicals remained within reach for most working people, and audiences were still coming to the Big Stem in throngs to pass the evening. (Theaters had actually lowered prices during the Depression; by 1940 the most expensive theater ticket was $4.40.) And even if Broadway in general was losing its influence, the musical was far from moribund; critics had, after all, been pronouncing its demise since its beginnings in the 1860s. So while the 1939–40 season was not an especially robust one for musicals, it was scarcely a bust, with *Leave It to Me, Streets of Paris, The Mikado* (revival, along with *The Hot Mikado* and *The Swing Mikado*), and Rodgers and Hart's *Too Many Girls* opening.

Enter Rodgers and Hammerstein

Every fan of musicals knows that the 1940s included one of Broadway's fetish moments: *Oklahoma!* With this 1943 musical, historians tell us, musicals became integrated, and songs now worked to develop narrative situations and provide insight into the emotional lives of stage characters. No longer aiming to present spectacle with a nod and a knowing wink to the always-acknowledged audience, integrated musicals aimed to establish self-contained fictional worlds that, however fantastic, operated according to rules and behavior appropriate to that world. Song-and-dance numbers emerged organically from emotional situations, not from an impulse to razzle-dazzle. All of this did not start with *Oklahoma!* of course. Predecessors included Jerome Kern's monumental *Show Boat* in 1927, and before that were the *Princess Plays,* all important examples of integrated musical shows that predated Rodgers and Hammerstein. But these shows' successes lacked the immediate *and* lasting influence of *Oklahoma!* whose impact was so great that no less a Broadway historian than Gerald Bordman refers to 1943–49 as the "Rodgers and Hammerstein Years."[46]

A Rodgers and Hammerstein musical tackled social issues with a trademark liberal idealism. Understating things a bit, that is *not* the typical Ethel Merman musical show. The more "serious" orientation of the integrated musical has led some historians to refer to it as the more "mature" theatrical form, in contrast to the revue-influenced musical comedy, leading critics to bring charges of vulgarity, outdatedness, and childishness unfairly against earlier musicals—and performers like Merman.[47] In a show with the Rodgers and Hammerstein imprimatur—almost a brand name—audiences could expect to find themes of community integration, tolerance, and assimilation (see *Oklahoma! South Pacific, The King and I, Flower Drum Song*, and *The Sound of Music*). That soft liberalism was hardly Merman's forte, personally or professionally, so it is scarcely incidental that she never performed in a Rodgers and Hammerstein show; she and Rodgers didn't even get along well. (He told Marilyn Cantor Baker that Ethel was "so cheap" she stored her artificial Christmas tree in a theater to avoid paying for storage, a falsehood disproved by her year-round enjoyment of her beloved Christmas tree, decorated in her foyer, at least in her later years.)[48] Others speculate that the frosty relationship began when Ethel refused to extend her contract for *Annie Get Your Gun*, which Rodgers produced, at the end of the 1940s.

Ethel's strong suit was always the light book comedy, those star vehicles whose songs Porter, Berlin, and George Gershwin wrote with her in mind. As their kind of music became dated, along with the old style of musicals, Ethel's professional wings would be clipped. And so despite Josh Logan's accolade of her being the best instinctive actress, Merman's work outside musical comedies never got her high accolades. Her few efforts to perform straight dramatic roles on radio, for instance, were met with almost unanimously unfavorable reviews. Ethel was surely aware of her limits as an actor and later was justified in cherishing her dramatic success in *Gypsy* as much as she did.

Not only was Ethel's standard material at odds with the new kind of musical theater, but her very style of performance chafed against it. She still sang her songs staring straight into the audience or camera. (Again, one is reminded of Mary Martin fluttering around, wrapping her arms around Ethel's shoulders, as Ethel stares straight ahead.) Ethel never unlearned that self-conscious, performative delivery. Why should she? It had brought her success for decades. Her stubborn adherence to it, though, not only made her an ill fit for the kind of theater that Rodgers and Hammerstein exemplified but arguably impeded her success in film and television as well. In a very real sense, Merman's acting style was simply too big, too much for the cameras.

As early as *Red, Hot and Blue!* a few critics were starting to tire of the old vaudevillian-styled musical comedy that had been the staple of Ethel's work. The perspective continued with later shows: "It is a strange thing to say of so bright and dashing a show as *DuBarry* that there is something nostalgic about it."[49] Whether as criticism, encomium, or simple description, the term *old-fashioned* started to be attached more often to Merman vehicles, even as her star was hitting new heights. Some Broadway critics found the more adult, nuanced fare proffered by *Pal Joey, Lady in the Dark,* and the work of Rodgers and Hammerstein more enticing; some found the light book musical to be inappropriate for a country at war (although others argued precisely the opposite). But for other writers and theatergoers, this form of musical entertainment had simply run its course, much as operetta had done fifteen years before.

Rodgers and Hammerstein also changed theatrical rules by not writing their musicals as star vehicles geared to a particular personality (a decision that helped simplify tours and revivals). Marketing, too, was changed. For *Oklahoma!* Richard Rodgers and Oscar Hammerstein made a deal with Jack Kapp, president of Decca records, to release an original cast recording of the show that contained its bigger numbers, and the record was such a hit that a second volume of songs from the show was released. These cast recordings not only made for a good source of revenue but also exposed Broadway musicals to the entire country. People who couldn't catch shows in New York or on tour could experience them through their songs sung by the original performers. And for people who had seen the shows, the recordings were powerful souvenirs that could be played over and over; in them listeners could also discover new performers or cement addictions to old ones. Insofar as they "captured" an element of historical productions, the recordings also gave Broadway historians and critics a means of preserving and documenting the notoriously ephemeral art of the stage.

On a related front, Broadway was also able to increase revenues and expand its influence through jukeboxes. This actually predated the Rodgers and Hammerstein "revolution," since jukeboxes were available as early as 1928 (though without mechanical amplification). By 1936, business was such that fifty thousand units were manufactured and sold in the United States, and the industry forecast even higher figures for the 1940s.[50] Marketing Broadway was changing, and war was only part of it.

Something for the Boys

Ethel's last wartime show was *Something for the Boys,* reuniting her with Cole Porter and Herbert and Dorothy Fields, who did the book. Three estranged, competitive cousins inherit a ranch near Kelly Field Air Force base in Texas. Ethel's character, Blossom Hart, a former chorus girl from Newark, kept the

Merman image close to New York. Paula Laurence (according to Charlie Chaplin, the "funniest woman in America") played her burlesque queen cousin; the third cousin, played by Allen Jenkins, is a pitchman. The trio converts the base into a working residence for wives of servicemen, and when a resentful local misinforms an official that they are running a brothel, the place is shut down as a Senate investigation looms. But in a deus ex machina even more absurd than *Panama Hattie*'s, Blossom realizes she's able to pick up radio messages through her tooth fillings and thus saves the day—and gets a guy to boot.

Vinton Freedley was set to produce, but on October 16, the *New York Times* announced his withdrawal due to creative differences with the rest of the team, and the Fieldses replaced him with Michael Todd. Todd (1909–58) was the wunderkind whose quick rise as a Broadway producer stemmed from his bigger-than-life personality and his lavish big productions such as *The Hot Mikado, By Jupiter, Star,* and *Garter,* and later, *Around the World in 80 Days.* The prototypical self-made man, Todd moved quickly from being a shoe-shiner to coproducing the 1940 World's Fair in Flushing. And though he was only in his mid-30s at the time of *For the Boys,* Todd's life was already moving with the bold strokes that would characterize everything he did. He would go on to marry Elizabeth Taylor before his untimely death in a plane crash in April 1958.

Hassard Short directed *Something for the Boys;* Billy Livingstone did costumes; and Jack Cole choreographed. But it was Ethel Merman's show all the way, even if it was the first time she'd been given the star's dressing room. "They might very well toss—or even heave—most of the book of *For the Boys* into the Charles River," wrote the Boston critics of previews there. "It wouldn't raise a riple [sic] . . . and [would still] emerge then as one of the most successful musical shows of the season."[51] It was Merman that was sure-fire. "An announcement that Miss Merman is to appear in a new musical seems to be sufficient guarantee that this will be a show to see, come gasoline rationing or higher taxes."[52] In Boston, the Fieldses tightened the book slightly to prepare for the New York opening.

Total production costs exceeded $175,000, high for Broadway at the time and Todd's most lavish show to date. "If you're going to produce a big musical, you've got to give the public its money's worth," he said. "When people put down good money [in wartime] to see a show they're not interested in excuses [about the unavailability of items due to shortages]."[53] One set, for instance, included a bomber plane coming nose-forward toward the audience. Todd's approach to theater brokered in a new way of doing business and presaged the blockbuster mentality that took shape on Broadway after the war and would saturate it completely by the end of the twentieth century.

For the Boys opened January 7, 1943, at the Alvin Theatre and ran for 422 performances. Although the show didn't garnish the highest accolades, viewers solidly cheered its production values. The consensus on Porter's score was that it was diminished but serviceable, with the usual objections raised: "As is frequently the case, Mr. Porter is guilty again of offending good taste in his lyrics";[54] or he was exhausted or a byproduct of "wartime ambience."[55] Nevertheless, Porter, even after his riding accident, was still on top. In its January issue, *Time*'s "New Musical in Manhattan" focuses exclusively on the composer, giving Ethel only a nod as his "Songblitzer."

The score includes an example of what has come to be known as one of Cole's "list songs," "Hey, Good Lookin'," the kind of tune he'd given to musical history with "You're the Top." The list in the lyrics of "Good Lookin'" includes an uncharacteristic reference to Ethel Merman as "the missing link between Lily Pons and Mae West." Porter normally avoided references to his singers in his work so as to discourage competition among them, but that obviously didn't stop him here—or earlier, when he declared that Ethel Merman was the singer he preferred to write for.

It was "By the Mississinewa," though, that was the show's hit, and it has gone down in Merman folklore for behind-the-scenes reasons. A second-act comic number, Ethel performs it in American Indian costume (more ethnic drag for laughs) in duet with Laurence, similarly attired. Its place in the Book of Merm came from a widely reported spat between the two. Initially, Ethel and Paula got along beautifully, but problems arose. "I had found some business swinging my braids that got a laugh," said Ethel. "The first thing I knew, Paula was swinging her braids. Then one night I accidentally lost a moccasin. It fell off and went into the orchestra pit. That got a yak and I kept the business in. Then Paula began losing her moccasins."[56] Laurence claimed that Merman was peeved about the response that she was getting, and, although Merman later denied having gotten her fired, she registered a complaint about the young player, and the producers took it seriously. It was crucial for the show's health to keep its star happy. And so Laurence left to take a role in *One Touch of Venus.*

As with *Panama Hattie,* Ethel depicts a woman who shows up the pretensions and hypocrisy of upper-crust society. American comedy of the 1930s and early '40s was filled with this sort of thing, and it remains a comic staple today. It is equally a trademark of Merman's own work and style. *Something for the Boys* also showcased Ethel's skill with the quick retort and her ability to deliver lines loaded with double entendre.

SOLDIER [LOOKING AT HER LEGS]: Boy, look at those drumsticks.

MERMAN: How would you like a kick in the teeth from one of those drumsticks?

S: How do you like that? And this is the womanhood I'm fighting to protect?

M: This is the womanhood *I'm* fighting to protect!

Reviewers continued to praise Ethel's comedic delivery as well as her vocal power. The show's nuttiness ensured that it would not be taken too seriously, and there were enough references to the war to shield it from critical arrows: it was lighthearted but not actually disrespectful; improbable, yes, but good-hearted and easy to follow. That formula, topped by Merman's energetic performance, provided another way to protect musicals like this from critique in a country at war and a musical theater tradition in transition. If the show's makers kept their sights low, they could offer theatergoers and critics a combination of zany fantasy and relief over political matters. Only Porter's lyrics attracted accusations of being inappropriate, too sexually overt or "blue."

Porter had five hit shows during World War II, and Ethel Merman was in three of them: *DuBarry Was a Lady, Panama Hattie,* and *Something for the Boys.* (The others were *Let's Face It,* the Danny Kaye vehicle, and *Mexican Hayride,* with June Havoc, the very talented sister of Gypsy Rose Lee.) When most people think about patriotic American composers, Irving Berlin comes to mind before Porter. And while Porter had his more personal obsessions about the "boys in uniform," he was happy to lend his work to the needs of a country at war. Audiences, moreover, flocked to his work at this time every bit as much as they had during the Depression. Biographer William McBrien describes Porter's "patriotism [to be] mixed with the epicureanism and wit that audiences continue to find so entertaining."[57] (Noel Coward's "Don't Let's Be Beastly to the Germans" offers another example.) Rather than reflecting social conditions overtly (as wartime songs that are about war do), some of pop culture's most effective work acknowledges such matters while not bowing down to them.

"Merman for the Boys" ran countless review titles. Not only did they aptly describe Ethel's activities to support the troops; they also shed light on her popularity with young male fans and, particularly, urban gay men. While it may seem easy to "queer" this commentary from today's perspective, it's important to acknowledge that it would have been read this way even at the time; the term *gay*, for instance, already had homosexual connotations, even beyond gay communities. (Walter Winchell, for instance, punningly called *Red, Hot and Blue!* "risgay.")[58] And other terms, from *queer* to *violet* or *lavender*, circulated widely, particularly in cities like New York and San Francisco with their vibrant gay cultures. Popular gay icons were well established, from individual stars (Mae West, Ethel Merman, Noel Coward) to fantasy figures of social groups ("men in uniform"), and all of this could be evident in the straightest of shows. As one gay historian writes of Irving Berlin's *This Is the Army*, for instance, it "did much to promote the wartime image of Army and Navy drag performers as normal, masculine, combat-ready soldiers. . . . But a gay spectator or actor . . . could read these same drag performances for their more implicit homosexual meanings."[59] Ethel's popularity with gay men is evident in numerous articles of the time, again, even those culled from mainstream sources. In 1935, she was photographed in the dressing room of a drag queen from Columbia University, and there was the reviewer who wrote that "from 30–110, the male gender is mostly nuts about her," maintaining that the male fans of Ethel and Mae West liked them for "different reasons; Ethel hasn't any of Mae West's direct and open appeal *to the purely physical desires of men*."[60]

Michael Todd's genius as a producer had a chance to shine during the run of *Something for the Boys*. One evening, when Ethel was not able to perform, ill with laryngitis, Todd wanted to avoid canceling the show but was aware that using her understudy (Betty Garrett) might cause a mass exodus. So he

> had leading man Bill Johnson come out in his U.S. Army uniform/costume right before the curtain and read a speech that said Merman was unfortunately ill; after the groans faded, he went on, "There's a little girl who has been waiting in the wings since the show opened. . . . Tonight that little girl, Betty Garrett, will have her chance. Perhaps you'll see a new star find her place in the Broadway galaxy." Then, before anyone could leave, Todd had the orchestra play "The Star-Spangled Banner," upon which (especially it being wartime) everyone stood at attention. Practically on the final note he ran up the curtain. Anyone heel enough to thwart the man in uniform announcing the Cinderella understudy story, and willing to barrel up the aisle during the national anthem—well, he was welcome to his refund.[61]

Over the course of the show, Ethel received countless personal accolades and sweet notes. During previews, producer Todd sent his star a gift, "To Miss Show Business—the best performer and the best trouper of my time. I love you. Mike Todd." (Ever the secretary, Ethel writes "opening in Boston,

December 18, 1942.") Cole sent his usual gifts with cards, lovingly signed in his inky scrawl. But the best message Ethel received during the entire run was a telegram on opening night: "Dear Mommy I am thinking of you tonight and wish you every success Grandma and Grandpa send their love told me you would be a sensation in your new show Love and Lots of Kisses Your Loving daughter Ethel." Because, after *Hattie* and before *For the Boys,* Merman was married for the second time and had become a mother for the first.

SIX

Forging a Family

> I met her in Dinty Moore's. I was in there having dinner with a guy and I ran
> into Walter Young, an associate publisher of the *Journal American*. . . . Walter
> and his wife, Ella, and some other people, very close friends of Ethel's . . . in-
> vited me to join them; they said they were waiting for her. I had never seen her
> before, even on the stage.

So recalls Robert Daniels Levitt, Ethel's second husband, about that night in
April 1940. There was a terrible, late-season snowstorm that evening, and in
general, the night was not filled with romance and roses. Levitt remembered
keeping quiet in the company of Miss Merman and Young, his business associate. It didn't help that Ethel's friends were there and that everyone seemed
to know the big star except him.

> We went to some nightclub somewhere, and as I recall it, she had to go home
> early because she had a matinee the next day. And Young asked me to take her
> home . . . it was a snow storm. We got to her house and we came to get out of
> the car . . . and there was a great big pile of snow. So I thought, this is friend-
> ship, not love, and made her plow through the snow herself.[1]

Bob Levitt was the promotion director of the *Journal-American,* the
Hearst-owned paper, at which he also worked as a staff writer—he had a col-
umn called "Cabbage and Kings." Levitt would go on to be associate pub-
lisher of the *Journal-American Weekly* and then its publisher. When he met
Ethel, Levitt was in his early thirties, two years younger than she, and he was
graced with a quick wit with sardonic edges. Bob Levitt came from a New
York family that produced a number of successful financiers: his brother,
Arthur Levitt, was a four-time state comptroller of New York, and his son

Arthur Jr. (b. 1931) was appointed chairman of the SEC in 1993 under President Clinton, a position he held until 2001. Bob graduated from Rollins College, in Florida, in the class of 1931. The family, according to Bob Jr., was not especially close—his father had had a break with brother Arthur—and he does not recall interacting with the Levitts while growing up.

Reports indicate that Levitt wrote articles under a pseudonym for *Cosmopolitan,* something his son believes but cannot corroborate. Ethel was less bookish, and when she told Pete Martin, "I tried to read a book once, but I fell asleep,"[2] she was only half joking. "She never read a book," Levitt Sr. told an interviewer. "But I read the books, and she'd take my word for it."[3] Despite his more intellectual proclivities, Levitt shared Merman's well-honed radar for b.s. and her disrespect for forced, haughty airs and misplaced authority. At the same time, they both respected institutions and authority they found legitimate, such as political leadership, the army, et cetera. And both had a great sense of humor and a special appreciation of impish, "naughty" jokes. While courting, Bob penned Ethel a number of X-rated limericks ("love letters," as she called them in her memoirs) that pleased her enormously. One that their son recalls—searching for an example that would not melt the page—was "The punk between your toes tastes fine / Won't you be my valentine?"[4]

And so Ethel and Levitt began their affair. "The more I saw of Bob the better I liked him. He wasn't just handsome and broad-shouldered. He was a darling guy with a wonderful sense of humor. His lack of interest in the theater didn't arise from the fact that he was unintelligent. . . . He just didn't care for actors." The journalist had never seen an Ethel Merman show: "Musical comedies bored the hell out of him and always made him sleepy," she wrote.[5] When Levitt and a pal went to see Ethel in *Panama Hattie,* they couldn't stay awake, their slumber having been facilitated by drink beforehand.

The first reference to Levitt in Ethel's scrapbooks is a September 26, 1941, published photo of the couple one evening after *Hattie* at La Martinique. The press describes him as "her constant companion these midnights," and in early reports like this, the poor man's name appears variously as Levitt, Leavett, Levabitt, and Lovett.[6] They were very much enjoying their time together, but there was a problem. Technically, Levitt told Pete Martin, "Ethel was married, and I was married—a marriage that I just never bothered doing anything about, and finally I had to get an annulment." William Smith was in the process of getting a divorce in California, but, as Levitt noted, "that takes a hell of a while. A year for an interlocutory. . . . I think he got it but there was a year gap." They ended up getting a Mexican divorce, but the divorce and Levitt and Merman's marriage were "all screwed up as to the dates."[7]

Fourteen years later, when Ethel's first autobiography was serialized in a magazine weekly, she offered a vague marriage date: October 1940, in Connecticut. Ethel kept the exact date (which was later) under wraps, not just because of the complicated divorce proceedings on both sides, but also because she was pregnant. Her baby would be born in July 1941, less than nine months after she and Levitt signed the papers, and she didn't want nosy journalists doing the math. After the wedding, Danton Walker and other columnists obligingly reported that Ethel's child was due in August. (Always one to push it, Winchell wrote, "sometime in July.") That spring, in 1941, Dorothy Fields threw a baby shower for Ethel, inviting Broadway gal pals such as Madeline Gaxton, Dorothy Kilgallen, Eleanor Holm, and Sylvia Fine.[8]

Little Bit

It was a girl. Following her mom Agnes's tradition, Ethel gave her daughter her first name, but for a first, not a middle, name. Little Ethel Merman Levitt was born on 5:32 p.m., July 20, 1941, in a difficult Cesarean birth. Her birth certificate lists her father as age thirty-two; occupation, "Captain, U.S. Army" (Levitt had signed up in May). Mother, "Ethel Agnes Merman," was thirty-one. Ethel seldom used "Merman" in her personal life, and, like many women of the time preferred being identified by her married name, Mrs. Robert Levitt. (Or, when making a point like "I haven't changed" to the press, she would say, "I'm just Ethel Agnes Zimmermann.") More surprising than the "Merman" on the certificate is that the mother's occupation is listed simply as "Housewife, at home," evidence, perhaps, of Ethel's desire to take part in a typical marriage and family life. And once Little Ethel was born, all of Merman's close professional acquaintances, from Cole Porter to Dorothy Fields, remarked on what a proud mom she was. And she was. She happily shared Ethel Jr.'s birth date with the press, although, as the Levitt interview suggests, that meant keeping the date of her marriage shrouded.

All that appears by way of announcement of this personal event in the scrapbooks is a brief reference from the *Washington Herald,* which announced on July 25 that Ethel Merman had a daughter, Ethel "Jr." Little Ethel was christened in October at St. Thomas Church in New York, with Eleanor Holm present as godmother and William Gaxton as godfather. At home, the baby was quickly dubbed "Little Bit," because Levitt, "who had never been around a new baby, thought she was so small,"[9] and the name also made her a bit off the old block. Little Ethel had her mom's wavy brown hair, soft pale skin, and beautiful brown eyes; as she grew up, remembers Tony Cointreau, "she looked just like her mother."

Big Ethel's first public appearance after giving birth was at an Army Emergency Relief show at Madison Square Garden, September 30, 1941. It was a long evening; a six-and-a-half-hour, sold-out extravaganza called "We're All in It Show," named after a song written by serviceman Kurt Kasner. A photo was taken of Ethel rehearsing with him: Kasner is in military uniform, and Ethel is wearing a frock dress with a girlish bow atop her head. Later, she would (understandably) complain about the horrible outfits pregnant women and new mothers had to wear back when maternity fashions often infantilized the mother as if she were the one being brought into the world.

All performers who become mothers have to endure predictable lines about now performing "her favorite or most challenging role yet!" and Ethel Merman was no exception.[10] In March 1942, the press announced that Ethel was "playing housewife since her memorable portrayal of *Panama Hattie*."[11] "Ethel Merman Scores as Always in New York . . . But Likes Most of All to Talk of Her Best Production—a Baby."[12] This last piece, from December 1942, is the first scrapbook item in which Ethel talks extensively about her daughter, showing a rather successful degree of keeping the press at bay.

When he and Ethel married, Bob Levitt was making about two hundred dollars a week, high pay for a journalist but peanuts to a Broadway star.[13] At home, he said, "She'd pay everything and I'd get an accounting and split it in half, when I could afford it. When I couldn't I'd give her all my money, less what I needed. . . . We had a cook, an upstairs maid, a downstairs maid. . . . I don't mean to imply that she was by any means profligate, but we did live on a scale that was excessive, for me."[14] The lifestyle was bumpy not only for Levitt. Ethel's relationship with domestic help was not smooth. Dorothy Fields thought that Ethel gave her maids and governesses too little to do, or kept them on too short a leash, or both. "She would out-talk the governess, or she would take the authority away from the governess, and barge in and do it herself, which is not good for the kids because they have an insecurity—they don't know where to go and who's the boss."[15]

In the early 1940s, the press continued to spike reports on Ethel's professional activities with details from her family life, some of them quite intimate. When Ethel left *Hattie* on January 3, 1942, for instance, Louella Parsons said it was because she was pregnant. When she left *For the Boys* on February 12,

1944, she actually was. Two months later: "Tragedy has changed Ethel Merman's nursery plans."[16] Wrote her pal Dorothy Kilgallen: "Ethel Merman is in a local hospital. The Stork cancelled its scheduled visit."[17]

Ethel's contract for *For the Boys* stipulated that after the New York run, she had to perform two weeks in Philadelphia. Ethel extended it to five, reportedly as a favor to Todd. Medical problems ranging from the miscarriage to the bout with laryngitis had kept Ethel from her usual "miss no show" record, and at one point Todd wrote urging her to stay home rather than jeopardize her health. Reports are mixed on how well he and Ethel actually got along, and she might have given him the "favor" of extending the Philadelphia run simply because he never docked her for performances missed in New York. When Ethel finally left the show, she was replaced by another brassy woman with moxie, Joan Blondell—Todd's wife at the time.

Reports soon circulated that Billy Rose was courting Ethel for his "Seven Lively Arts" revue, with music by Stravinsky (who would prove a devoted fan of Merman). But Danton Walker announced that she was going to take the role "to take her mind off her domestic differences."[18] Although Walker was wrong on the first point (Ethel never took the show), he was right on the latter. The Merman-Levitt marriage was already in trouble, and by June 1944, Ed Sullivan reported that Levitt and Merman were experimenting with a "very friendly" separation, language that Ethel probably fed him.[19] Gossipers said they were spotting Levitt alone, drinking. Ethel, for her part, avoided the nightclubs.

Sadie Thompson

Ethel was now pondering an upcoming role in a musical version of Somerset Maugham's classic story "Rain," about a hypocritical preacher trying to convert an exiled prostitute. The story had been done twice before on Broadway, in 1922 with Jeanne Eagles and in 1935 with Tallulah Bankhead; Gloria Swanson and Joan Crawford had starred in film versions. It was a role familiar to many. Should she do it? In June 1944, producer A. P. Waxman sent Ethel a personal note along with the script, buttering her up, writing that no less an authority than Moss Hart had proclaimed about her, "That girl really is a great actress!" and that Ethel Merman would be "perfect casting."[20] Columnists openly speculated about the show and the challenge of making a lighthearted musical out of such a tragic story. Ethel took it on.

And so on September 18, 1944, Ethel began rehearsals for *Sadie Thompson.* The book and lyrics were by Howard Dietz and music by Vernon Duke.

Rouben Mamoulian directed (and helped with the book), and Edward Caton choreographed. Rehearsals did not go smoothly. As Ethel tells it, she was asked to sing a song with a reference to "Mal Maison," and she asked Dietz to explain it. A kind of lipstick, he answered. Ethel had never heard of it, and, after polling some of her girlfriends, returned with the news that no one else had either, telling him, "Either that line goes or I do." Dietz wouldn't budge, and by the end of the month, after only five rehearsals, Merman withdrew from the show. (According to musical historian Gerald Bordman, Ethel demanded that they hire her estranged husband, Levitt, to repair the lyrics, but that is unlikely.)[21] Nor is it likely that a tube of lipstick broke the deal, especially in light of all the Cole Porter songs Ethel performed with references to all sorts of things most Americans—Merman probably among them—might not know. Given her good instincts about material, Ethel most likely didn't fight to stay on because she knew the show wasn't going to work. The story of Sadie Thompson was familiar, true, but so was its shock value. The music was an even bigger issue. "She feels she's a very good judge of a song," said a colleague at 20th Century–Fox. "She's not apt to pick a song that won't go over."[22] Recalled close friend Roger Edens, "After she did *Red, Hot and Blue!* [and] *Stars in Your Eyes,* she had this wonderful *Sadie Thompson* [show, but] the songs were wrong for her. When she said it was wrong, there was no possibility; she was so right."[23] *Sadie Thompson* would be the only show Ethel backed out of, and her lipstick defense has become a standard in her hall of legends. Later, Ethel maintained that the role of Sadie belonged to earlier dramatic heavyweights Gloria Swanson and Joan Crawford and that she didn't want to infringe on their territory.

We'll never know what Merman as Sadie Thompson would have been like (June Havoc took the part). Although the role seems an incongruous fit, aspects of the famous temptress lined up with the Merman persona. Who else could expose the pretensions of hypocrites or the upper crust with such gusto? In a way, Sadie would have been another in the series of earthy, good-hearted independent gals who had glommed onto Ethel's stage persona and to some people's perception of her offstage. Their very names—Hattie, Blossom, Flo, Nails—helped load it on thick.

Stage Door Canteen

In 1943, Merman made another appearance on the silver screen. With producers Sol Lesser and the American Theatre Wing War Service behind them,

United Artists gave director Frank Borzage "more stars than shine in the heavens of a clear, California night . . . an embarrassment of riches" to make *Stage Door Canteen*.[24] Proceeds were earmarked for the ATW's Stage Door Canteen and the Hollywood Canteen. Ethel was one of over seventy stage and screen stars who appear for a number or a quick cameo. Written by Delmer Daves, the movie's slight story follows a young soldier, Dakota, in New York City on a pass. He spends it with friends at the Canteen, where he meets a young woman and takes in the stars that movie audiences on both coasts would be happy to see: Lunt and Fontanne, Judith Anderson, Harpo Marx, Yehudi Menuhin, Vin Freedley, Ethel Waters, Ray Bolger, Peggy Lee, Marian Moore, Edgar Bergen, Katharine Hepburn, and the bands of Benny Goodman, Guy Lombardo, and Count Basie. Shot in New York, *Stage Door Canteen* made it easy for Broadway stars to put in their appearances without having to take time off from their shows; Ethel recorded her number, "Marching thru Berlin," in just one day at the Movietone Studios on West 53rd Street while she was in *Something for the Boys*.[25] With so many big performers coming together to help the war effort, the finished product was virtually critic-proof, and its success was enough that the following year, Elmer Fudd and Bugs Bunny sent it up in "Stage Door Cartoon," with Elmer chasing the famous rabbit into a vaudeville house.

Ethel was doing other appearances at the Canteen; one included an appearance on January 12, 1945, with her good friend Bill Gaxton, which was broadcast on radio. Her other war efforts continued apace. On Independence Day 1945 she joined Marlene Dietrich, Red Skelton, Paul Whiteman, and countless others at the Washington Monument in front of a quarter of a million people, selling over twenty thousand war bonds. Fox, Ethel's old studio employer, purchased $1.25 million worth alone.[26]

Ethel sang for FDR at the July 1944 Democratic Convention and again in October at the Madison Square Garden Party Rally. She saved ads for these "Liberal Party Rallies," at which she performed Yip Harburg's "Don't Look Now Mr. Dewey, but Your Record Is Showing!" and was joined by other performers such as Frank Sinatra, Victor Borge, and Bill Robinson. Like many New Yorkers, she was thrilled when Roosevelt won and saved a telegram thanking her for her help and hoping for "four more years of progressive government under FDR."[27]

In only five months, President Roosevelt would be dead. Ethel and Dorothy Kilgallen were joking together in a radio studio prior to doing Kilgallen's show in April when someone rushed in to tell them the news. Kilgallen went on the air: "Ladies and Gentlemen, this is Dorothy Kilgallen.

Because we have just heard the news of President Roosevelt's death, Ethel Merman and I will ask you to excuse us from the program which we had prepared for this time. Our hearts are too full to speak." When the two left the building, there was an eerie silence. The papers hadn't hit the streets, Kilgallen said, but "everyone seemed to know."[28]

That summer, things had changed on another front: Ethel and Bob Levitt reconciled. The couple was intent on making their life together with Ethel Jr. a success, and Big Ethel, unlike Levitt, was not one to be down and out very long. "Ethel Merman has had an unbroken stage success, with [only] temporary cardiac difficulties," wrote Ed Sullivan in a piece on female celebrities whose lives were stalked by tragedy.[29] Sullivan was genuinely pleased that Levitt had moved back to the 25 Central Park West compound, where Ethel promised her young family that she would take a break from the boards.

Life at Home

Soon, Ethel Merman Levitt was pregnant again. She told friends that she loved expecting, loved wearing a big black cape and waddling down to the corner drugstore for a milkshake. For his part, too, Levitt told interviewers that he adored Ethel when she was pregnant. Their second child, a son, Robert Daniels Levitt Jr., was born at Manhattan's Doctors' Hospital on August 11, 1945. Like Little Ethel, the baby was delivered by C-section, but Bobby's birth was more traumatic, gravely complicated by his RH negativity and need for a transfusion the moment he was taken from her. It was a life-and-death situation, and, to save the newborn, the obstetrician, who had delivered Little Ethel, used his own blood while waiting for a transfusion to arrive. The act saved the baby's life.

Bob Jr. considers the names he and his sister received as typical of the times, even though women didn't typically pass their names on to daughters. In his opinion, he said, it was a way for his parents to make "mini-me's" (evoking the *Austin Powers* character), miniature versions of themselves, just like "Little Bit." Levitt believes that their names allowed his parents to engage the myth of a harmonious, close-knit family, a myth that they, like many people, would find difficult to live up to. For the kids, Levitt was never "Dad"; he was "Big Bob" or "Big." "As I was often called 'Baby Bob' in a loving way, our father was always called 'Big' or 'Big Bob,' in a loving way. I almost never say the word *big* without evoking a wisp of my father's memory," Levitt Jr. writes today.[30]

Merman openly shared her views on child rearing with the press. Aware that these aspects of a female celebrity's life fascinate the public, she was also able in this way to control the information that went out. Big Ethel and Bob were committed to shielding Little Ethel and Bobby from the scrutiny of public life. Said Levitt, "We agreed that certain things should be done with respect to the children. . . . We used to have very strict policies about not letting the kids in any way participate in her career. . . . she wouldn't use them to pose for pictures or any crap like that. . . . it was not fair to the children to handicap them with that kind of notoriety, because they had to go to school with a bunch of kids who will not take kindly to their identification with a star. I think people who do that kind of thing . . . are doing the kids an injustice."[31]

Another reason that Ethel and Bob carefully monitored press reports on their family was Ethel's almost hard-wired concern for propriety, avoiding scandal, and doing things right. Certain things were expected of you as a wife and mother, and Ethel intended to adhere to those expectations. Moreover, in her case, the press might have been a little extra curious because her persona as Ethel Merman was not your standard-issue mom material: there were the near asexuality of her roles, her childlike affinity with animals and children, and the mothering given her by children in *Hattie.* Her voice, her personality, her bravura and self-confidence were hardly the stuff of your typical selfless, nurturing mom. Predictably, all sorts of "Mother Ethel" stories circulated: Ethel didn't care if her kids didn't follow her footsteps into show business (true), or she prohibited cursing in front of the kids (her son recalls only a few "Goddammits").[32] A very widely told Ethel legend still circulating in one variation or another is the following: Mama Ethel (in later versions, Grandma Ethel) is strolling in Central Park with a young child. The girl is screaming and clearly has been for some time. "Do you want to go do this?" asks Merman to no avail. "Do you want to do that?" More tears. "Well, do you want to do this?" Nothing. "Goddammit, I give up. What the [expletive] do you want to do?" Recounted from Dorothy Fields to Broadway divas and fans who never even met her, the rumor shows no sign of abating. Close friends and Merman's son find the tale completely implausible, but the story has taken on a life of its own, enabling Merman fans and detractors alike to reconcile the "real" Ethel Merman with the mother they imagined her to be, a trend that would peak when she depicted Rose in *Gypsy.*

Ethel's scrapbook entries are less frequent during this period, hardly surprising given her new family responsibilities; moreover, she had her personal home scrapbooks to fill. Still, the "career scrapbooks" reflect other shifts in Merman's life. For instance, although plenty of correspondence still came from "regular folks" and individual fans at this point, more came from fellow entertainers. Since Ethel was now circulating with them, this can only be expected, and it's hard to imagine anyone, no matter how famous, not eager to save fan mail from Katharine Hepburn, Joe Weber, Lew Fields (father of Dorothy), and former costar Tyrone Power (who penciled a note, "My dear Miss Merman—is it your general practice to come to this distinguished establishment without dressing? If you know what I mean. Alexander"—God only knows what happened).[33] That Ethel saved every artifact is slightly more surprising. Each memento was pasted into the bulging scrapbooks, testimony to the pleasure that father and daughter both shared in Ethel's success and her place in celebrity culture. Ethel helped by annotating clippings, circling reports or identifying photos or seating arrangements ("I met him that night!" "He is the Attorney General," etc.).

The young family was back at 25 Central Park West. Little Ethel, Bobby, and their governess lived at one end of the long hall on the twenty-first story, the second of their two floors. At the other end of the heavily carpeted hall were Ethel and Big Bob's bedroom and his office. When she was in a show, Ethel came home on nonmatinee days from 4:30 to 5:30 to see the young kids. But by and large, parents and children occupied separate worlds and separate spaces. Bobby and Ethel took their meals with their governess, except for the family meal that was taken together on Wednesdays, her day off. Then Gram, who still lived in the building with Pop Pop, would take the grandchildren to the five-and-dime. Bob has fond memories of her giving him tea and graham crackers out of a tin and her resting in bed with him, giving a physical contact he loved. "Although I was very young," he says, "I remember my mom at the time mostly as a 'presence.' "[34]

Help included Myron the maid, who delivered the tray of food to Mr. and Mrs. Levitt's bedroom ("She accidentally blew herself up in the stove," recalls Bob Jr.) and Margaret the cook.[35] Once Bobby was born, Ethel hired help for the two children, a beloved governess named Abba, who was replaced by a Miss Kopeman, whom Bob calls " 'Koppi the Fierce and Terrible,' our child-abuser governess."[36] Miss Kopeman would force the kids to recite the Lord's Prayer every night, in German, and beat them for the small misdemeanors that children routinely commit. Should they rest their elbows on the dinner table, for instance, Koppi grabbed their arms and smashed their elbows down hard onto the tabletop. They got the message.

Bobby and his sister formed the Gorilla Club, whose two other members were Dickie and Jill, children of Dorothy Kilgallen and musical comedy performer Richard Kollmer. Dickie and Jill also had a governess, Miss Muller, who was a friend of Koppi's. The chief aim of Gorilla Club members? To stay out of trouble and keep out of the way of grown-ups supervising them.

Young Bobby seemed especially prone to misadventure. His big sister would taunt him, calling the pudgy boy "Fatso" and tripping him as he was learning to walk. Bobby found himself repeatedly hauled off to the bathroom at the end of the hall, where Koppi would inflict her harsh discipline, spanking him with a hard hairbrush or washing his mouth out with soap. Merman, having no idea that this sort of thing was going on, kept Miss Kopeman in her employ until the mid-1950s. It took some time for Bob to come to terms with that experience with Koppi: "I'm sure my mother had no idea at the time, but we were able to talk about it later."[37]

If Merman was a "presence" to young Bob, it was a most welcome one. He has special memories of her saying good night before leaving to do her shows. Ethel would come into his room, and they sang a simple rhyming game, "Play Ball," back and forth together: "Play ball, play ball / Everybody likes to play ball / Sometimes you catch it / Sometimes you don't / When you miss / Remember this / Let the ball roll." It became a cherished ritual to the young boy, who deliberately altered words as they went along. "My changing the word *miss* in the rhyme 'when you miss, remember this' to the word *don't* was the funny, lightly desperate way I had of stopping the song with that wrong un-rhyming word so that we'd have to start over again, so that Mom would stay longer. So that she wouldn't leave for the theatre."[38]

He remembers little about his parents' marriage; it dissolved in 1951, when he was only six. He and Little Ethel kept pretty much to themselves, busy with their animal clubs and societies and trying to avoid Koppi's wrath. Of his parents, Levitt recalls that his dad would sometimes refer to his mom as "the Fearless Leader." From the early years, he remembers a lot of fighting and raised voices. After the marriage dissolved, his father told Pete Martin a bit about their differences:

> When I write "Life with Merman," my evaluation of her is that she is a very possessive woman and she has many possessions . . . the kind of woman that she must fancy herself in her fantasies, a woman who has got a distinguished

career, has handsome children, and a presentable husband, has a good looking automobile, good looking clothes, good church, and jewelry—and I don't
think she differentiates much among them. When a car gets scratched she
races to have it polished up; when the kids get sick, she calls in the best doctors to have them made well. When her husband breaks his leg, I'm sure she
mourns suitably and behaves in all respects as a dutiful wife should. What goes
on inside of the automobile, what goes on in the minds of the kids, and what
goes on in the mind of her husband or his feelings is something that she just
doesn't comprehend. . . . Ethel, she's crazy about the kids, but she's crazy because they're her children.[39]

Levitt's postdivorce cynicism is understandable. At the time of these remarks,
he was fighting a losing battle with depression and alcohol. However sardonic
or bitter, the remarks reveal an interesting insight, namely, that Ethel understood her life as wife and mother as things to *get right,* almost like a role—
not in the sense of a pretense or a falsehood, but as an out-of-reach image or
goal. His assertion that his ex-wife's understanding was superficial or that she
was a "lousy mother" remains harsh,[40] and their son assesses her abilities in
much more forgiving terms today. In Bob Jr.'s view, the "intensity of her
other demands as 'Ethel Merman' distracted her from attending to her children. She wasn't able to see it." That did not make her "a monster mother,"
he says, "quite the opposite."[41]

SEVEN

What Comes Natur'lly

Annie Get Your Gun

As a comedienne, Miss Merman is as American as the
Fourth of July. Hers is a sense of humor which ought to
sport a raccoon coat, wave pennants, wear slacks, or
send a juke box about its business . . . Miss Merman is
Broadway's idea of its own Beatrice Lillie. The difference
between the two of them as entertainers is the
difference between Times Square and Mayfair. . . . The
one is as much the mistress of nuance as the other is of
noise. Both are incredibly professional . . . and equally
hilarious.

WARD MOREHOUSE, *"Broadway after Dark"*

I was captured by the air of surprise and complete
disbelief with which she portrayed . . . Annie Oakley,
and the superbly ingenuous delivery of her lines in a
kind of a Bronx-Hillbilly dialect while looking into my
heart with a frankly baffled stare.

Esquire, *1946*

Annie Get Your Gun secured Merman's place as an all-American icon who embodied the vitality and can-do spirit of a nation. It also confirmed her reign
as queen of Broadway; a typical review ran, "Annie Gets Her Gun and Drills
a Bull's Eye in Broadway."[1] The show became one of the most successful popular shows of twentieth-century musical theater, and since its 1946 premiere,
it has been in endless local productions, tours, and revivals on Broadway and
around the world. Ticket sales outstripped all of Merman's previous hits and
convinced Irving Berlin that it was the best Merman show ever. Only *Gypsy*

rivals *Annie*'s impact on American culture and Merman's place in it, and when you ask fans today which is their favorite show or set of songs, it's a dead heat between the two.

The story is straightforward. It begins with the arrival of Col. Buffalo Bill's Wild West Show outside Cincinnati, Ohio, one summer day. The show boasts that it's "got the stuff that made the Wild West wild," including "the world's greatest sharpshooter," Frank Butler, and plenty of bloodthirsty Indians to stage "historical" battles. To promote it, sales manager Charlie Davenport puts up notices at the town inn, challenging the best local shot to a sharpshooting contest with Butler. Enter Annie Oakley. Merman entered less voice first than "shot first"; wearing a buckskin dress and moccasins, "bumpkin" hair and dirty face. Annie spots an artificial bird on the hat of Frank Butler's assistant, Dolly, and shoots it off. When Dolly explains, "It's not an eating bird, it's a wearing bird," Annie doesn't get it. She understands the world of nature and, with her "clan," a group of unscrubbed kids, sings "Doin' What Comes Natur'lly," which good-humoredly details the basic know-how of the uneducated folks at home. Annie takes up the show's challenge, boasting, "I shoot like a man!" but when the tall, handsome, supremely self-confident Frank Butler steps out, his charm locks Annie in its spell. Her eyes go wide as saucers, and the rest of her falls slack-jawed and limp in what quickly became known as Ethel's "goon look." After this, Frank sings "The Girl That I Marry," describing the wifely traits he seeks, and Annie, not finding herself in any of his criteria, then sings "You Can't Get a Man with a Gun."

Annie wins the sharpshooting competition, to Bill's bemusement and Frank's chagrin. Eager to increase revenues, Bill and Charlie convince Frank to let Annie join the show; a woman shooter will be a "novelty," they say. Butler concedes, as long as he remains the main attraction. The men encourage Annie to join them by exhorting their livelihood in "There's No Business Like Show Business."

The show continues its Midwest tour by train. Eager to be worthy of Frank's attentions, Annie slowly transforms her appearance and demeanor to become the kind of gentrified girl that Frank has described. He starts to warm to the ingenuous young woman, and they duet with "They Say It's Wonderful." Charlie and Bill suggest to Annie that she be part of the act to boost sales (sagging, thanks to rival Pawnee Bill's Wild West show), convincing the lovesick woman that Frank will be pleased if she surprises him in a dazzling new performance. And so Annie unveils her new routine, in which she shoots lights on a pole from a moving motorcycle. She is an immediate sensation, but Butler, furious over what he views as an attempt to upstage him, quits to join the rival Pawnee Bill Show. Distraught, Annie is comforted by Chief Sitting Bull, who was bowled over by her performance. "Papa Bull" reads Frank's good-bye letter to the illiterate woman and decides to adopt her as his tribal daughter in an elaborate Native ceremony ("I'm an Indian Too").

Buffalo Bill and crew go on an undepicted European tour in which Annie is a hit. But because of the unpaid command performances, the troupe fails to pull in much-needed money, and Annie is still preoccupied with Frank. Bill, Charlie, and Sitting Bull, now manager, all recognize the need to pair the two sharpshooters, not just for Annie's happiness, but also for the fiscal health of the show, all information that is telescoped at the beginning of the second act, which opens on a cattle boat on their trip back to the States. Their plan is to merge with the rival Pawnee Bill to boost their dwindling fortune; Pawnee Bill and Frank Butler, meanwhile, entertain the same scheme. Pawnee Bill throws a lavish party at which they hope to seal the deal, and Annie makes a grand entrance in an evening dress with a bodice covered by medals she's garnered from Europe, whose stones are worth a small fortune. Ultimately she offers to sell them to help the merger. When Frank appears, they embrace passionately but quickly grow competitive (singing "Anything You Can Do, I Can Do Better").

Another sharpshooting contest is held between the sparring lovers. On the sidelines, Papa Bull convinces Annie that she can win either the match or the guy—not both. She happily takes the bad gun he offers and feigns defeat. The show ends with her and Frank reprising "They Say It's Wonderful" and "The Girl That I Marry," then Annie leads the coupled western shows with "There's No Business Like Show Business."

Annie Get Your Gun omitted most of the hardships of the real-life Annie Oakley. Born Phoebe Annie Oakley Mozee (sometimes Moses) in a log cabin in Dark County, Ohio, in 1866 (some say 1860), "Annie" was the sixth of eight kids. At the age of four, stepfather Jake Mozee froze to death driving the family wagon home in a storm. The young girl probably witnessed his gruesome arrival: frozen solid, still clutching the reins of the horse that had brought the wagon home. The widowed mother and her children moved, but when Annie turned nine, she was sent off to live with a couple who put her to work. After they withheld food from her, whipped her, and locked her outdoors in winter, Annie ran away and went back home, helped by strangers who bought her a train ticket. Throughout her childhood, things went better when the young girl had a gun in her hand. At the age of eight, Annie took the family shotgun to kill a squirrel in the front yard. "It was a wonderful shot," she later boasted, "going right through the head from side to side."[2]

Oakley met sharpshooter Frank Butler at a shooting competition that she won, and the two married soon after and started touring together. Their act was much the same wherever they went: Annie's part consisted of ten minutes of shooting nonstop from either hand, hitting playing cards, pucks, or whatever else was thrown up into the air. One legend claims that in twenty-seven seconds, Oakley put twenty-five slugs through an ace of hearts without once hitting the white of the card.

Off season, she and Butler resided in Nutley, New Jersey, where they lived a tranquil life. She retired from performing in 1913 and died in 1926. A grieving Frank Butler died less than a month later. Interestingly, the female sharpshooter who claimed, "I have always maintained that outside of heavy manual labour, anything a man can do a woman can do practically as well,"[3] opposed the women's suffrage she lived to see.

Not all of Oakley's life was the fodder for a Broadway play. Laughed Dorothy Fields, who cowrote the book, "We did a lot of research on Annie Oakley and Frank Butler, and both of them apparently were about the dullest people in the world. Annie Oakley in real life used to sit in her tent and *knit,* for God's sake!"[4] It hardly mattered. Plenty of other details about the actual Oakley helped promote the show. Boasts one souvenir program, "Once she hit 943 of 1000 flying balls in a rapid fire demonstration and at the age of 56, using three double-barreled guns, punctured in midair six balls sprung from as many traps!" Free theater passes—called "Annie Oakleys"—were printed to look as if a bullet had scorched brown holes in the thick stock.

Staging Annie Oakley's Story

In 1935, Annie Oakley's story was made into an RKO film with Barbara Stanwyck, but the idea of turning it into a musical comedy on Broadway came a decade later from Dorothy Fields. "I was sitting next to my husband at Pennsylvania Station," she recalled. "Next to us was a woman from the Traveler's Aid Bureau—that was the aid that when boys in the war came in from the trains from Coney Island, Palisades and wherever, they could stay at the station until their trains left for camp. . . . She said, 'I had the cutest guy in the other night, this sharpshooter. The most brilliant sharpshooter with medals from here to here, and he was tight as a fool. But he'd been to Coney Island

and he'd won everything he could possibly win.' . . . And for the strangest reason I just thought: Annie Oakley and Ethel Merman."[5] The only other detail she had in mind at this point was that, for her entrance, Merman would shoot a bird off a woman's hat.

Summer 1945. Fields approached Mike Todd to produce. "We had to tell him first," she recalled. "Mike said, 'Ethel Merman as Annie Oakley? She's through, she'll never do another show.' " It was not the response Fields expected, nor was it a sentiment that Todd ever let on to Merman. "I don't know [why he said that]," Fields said later. "He was busy being a general at the time."[6] Undaunted and spurred by the success of Rodgers and Hammerstein's shows *Oklahoma!* and *Carousel* and their interest in producing, Fields approached Oscar Hammerstein at the next ASCAP meeting: "Ockie, what do you think of Ethel Merman as Annie Oakley?" "We'll do it," he said. "Tell Dick after the meeting." When Rodgers had the same reaction, the production team was set.

Ethel may have been ideal for the role of the talented sharpshooter, but Rodgers, Hammerstein, and the Fieldses couldn't be sure of her participation. The reason: that August, she was at Manhattan's Doctors' Hospital recuperating after Bobby's Cesarean birth. Fields went in to pitch the role to her friend two days after the surgery. "Frankly," recalled Ethel, "I was much more concerned about my stitches than I was about a show."[7] Moreover, she had promised her husband and young family to take a year off from the boards. But it didn't take Fields long to convince her, and Merman was signed on for the commanding salary of forty-five hundred dollars a week plus 10 percent of the show's gross. Before the month was out, the *New York Times* was announcing the deal, and five months after that, Dorothy Kilgallen reported that Rodgers and Hammerstein were purchasing a quarter-million-dollar insurance policy on their star.

Dorothy Fields was the daughter of veteran entertainer-producer Lew Fields, one-half of what they called the "Dutch" (Jewish, Yiddish) vaudeville comedy team of (Joe) Weber and Fields, one that generated the gag, " 'Who was that lady I saw you with last night?' 'That was no lady, that was my wife.' " When Fields turned from performing to producing, his Broadway shows included the all-black revue *Blackbirds of 1928*.[8] Producer Fields was credited with discovering the song-writing team of Richard Rodgers and Lorenz Hart.

Dorothy was one of Fields's four children, three of whom went into the theater. Of her two older brothers, the younger, Herbert, was a librettist.

He'd worked with Rodgers and Hart and, later, with Cole Porter, writing *Panama Hattie* and *Something for the Boys*. Although Dorothy was also a librettist *(Mexican Hayride, Let's Face It,* and, with brother Herb, *Something for the Boys* and *Annie Get Your Gun)*, she was known primarily as a lyricist. That's how her career started, with hits such as "A Fine Romance," "I Can't Give You Anything But Love," and "On the Sunny Side of the Street," the upbeat, flip side to Yip Harburg–Jay Gorner's sorrowful Depression anthem, "Brother, Can You Spare a Dime?"[9] In these and other works, Dorothy Fields used a deceptively simple combination of urbanity and unsentimentality, and her lyrics conveyed an affectionate, nonjudgmental humanity. She also had a great gift for internal rhymes and integrated vernacular language into lyrics with ease. "What I like best about Dorothy Fields," Stephen Sondheim later summed up, "is her use of colloquialism and her effortlessness."[10]

Fields achieved a rather remarkable level of success in the male-dominated world of Broadway, where women were expected to be big on the stage, not behind it. Fields was one of few exceptions, along with Betty Comden. "I must say," she said, "all the boys were simply wonderful. I was the little sister. They were very solicitous of me, very careful not to say anything wrong in front of me, and they got furious if anyone used improper language in my presence."[11] It helped that Dorothy was a relatively unthreatening figure. Neither glamorous, nor physically imposing, nor a prima donna in her behavior, she was reliable, respectful, and professional. The Broadway community was united in its adoration of Dorothy, responding not only to her talent but also to her wit, generosity, and warmth. Everyone knew her as a good egg.

"Dorothy was a gal who took time for friendship," said Merman. "She was a woman of great warmth and wide experience."[12] The two got along well professionally and personally and remained close until Dorothy's death in 1974. Today, her son, songwriter and performer David Lahm, recalls that whenever he or his mother saw Ethel, she greeted them with great warmth. He has a photograph of Merman congratulating him and his wife, singer Judy Kreston, at one of the cabaret shows they often do together.

Although Rodgers and Hammerstein are lionized as the creators of some of Broadway's most memorable musicals, their career as producers of other people's works—such as John van Druten's *I Remember Mama* in 1944—is less widely known, and for some reason, *Annie Get Your Gun* was the only *musical* they ever produced. They were as good with the business of Broadway as they were in creating its hits; they seemed to know every detail that was necessary to make a show a success.

For *Annie Get Your Gun,* they brought Jerome Kern in for the songs. He was the genius behind *Showboat,* which he had composed with Hammerstein, and Hammerstein was himself a respected mentor to young Dorothy Fields, who was slated to do song lyrics with Kern. The two had teamed up before, writing the beautiful Academy Award winner "The Way You Look Tonight" for *Swing Time* in 1936. Now, in 1945, Kern had not been on Broadway for six years, when his last show, *Very Warm for May,* had closed after fifty-nine performances, and he was understandably reluctant to return. Dorothy Fields pleaded with him, and Richard Rodgers telegrammed him, "It would be one of the greatest honors of my life if you would consent to write the music for this show."[13] Kern accepted.

Kern was never to enjoy his comeback. The day after returning to New York to start work, he suffered a severe stroke. Less than two weeks after that, on November 11, 1945, the maestro was dead at the age of sixty. Dorothy Fields, along with the rest of the Broadway community, was devastated. Not since the death of George Gershwin in 1937 (at thirty-eight) had the Big Stem grieved so collectively. Even Merman's scrapbooks—not prone to widely detailed context—convey this. Amid dozens of clippings about her upcoming show is a simple white card framed in black: "The family of the late Jerome Kern acknowledges with deep appreciation your kind thought and expression of sympathy."

Rodgers and Hammerstein did not panic long. What about Irving Berlin? After all, Berlin wrote fast and could seemingly pull show-stoppers out of his hat (or his trunk). And, as Kern had said, Berlin *was* American music and thus ideal for an American frontier story. But like Kern, Berlin had not had a success on Broadway for six years. His last had been *Louisiana Purchase,* which played at the beginning of the decade, when *DuBarry* was running. Since then, Berlin had been in Hollywood and then with the army, doing *This Is the Army.*

During Berlin's absence, however, Broadway had changed. *Oklahoma!* had taken it by storm, and the new character- and narrative-driven book musical was starting to eclipse the less "integrated" musical comedy, for which Berlin—and Merman—were known. Understandably apprehensive about doing what he called a "situation show,"[14] Berlin would be not only competing with Richard Rodgers on new turf but also working under Rodgers on his terms as the producer. Berlin was also concerned about the show's theme: what on earth did he know about what he called "Hillbilly music"?

With some nudging from his wife, Ellin, Berlin was in and, within two weeks, had written most of the show's classics, famously penning "Anything You Can Do" in a fifteen-minute cab ride. Recalled Ethel, "In eight days, he turned out ten great songs, ranging in form from sentimental ballads to risqué comedy. . . . With all due respect to the Gershwins and Cole, Irving had given me range, allowing me a kind of vulnerability that was missing in girls like 'Nails' Duquesne, Blossom Hart and Hattie Maloney."[15] Berlin's songs provide not only emotional range but musical variety as well, including a march ("Buffalo Bill"), a razzle-dazzle anthem ("There's No Business"), a romantic ballad ("I Got Lost in His Arms"), and a novelty number ("Anything You Can Do").

Ironically, Berlin didn't think "There's No Business Like Show Business" was going to be well received and pulled it until Rodgers and Hammerstein insisted he bring the song back in. Later, in previews, Hammerstein told reporters, "Irving Berlin . . . gave us a superb score. A score which never once deserts the mood or the story. The book didn't get in Irving's way. He strengthened it! . . . In fact, he really went overboard one day when he insisted that if a certain sure-hit song ["There's No Business"] didn't suit the situation he was going to yank it out! We had to be fanned."[16] Berlin wrote the number with the intention that Bill and his associates would sing it to convince Annie to join their show, but Richard Rodgers was so sure of its firepower that he insisted on finding a way for Ethel to sing it. The solution was to show Annie listening to a few verses and then saying, "You mean . . . ?" before singing the song back to them.

Of course, the kind of "show business" *Annie* champions was at the time retreating in the face of the new kind of show making that *Oklahoma!* helped usher in. According to Berlin's delightfully biased biographer Laurence Bergreen, "As Rodgers and Hammerstein repeatedly (and profitably) demonstrated, audiences responded to a treacly blend of self-conscious Americana and heartening liberal sermons with as much enthusiasm as an earlier generation had brought to the spectacle of flashing thighs and heaving bosoms."[17] Although *Annie Get Your Gun* acknowledges that new model, it hardly capitulates to it. Its self-conscious theatricality is in sharp contrast to the naturalized narrative worlds of Rodgers and Hammerstein musicals. *Annie*'s emphasis on putting on a show has more in common with an older, presentational style of musical comedy—the one that says, "Hey, look at all this fun we're having!" with entertainers such as Jolson, Cantor, Brice, and Durante— and Merman, in song.

Despite the emotional resonance given to Annie Oakley's character, both the show and her character are far from nuanced. The story makes few bids to social consciousness (compared with the later musicals of Rodgers and Hammerstein, *The King and I* and *South Pacific*), and the community it lauds is its own: the entertainment world. Moreover, it is less the personal or expressive dimension of performing that Berlin's show champions than the *business* in show business. There is no community of the "land" or region as in *Oklahoma!* In fact, as Andrea Most notes, the show positions the American West as nothing but a series of stage sets, a world of artifice, in which happiness and success are measured by personal achievement and profit. She writes, "As if in direct response to *Oklahoma!* this play rejects claims of naturalness . . . insisting that America is *theater,* and that only those who understand and embrace America's inherent theatricality are destined for success. Moreover, success in the play is financial, and American theatricality is intimately linked to capitalism."[18] Indeed, the precarious finances of Buffalo Bill's and Pawnee Bill's operations are crucial themes of the show and, as David Lahm notes, "drive a good deal of the comedy."[19] The show evokes another myth of Americana: the overnight success story, which was embodied by both Oakley and Merman and practically urged people to conflate Ethel Merman with the sharpshooting heroine she played. After all, their stories seemed to flow together: Annie, like Miss Zimmermann, moved from an untrained world in which she "does what comes naturally," using skills that enabled her and her partners to become successful in theater and commerce.[20]

For Broadway historian Cecil Smith, *Annie* was devoid of novelty or aesthetic risks, "a thoroughly standardized product produced . . . with the unerring comprehension of all the ingredients and proportions of the recipe for success."[21] Although a few critics at the time complained that *Annie*'s tunes were a string of hits rather than pieces integrated into story lines or that its characters were colorful but undeveloped, the criticism is not quite fair. Yes, it is stuffed with show-stoppers, but plenty of numbers help express Annie's feelings and thoughts ("I Got Lost in His Arms") rather than simply promoting gags. To be sure, "I Got Lost in His Arms" has not had the afterlife that "Anything You Can Do" has had, even though in 1946 it was the ballad "They Say It's Wonderful" that had most of the radio airplay.

Papers first reported that George Murphy would play Frank Butler, but then on January 4, 1946, they announced that the role had gone to Ray Middleton (1907–84) the tall, Juilliard-trained opera baritone who had arrived on Broadway via Hollywood, where he usually played bad guys *(Roberta, Lady from New Orleans, Lady for Night, The Girl from Alaska)* in a career that wasn't igniting. Sitting Bull was played by Italian American Harry Bellaver, who'd been an underemployed farmhand and coal miner in the Midwest before turning his sights to the stage.

The spectacular sets were by virtuosic Jo Mielziner (1901–76), and Helen Tamiris (1905–66), who'd done *Showboat* on Broadway, choreographed. In contrast to her contemporary Agnes De Mille, Tamiris did not use dance to advance the plot or a character's inner thoughts or dreams so much as to show off the songs. Her work in "I'm an Indian Too," the show's most elaborate number, was an audience favorite. There she westernizes indigenous dance movements and, when Annie joins the number, pulls those features back, partly out of respect for Ethel's limited dancing skills. Tamiris also mapped out Ethel/Annie's shooting numbers in the Wild West Show. Costumes— ranging from Annie's bumpkin garb to show biz cowgirl to evening gown to ceremonial Indian dress—were by Lucinda Ballard. Ballard had to respond to complaints Ethel voiced through management that her buckskin outfit was too heavy. After toughing it out for several shows, Ethel found herself exhausted and sweating profusely in the outfit, and Ballard found a lighter, look-alike fabric.

Joshua Logan (also a choreographer, writer, manager, and actor) was signed to direct. Ethel was still beaming with appreciation for his compliments about her acting when they did *Stars in Your Eyes* and was delighted to work with him again. Logan, like Berlin, had been in Europe during the war, serving in the U.S. Army Air Corps and, also like him, had not done anything on Broadway since then. *By Jupiter,* which closed in June 1943, had been his last show.

Juilliard graduate Jay Blackton (1909–94) arranged the score. A diminutive man who had been afflicted by polio as a child, Blackton quipped that his musical skills "meant he would be able to earn a living sitting down."[22] At the time of his appointment, Blackton was working with the New York Opera Comique when he was called in to replace arranger Philip Lang in a dramatic, last-minute switch. Blackton had also been orchestral conductor for *Oklahoma!* and would be paired with Merman again in *Call Me Madam, Happy Hunting,* and as her longtime accompanist when she turned to solo touring toward the end of her career. Conducting was Milton Rosenstock, who had toured in the army with Berlin as conductor of *This Is the Army;* he, too, would work again with Ethel on *Gypsy* (on Broadway and on tour). Ethel's understudy was Margie Knapp and later Mary Jane Walsh, both of whose primary role seemed to be causing columnists to speculate about another pregnancy for

Ethel Merman. The casting was finalized by early 1946, and calls went out for gypsies' auditions on February 8.

Ethel kept her usual busy balancing act as the show was being prepared, attending balls (e.g., the annual ball for the press photographers of New York in February), benefits (Red Cross), and hospital tours. She didn't see as much of her young children as she had intended. Rehearsals for the show were scheduled for February 18 and began a week later, one day shy of Buffalo Bill Cody's one hundredth birthday anniversary.

From Tryouts to Opening Night

Tryouts were in New Haven (March 28) and Boston (April 2). The first problem was that the show ran too long. Too much ground was covered in the first act, presenting the naive Annie, then the infatuated Annie, the successful Annie, the romantically involved Annie, the broken-hearted Annie. Even after adjustments were made, the first act remained much longer than the second, and Ethel, with no time for encores, could only blow kisses to an excited New Haven audience after singing "Anything You Can Do." (This was a song that both Ethel and Hammerstein liked as it was, but Berlin insisted on making some last-minute changes, which Merman, in an uncharacteristic move, agreed to adopt the same day. When the new version failed to ignite, "Anything" went back to the way it had been done before. Ethel's instincts were seldom wrong.)

Audiences loved her. In Boston, she received the following note: "Yesterday in the lobby of the Ritz Carlton Hotel, Mr John F. Royal was teasing me a bit in your presence about our 'great' art and yours. Believe me I am convinced that your performance of A Oakley is one of the greatest samples of theatrical art I have seen since a long time. In every respect: singing, acting, sincerety [sic] of conception—it's wonderful."[23] It was signed by Herbert Graf, the stage director of the Metropolitan Opera House in New York. So much for hillbilly music.

The show faced plenty of challenges and small curses: the unexpected death of Jerome Kern, the sudden change in orchestrators. In Boston, Ethel caught her finger in the gun catch and tore it open. She continued to sing all of "I Got Lost in His Arms" and, after the scene, saw the house doctor, who dressed her bleeding hand in the wings. Another crisis involved the theater where the show was scheduled to open in New York. *Song of Norway* had left the Imperial (moving to the Broadway) so that *Annie* could open there on

April 25. One day, after a dress rehearsal, the cast left, and as the crew was hoisting the show's heavy sets, a girder pulled right out from the brick wall, and things came crashing down with a tremendous boom. "If that girder had fallen during rehearsal, I don't know how many people would have been creamed," said Ethel.[24] The building's license was revoked immediately, and the Shuberts were forced to close it down for two weeks. *Annie* was quickly moved to Philadelphia from April 30 to May 11.

On May 16, 1946, a drizzly rain was falling on New York when *Annie Get Your Gun* opened at the restored Imperial Theatre at 8:30. Top-price tickets were a soaring $6.60,[25] the highest charge for a Broadway show since *Oklahoma!* In contrast to its warm receptions in New Haven, Boston, and Philadelphia, the show faced a distinct chill during the first act in New York. The $350,000 musical had had extensive advance publicity; perhaps the opening night audience was expecting a sophisticated, Rodgers and Hammerstein–styled affair? "What they got, to their initial dismay, was a knockabout Irving Berlin musical filled with bits, routines, shtick," writes Berlin's biographer.[26] Recalled Merman, "During the interval everybody must have reassured everyone else that it was okay to laugh, because when the audience returned it turned out to be a responsive group."[27]

She could not have understated it more. So successful was opening night that one critic proposed that May 16 should be made annual "Merman Day." *Annie Get Your Gun* would go on to make its producers a small fortune; Merman's annual income during the run was estimated at about $244,400.

Reviews were positive, and once again it was Merman all the way. "The big news about *Annie Get Your Gun* is that it reveals Ethel Merman in her best form since *Anything Goes,*" wrote Ward Morehouse. "Miss Merman, now wearing buckskins as the redoubtable sharpshooter from the Kentucky *[sic]* hills, is her own hearty, brassy, noisy self. She shouts the Berlin music with good effect. She often comes stridently to the aid of a sagging book. She has a great time all evening."[28] "Ethel is the shining star, and she's a new Ethel Merman, better than ever," wrote Elsa Maxwell.[29] Everyone loved her singing, and her acting was garnering praise as well. Wrote Robert Garland, "She's no longer Miss Merman acting like Ethel Merman. She's Miss Merman acting like Annie Oakley."[30] Musicals historian Stanley Green concurred: gone were the days when she played only a "big-hearted dame [incapable of] romantic expression."[31]

Ethel appreciated what the role did for her: "I have to thank Irving Berlin for making a lady out of me."[32] And it wasn't just his lyrics: ballads like "I Got Lost in His Arms" conveyed the change musically and gave Ethel a softer, vulnerable side missing from her earlier characters. The show "projected a less abrasive Merman,"[33] giving her more emotional and dramatic range, and Ethel openly thanked Josh Logan and the Fieldses as well as Berlin for that.

They, moreover, were as impressed by her as she was appreciative of them. In Logan's memoirs, he recalls the moment in the first act when Annie first catches sight of Frank Butler:

> The script read, "She looks at him and in a second falls in love with him for-ever." I felt that the only way I could show such an abrupt change was to have her collapse inwardly and outwardly as if she were a puppet whose strings had been cut quickly. I told Ethel to keep her eyes fixed on Ray but to let every-thing else in her body and mind go. She tried it. Her mouth dropped open, her shoulders sank, her legs opened wide at the knees, her diaphragm caved in. It was an unforgettable effect . . . and it won for me the eternal devotion of everyone, including myself.[34]

Again he praised Merman's innate acting know-how, telling Pete Martin he was awed by her ability to make transitions "without asking for cerebral rea-sons for those transitions."[35]

Theatergoers and critics were equally captivated, something evident even in the backhanded compliments: "Miss Merman is the country's most au-thentic comedienne. There was a time when Miss Merman's shouts and stage exercises seemed merely strident: last Thursday they were as tamed leopards, in leash by an actress who can not only project humor when it is written but create it when it is not. . . . Annie's humor was forthright, and apparently au-thentically American, a spirit which Miss Merman eminently preserved."[36] For *Newsweek,* Merman was "a sort of backwoods Beatrice Lillie. Practically every gesture she makes and every word she utters is funny, whether inten-tionally or not. She paddles around in moccasins and a tattered dress and is amusing in a pathetic sort of way."[37]

In June 1946, men's magazine *Esquire* took another angle, that of besot-ted critic. Noting the collective crush American men had on film star Ingrid Bergman—currently starring on Broadway in Maxwell Anderson's *Joan of Lorraine*—the writer states, "I would like to get in on it too, except that the girl I love best isn't Miss Bergman, but Ethel Merman." Building up to what he acknowledges might be an odd romantic preference, he says,

> I will tell you something strange, namely that this big and somewhat beamy girl with the moonface, flat nose and black-eyed-Susan orbs, who walks like a

cowpoke and whose singing is a kind of a lusty, strident yell, can get me all choked up in those moments [in *Annie Get Your Gun*] when the book calls for her to pretend to be sad and unhappy because she has been temporarily thrown over by the man she loves. She just gives one sort of forlorn look and a little sag, and I feel much sorrier for her than I ever do for Miss Bergman in her troubles; I want to climb right up on the stage and put my arms around her and comfort her.[38]

Other reviews used equally colorful prose to different ends. Reminding readers of the historical moment—and putting Merman at its boisterous middle—John Mason Brown wrote, "Even before the atomic bomb, there was Ethel Merman." (In Ethel's 1945 scrapbook, an article on the play's development is printed on the same page as an ad for a toy atom bomb.) Brown continued, "The Big Crash came in 1929. Being financial, it resulted in a depression. The Bigger Crash followed the next year [Ethel's debut in *Girl Crazy*]. Since Miss Merman was responsible for it, its victims knew only pleasure." With *Annie,* she "not only gets her clay pigeons; she gets her man, too. Since she is played by Ethel Merman, Annie also gets her audiences. She gets them with an accuracy the real Annie Oakley would have admired. . . . She shoots from the hips; from the tonsils, too."[39]

Merman took her success in stride. She said, the day after *Annie* opened, "I'd got up early. . . . I'd gone over the grocer bills and called to complain about being charged for two cans of grapefruit juice when I'd only received one."[40] Ethel's attitude toward her work was not blasé, just matter-of-fact. More than a personality trait, that worldview shaped the way she ran her life.

Ethnic Ethel

With *Annie Get Your Gun,* Merman's relationship with different ethnic figures continued to inform how the press and the public viewed her. One *Annie* reviewer wrote, "She has an abundance of black hair; long-lashed, dark-brown eyes; a nose that has a rather Semitic cast, although she is not Jewish, and a generous mouth . . . nature obviously intended her to have a rather inexpressive face, and the look of intense vivacity that adorns it is comic and unnatural."[41] This was not the first time Merman had been described as looking Jewish; an interviewer during the time of *Alexander's Ragtime Band* wrote, "Ethel is prettier in real life than she is in movies. She's Episcopalian. She looks Jewish. Weighs 118 pounds, has dark brown hair and brown eyes with long black lashes."[42]

Ethel was not the only one to generate an appearance of Jewishness in *Annie Get Your Gun*. In a stereotype of Jewishness—and Native Americans— Sitting Bull "begins to resemble more and more the earlier, self-consciously theatrical Jewish stage comics."[43] As Papa Bull becomes involved in the business aspect of Wild Bill's show, he reveals "instincts" for things entrepreneurial, advising, among other things, "Never put money in show business!" Whether as Jew or Native, his role had another function too, that of the non-Anglo sidekick who helps and watches the white couple form, a role that various nonwhite "ethnics" filled over time, from Indians to Jews—or here, the two fused together, just as had happened in *Girl Crazy*, where Willie Howard's Yiddish Goldfarb could magically communicate with the Navajos of Arizona.

In old musical comedy, ethnic figures like this were novelty characters, rarely played for anything but laughs. On this point there is little difference between Ethel disguised as a Chinese woman in *Anything Goes* and her work with Cantor in blackface or when she dressed up as an Indian with Paula Laurence in *Something for the Boys*. Her exaggerated portrayal of backwoods Annie Oakley—saying "cain't" instead "can't," giving stricken goon looks, and her difference from the "pink and white" girl Frank describes—is imbued with racial, ethnic, and regional overtones. Ethel was able to utilize these traits in singing Berlin's songs, adding a hiccup to her grace notes at the end of "too" and "Sioux" in "I'm an Indian Too," a Buddy Holly before his time. Later, she did the same thing in *Call Me Madam* when she needed to convey her character's middle-American roots.

Ethel's foray into nonwhite ethnicities shows the way that New York's musical worlds offered a fantasy in which ethnic, social, and national differences were believed to come together in one big American melting pot. From *Girl Crazy* on, Ethel had been in shows with stories of ethnic, national, and religious minorities and outsider groups who were guided into the mainstream of white, middle-class, Christian America. And it would be an error to say that the trend stopped with the Rodgers and Hammerstein musical, since the idea of integrating outsiders into a community endured, now with much greater dramatic gravitas and never as a source of gags. It has continued to this day, with shows still featuring unfairly outcast characters (ailing, overweight, cross-dressed, puppets) whose successes enable them to be folded into mainstream, ethnically integrated America.

Aligned with nature and "doin' what comes natur'lly," Annie and Panama Hattie, like other characters of Ethel's, were comfortable cavorting with the locals in their story worlds. *Annie* and each of these other shows shepherd their principal woman into the more urbane, genteel worlds of adulthood and heterosexual partnering. For Ethel, her on- and offstage images traded in being able to move in and out of those worlds. In other words, no matter how high her level of prestige and success, people were always able to place Ethel Merman alongside so-called regular people—people of color, munitions workers, folks down on their luck, illiterate children. Ethel could easily give off the image of bucking standard adulthood and grown-up restraints. At *Annie Get Your Gun*'s second anniversary party in June 1948, the child players played the show's adult parts and vice versa. Newspapers ran a photo of Merman good-naturedly kicking around in a frilly white toddler's dress.

Annie transforms this unconventional girl into the pinker and whiter feminine woman of Frank's fantasies, just as it transforms the character's natural skills to fuel the money-making machine of show biz. That success has its costs; the ending reveals just what Annie had to lay down in order to be romantically, economically, and culturally successful. At the same time and even as Annie forsakes her gun for Frank, there is something about Ethel Merman *playing* Annie that makes it difficult for her to be the docile girl Frank dreams of. For even in *Annie,* the show that "made a lady out of her," Ethel Merman never epitomized genteel/gentile femininity.

Even today, something about Merman's public persona doesn't fit in, something that was not quite straight, not quite middle class, not fully glamorous or credible as that "pink and white girl," something, in short, that the story line of *Annie* can't contain. It's not her losing to Butler or her desire to please him that most people remember—as we'll see in a moment—but rather her open spirit and force. Even in the show's romantic moments, she was far from the sweet thing that Butler swooned about: when Annie decides to go after him, she proclaims, "I'll wear my long, low-cut in the front dress; I'll show him a thing or two!"

That mix of ethnic, economic, and regional associations of *Annie* and her other shows stuck to Ethel in ways in which it seldom clung to other stars of her caliber. With the significant exception of Fannie Brice, most of the ethnically marked female performers with roots in the early musical comedy on the East Coast rarely went on to do much outside of comedy. But many of these associations stayed on with Ethel, even after the ethnic conventions of comic performance had changed.

Annie and Its Impact

After *Annie Get Your Gun,* Roger Edens said that "Merman wasn't a star, she was an institution."[44] As Annie Oakley, she conveyed not only good old get-up-and-go but also an updated version of Horatio Alger, and, for a country still recovering from World War II, it was exactly what was needed. The fact that the show featured a female sharpshooter added to its novelty, and that image was, moreover, fitting for the times. The war had generated a number of new images of women, not the least of which was Rosie the Riveter, and contemporary audiences could accept the idea of a woman holding a gun, of helping out the country, if not on the battlefield, at least in the munitions plants. Annie Oakley was a displaced Rosie, a self-sufficient working woman who could succeed in a man's world, just as women had been permitted to do during the recent war, for a few years at least.

Indeed, as we saw with the ad for the toy atom bomb, the shadow of World War II was hanging over the show. While it was still in preparation, Ethel accepted an invitation to a "Victory Ball" on November 1, 1945, where she joined high-ranking military guests to benefit the Westchester Victory Fund. Before, during, and after the show's run, Ethel continued her benefits for hospitals, the Red Cross, refugees, and various official military efforts. Because *Annie Get Your Gun* was set a half century earlier and was *not* about war, it managed to displace contemporary anxieties it might have provoked about the war, about guns, and, especially, about women performing men's tasks. It took an idealized moment in the American past in which things appeared simpler—people, gender roles, pleasures, and ambitions—to keep the fantasy rolling.

The original *Annie* has a huge place in the hearts of those who saw it. Stage and TV star Kaye Ballard recalls, "The very first musical I saw was *Annie Get Your Gun.* She was the *best.*"[45] A New York audiologist remembers, "Ethel Merman was so upbeat and came on so strong. I'd heard 'Anything You Can Do' as a kid at camp one summer and I adored it. The line 'Can you bake a pie? Well, neither can I' tickled me. It was so silly, I just loved it."[46] Loyal fan Marilyn Cantor was equally smitten: "Oh, I think I saw *Annie* at least thirty times during its three-year run. And every time I saw it, Merman never missed a beat."[47] Its impact was recorded as far away as Queensland, Australia, where a woman reported to the papers that Ethel's recording of "Anything You Can Do, I Can Do Better" "broke a 12-inch mixing bowl in two pieces."[48] Today, New York City Opera singer and Merman fan Jill Bosworth considers Annie Oakley to be Merman's quintessential performance, because it *wasn't* a typical Merman role. Consider "I Got Lost in His Arms," she argues. "It was not her kind of role, but she made it her own through sheer force. Her New York accent is everywhere in the songs."[49] Not everyone agrees. Another musical theater aficionado calls "I Got Lost" "ridiculous" from Merman's mouth; yet his partner insists it makes no difference, since Merman's persona fit the overall show and character.

The show left a special impact on young women and girls. Today, middle-aged New York women vividly recall *Annie Get Your Gun;* for many it was their first Broadway show. "I saw Ethel Merman in the original version of *Annie Get Your Gun* when I was a child," said one. "What a fireball! There hadn't been that kind of woman before on Broadway. She was out there, not sexual, and not punished for being ambitious"[50]—a reading obviously enabled by a later feminist perspective. In *Annie* this audience member saw a woman who didn't need a man, was self-sufficient, and, through Merman's powerhouse performance, was her own solar system. It's a powerful fantasy, one that has little to do with who Annie is or how she was written; as Fields's son David Lahm notes, "These fans are projecting onto Annie/Ethel their own independence, whether wished-for or actual."[51]

Other women who saw the show were frustrated by it, experiencing Annie's capitulation to Frank Butler as a cop-out. Given how extensively contemporary American culture was trying to coax female factory workers back into the home (recipes in women's magazines, for example, were growing more elaborate and requiring more prep time), their irritation is understandable. One historian goes so far as to read the show in terms of pop culture's suspicion of professionalized women in the early postwar era. That view was reflected in articles about the historical Annie Oakley that appeared during the show, invariably describing her as a tough and competent woman who willingly gave it all up for a guy—scarcely different from the expectations being placed on contemporary "Rosie the Riveters" to abandon their own careers.[52]

Yet to view *Annie*'s ending as sheer capitulation is to miss the point. For as Annie, Ethel Merman ate up the stage; she was the central character around whom absolutely everything in the show revolved. The force of both her performance and her star power trumped everything. After all, she even won the contest of the *whispering* response to "any song you can sing, I can sing softer." And for some fans, knowing that Oakley could outgun Butler if she wanted to was all that mattered.

For a Broadway musical, *Annie*'s influence could scarcely have been wider, and the country's interest in Merman was at a peak as well. But Dorothy

Kilgallen might have been going too far when she wrote, "A major film company is on the verge of bidding for the screen rights to Ethel Merman's life story."[53] In the end, not only was the Merman biopic never made, but also after Berlin, the producers, and Dorothy and Herbert Fields sold *Annie Get Your Gun*'s rights to MGM—in a record-smashing $650,000 deal[54]—Ethel would not resume her hit role. Instead, MGM gave the part to Judy Garland, their young star (who had earlier reprised Ethel's role in the film version of *Girl Crazy*). After shooting "Doin' What Comes Natur'lly" and "I'm an Indian Too," however, Garland, beset by fatigue and addiction problems, was let go. (Howard Keel, who played the role of Frank Butler, said it was "the only tacky thing MGM ever did.")[55] The studio replaced her with G-rated Betty Hutton, who had played Florrie in *Panama Hattie,* the young woman who spends the show chasing Arthur Treacher. Hutton may not have had the phenomenal performing gifts of Garland, but she didn't have her risks either. Production finished ahead of schedule and under budget, and the 1950 movie won several Academy Awards, including best adaptation. Reviewers praised Hutton's energetic performance, even though they inevitably admitted that she was no Ethel Merman. Predictably, dialogue like "I'll show him a thing or two" was excised.

If Ethel was upset, she did not say so publicly. She knew that other Annie Oakleys could not top hers. So did Irving Berlin. One evening while he was dining with Eddie Cantor and daughter Marilyn, Cantor teased, "You know, I think Dolores Gray (in the London run) is doing a great job. She's just as good as Ethel Merman." Knowing her dad was trying to get a rise out of them, Marilyn didn't take the bait. "But boy, Irving Berlin sure did!"[56] In her well-researched 1986 dissertation on the star, Sherri Dienstfrey argues that Merman's ego and professional experience were partly to blame for her lack of success in Hollywood.[57] As anyone who saw Ethel live will attest, she had an absolutely magnetic presence in front of a live audience. Merman was a performer who fed off the immediate energy and gratification audiences gave her, and motion pictures could not reproduce that. Even when doing live radio or television shows in front of small studio audiences, Merman, like any performer, had to pitch her delivery to the mikes and cameras, not to the people.

Merman was used to enthusiastic responses from New York audiences, and her success there had been relatively effortless. She might have been perplexed about not getting the same reception in other places and with other media. Dienstfrey maintains that, at some level, Merman was either too stubborn or too lazy to change. Like other performers who move from stage to screen, Ethel needed to tone down facial expressions (especially as someone lauded for her mugging, as in her "goon look") and had to reduce her voice and body movements to make them seem smaller. Given that people are always surprised today when learning that Ethel Merman was only five feet, five inches, it seems that that diminutiveness never gelled.

Ethel Equals Annie

So close were the associations between the Annie Oakley character and the star that fans and the press alike treated Ethel and Annie almost interchangeably. Although this had been the case since *Take a Chance,* when reviewers and fans addressed Ethel as "Eadie," the degree and duration of Annie's popularity formed a stronger, more enduring legacy. One paper ran side-by-side feature snapshots called "The Two Annie Oakleys."[58] Countless interviews were entitled "Doin' What Comes Natur'lly," burnishing Ethel's image as a homegrown talent, untrained and unpretentious. By now, Berlin's phrase "doin' what comes natur'lly" had fully entered the public vernacular; Edward Zimmermann even saved a photo from an agricultural magazine that used it as a caption for a sow suckling her piglets. Decades after *Annie* closed, "sharpshooter" Ethel posed with rifles for photo ops; as late as 1979, when she voiced *Rudolph and Frosty's Christmas in July,* a kids' animated movie, her character was dressed just like Annie Oakley and even operated a theme park—not so far off Buffalo Bill's traveling show.

During the show's run, family and fans of the actual sharpshooter sent Merman mementos such as photographs and cards that the real Oakley had shot through. For the hundredth performance on August 10, 1946, she was presented with one of Oakley's actual guns, a gold-and-silver-mounted .32-caliber Winchester rifle, loaned from a Mrs. Spencer Olin. The real Annie Oakley had used it in her 1887 European Buffalo Bill tour, the one depicted in the show. At another point, Oakley's granddaughter, Elizabeth Butler Hall, wrote Merman a note of appreciation.

Merman saved other mementos from the long run, including a fan letter from writer John Steinbeck, who'd been seated behind a chatty couple who explained all of the jokes to each other, which, he wrote, was a good thing, because it "not only meant that we heard everything twice but we understood everything."[59] When war hero General Dwight D. Eisenhower took in the show, he went backstage between acts; the delighted diva had had her scouts sleuth out his favorite drink (scotch), and she saved his unwashed glass afterward.

Merman produced a few singularly memorable moments of her own. One night at the start of the second act, when Annie shoots a seagull from the deck of the steamer, the bird failed to fall on cue, and later when it eventually did, Merman ad-libbed, "Must be apoplexy," to howls from the audience. Columnist Earl Wilson reported that on another night, Ethel played "a big hunk" of the show with her back to the rear wall after a dress zipper broke, exposing her back.[60]

Because of *Annie*'s late start in the 1946 season, Ethel didn't have a summer break. Next year, while the show was going strong, she took a two-week vacation early in August to undergo some undisclosed minor surgery—not much of a reprieve. But after two years with the show, when her contract was up, she went into discussions with Rodgers and stipulated that she wanted a six-week vacation if she was to continue. Rodgers happily complied, so on July 5, 1948, Ethel, Levitt, Little Bit, and Bobby went to Glenwood Springs, Colorado, where they stayed at the ranch home of some friends and began a lifelong love affair with the region.

So much a fixture had Merman and *Annie* become on Broadway that critics such as John Chapman defended her need to leave for a break: "Ethel Merman's very nice upholstery is deceptive, for she is really made of iron— a trouper if ever there was one. Yet even she needs a vacation, and assuredly she has earned it."[61] When understudy Mary Jane Walsh took over in the sweltering summer heat, however, ticket sales fell so precipitously—from a weekly intake of thirty-six thousand dollars to twenty-four thousand—that Rodgers begged Ethel to return early. She refused. The cast took a temporary cut in salary in one of the few times that Ethel made a decision for which the cast would "pay." When discussing the six-week break from the show in her memoirs, Ethel was at pains to say that the cast supported her in her right to a vacation. (Today, one is hard-pressed to imagine a star having to defend her right to time off.)

Before the break, Miss Walsh's services had scarcely been used. When Ethel underwent a minor procedure in 1947—reportedly for the removal of a mole from her foot—an infection extended the time she had to take off, so Walsh found herself playing Annie longer than expected: from September 29 to October 11. During that time, the young actress suffered an unexpected personal tragedy. Her fiancé, Ernie Holst, the high-society orchestra leader and violinist, died while riding in a cab with her, and that same evening, with

Mermanesque toughness, Walsh performed the entire show, collapsing afterward.

Annie's run was so long and robust that critics joked that Ethel would be doing the role well into old age, and she even quipped, "One of these days, I'm going to do the whole show in an iron lung."[62] Little did everyone know that she would star in its revival two decades later. The last performance of the original *Annie Get Your Gun* was on February 19, 1949, after two years, and nine months, and 1,147 performances. Ethel was proud but exhausted.

Annie played even longer (four years) at the London Coliseum with Dolores Gray. In 1950, *Annie du far-west* opened in France, with chanteuse Lily Fayol in a production that featured live elephants and that transformed Tamiris's Native American choreography into an African-American boogie-woogie. Over the years, dozens of larger-than-life figures have depicted Annie Oakley abroad, on Broadway, and in regional theaters, including Mary Martin, Ginger Rogers, Martha Raye, Bernadette Peters, and Reba McIntyre (who recalled singing "Anything You Can Do I Can Do Better" as a child). Even with the considerable talents of these actors, Ethel Merman remains the gold standard.

Some maintain that had Kern lived, Mary Martin would have been the first Annie Oakley.[63] Martin did end up being the first Annie Oakley to go on tour, and her performance gave a soft, adolescent vitality to the tomboy character. Later, Martin would describe the role as "the real me," but she consciously decided never to perform it on Broadway. "I would never do *Annie* in New York," she said in her memoirs. "That is the turf of my good friend Ethel Merman."[64] When casting preparations for the tour were under way, Martin had just finished her run in *Lute Song* and was two years away from the first of her own shows with Rodgers and Hammerstein, *South Pacific* (the other would be *The Sound of Music*). At first, the pair found Martin *too* demure to play the sharpshooter, but the Texas-born star was quite intent on getting the part—touring was her and husband Richard Halliday's idea, she claimed in her autobiography—and she wowed them. Ethel gave her blessing by applauding enthusiastically during Mary's last run-through in New York in 1947. The first stop gave the star a fond homecoming, in Texas.

Annie's Music

Berlin's music for the show did little to acknowledge changes in contemporary American popular music. He made no attempt to update or be hip as he did with *Alexander's Ragtime Band,* which delivered 1910s "ragtime with a swing." When someone complained to him that the score of *Annie Get Your Gun* was old-fashioned, he famously responded, "Yes, nothing but good old-fashioned hits."[65]

Innovative or not, he produced a wonderful, rousing score, with tunes that would be cemented to Merman's image even more firmly than Annie's traits were: "Doin' What Comes Natur'lly," "Anything You Can Do," "You Can't Get a Man with a Gun," and "There's No Business Like Show Business," a piece as indelibly associated with Merman as with the musical theater she embodies.

Berlin composed the songs within a relatively short range, just over an octave, as was his style, and with a tight tessitura. Ethel used the few leaps Berlin gave to great effect. Generally his notes are rather short, giving Merman little time to sustain them, as she'd done with "I Got Rhythm." Since *Annie* required her to sing in nine of its fourteen numbers, the pieces could not be too taxing, and Berlin's simple song structures worked well. Unlike other composers, such as Cole Porter, who liked to end songs for Merman with A natural, Berlin made no special accommodations for her voice; most of the score's "Merman effects" were produced by Merman. For instance, in "Doin' What Comes Natur'lly," her voice slid down from one note to the next, producing that slight hiccup when landing on words like *doin'*. The effect is suggestive of a cowboy's yodel, appropriate to the Wild West setting of the show. Yet neither the slide nor the yodel was written into the score.

In her rendering of "Natur'lly" and "Can't Get a Man," Ethel's singing voice exhibited almost no vibrato; its features overall were those of a young woman, as Annie was at this point before entering the more "adult" world of Frank Butler and Buffalo Bill. Her delivery remained youthful in "I'm an Indian Too," with little vibrato and no lingering on its short notes. That Ethel's vocalization while singing as an "Indian" suggested childlike features presents an unfortunate racial cliché, even if at the time it was intended as a relatively unself-conscious gag. The dialect that Merman used periodically (Su—ewww for Sioux) further enhanced her voice's childlike quality, and Berlin composed "Indian" in a slightly higher range than the others, making her work in a more youthful register.

The showiest song is "Anything You Can Do," although its effects are produced not through a dazzling melody but through lyrics. Its excitement is bolstered by the fact that it's performed as a competitive duet, with Frank and Annie challenging each other on various levels and terms. The lyrics dart from traits appropriate to their characters in the show (shooting sparrows with bows and arrows) to those tied to their images as performers, particularly Merman's: any note you can sing I can sing *higher/sweeter*—and, humorously, *softer.*

One of the show's ballads, "They Say It's Wonderful," is not unlike the male-female paired songs gaining ground in Rodgers and Hammerstein shows. *Oklahoma!*'s "People Will Say We're in Love" and *Carousel*'s "If I Loved You" hypothetically articulate the attraction between the couple in the early phases of their relationship. As implausible as they are—if one expects credibility in musicals—such paired songs are a brilliant device to convey a budding romance to the audience without slowing the story down with exposition. With *Annie*'s "They Say It's Wonderful," Ethel softened her delivery, swooping *up* to emphasize the first beat of *wonderful,* without the hiccups and grace notes she used in the more comedic songs.

On its own, the melody of "There's No Business" is not particularly innovative either: the verse is tightly composed, the range not wide. But by using the bright, twinkling key of C major, Berlin created a great sense of uplift, and during the bridge, the upward-step motion of the scale ("everything about it is appealing / everything the traffic will allow") generates a certain momentum and energy, rather than simply showing off. (It doesn't go too far into showier high ranges.) The piece's subtle but forceful syncopation also enlivens, and Merman came down hard on the notes to stress them as if to bring them all the more to life.

Merman's instinctive sense of getting the most out of every syllable is easily noted in *Annie*'s soundtrack recording. In "Doin' What Comes Natur'lly," she pauses, ever so lightly, on the word *sex* to give it a little extra punch. She flats notes, especially in the early comiclike "You Can't Get a Man with a Gun." And her many grace notes, as one writer put it, go "off like bombs."[66]

Just as Annie linked Ethel Merman's persona with Annie Oakley's, it would forever join her name with Berlin's, whose career it helped revitalize. (That same year, Hollywood released another movie of his, *Blue Skies.*) Berlin shrewdly told Broadway interviewers that he preferred writing for theater to the movies, and how could he not, with *Annie*'s runaway success? He made close to 1.5 million dollars during the run of the show, earning royalties for sheet music sales, the sale of film rights, and the release of an original cast recording.

By the time of *Annie*, original cast recordings were starting to become common practice—another byproduct of the Rodgers and Hammerstein revolution.

Decca's Jack Kapp explained that before that time, the prevailing wisdom had been that the general public would be interested in only hits from shows, not in every song, so the practice of releasing entire recordings by their original performers—even with *Oklahoma!*—developed unevenly. Kapp himself had started it earlier, with the July 1942 release of Berlin's *This Is the Army*,[67] and it proved an immediate success and source of revenue; Rodgers and Hammerstein would further the trend, which, within the decade, would be the norm.

Competition among record labels to secure contracts could be cutthroat, and releases weren't always granted for stars with existing contracts with other labels. Still, the original cast recording was a win-win situation, enabling fans to experience or reexperience the shows and generating extra revenue for producers, songwriters, and recording labels. And then there was the exposure that the recordings gave shows—and stars like Merman—well beyond Broadway. Even if Ethel Merman didn't tour as Annie, she could now be heard all across the States.

Berlin had made a deal with Decca to release the original cast recording for *Annie* before the show even started. Once it was released, the label promoted it robustly; Merman's scrapbooks are filled with ads and announcements. One writer speculates how "tragic" it would have been had Decca not secured her in the cast album.[68] But as one historian writes, "The truth was, Ethel had been with the label since *Panama Hattie* (for which she recorded four songs) and stayed with them through the mid-1950s."[69]

Life Offstage

Merman would later write that this period in the mid- and late 1940s was among the happiest of her life. She was a hit on Broadway and was enjoying her work. But more than that, her family life was stable, which gave her tremendous joy. Little Ethel and Bobby were like any kids, and, in some ways, Big Ethel and Big Bob were like any parents: proud and enjoying the stories they could tell about their children. Once a reporter coming out of a matinee performance at the Imperial noted a "tiny figure" who came out onto the dimly lit stage. "In a flat, lisping, one note baby-voice," this child sang "the chorus of 'They Say It's Wonderful'" while the audience of two usherettes and a man with a broom listen[ed] tenderly and appreciatively."[70] Little Ethel had gotten out of her mom's dressing room.

By the time she was three, Little Bit had other reactions to her mother's work. When she was watching *Annie* with her father, the first thing she witnessed was her mom killing a bird; the girl could not be convinced it wasn't real, becoming so upset that Levitt had to remove her from the theater. Her mother passed the story along to reporters, who printed it endlessly. Other Little Bit tales appeared: "When her mother's vivacity gets too much for her, as it sometimes does, she has been known to say, 'Let's get out of this. It's too noisy with her in here.' "[71]

When Ethel Jr. was three, Bobby was ten months old. Interviewers called him "a solemn child, reticent about showing strangers his eight teeth."[72] The time of *Annie Get Your Gun* evokes other memories for him; one comes from watching his mom from the wings, being held by someone he cannot remember. He remembers seeing his mom crying at the end of act I and Sitting Bull/Harry Bellaver comforting her. "To me, Sitting Bull took care of Mom. He sat next to her on a bench and told her that it was going to be OK when she cried."[73]

Merman kept up her typical busy pace off the boards. In June, soon after the show opened, she and others celebrated Jimmy Durante's thirtieth anniversary with Broadway. "It was just like old times, they said—this great night in tribute to the beloved Wizard of Schnoz, Jimmy Durante—and some folks around me, like Billy Rose and Ethel Merman, got real sentimental and almost weepy when Eddie Jackson, now a little grayer and heavier, joined Jimmy in singin' a song and then out trotted the aging Lou Clayton to plunge into a quick-step jig."[74] Merman also maintained her busy benefit schedule: for heart disease; for the Damon Runyon Cancer Fund (May 27, 1948); and for nurses, at Madison Square Garden ("Stars Shine Bright for Women in White," May 20, 1947). This last event was huge, with Ethel joining the Andrews Sisters, Bill Robinson, Margaret O'Brien, Carmen Miranda, Bert Lahr, Victor Moore, Milton Berle, Joseph Cotton, Duke Ellington, and others to entertain thousands of visitors.

Ethel proved a fantastic and popular radio guest and continued making numerous appearances, guesting several times on Bing Crosby's popular show. But she proved unable to carry a show on her own. When *The Ethel Merman Show* aired on radio on July 31, 1949, after *Annie* had closed, NBC almost pulled it at the last minute, and it was reviewed poorly. "Normally," wrote John Crosby, "Ethel Merman has more personality than seems quite fair, but it is seriously diminished by radio."[75] *Variety* complained that the program only "ostensibly" reflected her career (e.g., she sang "Some Enchanted Evening," the hit from *South Pacific,* which had just opened in April) and that it was, moreover, just not enough of a show for her to carry. Much has been said about Merman's lackluster career off the boards, especially in film and television, where there's a consensus that she was "too big" for the screen. Still, it's interesting that on radio, where one would think she'd excel because of her voice, she did best in supporting roles and guest appearances.

Although it was hard for Merman to cede center stage, when she had to—in radio, TV, and movies—she was a good sport about it. These venues were not only essential to her career but also less grueling than a long Broadway run. Unfortunately, her brief experience with *The Ethel Merman Show* on radio would become a harbinger for her other work in film and TV. Always the guest star, never the star.

EIGHT

Call Me Madam

After the long run of *Annie,* Ethel was tired but did not slow down. For a year and a half, she continued her guest spots on radio and television. Her very first TV appearance was likely to have been on March 22, 1949, on Milton Berle's *Texaco Star Theater.*[1] She was back on radio three months later on *The Ford Radio Show* with Berle. For the event, CBS president Frank Stanton sent her a telegram welcoming her to the CBS family.[2] Typically Ethel, like most guest singers on these shows, engaged in some repartee or brief comic skits with hosts or costars before singing a few numbers. During this time, she also continued her recording career; in 1950 and 1951, she and Ray Bolger went into the Decca studios to cut ducts such as "If I Knew You Were Coming, I'd Have Baked a Cake" and "Dearie." She also recorded "If You Catch a Little Cold I'll Sneeze for You" and other novelty songs with old friend Jimmy Durante.

World War II was over, but the Cold War was revving up, and certain off-stage appearances were expected now more than ever from America's celebrities. On April 29, 1950, Merman participated in a Fifth Avenue march as the "queen of the Loyalty Day Parade." In its third year, the march was held to defy the "reds" on the upcoming May Day, and that year, Ethel used the occasion to pay her personal respects to William Randolph Hearst, who was celebrating his eighty-seventh birthday. Ethel was now a full-fledged Republican, but she took part in these conservative events not out of a newly defined political allegiance but, once again, because of her belief that it was the right thing to do.

If her own political convictions were getting stronger, however, they were scarcely reflected in press reports. For it was the ideological leanings of their writers that seemed more in evidence than what the stories were reporting. As red-baiter Leonard Lyons wrote, "Ethel Merman, who will star in the show *[Call Me Madam]*, once appeared in a musical where a Red chorus-man

177

said: 'Comes the revolution, I'll play the lead opposite Merman.' Miss Merman told him: 'If you get the talent, that'll be the revolution.' "[3]

In her personal life there was little turmoil. Ethel had found domestic stability with Levitt, a sensible, strong-willed, unpretentious man, who, however troubled by his demons, was more or less able to stand up to her strong personality and her set ways. Most important, especially in light of their different personalities, he was as committed to the success of their marriage and the happiness of their children as she was. In a celebrity marriage in which he "was used to being called Mr. Merman," that was no small thing. Although it wouldn't take long for the realities to prove harder to manage than the image of a happy home, for now, domestic life was not a source of emotional trouble for Ethel. Little Bit and Bob Jr. were the apples of their mom's eye. "Ethel was always proud of whatever the kids would do. She never—like some people who show them off—she never did that. She's a very, very, very good mother. . . . she [just] doesn't have the chance to hover over them too much," said Dorothy Fields.[4]

Like many kids with preoccupied, loving parents, Bobby and Ethel played together constantly. They took refuge in their pets (fish, turtles, birds, a small dog) and complemented their Gorilla Club with two organizations, "E.A.U.N." and "B.A.U.N." (Ethel's Animals' United Nations and Bobby's Animals' United Nations). When the children weren't engaged in other activities, their two UNs were often "in session." In attendance were Ethel and Bobby's collection of toy animal delegates. (Levitt remains a passionate supporter of animal rights to this day, and Ethel remained deeply connected to animals all of her life.) The sessions, however, would be brought to an abrupt halt when they heard the chilling "Yoo-Hoo!" of Miss Kopeman. When the children heard the call, no matter where they were, "We knew too well what would happen if we didn't respond, pronto."[5]

Already young Ethel resembled her mother. Her face was slightly narrower and less oval, with beautiful, soft features. She shared Big Ethel's creative and outgoing nature, but she was a sensitive and emotionally delicate child. Bobby, also creative, was a more suspicious type. Like his mom, he was stubborn, and like both parents, he didn't go for pretense and airs. And although he would correct reporters interviewing Merman at home, the boy never felt like he was able to speak his mind. "Being without any sustained nurturing attention from my mother and father and being constantly constrained by the emotional and physical violence of a sadistic nurse, I hardly developed the balance and confidence a child needs to speak the truth to power," he says today.[6] And, as photos make clear, Bobby seldom smiled. But he got along well with his sister. "Ethel and I just tried to avoid getting in trouble for doing what kids do. It was later, when I became a young teenager, that I became the brat brother."[7]

Call Me Madam

Ethel's next hit on Broadway was *Call Me Madam,* written by Howard Lindsay and Russel Crouse, with Irving Berlin again composing the songs. Merman was cast as Sally Adams, a wealthy oil widow known for her popular parties in Washington, D.C., the "hostess with the mostes'." When the president appoints Mrs. Adams to be ambassador to the small, fairy-tale-like country of Lichtenburg, Sally eagerly sets out to perform her civic duty in a country she can't even locate. Before Sally departs, Kenny Gibson, fresh out of college, talks his way into joining her as her attaché. In Lichtenburg, Sally immediately falls for the dapper prime minister, Cosmo Constantine. Cosmo is the only member of his government not interested in the money that others expect Mrs. Adams to give the struggling nation. But she assumes he is, and after several misunderstandings and Sally's glum return to Washington, everything gets straightened out. In the end, two couples are formed: Cosmo and Sally, and the younger Kenny and Lichtenburg's young princess Maria.

Sally Adams was inspired by the real-life U.S. ambassador to Luxembourg, Perle Mesta, who was also renowned for her great parties. (She had none of Sally Adams's backward naïveté.) Lindsay claims that he got the idea for the show in the summer of 1948, during a vacation he and his wife, Dorothy (Stickney), were taking in Glenwood Springs, a spot Ethel had recommended. One morning, he was reading about Mesta in *Time* and, when glimpsing a sunbathing Ethel, made the connection.[8] Merman says that inspiration struck the moment he saw her, a bandanna'd sunbather, with a copy of the magazine at her side that had that picture of Perle Mesta. "He'd said to himself, 'Ethel as an ambassadress' . . . [and] he suddenly yelled out the window 'Hey, I've got a wonderful idea for a show for you!' 'What is it?' I yelled back. 'Perle Mesta!' he yelled. 'Who's Perle Mesta?' I shouted. 'Tell you later,' he said."[9]

Lindsay called up Buck Crouse, and the two worked out the basics over long-distance calls. Lining up talented, savvy producer Leland Hayward was a good start, and Hayward persuaded NBC to underwrite the show, putting up $250,000, all of the show's initial costs.[10] Radio had never before backed a Broadway show, and the deal gave NBC first call on important, lucrative television rights and, as the parent company of RCA, on recording rights as well. Berlin, onboard for the music, had committed recording rights to the RCA/Victor label prior to the brokering of the deal, and the arrangement caused Ethel problems. (In May 1950, she had renewed her contract with Decca for three years, and Decca would not release her for the original cast recording of *Madam,* replacing her with Dinah Shore.) Not to be outdone, Decca released its own studio cast album with Dick Haymes singing "You're in Love" in duet with Merman in Russell Nype's place.[11]

Ethel was an enterprising businesswoman and negotiated 8 percent of the gross; she'd received 10 percent for *Annie Get Your Gun.*[12] On top of that, she owned 10 percent of the entire property, earning royalties whenever the show was mounted, whether she was in it or not. Hayward, Lindsay, Crouse, and Berlin also owned shares, but it was less common at the time for stars to maintain partial ownership, particularly if they had not been investors. And Ethel didn't "believe in investing in shows."[13]

Hungarian actor Paul Lukas played the Lichtenburg envoy Cosmo, Sally's romantic interest; Illinois-born Russell Nype, who had just played in the musical *Regina,* was hired as young Kenneth Gibson and brought to the role a fresh new look of short crew cut and spectacles, which young men soon emulated. Directing was the legendary (and legendarily strict) George Abbott, whom everyone, Ethel included, called Mr. Abbott. The team approached Robert Alton to choreograph but, when they couldn't agree on terms, hired wunderkind Jerome Robbins, who had been in the chorus of *Stars in Your Eyes.*

Rehearsals began August 14, 1950, and tryouts were scheduled in New Haven and Boston for the following month. Advance sales sizzled: the entire New Haven run was sold out before the show even began. Opening night there was set back several days, to September 11, because Lukas, insecure about his singing role from the start, claimed to have throat problems. When the show opened, audiences enjoyed Berlin's score, which included "The Hostess with the Mostes' on the Ball," "Can You Use Any Money Today?" and "It's a Lovely Day Today," but act two dragged and generated only a lukewarm response.

The team took to endless revisions, excising two second-act numbers. One, "Mr. Monotony," was a tune Berlin had been trying to put into his shows for ages. According to Lindsay and Crouse, Ethel didn't like it from the start, predicting that it wouldn't go over, and, as usual, she was right. (The second was a tune called "Free.") But with two songs gone, the second act needed another tune, and what Berlin produced would go on to be *Madam's* show-stopper.

Accounts differ on exactly what happened. In her 1955 autobiography, Ethel said that the new song Berlin wrote was performed for the first time in New Haven, on the third night. In her second, she says it was on opening night in Boston.[14] Accounts also vary on what *kind* of song Berlin was instructed to write. The act needed something upbeat, that much was sure. But who would perform it? Some say that because Ethel was down two numbers, it had to be for her; others claim that Berlin was directed to compose one for Russell Nype on the basis of the enthusiastic response he was getting for "It's a Lovely Day Today" at the end of act one. Some say that Ethel herself pushed for a song her young colleague could perform. Cole Porter recalled that he'd heard that Berlin was told to write a comic number but simply didn't produce one.[15] Others said Berlin was instructed to write a duet so that Merman wouldn't get peeved over a new song being given to someone else, even Nype. Whatever the case, history was made when Irving Berlin knocked off the duet "You're Just in Love," which Ethel's Sally Adams sings in counterpoint with Nype's character during a lovesick moment of the latter. Beautifully exploiting their different vocal talents, the duet sets Ethel's rhythmic part against Nype's melodically driven one. Her voice moves energetically with the rhythms; he croons. We might not know what night they first performed it, but when they did, they brought the house down. Poor Paul Lukas had trouble making his entrance in the next scene—and would for as long as he stayed in the show.

The buzz on *Madam* was such that a half-hour preview was planned to air on NBC TV in September, but a series of fiascoes involving theater locations and degrees of readiness forced them to scrap it. In the Boston tryout, the Ritz Carleton there feted the crew with a "Call Me Madam" dinner menu that offered Ethel as the "Baby Steak Sauté" and Irving Berlin as the "Vienna Schnitzel." Ethel's family sent a telegram in time for the show, penned in characteristic Levitt wit: "Because you're the hostess with the mostess on the ball and a beauty with a cutey and a five alarmer charmer and a mudder with an udder for us all. We're not sick we're in love with you. Little Ethel. Little Bob. Big Bob."[16]

In New York, the office had been unable to handle the heavy advance demand for tickets, and Hayward had to go so far as to take out articles in local papers instructing patrons how to place mail orders, explaining how their orders would be processed, and pleading for their patience—all good publicity, to be sure. *Call Me Madam* ended up enjoying the biggest advance sale for a Broadway musical to date, with tickets going for as high as $5.40 *before* tax, pushing potential receipts for a full house to $40,000. (The show went on to surpass the previous record of $36,500, set by *South Pacific,* whose ticket prices topped at $4.80.)[17] During the run, Merman would be taking in over $5,000 a week, more than anyone else on Broadway.

Before *Call Me Madam*'s opening at the Imperial, another legendary Merman tale was born. After so much tinkering with new songs, lines, and choreography, she simply refused to accept additional changes. Merman claims to have told Lindsay and Crouse, "I won't do it," when they approached her with new material, but Pete Martin—and others in his wake—gave her a much more endurable line: "Boys, as of right now, I am Miss Birds Eye of 1950. I am frozen. Not a new comma."[18]

On opening night, October 12, scalpers on Broadway were charging as much as two hundred dollars a ticket, and it's hard to imagine that anyone doubted the troupe had a hit on their hands. Everyone involved with the production showered the star with notes, telegrams, gifts. Ethel avoided flowers because of her allergies, typically forwarding them to local hospitals. Telegrams came from a young belter named Judy Garland, whom Ethel adored and encouraged, especially in her early concert years. ("This was the greatest thing I've ever known," said their close mutual friend Buster Edens. "They were starry-eyed with each other," and the two women remained warm, dear friends.)[19] Mary Martin wired, "They may call you Madame, but I just think you're very great and very wonderful," and Rosalind Russell exclaimed, "They can only call you Great." Among scores of others, Lynn Fontanne later wrote to say that she and Alfred Lunt had seen the show several times and enjoyed it more every time.[20]

Audiences enjoyed the topicality of *Call Me Madam*. Lindsay and Crouse had inserted playful disclaimers into the program about the obvious real-world references: "The play is laid in two mythical countries," it read. "One is called Lichtenburg, the other the United States of America." And "neither the character of Mrs. Sally Adams, or Miss Ethel Merman, resembles any other person alive or dead." Regarding Miss Merman, Cole Porter said, "They [Lindsay and Crouse] couldn't have been righter about that."[21] (The filmed version would go for a vaguer reference about the story taking place "long ago," in what would be the recently ended Truman presidency.)

Not only is the book filled with contemporary references, but it also pokes fun at contemporary political figures. Sally has several long-distance phone conversations with "Harry," and at the curtain call an impersonator played by Irving Fisher, unnamed in the program, joins the crowd as the president to take a bow with the cast. The dialogue makes references to first daughter Margaret Truman and the infamously poor reviews she received when she tried her hand at singing. Berlin's rousing tune for the show, "They Like Ike," was later transformed into "I Like Ike" and, with modified lyrics, was used in Eisenhower's actual presidential campaign. As light and fanciful as *Call Me Madam* was—not unlike fairy-tale operetta in its setting and tale—it was very much a product of a specific political moment. At one point, Mrs. Adams says, "I'm so happy that I oughtta be investigated," referring to the activities of Senator McCarthy. One London critic said, "The theme of this smash hit . . . is the Marshall Plan" and went on to add how typically American another remark of Sally's is: "I've always followed the affairs of Lichtenburg closely. . . . by the way, where the hell is Lichtenburg?" In that, he writes, "the whole idealistic policy of the administration is held up to joyous ridicule."[22]

"To me," wrote an American critic, "the most heartening thing about this show is that it is the first political satire we have seen in the musical field for some time, and it comes at a time when people are getting neurotic about speaking critically for fear of misinterpretation. This show ribs Democrats and Republicans . . . [everyone] except, I dare say, those who hew to the Communist lie. As long as we can laugh at our own government's foibles right out in public without fear of being banished to Siberia, we are doing all right."[23] A somewhat less tolerant view was voiced in the *New York Journal American:* "The Sardi set hears Lindsay and Crouse will tone down the satire in *Call Me Madam* if the war situation gets worse. The theory being that this is not time for ribbing the government, even [in] a musical comedy way."[24]

As usual, the critics' focus fell on Ethel. "Give her a show," wrote Robert Williams and Vernon Rice, "and she'll carry it like a suitcase."[25] Everyone knew that the show's success was a result of her starring in it. Press reports and reviews made innumerable references to Merman as "the one and only" or "inimitable." Even tough guy Walter Winchell said, "Ethel is the undisputed musical comedy queen. No queen ever wore a crown more gracefully."[26] More surprising, Hollywood was trying to piggyback on the show's success, with Paramount re-releasing her mid-1930s movies, *We're Not Dressing* and *Anything Goes.*

Merman in Mainbocher

Part of the great success of *Call Me Madam* was its exquisite costumes. Raoul Pène Du Bois did general costuming, but the real coup was having Mainbocher, Manhattan's premiere haute couturist, designing nine outfits for its prima donna. Mainbocher (aka Main Rousseau Bocher or Main Bocher) had first designed for Broadway in *One Touch of Venus,* the show that launched Mary Martin's career. Of *Call Me Madam,* he said, "I wanted those clothes to do for Merman what the gong is supposed to do for a fire horse—get it ready to go out and give."[27] Ethel's gowns cost nearly twelve thousand dollars, and some outfits were so elaborate that it took hours to press them after every performance; it cost nearly thirty-five dollars just to clean her court gown alone.

Mainbocher was never known for outré designs or colors—he'd developed his "Venus pink" for Martin—and for Ethel in *Call Me Madam,* he went for a vibrant elegance that she appreciated. "In *Madam,* I was properly attired for the first time in my theatrical life. Until then my costumes had never been designed to accentuate any physical charms I may have had as Ethel Merman. . . . In *Madam* they were."[28] She especially liked the long, elaborate red dress he designed, which she described as having "yards and yards of lace," and later wore it to private affairs, even shipping it to a party in Denver by air freight at the rather extravagant cost of thirty dollars.[29] Mainbocher appreciated Ethel also, finding in the forty-two-year-old actress a well-proportioned, "perfect figure."[30]

An obvious part of the show's thrill was seeing ex-Queens stenographer Ethel Zimmermann-Merman portray a U.S. ambassador, a role in which Ethel could bring her down-home, straight-shooting Americana style into the high-class, formal dress and manners of old Europe. Although the show's comedy was derived from that incongruity, Ethel carried it off effortlessly and glamorously—no more *Panama Hattie* fashion errors here. As Brooks Atkinson noted, "Since Miss Merman is now moving in the best society, she is wearing dresses hemstitched by Main Bocher in his most lyric mood. They are expensive and look it. But," he continues, "they have not tempered the clangorous vulgarity of this phenomenal lady."[31] *Call Me Madam*'s book highlights that same disconnect between boisterous Ethel and her high-end wardrobe when Sally says, "I don't mind a train, but why'd they give me the Super Chief?" after taking a pratfall in a silver lamé gown.

While Annie Oakley might have begun the process of making a lady out of Ethel, it was Sally Adams who turned her into a sophisticated, attractive woman—without the airs of such. And although the latter role capitalized on her direct, boisterous style (especially in her speech), this glamorous, more respectful treatment of Ethel helped reinvigorate her stage persona. Ethel was now a good-looking *adult,* capable of romance, and for once boasted an emotional range that entailed more than just wisecracks, spunk, and a booming voice. Sally Adams took Ethel out of the woods and into the full blush of womanhood, without sacrificing her down-to-earth style and skills, and today it's a joy to watch Merman depict a simultaneously attractive and funny woman in the film version, a welcome departure from the clichés that Hollywood had usually assigned her.

Despite Ethel's new elegance onstage, a few contradictions and some detectable "edginess" started to emerge in some of the press's comments on her and her sartorial sensibilities.

> There was a time . . . when she heavily favored tight black dresses with jet bugles for daytime street wear. "Ethel had a lot of ideas about clothes in those days," one of her friends said recently with a reminiscent shudder, "mostly bad." Miss Merman has long since been persuaded out of such indiscretions and is now practically indistinguishable on the streets from any other woman. Her single eccentricity in matters of fashion is that she will not wear green, on stage or off, on the obscure theory that it will make her look "horrible."[32]

Still, at the time of *Call Me Madam,* most jabs were put to the back burner as Broadway celebrated its biggest star. And it was not just New York that was celebrating her, but also Washington, D.C., a city that was fully enjoying its ambassadress onstage. Dwight Eisenhower was among many politicians who attended the premiere, along with the usual high-profile theater and film stars. And that year Ethel, who was entered in the latest *Who's Who of the Theatre,* was given the chance to correct galleys to reflect a birth year of 1909.

Ethel's mounting success was evident according to countless New York standards and traditions. Al Hirschfeld's portrait of her splashed the cover of the Sunday *New York Times* Arts section; writer E. B. White mentioned her in a poem he wrote for the *New Yorker* about *Antony and Cleopatra,* then playing on Broadway with the soft-speaking Vivien Leigh:

> When actors speak the Bard's immortal words,
> Their mouths fill up with butterflies and birds.
> So great the love they bear for what they're playing
> It's frightf'ly hard to hear what they are saying.
> Let's have one other gaudy night, Miss Leigh,

When all is sweetly audible to me!
Some wine within! And for mine ear a trumpet—
When Egypt speaks, I want to hear the strumpet.
And if through Leigh I cannot hear Nile's sermon,
By Heav'n, I wish they'd give the role to Merman,
To whom my heart is ever tied by th' strings
Because I catch each syllable she sings!*

Successful though it was, no critic accused *Call Me Madam* of being cutting edge. "In some ways," writes Gerald Bordman, "*Call Me Madam* was a reversion to the topical musicals of the thirties."[33] Indeed, the play boasted old-fashioned references to contemporary political figures; the double couple romance, whose outcome was strictly by the numbers; and the old-school guffaws that banked on Sally's "gaucheries," double takes, and double entendres.

By now, Ethel the acting comedienne was garnering as much praise as she did as a singer. But there was also a growing awareness of the sense of history Ethel seemed to carry with her onto the stage or into a room.

Show biz is a mechanized industry these days, with a mass market. It depends on machine tools—the microphone, the camera, the tape recorder, the cathode-ray tube, the juke box, the gag writer—and the product is economy-sized, built-in . . . and, worst of all, homogenized. But Merman, she's still got the cream left on top. She's too bouncy to fit into machines. Cameras make her look like an overblown peony. . . . She's back in the great days of show business, the Palace Theatre days, the handicraft days, the days when an actor and an audience felt they knew each other personally and sparks flew between them. That's why she gives the people such a lift. When they watch Merman they can feel, for a change, that human beings are more attractive than machines.[34]

The critic Robert Rice's nostalgic appreciation appeared in *Flair*, a short-lived arts monthly whose trademark was cut-out covers printed in saturated colors on high-quality stock. (Ethel, Berlin, Crouse, Hayward, and the rest of the *Call Me Madam* team made the cover in October 1950—as so many elaborate, handmade dolls.)

*Reprinted by permission; © E. B. White, originally published in the *New Yorker*, all rights reserved, 19 January 1952 (MCNY, SC 15).

Fun Off the Boards

Ethel's life wasn't all work. The Duchess of Windsor and "the Boy," as Ethel called him, were constantly seeking her company, thanking her for tickets and for time spent together. Ethel kept a photo of them on her piano, signed to the Levitts. Ethel also socialized with Tallulah Bankhead, her old friend Madeline Gaxton, and Vivian Blaine, currently playing in *Guys and Dolls.* In 1951, Dorothy and Richard Rodgers held a big New Year's Eve party in which guests were asked to come as their favorite painting. Their invitation had Little Lord Fauntleroy on the front and, to "eliminate the horrid possibility of seven Mona Lisas turning up," instructed guests to okay their choices with a designated clearance person. Moreover, it advised, "there will be dancing, [so] if you are a 'Nude Descending a Staircase,' be sure the staircase is detachable."[35] Ethel and Levitt came dressed as a Spanish couple, posing with friends as the subjects of Goya's *Majas on a Balcony.*

Prior to *Call Me Madam,* Ethel's feelings about art, especially modern art, weren't too different from her love of books. As Lew Kessler recounts, "She goes to this art gallery with Eleanor [Holm] and Billy [Rose] and the bidding starts on this painting. So it's a still life, a bowl of fruit or something. And Merman sits there and it's going up [and up, to some] fourteen thousand. And finally Merman turns to Eleanor and says, '____ ____. Fourteen thousand bucks! I can buy all that fruit for thirty-five cents and eat it besides.' "[36] Cole Porter had once given her a painting by Grandma Moses, and later Ethel was unable to recall whether she had given it away or not.

By the time of *Call Me Madam,* however, the press was announcing Ethel's new interest in paintings by such masters as Manet and Renoir. She was buying art for her home, and Richard Rodgers's New Year's Eve party now seemed an apt way to celebrate her new fancy. Pals Lindsay and Crouse did not take Ethel's recently acquired interest too seriously, however, joking that she had once told them that she "had an original over the mantel in [her] apartment. And either Buck or Howard said, 'An original what?' And [Ethel] turned on the full power in [her] pipes and said, 'An Original. That's all.' "[37]

Ethel was hitting the late-night New York scene more than she had in the 1940s, frequenting the Casino, El Morocco, the Stork Club, and other popular clubs of the time. She would go out with friends alone or with Levitt, leaving Bobby and Ethel, no longer toddlers, in the care of their governess.

Her scrapbooks suggest that her level of socializing seemed to nearly rival that of Perle Mesta's.

Bob Levitt Sr. did not enjoy this period, later saying that Ethel was getting caught up in the high-society scene. If she was, the phase didn't last long. She still retained old friends from Queens, such as Josie Traeger, and even these newer celebrity friendships with people such as the Duke and Duchess of Windsor were based on genuine fondness, not name-dropping or social climbing. Their status didn't trip her up, and her high wattage energized the often lackluster Edward, whom she frequently brought out onto the dance floor. She and Levitt had a private joke about him—about his habit of humming to himself. "Why do you suppose he does that?" asked Ethel. Levitt: "Well you see, maybe he's AC and the Waldorf is DC."[38]

Throughout the run of *Madam,* Ethel constantly told reporters that her main happiness was her family, and indeed a strong, stable family life was her priority, even if she wasn't always capable of honoring it. One story that was frequently told explained why she and Levitt were an hour and forty minutes late for a dinner when they were to meet Perle Mesta for the first time: their physician was late in arriving at their home to treat Bobby's measles.

In early November 1950, Ethel was a hit on NBC's *The Big Show,* the popular radio show emceed by Tallulah Bankhead. (That particular evening Jimmy Durante started the proceedings by musing how hard it would be to translate his "good looks" into words for listeners.)[39] Merman and Bankhead were a riot together. Bankhead: "Well, DAHLINGS, we're forced to have Ethel Merman on the show again tonight." Ethel, very sarcastically: "Tallulah, I think you're the most divine woman." Another night, Bankhead drily noted to her guest, "I saw the movie of *Annie Get Your Gun,* and you're not in it." With radios in nearly 95 percent of American homes, these hilarious appearances expanded Ethel's audience—and her popularity with NBC brass. Other activities when *Call Me Madam* was running included fundraisers for Eddie Cantor's March of Dimes and the Actors' Fund of America as well as numerous benefit performances of the show.

Mrs. Adams in an Integrated Washington

After eighty-one weeks, Ethel's friend and fellow musical comedy performer Benay Venuta took over the role of Sally Adams, and Ethel's understudy,

Elaine Stritch, toured. Just before leaving, she telegrammed, like a gladiator to the emperor, "We who are about to die salute you." Although Ethel's run with *Call Me Madam* at the Imperial terminated on May 3, 1952,[40] she took the show to Washington, D.C., for a historic two-week run before her contract expired on May 31. The Washington run began on May 5, not too long before the start of the national political conventions. The event was historic not only because Ethel Merman was finally bringing a hit show outside New York but also because she was performing at the National Theatre, which was opening its doors to a racially mixed audience for the first time in its 117 years.[41]

Given Merman's "apolitical nature," the political dimensions of the National engagement might be brushed off as irrelevant. But the event shows again how complex her relationship to race and ethnicity was. Here was conservative Merman, appearing at a politically charged, progressive event. If Ethel wasn't always the most sensitive being ever to walk the planet, she had an innate sense of fairness that might have enabled her to make a pro-integration statement in those early days of the civil rights struggle.

Call Me Madam had been selected for reopening the National for a number of reasons: (1) Leland Hayward's skill as a producer, (2) the presence of Broadway's biggest star in the cast, and (3) the show's Washington setting. The way *Call Me Madam* was received—and, to some extent, written—shows how flexible the lines between theatrical entertainment and American political life were becoming. Of course, Washington was thrilled about the short run there; it had taken over twenty years to get Merman to perform there, and opening night attendees included congressmen of both political parties, members of earlier administrations, ambassadors and former ambassadors to dozens of countries, justices, military officers, and, of course, stars of the theater world, including Berlin, Lindsay, and Crouse.

Just as *Annie Get Your Gun* had produced two Annies, *Call Me Madam* gave the press the opportunity to draw constant comparisons between Mesdames Mesta and Merman. There were plenty of differences: Mesta was a well-rounded, educated diplomat appointed by President Truman; Merman was a self-made star whose public decorum was not always for the fainthearted. That hardly stopped the comparisons: Saks Fifth Avenue promoted leather portfolio bags by asking, "What famous Broadway ambassadress carries a portfolio just like this?"; Perle Mesta penned a piece in the *Journal American* called "Call Me Minister";[42] and Ethel was suddenly approached as an expert on throwing successful parties (although she rarely hosted them, especially when she lived in New York). In a piece for *Cosmopolitan* that had run several years earlier, during the show's preopening buzz, Merman offered advice as "the poor man's Elsa Maxwell": "Don't have too many seats"—people need to mill about. "Nooks and crannies have killed more good parties than Carrie Nation." Hosts should have a star guest list, with a "good line-up of hams" (her favorite was Jack Pearl) and then a large group of "semi-squares," appreciators who "can recognize a hilarious story, but they don't try to tell any." Always important to invite "a few unattached men of known wolfish tendencies. Their presence somehow makes the married men more attentive to their own wives."[43] Like other pieces, this was likely to have been co-penned by Levitt.

Marriage Troubles

Levitt, meanwhile, was having a rougher time. Although he had been promoted, his career was not moving in ways that gratified him personally or intellectually. He had reportedly declined a military promotion in order to stay in New York City as a Hearst journalist, but during the run of *Call Me Madam,* the corporation fired him when his drinking and depression were interfering with his work. They were not helping his marriage either.

Alcohol was no friend to Bob or to Ethel. As Bob Jr. recalls, "When Mom drank she could be intensely inappropriate as a parent to her children; as a friend to her friends; as a celebrity to her fans. . . . When she was loaded, she could be fiercely irrational and maudlin, carelessly and wantonly aggressive, and unyieldingly self-centered to the point of total emotional abandonment. . . . I dreaded an encounter with 'Mom, drunk' more than I dreaded an encounter with 'Koppi, mad.' Why? Because I learned to expect nothing [but trouble] from Koppi. And though Mom and I had no mother-child security established between us . . . I still needed it, yearned for it, and I believe that my mother needed it and yearned for it too. Alcohol inflamed the hurt and confusion around all that unfulfilled need and yearning."[44] Ethel's social drinking remained heavy all of her life and affected a number of people, although Tony Cointreau and his partner, her two closest friends, never saw her lose control. And despite its corrosive effects on her family, Merman was able to control her need for drink and could turn it off at will. She never drank alone. She never drank when she was working, and she did not tolerate it in colleagues who did. Her husband, though, lacked this iron will.

A few years later, the always-direct Dorothy Fields said, "Bob Levitt was an irritant to Ethel. He was so far above her intellectually. . . . He's a very, very bright guy. And Ethel is not an intellectual woman. She is a shrewd woman, but she's—she knows all the small talk, but you can't sit down and talk to her. You just can't."[45] (Fields made her remarks when Ethel was happily married to her next husband.)

And so two strong, stubborn, and loving personalities watched as their dreams began to wear out. After a long time of fighting and raised voices, Bob and Ethel separated for good in May 1951. Soon thereafter Levitt was seen around town escorting Linda Darnell, but he was hardly doing well. In August, he was involved in a horse-riding accident in which he suffered multiple broken bones, and the double lock of depression and alcoholism was taking its toll. Although he would remarry, twice (the first time to a fellow alcoholic), Levitt never really got his life back.

After their parents' separation, Bobby and Ethel Jr. spent summers and weekends with Big at his rented apartments in the city, and, after he moved, at houses he rented near the water, like Bell Island and Rye, and eventually at a home he bought in East Hampton. At first Little Ethel would take her brother to the window in Big's den to point out the building their father was going to move to. "All of a sudden," says Bob Jr., "there was no father in our underparented lives."[46] For Big Ethel and Bob, there was heartfelt regret on both sides, along with the usual acrimony, especially for the more cynical and introspective Levitt. Both never seemed to know exactly what had gone wrong.

NINE

A More Complex Image

Ethel Merman can lay no claim to great beauty, glamour or "legit" vocal quality, but she is a dynamic baggage with syncopation in every breath and gesture and a voice with the hard, clarion forthrightness of a jazz trumpet.

Time, *October 28, 1940*

She yelled for an ice bag and fought off attempts to stash her away in a hospital. Then she took the stage at the Waldorf party and, as usual, toppled the walls. When she was done, she took a cab to the hospital.

Scrapbook clipping by Bob Considine, November 14, 1949,
reporting that Merman suffered an attack of appendicitis just before
she was scheduled to sing at a Banshee Luncheonette. Above it,
in her handwriting, "This never happened."

By this point, Ethel Merman seemed to symbolize both wholesome, American dynamism and New York brashness, and however contradictory those things might appear, at the time they merely revealed the breadth of her impact. Scrapbook clippings attest that in the years between *Annie Get Your Gun* and *Call Me Madam,* no one disputed her reign as Broadway's great queen. Moreover, her image had more range now than ever before. If Annie Oakley had added softness to her persona, Sally Adams had given her sophistication, maturity, and class.

Still, "I Got Lost in His Arms" has never gone down as a Merman classic the way that "You Can't Get a Man with a Gun" and "There's No Business Like Show Business" have. *Annie* may have softened the Merm, but as vocal scholar Henry Pleasants says, by then "it was already too late."[1] Her image had already "hardened," the same word Barbara Geary uses to describe the public's conception of her grandmother. Bawdy and tough, onstage and off—that was the Merman legend that gelled, one that she would never shake, even after death.

Despite this hardening, the cracks and contradictions of Ethel's public persona had started coming into relief in the 1940s. "People disagree on many points in Ethel's character," an interviewer of the time noted. "She is stingy with money or extremely generous, depending on who's talking. She is difficult and temperamental—or the best working companion in show business. But nobody denies Ethel's strong will. Her work comes first, absolutely."[2]

And so although her status as the winningest star of musical comedies was affirmed and celebrated more than ever, less sympathetic aspects of Merman's onstage characters—and, now, her offstage personality—were raising eyebrows and starting to polarize people in ways that her early career had not. The postwar press was presenting Ethel Merman with less uniformity, and, as the contradictions around her intensified, boundaries between her public and private personae began to criss-cross as well. People knew that she had begun a family life with Levitt and their children, for instance, but while the papers were running pictures of Bobby and Little Ethel playing with Dorothy Kilgallen's children, they were also printing pictures of Ethel alone in clubs with hard-core partyers like Bankhead. Yes, she swore in front of her young children; no, she never did. All of this was both the source and the result of competing interpretations of Merman, and the tensions would provide the basis for interpretations and reinventions of Ethel to come. With the very same stories in their hands, fans and media could produce a delightfully irrepressible Ethel or a coarse, nasty egotist.

To be sure, tensions had always existed. In the 1930s, at the same time that the media offered up Ethel Merman as a girl-next-door and a dutiful daughter, she was portraying hardened women of experience onstage. Here was a young singer who couldn't cook but was dishing out recipes to women's magazines, giving instructions on preparing lavish turkey dinners at home.

Still, as late as *DuBarry*, the press did not confuse Merman with the characters she depicted, except in affectionately calling her "Eadie" and the like. No one saw her *as* DuBarry or maintained that DuBarry gave any insight into the real Ethel. But the brashness of roles *like* DuBarry was starting to wear off on the person the press wanted to believe Ethel Merman was offstage. One report, for instance, claimed that Merman "went prima donna" just before the opening of *Red, Hot and Blue!*: she "ripped off all the clothes and hats designed for her by a couple of Madison Avenue top-notchers and demanded a complete new wardrobe."[3] The tall tale likely emerged from a small incident: Ethel wanted a bustle (with a hen in a nest, for laughs) removed from a gown she wore during one of the numbers. "Any audience that gets a laugh out of me gets it while I'm facing them," she told Vin Freedley. She was also displeased that the gag might overshadow the musical mood of the song.[4]

One interviewer took a misstep and caught a glimpse of the star's fury:

"I know flappers were supposed to be unconventional and wild," Merman was saying, "but if they think a flapper was that way what do they think of girls nowadays? They sure travel at a faster rate than we ever did. . . . Huh? [to another question] Listen. I never had an outright proposition in my life." Miss Merman, the grown-up flapper, got her breath and looked out the window, and pretty soon she was smiling again and being the gay, gracious chatelaine. But the look she flashed there for a minute—whew! It would have pleated a battleship.[5]

It was with *Annie Get Your Gun* that the press started to blur the lines between Ethel and her stage role in earnest, if only to focus rather innocuously on her and Annie's "natural" skills and energy. Yet it was also around this period that Ethel's private and public lives started to give her all-American image a run for the money—even as that image continued to make her one of Broadway's wealthiest women. Yes, she was still the nice daughter who loved her folks, but now, after fifteen years in show business, words like *nice* and *sweet* were rarely used to describe her (unlike Mary Martin, for instance). As for Merman's inexhaustible energy, the press was not lauding her stamina anymore but using it to transform her into a powerhouse that crushed everything in its path, box office records, eardrums, and costars. "Ethel Merman Merely Mows 'Em Down," ran one review of the show.[6]

Such assessments never occur in a vacuum. In many ways the contradictions attributed to Merman reveal more about changing cultural values than they do about Merman herself. Ethel was always a lightning rod that reflected changes in the social landscape, and in her (and responses *to* her) we see evolving attitudes toward family, sex, celebrity, class, and age. For instance, although Merman's affairs with married men had never made the scandal sheets, now that she was a married mother, the press was intent on pointing up differences and similarities between "Miss Merman and Mrs. Levitt"— hardly singular treatment, to be sure. Still, when combined with other tensions emerging with more regularity, these stories made "Ethel Merman" into a more complex figure, more three-dimensional than she had been before or that many today believe her to have been. Some of the stories have found their way into her larger-than-life legacy; others have not. Others still, such as whether she swore in front of the kids, show that Ethel Merman was simply mortal, a woman trying to enjoy her career and maintain the semblance of a normal family life.

Ironically, one change emerged from a lack of change. Once the success of *Annie* had subsided, there was a sense that no matter how much she was at the top of her game, Ethel's successes were so familiar as to almost become old news. Thus, for all her celebrity and precisely for being at the *top* of her game, columnists evoked Merman less as "breaking news" than as a lesson in reliable old familiarity.

Because Merman was so established, her success so inevitable, some members of the press and some of her colleagues searched for some sign of imperfection and weakness. Her record was impeccable: seven shows by the time of *Annie Get Your Gun,* and none of them box office failures. Perhaps the only place to hunt for blemishes was in her personality or offstage deportment. It is impossible to ascertain which press attacks were provoked by Merman's perceived crassness and which were a result of simple resentment. The point is that, by now, negative claims and observations were increasingly out of Ethel's control, and she no longer had the tight, close reins over the press that she had before.

These shifts were abetted by changes in the postwar landscape beyond the entertainment world. There was a widening gap between public and private spheres: private and family lives were more guarded, seen as off-limits, and in the process became *more* attractive to gossip columnists. Media and reporting styles were changing as well. Gossip columns were more aggressive, intruding more openly (and with less discretion) into the private lives of their subjects. Celebrity was less a guarantor of respect, awe, or discretion; now it was prey for hunters to expose. When Merman's star was being groomed in the 1930s, gossip columnists such as Ed Sullivan, Louis Sobol, Dorothy Kilgallen, George Sokolsky, and Hedda Hopper ruled the press. All were New York–based, and Ethel easily and openly fostered their goodwill with small favors (thank-yous for favorable remarks; small gifts when they were in mourning). Again, although the practice was not uncommon, it shows that Merman knew how much of a role these media personnel played in sustaining not only her career but also her very image and reputation. But now, gossip had become more of a cutthroat business and, as such, was less dependent on cordial relations with celebrities or producers than it was on nurturing anonymous "sources." The wider practice of national syndication also made local sources, relationships, and communities less crucial to their writers.

Walter Winchell

It was Walter Winchell who personified the new, hard era of gossip, even though his career had started well before the war. His work showed the best and the worst of new reporting trends. Born in New York in 1897 to Jewish immigrant parents, Winchell's working-class roots would be a source of personal and public contradictions, just as Ethel's were to her. As a child, he sang and danced in vaudeville, giving him not only an insider's view of the entertainment world but also an awareness of the gritty realities of the people inhabiting that world. Winchell worked in Hollywood as a screenplay writer and an actor, and he was the subject of *Sweet Smell of Success* by 20th Century–Fox, whose films, like Winchell's work itself, were often torn from the headlines and relied on the lives of regular people. (Biographer Neal Gabler calls Winchell's "a column run for the masses in their own vernacular.")[7] His clipped, staccato writing self-consciously reflected the patter of the street; his creative slang was both contagious and influential. It was Winchell, for instance, who coined the term "the Big Apple."

He used the rough tactics of the street too. At once fearless and self-serving, Winchell thought nothing of blackmailing other reporters or sources to "make" or break certain stars. He cooperated with the House Un-American Activities Committee, turning people over for questioning. During the blacklist era, columnists were under pressure to cooperate, and most did: Sullivan, Jack O'Brian, Hopper, Sobol, Sokolsky—basically everyone but Kilgallen. (As Victor Navasky puts it, "For [them], the line between name-dropping and name-naming was so thin that they ended up as adjuncts of the blacklist process.")[8] Winchell also had an extremely ambivalent relationship to New York's subtle but very real anti-Semitism, at a time when Jews were barred from many of Manhattan's nicer residential areas and when some turned to careers as entertainers to leave behind their Jewishness. At times militating against anti-Semitism, at times capitulating to it, Winchell embodied an era's ambivalence.

Merman's scrapbooks contain few notes to and from Winchell, many fewer than for Kilgallen, with whom she had genuinely cordial relations. One can only guess about this, but perhaps Winchell viewed Merman as too established and redoubtable to mess with, yet also too homespun for his slick crowd. In all likelihood, Merman and Winchell held each other at slight remove, respecting each other's power but not eager to capitulate to it. Says Ethel's son, "I'm actually fascinated by my mother's self-protective deference to Walter Winchell. It contrasts dramatically with the more relaxed 'mutual admiration' that she shared so openly with women who were married to presidents and women who sat on thrones."[9]

Ethel recognized the media's role in putting out Ethel Merman lore and legends into the public eye and even acknowledged her own part in their production in an interview by Robert Garland in summer of 1947:

> "Which interview you want?" she asks.
>
> "Which interviews you got?" ask I.
>
> "The old reliable three . . . The Sure-Shot Merman in which I never had a failure. The Doin' What Comes Naturally one in which I revamp the 'I Got Rhythm' stuff of 'Girl Crazy' Days. And the Wife-Into-Mother-Into-Homebody-One in which I also loathe the country[side]."
>
> "I've used them all," I say. . . .
>
> "So has everybody . . . but they're true enough. . . . I guess there isn't any interview today."[10]

Changes in Popular Culture

For the musical comedy, new trends in popular music proved tough to negotiate, and for the most part, Broadway dealt with them by ignoring them. Musicals of the 1950s were only beginning to exploit rock (it would be another two decades before it really clicked), and in general, rock and roll split audiences generationally more than popular music had before. This too influenced theater audience demographics: Tin Pan Alley was out, swing was out, and Broadway show music, though widely available through cast recordings and new media outlets such as television, was losing its grip on the current hit scene. Berlin's and Porter's efforts had lost their impact, and even in the world of musical theater, it was Rodgers and Hammerstein who were mopping up. *Call Me Madam* was one of Berlin's last hits, and it was Merman's last before *Gypsy*.

It was a strange backdrop for one of the more innovative decades in Broadway musical history. For the '50s saw the rise of shows in which dance routines would be crucially important to the show's storytelling and provide insight into characters' inner lives and dreams. This was the decade of the "choreographer-director," and although Ethel would work with one of the most famous ones and in one of Broadway's most innovative shows, there was no doubt that her school of the old book musical was on its way out.

Popular culture was changing as well, primarily because of the speedy rise of television. With it, the rules of comedy were changing—they had to. Shows were broadcast into living rooms across the nation, and so tamer family fare ruled the day. Jokes were toned down and cleaned up. Industry was targeting "average" audiences, and that meant white, suburban, nothing identified with a particular region, such as New York's Lower East Side. Old-time performers like Cantor and Lahr had trouble adapting; others brought their old personalities onto TV (Groucho Marx, Durante). For female performers the transition was generally harder: singers like Kate Smith were reduced to one-trick ponies; comics like Gracie Allen transitioned well, successful as ever as a hilarious ditz; Imogene Coca was brassy but unthreatening; Lucille Ball flourished, even if most of her younger audience was unaware of her prior career as actress and dancer.

Female comics often experience longer careers than other female entertainers who have to depend on their looks or voice. Merman was enough of a blend of both to keep her career going: her voice was in fine shape, and she could capitalize on her instinctive comedic gifts in the new TV era. Yet while her energetic appearances kept her in the public eye for a long time, her performance style and mannerisms often marked her as from another era and another medium. Merman's ability to turn sex into a "good clean joke," for instance, had the vestiges of vaudeville and old music hall comedy and was readily available to a broad, working-class urban audience. Legitimate Broadway theater and, even more so, Hollywood film were now setting their sights higher, on the ostensibly more respectable middle class. Hollywood excelled at turning human sexuality into something transcendent and glamorous or at rendering it innocuous through jokes and caricature; TV whitewashed it even more. Such gentrifying trends didn't change the musical comedy Merman was known for, but Broadway itself was now becoming a leisure form for middle- and upper-class consumers; expenses and ticket prices skyrocketed after the war. With so much financial stake in every new show, producers were weaning themselves from "risky" ventures, a tradition that continued for decades, culminating late in the century with endless musical revivals or shows based on existing films, operas, and TV shows.

Staying with Her Roots

One thing that was starting to make Ethel stand out from other celebrities is that she didn't try to escape the worldviews into which she'd been born. Even if she enjoyed having one foot in the high-flying world of celebrity, she kept the other firmly in the lower-middle-class mentality she'd known since birth. High culture was not for her. "She's always been the kind of gal who'd rather have a rhinestone orchid than two tickets to Faust," said Lew Kessler.[11]

Ethel also kept a hands-on approach to the way her home was maintained. "A lot of women, for heaven's sakes, don't want to be bothered about the help, and [Ethel would] get down and scrub the g.d. bathroom floor herself when the help would quit," said husband Levitt after their divorce.[12] Like any woman of her station, Ethel preferred having the help, but, according to her son, working for Ethel Merman was not always easy, and she rarely enjoyed good relations with people hired to serve her. (Levitt has a vague memory as an infant of being wrenched from the arms of Abba, the nurse he loved so much and whom his mom fired, replaced by the cruel Miss Kopeman.) His mother's difficulty with her employees did not come from being inherently nasty; she just didn't think of them as people with feelings of their own: they were there for her. She was a terrible tipper, for instance. "Mom had attitude when it came to the people who served her, and she was hard on them," driving the doorman in one hotel to the point of near-murderous impulses. "Mom had very little empathy for other people's emotional needs or for their experience with the financial rigors of life. . . . Her own certainty in her own ability to sustain herself in life, at brilliant levels, seemed to create an attitude towards others made up, in part, of a general disinterest and, in part, from a general expectation that anyone else could do the same if they just applied themselves. I can't recall seeing Mom take any real pleasure in her generosity's impact on others. She really did believe, and rightly so, that Ethel Merman gave a lot to the world around her. Big tips not included."[13]

By the mid-1940s the star was complaining with surprising candor and frequency about not being able to keep good housekeepers. One *New York Herald Tribune* story was called "Ethel Merman Discovers Maids Are More Elusive Than Roles"; "Ethel Guns for a Baby Sitter" ran another. In one of her 1951 columns, Kilgallen noted, "If you can get her to do it, Ethel Merman's recital of her difficulties with her domestic help is the funniest one-woman sketch in town."[14]

Like many people tight with the penny, Merman was swift to spot cheapness in others, disdaining hucksters and gold diggers, and referred to an especially parsimonious acquaintance as a guy who could "squeeze a nickel until the Indian humped the buffalo."[15] The public started to circulate stories about Merman's reputed stinginess too; Richard Rodgers's comment on the Christmas tree was not the only anecdote out there. "Three things are important to Ethel," said Lou Irwin, "and the first is money, and the second is money, and the third is money." Ethel viewed her attitude toward finances as nothing more than common sense and was proud of her frugality and her attentiveness to expenditures. Talking with Pete Martin, Ethel told the story of the morning after *Annie* had opened; she was poring over the papers, noting to her husband that the price of canned peaches had gone up. Levitt, she told Pete Martin, "never got over that."[16]

There are just as many accounts of Ethel's acts of generosity. Her scrapbooks are filled with notes from fans, celebrities, and managers thanking her for notes, gifts, and other acts of kindness. If someone was sick, Ethel came through in abundance, even if theirs was just a casual working relationship: "Dear Ethel," began a letter from choreographer Bob Alton during *Panama Hattie*. "I cannot tell you how pleased I was with the beautiful basket you sent me. I was pretty sick when [it] arrived and I am most grateful to you for being so thoughtful. . . . I will drop backstage soon. Sincerely, Bob Alton."[17] Betty Hutton, also from *Panama Hattie* and MGM's future Annie Oakley, received a large topaz ring from Ethel when she left *Hattie*.[18] Many of Ethel's gifts sparkled with her impishness. To John Mason Brown, hospitalized in July 1947, she sent an arrangement of red carnations interspersed with packs of cigarettes and placed a phone call to him that he said had the hospital staff in stitches.[19] Ethel's little black book had notes for everybody's birthday or anniversary, and she never missed one.

A well-known Merm story is that every Saturday during the run of *Gypsy*, she brought a chocolate cake to the theater after discovering that costar Jack Klugman liked chocolate cake. A "gypsy" chorus member from *Call Me Madam* recalls running into Ethel at Bloomingdale's on a day off. He offered to help her take her bags out to the car, and she accepted, then offered him a ride, which he declined. At the theater the next day he found a pair of platinum cufflinks from Cartier's waiting for him with a thank-you card. Going to her dressing room, he said, "Oh, Miss Merman, I can't possibly accept these." Without even glancing up from her makeup table, she bellowed, "What's the matter, don't ya want them?"

"Mom never went for the trappings of celebrity," says her son today. "She enjoyed its perks, and she liked having things. But she was never ever caught up in her own fame."[20] Ethel prided herself on not having a secretary, on doing her own typing and correspondence, on supervising her finances (with accountants—starting with Pop—and investment advisers). In many ways Merman really did retain her modest roots, keeping records of *every* detail of her life as a celebrity, including the building floor plan for the 1954 Republican National Convention, and even typing up menus of important dinner parties. Her closest friends were not from the entertainment world; most intimates came from the days in Queens, like Josie Traeger and the Panzer family. Later, she relaxed in New Jersey with Kathryn Shreve, who looked after Ethel's elderly Pop. "Ethel was most comfortable when she was with people she knew weren't trying to use her for anything," says Cointreau.[21]

Ethel was not the first or last star to downplay her wealth and privilege; most entertainment figures try to present themselves as not all that different from their fans. Marlene Dietrich, for instance, swore that she was "just a hausfrau," dispensing cleaning and cooking tips. (She actually loved homemaking.) Merman, who *didn't,* "kept to her roots," as her *Call Me Madam* gypsy says; he recalls seeing her shooting craps with the crew.

Ethel mingled just as easily with heads of state and big celebrities, yet she never adopted or tolerated the airs or pretensions that might have made her a more seamless fit into the upper classes, and she seemed strikingly aware that that was a deliberate choice. To her granddaughter she later advised, "Don't fart higher than your ass."[22]

Backlash

For some, Ethel Merman was the gauche nouveau riche, the inappropriately landed celebrity—Horatio Alger stories tend to overlook the resentment that awaits the suddenly elevated. This perception was formed by roles and the reports of incidents such as her purported outburst over the wardrobe in *Red, Hot and Blue!* Later, during a *Call Me Madam* revival in the 1960s, a gypsy says that Merman barely interacted with anyone in the show other than Nype. But as early as the mid-1940s, the press was already hinting at her aloofness:

Unlike Tallulah Bankhead, who, offstage and on, is always and emphatically Tallulah Bankhead, Miss Merman has two personalities. In the theatre she is

Annie Oakley, Panama Hattie, or whatever part she happens to be playing, and such is the vehemence of her portrayal of these noisy, domineering girls that some of her colleagues are prone to credit her with similar qualities in private life. "I know Ethel gets terribly cozy with the audience," one of them remarked thoughtfully a little while ago, "but you can't help feeling that she's never been introduced to the cast."[23]

Ethel had quickly come to embody class tensions and disparities. For some people, her roots and her ongoing connection with "regular" Americans on and off the stage, coupled with stories about rough behavior and language, made for a distinctly unpalatable combination. Rather than adoring her blunt-edged joie de vivre, they recoiled from the crassness or lack of sophistication they perceived in, or projected onto, her. "My father," recalls a fortyish Italian American raised in working-class Queens, "*hated* her. He wouldn't let us listen to her when I was growing up, even though he adored show tunes. She came on too strong for him. Maybe it was a misogynist thing, but he thought she was vulgar."[24] And a middle-aged woman recalls how her father, born around 1920 in New Jersey, referred to Merman as "that loud-mouthed *Jew*."[25]

Jewishness was still sticking, and for some of the public, Merman's consummate New Yorkness clinched it. (Recall Wolcott Gibbs's comment about the "Semitic cast" of her nose.) Yet others are convinced that Merman was biased *against* Jews; Arthur Laurents remembers a day off during *Gypsy*'s run in Philadelphia, when he and Sondheim "ran into Ethel wandering around the city. We asked what she had been up to. 'Praying for the show,' she said, hastening to add, 'in church!'" For Passover, she not only brought a ham sandwich to the seder that Jule Styne held for the cast but also ate turkey sandwiches with Russian dressing in front of them during rehearsals, infuriating Styne.[26]

Whenever the press called her Jewish, Ethel wrote or called to correct them, and Laurents is right to note that she was rather obsessed about being mistaken for Jewish. Says Tony Cointreau, "You have to put it in perspective. In the 1920s and '30s, New York was a very anti-Semitic town. There were 're-stricted' areas. Jews and blacks did not live on the Upper East Side and other of the tonier addresses. And they accepted it."[27] In this way Merman was just a product of her time, neither rising above it nor forecasting more tolerant future attitudes. Levitt Jr. gives an indication of what those "treacherous, historical waters" were like when he discusses his own experiences. "For me, as a child, anti-Semitism was an unpleasant wisp of something that came and went, a bad smell, a different sounding name, a condemning tone. . . . Long before I knew its name, anti-Semitism was in my childhood as a 'vague something' that I felt within the distancing, disgust and disliking that I observed as it was acted out by some of the prominent adults in my world. Including, and especially, my mother and father."[28]

When Pete Martin interviewed Bob Levitt Sr., Levitt told him he believed his ex-wife had inherited the "bigoted prejudices" of her parents, whom he considered small-minded. (He would derisively refer to them as "Momsy" and "Floppsy.")[29] Yet Levitt hardly escaped those influences himself; Levitt Jr. refers to his father's "lifetime effort to cover-up the Jew he was in religions he wasn't—first Episcopal, then Presbyterian, while persistently, and aggressively, keeping his distance from his family and his Jewishness."[30]

The gypsy from the *Call Me Madam* revival who noted Merman's distance from the cast—a singer named Ed Zimmerman (no relation)—remembers an incident in Florida in the 1960s. Ethel came up to him out of the blue, asking, "So, how do *you* spell Zimmerman?" and when he told her, she said, " 'I spell it with *two n*'s,' as if to say, because I'm not Jewish."[31] Today it seems as many people believe Merman was Jewish as maintain she was anti-Semitic. That second misconception is somewhat more complex than the first: yes, Ethel joked about "kikes," jokes that are unsavory by today's standards—or even by genteel society of her time—but that might also suggest a relaxed attitude about ethnic difference as much as an insensitivity to it.

Cointreau says that Ethel corrected public reports of her being Jewish simply to set the record straight and wasn't motivated by strong feelings or biases. "Any anger wasn't out of anti-Semitism at all; it was her pride in being Episcopalian," he says.[32] Religious differences, for instance, were not an issue for her when she married the Jewish Levitt and their two children took his name. And then there was her frequent work alongside Jewish performers, businesspeople, and other personnel over her long career; there were also the benefits she did in the 1930s and '40s for Jewish war relief efforts, et cetera. In all, Merman's relationship to anti-Semitism was as complex and conflicted as it was in American culture more generally. After World War II, for instance, as the Cold War simmered, the government viewed the progressive activities of many liberal New York Jews with suspicion and, with the help of people like Winchell, targeted Jews for suspected Communist activities. Ironically, General Foods, the sponsor of Gertrude Berg's popular TV show *The Goldbergs*—the first to feature a Jewish family—pressured Berg to remove blacklisted Jewish actor

Philip Loeb from the cast, and when she refused, CBS canceled the program. (Loeb killed himself five years later.) Actor Farley Granger and choreographer Jerome Robbins also had their Jewishness—and the threat of being outed sexually—used against them. In McCarthy's America, being Jewish was a detriment to being a "true American"—ironic in light of the fact that the U.S. had just helped defeat a regime wanting to eradicate the Jewish race.

An Image of Toughness

Other features of Ethel's public image were changing. Her personal achievement and autonomy had always been part of her persona, but they were being interpreted differently. Ethel was no longer a stenographer sprinkled with Depression fairy-tale dust; now her success was seen as a product of hard work and an extremely strong sense of self. Ethel had made it *on her own,* and "Ethel was very proud of that," says Cointreau.[33] Unlike women such as Mamie Eisenhower, with whom she enjoyed good relations, Ethel had acquired her position not through connections to a man but through her own work and talent, and this was an important feature of the public Ethel Merman. Levitt Jr. believes that other celebrity women with whom Merman interacted also appreciated his mother's having achieved such success on her own. "Mom and Mamie Eisenhower talked on the phone, sometimes late at night, and my mother was pleased to do that, pleased to be a consoling friend who had enough self-generated status to make a President's wife feel comfortable."[34]

By midcentury, the image of Merman as ultraprofessional had also taken root. Here was a star who was always on time, who always gave 100 percent, who took notes during rehearsals and enjoyed working with other big talent. Betty Allen, the understudy in *DuBarry,* called her an "iron horse" for missing so few shows.[35] During the same show, an interviewer noted, "She has great respect of her ability to put over a song, but she doesn't think her talent gives her a right to be temperamental or late for appointments. . . . Ethel Merman is known as a 'good egg.' " Disciplined to extremes, Ethel was nononsense about her tasks and conserved her energy while working, not going out on nights before matinee days and not signing autographs between matinee and evening performances.[36]

Merman's work ethic scarcely made her an angel, and some of her astonishing discipline was centered around control issues, according to family members. Says Barbara Geary, "Ethel had trouble letting others be the center of attention, and when you're a kid, that's hard, because kids also need to be at the center sometimes."[37] Some people saw her refusal to make changes in rehearsals ("Miss Birds Eye") or getting "upstarts" such as Paula Laurence fired as forms of hostile indifference to her coworkers; to others, this behavior was simple self-preservation, which allowed Ethel to perform at her best. The latter seems closer to the mark, even if it did activate a truly tough part of Merman's personality. David Lahm describes her as "just like the Roman Empire, justifying conquests to protect her perimeters."[38]

To fans, Ethel said:

So far as I know, I only blow my top when someone hurts the show. Up there, I'm a working girl, just as much as I ever was in the old days when I pounded a typewriter from nine to five. If someone fluffs a cue, comes on drunk, or misses an entrance while I'm there beating my brains out—sure, I'll blow. And if I'm shredding my larynx over a song and there's horseplay in the ensemble or if a guy in the orchestra pit is rustling the Daily Racing Form, I'll damn well do something about it.[39]

According to Tony Cointreau, Ethel said she broke out of character only once, during *Annie Get Your Gun* when she chided two "loudmouth no-goods" who were drinking and being obnoxious in the audience.[40] More famous is a tale Elaine Stritch told in her 2002 show *At Liberty*, in which she claimed that once while Ethel sang "Can You Use Any Money Today?" in *Call Me Madam*, a heckler kept screaming smart-ass answers. After some time and no action on the part of the house management, Merman herself walked into the audience—midsong—and physically heaved the man out before returning to the stage to finish the note. Cointreau says Ethel denied that this ever occurred, but for the Merman legend, the truth is almost immaterial, for, by now after the war, the tale was fully compatible with the toughening Merman image.

Ethel's lack of stage fright was also assuming legendary proportions. Ethel never experienced it, not even as a child; that part of her fearlessness was the real deal. "Ethel sweats ice water," said agent Lou Irwin;[41] for producer Vinton Freedley, "She is so sure of herself she steadies the whole cast."[42] By the 1940s, the press was giving that lack of nerves even more coverage and started reporting the famous Merman lines in earnest: "Why should I be nervous on opening night? The people who paid $4.40 for a new play, they're the ones who should be nervous." Or, "What's there to worry about? I know my lines."

Or, "Mermo, aren't you nervous tonight?" "What the hell should I be nervous about, for Chrissake? They came to see me. I didn't come to see them."[43]

Her relaxed confidence stunned other professionals. After all, stars like Lily Pons in opera and Laurence Olivier in theater were known to get so nervous that they actually vomited before going on. Merman's guts seemed to be made of iron. A typical work day would have her resting in the late afternoon, after which she would dine on a steak sandwich or raw hamburger several hours before the show (as "enthusiastic with a knife and fork as she is with a song,"[44] said a pressman who interviewed her in her dressing room). Once at the theater, the ritual was simple. Belter Klea Blackhurst: "How did Ethel warm up? [clears her throat] That's it."[45]

Cole Porter explained Merman's lack of stage fright with charming simplicity: "She comes from very healthy stock."[46] Ethel knew there was no point getting worked up about what she did. Her self-confidence merged with her pragmatism: she arrived on time, did her work, and went home. "I sing honest," she said. Irving Katz, her investor and close associate, agreed, saying, "She was confident, not arrogant."[47] "[Ethel's] nerves were manifested differently," Tony Cointreau recalled later. "They came out in her perfectionism."[48]

Still, by the 1940s there was some grumbling and mixed responses. Some found Merman less than helpful to her colleagues and said she had trouble sharing the spotlight. In his "Little Old New York" column, the usually supportive Ed Sullivan wrote, "Paula Lawrence [sic], who started picking on Ethel Merman in Something for the Boys, is learning what other novices have learned."[49] Merman's habit of not looking at colleagues onstage was also receiving attention. George Abbott, her director in Madam, said, "She would take direction perfectly in rehearsal and play it that way on opening night. Then she changed to her old way to sing to the audience and did so, much to the distress of her leading men."[50] At the same time, people were noting the strong and very enthusiastic support Ethel was giving to other performers, especially emerging women singers. When Lena Horne sang Ethel's anthem, "I Got Rhythm," in a 1943 nightclub act, she was right there in the audience applauding; she also made a point of catching as many Judy Garland performances as possible and later supported a young, long-haired Liza Minnelli with visible affection and pride.

Another contradiction emerged from Merman's ability to combine a raucous, almost vulgar spirit with innocent wholesomeness—all in the name of a flaming good time. Characters like Eadie, Hattie, Nails—"dames" though they were—contained that same wholesomeness deep down, walking clichés of the tough gal with a heart of gold. Ethel carried off these roles effortlessly onstage, but after a while the public seemed to want to attribute those features to her persona off the boards. This was quite at odds with how Ethel thought of herself and how close friends such as Tony Cointreau describe her: as a shy woman at heart. "I remember in the 1970s, Ethel and I went to see a colleague of hers in a show," recalls Cointreau. "I had to convince Ethel that it would be all right to go backstage and say hello."[51] The stories with public sticking power, though, are the ones that make Ethel Merman into a brassy broad, ones that point to outrageous, obstreperous, often indecorous behavior or remarks that have taken on a life of their own. "That's probably what I spend the most time doing when people want to know about the 'real' Ethel Merman—talking about that reserved, shy side of her," says Cointreau.[52]

Family and Career

As soon as *Something for the Boys* was over, Ethel told reporters, "I'm going to have another baby right away."[53] Combining parenthood, romantic relations, and celebrity has always been hard for female celebrities, and the press didn't treat Ethel that much differently from other women, especially the women whom they viewed as "independent." In "Sobol Discusses Success Gals," Louis Sobol writes: "I suppose there will always be a place for a man in the lives of these ['highly capable sisters'] who don't need a fellow for the household expenses he can dole out—but it is a shuddery truth that we dominant males must face—they can do without us. . . . I tip my hat to these queens."[54] Along with Ethel, he singled out Martha Raye and Mary Martin, adding, however, that "probably the foremost anti-marriage career disciple on the Main Stem was Ethel Merman," showing how little Sobol knew the real Merm.[55] But that was the image that gained currency. In 1941, Sobol said that Ethel "was generally accepted as the typical bachelor girl—until her surprise marriage last year to Bill Smith, Hollywood agent."[56]

Merman's scrapbooks preserve conflicting, often hysterical accounts of her purported attitude toward men, marriage, and romance. One came from a simple card she received from "Doc Lou Clement" and Harold Hoffman, family friends who'd just taken in *Something for the Boys.* They wrote:

> We're here, dear Ethel, on the cuff
> To watch the way you do your stuff
> And see them lovely gals in scanties
> While Bob is changing Baby's panties.[57]

A social column had fun inserting a bit of romantic intrigue into Ethel's secretarial past:

> Ethel Merman, when a stenographer, fell in love with Rudolph Valentino. And she wrote Rudolph a five-page letter every day to which she received no answer. After she had written 1,142 five-page letters, all unanswered, Ethel became discouraged and included the correspondence with the following:
>
> > "Dear Rudy (my ex-dream man):
> > Roses are red,
> > Violets are blue,
> > Gosh, the postage
> > I've wasted on you."[58]

Even before she was married, Ethel was tight-lipped about her love life; "Her Life Is Private," ran one interview,[59] which seemed to ignite speculation all the more. In 1940, a palm reader forecast Ethel's future for readers: "DuBarry's to Marry, the Fates Indicate," predicting that Ethel was going to be mother to three kids.[60]

Ethel probably tossed off various remarks about men to the press, and she was at least partly responsible for some of the contradictions attributed to her. She gave conflicting lines according to the different moods she was in or depending on the activities she needed to promote at the time. In the mid-1950s, for instance, Ethel wrote a guest column, "Actress Dreams of Laws for a 'Perfect Husband'":

> Husbands should never be allowed to overwork and talk themselves out during their business day, so they're good for nothing but a grunt of greeting and a short goodnight when they get home. . . . Men [must] wear blinders at the beach. . . . Husbands [should] be forced to stay at home with the kids at least once a week . . . to take their wives out on a dress up date once a week. . . . Husbands [should] be forced to submit to a "perfume" detector test when they come home from "working late at the office."[61]

Although *some* of the lines attributed to Ethel on love, romance, and family life were heartfelt beliefs, most were not, and nearly all were heavily edited or outright inventions of writers and publicists going for an extra edge. In all, the press did not handle the issue of Merman and marriage with any consistency, again, unsurprising given that her celebrity depended less on her relations with men than on the powerhouse voice.

Managing Contradictions

Whether over the span of their careers or in a particular moment, public figures always generate different responses from different groups, audiences, and contexts. A star's image will inevitably produce a certain amount of contradiction; the question is how to manage it. Consistency on the part of the star is imperative, something needed to fulfill a kind of contract with his or her consuming public. For instance, it's comforting for audiences to believe that Ethel Merman had the same tough gusto offstage as on or that Bing Crosby was as easygoing at home as he seemed when he sang. When stars' inconsistencies or incongruous associations go too far, they risk imploding, and the industry, press, and fans will often try to come up with ways to absorb the contradictions or explain them away (a momentary indiscretion, an error in casting). But there's another way for fans to manage inconsistencies, and that is to highlight them, to turn odd juxtapositions into playful jokes. Twenty-first-century performers such as Jeffery Roberson have done just that with Merman; his stage name is Varla Jean Merman, a character who claims to be the "love child" from Ethel's brief union with Ernest Borgnine in the 1960s. Often, celebrities are little more than beloved source material that fans use for their own purposes, becoming part of a creative recycling process. This is especially common in camp, which thrives on unexpected juxtapositions and new contexts.

It's rare, however, for that kind of playful, inventive understanding of inconsistencies to win out, particularly in conservative periods or when entertainment industries stand to gain or lose considerable capital on their clients. And that accurately describes the business climate in which Merman moved at this midcareer point. As noted, the postwar period saw producers start to move away from "risky" ventures, a trend necessitated in part by economic constraints (it cost close to a quarter of a million dollars to mount a musical in the early '50s) and also ideological imperatives (with officials keeping watch for "un-American" signs in the entertainment world).

American entertainment was also changing and, as we've seen, comedy no less so than other forms. With every show, Ethel garnered more recognition for her comedic talents, and she had quickly joined the ranks of other "mouthy broads" of the '30s, '40s, and early '50s. "There are quite a few female comics, most of them very good," begins theater critic Burton Rascoe in 1943, "Ethel Merman, ZaSu Pitts, Gracie Fields, Una Merkel, Patsy Kelly and Eve Arden [who] get their effects by grotesquerie, contortions or horseplay. The comedienne, on the other hand, gets her effects largely by . . . a sense which involves an intelligent, critical response to almost any given situation, with . . . very subtle contortions of the facial muscles, in the glance and in involuntary movements of the body."[62] Into the latter group Rascoe puts Fannie Brice, Beatrice Lillie, Celeste Holm, Tallulah Bankhead, and others. The first group are comics, not witty romantic partners, not beauties. They don't exemplify glamour or display proper behavior; instead, it's "horseplay" and unelevated gags. The social and class connotations of Rascoe's remarks are painfully clear: unlike the "intelligent, critical . . . subtle" behavior of the second, gentrified, group of women, Ethel's comedy, according to him, anchored her in the lower depths. For people like Rascoe, Merman would never make it out of that comic group, despite her own razor-sharp wit and instinctive timing with zingers, on or off the boards.

The Merman Look

Because Ethel did not have exceedingly good looks and never aspired to WASPy glamour, reviewers were all over the place when they described her appearance. As a singer, she was expected to be attractive, but less so than women working in more visual media, such as movies. And because Ethel sang in a markedly animated style, the press seemed uncommonly interested in finding unusual features of her appearance. "Nature," wrote Gibbs in his *Life* article, "obviously intended her to have a rather inexpressive face, and the look of intense vivacity that usually adorns it is as comic and unnatural as the look of glassy distinction worn by the odd celebrities in those whisky advertisements."[63] A male fan at the time of *Something for the Boys* said, "She is funny looking—certainly not a pretty girl—but she makes all pretty girls of the stuck-up kind look like dehydrated potatoes. . . . There is a natural, uninhibited lustiness about her, something healthy in her brazen sureness of herself."[64]

To say that women's looks are under the microscope is not news, and the gaze on female entertainers is particularly intense. Young beauties are described in terms of otherworldly features or transcendent glamour, but as divas age, critics use new words to describe them, focusing on their suddenly fleshy, gravity-influenced bodies. (There are reasons why icons like Garbo and Dietrich refused to be photographed after a certain age.) American attitudes toward aging are famously harsh, portraying the sexuality of middle-aged and older women as desperate, ridiculous, or grotesque; their emotional lives as embittered, shrill, or destructive.

Even if Ethel never fell from the position of ethereal star to that of the somatically encumbered old woman, she was not immune from the attitudes that lurked behind these clichés. People who had reasons to resent her power and success probably felt some cheap delight in making pejorative remarks about her appearance when the star hit middle age. The undercurrents of the *New Yorker*'s rave comments about Ethel in *Annie Get Your Gun* convey that changing response to her: "As everyone knows, Miss Merman has a particularly charming and humorous appearance. Her face is large and her features seem somehow to be closely grouped down toward the bottom of it; her shoulders are square and wide, so that her arms hang away from her sides [not taking into account she might have been directed to swagger for the role]; her hips and legs, tho agreeable, were apparently designed for a much smaller woman; the whole effect, indeed, is queerly fore-shortened, as if you were looking directly down on her from a ladder."[65] (One wonders where this critic's seat was.) For the press, Merman's *voice* was still a natural phenomenon, but they were moving her looks and behavior *away* from naturalness. The icon that was Ethel Merman was moving into glitzier, professional terrain, mimicking the path of Merman's own career.

When she first started out, Ethel's weight was given as 115 pounds, but by the time she reached her late thirties, at around the time of *Something for the Boys,* critics felt free to say, "Now 130 seems more probable," and to refer to her as buxom or plump.[66] The tone is not always harsh but shows a turn nonetheless. A mid-1930s piece called "A Weighty Problem" reads, "On the same day that it was announced that Ethel Merman would play opposite Eddie Cantor in his next picture, the Johns Hopkins Hospital in Baltimore announced a new diet and somehow I cannot untangle the two dispatches in my mind. Patients reduce from 10 to 20 pounds in two weeks on a diet of bananas and milk. Ohoo, Miss Merman could you spare a couple of weeks before you go to Hollywood!!"[67] In 1940, Dale Carnegie snidely reported that Merman was an alumna of a "health and weight farm for women."[68] (Likely untrue. According to Dorothy Fields and Merman's own granddaughter, Ethel *did* struggle to keep her weight down, but desperate measures never interested her. "I don't believe in exercise," was her motto. "I believe it's unhealthy. In fact, I think having yourself massaged is too strenuous. It's liable to soften up your muscles.")[69]

Ethel always had an ample chest, narrow hips, and shapely legs, and when Pete Martin interviewed her for her first autobiography he asked her what she thought her better physical features were. It is hard not to be delighted by her response: Well, she said, her top teeth were absolutely straight. Pause. On to sexier things. When Martin asked about her legs, she said,

> "This is putting me on the spot, Pete, because most people think I've got pretty nice legs."
>
> Martin: "Well all right. Why don't you say, 'Most people think I've got pretty nice legs'? That's being honest about it."
>
> "Well I don't like to say those things."[70]

So much for the boisterous braggart Ethel. Not only would Martin omit her line about not liking to boast, but also, in her reference to her legs, he substituted *gams*.

Vogue noted, "Her pretty legs are rarely noticed in high-flown reviews."[71] It was true: Ethel's roles seldom showed off her legs or accentuated her figure, and not until the shorter dresses of the early '60s did TV audiences get to see her legs. To the public, Merman's body was neither erotic nor clumsy and was seldom the source of much attention either way; it was just there, in its vibrant earthy presence. Curiously, though, for female stars, that lack of fascination could produce a degree of desexualization, which might be linked to their comedic personae. Thus "desexed," was Merman less of a threat to men or to other women? Was she bucking gender roles onstage? (She certainly wasn't in her private life.) And do either of these things explain Ethel's appeal to gay and lesbian cultures then and now?

By the 1940s the press was commenting endlessly on Merman's makeup and features, giving special focus to her dark, round, twinkling eyes that "give her a perpetually astounded air," part of the faux innocence she put over so well onstage.[72] All Ethel had to do was roll her eyes and she had the audience in her hands. Josh Logan was not the only one who raved about the goo-goo eyes she made in *Annie Get Your Gun*. Ethel certainly knew what she was showing off; after all, she'd been placing small jeweled clips at the end of her sleeves since the late '20s, guiding the audience's attention to her twinkling eyes as she gestured. Her eyes, in fact, are one of the few aspects of the Merman vitality that come through on electronic media.

To accentuate her round "saucers," Ethel penciled in long, thin, raised eyebrows, a popular practice among women, especially those pursuing a glamorous look from the early '30s to the late '40s (think Lombard, Dietrich, Garbo). Ethel also beaded her lashes, applying small balls of melted black wax to the tips, a makeup practice that was popular in the late 1920s and '30s. In 1948, she said, "I'm probably the only person in the theater who still beads her eyelashes. I can't wear false lashes because they make me look droopy."[73] She was still beading her lashes into the 1960s, sticking with something she knew flattered her, well after that cosmetic trend had come and gone.

Merman's wide eyes weren't the only obsession of the press. It was also captivated by her mouth—hardly an unusual focus for a singer. For that was the mouth that gave voice to her clear, powerful energy onstage and to the offstage personality with a penchant for speaking her mind—all in a strong Queens accent. In many ways, the media used Merman's mouth not only to telegraph her force as a singer but also to point visually to the "mouthy" woman she was assumed to be.

Merman's shows, movies, and concerts were almost always promoted by a picture of her with her mouth wide open, be this from *Alexander's Ragtime Band* or most shows through *Gypsy;* the same was true of many of her appearances on magazine covers. Among the most famous of the promotional images is the one from *Call Me Madam.* Peter Arno's animated portrait of Merman's head highlights her high-piled curls, the beaded lashes, and, of course, the mouth agape. *Gypsy's Playbill* features a three-quarter photographic portrait with mouth open and a wide-eyed, upward gaze. It's almost like the rest of Merman's body didn't matter—she was all eyes, mouth, and spirit. One stunningly effective portrait of her was by legendary photographer Irving Penn during the run of *Happy Hunting.* Penn captured her mouth open in a perfect oval and visually echoed its shape by seating her behind the rounded curve of a French horn.[74]

The 1940s and early '50s also saw the press entranced by Merman's hair. The bobs of the late '20s and early '30s were long out of fashion, and all that she retained from the time was the auburn dye Hollywood had introduced her to. By the late '30s and '40s, shoulder-length coiffures were popular, and Ethel adopted the look, her thick, wavy hair well-suited for the trend. It was by the time of *Call Me Madam,* though, that Ethel settled on her signature "do": short on the sides with a mop of curls on top that bounced whenever she moved. Al Hirschfeld enshrined it in many of his sketches of her, and Ethel retained it through *Gypsy.* She wore it well; it gave her height, as she noted. And in 1957, Ethel was among the runners-up in the press's "Best Tressed Awards," after Mamie Eisenhower, for her bangs.

The most famous Merman hair story happened during the production of *Call Me Madam.* Mainbocher, pleased with his work on her outfits, turned to his star and said, "And now, Ethel, what do you plan to do with your *hair?*" "I plan to wash it," she said. That dialogue has been repeated without end, and Merman kept versions of it—along with other references to her hair—in her scrapbooks: "Other ladies fuss with their hair and change the mode of their coiffure from season to season. Ethel Merman has found nothing suits her apple cheeks and cheerful jowls except the hair-do of a golliwog. When she went to Hollywood to make the film *Call Me Madam* an esthetic *[sic]* hairdresser asked her what she intended to do about her hair. 'I intend to wash it,' said Ethel Merman, and went out looking like . . ."[75] Here, the clipping was abruptly cut off.

Interviewers' fascination with Ethel's pompadour lasted through the '50s and '60s. Was she planning to change it? No, she'd say, it is my trademark. "She's kind of a hair die-hard," said Dorothy Fields. "She won't change it unless it's absolutely necessary."[76] Aware of the scrutiny, Ethel said, "People criticize my hair. They say it's too thick. Well they can't say that now 'cause I wear it up. They criticize my pompadour. They say it's freakish looking. I told you that yesterday. I like it, so I wear it. . . . it's done all right by me so I'm going to keep it." Later: "I've been criticized for it, people have written it up in the columns here. What did they say? 'When will Ethel Merman *ever* get rid of that horrible hair?' . . . It doesn't make any difference but so—pooh! I don't care. It's all right for me and I'm going to stick with it. . . . And it's becoming. I . . . get some height in the front."[77]

Throughout most of the '60s, Ethel sported a lightly shellacked bubble, more demure than her pompadour but also more age appropriate. For a while, she wore a short, modest flip. (See her appearances on *That Girl,* with Marlo Thomas, queen of the flip.) By the time she retired from the boards in the '70s, Ethel turned to the big hair that ruled the day, teasing her hair in bold new directions. Every Friday, she maintained a standing appointment with her hairdresser.

Despite her personal distaste for hats, Ethel's work frequently required them, often in the form of very elaborate headpieces. *DuBarry, Annie, Hattie* (the name alone . . .) all used headpieces for comic effect. *Something for the Boys* featured one with an oversized dark bronze plume that was erect as a chainsaw, "creat[ing] the effect of an exclamation point" whenever Merman bobbed her head.[78] Offstage, Ethel participated in the "wild hat" craze in vogue in the '30s and early '40s. Photo shoots reveal that the hats Ethel wore were no more outrageous than those of other women of the time; this was a period of especially zany fashion in women's millinery. In New York's 1940 Easter Parade, Ethel wore "an inverted straw cashet *[sic]* with a 'handle' under the chin with two large pink camellias tucked under each ear."[79] But that was no match for another woman's clear cellophane pillbox hat with live ducklings munching on carnations inside it that Easter Day.[80] As the years pressed on, women's hats did finally tone down and eventually came off altogether, and offstage, Ethel's headwear followed suit.

Fashion excess and the Ethel Merman "image" go as far back as the luxurious costumes of *DuBarry,* a show whose sartorial opulence made sense for its story line; they also conveyed the impression of bounty when most audience members were experiencing scarcity and struggle. Clothes helped fulfill that show's fantasies of upward mobility or, by contrast, of ridiculing the wealthy. *DuBarry's* fashion excesses were thus not revealing any particular character trait of May Daly, much less anything about Ethel herself, so much as establishing social and historical place. In the next show, *Panama Hattie,* costumes functioned very differently. There, Ethel's sartorial extravagances conveyed her character's "unrefinement" and transformed the character into a source of gags rather than envy. As the star depicting her, Ethel risked offstage ridicule, but those onstage excesses were not yet carrying over to people's perception of her own image; for instance, "Panama Hattie Puts It On! What Not to Wear at One Time in Accessories—a Shining Example by Ethel Merman" ran alongside a photo with the caption "For your entertainment—consider here Miss Merman—huge lacy parasol; bird-trimmed hat with twin hatpins and veil; enormous lace collar; massive jangling necklace; two pairs of matching bracelets; ruffles on the sleeves; earrings; knotted ankle ties with jeweled ornaments."[81] Clearly, Hattie's flamboyance was part of the show, not part of Ethel, who, it spelled out, knew better. Ethel was still offering fans a critical link between glamorous appeal and day-to-day practicality. Earlier that summer, she'd modeled a Wilma gown that was used as a door prize for a publicity event; "chosen because it will be becoming to the average woman, the gown gives lovely slim lines and is perfect for a first Fall dress."[82] Merman's ability to convey celebrity *and* ordinary life was at work, here and in other product endorsements. During *Annie Get Your Gun's* run, she did ads for Piel's Light beer, Chesterfield cigarettes, Arrid deodorant, and the "ultra-glamorous" Lux soap.

But rumblings questioning the star's *personal* fashion sense were beginning. "Merman loves fur and jewelry, lots and lots of jewelry," wrote columnist Amy Porter.[83] In that sense, Merman seemed to embrace part of her onstage image. In actuality, her personal clothing remained relatively conservative and she was always impeccably groomed, but her choice in jewelry did prompt a few people to question her taste: "In addition to the star sapphires, aquamarines, etc.," wrote one writer, "she has a bracelet . . . which spells out Ethel A. Merman, the letters in baguette diamonds, the period after the A-for-Agnes in rubies. All it needs is to flicker on and off."[84]

None of this bothered Merman, who took real pride in her jewels. As friend and accompanist Lew Kessler said, Ethel "loved [her jewelry] because she worked like a dog to get it, and she'd make fun of it if she got it."[85] Among her most prized jewels was a broach from her mother and, more famously, her charm bracelet, on which she added a new charm for every show. (It also had one of a typewriter.) With each success, the bracelet grew clunkier, as if her mounting celebrity were slowly making her noisier and brassier. By the time of Stanley Kramer's *It's a Mad, Mad, Mad, Mad World* in the early '60s, Merman was playing up that garishness, wearing a clunky bracelet that was so heavily miked that its jingles can be heard every time she belts or shakes her hands at someone.

"She has a childish love for dressy clothes. . . . her favorite evening gown has an enormous black taffeta underskirt that swishes when she walks. Her idea of a simple street outfit consists of a black satin dress, short sleeved, with a gold kid belt, gold beads and gold bracelets, a satin off-the-face hat with a long veil, black suede slippers with French heels, a pair of long black suede gloves, a black broadtail coat, w/ the full sleeves pushed over her wrists. She uses perfume liberally."[86] Why were critics like Amy Porter here making Merman into a fashion monster, and a cheap one at that? Wolcott Gibbs quotes a "fashion expert" (conveniently unidentified) who says that Ethel had few made-to-order dresses. (True—Ethel did buy most things off the rack.) But the unnamed source goes further, complaining, " 'She is not really a very lucrative customer. She likes dresses to cost $39.95, $49.95, or $60 or $70 at the most, getting wary if they cost over $100. . . . She tends to stick with 'black and navy,' but goes nuts with wild hats, jewelry and fussy shoes.' "[87] Another writer ventured, even more cruelly, "When she tries to say she likes conservative clothes, the folks that know her burst out laughing."[88]

Such reports don't put Merman's tastes into any context; plenty of women enjoyed going nuts with wild jewelry and hats, and Ethel's preference for ready-to-wear clothing could have been a holdover from growing up and a way of refusing celebrity excess or a desire *not* to match the flash of her accessories. In all, however, the effect of these comments was to shift Ethel's image away from the natural girl she had been in the early to mid-'30s to something rather more caricatured. Sure, she was still appearing in fashion shows, such as one for Eddie Cantor's March of Dimes benefit in 1947, but at the same time, even Dorothy Kilgallen described her in an appearance at the elite 1-2-3 Club as resembling a "mermaid, her chassis wrapped in a gown of green sequin scales."[89] Ethel probably got a laugh out of it, but underneath a friendly and playful description, some serious shifts were under way.

Merman's evolution from a "natural" icon to one of artifice carried certain economic and symbolic repercussions. On the one hand, it impeded her success on TV and film, where she was deemed "too much," but on the other, it helped Ethel move into new and evolving fan bases. This ostensibly "made-up" look after the war helped set the stage for some of Ethel's subsequent transformations, not the least of which were her ever-expanding roles as queen of musical theater and, especially, gay camp icon. Most camp practices celebrate artifice over authenticity, the performance of intense feelings over their realistic expression, excess and fantasy over conformity and restraint. These features help explain not only Ethel Merman's importance as a camp figure but also how the often extravagant forms of musicals, opera, and other fantasy-driven forms of mass culture appeal to so many of us.

TEN

Madam in Hollywood

It was her forthright charm, and native common sense,
that made her Washington's number one hostess.

Narrator in Call Me Madam

It was in January 1952 that Ethel and Bob Levitt ended their marriage after their half-year separation. As the marriage started to shipwreck, tongues wagged, yet once again Ethel received little vitriol from the columnists, and her cordial relationships with them, and with Sullivan and Kilgallen in particular, paid off. Kilgallen referred to the newly single Ethel as "Broadway's most enthusiastic mother" and described her running, one Saturday morning at nine o'clock in "casual dress, bandana'd and bobby pinned," across Grand Central to meet Bobby and Little Ethel on the train, returning from a vacation with their father in Colorado.[1] Both parents were doing their best to shepherd the children through a difficult period.

Though at heart a homebody, Ethel was free to enjoy Manhattan's social scene now that she and Levitt had split, and that she did. The recent success of *Madam* had widened her social circle, and new friends joined old friends and family to look after the newly solo Ethel; "love to *one* and all," critic Robert Garland wrote in a note subtly acknowledging the transition.[2]

The Duke and Duchess of Windsor were especially intent on keeping Merman occupied; they'd always adored her company. It was the Windsors who introduced Ethel to investment banker Charlie Cushing, whom she dated—uncharacteristically acknowledging that relationship in her second autobiography. The two were spotted at El Morocco and other hot nightclubs. The millionaire Cushing hosted big parties for Ethel and her friends, whether to fete Celeste Holm's birthday, honor the Duke and Duchess, or mark other events. Guests included future *Gypsy* figures Rosalind Russell, Freddie Brisson, and Gypsy Rose Lee, along with Sid Caesar and Ethel's frequent party companion, protégé Russell Nype. Sparing no expense, Cushing provided hundred-dollar bottles of perfume as party favors at one bon voyage party for the Windsors in May 1951.[3]

During the early part of the year, Ethel resumed her romance with Sherman Billingsley, though they remained extremely discreet. One telegram, for instance, invites her to a Stork Club event "on behalf of Walter [Annenberg]," another of Ethel's escorts.[4] Like Cushing, Billingsley showed his appreciation by throwing pricey parties at his Stork Club for Ethel and her friends in show business, such as Ginger Rogers and Joan Crawford. (Crawford was Ethel's favorite actress when she was a young stenographer; now Crawford was sending Ethel fan letters joking about their "mutual admiration society.") During Crawford's party, Ethel went to the stage, where she mouthed the words to "You're Just in Love." Behind her was impersonator-comic Mary Healy, who, along with husband Peter Lind Hayes, was making the rounds of New York clubs and parties, sending up the Merman-Nype duo to peals of laughter in a skit called "Call Me Merman, Starring Ethel Madam."[5] (Berlin's song was so popular at the time that other singers, such as Pearl Bailey, were featuring it in their nightclub acts as well.)

Ethel remained the apple of New York's eye. In the spring of 1951, tickets for *Call Me Madam* were booking six months to a year in advance; in May, a journalist reminded readers that when *Annie Get Your Gun* opened in 1946, "we declared May 16 Merman Day, in perpetuity"[6] and that it was high time to renew the proposal. Musicals were as popular with critics as they were with audiences; ticket sales for *Guys and Dolls, The King and I, A Tree Grows in Brooklyn,* and *South Pacific* were as brisk as *Madam*'s. Ethel was acquiring new fans every day; a young comic named Jerry Lewis was sending telegrams on her birthday or whenever he and his wife took in her show; Judy Garland, Ethel's favorite young singer, was a frequent companion and coperformer at events around town. (It was Garland who reopened the famous Palace Theatre in December 1951 for the first live show there in eighteen years.) Noncelebrity fans continued to stack up, and Merman saved poignant messages from many of them—from parents whose ill children she had cheered up and from a man who'd appreciated a visit she'd made to a military hospital where he was recovering from war wounds. For many fans, Ethel Merman had evolved from being a personality that ordinary young girls could emulate into a star who came down to visit from on high.

In July 1951, when Russell Nype took temporary leave from *Madam* to pursue work in Hollywood, receipts took a small plunge. But the bigger news that month was when Merman announced a pending deal with 20th Century–Fox for her to star in the filmed version of *Call Me Madam,* reprising for the first time in Hollywood her lead role on the boards.[7] Even better, it would actually come to pass.

In just a couple of months, though, something happened that would change her life even more than filming *Call Me Madam.* On October 20, 1951, producer Leland Hayward threw a lavish dinner party at L'Aiglon to celebrate the one-year anniversary of *Madam,* which had now grossed over $2.7 million. One of the guests was Robert Foreman Six, a charismatic Denver business executive whom Hayward had met while serving in the army in World War II. Six would become Ethel Merman's third husband, the man who inspired her to leave the Broadway stage and New York for over five years.

Robert Six

Large-framed and tall, Six cut an imposing figure. His face was long and rugged, almost horselike. Just a year younger than Ethel, Six had made aviation history by single-handedly presiding over Continental Airways, a company he'd founded in 1937, a time when only 1 percent of the nation's population had ever taken a commercial flight.[8] Along the way, Six repeatedly defied rules of the trade with an almost uncanny ability to suss out future trends, anticipating three-class service, the importance of an all-jet fleet, decent food, "no-frills flights," and the financial potential of Asian routes. He surrounded himself with knowledgeable advisers, demanding and receiving loyalty in abundance. And by running his comparatively small company efficiently, he defied the odds and held a profit against larger airlines, such as TWA, Pan Am, and United, companies with much larger budgets, more planes, and more lucrative routes. (Throughout the '50s, Continental operated with just four jets. Six kept them in the air almost continuously, maintaining them at night rather than wasting daytime hours, to maximize profit.) Entirely driven about his work, Six was notoriously hands-on, famous for surprise visits on flights, which would terrify crew members if he found the smallest detail not to his liking. Once, a martini served with both a lemon slice and an olive provoked an outburst: passengers should choose one or the other, not be offered both—too expensive.

Although the scrapbooks contain scores of photos of Merman and Six together during the early and mid-'50s, one taken about fifteen years later shows the man at his best. He is in his sixties, surveying his ranch with guest John Wayne, cowboy hats and all, the two resembling each other like uncanny mirror images.

Indeed, Bob Six was the iconic westerner. An adept barbecuer and an avid fisherman and hunter, he stocked his home and office with gun collections and formed the "Six Guns" fast-drawing club with some close colleagues from work. The Six Guns actually participated in regional competitions, and once Six even took part in a duel, to the understandable anxiety of his mates. The archetypal self-made man, Six had dropped out of high school and risen to the top through hard work, shrewd skills, and sheer moxie. In a way, Six was the business world's male counterpart to what the public took Ethel Merman to be: brash, talented, supremely self-confident, and obsessive about his work. Unlike Ethel, though, Six was gruff, moody, and volatile, and colleagues attested that his language was as foul as his temper, which could take dark, violent turns. He was a difficult man to stand up to, impossible to intimidate.

If there ever was a man's man, Six was it. He could be awkward around women—again, think John Wayne—but had a magnetic personality that for some women could be very seductive. And while he was too distracted by work to be reckless in that regard, by the time he met Ethel, Six had been around the block. He'd been married once, to Pfizer pharmaceutical heiress Henriette Erhart Ruggles, for some ten years. Evidently, his preoccupation with work was more than the marriage, or Henriette, could bear. Six had broken from his parents early on, leaving them while still in his teens, and when they died, he did not attend their funerals. Six knew he was hardly predisposed to being a family man and never claimed to be great around kids. He never became a father himself, although Henriette had two children from a prior marriage; they met an awful fate, perishing in a house fire that happened one evening. (Miraculously, the children's nursemaid got out alive.) The event traumatized the young Mrs. Six, and the gruesome tale would be heard again well after that marriage was over.

In contrast to Merman, whose relationships with politicians were for the most part social, pleasant, polite, and mutually appreciative, Six, a businessman in a cutthroat industry whose policies, practices, and routes were determined by government agencies, had to be more closely entwined with them, able to balance hardball negotiations with smooth relationships. A registered Democrat, he felt a special kinship with LBJ, the larger-than-life Texas maverick who, just like Six, was legendary for his gruffness, sharp tongue, and deep appreciation of loyalty. But Bob Six got along well with members of both political parties, favoring whichever policy makers helped his business.

Between his high-flying business profile and the contacts made through Merman, Six had easy access to influential politicians of all stripes: President

Eisenhower invited the two of them to attend the launching of the first nuclear submarine, the USS *Nautilus,* on January 21, 1954, in Groton, Connecticut, when even people who'd developed the sub were kept off the list.[9] These were the kinds of connections that over the 1960s would help Six acquire several lucrative government business deals.

During that decade, Continental created a spin-off company called Air Micronesia ("Air Mike"), which flew routes within Southeast Asia, an area that had long fascinated Six. The government awarded Air Mike and Continental Military Air Transport contracts involving military loads between Guam, Majuro, and Okinawa for tasks that were deliberately undefined. With Kennedy insiders like Pierre Salinger, Bob Six was in on the formation of Continental Construction, a corporate venture—a Halliburton of its time, as Bob Levitt Jr. describes it—that prospered enormously from the carnage of America's war with Vietnam. "It was war profiteering plain and simple," Levitt says.[10]

Even before Vietnam, Six had politics that would hardly square with progressive sensibilities. Before his days with Continental, the young man drove delivery trucks for the *San Francisco Chronicle,* and when a general strike was called, Six "earned a gold medal from the *Chronicle* for driving his truck through rock-throwing picket lines."[11]

Back at the *Call Me Madam* party in October 1951, Six was enjoying himself. Separated from Henriette, he had arrived with a date—just a friend, he said—and quickly spent time with others. Six and Ethel hit it off immediately, chatting for most of the evening; she would write, "He takes an interest in my work. He doesn't expect anything out of it. He's just interested in me and in what happens to me. . . . I simply adore the guy."[12] Opting to leave for quieter grounds at the Hamburger Heaven, they brought along Ethel's escort, a last-minute replacement for Charlie Cushing, who fell asleep while the Broadway star and the airline executive talked the night away.

In contrast to Bob Levitt, Bob Six was well aware of who Ethel Merman was before he met her. While in New York on business, he had taken in *Red, Hot and Blue! DuBarry Was a Lady, Annie Get Your Gun,* and now *Madam.* He was not intimidated by her success; in fact, he was drawn to it; and unlike the introspective Levitt, Six enjoyed basking in the limelight of celebrity. Says Six's biographer, Robert Serling, "Bob never would have married [Ethel] if she hadn't been a glamorous entertainment personality—show business fascinated him and she was absolute tops in that field."[13]

Six phoned Ethel often after that first night, and the two started seeing each other during his weekly visits to New York. "Something serious is going to come of this," said Ethel.[14] She tried to be discreet about the affair, but the secret was hard to protect. "Ethel Merman's current dinner escort is Continental Airlines biggie Bob Six of Denver. Such muscles!" Walter Winchell gushed in the first published report on November 5, 1951.[15] After that, the proverbial dam burst, and papers were filled with the couple's nightclubbing activities.

Ethel's Return to Hollywood

It had been nearly fifteen years since 20th Century–Fox had elected not to renew Merman's film contract. Now, with *Call Me Madam*'s record-breaking ticket sales on Broadway, Lindsay and Crouse's strong script, Berlin's score, and, of course, Merman's take-charge performance, they opened the doors.

On June 11, 1952, Fox acquired the rights for $250,000 of which $100,000 was for the book. A good negotiator, Irving Berlin received as much as composer and publisher as Lindsay and Crouse did combined. He also won the following: "Credit will be given to Irving Berlin on a separate frame, on which no other name shall appear and with exposure long enough to be conveniently read by the average audience."[16] (The film is actually introduced as *Irving Berlin's Call Me Madam,* which remains its official release title.) Even more astonishing, the first shot of the movie commenced with Berlin's tunes, not the studio's musical fanfare that typically opened 20th Century–Fox movies.

Fox regular Walter Lang (1896–1972), the able director of films such as *The Little Princess, State Fair, With a Song in My Heart, The King and I,* and *Week-End in Havana,* was signed on. Lang had a great eye and was a natural at musicals and other visually spectacular genres. New York–born Sol C. Siegel (1903–82) produced. Siegel's extensive career in Hollywood included cofounding Republic Studios, where he worked for six years as producer and executive producer.[17] (He helped get John Wayne cast as the lead of *Stagecoach.*) Siegel left Republic in 1940 and began producing for his own unit at Paramount, where he stayed before starting his position at Fox as producer–associate producer in early January 1947 at a salary of $156,000. His production credits there included *I Was a Male War Bride, Gentlemen Prefer Blondes,* and *Three Coins in the Fountain.* In the '50s, Siegel served as president of the Screen Producers Guild.

Although Fox was counting on casting Merman from the start, it was Russian-born, British-trained George Sanders (1906–72) who was secured first, as Cosmo. This was an entirely new role for Sanders; he usually depicted world-weary villains with a brooding edge. (This was the actor whose suicide note said, "I was bored," after all.) He had played one of the title character's lovers in Hitchcock's 1940 film *Rebecca* and the sardonic Addison De Witt in *All about Eve* (1950). Off-screen, he had gone on record declaring women "little beasts."[18] Happily, none of these brooding, misogynistic features surfaced in *Call Me Madam*—a musical was a "women's genre," after all—in which Sanders was mainly called on to exude the charm of old Europe, and that he did. Sanders was able to give his character the formal, debonair style needed to contrast his role with Ethel's outgoing, relaxed Sally Adams. Sanders also had his first opportunity to sing in film—the musically trained performer had a pleasant baritone—and spoke in a generic, unplaceable Euro accent that might have been drawn from his Slavic roots.

Sanders received $60,000 in a contract dated January 4, 1951–November 21, 1952. At the time, his track record in Hollywood was better than Merman's (who nonetheless received $125,000), but he had no experience in musicals and was not going to be the one carrying the picture. Besides Ethel, the only other person reprising a role from the Broadway production was Lilia Skala, who played the Archduchess of Lichtenburg, getting very little screen time.

To Ethel's dismay, Russell Nype lost the role of Kenneth. Nype just wasn't an established name, especially to West Coast executives, who in addition were looking for an actor who could dance. They decided on rising star Donald O'Connor, fresh from the success of *Singin' in the Rain* (1952) for $75,000. Fox had to borrow him from MGM, where delays pushed back his start date for *Madam* nearly a month, to August 11, 1952. When wasp-waisted dancer Vera-Ellen was cast as Princess Marie—Kenneth's partner in the secondary young romantic couple—casting was set. Because of these decisions, the movie was free to feature dancing much more than the play had.

Vera-Ellen had crossed paths with Merman before, as a chorus member in *Panama Hattie*. Zanuck had her in mind to play Maria from the start, and choreographer Robert Alton was delighted to work with her. (They'd worked together before.) Alton and Merman's working relationship went back to *Anything Goes* and *DuBarry;* he had been approached to stage the dances for *Call Me Madam* before the job went to Robbins. Alton was a top choreographer in musical theater and film, and many feel that his short career has been unjustly eclipsed by Robbins, De Mille, Fosse, Gene Kelly, and others. (Alton died in 1957 at the age of fifty-one.) His Hollywood credits include *Showboat, Easter Parade, Annie Get Your Gun, Broadway Rhythm,* and *The Barkleys of Broadway.* Alton was versatile, as adept at staging romantic duos as group scenes, which he could choreograph with dazzling degrees of activity, balance, and color. His work with *Call Me Madam* contributed greatly to its success.[19]

The last time Ethel Merman had lived in Los Angeles was 1938, but now, in the summer of 1952, she was finally back in Hollywood, going between her favorite hotel (the Beverly Hills) and a home she rented during the film's production. Her language to the press balances candor about her previous experiences out west and care in maintaining an upbeat, professional tone about her new project there:

> When I was here before I had to step back in favor of people who were established in the films. At 20th during *Alexander's Ragtime Band,* Alice Faye was the reigning star of the lot in musicals. . . . The best I could hope for was a featured role in a picture, singing spots, but I wasn't in a position to carry a film.
>
> I resolved then that my next trip to the Coast would be on a different basis. It would be in some story specially designed for me, with which I was definitely identified, and that would also be right for me in pictures.
>
> The perfect format has been reached, I feel, in *Call Me Madam.* It was written for me on the stage, became an established and very personal sort of success.[20]

LA hosted no shortage of New York talent that summer: Mike Todd, Robert Sherwood, Howard Dietz, Dorothy and Herb Fields, among others. Ethel's kids ("I call them Little Bit and Stinker")[21] spent days swimming with a young Liza Minnelli at the home of Sidney Luft and Judy Garland. Her July and August evenings were filled with parties, and Louella Parsons commented, "The hit Broadway's darling, Ethel Merman, has made it in Hollywood just being herself—which is really swell."[22] Ethel mingled with studio heads (Louis B. Mayer), prominent businessmen (Conrad Hilton), and stars at one party;[23] at another, hosted by the Screen Producers Guild honoring Mayer; and at several by actress and Hearst partner Marion Davies, whose guest lists ran as high as five hundred. On October 2, Davies transformed three rooms in her mansion to resemble New York's Stork Club, El Morocco, and 21. Ethel enjoyed visiting other celebrities, among them new parents Lauren Bacall and Humphrey Bogart.

July 28, 1952, was a warm summer day when Ethel first reported for work at Fox's studio on 10201 West Pico Boulevard. Her first task was to record songs for *Madam*. As was typical for musicals, the show's songs were prerecorded, and actors later lip-synched to their own vocals. (Vera-Ellen's vocals in the film were dubbed.) Shooting wasn't scheduled to begin until close to September.

The local press learned quickly that Merman's voice made for good copy: "Ethel had only started song rehearsals at the studio when she got a phone call from friend Robert E. Sherwood, working at the studio on the screenplay of *The Man on a Tight Rope*. 'Sure glad you're with us,' said Robert E., explaining that his office was only a few hundred yards from her rehearsal stage. 'And Ethel, I know you'll be happy to learn,' he said, 'that you're coming in fine.'"[24] Said *Variety*, "Studio microphones will be fitted with 'ear muffs' when brassy-voiced Ethel Merman begins recordings today for 20th-Fox's *Call Me Madam*. Decibel-stacked delivery of singer star necessitates use of special baffles to protect the mikes."[25]

The studio gave her the dressing room of Betty Grable, who was under suspension at the time, and Merman decorated it in a Victorian theme; she told reporters she had filled it with "beautiful antiques," joking that she hoped not to be confused with them, "because I haven't been here for so long."[26]

Press and crew were impressed by Merman's professionalism on the set, and Walter Lang especially enjoyed working with her. "She's a real trouper," he said, lauding her hard work and lack of moodiness.[27] O'Connor said much the same: "She has a great deal of warmth. . . . She's herself off the screen with many of the qualities which you would expect her to [have] on the screen or on the stage but at the same time, it is a human functioning person. She's real, she's nice," he added, implying "unlike other performers."[28] "She works hard. She is never late," summed up a reporter. "She will argue with a director about a piece of business until she understands it and it is successful. Then she loves the director forever. She is a perfectionist, but having achieved what she wants, she relaxes and enjoys it."[29] Sol Siegel remembered that the star became "fidgety between takes, having little to do compared with the split second activity required when working on stage,"[30] all the more understandable, given that she was forced into more inactivity than most of her costars. Merman's elaborate gowns required that between takes she had to prop herself on a board placed at a seventy-five degree angle to keep from wrinkling them. (Duplicates had been made so that she always looked fresh.) It is hard to imagine someone with her energy in such a position, but Hollywood would again require this of her in her next picture.

Madam's daily rushes did not interest Merman, who still didn't enjoy watching herself, obviously unable to follow Tyrone Power's advice to consider it someone else's work. Part of this derives from Ethel's shyness or modesty and perhaps her fundamental pragmatism as well: once she was done and the calls were out of her hands, Ethel didn't waste energy worrying about them.

The shooting schedule went along without great incident. No falls or hurt ankles, as there had been in *Happy Landing*. At the end of October, though, low-risk Merman—who hadn't missed a single performance of *Call Me Madam* on Broadway—missed a few days of work because of flu; but generally, her usual high-octane energy was uncompromised. ("High Ethyl," the press punned.) In October she did a benefit for the Shriners, scribbling on the program, "It was really something! I had been asked to appear as representing The 20th Century–Fox Studio and could not very well turn it down."[31]

There was a lot of activity at Fox studios during the filming of *Call Me Madam*, with many other projects in or nearing production. The studio was planning to shoot nine pictures by the end of September 1952 (which would break its own production record),[32] and the pace and kinds of projects being developed might have been too much for Sol Siegel, the producer of several simultaneous projects.[33] On September 13 he stepped down as executive producer of the studio's musicals unit, he explained to *Variety*, to avoid being typecast as a musicals producer and because financial pressures for musicals were simply growing too intense. The budget per picture now pushed two million dollars, and with that came the special pressures such budgets entail. It's unclear how confident Siegel really was about the future of musical comedies; he expressed concern that "musicals don't do well overseas," with the exception of those with "universal talents, like Danny Kaye or Esther Williams."[34] These remarks indicate the extent of the stakes his studio was putting into *Madam*.

From Stage to Screen

The main task of screenwriter Arthur Sheekman was to reduce the play's running time of over two and a half hours to under two, and he was able to streamline the book without sacrificing its spirit, for instance, by telescoping the developing affection between Kenneth and Marie while adding several dance scenes. The book stayed much the same, retaining its gags ("You do not strike me as a cold woman, Sally." "Oh, I'm not. I've got a woolen sweater.") and the joke about being investigated. Sheekman, incidentally, had worked as a writer on *Kid Millions*.

On Broadway, Sally Adams had been a Democrat. Hollywood was more concerned about selling a product to the entire country and demurred from assigning particular political affiliations to its characters, even though Sally Adams was appointed by a Democratic president. The story was depoliticized in other ways as well, going from giving Lichtenburg a coalition government (shades of the Marshall Plan) to making it a monarchist nation that supported democratic elections. Kenneth's expertise (a Harvard degree in international relations) and his plans to modernize and industrialize Lichtenburg by turning a waterfall into a power plant were dropped, as was Kenneth's social stature: in the play, he had landed the job with Mrs. Adams because he was the son of a senator; in the movie, he is a self-made journalist, peddling the image of self-made men over that of political insiders.

As soon as Sheekman produced his first working script in March 1952,[35] Zanuck expressed concern over its political satire and its many tongue-in-cheek moments. He agitated for something less edgy and was particularly concerned about giving the story, especially the romance between Sally and Cosmo, credibility: "We should root for them to get together." He urged the writer to give a "little more depth" to their scenes together: "I feel that she now shrugs off too easily her loss of Cosmo" before their final reunion.[36]

Zanuck had worked on plenty of musicals, but he preferred films with strong story lines, driven by compelling, interesting characters. He was most at home with social issue films that lent themselves to credible character psychology and clear motivation, features at odds with most musicals. In an April 2, 1952, conference on *Call Me Madam*'s first treatment, for instance, he expressed trepidation about "chorus numbers": "I think it is wrong to have secretaries, reporters, tourists, singing."[37] In short, Zanuck was more interested in personality over spectacle. That he could make a musical at all, especially one as fantastically set as *Call Me Madam,* is something of a marvel, especially since he said he wanted "no great splendor . . . or grand scale."[38]

Two songs were deleted from the Broadway show, "Once upon a Time" (sung by Kenneth) and "They Like Ike" (sung by three U.S. senators). The latter was not only too sectarian but too actively political with its afterlife as Eisenhower's presidential campaign song. Berlin added two in their stead, "What Chance Have I with Love?" and "The International Rag." Neither was new: "What Chance?" had appeared in *Louisiana Purchase* (1940), and "The International Rag" had been composed in 1913 for Sophie Tucker. Audiences didn't seem to mind the recycling, if they noticed it at all. Certainly the final film allowed knowing viewers other traces of Berlin, providing a glimpse of him in his photo that appears on sheet music held by Marie/Vera-Ellen during "It's a Lovely Day." (The in-joke went even further when Kenneth tells her that the song was a hit in a Broadway show a few years back.)

The picture's big budget enabled it to depict Lichtenburg as an even more lavish, quaint place than the play had, a fictive meeting ground of Monaco, Luxembourg, and Switzerland. Filled with tradition, royalty, and not one but two love stories triumphing over national and cultural differences, it offered a fairy-tale world steeped in the myths of high Europeanness with which Sally's Americana was contrasted. True, her dresses weren't lowbrow "American" like those of Panama Hattie or Annie Oakley, but her mannerisms were, and her dialogue and songs were filled with references to a whirring American economy and up-to-date way of life. Both play and film play the tension for laughs in scenes with Sally's chargé d'affaires, whom she calls "Fancy pants," contrasting Ethel's down-to-earth, tough persona with Maxwell's upper-class, more feminized European one. The contrast also informs the scenes between Sally and Cosmo, though to more poignant effect.

In many ways, it is impossible to tell where Ethel Merman's public persona ends and Sally Adams's begins. Her Americanness is established through a variety of means: like a good Jewish mother, she promises to deliver some chicken soup to the archduke for what ails him (a weakened economy); she has to defend herself against the advances of political officials (with her comment about a sweater); et cetera. Like the play, the film capitalized not just on Ethel playing an American abroad but also on Ethel being a *New Yorker* out of her element, comparing the size of Lichtenburg with Brooklyn. And when she is told on first arriving in the duchy that she is to be presented at the palace that night, she says, "The Palace? Who's playing there?"[39]

Like a Rodgers and Hammerstein show or even previous Merman vehicles such as *Girl Crazy,* assimilation was an important theme in *Call Me Madam;* here, however, Americanness is *exported* to the economically vanquished postwar European "colonies," and Sally Adams is its ambassador: "You are the most American American I've ever met," George Sanders tells her, and she thanks him for the "best compliment" she's ever had. Sally's infatuation with Cosmo dramatically literalizes the notion of winning hearts and minds, something that had occurred onstage, but now, in a film that would appear all across the country, the stakes were higher. Moreover, in the few years since the story's Broadway run, the Cold War had intensified, and the United States, an isolationist country to begin with, was even more suspicious of foreigners.

Partly to show off the movie's Technicolor technology, Irene Sharaff's costumes were vibrant and colorful, less subdued than Mainbocher's had been. (The studio's Charles LeMaire also worked on their designs but had to waive his credit, "Wardrobe direction by," in order for Fox to procure Sharaff's services.)[40] Sharaff (1910–93) had a long, distinguished career both on Broadway and in Hollywood. She excelled at gowns for dance sequences; it was Sharaff who created Gertrude Lawrence's full-skirted gown for the stage production of *The King and I* and Deborah Kerr's in the film. Like Mainbocher's in New York, Sharaff's work gave Merman a dignified glamour, though here too it is sent up once when Sally takes up her "supertrain" between her legs to move about the room more easily.

In *Madam,* Ethel's outfits have a glamour missing in other film roles; their very colors show a "new Merm, more subdued and elegant." Stateside, her character is clad in black dresses, with diamond jewelry and tastefully placed sparkles in her hair. In Lichtenburg—where most of the movie takes place— she wears pastels: two pink gowns, one pale blue, a gold-colored dress, and the pale silver lamé "Super Chief." Such care was given to her look that, at the end, when Cosmo bestows Lichtenburg's ribbon on Sally, its deep pink is an exact match of her lipstick.

When a reporter asked Merman how she looked on-screen in Technicolor, she pointed to house cinematographer Leon Shamroy (1901–74) and said, "Ask him!" When he responded, "She looks great and will surprise everyone," she laughed and said, "I could take that for a dirty crack!"[41] Ethel loved Shamroy's work; his lighting made her look radiant, and she insisted on his services in the forthcoming *There's No Business Like Show Business.* Shamroy had an impressive track record in musical and other spectacle pictures, working on *South Pacific, The Girl Can't Help It, The Robe, Love Is a Many Splendored Thing, Daddy Long Legs, The King and I, Porgy and Bess, Cleopatra, The Agony and the Ecstasy,* and others. "[Ethel] attributes much of her success in Hollywood to Leon, she's very quick to say so," said Lou Irwin. "She feels that Shamroy is a very knowing cinematographer, that he paints with colors and knows what colors she looks best in. He sees that the sets are dressed with beautiful flowers which must compliment her beauty and she has very beautiful coloring, and this accentuates it. Walter Lang swears by him. He's one of the most sensitive directors in Hollywood."[42] And so the combined work of Shamroy, Lang, and Sharaff produce a very attractive Ethel. They did not try to make her look younger or steamily glamorous; she was presented as a high-society adult woman with a womanly figure to show off. (Remarked Kilgallen of her friend's appearance, "Not a day over 25 in any shot!")[43]

Censorship

Although Hollywood studios had been submitting their scripts and lyrics for the approval of the industry's self-censoring agency since 1934, it was probably Zanuck who axed the modest offenses of all the *hells* and *damns* in Lindsay and Crouse's book. ("Where the hell is Lichtenburg?" became "Hey Kenneth, where the—where IS Lichtenburg?" and "Hey boss, where the heck is Lichtenburg?") But there was distress up the chain as well: Fox received this notification: "In the lyric 'The Hostess with the Mostes' on the Ball,' we believe the following [italicized] words should be changed: 'He can come and let his hair down / Have the best time of his life / *Even bring his new affair down / Introduce her as his wife / But she mustn't leave her panties in the hall.*' "[44] When Sally was establishing her authority to her chargé d'affaires, Pemberton Maxwell (Billy De Wolfe), Lindsay and Crouse had her say, "I'm the madam and you're just one of the girls." Not surprisingly, Breen did not approve the line but remarkably accepted it when changed to the equally sexed-up "I'm the madam and you're just one of the boys."[45]

Zanuck was on guard about other items: "About the phone calls to Harry," he said in a script meeting, "please watch this carefully. We don't want to be in the position of poking fun of an ex-President of the U.S." Also axed was a discussion about potatoes and powdered eggs (as a form of foreign aid), which he dropped so as not to appear to be ridiculing the Marshall Plan.[46]

A check-off sheet was required for each of the film's characters. Foreign nationals had to be cataloged as either "sympathetic" or "unsympathetic." (Cosmo received an "indifferent" rating.) The procedure was not unique to Fox, or to musicals, and reflects conflicting mandates. Cold War fever required that foreigners, even fictional ones, not be depicted too sympathetically, yet the concern about profits abroad could not permit foreign characters to be too unsympathetic. Other items that had to be checked were scenes depicting drunkenness, violence, gambling, courtrooms, prayers, oaths, divorces, weddings, adultery, illicit sex, and illegitimacy.

Costumes had to be cleared ahead of time before a film was okayed, and Fox was told: "The greatest possible care [is needed] in the selection and photographing of the dresses and costumes for your women. The Production Code makes it mandatory that the intimate parts of the body—specifically, the breasts of women—be fully covered at all times. Any compromise with this regulation will compel us to withhold approval of your picture."[47] Usually a studio submitted 8½×11 still photos of actors in each of their outfits. Ethel's dresses—largely gowns or light formal wear—feature a lot of exposed chest. But not to worry—a nearly invisible flesh-colored net was sewn into garments to cover any excess skin or cleavage that might have sexed up the proceedings too much.

News Reports

While *Call Me Madam* was in production, entertainment columnists noted other milestones. In September, Broadway lost Gertrude Lawrence, the incomparable talent who had been appearing in *The King and I*—and teaching a weekly drama class at Columbia University—while gravely ill with hepatitis. Ethel sent her condolences and saved the thank-you card from Richard Aldrich, annotating it, "This is Gertrude Lawrence's husband."

Outside the entertainment world but included in the scrapbooks was a letter from Tennessee senator Estes Kefauver, who spearheaded a crackdown on organized crime in the early 1950s and then went after purveyors of images that were purportedly pornographic. The letter thanked Ethel for her note commending him on his work—one of the few scrapbook clippings that ventures into explicitly political terrain.

Ethel pasted in the usual misreports, such as one from Mike Connolly, the *Hollywood Reporter*'s "Rambling Reporter," who said Merman was dating Alan Campbell, Dorothy Parker's ex.[48] Other Merman escorts in the gossip sheets included Charles Cushing and James Polk; as late as December 6, after *Call Me Madam*'s shooting had finished and Ethel was back in New York, a photo shows her with her "escort Cesar Romero," sharing her faux lover with Joan Crawford.[49] Ethel was a "single girl again after her recent divorce," ran the story, and here, even the most reliable Merman columnists such as Sullivan and Kilgallen were off the mark.

The more accurate reports asked when wedding bells would ring for Ethel and Bob Six. "Airlines president Bob Six, whom Ethel Merman is supposed to marry, just put $10,000 into a bachelor apartment which, his friends say, isn't big enough even to hold Ethel's voice."[50] In truth, they were planning to wed as soon as his divorce from Henriette was final, but between Ethel's inborn discretion and Six's marital status (along with his strange insistence on keeping their union secret after he and Merman actually married in a civil ceremony), we can see why Ethel might have encouraged false reports of other romantic partners. Part of it was to keep the press off her back, part to keep Bob Six happy.

When the West Coast press wasn't speculating on Ethel's marital status, it was marveling about the possibility of her staying in town for a while. This, after all, was the "first time she's not got something lined up back in New York,"[51] and her new colleagues seemed eager for her to make her mark there:

> La Merman received her first fan letter since she started the film *Call Me Madam* at Fox. It was a glowing note her next-door neighbor at the Beverly Hills Hotel slipped under her door after overhearing the musical sound track. The neighbor happened to be Rosemary Clooney. . . . "Dear Miss Merman— I have a confession to make before I leave town—I'm just down the hall from you, and I'm afraid I've been guilty of eavesdropping whenever you play your wonderful sound tracts *[sic]*. I just wanted you to know how much I enjoyed them and how anxious I am to see your picture."[52]

The report was not a publicity stunt; Merman sent Clooney's note to Pop to save in the scrapbook.

End of Production

Shooting wrapped near Thanksgiving, and Ethel told the press she was tired and looking forward to taking a break with her children. Within four days, she was booked to go back to New York, and George "Rosie" Rosenberg, Merman's film agent at the time, threw a going away party for her at Romanoff's Crown Room. Sitting with Ethel and Bob Six at the first table were Fox heavyweights Zanuck, Siegel, Lang, Pauley, and their wives, and a solo Bing Crosby, recently widowed from wife Dixie.

With *Call Me Madam* now in postproduction, Merman took advantage of life back in New York. An early event was a huge party thrown by Elsa Maxwell—another "hostess with the mostes'"—to honor Mary Martin for her success in *South Pacific.* Merman was one of hundreds of stars in attendance. Radie Harris noticed that Ethel's ten-pound weight loss for her recent film "doubled her dynamism,"[53] and other columnists were noting how low-cut many of Merman's evening dresses now were. Ethel was pleased with her figure and was justifiably feeling more "womanly" and sexually attractive than either the media or her career had allowed her to be before. And then there were the attentions of Bob Six, whose frequent visits to New York she was happy to accommodate.

Advertisements of the time also showed a softer, more glamorous woman. A special color magazine ad featured "Ethel Merman, famous star of radio, stage and screen," posing with monogrammed green luggage and wearing a sharp business suit, gloves, and her own famous charm bracelet.[54] The worldly elegance of Sally Adams helped companies pitch their products, even as Ethel continued to promote more down-home products such as Knickerbocker beer, Carling's Ale, and—on a page with lyrics from "Can You Use Any Money Today?"—Macy's clothing purchased with the store's cash-installment plan.

Ethel was allowed to be glamorous and classy in a way she hadn't been for nearly twenty years. Lydia Lane's syndicated "Hollywood Beauty" column, while not pretending Merman was a pinup (it starts with "she offers a word of cheer to every girl who doesn't like what she sees in the mirror"), features Ethel sprinkling advice with references to her upcoming film: "If you have something on the ball . . . and you develop your individuality, you don't have to be beautiful. The less beautiful a person is the more important it is to stress other things. I don't think regularity of features means much. You can't just sit and stare at a pretty face without soon getting bored. Beauty has to be accompanied with something else." What compliment does she get the most? "I think it's about my hands being graceful and expressive," at which point Ethel shows her nails and gives readers manicuring tips. The article moves on to a discussion about makeup in general, giving tips that were rarely solicited from stars her age.[55]

Even her outlook and vitality were tied to beauty and health. Asked where her energy came from, she replied, "People are always asking me that. . . . I think part of it comes because I'm happy in what I'm doing. Boredom and fatigue go together, you know. But I also believe that diet has a lot to do with it. I love raw meat—I can eat it by the pound. . . . And I find tea quite a stimulant. During a show when I drink 8 or 9 cups of tea in my dressing room, I find I don't get tired." Worrying, she said, is what makes people tired. "When I go home, I leave the show with all its problems behind me."[56]

Ethel spent Christmas 1952 in New York with family and then left for a vacation in Palm Beach. Walter Lang had a big bottle of Bollinger champagne delivered to her there to celebrate New Year's Eve, which she feted at a party hosted by Jayne and Charles Wrightsman, joining guests Joseph, Jack, and

Bob Kennedy and members of the Detroit Ford family. The Duchess of Windsor had invited Ethel to perform at a charity ball on January 5 at the Waldorf-Astoria to benefit war veterans, which Ethel canceled when a cold kept her down in Florida.

The big event that month for Ethel, like for many Americans, was the inauguration of war hero Dwight Eisenhower, the first Republican president since Herbert Hoover. His election was settled back in November, when Ethel was still working on the film, but once she was free she became an active part of the plans for the January 19 pre-inaugural festivities. (Eisenhower declined to attend, announcing that he wouldn't be making any public Washington appearances before being sworn in on the 20th.) *Variety* published the event's confirmed list: "Merman, Lily Pons, Edgar Bergen, Fred Waring and his Pennsylvanians, Helen Hayes, Hoagy, Walter Pidgeon, Menjou, Jeanette MacDonald, Gaxton, Allan Jones, et al."[57] Ethel's first place on the list indicates how bright her star was shining at the time.

Bob Six accompanied Ethel to Washington on a special flight of the Continental flagship, along with Colorado governor Thornton and other state officials. The inaugural ball, where Ethel performed "There's No Business Like Show Business," proved one of the most lavish of the century and was broadcast on television. In all there were five bands, a thousand military aircraft flying overhead, a parade, and a second ball to handle overflow from the main one at Georgetown's National Armory. (Earl Wilson grumbled the next day that "It was all just too big.")[58] As for Merman's performance, "Ethel could have even made the Democrats happy."[59]

With *Call Me Madam* behind them, Irving Berlin and Leland Hayward now acquired rights to Cleveland Amory's *The Last Resorts: A Portrait of American Society at Play.* They wanted Merman to agree to the project, which they would set in Palm Beach, but it seems that she was too busy *being* in Palm Beach to consider it, and by March, papers announced she was turning it down to pursue nontheatrical ventures: "You get no time to go off and have a vacation on Broadway," she said. "But gee! You do one or two pictures a year in Hollywood, and the rest of the time you can have a life of your own."[60] Over the following years, she'd be using that line more and more, and press reports would appear: "Merman won't do a Broadway show. She's tired, Hollywood is less work," but one variation that appeared was significant: "Also, she would like to have time for a honeymoon."[61] Ethel was denying her actual March marriage with Six well into the spring, and it wasn't until June that Walter Winchell spilled the beans, claiming in his column that "someone in Colorado" had beaten Ethel Merman to announcing her own wedding.

After February, when the soundtrack was cut, 20th Century–Fox prepared *Call Me Madam* for release and put its publicity machines in gear. The whirring was especially loud in New York, where on March 2 there was an advance screening at Fox's home office on 56th Street, followed by a party at which Irving Berlin gave Ethel a big kiss for the cameras, and they happily hammed it up with a rendition of "You're Just in Love."[62]

The official premiere was in Los Angeles, where the Miracle Mile Fox Ritz Theater charged a whopping two dollars per seat and took advance reservations. Ethel stayed in New York, and it is unclear why she wasn't in LA for the opening night gala. (Of the four leads, only Donald O'Connor attended.) The Zanucks and other West Coast glitterati were present, though, as were plenty of fans. "Most of the fans were women, from 10 to 70 years old. . . . Screams of delight rang out when favorite stars stepped from their big limos."[63] Joan Crawford, Cesar Romero, Janet Leigh and Tony Curtis, Dinah Shore, Dorothy Lamour, Clifton Webb, Mitzi Gaynor and Hugh O'Brian, Farley Granger, Louella Parsons. That first week, *Call Me Madam* broke records, grossing $15,900, surpassing industry estimates of $13,000, which itself would have been strong business.[64]

As Ed Sullivan reported, "For the first time in her spasmodic movie career, Miss Merman . . . is the 'take-charge femme.'"[65] And Cole Porter told Ethel that this was the first movie in which they allowed her to be herself successfully. This was the consensus, and it was easy to see why Ethel was telling the press, even in New York, that she preferred the film version to the play. The movie, she said, provided "broader and more authentic background" and reached broader audiences. But one thing wasn't changed from the stage: *Madam*'s highlight remained the duet "You're [Just] in Love." Read one telegram she received soon after it opened: "Dear Ethel, as per our promise, my daughter and I will be singing the duet from *Call Me Madam* Thursday night, on my television show, and if you don't listen to it, I will never buy any of your records again. Love, Groucho."[66]

On March 12, Ethel flew with Six to Miami for the opening there at three different theaters at eight, nine, and ten P.M., going from one to the next. The city honored her with a parade that included a 150-piece drum and bugle corps and an official welcome with keys to Coral Gables. She stayed in Miami Beach at the Kenilworth Hotel.

Ethel and Pop saved all these items, along with all of the movie's reviews— and even theatrical playing times—highlighting the positive reviews in red crayon. In general, *Madam* was well, if not enthusiastically, received, with critics consistently praising the picture's lavish production values. *Variety* called it "a literate musical, and it avoids most of the common clichés."[67] Because *Madam* was not a widescreen production—common for spectacle films at this juncture—several reviewers quipped, predictably, that the big Broadway star might have needed 3D. She and Donald O'Connor were usually singled out for praise, sometimes getting more kudos than the picture itself. Wrote Hy Gardner, "Ethel Merman, the gal with the 3-dimensional personality, makes such a lark out of the Fox tickle-colored version of *Call Me Madam* you almost get the feeling that you're watching an in-the-flesh performance. Never have we seen any actress who was so much the master of the situation so much of the time."[68]

Time magazine accurately summed up Ethel's current status in the business:

> For years, Hollywood has seemed unable to make effective use of Ethel Merman. . . . She has appeared in a number of second-rate movies (the best: the 1936 Eddie Cantor musical *Strike Me Pink;* one of the worst: the 1936 movie version of her own Broadway hit *Anything Goes*). But the moviemakers, fearing that the rowdy Merman personality was too strong for the screen, usually tried to tone it down. When she arrived at the studio to begin *Call Me Madam,* she finally had a film tailored to her dimensions. . . . [And] she was told to be herself.[69]

Call Me Madam had given Ethel a chance to transform into a glamorous, mature woman without losing any of her joie de vivre. With its tight, escapist story, bouncy score, and the vibrant Sally Adams, it seemed the perfect vehicle to "introduce" her to America's moviegoing public. Film attendance was at a historical high in the immediate postwar period (although it quickly tapered off with the rise of TV), and this picture gave Ethel what she thought was an entrée into a strong career in pictures. She became increasingly firm when she told reporters that she wanted "a life" and was not considering opportunities on Broadway. "You might say," she said with characteristic optimism, "Hollywood and me—we've discovered each other."[70] Given that she was already involved in the preproduction of *There's No Business Like Show Business,* her next musical with Fox, Merman had every reason to be confident.

Ultimately, however, *Call Me Madam* would not prove as successful as either the studio or Ethel had hoped. There were a number of reasons. Yes, it was fun, but the movie was old-fashioned, and its main stars (O'Connor aside) lacked the youthful draw audiences seemed to crave. And Ethel might not have had the kind of national star power to carry it; even in a film in which she is wonderful, she doesn't ignite the screen the way she could the stage.

Over the decades, *Call Me Madam* has aired on American television from time to time, and in 1981, it was licensed to air in Italy, Australia, and Canada. The next year, Irving Berlin negotiated 10 percent of all gross receipts "for all media other than video and the same figure for wholesale worldwide home video,"[71] but *Madam* was never released on video, and it remained effectively out of print until a DVD version was released in 2004. If its afterlife was not what she hoped for, *Call Me Madam* remains the "biggest" movie of Merman's career, and, truncated role in *Anything Goes* aside, it would be the only time she reprised one of her stage roles on the silver screen.

ELEVEN

_____

Life with Six

I don't think I've ever been happier in my life. The air is
simply wonderful; it's the mile-high city, you know. I
was in New York last week, and oh, it was terrible. The
smaze or smog or whatever you call it. You can hardly
breathe. Yes, I miss the theatre a little, but happiness is
more important.

What about doing a Broadway show?

Never again. Nobody is indispensable.

Merman to the Denver Post, *8 December 1953*

Ethel gives conflicting dates for her divorce from Levitt and Bob Six's from
Henriette. In her first autobiography, she writes, "Six got his divorce in Colorado a month before mine was filed. His divorce became final in September of 1952. We married in March 1953."[1] In her second she says, "I flew to
Mexico City on 7 June 1952, for a quickie Mexican divorce. Finding the procedure complicated, I went to Juarez, where a mutual consent decree was
granted not more than thirty minutes after the petition was filed."[2] Whatever the case, Merman and Six did indeed marry in Mexicali in a "quickie"
ceremony on March 9, 1953, which was, of course, just as quickly found out.
For all the high-flying publicity about their courtship, Six remained adamant
about keeping their actual marriage a secret, and Ethel claimed never to have
understood why. It may well have had to do with his terminating the union
with Henriette, whose fortune might have required delicate treatment. Or
there may have been taxes and other financial issues that Bob Six didn't want
to raise with his new bride.

So now Ethel Merman had remarried. The world received the news with fanfare: friends and strangers alike sent congratulatory notes, letters, and gifts, none
of which made it into her scrapbook (unusual, since letters of congratulations

from work colleagues were usually preserved). The couple honeymooned in her beloved Beverly Hills Hotel and then rented out Stewart Granger's home while she was doing *Madam*. In the meantime, Six was working on purchasing the new family home in Cherry Hills, outside Denver, Colorado.

It was soon after *Call Me Madam*'s release that Ethel Merman made the stunning announcement that she was leaving Broadway indefinitely. The superstar was now asserting the role of superwife: "My husband works out of Denver. Why should I spend my life in New York when he's all the way out here? I'll go to New York when my husband's business takes him there."[3] Ethel, Bobby, and Ethel Jr. had had plenty of time to develop a fondness for Colorado from their earlier family vacations there. New Yorkers were aghast, betting whether Ethel really meant it or not, assessing their loss, her marriage, and the probability of her returning to the boards. Colleagues who knew her rather well, such as Dorothy Fields, Cole Porter, Irving Berlin, and Jule Styne (who would soon produce a TV version of *Anything Goes* with her), were convinced by Ethel's radiant happiness, although Styne expressed a caveat: "She has no right to bow out. Deep down in her heart, no matter what she tells you, one of these days she's going to say, 'I'm going back to it.'"[4]

Of course, Ethel could no more abandon her career than she could stop breathing. She still enjoyed working, earning money, and being in the spotlight. Now she was just ready to throw her energy westward, and given the promise first shown by *Call Me Madam*, it was not an unreasonable expectation. Film and TV were easier work than the stage, and Ethel loved the idea of not being tied down for months or even years on end, in contrast to life during the run of a show, which she likened to "taking the veil." Plus, as entertainers who'd left New York behind had known since the great Depression, Hollywood products reached more people and paid much better than Broadway.

Although the movie version of *Call Me Madam* had slightly underperformed, Ethel was still able to view Hollywood as a land of opportunity, and she was as close to "hot" as she would ever be on the West Coast. She was sought after as a guest on television and radio shows with Bing Crosby, Dinah Shore, Ed Sullivan, Milton Berle, and Eddie Cantor, and, in January 1953, Leland Hayward asked her to perform in a television special that would be produced *jointly* by NBC and CBS, commemorating the fiftieth anniversary of the Ford Motor Company, the sponsor. What Hayward didn't tell her was that he was also approaching Mary Martin with the same request. It all worked out rather quickly, by today's standards, and on June 15, 1953, the show in which Merman and Martin sang their famous thirteen-minute, thirty-one-song medley went down in history. The two sat on stools in a minimally decorated set that favored neither one performer nor the other, its simplicity guiding viewers' attention to where it belonged in the first place, on the two singers. Everything about the production was carefully balanced. When a record of the special was issued, one side of the jacket front features Mary Martin on the left, with her name first, and on the other half the image is simply flipped, with Merman on the left appearing first. In 2004, a short DVD of the special came out, and Merman's side was the one that was printed, to the sure delight of her fans.

With the Denver location so convenient to Los Angeles, Ethel knew that a home base there wouldn't intrude on her family life as much as one in New York. "I do miss my Mom and Pop," she said.[5] (They were afraid to fly.) She wrote and called on a regular basis, sending postcards when she traveled or using hotel cards and stationery, circling pictures of the rooms she'd stayed in.

Merman's public learned something important about her when she moved west: Ethel Merman was not so enslaved or entranced by her Broadway successes that she was unable to walk away from the stage. To her fans she explained, "Oceans of hooey have been spilled about living up to the 'Show Must Go On' slogan. To me, that's an overplayed cliche. Show biz is no more important than any other business. In other business, there's no question about 'going on.' The work goes on in spite of toothache, heartache, and losing loved ones. There's no point of singling out show biz and making a big dramatic thing about it."[6]

Six Acres

And so Mr. and Mrs. Robert Six, Bob Levitt Jr., and Little Ethel moved to 26 Sunset Drive in the prosperous, exclusive Cherry Hills suburb less than eight miles from Denver. Their 5.8-acre lot quickly earned the nickname "Six Acres" from Little Ethel. Their home cost seventy-nine thousand dollars, a price publicized with puzzling frequency, and it had been built in 1927 in the Tudor style. It was massive—Levitt Jr. compares it more to a castle than a home, replete with a dungeon-basement. Its twenty-eight rooms included eleven bathrooms; its floor plan included two two-story wings, in between which was a large midsection that served as a living room and area for entertaining. The area featured a large fireplace and was topped off with a vaulted, wood-beamed ceiling, and adorning the house in general was plenty of hand-carved oak and stone. Ethel, along with decorator Ed Stanton, had the beige walls painted turquoise, crimson, and white and covered one of the living room windows in a bright floral print. There was a large, twelve-foot couch and, scattered around the home, five television sets. Ethel combined her small art collection of Renoirs and Monets with Six's.

Along with the Merman-Levitt family came the dreaded Miss Kopeman, the black poodle, Midnight, and Little Ethel's menagerie of small animals, including Uncle Ned and other birds, whose feathers were the worse for wear after the trip. The family was unable to move in right away, awaiting approval by the Cherry Hills Land Association, whose dozen members controlled the area's utility, water, and road facilities—and controlled the kinds of people who could "buy into" the elitist enclave.[7] On the list of undesirables were Jews, and the moment that the last name of Ethel's children came up, the association balked, and, as Bob Jr. says, "the grown-ups had to figure some way around the 'no, NO Jews' problem."[8] While appeals were made, the family lived in a nearby rented property that Ethel dubbed "Uncle Tom's Cabin" to the press because of the proprietor's name.[9] If, in the early to mid-'30s, Merman's public persona was bathed in a relaxed, even playful ethnic mix in the musical styles and performance of the time, now the realities of racist America, on whose values communities like Cherry Hills were founded, were anything *but* relaxed or playful.

The newlyweds kept their financial matters separate, just as Ethel had done with Levitt. Monthly bills were totaled up and divided between them, with Ethel paying for the children's expenses. On this front, Ethel had met her match with Six, who counted pennies every bit as much as she did. Both were prosperous businesspeople who had acquired their wealth through their own hard work, and both guarded their fortunes carefully. In all probability, Ethel was constitutionally incapable of merging finances, but her painfully scrupulous arrangement with Six would prove to be a sore spot and source of bitterness to come, emerging in her final autobiography in petty tales about her third husband's cheapness.

For the moment, however, everything was great. The Sixes threw a housewarming cocktail party on December 11, 1953. Ethel enjoyed the clear Colorado sky and the fresh start she had with a new home, a new husband, and, she hoped, a new career before the cameras. She made appearances at local events, posing with Colorado business leaders and politicians with a sharpshooting rifle, ever Annie Oakley, hosting parties—which she did not do in New York—and attending events with Six's business associates and community leaders, who were delighted to have a Broadway legend in their midst.

To the world she was now Mrs. Robert F. Six, not Miss Ethel Merman. ("Call Me Mrs. Six," ran interview titles.) This seemed the role to play for Six as well as for herself; at any rate, Merman fueled that perspective in interviews. And Bob Six's biographer, who didn't interview her, wrote that Ethel now "played ping pong with the children, cooked her husband's favorite dishes, and got involved in Six's considerable activities on behalf of the Boy Scouts. . . . She did her own shopping at a nearby supermarket, learned to garden and got to enjoy hunting and fishing in the mountains—or claimed she did."[10] Six Acres had given Ethel the opportunity to play a traditional wife who, within limits, was eager to please and let the man be the boss. She was still a woman of no small fortune, however, and so many standard domestic duties were passed along to others, and by this point, Ethel was making few public claims of being able to cook, as publicists had claimed in the 1930s.[11] Ethel never took to hunting or fishing, and her son says she never even played ping-pong with the kids. Still, Ethel thrilled to the idea of playing mom and publicly reveled in the pleasure the family's new environs brought to her children, Little Ethel in particular.

Bob Levitt Jr. calls life in the Colorado outdoors "the biggest liberation" he could have had as a boy, and, after a year and a half, Koppi went back to Germany! It seemed a delirious freedom for the young boy. "Denver gave us an escape into nature. At Six Acres, I could ride my bike wherever I wanted; there was Little League, A&W. It was a regular American life—except our house was a castle," a castle filled with proscription and prejudice.[12] Bobby's first good friend there was a Mexican boy, the son of their neighbor's chauffeur, and when the two boys were told they could no longer play together, the class and racial prejudices of the community hit home with weighted force. Many of Bobby's friends had been from tract homes in Hampton Hills, another part of town, he remembers, along with the community's rigid pecking order, which was absorbed by the children, who singled out kids from farms for the worst ridicule and abuse.

Such distasteful prejudices and violence informed the family's life there, even in Bobby's joyous "escape into nature." Although his stepfather never taught the boy to hunt, Six gave the young boy a number of guns, and Bobby would go outside on his own, in his words, to "kill helpless creatures [squirrels, rabbits, birds, other small prey] wantonly and indiscriminately."[13] It may have been freedom, but it was chaotic and unguided, filled with ruthless violence. Needless to say, the United Nations of Animals dissolved.

Little Bob and Ethel were still united against the tyranny of the adults around them, but they played separately more, with their respective groups of friends from school. Young Ethel was still passionate in her love for animals and was not favorably impressed by her stepfather's enthusiasm for hunting or for Jumbo's elaborate collection of animal heads and trophies. Bob recalls a party she threw with some of her high school friends, and one of them put a cigarette in the mouth of a huge swordfish, stuffed and mounted with lifeless glass eyes on the wall. Her stepfather, unsurprisingly, hit the roof. "Messing with Jumbo's trophies was a sneaky hand's way of disrespecting the Big Man himself, behind his back, and that cost Ethel the right to have any more parties . . . Jumbo [the brother and sister's secret nickname for their stepfather] ran a tight, no slack ship when it came to 'respect and disrespect.'"[14] Little Ethel took an almost instinctive dislike to their new stepfather and never got along with him. From the start, Bob Six did nothing to foster any closeness or relationship with his wife's children, who were never invited to call him Dad and, in fact, were instructed instead to address him as "Mr. Robert."

So although Koppi's departure and the Colorado wilderness were giving the children some newfound freedom, their domestic environment was not. The castle crackled under the repressive hand of Six, who tried to coerce the children's respect rather than earn it. To Bob, Six's parenting skills were little more than bullying, and he experienced the authoritative man as a "hypocrite."[15] The name "Jumbo" had absolutely none of the love that infused "Big" or "Big Bob," their endearing names for their own father, Bob Levitt. Quite the opposite. "The many small and wonderful, early childhood meanings of him trump the size-oriented meaning of . . . 'big.' The opposite was true of Mr. Robert. His large size, his large meanness, and his large negative impact on our hearts were, all together, the truth within our secret naming of him. Saying the name Jumbo, for my sister and I, was something akin to the way victims in his namesake movies say the name 'Dracula.'"[16]

Worse, Mom was taking Mr. Robert's side. To ensure that Little Ethel and Bobby heeded their new stepfather's authority, Ethel would scare them with "Remember what happened to the last stepchildren—only the nurse made it out alive."[17] Today he calls those words an "advisory condemnation" that contributed to the sense of the big man's threat and violence saturating their home.[18] In time, Bob's mom gave a sexual dimension to the story, making it even more strangely ominous to the young boy. When she thought he was old enough a little later, Ethel told Bobby that at the time of the incident, Six was "boffing the nurse," assuming her son would understand what that meant. He didn't.

> I had zero information about birds, bees, sex, reproduction, procreation. . . . Boffing, then, was just whatever Mr. Robert and the nurse were doing instead of saving those children, and whatever it was, it was *bad,* because I knew very well what burning up in a fire would be like, and I knew what nurses and stepfathers *should* be doing in such circumstances; they should be doing the same as firemen do, not boffing, whatever that was, and not running out of the house without the children, no matter what.[19]

On the surface, the family's routines weren't so different from ones they'd had in New York. Little Ethel and Bobby took their meals early, apart from the grownups, in the little dining room, at the kitchen countertop, or in front of the TV. Big Ethel and Six ate later, around 7:30 or 8:00, by themselves in the bedrooms with trays, or they would go out. On Sundays, the main meal was taken *en famille,* and Six would grill one of his famous steaks or hamburgers. ("He and mom ate a lot of meat, like a lot of people did at the time," recalls Bob.)[20] The children were carefully instructed to compliment Six's barbecuing. Whenever protests were registered, horrific scenes ensued, and so not wanting to cause trouble, Little Ethel and Bobby participated in the ritual while holding their tongues about Jumbo and his meals.

In February 1954, the family took a vacation to Hawaii, where they stayed at the home of Charles Boetticher. A local journalist arrived to take pictures of the newly arrived star and her family and described the entourage. First, he said, a housekeeper came to the door and told him to wait; then Bobby emerged. "He had an airplane on a string and he was swinging it around his head to make it fly," wrote the journalist. "He seemed like a normal, reasonably ornery sort of kid." After Bobby, Bob Six emerged,

> wearing shorts. . . . I got the impression the picture-taking idea was his wife's idea and he was still sort of confused by the whole thing. . . . He kept telling us to wait till she got there and then decide what to shoot. . . . Ethel Merman came out of her house with her eleven year old daughter Ethel. They were both wearing shorts. Miss Merman—or Mrs. Six—also had on a bright red blouse and earrings that look like Chinese gongs. I tried to decide how to describe her. What she looked like. I finally decided she looked like a tourist.

He took pictures of the "tourist" family, and of the boxer, fox terrier, cat, and other pets surrounding them. "Mr. Six said they came with the house. Bobbie *[sic]* immediately corrected him. '[The fox terrier] and [the cat],' he said, 'belong to the maid's daughter.' "[21]

Family life was documented again by the press in September 1954, when Edward R. Murrow televised one of his live half-hour *Person to Person* TV shows on CBS. The shooting preparations included a sixty-foot scaffold to enable transmitting the broadcast signal from Denver to New York, and mikes were placed throughout the house and on each of the family members. Everything was carefully staged in advance: audiences watched Bob Six barbecuing in a scene that prompted fans to write to question whether such large, succulent steaks were authentic. At another point Murrow was talking with Ethel about her latest album when, with her arm around Bobby, she spontaneously sang a few bars of "Boy o' Mine." But it was another moment that left its deepest impression on the underparented boy. Somehow, Levitt recalls, Murrow had heard about an owl that he had killed, and Murrow broke from the careful script to "bust" the young boy—"saying, 'No, you mustn't do that, son,' and there it was—suddenly and totally by surprise—a crystal-clear, nationally televised boundary put up in a place where I was crazy, running wild, shooting owls out of trees."[22] It took an off-site national broadcaster to give the boy desperately needed and yearned-for paternal guidance.

Overall, the picture of the Six family broadcast into American living rooms was one of domestic bliss, despite the tensions running wild under the surface. Six, for his part, didn't even enjoy interviews, regardless of his outgoing personality, though he appreciated the attention they gave Continental. Ethel, more accustomed to performances, was unfazed by such events, considering them part of her professional duties. In fictional formats, she even continued to send up the idea of domestic bliss, just as she had twenty years earlier in *We're Not Dressing,* singing "Let's Play House!" For a magazine, she wrote "Why I Would Like to Send Men to the Moon," hamming up clichéd frustrations of married life. In a TV appearance on *The Frank Sinatra Show* in 1958, she and Sinatra, who had just been paired in a shortened TV version of *Anything Goes,* depict a married couple caught unawares by a television camera doing an "at home with" interview à la Murrow. The couple they portray had been up late the night before partying, the debris of which is in evidence everywhere. The show was filled with inside jokes. When the unseen announcer asks Ethel of her decor, "Is that a Picasso?" she responds, "No, it's a painting. You see, you can always tell from the frame around them."

Ethel continued to paint her family life in bright colors. When the *New York World Telegram* asked her, "Would You Marry Your Mate—If You Had

Another Chance?" Ethel replied, "Which one? I've been married three times. My only regret is I did not marry my present husband, Robert Six, first. I feel I wasn't married until I married Bob."[23]

Autobiography I: The Dame She Was

In 1954, Merman published her life story, "That's the Kind of Dame I Am," in four installments in the *Saturday Evening Post*. They were actually written by Pete Martin, a *Post* writer who had ghosted autobiographies for Bing Crosby, Bob Hope, and other film stars. The *Post*'s Merman series was illustrated with personal and professional photographs of Ethel and her family and written in the brassy language and with the gusto people had come to expect of her: "I've sung some hard-boiled songs in my life and I've acted some hard-boiled roles, but I'm a soft-boiled gal."[24]

The *Saturday Evening Post* was a popular weekly whose wide circulation enabled it to find its way into middle-class and suburban homes all across the country. Most readers were likely to have known Ethel as a name, a voice, a celebrity image that they experienced through TV, radio, or recordings and not as a musical star experienced firsthand. Publishing the memoirs in the *Post* gave her a chance of exposure far beyond New York and might also help boost her film career too.

The month-long series of articles was excerpted from a book published by Doubleday in 1955, *Who Could Ask for Anything More?* (in the United Kingdom, *Don't Call Me Madam*). The less bawdy American title reconnected her to the Gershwin song crucial to securing her fame; it also gave an indication of how Ethel wanted her professional achievements—and present domestic life—perceived. Who *could* ask for anything more? This may well have been how she was wanting to view life at that point: there *was* much to be grateful for, even if the book's dreamy depictions of Six had little to do with the realities of living with him.

Pete Martin based *Who Could Ask for Anything More?* on taped interviews conducted with Merman, her family, friends, and associates. ("If Pete Martin hasn't interviewed you yet about Ethel Merman you're the only one he's missed," ran the *Hollywood Reporter* at one point.)[25] Ethel gave him access to photographs from her own collection, and his task was made even easier by the copious materials she and Pop had kept in the scrapbooks over the years, clippings that enabled Ethel, the book's narrator, to cite reviews, lines, and articles as if from memory.

With these materials in hand, Martin had the task of transforming remarks that Ethel's colleagues and reviewers had made about her into her own, first-person voice. Typical are lines like "There's a belief in some quarters that I am one of the symbols of Broadway"; and "Then I love something Buddy DeSylva said: 'Watching Merman in a show after she's got her lines and her songs and her stage business all set is like watching a movie after it's been filmed and edited. After that, no matter how many times you see it and hear it, it's always the same'"; and "Irving Berlin once said, 'If you write lyrics for Ethel, they better be good, for if they're bad everybody's going to hear them anyhow.' And Cole Porter said I sound like a band going by."[26]

Unfortunately, the net effect of this created a sense of name-dropping that put off more than a few reviewers, who concluded that the book's "author" was self-aggrandizing and self-absorbed: "After Ethel's book, printers must be about out of personal pronouns."[27] "It is difficult to believe that Ethel Merman, as dynamic a stage personality as Broadway has ever produced, could possibly be the dull-witted, tiresome egotist offstage that this book makes her appear to be. . . . Add to it the inclusion, in quotes, of almost every bouquet that has been thrown her way in the last 25 years and one comes up with the sum total of what is to be found in this book."[28] Thick-skinned and thorough, Ethel kept even those reviews.

To interviewees, Pete Martin often presented himself as a writer with a problem on his hands: people weren't responding enough to help him out. To the estranged Bob Levitt, he complained that his interview with Ethel's old friend Josie Traeger for information on her youth was a waste of time; to Lew Kessler he said, "Cole was a great disappointment"; and to everyone, he agonized over how to represent Ethel's fallout with Al Siegel, about which Ethel consistently remained mum. And he was especially surprised to find Ethel less forthcoming than he had hoped. "I can't get anything out of this girl; other people, like Bob Hope, just need a prompt, but you can't get her to say anything. It's not like she's uncooperative, she's. . . . but she just doesn't seem to like to talk about herself."[29] Martin might not have realized it, but his remark was on the mark: Ethel Merman was uncomfortable boasting.

Reviewers responded with the predictable stream of adjectives: *lusty, uninhibited, brash.* Some found the book rambling and disjointed; others found it refreshing. Responses were similarly mixed about Ethel's apparent lack of modesty—some admiring it, others finding it boorish—and that strange mix of attitudes appears even in the same review: "Miss Merman ain't my type of woman; she scares me. [But her book] is well worth reading."[30]

Despite its "Mermanesque" style, the voice in *Who Could Ask for Anything More?* was not at all Ethel's voice but Pete Martin's rendering of what he thought "Ethel Merman" should sound like: "I'm a dame who can take a naughty situation and make it seem as plain and natural as bread and butter. At least, I've been told that I can."[31] His autobiographies of Crosby and Hope had been written in styles appropriate to them and their public personae: Crosby's was breezy, whereas Hope's was clipped and filled with one-liners.

The process of Mermanization is clear in changes Martin made to the transcripts of his interviews. It's in the final book that Ethel says of her success, "The way it worked out, I made Cinderella look like a sob story. My role in *Girl Crazy,* when I became a success, was handed to me on a silver platter. After that, I went into George White's *Scandals* and *Take a Chance,* and both of them helped me. So the way I figure it, Cindy's tale is a downbeat one compared to mine."[32] Here is how the actual interview went:

MARTIN: Ethel, would you say you had to struggle or was it a little like Cinderella?

ETHEL: I think it was a little like Cinderella because *Girl Crazy* was given to me on a silver platter. . . . I mean that part made me overnight.[33]

This is also where Ethel identifies The Little Russia as her first singing gig (whereas she had told Martin that it was Keens English Chop House) and where she claims to like bows, frilly accessories, and so forth. The change produced the Ethel Merman that the public expected. Observed Broadway columnist Danton Walker, "La Merman's talk is as brassy as her voice, but I suspect the language is more [Pete] Martin than Merman (I've known Ethel a long, long time, and I never heard her talk like that)."[34]

It would be wrong, however, to say that Ethel was not complicit, for not only did she sign off on Martin's final work, but she also made corrections to promotional copy. "This is the story of Ethel Merman and her fabulous success on Broadway and Hollywood; as a personality in show business, and as a singer known the world over for her interruption of song." Merman corrected the typo on the document, crossing out "interruption" and inserting "interpretation." Then she added "and trumpet-like delivery" to the line, showing her awareness of what people expected of the "Merman voice."[35]

Doubleday promoted the book well, and Ethel energetically attended signings and other publicity events. A reviewer at one of the Doubleday parties expressed surprise to find a star "so courteous and considerate that she smiled and chatted with everyone who came up to her. . . . she has the rare quality of making each person feel she is particularly pleased to be talking to him."[36]

In Transition

Now that Ethel was quasi-retired from Broadway, her value as a news item began to diminish. Stories about her were being pushed into smaller corners of the page, in paragraphs that were farther down in articles like "Would You Marry Your Mate?" in which Ethel is among a long list of celebrities asked this question but, unlike the others, gets no photo and only a few lines. After all, Ethel was a theatrical star no longer working on the boards, a transplant in the West who wanted to make it in newer media and who, moreover, seemed as resistant to changing her style of performing as they were to accommodating it. Her hopes remained characteristically high, though, and her new situation gave her opportunities to travel, which she was now enjoying more. Freed from the grueling schedule of a long-run show, Ethel was pursuing career opportunities as they became available, along with the hope of achieving a seemingly normal family life. Whenever business took her or Six to New York, they stayed at the seven-room apartment they maintained at the Park Lane Hotel, then still on Park Avenue.

"Undoubtedly, Six was happy in those early years with his vivacious wife," says biographer Robert Serling,[37] and Ethel radiated contentment to her friends as well. Said Dorothy Fields: "I think she's really happy for the first time in her life. . . . He's really crazy about her, [and] she's mad about him. . . . he's not a wise guy like Bob [Levitt], and he isn't a dope like poor Bill Smith. [He's a] nice, big, easy-going guy, not too bright, but sweet and wonderful with her. And he makes her feel young and he makes her feel beautiful. . . . She's never looked so well, so thin and so young."[38]

After two or three years, however, cracks became apparent, at least to some people who knew the couple in Denver. A friend of Six claimed that Ethel was critical of some of his closest colleagues at work, all of whom he'd personally appointed, and that he didn't take kindly to having his judgment impugned. As for Six, he didn't like it when Ethel's own work took her out of town. "Six," writes Serling, "was a brooder capable of immense loneliness, need[ing] almost constant companionship as he grew older."[39] Business required him to travel a fair amount of time, even more than it did for Ethel, and this began to wear on her. As his trips became more and more prolonged, she began to grow suspicious. "Mom grew to believe that Six was using her, for her name, her money, and her connections to famous people and politicians that would be useful to his business."[40] Although Six's finances, including significant oil property investments, never really suffered during their marriage, some of Continental's worst years coincided with their years together. Whether this added to the tensions is hard to say, but it didn't stop Six from his constant search for ways to expand, increase profitability, and test new opportunities. For him, those things came first.

In that regard, Bob Six and Ethel could not have been more different. According to Bob Levitt Jr., Ethel may not have been the best mother in terms of her choices or her behavior, but she was devoted in her heart, just as she always was to her own parents. One summer, he recalls, Ethel's mom and Pop came out to visit, a welcome treat for Bobby and his sister, who were craving adult attention that was given to them at their own level. "Pop was the only grown-up who played with me there. He was kind of old, but he'd throw a baseball and we'd play catch."[41] During this visit, though, the violence that infused Six Acres erupted and showed the family members' terrorized powerlessness to it. Levitt, a young boy, watched helplessly as Gram and Pop, both in their seventies, were brutally battered by the six-foot-four-inch Bob Six. He beat them "in the library, downstairs on the ground floor of our house, in front of my mother, while I stood still on the balcony above, listening, trembling, and clutching a baseball bat that I didn't have the courage to use." The next morning, he recalls "all of us pressed into silence by the weight of *big* trouble, all of us pretending that [the] bruises were invisible" at the family's breakfast counter.[42]

In another instance, an inflamed Bob Six pulled a loaded .45 Colt on his wife, ramming it into her belly. Merman screamed at him, "Go ahead and shoot! You don't have the nerve. You'll end up in the papers." Years later, Ethel told her son that she knew Six didn't dare, if only to protect himself against the bad publicity it would give him and his airlines. As awful as it is to imagine Ethel Merman (or anyone) thrown into a chair with a husband holding a gun to her, Ethel's defiant response upholds what many consider to be the quintessential Merman, giving a defiant dare in extraordinary circumstances.

But Merman's situation with her husband was far from extraordinary, and, like the majority of abused women of the time, she kept the experience a secret. Bob Six was a powerful public figure, and many outsiders perceived his authority and influence as bigger than life and something to be admired. (One woman who scarcely knew Merman tried to convince me that by marrying him, Ethel "made it into big society. He gave her class.") And even Six's biographer believes that Six, whose hot temper he notes, could never have been capable of physical and emotional violence. For Levitt, the many strands of violence that Robert Six came to represent for him as a boy were reinforced along other lines, in and outside their home in Cherry Hills:

> The impact on us from the relentless family violence of military industrialist Bob Six was our personal share of his larger impact on American families and the people of Vietnam. Way back then, the men who orchestrated and profited from the Vietnam War were not known to my sister and I as the "patriarchs" who create and control a "military industrial complex" through waging war. We knew nothing of such complexities. But we knew very well that "Jumbo" Six and all the men like him were the kind of men who hurt people. From our children's perspective, Jumbo and his pals were fake on the outside and mean on the inside. We didn't know what to call it, and we certainly didn't know what to do about it. And neither, it seemed, did Mom.[43]

Ethel was ill-inclined to report him; this was not a historical moment where women were encouraged to make abusive marriages public. Before the women's movement, before women's shelters, there were very few social and institutional supports for women in Ethel's predicament, and spousal abuse had not yet entered the public eye as an epidemic or even a legitimate problem. And, as the lesson of Rosie the Riveter was instructing Americans, a wife in this postwar era should cede her economic and psychological autonomy to her husband (never mind working-class women who never had the *choice* of returning to unpaid work in the home). A man's status as breadwinner and king of the castle was, it seemed, irrefutable. And Six Acres did not seem like the sort of castle where challenges could be played out.

"Mom suffered male violence and covered it with a veneer appropriate to her class," says Bob Levitt today. Lower-income women may have had no choice but to show up to work in sunglasses and tell tales of falling down steps, but as a celebrity, Ethel selected the response pervasive to those in the upper class: saying nothing. Given her upbringing, the historical times, her gender, and her celebrity, it would have been most difficult for Ethel, cautious and private to begin with, to break with the tide and publicize her domestic problems.

Although her silence may have enabled her to feel like she was protected, it was a form of complicity that did nothing to dispel the toxic atmosphere of the Six-Merman household. "Mom gave her collusion its own special spin," Bob reflects. "'Just remember [what happened to Six's last stepchildren]' was just one example."[44] Despite the violence she and her family would experience in years to come, the abuse from Six was one thing Ethel never, ever discussed. "Mom referred to his stewardesses as his 'hookers'; she would be public about Six's sexual and economic abuse, but not his violence," says Bob.[45]

Even among those who knew her well, Ethel kept Six's emotional violence and threatening behavior to herself. Her parents had had firsthand experience with his temper, but Ethel obviously couldn't discuss her situation with them and restricted her confidences to the most discreet and trusted of her friends. Within that very small circle was Roger Edens. Now at MGM's prestigious Freed unit, where he'd helped develop the career of Judy Garland, Edens was but a phone call away. After the attack on Pop, Bob recalls, Ethel called Edens from Denver to tell him what happened, asking for advice, asking him not to tell anyone. And so things stayed in the family.

While class and celebrity informed Merman's silence, other postwar changes made it easy for Ethel and Six to hide their secret of family violence from view. Americans were leaving rural and urban areas in favor of suburbs, which held the lure of calm, atomized living, in self-sufficient family homes. The layout of these new suburbs reduced, if not out-and-out discouraged, casual contact with others, and there was a physical sense in which experiences—from the trivial to the life-threatening—could not be easily shared. This contrasts sharply to the kind of neighborhood in which Ethel had grown up, where residents mingled freely out of doors.

This is not to say that old neighborhoods had vanished; plenty of families still relaxed on city stoops, gossiping or keeping neighbors up to date in informal community. And clearly, the wealthier the neighborhood—like Cherry Hills—the greater the insulation. But what was changing was the mass public's idea of the "ideal" neighborhood; the suburban family-unto-itself now prevailed in the middle-class imagination and in mass culture images. It was hard to imagine a daughter's big voice heard singing throughout the neighborhood anymore. For the Levitt-Six family and others, this meant that experiences of violence could be sequestered behind family walls and walls of psychological shame. Moreover, few structures were in place to help expose Six's abuse, and Ethel was so much a product of her time that over a decade later, when the women's movement emerged (with its slogan "the personal is political") and domestic abuse entered the public arena—along with women's shelters and protective legislation—she would refuse to identify with "women's libbers." Curiously, as Tony Cointreau points out, Merman did *not* tolerate the abusive partners or marriages of her friends.[46]

Ethel's attitude emerged against the backdrop of the 1950s, a contradictory, even schizophrenic, decade as far as women were concerned. These were the sexually charged years of *Playboy* magazine, the aftershock of the Kinsey Report, of mammary madness and icons like Jayne Mansfield, Marilyn Monroe, and Jane Russell; it was also the time of "professional virgins" like Doris Day and Sandra Dee and of white wives without professional careers who maintained sanitized families on TV shows like *Father Knows Best* and *Leave It to Beaver.* Moms seemed to reign supreme. Popular press, magazines, news and medical reports all vaunted the values of domestic motherhood.

Yet this was also the period of "Momism," the invention of pop psychologist Philip Wylie, who argued that the moral fiber of American life was being eroded because the role of mothers in psychological, social, and practical matters had become too large and too influential. America, he maintained, had become obsessively subservient to a domestic function (and a sex) that had been wrongfully elevated: for him, even the country's obsession with large breasts was a sign of mommy pandering. Were it not such a hateful diatribe, his misogyny would be almost comic.

Eccentric though he was, Wylie had his pulse on a simmering resentment of women and mothers that would shape the way Ethel Merman would be understood. Although that sentiment would culminate with *Gypsy,* it is evident earlier, particularly in the growing scrutiny with which she was assessed in the '50s, both as a real mother and as a performer who depicted one.

TWELVE

There's No Business Like
Show Business

Ethel's next movie project with Fox studio was the gala *There's No Business Like Show Business,* a widescreen color musical with a six-million-dollar budget and big-name costars: Marilyn Monroe, Dan Dailey, Donald O'Connor, Mitzi Gaynor, and Johnnie Ray. Like *Alexander's Ragtime Band, There's No Business Like Show Business* was planned as a vehicle to showcase Irving Berlin's songs, lavishing attention on the movie's spectacle value and placing story and characters at the service of the numbers rather than the other way around.

There's No Business Like Show Business was Ethel's first of a two-picture deal; the second was an unspecified follow-up. Buoyed by the experience of *Call Me Madam,* she entered negotiations making tough demands, with her attorneys writing Lew Schreiber, Fox's legal counsel, to say that Merman's name must be positioned as "first costar" and that the type would be the same size as Berlin's, whose name was part of the official U.S. release title: *Irving Berlin's There's No Business Like Show Business.*

The sealing of the deal ended up becoming a family affair, with Pop notarizing the final contract between his daughter and the studio, dropping an *n* as the notary Edward Zimmerman, just as his daughter had in "Merman." Down the road, Bob Six would throw his weight around when the contracts had to be redrawn, demanding that his wife receive an official letter concerning changes, "Otherwise, she will submit a bill . . . for the expense and loss taken due to Twentieth's postponement of the picture."[1] Merman knew how to protect herself; says Eddie Cantor, "Ethel is one of the shrewdest gals in show business. She can see the small print in a contract from twenty paces."[2] Some of her concerns revolved around the fact that she was not carrying the show and would be sharing the spotlight and billing with four other "leads," of whom Marilyn Monroe was a particular concern.

Ethel's remuneration for *There's No Business Like Show Business* was $130,000, a high figure for someone with her less-than-"boffo" box office record. She insisted on being paid at a rate of a thousand dollars a week beginning March 8, during preproduction and rehearsals, rather than July 6, when actual shooting began, and even though this deviated from standard procedure, Fox agreed. She also insisted that the studio pay for her shoes, even for those in scenes taking place in "modern settings," when actors usually provided their own. And, Ethel notified the studio, "I would like a clause inserted as I contemplate an Ethel Merman enterprise from promotion of certain products under an Ethel Merman label or sticker. I do not anticipate conflict, but believe 20th Century Fox should be notified of this."[3] In addition to Six, Ethel had her LA attorney Bob Coryell and her agent, George Rosenberg, working on her behalf. It was during this time that Irving Katz joined Ethel as her New York attorney and later would become her financial adviser. Their association continued for the rest of her life.

The Story and Its Production

The story of *There's No Business Like Show Business* follows an old vaudeville family who in treatments were called the Monahans; once shooting began, they became the Donahues. Molly (Merman) and Terry (Dan Dailey) meet, marry, and within quick succession have three children—Steve, Katy, and Tim—who join their act, "The Five Donahues." The movie conveys this information economically in a near-continuous scene on a vaudeville stage with placards announcing "The Three Donahues," "The Four Donahues," "The Five Donahues," giving truncated performances of numbers, such as Berlin's 1912 "When That Midnight Choo Choo Leaves for Alabam'."

Present tense, Depression America. Vaudeville falls on hard times, and so do the Donahues. They split up their act to get by and are plagued by internal tensions. Tim (Donald O'Connor) is smitten with hatcheck girl and aspiring singer Vicky (Monroe), whom he helps out by handing over "Heat Wave," the featured number of his mother and his family. Molly resents the young, ambitious woman, believing she is not only stealing their hit but also her son. Meanwhile, two of the young Donahues, Tim and Katy, splinter off into their own group and eventually perform onstage with Vicky in New York.

Daughter Katy, the most stable character of the family, marries, happily. The male family members, by contrast, are dogged by problems. Unsure about his place in Vicky's heart, Tim takes to drinking heavily, Steve turns his back on vaudeville to become a priest, and Terry is depressed. Molly remains the dominant force in the family, particularly in keeping their show alive, and several scenes are devoted to dramatizing the extent of her maternal concerns: it is Molly who bucks up her husband, sobers up Tim, and has to deal with the effective loss of her other son to the ministry.

The low point comes one night when a drunken, hospitalized Tim has a fight with his father and takes off for parts unknown. Shaken, Terry goes off to find his son, but it is clear that he too has lost his way. Molly and Katy are left to carry on the family act, doing so in numbers in which Molly plays Tim's role with Katy ("A Sailor's Not a Sailor"). In the meantime, Katy convinces her mother that Vicky's feelings for Tim are genuine and makes sure that Molly and Vicky patch up their differences. The film ends with Molly/Ethel performing a rousing rendition of "There's No Business Like Show Business" at the Hippodrome, the 1905 New York vaudeville theater that was demolished in 1939. Terry, Tim, and Steve return, Tim in a military uniform, Steve as a military chaplain, arriving at the theater while Molly is in the middle of singing the song. When she catches sight of them in the wings, she chokes back tears to finish the song and "go on with the show." Everyone makes peace, and the six leads walk down a lavish staircase to close the show with the rest of the song.

The production team was a virtual repeat of *Call Me Madam*. Walter Lang directed, Leon Shamroy was cinematographer. Publicly Merman expressed her delight; privately, she refused to do the picture if Lang and Shamroy were *not* involved. Sol Siegel again produced, although from the start he found it less compelling than *Madam*, telling Zanuck of his "dislike of the material" on first receipt.[4] Writing duties were assigned to Lamar Trotti (1900–1952), whose work included stories and screenplays for movies as diverse as *Young Mr. Lincoln, The Oxbow Incident, The Razor's Edge, Cheaper by the Dozen, With a Song in My Heart,* and *My Blue Heaven.* Work on the story was under way in 1952 while *Call Me Madam* was in postproduction.

No sooner had preproduction begun than serious setbacks intervened. One involved Walter Lang, who in June 1953, a month after his contract began, was rushed to the hospital with a perforated ulcer. Ensuing complications, including pneumonia and several infections, were so grave that for a while, the director was not expected to live. Understandably nervous about postponing such a big picture for more than six months but aware of the great skill and stability Lang brought to it, Fox's Frank Ferguson eventually declared, "It is a project which only Walter Lang can bring off with any degree of satisfaction."[5] Lang pulled through, but the production schedule was set back nearly a year, to the spring of 1954.

The second tragedy involved screenwriter Trotti, who had begun work on the project by December 1951. After a six-month leave from the studio, in August 1952, Trotti died unexpectedly. When he passed, the basic story was in place (Trotti retained the final credit "story by"), but secondary plots, characters, and relationships would be altered substantially. Fox gave the assignment to I. A. L. Diamond *(Love Nest, Monkey Business,* and later, *Some Like It Hot* and *The Apartment),* but Zanuck's concern quickly mounted about Diamond's ability to produce the "combination of comedy and pathos" that he wanted, and he soon replaced him with Phoebe and Henry Ephron (parents of Nora). They were not excited. Phoebe said, "I won't go to see it, why should I write it?"[6] But the Ephrons stayed on.

Trotti had sketched out the story: "Here is the sort of family we are thinking about . . . a 'Royal Family' of Show Biz. They are not Barrymores, but they are people who, for two, three or even four generations, have been in the business, who know nothing else. They are Irish. They are a fighting, sentimental, humorous, lovable and loving group of people."[7] The mother would be "a Thelma Ritter type, the central figure who holds the family together." Dad would be a "hoofer," Danny, the eldest son would be "a Dan Dailey type"; daughter Betty (later, Katy) a "Betty Grable type"; the younger son would be a "Donald O'Connor type, in love with Mitzi Gaynor" (in the role that eventually went to Marilyn Monroe), to whom he is ready to give his sister Betty's spot. Betty would be hooked up with an outsider, a famous dancer named Al Garbey (a "Fred Astaire type"), a partner who would bring Betty to new career heights.

One of the challenges faced from the start was how to repackage Irving Berlin's songs, some of which were close to half a century old. Although *Alexander's Ragtime Band* had been a bit of a musical throwback, *There's No Business Like Show Business* was even more so: set in the past, with few attempts to update the material, as *Alexander* had done by turning ragtime numbers into swing. In the final picture, the only exceptions to this were Monroe's numbers, which were set in a jazzy present. After *Alexander,* Hollywood had released other Berlin tributes, such as *White Christmas* and *Easter Parade,* but there was no denying that the postwar music scene was in transition. Slightly blind to this new arena—or defiant of it—the studio was planning to open the picture with chestnuts like "Alexander's Ragtime Band," a flashback of the family singing "Mandy," or a minstrel act they performed "in Uncle Tom costumes."

Although blackface was part of vaudeville during its heyday, by the early to mid-1950s, it was no longer a mainstay of American popular entertainment and was in dubious taste in these early days of civil rights, which Zanuck openly supported. For Merman, fresh from her triumph in reopening the National Theatre in Washington, doing blackface would have added an odd new layer to the racial and ethnic associations that already swirled around her image. (The ethnic and class associations of Molly already marked a return to Ethel's pre-*Madam* persona.) Although the blackface finally did not come to pass, the minstrel act stayed in draft after draft of the film's screenplay, used variously to establish Molly and Terry's first meeting, their wedding ("And so they were married," Berlin was to voice-over, "the dancing teacher and the minstrel man"),[8] or the birth of their first child ("while playing 'Uncle Tom's Cabin,' Molly, playing Eliza, goes into labor").[9] Even the Donahue children were written into the blackface act, with "Mandy." The scenes continued after the Ephrons came onboard, and it wasn't until late May 1954—very late in the game—that the detail was dropped. No explanation was recorded.

Berlin was paid four hundred thousand dollars for the picture and was required to prepare only six new songs; the rest would come from existing material. (Once again, he tried to use "Mr. Monotony," but to Ethel's relief, it didn't make it in.) A few attempts were made to update his music. Said Zanuck about the songs scheduled in one script version: "I would like to eliminate Scene 124 on page 88, which is a repeat of the number we used in *Alexander's Ragtime Band*.[10] I think we would be criticized. . . . It is too well remembered from *Alexander's Ragtime Band* . . . and we must not do anything that will take away from the musical punch at the end of our picture."[11]

In the final film, "Alexander's Ragtime Band" is performed midway through by combinations of the Donahues, each combination with the costumes, backdrops, accents, dance, and musical styles evocative of different nations and cultures. Katy performs a jazzy version, sprinkled with pidgin French; O'Connor, a Scottish version; Ray, a rock-gospel version; and Mom and Dad do a kitschy Swiss-German rendition in lederhosen and braids, "*Commen Sie hier! Commen Sie hier!*" For some reason, producer Sol Siegel liked doing the song that way: "[To] stress its international appeal, it will be done partly in a middle Europa accent. The whole number now becomes a new number since it is a showcase and in truth has become an international jazz piece since it was written 43 years ago."[12]

Other changes included dropping a long, overwrought subplot in which Tim enlists and goes to battle in Europe, where he is killed. The family arrive, and Steve, now a military chaplain, blesses Tim's remains as they perform "There's No Business" for the soldiers at the finale. The military story in Europe was deemed too expensive and dropped. Zanuck's instincts might also have told him that in 1952, an era of perceived peacefulness in the United States, it was time to move beyond reminders of the recent high costs of patriotism. In the final picture, Tim enlists, but all of the military activity occurs off-screen; he is the family's "black sheep" not because of military ambitions but because of a drinking problem—showing that the 1950s social-problem film was trumping the patriotic one of the '40s.

Initially, there were opposing ideas about the kind of musical that *There's No Business Like Show Business* should be. Zanuck said, "We should avoid so-called elaborate production numbers, mainly because they have worn out their usefulness and audiences are becoming sick of them. We should only use production numbers where they are *essential* in the telling of our story [and the aim of the music should be for] realism and personality effect rather than scope and size."[13] (Trotti's brief treatment, on the other hand, planned on twenty-five to thirty production numbers!)[14] Zanuck was most concerned about building up to a big finale that packed an emotional punch: "Almost every great musical has contained an emotional last act. The really great musicals make you cry: *Show Boat, Alexander's Ragtime Band,* etc. I believe our new last act can top them all and that we can emerge with a four star picture as well as a 'four handkerchief' picture."[15]

Siegel disagreed. "I have always felt that in a story of this kind, the basic story . . . is not the prime consideration. . . . The title *There's No Business Like Show Business* gives the promise of great entertainment and in a sense sounds like it ought to be 'the greatest show on earth' of musicals. [A better story] might help . . . but the musical and entertainment content ought to far outbalance the story values."[16] As the script was being written, Siegel complained that there was "more story than we need." It was his intervention that excised a number of complex "twists and turns," producing, in the end, a tighter story.[17]

Despite the similarities between the production teams on *There's No Business Like Show Business* and *Madam,* the studio did *not* perceive the new picture as a star vehicle for Ethel Merman. Siegel, Zanuck, and others were at pains to divide the leading roles evenly and to balance the two older stars with the younger ones. "It is not a solo picture for anyone," Zanuck told Berlin, adding, to Ethel's certain horror if she'd ever known, "Like *Call Me Madam,* it will have five or six roles of almost equal importance."[18]

Ethel was not even on the producers' minds when the project got under way. Berlin, a champion for her if there ever was one, initially proposed box office stars Betty Grable and Fred Astaire for the leads,[19] and as late as December 1952, no less than Zanuck himself was envisioning Fox contract player Jane Wyman as Molly. Other players in his "ideal cast" were Robert Wagner as Tim, Johnnie Ray as Steve ("we will have to convince him"), and "Mitzi Gaynor or June Haver" as Katy.[20] Zanuck liked Dan Dailey for Terence and O'Connor for the "Fred Astaire role" as Katy's love interest. Eventually, O'Connor landed the role of Tim, Katy's brother, so that angle was changed. No stranger to vaudeville, O'Connor had been a child star in his own family act. And he had actually played a similar role on film before, in a 1944 Universal picture about a fictional vaudeville family called *The Merry Monahans,* necessitating Fox's transformation of the Monahans into the Donahues for *There's No Business Like Show Business.*

Ethel was onboard by late February 1953. Siegel worked to "keep her alive even in scenes in which she is not the dominant personality. I want to borrow the character of Minnie, the Marx Brothers' mother. She was the business agent and the brains of the combination,"[21] not a far cry from Merman's stage image either, but again one that eschewed the glamour of Sally Adams. Siegel was also writing the Denver resident independently, requesting photos of her Broadway shows to give him "costuming ideas."[22]

Mitzi Gaynor, who played daughter Katy, was born Frances Gerber.[23] Fox changed her name on the basis of the popularity of Janet Gaynor. Level-headed, well-adjusted, and talented, Mitzi Gaynor was a trained dancer, gifted with a great body and good skills at light comedy. Studio publicity talked up the young star as a "stripper without removing clothes," and, as Oscar Levant said of her, "There's nothing wrong with being an exhibitionist if you've got something to exhibit."[24] In addition to her sexiness, Gaynor exuded a wholesome sparkle that easily carried over to her public persona. She had a private life that was without scandal, marrying Jack Bean in 1954, and ever since has been able to give the press views on being a good homemaker and maintaining a successful marriage. Gaynor's ability to combine unneurotic wholesomeness and sex appeal served her well when she reprised Mary Martin's role in filming *South Pacific.*

Popular singer Johnnie Ray was fresh off his huge 1951–52 successes with "Cry" and "Little White Cloud That Cried," songs that fused the music of country ballads, gospel, and rock and roll. An emotionally intense performer nicknamed "the Prince of Wails," Ray would contort his face and weep while he sang. At the time of *There's No Business Like Show Business,* Ray was freshly divorced. He was also a closeted gay man, which makes his "coming out" to his parents in the film as a man of religion interesting, since both Molly and Terry had earlier been worried about Steve's lack of interest in women: "It's like he's a poet or something," says Molly. (Even when Steve was a child, the Father of the children's school talks about him as studious and contemplative, whereas Tim, by contrast, is "all boy.") Ray was not to everyone's tastes, but among young middle-class teenagers, "bobby soxers," he was insanely popular. Girls would whip themselves into a frenzy when Ray removed the mike from its stand to deliver one of his overwrought performances. Older women were not necessarily immune, either; Tallulah Bankhead was so smitten that one night she left a Manhattan club in the wee hours of the morning to search him out.

Zanuck was certain Ray would give the film some needed appeal to younger audiences. Lang was less convinced, writing Ethel from his recovery bed: "J. Ray would play the priest but I am secretly hoping that something happens where we won't have to use him at all. However, he might be good in that part since I understand he is something of a religious fanatic."[25] Ray had a nasal speaking voice and a weak, rather awkward presence when not singing, and in the final picture, he rarely looks comfortable.

Marilyn Monroe was added late in the game. Initially, O'Connor's love interest had been written with Gaynor in mind in a pairing that would have been easily convincing. But once Fox settled on Gaynor as his sister, the role of the girlfriend opened up for Monroe—or someone like her—and things changed. The first reference to Monroe actually appears in the January 1953 draft: "Tim is having himself a time with a curvaceous Mona Dawn star, a Marilyn Monroe of the 1930s."[26] Different tales relate how Monroe finally won the part. One attributes the choice to Berlin, who had seen a photograph of her at the home of Fox executive and fellow New Yorker Joe Schenck. Berlin's biographer writes, "He was seized with the inspiration that just as Merman had personified the thirties in *Alexander's Ragtime Band* . . . Monroe could enliven this cavalcade and bring it into the spirit of the fifties. He insisted that Schenck call Monroe, even though it was two in the morning."[27] Monroe, however, was not even remotely interested and accepted the part only after Zanuck offered her the lead in Billy Wilder's upcoming sex comedy, *The Seven Year Itch*. (Like Merman, Monroe shines less brightly without a solo spotlight. And like Merman, she knew it.)

Once Marilyn was signed on, the writers toned down the role of Tim's girlfriend. Before, she had undergone various permutations that all added up to the same thing: a floozy. Initially, she was the punningly named "Mona

Dawn," then a hard-boiled "Peggy," and then "Lilly Sawyer," a woman who had been "married three times and divorced once"—so Molly wouldn't need to worry if Tim proposed to her, according to the script.[28] Her final incarnation was as the sexy and ambitious, but ultimately harmless and wholesome, singer, Vicky Parker.

Costumes were by the beloved and respected Broadway and Hollywood talent Miles White, whose credits included Broadway's original productions of *Gentlemen Prefer Blondes* and *Pal Joey*. Ethel adored his work, and the two developed a cordial relationship; Monroe, on the other hand, refused to be outfitted by him, bringing in (William) Travilla to do her outfits. White did everyone else's. The behind-the-scenes battle is actually referenced in the movie, when Vicky refuses to wear a fourteen-hundred-dollar purple dress that had been designed for her.

Rounding out the talent was Bob Alton, also retained from *Call Me Madam*. Zanuck had considered assigning Jack Cole as choreographer but preferred Alton, "because there must be a nostalgic quality to the numbers and there must be nothing that looks too very sophisticated or that resembles 'fantasy.'"[29] *There's No Business Like Show Business* was one of the last jobs Alton did in his career, which was cut short by his early death. Ethel had worked with Jack Cole on *Something for the Boys*. Monroe had just completed *Gentlemen Prefer Blondes* with him, and once again she was emphatic: she would not work with Robert Alton on *There's No Business Like Show Business*, persuading Fox to procure Jack Cole to choreograph her numbers only, giving her work an entirely different feel from everyone else's.

Production started in the spring of 1954. Although the film had been hurt by Lang's medical problems and Trotti's death—not to mention the writers' and Sol Siegel's lack of conviction—the actual production went smoothly. Ethel wrote in her memoirs that there was "little emotional stress and strain involved in working in a Walter Lang picture—you're surrounded by people you like."[30] Only a few complications came into play: Gaynor sprained her ankle and couldn't dance for several days. Ethel had to take time off to "stave off an appendectomy."[31] (Fresh from doing *Person to Person* with her, Edward Murrow sent roses.) O'Connor—who had been so ill on *White Christmas* that producers replaced him at the last minute with Danny Kaye—missed only a few days' work.

Then there was Marilyn Monroe, whose "difficult" behavior on set was already legendary. On this project, she did not endear herself to colleagues, keeping to herself and complaining openly about being paired with O'Connor, whose small frame and youthful looks, she claimed, "would make people think I was his mother." (Monroe was a year younger than he.) In "Lazy," a number she performs with O'Connor and Gaynor, Monroe defied directions to do it barefoot, insisting on high heels that made her tower over her male costar.

Decades later, Gaynor said, "[Marilyn] didn't seem to be aware of the rest of us." She went on to describe what happened before one of her lunches with Ethel: "One day we asked [Marilyn] if she'd have lunch with us. She said, 'No, I'm going to have lunch off the lot.' She seemed very moody and depressed. When she came back after lunch she was smiling and friendly and said, 'Hi!' to everybody. Ethel said, 'Girl, do you know what happened? Why, she went home and had *lunch* with Joe!'"[32] Thirty years later, in Bob Thomas's biography on Merman, Gaynor said that those naughty stories were how she "managed" Ethel's growing impatience with Monroe. "I found a way to keep Ethel cool. . . . Whenever Marilyn wouldn't come out of her dressing room, I gave Ethel a wink, hinting that something naughty was going on in there. Of course that wasn't true, but if Ethel thought maybe some hanky-panky was going on, she could enjoy the situation."[33]

The press circulated endless reports about the young star: Marilyn was collapsing on the set, was not showing up, was not releasing her phone number to the studio. Her husband at the time, baseball legend Joe DiMaggio, had to accompany her, both to quell rumors of their spatting and to lend her moral support. When he posed in photos with Ethel on the set, one gossip columnist speculated that he had been more eager to come and watch her, not his wife.[34] Monroe's moods swerved from one extreme to the other. Some days she was garrulous and charming, but most of the time she kept to herself. Merman and Gaynor eventually gave up asking her to lunch.

Reports flew that Monroe was too fragile, too tough, too combative, too scared. Apparently she was at once too cold and too hot for the crew to handle. (Nonessential personnel were sent away when some of her dance numbers were filmed.) Such was the press that wanted to keep Marilyn Monroe as the too-much-for-mere-mortals icon she had already been made into. Unsurprisingly, lines in the final movie serve up that Monroe to audiences: When Tim meets Vicky at the hatcheck room where the aspiring singer works, she speaks in heavily studied elocution, and he jokes, "Once again, more from the chest." Then, "Tell me, what's a girl with such pear-shaped tones doing checking hats?" (Censors warned that that line "should not be delivered in such a way as to indicate that the pear shaped tones are her breasts.")[35]

The Dress That Broke the Censor's Back

Even though Hollywood's Production Code was losing its teeth in the 1950s, Fox still submitted material to the Breen office for approval during early stages of film production. This included lyrics to Berlin's new numbers, "After You Get What You Want You Don't Want It," "Lazy," and "A Man Chases a Girl," to be sung by Monroe, along with "Heat Wave," the 1931 number whose lyrics had been changed for Ethel's rendition of it in *Alexander's Ragtime Band,* when thermometers peaked from the waving of a woman's *feet,* not her seat.

Religion proved a dicier issue. As Steve, Johnnie Ray celebrates his departure for religious studies by performing a rock-gospel ballad, "If You Believe," a number ideally suited to his performance style. The subsequent ordination scene generated a barrage of letters back and forth between Breen's office and the studio, and Fox brought in a Catholic authority to supervise the scene for accurate and respectful treatment. Lines had to be changed, particularly when Steve tells his parents that he's leaving the act to become a cardinal. Terry's response was modified from "The only Cardinal I want in this family is one that plays ball with St. Louis!" to "the only Cardinal I *expected* to see."

There were other concerns. "As we interpret it, the character of Geoffrey [the designer with whom Vicky spats] would appear to be suggestive of a pansy. We are sure you realize we cannot approve a characterization of this kind."[36] (This was hardly the only gay moment in the picture, just one that they caught.)[37]

One of the most ironic battles in the filming of *There's No Business Like Show Business* involved Merman and Marilyn, but probably neither of them knew anything about it. In April and May 1954, Fox submitted photographs of their planned costumes for the approval of the censorship board. The board approved a chorus girl's outfit that consisted of a sequined bra, exposed midriff, and high heels, as well as an outfit for Vicky (for "After You Get . . ."), a risqué form-fitting flesh-colored dress with design work strategically placed at the tips of the breasts. Gathered satin material was placed at the hips to cover some of that area, although it didn't hide the skirt's slit to the upper thigh. The studio's caption: "The cloth of the garment which fully covers Miss Monroe's torso under the net is a heavy flesh colored crepe which is in no sense transparent."[38] Approval was not a problem.

A glossy of Merman posing in a matronly but dazzling "black evening gown, feather skirt" was also submitted. Responded Breen's office, "While this photograph itself does not indicate any unacceptable exposure of the lady's body, the costume is one that could possibly become troublesome. . . . We therefore respectfully urge that you handle the photographing of the costume with the possibility in mind that it could result in unacceptable breast exposure which we would be unable to approve in the finished picture."[39] Only in Hollywood could Marilyn Monroe be passed for approval but Ethel Merman be deemed indecent.

Shining Star

Although Merman is not as central to the movie's story as she was to *Madam's*, she is almost as commanding a presence. Part of this is due to what she *doesn't* do well, relinquishing the spotlight, and in that regard she is every bit Marilyn's match. In her numbers with Dan Dailey ("Midnight Train," the kitsched-up "Alexander's Ragtime Band") and with Mitzi Gaynor ("A Sailor's Not a Sailor . . ."), Merman injects a firm comic touch, and their upbeat, in-your-face energy is a study in contrasts with Monroe, who performs as if on drugs, with "Lazy" accentuating her languorous style. (She performs the piece reclining on a couch.) Since *There's No Business Like Show Business* is about show business, most of the numbers are very stagey, and the cast, especially Merman and Dailey, were directed to ham it up, just as they might have done in their early stage careers. That energy and sense of fun are contagious; one film viewer wrote that it's the "old timers" like Merman and Dailey who always "mop up the proceedings" in '50s musicals like this.[40] Theater historian John Clum takes a different view:

> The film offers one of the weirdest smorgasbords of performing styles of any fifties musical. . . . The camera avoids close-ups—this is a Cinemascope movie—which benefits Merman. She can perform as if she were on stage. The dialogue scenes are another matter. Merman has a veteran stage performer's habit of looking straight ahead when listening or talking to another character. . . . With Merman's indifferent but loud line delivery, Monroe's offbeat delivery with her eyes moving back and forth as if she thought someone would pull a gun on her, and Johnnie Ray's spacy, smiley acting . . . combined with the chronic perkiness of O'Connor and Gaynor, this is a camp classic.[41]

Camp or not, Ethel radiates when performing "There's No Business Like Show Business" at the finale. (Ironically, it was not the studio's first choice of numbers; "God Bless America" had been.) It was, of course, Merman's anthem as much as Berlin's, and in this way she lays claim to the entire picture, and it is one of her best performances captured on film. She is completely on voice, sustaining notes without sliding off pitch, performing with vocal force and clarity, considerable chest depth, and control. Most striking, however, is the emotional depth of the performance, and what she creates is more than her usual vitality and spirit, for she is also able to convey the sadness that usually lurks behind the task of "going on with the show." ("There is no such a thing as the *show* must go on, but *you* have to go on," as Roger Edens said.)[42] Ethel channels the loss Molly experiences as a mother, doing so with a song that normally does not lend itself to pathos. We catch the choked-up joy Molly feels when her eye catches her lost son and husband in the wings. Molly/Merman doesn't miss a beat, but it is hard for the audience not to, if only for a moment. It is a shining example of Merman performing while vocalizing, and her work here as both vocalist *and* actor gives a hint of the power she would bring to her role in *Gypsy* five years later.

While the film was being shot during the spring of 1954, Bobby and Ethel Jr. visited their mother when they could get away from school. But what to do over the summer? The estranged Bob Sr. stepped in. A confirmed Manhattanite, Levitt rented a house north of the city in Rye, New York, so that Ethel and Bobby could spend the warm summer months with him. Ethel knew that this was a sacrifice and appreciated it, joking that Levitt "refused to move any farther up than Seventieth Street. . . . so leasing a house as far north as Rye was like renting a sod cottage on the tundra to him; it was quite a gesture."[43]

While his mother was working on the film, Bobby was often on the *No Business* set or, more frequently, playing on the studio's *Prince Valiant* set, replete with an old castle, where he enjoyed brandishing his cherished sword about. But another place on the Fox lot left memories infused with the realities of an adult world. The studio's barbershop was where men gathered, watched TV, chatted, and hung out. This was all happening in a period Lillian Hellman later immortalized as "scoundrel time," during which Senator Joseph McCarthy was hunting down Communists in Hollywood, the military, and finally, the U.S. Congress. Levitt recalls that whenever the HUAC proceedings appeared on the black-and-white screen in that barbershop, the room would go deadly quiet. "I was too young to know what was going on, but I sensed a chill in the air that was palpable."[44]

The film brought out a cool competitiveness between Merman and Monroe behind and in front of the cameras. Merman's scrupulous attention to billing had been in place before Monroe came onboard, but once she was signed, Merman's vigilance was sharpened by the competition Monroe posed; audiences were crazy for the blond bombshell, and everybody knew it, including Ethel's friends. When *There's No Business Like Show Business* was in release, a friend jokingly sent Ethel a snapshot of a billboard ad for it in Madrid, where Monroe's large face was dead center; Merman's, but one of the floating satellites off to her side. Stateside, Ethel's attorneys stayed on high alert, looking for breaches of contract; in one ad, they complained, "The name of Marilyn Monroe precedes the name of Ethel Merman," and Berlin's font is bigger than hers, registering their protest to the studio.[45]

"Heat Wave"

Merman and Monroe's onstage antagonism was propelled by several plot contrivances, which had Molly "losing" her son to Vicky and also had Merman losing her big act, "Heat Wave," to Monroe. That number is what best encapsulates the gulf between the two divas.

Sol Siegel boasted that "Heat Wave" was the "hottest thing that Berlin has written in exotic music." Initially Siegel wanted to use it in a dance sequence with Tim, O'Connor's character, and in the first draft continuity, Tim was to perform it with Gaynor's character, but no sooner had Siegel proposed O'Connor than he took him off: "Let Merman do 'Heat Wave,' which is a perfect song for her."[46] Indeed it was, as people had noted with her performance of it in *Alexander's Ragtime Band* fifteen years earlier.

In *There's No Business Like Show Business,* "Heat Wave" was still supposed to be her number, a chance for Molly to solo in the family act. When the Donahues are booked at the Tropical Room in a Florida nightclub, Molly hums the song while unpacking what the script calls her "brilliantly colored Cuban costume" and taking a couple of spirited rumba steps with the dress as her partner.[47] (Tim quips: "If the number doesn't go, we can always eat the act.") We hear "Heat Wave" from a second source in the background, and as Tim leaves, we learn quickly that the band playing the number was rehearsing it not for the Donahues but for Vicky, who is rehearsing with them in the room. Alarmed, Tim tells her that that's his family's big number, and she pouts, "But Heat Wave's *my* big number too, I have boys working for me and everything. [sullen, softer] But of course, *you're* the headliner." And so Tim gives it to Vicky/Marilyn.

Siegel's remarks about the exoticism of "Heat Wave" are hardly confined to the song. Before we even hear it, it's aligned with the Tropical Room, with colorful, edible costumes, and the like. And in her rendition of it, Marilyn, who may have been the whitest and blondest bombshell ever, carries on as if she were tropical heat itself. Overall, the sensuality here is painted in wild, almost comic ethnic strokes. Monroe performs on a darkened set that's illuminated by hot pink and red colors, and several abstract forms suggest burning tree trunks in a steamy, primitive environment that seems to be partly in flames. Vicky/Marilyn arrives onstage in a Flintstone-like vehicle carried by four shirtless, sweating men of color. When the Anglo goddess steps out, she calls out, "Pablo, Chico," before launching into the number.

Her costume is pure sex: a two-piece outfit consisting of a black bra and a ruffled black, white, and hot pink skirt, which is split up the middle to expose the full length of Monroe's legs, much like a two-piece sun or bathing suit with skirt panels attached. She is also wearing a big tropical hat and large droop earrings.

Said Merman later of the choreography, "Alton had had her whole number laid out. . . . he had . . . four guys slappin' the tom-toms for Marilyn, but she didn't like it. . . . she 'wanted more movement in it.' " And so in came Jack Cole, who knew how to mix exotic styles and jazzy, sensual movement.

> Storywise, Alton didn't want her dancing to be *that* broad. . . . if her dancing got a little too sexy with the bumps and grinds the audience would think (and it would be natural for Dan and me as Donald's parent to think it too), *This is not the girl for our boy.* After all, Dan and Donald and I were supposed to be a real, down-to-earth, good American vaudeville family, so for the picture's sake Alton didn't want her dance to be too sultry. But Marilyn wanted it the other way, and at that point the studio was doing its goldarnedest to keep her happy. Oh well.[48]

Merman is not off the mark. Cole's erotic, jazz choreography makes the number seem to emerge from a completely different world from the rest of the picture.

Monroe's "Heat Wave" retains and exaggerates the calypso rhythms the song always had, highlighting them through conga drums marking the beat. The song's performance history had always given it additional "Caribbean" overtones, starting with Ethel Waters, who was outfitted in bright "island" colors. But she sang the song without any attempt to exoticize it, and her voice—with its putatively "Anglo" enunciation—helped strip the number of the clichés of color. Fast-forward to the Ethel Merman version in *Alexander's Ragtime Band,* a performance that seemed to rise only then to efface any Caribbean or African-American component of the song. In *There's No Business Like Show Business,* however, "Heat Wave" morphs into something new altogether. In contrast to the earlier versions, Monroe sings in the first person, referring to "I," not "she," as the woman who started a heat wave, as if Marilyn were singing about the effects of her own star power. The song was made all the hotter when, astonishingly, the censors allowed Berlin to restore the "seat waving" line (from the 1933 version), rather than substituting "feet waving," as he'd had to do in 1938. Fox hired Hal Schaefer on special assignment to arrange (he also did "Lazy" and "After You Get What You Want You Don't Want It" for Marilyn), and he slowed the tempo of "Heat Wave" considerably, transforming it into a steamy jazz number that was most unlike the upbeat swing rendition Merman performed.

Gone also is the playfulness Ethels Merman and Waters brought to the piece. The focus is strictly sensual and placed squarely on the singer's body—something that a pronoun change alone wouldn't accomplish. Monroe throws her entire body, pelvis most conspicuously, to accentuate rhythmic breaks, gyrating at her waist left to right, back and froth. At one point she bumps and grinds against a pillar, and at another, when she coos that the heat wave comes from the "deep south," she pulls up her split skirt to uncover her crotch. The performance turns a lightly suggestive and comic song about the weather into a steamy discourse about her own body.

"You haven't heard 'Heat Wave,'" wrote Hedda Hopper, "until you watch Marilyn sing it. . . . I counted 52 people on the set of *There's No Business Like Show Business* watching her rehearse her 'Heat Wave' number. Some were on business, but most of the visitors come to ogle Marilyn."[49] The audience within the film seems to invite that very reaction. While Vicky performs, the Donahues observe from the wings. A fuming Molly watches as her husband and son are enjoying it, a bit too much:

TERRY: Easy, Molly, take it easy. You'll explode.
MOLLY: Terry, I think they switched babies on us in the hospital. I mean, he couldn't be mine.
TERRY: Well, maybe he's not yours, but I know he's mine. *I* can see why he did it.

"Heat Wave" would be the one scene that reviewers always mentioned, the one that often made or broke personal responses to *There's No Business Like Show Business,* especially for those coming into it with little knowledge about Merman, Broadway, or vaudeville. Critics were rather amazed by Monroe's openly seductive performance—the *New York Herald Tribune* called her "animated cheesecake";[50] others deemed it obscene. No one commented on its racism.

In the story line, Molly's grudge intensifies against Vicky after "Heat Wave." In one scene, Molly takes a phone call from Vicky in a way described in the script as "an iceberg is a lot warmer than her tone of voice."[51] Throughout the picture, Molly is deeply suspicious of Vicky's interest in her son. After Tim has run off and Katy puts the two women in the same dressing room for a show, a press photographer says, "I think a picture of you [together] at your dressing room tables would be [significant pause] noteworthy." Molly responds, "Wouldn't it be more newsworthy if we pulled each other's hair out?" perhaps a line that gave Ethel secret pleasure.

Given the trouble Ethel had had being photographed with Shirley Temple fifteen years earlier, how could she have enjoyed sharing the screen with Marilyn Monroe, a woman who was whipping an entire nation into a frenzy? It was not that Merman couldn't handle young beauties—consider her rapport with Gaynor—but given her instincts of self-preservation and her vigilance about professional behavior, it would have been extremely difficult, if not impossible, for her to enjoy her experience with Monroe. Over half a century later, the rivalry has become interesting in another way, as two divas who have become important icons for men all over the world, straight and gay.

Mitzi and The Merm

If Merman had trouble with Monroe, her relationship with Gaynor was terrific. Both were unpretentious women with plenty of talent and spirit. Gaynor recalls meeting Ethel for the first time: "She walked into the room . . . and proceeded to tell me the dirtiest story I ever heard. . . . I fell on the floor, and we became fast friends."[52] Merm would call her "Mitzallah," playing a faux Jewish mother. Their on-screen affection is evident in their cross-dressed duo, "A Sailor's Not a Sailor." (Merm gets the butch sideburns and tattoos; Mitzi is the femme.) Their friendship lasted over twenty years, documented in Merman's scrapbooks through dozens of affectionate notes and telegrams, many addressed to her as "Mom." Mitzi hosted dozens of parties for "Mom" whenever Ethel came to Hollywood, and Ethel in turn sent telegrams congratulating Mitzi on her own shows and various successes.

Marilyn Monroe's odd behavior only fortified Ethel and Mitzi's bond. "Ethel and I would go to lunch and dish dirt about everybody," said Gaynor. "We'd cut everybody up and put 'em back together again." "One day," writes an interviewer, "Mitzi, a gifted mimic, couldn't resist doing an impression of Marilyn Monroe, chest thrust forward and mouth open, as she walked into the studio commissary. Ethel Merman then did an impression of Mitzi doing an impression of Marilyn."[53] Forty years later, Gaynor reprised her impression for A&E's biography of Merman, amusingly mimicking Monroe's breathy, soft, feminine voice and joking about her behavior. Apparently Marilyn would hide in her dressing room or go off the set, and when she finally returned, she'd say, " 'And I was so confused,' and she was all dewy eyed. . . . and Ethel just looked at me, as if to say, 'What was *this* routine?!' "[54]

Viewers in the know can appreciate *There's No Business Like Show Business*'s many in-jokes and references concerning most of the players. Richard Eastham, who portrays Vicky's manager and producer, replaced Paul Lukas as Merman's costar in Broadway's *Call Me Madam*. Donald O'Connor plays a character with a drinking problem and would himself come out later as an alcoholic; Mitzi Gaynor is the happily married young bride on- and off-screen; Johnnie Ray's deeply held religious views off-screen are reflected in his character's turn to the church (which can be read as an escape from heterosexuality as well); Geoffrey Miles, the designer with whom Vicky argues, is a transparent reference to Miles White; and Dan Dailey, like his character Terry, was a veteran hoofer (he'd had a small role in *Stars in Your Eyes* as the show-within-a-show's "fifth assistant director"). Molly's character borrows liberally from Merman's established persona and even from her family history. At one point, Molly asks her family, "Do you know who was in the audience tonight?—Flo! . . . No, not Flo Ziegfeld, Flo Zimmermann, my cousin from Passaic!"

A Wrap

Ethel's contract for the picture expired on August 7, 1954, but after some haggling was extended to the 27th. To allow for inevitable retakes, recordings, and re-recordings, it had to be extended further, to the 31st, landing the star an extra twenty thousand dollars in the process. The battles between Ethel's lawyers and the studios regarding other additional work started growing nasty. After filing a complaint, producer Siegel wrote Lew Schreiber, "We brought Miss Ethel Merman in long before shooting time for very necessary preparation," and spent thirty thousand dollars "testing Miss Ethel Merman for gowns, costumes and the remedying of facial characteristics. It is an ironic comment that we were paying her her usual weekly salary and at the same time spending a fortune trying to enhance her attractiveness." (That Siegel had courted Merman in personal letters at the time, asking her to send pictures as they explored ideas for outfits brings a certain cruelty to the proceedings.) Hollywood seemed continually unashamed when it came to challenging Merman's looks.

Ethel was, as always, enthusiastic about the project and happy to talk about it, making special ado of the last scene, in which she and her costars descend a gigantic staircase at the Hippodrome. Hidden behind the wide—and steep, she reminds you—staircase was a ladder they had to climb first in order to move down the stairs. Merman, wearing a scalloped white gown that weighed "fifteen or twenty pounds," told the press that there were some "thirty" rehearsals and retakes, and she good-naturedly opined about her "jaggy icicle" dresses that poked her whenever she sat down, clearly relishing such "complaints" about her glamorous wardrobe.[55]

The film's six-million-dollar budget was three times that of *Alexander's Ragtime Band* and was substantial enough to become part of its advertising campaign, announced, for instance, in the movie's trailer. In a decade of big spectacle movies, *There's No Business Like Show Business* fit right in. Predictable jokes were made: Gaynor described Merman's walk: "Like Marilyn Monroe's, without the widescreen." Ethel said after a screen test, "Turns out I was three dimensional." (She preferred Cinemascope, she said, since the wider frame gave her more room to move around, and she'd always been frustrated by Hollywood's tight chalk lines.)[56] Ethel nursed big hopes for the big picture.

Unfortunately, Merman had no way of knowing what was going on behind her back, even before cameras had begun rolling. There was Zanuck's rather amazing assertion that she had had a *co*starring role in *Call Me Madam*. And her agent, George Rosenberg, didn't take long to realize that Zanuck and Fox had no plans to meet some of her demands when she was finishing up the picture and establishing the terms for the next, unidentified film in her contract. There was a question about expenses Merman would incur between *There's No Business Like Show Business* and the next one; when

Ethel insisted on ten thousand dollars, Fox was ready to walk. Rosenberg cut what memos identify as a "strictly confidential deal" with the studio, fronting five thousand dollars of his "own" money (likely fees charged to Merman) to reach that figure.[57] Merman never knew about it. Moreover, Fox's perception of her prestige and star power continued to be vastly different from her own. For the next project—tentatively entitled *Star in the West*—they were thinking of giving the role to Merman—"unless Susan Hayward" was available.[58]

Worse, as contracts were redrawn for *There's No Business Like Show Business* (due to Lang's illness, shooting delays, postproduction schedules, etc.), Fox was hedging its bets on that second picture. By this point, they knew that *Call Me Madam* was underperforming, and the studio brass was displeased about her considerable demands for the next feature. In a letter to Frank Ferguson, Lew Schreiber wrote, "She is insisting on so many approvals . . . such as story approval, definitely agreeing that it would be made in Technicolor, wanting a definite starting date now and a stop date, and many other approvals, that the making of the second picture would actually be in her hands. We would have no controls and we would be committed to make the second picture, whereas she would not be committed."[59] Fox scored a considerable coup when it was able to persuade Rosenberg only to finalize terms for *There's No Business Like Show Business*.

The movie premiered December 1954, in time for the holiday box office surge. Ethel flew to Los Angeles with Bob Six, where she joined Mitzi and Jack Bean. The four also attended the Denver premiere together; Six quipped, "That makes four times I've seen it now." Mr. and Mrs. Six were also invited to a private screening at a gala Christmas party hosted by the Duke and Duchess of Windsor, also attended by Grace Kelly, Henry Ford Jr. and his wife, and assorted ambassadors and counts, all of whom dined on caviar, crabmeat, green turtle soup with sherry, roast pheasant, endive and avocado salad, and crepes. (Ethel kept the menu.)

It was widely reviewed, though most were mixed, reflecting the film's highs and lows and its strange fusion of stars and performance styles. Ethel "socks home every number," said one East Coast paper;[60] another reviewer wrote that the best scenes were those with Merman and Dan Dailey and that things weakened considerably whenever the younger players were involved:

> It is always horrible to see or hear a human being make a public exhibition of his weaknesses, and the agonies of watching Mr. Ray and Miss Monroe apply themselves to song were to me almost unendurable. Both seemed to be in agony; he, approaching God with a desperate piston-action of the jaws; she,

in urgent need, perhaps, of a nice, quiet "lay-down" and a comb run through the voice. At the risk of seeming prim, I would call *There's No Business Like Show Business* a vulgar picture; suggesting to me at least an insult to intelligence, religion, music, Ethel Merman, good taste and the human soul.[61]

Predictably, Ethel's scrapbooks bulge with reviews, especially from West Coast papers. Although she was the denizen of a new region working in a new entertainment industry that was more profit-driven, institutionalized, and industrialized than Broadway ever was, correspondence shows that the human element was still not lacking. Telegrams stacked up from friends from all over the country when the film opened, including the sweet "faux family" notes: "Dear Mom, You're not only the best of Broadway you're the best of the whole world. . . . Love and Kisses, Your daughter Katie."[62] Back in New York with the film, Ethel attended a special benefit screening for the Actors' Fund at the Roxy Theatre on December 11.

Ethel's evolving persona—and its relation to "Momism"—is apparent in reviews that placed considerable weight on her role as materfamilias. *Call Me Madam* was great, began one, but now with *There's No Business Like Show Business,* "Miss Merman spends much of her screen time as a bereaved mother, spurred by the old tradition that the show must go on even though one's heart is breaking. It seems odd that someone missed the fact that Miss Merman is more of a comedienne than an emotional actress."[63]

Given Ethel's cultivation of her offstage image at the time *as* a wife and mother, the remark suggests just how much her public did *not* want to see singer Ethel Merman as a domestic figure—or even, apparently, as an emotional one. Sol Siegel seemed to have anticipated this reaction while the story was in development: "If more [emphasis] is shifted to the role of the mother, then we will not get Donald O'Connor to play Al or Dan Dailey to play Tim. The whole idea that we talked about was based on this being the story of a 'family.' If it becomes just a 'mother' story then I think we narrow the dimensions."[64] And in a review that extols the efficiency with which the film introduces the Donahues, the *Hollywood Reporter* adds, "By this time, you like them so much that you don't resent the fact that the very first line that Ethel Merman delivers in the picture is a petulant line that chops her husband. . . . [She] leaps right into the role of the tart and lovable bickerer that is to be her character throughout the picture."[65] Momism, anyone?

Decca had contractually arranged to release the movie soundtrack, and, since Decca was Berlin and Merman's label, there was no problem getting their work. Johnnie Ray, however, had to be borrowed from Columbia, and

Marilyn Monroe's voice never made it to the final recording, since no agreement was ever reached with her recording company, RCA/Victor. Zanuck proposed replacing her with Peggy Lee but finally okayed Dolores Gray.

End of an Era

In many ways, *There's No Business Like Show Business* is Fox's bookend to *Alexander's Ragtime Band.* Both are tributes to earlier musical eras, but whereas *Alexander's Ragtime Band* shows the reinvigoration of that era, *There's No Business Like Show Business* marks its passing, something apparent even by having the grand finale occur at the Hippodrome, a building that was now gone in reality. This was where the cinematic family enjoyed its first big success, and now it provides the locale where the Donahues reunite as a family, but *not* as a show biz act. For a movie called *There's No Business Like Show Business,* the ending is infused with a surprising sadness, even if it lacks real emotional punch. In order for the Donahues to move forward, vaudeville has to be left behind, and, by this time, the three children are moving into different careers and futures. There will be no more "family business," something that many real family-run businesses were experiencing in the postwar boom of corporate life. American society and economics were in the middle of a shift away from the family business model, like the Donahues', to a system in which individuals worked for large firms owned by other organizations.

If Monroe's Vicky was a thorn in the side of Merman's Molly, she also gave Merman a run for her money in this larger cultural arena. For *There's No Business Like Show Business* self-consciously uses Ethel as a figure to symbolize old Broadway or vaudeville performances or both. She is, moreover, a star whose magic doesn't transfer to the camera, whereas in the supremely photogenic Marilyn Monroe, the film offers the young forward-looking model of Hollywood itself. The transfer of Molly/Merman's "Heat Wave" to Vicky/Monroe cements that connection all the more. In all, Zanuck biographer George Custen says of both the film and its casting, "New Hollywood has triumphed over old."[66] Nearly thirty years later, when Fox released *There's No Business Like Show Business* on video, it would be as part of its "Marilyn Monroe Diamond Collection," with only Monroe depicted on the box.

For many audiences, *There's No Business Like Show Business* doesn't work, even now, decades after its release. Viewers of all ages say they are unable to sit through it, that they either love or hate one of the principals (Merman,

Monroe, Johnnie Ray—performers who all elicit strong responses); many find the story dull, corny, or overstuffed. Even for those who enjoy *There's No Business Like Show Business*'s numbers and performances—myself included—the movie just does not satisfy. One reason might have something to do with what *There's No Business Like Show Business* leaves behind: in many ways, *that* entertainment world is more compellingly depicted than either the movie's own story line or the characters drawn around it.

When *There's No Business Like Show Business* failed to do as well as the studio had expected, 20th Century–Fox chose not to pursue its option of a follow-up picture with Merman. Ethel turned her hopes elsewhere, to TV, as she returned to the Denver suburbs.

THIRTEEN

From Mrs. Six to Mama Rose

In 1956, Ethel had not yet given up on her marriage with Bob Six and took advantage of a new career opportunity to reinvigorate it. Stunning everyone, she announced her return to Broadway for the upcoming *Happy Hunting*. The news began to trickle in during February, when Sam Zolotow, Earl Wilson, and Walter Winchell announced separately that Ethel was back in New York "to discuss a musical version of the film *All About Eve*"[1] (eventually, *Applause*). Explaining her change of heart, Ethel tried to manage the inconsistencies of earlier statements she'd made:

> I've been misquoted about giving up the stage. . . . I did move out of New York . . . to live in Denver and it did force me to give up Broadway temporarily. But I did manage to make a couple of movies and appear on some TV shows. . . . Please get this for the record. If I do come back and do a show it's because my husband's business will keep him in the East. I'll work only to be near him and that's the only reason. . . . This is strictly a one-show deal, because we're still keeping our home in Denver.[2]

She claimed to be mulling over "about three shows," but in truth she grabbed onto *Happy Hunting* to keep the marriage together. Now that Six was spending more time in New York, perhaps a return to the spotlight would rejuvenate the ailing relationship. It was not a decision Ethel made to regain her autonomy and independence; that would come later. Together, she and Bob Six had pooled resources to found the "Mermsix" Production Company, which eventually became one of the backers of the new show, despite Ethel's professed aversion to the practice.

Colorado reluctantly said farewell to its colorful guest. Associates threw parties, and the local press announced, "Ethel Merman Packing—Back to

278

Broadway." Ethel told them she had had "three great years here, loved it," but had just changed her mind. She was simply unable to resist the new show, she averred, talking up its thin story line.[3]

After a late-winter Florida vacation, during which papers announced that she (actually, Six) went deep-sea fishing, and after several more TV appearances—Ed Sullivan on March 18; *The Arthur Murray Party* on April 5—Ethel sold her two-door 1950 Ford to the wife of Six's assistant Stewart Faulkner, and the family moved back to their Park Lane apartment in New York. The city welcomed its diva back with open arms. On May 19 the *Journal* ran a full-page, five-photo story of Ethel and Bob Six. In one photo, Six embraces his wife as they gaze out the window at the horizon, and we read in the caption under Ethel, "That's my town, Broadway."[4] "Ethel Merman Returns Shouting 'I Love Broadway,'" ran another.[5] New York was also abuzz about the new show, whose tickets were topped at a sky-scraping eight dollars. Scalpers were on the make before the show was even written.

Happy Hunting would prove to be, if not Ethel's least favorite show, her least favorite time spent on the boards. "*Happy Hunting,*" she said, "rivaled *Sadie Thompson* as my most miserable theatrical experience."[6] The show was the twenty-second written by the team of Lindsay and Crouse, and the program rightfully boasted that "Mr. Lindsay and Mr. Crouse hold another record. They . . . are still speaking to each other." They had worked with Ethel on *Anything Goes, Red, Hot and Blue!* and *Call Me Madam.* The three were a great trio and knew it. Lindsay and Crouse ended up dedicating their published script "To Ethel Merman, to whom we, too, are dedicated."

Happy Hunting

Happy Hunting was a simple musical comedy written around a star persona, like musicals of old. It borrowed tidbits from the team's previous successes. Like *Call Me Madam,* the story centers around a current event—here, the excitement over actress Grace Kelly's "defection" from Hollywood to wed Prince Rainier of Monaco, whom she had met while filming *To Catch a Thief.* (Before the April 19 marriage, a piece called "Merman Eyes Monaco" was already announcing the premise of the new show.) Ethel's character was a curious amalgamation of previous roles, reprising Sally Adams as a mildly uncultured American in Europe, the protective Molly Donahue, and the scheming Nails Duquesne.

In *Happy Hunting*, Ethel plays wealthy widow Liz Livingstone. Arriving in Monaco with her daughter, Beth, Liz anticipates an invitation to the imminent royal wedding, at which she intends to snag a rich husband for Beth. To her deep chagrin, she is not invited, so to save face, she feigns a hotel burglary of all of their clothes, since without clothes, they obviously can't attend. Beth sees through her mother's ruse, as does a puzzled Duke of Granada—a kind of Latin Cosmo—who happens to catch Liz hiding her wardrobe. (She goes to bed in layers of clothing and jewels to protect them from the fake theft.)

The ruse brings Beth and Liz closer, prompting them to sing "Mutual Admiration Society." And Liz gets to know the Duke, who has a title but no money, whereas she has plenty of money but no title and, hence, no respect from Philadelphia's "Main Line." They arrange for the Duke to accompany the Livingstone women back to the United States as Beth's fiancé, resolving several dilemmas at once.

On the trip back, Liz discovers she has more than the feelings of a *belle-mère* for the Duke. (At first Liz thinks this term refers to a horse with a bell— a confusion enhanced by the onstage presence of Daisy, a horse to whom Liz confides her feelings for the Duke.) But she refuses to act on them: "Let's not add incest to injury."[7] Meanwhile, Beth has fallen in love with Sanford "Sandy" Stewart Jr., a blue-blood lawyer from Philadelphia.

In a fox hunt scene back in the United States, Liz, who is not a horsewoman, is thrown from her saddle. (Any wonder why the role of Auntie Mame—on Broadway at the same time—seemed right for Ethel?) Best friend Maud Foley insists they go to a ball dressed as a Goya painting, like the costume party that Ethel and Bob Levitt had attended several years back. Both the hunt and the ball scene afterward work to show high society as hypocritical and pretentious.

Eventually Liz decides to straighten out matters: she'll marry the Duke, singing, in a softer mood, "I'm a Funny Dame." Beth elopes with Sandy with the Duke's assistance. The Duke, whom Liz now calls "Hymie" in another ethnicity-bender, realizes he has feelings for Liz, even though, like another Duke of the time, he learns that if he marries her, he cannot accede the throne. He marries her anyway, allaying Liz's fears that he is only interested in her money. The two end by reprising "Mutual Admiration Society."

Happy Hunting abounds in references to the Monaco wedding, with Liz even sharing Grace Kelly's hometown of Philadelphia. But it makes almost as many references to Ethel Merman's life, giving insiders a wink or two. Liz moved to Philadelphia from Colorado, where her husband (in the play, departed) had made his fortune in the transportation business—railroads, not airplanes. Liz's quick entry into the upper class keeps her at arm's length from the older society mavens, who perceive her as a nouveau riche among blue bloods.

Happy Hunting was not an unusual Merman musical; it was basically an unambitious vehicle for her vocal and comic talents, boasting the usual Lindsay-Crouse gags, funny, if slightly old-school:

> DUKE: I am what is called a pretender.
> LIZ: I like you all the better for admitting it.[8]

and

> DUKE: Do you know the difference between Bourbon and Hapsburg?
> LIZ: Sure, one's whisky and one's beer.

(The latter surely pleased the executives at Rheingold, whose product Ethel and costar Fernando Lamas were both shilling at the time.)

Lindsay and Crouse's book plays off established aspects of Merman's persona, taking advantage of her comic skills and purportedly tough femininity. In act II, after the Duke tells Liz to "stop trying to be feminine":

> LIZ (more determinedly feminine): Hasn't a woman the right to be feminine?
> DUKE: Not your kind of woman. Leez, there are two kinds of women, feminine and female, and you're female.
> LIZ: Female! That's a hell of a thing to call a woman.[9]

There was widespread speculation about who would finance and produce—David Merrick or Jo Mielziner, who at the time was bidding on *Long Day's Journey into Night?* NBC/RCA? It was NBC/RCA Victor and, eventually, Mermsix that finally put up the show's $350,000 budget, and Mielziner received credit as producer. Ethel and Bob were characteristically mum when journalists asked about their financial involvement, not even announcing the formation of Mermsix until February 13. *Variety* called their production company an "outfit [with] no immediate production plans but has been established to permit launching operations when desired."[10]

Hunting attracted a team of Broadway greats. Mielziner also did sets and lighting; Irene Sharaff, who had outfitted Ethel so well in Fox's *Call Me Madam,* did costumes; and Abe Burrows, fresh from *Guys and Dolls, Can Can,* and *Silk Stockings,* directed. Jay Blackton was musical director. But there were no big stars behind the music; no Irving Berlin, no Cole Porter onboard. The songs were penned by two gentlemen from Philadelphia, Matt Dubey and Harold Karr, who had composed a few popular tunes but had never written a complete Broadway musical before. (Karr was a former dentist, which so tickled the Broadway community that *Bells Are Ringing,* another 1956 musical, featured a dentist who longed to write songs for Broadway.)

According to Louella Parsons, Ethel wanted Anthony Quinn to portray the penniless Duke. Whether she did or not, it was Fernando Lamas who was actually signed. Born in Buenos Aires, Lamas (1915–82) was a well-known film star in Argentina. In Hollywood, he was most well known for playing the dashing foreign Count Danilo in the recent *Merry Widow. Happy Hunting* would continue Lamas's run as the stereotypical Latin lover, and Lamas was happy to comply, telling reporters that "Latins are temperamental" as a way of explaining what made his female fans swoon so.[11] (The show's program added a dash of political spice by describing him as "one of the most popular stars in our Good Neighbor Countries.") Athletic and good-looking, Lamas was also a former boxer and swimmer with large sexual appetites; his wife at the time was actress Arlene Dahl.[12]

Merman stunned the industry by permitting Lamas, a newcomer to Broadway, to share top billing in lettering of equal size to hers. "It's the first time in twenty years that Ethel allowed herself to be costarred with anyone," wrote Sheila Graham.[13] But it was hardly an act of wild benevolence: Ethel's name appeared above the show's title, and the sole photo promoting it depicted her face alone. The young lovers Beth and Sandy were played by Virginia Gibson and Broadway tyro Gordon Polk. Gene Wesson played Harry Watson, an American reporter in Monaco.

As early as April 3, 1956, Merman's "new Broadway show" was officially announced, though its story line remained "undetermined." (The *Rocky Mountain News* printed that report next to the story "Grace's Royal Marriage Is Termed a Gamble.")[14] Rehearsals were scheduled to start April 29, but nearly four months later, Lindsay and Crouse wrote to Ethel: "Abe tells us the first act will be typed by tomorrow and airmailed to you. . . . We think this is going to be the best book we have ever written. . . . Howard and Buck."[15]

None of this deterred advance sales, which came in at over one and a half million dollars,[16] and the show's three-week Philadelphia tryout was sold out well before doors opened on October 22. The Shubert Theatre there broke records, with the musical grossing $180,000, and, when it moved to Boston for three weeks, it beat house records there too.

Happy Hunting's Broadway opening was December 6, 1956, at the large 44th Street Majestic Theatre. Once again Merman's entrance was grand: several journalists mingle in a crowd and spot a woman behind a big hat, asking hopefully, "Miss Kelly?" to which she responds, "All right, all right, so it ain't a Kelly under the Kelly."[17] The playful hide-and-seek tickled Broadway audiences, and their response was clinched by her first song, "It's Good to Be Here." It might have been Liz Livingstone singing for all of Monaco to hear, but New York audiences knew better. Their Ethel was back.

"Happy Feuding"

Happy Hunting has gone down in Merman musical history for the clashes between her and Lamas. Even at the time, reports stated that their dislike was both mutual and immediate. It could have been the billing arrangements or the fact that Lamas sang one song to Ethel's nine. Biographer Bob Thomas maintains that it started the first day of rehearsal, according to an unidentified witness:

> The two stars greeted each other with a degree of formality and immediately began reading their first scene together. After ten minutes, Lamas held up his hand to halt the proceedings.
>
> "Excuse me," he said in his mellow Argentine accent, "but I would like to ask a question. Is this the way it's going to be?"
>
> "Is what the way it's going to be?" Burrows asked warily.
>
> "What I mean is, am I going to read my lines to Miss Merman and Miss Merman reads hers to the audience?" . . .
>
> Merman's eyes narrowed, her jaw tightened. "Mr. Lamas," she began, her voice growing edgy, "I want you to know that I have been playing scenes this way for twenty-five years on Broadway."
>
> "That's *[sic]* doesn't mean you're right," Lamas replied. "That just means you're old."
>
> A witness to the exchange comments: "From that moment on, it was World War III."[18]

Lamas would do the show with garlic breath to annoy her, and she would mutter, just loud enough for him and the cast and crew to hear, "toilet mouth." She accused him of "stepping on her laugh lines," obstructing her entrances, and upstaging her.[19] Their glacial silence was widely noted, and the two did not speak to each other offstage unless absolutely necessary, which proved awkward for people such as Benay Venuta, who was a friend of both. Two incidents inflamed the situation. One night, after Lamas and Merman exchanged an onstage kiss, he wiped his mouth with his hand in full view of the audience. Enraged, Merman went to Equity, which gave Lamas an official reprimand for "making unauthorized changes in his performance and stepping on Miss Merman's laugh lines."[20] Lamas retaliated by suing for damages of a hundred thousand dollars for improper censure. He lost. Director Burrows quickly changed the onstage kiss to an embrace. (Unapologetic, Lamas later told an interviewer, "Have you ever kissed Ethel Merman? It's somewhere between kissing your uncle and a Sherman tank.")[21]

The second incident involved Gene Wesson, the actor who played the young reporter. One day Wesson showed up for work with his hair dyed gray. He did it to appear older for a part he was trying out for in *Too Much Too Soon* and refused to change it back. Ethel went "insane," as she said, convinced that Lamas had egged him on, and a barrage of official complaints and countercomplaints ensued.

With all this backstage bickering, it was small wonder that columnist Marie Torre referred to *Happy Hunting* as "Happy Feuding."[22] The press was having a field day. The *New York Journal American* reported that after Equity's verdict, producers took down a portrait of Lamas in the Majestic lobby and replaced it with a shot of the less controversial juvenile leads.[23] Columnists such as Leonard Lyons and Ed Sullivan lined up behind the extremely public war, defending Ethel. Wrote Sullivan, "The Merman . . . has been so nice to performers, that I can't go along with any attacks on her from Gene Wesson or Lamas."[24] (Ethel thanked him, keeping Sullivan's two-line response, "Dear Ethel, You're m'gal! Say hello to Bob for me.") Lyons extolled her "exemplary behavior" in the spat with Wesson.[25] For her part, Ethel kept quiet about Wesson, simply filing another complaint to Equity, which, after its unanimous decision, tendered her an apology on behalf of Wesson, who refused to produce one himself. (Its decision also barred Wesson from making further public statements about her.) Bill Fields, Merman's press agent, offered suggestions for dealing with the press during the legal battles. Specifically, he asked her to write to columnist Hobe Morrison, providing her with a sample letter that was "very short and simple, like your wire to Ed Sullivan."[26] In the end, Wesson was let go from the show.

Reviews

Critics were aware that *Happy Hunting* was a rather generic production: "As musicomedy, it is more than just not out of the top drawer, it is from a discontinued line of furniture. . . . Where she can, Ethel outflanks her material; where she cannot, she outstares it."[27] *Variety* wrote: "She is a spectacular performer, even when her show is otherwise mediocre. . . . [She] has a voice like a calliope, the energy of a bulldozer and the comedy touch of an old pro." But then the review qualified with, "It remains to be seen . . . whether an Ethel Merman, not quite as svelte or sprightly after several years of retirement, can tote the production in the money."[28] The troubled show didn't exactly tank—it grossed $3.2 million on the $500,000 investment,[29] closing on November 30, 1957. Few people suggested that *Happy Hunting*'s slightly disappointing performance had anything to do with Ethel, since she had carried weak shows before. When *Variety* made its remarks, for instance, it wasn't trying to be mean-spirited, but its shot at Broadway's diva does hint that Ethel's cultural capital was not as solid as it had once been. While some detractors had been looking for such signs for years, the difference was that now the shot was taken at work in New York, her home turf. Were stars now something to be shot at rather than aspired to?

Partly because of the unpleasantness with Lamas and Wesson and partly because of the reviews, Ethel later referred to *Happy Hunting* as "a jeep among limousines."[30] She especially regretted working with inexperienced songwriters, something that would limit her working relations with a young Stephen Sondheim in *Gypsy*. There wasn't much to celebrate in the play itself: "In spite of Merman's hard sell, the charm of Fernando Lamas, the fresh spirit of Virginia Gibson, and two hit songs by Harold Karr and Matt Dubey ('Mutual Admiration Society' and 'Newfangled Tango'), audiences realized they had seen and heard this all before."[31] Critics complained that the show's tunes were substandard, and indeed, some songs are rather painful to listen to. Even the "Mutual Admiration Society" duet, the show's standout number, fails to take hold as Porter's "Let's Be Buddies" had in *Panama Hattie*, and its melody is undercut by an abundance of short notes and a hiccuping syncopation that gives strange comic edges rather than the emotional punch it needs. The piece was much like a prewar musical tune going for gags and showmanship over emotional engagement.

Ethel utilizes a variety of clever vocal tricks. Her numbers are filled with grace notes, but here she twangs at the beginning of sounds rather than at the end, as she usually did (e.g., "blo-ow, Gabriel, blow"). She also exaggerates her American accent, especially in lyrics referring to the late Mr. Livingstone, to deepen the incongruity of an American staying in a European kingdom. Interestingly, her Queens accent is allowed to be full out in the show, as if Ethel is finally claiming ownership of her songs in a way she hadn't before. The combined effect is quite comic, revealing a performer who understands her value not simply as a singer or as a comic actress but as a *comic singer.*

Tony Cointreau maintains that Merman may not have been singing her best material with the show but that technically her voice could not have been richer or more solid. "Ethel had *so* many more harmonics than most singers," he says, referring to the additional overtones produced when a given pitch or note is sounded, "and these things thrill audiences. This is especially so in *Happy Hunting,* where her harmonics are at their peak."[32] Others, however, complained that, despite the technical skills Ethel had at her disposal, her vocal performance for *Happy Hunting* reveals little pleasure or emotional depth for them. One scholar of the cast recording says, "The range she had displayed in *Annie Get Your Gun* and *Call Me Madam* had disappeared. All I heard was a loud, energetic voice. Naturally, her style remained the same but there was no depth . . . not a sense of enjoyment in what she was singing."[33] Given her experience with the show—and the awareness of that experience among most informed listeners—it is hard *not* to hear Ethel singing that way.

Happy Hunting did not develop the Merman persona so much as bank on its established traits. The story sets up high society as an elite, pretentious affair deftly deflated by Liz/Ethel's zip and faux naïveté. Whenever someone knocks at her hotel door, for instance, Liz launches into the local language with a "*N'est-ce pas?*" Later, she complains, "This whole place isn't as big as Franklin Field!"[34] The character is the consummate American adrift in a mythic old country, just as *Call Me Madam* required, and indeed, Liz Livingstone mixes the newfound elegance of Sally Adams with the sartorially inappropriate figure of earlier shows. (At one point, Liz is described as a "walking Christmas tree.")[35] And the defiant Merman pompadour is highlighted on and off the boards; here, as in *Madam,* the star's floating head was the chief image used in publicity materials.

Happy Hunting came out at a time when Merman's fans, critics, and audiences could be broken down into three principal groups. First were the enthusiastic worshippers, who adored all that Ethel was and what she represented, who loved the locked-in "Merman qualities." Then there was the jealous or resentful group, people who were connected to the industry with some stake in her fame and who were eager to chip at her success. This group had found Merman's power too solid and her reputation too daunting ever to be challenged before. The third group found in Merman nothing less than a living piece of Broadway, an icon of an old performance style and golden era that was met with appreciation and awe. One thing is certain, however: *Happy Hunting* shows a more deliberate melding of "Ethel Merman" and the character she plays than most of her earlier shows did. (It would take three years, in *Gypsy*, for even more people to confuse Ethel's performance as Mama Rose with the "real" Ethel Merman.)

That said, it's a domesticated, genteel Merman that prevails as Liz in *Happy Hunting;* she is tastefully clad in respectable suits, wearing pearls, hair swept up on and off the stage.[36] A frequently reproduced production picture has Ethel/Liz tilting her head with eyebrows raised in a look that suggests that Liz is going to move cautiously into this group of high-society folks; a little bit of hurt is in the look and a little mischief as well. It captures the status of an outsider and lets us know that Liz is a bit of schemer, suspicious of bullshit or shenanigans. Ethel would use the same look, the same tilt, in *Gypsy*, but had her eyes reflect a steady, shining gleam.

Ethel pursued other projects while in *Happy Hunting*, appearing on television's *The Ed Sullivan Show*. Phil Silvers, who was enjoying a successful run on TV's *You'll Never Get Rich*, was said to be in "discussions" with her about doing a new show together, but it never materialized. More troublesome was the prestigious *Crescendo* television special sponsored by DuPont. Ethel was to appear with Rex Harrison, the star then wowing Broadway with his turn as Professor Henry Higgins in *My Fair Lady*. Harrison's asking price was forty-five thousand dollars; Ethel's, twenty-five thousand. (Next to this figure in the scrapbook appears a rare editorial notation: three inked-in exclamation points.) Ethel withdrew from the show at uncharacteristically late notice, dissatisfied with the lower pay and concerned about her weakly written supporting role. (All she did was perform as a singer.) "Something MUST be wrong with [Ethel's] role," said one bitchily sympathetic producer. "Merman's usually not very finicky about her parts."[37] Harrison reportedly didn't like his lines either and hired Peter Ustinov, at an expense of ten thousand dollars, to doctor them. Other problems dogged the show, including a behind-the-scenes incident with guest Louis Armstrong that almost caused a racial boycott.[38] After it aired, most reviewers complained that it used too many stars and rushed through too many numbers, and most were sympathetic with Ethel about withdrawing. *Variety*'s front-page story ran, "It's no longer a case of money," saying that dollars alone could no longer buy good name guest stars on TV, "as Ethel Merman's case demonstrated."[39]

For years, Ethel had wanted to stretch her legs as an actor and tackle dramatic, nonsinging work. *Reflected Glory* gave her that opportunity. A dramatic play by George Kelly (*Craig's Wife, The Show-Off*), *Reflected Glory* starred Tallulah Bankhead when it opened on Broadway in the autumn of 1936. Another version aired on the *Broadway Television Theatre* in 1954 that starred Clare Luce. On March 25, 1956, Ethel's version was broadcast on CBS's *General Electric Theater,* hosted by her friend Ronald Reagan. Merman played Muriel Flood, a popular actress who can't decide whether to leave the theater to marry and settle down or to continue with her career—not a big leap for Ethel the Denverite, as several reviewers noted. Costarring were Walter Matthau and Philip Bourgneuf. The play had been boiled down to half an hour, and, as most reviewers argued, it was a crippling cut. Reviews were poor, and in addition to complaining about the truncated story, many wrote that Merman was overextended and out of her league with the material. (A few suggested that she should have picked less corny material for her dramatic debut to begin with.)

End of the Sixes

Reflecting back on the period, Ethel said she had been able to forestall marital disaster by making a point of defining herself "in wifely terms" in interviews, indicating that she was rather well aware of her performance as Mrs. Robert F. Six.[40] In the summer of 1957, when she reprised her role as official hostess of the New York City festival, the press dutifully played up that wifely role, discussing the "Summer Festival hostess, playing to her husband, Bob Six, the airline executive, who flew into Gotham for one of his infrequent trips here." "No one," they added, "ever calls him 'Mr. Merman.'"[41]

That same year, a reporter quoted Six. "I suppose [my wife] is the old fire-horse that paws the ground at the sound of a siren. She says that show business means nothing to her but work. We know that isn't true. . . . Ethel and I are mature people. We have both been married before and we understand each other very well. In the evenings I sit at home and watch television or go through business papers. Then she comes back after the show and we get to bed around midnight."[42] Hindsight or simply the passage of time may make it seem odd to refer to one's wife as an old firehorse or to omit any mention of one's stepchildren, who were still minors at the time. But Ethel was hardly saying anything much different, explaining to the press, "My children don't like it in New York. Why should they? There's nothing for them here. At home in Denver, they have lots of friends and so much freedom. It's just a better life for kids there."[43]

Happy Hunting ran for 412 performances and, contrary to Ethel's hopes, did not revitalize the marriage with Six. When they first returned to the city in 1956, they were welcomed back with open arms, and the press reported on their every move: their social life at clubs such as El Morocco; their trip to England, where Ethel performed for the queen and Six landed a deal to purchase several aircraft. But now that Bob Six was increasing his out-of-town trips and reducing his phone calls back home ("I'd rush home to wait for the call and it wouldn't come"),[44] *that* was the kind of Merman-Six news finding its way into the press.

Ethel's home life was losing its sense of family all over again. Bobby recalls spending a lot of his time at the Park Lane Hotel in New York, accompanying elevator man Bob "Duddy" Duddleson, riding up and down as famous people came and went. Duddleson was a natural comic, a good man, and quickly became an important "friend and teacher" to the preteen boy: "Bob could confirm the presence of a meany or a phoney even before he'd shut the elevator doors. . . . I'd be tickled to the exploding point exploring the airs and natures of the Park Lane's guests and visitors . . . in each and every ride. . . . Imagine a perfectly liveried, *perfectly covert,* clowning, mimicking, elevator man: ⅓ Charlie Chaplin, ⅓ Jerry Lewis, and ⅓ himself, Duddy Duddleson."[45] Bob Duddleson hailed from a lower-working-class part of Brooklyn, where the ascending stage and TV star Jackie Gleason had also grown up and where Gleason found the basis for many of his TV characters, notably crabby bus driver Ralph Cramden. Clearly Duddleson touched Gleason as well, for at the end of every episode of *The Jackie Gleason Show,* the comic paid homage to the gentle man. Playing a bartender wiping up the counter at closing time, Gleason bid his audiences good night, adding, "And good night to Duddy Duddleson, wherever you are."

Gossip columnists had a feeding frenzy on the deteriorating Six marriage. Ethel may not have been the front-page news she had been before, but small matter. In the world of postwar gossip columns, scandal was blood to the shark, and the colorful Robert Six was bigger game than either Bob Levitt or William Smith had been. Moreover, unlike in her relationship with those men, Ethel Merman's hackles were up in this one, and while silent on many matters, such as his violence, once she suspected that she no longer had her husband's full affections, she made noises to friends in the press corps. Columns now included tidbits like "Why was Bob Six now taking so many long stopovers in Hawaii?" items that could have been fed to them only by her. Small jabs aside, however, Ethel did her best to keep a sense of dignity about her marriage She had no interest in inviting scandal or in making things more unpleasant than they already were.

In January 1958, life would change dramatically when Robert Levitt Sr. was found dead in his home of an overdose of sleeping pills. Although Ethel had put the marriage behind her by this point, there was no way around the horrific impact his suicide had, especially on her sixteen- and twelve-year-old children, who were unable to cope with the threats and violence of their new home. To manage the news publicly, Ethel reminded interviewers that she and Levitt had been divorced for years, saying, in effect, that it wasn't the dissolution of their marriage that had caused the tragedy. (Levitt had since remarried, twice—most recently, three months prior to his death.) Bob Jr. remembers how his mother broke the news to his sister and him: there was "Mom's phone call that took us out of school and mysteriously home only to learn that our father was dead. . . . hearing that news, both my sister and I dropped our phones on the floor. I can't recall who hung them up. I do recall that there was no comforting, maternal presence ever to follow," adding that their cook, Venus, gave the children deeply needed loving and mothering in the months following the news.[46] There was no service for their father. Today, Bob Jr. says his mother gave them "all kinds of reasons . . . why it must have been true that Big *intentionally* killed himself on Bill Hearst's birthday ['to get back' at Hearst, she would say]. But I never—ever once—heard Mom give *any* reason or even a comment—much less any consolation—about why Big killed himself in the middle of our childhoods." It was Venus, he said, who "let me sit in her lap and cry."[47]

Tony Cointreau, who was dating young Ethel at the time, recalls, "Her tone was flat when she told me. There was no outward grieving—Bob did more of that. I think Little Ethel just swept it under the rug."[48] Bob agrees and says that by swallowing her grief, his sister did herself some real harm. At the time, though, neither of the children had much opportunity to wade through their feelings, with a family falling apart and a mother who, despite her good intentions, was dealing with the tragedy through the cover of repression. Six was publicly supportive of his wife, but that could hardly have provided any meaningful succor. Cointreau recalls that Six never spoke to him and that Little Ethel told him her stepfather was even now constantly threatening to harm her beloved poodle, Midnight.

According to Robert Six's biographer, "Those who knew Merman and Six intimately are convinced that her decision to do *Gypsy* made their breakup inevitable, even though Six apparently didn't try very hard to stop her."[49] That might have been the view of Six's friends, but not of Ethel's. There were the visceral incidents that Roger Edens and her parents knew about and the troubles that even average New Yorkers were starting to glean from local gossip sheets. The truth was, their marriage was already well past repair before Ethel went from being Mrs. Six to Mama Rose. But at last, Ethel's instincts finally kicked in, and she opted to embrace her stage career anew and live in a more supportive world of family, friends, and fans in a city that still adored her.

For a few years, Ethel had grown suspicious that Six was having an affair. Whether he was or not will never be known; he died in 1985 and hardly would have wanted to make such an admission to begin with. In all, it seems likely that Six was most probably trying to avoid a crumbling marriage rather than actively seeking refuge in another woman's bed. Nonetheless, Bob Six started seeing Audrey Meadows, the costar of Gleason's current TV hit, *The Honeymooners,* immediately after separating from Merman, if not before. A gifted comic, Meadows played Alice, the long-suffering but fiery wife of Gleason's bus driver Cramden. Meadows would turn her back on show business to become the third and final Mrs. Robert F. Six, and the couple remained together for the rest of their lives.

It was in 1959 that Ethel, still living at the Park Lane, announced to the press that she and the Colorado maverick were officially separated. (Evidently, that was how Six found out.) Now, whenever business took him to New York, he and Ethel met only to settle their holdings, prompting the press to speculate uselessly about a reunion. Their talks lasted for months. The two did keep a promise they'd made to the children, taking a family vacation to the Caribbean that winter, but soon after that, Six and Ethel went their separate ways. During a short break from *Gypsy,* Ethel flew to Mexico City for a divorce.

While the failure of Ethel's second marriage to Bob Levitt had been a disappointment, her trust had not been abused. "I imagine they just let it go," says Cointreau, who by now was a second son to Ethel, long after he and Little Ethel had stopped dating. "They might have been able to make a go of it, but like a lot of couples, they reached a point where the relationship could either go on or not. In later years, she never seemed to understand what went wrong and considered him to have been the love of her life."[50] The divorce from Six was different. Although Ethel was too life-affirming to dwell on the marriage, she was, according to her son, very bitter about Bob Six and never forgave his abuse. For her, the relationship was a profound betrayal, one that left her guarded when it came to financial and romantic matters in the future.

FOURTEEN

Gypsy

Ethel Merman's Musical Fable

At 7:25 P.M., May 21, 1959, the curtain went up at the Broadway Theatre. The house was packed. Mama Rose/Ethel Merman entered from the back, marching down the stage-left aisle, screaming out, "Sing out, Louise!" to one of the children onstage. An ecstatic Broadway audience exploded. Ethel Merman had announced her return.

Ostensibly *Gypsy* is the story of stripper Gypsy Rose Lee. But from that moment of her grand entrance, Merman made it clear just whose show *Gypsy* was. Merman as Rose lords over everything, and the show was indeed something to lord over. *Gypsy* was easily her most ambitious musical, demanding more work and nuance in terms of acting than all of her previous roles put together; her triumph was such that even hard-to-please critics consider it perhaps the greatest performance in musical history.[1] *Gypsy* would leave a permanent imprint on Ethel's persona, and Mama Rose's impact was so great that, as one Broadway historian said, it "swept aside all [of her] other characters."[2]

Rose's Story

Rose is the mother of two girls, Baby June (her clear favorite) and Louise. Their success on the vaudeville circuit means everything to her, and there is nothing she won't do to procure it. In this opening scene, she threatens to tell the press that "Uncle Jocko's Kiddie Show" talent contests are rigged if he doesn't feature her girls more prominently. When she gets her way, Rose exhorts, "Smile, girls, smile!" as the girls sing "May We Entertain You."[3]

From there we meet Rose's disapproving father, who refuses to support her. After chiding him for his lack of adventure in "Some People," Rose makes off with a gold plaque he received at work and then lands in Los Angeles, where she soon meets candy salesman Herbie. After they exchange a "sexual look," Herbie asks the thrice-married woman whether she would marry again. No for her; yes for him. In the bittersweet "Small World," their differences and their mutual attraction are made evident, and Herbie becomes the family's agent and Rose's lover.

Daughter June is still the star performer. Louise, younger and less confident, is shunted to the back, something that continues as the two become young women. The girls lament life on the road, the inability of their mother to settle down ("If Momma Was Married"),[4] and the fact that their lives are dominated by life on the stage, their mom, and a vaudeville act that everyone has outgrown. The teenage June elopes with Tulsa, one of the young men Rose had brought into the troupe and the only male in the entire show with a solo number ("All I Need Is the Girl"). Louise, whose crush on Tulsa had gone unnoticed, is now stuck with a family act and working for a mother who doesn't think she has the chops to make it. But in the rousing "Everything's Coming Up Roses," Mama Rose's instinctive determination kicks in, cheering Louise and Herbie on and converting despair to optimism.

Rose is grooming Louise for the starring role, but the shy, gangly girl lacks the innate talents of her sister. Rose rallies the troupe again in "Together, Wherever We Go," an upbeat, jaunty tune with lyrics that assure and threaten all at once. ("You'll Never Get Away from Me" conveys that same tension, with lyrics recalling the actual words Rose Hovick [sometimes Havock] said to her daughters on her deathbed.) But the family acts are getting hokier, the Depression has taken its toll, movies are popular, and vaudeville is not. Rose refuses to bend. When the family is booked into smaller and seedier venues, the end of the road comes to them in the form of a burlesque house. At first, Rose is horrified that her "family act" has been booked in a house featuring strippers, but then she quickly offers up Louise as a replacement when one of them can't go on. Strippers Mazeppa, Tessie, and Electra had earlier instructed them with "You Gotta Have a Gimmick," and now Louise, suddenly onstage as "Gypsy Rose Lee," decides that *hers* is to minimize the stripping while bantering with the audience with wisecracks about the act. Herbie, meanwhile, finally realizes that Rose cannot change and walks away. Louise, too, has also taken leave of her mother; after her "Let Me Entertain You" act, she comes into her own and ascends into stardom, a process conveyed in montage.

"Rose's Turn" is performed solo on a darkened stage. The cast-aside mother performs as if for herself, reflecting on her life and all that she has done for her children, both of whom are now gone. The moods of this number range from vulnerability ("M-m-momma's letting go . . .") to defiant self-preservation ("I did it for *me!*"), after which the delusional Rose bows to an imagined audience. Louise, who'd been watching from behind, tenderly invites her estranged mother out, draping her fur stole over her mom's shoulders with maternal care.

Producing the Fable

Both *Gypsy: A Musical Fable* and the story of its production have become the stuff of legend. In 1994, the full-length book *The Making of Gypsy* was published, and Arthur Laurents's play and the original cast recording have remained in print steadily, keeping the original show in the public eye. Its bigger revivals have done the same thing, notably Angela Lansbury's in 1973, Tyne Daly's in 1989, Bernadette Peters's in 2003, and Patti LuPone's in 2007. Bette Midler played Rose in a high-budget TV movie in 1993. Surprisingly, the recollections of the musical's original creative team and performers lack most of the usual contradictions that shape the afterlives of so many shows. Their stories have circulated and recirculated with each revival or with each new biography, and so the accounts are for the most part reliably well-worn. This is not to say that the initial production went smoothly, however, or that the show was without its tensions.

Gypsy began as the quasi-factual memoir that Gypsy Rose Lee published soon after the death of her mother, Rose, in 1954. A gifted storyteller, the charismatic stripper was less concerned with accuracy than with telling a tale with flair. It was David Merrick who had come up with the idea of turning the stripper's memoir into a musical after reading excerpts published in *Harper's* and *Town and Country*. Merrick (1911–2000) was one of Broadway's biggest and most formidable legends. In a thirty-year career, he produced such shows as *The Matchmaker* (and its musical reincarnation, *Hello, Dolly!*), *I Can Get It for You Wholesale, Stop the World—I Want to Get Off, One Flew over the Cuckoo's Nest,* and *I Do! I Do!* An odd-looking man with a "cheesy, lopsided toupee,"[5] Merrick was gruff and ruthless and made no bones about being in show business for the money. The producer was extremely gifted with promotional savvy and daring; he'd been known to plant shills in the audience, feed fake stories to the press, and encourage fights among his stars.

An "abominable showman," Merrick thought nothing of promising more than 100 percent of a show's take to get people onboard, breaking the backs of unions, squaring off with Walter Winchell, whatever it took. He may have been an admired man, but he was not a beloved one. Asked at one point whether he was on speaking terms with Merrick, actor Peter Ustinov replied, "We speak but we do not talk."

Competing with him for the rights to Miss Lee's book were Alan Jay Lerner and Frederick Lowe, the *My Fair Lady* duo who were also in discussions with Lee, as was Warner Brothers, which offered her two hundred thousand dollars. In the end, she accepted Merrick's much smaller offer. Not only did she like him (according to her son, Erik Preminger, he reminded Lee of her ex-lover Mike Todd), but she also understood that his offer, which included film rights, would be more lucrative in the long run if the play became a success.

Merrick's coproducer was Leland Hayward, a less gimmick-driven producer than Merrick but one who was no less shrewd. His films had included *Mr. Roberts, The Old Man and the Sea,* and *The Spirit of St. Louis,* and he had produced shows such as *State of the Union, Mr. Roberts, South Pacific, Anne of the Thousand Days,* and, of course, *Call Me Madam.* It was Leland Hayward who had produced the classic *Ford 50th Anniversary Show* with Ethel, and her appreciation for him was enormous.

Betty Comden and Adolph Green signed on to do the book but soon changed their minds, preoccupied with another project—the film script for *Auntie Mame,* Rosalind Russell's reprisal of her stage role. When Comden and Green backed out, the producers turned to Arthur Laurents, the gifted young writer of *West Side Story* and recent Hollywood movies such as *Snake Pit* and *Rope.*

Hayward procured Jerome Robbins as choreographer-director. Robbins's and Merman's paths had crossed before, in *Stars in Your Eyes* and *Call Me Madam.* A notoriously difficult personality ("bastard" is how most associates describe him), Robbins was brutal to his dancers and to people who challenged his artistic decisions. During *Gypsy's* production, Broadway tongues flapped over possible clashes between him and Merman, both strong personalities, but their professional areas were different enough that he likely didn't feel competitive with her; besides, this woman was carrying the show. The two enjoyed a good working relationship, and when a reporter suggested to Ethel that "it was her own box-office appeal that made Merman so sure of [the show's] success," she corrected him: "That's bunk. I read the book. I heard the music. And then I learned Jerome Robbins would direct. That was the end, honey. Jerry Robbins directing—on Broadway, that's like working for God."[6] Ethel referred to Robbins as "Teacher" for what she gained from him during the project.

Along with Agnes De Mille, Gene Kelly, Michael Kidd, Robert Fosse, and Robert Cole, Robbins was a key figure who made the '50s the "choreographer's decade"; *West Side Story,* directed and choreographed by Robbins, is unimaginable without its dance routines. The decade saw musical dance routines utterly transformed, a period when, in the words of the *New York Times,* the "high-kicking chorus cuties have been replaced by an eager, earnest *corps de ballet.*"[7] Dance sequences were now used to express complex emotional, psychological, and narrative situations across musical hits like *Carousel* and, of course, *West Side Story.*

Arthur Laurents had been left raw from the experience of working with Jerome Robbins on *West Side Story* before *Gypsy* and vowed never to work with him again. (He was also infuriated that Robbins had caved to pressure and named names during the HUAC-McCarthy hearings.)[8] But for all his rancor, Laurents knew that "no one could choreograph a scene like Jerry," and Robbins, for his part, insisted that he wouldn't do *Gypsy* without Laurents onboard.

Enter Stephen Sondheim

Also fresh from the critical success of *West Side Story* was Stephen Sondheim, a composer and lyricist who came to the project with all the promise in the world. But Ethel did not care to entrust the show's music to a relatively inexperienced songwriter; the disappointing *Happy Hunting* was too fresh in her mind. The producers offered no resistance; after all, their first choice of composers had been old Merman favorites Irving Berlin and Cole Porter, before turning to Jule Styne, the versatile popular composer for *Gentlemen Prefer Blondes, High Button Shoes, Peter Pan,* and *Bells Are Ringing* and who had worked on film and TV projects involving Merman for decades—in the '30s, he had provided some of the music to *Straight, Place and Show* at Fox. Styne's was an established, mainstream track record, something the young Sondheim lacked. Styne also knew how to write with particular stars in mind, another thing Sondheim had little experience with at the time. Said Styne, "This is not denying Steve's musical talent, but to write for Ethel Merman was a kind of bag he didn't know much about. . . . When you write for a star you've got to take in what the star has to offer. If you don't, you're not doing what the people want to hear. . . . Steve didn't have to tailor, he had to write only character."[9] At the same time, some of *Gypsy*'s production team was concerned that Styne might be too commercial for the show and unable to convey its tangled, intricate themes. Styne's songs were usually simple and straightforward, with memorable, hummable refrains ("Diamonds Are a Girl's Best Friend," "The Party's Over"), and his musical phrasing was geared to lyrics rather than offering elaborate melodies to which his lyrics might conform. Pairing him with Sondheim, a composer and lyricist of much more complexity, did not seem a likely match, a point that cast further doubt. The *Gypsy* team was glad to be proved wrong when Styne—a man most remember as a person of talent and decency—played some of his ideas. They were also struck that the composer's pride was unruffled by having to audition.

Sondheim was understandably chaffed by the decision to give him the job of lyricist at a time when he wanted to develop his career as a composer. Taking on *Gypsy* would mean interrupting *A Funny Thing Happened on the Way to the Forum*, which wouldn't debut until 1962. "The worst thing about being a lyricist is that everyone else is in rehearsal, whereas you are back at the hotel, trying to fix those two terrible lines."[10] Sondheim asked his mentor Oscar Hammerstein what to do, and Hammerstein advised him to take the job, that the experience would be worth it. Instead of writing Madame Rose, Hammerstein told him, you write for Madame Rose as played by Ethel Merman: "It's not so much that you tailor the material, but you hear the voice in your head whether you want to or not."[11] On signing, Sondheim was compensated in part by receiving a larger percentage for the lyrics than was standardly given: "My guess is that I had two and a quarter, going to two and a half once the show made a profit. I don't remember what shows grossed in those days, but let's say it was $100,000. That amounts to $2500 a week, or $2250. That was a lot of money for those days, when theater tickets cost four dollars and ninety cents."[12]

Laurents, meanwhile, was working on the book and checking in with Gypsy Rose Lee from time to time to verify the accuracy of events and characters. Every time, he says, she'd give him different accounts, different lines and details, and was clearly much more focused on a good tale than on historical fidelity. For example, when he invented the character of Herbie, she said, "I wish I'd thought of him for my autobiography!"[13] Laurents quickly realized that he had carte blanche; all that Lee insisted on was retaining *Gypsy* as the title.

With sister June Havoc, however, things were not so simple. Havoc was understandably peeved with the unflattering and dismissive treatment her character received in her sister's account; and it was not much better in the final show, which urges audiences to pull for Louise from the very start. Later, when June runs off to elope, it's as if she's fallen off a cliff; audiences would have no way of knowing that "Baby June" turned into a successful musical star in her own right. Producers worked overtime to deal with Havoc, although correspondence shows that they were prepared to proceed even if she refused to sign the release. Havoc went through Laurents's book, and for the most part he agreed to her changes. (He refused to accommodate her request to say that she was thirteen when she left the show, however.) Just to hedge his bets, Merrick decided to change her character's name from June to Claire at one point, a decision Dorothy Kilgallen reports as having been made at Havoc's insistence.[14]

Ethel Prepares

Ethel's desire to widen her range as an actress was no secret in New York, and gossipers wrote that Ethel had said to Gypsy Rose Lee, "I've read your book. I love it. I want to do it. I'm going to do it. And I'll shoot anyone else who gets the part."[15] (This anecdote, likely apocryphal, already has Merman channeling Rose's bulldozing determination.) The pleasant and rewarding working experiences Ethel enjoyed with Hayward ("My favorite producer," she inscribed a copy of one of her plays to him) made her decision to sign on very easy. "She's the easiest person in the world to get along with so long as you tell her the truth," Hayward told the press. "You must never stall her. If you kid her, you're dead. Of course, like any one else, if Ethel is unhappy, she's very difficult." Of the role itself, he said, "I told her that if she played the part she couldn't go back to other types of roles, but she laughed, and asked me who was kidding whom? She knows she is no longer a romantic leading lady."[16]

Laurents recalls his first sit-down with Merman late one afternoon at Sardi's: "'Rose is a monster,' I told her. 'How far are you willing to go?' 'I'll do anything you want me to,' she said."[17] Ethel told the same story in interviews at the time, that she was in fact willing to do as much as it took, accurately predicting that *Gypsy* would show off her acting skills as nothing had before. Laurents was privately skeptical, however, about her talents as an actress, especially a dramatic one. He later said that, to him, Ethel Merman was "a voice, a presence, and a strut, not an actress."[18] In public, Laurents treated Merman with respectful care. "Knowing that she went along with my ideas was tremendously helpful in writing the book," he told an interviewer. "I have more admiration for her than any actress I've ever worked with. She is very professional and a terribly nice woman. She doesn't equivocate, and that's what wins over sympathies of audiences."[19]

Merman had personal reasons to long for the part. She was eager to put the unpleasantness and poor performance of *Happy Hunting* behind her, and what better way than a powerhouse of a new show? Even more important, though, was getting past the experience with Six, the man for whom she had left New York and for whom she had, in a sense, left Ethel Merman. She had been used, financially and socially, cheated on, and there had been Six's appalling physical and emotional abuses. It had taken awhile, but she was now prepared to declare the marriage a loss and move on. Says her son,

> One of the ways I see that period is as Mom taking back her power that Bob Six had tried to contain and control in our castle at Six Acres. *Gypsy* brought Ethel back to her own world where she was a queen and though Bob Six tried his best to play the king in her realm, by *that* time Mom was painfully immersed in her reality that whatever kind of kingly husband she'd hoped Bob Six would turn out to be—he wasn't doin' so good, to say the least. . . . Once *Gypsy* started happening, from the get-go Mom was back on top and "Jumbo" had gotten shrunk to number two.[20]

Merman first announced that she was working on *Gypsy* on the November 11, 1958, *Eddie Fisher Show*.[21] Rehearsals began early next March. By then, Robbins had already been working for nearly a month with dancers and set designer Jo Mielziner and was going "slightly cuh-razy, trying to cast three June Havocs and three Gypsy Rose Lees because Laurents's book calls for them to appear at three different stages of their lives."[22] The role of the adult Gypsy came down to two young actresses, Sandra Church and Suzanne Pleshette. "Suzanne was perfect for the second act because she could be a strong, sexual, fearless woman. But the first act called for an asexual, yearning, timid girl: that was Sandra."[23] So twenty-four-year-old Sandra Church got the part. Baby June and Baby Louise were played by Jacqueline Mayro and Karen Moore, respectively.

Casting Herbie took awhile. The producers approached stars like Robert Alda before finally turning to Jack Klugman, a nonsinger known mostly for his turn in *12 Angry Men* (1957) and for TV appearances, including a small part in *Kiss Me Kate*. Klugman's greener status and relaxed, everyman persona made him a perfect match for the hard-to-partner icon. Tony Randall recalled what his future costar on *The Odd Couple* told him about working with Merman. Jack didn't know his way around Broadway musicals, and Ethel "introduced" him by singing a number of songs from her shows for him, giving him a history lesson all alone in the theater. It was a generous side he didn't see at first. "I was certainly aware of her fearsome reputation," Klugman recalled about the early days. "And so I kept my distance. I'd call her Miss Merman." Then, one day, she said, "What's this Miss Merman stuff?" and he said, "I don't want to be disrespectful, you're the star." Merman: "Have I ever acted the star with you?" Soon she'd taken him in as a confidant, and Klugman became close to her family as well. She even dropped the discretion performers usually maintain when discussing their preferred colleagues, telling reporters long after the show had closed that Jack Klugman was her favorite costar.[24]

A solid dramatic actor, Klugman did not have the panache of a romantic leading man and also lacked Merman's commanding stage presence. In a way, those differences, coupled with his distinctive, nonsinging voice, gave a real pathos to their stage relationship, but at the same time, as Laurents notes, casting Klugman as Herbie removed what he called their "very sexual subtext,"[25] although traces of it remain in "You'll Never Get Away from Me." Klugman, moreover, was fourteen years younger than Ethel, so theirs was a less credible romantic relationship that way. And, more important, the Rose-Herbie relationship has only a supporting role in *Gypsy*'s story, whose real pathos depends on the mother-daughter pairing.

Klugman brought out Ethel's affectionate, generous side, and she was able to boost his confidence about his role and his singing, even though he'd been ready to throw in the towel: "I just wasn't very good. I was totally humiliated [at the audition]. . . . Jerry asked me to sing 'Small World' with her and I warned them, 'If she belts it, I'm going to walk right out!' Well, she sang it so softly that her voice cracked—there was so much love in it, such concern, that I picked up and sang the second chorus and sounded like Pinza. . . . When I got home, they called and told me I had the part."[26]

Most of the show and songs were written during the fall of 1958. Ethel was so taken with Styne and Sondheim's work that she got them to perform the songs at Cole Porter's apartment in the Waldorf-Astoria in an attempt to get the ailing composer to start working again. By this time, Porter was almost a total recluse, relying increasingly on painkillers and drink after the death of his wife, Linda, and the amputation of his leg. Said Sondheim to biographer Meryle Secrest:

We went for dinner up in his apartment at the Waldorf-Astoria Towers, Jule, myself, Merman and Anita Loos. By then he was being carried around by his strong servant piggyback. My memory is that when we sang "Together," the song from *Gypsy* that has a quadruple rhyme "wherever I go, I know he goes / Wherever I go, I know she goes / No fits, no fights, no feuds and no egos / Amigos"—and when I said "amigos," I heard him go "Ah!" right in the corner of the room. It's a very Cole Porter line, because he would use these foreign languages for rhyme, for effect, and he didn't see it coming.[27]

Too weak to applaud, Cole tapped a spoon against his glass in approval. Later, Jule Styne said that he was relieved his piano was facing the other way, since tears were streaming down his face.

Klugman recalls the moment that "Rose's Turn" was unveiled. Styne was at the piano, and Sondheim "sang it with such feeling and such awareness of what it was about that I just fell apart and bawled like a baby. It was so brilliant. I will never forget that moment. When Steve did 'M-m-momma, M-m-momma,' and couldn't get it out, Ethel and I just burst into tears."

Sondheim's lyrics to "Some People" included a line in which Rose tells her father to "go to hell." Ethel refused to do it. She also did not want to sing, "I guess I did it for me," toward the end of "Rose's Turn." "It would make her Rose awful, a monster," explains Laurents, and that was something Merman was loath to do.[28] The team had to convince Ethel that the line was pivotal to unlocking both the show and her character.

More extensive were group discussions about how to follow the climax of "Rose's Turn." As Sondheim said, "A woman having a nervous breakdown should not get applause from the audience."

To have a mad scene and then have a bow violated everything I thought I had learned from Oscar Hammerstein, who taught me to be true to character and . . . the situation. So I forced Jule not to put a [musical] ending on it, but to have it fade out with high screech violin sounds with those last chords when she's screaming—not singing, but screaming—"For me, for me, for me!" And there would be this chilling . . . moment in the theatre and then, as Arthur wrote it, the daughter would come out of the wings applauding her, and they would go on.[29]

Again, they approached Hammerstein for advice. "Oscar argued that the audience was so eager to applaud Merman, who deserved her bow, that they didn't listen to the last scene which was what the entire play is about," he told them when the show was in Philadelphia tryouts.[30] "I know it's dishonest, but *please,* fellows, put a big ending on that number if you want the rest of the play to play. Or bring the curtain down there."[31]

"Rose's Turn" is nearly five minutes long and comes at the end of a show in which Rose has already sung seven songs. Filled with a great deal of movement and shifts in melody, style, and tone, it demands unusual vocal control, timing, and dexterity. Ethel's voice was more than up to it, hitting notes so hard on the soundtrack that she generates a yodellike sound, especially in the reprised fragments of "Everything's Coming Up Roses." Yet unlike the comic result of those effects in *Annie Get Your Gun,* nothing here was for laughs; rather, the result was intensity. "In classical singing, you would never allow someone to do that, never. And it would be questionable from the standards of vocal health as well," says singing voice specialist Jeanette LoVetri.[32] LoVetri calls "Rose's Turn" a "gut-buster," and Ethel was only too aware of this, telling friends privately that it was a "motherfucker to sing,"[33] and the singer was left uncharacteristically tired after each performance. "Rose" is the one song that makes or breaks *Gypsy* and is the yardstick by which critics and fans measure the performance of all Mama Roses.

Ethel was amenable to most changes, up to a point. Sondheim recalls, "Two weeks before the opening I thought that 'Some People' needed a verse because the dialogue that precedes the song is on a high pitch and the song starts low. It needed the verse to bring it down. The cue-in is clumsy and it would have helped the song a lot. After it was written, however, she said that she felt it was too angry and refused to learn it."[34] Flora Roberts, Sondheim's agent, called the Dramatists Guild and said, "If there's an unnamed star who doesn't want to sing a verse, what are the writer's rights?" And the man at the guild said, "Let's put it this way. There was a star named Ethel Merman and she was in a show called *Call Me Madam,* and she sang a dummy lyric for 'Hostess with the Mostes' on the Ball' for many weeks out of town and just as she got into New York, Irving Berlin came into her dressing room and said, 'I've finally perfected the lyric!' And she said, 'Call me Miss Birds Eye. The Show is frozen!' So for three years, she sang the dummy lyric."[35] Sure, Sondheim was told, a singer was obliged to sing the song as it was written, but if that singer was Ethel Merman, he didn't have a chance.

"Little Lamb" caused more tension: Robbins didn't like it, saying it didn't have much to do with the show (and it didn't, in terms of pure story line), and then announced that he was planning to excise it. The next day at rehearsal, Jule Styne took charge; he went onstage and, facing front, said, "Mr. Robbins . . . I have informed the Dramatists Guild and my lawyers. Unless 'Little Lamb' is back in the show, tonight, I am withdrawing my entire score.' He bowed and walked off."[36] It was restored. Some of the show's songs came out of the Jule Styne trunk. One had been written for an unfinished movie called *Pink Tights*, "Why Did You Have to Wait So Long?" for which Sammy Cahn had not finished the lyrics; Styne revisited it as "You'll Never Get Away from Me." ("What Jule had *not* told me," recalls Sondheim, "was that Leo Robin had subsequently written a set of lyrics to it for a TV musical, *Ruggles of Red Gap*, with the title 'I'm in Pursuit of Happiness.'"[37] Sondheim was understandably displeased, but apparently nothing came of it.)

It's hard to believe, but the melody of "Everything's Coming Up Roses" also came out of Styne's trunk. Initially, it was going to appear as "In Betwixt and Between," with lyrics again by Cahn, for *High Button Shoes*, but was put in the trunk. It ended up being the perfect vehicle for Merman: upbeat and brimming with high-octane optimism, showcasing one of Merman's distinguishing vocal techniques, coming at notes from above. As singer Klea Blackhurst says, "Ethel Merman's notes just *land* from above, and it's a clear bing."[38] She starts "Coming Up Roses" this way, and the effect is even more striking, since she doesn't even hit the title lyrics until the end of the first quatrain. Robbins didn't see the innovativeness of the song and was even puzzled by the title. Recalls Sondheim, "And Jerry says, 'I just don't understand that title.' I say, 'Why not, Jerry?' And he says, 'Everything's coming up Rose's *what?*'"[39]

Previews and Premiere

Gypsy previewed at the Shubert Theatre in Philadelphia from April 13 to May 16. The sold-out run brought in $65,916 the first week alone.[40] About Ethel critics raved ("She is close to brilliant in an assignment that demands as much of her dramatically as it does vocally!"),[41] but reviews said that the show needed trimming, especially the first act, asymmetrically heavy compared with the second one. Forty-five minutes were cut, a solo by Merman ("Smile Girls") and one by Klugman ("Nice She Ain't") along with children's numbers such as "Mama's Talking Soft." (This is when Robbins tried to excise "Little Lamb.") Styne also had to fight Robbins to retain the overture, and happily he won; *Gypsy*'s score would not have been the same without it.

When the show was in previews, Dorothy Kilgallen was dishing dirt that Robbins and Merman were "at odds" over last-minute changes, saying, "The smart money, as usual, is betting on Merman."[42] It's hard to imagine that Merman and Robbins would agree on every detail, and given Robbins's mercurial behavior, it seems a logical enough report, but whatever Kilgallen might have been referring to didn't amount to anything. Most of Robbins's battles were with Styne and Laurents, not Ethel Merman.

Did the press want Ethel to be difficult? Kilgallen, her friend, was probably going for something else, lauding Ethel for her tough professionalism, but other reports were aiming to ramp up the rough, brassy image. Of course, Ethel *could* be difficult, often displaying a harsh perfectionism when she worked on shows ("not to get her way, but to get the best show," Levitt notes).[43] A notorious Merman chapter from *Gypsy* was her reported dislike of Sandra Church (Gypsy) and her pleasure when Church was replaced later in the run. Church has publicly affirmed how unpleasant Merman eventually made things for her, but for a time at least, their relationship was cordial. Ethel saved over half a dozen cards from the young star, who thanked her for various gifts and expressed her love for the Broadway icon. Merman had no reason not to support Church, and even when she believed that the young woman was having an affair with Jule Styne—a much older, married man— Ethel kept still.

Gypsy was scarcely helped by David Merrick's obstreperous pessimism. During the previews, he kept saying that if the show didn't start generating better buzz, *Gypsy* wouldn't last a month on Broadway. Although this was hardly strange behavior, it hurt the morale of the group, and, Laurents recalled, the show "came into New York facing death."[44] Perhaps Merrick didn't want to treat the show as his own, or maybe he didn't think *Gypsy* was under his control as much as he wanted, so why stick his neck out for it? At the same time, Merrick thrived on stirring things up. Whatever his motives, matters peaked when a frustrated Hayward, almost on a dare, offered to buy out Merrick's portion of what Merrick was calling "this bomb." Merrick backed off.

Variety was of a different opinion, predicting in a headline, "*Gypsy* Could Do $81,000 a Week."[45] And now, after the Philadelphia previews, *Gypsy* was rehearsing at Broadway's Winter Garden one week before the premiere. *Variety* was right: tickets, priced between $2.50 and $9.40, were moving like hotcakes.

And so, on the evening of May 21, as New York geared up, *Gypsy*'s cast, crew, and producers were trying to calm their jitters. Ethel had been flooded with notes from figures as diverse as Bill Fields, Mary Martin, Johnnie Ray, Gertrude Berg, Meredith Willson, and Oscar and Dorothy Hammerstein. Among the sweetest is a greeting card with roses all over it: "With Love to Mother on Mother's Day" and a handwritten note inside: ". . . and tonight it *is!*" Under a sketch of an arrow-pierced heart, it is signed "Teach." From Mitzi Gaynor: "Dear Mom, we are thinking of you and already sharing your great success in *Gypsy*." Ethel's scrapbooks also have pages of spirited notes from fans who took in *Gypsy* in the months to come, such as an office worker from South Bend, Indiana, and a woman who worked on an ocean liner who said she was moved by Ethel's hard work and the show's message that stage moms shouldn't push too hard. Not every viewer saw the monster in Rose.

Just hours before the curtain went up, what was Ethel Merman doing? Polishing her jewelry. "She's got no nerves," said an amazed Benay Venuta.[46] In retrospect, there was little to worry about. As Arthur Laurents said later, "In theatre paradise, every opening night would be like the New York opening night of *Gypsy*. From overture to curtain calls, the audience was madly in love—with every word, every note, every player, every moment. They roared their love."[47]

Other legends were made that night, including one that took place in the audience. As Laurents tells it:

> At the end of Gypsy's strip, Walter and Jean Kerr came up the aisle, clearly on their way out because there was no place to stand in back. Everyone feared Walter Kerr [*New York Times* drama critic]; even Jule had begged me to cut a joke about the Vatican because Kerr was a Catholic. I wouldn't, and I wouldn't let him out of the theatre until he had seen the whole show. I blocked the Kerrs at the head of the aisle: "Go back to your seats," I ordered. "It isn't over." Startled, they dutifully turned around.[48]

Robert Serling, biographer of Robert Six (who was still married to Ethel, though barely), gives another version: "Six was present on opening night, occupying an aisle seat just behind a prominent New York theater critic. After the curtain came down on a particularly effective and climactic scene, the critic rose and started to leave. Standing in the aisle, blocking his path and with arms folded across his broad chest, was Six. 'Where the hell do you think you're going?' he growled. 'The show's over,' the critic insisted. 'The hell it is. Ethel's best scene is coming up. Sit down!' The critic did."[49] The next day, Kerr's review ran in the *Times:* "I'm not sure whether *Gypsy* is new fashioned, or old fashioned, or integrated, or non-integrated. The only thing I'm sure of is that it's the best damn musical I've seen in years."[50]

New York was enthralled. For Kenneth Tynan: "The first act is perfection. The second mere brilliance."[51] For Winchell, "Ethel Merman, who rockets songs and roman candles, demonstrates her explosive radiance in the grandest musical since *My Fair Lady.* Everything about the show is fodder for superlatives . . . the bright satellites revolving around the star are Jack Klugman, Sandra Church and Lane Bradbury. As for Queen Ethel, this show is the brightest gem in a career crowned with hits."[52]

Gypsy in Perspective

Gypsy is a musical lover's musical. The title alone, in addition to referencing Gypsy Rose Lee, pays tribute to the hardworking dancers and singers who move from show to show. What distinguishes it from other musicals about show business (such as *Annie Get Your Gun*) is that *Gypsy* wasn't out to *celebrate* that world so much as use it for story material, casting a reflexive look at show biz that captures it not in its glory days but in a difficult transition. In a way, the show provided an emotionally layered rendering of what *There's No Business Like Show Business* tried to capture in "going on with the show."

Although *Gypsy* was a product of the moment, integrating song and dance in a sophisticated story of complex characters and issues, as most '50s musicals did, it was at the same time a step apart from musical theater of the time. Its protagonists were atypical—a pushy stage mother and stripper daughter—and it boasted only the most perfunctory of heterosexual romances. Historians have subjected the show to a number of assessments, placing it against different backdrops. For Mark Steyn, "It's the most Broadway of Broadway musicals, fusing the two strains of American musical theater, seizing the principles of the R&H [Rodgers and Hammerstein] musical play and setting them to gorgeous, vulgar rhythms of musical comedy—the dramatic ambitions of the former, the sass of the latter."[53] For Ethan Mordden, *Gypsy* and *West Side Story* weren't so much "climaxes of the R and H era as much as the first strikes in the next era, one in which the musical finally gives up its membership in the popular arts to confront its audience."[54] Yet even while it followed Broadway's move from diversionary spectacle to "integrated" musical, *Gypsy* was savvy enough not to leave the razzle-dazzle world of old entertainment behind.

Merman fans usually turn to either *Gypsy* or *Annie Get Your Gun* for the "best" Ethel Merman role. In some ways, *Gypsy* repeated what *Annie Get Your Gun* had done nearly fifteen years earlier: it reestablished Merman as Broadway's most vital star. Yet *Gypsy* achieved this not only in a completely new era of musical theater but also on completely different terms. For Rose is a demanding role in a demanding, innovative musical. She may have some of the same toughness as Nails Duquesne and others, but she is a character, not a caricature. Unlike Annie Oakley—who is not a caricature either, to be sure—Rose is psychologically complex and attracts (or repels) people for a variety of reasons. People are drawn to Rose not out of likability but, depending on whom you talk to, out of her defiance toward tradition, her chutzpah, her dedication, even, for some, her delusion. Especially in Merman's hands, Rose bristles with energy, and if Ethel's performance as Madame Rose is not every fan's favorite, it is certainly her most accomplished.

Reviewer Tom Donnelly agreed: "As far as I'm concerned, Ethel Merman playing Ethel Merman has been the ultimate peak in Show Business. Now, in *Gypsy*, a 'musical fable' based on the memoirs of Gypsy Rose Lee, Miss Merman not only blows her glorious bugle as of yore but also offers a characterization that is better than three-dimensional. It's 4-dimensional. Lynn Fontanne, Helen Hayes, Judith and Dame Edith Evans will have to move over."[55] *Newsweek,* the national weekly, made much the same point, reporting that while Merman's voice had been great in previous scores, when her librettists seemed most interested in her vocal dynamics, now, "the voice is still here, as commanding as Gabriel's horn, but this time, Miss Merman can make you weep between cheers."[56]

Encouraged by such raves, producers rushed out the cast recording earlier than planned, and it was well received. (With "Rose's Turn," wrote one reviewer, Ethel "rises to such heights of intensity that the record machine seems in danger of splitting.")[57] In June, *Variety*'s 21st Annual Critics Poll for best woman lead in a musical gave Merman more votes than Gwen Verdon in *Redhead* or Lotte Lenya in *Seven Deadly Sins* combined. And she was also nominated for the Tonys. (Curiously, three of the nominees that year—Merman, Mary Martin, and Dolores Gray—had all starred in *Annie Get Your Gun* at one point.) Justifiably proud of her work, Ethel was confident that this would be her year; her only other previous win had been for *Call Me Madam.* As the city geared up for the awards, Sherman Billingsley planned to host a Stork Club party for more than two hundred Tony nominees and former recipients, but a boycott organized by Angus Duncan, the director of the Theatre Wing, hurt the event. Citing labor problems at the Stork Club, Duncan urged those on the huge guest list to boycott the event. Ethel sent her close friend her regrets, something few others bothered to do. Fifteen people showed up.

In the end, there was not much to celebrate. Just as *West Side Story* had lost out to the more commercial *Music Man* two years earlier, *Gypsy* lost to *The Sound of Music,* also coproduced by Leland Hayward. Merman lost to Mary Martin, and when she heard the news, her now-fabled response was a supposed shrug of the shoulders and, "Well, how do ya buck a nun?"[58] When it learned that *Gypsy* had been shut out of the awards, the show's contingent, including Hayward, stayed away from the awards, and Leonard Lyons noted the irony that the ceremony that year opened and closed on the strains of "Everything's Coming Up Roses."

Fans lodged an official protest with the American Theatre Wing. Critic John Chapman wrote that when he voted for Merman, he wasn't voting against Mary Martin. What influenced his vote, he said, was that Martin wasn't doing anything new, whereas Merman was performing a new kind of role for Broadway and a new one for her.[59] (A Chicago fan sent his copy of that article to Ethel, writing under the photo of Martin as Maria von Trapp, "good," and under Ethel's as Rose, "excellent.") Much of the East Coast entertainment world found it perplexing that Martin and Merman weren't at least given a joint award, especially since *The Sound of Music* shared its best musical award with *Fiorello!* and, as one columnist wrote, "Mary . . . would have loved sharing the glory."[60]

For one Broadway historian, the Tony Awards that year were "a decision that clarified mainstream cultural values by rewarding a nun-turned wife over a relentlessly ambitious stage mother."[61] Stephen Sondheim was philosophical:

What makes smash-hit musicals are stories that audiences want to hear—and it's always the same story. How everything turns out terrific in the end and the audience goes out thinking, that's what life is all about. . . . *The Sound of Music* says you can eat your cake and have it—you can get away from the Nazis, marry the man of your choice, *without* compromising your religious goodness. . . .

Gypsy says something fairly hard to take: that every child eventually has to become responsible for his parents. . . . It's something that everybody knows but no one likes to think about a lot. And that's why *Gypsy,* at base, in spite of the terrific reviews, wasn't a smash hit.[62]

Rosalind Russell: The Anti-Merm

Worse for Ethel was what happened when Hollywood decided to adapt *Gypsy* for the screen. Sol Siegel had expressed interest, as had MGM's Arthur Freed. Warner Bros.' Mervyn LeRoy saw the Broadway show numerous times and was in discussions with Ethel about resuming her role on the screen, and, indeed, it was Warner Bros. who picked up the film, paying $650,000 against 10 percent of the picture's gross. But Ethel was not part of the deal. In early December 1960, writer George Oppenheimer was in the room when Merman learned that LeRoy had given the part of Rose to Rosalind Russell: "I happened to be in Jule Styne's office that day and Jule came in and the phone started to ring. . . . he answered it and his face turned white. It was Ethel, who had just found out that Rosalind Russell's husband, Freddie Brisson . . . had somehow gotten his wife signed for Ethel's part in the movie. Ethel was screaming at poor Jule over the phone."[63] Jack Klugman says, "[LeRoy] really screwed Ethel. He was constantly with her and *promised* that he wouldn't do the picture without her. Then he went and signed Roz Russell for the role. Mr. LeRoy is not a very nice person."[64] After learning that she'd been passed over, Ethel fired her agent, replacing him with Milton Pickman, who remained with her for the rest of her career. And she quickly went into negotiations with Merrick about doing a tour with the show, "to show how it oughtta be done," as legend has her saying. (Her actual public words were more subdued: "It's my favorite role and I want people to see me do it. My two kids are grown, I'm not married and have no ties right now.")[65]

Russell's and Merman's careers had circled each other's—almost like distant relatives—for over twenty years. Both women were known for playing strong, independent, colorful characters. Russell was gifted with a sparkling presence and great comic timing *(His Girl Friday),* but her being an established screen star didn't endear her to Broadway critics, especially when she appeared in adaptations of plays that other women had introduced onstage, "taking" Gertrude Berg's role in *A Majority of One* for Warner and Jessica Tandy's in *Five Finger Exercise* for Columbia. "Roz's next 'exercise' in versatility is still an official secret," speculated Radie Harris. "But I suspect it's *Gypsy,* which I know will break Ethel Merman's heart just as it broke Gertrude Berg's heart to lose *Majority of One.* . . . Roz's screen name is considered more potent box office to the Hollywood top brass, who make the decisions."[66]

Up to this point, Ethel and Russell had enjoyed a cordial relationship, exchanging congratulatory gifts and telegrams on opening nights, greetings at Christmastime, and so on. A reading of Russell's notes in hindsight, though, suffuses them with bitchy irony. For *Gypsy:* "Dearest Ethel, A wee note to tell you how fantastic you were on opening night. Freddie and I were heartbroken we didn't get to see you at the Stein's *[sic]* to tell you in person how terrific you were."[67] Today, Merman lovers delight in taking potshots at Russell. It's become a way to show their loyalty to Queen Ethel and to celebrate her misunderstood power. Forty years later, Elaine Stritch relayed in her one-woman show that Merman privately referred to Freddie Brisson as "the Lizard of Roz."

Pop saved reviews not only of his daughter's performances on the *Gypsy* tour but also of Russell's performance when the movie was released in November 1962. After all, his daughter was mentioned in most of them—and usually fared better than Miss Russell. From the *Toronto Globe and Mail:* "The chief fault for the debacle must rest on Miss Russell . . . and the result is, in a word, disastrous. . . . [Miss Merman had] stopped the show, and rightly so. What can Miss Russell do with this part? She can only pick up the crumbs that her limited talents in this area allow her. She plays Rose at a mile a minute."[68] To reporters Ethel was acidly diplomatic. "I haven't seen it," she told one who dared to ask her. "But I'd like to say that . . . it was a great personal tribute to have my name mentioned by nearly all the movie critics."[69] Other stock answers were: "Why didn't I? I wasn't asked"—"If the movie didn't do as well as the stage version, I would have taken the rap"—"No comment"—and (a favorite of fans, though only *attributed* to Ethel), "I hear it's being done more as a play rather than a musical."

In her column, Dorothy Kilgallen reported that someone had given Ethel a tape of Miss Russell's attempts to sing as Mama Rose (in the end, Russell was dubbed by Lisa Kirk), a story that has had the half-life of a nuclear explosion.[70] In 1998, a Broadway historian wrote, "After Merman's death, her knickknacks closet gave up discs of the *Gypsy* movie's prerecorded vocal tapes—not the improved Lisa Kirk tracks dubbing for an overparted Russell, but Russell's inadequate originals. Party records at Merman's *je m'en fiche* soirees?"[71] Tony Cointreau, who helped settle Ethel's belongings after her death, said he never encountered those recordings.

Three months into the run, Merman had throat trouble, missing seven performances. On the first night that understudy Jane Romano took over, she got a standing ovation—for her bravura if nothing else—but within a week, house receipts went from $82,900 to $71,800. Mary Martin wrote Ethel a handwritten note to say how glum her producers were looking.[72]

Dear Queen!
We heard you were "out"—! This is like hearing that Gabriel has stopped
blowing you know what! . . . Take it easy "boy" (as our darling Doctor Craig
would say) "try not to worry" and know that you truly are "The One and
Only" Merman, horn or no horn!!
Love always, Mary and Richard[73]

The ailing voice made for much, much bigger news than her tonsillectomy
had in 1929. Speculations abounded about whether Ethel had laryngitis or
had burst a blood vessel. (The latter was the case.) Everyone in the show sent
get-well notes, and while Ethel was recovering at home at the Park Lane,
Benay Venuta presented her with the oil portrait she'd done of the star as
Mama Rose. In it, Ethel/Rose is wearing her makeshift plaid coat, big bow
in hair, holding her small dog. Tony Cointreau was there when the gift was
presented and remembers that "even when she was unable to speak, [Ethel's]
energy took over the room." (He recalls Little Ethel once telling him, "Even
when Mom is sick, she's not like everyone else.")[74] When Ethel and her
slightly altered voice returned to the show, Styne sent a note, "Welcome back
in any key."[75]

Gypsy was now grossing over $80,000 per week, breaking records at
$86,472.26 in January 1960. The big take was facilitated by the 1,765-seat ca-
pacity of the Broadway, the largest theater in town (and originally a movie
theater palace). At an initial cost of about $420,000 to produce, *Gypsy* was
able to distribute a profit of $285,864 by April 23, 1960. Individuals such as
Gypsy Rose Lee owned about 23 percent; Merman and Six, 15 percent; Robbins, 5 percent; and so on down the line.

Ethel left the show for three performances to attend Ethel Jr.'s com-
mencement at Cherry Creek High School in Colorado on June 3. She graduated a year early and then stayed in Colorado, where her sense of independence was greater. Merman had negotiated the time off in her contract, and
when she left, papers rumored that David Merrick had purchased a three-
million-dollar insurance policy on Merman's flight. A syndicated photo from
Colorado showed the beaming star next to her daughter, now a beautiful
young woman. Her brother, meanwhile, had been unhappily shuffled off to
the Hackley School, a boarding school in Tarrytown, New York.

Ethel may have felt tired from performing each night in *Gypsy,* but she
kept a level of activity of someone half her age. While *Gypsy* was running, she
recorded "An Evening with Ethel Merman"—later changed to "Merman on
Broadway"—which NBC broadcast on television on November 24, 1959, as

part of its *Startime* series. Roger Edens, now working at Columbia Studios in Hollywood, returned to New York to produce it at Ethel's request and opened it with Merman singing "Lady with a Song," which he had composed for her in 1953 when Ethel appeared at the Texas State Fair. Her costars on the show were Fess Parker, Tab Hunter, and Tom Poston; Ethel and Hunter sang "You're Just in Love" in a skit in which Hunter played a psychiatrist and she the patient who ends up dispensing her advice to him.

The telegrams Ethel received for this appearance provide an informative look into the entertainment scene of the day, one that, like everything else, seemed to be growing ever more corporate and professionalized. More than ever, notes and telegrams were coming from TV executives such as the president of NBC and the director of special programs at MCA, and fewer—or fewer that she saved—came from colleagues and fans. It was a different world from the one of even ten years earlier, part of the shift away from Broadway's intimate, if squabbling, family. One colleague from the old days who remained true throughout, however, was Cole Porter, who sent a wire the day after "Merman on Broadway" aired: "I saw your television show last night you were stupendous all my congratulations and love."[76]

For her mother's TV special, Little Ethel sent a very long piece of tissue—possibly toilet paper, it is hard to tell—on which "Congratulations" was written in red, with a return address announcing, "From Ethel's classmates in Colorado College." Big Ethel's peers and colleagues may have been writing a little less, but her kids were writing more; during this same time, Bobby sent a number of (usually humorous) cards for her openings, birthdays, and Mother's Day, signing them with affection in a childish scrawl.

Nineteen fifty-nine saw Kay Kendall, Mario Lanza, and Maxwell Anderson pass away and Brooks Atkinson announcing his retirement. *Some Like It Hot, Exodus,* and *Suddenly Last Summer* lit up the screen; *A Majority of One, Raisin in the Sun,* and *The Miracle Worker* opened on Broadway, along with the musicals *Sound of Music, Fiorello!* and *Once upon a Mattress.* Ground in Manhattan was broken for Lincoln Center. Liz Taylor married Eddie Fisher, and at the end of the year Ethel and Bob Six finally made their "amicable" split public. "New Yorkers," said an unsurprised Kilgallen, "had often observed her paying more than just polite attention to another chap while Mr. Six sat at the same table, apparently not minding a bit."[77] Ethel was not romantically close with anyone, but journalists continued to identify partners, often the escorts filed under "dates" in her address book: Charles Wacker, Spencer

Martin, Peter Arnell, designer Donald Brooks, and songwriter Jimmy van Heusen (a frequent companion). Ethel still resided at Park Lane, where Judy Garland and Sid Luft were neighbors; Six was in Los Angeles in Bel Air. Six Acres was gone, having been purchased by an oilman whom the neighbors okayed. Whenever the press mentioned Bob Six with a date, it was Audrey Meadows.

By this time, Ethel's manager, William Fields, was sending her most of the clippings she passed along to Pop for the scrapbooks. One was to "have appeared on Friday, Dec. 18 [1959] which is the day the separation story broke in this and other newspapers." It was called "What Christmas Means to Me," by Ethel Merman, in which she says how much she loves "the bustle and the crowds and the happy preparations," adding, "Christmas carols cause me to cry like a fool." She wonders about what children think when they see all of Santa's different "understudies" at every street corner and tells readers that this year "this 'Gypsy,' her husband and two children will be having a green Christmas, in Jamaica. It's my week off from work, but I'll be thinking of New York, its glitter, glamour and happy faces."[78]

Christmas was Ethel's favorite holiday, but in 1959 it could hardly have been a joyous one. During her break (*Gypsy* closed for a week for the holiday, as did *The Sound of Music*), she and Six went through the motions of that trip they'd planned to the Caribbean for the kids. The new year would see her lose the Tony, lose the film part of Mama Rose, and see the divorce from Six finalized. But at the same time, with *Gypsy* Ethel's career was reinvigorated, and it was on her terms now, not Six's.

She stayed busy. That same Christmas break, she took part in a city charity drive and recorded the 1960 American Red Cross theme song, "Good Things Happen When You Give." On January 16, the cast and crew of *Gypsy* gave Ethel an oversized birthday card, and Gypsy Rose Lee sent a card with "a toast to you and the cast with love and gratitude from Gypsy." (On the back, over Lee's name, Ethel notes for the scrapbooks, "She sent over a chilled bottle of champagne—a Jeribom, which is six ½ quarts. We served it in paper cups when the curtain went down Saturday night.")[79] The show was still going strong, and now some of the child extras had to be replaced because they were outgrowing their roles.

Less than two weeks later, on the 29th, Ethel appeared on TV on NBC's *Bell Telephone Hour* with Beatrice Lillie, Benny Goodman, and Ray Bolger, all show biz veterans, in a special called "The Four of Us." The gimmick was to give each performer a chance to do something new and different; as was said on the show, "Why should we do what the public expects of us?" (Benny

Goodman, for instance, performed a piece by Carl Maria von Weber.) But Ethel didn't behave and sang "Alexander's Ragtime Band," "When My Sugar Walks Down the Street," "Sweet Georgia Brown," and "After You've Gone," all of which she had recorded earlier. To be sure, given the short memory of young TV audiences, perhaps she *was* showing viewers an unfamiliar, new (i.e., non-*Gypsy*) Ethel Merman, but the effect is odd nonetheless.

In May, Ethel was on television again, in a special honoring Cole Porter. Once more, she tried to lure her old friend out of seclusion by telling producers that she would appear only if he did, but he wouldn't budge. Ethel performed anyway, and the show was well received by critics—a warm, nostalgic tribute to a musical giant.

The Fable Winds Down

After a year and a half, *Gypsy*'s drawing power was starting to cool slightly. *Variety* reported that it was pulling in $53,500 out of the possible $82,900 it could at the Broadway, and so, in the summer of 1960, the producers relocated it to the smaller Imperial Theatre, where it stayed until the end of Ethel's contract in March 1961.[80]

While *Gypsy* was being moved to the Imperial in July, Ethel went to visit Ethel Jr. in Colorado, where she was acting in a local production of *Brigadoon*. On July 10, she headed for Europe with Benay Venuta and Bob Jr. (Ethel circled what she and Bobby ordered from the Pan Am menu.)[81] The trip included a visit to Florence, where Ethel attended a performance of Liliana Poli. She and Bobby also spent four days in London, where, after she landed incognito in her trademark big dark sunglasses and kerchief, a photographer found her; Ethel saved the tabloid clipping.[82] There she took in the premiere of *Ross,* in which Alec Guinness portrayed adventurer T. E. Lawrence. Pop and Agnes saved various postcards, photos, and souvenir pamphlets of the places Ethel visited, stayed, and shopped.

In the fall of 1960 during her time off from *Gypsy,* Ethel stumped vigorously for presidential candidate Richard Nixon. On the Wednesday before election day, she sang at three different downtown rallies, in addition to performing her matinee and evening show. Although Nixon lost, Ethel accepted an invitation to perform at JFK's pre-inaugural ball. ("Why shouldn't I sing at the gala? I helped put them in debt," she quipped, referring to the Democrat's campaign deficit.)[83] Smart remarks aside, though, Merman was delighted and proud to be part of the event.

At the time, Frank Sinatra was still an avid Democrat and coproduced the extravaganza with President Kennedy's brother-in-law Peter Lawford. By agreeing to perform for scale (two hundred dollars) on Leland Hayward's upcoming CBS TV special, *The Gershwin Years,* Sinatra was able to negotiate the releases of guests such as Laurence Olivier and Anthony Quinn (then in *Becket*) from their Broadway runs for the day. But that earlier inaugural event did not go smoothly. A blizzard upset people's travel plans, and Ethel was separated from her luggage. Forced to perform in her street clothes—a respectable but plain wool suit—a displeased Merman told Leonard Bernstein to explain what was going on to audiences before she sang "Everything's Coming Up Roses." To her, the situation compromised professional standards; yet, to one of the musicians playing, she was just a badly behaved diva. "Ethel Merman was furious," she said. "And she wasn't shy about making her dissatisfaction known!"[84] But none of this hurt her performance, and after her last notes, Sinatra cooed, "Absolutely glorious, Ethel!"[85]

When Ethel teamed up with Sinatra a few months later for *The Gershwin Years,* they were joined by Maurice Chevalier, Julie London, and other guests. The special aired the following year on January 15, 1961, with Richard Rodgers as host. Ethel promoted it in advance interviews by reminiscing about working with the Gershwins and the importance of the Gershwins' music to her career. On the special itself, she sang a medley from *Of Thee I Sing.* A few reviewers grumbled that more time should have been spent conjuring up the lost era, presumably to situate younger TV audiences, but the overwhelming response to the show was strong, and Ethel was well received.

Ethel turned fifty-three the day after the Gershwin tribute aired, and she saved the oversized birthday card that the cast of *Gypsy* again gave her. January gave her another special moment when Judy Garland flew in from London and "was given Miss Merman's house-seats on the aisle." The reporter added, "She didn't know the star made her entrance into the show from the rear of the theatre. Merman stopped at Judy's seat, embraced her, then went up onstage."[86]

Gypsy's run was now drawing to a close, and Ethel did not extend her contract. Jimmy Gardiner threw her a farewell cocktail party at the Sherry Netherland on March 19, for which he had a red-inked "One for the Road with Ethel" printed on cocktail napkins stapled to the invitation. Attending were Laurence Olivier, Joan Plowright, Lucille Ball, Elaine Stritch, and Bob Jr., whose note said, "Dear Mom, You were the prettyest *[sic]* girl at the party!!! Love, Me." On March 25, 1961, *Gypsy* closed, but not before a number of critics and reporters remarked that Ethel was as solid and powerful for the *n*th time as she had been opening night. To close out the last show, the orchestra played "Auld Lang Syne."[87]

Strong Women and Monster Mothers

Rose was not the only dominant woman on Broadway that season; that same year saw a revival of *Lysistrata* on the boards. In fact the entire decade had been filled with them, especially in musicals, whose stars were powerhouses in themselves. Mary Martin in *South Pacific,* Gwen Verdon in *Damn Yankees,* Rosalind Russell in *Wonderful Town,* and even Judy Holliday in *Bells Are Ringing* had audiences in the palm of their hands. Of course, Ethel was no stranger to playing strong figures, but by the late '50s, the lambent feminist spark of her roles like Annie Oakley had exploded into something larger and, presumably, scarier. And that scary thing was mother. For Mama Rose partakes of more than the musical comedy traditions of the decade's strong female leads; in her, we see the time's conflicted attitudes toward motherhood reach a fever pitch.

Although Philip Wylie's Momism offered an extreme manifestation of it, some of the misogyny circulating in the United States seemed to take aim at mature women, career women, and mothers. It can be detected in an August 1958 interview with Leland Hayward, when *Gypsy* was being written, in which the producer discusses his work on the picture *The Old Man and the Sea.* The interviewer writes that Hayward believes that Americans have already lost out in the world struggle "because we let ourselves get too soft. . . . Our culture is against the male. I think women are more honest and realistic and less sentimental than men. But I don't think as a rule American women are as attractive as other women. We ruin them by spoiling them. We men have corrupted them by killing ourselves working for them. They are now 60 [percent] of the population, live several years longer than men, own 80 per cent of the wealth. In another 20 years they will own everything. I am a pessimist about what they will do with total power, when they get it."[88]

Hayward's remarks, in their casual (though unjoking) expression of his concern about women's supposed dominance over men, establish just how routine that anxiety was and how unproblematic its public articulation was. Two decades earlier, during the Depression, gendered anxiety didn't play out much (men and women were not pitted against each other; anyone was lucky just to have a job), nor did it during the war, another time when a certain autonomy was expected of most women. But after the war, it seemed that women were damned if they worked outside the home ("they will own every-thing") and damned if they didn't ("We ruin them by spoiling them"). "Smothering-mother" Madame Rose was more off-putting and threatening than working women could have been in those earlier periods, and probably she could not have been invented in those times. Like the increase in time-consuming recipes in women's magazines, there were now more articles about the psychological hazards of child rearing, especially if the mom worked outside the home: if mothers were "training" the country's youth and the kids came out wrong, who was to blame? Countless films of the time re-flect these anxieties, Hitchcock's *Psycho* (1960) most violently,[89] but putting the blame on mom quickly became a staple of pop psychology that has lived on for decades.[90]

Rose received more than her fair share of blame, and she still does, even when there is a sweetness giving cover to the barbs. Laurents describes her as "a mythic mesmerizing mother, a monster of a mother sweetly named Rose."[91] To Keith Garebian she "is a larger-than-life representation of American Mom-ism, that syndrome that so bedevils many a generation that feel smothered by the hand that rocks the cradle. . . . Yet Rose is not grotesque, she is a human being, subject to her own chimeras of pain and travail."[92]

As huge a triumph as *Gypsy* was for Merman, especially in reinvigorating her iconic place on Broadway, the less adoring side of Mama Rose also took its toll on her, particularly in terms of what the public imagined her to be in her public and private life. As one review put it, "The view of America as the prime matriarchy, hog-tied and talked to death by mothers, wives, mothers-in-law, and female executives, is powerfully embodied and voiced by *Ethel Merman*."[93] Another critic famously referred to the show as "the Medea of Musicals."[94] To be sure, *Gypsy* was not alone in attracting such comments; an-other article of the time was entitled "Mother—It's Murder / Stage Holds Up Mirror to a Tarnished Image," calling the mothers of several recent Broad-way shows "a traumatic experience to her little ones and perhaps to the more sensitive members of the audience." But why some authors took aim at Ethel Merman personally is harder to fathom: "Miss Merman was given every op-portunity one recent night to give America a stirring Mother's Day message by denouncing the likes of Madame Rose and coming out for the Mom who bakes apple pies and has a kindly light in her eyes. But she declined. 'Why should I say anything bad about Madame Rose?' Miss Merman said."[95]

So Ethel Merman was a bad mother for not hating Rose, and hate Mother Rose you evidently should: "If *West Side Story* is about how bigotry destroys you," writes Ethan Mordden, "*Gypsy* is about how your mother destroys you. This show is The One That Got Away With It, shattering a cultural given, that all mothers are nurturing, loving and self-sacrificing. *Gypsy* is about a mother who is a selfish, stupid, destructive piece of junk."[96] It could be said that in Merman's career, Rose is a sort of bookend to Annie Oakley, at once Annie's complex counterpart and her unhappy outcome, a cautionary tale of what happens when career women try to fuse personal reward and family life with professional success.

Mama Rose Equals Ethel Merman

"Ethel was so strong and overwhelming onstage that people believe she was that person. It was the role of Mama Rose that shaped the way the public perceived who Ethel really was," reflects Tony Cointreau.[97] Indeed, Rose was everything that Ethel Merman was assumed to be at this point in her career: brash, vulgar, obsessed by her career, and oblivious to the feelings of others. Merman's determination and drive, her rough mouth and tough style were the "real" Ethel Merman, right?

Arthur Laurents believes that Merman's "personal qualities made her right for Rose: not very bright but shrewd, common but charismatic, able to defeat you before you could get a swipe at her and pure Rose, a walking, exuberant advertisement for Self-ignorance is bliss."[98] There was Rose—and, evidently, the big star who portrayed her—clueless, defiantly stubborn, unwilling to see the truth around her: that her kids had grown and her career was stuck in the past.

Ethel was assertive about standing up for herself and in exacting a good performance from colleagues. She made her demands overtly and would not be underhanded or devious about them. Merman was also known to dish out invective if she felt used or betrayed, and that side could be unpleasant and vulgar. But as Tony Cointreau notes in deliberate understatement, "It's interesting that in twenty-five years, I never saw that [abrasive, vulgar] side. She wasn't like that." He added, "The only times offstage that Ethel would ever go into that [brash] stage persona was when there was a chance for a good joke."[99]

Bob Levitt says today that the legacy of his mother has produced a "cartoon caricature" of Merman's vulgarity and love of off-color jokes. Her vulgar side, says Levitt, "did exist, but it was a small fraction of her true humor." She had an almost juvenile love of dirty jokes, he says, but "it was a kid's delight my mom had in them. She thought they were just so funny, and she would say, 'Oh, isn't that awful?!' after telling them."[100] Levitt understands those jokes as coming from a place of innocence, a place of almost juvenile pleasure and enthusiasm, and a way for his mom to break from the rigidity of her parents.

As for *Gypsy*, Hayward says, "It was Ethel who saw the book as a story for the mother, not the kids,"[101] and Merman took that view seriously, refusing to tell her stage father to "go to hell." She played Rose without irony and never viewed her as a monster, telling the press, "She yells and screams but she loves her children. Everything she does, she does because she loves too much."[102] The actual Rose was nothing like this, as Gypsy Rose Lee wrote in her memoirs: "Mother had been many things, but she had never been 'nice.' . . . Charming, perhaps, and courageous, resourceful and ambitious, but not nice."[103] But there is a compelling force to Ethel's compassion for Rose, and later in 1965, when she was a guest on Gypsy Rose Lee's San Francisco–based TV talk show, she said of Rose, "How can you not love her? She's a mother."[104] Lee simply smiled and agreed.

As Rose, Ethel was able to produce some of the "mother love" she wanted to bring to the complex role. As the letter from the female fan on the ocean liner revealed, Rose was not Medea for everyone, and Merman's own presence in the role led one reviewer to comment that "she was rather like the mother of us all (if mothers had such talent)."[105]

Arthur Laurents was able to catch a glimpse of the more innocent side of Ethel during an exchange while working on *Gypsy*. When he asked Jack Klugman if Tab Hunter was gay, "Jack replied, 'Is the Pope Catholic?' 'Yes,' said Ethel, waiting for the answer. Not bright, no, but endearing and despite a life spent in saloons, childlike."[106] Laurents's appreciation, of course, is offset by the saloon jab (and he writes this after saying that "four letter words were as at home in her mouth as saliva"), but divas are often swiped at at the same time they are adulated. Even so, Laurent's note about Ethel's childlikeness is on the mark, as Levitt and Cointreau both maintain; Cointreau, in fact, wonders if Ethel's nonresponse to Klugman's gag might have been intended as a joke.[107]

Cointreau goes on to note that Ethel's desire to bring dignity to Rose not only brought depth to the role but also generated sympathy for it. "Ethel never thought that Mama Rose was horrible or filled with dementia. You loved her because she did it from a place of innocence," he says.[108] Historian Gerald Bordman agrees: "Her electric personality made the abrasive, almost unpleasant Rose seem a little lovable."[109] Merman's belief in the inherent goodness of a relatively unsympathetic character makes her depiction of Rose all the more potent.

Still, portrayed in a decade of Momism, Rose was far from universally loved. One woman, who had seen the show as a young teenager, found the character outmoded, out of sync with what mothers were "supposed" to be like in the world at the time and when relating to their children. She perceived Rose as out of touch, over the top, and a bit camp, features that, again, fans or critics may have imposed on Merman herself. Clearly for that viewer, the values and brand of motherhood that Merman depicted as Rose were as passé as vaudeville itself.

Ironically, Merman's ability to convince people that she was Madame Rose, in the standout performance of her career, convinced some that Ethel was not performing at all but was simply playing *herself.* That her persona could be so "Rosified" points to changes not only in Merman's persona but also in larger cultural attitudes toward women, family, ambition, and fame.

Gypsy came out nine years after Billy Wilder's movie *Sunset Boulevard* was released and three years before Robert Aldrich's *Whatever Happened to Baby Jane?* Both movies tell the stories of older female celebrities whose successes and productivity were well behind them. The stars who played them—Gloria Swanson, Bette Davis, and Joan Crawford—were cast for that reason and were lauded for their "bravery" in taking such unflattering roles. The women played their characters with verve, and the direction of both films highlights the physical signs of their aging—faux-glamorous clothing, excessive makeup and wigs—as indications of their deluded desires to recapture lost youth and fame. Although these characters stood outside the category of Philip Wylie's mothers, they were no less victimized by its scorn, although less for their putative power than for having once been beautiful stars. Rose didn't prompt many critics to comment on her physical appearance; it was her *psychological* makeup that was deemed out of whack and past its prime, since this was a character who refused, like Norma Desmond of *Sunset Boulevard,* to move with reality or the times. (For many, of course, that stubbornness is part of Rose's allure.)

Merman's magnetic performance as Rose inspired other stars, such as Kaye Ballard and Liza Minnelli, to go into musical theater themselves. Ballard would go on to play Madame Rose (but "no one came *close* to Merman," she insisted),[110] and when Liza Minnelli performs, she performs "Some People" to acknowledge these historical "roots." Other stars have been just as awed by Ethel's Rose. One wrote: "Dear Ethel: I guess every once and a while we all get kinda blasé and tired of our business. Hence this note. I want to thank you from the bottom of my heart for inspiring me so very much, I can't wait to get before an audience again. You're the true champ of all time. God bless you, and I love you and everything you stand for. Most humbly, Jerry [Lewis]."[111]

Today, middle-aged women recall seeing *Gypsy* as children with their mothers. Many now are mothers themselves who take their daughters to revivals or play them the original cast recording, handing down an important memory. One says she and her eleven-year-old always sing along to the album and attended the Bernadette Peters revival together. "It's fun passing along my love for this show by sharing it with her. The songs are my favorite. I never saw Merman—I [first] saw Tyne Daly, who was amazing, but we listen to the Merman recording. It must have been great to see her do it."[112] Diane, a businesswoman, recalled: "Ethel Merman simply blew me away. It was electrifying in that audience. . . . I remember how her voice enveloped me in that theater. My strongest memory was 'Everything's Coming Up Roses'; I thought it was a really happy song. 'Rose's Turn' was lost to me—I must have thought it was too grown up, but I remember the intensity she gave off when she was doing it."[113]

Other women were less wowed. The manager who worked at the Broadway Theatre during *Gypsy*'s run there recalls that many middle-aged and older women didn't care for the show at all. They had grown up with Ethel Merman and had followed her career, and now these women were mothers themselves. Here she was, playing this horrible "jungle mother." "They felt betrayed by Miss Merman," theater historian Miles Krueger remembers the manager saying,[114] as if the star were attacking them and their life choices, even though their Mama Rose was a world away from Merman's intentions.

The *Gypsy* Tour

Ethel was able to spend several weeks relaxing before preparations began to take *Gypsy* on the road, seeing family and friends from Queens, spending time at home, socializing at nightclubs, attending events. In April she attended the opening night of Vivien Leigh's return to Broadway in *Duel of Angels;* in May, she took in jazz pianist sensation Frances Faye. She attended dinners honoring the widely liked Dinah Shore and another for Bob Hope, a luncheon at the Friar's Club and one for the Banchees, the group that honored journalists. The following month, when Hedda Hopper reported that the single Ethel had "slimmed down," it might well have been from going to all of these engagements.

Rehearsals for Ethel's tour of the show began early in 1961; Merman's old friend Lew Kessler would be continuing as pianist for the tour. Jule Styne helped with the initial conducting and arranging, and Milton Rosenstock would conduct on tour. Cast changes included Julienne Marie who played Louise; Herbie was played by Alfred Sandor.

Conserving her energy, Ethel avoided booking matinee and evening shows on Wednesdays, making Saturday her only two-performance day. The tour opened on Wednesday, March 29, 1961, at the Auditorium Theatre in Rochester, New York, and there it remained through April 1. Although *Gypsy* didn't perform quite as well there as the tour of *The Sound of Music* had, it did well. The next stop was Detroit's Riviera Theatre (April 3–15), where Shirley Eder, the gossip columnist based there, attended with her husband, Edward Slotkin, and threw a party for Ethel. The local press reported, "Miss Merman was amused at comments that she was 'holding up very well.' 'I get lots of sleep,' she laughed, 'and lead what I guess you'd call a normal life. But I've been around so long that a lot of people expect me to come onstage in a wheel chair. They should remember,' and her eyes twinkled impishly, 'I started very young.'"[115]

Everywhere the show went, reviewers took note of the overwhelming, sustained applause of crowds when Ethel took the stage. To calm the pandemonium, Merman often had to do something she didn't want to—break out of character and bow.

From Detroit the show went to the Cleveland Public Music Hall, where it played for six days, starting April 17 during a late-season snowstorm. The weather did not dampen her reception. Harlowe Hoyt of the *Cleveland Plain Dealer* wrote: "It is a new Merman who plays Rose Hovac [sic], mother of June and Louise. . . . And some way or other, it is a more mature Merman, as though the duty of introducing her two youngsters into the theatrical world imbues her with a responsibility that has toned down her ebullient spirit to characterization more sincere than any of her previous roles."[116] The next stop was three weeks at Boston's Colonial, a sixty-year-old theater whose records the show broke. Its grateful management ran a huge public thank-you to Ethel Merman in *Variety* on behalf of "the legitimate theatre ticket agencies of Boston and New England," predicting that *Gypsy* would gross two hundred thousand dollars during its run. (On this ad Ethel wrote, "This has never been done before by the ticket men.")[117] The day before Mother's Day, *Gypsy* closed in Boston.

From there it went to Toronto's O'Keefe Performing Arts Centre, where it—and Merman especially—were well received. The press complimented her for "toning down [Rose's] cannibalism" and "offering the impression that Rose basically has only her children's interest at heart."[118] Two days before the show opened, a Toronto TV channel broadcast *Straight, Place and Show* in honor of the arriving star, and *Gypsy* stayed in Toronto from May 15 to 27.

The next stop for the *Gypsy* train was Chicago. Mayor Richard Daly wrote in advance to welcome Ethel, just as Toronto's mayor, Nathan Phillips, had done. Chicago was a bigger deal than Toronto, though, since Ethel had last performed there in April 1937, in *Red, Hot and Blue!* The start of that show had been postponed a day because the scenery was late in arriving, and Merman had found the crowds distant and cool. Apparently they'd had a chance to warm up, for *Gypsy* ran there from May 29 to August 3:

> They're wrong about Ethel Merman. She's not like a brass band. She's like a symphony orchestra. When the vivacious 51 year old star talks about her children or her four month old granddaughter, she's all violins and cellos—warm, mellow, and affectionate. When she talks about her long (5,000 performances) career, she's woodwinds and French horns, full of love for her work and gratefulness for the warmth of her public. And when she talks about how Chicago has received her in *Gypsy*, her 12th hit and the first time she's ever been on the road, she beats the drums and clashes the cymbals.[119]

Merman returned the favor by calling Chicagoans a "hep audience."[120] While there, Ethel did local benefits for Easter Seals and area hospitals; she socialized with local figure Eddie Bragno (whom she still called "a friend and a most enjoyable escort," but informed the press not to consider them "a romantic duo").[121] Benay Venuta was there for part of the run, as was Bobby, and again Merman saved city maps for her parents, marking out "my hotel" and "theater." As she happily told Radie Harris, "This '*Gypsy*' life is for me. You suddenly discover that ALL the people aren't at El Morocco and the Stork, and because they don't live in N.Y. they must be 'square.' And everything really comes up roses on the road, with a Mayor to present them in each city!"[122]

Ethel was enjoying new fans and colleagues: a card and flowers from clothing designer Danny MacMahon; a long letter from an "usherette" at the Chicago Shubert, who thanked her for coming to Chicago (Merman writes, "I have answered this"); and other cards, one from the Chicago crew depicting an audience weeping, another of elephants never forgetting. *Gypsy* closed two days earlier than planned in the Windy City to allow extra time for the gear and crew to get to San Francisco, where it was to open Monday, August 7.

Reviewers across the country often started by saying that they had never been Merman fans or had understood what the fuss was all about, though after seeing *Gypsy*, many wrote they were ready to take it all back. It's as if seeing her live gave them a conversion experience. In that regard, touring gave Merman a way to show that she was more than the one-dimensional performer that circulated in the national imagination. By now, references to Ethel—and her voice—were downright predictable: "one of a kind," "inimitable," "leather-lunged." If the show itself received some criticism from the out-of-town critics, Merman still reigned supreme with them. Still, no one was prepared for the reception Ethel got in San Francisco.

That August, the curtains at the Curran Theatre were half an hour late going up because the scenery and props, which had arrived ten hours late, were still being hung. When Rose finally went down the theater aisle, a long, deafening ovation greeted Merman. Neither she nor the city recalled anything like it. "Not since the San Francisco earthquake," wrote Radie Harris.[123]

The overwhelming reception was not just from an audience grateful that Ethel had gone "west of the Hudson," although that was a tremendous part of it. Much was specific to San Francisco, a culturally savvy town that appreciated theater and a visit from Broadway's living legend. (Chinese- and Russian-language papers in the city even reviewed the show.) The city's large gay population was a significant part of the welcoming chorus as well, appreciative of a living theater icon who had come to visit.[124]

Several slightly gender-bending *Gypsy* artifacts are included in Ethel's scrapbooks. A local columnist challenged his readers to "list ten stars . . . who could replace Ethel Merman in *Gypsy*. Noel Coward is ineligible." Another comes from a postcard Ethel received while staying in San Francisco. Glued to the back of it is a newspaper clipping of the publicity portrait of her in *Gypsy*, and under it the caption reads "Zero Mostel." "Something wrong here?—F," wrote the sender, possibly Fred Clark, Benay's husband, who often sent Ethel gag notes. Another clipped newspaper photo has Ethel putting on her eye makeup, the caption missing an *s* so that it read "TARRY EYED." Merman had the humor to save them all.[125]

In San Francisco, Ethel also had a chance to visit with Ethel Jr. and Bobby, who had both come in for the show. She had time to shop and was spotted once at a local Woolworth's. There were the usual social engagements—

before she even arrived, Ethel told an interviewer, "I have been invited to 61 black tie dinners and 103 barbecues."[126] She stayed in the exclusive Nob Hill area and on one occasion had the chance to express her appreciation of the staff at the Mark Hopkins Hotel there. Buddy Hackett, Ethel's upcoming costar in *It's a Mad, Mad, Mad, Mad World,* told the press, "Last night we had three cartons of leftovers from a Chinese dinner delivered to her [because *Gypsy* features Chinese food] at the Mark [Hopkins]. . . . It was 4 am. . . . It seemed like a great idea then. I hear Ethel's fired the whole staff!"[127] Merman's handwritten note is stapled to the clipping: "He *did* send over the food, but I never saw it— I had put in my 'Do Not Disturb' at 1 o'clock and was awakened by the operator. She got hell from management for disturbing me and I got a letter of apology from management, but no one was fired—that's what Buddy made up."

Toward the end of the San Francisco run, Merman experienced a slipped spinal disk and was in excruciating pain. Her physicians insisted she not perform, but she refused and took spinal injections before each show. When she was not on the stage, Ethel was effectively in traction. ("I was in pain but kept my hair appointments," she wrote in her autobiography.)[128] The star insisted that the public not be told she was playing injured, and her problems weren't revealed until the tour was over.

After seven weeks, *Gypsy* ended its San Francisco run on September 30, and Ethel went on to Los Angeles in a brace for the penultimate stop. Agnes and Edward had flown out, aware that Los Angeles would be a particularly special event and also eager to help their injured daughter. Despite her back trouble, the day before opening, Ethel went flea marketing with them (a favorite pastime). When she opened at LA's Biltmore Theatre, she received a thunderous ovation (and a bouquet of flowers from Rosalind Russell—did she know Ethel had allergies?). Sidney Skolsky wrote of the night, "I tell you, you don't see a scene like this except in a movie. Considering the fact that the majority of the audience were movie people, they acted like people in movies."[129] The audience was a who's who of celebrities, and most of Ethel's colleagues outside New York had actually waited to see her there. Styne, there for the opening, telegrammed in advance to joke, "By the way, I am sending Mervyn LeRoy San Francisco reviews."[130] Another fan wired, "Let them hear it tonight, Ethel. Affectionately, Cary Grant."[131] Merrick threw an opening-night party at Romanoff's, with partygoers then making their way to the home of Mitzi Gaynor and Jack Bean to continue celebrating.

Despite hobnobbing with the royalty of the entertainment world, Ethel never lost herself to it. And judging from at least one fan, not everyone was convinced that she was a "Medusa Mother":

Please let me begin this letter by thanking you so very much for the $5.00 gift you gave to Barry [Kemp, one of the children in the San Francisco cast] for his birthday. . . . I will be eternally grateful to you for being so wonderful to my child all these months. Barry would have been a very unhappy little boy during a good part of these last months, had it not been for the friendship and kindness you extended to him. As Barry has said, "Mommy, I think Miss Merman *really* likes me." Being a Mother yourself, you must know how very good all this makes me feel.[132]

Another missive from Los Angeles read:

When I was growing up back East my father was a great fan of musical comedy, especially those in which you appeared. . . .

Yesterday my husband and I saw you in *Gypsy*. I must confess, without shame, that I cried like a baby. Not only because your portrayal of Madame Rose was tremendously moving, but because after twenty years, the last time I saw you on stage, you still thrilled me to my fingertips. . . .

One more thing. Whoever is responsible for not casting you in the film version must be out of his cotton-picking mind.[133]

After breaking records at the Biltmore, *Gypsy*'s run was extended from November 11 to the 25th. From Los Angeles, the tour's final stop with Ethel was ten days at the American Theatre in St. Louis. The *Gypsy* tour continued from there to Denver, but Ethel was eager to get back to her regular life, to enjoy her freedom and her family, so a new Madame Rose took her place, played by Mary McCarty, who had also done the role in Las Vegas. After taking the country by storm, Ethel now could go home.

New Turns for Rose

Rose's unconventional aspects have triggered responses that reshaped Ethel's image for years to come, manufacturing new Ethel Mermans as well as revising old ones. Not only was there the belief that Rose "was" Ethel Merman but also that the role revealed some of the ostensible "Jewishness" of Merman's persona. Rose Hovick was in actuality Jewish, a detail that enters the play, according to historian Stacy Wolf, only through the backdoor, in character names like Mr. Goldstone and Herbie and in lyrics such as the stripper's "Once I was a schlepper / Now I'm Miss Mazeppa." It also resides in the clichéd aspects of Rose as a pushy show biz mom. Adds Wolf,

But it's not only that *Gypsy* powerfully evokes Jewishness without naming it as such. In the musical, Jewishness works with queerness, another marginal, malleable, not-quite visible identity; they both inflect each other. Merman's Momma Rose, on Broadway in 1959, not only reads as Jewish but is the quintessential Jewish mother, queered. . . . The show refuses a musical's expected heterosexual romantic resolution. Instead, *Gypsy* eschews heterosexual marriage for a gynocentric world, comes forth as a star vehicle for a single woman's performance and develops a primary relationship between two women.[134]

Gay critic D. A. Miller also finds it significant that *Gypsy* gives little time to male characters, maintaining that the show acknowledges a key mechanism of the postwar musical: shows revolve around women who have the central, most colorful roles. In *Gypsy*, he says, we see a full "swerve away from men,"[135] and hence a strong feminization of the entire spectacle that audiences take in on the stage. To be sure, the stage (and performing itself) has been feminized in North America for over a hundred years; as recently as the early twentieth century, theater work was considered disreputable, glorified whoring.

There are plenty of reasons *Gypsy* has the iconic place it does within gay and lesbian cultures. Like many other musicals, it is about fantasy and the potentials of people with different worldviews and experiences, of people who don't fit tightly defined norms and who fight for fulfillment in a world at odds with them. If material and cultural conditions cannot make our fantasies possible "in real life," what better way to acknowledge or announce them than with the extravagant, dramatic, openly emotional journey of a musical? (Opera has much of the same appeal.) For as unrealistic as musicals are aesthetically, the fantasies they provoke in us are deeply tied to the social and historical realities underpinning them.[136] Even the space of the theatrical house has importance as a historically safe place for different gendered and social communities to meet.

It is the diva's commanding presence in these worlds—her on- and off-stage sufferings (actual or perceived), her soaring voice, her materiality—that gives everything its potent "reality." She is what enables fans to transport the onstage passions offstage, bringing them into her image and all that she seemingly blesses. And while Miller and other gay critics have discussed the importance of divas specifically to gay men,[137] it is apparent that divas and their musical worlds have considerable stakes for all viewers, including lesbians and other female viewers. In postwar American popular culture, for instance, stage and screen musicals offered girls and young women a certain sanctuary from the male-dominated world of rock music, and, unlike opera, the musical gives women and other viewers a form that avoids opera's studied world and rarified talents.

For one middle-aged lesbian fan from a Los Angeles suburb, *Gypsy*'s "Some People" has particular resonance and remains her favorite Merman song. Rose is not like regular people; she's an outsider who is impatient with the staid, stay-at-home, straight, middle-class existence her dad represents. Laurents was well aware of the sexual subtexts of *Gypsy*'s real-life characters: "There had always been speculation that Gypsy [Rose Lee] was a lesbian, but . . . Gypsy Rose Lee's mother?"[138] (Rose was actually bisexual, and June Havoc wrote about the lesbian cocktail parties her mother and sister hosted, for which they sometimes charged people admission.)

Theater historian Wolf describes Merman's performance of Rose as "butch Jewish force."[139] Less concerned with strict biographical fact, Wolf focuses on features of the performance that have adhered to Merman over time, acknowledging the importance of speculative stories, appearances, and long-standing rumors that make of Merman an icon who is not your run-of-the-mill heterosexual woman. Wolf points out that in TV appearances such as the one playing house with Frank Sinatra, Ethel only "plays at femininity," producing a "Merman-as-femme,"[140] and other queer critics have similarly noted that Ethel's drag as a man ("A Sailor's Not a Sailor . . .") seems less like drag than when she is asked to play genteel femininity.

The Jacqueline Susann Story

It wasn't just subsequent critics who "queered" Merman in *Gypsy*. At the time, Jacqueline Susann, an attractive second-tier actress who had been in shows such as *The Girl from Wyoming, Banjo Eyes, Blossom Time,* and *Lovely Me* and the TV series *Open Door,* developed a "fixation" on Merman.[141] Susann, who was bisexual, was wowed by Ethel's depiction of Rose and was "intrigued with the kind of magnetism Ethel had," said Benay Venuta.[142] According to Susann's biographer, Susann's erotic interest was clinched when she reportedly performed a bump and grind at Ethel's Park Lane home one night while helping her prepare for *Gypsy*.

Two other stories fan the infamous fire. The first involves an incident that purportedly occurred one night at a party hosted by Lynn Loesser on Central Park West, where a very drunken Merman and Susann had a make-out session on the couch. The second describes an incident that began at a nightclub where Merman, Venuta, and their dates were dining after a performance of *Gypsy.*

> Irving [Mansfield, Susann's husband] wanted to take Jackie home, and Jackie was having none of it. . . . "Fuck you! Get the hell out of here!" she [screamed]. Jackie later remembered Ethel saying, "I don't ever want to see you again. You're as crazy as your son [who was autistic]." Benay doesn't recall that remark, but she does remember Ethel leaving the restaurant with Jackie following her. Jackie followed her all the way home and then stood outside her apartment, banging on the door and yelling, "Ethel, I love you!" Ethel said later that this went on for hours, until she at last threatened to call the police. [143]

Soon after the drunk stalking incident, Susann was admitted to a sanitarium. She exacted revenge in her novel *Valley of the Dolls,* in which she drew the nasty, drunken, middle-aged stage diva Helen Lawson with exaggerated features of Merman, down to her drink of choice, champagne on the rocks. Ethel never spoke to Susann again.

The afterlife of this tale has taken on huge and conflicting proportions, giving both Merman and Susann strangely unattractive features as they both get "queered." Susann's biographer, for instance, considers her attraction to Merman a sign of inner instability, as if lesbianism were a sign of sickness: "Jackie seemed to follow Ethel almost everywhere. . . . Jackie was past forty now, a bit old for those adolescent 'star crushes' she'd had [on other women]. It just wasn't right for her to be tagging around after Merman so blatantly."[144]

But if these stories make Susann immature, they make Ethel into a grotesque lowlife: "[Jackie] knew Ethel was coarse and vulgar, a woman who described Benay's important Jewish society friends as 'dull as pig shit.' . . . When she starred in *Gypsy,* Ethel was turning fifty, overweight, physically unappealing, and an intellectual lightweight to say the least. . . . She drank too much, and she was often abusive when she'd had too much to drink. . . . Dumpy and vulgar though she might be, and bigoted as she certainly was about 'niggers' and 'commie Jews,' she was the undisputed star of the musical stage."[145] The biography offers no sources for the unsavory remarks attributed to Ethel here; one is supposed to take them as truth, along with the vicious description of her. It's strange that people buy into this Ethel Merman, one who is anti-Semitic for not liking the upper crust and homophobic for shunning Jackie's unwanted advances.

The less mythic, ordinary Ethel Merman had no trouble interacting with lesbians; her agent and many close friends and associates were lesbians, recalls

Levitt. And Cointreau recounts a time at a party where Ethel said that she found that gay and lesbian couples were among many of the happiest long-term relationships she knew—and that included Cointreau and Jim Russo. Cointreau also remembers her saying, "I just like men. Never liked women, never have," no big deal.[146] It's unlikely that her matter-of-fact attitude was anything she'd want to make a big fuss over. And she was, understandably, furious about the Susann story. What remains interesting—and deeply ironic—about that legend-that-won't-die is that people seem to take it as an indication both of Merman's homophobia *and* of her latent lesbianism, neither of which she had anything to do with.

Why have so many gay and lesbian critics insisted that Ethel Merman was homophobic? Wolf, for instance, states matter-of-factly that Merman was "very rude to lesbians." Merle Louise, who as a child played the replacement Baby June, is quoted as saying: "They used to say Merman never liked gays. But we went to this club once in Detroit, and it was a gay club—and everyone was surprised she went in the first place. One of the men asked her if she would please sing a song and I thought, 'Oh, Jesus.' But she said, 'Sure.' They had this piano that wasn't in the greatest tune, and she sat on top of that piano and sang 'There's No Business Like Show Business.' And those guys wept. We all did."[147]

Merman's not-quite-straight public image in midlife is as complex as the overlapping layers she had with her not-quite-white image in the late 1920s. Neither has much to do with the facts of Ethel Merman's life. The historical record does not bear out the claim of her homophobia, but what remains significant is the force with which its association—along with her purported lesbianism—has stuck to her. Obviously, a lesbian is what many fans *want* Merman to be. No disrespect to her is intended by many of these people or by critics like Wolf, who argues that Ethel might have been playing a lesbian, or someone like a lesbian, or a figure that lesbians could take to their heart. In fact, even if the role of Mama Rose caused Ethel to lose some of her older female fans, it helped usher in new, younger ones. To some of the lesbians and gay men who adore her to this day, that "queerness" resides in Ethel; for others, it does not. For many, it is enough that the show made Ethel Merman Broadway's top figure, Mama Rose its shining crown.

What *Gypsy* finally reveals is the emergence of Ethel as a more malleable icon than ever before, something that would only intensify in the remaining two decades of her life. "When Merman made her entrance as Dolly Levi [on Broadway in 1970], the ovation was thunderous, not only from homosexuals who saw her as a kind of superwoman, but from Broadway theater fans who considered her an icon. Predictably, their outpourings irritated the critics." This discussion, from biographer Bob Thomas, then goes on to quote Walter Kerr about the same audience: "They stand up and scream on the first number, they stand up and scream louder on the second and by the time she gets to the 'Hello Dolly!' number they don't bother to sit down between notes. I'd like to make a deal with them. Equal time for Miss Merman."[148] Merman had moved into the rich emotional lives of people's fantasies; all of her fans wanted to own her, to lay claim to "their" Ethel, their personal and collective icon. Ethel Merman was now being received with many of the same complex, competing, and intense reactions as Madame Rose.

FIFTEEN

It's a Mad, Mad Schedule

On October 27, 1963, Ethel appeared on the TV quiz show *What's My Line?* as its mystery guest, whose identity panelists Dorothy Kilgallen, Bennett Cerf, Allen Ludden, and Arlene Francis, sporting his-and-her blinders, tried to ascertain through a series of yes/no questions. To disguise the famous voice, Ethel lowered it and answered questions with husky, monosyllabic *oui*s or *non*s. The panelists didn't understand that the guest wasn't male until Ludden asked the question outright, and Merman, with her shoulders rising up to her ears and eyes widening in feigned shock, boomed a "*non!*" with girlish delight. When friend Kilgallen asked with a grin, "Are you in the upcoming *Mad, Mad, Mad, Mad World*?" the panelists zeroed in and quickly named her.

Such was the buzz on the movie. Ethel was telling reporters, "I've got no regrets about not doing *Gypsy*. If I'd had to make the film, I wouldn't have been free to do *A Mad, Mad, Mad, Mad World*," and she wasn't the only one talking it up.[1] United Artists was boasting it would be "the biggest grossing film ever,"[2] the biggest, best comedy ever made. It was the first time that Stanley Kramer, the independent producer known for message pictures like *Inherit the Wind* and *Judgment at Nuremberg*, ventured into comedy, and he was determined to do it with gusto. Kramer stuffed the picture with rambunctious physical comedy, which was pay dirt for Universal executives, because the less dialogue in a film, the greater its chance for success abroad.

The huge, star-studded cast included, among others, Spencer Tracy, Milton Berle, Sid Caesar, Carl Reiner (who also cowrote), Jonathan Winters, Phil Silvers, Terry-Thomas, Dick Shawn, Mickey Rooney, and Buddy Hackett, with cameos from Jack Benny, Buster Keaton, Eddie "Rochester" Anderson, Jim Backus, Edward Everett Horton, and Jimmy Durante. So filled with comic talent was it that comedians who were *not* asked to take part felt left out; Groucho Marx said that since the role he'd been promised in *It's a Mad, Mad, Mad, Mad World* went to Ethel, he planned on taking her role in the upcoming tour of *Gypsy*.[3]

The story is simple. After a road accident, Durante lies on a hillside, mortally wounded. Before literally kicking a bucket (what do you expect from an old vaudevillian?), his last words impel a group of greedy travelers to race to uncover a buried treasure. The movie is largely a series of madcap antics with characters trying to outwit or sabotage one another in order to be the first to find the loot, but the second they do, cop Spencer Tracy swoops in, confiscating the treasure so that he can retire early from the force. Another chaotic chase ensues, now with the travelers pursuing *him*. In the process, the money flies off to the winds, chaos ensues, and nearly everybody lands in the hospital, groaning in traction.

Ethel played the "distastefully shrewish mother-in-law" of Milton Berle, who was actually a mere seven months younger than she.[4] Merman was a good sport about the role, cracking jokes with the same big heart she had when she was the butt of them. Describing her work to the press, she said,

> It is also the first time I ever played a role 50% bottom-side up. There was nothing in the script about this southern exposure. I got my first inkling when I reported for work and found little interest in my facial makeup but great concern about fitting me for thigh-length drawers. I began to understand after shooting started and I was:
>
> 1. Tossed into a top-down convertible and left standing on my head;
> 2. Picked up by the feet by Berle and Terry-Thomas and shaken like a pair of dice until a key they were seeking fell from the hiding place in my dress-front;
> 3. Pulled feet first, head down, from a tow truck by Jonathan Winters;
> 4. Skidded on a banana peel in a jail hospital corridor and landed head down, feet up;
> 5. Tossed into a trash can head first, legs up, by Spencer Tracy.
>
> This is the way you become a great dramatic actress, that fellow (Kramer) said.[5]

The working title was *Something a Little Less Serious*. Kramer began by shooting scenes that didn't require the featured players, such as stunts, long shots, and masters, bringing the stars to the California desert only after preliminary shooting was done. Cast members said that with all the footage he'd filmed, Kramer had almost a complete picture on his hands before they ever arrived and remarked how impressively sequenced, paced, and designed it was. Shooting with the featured players, however, was grueling during the hot months between April and December 1962, when desert temperatures were often upward of a hundred degrees.

Kramer shot in Cinerama, Universal's widescreen format, which enabled the picture to be projected by one projector, replacing the previous three-projector system with panels. The new system, he said, would save exhibitors and producers money, even though the up-front cost was considerable: theaters had to be modified, their screens curved. In anticipation of the success of *It's a Mad, Mad, Mad, Mad World,* a "specially built geodesic dome theater for Cinerama attractions" went up on Sunset Boulevard, and in New York the Stanley Warner Theatre was refurbished on Broadway.

Kramer spared no expense promoting the picture, mounting a record-breaking, 210-foot billboard that covered nearly a full block on Sunset Boulevard, and United Artists spent over four hundred thousand dollars to bring in 250 foreign correspondents for a five-day visit for the premiere.[6] Its entire budget was six and a half million dollars—an enormous amount.

On the last day of filming, Ethel, following a tradition she had always kept on Broadway, gave jewelry to crew members, and to celebrate the wrap, Milton Berle, Phil Silvers, and their wives hosted a huge party in September at the Beverly Hills Hotel, with Ethel as the guest of honor. (Ethel kept the invitation and typed up a report of the food that was served.)[7] All of the stars from the film were there, in addition to Warren Beatty, Natalie Wood, Sammy Cahn, Gladys Cooper, Fred DeCordova, Buster Edens, James Garner, Gene Kelly, Walter Lang, Vincente Minnelli, Mitzi Gaynor, Cyd Charisse, and many others. The hotel's patio, decorated to resemble an over-sized dressing room door, featured "a giant enlargement of the still picture of the guest of honor's backside after being dumped in a trash can by Spencer." Under the photo was the caption: "The First Lady of Broadway—Merman Flops." Ethel roared.[8]

In spite of its up-to-date technology and high-end promotion, *It's a Mad, Mad, Mad, Mad World* was at heart quite old-fashioned, "a throwback to the wild, wacky and wondrous time of the silent screen comedy, a kind of Keystone Kop Kaper with modern conveniences."[9] Kramer said he intended the picture as an homage to silent film comedy, and Ethel, for her part, described it as being "like one of the old Marx Brothers pictures."[10] Many of its characters were built on shopworn figures, such as the "repulsive old battle-ax" mother-in-law and her son (Dick Shawn), a newer cliché, the California "beatnik."[11]

The picture premiered at a whopping 190 minutes, opening to great fanfare in Los Angeles on November 7, 1963.[12] Although *It's a Mad, Mad, Mad,*

Mad World was ultimately not the earthshaking hit Kramer was hoping for, it did well and remained a cultural reference point through much of the '60s and, after that, was shown frequently on late-night television for decades.

Ethel had a blast making the movie, delighted to be in the company of so many skilled comedians and to be given the opportunity to appear in such a high-profile project. It gave her another chance of trying her hand at new things and reinventing herself. And after *It's a Mad, Mad, Mad, Mad World,* Dick Shawn and Milton Berle joined Mitzi Gaynor, Eddie Cantor, Johnnie Ray, and others in calling Ethel "Mom." Berle sent a note signed "your almost loving illegitimate son, Berle";[13] Shawn shouted, "That's my mother!" seeing Merman later at a nightclub. After *Gypsy,* it seemed her "momification" was never going to unravel, and by all accounts, she loved it.

Off-camera Merman was as much of a practical joker as any of the movie's comic stars, and she used a still from the movie for her Christmas cards that year. She was upside down, stuck in a trash can in a Long Beach alley. Friends loved it. Wrote Stanley Kramer,

> . . . Your Christmas card was a panic.
> "Gypsy" as a movie, is a disaster. Miss Russell flounders around like a gym teacher. You would have been so great. I suspect they won't make a penny on the film. I did think Betty Bruce gave the picture its only bright moment. Mervyn's direction was calamitous. . . . I lunched with Roger Edens yesterday . . . and we spoke fondly of you. All my love for my favorite star, S.[14]

One of *A Mad, Mad, Mad, Mad World*'s running gags involved the heavy handbag Ethel carried and frequently used as a weapon, primarily against son-in-law Berle. One day, she filled the purse with some of her heavy jewelry and swung it into Berle as the script required, but with an unexpectedly big punch. For years, when they ran into each other, Ethel inquired about the bump on Berle's head.

Bob Levitt recalls that it was Jonathan Winters's comedy that really tickled his mother. Winters did impromptu routines in the cast trailer between takes, leaving the cast in stitches and Ethel raving about his work. Berle, for his part, was a bit of a ham who made a point of lingering in shots to squeeze in extra moments of screen time. Kramer seemed to relish challenging the rather sizable ego of "Mr. Television" and chuckled that "Ethel Merman was a powerful woman, a worthy antagonist for Berle. It was the Big Mouth against the Big Ego. And to see Berle henpecked by his mother-in-law was a pleasure I never ceased to enjoy. Merman managed to hold her own and then some, not only with Berle but with the others as well, despite the fact that her role subjected her to endless indignities . . . she never complained about the way the script or her fellow actors treated her."[15]

In August 1963, when Ethel was off the production schedule, she took a trip to the Edinburgh (Film) Festival to promote the movie and to join son, Bob, who was traveling solo to study the repertory theater of the United Kingdom, a trip that would give him direction as he entered the Directors' Unit at Carnegie Tech that fall. Meeting his mother overseas, as an adult now with an awakened appreciation of theater, gave him a connection to her world, and her to him, and it was a special visit. To be sure, many of his activities traveling there had been of the "sowing wild oats" variety, things that he knew were made possible with his mother's money but without her knowledge.

Leaving New York on a Pan Am flight, Merman spent the night in London before traveling north. United Artists had made sure the trip would be well covered, sending out a press release: "Note to Editors: Ethel Merman leaves Idlewild [now JFK] Friday, August 16 . . . at 8.15 P.M. *Photo coverage will be appreciated.*"[16] She didn't have to worry about lack of coverage. To the Scottish press she said, "My mother's mother was born in Glasgow, and her name was Gardner. Actually when I started in the theatre I wanted to call myself Ethel Gardner."[17] Fans were excited that Broadway's big star was finally among them:

> May one of your real admirers bid you welcome to Scotland? . . . I have long admired your sheer professionalism—in fact ever since you swiped *Alexander's Ragtime Band* from under the snub nose of Alice Faye! But, Miss Merman . . . what on earth happened to *"Gypsy"*? . . . Kept hoping that you would do the film version—or, if not you, then Judy Garland. However, the Rosalind Russell movie was, to my mind, a complete botch. All due respect to Miss Russell—a fine Auntie Mame—but *not* Rose. I have the LP of your Broadway production. . . . A superb record and one I never tire of playing, even though it is now beginning to show signs of wear!

At the top of the letter, Merman writes, "I answered this nicely."[18]

A Scottish interviewer asked for Merman's views on the advantages and disadvantages of fame. For the former, she briefly replied, "Independence," but reflected on the latter: "It makes people have some kind of awe and they are usually the kind of people I know I would like. My son is a bit [shy] of my success too. In all his travels around the repertory theatres in Britain, to all the people he has met he has never disclosed that I am his mother. I think he wants to stand on his own feet, and that's fine, isn't it?" It was Bobby, she told them, who was "getting a kick out of sitting unnoticed in her hotel lounge." And she enjoyed being "free as the wind," untrammeled by marriage, a Broadway run, or young children.[19]

Ethel the Comic

Reviewers of the film praised Ethel for holding her own among so many renowned comedians. For those tracking her career, this may not have been surprising. Although this was her first nonsinging role in a movie, theater critics had, after all, been praising her comic abilities for over thirty years. And now, as the "plump but comely 53 year old," as one interviewer in the United Kingdom described her, she knew that comedy enabled her to branch out from the tiring long runs of stage musicals. (On the clipping, Ethel underlined the word *plump*, writing "that's the English press, they're murder!")[20] Without any real desire—or need—for another long Broadway run, Ethel was able to bank on her established *comic* persona in other media, and *It's a Mad, Mad, Mad, Mad World* marked an auspicious foray.

Her relaxed sense of play is evident in the movie's final scene. All the male characters lie immobilized in traction in a hospital room, punished for their greed. *Variety* writes, "Along comes Ethel Merman, an 'old bag' mother in law detested by all parties present. . . . Miss Merman flops head over heels [on a banana peel], landing with a resounding thud on her derriere. The room is instantly filled with convulsive laughter, and the picture ends on this optimistic note."[21]

The mother-in-law gag was an old staple in comedy, of course, and *Variety*'s remark about optimistic closure suggests that mothers-in-law (and perhaps the funny women who played them) seemed not altogether different from the more serious judgments against mothers at the time. And the women who played them had a rough time of it, too. Female comics enjoyed less celebrity, less salary, and less success than their male counterparts, especially on TV and film screens (Lucille Ball being a significant exception); the problem was somewhat less marked on Broadway. Was there something wrong with being a bawdy, funny woman? One review of *A Mad, Mad, Mad, Mad World* extends praises to Jonathan Winters and, "in descending order, Buddy Hackett, Phil Silvers, and Terry-Thomas," adding that "the effects [of other performances] range from brief smile (Milton Berle) . . . to outright disgust (Ethel Merman, showing off her bloomers)."[22]

Ethel could not only take this sort of thing but could take part in it, describing her character to an Edinburgh reporter, "She wears about a hundredweight [ton] of costume jewelry and bangles all the way up her arm so you can hear her clanking toward you before she's even in sight. And she has this big, white purse she hits everybody with. It's kind of a running gag."[23] She was sure enough of herself as a performer to be unfazed, no matter how déclassé or ridiculous her character was supposed to be. It had nothing to do with her or the way she lived at home or interacted with friends; the image was "just a joke."

During the 1960s and '70s, Ethel's choice of roles was not entirely different from other stage divas who were taking up TV and film parts and cameos. Ann Miller and Carol Channing were also playing up aspects of their established personae in guest spots. In Ethel's case, though, there is a discernible difference of degree. The cameo roles she took and the way that she depicted them were full-out, lusty (though clean), and she seemed to delight in parodying the icon that was "Ethel Merman," playing up the brash, direct speech, the big hair and jewelry, and, of course, the voice. Few stars of her generation appear as willing to poke so much fun at themselves, culminating in her turn as *Airplane!*'s hysterical Lieutenant Hurwitz. Also unlike many other female stars, Ethel kept on singing throughout this entire period, and soon, in fact, she would be embarking on a new concert career phase.

Well before this and before *It's a Mad, Mad, Mad, Mad World* even began shooting, Merman's work schedule found her all over the country. In 1962, she had visited San Diego, where a young Marlo Thomas was performing in *The Yum Yum Tree*. (A few years later, Thomas twice invited Ethel to guest star on *That Girl*.) Ethel taped a TV show with Bob Hope in February 1962 in their first work together since *Red, Hot and Blue!* In April, she participated in New York's big Easter Day parade. That same year, Ethel was awarded "Actress of the Year" by the Troupers, a charitable New York organization that looked after needy theatrical children; of the April 8 ceremony, Bobby penned, "You are a good girl—and I was so proud of you tonight, Love Bobby." Bobby was sending his mom many billets-doux now, some scrawled on hotel stationery, giving touching signs of a son reaching out to a busy mom.

Merman in Las Vegas

Ethel had never expressed much interest in doing a Las Vegas show. Nonetheless, the generous pay of the casinos and the novelty of the venue were nothing to turn your nose up at. By this point in her career, Ethel's antipathy against working outside New York had softened, if not altogether evaporated; doing a twice-nightly club act for a few weeks was certainly less taxing than working in an indefinite run of a Broadway musical. And so on October 25, 1963, La Merm opened her one-woman show in Las Vegas at the historic Flamingo Hotel, where her salary was top-of-the-line (forty thousand dollars per week). Demand for the show was such that the hotel had to remodel to expand seating capacity by 250, and Ethel received so many flowers that one critic compared her dressing room to a gangster's funeral. (The bouquets were sent to local hospitals to avoid sneezing fits.) Planeloads of friends and reviewers descended for opening night and the following celebration. Edward and Agnes Zimmermann had flown out from New York, and Judy Garland, whose own show at the Flamingo had closed just days before, sent a card— "Darling Ethel, Know you will be a great success tonight. . . . I love you very much. Judy."[24] It was there that Dick Shawn boasted to the crowd, "That's my Mother!"[25] and Ethel's other movie offspring, Mitzi Gaynor, expressed her delight as well, along with Jule Styne, Eddie Cantor, Stanley Kramer, Spencer Tracy, and Dinah Shore. Roddy McDowall, who was working on George Stevens's biblical epic *The Greatest Story Ever Told,* flew in from Los Angeles with several cast members to take in the show and party. According to columnist Sheila Graham, Ethel said, "It's the first time a Jewish girl ever had St. Matthew, Judas, Nathaniel and St. Peter as her escorts," in a story that was obviously not cleared by Miss Merman.[26]

The show consisted of twenty-three songs, most from her Broadway shows, and was later released on LP. Reviews of the debut were enthusiastic; one called Merman—ever the force of nature—"the happiest earthquake ever to hit Las Vegas."[27] By now, the voice was always cast as a force, the vocal delivery a "belt."

For one local reporter, interviewing Ethel proved comic but embarrassing. After their conversation, Ethel asked him to play some of it back on his tape recorder. The thing didn't work. "I tried explaining to Merman that I was unskilled with mechanical gadgets. . . . She just glared at me in a slightly homicidal manner. . . . Yesterday I got a year's subscription to *Popular Mechanics* with a note from Ethel Merman which read: 'Maybe you'll learn how to operate that machine of your's [sic] now.' "[28]

Ethel on Television and around Town

During the filming of *It's a Mad, Mad, Mad, Mad World*, Ethel entered negotiations to launch her own half-hour TV sitcom. On February 4, 1963, Ethel went to Desilu Studios in Cahuenga, Los Angeles, where good friend and Desilu co-owner Lucille Ball, her husband, Gary Morton, and Mitzi Gaynor watched as the pilot for *Maggie Brown* was shot in color. The script was by Bill Manhoff,[29] and the show's premise made clear nods not only to Merman's *Panama Hattie* but also to the *Titanic*'s fabled unsinkable Molly Brown, recently the subject of the 1960 musical. Ethel portrays Maggie Brown, a club owner on Lobster Island, a naval atoll in the South Pacific used largely for refueling planes, where she is a solo mom to teenage daughter, Linda. The pilot episode concerns the island's beer supply, which has been temporarily cut off. With a still operating under the saloon floor, Maggie's saloon remains in business, but then when a rival bar owner tips off local authorities, they uncover it. This is not before young Linda nearly runs off with the handsome sailor whom Maggie had hired to help repair the contraption. Over the half-hour running time, Ethel reprises two Broadway tunes, "Friendship" (singing to the sailors in her establishment at the beginning) and, with her daughter at the end, "Mutual Admiration Society." In between, she does a rushed, comic medley of fragments from numbers such as "The Trolley Song" and "Steam Heat" to hide the noises of the ailing still during the inspectors' surprise visit.

Maggie Brown has its moments. Ethel's voice is used to compelling effect, whether speaking or singing. Its gags are no worse than most other TV shows of the time: As Maggie stares wide-eyed at the legs of her rival restaurateur, a kilted Scotsman, he says, "You've seen me in my kilt before." "Yeah," she says, "but not since you raised the hemline." The characters—a protective single parent of a hormonally challenged teen with suitors—were standard issue sitcom ingredients. But the show was able to appeal to longtime Merman followers and fans by exploiting her established trademarks, like her easy camaraderie with working-class people, the military, and people of various ethnicities; here she was playing yet another spirited saloon woman with a brassy, can-do attitude and a mother with tough love and a sentimental heart. Unfortunately, what *Maggie Brown* lacked was much of anything new.

Ethel was the usual go-getter talking up the pilot's future, and she deeply wanted the stability that a weekly series would give her. "There's nothing like it on TV now," she told reporters about *Maggie*. "It's a half-hour that's partly situation comedy and partly musical comedy. I'll be able to sing two songs each week." Each of the networks, NBC, CBS, and ABC, considered it, but they all took a pass, and *Maggie Brown* was in the end never picked up. Even Lucille Ball's appreciable clout wasn't enough to get the show on the air. *Maggie* was beset by conceptual problems from the start. The brass, nervous about Merman's star power, first called it *The Ethel Merman Show*, which then became *Trader Brown* (surely to Ethel's consternation) before becoming *Maggie Brown*.[30] Studios were clearly not sure about how to package it or its star.

A West Coast insider speculated, "I figure the pilot didn't sell because of the setting; take Ethel out of that musical comedy–type island and put her in a big city saloon and I'll bet even a presentation without a pilot will make an easy sale."[31] Evidently, Ethel's affiliation with New York City was not helping her success in television. (Fifteen years later, though, another Merman sitcom was placed squarely in Manhattan and fared no better.) Ethel, who lobbied for *Maggie* for years, seemed circumspect but slightly peeved about the whole affair, complaining to the press as late as 1966 that the show was "killed" by one CBS executive in particular, "who," she added, "was later fired."[32]

During this time, Ethel was enjoying a healthy personal life, going out with different men. ("I'm not a nun, you know.") Some were lovers, some simply escorts. Among the latter were several gay men who ranged from trusted, charming, and discreet confidants, such as Eric Palm, to dissimulating types who "led Ethel on, just to say they'd been with her," according to Cointreau, who knew some of them.[33] Ethel was reported to be in the frequent company of songwriter Jimmy van Heusen, whom she called Chester (his birth name was Chester Babcock) and was also escorted by Woolworth heir Jimmy Donahue. Her name was frequently tied to Jimmy Gardiner, an oil businessman and producer whose cards and letters suggest a solid friendship, and to screenwriter Ernest Gann, a friend from the West Coast. The press still speculated that she had a romance going with Chicago friend and escort Eddie Bragno, and she still wrote them to deny it. Ethel also resumed her relationship with Sherman Billingsley, under the radar as always, sleeping at girlfriends' apartments. In 1966, Billingsley passed away without ever having divorced his wife.

Most of the time when reporters asked Ethel about the prospect of remarriage, she laughed it off with a "Why jump back into the frying pan?" or "What, with my track record?"[34] Occasionally, interviewers coaxed Ethel into admitting that she would like to have a man to take care of her, which close friends and family knew to be the case, even though she handled being alone well. But she was tired of men who "wanted to be linked with me just because I'm Ethel Merman" and of others who took her heart. "The truth is I'm very unhappy when I'm in love. I'm basically a one-man woman," and when the men start to stray, "I go right up the wall."[35] So Ethel had various escorts and didn't actively seek serious new romance.

During this period of a relatively active nightlife, Ethel was spotted doing the twist with no less a partner than Jerome Robbins, attending dinners with Perle Mesta, and serenading at the party for Jule Styne's wedding. She wrote to her parents: "At the dinner to Jule Styne and his bride Maggie last night—*everyone* was there, including Jack Warner, Mervyn LeRoy, even Groucho Marx—[I'm] packing now. Love, Ethel."[36] She sang "Everything's Coming Up Roses" with special lyrics that Sammy Cahn had penned for the occasion:

> As you read, they were wed
> And most natur'ly they went to bed
> And I'll state, it was great—Frankly,
> Everything's coming up—Thank God![37]

In public, Ethel altered the lyrics of the songs she sang only once, out of respect for their creators and out of her deep sense of professionalism. At private parties, though, she sometimes sang blue renditions of her hits for laughs; few records of those were kept.

In 1963, Ethel performed twice at Harrahs' South Shore Room, a popular nightspot in Lake Tahoe. Before the April appearance, Van Johnson sent a telegram pleading, "Please don't take this coast too. It's all we have left."[38] She sang at the spring Oscars telecast that was hosted by Frank Sinatra. For that, Ethel's adored designer from *There's No Business Like Show Business,* Miles White, sent a handwritten card: "Dearest Ethel—That was the most superb and exciting version of 'Show Biz' I have ever seen you perform! You were so magnificent and beautiful on The Academy I am still thrilled—Thank you—with my love Miles."[39]

By this point Merman's activities were more diverse than they'd ever been when she was working on a show, and she was free to appear in different venues, media, and events. On May 6, 1963, *Time* invited Ethel and all of the other people who had graced the magazine's covers to attend an enormous dinner commemorating the publication's twenty-fifth anniversary at the Waldorf-Astoria. Later in the month she appeared on *The Red*

Skelton Show, and she was also performing in live shows throughout New England. Reviews for these shows on the road were mostly positive, if less consistently adoring than those from New York. After noting that the Merman voice was in fine shape, a Boston critic wrote that "There's No Business . . ." aside,

> without the friendly cover of costumes and sets, [the other pieces] seem strangely old-fashioned. Cole Porter's "You're the Top" is a period piece, and needs to be treated that way. In its day, it represented a high kind of nervous sophistication; now its slick lyrics are out-of-date and its rhythms, too. "Down in the Depths on the Ninetieth Floor" was pretty moving it its day; now it is desperately old-fashioned. . . . Whoever put [the show] together made a basic mistake, presenting her as though she were an old-timer making a farewell appearance.

Although this reviewer insisted that Merman herself was no old-timer, he closed with the line "her glow is, alas, dimmed."[40]

Soon after that, the woman with the ostensible "dim glow" performed at the Washington Amphitheater in June, where a critic there said, "That was no siren pealing across town last night. That was Ethel Merman opening. . . . And she blasted it [the amphitheater] open."[41] Critics seemed intent on finding in Ethel Merman either a trip down memory lane or a delightfully overpowering force of nature; the range of her public image was by now narrowing and losing the nuance and complexity it had enjoyed earlier.

That summer—still 1963—Ethel recorded a song for the U.S. Post Office to promote the new zip code system it was introducing and did publicity shots standing next to a cardboard cartoon of a smiling postman holding up envelopes with zip codes written boldly across them. In August a big performance at the Hollywood Bowl was scheduled but, after an extensive advance publicity campaign, was canceled, a casualty to either conflicts with Ethel's shooting schedule or, more likely, competition feared from a Dodgers' baseball game the same night. No matter. On September 22, Ethel, back in New York, appeared on a live special televised by CBS from Lincoln Center, celebrating its first anniversary. The special was so big that it preempted the extremely popular *Ed Sullivan Show* that night. The special, hosted by Alistair Cooke, included classical, popular, and show performers, and after her introduction by Richard Rodgers, Merman sang "Everything's Coming Up Roses," "They Say It's Wonderful," and "Blow, Gabriel, Blow."

Three Divas on *The Judy Garland Show*

October 1963 saw more TV work, including another appearance on Red Skelton's variety show. While she was taping it, Merman made a TV appearance that would become almost as celebrated as her work with Mary Martin on the *Ford 50th Anniversary Show*. Elsewhere in the CBS building, where Merman was doing the Skelton show, Judy Garland was taping her show, hosting guests the Smothers Brothers and a young Broadway star named Barbra Streisand. ("I'm doing *Funny Girl* next with Jule Styne.") Streisand—barely twenty-one years old and wearing a long slit skirt and a sailor-style top—sings "Bewitched, Bothered and Bewildered" from *Pal Joey* before responding to some diva chatter initiated by her admiring host:

> GARLAND: You're so thrilling, so absolutely thrilling, I must say you're so good . . . that I hate you!
>
> STREISAND: You're so great, that I've been hating you for years, and my ambition is to be great enough to be hated by as many singers as you.

After dueting with "Get Happy" and "Happy Days Are Here Again," the two women chat about singing, and as soon as Judy tells Barbra, "You really belt a song, and there are very few of us left," Ethel's recognizable voice comes up from the audience singing the first few bars of "You're Just in Love." Ethel joins them onstage to great applause, telling them she'd been across the hall recording for Skelton and "*you* guys were belting!" Barbra is introduced as the new big belter and appears rather shy and overwhelmed by the two old pros, especially when all three team up for "There's No Business Like Show Business." Merman stands in the middle, sandwiched between an appreciative, glowing Garland and an awkward, bemused Streisand, who allow her the center stage vocally as well. Merman and Garland's affection for each other is transparent in the footage. At one point Ethel says, "You look great!" Garland responds, "I finally lost a few . . . ," and Merman blows out air on her, as if she could knock her thin friend over. The show aired on October 6, and to this day remains a classic; every fan of big belters—from Merman to Garland and Minnelli and Streisand—refers to this show as a near holy moment of the trinity of Belt.

In November, Ethel sang live at the prestigious supper club the Persian Room, to the delight of New Yorkers; it was her first Manhattan nightclub engagement since the Central Park Casino when *Girl Crazy* was running three decades earlier. Like other contemporary singers, Ethel wore a mike, as she did for all her concert appearances (but never her stage work), but that scarcely stopped the jokes about the big Merman voice. One ad announced, "A war is about to be unleashed!" Ethel the Singing Warrior was too happy with her new work to be missing old Broadway much.

SIXTEEN

The Sixties and the Art
of Love

Ethel would be photographically teamed with her fourth and final husband nineteen months before they ever met. On April 22, 1962, papers announced NBC's plan to broadcast *Call Me Madam* with a photo of Merman dancing with George Sanders in the film.[1] Below it on the same page is a picture of Ernest Borgnine from *Marty,* his 1955 film, which, like *Call Me Madam,* was now making its debut on the small screen. Quite unlike Sally Adams, Marty was ordinary, an overweight Italian-American butcher who lived in the Bronx with his lonely and overbearing mother. Borgnine's depiction earned him an Academy Award.

Merman and Borgnine met at a party on November 30, 1963, given by Ethel's good friend Temple "Texas" Schribman. "Right away Borgnine began paying a lot of attention to me. I thought he seemed pleasant, but I wasn't any more interested in him than I was in Ernie Gann. . . . Next day Borgnine began calling. We started going out a lot, but I was due back in New York."[2] Soon after that, when an interviewer spotted a ruby on her left finger, Merman told her that it "did not signify her engagement. I have romances," she said, "but no serious ones. IF I were engaged, this would be one big diamond. I wouldn't be fussing around with rubies."[3] Four days later, the day after she'd spent Christmas with her parents and Bobby, Merman says that Borgnine appeared unannounced at her door in New York and proposed on the spot. "Don't ask me what I was thinking about when I said yes."[4]

It was an unusual pairing, but in truth, several aspects of even their public images intersected rather well. Both were down-to-earth, working-class figures on- and offstage. Neither was a glamorous, refined celebrity, and both were more appealing for not having tried to be. Yet at the same time, these two people came from utterly different solar systems: Merman was a stratospheric Broadway star, with a longer, brighter career, which outshone Borgnine's film and TV successes in the '50s and early '60s. Borgnine was at the end of a second marriage and was nine years younger than Ethel. The flattery of a younger man's attentions, especially at this time in her life, doubtlessly intoxicated her. But intoxicated she was. Over the holidays, Ethel gave Borgnine a private recording she made of the Gershwins' "Someone to Watch Over Me" (coupled with "White Christmas") at Nola's in New York City, a place where nonprofessionals could cut their own records. "Her heart was really into it," remembers Bob Levitt. "It was not a performance but an authentic expression of her longing and her vulnerability."[5] Those feelings resonate deeply for him to this day; for him that recording conveys what he calls his mother's "inner yearning" for the love and stability that a man and family—so idealized in her heart—were supposed to provide.

Her heart was as full as it was serious, but the entertainment world was stunned by what they viewed as an unlikely engagement. Marilyn (Cantor) Baker remembers learning about it in Los Angeles, where she was visiting her father. "Daddy was watching the news and called up to me, 'Marilyn, your Ethel has married the plumber.'"[6]

The press printed an interview humorously called "Must Be Love: Ethel and Ernie Unfamiliar with Each Other's Work," accompanied by a decorous portrait of the couple. Here Ethel repeats the line she'd used when she was with Six, that this was the first time she was "really in love." There was tenderness both didn't shy from. Borgnine: "Everybody thinks she is loud and brash. She's just the opposite. She's soft, gentle and shy. And you know me, I'm 'Marty.'"[7]

Of course, Borgnine's image as Marty was every bit as fabricated as Merman's "loud and brash" one. In fact, although newer on the scene, Borgnine's image had probably undergone more media cultivation than hers, since Hollywood is and always was more aggressive than Broadway in producing and marketing "stars." (To promote *Marty*, for instance, Borgnine appeared at the opening of a Santa Monica supermarket as a guest butcher, and starlets in bathing suits greeted him there, holding signs reading "I love Marty.") *Marty* was considered an iconoclastic film for depicting an unglamorous hero in a slice-of-life story and seemed to have more in common with Italian neorealism than with studio slicksterism, despite its well-oiled marketing campaign.[8] *Marty* ended up sweeping four Academy Awards for best picture, director, screenplay, and actor.

Marty's Anglo-American girlfriend, played by Betsy Blair, is as intriguing as he is, perhaps all the more because of the attention the character and actress *didn't* receive. Blair plays a perfectly attractive if unglamorous woman, but throughout the story, male characters refer to her as a "dog." In fact, Marty's transformative moment—one that implies a future in which he can move on from his mother—is when he pursues this dog not out of sympathy but from real desire. Given the derision of his buddies and the disapproval of his lonely, self-serving mother and her friends (shades of Momism?), Marty is depicted as downright heroic for daring to like such a woman.

The role imbued Borgnine with a gruff but ethical working-class image for the rest of his career, from the 1960s sitcom *McHale's Navy* to his role as a grieving widower in Sean Penn's portion of the movie *11'09"01* (2002). Like any star, though, Borgnine's public persona was not restricted to this one character trait, and other roles, such as those in westerns from the campy *Johnny Guitar* (1954) to the testosterone-fueled *Dirty Dozen* (1967), made him into a tough guy easily roused to vicious behavior.

That tough side was enhanced by press reports of the temper Borgnine purportedly displayed with Chicana actress Katy Jurado, his second wife, whom he'd married in December 1959. Tabloids had a field day with the volatile relationship: "Ernest Borgnine and Katy Jurado have wound up fine, too—at least until the next explosion."[9] In a May 16, 1962, interview, Hedda Hopper jumped right in: "Are you divorced, separated, or what?" Said Borgnine, "Just separated. . . . I haven't heard from her since last August. I'm so engrossed in my work now *[McHale's Navy]*, I couldn't care less," he said, not referring to Jurado by name.[10] Later, Sheila Graham—never a reliable reporter of Mermania—queried: "Is the engagement between Ethel Merman and Ernie Borgnine still on? I pose the question because Ernie has just sent in a request to see *It's a Mad, Mad, Mad, Mad World,* in which his intended plays the kind of nagging shrew that Ernie has spent all his life avoiding."[11]

Years later, Benay Venuta claimed to have warned Ethel against Borgnine's alleged volatility and said that Ethel refused to hear it, remaining proud about and devoted to her new lover. After the loss of Levitt and the abuse of Six, it was only human that Ethel would protect and defend the romantic choices she made, and at this point there was nothing wrong with the relationship. To Ethel's intimates, the feelings they had seemed both strong and ingenuous. "I thought they made a lovely couple," says Tony Cointreau. "They were made for each other; they were both so down to earth, and they truly enjoyed each other's company."[12]

After a six-month courtship, Ethel and Ernie exchanged vows on June 27, 1964, five days after Borgnine's divorce from Jurado was finalized. Ethel wore a chiffon dress in three shades of yellow at the wedding, which was held at Borgnine's Beverly Hills home. Reception guests included many of Hollywood's who's who, including the cast of *McHale's Navy* and Merman colleagues such as the Bob Hopes, Jack Bennys, Carl Reiners, and Stanley Kramer, Gypsy Rose Lee, Ethel's mom and Pop, Bobby, and Little Ethel and her young family. Granddaughter Barbara Geary recalls, "I mainly remember being a kid surrounded by grown-ups. Here was Grandma Ethel getting married at a really big party. There were flowers all over the place, and I went over to pick one from an arrangement on a trellis. One of Ernie's associates spotted me and made me go up to him to apologize and give it back. I did and he got furious. There's a photo of me running back to the trellis in silent mortification to put the flower back on."[13] When Uncle Bob saw what had happened, he went over to play with the girl, lifting her up and down by the arms. Somehow she dislocated her shoulder, and her howls disrupted the proceedings. Grandma Ethel, newlywed, accompanied the child to the emergency room.

The plan was that after their honeymoon to Hawaii, Japan, and East Asia, Ethel would move into Borgnine's house. Living in Los Angeles made sense; as she kept saying, she was through with long-running Broadway shows, so she had her belongings shipped out west. The press was releasing reports about Merman's new career options; even before their wedding, Sheila Graham reported that

> Ethel Merman will appear in one of Ernie Borgnine's "McHale's Navy" [episodes] if they have to re-write the whole format to get her aboard. No TV show in its right mind is going to let all that Ethel-Ernie engagement publicity go to waste. Ethel drops anchor here over the weekend to visit lover boy on the set—why not put her to work? The day Ernie returned to work after shore leave with the "Merm" in New York, the whole cast and crew pelted him with old shoes and rice. And not for a minute have they let him forget that he's now a sailor with just ONE girl in port.[14]

The marriage to Ernie Borgnine is one of the most stupendous chapters in the Book of Merm. Very early into the honeymoon, Ethel suddenly wanted out and wanted out immediately. She called her agent, who told her that it would be a public relations disaster bailing so soon and that the couple needed to go through with the honeymoon and maintain the marriage for a few weeks for appearance's sake. "What should I do with the gifts? I can't return them," she reportedly asked Earl Wilson.

When the papers ran an interview with the lovesick Merman and Borgnine in July, it was already out of date, although readers had no way of knowing that at the time:

[INTERVIEWER:] The two keep busting up together, like love birds.

ERNIE: I'd sort of given up marriage.

ETHEL: I had, too. After the last one, particularly, I was afraid to try it again. But with Ernie everything sort of fell into place, it came so naturally.

ERNIE: It's the most natural thing we've ever done.[15]

Soon after this, the news broke. On August 4, Louella Parsons proclaimed, "Ethel Quits Honeymoon Cottage."[16] The *Los Angeles Times* wrote that the marriage lasted thirty-eight days; the *Daily News,* five weeks.[17] One reporter called the marriage "World War III"; Ethel sometimes referred to it as "that thing" and refused to discuss it. Between March and September 1964, the Borgnine months, her scrapbooks are uncharacteristically blank.[18]

Ethel never disclosed the reason for the split to anyone, including her parents, her son, or close friends such as Cointreau, who today says, "I have a lot of respect for both Ethel and Ernie for keeping the reason to themselves."[19] For strangers, that silence has fueled much speculation, almost all of it based on the myth of "Merman," or the simple incongruity of the match, or both. In 2005, during an airing of "Shortest Celebrity Marriages" on an entertainment channel, Merman and Borgnine still made the "top ten." The show's explanation was catty invention: by the time of the marriage, it said, Borgnine was more famous than Ethel, and wherever they went, people were recognizing him, not her, and she couldn't stand being in anybody's shadow.[20] This could not have been further from the truth, for both stars enjoyed a great deal of visibility from TV and their appearances. According to Cointreau, the two of them actually kidded each other, affectionately, about being the real apple of the media's eye. Whatever the private reasons of its demise, the notoriously short union has played a substantial part in Ethel's afterlife as a camp icon. Broadway royalty marrying working-class "Marty" the butcher could hardly seem more incongruous, as Cantor's "plumber" comment indicates, and then there is Jeffery Roberson's act as "Varla Jean Merman," which shows how the legacy of the marriage endures.

Columnist Radie Harris gives a sense of how Merman treated the break-up in public: "Ethel Merman, one of the staunchest of Republicans when Mamie and Ike [were] in the White House, will be a visitor at 1600 Penn. Ave. again today as the guest of Lady Bird and LBJ. She will lead a committee of 'Republicans for Johnson. . . . ' After that she takes off to Sydney and Melbourne. Won't play *Gypsy* and has vowed she'll never do another show. And when Ethel shuts a door, she really slams it. Ask Ernie Borgnine, he knows!"[21]

Merman's second autobiography contains the infamous "My Marriage to Ernest Borgnine" chapter that consists of the hilarious single blank page. Early in the next chapter, she writes, "I'm a lover, not a fighter," words that may be more suggestive now than they were at the time.[22] Some of Ethel's associates do, in fact, speculate that it was physical abuse that ended the stormy union. (One fan ventured that Ethel was the batterer; after all, "Ethel Merman" was supposed to be an indomitable superpower, not anyone's victim.) For some reason, rumors of abuse have been stubbornly held. One fan/colleague, who was not an intimate friend, reported gossip to the effect that Merman considered Borgnine's sexual demands excessive and unreasonable. Another person who knew Merman vaguely from the 1970s states flatly, "He beat her, you know," as if that were the self-evident and absolute truth; and some of the people who looked after Pop in New Jersey late in his life seemed to believe the same thing. It is a lot of talk for something Merman never discussed.

Tony Cointreau says, "The only thing she ever told me was that it came down to money."[23] After Six, he says, Ethel was sensitive to being chiseled, and in her autobiography Merman does complain that Borgnine had acquired the tickets for their Pacific honeymoon as freebies from a promotional campaign.

The divorce was a protracted, unpleasant affair. After a series of suits and countersuits, the courts awarded Ethel the divorce on grounds of extreme cruelty. Waiving all alimony and support, she made Borgnine cover the expense of shipping her personal effects back to New York. To the press she readied her lines. Jack O'Brian reported that when Winchell playfully "dared the impudent question, 'What happened?'" at the Stork Club Room, she retorted, "I forgot to duck." Elsewhere, "Why did I do it? I don't know. I certainly didn't marry him for his looks."[24]

Wanting to cleanse herself of the relationship, Ethel took Bob Jr., now nineteen, to Hawaii, Asia, and Russia on a trip that traced the exact path of the honeymoon, step by step. "It was a rerouting of Mom's heart," says Levitt, "to undo things with Borgnine."[25] It was also a chance for mother and son to keep up what Levitt calls their shared "yearning" to try to connect and make things between them and with their family right. In spite of their mutual estrangement for most of their lives, Bob says that he and his mother "never strayed" from that hope of closeness with each other in their hearts.

Ethel with Ethel Jr. and Bob Levitt Jr., 1946.
Look magazine photograph; courtesy of Sydelle Kramer.

An abundantly dressed Ethel in *Panama Hattie,* 1940.
Photograph by Lucas & Monroe; courtesy of Sydelle Kramer.

The Merman performance style (as Panama Hattie). Courtesy of the Museum of the City of New York.

The cast of *Panama Hattie.* Photograph by Lucas & Monroe; courtesy of Sydelle Kramer.

Ethel the Riveter, 1943.
From *New York Mirror;*
courtesy of the Museum
of the City of New York.

The Merman mouth and eyes.
Courtesy of the Museum of the
City of New York.

High-hatted Ethel, 1943.
Courtesy of the Museum of the City of New York.

Ethel and Harry Bellaver in *Annie Get Your Gun*, 1946.
Author's collection.

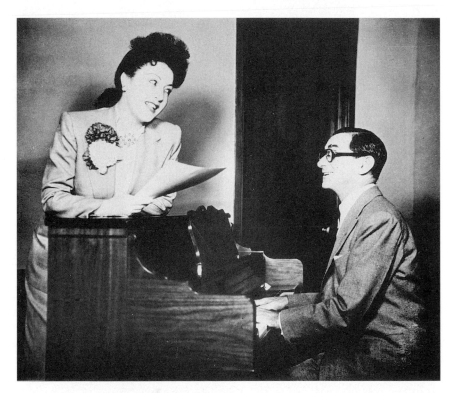

· Rehearsing with Irving Berlin, c. 1946.
Courtesy of the Museum of the City of New York.

Ethel and Russell Nype sing the show-stopping "You're Just in Love" in *Call Me Madam* on Broadway, 1950. Courtesy of the Museum of the City of New York.

Call Me Madam dolls used on the cover of the arts monthly *Flair*.
Courtesy of the Museum of the City of New York.

Ethel, standing with George Sanders, holds her "super train" in the film version of
Call Me Madam, 1953. Courtesy of the Academy of Motion Picture Arts and Sciences.

Ethel sings the poignant finale in *There's No Business Like Show Business*, 1954. Courtesy of the Academy of Motion Picture Arts and Sciences.

Ethel's banned outfit in *There's No Business Like Show Business*. Courtesy of the Academy of Motion Picture Arts and Sciences.

Performing with Mary
Martin at the famous *Ford
50th Anniversary Show,* 1953.
Courtesy of the Museum
of the City of New York.

Ethel and Bob Six, 1950s.
Courtesy of the Academy
of Motion Picture Arts
and Sciences.

Herb (Jack Klugman) takes leave of Rose in *Gypsy*. From souvenir booklet; courtesy of Al F. Koenig Jr.

Encouraging Liza Minnelli at her premiere at the Person Room, February 1966. Courtesy of the Museum of the City of New York.

Poster for *The Art of Love,* 1965. Courtesy of the Museum of the City of New York.

Ethel and Ernest Borgnine, 1963 or 1964. Courtesy of the Academy of Motion Picture Arts and Sciences.

Hasty Pudding visit, 1966. Courtesy of the New York Public Library.

Promotion for the disco album, 1980.
Courtesy of the Academy of Motion Picture Arts and Sciences.

Performing with Jule Styne after receiving ASCAP's Pied Piper Award at Carnegie Hall, May 1982. Courtesy of Al F. Koenig Jr.

Ethel and Bob Levitt Jr. vacationing near Catalina Island, early 1980s. Courtesy of Bob Levitt.

Edward and Agnes Zimmermann, 1973. Courtesy of Al F. Koenig Jr.

Ethel at home in her Surrey Hotel apartment with her ceramic bassett hound, George, 1982.
Courtesy of Al F. Koenig Jr.

The Art of Love

When Ethel reflected on her next film, 1965's *The Art of Love,* she called it "a featherweight comedy that sank like lead."[26] It was an apt description for a picture whose outcome didn't match up with all the talent behind it. *The Art of Love* was produced by Ross Hunter, Universal's star producer of vehicles for Rock Hudson, Douglas Sirk, and others in the '50s; Cy Coleman scored; Don Raye wrote lyrics; Carl Reiner did the screenplay; and Norman Jewison directed. The cast was equally stellar, with Dick Van Dyke, Elke Sommer, James Garner, and Angie Dickinson taking leads.

Van Dyke portrays Paul Sloan, a struggling American painter living in Paris. When Sloan's art dealer tells him bluntly, "Dead artists sell more," Paul and his roommate, Casey (Garner), a frustrated writer, head to a bridge and get drunk. Casey writes a dramatic fake suicide note that Paul signs at the moment he sees a woman jumping into the water (Elke Sommer as Nikki). When he jumps in to save her, the drunken man lands on a barge that floats him out of town. Eventually he catches up with her, and she tells him she'd despaired after receiving sexual overtures from her boss.

When he reads about his own death in the papers, Paul returns to Paris to witness a veritable bidding war over his paintings and his estate, all managed by Casey, who urges Paul to keep up the pretense. Reluctantly, Paul disguises himself in a ridiculous Andy Warhol–like wig and hides out in the house of Madame Coco La Fontaine, Ethel's nightclub for gentlemen. Casey, meanwhile, is making a fortune without him and is now putting the moves on Paul's rich American fiancée, Laurie (Dickinson), who has unexpectedly come to Paris. (She spends most of the picture fainting from shocking news.) Casey bribes Paul's cohorts to intimate that Paul has been cheating on her. Meanwhile Paul, oblivious that his fiancée is even there, tries to hide his feelings for Nikki, who is aggressively going after him.

The gendarmes ultimately finger Casey and the art dealer for the murder of Paul Sloan. Paul, after finally learning that Casey has taken both his earnings and his girlfriend, attends the trial disguised as an elderly man, making no attempt to intervene when Casey is pronounced guilty. After Casey is sentenced to the guillotine, however, Paul tears off and is involved in a car race to save him. Arriving at the gallows at the last moment, Paul "explains" his own death as a result of amnesia to police and onlookers. The film closes with a set of new couples: Laurie and Casey, Paul and Nikki, and Madame Coco/Ethel and Pepe, a wealthy elderly man on whom she has forced herself.

Universal's unpublished plot synopsis concludes with the line, "Quite a place, Paris, *n'est-ce pas?*"[27]

Despite the comic gifts of writer Carl Reiner, *The Art of Love* is not the stuff of literary giants. It borrows heavily from other successes of the time, especially *An American in Paris* (the story line) and the Pink Panther spy caper spoofs; not only is there a Clouseau-like character named Carnot, but when Carnot accuses Garner of Paul's death, Garner dismisses him with "You've seen too many Peter Sellers movies." The final chase is straight out of a Jacques Tati picture, and in the trial scene, Dick Van Dyke reprises the look of the elderly Mr. Banks, whom he played a year earlier in *Mary Poppins.* This is only one of many disguises Van Dyke undergoes in this picture; only Merman changes her wigs more often than he.

In fact, the most attention-grabbing aspect of Ethel's role is the assortment of odd-colored wigs she wears. All were styled in a short, wavy bubble, a hairstyle that Ethel wore, in less exaggerated forms, for most of the decade. (Louella Parsons approvingly reported that, along with her blond highlights, the cut made the star "look ten years younger.")[28] As seen in the film, the wigs are right out of Oz's Emerald City: the first is a frosted pink to match Madame Coco's pink shirt; later versions are blue- and green-tinged platinum. It's tempting to see the wigs as a sign of people's well-documented fascination with Merman's hair, but their presence here seems motivated by the character she plays—a madam, after all—rather than by Ethel's own star image, which barely scratches the picture. The wigs, like much else, don't really add up, except to contribute to the picture's general zaniness.

Elke Sommer recalls of the shoot:

> Everyone got along making the movie—it was fun. I didn't have the opportunity to form an impression of Miss Merman one way or another, though, since my scenes were mostly with Dick Van Dyke. To me, Miss Merman seemed to be of an entirely different generation and background. My only impression of her at the time was that she had this bright red hair, and that she was carrying a lot of weight on her body. But I can't say whether I learned from her or I didn't learn from her. . . . we just didn't have much chance to interact.[29]

Like Sommer, the movie's intended audience would likely have known little or anything about this older woman who, indeed, seemed to come from another world. By contrast, older or East Coast viewers could see in the brassy, mercenary "madam" a throwback that went as far as Ethel's roles in 1930s movies. And, just like that work, *The Art of Love* underuses her. Universal publicists tried to hype her presence for what they could. "When Merman belts a number in French, you'll find out that fifty million Americans can't be wrong,"[30] said Ross Hunter; the studio talked up what it called the "flashy French tune" ("M'sieur"), which she sings as part of the show in her establishment. "M'sieur" is a strong candidate for being the strangest song Ethel ever recorded on film. It's certainly a little camp but too unfocused to be enjoyable as such, mixing English with pidgin French ("C'est si bon, pourquoi pas le love?"), and the combination of Ethel's Queens accent and the French is not particularly euphonious. Don Raye, a 1985 inductee into the Songwriters' Hall of Fame and writer of "Irresistible You" and "Boogie Woogie Bugle Boy," produced surprisingly trite lyrics, an effect that is only enhanced by the chorus girls, who prance around Ethel in strange outfits that are little more than dress hoops.[31]

There is, however, a momentary glimpse of what seems to be "Ethel Merman" that survives the strange proceedings. Near the end of the number, she glances over her shoulder and raises an arm in triumph, shooting a twinkling look directly at the camera. In that microsecond glance we see a vivacious Ethel Merman, not Madame Coco executing a bizarre floor show.

During production, *The Art of Love* encountered censorship problems, even though the actual power of the MPAA was decidedly on the wane by the '60s. It wasn't just the bumps and grinds of Madame Coco's "girls" that raised eyebrows but also her cathouse, which had to be clearly established as a nightclub. The lyrics of "M'sieur" required modification, with all of the references to the lips, arms, and hearts of the women of the "maison" transformed into a vaguer, more palatable celebration of love. There could, moreover, be no suggestion of sexual activity between any of the couples, including a nude mannequin that bare-chested James Garner wakes up with in the opening scene. (It caused a veritable avalanche of letters from censors to producers.)[32]

Top billing went to Garner, Van Dyke, Sommer, and Dickinson in that order, and Ethel's credit usually appeared at the bottom of the ads used in promotion, with her photograph off to the side rather than with the images of the bigger stars. Her billing, though, is in larger type than that of other bit players, such as Carl Reiner, who is superb as the French lawyer. It's clear that Universal's marketing machinery didn't spend much energy on Merman, and a reading of their publicity sheets now makes it hard not to think that the industry had more or less given up on her. Pop diligently cut out every published reference to his daughter with the new picture, though, and pasted them in his scrapbooks—now numbering over twenty-five volumes.

Ethel talked up the forthcoming flick: "I have a straight dramatic role in a Ross Hunter film that hasn't been released yet—I play a French broad that has a café in Montmartre. This is what I've wanted to do for a long time, straight dramatic things," she said, probably referring to the fact that *The Art of Love* wasn't a musical.[33] Generally, the New York press was good about plugging the picture. Louis Sobol's column included a note from Hunter: "I know how fond you are of Ethel Merman—well, on our tour with my new picture, *The Art of Love* (Forgive the plug, Louis), you should see the reception she gets. Wild—just wild. She's really been rediscovered by the teenagers,"[34] showing sensitivity to the idea that Ethel came, if not from another world, at least from a different entertainment era. Another New York review touted the film as a personal triumph for the local star: "Fresh from a marital disaster and a tour of Australia and Europe to get over it, Ethel Merman is back in town sporting a new hairdo, a new apartment and a new movie, *The Art of Love*."[35]

At this point, Ethel was still was insisting that she had no intention of returning to Broadway. "'But if I should come back,' she hedged, 'it would be in a blockbuster. That's the only way I'd do it.'"[36] It was true that when Ethel made a decision, whether professional or personal, she stuck to it; at the same time, she was never one to shut doors on professional options. During her short time with Borgnine, for instance, she taped two appearances on Judy Garland's TV show; in February, she performed in London's Piccadilly Circus, where the review read, "The M (for Merman) bomb exploded her last night."[37] (The year before, a U.S. Air Force general had given Ethel the official designation of "Miss Sonic Boom.")[38]

Woman of the Year

The mid-'60s were filled with events and appearances for Ethel all over the country. On March 11, 1966, Harvard University's Hasty Pudding Club awarded Merman its annual "Woman of the Year" award "in recognition of great acting skill and feminine qualities."[39] Founded in 1795 as a satirical secret society, Hasty Pudding (so named because, initially, "each member in alphabetical order provides a pot of hasty pudding to each meeting") had been producing student-written shows in drag since 1891, and every year since 1961, the club had invited an actress to join them in their annual parade, show, and merrymaking. Recipients included Grace Kelly, Gertrude Lawrence,

Jane Fonda, Lee Remick, Joanne Woodward, Shirley MacLaine, and Rosalind Russell.

In Ethel's year, the show was *Right Up Your Alley,* with lyrics written by Mo Hanan.[40] As soon as Merman arrived in Cambridge, the students surprised her with a rousing rendition of "There's No Business Like Show Business," which she sang right back to them. Ethel posed for photographs in a chorus line, merrily kicking up her legs with the Ivy League drag queens. This was certainly not the first time Merman had been photographed in the company of cross-dressed men (this went back to the mid-'30s), but given her status now as an oft-impersonated drag icon, it is exhilarating to see photos of her having a great time, ripping it up with the men.

Those months in early and mid-1966 witnessed a few critical passages in the world of show business: March saw Richard Rodgers receiving the National Performing Arts Award. On April 3 came the sad news that the widely beloved Buck Crouse had passed away. Howard Lindsay was himself too ill to attend Broadway's gala tribute to Crouse in late May, so Lindsay's wife, Dorothy Stickney, stepped in to relay his sentiments, expressing his sense of failure in not writing "a proper message" for her to bring because, in his words, "Buck isn't here to help me." The two had worked so closely, she explained, that neither knew who had created a particular joke or line, and she told the group that once she had overheard her husband absentmindedly answer the phone, "This is Buck."[41] Ethel kept the thank-you that Lindsay later wrote her for helping out with the memorial service for their colleague.[42]

That fall, Ethel performed at the inauguration of New York mayor John Lindsay, singing "The Star-Spangled Banner" with unusual group accompaniment—the New York City Sanitation Department Band, conducted by John Celebre, all members of the professional musicians' union. For two years, they had performed at the city's World's Fair and at hospitals, parades, and a variety of other municipal events. After working with Merman, the band sent Ethel a "certificate of appreciation," which she kept. What better way to live up to her own advice: "Don't fart higher than your ass"? Her connections with regular working people of New York were still strong.

Nineteen sixty-six saw Merman making plenty of high-profile appearances on TV as well, with hosts such as Ed Sullivan, Johnny Carson, and Mike Douglas; she also joined Fred Astaire live at the Hollywood Palace that year. For every radio, stage, concert, and television appearance, Ethel hand-labeled and filed the accompanying acetates. Says their handler today, Al Koenig Jr., "When she sang a Porter medley on 'The Bell Telephone Hour,' she noted that it ran nine minutes. When she performed with Carol Burnett, she noted the location of the sketch. When her grandchildren appeared with her on a Mike Douglas afternoon, she marked 'with the children.'"[43]

Annie Get Your Gun Revival

Since Ethel was now turning down musical proposals for shows as big as *Mame* and *Hello, Dolly!* (the latter was written with Merman in mind), it was no small feat to get her back on the boards.[44] But in 1966, she received a phone call from Irving Berlin. Might Ethel be interested in starring in a revival of *Annie Get Your Gun?* It didn't take long to convince her, and her response was positive and public: "I'm glad to have this chance to straighten something out. You may have read that I don't want to do another Broadway show. Wrong. I've been misquoted—again. Here's the story the way I told it and the way it should have read: Yes, I'd do another show on Broadway but I do not want to play in it for two or three years. Get the difference? It's a big one. Long runs are not for me anymore."[45] To preserve her freedom along with her stamina, Ethel signed on for a thirteen-week run—nine in Toronto and New York and four at Detroit's Fisher Theatre.

In Manhattan, the show was scheduled to play not on Broadway but at the New York State Theatre at the prestigious new Lincoln Center. Richard Rodgers, producer of the original *Annie Get Your Gun,* was now president of the center's Music Theatre and was an energetic force behind the new production. (Partner Oscar Hammerstein had died in 1960.) Along with Merman, one other original cast member was Harry Bellaver, the man whose Sitting Bull had made such a strong impression on young Bobby. Dolly Tate would be played by Benay Venuta, who also played Dolly in MGM's adaptation of the show. (Venuta was the only person from the film who was cast in the revival.) By this point, Venuta's career had intersected with Merman's for nearly three decades, whether as her understudy or touring in roles Ethel had originated, but this was the first time they worked together. Jerry Orbach (1935–2004) played Charlie Davenport. The role of Frank Butler was given to Bruce Yarnell, a baritone who'd been introduced to Broadway several years earlier in a small role in Lerner and Loewe's *Camelot.* Critics were quick to jump on Yarnell's age, thirty, in contrast to Ethel's, fifty-eight, even though it was commonplace to pair aging male screen stars such as Fred Astaire (1899–1987) and Cary Grant (1904–86) with women less than half their age. Maybe the critics felt a cheap thrill of getting their talons into the star who'd been invincible for so long; some New Yorkers referred to the revival as "Annie Get Your Son" or "Granny Get Your Gun."

To dress up his classic, Berlin added a new duet for Merman and Yarnell, "An Old-Fashioned Wedding," which was a smash in previews. He'd also written a new song for Venuta's Dolly, which was cut before the show came to New York, and scrapped two others from the original ("I'll Share It All with You" and "Who Do You Love, I Hope"). In all, the composer was delighted about *Annie*'s prospects, especially at this post-*Gypsy* phase of Merman's career.

Work on *Annie Get Your Gun* went relatively smoothly when rehearsals began in April, and Merman enjoyed getting to know Yarnell, for whom she showed great affection, enthusiastically telling the press what a good career the young singer had ahead of him. *Annie* previewed in Toronto's O'Keefe Performing Arts Centre on May 9, 1966, to robust reviews. When it closed on the 21st, it traveled to Lincoln Center, where the premiere followed ten days later. Bob Levitt recalls the evening of the show and says that once the show—and his mom—began, any notion that Ethel was too old for the part, any snide "Granny" sentiment, was dissipated in minutes. When Ethel came onstage, the audience went wild, and she had to wait them out before she could even start. Everyone seemed to be aware of the historical weight of the occasion. Ethel did the show unmiked, even though miking was now standard practice, and critics delighted in calling her "the lady with the built-in amplifier."[46]

When the show moved to Detroit, Merman gave a long interview to Shirley Eder, the columnist with whom she had warm, cordial relations. Said Eder,

> The offstage Merman is soft and sensitive. Her feelings are tender and she has developed an elephant hide to keep from getting hurt. One day recently she said, "I'm pretty sensitive when it comes to relatives and close friends. Sure I depict the brassy type on stage, but if I'm spoken to in the wrong way by someone I love, I bruise easily. In private life, a person needs love and affection. I guess we all need that. And I have many good and loyal friends who know my true feelings. And I'm so fortunate that I still have my mother and dad and two wonderful children and two grandchildren."[47]

(On opening night at the Fisher, Ethel received a wire: "Be as great as you are. Love, Bobby.") Eder later thanked Ethel for her "charm," adding, "Anything I can do for you in 'print,' let me know."[48]

A small problem occurred one night at the Fisher, just before the big "I'm an Indian Too" number at the end of act I. Merman went to sit down on her chair to change her shoes and stockings, but someone had moved it, and she fell hard onto the floor. No time. She went back onstage and performed the number, "tears of pain streaming down her face. She also did the whole second act not knowing whether the pain meant a broken hip or back," Eder later reported.[49] X-rays revealed that nothing had been broken, but Merman was quite badly bruised. Ethel suppressed the story until the Detroit run was over, just as she'd done in California with her back injury in *Gypsy*.

The *Annie Get Your Gun* revival went well, and Ethel agreed to the producers' request to extend the length of the run, moving it to the Washington National Theatre until August 27 and from there to Philadelphia's Forrest Theatre from August 30 through September 17.[50] After that, the show returned to New York, and in March 1967, a truncated, ninety-minute version was broadcast by NBC.

Annie Get Your Gun was exactly twenty years old and reaching new generations of fans, something that delighted Ethel: "Kids that never saw me before will see me. Maybe I'll start a whole new following."[51] But the changes on Broadway struck her too, especially the competitive business mentality that nobody seemed to escape. More than once, she took aim at what she perceived as the overprofessionalization of child actors ("acting like midgets, not children") and mimicked them to an interviewer.[52] Merman expected kids to be kids, not miniaturized professionals, and she vocally disapproved of parents who pushed adulthood onto them that way.

Outside New York, reviewers responded to Merman enthusiastically, although they retained bits of the same ambivalence they'd always had, an ambivalence that could seem more acute with the press's diminished sense of public respect, not for Merman per se, but for celebrity and public figures in general. For instance, an issue of *TV Guide* came out when the show was televised, and Edith Efron opens it by saying that "Doin' What Comes Natur'lly" "captures the essence of Merman herself," just as everyone said it had in 1946. Then, however, she goes on to describe the star's audience in terms of Merman lovers and Merman haters, a remark that would never have accompanied a 1946 review: "Criticism ranges from relatively mild complaints that her voice is 'terrible' to vehement statements such as 'The very sound of that raucous yelling sets my teeth on edge.'" Although the piece refers to the star as "The Voice," it says little about Merman's importance to Broadway musicals, instead focusing on rumors about her personality: "Historically, Merman *is* said to be difficult to work with. Stage rumor has it that she's a touch over-concerned with the spotlight and is inclined to stomp on lesser performers if she has the slightest suspicion of being upstaged. She somewhat confirms this herself." Then the discussion offers strange support in a quote from Merman, saying she can't stand lazy folks or people who step on her lines.[53]

Efron, like other commentators, was still relying on class distinctions when she discussed Merman's appearance: "She's not a glamorous human being. . . . There's a crudity of manner which contradicts the good-looking, expensive clothes, and the gallery of delicate impressionist pictures which line her hotel living room. She's given to heavy name-dropping, almost compulsively quotes what the 'greats' have said about her, at one time or another." After comparing her to the nouveau riche, "without having undergone any social polishing," Efron goes on to say that Ethel is "a unique woman—brassy, boastful, uneducated, bawdy, sentimental; and a tough, disciplined trouper, who, at this point, is a fixed star in the show-business firmament and a 'living legend.' As a star, she's the real explosive thing—not the kind that's manufactured by mimeographed press releases."[54] On this last point Efron was right, by dint of both Merman's personality and the history of the star system when her career began. But when Efron concludes by saying both sides are right—the Merman lovers who call her "earthy" and "natural" and the detractors who find her "ignorant" or "anti-intellectual"—we see that Ethel Merman was little more than a collective projection screen, mirroring contradictory attitudes and fantasies that had little to do with her actual life.

Little Bit of Ethel

So New York had welcomed Merman back after her most recent "marital disaster." And while Ethel's disappointments on that front were put on the back burner after her latest professional triumph, other family events in the mid-'60s would prove tougher to reconcile. Ethel was still phenomenally loyal to Mom and Pop and enjoyed frequent contact, but her own family's history had not experienced any of that kind of stability. Ethel was zero for four in marriages, her second and third scarred by violence; Bobby, though loving, was detached and full of attitude. And Ethel Jr. was moving quickly into adulthood.

Little Ethel was enrolled in Colorado College, and in her first year she became involved with a handsome football player named Bill Geary. The two married in Juárez, Mexico. On February 18, 1961, Ethel Merman became a grandmother when Barbara Jeanne (often misspelled Jean) was born. The new mother, Ethel Geary, sent her mom a card, "'A Valentine, MOM, for you,' Love, Bill and Ethel and Fatso," the term of endearment that she and her mother had used for Bobby as an infant.[55] Son Michael Lee Geary followed in short order, coming into the world while Grandma was engaged at the Las Vegas Flamingo. The proud grandmother carried pictures of them, showing them off to everyone. "Call Me Grandma" ran the newspapers, especially for the first grandchild, in which a widely syndicated photo shows Grandma Ethel beaming through a hospital window at infant Barbara Jeanne.[56]

The Geary couple set up house in Colorado Springs, where Bill supported his family as an insurance agent, a line of work he kept throughout his life. Bill's family hailed from Pennsylvania, and, according to Barbara, his parents were not overly fond of their son's mother-in-law: "They didn't like Ethel in person—they thought she was too pushy. But then, we [she and her brother] would complain that 'She criticizes us *all the time!*' so they were not really predisposed to liking her." Barbara describes the relationship between Ethel and Bill Geary (from whom Barbara is currently estranged) as one of "mutual tolerance."[57]

Despite the joy her young kids gave her, Little Ethel's emotional problems could not be disguised. She'd always been a sensitive child (recall her response to the bird in *Annie Get Your Gun*), and her chaotic upbringing and family situations only exacerbated a sense of instability. "My mother always seemed overwhelmed," says Barbara. "I remember her as having no strength, no way to find a center."[58] And Grandma Ethel wanted everything to be right and wanted to make it *look* right. Bob Levitt recalls Jack Klugman, now a close friend of the family, saying, "Little Ethel's hair was on fire and all Ethel saw was that her shoelaces were untied."[59]

Life was not going smoothly for Ethel Jr.—wanting to be called Nicole as she made her push for greater autonomy—and the marriage with Bill Geary deteriorated quickly. "All I remember is my parents fighting," recalls Barbara, "and then they separated. My father was weeping when he left, and told me how sorry he was, but he just couldn't stand being so unhappy anymore."[60] Ethel Geary was treated for depression and insomnia, and, without clear options in sight, she drank. Says Barbara, "I had to help out with my brother. We would walk the dog in the middle of the night because no one else had. We were little wild children. No one told us anything. My brother and I would come home from school and the family dog would be gone. Or we were moving again. There'd be no explanation."[61] Some were the result of

Ethel Sr.'s interventions, some her father's decisions, but the net effect was a chaotic—though not at all unloving—home life. Grandma tried to help out and would give things to them and their mother, but always with instructions and strings attached, says Barbara.

When Ethel and Bill Geary divorced, Bill was given primary custody of the kids, to Little Ethel's great distress. Big Ethel was understandably concerned about her daughter's lack of direction and tried to help where she could, pulling strings so that Little Ethel, now living in Los Angeles, could find work in theater, something Big Ethel had never pushed on her but an interest young Ethel developed on her own. In a 1965 revival of *Call Me Madam,* for instance, Ethel Jr./Nicole played the small role of the ambassador's secretary, Miss Phillips. (Merman's costar remained Nype, still a good friend along with his wife, Diantha.) Despite her occasional forays into acting, young Ethel seemed to experience this particular job—and much of her mother's help—as a form of domination over her. When the two appeared together on a Johnny Carson show, she started a spat that prompted Carson to cut the interview short.

Merman was intent on getting her daughter's life on track and tried to put a happy face on the situation. In a guest-authored column called "Memo to Teen-agers" in a syndicated newspaper magazine, she wrote:

> Last June, my daughter Ethel graduated from high school, and before we even had time to frame the diploma, she came to me and said: "Mom, I want to be an actress." Well, at first I thought she was kidding. She'd been a sensational student, and I'd always had fond dreams of her going on to bigger things in college. . . . But she wasn't kidding—she had it all figured out. "I'll go to college for *one year,*" she said, "because I think I owe that much to the man I marry some day. But then I want to be an actress. And, Mom, I want to do it all on my own." "Well, angel," I said, "*that* part I like anyway."[62]

The article containing this revised bit of history was called "How to Be a Hit." Along with a lovely picture of Ethels Sr. and Jr. was the following advice:

> Ethel Merman belts out a few rules for success:
>
>> Stand tall [and "do it on your own"]
>> Give it all you've got ["whatever part you get"]
>> Be yourself . . .
>> Go ahead on your own—The guy who marries the boss's daughter just winds up with two bosses.

Don't "stay on too long" . . .

. . . Work hard, loaf hard. Take the money you save on sleeping pills and put it into A.T.&T.

In the fall of 1963, her brother, Levitt, started college at Pittsburgh's Carnegie Mellon University (later Carnegie Tech) as a student in the drama program. He never graduated but was able to bring the experience he acquired there to his subsequent work at different theaters across North America, including the Stratford Shakespeare Festival in Ontario, the American Conservatory Theatre in San Francisco, and the Theatre of the Sea in Hawaii. As a young adult, Bob's sardonic edges, considerable intelligence, and ability to detect b.s. kept him at arm's length from many things, including, it must be said, his mother. The '60s, of course, were a tumultuous time for anyone to come of age, a period of social upheaval and intense, layered challenges to authority and official policy in general. This was a time when "the generation gap" was a common expression and defining oneself against one's parent was extraordinarily easy to do, especially if one's parent was as strong and iconic as Ethel Merman.

When Levitt reflects on his mother's parenting today, he says the problems she faced were a built-in effect of her celebrity and class, and these things helped produce what he calls a "disservicing to the kids," such as when she hired Koppi or shuffled him off to boarding school when he was still grieving over the death of his father. But Levitt says there was never any outright neglect, abuse, or lack of love from his mom. (His niece Barbara says much the same thing; in her experience, "Ethel really didn't know what to do with kids" and was someone simply accustomed to an adult world.)[63] As Bob was growing up he found himself looking to sources *beyond* the family for guidance, finding his bearings through people like Venus and Duddy Duddleson. "My emotional experience," he says, "I got in solidarity with regular people. . . . Mom did the same thing," referring to her relationships with people like Anna and Fritz Panzer and their daughter Carol Freund (old friends from Queens) and his mom's old coworker from the days at Bragg, Josie Traeger.[64]

Bob stepped up to help his sister after her divorce, hiring an attorney to help her obtain her share of their late father's inheritance, which was being withheld from her, ostensibly because of her emotional problems. This enabled her to leave Los Angeles, where she'd been living, and return to Colorado. It gave her a certain amount of freedom and the autonomy to consider her options without being under pressure from her mother or from Bill Geary. After a long stay at a dude ranch, Little Ethel moved into a small place where she could ride. Soon after, she reenrolled in Colorado College. This was 1967. The bonds and affection between brother and sister remained: her nickname for him was Burt; he called her George.

Young Ethel still struggled in her Rocky Mountain sanctuary, but she was very intent on getting her act together and especially on regaining custody of Barbara and Michael. In the summer of 1967, she convinced Bill, who was living in LA, to give her the kids for a month. Beginning July 24, she rented a two-bedroom cabin in Green Mountain Falls, where the three of them stayed. Toward the end of the visit, locals saw Ethel's distress grow at the prospect of having to relinquish them to their father again.[65] The morning before they left, Barbara and Michael awoke to find their mother still sleeping in the next room, and they weren't able to wake her up. Barbara, age six, ran out of the cabin to find the nearest grown-up, a woman named Carol Friesen, there on her honeymoon. Friesen was waiting in the car while her husband checked them out of the Green Hill Motel and remembers the girl approaching her and saying, "Can you help me? I can't wake up my mama, and she's all blue." She accompanied Barbara up to the cottage and found the stiff body of Ethel Six Geary; she also remembers that vodka and medicine bottles were scattered around the room but no note of any kind. Mrs. Friesen called the fire department, and at 10:30 the county coroner arrived and pronounced Ethel Geary dead, giving the time of death as between 12:30 and 1:30 A.M.

Mrs. John Geary, Bill's sister-in-law, came to identify the body. Friesen remembers a black limo pulling up and the two kids being whisked away, and that was it.[66] On the scene, Detective Sgt. Franklin Ripley of the sheriff's office told Friesen that Ethel Geary had been upset ever since her February divorce and that people in the area understood their custody battle had been especially nasty. Ethel, he said, got the kids just one month out of the year, and he told Friesen that Barbara and Michael were supposed to go back to Bill Geary the following day.

There was no evidence of any foul play, but the El Paso County coroner had to make the call about whether Geary's death was a suicide. After performing the autopsy, Dr. Raoul Urich determined that the cause of death was an accidental overdose, a fatal interaction of drink and pills. His report noted that traces of three different prescriptions had been found in Geary's body, and although no single medication exceeded the limits of the doctor's prescriptions, their combination was lethal. Not only were the medications prescribed by different doctors, but they included diet pills (speed). "There was no question it was an accident," Tony Cointreau says today. "This was at a time before people knew just how deadly those interactions were [between drugs and alcohol]. A lot of people died that way."[67] Bob recalls that his sister had had her prescription levels upped precisely to be better equipped to handle her children's visit.

Ethel Sr. flew immediately to Colorado with friend Benay Venuta. In her memoirs, she writes that Bob Jr. took care of the final arrangements; Levitt says that he didn't.[68] There was no memorial. Daughter Barbara recalls that at first, she and Michael were told that their mother was sick and staying in the hospital, but a little later, Bill Geary and a priest went with them to a park where they told the children the news. Barbara recalls the priest's involvement being a little strange, since "we hadn't gone to church in ages," but imagines he attended for her father's moral support.[69] Geary's cremated ashes were placed in a family alcove in a small mausoleum in the Colorado Springs area, and Merman started an Ethel Merman Geary Scholarship at Colorado College, asking people to make donations there in lieu of flowers.

Barbara suggests her mom's death was like a "willful accident."[70] She believes that just before her mother died, she had lost her optimism about being able to move forward and make a new start. In a certain sense, Barbara says, she believes that her mom did kill herself, but "not in a deliberate way or to make a statement," because she would never have done that with her children right there. Merman understood it this way as well, writing, "No mother contemplating such an act would have brought her children to her and then have left them behind."[71] Cointreau agrees and says that at the time, young Ethel was "less depressed than frightened about getting her life back together and back on track."[72]

Given the circumstances of Geary's death—and the whiff of celebrity scandal around it—the media widely reported it as a suicide. Merman denied it, taking the uncharacteristic step of writing or phoning to correct erroneous press reports. Her scrapbooks are understandably silent on the topic; the one exception is a March 30, 1968, clipping that retracts an earlier report, apologizing to Merman and stating a correction that Ethel Jr. died "after a brief illness."[73] Still, for the rest of Merman's life, rumors of Ethel Jr.'s purported suicide dogged her, and some people went so far as to claim that late in her own life, Ethel confided to them that her daughter did deliberately die by her own hand.[74]

Losing Ethel was the biggest tragedy of Merman's life, as it would be for any mother. Bob believes that afterward, his mom—again, like so many others—preferred the fantasies she had about her two children over their actual realities, overstating Bob's professional accomplishments, for instance, or failing to notice that her daughter's "hair was on fire." Barbara Geary says that after her mom's death, "Grandma created a kind of shrine based on her memories of young Ethel. She'd only discuss her as a child. I remember once when I was a kid chasing butterflies, she said, 'You look so much like your mom!' That was the sort of way she remembered my mother."[75] After the death, Ethel began to turn more deeply to religion for solace and was even briefly taken in by a corrupt TV evangelist. She kept a lock of Ethel's hair in her possession and would often speak to her daughter's ashes when they were later removed from the mausoleum, finding great comfort in knowing someday she would be able to join her and Bob Levitt again. "She was always convinced she'd go to heaven," said Bob.[76]

Ethel showered Barbara and Michael with the same punctual devotion she did her parents, calling them weekly in Los Angeles, where they lived with Bill Geary. Says Barbara, "She'd take us out, and we'd get sent home early. I remember going to places where there were usually just adults. My brother and I didn't have anything to do, and so we'd get in trouble," just as Bob Levitt remembered his childhood. Barbara remembers being too young to have a sense of who her grandmother was or the extent of her fame in the '60s. "I remember going to Lucille Ball's house and swimming with her and the kids. It was no big deal—Oh, here's this other red-head. I see her on TV too; that's just like Grandma!"[77] (It was later, during a *Call Me Madam* revival, when she first had a sense of her grandmother as a big star and personality.) The Geary family stayed in Los Angeles until the early 1970s, when they moved to Pennsylvania, closer to Bill's family. Bill Geary remarried several months after Ethel's death to the governess/au pair whom he'd hired to look after Michael and Barbara. In the early 2000s, after his retirement, the couple relocated to Sweden, his wife's birthplace.

That Girl and Lola Lasagna

When Little Ethel died, Merman canceled all of her professional obligations, withdrawing from rehearsals for a George Cohan tribute (replaced by Kaye Ballard). At the time, Merman had just wrapped filming three television appearances.

On September 7, the first of Ethel's two guest appearances on Marlo Thomas's popular comedy series, *That Girl,* aired. In this show Thomas played Ann-Marie, a young woman trying to make it as an actress. At the heart of the series was Ann-Marie's relative self-sufficiency as a single professional, the kind of role Mary Tyler Moore would develop in her '70s series. Satellite characters included Thomas's steady beau, Donald, and her two parents.

Ethel guested as herself. Ann-Marie is trying out for a walk-on in a show with Merman. She's shocked when selected ("let's use . . . that girl!"), and tongue-tied and starstruck when trying to approach Ethel. Donald catches the star alone in her dressing room, eating a hamburger for dinner, and invites her over for a home-cooked meal. But Ethel hates what they're planning, macaroni and cheese, so she ends up making stuffed cabbage, arguing with Ann-Marie's dad about how to prepare it: "If you think this is yelling, you ain't heard nothing yet!" After eating, Ethel chats with her hosts: "It was never easy for me," she starts. "I remember my first gig. I sang 'After You've Gone' and was fired for being too loud! Have you ever heard anything more ridiculous?" The advice she passes on to Ann-Marie: "Always let 'em know you're enjoying yourself. And reach out to the audience, sing!"—vintage Merman.

She sings briefly several times: At the very beginning of the show, she is finishing up "Everything's Coming Up Roses" in a rehearsal. Later, as fans and neighbors gather outside Ann-Marie's apartment door, she sings a line from "There's No Business . . ." to appease them. Ethel is on the screen for the majority of the show's half-hour format, suggesting how much Marlo Thomas, who was the show's producer as well (under the pseudonym Danny Arnold, so as not to appear too much the woman's libber) revered Ethel. Even the background music—barely noticeable—plays tunes of Ethel's hits on Broadway. Ethel's character is utterly devoid of diva attitude. Down-to-earth, she cooks cabbage just like her mother, Agnes, might have done; in fact, the show spends as much time on food as on show business: the title of the episode is "Pass the Potatoes!"

Ethel's second spot on *That Girl* aired in February 1968 and was called "The Other Woman." Starting off with the food theme again, Merman meets up with Ann-Marie and Donald at a delicatessen, where they reminisce about their previous encounter and the cooked cabbage. But a domestic crisis is brewing: Ann-Marie's mother is certain that her husband has "another woman," and that other woman, she's convinced, is Ethel Merman, with whom her husband has become rather celebrity-struck. The characters have fun with cracks like, "Lana Turner I ain't" and "*He* ain't Gregory Peck." Eventually, Mom is persuaded that no funny business is going on between her husband and the star. "The Other Woman" spends more time with Merman's wisecracking side than the first episode did, and it also presents Ethel as a magnetic and desirable woman who, like Ethel herself, was able to turn that appeal and tension into a good-natured joke.

The second series Ethel had shot in June was *Batman,* the deliriously camped-up version of the dark superhero comic strip featuring Bruce

Wayne, mild-mannered millionaire, and his alter ego, Batman. With his "boy wonder" sidekick, Robin, they form the crime-fighting duo who keep the citizens of Gotham City safe from evil. The series had a spirited tradition of featuring celebrity villains—Cesar Romero as the Joker, Vincent Price as Egghead, Julie Newmar and Eartha Kitt alternately as Catwoman, Burgess Meredith as the Penguin, Milton Berle as Louie the Lilac, Tallulah Bankhead as the Black Widow, and George Sanders as Mr. Freeze. Among these villains, Romero, Berle, Bankhead, and Sanders had been Merman's costars. *Batman* used the "old-timers"—schooled in stagy showmanship and abundant personality—to great effect, and the veterans played their roles with gusto.

Ethel appeared in two back-to-back episodes that aired in October, "The Sport of Penguins" and "A Horse of Another Color." She is Señora Lola Lasagna, the Penguin's co-conspirator. They join forces to fix the Bruce Wayne Foundation Handicap horse race. Ethel's steed, Parasol, is a clear favorite, and to boost their betting odds they disguise it as a horse of another color, with the help of Lola's makeup and some spray paint, and run it under another name. Of course, their criminal plot is foiled by the dynamic duo, with help from Batgirl, the heroine alter ego of the police commissioner's librarian daughter.

Batman is a sparkling romp, filled with brightly colored sets and artifice. Batman and Robin rely on a "bat shield" for protection; the hokey male voiceover creates faux suspense ("Will the duo get out?"); Robin exclaims, "Holy Time Bomb!" when they learn that the Penguin left a loaded parasol at the library; fights are interrupted with cartoon-styled *Pows, Bams, Biffs,* and *Splats,* and canted film angles abound. Merman as Lola Lasagna seems at home in this colorful world.

Decked in colorful outfits, broad-brimmed hats, parasols, gloves, and handbags, Ethel's character recalls the mother-in-law in *Mad, Mad World.* The show makes other indirect nods to her established persona, including even a reference to marital woes. (Lola had been married for three weeks to a "billionaire South American playboy. . . . Instead of dying, he divorced me!") Her role in *Panama Hattie* is suggested by her garish dress, especially the prominently displayed parasol; *The Art of Love* and *Happy Landing* are invoked in the gold-digging themes; and even *Straight, Place and Show* casts a shadow on the episodes' racetrack theme. Other Merman leitmotifs include her communing with animals, gambling, and scheming with morally dubious people to get rich quick (*Kid Millions,* etc.). Such roles and traits reach far back and give Merman fans "bonus material" that enhances her performance, just as her performance enhances the lighthearted camp of the series.

At the heart of comic-strip heroes like Batman (who at first was a dark and brooding figure) is something both serious and camp. For in camp, disguise and role playing are crucial, and in *Batman,* the superhero and Bruce Wayne's only go-between is the grandfatherly servant, Alfred, who also shields Batgirl's real identity from everyone. Secret identities are potent fantasies, and the show's various disguises and self-conscious role playing were pivotal to its success. Viewers could enjoy vicariously winning out over forces of evil that in real life were too powerful to correct, much less conquer. *Batman*'s camp is also derived from its sundry mismatched pairings: the waddling Penguin is angry at Miss Gordon, the young, attractive human who declined the bird's offer of marriage; there are odd remarks (like Merman telling her horse, "Looks and your legs are all we've got left!"); and there are numerous homoerotic subtexts between Batman/Bruce and Robin/Dick. (When the millionaire enters his own horse in the race to thwart the villains, he tells Dick, "I couldn't allow my ward to ride my own thoroughbred. People might think it was funny.")

In December 1967, the last of the summer work aired that Merman had done before Ethel Jr.'s death. In one of her most far-fetched roles, she played a missionary on *Tarzan.* Radie Harris wrote, "Do you believe that Julie *[sic]* Styne called Ethel Merman and asked her to play the head nun in a musical version of 'Lillies of the Field'? Retorted Ethel, 'What's with this new image of me? . . . I'm just waiting for someone to offer me the role of Mother Cabrini.'"[78]

Back to Work

By 1968, Ethel was back on a full schedule. "My daughter Ethel died last year," she told an interviewer, "I was in such a state of shock. But I don't ever feel she's dead. I feel she's going to walk in my door any minute. Working helped me so much to relieve a terribly emotional situation."[79] She started recording television work for the upcoming months and took part in a birthday tribute to Irving Berlin that aired on *The Ed Sullivan Show* in May. By the following year, April 1969, Ethel was presenting the Best Director Award of a musical at the Tony Award ceremonies. ("I've been wanting to give it to directors for years," she said, playing Ethel Merman like a pro.)

During this period several short-run revivals of *Call Me Madam* toured to various parts of the country with Merman and Russell Nype, who always resumed his role as Sally's attaché. Richard Eastham played Cosmo, and he and Nype were squabbling over who was to get better billing. Outside of that small incident, these tours were largely enjoyable affairs for Ethel, and she also enjoyed traveling now. "She loved packing, and was really good at it," recalls her son.[80] She never had an entourage and was so practical that she brought her own stain remover whenever she was on the road, as well as her own lunches and snacks, using the bottom of lunch bags to hide her most expensive jewelry to deter thieves. Ethel enjoyed spending time with Nype and during the summer often joined him and his wife at their second home in Kennebunkport, Maine, where they would play cards, go antiquing, and sunbathe.

During the same period, Ethel also made club appearances in cities such as Chicago and Fort Lauderdale. She described the work matter-of-factly: "I'm on for 60 minutes in my act. I conclude the first half with a medley of my big hits, then bow off and come back to do some more big numbers. I find I've had to cut some tunes [her act had been longer before], like 'Down in the Depths,' for instance. I love it, but the public doesn't know [the song], and you've got to be commercial in night clubs, give 'em what they like."[81]

By this point, the media were acknowledging Merman as a living legend, with many good-naturedly complaining that all of the words to describe her had been used up: *singular, incomparable, indestructible, lusty-lunged.* It seemed that now it wasn't just Ethel's voice that was defying description, but the woman herself, "Still 'Klass with a Capital K,'" as one review ran.[82] (Ethel's clippings are less organized than usual during this time, whether a result of dealing with her daughter's death, fallout from the Borgnine marriage, or simply from the problems Pop was having with his eyesight is impossible to say.)

Press reports often commented on the difference between the iconic woman they witnessed doing her show and the one they encountered offstage. "She is a warm delightful lady who wears her 59 years beautifully. The figure is lithe, even when enveloped in a black and polka-dotted tent dress."[83] "Of her own fame, she says she's 'really very shy.'"[84] Back onstage, though, Merman prompted the same familiar rush of lines:

What a broad! What a belter! What a Merm! Ethel the Great opened the Empire Room Thursday night, and a lot of us are still weak in the knees. Merman doesn't tell you her age, or how long ago she first sang 'You're the Top,' or about her troubles. . . . She just stands there and clenches her fists, and tauts her muscles, and opens her mouth and blows the roof off the joint. And then she struts around the room, and opens her mouth, and blows the roof off the roof. Ethel Merman is one of the great national wonders, ranking somewhere between the Grand Canyon and the Los Alamos Proving Grounds. Given a choice of the three, put your money on Merm.[85]

Ethel was more circumspect, though still maintained her endless enthusiasm and optimism. "Today I have a whole new audience. The kids who come to see me weren't around when I did the original *Annie Get Your Gun* or *Call Me Madam.* Everything seems new to the young people and it's great fun for me."[86]

She spent more time with Barbara and Michael. Barbara, recalling how much trouble she and her brother got into, remembers that when Grandma took them to St. Martin, in the Caribbean, they'd relate mostly with the servants there.[87] In June 1968, one of those Caribbean trips turned into a fiasco; the house Ethel had rented was so remote that it was impossible to feel safe or have a good time. As Merman told the press, the "nearest neighbors were fifteen miles away. . . . We couldn't stand the loneliness"; the landlord had provided them with a guard dog for protection, "but when the big frightened animal also joined us in the one bed . . . we panicked and came home."[88] Barbara remembers one time in Puerto Rico, on their way down to St. Martin; she was about eleven, and she snuggled in bed with Grandma, who told her all sorts of show stories. It's a memory she loves.

Uncle Bob started coming into Barbara and Michael's life more after their mom's death. "He always represented *fun* to us. It was irregular contact, but we'd be right back as soon as we got together again. It's still like that," says Barbara, who remains very close with her uncle. "Bob was my best friend, and I think my father resented that."[89] At this time, Levitt was living in the San Francisco Bay area. "He's 22 and unmarried," said one press report, "and, according to Mom, bought his house in Sausalito just so his dog would have plenty of room." (Ethel underlined "bought" with several firm ink strokes followed with an editorializing question mark.)[90] Better yet for Ethel, Bob was in a committed relationship with someone, living with a young actress named Barbara Colby, nine years older than he. By the age of twenty-nine, Colby was a nationally acclaimed and respected stage actress; in 1965 she'd already appeared on Broadway with Anne Bancroft in *The Devils.* "Barbara was a vibrant human being, on and off the stage," Levitt says. "And the most amazing thing about her brilliant vibrancy was its core: she had natural balance. That's what first attracted me to her. She was a radiant person, with radiant balance."[91]

In December 1967 Ethel was in the Bay Area doing a benefit for the American Conservatory Theatre, where Bob and Barbara worked, and at the Geary Theatre, where the star received a telegram from Sausalito. "Have a good time tonight, we love you, Ganky, Barbara, and Bob."[92] (Ganky was the young couple's dog, whom Ethel adored.) Merman was delighted that her son was "settling down" and genuinely liked Barbara. "When we got married," Levitt adds, "she liked her even more."[93]

SEVENTEEN

After the Big Stem—the Seventies

One of Broadway's longest-running musicals, *Hello, Dolly!* had been written with Ethel Merman in mind for the part of Dolly Gallagher Levi, widow of Ephraim Levi, trying to land "half-a-millionaire" in the form of one Horace Vandergelder. The show, a musical version of Thornton Wilder's *The Matchmaker* was called *Dolly Levi: The Exacerbating Woman* before becoming *Hello, Dolly!* The book was by Michael Stewart, and Jerry Herman did the score. MCA's David Harker had sent Ethel a copy of *The Matchmaker* almost as soon as her tour with *Gypsy* had ended late in 1961, asking if she would be interested in helping this become a musical. No, she wouldn't: she had sworn off of long-term runs.

A decade later, David Merrick, who owned rights to the material, tried to get Merman back, and when he approached her, she demurred, telling him that she always opened in new shows and although *Hello, Dolly!* was a new musical, its initial dramatic lead was played by Ruth Gordon, and Ethel believed that the role should stay linked to her. Her second reason was familiar: Ethel's long runs on Broadway were behind her. "Sure, Broadway's been good to me," she'd frequently say, "but I've been pretty good to it"—at times adding, "From now on, I'm living for Ethel."

The first musical that New York songwriter Jerry Herman ever saw was the original *Annie Get Your Gun:* "It honestly changed my life. . . . I couldn't have been more than fifteen or sixteen. . . . I came home, and I remember being able to play—because I play by ear—four or five songs that I had never heard before in my life. I thought, 'What a gift . . . what a lovely gift this man named Irving Berlin has given me!' It made me want to do the same thing."[1] Born in the early '30s, Herman was a relative baby on Broadway when Merrick approached him to work on *Dolly!* Herman had done *Nightcap* in 1958, a very well-received revue, but his only show on Broadway had been *Milk and Honey* in 1961. Partly because of this record and partly because *Milk and Honey* contained as much Yiddish music as it did, Merrick gave him a homework assignment: produce some full-out "American" songs for *Dolly!* Over the course of a weekend, Herman generated four tunes, and Merrick, impressed, kept him on. Three of those songs stayed with the final show.

Herman knew how to write memorable, hummable tunes, the kind that could be released as singles—like "Hello, Dolly," which for some reason Herman never expected to be a hit. After *Dolly!* Herman went on to write *Mame* (another musical with a strong middle-aged woman), whose score, he said, wasn't written with anyone in mind, despite the theater world's legends of all of the actresses supposedly approached early on for the role, from Merman to Garland to Bette Davis. It was in fact Angela Lansbury who, in 1966, introduced *Mame* to Broadway; after *Mame,* Herman wrote other shows, notably *La Cage aux Folles* in 1983.

Merrick eventually found his first Dolly—Carol Channing—and when the show opened on Ethel's fifty-sixth birthday, January 16, 1964, at the capacious St. James Theatre, it was a smash, going on to play continuously for nearly seven years. When Channing took it on the road, she was replaced in New York, in succession, by Ginger Rogers, Martha Raye, Betty Grable, Pearl Bailey (in an all-black production), and Phyllis Diller. Artist Al Hirschfeld commented on Broadway's most famous rotating door by doing a cartoon of Merrick as a scowling ringmaster holding up a hoop through which Channing, Bailey, and Merman all cascaded. (The producer had even approached Jack Benny to do the role in drag, opposite George Burns; evidently Benny was amenable but couldn't commit himself for more than a week.)[2] Mary Martin toured in *Dolly!* when it played for audiences in London, Tokyo, and war-torn Vietnam.

When Merman came onboard as the seventh Dolly, Herman reintroduced two songs that had been dropped when she first turned the show down, "World, Take Me Back" and "Love, Look in My Window," tunes that showed a softer side of her. Recalled Herman, "Both of them stopped the show cold."[3]

To play Cornelius Hackl, Ethel procured friend Russell Nype; Jack Goode played Vandergelder. And so on March 28, 1970, the Ethel Merman *Dolly!* opened at the St. James. So thunderous was the applause that Ethel uncharacteristically needed a moment to regain her composure. Countless theater reviews said that their Ethel was "back where she belonged." Ethel was the only Dolly to perform unmiked, and when *Detroit News* theater critic Jay Carr reported otherwise, she wrote to correct him. The issue was a small blip. Most cities simply reveled in the Ethel Experience. "Like Brunnhilde, sans horned helmet, she plants herself solidly at stage center and cheerfully bellows chorus after chorus in a contrary contralto that can still crack a water glass at 10 paces. Dolly Levi? Hell, she is Annie Oakley, aiming at the customers in the last row of the balcony; an institution, like the Statue of Liberty or Winged Victory."[4] Some sneaked in a few racist and anti-Semitic hits, noting that Streisand "had given Dolly a sense of greed [in the film] and Pearl Bailey a lack of inhibition," whereas Merman gives the character "a gentle touch."[5] Said Walter Kerr in the *Times,* "Missing Merman in the role would be like waiting until . . . Bernhardt had called it quits with *Camille.* You've got to come when the siren calls."[6] That year, Ethel received the 1969–70 Drama Desk Award.

Hello, Dolly! was trading in the kind of musical theater of Broadway's golden age, which was well over by the 1960s and certainly before 1970. By now, few musicals were attempting to emulate the old-time spirit and earlier ways of show making; this was the era of the "message musical"—with the significant exception of *Funny Girl,* in which Barbra Streisand played Fannie Brice and which opened the same season as *Dolly!* Ever since its opening in 1964, *Dolly!* had been a feel-good show for a nation reeling from the assassination of President JFK and moving into tumultuous times at home and abroad.

Like *Gypsy* before it, *Dolly!* was pure show biz, but unlike *Gypsy,* it was not ambitious, just an old-fashioned good time. Set further in the past than *Gypsy*—the 1890s—it depicted marriage and courtship rituals that were so far out of vogue as to seem charming rather than out-of-step, as Rose/Merman's motherhood had been for some. *Dolly!* offered a welcome salve for Broadway, with all its principal characters middle-aged and cast with celebrated "old-timers," whom audiences were delighted to pay to see onstage. Merrick's biographer calls it "the last of the innocent American musicals, the last musical to reflect the unbounded optimism that characterized America before it plunged into the Vietnam war."[7]

Merman accepted the role because Merrick's terms were good, and so was the show, with character and songs ideally suited for her. As the last in a long line of ethnically mixed figures that influenced Merman's on- and offstage persona, Dolly offered her a way to give some unintended commentary on her career. Like the Irish Gallagher, Ethel was a gentile who had become

"Jewish" by choice, through marriage. (And by the time the show came out, Ethel was referring to the late Bob Levitt as the love of her life.) Also, playing Dolly Levi gave Merm a chance to—voluntarily and publicly—enact a Jewish identity, rather than deny it, even if that motivation was the furthest thing from the star's mind.[8]

From the start, Merman had been insistent that the run be kept short, signing on for just three months. When the three became six and, then in September, when it became was clear that *Dolly!* would surpass *My Fair Lady*'s record run for a musical comedy, she agreed to stay on until just after Christmas, to help make musical history. Said the press, "She's all set to break the long-run musical record. 'That's mainly why I'm back,' proclaims the star whose intuitive sagacity about being in the right show at the right time ranks only a little lower than her calliope pipes as a show world wonder."[9] But "her reward for staying on and helping Merrick break the record," writes Merrick's biographer, "was a closing night gift of two bottles of indifferently chosen champagne."[10] *Hello, Dolly!* closed on December 27, 1970, indeed surpassing *My Fair Lady*'s 2,717 performances with its 2,844. Merrick knew that, with Ethel Merman, the new record had been guaranteed and that many other Dollys would follow her—strong, iconic actresses all. Recognizing what kind of personality the role needed, Merrick, when asked about future casting prospects, shrugged his shoulders, "Mae West? Liberace?"[11]

Conscious of the momentous nature of the occasion—very likely the last time that La Merm would be in a Broadway show—one fan attending the Sunday afternoon finale committed every detail to memory: "Merman gave an abridged curtain speech after that Sunday matinee, 'I don't know about you, but I'm going out for some Neapolitan ice cream!' and backstage confessed that she was too emotional to continue her remarks."[12]

Settled but Indefatigable

Ethel was now living at the Hotel Berkshire on Madison and 52nd Street, in an apartment that was quite modest for someone of her stature. The walls and shelves were covered with mementos of a long career—framed pictures of her with the Duke of Windsor, Queen Elizabeth, Bobby Kennedy; signed photos of Gershwin, FDR. Her royal blue bedroom featured a heavy Victorian bureau that Dorothy Hammerstein had given her in 1941 and that Ethel had had shortened to move in. An interviewer described the large Victorian brass bed as being covered with "bright chintz coverlets and a sleeping doll collection."

(Merman enjoyed her dolls.) Also in the bedroom was a crystal chandelier, porcelain lamps, and a writing and bill-paying desk—the last had reportedly belonged to Henry Wadsworth Longfellow, something she'd bought on one of her antiquing forays. The living room was red, white, and blue, all-American even when not trying to be. The reporter summed up, "Her taste is lady like, but honest and strong, dashed through with imaginative twists and turns that make it pure one of a kind Merman; who doesn't allow one smidgeon of artificiality to creep into her surroundings—or her life."[13] Everyone close to the offstage Ethel speaks of her in just those terms; she was "real people" is nearly everyone's description of her.

One of the challenges Ethel faced in her personal life in the '70s was her aging parents. Both in their nineties, Agnes and Edward Zimmermann had followed their daughter to the Berkshire Hotel; they resided on the seventeenth floor, Ethel on the fourteenth. Pop was relatively healthy but was losing his sight; Agnes was much more frail and, in 1971, not long after her daughter had finished *Dolly!* suffered a severe heart attack. When Agnes was released from the hospital, Ethel hired a full-time nurse, named Kathryn Shreve, to help Pop take care of her mother and enable them to continue living independently. Shreve, a retired nurse living in Kenilworth, New Jersey, had been recommended by the family's former physician. When Merman first called her to ask if she'd be interested, Shreve declined. "An hour later she called back and said she had always been fond of Mom and Pop and she'd take the job," said Ethel. "There was only one problem—she had a dog. I was so happy to get her, I told her, 'I don't care if it's a Great Dane, just come.'"[14] The arrangement worked out well, and Ethel became genuinely fond of Shreve, who became much like an extended family member.

Aware that it had been lucky to lure Ethel back on the boards for *Dolly!* the entertainment world began to pay homage to a performer whose career had intersected, in some form or another, with all of the giants of twentieth-century music and musical theater: George and Ira Gershwin, Cole Porter, Irving Berlin, Vernon Duke, Buddy DeSylva, Dorothy Fields, Jule Styne, Jerry Herman, Stephen Sondheim, Jerome Robbins, Roger Edens, George Abbott, Josh Logan, Lindsay and Crouse, Leland Hayward, David Merrick, Jimmy Durante, Bing Crosby, Eddie Cantor, Bert Lahr, Ray Middleton, Ginger Rogers, Alice Faye, Judy Garland, Barbra Streisand, and others. At times, she was received with such praise that TV recordings show an Ethel Merman who, while clearly honored, registers a little embarrassment, a shy discomfort on her face. For as much as Ethel enjoyed—and, indeed, demanded—respect, she really was uncomfortable about generating a fuss, and when she thought people were going too far in their enthusiasms or were intrusive in making them, especially offstage, she became uneasy or even unpleasant. Most of the time, though, she just took it like a pro.

When Merman was asked to revive *Gypsy* in London, she turned it down because of her parents' health, even after the producers offered to fly them over with her. A special honor occurred at the April 1972 Tony Awards, in which Ethel appeared not as a presenter but as the recipient of a lifetime achievement award. Half a year later, in October, Ethel was inducted into the Theatre Hall of Fame. Two years after that, in 1974, she played London for two weeks at the Palladium Theatre, and in August 1977 she played the Hollywood Bowl.

A frequent guest on *The Merv Griffin Show,* Merman also joined Ed Sullivan, Johnny Carson, Mike Douglas, and Dinah Shore on their talk shows during this time. When one 1969 appearance coincided with Ethel's sixty-first birthday, Dolores and Bob Hope wired their telegram: "Dear Ethel: It's hard to believe . . . you sure don't look it. Whatever you're doing, double up and send me your diet. . . . [The next sentence she inked out: "I was astounded when I heard the figure."] I wish I was there to do 'De Lovely' with you 'cause that's what you are. Lots of love. Dolores [and] Bob Hope."[15]

Watching tapes of these shows today drives home just how indefatigable (and patient) Merman was about her work. Appearance after appearance, she sings the same songs, tosses off the same lines, responds to the same questions, and performs in the same style she always had, looking right out into the crowd or camera, throwing off enthusiasm and pep in a way that must have made colleagues her age tired just watching. Instinctively, she knew where to direct her gaze, when to pace, what to say. ("I'm still new at this. . . . I'm used to being on the other side of the highballs.") The tapes verify Buddy DeSylva's claim that watching Ethel was like watching a movie, so effortlessly did she repeat every detail, giving everything the same vitality as if she were doing it all for the first time.

By far Merman's most moving TV appearance aired on May 20, 1971. Once again she was a guest on Merv Griffin's show, along with Jerry Herman of *Dolly!* and Ralph Edwards, the host of the long-running radio and TV hits *This Is Your Life* and *Truth or Consequences*. Griffin tried to persuade Edwards to reveal how he always surprised his guests on *This Is Your Life*. The show's formula involved bringing a guest—often a celebrity—into the studio under some pretense, and then when Edwards announced, "John Doe, this is your life!" the person would be reunited with various real-life players—family members, lost friends, former high school teachers—who would wait behind the stage curtains. It wasn't hard to do, said Edwards. "For instance, I could say to you, 'Merv Griffin, this is your life,' or 'Jerry Herman, this is your life.' But what I'm *really* going to say is, 'Ethel Merman, queen of musical comedy, this is *your* life!'" Ethel was floored. Josie Traeger was there, as were Texas Schribman, Benay Venuta, Perle Mesta, and, most important, son-in-law Bill Geary with Barbara and Michael, whose heads Ethel kissed passionately, clutching them for the rest of the show. Emotionally overwhelmed, Merman was onstage as just herself, a regular grandma. And although she kept saying "I can't *believe* it!" (as in *How could you trick me?*), Ethel made no attempt to hide her tears.

In March 1973, Merman went on a short vacation to see her grandchildren. The trip had been planned in advance, and when Broadway organized a special tribute to Stephen Sondheim during the same time (for which Angela Lansbury, preparing for *Gypsy* in London, flew in, as did most of Broadway's royalty), Ethel chose not to cancel. (Both she and her son, Bob, were spending more time with Barbara and Michael.) Merman's focus on her family intensified even more the following month, when Agnes suffered a severe stroke that left her hospitalized for the rest of her life. Ethel pared back professional activities to the bare minimum so that she and Pop could make daily visits at Roosevelt Hospital, the prestigious West Side facility. Agnes Zimmermann died there on January 14, 1974, two days shy of Ethel's sixty-sixth birthday. Her ashes were flown to Colorado Springs, where they joined Ethel Jr.'s in the family's small section of the mausoleum there. A modest service was held.

Mother and Son

Bob Jr. was still distant but devoted. The mother-son relationship was still not especially close during this time, and his absence on the *This Is Your Life* spot is conspicuous. (Levitt has not been predisposed to heavily media-oriented celebrations of his mother.) "Ethel and Bob have so many similarities—that's why there was often so much friction," says Tony Cointreau. "He has his mom's humor and impishness. Both have a stubborn streak. Bob gets his generosity and trust from his mom. . . . They'd lock horns a lot, and he played the rebel with her. But they adored each other."[16] Bob shared his mother's suspicion of show-biz fakery; he just pushed that world further away from him than Ethel could. "We didn't see each other too often, a couple times a year," he says.[17] In some regards their values were different; Ethel's conservative views and positions made it impossible for her to embrace what she considered her son's "counterculture" lifestyle, and Bob's lack of professional ambition and focus was a source of disappointment to her. Ethel was proper and organized; her son, by contrast, had the disheveled "hippie" look that many of his generation had. But she adored new daughter-in-law Barbara, and loaned the young couple money to buy a residence in New York City.

It would be difficult for any son to know how to navigate the world of his mother when that mother is Ethel Merman. Bob constantly struggled with how to appreciate her celebrity while trying to stand down from that celebrity himself. An illuminating encounter shows that struggle, as well as mother and son's eagerness to get along:

> Long ago, there was a blackout in New York City one night . . . and I got "stuck in the dark with mom" in her apartment for *much* longer than I usually stayed. . . . We had a great time, talking about this, that, and the other thing; going a bit deeper than we usually did in normal conditions. . . . My mother *loved* the thought of being a spokeswoman. . . . What [she] *really* wanted was something like the role of spokeswoman for NASA. She was quietly disappointed when her friendship with the Nixons didn't shake that loose.
>
> So there we sat in the blackout, on her big brass bed, and Mom introduced the subject of . . . "another spokeswoman opportunity." . . . "[But] I'm not going to tell you because you'll tease me, and this is *very important* to me." I *had* teased her about the NASA thing; ribald stuff about riding the rockets with astronauts. She *loved* it. . . . Until it all fell through. Then there was a sore spot, so I promised I wouldn't tease. And after a few rounds of "I *really, really* promise!" Mom took a chance and broke the news that she was being considered, "*just considered* . . . for the spokeswoman . . . for SEARS!" I was bound to my promise to be very careful how I said "Sears?"
>
> "Yes Sears! . . . Wouldn't that be wonderful? . . . Sears is all across America! If I were the spokeswoman . . . I'd be all across the country." . . .
>
> "But why do *you,* the Queen of Broadway, need to beat the drum for Sears?" We were talking in circles. . . .
>
> "Why not? What's the Queen of Broadway got to do with it? . . ."
>
> My mother set me straight. . . .
>
> "Look, classy is classy, and Sears is Sears, and I know the difference. And I'm not worried about it. So don't you be. I've got lots of opportunities in this world to be 'classy.' . . . If [the work with Sears is] done right, like an Aunt Ethel character, but *real,* just me, I'd find *that* very satisfying."[18]

Later, Bob came to respect and understand his mom's decision more. "She always wanted to be in touch with regular people. She didn't need the airs. . . . I think that's the reason so many fans are still delighted by her."[19] That openness to "regular" opportunities—from Sears to singing with the New York Sanitation Department Band—shows that Merman was never one to find things beneath her station, something that fans might overlook when they attribute aspects of the ambitious, celebrity-obsessed "Mama Rose" to her. There was a comforting friendly neighbor or aunt in this real-life Ethel.

One fan, an acquaintance of Bob Levitt's, remembers:

> My most vivid memory was actually the first time I rang the bell and Ethel opened the door, standing there in a pink housecoat and bunny slippers. She was so warm and gracious and unpretentious. . . .
>
> Behind a set of French doors was a small room lined with oil paintings of Ethel in roles going back to Panama Hattie. That's where Bob and I sat to discuss a project we were working on, and at one point that unique voice said, "Bob, open the door, my hands are full." She was standing on the other side with a dish of Haagen-Dasz [sic] coffee ice cream in each hand. It was overwhelming for a young fan like me to be served by this legend. Another time she was going out with friends for the evening, and when she was ready to leave, she stopped by and introduced us to them. They were all around her age, but I was especially tickled that one of them was "Mrs. Gaxton," presumably the widow of her *Anything Goes* co-star.[20]

Ethel's business instincts had noted in Sears an opportunity to boost her name recognition across the country. "I'll be in everybody's living room, on the TV, in the papers, I'll come through their *mail,* and everybody will get to know me better as the person who welcomes them to where they shop," Ethel told her son when he asked her what made her think the job would be gratifying. Although Ethel never became their spokeswoman, she did a number of commercials for Texaco, Canada Dry, and Friendship Cottage Cheese. Knowing full well the difference between classy and "unclassy" and maintaining a strong sense of herself as a regular "Aunt Ethel" figure, her ability to redirect that image was as unconventional in the '70s as it had been fifty years earlier, when she was just starting out.

With more time away from professional activities, Ethel didn't need to spend as much time maintaining "Ethel Merman," and she enjoyed this new phase of her life, living it fully if rather quietly. She enjoyed "rooting around [her] place,"[21] watching TV, answering mail, talking on the phone. ("Ethel *loved* talking on the phone," recalls Cointreau. "And she loved gossiping!")[22]

She enjoyed listening to records by Perry Como, Tony Bennett, Frank Sinatra, Eartha Kitt, and especially Christmas carols. "Mom was very comfortable as a solo homebody," says Levitt. "And she was also very comfortable with old friends like the Panzers [from Queens], or with Tony and Jim [Russo, Cointreau's partner]." She loved being "Aunt Ethel," he says, adding, "she was less comfortable with her own kids and grandkids because of the history."[23] (Ethel often referred to her two grandchildren as "those *monsters!*")[24]

Today, Levitt admits that the larger-than-life production that was "Ethel Merman" "could be nasty. Mom was under a lot of pressure to animate that figure and [then there were] the pressures of celebrity—plus the histories of her own abuse," especially from Six. But he adds that "it was not her essential nature to be mean." Levitt is wholly aware that people did, in fact, experience her that way, since he witnessed firsthand how cruel his mother could be. But he says, "Her cruelty—which could be vicious—was never calculated. She was mean like a little girl could be mean." (Barbara remembers how Grandma Ethel would tease her brother about a speech impediment he had.) Levitt describes his mom as "adolescent by nature," with that petulant, immature side—along with a positive, innocent side that was filled with playfulness. He remembers that when he visited her at her apartments, she delighted in playing peekaboo at the door, pulling her pink nightcap over her eyes and making squeaky noises like a small animal. When Bobby teased her in rhyme about her various beaux ("Eric Palm . . . is a bomb!")—reprising the chimed rhymes they had shared when she put him to bed as a youngster—she loved it: "Oh, *stop it!*" she'd giggle. "Mom was willing to be foolish with people she trusted," he says.[25] Merman did a great deadpan and was good at feigning outrage and indignation; he also remembers the impromptu imitations she'd do behind the backs of folks she thought were pompous. She and Betty Bruce—a close friend who shared Ethel's wicked sense of humor—delighted when, at the Korvettes store on 47th Street, they would hear a "Carolyn Cooze" paged frequently. Whenever they heard the name over the loudspeaker, Bruce and Merman would break up.

That childlike side of Ethel is evident in her appearance on *The Muppet Show* in the 1970s. "Her true humor," says Bob, was brought out in this work, and both he and Cointreau report that Ethel said this was the TV appearance that gave her the most pleasure. It is not Ethel Merman, Broadway superstar, who appears here, as she does on *The Bobby Vinton Show, The Jack Jones Show,* and *The Sha Na Na Show* at the time, nor is it Ethel Merman the comic or camp icon, as on *Batman. The Muppet Show* reveals a sweet Ethel, and since that feature played no part in forming the public Merman, as her voice and wisecracks did, its signs may be harder for nonintimates to detect. The show introduces Merman wearing a tall red-and-black-feathered headpiece, à la Dolly Levi, seated as if in a still portrait and surrounded by her excited Muppet costars. Later, in front of a mock makeup mirror, Ethel performs a medley of her hits in duets with the different puppets, saving the competition number "Anything You Can Do, I Can Do Better" for Miss Piggy, the diva with attitude toward her human rival. In this and the other numbers, Ethel's eyes twinkle in evident pleasure.

She took what Cointreau and Levitt describe as an "innocent delight" in those puppet characters, something the camera was able to capture. She is not "on" in any sense; nowhere else on tape does she appear so relaxed as she does here serenading Kermit the Frog or dealing with the difficult Miss Piggy. And she genuinely enjoyed the Muppets as characters. "She saw them as little people," says Cointreau.[26] At home, her big brass bed was covered with the little Muppet characters.

The decade brought more troubles and sadness. At the end of November 1973, Bruce Yarnell, her costar in the *Annie Get Your Gun* revival, of whom Ethel was very fond, died in a plane crash, and she took the news hard. Violence hit again in the summer of 1975, in a loss that was much closer to home. On the evening of July 25, Ethel's daughter-in-law, Barbara Colby, was shot dead while returning to her car at a drama studio where she'd been teaching, in the Palms district of West Los Angeles. She died instantly, and her companion, actor Jim Kiernan, died a few hours later. It was a bizarre, unmotivated killing, but the area had recently seen several bold and strangely random robbery-murders. The day after the incident, six youths were brought in for questioning, but there was no proof of their involvement.

By this point Bob Levitt and Barbara Colby were separated. Their 1972 marriage had lasted just two years, but their commitment and closeness to one another remained deeply bonded. Says Levitt today, "In our seven years together Barbara endured so many hurts from my young man's imbalances that my heart winces for her as I remember them. Contrarily, I can't think of one single hurt that she inflicted on me, ever."[27] When they made the decision to end the marriage, the two of them split their assets 50-50, moved Barbara into a rental on the beach in Malibu, and then "went on a dissolution honeymoon." On their return, their beloved cat, Spike, who was to stay with Barbara, went missing—a painful sign of the sadness of the split. Yet many months later, in July 1975, when Bob came to visit Barbara for her thirty-seventh birthday, the missing cat miraculously reappeared. Just as Bob was unpacking his car outside of her home, "Spike came meowing his way off the hills of Old Mailbu Road into my arms. In keeping with the theatricality of our family, Spike made himself into Barbara's surprise birthday present," an event of "amazing grace," he says, "one more in a steady stream of such events that saturated our seven years together."[28] In spite of giving up on their marriage, Bob and Barbara had hoped to find a way of sharing what Levitt calls their "eternal union." Shortly after this, however, Barbara was gone.

Her death closed down a promising career. Colby had moved from theater work on the East Coast to reside in California, where she was branching into television, including guest roles on popular '70s shows such as *Colombo, Gunsmoke,* and even an appearance on *The Odd Couple.* She had done two well-received guest appearances on *The Mary Tyler Moore Show* as Sherry, a woman Mary gets to know when she does jail time. That engagement had led to Colby getting a featured role on *Phyllis* (Cloris Leachman's spin-off from the *Mary Tyler Moore Show*), where Colby played Julie Erskine, Phyllis's boss. Colby had appeared in one episode before her death (she was replaced by Liz Torres). MTM's CEO Grant Tinker and, especially, costar Cloris Leachman grieved for the warm, talented actress of whom they had become fond, and Leachman prepared a eulogy that, in the end, was not aired.

Bob Levitt immediately flew to Los Angeles. Because he and Colby were still legally married and he stood to benefit financially from her death, he was briefly considered the prime suspect. Although the case was never resolved, the police ultimately suspected gang or gang-related activities behind this and other murders in the area. At Paradise Cove, just off the Malibu Coast, Levitt; Colby's mother, Estelle Galliano; and a huge boat full of her closest friends gave Barbara's ashes to the sea.

It is hard to imagine how Bob and his mother were able to handle yet more violence and loss. Ethel grieved deeply for the woman who had become a second daughter and attended ceremonies memorializing her. But a large part of her response was familiar, and she shielded much of that tragedy. In her second autobiography, for instance, Merman not only omits the incident, but never mentions that her son had ever been married.

At the time Colby was in Los Angeles, Bob Levitt was living in the San Francisco area, where he was working at the American Conservatory Theatre, training actors (he was not the lighting electrician, as his mother claimed). "Bob is an extremely gifted acting teacher," says Cointreau.[29] A little later, in 1978, Bob relocated to Maui, Hawaii, to live communally on a boat with a ceremonial theater group, the Teatro Mare, or Theatre of the Sea. Life with the group gave the young man focus, and it also gave him family. "We raised one of my goddaughters, Bella Rosa, on our boat," says Levitt. "She started walking on sea legs [and] when she came ashore with us, she'd wobble for the first few minutes of walking on land."[30]

Concert Years

Ethel had been doing revivals of *Call Me Madam* across the States for years, most recently in Kansas City in September 1969. But in the 1970s, she began a truly new phase of her career on the road. With her back to Broadway, Merman embarked on a fast-paced series of cross-country concerts. She said that it was a TV special that started it. On July 4, 1976, Ethel performed with Arthur Fiedler conducting the Boston Pops Orchestra to commemorate the American bicentennial. Merman found the experience so enjoyable that she decided, with her manager, to explore concert touring on a regular basis.

As Ethel repeatedly explained to interviewers, the timing was good: she was single, with no kids at home, and Pop was well taken care of. Kathryn Shreve, now partnered with neighbor Ona Hill, stayed on with the family after Agnes died. Merman was free to travel, and touring gave her the opportunity to enjoy her autonomy in a new way. She could now give Americans outside New York the experience of hearing her live for the first time, even if performing her songs without the context of a show or show character lowered the overwhelming effect Merman had on stage audiences. Still, the electricity Ethel could generate turned many Merman agnostics into believers. "I wasn't expecting to like her," ran the typical review, "but there was something amazing about this living legend with big hair. Her voice would shake the rafters, but it would also reach out and grab you deep inside." Merman used the stage to full advantage, as always, lifting her arms, snapping her fingers, and moving to the rhythm of her numbers while giving a flash of her still-shapely legs with a snappy twirl of her skirt.

Her first concert appearance was with the Wichita Symphony Orchestra on March 16, 1977, during which she performed a dozen hits, most from her Broadway repertoire. She loved it. One member of the symphony, though, who now plays with the New York Philharmonic, was less excited: he says that Merman's offense was not unprofessional behavior or anything like that, but he opines, "By this time, her vibrato was so large you could drive a truck through it." The voice had indeed acquired a vibrato as well as a slightly lower register—common changes with age—but for a vocalist with a half century of steady performing behind her, Merman's vocal health and skills remained rather remarkable. All of her life, Merman never lost her ability to convey lyrics clearly and powerfully.

The peak concert years were 1977 to 1979, when Ethel's itinerary included a range of cities that would daunt a performer half her age: Dallas; Seattle; Denver; Indianapolis; Springfield, Massachusetts; Hamilton, Ontario; Norfolk; Detroit; Kansas City, Kansas; Milwaukee; Atlanta; Baltimore; and Syracuse and Chautauqua, New York. Eric Knight was her conductor of choice, and under his baton, her repertoire now, in contrast to the beginning of her career, did not vary, but small matter: few singers of any generation could assemble as many hits that they could call their own. As Kaye Ballard put it, "Ethel Merman, are you kidding? She *invented* the ASCAP repertory!"[31] Every evening, she'd play with the local symphony orchestra in two shows of seventy-five minutes each, going as far back for material as "Life Is Just a Bowl of Cherries" (1931) and "Alexander's Ragtime Band" (1911)—all this at a time when the Beatles and the Rolling Stones had been working for over a decade; Chuck Berry and Little Richard, for two.

Aging Pop

Ethel may have doing a good job defying Old Man Time, but the struggle was harder for her father. Now legally blind and extremely frail, Pop told her shortly after his ninety-seventh birthday, "I'm lucky, Ethel, to be ninety-seven and still have all my marbles."[32] He dutifully tried to maintain the scrapbooks, preserving mementos of his daughter's appearances, pasting them into the pages with a new erraticism—the scrapbooks preceding this period testify more to his failing sight than to his daughter's career: clippings are glued on top of others, some are cut or torn so that the references to Ethel are obscured. By the early '70s, the duty of maintaining the scrapbooks was increasingly shared with Pop's caregivers in New Jersey.

Summers, Ethel brought Pop out of the sweltering city to a nice, airy room in a suburban home in Kenilworth, a block away from Kathryn Shreve, where she, Ona Hill, Ona's sister Edna, and Al Koenig Jr., a local high school teacher, all took care of him. They would play cards, work on the scrapbooks, take car rides, sit in the yard, chat, listen to records ("Pop was partial to 'You Can't Get a Man with a Gun," recalls Koenig),[33] and Pop would take his daily scotch. On some days, if the Hill sisters let Edward sit around a bit too much on his own, Koenig took him out for a ride or to get some ice cream so that he always had activities to recount to his daughter when she came. Whether in Kenilworth or at the apartment he still kept at the Berkshire in the city, Ethel made sure to have Pop's possessions arranged the way they'd always been so that the elderly man could make his way around his place by touch.

"Both Kathryn and Lucy [Ona] were so good to Pop," said Ethel, "that they have become almost like sisters to me."[34] When Ethel visited, they gossiped, had tea, and, circumstances permitting, went antiquing or flea marketing. Ethel felt at home with them, and their loyalty and reliability meant a lot to her. (After Pop passed, Ethel still went out to Kenilworth for visits, and when Shreve became ill some years later, Ethel bought her a wheelchair that the retired nurse was unable to afford.) Still, it was a business arrangement: their pay for looking after Pop was seventeen dollars a day. One day, Koenig recalls, Merman came out to New Jersey with an LP she'd just released: "Here," she said, "here's today's pay!" Ona, he reports, was not amused.[35]

Even before Pop began losing his sight, Ethel was doing charity work for organizations that helped the blind and the visually impaired, such as the Lighthouse International Organization and the "Fight for Sight" campaigns. Although she'd been doing this since the '30s, her zeal for this kind of charity work had greater focus and personal motivation now. On Wednesdays, Ethel also began volunteering at the Roosevelt Hospital gift shop, a decision she'd made when she and her father were spending so much time there while Agnes had been ailing. Finding herself restless, Ethel said, "After a few weeks I asked whether I could be of some service. At first they put me on escort duty, taking patients in wheelchairs and on stretchers . . . but as Mom faded I reached the point where I couldn't bear seeing people on stretchers."[36] So she moved into the store. Bob Levitt recalls, "She liked working with regular folks, and she really loved working with the cash register and having daily receipts."[37] ("If I hadn't been a singer or a secretary," wrote Merman in her second autobiography, "I think I'd have loved being a saleslady.") Needless to say, sales at Roosevelt's gift shop shot up, but Ethel was not thrilled about the attention she got, especially when the hospital decided to move the shop closer to the entrance on the ground floor, where there was more traffic. Still, she took it in stride. One day she wrote, "I was riding an elevator, wearing my Pink Lady uniform, with this middle-aged couple. The woman looked me over and then asked, 'Has anyone ever told you that you look like Ethel Merman?' Before I could answer, the man piped up. 'Ethel Merman just wishes she looked like you.' I grinned and said, 'I *am* Ethel Merman.'"[38]

Ruth Munson, a New Yorker born two years before Ethel, was another volunteer at the hospital at the time. She remembers that, in addition to doing her work in the gift store, Ethel would visit all the entertainers who were patients at Roosevelt. And "anybody who didn't have anybody, people on their own, she would visit them too." Ethel sang to them, she remembers. "You know, she could sing very low, very sweet." Munson vividly recalls not liking Ethel's hair ("Oh, it was terrible, so scrawny"); and she also had an opinion of what caused the Borgnine marriage to fail, stressing what a "sad, tragic" life Merman had had. At the time of our interview, Munson was still pushing gurneys for Roosevelt Hospital on Mondays and Wednesdays; she was ninety-five when we spoke.[39]

After her mother passed away, Merman had a small ivy garden put into Roosevelt's 9th Avenue entrance with a plaque commemorating Agnes Zimmermann, and on November 3, 1976, an ailing Pop was able to attend its dedication ceremony. (By 1974, he had suffered two massive heart attacks.) The garden was set off from the street by a short black iron fence, and with this memorial Ethel was not only able to commemorate her mom but could also acknowledge the good care that Agnes had received at Roosevelt. Today, at the beginning of the twenty-first century, the bronze plaque and small garden no longer exist, casualties of Roosevelt Hospital's having moved several city blocks from its original site; all that remains of the hospital's initial location is the Surgery Theatre, which was preserved by the city as a historic building. In the Volunteer Service Department, however, people today still have stories of when Ethel Merman worked there.

With Mary Martin *Together on Broadway*

Ethel continued doing benefits for other charities, such as the Easter Seals and a number of groups and organizations involved in preserving theater history. In the fall of 1976, Arnold Weissberger approached her to do a benefit for one of them—the Museum of the City of New York, a small gem located on the city's Museum Mile on upper 5th Avenue. Weissberger, chair of the museum's board of directors, had the idea to reunite Ethel and Mary Martin for an evening together on Broadway. There was some question whether Martin would agree to do it, since her husband, Richard Halliday, had died recently, and even before, she'd not been performing much. But she agreed, as did Merman, and *Together on Broadway* was planned for Sunday, May 15, 1977, at the Broadway Theatre. Produced by Anna Sosenko, the event was careful to give the stars equal treatment. Its program was designed with the same exact balance as the record jacket for their 1953 TV appearance had been: turn the program one way, and Merman is the cover girl with top listing; the other, and it's Martin. Every detail is identical: the size of their names, page layout, design, et cetera.

Together on Broadway was a historic, momentous evening for Broadway. Ticket prices (unscalped, that is) ranged between $25 and $150 and were sold out as soon as the first ad appeared. "Even Lauren Bacall had to stand by until almost curtain time," Ethel later remembered.[40] The divas' entrance was playfully dramatic: Martin was dressed in a large sailor suit as Nellie Forbush (from *South Pacific*), Merman was Mama Rose, and the pair came crashing through paper circus hoops to Stephen Sondheim's song "Send in the Clowns," an effective and neutral choice, since it came from a show that neither had performed in, *A Little Night Music*. Together Ethel and Mary sang many of the tunes they'd done on the *Ford 50th Anniversary Show* twenty-four years earlier, reprising the now-famous medley in full. At one point, they appeared as two "Dollys" on the arms of Cyril Ritchard, "Captain Hook" from Martin's *Peter Pan*. For three hours, they sang to ovation after ovation; one audience member describes "audience bedlam" when Ethel launched into "Gee but It's Good to Be Here" and "Blow, Gabriel, Blow."[41] "There was such an outpouring of love," Ethel reflected later, "I felt as if they were unconsciously repaying us for all the years we'd sacrificed our social lives to give performances and shown up when we were ill or someone near and dear to us was ailing."[42] Reviewers dug deep for praise, recognizing the joyous weight of the evening.

In 1973, Ethel Merman and Mary Martin had appeared in the trendy Blackglama fur ads in which celebrities were put into poses appropriate to their persona, with the tagline "What becomes a Legend most?" Merman's and Martin's images could not have been more different. Mary Martin is wearing a short-length light-colored fur jacket, without slacks or skirt, legs clad simply in dark stockings. She is shot from the side, legs together, giving a slightly coy look to the camera in a pose that recalls her breakthrough hit, Porter's "My Heart Belongs to Daddy." Merman, by contrast, looks as if she were sweeping across the room, not standing still so much as caught midmovement. Her longer, asymmetrical black fur coat is shaped almost like a bell pepper, with her legs and arms outspread, head tilted up, and a beaming face—clearly enjoying herself. Perhaps it was a way for Merman to have some fun with the upscale glamour of the Blackglama campaign.

After *Together on Broadway* the two stars wrote each other in letters filled with the ingenuous affection and pride each felt for the other; Mary, as she often did, referred (deferred?) to Ethel as "Dear Queen"; Ethel's note to Mary enthused about how great it was to work together again.[43] Correspondence between them had been strong for years, and they still kept sending each other notes, gifts, and plants whenever the other was sick, if one of them made an appearance, or if there was a family event of note. Ethel and Mary also shared a passion for needlepoint; Mary made the patterns, and Ethel did the stitching. Ethel kept the needlepoint work all over her apartment on many pillows and cloths and displayed some of her work in the 19th Biennial Exhibit of Amateur Needlepoint of Today in 1975. (Kaye Ballard has a pillow that Ethel did "with two frogs doing something rude" on it.)[44]

Mary Martin was the only Broadway musical star whose career and stature came close to rivaling Ethel's. In fact, the two were never rivals, although fans and the press salivated for a bloodthirsty rivalry between them, the kind of competitive diva situation Judy Garland and Barbra Streisand had mocked up with their "I hate you" comments/compliments. Divas Merman and Martin were competitive, to be sure, but they were too professional to feed into any petty rivalry. And besides, their mutual respect was very much ingenuous. There were enough differences between what each of them did that competition wasn't as ferocious as it might have been: yes, Mary Martin toured as Annie Oakley, but she could never have pulled off Mama Rose, just as Merman could have played Peter Pan or Maria von Trapp only in some wild, parallel universe. Ethel assessed their distinctive styles in her second autobiography:

> I like to look after myself. . . . I enjoy keeping a part of my time for myself alone. And if anyone shoves me, I'll shove back. Mary is just the opposite. Not that she is without convictions or bland. Her way is just quieter. Nobody pushes her around, because she always sees to it that she has someone looking after her interests [notably, manager-husband Halliday]. She has by delegating responsibility retained a lovable fey quality (Is it any wonder that Peter Pan is her favorite role?) to which audiences respond. She also has it in real life. . . . One matinee afternoon during the Broadway run of *South Pacific,* Richard was indisposed and could not accompany her to the theater as he always did. The apartment doorman secured a taxi for Mary, and when she got in she told the driver that she wanted to go to *South Pacific.* Pressed for the name of the theater, Mary, who had been playing in the show for a year, couldn't recall it. In all that time, she'd just never bothered to look, depending upon Richard to get her there.[45]

Changes in the Family

Pop was well enough to spend the summer of 1977 in New Jersey, but that fall his health deteriorated, and he was admitted into Roosevelt Hospital. Edward did not want to stay there any longer than necessary, so he moved back into his Manhattan apartment, which Ethel had "converted into a tiny hospital, with twenty-four hour nursing care."[46] Pop Zimmermann had always said he expected to make it to one hundred, and he almost did, passing away on December 22, 1977, at the age of ninety-eight. Toward the end of his life, Ethel wrote, he spoke more and more of seeing Agnes again; "tears would course down his cheeks and he'd talk about joining Mom."[47] His ashes joined hers and Ethel Geary's in Colorado. In Kenilworth, family members and caregivers planted a red maple tree in the yard to commemorate him, and the tree still flourishes today.

Most everyone remembers Pop as an affectionate, warm fellow and remembers that it was Agnes who had the tougher side. Neighbor Al Koenig remembers a time when Agnes, with her sharp eye—guarded to the point of suspicion—failed to locate a silver frame and promptly accused him, Shreve, or Hill of taking it. "'That's funny, that's *real* funny. It was just here,' she said, looking at each of us."[48] (Ethel had the frame all along.)

Throughout the '70s, grandson Bob was still the rebel, and the political differences between him and the other family members weren't bringing them any closer together. Agnes and Edward were lifetime Republicans; Bob's own political inclinations went in the opposite direction. During the 1972 election, he recalls, Pop—now blind—asked for a Nixon campaign button, and Bobby complied by pinning a "Fuck Nixon" button to his lapel, causing his mother to hit the roof. Of course Levitt's rebellions against his mother and grandparents—even adolescent pranks like the button—were but a moment in a specific time of American history, when generational, racial, and economic divisions were pulling far more than families in entirely different directions. But the tensions may have been experienced more profoundly in the Levitt-Zimmermann clan, given the compounding factors of Merman's great celebrity and the considerable violence, tragedies, and noncommunications they suffered as a family.

As the '70s wore on, though, the mother-son relationship saw some softening, and Levitt and Merman seemed intent on at least *trying* to accept and respect each other more. Today, Bob expresses his gratitude for all that his mother did (and attempted to do) for him with an exceptional degree of openness, candid critique, and forgiveness.

You're Gonna Love It Here

Before Pop's passing in December, Merman experienced a number of lighter milestones and activities in 1977. She was the celebrity "team leader" on *The Match Game,* the popular TV game show hosted by Gene Rayburn. (Regular Charles Nelson Reilly remembers the fun he had working with her.) More important, the year saw *You're Gonna Love It Here,* Merman's second stab at her own sitcom on television. Written by Bruce Paltrow (Gwyneth's father), the half-hour pilot features Merman as "big Broadway star" Lolly Rogers, another brassy broad with a name somewhere between Lola Lasagna and Dolly Levi. Lolly has a busy life; she's preparing for a fifteen-city tour in *Mame.* When an undepicted daughter and son-in-law are jailed for tax evasion, Lolly has to find a home for her smart-mouthed grandson (who tells grandma things like "your peroxide has gone to your brain") and convinces her unmarried son, Peter, a New York press agent with "crazy hours," to take in the boy. The pilot follows the ambivalence of uncle and nephew as they adjust to their new union. Peter is played by Austin Pendleton, who'd played Motel, the tailor in *Fiddler on the Roof,* on Broadway, bringing a light touch of Jewish luster and humor to Merman's TV family.

The show was never picked up; said Ethel later, it lacked "zing." But it was put together with considerable forethought: had *Love It Here* gone forward, Ethel's role could easily have been scaled back to that of featured guest star to accommodate her schedule or wishes, or it could have just as easily been moved in the other direction, giving her the lead. But in most ways, *You're Gonna Love It Here* is standard '70s sitcom family fare, filled with mouthy, disrespectful kids, with a slightly more adult and cynical version of domestic life than sitcoms of the '50s and early '60s. The nuclear TV family was no more; by the '70s, it was fractured, with one or two parents usually missing and alliances patched together across different blood and generational lines. Authority figures were flawed (Beaver Cleaver's dad would never have done jail time), and character behavior and language were more irreverent. *Love It Here* seems far more relaxed than *Maggie Brown,* even though it was no less formulaic for its time than *Maggie* had been for its.

In marked contrast to *Maggie,* though, *You're Gonna Love It Here* banks heavily on Merman's New Yorkness. Before the show even begins, the opening credits appear over an aerial view of Manhattan's skyscrapers while Ethel sings Peter Matz and Mitzi Welch's jaunty title song. The theme is sustained throughout the episode; at one point, when the unhappy grandson opines, "My home is in Philadelphia," Grandma Ethel replies, "Philadelphia is only good for out-of-town tryouts." The shift in locale not only made the show more compatible with Merman's image but also reflected a change in TV comedies. Earlier family sitcoms, especially from the '50s, standardly took place in unidentified generic suburbs so as to appeal to an invisible "everyone," but by the '70s, after the sitcom had been firmly established as a TV staple, producers were turning to regional differences as a way to differentiate their otherwise standardized product. This hadn't occurred overnight; in between, there'd been *Mayberry, RFD* and *The Andy Griffith Show* (in the not-too-deep South). *The Beverly Hillbillies* banked on another generic formula—the improbable "match," in this instance among people, class, and place; there was also Lucy and Desi's interethnic marriage and the odd pairing of Eva Gabor's and Eddie Albert Jr.'s cross-class characters on *Green Acres*. Regional and class differences were no longer erased in favor of a white-bread, suburban middle-class soup, but could be counted on for flavor, as if from a spice rack. Areas and regional "types" provided the main source of gags, suggesting in some cases that not much had changed from silent film culture or stage shows such as *Girl Crazy*, which, like *The Beverly Hillbillies* in the '60s, used "country rubes" in exactly the same way.

You're Gonna Love It Here references other features of Merman's established persona. Lolly's planning a tour as *Mame*, a role Ethel never played but could easily have brought to life. There is also Lolly's down-to-earth demeanor and her quirky contradictions: in some situations she is unbothered by propriety (beating her young grandson at poker); in others, she shows outright scandal ("Chinese takeout for breakfast?"). Lolly wears Ethel's take-charge attitude like a glove: in the middle of arguing with her son during a fitting, for instance, she barks in split-second timing to the tailor, "I wanna show more leg!"

The show makes some noteworthy, though surely unintentional, references to Ethel's personal life. Some seem to mirror events; others contradict them. Not since *Gypsy* had a Merman vehicle offered up so many possible analogies, even if the show's small viewership left them hidden from sight. With a curious frankness, Lolly says, "As a parent I'm hit and miss." When Peter complains, "What do I know about raising a kid?" she responds in singsong, "There's nothing to It / Didn't I do it?" almost like her rhyming games with Bobby. The TV mother-son relationship is affectionate, as it was between Merman and Levitt, but tensions are evident as well. Trying to get Peter to take the child off her hands, Lolly pulls out all the stops with faux theatrics, turning into a clichéd Jewish mother: "Didn't I spend my entire life sheltering you, protecting you, sacrificing my entire career for you. . . . [fake sobs] I've been *too generous*."

Merman plays it to the hilt and is very funny. But in addition to the private Ethel that her role vaguely invokes, one can see a certain sense in which Mama Rose's ghosts haunt the edges of the role. A few of Lolly's lines nearly suggest a public response to Rose, if not to Ethel's own experiences with motherhood, by being more relaxed, more "hit and miss" in her approach to child rearing than the severe model Rose offered twenty years earlier.

Visually the show made a few modest attempts to capture "the real" Ethel, notably, in scenes inside Lolly Rogers's apartment, where we see photos of a young Ethel Merman barely discernible on top of her piano. Although in some ways this isn't unlike Merman's actual apartments, whose walls were covered with photographs and career mementos, in other ways, her fictional abode couldn't have resembled Merman's less. By now, Ethel was residing at the Surrey Hotel on 20 East 76th Street, after a somewhat public dispute with the owners of the Berkshire about increases in rent and service charges. When she moved into her eighth-floor unit, Ethel had the stove taken out of the kitchen, keeping a small toaster-oven in which she could reheat Chinese takeout or cook chicken hot dogs, about all the food preparation she cared to do. Again, it was a modest residence, just three and a half rooms. In the foyer she kept her miniature Christmas tree, whose tiny lights were illuminated all year long; in the lime-green living room was a fireplace whose mantel held a clock she'd been given by the Civic Light Orchestra of Pittsburgh. A ceramic basset hound named George guarded the room at ankle height, and all over the apartment Merman kept her needlepoint work, some of it in the bed pillows alongside her beloved Raggedy Anns and Muppet friends.

Autobiography II

In 1978, Simon and Schuster published Ethel's second and final autobiography, *Merman: An Autobiography.* Unlike the first, this was not first serialized in a magazine but appeared in its entirety in book form. *New Yorker* writer George Eells—the biographer of Cole Porter, Hedda Hopper, and Louella Parsons—taped a number of two-hour sessions with Ethel. Eells handled the final transcripts very differently from Pete Martin and did little editorializing to "Mermanize" his subject. Even the most casual reading of *Merman* reveals less of a "tough broad," with fewer hokey colloquialisms, though still maintaining Merman's directness and humor. "George really captured Ethel's voice," appreciates Cointreau. "Of course, all he had to do was transcribe his interview tapes with her!"[49]

Much had happened in Merman's life since the first autobiography, most notably, the divorce from Six, whom the earlier book paints as the love of her life. It's not unreasonable that Ethel would have wanted to update and correct the public record. At this point, she was near seventy, and *Merman: An Autobiography* paints a portrait of a highly successful, mature woman looking back on a full and unusual life. There is more candor in this tome, and although Merman seems less guarded than she did in Martin's account, the autobiography is by no means "no holds barred." Bobby's adult life barely skims the pages; Bob Six comes off as appallingly cheap but not violent; the Borgnine story is consigned to its blank-page prison (which infuriated more than a few reviewers).[50] Even the way she talks about the late Bob Levitt shows some reflection, nuance, and guardedness. Around the time of *Annie Get Your Gun,* she wrote, "I enjoyed my home life as fully as the demands of my job would allow. Bob had long ago adjusted to being 'Mr. Merman' and had enough inner resources to live as comfortably as anyone could under the circumstances. Luckily, at work or out having cocktails with newspapermen, he was regarded as a successful and amusing fellow in his own right. I wasn't any crutch. I don't really know, but there may have been some hidden stress."[51]

Like *Who Could Ask for Anything More?* Eells's *Merman* leans heavily on the scrapbooks for details concerning the historical record and reproduces telegrams, reviews, and quotations from fellow celebrities word for word. The effect is still striking, and, while *Merman* doesn't name-drop with the heavy hand of *Who Could Ask?* the later book is not free of this either, and reviewers again took note. Some of them still found a gauche, boastful star at work here, but those who knew Ethel well knew that the frequent quotations from others reflected her concern for accuracy and the pride she had in her achievement—not pride in her celebrity. Moreover, Merman was not one to feign modesty any more than she liked to exalt her successes.

After Eells was finished, Ethel handed over her scrapbook collection to the Museum of the City of New York in two large installments, and there they remain today in the Theater Collection. The earliest volumes are now ravaged by age, and many book signatures are illegible from mold and deteriorating paper. A few portions have had to be tossed out and are lost to posterity, and the museum is constantly looking for the means to preserve the remaining ones.

The Last of a Kind

By the 1970s, Ethel was a walking piece of Broadway history, a figure who was both standing still and moving forward, recalling old contexts as much as she was brushing up against new ones. She made no bones about the disparity between her own work and tastes and current entertainment trends, disapproving of Broadway stars who were signing on for only short runs and refusing to do matinees. "We used to do movie shorts in the day, and double-in to a late show after curtain," she said. "That's three jobs. Now you can't get people to do eight shows a week—and they're young!"[52] She openly disdained the "message musical" and complained of leaving theaters without any hummable tunes going through her head. Shows like *Hair*, needless to say, appalled the conservative star, who found much of current popular music abominable, especially rock and roll ("method acting for musicians"). Merman openly lamented that her kinds of songs—and their songwriters—were no longer on the scene.

Given that Merman's music, like any popular music, is more emphatically tied to moments, trends, and fads than "art" music is (however weak that high-low distinction is), most forms of popular music (and their singers) are lucky to retain audiences for a generation, and in that regard, Merman might be the exception that proves the rule. Over a half-century career, she moved in and out of wildly different media and performing venues. Yet at the same time, she never left the older entertainment world behind, sticking to its energetic presentation, rigid work ethos, and audience-directed performance style. "Ethel Merman always gave you Ethel Merman," says Tony Cointreau. "Even when she was a little girl doing 'When Maggie Dooley Did the Hooley Hooley,' you got the same Ethel. She never changed."[53]

How audiences and the press responded to her over time reveals more about the attitudes toward entertainment and leisure, music, women, and celebrity at a given time than anything about Ethel Merman herself. When she made her appearance at the Hollywood Bowl in 1977, for instance, one reviewer applauded the Merman voice in order to complain about current trends: "In an era when a Bette Midler . . . isn't able or motivated to sing on pitch, the indomitable accuracy of Merman's vocalism can't be discounted."[54] (Midler is a curious figure with whom to make the point, since so many people consider her as keeper of the Merman flame.)

Ethel was fortunate that during her late-career concert phase, the belt in her voice, the force of her spirit, and her place in musical history were all substantial enough to engage young people, including performers *like* Midler, as

much as they did. At the same time, it would be wrong to attribute her lon-
gevity and appeal to the concert tours. According to many of the younger fans
that I spoke to, what drew them in came earlier: seeing *Gypsy* or the *Annie* revival or *Call Me Madam*—those were the "Ethel encounters" with terrific
meaning. Time and time again, people said how important it was to hear her
perform her songs as a *character,* a personality, and those character traits often
rubbed off on Ethel just as much as she imposed her stamp on them. The concert performances didn't have this force. They tended to attract an older, established fan base, one already familiar with her work and happy to enjoy the
evenings as a tour of song hits of their youth. (Younger listeners might have
stayed away also because Merman was backed by symphonic orchestras; this
was a time when young fans were turning to rock, pop, and disco, and for
them, orchestras like the Boston Pops were little more than old squares trying
to make their old music hip, much like high school English teachers were trying to appeal to their classes by teaching Bob Dylan lyrics.)

Those kinds of splits in the musical tastes of Ethel's fan bases are evident
in several tapes of her televised work. In a 1971 appearance, *Super Night at
Forest Hills* at the U.S. Open in Queens, Ethel entertains the crowds in the
bleachers as tennis superstar Ilie Nastase sits on the stage wearing tennis
shorts, sneakers, and a shirt that says "Nasty." Ethel mills among the crowd,
singing "Everything's Coming Up Roses" to the clear bemusement of some
of the younger members, who don't seem too sure of what to make of this
older woman so full of confidence and show biz energy. And Nastase, for his
part, just looks awkward about the whole affair. Merman, of course, is not
there for him and does not have as much meaning for the young tennis fans
as for older viewers, especially in this Queens locale. Merman herself seems
to have no trouble disregarding all this, handing out roses to audience members while she sings full-out.

Her guest appearance on *The Sha Na Na Show* plays up the same generational discrepancy but with more self-awareness and fun. Ethel is relaxed but
professional: "Instead of calling me Miss Merman," she tells them, "just call
me Ethel." The group is wearing its signature '50s greaser gang outfits—tight
jeans, cutoff T-shirts, and slicked-back hair; Ethel wears an age-appropriate,
but still hip for the '70s, large, splashy caftan ("Grandma was always wearing those," recalls Geary) and lacquered teased hair. If Sha Na Na were banking on the nostalgia for '50s rock and roll, Ethel is there as if visiting from an
even older era ("another world," as Elke Sommer had put it), a good sport
who plays the cultural disconnect for a rocking good time. In the skits, her
clear, booming voice is pitched against their playfully macho ones, and

significantly, the band joins her in singing Merman's music, not she in theirs, with Bowser, the group's lead singer, going head to head with her in a version of "Anything You Can Do, I Can Do Better."

Predictably, the media continued to have conflicting attitudes toward Ethel. By now, most of the New York press, especially the entertainment writers, knew that with Ethel Merman they had a piece of theater history on their hands and treated her with respect and awed affection. Most were delighted that Ethel never stopped performing and noted that her endurance made her not only a legend but also a survivor. Others saw in Merman a woman who "was staying on too long," as if the proper thing to do at a certain age was to hole up in a dark room and shield one's face from the press, as Dietrich and Garbo had. Merman proved quite the opposite and never took cover; in that regard, she was more like film diva Bette Davis. The '70s in fact gave Merman opportunities to widen the scope of her visibility and her "worth" all the more; making herself scarce was not what she was about. "When they stop asking for autographs," she said, "is when I'll think about retiring."[55]

The Love Boat

The year 1979 was especially busy for Merman with television appearances, among them *American Pop: The Great Singers* in January; May and October appearances on *The Merv Griffin Show;* a PBS special in October; and a Christmas movie for children, *Rudolph and Frosty's Christmas in July,* in which Ethel voices a Claymation character who manages a sea theme park and wears an outfit that makes her look just like a middle-aged Annie Oakley. In addition to giving Ethel a chance to work for children, as she had with the Muppets, the movie also gave her a chance to celebrate her favorite holiday. She closes out the special singing "Rudolph the Red-Nosed Reindeer," hitting the notes hard with her characteristic twangs and grace notes.

At the end of the year, Ethel shot a television show that quickly became legendary in the Book of Merm. It was *The Love Boat,* in which Ethel was joined by Carol Channing, Della Reese, Ann Miller, and Van Johnson for a special musical pair of episodes. In them Ethel plays the mother of cruise ship regular Gopher and, like the other stars, performs a number onboard the ship. Given all of its famous guests, *The Love Boat's* producers, agents, and writers were busy keeping everyone on a relatively level playing field and not advantaging one star more than another; each guest, for instance, did one song or dance number in the episode. But Merman had a little edge. Not only was hers the final song, but hers was also the only female character who was given an on-screen romance, with Van Johnson, and her character ends up being more rounded out and developed than the others.

Ethel prepared for the show as she prepared for her other appearances, learning only the script scenes in which she appeared. "It could be read as egotistical," says Cointreau, "but it worked! She had incredible instinctive gifts. Ethel relied on total instinct, and she never made any mistakes in the roles or songs she chose. Everyone in the business is so afraid of instinct, and it's all Ethel knew."[56] The episodes were shot in Los Angeles, and Ethel was able to stay at her long-preferred Beverly Hills Hotel—the same spot where, during *No Business,* little Bobby had caused an uproar by burning some candy wrappers in his mother's wastebasket and accidentally igniting the drapes in the room.

For any viewer of the "Love Boat Follies," it's clear that the elder guest stars are enjoying themselves immensely; they perform their hearts out and sparkle with appreciation as they watch one another. If there was any rivalry on the set, it doesn't come through. Channing recalls working on the show:

> When we were rehearsing a musical number of an episode of "The Love Boat," Ethel was supposed to be "Miss Mexico," dressed in a big black sombrero and a black shawl [ethnic cross-dressing again], Ann Miller was "Miss Panama Canal" with a parrot on her shoulder and I was "Miss Alaska." They had me dressed in a long white diamond dress with a white fox stole, white everything. When I was at the top of the staircase to do my number, Ethel yelled out, "What the hell is this? I'm dressed like a Mexican señora, but you look like a big bottle of Maalox!" I worshipped her.[57]

The episodes have become an affectionate camp classic, though quite devoid of camp's sometimes vicious side, especially where aging divas are concerned. For Ethel, playing the character gave her a chance to exhibit her familiar firm, brassy side through the character's banter, along with a sense of genuine softness and wisdom. (Her character demurs to act on the feelings she and Van Johnson's character have for each other.) For people growing up at the time, *The Love Boat* was their introduction to Ethel Merman, and to this day, "their Ethel" remains Gopher's mom.

EIGHTEEN

Twilight and Transformation

Twenty years after *Gypsy,* Kip Cohen of A&M Records contacted Merman to see if she would be interested in recording a disco album with them. Ethel thought it was a great opportunity for something new and took one day to say yes. *The Ethel Merman Disco Album* was produced by songwriter-arranger Peter Matz (1928–2002), whose work had intersected with hers before when he composed the theme song for *You're Gonna Love It Here.*

Ethel spent two days at A&M's Studio B in Los Angeles laying down the vocal track, singing with minimal accompaniment; the instrumentation was laid down after she finished her session. While she was there, Ethel was introduced to A&M's disco star Donna Summer ("She Works Hard for the Money" and "Hot Stuff"), and the press released a photo of the two in wide syndication. Reportedly, Summer greeted Merman with, "If I'm the Queen of Disco, You're the Disco Diva."[1]

Though hardly the music of Merman's heritage, disco's synthesized, repetitive style was actually not unsuited to her—after all, her voice, with its innate sense of rhythm, could practically syncopate itself—and A&M label owner and trumpeter Herb Alpert enthused, "It's almost as if disco was made for her."[2] But the response to the venture was sharply and wildly divided, and people remain touchy about *The Disco Album* today, loving it, hating it, celebrating it, wanting to downplay it, championing it, and so on.

In its review, the *New York Times* wrote: "The results are not quite so embarrassing as might have been feared."[3] Others called the enterprise out of touch, the singer and her producers oblivious to changes in popular tastes. Some found the idea of a septuagenarian singer trying to update herself through disco nothing short of ludicrous. For many musical theater purists, Ethel Merman had betrayed her "audience" and sold out: "Et tu, Ethel?" ran one review.[4]

Giving fuel to this hostility was Ethel's voice, which was not in peak form. Although she still hit the pitches very well, and to Cointreau, her "soft voice in 'I Got Rhythm' was very powerful,"[5] her vibrato was relatively open, and the voice had a wobble and a harshness to it that wasn't there in earlier years. The disco recording shows the late-life voice that people parody as the "Merman" belt today, forgetting that she ever handled ballads and complex jazz without a trace of harshness or vibrato and with absolutely clear diction.

The Ethel Merman Disco Album is a fun if strange LP, full of disconnects and incongruities. Unlike disco recording artists such as Summer, Thelma Houston, and the Bee Gees—and the countless pop, folk, and rock singers who were suddenly cutting disco albums—Ethel chose songs that were *not* contemporary. It is indeed strange to hear "Alexander's Ragtime Band" performed to a disco beat and instrumentation. Yet despite the strangeness, there are some points of connection: "Alexander," first released in the early 1910s, was riding the ragtime wave sweeping the country, when ragtime generated some of the same criticisms that disco faced sixty years later. Traditional white critics feared that left unchecked, the ragtime fad could lead to mass hysteria, simplemindedness, and the wholesale enslavement of white women, and in the 1970s, disco was accused of being numbingly repetitive, too commercial, artificial, decadent—just as its urban, gay, and African-American consumers were believed to be. For critics, the dance-halls of both ragtime and disco were nothing more than dens of iniquity where drugs and illicit sex mingled freely. For all this critical opprobrium, though, both genres were widely popular: ragtime was one of the country's earliest forms of mass-distributed pop music, and disco was an important expression of a number of urban cultures that were repudiating the bogus authenticity of rock or the saccharine taste of pop. Disco, in fact, remained popular for most of the '70s—until about the time of Merman's LP, alas.

She promoted the album with characteristic zeal, appearing on Merv Griffin's and Johnny Carson's talk shows, talking to national and local print journals, confiding to reporters that "she loved the beat" even if she "didn't understand the lyrics" to the disco songs she knew.[6] When columnists asked her what Irving Berlin thought, she told them that the ninety-three-year-old composer had said that her disco rendition of "Alexander's Ragtime Band" was the best version he'd ever heard. To the reviewer who asked if she'd do another disco LP, she said, sure, she was ready; she'd had a blast and "there are plenty of showtunes left." "She loved making that album," recall both Levitt and Cointreau.[7] She saved the promotional T-shirts that said "Disco Diva."[8]

The largely poor reviews of *The Ethel Merman Disco Album* show enormous prejudice involving class and taste, and some reviewers seemed to gloat over how low Merman's star seemed to have fallen. A&M, they said, "forced" her to appear at the New York–based discount store Korvettes to sign copies of the LP. This is what the queen of the Great White Way had been reduced to! Even worse, they reported, the queen was behaving poorly:

> For nearly two hours, she greeted fans with the warmth of a fjord. . . . If you didn't have the disco album, you couldn't meet Ethel. Those were the rules. Here is the dialogue (some of it). Reported verbatim:
>
> FAN: I play your records every day. You're my favorite.
> MERMAN: Yeah . . .
> FAN: I saw your concert in Saratoga Saturday night. It took my breath away.
> MERMAN: Good for you.[9]

Jim Russo, Cointreau's partner, who was with Ethel at the album signing, does not find anything real in these words. Neither does John Kenrick, a young gay man who had waited for hours at Korvettes to get Ethel Merman's autograph. To this day, Kenrick prides himself in being the first in line and bristles at reports that he wasn't; one claimed an elderly woman was. The Ethel Merman he encountered had nothing in common with the one produced by the press. After greeting the teenager warmly, he said, Ethel signed his LP, asked how long he'd been waiting in line, and was surprised it had been for so long. She seemed genuinely happy to be there, he recalls, although he remembers she was frustrated by A&M's restriction allowing her to autograph only the new disco album and nothing else that fans might have brought in.

The experience of *The Ethel Merman Disco Album* gave young fans and self-professed "musical theater queens" like John Kenrick a chance to encounter the Broadway legend firsthand. Moreover, in going disco, Ethel seemed to be acknowledging her gay fan base in a way that she'd not done before. Although this was not the reason she actually chose to do the LP ("Ethel just wanted to do something new," says Cointreau, "there was no deeper motivation than that"),[10] many fans readily find in this recording a way that Ethel Merman might be speaking to them.

Over the '60s and '70s, Ethel had good-humoredly hammed it up (Hasty Pudding, *Batman*), nurturing her status as a gay man's diva. In truth, it's unlikely that Ethel appreciated or understood herself as a camp icon as such, but it's equally unlikely that she had no clue at all about her place in the hearts of gay male fans. Today, there probably isn't a gay Merman maven anywhere who doesn't know his way around her disco album, and other appreciators, including this author, play it at dinner parties to capture the reactions of unsuspecting guests. *The Ethel Merman Disco Album* remains easy to love, in all of its full-blooded, goofy spirit. Before a CD of it was pressed in 2003, vinyl copies were going for as much as fifty dollars on eBay and at used-record shops, a remarkable afterlife for an LP that was not a big deal for Merman anymore than it was a big deal for her to promote it at a store like Korvettes. It was only the press that interpreted such appearances as "beneath" the star; for her, the appearances were fun and gave her ways to reach all her different fans.

And so in 1980, Ethel Merman was transformed anew, even as she entered the last few years of her life. It had been exactly half a century since her debut in *Girl Crazy,* and Broadway was beyond its golden days as well. On August 25, 1980, it held what was arguably its last old-time gala premiere at the Winter Garden for *42nd Street,* a musical produced by David Merrick. Audience luminaries that night included Merman, Josh Logan, Bob Fosse, Ruth Gordon and Garson Kanin, Neil Simon, Joseph Papp, Joan Fontaine, and Henry Kissinger.[11] But it *was* the end of an era, and the upcoming years would not prove to be a boom time for the musical stage. Production costs were skyrocketing, and so were ticket prices, and although both of those trends had been decades in the making, they'd become so excessive that most musicals were now priced out of the range of all but upper-middle-class and wealthy patrons or out-of-town tourists willing to splurge on recognizable, big-name shows. Under those conditions, small innovative shows were not going to pay off. Big-budget productions ruled the day, and unestablished works or creators were simply deemed too risky. In the 1979–80 season, for instance, many of the musicals that "opened" were actually revivals, such as *Peter Pan, Oklahoma!* and *Brigadoon.* By this point, Hollywood had Broadway under its heels, at least in terms of generating wide public excitement over new shows. And even on-screen, the musical was a genre in steep decline. Gone too was the time when Broadway songs dominated the national scene; the truly *popular* music that most Americans were listening to did not come from shows anymore, and a deep schism separated Broadway music from other popular music. The entertainment world of 1980 could scarcely have been more different from 1930, when Ethel opened in *Girl Crazy.*

Still, Ethel ushered in the sixth decade of her career with high-voltage energy, still doing concert tours and performing at different events across the country. One invitation was extended by Frank Sinatra, now a die-hard

Republican, who asked her if she would perform at Ronald Reagan's presidential inauguration. Merman was thrilled to be asked. Levitt recalls his dismay over how much his mother admired Reagan; she liked his traditional and conservative values and what she perceived as his personal integrity. Levitt adds that she was especially impressed by Reagan's long-term, stable marriage with the former Nancy Davis.[12]

Reagan was inaugurated on January 20, 1981, and the show featured a pyramid-like stage at the center. That evening, Ethel mounted the stairs and serenaded the new president, who beamed in obvious appreciation. It was here, in singing "Everything's Coming Up Roses," that Ethel broke one of her professional vows, uncharacteristically modifying the lyrics at one point to "everything's coming up *jelly beans*," a favorite treat of the new president. The crowd applauded wildly, none more so than Reagan himself.

Just prior to this, Bob Jr. left his home in Hawaii to spend the year in New York City. "Privately," he says, "I came to celebrate my mother's fiftieth Broadway anniversary and to try to woo her to move back to Maui. I had my first warm family experience there; there was family harmony." He hoped that with neighbors on the island such as Jim Nabors and Carol Burnett, his mother might be enticed into moving back there with him. But Ethel was not going to leave Manhattan, and Bob realized that, although they "loved the idea—if not the practice, of being with each other," that vision was a fantasy. Now, when he looks back on the earlier times when he'd been the "bad boy" and had abused either his mom's trust or her money, he says, "What I regret the most about those stories is not the ill deeds and bad moves within them, but more, how much opportunity and trust was lost in those moments that we . . . needed for living a more fulfilling life of Mother and Son."[13] So he stayed on the West Coast and she on the East. They enjoyed a number of visits and vacations together in New York and in Northern California, where Levitt would be spending much of his time with a new partner. One particularly special vacation they took together was in Southern California, on Catalina Island, where Ethel had filmed *We're Not Dressing* nearly fifty years earlier.

Everything's Coming Up Merman

In 1980, *Airplane!* the spoof of the 1970 disaster film *Airport,* was released. Ethel's cameo as Lieutenant Hurwitz, the traumatized soldier who's convinced he's Ethel Merman, had taken a quick two hours to shoot and earned her fifteen hundred dollars. Cowriter-codirector Jerry Zucker recalls her as "a sweet lady" who was unusually cooperative. Ethel had made only one stipulation, he said, which was to use her own hairdresser. ("When she arrived, she had the familiar Merman beehive—which made us wonder why she needed a hairdresser.")[14] It is a great appearance for Merman fans; it is a hysterical cameo, and it speaks volumes to her playfulness. "I enjoyed that she could make fun of her own persona (e.g., her roles in *It's a Mad Mad World* and *Airplane*)," one fan wrote me.[15] Even people who *don't* like Merman love the *Airplane!* appearance. Two men of very different backgrounds (neither of whom was especially interested in Merman or her music) told me they have the scene committed to memory and think it's one of the funniest moments in an extremely funny movie.

By now, Merman was becoming an affectionate pop-culture reference point. In *Dead Men Don't Wear Plaid* (1982), a film noir parody directed and written by Carl Reiner, Ethel's colleague in *It's a Mad, Mad, Mad, Mad World* and *The Art of Love,* Steve Martin stars as a private eye who's hired on a case. The picture intercuts clips of actual 1940 films noir into the story, giving the illusion that gumshoe Steve Martin is getting advice from the likes of Humphrey Bogart, Jimmy Cagney, and others. At one point, after a femme fatale slips a Mickey Finn into his drink, Martin starts to mumble about a boat full of dangerous Germans, and as his speech blurs, "Germans" become "Ger-mermans," then the "Ger-mermans" becomes "Ethel Mermans," and finally he asks the beautiful woman if she wants to join him at an Ethel Merman concert.

Even though Broadway's influence may have been waning nationally, its history and legends were still robustly celebrated in plenty of venues around New York. One was *Forbidden Broadway,* the annual parody of skits, legends, and songs, which had its beginnings in the gay piano bars of Greenwich Village that were popular in the '80s (the Duplex, Eighty-Eights, the Monster, and later, Rose's Turn). The show caught on and eventually made it to off-Broadway, a symbol of well-earned success (and of gay culture's mainstreaming). One year, Ethel caught the send-up of her famous medley with Mary Martin and loved it. Recalls Cointreau, "She was too shy to go backstage to compliment the performers. I had to go with her before she'd go."[16]

For the most part, Ethel was leading a relatively quiet life. She still lent a hand to various charities, churches, and theater groups; one very public—and celebrated—event occurred on May 10, 1982, when she did a second benefit for the Museum of the City of New York. This time the venue was Carnegie Hall. The evening, *Ethel Merman at Carnegie Hall,* was produced by Anna Sosenko, the same producer of *Together on Broadway.* As invitations promised viewers, "We are sure this will be . . . magical. . . . Please be with us for this night that will make theatre history."[17]

The American Symphony Orchestra accompanied Ethel that night under the baton of her favorite conductor, Eric Knight. Ethel arrived onstage in a dress designed by Barbara Matera—semiformal, knee-length, sequined, and lavender, her favorite color, with shoes to match—and opened with "I'm Just a Lady with a Song." After some talk with the audience, she sang a medley including "Life Is Just a Bowl of Cherries," "It's De-Lovely," "Doin' What Comes Natur'lly," and "I Got Rhythm." "There's No Business Like Show Business" was her finale. Merman then shared the stage with ASCAP president Hal David, there to give her the ASCAP's prestigious Pied Piper Award for lifetime achievement in the musical field. (The only prior recipients had been Frank Sinatra, Barbra Streisand, and Fred Astaire.) When Ethel accepted the statue from him, she said gratefully, "You know, they say you're only as good as your material," before giving a more Mermanesque quip, "I can get a lamp made out of this!" Accompanist Jule Styne ended with "Everything's Coming Up Merman." The event raised sixty thousand dollars for the museum's Theater Collection, and a proud Bob Levitt escorted his award-winning mother to the party afterward.

The following morning Clive Barnes wrote his now-famous, open love letter. "Dear Miss Merman," it begins,

> How do I start? I know I'm far too old to be writing a fan letter. . . . But I just had to write and tell you how fantastic I thought your Carnegie Hall debut was last night. . . . You were a strange muse for the likes of George Gershwin, Cole Porter, Irving Berlin, and Jule Styne. You also became the embodiment of musical comedy when people knew what musical comedy was. Your voice was the clarion call for a kind of theatre. . . . Not everyone *liked* your voice, you know. In fact, I don't think *anyone* actually liked your voice. It was a voice the happy majority—blissfully including me—love, and a mealy-eared, frost-bitten minority, hate.[18]

Another gratifying appearance involved a second reunion with Mary Martin. In the early 1980s, Martin had taken over as host of a popular PBS talk show called *Over Easy,* which was geared for older audiences.[19] It was an ideal format for Martin's casual charm and warmth, and she attracted viewers easily. When Mary asked Ethel to appear in the spring of 1982, Ethel happily packed her bags and flew to San Francisco to tape the show. For two days, the two of them rehearsed "Anything You Can Do" and enjoyed themselves so much that Ethel extended her visit. In her autobiography, Martin said that during the visit, she screwed up the courage to ask her friend if she had ever really said, "Mary Martin's okay—if you like talent." " 'Of course not,' said Ethel. 'A press agent dreamed it up.' "[20]

The episode of *Over Easy* delighted fans of both stars, and Hollywood also took note. Would Mary Martin and Ethel Merman agree to perform together again for the Oscar Awards ceremony next spring? They accepted. That engagement, though, wouldn't take place. In September 1982, Martin was in a terrible car accident in San Francisco that killed her manager, Ben Washer, and gravely injured actress Janet Gaynor, who later died of complications.[21] Martin herself was seriously injured, and her recovery lasted months. Ethel called and wrote affectionate notes urging her friend to a speedy recovery.

Diminished Health

Ethel's own health was relatively good, although her eyesight was diminished. In 1981 she'd been diagnosed with macular degeneration, the retina disorder that usually leads to blindness. Levitt remembers being in Los Angeles when his mother was on a break, and "when it came time for Debbie Reynolds to rehearse her number the lights came on, the intro music began, and the set appeared," with large images of Reynolds lowered onto the set. "Mom said, 'What's with the bunnies?' I replied, 'They're not bunnies, they're big caricatures of Debbie Reynolds.' Mom, swallowing her disgruntledness [sic] about her ever-worsening vision, said, 'Oh.' And then, bouncing back, added, 'Same thing.' "[22] Borrowing a big-print typewriter from the Lighthouse for the Blind, Bob typed out his mother's address book in big print so she could read it with a magnifying glass. Entries for some people were still listed by function—*D* for dates, *T* for her throat doctor—and she kept scrupulous records of everything. "She even wrote out a recipe for [a] grilled cheese sandwich," says Cointreau.[23] But when she was taping TV shows, Merman no longer could read her lines. One time, Bob remembers, when they were out at a restaurant, her friend Lucille Ball yelled when she saw her, "Hi, Ethel!" and Ethel was looking everywhere for the bright red hair and had to call out, "Lucy! Where are ya?"[24]

Ethel was also starting to say words and phrases backward, and when she tried to repeat them correctly, could not. At times, she wasn't able to recognize old friends, and once, in 1979 while taping a PBS special, *Musical Comedy*

Tonight, with Sylvia Fine, she looked at the music for Porter's "Anything Goes" and reportedly told Fine that she'd never seen the song before. Less than an hour later, she recognized it without incident and recorded it flawlessly, but it was cause for alarm.[25] Friends and colleagues knew something was not right.

Merman's 1985 biographer, Bob Thomas, interviewed a number of her friends and colleagues who commented on Ethel's growing erratic, sometimes hostile, behavior in her later years, another possible indication of medical problems. Ethel was questioning the motives of longtime friends and colleagues and was cutting ties or firing more and more associates. Although Thomas writes sympathetically about Ethel's confusion and lapses of memory, he doesn't connect Ethel's increasingly strange behavior with the health problems that would soon strike, instead painting a picture of a woman whose vicious side had gone haywire with bitterness and age, someone who was scattering her trusted friends and coworkers like so many rabbits with a shotgun. Friend and colleague Russell Nype, for instance, told Thomas that he had a falling-out with Merman was because he "got tired of trying to deal with a twelve-year old mind";[26] Merman and Mitzi Gaynor were no longer like "mother and daughter"; and Ethel had withdrawn the trust she'd had in her friend of fifty years, Benay Venuta.

Many of these fallings-out were not accidental. "Benay wanted to *be* Ethel Merman," says Tony Cointreau, with some sympathy, adding, "That was a problem with a lot of Ethel's female friends." He maintains that Ethel was letting go of many of her associates at the time for a reason. "She was absolutely right about most of these people," he says. "A lot of people used her. And Ethel was not capable of letting b.s. fly. She wouldn't let it pass, like many people do. She had the same laser-beam focus on that [issue] that she had [when she was performing] onstage."[27]

In January 1983 Ethel Merman sat down with TV host Gene Shalit to shoot an in-depth interview in which she recounted the stories of her life: Gershwin's advice against taking singing lessons, working with Porter and Berlin, being single after four failed marriages. Tapes show her at once relaxed and professional, filling the time with the usual stories and down-to-earth responses she'd been offering the press for decades. Producer Marie Marchesani remembers, "The Gene Shalit interview was for a special exhibit of the MCNY that Mary Henderson [of the museum's Theater Collection] put together, called 'Show Stoppers.' The video played in a darkened room at the museum. Ethel sat and watched it, occasionally looking down and sad at parts. [But] she loved it," recalls Marchesani of watching it with her on March 15.[28]

Final Illness

Three weeks later, on April 8, 1983, Ethel was preparing for a flight to Los Angeles, where she was going to tape her part of the tribute to Irving Berlin on the upcoming Academy Awards. Mary Martin was still on the mend and wasn't going to be sharing the stage with her, so Ethel was scheduled to go on as a solo performer, doing "There's No Business Like Show Business." In her Surrey apartment, she was busy packing, making calls, jotting notes to colleagues. In a quick memo to Marchesani, Ethel wrote, "Dear Marie, The enclosed is self-explanatory [a postcard from Robert Gardiner outlining plans for an engagement in Richmond, Virginia]. I'll be in touch upon my return—am leaving in about two minutes. I'll arrange for the tickets. It's the opening of the new performing arts center." The writing is uncharacteristically shaky, especially the last two lines.[29] According to Ona Hill—who did not share especially warm feelings with the star—Ethel called her in New Jersey to report that she was feeling "dizzy" from a bad headache and was planning to call a cab to go the hospital; Ona was not to worry about whatever she might read in the papers the next day, Merman purportedly told her.[30] To friends and family, Ethel never mentioned making this call.

It was when Ethel was applying lipstick in front of her mirror that the seizure struck, and the force threw her violently to the floor. Although she was able to move herself to a phone and lift the receiver, she wasn't able to speak. The Surrey management saw that the call was originating from Merman's apartment and went up, but their master keys couldn't open her door; Ethel had had a special security lock made. Merman had to crawl to the door through the lipstick and other debris from the fall to let them in. The medics arrived shortly, and by then she was able to convey to them that she wanted them to call Irving Katz, her trusted friend and financial adviser since the early '60s, and have him come over. Katz arrived, and the medics continued to work on her. Later that evening, after they'd stabilized her, Katz took Ethel by cab to Roosevelt Hospital, where she was admitted.[31]

Three days later, on April 11, Mary Martin was at home watching the Oscars, and when she didn't see Ethel, she worried that something was wrong. There was. Initially, hospital doctors had thought that she had suffered a stroke, but after extensive tests and a long surgery on April 15, Merman was diagnosed with an inoperable brain tumor. Neurologists gave her eight and a half months to live.

"When Ethel got sick, Bob was right there," recalls Cointreau. "No son could do more. He gave his whole heart and soul every single moment."[32]

One of the first things Levitt needed to do was make her environment as pleasant as possible. When she was ready to leave the hospital, he got things set up for her at her home, making sure his mom would be surrounded by the personal objects that comforted her. Part of his job entailed shielding his celebrity mother from the press. He downplayed the severity of her condition to them, and, after she came home, he worked to minimize the chance of encounters: "Dealing with surprise photographers would [have been] awful."[33] He recalls one reporter from the *New York Star* who was on his mother's trail. Levitt spent forty-five minutes talking to her, explaining the difficult situation to her. Amazingly, Levitt was able to get her to pull back, an act he still appreciates today (when such journalistic restraint seems unfathomable).

Now it was Bob Levitt's turn to protect the Merman-Levitt family life from public scrutiny, a self-preservation strategy his mother had developed before he'd even been born, as in the 1939 interview, "My Private Life Is Private." As he put it, "Mom truly appreciated [her fans'] presence and their applause. But you shouldn't attempt to be personal—she drew lines, and she could cut you off."[34] Levitt preserved Merman's privacy with a hard-to-balance mix of compassion, empathy, and some real, no-nonsense toughness—more traits he had in common with his mom.

The illness affected Ethel's ability to talk. At the beginning, she was able to speak, but her speech was slurred, and as the tumor ran its course, she became increasingly aphasic. Toward the end, there was no Merman voice left at all. Tony Cointreau recalled a rather miraculous occasion during this time, involving a small needlepoint pillow he'd given her with the words "She's Me Pal" stitched on it, one of the songs she'd performed at Camp Yankhank. Tears were streaming down Ethel's cheeks, and holding the pillow to her, the "speechless" woman then started to sing "She's Me Pal." Says Cointreau with astonishment, "And Ethel sang the entire song from start to finish."[35]

At first Ethel's health benefited from a healer Bob brought in, who had reduced her brain tumor mass by a third. At a certain point, however, his mother refused to allow the healer in to see her anymore, and Bob made the agonizing choice to acquiesce to her wishes and confront a situation in which his mother now faced certain death rather than a miraculous, if temporary, recovery. This sad and wrenching period did, however, provide moments of sweet intimacy and bittersweet illumination. Bob notes that this twilight period gave him insight not just into his mother's life, her friends, and her nature but into human nature. "That big, Ethel Merman persona was shrinking from the impact of a brain tumor, and as it disappeared so did many of

Mom's more limited friendships." It's the rare person with skills to act with respect, understanding, and helpfulness in the face of such finality and in the face of the suffering of a loved friend or colleague. Mary Martin was one of the few who could, and did so with warmth and grace. "She would sit by my mother's bed and hold her hand," recalls Levitt. "She would talk to her softly and even cry with her gently. She was not afraid to share the woe of Mom's terrible predicament, but she never bottomed out there. She had the courage and loving presence to go into that woe, but she had the skillful grace to rise up through it again and return with Mom to the relief of more soft talk and silent smiling."[36] Mary encouraged Ethel to keep moving, to stay active and alert, explaining to her friend that she'd had to do the same thing during her recent rehabilitation. In addition to son Bob, family "members" Tony Cointreau and Jim Russo were at Ethel's side constantly; from Queens, old family friends Fritz and Anna Panzer, Carol and Joe Freund came every week, as did Madeline Gaxton.

Ethel was able to cheat the neurologists on their predictions but not by much. On Wednesday, February 15, 1984, ten months after her diagnosis, she died in her sleep. She had left precise instructions in her last will and testament, and in accordance with her wishes, a small, private funeral service was held at St. Bartholomew's, the Manhattan Episcopalian church that Merman liked to attend. At the service, close friend Dorothy Strelsin brought seventy-six roses, one for each year of Merman's life, and afterward, Levitt, Cointreau, and other intimates scattered the petals on Ethel's brass bed, interspersing them among her beloved Muppet dolls. For several days, they let them dry there and then distributed handfuls to Ethel's inner circle of close colleagues and loved ones. Levitt made a special trip to bring these and other mementos to Irving Berlin, who, in his nineties, had been too frail to attend her service. At the maestro's apartment, Berlin shared his affectionate and touching appreciations of Ethel and her work with her son.

New York knew that with Merman gone it had lost a part of itself. As Carol Channing said, "It's like the Statue of Liberty has fallen." The *New York Times* observed, "Offstage, as well as in the theater, Miss Merman was a sort of symbol of the Broadway of her era, with her New York speech, gaudy jewelry, flamboyant, gum-chewing manner."[37] On the evening of February 16, 1984, theaters along Broadway dimmed their lights in homage to her. At the time, Bob Levitt was returning from picking up his mother's cremated remains from a crematorium in the Bronx. Riding in his friend's car, heading downtown on Broadway, he had his friend stop the vehicle so he could place the urn with his mother's ashes onto a sidewalk on Broadway to "take in" the tribute as it was happening—he would soon understand how his mom could have spent time talking to the ashes of their other family members. (Several years earlier, Ethel had closed out the family mausoleum in Colorado Springs and had taken possession of her daughter's ashes, her parents, and later those of Bob Levitt Sr., whose widow gave them to her. Today all of their cremated remains, including Ethel Sr.'s, remain in the possession of Merman's family intimates.)

Ethel left a private set of instructions along with her official will of November 18, 1980. She wished to have her body cremated and the ashes given to Bob Levitt Jr. Her estate was to be divided largely between Levitt and the two grandchildren, Barbara and Michael Geary. It was valued at eight hundred thousand dollars—a very low total, the press noted. In fact, most of her assets were held by the American Entertainment Enterprise, the company Merman had formed under the guidance of her close associate Irving Katz, who was its CEO.

Merman's will stipulated that son-in-law Bill Geary receive the marble urns that had once stood at the Colorado mausoleum, along with five thousand dollars. To the Actors' Fund of America she gave a thousand dollars; twenty-six thousand more was distributed among friends and family caregivers. Granddaughter Barbara received nothing in the way of personal items through the will, since the two were not on speaking terms. A couple of years earlier, there'd been an incident when Barbara brought her soon-to-be-husband to have a meal with Grandma, and Ethel pitched a fit about his unkempt hippie appearance. Barbara dashed off a " 'How dare you!' letter" ("It was a function of being twenty-two," she says now), and the two never reconciled.[38]

Merman's will also specified that her personal effects were to be auctioned off, which disappointed MCNY's Theater Collection curator, Mary Henderson, who had approached Levitt about obtaining some memorabilia for its collection. Since Ethel had donated her father's scrapbook collection to the museum and done two high-profile benefits on its behalf, she was certainly aware of the museum's role in preserving her legacy, and it's rather odd that she didn't set a few items aside to give to its collection. It is also odd that Ethel identified so few items for friends and family. Before Christie's auction, Levitt, who had gone through his mother's things, set aside several things he wanted to stay in the family: Barbara was given Ethel's big brass bed and a broach that had belonged to Agnes Zimmermann—an item that Levitt wanted to keep on the women's side of the family.

On October 10, 1984, nearly everything else of Ethel's went up for auction, including the special Tony Award she received in 1972, the rifle from the *Annie Get Your Gun* revival, her "Sarah Bernhardt cup" from Josh Logan, her furniture, clothing, and jewelry, including the famous gold charm bracelet. A few people bought items to preserve them: Marie Marchesani purchased a watch of Bob Levitt Sr.'s and gave it to Levitt Jr.; Benay Venuta purchased the oil painting she'd done of Merman as Rose and donated it to the Museum of the City of New York. Katz, to whom Ethel had bequeathed a beloved *Panama Hattie* portrait, purchased her iconic charm bracelet.

Radie Harris, the gossip columnist who had followed Merman's career for decades, described the auction:

> It certainly was the first time within my memory that a Tony Award winner has shown such a lack of sentiment in this highly coveted honor. But Ethel was totally unsentimental about any of her personal possessions. I find this especially depressing, since some of these mementos would have been greatly treasured by her son, Bob Levitt, her grandchildren and close friends, like Madeline [G]axton, . . . and so many others. Perhaps that is why . . . so few of her fellow co-workers . . . were represented in the Christie's East turnout. Joshua Logan was among the few exceptions, but he made no bids.[39]

Soon after Ethel's death, a film producer who wanted to make a biopic of Merman's life approached the American Entertainment Enterprise. Would Bob okay it? When Levitt discovered that "the producer had been responsible for throwing the inaugural ball for George Bush, Sr., I lost all interest in placing my mother's life story in his hands."[40] Since then he has kept his mother's memory largely out of the hands of entrepreneurs and has celebrated her memory through more informal and personal venues. It would prove impossible for him (or anybody else) to keep Ethel Merman from living on with others who would memorialize her, in so many ways.

NINETEEN

Afterlife

Ethel Merman was "not just performing all the time.
She's been in the middle of things that have *made history*."

JULE STYNE

Merman's most immediate personal legacy is her family. Today her son, Bob
Levitt, lives in a small, close-knit community north of San Francisco, where he
keeps up with business affairs involving his mother and mentors children in programs in which they write short plays. He devotes considerable energy to his
community and to various other social and political activities. He has an adult
son, Richard. Ethel's son-in-law, Bill Geary, is retired and resides in Sweden with
his wife of forty years. Bill and Ethel Jr.'s son, Michael Geary, lives in Florida,
where he maintains a swimming pool business. His sister, Barbara, works at a
small, innovative theater school in Northern California. At night she sleeps in
her grandma's big brass bed. Tony Cointreau, Ethel's "second son"—and the
family's "historian and archivist," as Levitt puts it—keeps the Merman flame
alive in Manhattan, where he lives with Jim Russo, his partner of four decades.

Of course, Merman's legacy extends far beyond her family. By the time of
Gypsy, Merman remarked she was "turning into a landmark of sorts."[1] It
therefore made sense that several years before her death, this human Broadway "landmark" entered negotiations about renaming the 46th Street Theatre after her,[2] plans that, according to her son, came quite close to material-
izing before she died.

There may be no Ethel Merman Theater today on Broadway, but the star
is far from absent. Just a year after her death, shows and tributes started popping up across the globe. During the mid-1980s, three Japanese women performed as Ethel Merman, reversing the tradition of whites donning the "yellow mask" for gags, as Ethel had done with William Gaxton in *Anything Goes.*
Their "Japanese Ethel" was not a serious homage so much as a good time set

to music. In July 1985, Jack Tinker, theater critic for London's *Daily Mail,* wrote a show called *Call Me Miss Birds Eye,* in which he performed as narrator. This was a tribute that moved chronologically from *Girl Crazy* through *Gypsy* and presented Ethel's hit songs (sung by Libby Morris) interspersed with colorful Merman anecdotes—such as the one that gave *Birds Eye* its title. Reviews were positive: Christopher Edwards, Tinker's colleague at the *Daily Mail,* said it was "staged with wit, skill and professional pride. . . . This is Class with a capital K."[3] Said Clive Hirshorn, "Only one thing is missing . . . Ethel Merman!"[4]

Three years later, U.S. singer Rita McKenzie starred in a one-woman tribute, *Ethel Merman's Broadway: Call Me Ethel!* which ran off-Broadway at the John Houseman Theatre. McKenzie wrote the show with director Christopher Powich, who had interviewed Merman several years before. To spice up the proceedings, they too mixed songs from Merman's career with autobiographical elements and anecdotes (such as her keeping a swear box). McKenzie performed Merm with panache: during "Hostess with the Mostes'," for instance, she treated the audience to 1950s-styled hors d'oeuvres. Tony Cointreau recalls how carefully *Ethel Merman's Broadway* had been researched, and Bob Levitt, in New York for the initial run, told McKenzie he enjoyed it. Others did too; the *New York Times* called it "A Don't Miss!" and Rita McKenzie has been doing the act periodically in venues across the country ever since.

The Myths Take Over

In the years since her death, various mythic images of Merman have taken hold. A prominent iconic image is of Merman as survivor: a woman who lived a long life, lived it loudly, and possessed an unquestioned sense of self and place in that world. This is the singer who introduced Depression audiences to the lines "Don't take it serious / it's too mysterious" in "Life Is Just a Bowl of Cherries." In a way, this is one place where Merman the person and Merman the personality intersect: on being matter-of-fact and optimistic. Another was her ability to remain ordinary in the face of an extraordinary career. To June Squibb, Electra the stripper in *Gypsy,* "Working in the theatre was the most natural thing in the world for Ethel Merman. . . . It was like someone saying, 'Yeah, I dusted today.'"[5] That style has burnished Merman's image with approachability—she is not just Aunt Ethel, but someone comfortingly regular. This is the Ethel who never viewed herself as being "above" working for Sears, singing with a Sanitation Band, doing signings at Korvettes, and so on.

But the extraordinary side of Merman is even bigger. And as a singer and performer she was extraordinary, even if as a person she was not: this Ethel Merman is a kind of superheroine, an Ethel who could not be put down by anybody or, it seemed, by any earthly force; she was the "Atomic Bomb" that headlined clubs in the '60s. Despite Ethel's great physical stamina, this myth of her as woman warrior flies in the face of biographical fact; family members do not forget the men who took advantage of her celebrity, abused her trust, abused her. But that mythic Merm is half saint, half soldier, a figure people summon to come to their aid. In a 2004 song "Change the World," pop singer-satirist Nellie McKay asks who she "should . . . be today" and then sings, "Have to have a plan / Please, Ethel Merman / help me out of this jam!"[6]

Although these iconic Ethels overlap with the "Real Ethel," they rarely coincide fully. Some of the Merman myths, especially those regarding the big voice and big behavior, have utterly outstripped reality. People tend to adapt Ethel Merman to suit whatever they need her to be: pure Broadway queen and musical triumph; Jewish, anti-Semitic, or both; homophobic, lesbian, or both; generous or cheap; loud, sweet; or all of these things at once. So fans make Ethel Merman into or out of their own image.

If the Merman icon is varied, her appreciators are even more so. There are the professional consumers (critics, experts, people in the entertainment industry) and the fans (the regular, ordinary people). Of course, the two groups overlap, but the professional appreciators are assumed to be reasoned, detached observers, while the fans are often considered overinvolved adulators. (*Fans,* after all, are by etymology fanatics.) Supposedly, experts and fans are separated by levels of professionalism, education, and expertise, but with Ethel Merman we can see just how feeble that opposition is. After all, "serious appreciators" can brilliantly assess Merman's place in Broadway history, or give concrete specifics about every show she ever did, or analyze the details of her voice's belt and diction, but so too can many of the "ordinary" fans. These fans, with their unofficial museums of legitimate and pirated recordings, tapes, kinetoscopes, letters, autographs, auction items, and memorabilia, are themselves expert historians. Get one error wrong, and you will hear about it; Ethel devotees love to correct one another, sometimes out of respect for the historical record, sometimes with an eye toward bitchy one-upmanship. What's more, professional appreciators, such as Walter Kerr and Walter Winchell, have often written as if they were nothing more than excited fans themselves, gushing out praises with unabashed enthusiasm.

Merman has never generated neutral responses, and today the intensity of fans' devotion can reach insane, even toxic, levels. Given that Merman was such an overpowering figure to begin with, it's perhaps not surprising that even now she seems to demand intense involvement—despite her actual distaste for that kind of attention from fans. For some followers, competitive zeal is a measure of one's level of devotedness or presumed expertise, providing entrée into a club to which one is either rewarded with or refused membership. Such extreme fandom is particularly vibrant in New York and on Broadway-themed Internet sites, where possessive and peculiar behavior has a flair all its own.

Fans' interactions with one another range from big-hearted generosity to spiteful challenges, and writing this book exposed me to a delirious range of Merman-driven humanity. More than once, people communicated passionately about "their" Ethel or their "Ethel collections" and then shut off like a switch when I said I was writing a book. It was not that they didn't want to go on record, it seemed, but that they were irritated that it was not *their* record. (One of Merman's costars asked me, "How can you write a biography on Ethel Merman if you never *knew* her?") A few people spoke only after learning that this book was contracted by a university press, that is, by one less profit-driven than a commercial press. Others seemed agitated, even to the point of silliness, when this biographer's perspective didn't duplicate their own, such as in not disliking Mary Martin enough or in believing that Merman's importance to gay fans and drag queens merited discussion. The reasons for these strange relations among Ethel's devotees are as varied as the devotees themselves, for fandom—despite its communal nature—is a highly personal affair, and the affair between Merman and her lovers features some rather amazing turf wars.

When money is involved, the Merman universe is as nasty as any other business, and many of the people whose livelihoods depend on the Merman name can be especially touchy. Several performers whose shows announce some homage to Merman, from vocalists to male drag artists, simply refused to discuss someone whose name and image were earning them a living. Thus invested in Ethel Merman, why should they give anything away? These are people who have their own piece of the Merm, just as others hold on to her via a trinket or a souvenir of an encounter (emotional "possessions," which seem a more appropriate way to honor a woman ultimately so detached from her own possessions). Curiously, Merman's family, which stands to have more to gain or lose than anyone in memorializing Ethel Merman, is not part of this competitive world, despite its constant incursion into their lives. Says granddaughter Barbara Geary, "Personally, I think there's room for everyone. My grandmother touched so many people, and there is plenty of her to go around."[7] From Bob Levitt: "In my heart, I know that her memory is served best and enjoyed *more* in an open atmosphere; in sincere, non-proprietary celebration."[8]

In Ethel's Spirit

One professional "Merman lover" who celebrates Merman in an honest, open way is singer Klea Blackhurst. Her passion for Merman is such that, when Ethel died in 1984, a friend had to call her to break the news to her personally. Today her Web site features "The Book of Merman,"[9] a short, well-researched bio that makes clear Blackhurst's respect for the tradition and roots Merman represents to her. (It puns on Blackhurst's Utah origins.) She is an ardent fan of belting: "I will defend that sound to the end." Her mom, she says, was also a belter, adding that while growing up, "I just thought every woman sang like her and Ethel."[10]

In 2001, Blackhurst opened her show of about twenty Merman songs—some famous, some less known (such as *Happy Hunting*'s "Just a Moment Ago") in *Everything the Traffic Will Allow* at Danny's Skyline Room, a New York cabaret club. Response was great: the *New York Times* subtitled its review "Nothing to Hit but the Heights."[11] Like *Call Me Ethel* and *Bird's Eye*, Blackhurst's show consisted of songs peppered with anecdotes in between. In addition to stories about Ethel were stories of her own travels down the Ethel trail, such as her thrill of working with Dody Goodman, an original cast member of *Something for the Boys*. Even the vase of artificial roses on the piano was a show of respect to Ethel and her allergies to flowers.

Her contagious enthusiasm and humor make it easy to like Blackhurst, whose vitality fully conjures up Merman's spirit. Vocally, she shares Merman's great belt and crisp enunciation, her astonishing phrasing, breath, and vocal control. She can also hold the long notes and handle the complex rhythms of Gershwin and the fast pace of Porter, and she works well in slower ballads and love songs as well. (Blackhurst's rendition of "Blow, Gabriel, Blow" is terrifically slower and softer than Merman's.) When I asked her how she prepared for *Everything the Traffic Will Allow*, Blackhurst said she was intent on capturing the Merman *spirit* rather than actually matching the *voice*. "I chose not to imitate Merman," she says. "Rita McKenzie had done it before, and done it very well. I don't think I would have been that good."[12]

Although vocally Bette Midler has less in common with Merman than either Blackhurst or McKenzie, she is widely perceived as quasi-official carrier of the Ethel Merman torch. Midler's persona shares Merman's physical, earthy qualities, her purported "Jewish" ethnicity, and seems to channel the vibrant, lusty chutzpah of Ethel's public image. Like her, she is ample-figured and short and has a robust, down-to-earth presence. Miss Midler has never tried to be a glamour queen and also shares the same lack of upper-crust pretensions Merman was known for. There is also the near-constant twinkle in her eye and her readiness for a naughty joke: after marrying German performance artist Martin Von Haselberg, Midler told the press, "Every night I get dressed up like Poland and he invades me."

Midler's career is an open acknowledgment of predecessors like Merman. She has recorded songs made famous by Ethel and other vocalists from the '40s and '50s, such as Peggy Lee (an entire CD) and the Andrews Sisters ("Boogie-Woogie Bugle Boy"). And she has even walked in some of their very same footsteps, performing, as Merman and Judy Garland had done, at the old Palace Theatre in 1973; she starred in the film *For the Boys* (recalling *Something for the Boys*), and portrayed Jacqueline Susann in *Isn't She Great?* Perhaps the most overt connection to Merman was Midler's role as Mama Rose in the 1993 TV film of *Gypsy.* (Yes, she is better than Rosalind Russell!)

As much as Midler may recall Merman, however, she also reminds us that Ethel can never be reproduced; the two women are products of completely different eras. The Divine Miss M delivers her off-color remarks more publicly than Ethel ever could (or would) have. Her relationship with gay fans, moreover, existed before she was even out of the gate; after appearing on Broadway in *Fiddler on the Roof,* many of Bette's early singing gigs were in New York's gay bath houses popular after Stonewall and before AIDS. And Bette overtly courted a campy persona, doing early performances dressed as a wheelchair-bound mermaid, dedicating a TV special to "truth and beauty," cracking jokes about her aging body (with upper arms taking on a life of their own), all things that may evince the *spirit* of Merman but would never have been possible in the actual circumstances of Ethel's own life and attitude toward her career.

Impersonations

Mimicry and impersonation don't always give the impression of homage, and some performances done in Merman's image don't escape the whiff of ridicule.

These are often the campier Ethel Mermans, versions that invoke not just the voice but also the characteristics attributed to her character and look. Most typically, the performances take her appearance from later years, big bouffant hair, full figure, and colorful dresses and jewelry. Blackhurst explains why this particular Ethel remains stuck in the popular imagination today: "What eventually got remembered about her is what she looked like and sounded like late in life. People aren't really listening; they're remembering her hair style on *Ed Sullivan*, which she shouldn't be memorialized for."[13]

Some of the incarnations suggest that Merman herself resembled a drag queen. Interestingly, as gay theater historian John Clum observes, Merman was "not good" when she did *male* drag ("A Sailor's Not a Sailor . . ."); she was better in "female drag, [as] a pumped-up version of a sassy, tough woman."[14] A&E's *Biography* episode addressed the "camp icon" part of Merman's legacy, showing the kitschy, quasi-drag performance she did as a braided "Swiss Miss" performing a verse of "Alexander's Ragtime Band," from *There's No Business Like Show Business.* Ethel's relation to subsequent drag performers is complex.

Clum maintains that when drag queens "do Garland," it's "an homage": "You can't parody Garland. . . . You can only imitate the physical manner-isms, but not as the sort of parody one does with Merman or Channing,"[15] suggesting that some degree of ridicule—whether affectionate or barbed—always works behind Merm impersonations. It's a curious assertion, given that many drag queens meticulously research "their" Merman in order to portray details accurately in a meaningful homage, not a send-up. David, a drag actor in the American Southwest, says, "Oh, I would *never* do Ethel on the spur of the moment. I would need to go back and look at how she moves her arms, hands, her whole body. She's been done to death, and done so badly it's a shame."[16]

One impersonation of Merman that had special resonance for her son was produced collectively:

> I don't enjoy the experience of watching impersonations of my mother as much as I enjoy their "reasons for being." Ethel Merman is *everybody's* Ethel Merman, but she's only one (living) person's mother, and that's me. When it comes to viewing impersonators, I try to get into a "mermish" frame of mind, but no matter how I approach it, Mom always trumps Merm, and all the im-personations I've seen to date have evoked a slightly uncomfortable, "funny feeling" when I see them. Nothing awful. Sometimes even entertaining. But still—it's never quite comfortable for me. Not since my mother died. When she was alive it was different.

The single exception to this is the Ethel Merman Chorus based here in the [San Francisco] Bay Area. Watching a whole chorus of Ethel Merman "impersonators" lifted me way beyond any feelings I ever had watching one person imitate my mother. Presenting their tribute through over-the-top humor, with everyone singing their hearts out in full voice à la Ethel Merman, the chorus's many impersonal persons capture some of the essence of my mother's astounding style and bravura better than any single-person impersonation I've ever seen.[17]

There is something about impersonating Merman that many people find irresistible. Mention her name, and the most casual fan will give you the brassy voice, perhaps peppered with a saucy anecdote or two. "It is the easiest thing in the world to imitate a *caricature* of Ethel," says Tony Cointreau. He remembers Merman's response to a show they attended in which Carrie Fisher impersonated her. Poking him, Ethel asked, "Is that me?"[18]

Queer Fantasies

More than the actual details of Merman's personality as life story, it's her *assumed* attributes that matter to people. Fans use them as reference points, a sort of celebrity glue that lets them form some kind of community with others. Merman's own heterosexuality hasn't stopped queer perceptions of her from taking on a life of their own, giving people a way to overlay her iconic "toughness" with various sexual meanings and expectations. Merman is an especially pivotal magnet for the cultures of gay male "musical queens," but she is no less important among women of all sexualities. Unlike queer icons such as Garbo, Dietrich, Doris Day, and Barbara Stanwyck, Ethel hardly transgressed conventional gender roles, but something about the earthy autonomy that Merman conveyed in performance gives her a strong, unconventional sexual edge. Said Bob Fosse, "Everyone thought Ethel was butch and maybe a lesbian, but she wasn't. And everyone thought that lovely little Mary [Martin] was Miss Femme, and she was—except next to her gay husband." Clum agrees, "There's always something butch about Merman," as does Stacy Wolf, who found in Mama Rose a Jewish butch performance.[19] For one lesbian fan, Ethel gave her a way to connect to other women: "In about 1987, I placed a personal ad in the *Washington Blade* (the local gay paper in Washington, DC). . . . I included Ethel Merman as one of my 'likes' in the ad. One woman wrote back saying how much she enjoyed Ethel's rapport with Lucy [apparently confusing Ethel Merman with Ethel

Mertz, the character on *I Love Lucy*]. Another woman wrote back who was also a fan of Ethel Merman's. We became friends and exchanged tapes of Merman records."[20]

One of the more aggressively queer reinventions of Ethel Merman is given by Madge Weinstein, a male podcaster. Madge is a fictional mix of flamboyance, pathos, and flatulence in a deep voice, strong New York accent, and attitude. In a 2004 podcast, Madge relayed her fantasized encounter with Ethel Merman, opening with "How I fell in love with a very famous person." Here is some of the printable dialogue: "I had seen *Gypsy* three times and had worn out my record needle playing it. . . . Ethel Merman was *hot*. . . . I knew she was a dyke too, having married and divorced Ernest Borgnine in less than a year. And I saw the way she looked longingly at Gypsy Rose Lee in the show."

Madge sees the name of Ethel's daughter at her father's Bronx funeral home and goes insane. More insane is what follows: Arriving alone at the funeral home, Ethel Merman makes eye contact only with Madge ("a knowing gleam is how I'd describe it"). Madge says, "I felt love. . . . I pictured us growing old together." At a coffee shop, Merman gives Madge a rose pendant that she was planning to give her late daughter for Hanukkah, explaining, "because you remind me of her." Madge asserts, "Ethel was the love of my life . . . she taught me to be strong, to deal with life, and she taught me to be weak, in order to love."

"Madge" makes no attempt to professionalize her account, nor does she try to authenticate the story (e.g., the time and place of Little Ethel's death). It's a tale of hokey erotics that has an appalling crudeness and a strangely poignant pathos that ascribes the fictional lesbianism and Jewishness to Merman so many others have. But more than anything, Madge's podcast knows it's "made up," it's a rewriting of Ethel's history to bring the icon into Madge's own life. This small bit of Web culture (and Ethel is everywhere on the Web) suggests that Ethel Merman could be the mother or the lover of us all.[21]

Remembering Her Voice

Because Ethel Merman is indistinguishable from the Broadway musical, part of the pleasure people take in reinventing her is in considering her performing *other* kinds of music. For instance, when Blackhurst introduces her rendition of one of Merman's ballads on *Everything the Traffic Will Allow,* she says, "Now, for make-out music, I know that Ethel Merman usually isn't on the top of the stack of most people's CD changer." Merman herself gave people the chance to speculate about the big voice of the stage performing music from other worlds when she released *The Ethel Merman Disco Album*. Twenty years later, in fact, when that LP was re-released on CD, a reviewer mused about a possible "Ethel Merman Hip Hop CD" coming out soon. Other fantasy CDs, culled informally from fans familiar with the recording *Merman Does Merman*, include "Merman Does Mitchell" (Joni) or "Merman Does *Carmen*."

When Ethel's friend Roger Edens composed "Lady with a Song" for her, he acknowledged the gap between the typical Merman repertoire and opera in his lyric "you wouldn't want to see me / play Mimi in Bo-he-me." Yet, plenty of vocal experts believe Merman's voice was good enough for opera, and during her lifetime she had plenty of fans in high musical places. Among them was Igor Stravinsky. Lillian Libman, the composer's personal manager and press representative from 1959 until his death in 1971, recalls, "Ethel Merman was one of Stravinsky's favorite 'legit' stars, and when we went to see *Gypsy*, I had to secure seats that practically made us members of the percussion section so that he could satisfy himself that her voice— *'What an instrument! It could fill Madison Square Garden without a microphone!'*— was capable of conquering the liveliest combination of sound."[22] When Arturo Toscanini heard her sing "I Get a Kick out of You" and proclaimed "Castrato!"[23] he gave Merman entrée into not only a different musical world but a differently gendered one as well. Tenor Luciano Pavarotti told Merman that he admired her tessitura, to which the George Eells Ethel added, "Whatever that is."

Merman's voice continues to be reproduced whenever costars reminisce: "Singing a duet with her is thrilling and exciting—and it melts all the wax in your ears" (Jack Klugman).[24] Donald O'Connor said that after recording their duet in *Call Me Madam*, he couldn't hear for three days.[25] Music critic Henry Pleasants, who said that on its own Ethel's voice was "godawful," goes on to note that, like Judy Garland's, Merman's voice was somewhat limited, but both were "natural and exuberant belters." It was not their vocal range that impressed, he writes, but the fact that "their voices sounded bigger than they actually were. . . . They sang with an unfeigned ardor, with an irrepressible joy in singing, especially when they were belting, that persuaded even sophisticated listeners to countenance and applaud sounds not normally considered becoming to well-behaved females."[26]

Media Tributes

The year after Merman's death, Bob Thomas's 1985 biography, *I've Got Rhythm: The Ethel Merman Story*, appeared—surprisingly, the first one ever on the star. The Ethel Merman that Thomas produced, he announced, was not "the Merman that everyone knew: Shoulders squared, feet planted firmly on the stage, tossing her defiant heart all the way to the balcony," but rather "another Ethel Merman: frightened, erratic, explosive, a woman of great sorrows and high achievement."[27] Thomas's biography is not unsympathetic, but the sympathies take a backseat to the sensational copy they give. His research was drawn primarily from interviews with people fresh from Ethel's late-life phase, which he labels the "Angry Years." Bob Levitt finds the portrait of his mother of the time perplexing: "Mom was as proud of herself as ever. She never experienced her life in a diminished way. . . . The sense of her being lonely, bitter, tragic, withdrawn, etc., is simply untrue to what she was really about."[28]

A slightly fuller, if light, appreciation was offered in a 1999 TV bio of Ethel Merman that aired on A&E's *Biography* series. The hour-long show was hosted and narrated by Peter Graves (an odd choice for a Broadway diva but her lead in *Airplane!*), who traces the arc of Merman's life with help from interviewees including Barbara Geary, Tony Cointreau, Jack Klugman, Jerry Orbach, and Mitzi Gaynor (who judiciously does not share the dirty joke Ethel told her when they first met).

In the early 2000s, DVDs appeared for the first time of *Call Me Madam*, the *Ford 50th Anniversary Show*, and other long-unavailable recordings. CDs as well have been reissued and newly anthologized, ranging from *Alexander's Ragtime Band* to a new collection called *Mermania!* One expects more to come, since, as Al F. Koenig Jr. notes, Merman's death effectively coincided with the advent of compact discs. Merman continues to appear to us in every tome that has been published on musical theater, but strangely she remains the solo star of only a handful of books: after Thomas's biography, George Bryan published a "bio-bibliography" reference book in 1992; a second bio, by Geoffrey Mark, came out in 2005;[29] and another is being prepared by an opera critic. Ethel has many other half-lives, sometimes in odd corners: one very tiny Ethel tribute emerged on September 1, 1994, on a postage stamp in which a colorful, 1950s-era Merman joined fellow honorees Ethel Waters, Nat "King" Cole, and Bing Crosby in a series called "Popular Singers"; at the turn of the century, viewers could catch Ethel and Ray Middleton singing

"Anything You Can Do" on TV in commercials for Tide detergent. On the Internet on any given day, eBay offers scores of Merman memorabilia, and dozens of fan sites are devoted to her. (Curiously, the Ethel Merman domain has been purchased by an anonymous San Francisco resident, presumably for resale.) Today, fans have so many options for consuming Miss Merman that one can do so literally: there is an American gourmet chocolate brand called "Ethel M."

Every year without even trying, Ethel's in the Tony Awards ceremony, since celebrating the Broadway theater is impossible without her, whether referencing a show she starred in or playing a song she made famous, usually "There's No Business Like Show Business." In 2003 the Academy Awards ceremony—usually not a big promoter of New York culture—ran a brief kinetoscope of Ethel performing that same song.

—

As a historical figure, Ethel Merman towers over Broadway. With no flops in a forty-year stage career that paralleled the golden age of the American musical (her retirement and death roughly coinciding with its demise), she seems Broadway's human embodiment. For Tony Cointreau, Ethel's role as Broadway legend and great belter is what she will be remembered for in twenty years.[30] Conditions now are such that another Ethel could not come into being again. Her performance style, the songs she sang, and the light book musicals that showcased Merm are gone to history; so, too, the shows written for individual stars. The business of show business has been utterly transformed, and the nature of the entertainment industry doesn't line up with anything of Merman's time. Still, Broadway Ethel will always be around, as surely as other "Ethel Mermans" will continue to be regenerated. Moreover, what's special about Merman's image in afterlife is that it's one people can venerate and also have fun with, opening it up to new appreciations, respectful and playful all at once.

It seems only fitting that Ethel continues to be remade—this woman with a media savvy precocious enough to appreciate how public a production "Ethel Merman" always was. And so for as much as Ethel "stayed the same," as Cointreau and other intimates say, and for as much as her vocal and performance style stayed constant, her long career spanned so many American contexts and periods that Ethel Merman was continually born in new forms, even during her life. As much as she is lost to the historical moment, there is still plenty of "Ethel Merman" to go around. With so many Ethels around us today, she remains as vital and boisterous as ever.

ACKNOWLEDGMENTS

Brass Diva has taught me that writing a biography is a group effort. I've been fortunate that the Ethel Merman world I've inhabited for the last four years has been filled by mostly generous, open-hearted people who shared memories, stories, gossip, and multifaceted appreciations of the Merm.

Without three sources in particular, this book could never have come into existence. First is the Museum of the City of New York. The Theater Collection there is home to Ethel Merman's extensive scrapbook collection and was where I spent over a half year as a visiting scholar going through those scrapbooks—the first writer to tap them in their entirety. My thanks to those who invited me there: Sarah Henry, Debbie Waters, and everyone who made it a pleasure to go in every day in the summer and fall of 2003. Special thanks go to Eileen Kennedy Morales, Marguerite Lanvin, and to volunteers, such as Mary Cope and John Kenrick. Without question, though, my deepest appreciation goes to theater curator Marty Jacobs, a man whose knowledge of Broadway and theater history is outstripped only by his love for cranky, overweight cats.

Al Koenig Jr. is a high school teacher in New Jersey who has spent his adult life researching Merman's career and achievements. When Edward Zimmermann was ailing, Mr. Koenig helped him sustain his daughter's scrapbooks when his vision made it impossible to do so alone. I am grateful to Mr. Koenig for sharing his research collection, his images, contacts, and countless written appreciations. Without his contribution, the appendices—especially the discography—would be but a shell of what they are here, and his eagle eye helped detect errors in other portions of the book as well. Mr. Koenig's enthusiasm for Merman and this project was nearly superhuman: for over four years, hardly a day went by without my receiving multiple communiqués, lists, and essays from him. Thanks in large part to that level of energy, this book sees the light of day now.

Merman's family proved a warm and spirited group who shared their vantage points on an Ethel to whom very few outsiders were privy. I thank Merman's granddaughter Barbara Geary, who relayed Grandma Ethel stories with refreshing candor and good cheer. "Archivist and extended family member" Tony Cointreau spent hours with me on the phone, sharing his memories of life with Merman; his eye for exactitude, moreover, saved this book from several embarrassing inaccuracies. His dedication to the Ethel Merman he knew is a model of loyalty and love. Ethel's son, Bob Levitt Jr., graciously communicated for several years during the writing of this book in long letters, e-mail, and, in July 2004, a personal interview in his small community in Northern California. I appreciate the intricate picture Mr. Levitt shared of his mother; it is my hope that this book illuminates for others the woman he loved and lived with in real time.

I'm happy to express thanks to the helpful staff at the following institutions: everyone at UCLA Arts Special Collections, especially Lauren Buisson and Julie Graham; Jennifer Miller at UCLA's Film and Television Archive; Ned Comstock at the Cinema-Television Library at USC; everyone at the Academy for Motion Picture Arts and Science's Margaret Herrick Library, particularly Stacey Behlmer, Barbara Hall, Val Almenderez, and their dog June, veterans all of the art of love. My gratitude to the inimitable Miles Kruger and the Institute of the American Musical in Los Angeles, and to the staff at the New York Public Library for the Performing Arts, especially Jeremy Megrah, and the Billy Rose Theatre Collection.

I received generous feedback on drafts of *Brass Diva* from Al F. Koenig Jr., Tony Cointreau, Stacy Wolf, Gary Goertz, Barbara Geary, David Lahm, Klea Blackhurst, Jeannette LoVetri, and Bob Levitt. Errors or inaccuracies that remain are my own. Diane Meyer and Arlen Fast provided expert photographic assistance with images. For various other tasks such as typing, fact checking, and bibliographic work, I need to thank Lauryn Bianco, Dale Steiber, James Reel, Teresa Simone, Joy Wilcox, and Diane Weiner.

This biography put me in touch with singer Klea Blackhurst, to whom I'm grateful for our long and lively Merman talks; Miss Blackhurst is a walking Merman archive in her own right and had much to contribute about Merman and the powerhouse voice. Thanks to her I was also able to view many unavailable Merman film and TV recordings. I was also fortunate to talk at length to the onetime president of the Ethel Merman Fan Club, Marilyn

Cantor Baker. Mrs. Baker is the undisputed queen of Merman memories, and she shared recollections that stretch back to the 1930s; I thank her for her generous and spirited discussions and for the *Gypsy* picture that looked down on me in my office as I wrote.

I obtained other Merman recollections and thoughts from the talented Kaye Ballard (a fan of Merm and fellow *Gypsy* performer) and Ethel's *Art of Love* costar, Elke Sommer, both of whom graciously spoke on short notice. At Manhattan's Roosevelt Hospital, Susan Fenton (director of Volunteer Services) spoke of Ethel's long-running history with the hospital, and it was she who put me in contact with Ruth Munson, the volunteer who worked at Roosevelt with Merman during the 1970s—and who still volunteers at the hospital today, as she enters her tenth decade.

Carol Frieden and her husband, Jerry, interrupted their holiday to speak about their firsthand experience with the late Ethel Geary. Various voice and music professionals in New York shared their observations about Ethel Merman's voice and career. Special thanks to Gary Thor Wedow, chorus master of the New York City Opera, and to chorus members Ed Zimmerman and Jill Bosworth, for our lively discussion. Vocal expert Jeannette LoVetri shared her thoughts on the Merman belt and offered a welcome historical and physiological perspective; I thank her for her insight and generosity. Voice trainer William Riley and voice therapist Linda Carroll offered ideas, and David Lahm, the son of Dorothy Fields, exhibited both patience and generosity in discussing Merman, his mother, and *Annie Get Your Gun*.

A host of other people shared thoughts on Ethel and on the work involved in producing a biography such as this. For their stories, guidance, and helping hands, I thank (among others): Charles Affron, Kay Armatage, Cari Beauchamp, Jerry Beck, Arthur Boehm, Ralph Bravaco, Donna Cozzo, the late George Custen, Mary Driscoll, Arlen Fast, Krin Gabbard, Darlene Goertz, Gary Goertz, Kristin Graves, Stephen Mo Hanan, John Haskell, John Henrick, the late Edna Hill, Marty Jacobs, Miguel Juarez, Kay Kalinak, Liz Kennedy, John Kenrick, Louise Koehn, Skip Koenig, my agent Sydelle Kramer, Miles Krueger, Mark Langer, Marguerite Lanvin, David Lugowski, Bill Luhr, Sharon Mazer, Richard McQuillan, James Parish, Robert Parish, Joseph Patton, Kathleen Powers, Bobbi Prebis, James Reel, Morgan Sills, Charles Slocumb, Eric Smoodin, Chris Straayer, Liz Weis, Diane Wiener, Stacy Wolf, and Sande Zeig. I would also like to thank the people I received tremendous help from at the University of California Press, especially Mary Francis, Sue Heinemann, and Kalicia Pivirotto.

Heartfelt thanks to my friends, colleagues, family, and students for all of their suggestions, stories, and support during the time it took to write this book. And finally, I want to express my enormous gratitude to the large and lively communities of Ethel fans and appreciators for sharing all of their stories and encounters—some real, some imagined—about La Merm.

A WORD ON THE SCRAPBOOKS

From the start, it was both the press and the public that "made" Ethel Merman, Broadway supernova, out of the Astoria stenographer who was born Ethel Agnes Zimmermann. In a way, this is an oddity, because in early Depression-era America, media and promotional industries weren't mass-marketing stars to the extent that they did later, *particularly* for stage players; Broadway has never been as fully under the grip of national publicity machines as Hollywood studios. To an extent, Merman's celebrity was allowed to develop organically, especially at the outset. (Again, this is not to say the mass media weren't involved, for without them, "Ethel Merman" couldn't have been produced at all.) But Ethel's appointment of ten-year-old Marilyn Cantor as president of the Ethel Merman Fan Club in the mid-1930s clearly indicates that we are talking of another era. No publicity department oversaw this Merman, nor could it have anticipated the other Mermans to come or her place outside Broadway, living in the recordings owned by middle-class Americans, in her guest spots on their TV sets, and in the imaginations of fans who never even encountered her.

The single most important document I found that shows the process of "the making of Ethel Merman" is the fifty-plus-volume scrapbook collection that details her professional life. Housed at the Museum of the City of New York, the largely intact collection runs from the early '30s through the '70s. Portions have found their way into other institutions such as the Library at Lincoln Center and into the hands of individuals; the 1970–83 books are with a private collector who helped Merman maintain them late in her life. It was easily the most compelling source consulted for this project, showing the processes and mechanisms that produced Ethel Merman. These volumes contain every public piece of information printed about her, flattering or unflattering, with as many as seventy-five copies of the *same* syndicated photo from papers around the country pasted on adjoining pages. For the peruser who believes Merman maintained them, reading the scrapbooks transforms the star into nothing short of a self-absorbed egomaniac. But their actual caretaker was Ethel's father, Edward Zimmermann, and this knowledge lends them a very different meaning, painting a compelling portrait of paternal devotion and love, however compulsively enacted. Edward included *any* published reference to his daughter, no matter how trivial or repetitious: one-sentence announcements comparing new singers to Ethel, erroneous gossip reports, Ethel advertising shoes "like you can get in Hollywood!" in a Manhattan dress shop. Tabs glued onto newspaper clippings indicate that Zimmermann subscribed to a national clipping service to obtain all print stories that mentioned his daughter, items he meticulously arranged in chronological sequence.

From the outset, Edward Zimmermann seemed to know that the scrapbooks were recording the history of a celebrity whose life would interest more people than the immediate family and seemed to be aware that the scrapbooks could help memorialize his daughter's fame. He wasn't keeping family records; these big, green clothbound books of her career are separate from the extensive private ones in which Merman maintained personal and family events. In that scrapbook series, each of her children received his or her own black-bound volume.

To an extent, Ethel was eager to control the way she was produced publicly. Over her life, she dictated two autobiographies: the first, *Who Could Ask for Anything More?* in 1954 to Pete Martin, and the second, *Merman: An Autobiography,* six years before her death, in 1978, to George Eells. (A biography by Bob Thomas appeared shortly after her death.) Once in a while, the scrapbooks reveal her desire to control the material. Three photos of her from the younger days, for instance, have her stern handwriting on the back: "Do not reproduce without my permission!"[1]

Hardly unique for wanting to guard her private life, Ethel was more unusual for considering it so fully distinct from her public one, especially at this early point in her career. For in the late 1920s, the star system, even in Hollywood, was just getting off the ground. Ethel's attitude toward her celebrity status was as atypical as it was ahead of its time. So was her awareness that "Ethel Merman" was someone created out of a meshing of stage and film roles, interviews, songs, public appearances, endorsements, reviews, and rumors. The scrapbooks, for instance, contain dozens of misreports about the beaux she was reported to be dating, the fights she was supposed to have started, the smart-assed remarks she was supposed to have made. Ethel seldom corrected them, and the public record rarely bothered her. She knew that Ethel Merman was *not* Ethel Agnes Zimmermann.

Today, most Americans of a certain age, and almost anyone who lives in New York, remember Ethel Merman, as does anyone interested in theater and musical comedy. For other people though, her star power—like that of the Broadway musical theater more generally—has faded away, to the point that this amazing singer is confused with Esther Williams or even Ethel Mertz. Yet Ethel Merman is still with us more than we know. Every time an awards ceremony plays "There's No Business Like Show Business," there is a bit of her in the air; any show or study of Broadway musicals features her; and anytime there is a reference to a vocalist belting out a song, Merman is there, firmly on her throne. Decades after her death in 1984, stories about Ethel Merman continue to run through the streets of Manhattan just as surely as the Hudson hugs its West Side.

DISCOGRAPHY

This discography was produced primarily by Al F. Koenig Jr. with additional assistance from James Reel. The author is grateful to both.

This list of Ethel Merman's audio recordings focuses on first releases of material commercially available to the public. The discography consequently disregards test pressings, acetates of radio and television broadcasts, a V-Disc, and radio discs used to promote films. Nor does it include decades' worth of reissues, including major ones such as Decca's *Ethel Merman: A Musical Autobiography* (1956). With the advent of the LP in the 1950s, album releases, rather than nearly concurrent singles, take precedence here.

Items are given chronologically by date of recording, although several did not receive official release until many years later (notably the material on *Merman in the Movies* and prewar songs included in retrospective compilation albums in the LP era). In a few instances in which radio or television material was issued years after the broadcast, such as the radio duets with Bing Crosby, the most complete album has been included here, even if excerpts had already been issued. For original cast recordings and compilations, only songs featuring Merman and artists singing with her are listed.

"Wipe That Frown Right off Your Face," from *Ireno* (1931). On *Legends of the Musical Stage.* Take Two TT 104.

"Satan's Li'l Lamb," "I Got a Right to Sing the Blues" (1932). RCA Victor VIC 24145.

"How Deep Is the Ocean?" "I'll Follow You" (1932). RCA Victor VIC 24146.

"I Surrender, Dear" (1932). On *The Thirties' Girls.* Totem 1026.

"Eadie Was a Lady" (1932). Brunswick 6456.

"You're a Builder Upper," "An Earful of Music" (1934). Brunswick 6995.

"I Get a Kick out of You," "You're the Top" (1934). Brunswick 7342.

"He Reminds Me of You," cut from *We're Not Dressing* (1934). On *Personalities on Parade,* vol. 2. PP-2.

"An Earful of Music," "Mandy," "Ice Cream Fantasy," from *Kid Millions* (1934). Classic International Filmusicals CIF 3007.

"The Lady in Red," "It's the Animal in Me" (1935). Brunswick 7491.

"Down in the Depths," "It's De-Lovely" (1936). Liberty Music Shop 206.

"Anything Goes," from *Anything Goes* (1936). Caliban 6043.

"Ridin' High," "Red, Hot, and Blue" (1936). Liberty Music Shop 207.

"Satan's Holiday," from *Follow the Leader* (1930); "It's Just a New Spanish Custom," from *We're Not Dressing* (1934; with Leon Errol); "It's the Animal in Me," from *The Big Broadcast of 1936* (1935); "I Get a Kick out of You," "You're the Top," "Shanghai-De-Ho," from *Anything Goes* (1936; with Bing Crosby); "First You Have Me High, Then You Have Me Low," "Calabash Pipe," from *Strike Me Pink* (1936; with Eddie Cantor); "Hot and Happy," "You Appeal to Me," "You Are the Music to the Words in My Heart," from *Happy Landing* (1938); "With You on My Mind," "Why Not String Along with Me?" from *Straight, Place and Show* (1938); selections from *Alexander's Ragtime Band*. On *Merman in the Movies: 1930–1938* (compiled from original soundtracks). Encore Records ST 101.

"With You on My Mind" from *Straight, Place and Show* (1938; unedited, fuller version than on Encore ST 101). Choice Cuts ST 500/1.

"Why Not String Along with Me?" from *Straight, Place and Show* (1938; fuller version than on Encore ST 101). Radiola 2MR 1718.

"With You on My Mind," "Why Not String Along with Me?" from *Straight, Place and Show* (1938). Vertinge 2000.

"Say It with Music," "A Pretty Girl Is Like a Melody," "Blue Skies," "Pack Up Your Sins and Go to the Devil," "My Walking Stick," "Everybody Step," "Heat Wave," from *Alexander's Ragtime Band* (1938). Hollywood Soundstage 406.

"Marching along with Time" (1938). On *Girls of the 30s*. Pelican LP 122.

"A Lady Needs a Change," "I'll Pay the Check" (1939). Liberty Music Shop 256.

"This Is It," "Just a Little Bit More" (1939). Liberty Music Shop 257.

"It's All Yours" (1939; with Jimmy Durante), "Little Lamb" (unknown recording date). On *Forgotten Broadway*, vol. 2. Forgotten Broadway T 102.

"Friendship" (1940; with Bert Lahr). On *Stars over Broadway*. Star-Tone ST 214.

"Let's Be Buddies" (with Joan Carroll), "Make It Another Old Fashioned, Please," "My Mother Would Love You," "I've Still Got My Health," from *Panama Hattie* (1940). Decca A-203.

"I'm Throwing a Ball Tonight," "Make It Another Old Fashioned, Please," from *Panama Hattie* (1940). On *Cole Porter Live*. JJA 19745.

"Marching thru Berlin," from *Stage Door Canteen* (1943). On *Curtain Calls*. 100/11–12.

"Marching thru Berlin," from *Stage Door Canteen* (1943; version with male quintet), "Move It Over." RCA Victor 20–1521.

"Something for the Boys" (1944). On *Cole Porter 1924–1944*. JJA-19732.

"Something for the Boys," "Hey, Good Lookin'," "He's a Right Guy," "I'm in Love with a Soldier Boy," "There's a Happy Land in the Sky," "By the Mississinewa," "Finale," from *Something for the Boys* (1944; with Bill Johnson, Allen Jenkins, Betty Bruce). AEI 1157.

"Doin' What Comes Natur'lly," "Moonshine Lullaby," "You Can't Get a Man with a Gun," "I'm an Indian Too," "They Say It's Wonderful," "Anything You Can Do," "I Got Lost in His Arms," "I Got the Sun in the Morning," from *Annie Get Your Gun* (1946; with Leon Bibb, John Garth, Clyde Turner, Ray Middleton). Decca DL 8001 (also issued as 78-rpm album A-468 and 45-rpm album 9–12).

"You're the Top," "I Get a Kick out of You," "Eadie Was a Lady," "Blow, Gabriel, Blow," "I Got Rhythm," "It's De-Lovely," "Life Is Just a Bowl of Cherries" (1947). On *Ethel Merman: Songs She Has Made Famous*. Decca DL 5053 (also issued as 78-rpm album A-681).

Medley ("Love in Bloom," "I Got Rhythm," "Mexicali Rose," "I Get a Kick out of You"), "Your All-Time Flop Parade" (two versions), "Dearie," "Anything You Can Do" (1947–50; with Bing Crosby). On *Bing Crosby and His Hollywood Guests*. Avid 626.

"The Hostess with the Mostes' on the Ball," "Washington Square Dance," "Can You Use Any Money Today?" "Marrying for Love," "The Best Thing for You," "Something to Dance About," "You're Just in Love," from *Call Me Madam* (studio cast; 1950; with Dick Haymes). Decca DL 8035 (also issued as 78-rpm album A-818 and 45-rpm album 9–166).

"A Little Girl from Little Rock," "Diamonds Are a Girl's Best Friend," "Dearie," "I Said My Pajamas," "It's So Nice to Have a Man around the House," "(If I Knew You Were Comin') I'd've Baked a Cake," "Calico Sal," "She's Shimmyin' on the Beach Again," "Hawaii," "Ukulele Lady," "The Lake Song," "Don't Believe It," "Once upon a Nickel," "Oldies," "Love Is the Reason," "The World Is Your Balloon," "Make the Man Love Me," "You Say the Nicest Things," "A Husband; A Wife," "If You Catch a Little Cold." On *Ethel Merman: The World Is Your Balloon* (1950s, from Decca singles; with Ray Bolger, Jimmy Durante). MCA 1839.

"The Hostess with the Mostes' on the Ball," "Can You Use Any Money Today?" "The International Rag," "You're Just in Love," "The Best Thing for You," "Finale: You're Just in Love / Something to Dance About," from *Call Me Madam* (film cast, 1953; with Donald O'Connor, George Sanders). Decca 5465 (also issued as 78-rpm album A-936 and 45-rpm album ED-508).

"Ethel Merman and Mary Martin Duet from the *Ford 50th Anniversary Television Show*" (1953). Decca DL 7027 (also issued as 78-rpm album DU-999 and 45-rpm album ED-593).

"There's No Business Like Show Business," "When the Midnight Choo-Choo Leaves for Alabam'," "Play a Simple Melody," "A Sailor's Not a Sailor," "Alexander's Ragtime Band," from *There's No Business Like Show Business* (1954; with Dan Dailey, Mitzi Gaynor, Donald O'Connor, Johnnie Ray). Decca DL 8091 (also issued as 78-rpm album DAU-957 and 45-rpm album ED-828).

"Anything Goes," "You Do Something to Me," "I Get a Kick out of You," "You're the Top," "Just One of Those Things," "Blow, Gabriel, Blow," "Friendship," from *Anything Goes* (TV cast, 1954; with Frank Sinatra). "Ridin' High," "Fresh as a

Daisy," "Let's Be Buddies, "Make It Another Old Fashioned, Please," from *Panama Hattie* (TV cast, 1954). Larynx 567.

"The Band Played On," "The Bowery," "On a Saturday Night," "While Strolling through the Park One Day," "I've Got Rings on My Fingers," "In My Merry Oldsmobile," "In the Good Old Summertime," "Waltz Me around Again, Willie," "On a Bicycle Built for Two," "She'll Be Comin' 'Round the Mountain," "Put on Your Old Gray Bonnet," "M-I-S-S-I-S-S-I-P-P-I," "Listen to the Mockingbird," "You Tell Me Your Dream (I'll Tell You Mine)," "School Days," "Memories," "Way Down Yonder in New Orleans," "Somebody Stole My Gal," "Smiles," "Sweet Georgia Brown," "Take Back Your Gold," "Frankie and Johnny," "On Moonlight Bay," "By the Light of the Silv'ry Moon," "Shine On, Harvest Moon," "That Old Gang of Mine," "Sweet Adeline," "Oh, Johnny, Oh, Johnny, Oh!" "Dear Little Boy of Mine," "Forty-five Minutes from Broadway," "Mary's a Grand Old Name," "Give My Regards to Broadway." On *Memories: 40 Great Songs from the Gay '90s to the Roaring '20s* (1955; with the Mitchell Boys' Choir, Old Timers' Quartet). Decca DL 9028 (45 rpm released as 2276–2278).

"You're Just in Love," from *Call Me Madam* (1955; with Russell Nype, from Ed Sullivan's TV series *Toast of the Town*). On *Original Performances from the Best of Broadway Musicals*. Columbia House P6S 5936.

"It's Good to Be Here," "Mutual Admiration Society," "Mr. Livingstone," "This Is What I Call Love," "A New-Fangled Tango," "The Game of Love," "Happy Hunting," "I'm a Funny Dame," "Grand Finale," from *Happy Hunting* (1956; with Virginia Gibson, Leon Belasco, Fernando Lamas). RCA Victor EOC/LOC-1026.

"Have Yourself a Merry Little Christmas" (1958). On *Greetings from Broadway!* AEI 1176.

"Some People," "Small World," "Mr. Goldstone, I Love You," "You'll Never Get Away from Me," "Everything's Coming Up Roses," "Together," "Rose's Turn," from *Gypsy* (1959; with Jack Klugman, Sandra Church). Columbia OL 5420/OS 2017. 45-rpm set A-5420.

"I Got Rhythm," "This Is It," "Do I Love You?" "Sam and Delilah," "Life Is Just a Bowl of Cherries," "Blow, Gabriel, Blow," "You're an Old Smoothie," "Down in the Depths on the 90th Floor," "But Not for Me," "Friendship," "You're the Top." On *Merman . . . Her Greatest!* (1961). Reprise R/R9–6032.

"It's De-Lovely" (1962; with Bob Hope). On *Cole Porter Live.* JJA 19745.

"Just a Lady with a Song," "I Got Rhythm," "This Is It," "A Lot of Livin' to Do," medley ("Doin' What Comes Natur'lly," "The Hostess with the Mostes' on the Ball," "I Got the Sun in the Morning," "Life Is Just a Bowl of Cherries," "You're the Top," "You're an Old Smoothie," "Let's Be Buddies," "Anything Goes," "It's De-Lovely," "Small World," "Everything's Coming Up Roses"), "They Say It's Wonderful," "Make It Another Old Fashioned, Please," "You Can't Get a Man with a Gun," "Blow, Gabriel, Blow," "There's No Business Like Show Business." On *Merman in Vegas* (1962). Reprise R9–6062.

"Be a Witch!," "Keep a Gloomy Thought," "An Elephant Never Forgets." On *The Return to Oz* (1962). RFO 101.

"There's No Business Like Show Business" (1963; with Judy Garland, Barbra Streisand). On *The Judy Garland Show: Looking Back*. Kismet 1002.

Medley ("Friendship," "Let's Be Buddies," "You're the Top," "You're Just in Love," "It's De-Lovely," "Together") (1964; with Judy Garland). On *The Judy Garland Show: The Greatest Duets*. Broadcast Tributes BTRIB 0002.

"Everything's Coming Up Roses," with new Sondheim lyrics supporting John Lindsay's New York mayoral candidacy. On *The Lindsay Record* (1965). Columbia CSP 261.

"An Old-Fashioned Wedding," "Doin' What Comes Natur'lly," "You Can't Get a Man with a Gun," "There's No Business Like Show Business," "They Say It's Wonderful," "Moonshine Lullaby," "I'm an Indian Too," "I Got Lost in His Arms," "I Got the Sun in the Morning," "Anything You Can Do" (with Bruce Yarnell, Ronn Carroll, Rufus Smith). On *Annie Get Your Gun* (1966 revival cast). RCA Victor LOC/ LSO-1124.

"Love, Look in My Window," "World, Take Me Back." On *Ethel Merman Sings the New Songs from Hello, Dolly!* (1970). Bar-Mic Records (no number).

"You're the Top," "I Got Rhythm," "You're Just in Love," "Alexander's Ragtime Band," "I Got Lost in His Arms," "Eadie Was a Lady," "There's No Business Like Show Business," "They Say It's Wonderful," "It's De-Lovely," "I Get a Kick out of You," "Everything's Coming Up Roses," "Blow, Gabriel, Blow." On *Merman Sings Merman* (1972). London XPS-901.

"An Old-Fashioned Wedding," "Doin' What Comes Natur'lly," "You Can't Get a Man with a Gun," "There's No Business Like Show Business," "They Say It's Wonderful," "Moonshine Lullaby," "I'm an Indian Too," "I Got Lost in His Arms," "I Got the Sun in the Morning," "Anything You Can Do" (with Lesley Fyson, Neilson Taylor, Benay Venuta). On *Ethel Merman Sings Annie Get Your Gun* (1973). London XPS-905.

"Gee, but It's Good to Be Here," "Whispering," "Some People / People," "Sunrise, Sunset," "What Kind of Fool Am I?," "Ridin' High," "Someone to Watch Over Me," "The Impossible Dream," "On a Clear Day," "Nothing Can Stop Me Now." On *Ethel's Ridin' High* (1974). London PS-909.

Medley ("Doin' What Comes Natur'lly," "The Hostess with the Mostes' on the Ball," "I Got the Sun in the Morning," "Life Is Just a Bowl of Cherries," "I Got Rhythm," "You're an Old Smoothie," "Let's Be Buddies," "Anything Goes," "It's De-Lovely," "Small World," "Everything's Coming Up Roses"), "There's No Business Like Show Business." On *A Gala Tribute to Joshua Logan* (1975). Friends of the Theatre Collection (no number).

"Send in the Clowns" (with Mary Martin), medley ("It's Good to Be Here," "Blow, Gabriel, Blow," "Hello, Dolly!") (with Martin), "There's No Business Like Show Business" (with Martin). On *Together on Broadway* (1977). Friends of the Theatre Collection (no number).

"There's No Business Like Show Business," "Everything's Coming Up Roses," "I Get a Kick out of You," "Something for the Boys," "Some People," "Alexander's Ragtime Band," "I Got Rhythm." On *The Ethel Merman Disco Album* (1979). A&M SP-4775.

"Lady with a Song," "It's Good to Be Here," medley ("They Say It's Wonderful," "Some People / People," "Alexander's Ragtime Band," "I Get a Kick out of You," "Blow, Gabriel, Blow," "There's No Business Like Show Business"), and encores "What I Did for Love," "Someone to Watch Over Me." On *Ethel Merman at Carnegie Hall* (1982). Friends of the Theatre Collection (no number).

Girl Crazy (1930)

Book by Guy Bolton and John McGowan; music by George Gershwin; lyrics by Ira Gershwin; produced by Alex A. Aarons and Vinton Freedley; directed by Alexander Leftwich;[1] dances by George Hale; settings by Donald Oenslager; costumes by Kiviette; Antonio and Renee DeMarco (dancers); Red Nichols and his orchestra, Roger Edens at the piano (replacing Al Siegel); orchestra directed by Earl Busby.

Opened at the Alvin Theatre on October 14, 1930. 272 performances.

PRIMARY CAST

Allen Kearns	Danny Churchill
Ginger Rogers	Molly Gray
Willie Howard	Gieber Goldfarb
Peggy O'Connor	Patsy West
Ethel Merman	Kate Fothergill
William Kent	Slick Fothergill

MUSICAL NUMBERS

Act I

Bidin' My Time	The Foursome
The Lonesome Cowboy	Cowpunchers
Could You Use Me	Ginger Rogers and Allen Kearns
Bronco Busters	Dudeens and Cowboys
Barbary Coast	Peggy O'Connor, Eunice Healey, Olive Brady, Chorus
Specialty	Eunice Healey
Embraceable You	Ginger Rogers and Allen Kearns

Finaletto	Willie Howard, William Kent
Sam and Delilah	Ethel Merman
I Got Rhythm	Ethel Merman and Chorus

Act II

Land of the Gay Caballero	Ensemble
Specialty Dance	The DeMarcos
But Not for Me	Ginger Rogers and Willie Howard
Treat Me Rough	William Kent and Chorus
Boy, What Love Has Done to Me	Ethel Merman
Cactus Time in Arizona	Ginger Rogers and Chorus

George White's Scandals (1931)

Sketches by George White, Lew Brown, and Irving Caesar; songs by Lew Brown and Ray Henderson; produced and directed by George White; settings by Joseph Urban; costumes by Charles LeMaire; orchestra directed by Al Goodman.

Opened at the Apollo Theatre, September 14, 1931. 202 performances.

PRIMARY CAST

Ross McLean, Rudy Vallee, Hazel Boffinger, Everett Marshall, Ethel Colt, Willie and Eugene Howard, Alice Frohman, Ethel Merman, Ray Bolger

MUSICAL NUMBERS

Act I

The Marvelous Empire State	Ray Bolger
Life Is Just a Bowl of Cherries	Ethel Merman
Beginning of Love	Loomis Sisters
The Thrill Is Gone	Everett Marshall
This Is the Missus	Rudy Vallee
Ladies and Gentlemen, That's Love	Ethel Merman
That's Why Darkies Were Born	Everett Marshall

Act II

Song of the Foreign Legion	Everett Marshall
Here It Is	Joan Abbott

My Song	Rudy Vallee and Ethel Merman
Back from Hollywood	Barbara Blair, Julia Gorman,
	Hilda Knight, Betty Allen
The Good Old Days	Rudy Vallee, Willie Howard,
	Ethel Merman
The Wonder Bar	Entire Company

Humpty Dumpty (1932)

Book by B. G. DeSylva and Laurence Schwab; additional dialogue by Sid Silvers; songs by Nacio Herb Brown and Richard A. Whiting; produced by Laurence Schwab and B. G. DeSylva; directed by Laurence Schwab; dances by George Hale; settings by Cleon Throckmorton and Charles LeMaire; costumes by Kiviette; orchestra under the direction of Lou Silvers.

Opened at the Nixon Theatre, Pittsburgh, September 26, 1932. Closed in Pittsburgh.

PRIMARY CAST

Lou Holtz	Sam Moscow
Sid Silvers	Louis Mosco
June Knight	Irene Parker
Ethel Merman	Wanda Brill
Oscar Ragland	Jay Gordon

Take a Chance (1932)

Book by B. G. DeSylva and Laurence Schwab; additional dialogue by Sid Silvers; songs by Nacio Herb Brown and Richard Whiting; additional songs by Vincent Youmans; produced by Laurence Schwab and B. G. DeSylva; directed by Edgar MacGregor; musical numbers directed by Bobby Connolly; settings by Cleon Throckmorton; costumes by Kiviette and Charles LeMaire; orchestra under the direction of Max Meth; Sam Gurski's Recording Orchestra.

Opened at the Apollo Theatre on November 26, 1932. 243 performances.

PRIMARY CAST

Jack Haley	Duke Stanley
Sid Silvers	Louis Webb
June Knight	Toni Ray
Ethel Merman	Wanda Brill

Jack Whiting	Kenneth Raleigh
Douglas Wood	Andrew Raleigh
Mitzi Mayfair	Consuelo Raleigh

Act I

The Life of the Party	Nightclub Girls and Guests
Should I Be Sweet	June Knight
So Do I	Jack Whiting, June Knight, Guests
I Got Religion	Ethel Merman
She's Nuts about Me	Jack Haley
Tickled Pink	Jack Whiting and Girls
Turn Out the Lights	Sid Silvers, Jack Haley, Jack Whiting, Girls
Charity	Guests
I Long to Belong to You	Jack Whiting and June Knight
Rise and Shine	Ethel Merman and Ensemble

Act II

Tonight Is Opening Night	Ensemble
You're an Old Smoothie	Jack Haley and Ethel Merman
Eadie Was a Lady	Ethel Merman and Ensemble
Should I Be Sweet (Revue Version)	June Knight and Girls

Anything Goes (1934)

Book by P. G. Wodehouse and Guy Bolton; revised by Howard Lindsay and Russel Crouse; music and lyrics by Cole Porter; produced by Vinton Freedley, Inc.; directed by Howard Lindsay; dances by Robert Alton; settings by Donald Oenslager; gowns by Jenkins; musical direction by Earl Busby.

Opened at the Alvin Theatre on November 21, 1934. 420 performances. Benay Venuta replaced Merman beginning July 22, 1935.

PRIMARY CAST

William Gaxton	Billy Crocker
Ethel Merman	Reno Sweeney
Leslie Barrie	Sir Evelyn Oakleigh

| Bettina Hall | Hope Harcourt |
| Victor Moore | Rev. Dr. Moon |

MUSICAL NUMBERS

Act I

I Get a Kick out of You	Ethel Merman and William Gaxton
Bon Voyage	Ensemble
All through the Night	Bettina Hall and William Gaxton
Sailor's Chanty	The Foursome
Where Are the Men?	Vera Dunn, Angels, Petty Officers, Girls
You're the Top	Ethel Merman and William Gaxton
Anything Goes	Ethel Merman, Foursome, Ensemble

Act II

Public Enemy Number One	Passengers
Blow, Gabriel, Blow	Ethel Merman and Ensemble
Be Like a Bluebird	Victor Moore
All through the Night (Reprise)	Bettina Hall and William Gaxton
Buddy, Beware	Ethel Merman
I Get a Kick out of You (Reprise)	Ethel Merman
The Gypsy in Me	Bettina Hall and Girls

Red, Hot and Blue! (1936)

Book by Howard Lindsay and Russel Crouse; music and lyrics by Cole Porter; produced by Vinton Freedley; directed by Howard Lindsay; choreographed by George Hale; settings by Donald Oenslager; costumes by Constance Ripley; orchestra under the direction of Frank Tours.

Opened at the Alvin Theatre on October 29, 1936. 183 performances.

PRIMARY CAST

| Ethel Merman | "Nails" O'Reilly Duquesne |
| Jimmy Durante | "Policy" Pinkle |

Vivian Vance	Vivian
Bob Hope	Bob Hale
Thurston Crane	Sonny Hadley
Polly Walters	Peaches La Fleur

Stars in Your Eyes (1939)

Book by J. P. McEvoy; music by Arthur Schwartz; lyrics by Dorothy Fields; produced by Dwight Deere Wiman; directed by Joshua Logan; choreographed by Carl Randall; set design by Jo Mielziner; costumes by John Hambleton; musical direction by Al Goodman.

Opened at the Majestic Theatre on February 9, 1939. 126 performances.

PRIMARY CAST

Ethel Merman	Jeanette Adair
Mildred Natwick	Bess
Jimmy Durante	Bill
Robert Ross	Darrow
Richard Carlson	John Blake
Tamara Toumanova	Tata
Richard Barbee	Dawson

MUSICAL NUMBERS

Act I

Places, Everybody	Company
One Brief Moment	Walter Cassel, Paul Godkin, Ensemble
This Is It	Ethel Merman, Walter Cassel, Edward Kane, Robert Shanley, Davis Cunningham
All the Time	Richard Carlson and Tamara Toumanova
Self-Made Man	Jimmy Durante
Okay for Sound	Rennie McEvoy, Dawn Roland, Ensemble
A Lady Needs a Change	Ethel Merman
Terribly Attractive	Jimmy Durante and Mildred Natwick
Just a Little Bit More	Ethel Merman
Nightclub Ballet	Tamara Toumanova, Ted Gary, Dan Dailey Jr., Ensemble
Just a Little Bit More (Reprise)	Richard Carlson

Act II

As of Today	Rennie McEvoy, Frances Rands, Mary Wickes, Davis Cunningham, David Morris, Kathryn Mayfield, Betty Hunter, Dan Dailey Jr., Ensemble

He's Goin' Home	Jimmy Durante and Ensemble
I'll Pay the Check	Ethel Merman
Never a Dull Moment	Dawn Roland, Ted Gary, Dan Dailey Jr., Rennie McEvoy, Ensemble
This Is It (Reprise)	Ethel Merman
Court Ballet	Tamara Toumanova, Corps de Ballet and Walter Cassel, Edward Kane, Robert Shanley, Davis Cunningham
It's All Yours	Ethel Merman and Jimmy Durante

DuBarry Was a Lady (1939)

Book by Herbert Fields and B. G. DeSylva; songs by Cole Porter; produced by B. G. DeSylva; directed by Edgar MacGregor; choreographed by Robert Alton; settings and costumes by Raoul Pène Du Bois; orchestra under the direction of Gene Salzer. Opened at the 46th Street Theatre on December 6, 1939. 408 performances.

PRIMARY CAST

Bert Lahr	Louis Blore
Ethel Merman	May Daly

MUSICAL NUMBERS

Act I

Where's Louie?	Ensemble
Ev'ry Day a Holiday	Betty Grable, Charles Walters, Ensemble
It Ain't Etiquette	Bert Lahr and Jean Moorehead
When Love Beckoned	Ethel Merman
Come On In	Ethel Merman and Ensemble
Dance	Betty Grable and Charles Walters
Dream Song	Four Internationals
Mesdames and Messieurs	Dames de la Coeur
Gavotte	Betty Grable and Ensemble
But in the Morning, No!	Ethel Merman and Bert Lahr
Do I Love You?	Ronald Graham and Ethel Merman
DuBarry Was a Lady	Entire Company

Act II

Danse Tzigane	Betty Grable, Ballet
Give Him the Oo-La-La	Ethel Merman
Well, Did You Evah!	Betty Grable and Charles Walters
It Was Written in the Stars	Ronald Graham and Ensemble
L'apres midi d'un boeuf	Benny Baker and Harold Cromer
Katie Went to Haiti	Ethel Merman and Ensemble
Friendship	Ethel Merman and Bert Lahr

Panama Hattie (1940)

Book by Herbert Fields and B. G. DeSylva; songs by Cole Porter; produced by B. G. DeSylva; directed by Edgar MacGregor; choreographed by Robert Alton; settings and costumes by Raoul Pène Du Bois; orchestra under the direction of Gene Salzer; accompanist to Ethel Merman, Lew Kessler.

Opened at the 46th Street Theatre on October 30, 1940. 501 performances.

PRIMARY CAST

Ethel Merman	Hattie Maloney
Phyllis Brooks	Leila Tree
Elaine Shepard	Mildred Hunter
Ann Graham	Kitty Belle Randolph
James Dunn	Nick Bullett
Betty Hutton	Florrie
Joan Carroll	Geraldine Bullett
Rags Ragland	Woozy
Arthur Treacher	Vivian Budd

MUSICAL NUMBERS

Act I

Join It Right Away	Rags Ragland, Frank Hyers, Pat Harrington
Visit Panama	Ethel Merman, Ensemble
American Family	Janis Carter, Al Downing, June Allyson
My Mother Would Love You	Ethel Merman and James Dunn
I've Still Got My Health	Ethel Merman
Fresh as a Daisy	Betty Hutton, Pat Harrington, Frank Hyers

Welcome to Jerry	Singing Boys and Girls and Ensemble
Let's Be Buddies	Ethel Merman and Joan Carroll
They Ain't Done Right by Our Nell	Betty Hutton and Arthur Treacher
I'm Throwin' a Ball Tonight	Ethel Merman and Ensemble
Conga	Ethel Merman, Nadine Gae

Act II

I Detest a Fiesta	Singing Boys and Girls and Ensemble
Who Would Have Dreamed	Janis Carter and Lipman Duckat
Make It Another Old Fashioned, Please	Ethel Merman
All I've Got to Get Now Is My Man	Betty Hutton and Ensemble
You Said It	Ethel Merman, Arthur Treacher, Rags Ragland, Pat Harrington, Frank Hyers
Let's Be Buddies (Reprise)	Ethel Merman and Joan Carroll
God Bless the Women	Rags Ragland, Pat Harrington, and Frank Hyers

Something for the Boys (1943)

Book by Herbert and Dorothy Fields; songs by Cole Porter; produced by Michael Todd; directed by Hassard Short; book directed by Herbert Fields; dances by Jack Cole; settings by Howard Bay; costumes by Billy Livingston; orchestra conducted by William Parson.

Opened at the Alvin Theatre on January 7, 1943. 422 performances.

PRIMARY CAST

Paula Laurence	Chiquita Hart
Jed Prouty	Roger Calhoun
Allen Jenkins	Harry Hart
Ethel Merman	Blossom Hart
Bill Johnson	Staff Sgt. Rocky Fulton
Stuart Langley	Sgt. Laddie Green
Betty Garrett	Mary-Francis
Betty Bruce	Betty-Jean

Act I

See That You're Born in Texas	Bill Johnson and Ensemble
When My Baby Goes To Town	Bill Johnson
Something for the Boys	Ethel Merman and Boys
When We're Home on the Range	Ethel Merman, Paula Laurence, Allen Jenkins
Could It Be You	Bill Johnson
Hey, Good Lookin'	Ethel Merman and Bill Johnson
He's a Right Guy	Ethel Merman
Assembly Line	Allen Jenkins, Betty Garrett, Betty Bruce and Girls
The Leader of a Big Time Band	Ethel Merman

Act II

I'm in Love with a Soldier Boy	Betty Garrett, Girls and Boys
There's a Happy Land in the Sky	Ethel Merman, Paula Laurence, Allen Jenkins, William Lynn, Bill Johnson
He's a Right Guy (Reprise)	Ethel Merman
Could It Be You (Waltz Reprise)	Bill Johnson and Ensemble
By the Mississinewa	Ethel Merman and Paula Laurence

Annie Get Your Gun (1946)

Book by Herbert and Dorothy Fields; songs by Irving Berlin; produced by Richard Rodgers and Oscar Hammerstein; directed by Joshua Logan; choreographed by Helen Tamiris; settings by Jo Mielziner; costumes by Lucinda Ballard; orchestra under the direction of Jay Blackton.

Opened at the Imperial Theatre on May 16, 1946. 1,147 performances.

PRIMARY CAST

Marty May	Charlie Davenport
Lea Penman	Dolly Tate
Ray Middleton	Frank Butler
Ethel Merman	Annie Oakley
William O'Neal	Col. William F. Cody (Buffalo Bill)

| George Lipton | Maj. Gordon Lillie (Pawnee Bill) |
| Harry Bellaver | Chief Sitting Bull |

MUSICAL NUMBERS

Act I

Buffalo Bill	Marty May and Ensemble
I'm a Bad, Bad Man	Ray Middleton and Girls
Dance	Duncan Noble, Paddy Stone, Parker Wilson, Ensemble
Doin' What Comes Natur'lly	Ethel Merman, Nancy Jean Raab, Camilla De Witt, Marlene Cameron, Clifford Sales, Art Barnett
The Girl That I Marry	Ray Middleton
You Can't Get a Man with a Gun	Ethel Merman
There's No Business Like Show Business	William O'Neal, Marty May, Ray Middleton, Ethel Merman
They Say It's Wonderful	Ray Middleton and Ethel Merman
Moonshine Lullaby	Ethel Merman, John Garth III, Leon Bibb, Clyde Turner
I'll Share It All with You	Betty Anne Nyman and Kenny Bowers
Ballyhoo	Lubov Roudenko and Ensemble
There's No Business Like Show Business (Reprise)	Ethel Merman
My Defenses Are Down	Ray Middleton and Boys
Wild Horse (Ceremonial Dance)	Daniel Nagrin and Dancing Boys and Girls
I'm an Indian Too	Ethel Merman

Act II

I Got Lost in His Arms	Ethel Merman and Ensemble
Who Do You Love, I Hope	Betty Anne Nyman and Kenny Bowers
I Got the Sun in the Morning	Ethel Merman and Ensemble
Dance	Lubov Roudenko and Daniel Nagrin

They Say It's Wonderful (Reprise)	Ethel Merman and Ray Middleton
The Girl That I Marry	Ray Middleton
Anything You Can Do	Ethel Merman and Ray Middleton
There's No Business Like Show Business (Reprise)	Entire Company

Call Me Madam (1950)

Book by Howard Lindsay and Russel Crouse; songs by Irving Berlin; produced by Leland Hayward; directed by George Abbott; choreographed by Jerome Robbins; costumes and settings by Raoul Pène Du Bois; Miss Merman's costumes by Mainbocher; orchestra under the direction of Jay Blackton.

Opened at the Imperial Theatre on October 12, 1950. 644 performances.

PRIMARY CAST

Ethel Merman	Mrs. Sally Adams
Russell Nype	Kenneth Gibson
Paul Lukas	Cosmo Constantine
Galina Talva	Princess Maria

MUSICAL NUMBERS

Act I

Mrs. Sally Adams	The Company
The Hostess with the Mostes' on the Ball	Ethel Merman
Washington Square Dance	Ethel Merman and Company
Lichtenburg	Paul Lukas and Singers
Can You Use Any Money Today?	Ethel Merman
Marrying for Love	Paul Lukas and Ethel Merman
The Ocarina	Galina Talva, Bobby Tucker, Potato Bugs, Company
It's a Lovely Day Today	Russell Nype and Galina Talva
It's a Lovely Day Today (Reprise)	Russell Nype, Norma Kaiser, Arthur Partington, Company
The Best Thing for You Would Be Me	Ethel Merman and Paul Lukas

Act II

Lichtenburg (Reprise)	Paul Lukas and Singers
Something to Dance About	Ethel Merman, Tommy Rall, Muriel Bentley, Norma Kaiser, Arthur Partington, Company
Once upon a Time Today	Russell Nype
They Like Ike	Pat Harrington, Ralph Chambers, Jay Velie
You're Just in Love	Ethel Merman and Russell Nype
The Best Thing for You Would Be Me (Reprise)	Ethel Merman and Paul Lukas
It's a Lovely Day Today (Reprise)	Russell Nype and Galina Talva
Mrs. Sally Adams (Reprise)	The Company

Happy Hunting (1956)

Book by Howard Lindsay and Russel Crouse; music by Harold Karr; lyrics by Matt Dubey; produced by Jo Mielziner; directed by Abe Burrows; dances by Roger Adams; musical staging by Alex Romero and Bob Herget; settings by Jo Mielziner; costumes by Irene Sharaff; orchestra under the direction of Jay Blackton.

Opened at the Majestic Theatre on December 6, 1956. 412 performances.

PRIMARY CAST

Gordon Polk	Sanford Stewart Jr.
Virginia Gibson	Beth Livingstone
Gene Wesson	Harry Watson
Ethel Merman	Liz Livingstone
Mary Finney	Maud Foley
Fernando Lamas	The Duke of Granada

MUSICAL NUMBERS

Act I

Postage Stamp Principality	Tourists and Monegasques
Don't Tell Me	Gordon Polk and Virginia Gibson
It's Good to Be Here	Ethel Merman, Estelle Parsons, Robert Held, Carl Nicholas
Mutual Admiration Society	Ethel Merman and Virginia Gibson
For Love or Money	Girls

Bikini Dance	Virginia Gibson
It's Like a Beautiful Woman	Fernando Lamas
Wedding-of-the-Year Blues	Mary Finney, Gene Wesson, John Craig, Clifford Fearl, George Martin, Jim Hutchison, Estelle Parsons, Robert C. Held, Carl Nicholas
Mr. Livingstone	Ethel Merman
If'n	Virginia Gibson, Gordon Polk, Passengers
This Is What I Call Love	Ethel Merman

Act II

A New-Fangled Tango	Ethel Merman, Virginia Gibson, Leon Belasco, Guests
She's Just Another Girl	Gordon Polk
The Game of Love	Ethel Merman
Happy Hunting	Ethel Merman, Fernando Lamas, Members of the Hunt
I'm a Funny Dame	Ethel Merman
This Much I Know	Fernando Lamas
Just Another Guy	Ethel Merman
Everyone Who's "Who's Who"	Seth Riggs, Gene Wesson, Footmen
Mutual Admiration Society (Reprise)	Ethel Merman and Fernando Lamas

Gypsy (1959)

Book by Arthur Laurents; music by Jule Styne; lyrics by Stephen Sondheim; produced by David Merrick and Leland Hayward; directed and choreographed by Jerome Robbins; settings by Jo Mielziner; costumes by Raoul Pène Du Bois; orchestra under the direction of Milton Rosenstock.

Opened at the Broadway Theatre on May 21, 1959. 702 performances.

PRIMARY CAST

Karen Moore	Baby Louise
Ethel Merman	Rose
Jacqueline Mayro	Baby June

Jack Klugman	Herbie
Sandra Church	Louise
Lane Bradbury	June
Paul Wallace	Tulsa

MUSICAL NUMBERS

Act I

May We Entertain You	Karen Moore and Jacqueline Mayro
Some People	Ethel Merman
Small World	Ethel Merman and Jack Klugman
Mr. Goldstone, I Love You	Ethel Merman and Ensemble
Little Lamb	Sandra Church
You'll Never Get Away from Me	Ethel Merman and Jack Klugman
If Momma Was Married	Sandra Church and Lane Bradbury
All I Need Is the Girl	Paul Wallace and Sandra Church
Everything's Coming Up Roses	Ethel Merman

Act II

Madame Rose's Toreadorables	Sandra Church and the Toreadorables
Together, Wherever We Go	Ethel Merman, Jack Klugman, Sandra Church
You Gotta Have a Gimmick	Maria Karnilova, Faith Dane, Chotzi Foley
Small World (Reprise)	Ethel Merman
Let Me Entertain You	Sandra Church and Company
Rose's Turn	Ethel Merman

Annie Get Your Gun (1966)

Book by Herbert and Dorothy Fields; songs by Irving Berlin; produced by Music Theatre of Lincoln Center; directed by Jack Sydow; choreographed by Danny Daniels; settings by Paul McGuire; costumes by Frank Thompson; orchestra under the direction of Jonathan Anderson.

Opened at Lincoln Center's New York State Theatre on May 31, 1966; reopened at the Broadway Theatre, September 21, 1966. 78 performances.

PRIMARY CAST

Jerry Orbach	Charlie Davenport
Benay Venuta	Dolly Tate
Bruce Yarnell	Frank Butler
Ethel Merman	Annie Oakley
Rufus Smith	Col. William F. Cody
Harry Bellaver	Chief Sitting Bull

MUSICAL NUMBERS

Act I

Buffalo Bill	Jerry Orbach, Benay Venuta, Ensemble
I'm a Bad, Bad Man	Bruce Yarnell and Girls
Doin' What Comes Natur'lly	Ethel Merman, Ronn Carroll, Children
The Girl That I Marry	Bruce Yarnell
You Can't Get a Man with a Gun	Ethel Merman
There's No Business Like Show Business	Ethel Merman, Bruce Yarnell, Rufus Smith, Jerry Orbach
They Say It's Wonderful	Ethel Merman and Bruce Yarnell
Moonshine Lullaby	Ethel Merman, Trio, Children
Show Business (Reprise)	Ethel Merman
My Defenses Are Down	Bruce Yarnell and Boys
Wild Horse Ceremonial Dance	Jaime Rogers and Braves
I'm an Indian Too	Ethel Merman
Adoption Dance	Ethel Merman, Jaime Rogers, Braves

Act II

I Got Lost in His Arms	Ethel Merman and Singers
There's No Business Like Show Business (Reprise)	Bruce Yarnell, Benay Venuta, Jack Dabdoub, Ronn Carroll, Patricia Hall
I Got the Sun in the Morning	Ethel Merman and Company
An Old-Fashioned Wedding	Ethel Merman and Bruce Yarnell

The Girl That I Marry (Reprise)	Bruce Yarnell
Anything You Can Do	Ethel Merman and Bruce Yarnell
There's No Business Like	Ensemble
Show Business (Reprise)	
They Say It's Wonderful	Ethel Merman and Company

Hello, Dolly! (1970)

Book by Michael Stewart; songs by Jerry Herman; produced by David Merrick; directed and choreographed by Lucia Victor, after *Dolly*'s original direction and choreography by Gower Champion; settings by Oliver Smith; costumes by Freddy Wittop; orchestra under the direction of Saul Schechtman.

Opened at the St. James Theatre on January 16, 1964; Ethel Merman joined cast on March 28, 1970. 2,844 performances.

PRIMARY CAST

Ethel Merman	Mrs. Dolly Gallagher Levi
Jack Goode	Horace Vandergelder
Andrea Bell	Ermengarde
Russell Nype	Cornelius Hackl

MUSICAL NUMBERS

Act I

I Put My Hand In	Ethel Merman and Company
It Takes a Woman	Jack Goode and the Instant Glee Club
World, Take Me Back	Ethel Merman
Put on Your Sunday Clothes	Russell Nype, Danny Lockin, Ethel Merman, David Gary, Andrea Bell
Ribbons down My Back	June Helmers
Motherhood	Ethel Merman, Jack Goode, June Helmers, Georgia Engel, Russell Nype, Danny Lockin
Dancing	Ethel Merman, Russell Nype, Danny Lockin, Georgia Engel, June Helmers, Dancers

Love, Look in My Window	Ethel Merman
Before the Parade Passes By	Ethel Merman, Jack Goode, Company

Act II

Elegance	June Helmers, Russell Nype, Georgia Engel, Danny Lockin
The Waiters' Gallop	James Beard and Waiters
Hello, Dolly!	Ethel Merman, James Beard, Cooks, Waiters
The Polka Contest	David Gary, Andrea Bell, June Helmers, Russell Nype, Georgia Engel, Danny Locklin, Contestants
It Only Takes a Moment	Russell Nype, June Helmers, Danny Lockin, Contestants
So Long, Dearie	Ethel Merman and Jack Goode
Hello, Dolly! (Reprise)	Ethel Merman and Jack Goode

FILMOGRAPHY

Shorts

The Cave Club (1930)

Warner's Vitaphone #999. No known copy exists.
Cast: Marjorie Leach
      Frank Tinney
      Ted Lewis
      Ethel Merman
      Frank Pierlot
      Harriet Harbaugh

Her Future (1930)

Paramount
Written and directed by Mort Blumenstock. Musical
arrangements by Al Siegel.
Songs: "My Future Just Passed" and "Sing, You Sinners"

Devil Sea (1931)

Paramount
Written and directed by Mort Blumenstock. Musical
arrangements by Al Siegel.
Songs: "Devil Sea" and "I've Got My Man"
Cast: Ethel Merman
      Leslie Stowe

Roaming (1931)

Paramount
Written and directed by Casey Robinson. Songs by Johnny
Green.
Songs: "Hello, My Lover, Goodbye" and "Shake Well before
Using"

Ireno (1931)

Paramount
Directed by Aubrey Scotto. Written by Aubrey Scott and
Andrew Bennison.
Songs: "Shadows on the Wall" and "Wipe That Frown Right off
Your Face"
Cast: Ethel Merman as Irene

Be Like Me (1931)

Paramount
Written and directed by Aubrey Scott
Songs: "After You've Gone" and "Be Like Me"

Let Me Call You Sweetheart (1932)

Paramount
Directed by Dave Fleischer
Song: "Let Me Call You Sweetheart"
Cast: Ethel Merman
    Voice of Mae Questel as Betty Boop

You Try Somebody Else (1932)

Paramount
Directed by Dave Fleischer
Song: "You Try Somebody Else"
Cast: Ethel Merman
    Voice of Mae Questel as Betty Boop

Time on My Hands (1932)

Paramount
Directed by Dave Fleischer
Song: "Time on My Hands"
Cast: Ethel Merman
      Voice of Mae Questel as Betty Boop

Old Man Blues (1932)

Paramount
Directed by Aubrey Scotto. Written by J. P. Murray, Barry
Trivers, and Ben Oakland. Set design by Max E. Hayes.
Songs: "Old Man Blues" and "He Doesn't Love Me Anymore"

Cast: Ethel Merman	Helen
Hal Forde	Old Man Blues
Hal Young	Paul

Song Shopping (1933)

Paramount
Directed by Dave Fleischer
Songs: "I'm Yours" and "Sing, You Sinners"
Cast: Ethel Merman, accompanied live on piano by Johnny
      Green

Features (Theatrical Releases)

Follow the Leader (1930)

Paramount
Directed by Norman Taurog. Screenplay by Gertrude Purcell,
Sid Silvers. Based on the musical play *Manhattan Mary,* by
William K. Wells, George White (with music and lyrics by
B. G. DeSylva, Lew Brown, and Ray Henderson), Yip Harburg
and Arthur Schwartz, Irving Kahal and Sammy Fain.

PRIMARY CAST

Ed Wynn	Crickets
Ginger Rogers	Mary Brennan
Ethel Merman	Helen King

We're Not Dressing (1934)

Paramount
Directed by Norman Taurog. Produced by Benjamin Glazer.
Screenplay by Horace Jackson, Frances Martin, and George
Marion Jr. Based on stories by Walton Hall Smith and
Benjamin Galzer, and J. M. Barrie's *The Admirable Crichton*.
Music and lyrics by Harry Revel and Mack Gordon.

PRIMARY CAST

Bing Crosby	Stephen Jones
Carole Lombard	Doris Washington
George Burns	George
Gracie Allen	Gracie
Ethel Merman	Edith
Leon Errol	Hubert

Kid Millions (1934)

Samuel Goldwyn–United Artists
Directed by Roy Del Ruth. Written and adapted by Arthur
Sheekman, Nat Perrin, and Nunnally Johnson. Songs by Gus
Kahn and Walter Donaldson, Burton Lane, and Harold
Adamson. Dance ensembles by Seymour Felix.

PRIMARY CAST

Eddie Cantor	Eddie
Ann Sothern	Jane Larrabee
Ethel Merman	Dot
George Murphy	Jerry Lane
Jesse Block	Ben Ali
Eve Sully	Fanya
Burton Churchill	Colonel Larrabee

The Big Broadcast of 1936 (1935)

Paramount
Directed by Norman Taurog. Written by Walter DeLeon,
Francis Martin, and Ralph Spence.

Strike Me Pink (1936)

Samuel Goldwyn–United Artists
Directed by Norman Taurog. Screenplay by Frank Butler,
Walter DeLeon, and Francis Martin, with additional dialogue
by Phillip Rapp. Based on a story by Clarence Budington
Kelland. Music and lyrics by Harold Arlen and Lew Brown.

Anything Goes (1936)

Paramount
Directed by Lewis Milestone. Taken from the musical comedy
by Howard Lindsay and Russel Crouse; music and lyrics by Cole
Porter, with additional songs by Leo Robin, Richard A. Whiting,
Frederick Hollander, Hoagy Carmichael, and Edward Heyman.

Happy Landing (1938)

20th Century–Fox
Directed by Roy Del Ruth. Produced by Darryl F. Zanuck.
Screenplay by Milton Sperling and Boris Ingser. Music and
lyrics by Sam Pokrass, Jack Yellen, Walter Bullock, Harold
Spina, and Raymond Scott.

PRIMARY CAST

Sonja Henie	Trudy Ericksen
Don Ameche	Jimmy Hall
Jean Hersholt	Herr Ericksen
Ethel Merman	Flo Kelly
Cesar Romero	Duke Sargent

Alexander's Ragtime Band (1938)

20th Century–Fox
Directed by Henry King. Produced by Darryl F. Zanuck.
Screenplay by Kathryn Scola and Lamar Trotti, adaptation by
Richard Sherman. Music and lyrics by Irving Berlin.

PRIMARY CAST

Tyrone Power	Alexander/Aleck (Roger Grant)
Alice Faye	Stella Kirby
Don Ameche	Charlie Dwyer
Ethel Merman	Jerry Allen
Jack Haley	Davey Lane

Straight, Place and Show (1938)

20th Century–Fox
Directed by David Butler. Produced by Darryl F. Zanuck.
Screenplay by M. M. Musselman and Allen Rivkin, with
additional dialogue by Lew Brown. Based on the unproduced
play *Saratoga Chips,* by Damon Runyon and Irving Caesar.
Music and lyrics by Lew Brown and Lew Pollack.

Ritz Brothers	(Themselves)
Richard Arlen	Denny Paine
Ethel Merman	Linda
Phyllis Brooks	Barbara Drake

Stage Door Canteen (1943)

Sol Lesser–American Theatre Wing, United Artists
Directed by Frank Borzage. Screenplay by Delmer Daves. Songs
by Jimmy Monaco, Richard Rodgers, Lorenz Hart, Johnny
Green, and Gertrude Lawrence.

PRIMARY CAST

Cheryl Walker	Eileen
William W. Terry	"Dakota" Ed Smith

plus some seventy guest stars, including Ethel Merman

Around 1944, Merman also appeared (as herself) in *Sing with
the Stars,* produced by the Army Pictorial Service. The short
film has no date.

Call Me Madam (1953)

20th Century–Fox
Directed by Walter Lang. Produced by Darryl F. Zanuck/Sol C.
Siegel. Screenplay by Arthur Sheekman. Based on the stage
musical comedy by Howard Lindsay and Russel Crouse. Songs
by Irving Berlin.

PRIMARY CAST

Ethel Merman	Mrs. Sally Adams
Donald O'Connor	Kenneth
Vera-Ellen	Princess Maria
George Sanders	Cosmo Constantine
Billy De Wolfe	Pemberton Maxwell

There's No Business Like Show Business (1954)

20th Century–Fox
Directed by Walter Lang. Produced by Darryl F. Zanuck/Sol C. Siegel. Screenplay by Phoebe and Henry Ephron. Based on a story by Lamar Trotti. Songs by Irving Berlin.

PRIMARY CAST

Ethel Merman	Molly Donahue
Donald O'Connor	Tim Donahue
Marilyn Monroe	Vicky Parker
Dan Dailey	Terence Donahue
Johnnie Ray	Steve Donahue
Mitzi Gaynor	Katy Donahue

It's a Mad, Mad, Mad, Mad World (1963)

Stanley Kramer—United Artists
Directed by Stanley Kramer. Screenplay by William and Tania Rose.

PRIMARY CAST

Spencer Tracy	Capt. C. G. Culpepper
Milton Berle	J. Russell Finch
Sid Caesar	Melville Trump
Buddy Hackett	Benjy Benjamin
Ethel Merman	Mrs. Marcus
Mickey Rooney	Ding Bell
Dick Shawn	Sylvester Marcus
Phil Silvers	Otto Meyer
Terry-Thomas	J. Algernon Hawthorne
Jonathan Winters	Lennie Pike
Edie Adams	Monica Crump
Dorothy Provine	Emmeline Finch

The Art of Love (1965)

Universal
Directed by Norman Jewison. Produced by Ross Hunter. Screenplay by Carl Reiner, from a story by Richard Alan Simmons and William Sackheim.

James Garner	Casey
Dick Van Dyke	Paul
Elke Sommer	Nikki
Angie Dickinson	Laurie
Ethel Merman	Madame Coco

Journey Back to Oz (1971)

Warner Bros.
Directed by Hal Sutherland. Written by Fred Ladd and Norm
Prescott, based on L. Frank Baum's *The Marvelous Land of Oz.*
Animated feature—produced in 1964 but not released until 1971.

PRIMARY CAST

Milton Berle	Cowardly Lion
Liza Minnelli	Dorothy
Mickey Rooney	Scarecrow
Margaret Hamilton	Aunt Em
Ethel Merman	Mombi, the Bad Witch
Danny Thomas	The Tin Man

Won Ton Ton, the Dog Who Saved Hollywood (1976)

Paramount
Directed by Michael Winner. Screenplay by Arnold Schulman
and Cy Howard.
Merman has a bit role as "Hedda Parson," along with scores of
other celebrities, in a story following a woman who arrives in
Hollywood to become a star with her dog in the mid-1920s.

Airplane! (1980)

Paramount
Written and directed by Jim Abrahams, David Zucker, and
Jerry Zucker. Produced by Jim Abrahams.
Merman has a cameo appearance as traumatized fighter pilot,
Lieutenant Hurwitz.

NOTES

ABBREVIATIONS

A1   (autobiography 1): Ethel Merman and Pete Martin, *Who Could Ask for Anything More?* (New York: Doubleday, 1955)

A2   (autobiography 2): Ethel Merman and George Eells, *Merman: An Autobiography* (New York: Simon and Schuster, 1978)

AMPAS   Academy of Motion Picture Arts and Sciences: files and folders from the Margaret Herrick Library

BG   Barbara Geary

CP   Cole Porter

DF   Dorothy Fields

EM   Ethel Merman

IB   Irving Berlin

JS   Jule Styne

KB   Klea Blackhurst

LAT   *Los Angeles Times*

MCNY   Museum of the City of New York:
             Ethel Merman Scrapbook Collection and Boxes, Theater Collection

MPAA   Motion Picture Association of America

NYDN   *New York Daily News*

NYHT   *New York Herald Tribune*

NYJA   *New York Journal American*

NYM   *New York Mirror*

NYP   *New York Post*

NYPL   New York Public Library collections:
             Billy Rose Theatre Collection
             Music Division

NYT	*New York Times*
NYTM	*New York Times Magazine*
NYWJT	*New York World Journal Tribune*
NYWT	*New York World Telegram*
NYWTS	*New York World Telegram and Sun*
PM	Pete Martin
RE	Roger Edens
RL	Robert Levitt Jr.
RLS	Robert Levitt Sr.
SC	Scrapbooks at the MCNY
TC	Tony Cointreau
UCLA	University of California, Los Angeles
	Special Collections
	Arts Special Collections
	Paramount Picture Corporation Collection, Paramount Studio Production Stills, MC 448 2529, Collection 009
	20th Century–Fox Legal Records, Collection 95
	20th Century–Fox Production files, MC 461 4854, Collection 051
	20th Century–Fox Scripts Collection, MC 461 4853
USC	University of Southern California Archives of Performing Arts
	Fox Scripts
	Hollywood Museum Collection (HMC), Pete Martin Collection

PREFACE

1. Cole Porter, "Notes on the Morning after an Opening Night," *NYT,* 8 November 1936, n.p.

2. KB, phone conversation with author, 5 October 2004.

3. A1, 10.

4. John Mason Brown, "Ethel Merman Excellent in *Panama Hattie,*" *NYP,* 31 October 1940, MCNY, SC 8.

5. Anonymous fan, personal conversation with author.

6. Anonymous fan, personal conversation with author.

7. "Stage Door Johnny, Esq.," *Enquirer,* NYPL, Billy Rose Theatre Collection: Ethel Merman folder, early 1930s.

8. Anonymous fan, personal conversation with author.

9. A2, 80.

10. TC, phone conversation with author, September 2004.

CHAPTER 1: BEGINNINGS

1. Nancy Beth Jackson, "Accessible, Affordable and Highly Diverse," *NYT*, 19 October 2003.

2. RL, interview with author, July 2004.

3. Edward's own municipal records are elusive. Because he was born before the borough of Queens was established, his certificate should be included in the records for the city as a whole, where other births in Queens at the time are stored. But it is missing.

4. MCNY, box 2.

5. A1, 53.

6. EM, interview with PM, transcript, USC, HMC: Pete Martin Collection. In Ethel's 1955 autobiography, Martin changed this to "Mom was sharper than my dad," teaching her how to look after herself and her money. "Mom is the one with the hard head and the shrewdness, the one who wouldn't let anybody cheat her." A1, 54.

7. EM, interview with PM, transcript, USC.

8. A2, 21.

9. A2, 20–21.

10. A1, 54.

11. RL, interview with author, July 2004.

12. A2, 232.

13. A2, 22.

14. EM, interview with PM, transcript, USC.

15. MCNY, box 5.

16. A1, 52.

17. RL, interview with author, July 2004.

18. RL, letter to author, 28 January 2007.

19. Dorothy Fields, interview with PM, transcript, 27, USC, HMC: Pete Martin Collection.

20. Unidentified newspaper article, NYPL, Billy Rose Theatre Collection, file 2.

21. A1, 79.

22. A2, 21.

23. Roger Edens, interview with PM, transcript, USC, HMC: Pete Martin Collection, box 20, folder 1. Pianist Lew Kessler agrees. "If you give her a lyric, this dame, she takes this little black notebook and she's got everything systematically written out. Like I say, she's so organized. . . . She's got this lyric, and if you give it to her in the afternoon and she goes home to dinner, she comes back and she just closes the book. She knows it word for word [and she never looks at it again]. That's the end

of it. And if you change two words in that lyric, like 'so' to 'but' and you go remind her when she's very occupied mentally, if she sings that song two hours later she'll have that changed." Lew Kessler, interview with PM, transcript, 17, USC, HMC: Pete Martin Collection, box 19, folder 3. Al F. Koenig Jr. remembers much the same thing. Edens sent Ethel privately recorded discs, which she would play until she mastered the arrangement. "That is precisely how she learned Edens' seat arrangement of '[Blow,] Gabriel [Blow].'" Correspondence with author, December 2005.

24. EM, interview with PM, transcript, USC.

25. A2, 9.

26. EM, interview with PM, transcript, USC.

27. A2, 19.

28. A2, 22.

29. A2, 23.

30. The phrase is Barry Goldberg's, though popularized by David Roediger and other scholars. Goldberg quoted in Roediger, "In Between Peoples: Race, Nationality and the 'New' Immigrant Working Class," *Journal of American Ethnic History* (Spring 1997): fn. 11.

31. Mark N. Grant, *The Rise and Fall of the Broadway Musical* (Boston: Northeastern University Press, 2004). See especially the chapter "Before the Microphone" and pp. 20–21. Grant argues that "somewhere between 1900 and 1920, long melodic verses [e.g., of Victor Herbert] were replaced by short, simple tunes not requiring vocal agility" (26); the chorus, not the verse, became the hook for audiences; songs were written in lower ranges (average height of pitch), in shorter vocal compasses (distance from low to high notes), and with slightly lower tessitura (with mezzos and belters now dominant over sopranos). None of this was conscious but, rather, part of an evolution that Grant charts that began to establish the popular musicals, nonlegitimate song, and vocal style that soon prevailed on Broadway for nearly half a century.

32. Isaac Goldberg, *Tin Pan Alley: A Chronicle of the American Popular Music Racket* (New York: John Day Co., 1930), 150.

33. "Stage-Door Johnny, Esq," *Enquirer,* NYPL, Billy Rose Theatre Collection, Ethel Merman folder: early 1930s.

34. Stacey Wolf, *A Problem Like Maria: Gender and Sexuality in the American Musical* (Ann Arbor: University of Michigan Press, 2002), 102.

35. Stanley Crouch made this point in *Broadway: The American Musical,* episode 1: "Give My Regards to Broadway," PBS, 19 October 2004 broadcast.

36. A1, 57.

37. A1, 58.

38. Merman claims to have been six (A1, 56).

39. A2, 19.

40. A1, 59.

41. EM, interview with PM, transcript, USC.

42. Ibid.

43. A2, 21.

44. EM, interview with PM, transcripts, USC.

45. Louis Sobol, "Down Memory Lane with Ethel Merman," *Evening Journal,* 14 July 1934, USC, HMC: Pete Martin Collection, folder 3.

46. A2, 21.

47. EM quoted in unidentified article, NYPL, Billy Rose Theatre Collection, Special Collections.

48. RL, interview with author, July 2004.

49. Louis Schurr, interview with PM, transcript, USC, HMC: Pete Martin Collection.

50. A2, 28.

51. Hilda Cole, "The Past of Ethel Merman: How a Stenographer Led Double Life and Won Fame," supplement to *Sunday Ledger,* 9 June 1935, USC, HMC: Pete Martin Collection, folder 3.

52. EM, interview with PM, transcript, USC.

53. EM, interview with PM, transcript, USC.

54. *Chicago Daily News,* "Ethel Once Wrote Own Reference," 17 April 1937, NYPL, Billy Rose Theatre Collection.

55. Wolcott Gibbs, "Seasons in the Sun and Other Pleasures," excerpted in *Reader's Digest,* October 1946, 84–88 (quote from 86), NYPL, Music Division: Ethel Merman folder.

56. Lew Kessler, interview with PM, transcript, 2, USC, HMC: Pete Martin Collection, box 20, folder 1.

57. Anonymous coworker, personal conversation with author, summer 2003.

58. KB, interview with author, 5 October 2004.

59. Marilyn Cantor Baker, interview with author, June 2004.

60. Martin, notes on EM interview, 11 September 1950, transcript, 3, USC, HMC: Pete Martin Collection.

61. Al F. Koenig Jr., "Ethel Merman," in *Notable American Women,* ed. Susan Ware and Stacy Braukman (Cambridge, MA: Belknap Press of Harvard University, 2005).

62. Irving Drutman, "Eternal Merman," *NYWJT,* 18 September 1966, Theater sec., NYPL, Billy Rose Theatre Collection: MWEZ, nc 26.491, 1960–69.

63. A1, 74.

64. Al F. Koenig Jr., "The Merman Story," unpublished essay, 2004, 1.

65. Most accounts, including Merman's, refer to the establishment as "Little Russia"; extant menus indicate "The Little Russia."

66. A1, 70.

67. Press clippings and announcements spell the Pavilion club variously as "Pavilion Royale" and "Pavillion Royal/e."

68. Buck Lindsay and Russel Crouse, interview with PM, transcript, USC, HMC: Pete Martin Collection.

69. RE, interview with PM, transcript, 5, USC, HMC: Pete Martin Collection.

70. Lew Kessler, interview with PM, transcript, 23–24, USC, HMC: Pete Martin Collection.

71. ProArte compact disc liner notes for *Ethel Merman: You're the Top,* courtesy of Al F. Koenig Jr.

72. KB, interview with author, 5 October 2004.

73. Robert St. John, "Dream Tunes Are What US Wants: Ethel Merman Changes Her Ballads and US Claps Hands," unidentified source, MCNY, box 2.

74. Gary Wedow (choir master of the New York City Opera), interview with author, November 2003.

75. Ibid.

76. Jeannette LoVetri (singing voice specialist), interview with author, 7 November 2003.

77. Linda Carroll, "Topic: The Broadway 'Belt': Can Belters Avoid Injury in Exciting Performances?" in *Laringologiea e Voz Hoje, Temas do IV Congresso Brasileiro de Laringologia e Voz,* ed. Mara Behlau (Rio de Janeiro: Livraria e Editora Revinter Ltda. 1998), 99.

78. Jeannette LoVetri, interview with author, 7 November 2003.

79. KB, interview with author, 5 October 2004.

80. Ibid. Jeannette LoVetri objects, saying, "No opera singer I know has that idea. None!" Correspondence with author, 7 April 2007.

81. Linda Carroll and William Riley, interview with author, 17 November 2003.

82. "A Pair of Ethels Thrill Broadway: Ethel Waters and Ethel Merman," *Buffalo News,* 2 November 1940, MCNY, SC 8.

83. Marj Cherry, "Life Story of the 'Doll from Astoria with a Trumpet in Her Throat'—Merman," *Daily Press* (VA), 4 September 1955, MCNY, SC 19.

84. Linda Carroll and William Riley, interview with author, 17 November 2003.

85. KB, interview with author, 5 October 2004.

86. Lou Irwin, interview with PM, transcript, USC, HMC: Pete Martin Collection.

87. Ibid.

88. EM, interview with PM, transcript, USC. There is inconsistency on this; in her second autobiography, Ethel says she remained at the Booster Brake Company, making thirty-five dollars a week.

89. Louis Notarius, "Short Reviews of Short Features," *Publix Opinion,* 27 June 1930, 7, AMPAS.

90. A1, 70. Although the film was recorded as number 999 in the Vitaphone archives, neither it nor the sound discs have ever been found. Some say that Merman's number in *The Cave Club* was "Sockety-Sock" and that she performed it clad in animal skins.

91. Lou Irwin, interview with PM, transcript, USC.

92. A1, 72.

93. KB, interview with author, 5 October 2004.

94. EM, interview with PM, transcript, USC.

95. Both dates verified by Al F. Koenig Jr.

CHAPTER 2: FROM STENOGRAPHER TO STAR

The epigraphs are from Guy Bolton, "Merman Debut Is Recalled," *NYHT,* 19 June 1960, NYPL, Billy Rose Theatre Collection: Ethel Merman folder; and Will Friedwald, *Stardust Memories: The Biography of America's Most Popular Songs* (New York: Pantheon Books, 2002), 185.

1. EM, interview with PM, transcript, USC, HMC: Pete Martin Collection, box 19, folder 3.

2. RE, interview with PM, transcript, 52, USC, HMC: Pete Martin Collection.

3. PM, interview with EM, transcript, USC.

4. Willie and his brother Eugene Howard had appeared recently at the Palace as "Two Hebrew Humorists Who Hail from Harlem." See Howard Pollack's *George Gershwin: His Life and Work* (Berkeley: University of California Press, 2006).

5. Deena Rosenberg, *Fascinating Rhythm: The Collaboration of George and Ira Gershwin* (Ann Arbor: University of Michigan Press, 1997), 182; Arthur Ruhl, review of *Girl Crazy, NYHT,* 15 October 1930.

6. Ira Gershwin quoted in Rosenberg, *Fascinating Rhythm,* 184.

7. Friedwald, *Stardust Memories,* 184.

8. The higher number is repeated in Friedwald, *Stardust Memories,* 182.

9. RE, interview with PM, transcript, 4–5, USC.

10. DF, interview with PM, transcript, 4–5, USC, HMC: Pete Martin Collection.

11. Alex Aaron quoted in Guy Bolton, "Merman Debut Is Recalled," *NYHT,* 19 June 1960, NYPL, Music Division.

12. Al F. Koenig Jr., "Merman: Solid New York," *Joslin's Jazz Journal,* 1998, quoting from original reviews in *New York Daily Mirror.*

13. Unidentified article, MCNY, box 2.

14. Review, *NYHT,* 29 October 1930, MCNY, box 2.

15. Unidentified review of *Girl Crazy,* 1930, MCNY, box 2.

16. *Time,* 27 October 1930, MCNY, box 2.

17. Baird Leonard, "Theatre," unidentified source, MCNY, box 2.

18. Bolton, "Merman Debut Is Recalled."

19. RL, letter to author, 16 January 2004.

20. John T. Casey, "Singing Her Way to Stardom," *New Movie Magazine,* October 1934, NYPL, Billy Rose Theatre Collection, Special Collections.

21. EM, interview with PM, transcript USC; "revision" in A1, 33.

22. Casey, "Singing Her Way to Stardom."

23. RE, interview with PM, transcript, USC.

24. DF, interview with PM, transcript, 2–3, USC.

25. See, for instance, " 'Rhythm Girl' Joins Benefit," *Los Angeles Examiner,* 14 December 1933, MCNY, box 3.

26. *NYHT,* 29 October 1930, MCNY, box 2.

27. He did this in the 2004 biopic of Cole Porter, *DeLovely.*

28. RL, letter to author, 16 January 2004.

29. A2, 50.

30. RE, interview with PM, transcript, 12, USC.

31. RL, letter to author, 16 January 2004.

32. *Evening Journal,* 6 March 1931, MCNY, box 2.

33. Unidentified article, early 1930s, MCNY, box 2.

34. Unidentified newspaper article, *NYJA,* 13 December 1931, MCNY, box 2.

35. The other was in 1926. Louis Botto, *At This Theatre* (New York: Applause Books, 2002), 4.

36. For the description of Bolger, see J. Brooks Atkinson, review of *Scandals, NYT* [1931], MCNY, box 2.

37. Unidentified newspaper article, *NYT,* MCNY, box 2.

38. "The Theatre," *New Yorker,* 26 September 1931, MCNY, box 2.

39. "And Now the 'Scandals,' " *NYJA,* 16 September 1931, MCNY, box 2.

40. Letter, undated (probably late 1931), in MCNY, box 2.

41. Walter Winchell, "Winchell of New York," *NYM,* 5 August 1931, MCNY, box 2.

42. "Who's Who in the Cast," *Playbill* for *Scandals,* 28, NYPL, Billy Rose Theatre Collection: MWEZ, nc 9606, "Programs."

43. When Warner Bros. approached Merman, now the toast of Broadway, offering another contract at fifteen hundred dollars a week, she declined, still steamed over her previous experience.

44. My thanks to Jerry Beck at Cartoon Research for letting me see *Song Shopping.*

45. Gary Wedow, interview with author, November 2003.

46. A Columbia University graduate, Blumenstock entered the film industry as an editor and a title writer. He directed shorts from 1927 to 1931 and then went over to Warner Bros.' Advertising and Publicity Department. There is no evidence of where his aesthetic influences were derived.

47. KB, interview with author, 5 October 2004.

48. TC, interview with author, 11 September 2004.

49. Ann Pinchot, "—And Just whaT Has Ethel Got? Answering the Query about Lively Miss Merman," *King Features* syndicate paper, 1937, NYPL, Billy Rose Theatre Collection: Special Collections folder: C. and L. Brown Collection.

50. Ashton Stevens, *Chicago American,* 1 August 1933, MCNY, box 3.

51. Alma Whitaker, "Mae West Old Story Says Ethel Merman," *LAT,* 24 December 1933, MCNY, box 3.

52. In 1933, Ethel, during the filming of *We're Not Dressing* in Los Angeles, rented an apartment in the same building that West lived in; seventy years later, in 2004, eBay sold a photograph of Merman and West from the late 1950s or early '60s, standing alongside fellow icon Judy Garland. In all fairness to West on the question of who was imitating whom, if anyone, it should be stated that Mae West's act was secured well before she moved into pictures and even before Ethel hit the Broadway stage.

53. Sidney Skolsky, "Skolsky's Hollywood" (syndicated), 12 December 1935, MCNY, box 5.

54. Bernard Sobel, "Gay 90s Ghost Rules Broadway," *NYM,* 19 February 1933, MCNY, box 3.

55. Lloyd Lewis, "Stage Whispers," *Chicago Daily News,* 13 July 1933, MCNY, box 3.

56. John Mason Brown, "Two on the Aisle: Actors Who Work Too Hard to Win Attention," *NYP,* 26 June 1933, MCNY, box 3.

57. Remie Lohse, "Caught in the Act," *Stage Magazine,* May 1933, 34–35, MCNY, box 3.

58. Ibid.

59. Ashton Stevens, "Olssen and Johnson and Ethel Merman Strike 12 in 'Take a Chance,' " *Chicago American,* 11 July 1933, 15, MCNY, box 3.

60. "Filming of 'Chance' Set?" *Variety,* 13 June 1933, MCNY, box 3.

61. *Variety,* 27 September 1932, MCNY, box 4.

62. Unidentified clippings, *Variety* and *New Yorker,* May 1933, MCNY, box 3.

63. Unidentified clipping, MCNY, box 3.

64. Frank Meehan, *NYJA,* May 1933, MCNY, box 3.

65. A1, 34.

66. TC, interview with author, 11 September 2004.

67. Marilyn Baker, interview with author, June 2004.

68. Maurice Zolotow, "Ethel Merman Hit Parade," *Cosmopolitan,* October 1950, NYPL, Billy Rose Theatre Collection: Merman folder: "Mid-1950s."

69. Ibid.

70. RE, interview with PM, transcript, 13, USC. Edens's comment actually refers to vaudeville engagements Merman had had the summer before, when *Girl Crazy* went briefly to the World's Fair.

CHAPTER 3: THE EARLY THIRTIES

1. RL, letter to author, 16 January 2004.

2. Mitzi Gaynor, in *Biography* episode: "Ethel Merman: There's No Business Like Show Business," A&E, 1999 broadcast.

3. John Mason Brown, "Seeing Things," *NYP,* 28 October 1950, MCNY, SC 14.

4. "The Theatre," *Time,* 65, 28 October 1940, MCNY, SC 8.

5. John Chapman, "New Tops for Old Vic and Young Ethel," *New York News,* Sunday edition, 26 May 1946, MCNY, SC 12.

6. Wolcott Gibbs, "Ethel Merman," *Life,* 8 July 1946, 87, MCNY, SC 12.

7. Bosley Crowther, "New Angles on an Old Smoothie," *NYT,* Sunday edition, 1 May 1938, MCNY, box 7.

8. "Actress Can't Get Trunk Damage Pay," unidentified clipping, January 1934, MCNY, box 3.

9. Sidney Skolsky, "Hollywood: Watching Them Make Pictures," unidentified Los Angeles newspaper, 26 January 1934, MCNY, box 3.

10. "Ethel's Songs Guarded," *Hollywood Citizen News,* 10 February 1934, AMPAS.

11. The quote comes from a 30 January 1934 letter from Will Hays to Zukor, in which Hays quotes Joseph Breen. In the same letter, Hays adds, "Pursuant to the action of the Board of Directors at the meeting of 10 December 1930, it is suggested that the above title not be used." AMPAS: *We're Not Dressing* Paramount Production file.

12. AMPAS: Paramount press sheets for *We're Not Dressing,* 1 August 1933–31 July 1934.

13. Unidentified clipping, MCNY, box 7.

14. "Film Newcomers Assert Hollywood 'Tame Town,' " *Los Angeles Post-Record,* 13 March 1934, MCNY, box 3.

15. Quoted in William McBrien, *Cole Porter: A Biography* (New York: Knopf, 1998), 172.

16. Lucius Beebe, "Ethel Merman: Her Day Is Occupied," *NYHT,* 2 December 1934, MCNY, box 13.

17. Recently, Broadway historian Ethan Mordden disputes this "popular misconception" about this change to the story, saying, "In fact, that wasn't true at all. What had to be changed was a subplot involving a mad bomber loose on a boat." Web broadcast, 6 April 2007, *NYT,* "Musical Milestone," www.nytimes.com/packages/khtml/2007/04/08/06/theater/20070408_MORD_FEATURE.html.

18. Nunnally Johnson, interview with Tom Stempel, 1969, transcript, 202, UCLA: Special Collections.

19. *World Telegram,* 5 January 1935, MCNY, box 4.

20. A1, 106.

21. *Hollywood Reporter,* 9 March 1954.

22. A1, 109.

23. George Holland, "Sterling Quartet of Stars in Best Musical Comedy to Open in Recent Years," *Boston Evening America,* November 1934.

24. Unidentified clipping, MCNY, box 4.

25. Brooks Atkinson "Catching Up on Song: Ethel Merman, Cole Porter and a Couple of Tunes from Anything Goes!" *NYT,* 15 September 1935, MCNY, box 5.

26. Untitled review, MCNY.

27. Bige, *Variety,* 27 November 1934, MCNY, box 13.

28. CP, interview with PM, transcript, 8, USC, HMC: Pete Martin Collection.

29. A2, 74.

30. "Questions to Ask Merman," PM transcripts, 2, USC, HMC: Pete Martin Collection.

31. CP, interview with PM, transcript, 4, USC.

32. Ibid., transcript, 5.

33. Cole and Linda Porter, thank-you note to EM, MCNY, SC 13. My thanks to Al F. Koenig Jr. for verifying the words on his collection of Merman's acetate recordings.

34. CP, interview with PM, transcript, 2, USC.

35. Ibid., transcript, 14.

36. Al F. Koenig Jr., "The Last Scrapbook," unpublished essay (in author's collection).

37. *NYM,* [18] December 1934. The *Mirror* misreports this as Porter's first song.

38. The earnings were reported by Vinton Freedley, interview with PM, transcript, 23, USC, HMC: Pete Martin Collection.

39. Unidentified source, 9 December 1934, MCNY, box 4.

40. Unidentified source, 1934, MCNY, box 4.

41. "From the Pit," *The Princetonian* (NJ), 22 February 1935, MCNY, box 4.

42. Harriet Von Horne, "Merman Unveils Own Air Show," *NYWT,* 1 August 1949, MCNY, SC 13.

43. Winston Burdett, "Ethel Merman's More Than Unaffected—She's Untamed," *Brooklyn Eagle,* 20 February 1935, loose clipping, MCNY.

44. *New Yorker,* 16 February 1935, MCNY, box 4.

45. *New York Evening Journal,* undated, MCNY, box 4.

46. Beebe, "Ethel Merman: Her Day Is Occupied."

47. Paul Harrison, "What's in a Name? Nothing So Far as Play Titles Go," *Laredo Texas Times,* 5 December 1934, MCNY, box 4.

48. "Questions to Ask Merman," PM transcripts, USC.

49. Atkinson, "Catching Up on Song: Ethel Merman, Cole Porter, and a Couple of Tunes from Anything Goes."

50. *Variety,* 15 January 1935, MCNY, box 4. Other sources claimed that movie rights exceeded $125,000.

51. Unidentified newspaper article, August 1935, MCNY, box 5.

52. Burdett, "Ethel Merman's More Than Unaffected—She's Untamed."

53. "Hollywood Is Crazy; Broadway More Fun, Declares Blue Star," *Cornell Daily Sun,* 7 December 1934, MCNY, box 4.

54. Letter signed K. L., 29 July 1936, AMPAS: MPAA Production Code Administration Files, *Anything Goes.*

55. Letter from Vincent Hart to Joseph Breen, 10 January 1935, AMPAS: MPAA Production Code Administration Files, *Anything Goes.*

56. *Daily Variety,* 4 January 1936, AMPAS.

57. Paramount press sheets, *Anything Goes,* 1 August 1935–31 July 1936, AMPAS.

58. "Sidney Skolsky's Hollywood," *NYDN,* 7 September 1935, MCNY, box 5.

59. Eileen Percy, "In Hollywood," *Newark Star Eagle* (NJ) (syndicated), 1 October 1935, MCNY, box 5.

60. Unidentified source, April 1934, MCNY, box 12.

61. The advertisement goes on to promote high-end cars in which "Safety Glass is supplied in windshields and windows at no extra charge." Advertisement for Libbey Owens Ford Glass Co. (Toledo, OH), in Apollo Theatre Program, 15 May 1933, MCNY, box 3.

62. Correspondence for all events in MCNY, box 2.

63. Louella Parsons, "Eddie Cantor's 'Kid Millions' Musical Opens," *Playfilms,* 1 January 1935, unpaginated.

64. "Star, Cast, Writers, Production, Swell," review of *Kid Millions, Hollywood Reporter,* 27 October 1934, unpaginated.

65. Nunnally Johnson, interview with Tom Stempel, 1969, transcript, 59–60, UCLA: Special Collections.

66. The quote is from the *Ridewood Times* (NY), 16 November 1934, MCNY, box 13.

67. "Hollywood Is Crazy," *Cornell Daily Sun,* 7 December 1934.

68. These last two songs were released in a later collection titled *Merman in the Movies: 1930–1938.*

69. This quotation and all those that follow from Marilyn Cantor Baker are taken from her interview with the author, June 2004.

70. Unidentified clipping, December 1936, MCNY, box 15.

71. Deposited at the MCNY as "Scrap book created by Merman fan Esther Hader," MCNY, box 7.

72. Burton Rascoe, "Why Gentlemen Prefer Brunette La Merman," *NYWT,* 21 January 1943, MCNY, SC 10.

73. Undated clipping (ca. 1938), NYPL, Billy Rose Theatre Collection: Special Collections folder: C. and L. Brown Collection.

74. "Why Men Adore Ethel Merman," *Romantic Stories,* November 1935, MCNY, box 5.

75. Joyce Anderson, "Beauty a la Ethel Merman," *Radio Mirror,* NYPL, Billy Rose Theatre Collection: Special Collections folder.

76. Arthur Pollock, "Jimmy Durante and Ethel Merman Appear in *Red, Hot, and Blue* at the Alvin Theatre," *Brooklyn Eagle,* 20 October 1936, MCNY.

77. Cole Porter, "Notes on the Morning after an Opening Nite," *NYT,* 8 November 1936, MCNY, box 6.

78. Brooks Atkinson, " '*Red, Hot and Blue*' with Ethel Merman, Jimmy Durante, Bob Hope and a Musical Show," *New York Times,* 30 October 1936, MCNY.

79. Jimmy Durante, *NYHT,* 22 November 1936, MCNY, box 6.

80. Koenig Jr., "The Last Scrapbook."

1. Unidentified newspaper article, 18 January 1938, MCNY, box 7.

2. The studio's language about options for the third picture was noncommittal—standard procedure.

3. Contract, 7 August 1936, UCLA: 20th Century–Fox Legal Records, box 371.

4. UCLA: 20th Century–Fox Legal Records, box 107, Fan Mail.

5. Ibid.

6. Other titles included *Bread, Butter, and Rhythm* and, briefly, *Hot and Happy*, after a song in the film. *Hot and Happy* was a curiously suggestive title for a family picture, all the stranger for one that took place in snowy weather.

7. Darryl Zanuck, internal memo to Jerry Hoffman, 15 April 1937, USC: Fox Scripts "Happy Landing," file 1865.

8. *Bread, Butter, and Rhythm* conference with Darryl Zanuck, 24 July 1937, USC: Fox Scripts, file 1765.2.

9. Ibid.

10. Unidentified review, 1938, MCNY, SC 5.

11. 24 July 1937 treatment to script, 9–10, USC: Fox Scripts "Happy Landing," file 1765.1.

12. *Chicago Times,* 31 January 1938, MCNY, SC 5.

13. Herb Sterne, "The Movies" (source illegible), 29 January 1938, MCNY, SC 5.

14. Ed Sullivan, "Hollywood," *NYDN,* 3 March 1938, MCNY, SC 5.

15. Darryl Zanuck, letter to Ray Griffith and Richard Sherjan, 28 December 1936, UCLA: 20th Century–Fox Legal Records, box 937.

16. Ibid.

17. Irving Berlin to Darryl Zanuck, "Origin of Alexander's Ragtime Band Picture," 23 October 1941, UCLA: 20th Century–Fox Legal Records, box 937.

18. *Hollywood Reporter,* 25 May 1938, 3.

19. A2, 91.

20. EM, interview with PM, transcript, USC, HMC: Pete Martin Collection.

21. Fox preserved the outtakes, and they have aired from time to time on television specials.

22. A1, 123.

23. Joseph Breen, letter to Jason Joy, 18 February 1938, AMPAS: MPAA Production Code Administration Files, file number 283.

24. Joseph Breen, letter to Jason Joy, 23 March 1938, AMPAS: MPAA Production Code Administration Files, file number 283.

25. EM, interview with PM, transcript, USC.

26. 3 March 1937 treatment to script, 10 and 12, UCLA: 20th Century–Fox Scripts Collection, box PRS-405.

27. C. William Duncan, "Swing Music Is on Way Out Says Young Song Writer," *Philadelphia Evening Public Ledger,* 1 April 1939, MCNY, SC 6.

28. *NYHT,* 14 May 1938, MCNY, box 9. Alongside this article is a piece about armed vigilantes chasing WPA strikers out of Camden, New Jersey, but it's crossed-out to make sure our focus goes to the right place.

29. Laurence Rex D'Orsay, letter to Fox, 20 May 1944, UCLA: 20th Century–Fox Legal Records, box 937.

30. Louella Parsons, *Los Angeles Examiner,* 25 May [1938], MCNY, box 9.

31. Ruth Arell, "From Rhythm to Riches: Ethel Merman's Effervescence Paved the Way to Swing-Song Success!" *Modern Magazine,* August 1938.

32. *Zit's Theatrical Newspaper,* 30 April 1932, MCNY, box 4.

33. Conference notes, 27 April 1938, 2, USC: Fox Scripts "Straight Place and Show," folder 1.

34. Notes of First Draft Continuity, 8 April 1938, USC: Fox Scripts "Straight Place and Show," folder 1.

35. Main unit filmed on the Santa Anita racetrack with two hundred extras and bit players; second units shot at the Wrestling Arena in LA.

36. *Chicago American,* 8 October 1938, MCNY, SC 4.

37. On 25 July 1938, Fox Associate legal counsel Emilio C. de Lavigne wrote Merman, "The term of your employment thereunder shall be deemed to have expired on June 25, 1938, the date of completion of your services in the production *Straight Place and Show.*" In a private memo of the same day, de Lavigne notes that her option would have been for three more pictures in a year, "payment $32,500 per picture, six weeks employment guaranteed. . . . It is our understanding that this option will not be exercised." Both files in UCLA: 20th Century–Fox Legal Records, box 1374.

38. A2, 92.

39. "Hollywood Is Crazy; Broadway More Fun, Declares Blue Star," *Cornell Daily Sun* (NY), 7 December 1934, MCNY, box 4.

40. David J. Hanna, "Hollywood Editorial: Musical Talent" (unidentified magazine), 10 September 1938, MCNY, SC 4.

41. "Broadway a Snap to Movies," *Philadelphia Evening Bulletin,* 8 September 1938, MCNY, SC 4.

42. Alexander Kahn, "Ethel Merman Has Decided to Make Her Home in Hollywood," *Dallas Dispatch,* 10 September 1938, MCNY, SC 4.

43. "Merman Loyal to New York," *Washington D.C. Herald,* 6 February 1938, MCNY, SC 5.

44. Richard Watts, "Review of *Stars in Your Eyes,*" *NYHT,* 11 January 1939, MCNY, box 7.

45. "Review: Boisterous Energy of Jimmy Durante and Ethel Merman," *NYT,* 5 March 1939, MCNY, box 7.

46. Jack Stinnet, "What's Doing on Broadway," *El Paso Times,* 4 October 1938, MCNY, SC 4. George Jean Nathan was making similar observations.

47. *Life,* [29] February 1939, MCNY, SC 6.

48. John Mason Brown, "Ethel Merman and Jimmy Durante in Superb Form," 10 March 1939, *NYP,* MCNY, box 7.

49. Unidentified review of *Girl Crazy,* 1930, MCNY, box 2.

50. Elinor Hughes, "In Praise of Ethel Merman and of Musical Comedy Today," *Boston Traveler,* 4 January 1943, MCNY, SC 10.

51. "Hollywood Is Crazy," *Cornell Daily Sun,* 7 December 1934.

52. John Anderson, "Lahr, Merman Musical Opens," *NYJA,* 7 December 1939, MCNY, SC 7.

53. See Stanley Green's impeccably researched *Ring Bells! Sing Songs! Broadway Musicals of the 1930's* (New York: Galahad Books, 1971), 188.

54. John Mason Brown, "Two on the Aisle: Review of *DuBarry Was a Lady,*" *NYP,* 7 December 1939, MCNY, SC 7.

55. During the run of the show, the two appeared together on a radio program and led into "Friendship" with the following:

> LAHR:. You can't compare me with Mickey Rooney—I played in *The Wizard of Oz.*
> MERMAN: Yeah, what did you do?
> LAHR: Oh, I just made an Oz of myself.
> MERMAN: Cheer up, Bert, you're still the man in *DuBarry Was a Lady.*
> LAHR: Aw, Ethel, you're wonderful. You're the best performer I ever worked with.

Courtesy of Al F. Koenig Jr. from Merman's acetate collection. Show undated.

56. *Time,* 18 December 1939, 45, MCNY, SC 7.

57. *New York Cue,* 16 December 1939, MCNY, SC 7.

58. Libbey, unidentified Boston newspaper, 8 October [1939], MCNY, SC 1.

59. Edwin Schloss, "Review of *DuBarry Was a Lady,*" *Philadelphia Record* (unidentified date), MCNY, SC 7.

60. Robert Rice, *New York Telegraph,* 8 December 1939, MCNY, SC 7.

61. "Review of *DuBarry Was a Lady,*" *Boston Globe,* 19 November 1939, MCNY, SC 7.

62. Alicia Hart, "Ethel Merman Avoids Any Glamour Tricks," *Salt Lake City Telegram,* 29 February 1940, MCNY, SC 7.

63. Richard Lockridge, "Review of *DuBarry Was a Lady,*" *New York Sun,* 7 December [1939], MCNY, SC 7.

64. Peggy Doyle, "Review of '*DuBarry Was a Lady,*'" 14 November 1939, unidentified New Haven (CT) newspaper, MCNY, SC 7.

CHAPTER 5: BROADWAY'S BRIGHTEST

1. William F. McDermott, "Girl Shows in General Are Doing Better Than the Heirs of Shakespeare," *Cleveland Plain Dealer,* 23 February 1941, MCNY, SC 9.

2. DF, interview with PM, transcript, 25, USC, HMC: Pete Martin Collection.

3. RLS, interview with PM, transcript, 23, USC, HMC: Pete Martin Collection.

4. DF, interview with PM, transcript, 7, USC.

5. TC, interview with author, 11 September 2004.

6. RLS, interview with PM, transcript, 11, USC.

7. "Inside Stuff—Legit," *New York Variety,* 19 June 1940, MCNY, SC 7.

8. Barclay Hudson, "So This Is Broadway," *NYWT,* 23 July 1940, MCNY, SC 8.

9. Gerald Bordman, *American Musical Theater: A Chronicle* (New York: Oxford University Press, 1978), 518.

10. "Musical Comedy Is Written to Feature Shirley Temple," *Buffalo News,* 25 July 1940, MCNY, SC 8.

11. Unidentified clipping, MCNY, SC 8.

12. *Variety* (date unidentified), MCNY, SC 8.

13. Elliot Norton, "Two More: Ethel Merman Merely Mows 'Em Down," *Boston Post,* 13 October 1940, MCNY, SC 8.

14. All in MCNY, SC 9.

15. Brooks Atkinson, *NYT,* 11 November 1940, MCNY, SC 8.

16. Arthur Pollock, "Panama Hattie Provides Ethel Merman with a Hit," *Brooklyn Eagle* (date unidentified), MCNY, SC 8.

17. John Mason Brown, "Ethel Merman Excellent in Panama Hattie," *NYP,* 31 October 1940, MCNY, SC 8.

18. Columbia released a recording of the song by Eddy Duchin, the beloved New York pianist. Later in the year, Ethel recorded it with other *Hattie* songs.

19. Louis Kronenberger, "Down in Panama with Ethel Merman" (unidentified source), 31 October 1940, MCNY, SC 8.

20. Ira Wolfert, "Song Hits—and Misses," *NYTM,* 19 January 1941, MCNY, SC 9.

21. Burns Mantle, "Review of Panama Hattie," *New York News,* 31 October 1940, MCNY, SC 8.

22. Sidney Whipple, *NYWT,* 3 October 1940, MCNY, SC 8.

23. Hattie's ostensibly backward class is also coded in ethnic and national terms. She gets along effortlessly with the American sailors and the working men and women of Panama, just as Ethel did when appearing in the southwestern bar in the short *Be Like Me.*

24. Dorothy Kilgallen, "Voice of Broadway" (syndicated), 4 November 1940, MCNY, SC 8.

25. *Hollywood Reporter,* 29 November 1940, MCNY, SC 8.

26. "Ethel Merman Now Mrs. W. B. Smith: Blues Singer Becomes Bride of Local Actors' Agent," *Los Angeles Examiner,* 16 November 1940, AMPAS.

27. "Individuality Brings Ethel Merman Fame," *Philadelphia Inquirer,* 20 January 1944, MCNY, SC 11.

28. Telegram from Buddy DeSylva to EM, 18 February 1941, MCNY, SC 9.

29. TC, interview with author, July 2006.

30. *NYJA,* 30 January 1940, MCNY, SC 7.

31. *Brooklyn Eagle,* 1939, MCNY, SC 7.

32. "Comedians Take Broadway's Mind off World Strife," *Hartford Times,* 1 June 1940, MCNY, SC 7.

33. RL, interview with author, July 2004.

34. *Staten Island Advance,* 10 May 1940, MCNY, SC 7.

35. Alexander Woollcott, *The Story of Irving Berlin,* quoted in Laurence Bergreen, *As Thousands Cheer: The Life of Irving Berlin* (New York: Viking, 1990), 223.

36. Walter Cronkite quoted in Bergreen, *As Thousands Cheer,* 580.

37. CP, interview with PM, transcript, 3, USC, HMC: Pete Martin Collection.

38. Bergreen, *As Thousands Cheer,* 450.

39. *NYP,* "Stars to Act in 'Fun to Be Free,'" 13 September 1941, MCNY, SC 9.

40. Unidentified article, [11] May 1931, MCNY, box 2.

41. RL, interview with author, July 2004.

42. Ibid.

43. *News-Organizer* (Raleigh, NC), "In Broadway Theatres," 24 January 1943, MCNY, SC 10.

44. Helen Harrison, "Pull Down Your Vest, Lady!" *NYWJT,* 7 September 1940, MCNY, SC 8.

45. Dorothy Kilgallen, "Voice of Broadway," *NYJA,* 14 November 1939, MCNY, SC 7.

46. Bordman, *American Musical Theater,* 518.

47. For an extended discussion of this, see Andrea Most, *Making Americans: Jews and the Broadway Musical* (Cambridge, MA: Harvard University Press, 2004).

48. Marilyn Cantor Baker, telephone interview with author, June 2004.

49. Richard Watts, "Review of DuBarry," *NYHT,* 7 December 1942, MCNY, SC 7.

50. By 1940 the average price of a jukebox was $285, and owners expected average weekly returns of $3.50 per machine. The amount was split with location owners, and the jukebox owners soon tried to change profit percentages to 65/35, arguing that disc replacement was costly, with records wearing out after about sixty playings. "The Story behind a Hit," *Boston Sunday Advertiser: "Green Magazine,"* 21 January 1941, MCNY, SC 8.

51. Elliot Norton, *Boston Post,* 19 December 1942, NYPL, Billy Rose Theatre Collection: Special Collections.

52. "Ethel Merman Is Getting Big Laughs on Broadway in Her Newest Musical," *Milwaukee Journal,* 25 January 1943, NYPL, Billy Rose Theatre Collection: *Something for the Boys* file.

53. Mike Todd quoted in John Anderson, "Merman in New Hit Musical," *NYJA,* 24 January 1943, NYPL, Billy Rose Theatre Collection: *Something for the Boys* file.

54. Elliot Norton, *Boston Post,* 19 December 1942, NYPL, Billy Rose Theatre Collection.

55. Unidentified article, ca. December 1942, MCNY, SC 10.

56. A2, 129–30.

57. William McBrien, *Cole Porter: A Biography* (New York: Knopf, 1998), 241.

58. Unidentified clipping, ca. November 1936, MCNY, box 15.

59. Allan Berube, *Coming Out under Fire: The History of Gay Men and Women in World War Two* (New York: Free Press, 1990), 70, 72.

60. Burton Rascoe, "Why Gentlemen Prefer Brunette La Merman," *NYWT,* 21 January 1943, MCNY, SC 10; italics added.

61. Deborah Grace Winer, *On the Sunny Side of the Street: The Life and Lyrics of Dorothy Fields* (New York: Schirmer Books, 1997), 129–30.

CHAPTER 6: FORGING A FAMILY

1. RLS, interview with PM, transcript, 1–2, USC, HMC: Pete Martin Collection.

2. EM, interview with PM, transcript, USC, HMC: Pete Martin Collection.

3. RLS, interview with PM, transcript, 13, USC.

4. RL, interview with author, July 2004.

5. A2, 121.

6. Various sources, MCNY, SC 7.

7. RLS, interview with PM, transcript, 5, USC.

8. *Variety,* 3 June [1942], MCNY, SC 10.

9. A2, 125.

10. In *Biography* episode: "Ethel Merman: There's No Business Like Show Business," A&E, 1999 broadcast. For as common as the vocabulary of new "productions" and "roles" was, Ethel's own family deployed the same metaphors: granddaughter Barbara Geary refers to Ethel's time as housewife and mom as her "best performance."

11. *NYWT,* "Navy Relief Show," 10 March [1942], MCNY, SC 9.

12. M.L.A., "Ethel Merman Scores as Always in New York," *Boston Morning Globe,* 27 December 1942, MCNY, SC 10.

13. Danton Walker, "Broadway: Bob Levabitt [*sic*] Is Assigned to the Quartermaster Corps in Brooklyn," *New York News,* 26 May 1942, MCNY, SC 9. As a member of the military, Levitt's nonjournalist salary would be cut as a result of payroll cutbacks affecting all Americans from President Roosevelt on down.

14. RLS, interview with PM, transcript, 30, USC.

15. DF, interview with PM, transcript, 28, USC, HMC: Pete Martin Collection.

16. "The Rambling Reporter," *Hollywood Reporter,* 17 April 1944; also in Hal Eaton, "Going to Town," *Long Island City Star-Journal,* 24 April 1944; both articles in MCNY, SC 11.

17. Dorothy Kilgallen, "Voice of Broadway," *NYJA,* 10 April 1944, MCNY, SC 11.

18. Danton Walker, "Broadway," *New York News,* 21 June 1944, MCNY, SC 11.

19. Ed Sullivan, "Little Old New York," *New York News,* 19 June 1944, MCNY, SC 11.

20. A. P. Waxman, personal note to EM, MCNY, SC 11.

21. Gerald Bordman, *American Musical Theater: A Chronicle* (New York: Oxford University Press, 1978), 543.

22. Unidentified "Publicity Man from Fox on Lou Irwin," interview with PM, transcript, 12, USC, HMC: Pete Martin Collection.

23. RE, interview with PM, transcript, 19, USC, HMC: Pete Martin Collection.

24. Louella Parsons, " 'Stage Door Canteen' Film Dazzles with Star Galaxy," *Los Angeles Examiner,* July 1943.

25. A2, 132.

26. "Film Bond Drive Extended as Battle Costs Increase," *Variety,* 6 July 1944, MCNY, SC 11.

27. Telegram, 6 November 1944, MCNY, SC 11.

28. Dorothy Kilgallen, "Voice of Broadway," *NYJA,* 14 April 1945, MCNY, SC 11.

29. Ed Sullivan, "Little Old New York: Weep No More My Ladies," *New York News,* 16 July 1944, MCNY, SC 11.

30. RL, letter to author, 28 January 2007.

31. RLS, interview with PM, transcript, 13, USC.

32. RL, interview with author, July 2004. Dorothy Fields says that Levitt Sr. was the one with the mouth in front of the kids; it was people who didn't know Ethel who insist that Ethel used her salty language everywhere she went.

33. Tyrone Power, letter to EM, 3 March 1940, MCNY, SC 7.

34. RL, interview with author, July 2004.

35. Ibid.

36. RL, letter to author, undated, received 11 February 2004.

37. RL, interview with author, July 2004.

38. RL, letter to author, 28 January 2007.

39. RLS, interview with PM, transcript, 21–22, USC.

40. Ibid.

41. RL, interview with author, July 2004.

CHAPTER 7: WHAT COMES NATUR'LLY

The epigraphs are from Ward Morehouse, "Broadway after Dark," *New York Sun,* 29 September 1946, MCNY, SC 13; and author unknown, unidentified *Esquire* article, [1946].

1. Julia McCarthy, "Review of *Annie Get Your Gun,*" *NYDN,* 20 May 1946, NYPL, Billy Rose Theatre Collection: MWEZ, nc 1, "Annie Get Your Gun."

2. Michael Kesterton, "Sharpshooter Was Always a Lady," *Toronto Globe and Mail,* 4 November 2000.

3. Ibid.

4. Deborah Grace Winer, *On the Sunny Side of the Street: The Life and Lyrics of Dorothy Fields* (New York: Schirmer Books, 1997), 149.

5. DF, interview with PM, transcript, 9, USC, HMC: Pete Martin Collection (slightly modified for grammar).

6. Ibid., transcript, 10.

7. June Herder, "Ethel Met 'Annie' in Hospital," *Philadelphia Record,* 5 May 1946, NYPL, Billy Rose Theatre Collection: MWEZ, nc I, "Annie Get Your Gun."

8. Winer, *On the Sunny Side of the Street,* xvii.

9. The powerful, brooding song would be a hit by Bing Crosby but was later banned from radio broadcasts for its downbeat message.

10. Winer, *On the Sunny Side of the Street,* 58.

11. Ibid., 28.

12. A2, 138.

13. Laurence Bergreen, *As Thousands Cheer: The Life of Irving Berlin* (New York: Viking, 1990), 448.

14. Ibid., 450.

15. A2, 139.

16. Herbert and Dorothy Fields, "Authors of 'Annie Get Your Gun' Come Clean," *NYHT,* 21 April 1945, MCNY, SC 11.

17. Bergreen, *As Thousands Cheer,* 446.

18. Andrea Most, *Making Americans: Jews and the Broadway Musical* (Cambridge, MA: Harvard University Press, 2004), 119.

19. David Lahm, interview with author, November 2003.

20. See the discussion by Most, *Making Americans,* 122 ff.

21. Glenn Litton and Cecil Smith, *Musical Comedy in America: From the Black Crook through Sweeney Todd* (New York: Routledge, 1978), 185.

22. Bergreen, *As Thousands Cheer,* 455.

23. Note from Dr. Herbert Graf, 11 April 1946, MCNY, SC 11.

24. A2, 140–41.

25. Recently, the 10 percent federal admissions tax on all theater tickets had been doubled. According to *Variety* (10 April 1946), *Annie*'s $6.60 ticket price reflected a $5.50 base with $1.10 tax. Walter Winchell, reliably unreliable about money when gossiping about the stars, reported $7.20 as the top price (various sources in MCNY, SC 11).

26. Bergreen, *As Thousands Cheer,* 458.

27. A2, 141–42.

28. Ward Morehouse, "*Annie Get Your Gun* Hit at the Imperial: Merman Overcomes Flimsy Book," *NYWTS,* 17 May 1946.

29. Elsa Maxwell, "Elsa Maxwell's Party Line: Review of *Annie Get Your Gun,*" *NYP,* 8 August 1946, MCNY, SC 12.

30. Robert Garland, "'Annie Get Your Gun' at Imperial Theatre," *NYJA* (unidentified date), NYPL, Billy Rose Theater Collection: MWEZ, nc I, "Annie Get Your Gun."

31. Stanley Green, *The World of Musical Comedy,* 4th ed. (San Diego, CA: Da Capo Press, 1980).

32. A1, 187. Martin actually took the remark from his interview with Jule Styne, who said, "I think Berlin made more of a lady out of Ethel" in *Annie Get Your Gun.* "He showed her softer side . . . because the other type of girl [she usually played] is a cliche character . . . [who] was good in the 20s and 30s, the gangster moll, the 'hey hey' girl." JS, interview with PM, transcript, 9 (?), USC, HMC: Pete Martin Collection.

33. Henry Pleasants, *The Great American Popular Singers* (New York: Simon and Schuster, 1985), 342.

34. Joshua Logan, *Josh: My Up and Down, In and Out Life* (New York: Delacorte, 1976), 184–85.

35. A1, 190.

36. Richard P. Cooke, "A Perfect Score," *Wall Street Journal,* 20 May 1946, NYPL, Billy Rose Theatre Collection: MWEZ, nc 1, "Annie Get Your Gun."

37. *Newsweek,* "Annie Scores a Bull's Eye," 27 May 1946, NYPL, Billy Rose Theatre Collection: MWEZ, nc 1, "Annie Get Your Gun."

38. Unidentified clipping, USC, HMC: Pete Martin Collection, box 19: 2–3, 6, and 194.

39. John Mason Brown, "Seeing Things: La Merman," *Saturday Review,* 15 June 1946, NYPL, Billy Rose Theatre Collection: MWEZ, nc 1, "Annie Get Your Gun."

40. A2, 143.

41. Wolcott Gibbs, "Ethel Merman," *Life,* 8 July 1946, 92, MCNY, SC 12.

42. Unidentified article, ca. 1938, NYPL, Billy Rose Theatre Collection: Special Collections.

43. Most, *Making Americans,* 136.

44. RE, interview with PM, transcript, 11, USC, HMC: Pete Martin Collection.

45. Kaye Ballard, conversation with author, 28 June 2004.

46. Anonymous fan, informal conversation with author.

47. Marilyn Cantor Baker, interview with author, June 2004.

48. *Chicago Daily News,* "Ethel's Voice Can Bowl 'Em," 2 August 1948, MCNY, SC 13.

49. Jill Bosworth, interview with author, November 2003.

50. Anonymous fan, informal conversation with author, spring 2004.

51. David Lahm, letter to author, November 2005.

52. See Most, *Making Americans,* the chapter "The Apprenticeship of Annie Oakley," 142 ff.

53. Dorothy Kilgallen, "Voice of Broadway," *NYJA,* 25 July 1946, MCNY, SC 12.

54. Berlin would receive 4.5 percent of gross box office receipts; the Fieldses would each receive 2.25 percent.

55. Thanks to Al F. Koenig Jr. for this quote.

56. Marilyn Cantor Baker, interview with author, June 2004.

57. Sherri R. Dienstfrey, "Ethel Merman: Queen of Musical Comedy," Ph.D. dissertation, Kent State University, 1986.

58. G. A. Falzer, "The Two Annie Oakleys," *Newark Sunday Call,* MCNY, SC 12.

59. A1, 196.

60. Earl Wilson, "The Midnight Earl," *Daily Mirror,* 30 March 1946, MCNY, SC 11.

61. John Chapman, "Holiday Time along Rialto Finds Actors Ready to Take Over," 23 June 1948, *New York News,* MCNY, SC 13.

62. William Hawkins, "'Annie' Still Shoots 'Em Dead," *NYWT,* 17 May 1948, MCNY, SC 13.

63. Pleasants, *The Great American Popular Singers,* 338.

64. Mary Martin, *My Heart Belongs* (New York: William Morrow, 1976), 147.

65. Bergreen, *As Thousands Cheer,* 458–59.

66. Ethan Mordden, *Beautiful Mornin': The Broadway Musical in the 1940s* (New York: Oxford University Press, 1999), 36.

67. George Frazier, *Holiday Magazine,* October 1947, 132–33, MCNY, SC 12.

68. Ibid.

69. Correspondence from Al F. Koenig Jr. Koenig wrote liner notes for the subsequent releases of her Decca singles on LP and CD.

70. Louis Sobol, "New York Cavalcade," *NYJA,* 28 October 1946, MCNY, SC 12.

71. Wolcott Gibbs, "Seasons in the Sun and Other Pleasures," excerpted in *Reader's Digest,* October 1946, 88, NYPL, Billy Rose Theatre Collection: Special Collections.

72. Gibbs, "Ethel Merman."

73. RL, letter to author, 28 January 2007.

74. Louis Sobol, "New York Cavalcade," *NYJA,* 8 June 1946, MCNY, SC 12.

75. John Crosby, "Radio in Brief," *NYHT,* 11 August 1949, MCNY, SC 13.

CHAPTER 8: *CALL ME MADAM*

1. Records for Berle's show do not give precise dates of her appearance, and Berle himself, according to Al F. Koenig Jr., was unable to find them. In her first autobiography, Merman states that her TV debut was 15 June 1953—the famous *Ford 50th Anniversary Show,* which is probably not the case. Thanks to Al F. Koenig Jr. for noting the conflicting dates.

2. Frank Stanton, telegram to EM, MCNY, SC 13.

3. Leonard Lyons, "The Lyons Den," *NYP,* 15 August 1950, MCNY, SC 14.

4. DF, interview with PM, transcript, 28, USC, HCM: Pete Martin Collection.

5. RL, letter to author, 28 January 2007.

6. Ibid.

7. RL, interview with author, July 2004.

8. USC, HMC: Pete Martin Collection.

9. A1, 200.

10. Other reports give a figure of two hundred thousand dollars, but either way, only six outside investors were approached.

11. MCNY, SC 14.

12. AI, 202.

13. EM, interview with PM, transcript, 3, USC, HMC: Pete Martin Collection.

14. An insert in the program for the Boston tryout reads, "Tonight Miss Merman and Mr. Nype will sing 'You're Not Sick, You're in Love," the title that was later shorted to "You're Just in Love." Insert located by Al F. Koenig Jr.

15. CP, interview with PM, transcript, 4, USC, HMC: Pete Martin Collection.

16. RLS, telegram to EM, MCNY, SC 14.

17. *NYT,* 21 August 1950, MCNY, SC 14.

18. AI, 208.

19. RE, interview with PM, transcript, 21, USC, HMC: Pete Martin Collection.

20. All from MCNY, SC 14.

21. CP, interview with PM, transcript, 3, USC.

22. Beverly Baxter, *London's Evening Standard* (unidentified date), MCNY, SC 15.

23. Mary Sullivan, "Two on the Aisle: Review of *Call Me Madam,*" *Boston Advertiser,* 24 September 1950, MCNY, SC 14.

24. *NYJA,* 18 September 1950, MCNY, SC 14.

25. Vernon Rice and Robert Williams, "Call Her Magnificent," *NYP Weekend Magazine,* 14, MCNY, SC 14.

26. Walter Winchell, *NYM,* 4 February 1951, MCNY, SC 15.

27. Al F. Koenig Jr., "Merman—Solid New York," *Joslin's Jazz Journal* (Parsons, KS, 1998). The quote is taken from an unidentified 1950 clipping found in Edward Zimmermann's belongings.

28. AI, 210.

29. AI, 219.

30. KB, live dialogue recorded on the album *Everything the Traffic Will Allow: The Songs and Sass of Ethel Merman,* Lunch Money Productions, 2002 (compact disc). Blackhurst goes on to say that Mainbocher singled out Ethel's torso, legs, ankles, and feet for appreciation.

31. Brooks Atkinson, *NYT,* 22 October 1950, MCNY, SC 14.

32. Gilbert Millstein, "Madam Ambassador from and to Broadway," *NYTM,* 1 October 1950, MCNY, SC 14.

33. Gerald Bordman, *American Musical Theater: A Chronicle* (New York: Oxford University Press, 1978), 574.

34. Robert Rice, "Call Me Merman," *Flair,* October 1950, MCNY, SC 14.

35. Invitation, MCNY, SC 15.

36. Lew Kessler, interview with PM, transcript, 6, USC, HMC: Pete Martin Collection.

37. PM, "Questions to Ask Ethel Merman Based on Crouse and Lindsay Interview," typed notes, 2, USC, HMC: Pete Martin Collection.

38. EM, interview with PM, transcript, USC.

39. NBC, *The Big Show,* quoted in Jack Gould, *NYT,* 6 November [1950], MCNY, SC 14.

40. There is some doubt about the date. Most sources indicate the show closed in April, but according to the *NYT,* it closed on May 3. Thanks to Al F. Koenig Jr. for the research on this.

41. The last show to play there had been *Oklahoma!* on 31 July 1948. The National closed as a result of a dispute between Marcus Hieman, who leased the theater, and the Dramatists Guild and Actors' Equity, which said they would withhold their works and their members if the National Theatre continued its policy of racial segregation. Rather than change, Hieman used the theater as a film house. When his contract expired, the new lessees changed the policy.

42. Perle Mesta, "Call Me Minister," *NYJA,* 10 September 1950, MCNY, SC 14.

43. EM, "How to Give a Good Party," *Cosmopolitan,* August 1949; quotes reprinted in *Minneapolis Tribune,* 9 October 1949; both in MCNY, SC 13.

44. RL, letter to author, 28 January 2007.

45. DF, interview with PM, transcript, 17, USC.

46. RL, interview with author, July 2004.

CHAPTER 9: A MORE COMPLEX IMAGE

The epigraphs are from "The Theatre," *Time,* 28 October 1940, MCNY SC 8, and Bob Considine, "On the Line" (unidentified source), 14 November 1949, MCNY SC 13.

1. Henry Pleasants, *The Great American Popular Singers* (New York: Simon and Schuster, 1985), 342.

2. Amy Porter, "Sureshot Merman," *Colliers,* 10 August 1946, NYPL, Billy Rose Theatre Collection, *Annie Get Your Gun* file.

3. Alice Hughes, "Little Items about Big Store Chiefs," *New York American,* 2 November 1936, MCNY, box 6.

4. A2, 81.

5. Edd Johnson, "Ethel Merman Tells—All about Herself," *NYWT,* 13 August 1938, MCNY, box 7.

6. Elliot Norton, "Two More: 'Ethel Merman Merely Mows 'Em Down,' " *Boston Post,* 13 October 1940, MCNY, SC 8.

7. Neal Gabler, *Winchell: Gossip, Power and the Culture of Celebrity* (New York: Vintage, 1995), 63.

8. Victor S. Navasky, *Naming Names* (New York: Viking Press, 1980), 152.

9. RL, letter to author, 3 February 2007.

10. Robert Garland, "The Drama," *NYJA* [summer 1947], MCNY, SC 12.

11. Lew Kessler, interview with PM, transcript, 25, USC, HMC: Pete Martin Collection.

12. RLS, interview with PM, transcript, 23, USC, HMC: Pete Martin Collection.

13. RL, letter to author, 28 February 2007.

14. Helen Ormsbee, "Ethel Merman Discovers Maids Are More Elusive Than

Roles," *NYHT,* 28 April 1946, NYPL, Billy Rose Theatre Collection: *Annie Get Your Gun* file; "Ethel Guns for a Baby Sitter," *NYJA,* "Saturday Home Magazine," 12 June 1948, MCNY, SC 13; Dorothy Kilgallen, "Voice of Broadway," *NYJA,* 9 September 1951, MCNY SC 15.

15. RL, interview with author, July 2004.

16. EM, interview with PM, transcript, USC, HMC: Pete Martin Collection.

17. Robert Alton, letter to EM, 4 May 1940, MCNY, SC 7.

18. Betty Hutton, thank-you note to EM, MCNY, SC 9.

19. John Mason Brown, thank-you note to EM, 15 July 1947, MCNY, SC 12.

20. RL, interview with author, July 2004.

21. TC, interview with author, 11 September 2004.

22. BG, interview with author, July 2004.

23. Wolcott Gibbs, "Ethel Merman," *Life,* 8 July 1946, MCNY, SC 12.

24. Anonymous fan, informal conversation with author, summer 2005.

25. Anonymous fan, informal conversation with author, March 2005.

26. Arthur Laurents, *Original Story by Arthur Laurents: A Memoir of Hollywood and Broadway* (New York: Applause Books, 2001), 394.

27. TC, interview with author, 11 September 2004. He goes on to say that Billy Rose, whose wife, Eleanor Holm, was a good friend of Ethel's, was furious when Holm commented once that one of his hats looked "too Jewish."

28. RL, letter to author, 3 February 2007.

29. RLS, interview with PM, transcript, 11, USC.

30. RL, letter to author, 3 February 2007.

31. Ed Zimmerman, interview with author, November 2003. The only other time she acknowledged him, he recalls, was when she noted approvingly to costar Russell Nype that Zimmerman took both "ketchup and mustard" on his hot dogs and "that's why he sings so well!"

32. TC, interview with author, 11 September 2004.

33. Ibid.

34. RL, letter to author, 27 February 2007.

35. Unidentified clipping, MCNY, SC 9.

36. RL, interview with author, July 2004.

37. BG, interview with author, July 2004.

38. David Lahm, interview with author, 22 December 2003.

39. "Smile When You Call Merman Madam," *Collier's,* 21 October 1950, MCNY, SC 14.

40. TC, interview with author, 11 September 2004; recounted by EM in A1, 194.

41. Reported by Lewis Funke, "First Night Flutters" (unidentified source), MCNY, SC 15.

42. Vinton Freedley, interview with PM, transcript, USC, HMC: Pete Martin Collection.

43. Quotes are taken from Lew Kessler, interview with PM, transcript, 46, USC;

various clippings in MCNY; A1; A2; and Edward Baron Turk, *Hollywood Diva: A Biography of Jeanette MacDonald* (Berkeley: University of California Press, 1998), 295.

44. Mel Heimer, "My New York," 13 May 1947 (syndicated), MCNY, SC 12.

45. KB, live dialogue recorded on the album *Everything the Traffic Will Allow*, Lunch Money Productions, 2002 (compact disc).

46. CP, interview with PM, transcript, 19, USC, HMC: Pete Martin Collection.

47. Sherri R. Dienstfrey, "Ethel Merman: Queen of Musical Comedy," Ph.D. dissertation, Kent State University, 1986, 9.

48. TC, *Biography* episode: "Ethel Merman: There's No Business Like Show Business," A&E, 1999 broadcast (slightly modified for grammar).

49. Ed Sullivan, "Little Old New York," *New York News,* 6 February 1945, MCNY, SC 10.

50. From correspondence quoted in Dienstfrey, "Ethel Merman," 130.

51. TC, interview with author, August 2004.

52. Ibid.

53. Julia McCarthy, "Ethel Admits Love, Career Can Mix," *New York News,* 31 January 1943, MCNY, SC 10.

54. Lewis Sobol, "Sobol Discusses Success Gals," *American Weekly,* 6 June 1950, MCNY, SC 14.

55. Louis Sobol, "Louis Sobol Asks: They Hold Their Audiences, Why Not Their Men?" *American Weekly,* undated clipping [1941], MCNY, SC 9.

56. Ibid.

57. Doc Lou Clement and Harold Hoffman, letter to EM, 22 April 1943, MCNY, SC 10.

58. E. V. Durling, "On the Side," *Detroit Times,* 29 July 1940, MCNY, SC 8.

59. "Hides Romance" (unidentified writer), 1932, MCNY, box 7.

60. "DuBarry's to Marry, the Fates Indicate; but the Lady's Not Saying 'Whom' or 'Date,'" *New York Telegraph,* 31 March 1940, MCNY, SC 7.

61. Drew Pearson, "Ethel Merman, Marilyn Monroe on Merry-Go-Round," *LA Daily News,* 30 August 1954, MCNY, SC 4. Ethel's rival-to-be, Marilyn Monroe, wrote the other half of the guest column, relaying not sarcastic proclamations on marriage but opinions on glamour.

62. Burton Rascoe, "Theater," *NYWT* (date unidentified), MCNY, SC 11.

63. Gibbs, "Ethel Merman."

64. Quoted in Burton Rascoe, "Theatre: Why Gentlemen Prefer Brunette La Merman," *NYWT,* 21 January 1943, MCNY, SC 10.

65. *New Yorker,* "Ethel and Anton," 25 May 1946, 42, MCNY, SC 12.

66. Quote from Gibbs, "Ethel Merman."

67. "A Weighty Problem," *Picture Play Magazine,* April 1933, MCNY, box 7.

68. Dale Carnegie, *Pittsburgh Press,* 3 December 1940, MCNY, SC 8.

69. EM, interview with PM, transcript, 2–3, USC.

70. Ibid.

71. *Vogue,* August 1946, 140, MCNY, SC 12.

72. Gibbs, "Ethel Merman."

73. William Hawkins, "'Annie' Still Shoots 'Em Dead," *NYWT,* 17 May 1948, MCNY, SC 13.

74. When contacted, Penn did not want the photograph reproduced. It is not among his favorites, he said, because the piece relied on a prop to convey character.

75. Lee Rogow, "Brassy Dame: Review of *Who Could Ask for Anything More?*" *Saturday Review,* 2 July 1955, MCNY, SC 18.

76. DF, interview with PM, transcript, 19, USC, HMC: Pete Martin Collection.

77. EM, interview with PM, transcript, 19, USC.

78. John Beaufort, "*Something for the Boys* at the Alvin," *Boston Christian Science,* 8 January 1943, MCNY, SC 10.

79. Maybelle Manning, "Live Ducks on Hat Prove Amusement for New Yorkers," *Miami News,* 1 April 1940, MCNY, SC 7.

80. Ibid.

81. "Panama Hattie Puts It On!" *New York Women's Wear Daily,* 25 October 1940, MCNY, SC 9.

82. *NYJA,* "New York World's Fair's 'Free Milk Fund for Babies Day,'" 11 August 1940, MCNY, SC 8.

83. Amy Porter, unidentified clipping, NYPL, Billy Rose Theatre Collection.

84. Gibbs, "Ethel Merman."

85. Lew Kessler, interview with PM, transcript, 25, USC.

86. Amy Porter, unidentified clipping, NYPL, Billy Rose Theatre Collection.

87. Gibbs, "Ethel Merman."

88. Unidentified clipping.

89. Dorothy Kilgallen, "Voice of Broadway," *NYJA,* 6 March 1946, MCNY, SC 11.

CHAPTER 10: *MADAM IN HOLLYWOOD*

The epigraph is from dialogue transcribed from film box PRS-405, file 25235, 20 February 1953, UCLA: Arts Special Collections.

1. Dorothy Kilgallen, "Voice of Broadway," *NYJA,* 2 September 1951, MCNY, SC 15.

2. Robert Garland, note to EM, MCNY, SC 15.

3. *NYDN,* "Vintage Bon Voyage for Windsors," 24 May 1951, MCNY, SC 15.

4. Sherman Billingsley, telegram to EM, 2 July 1951, MCNY, SC 15.

5. Various clippings in MCNY, SC 15.

6. William Hawkings, "Merman Report: Fine as Ever," *NYWT,* 16 May 1951, MCNY, SC 15.

7. *Daily Variety,* 25 July 1951, MCNY, SC 15.

8. Robert Serling, *Maverick: The Story of Robert Six and Continental Airlines* (New York: Doubleday, 1974), 11.

9. Invitation to EM, MCNY, SC 17.

10. RL, interview with author, July 2004.

11. Serling, *Maverick*, 11.

12. AI, 225.

13. Serling, *Maverick*, 104.

14. AI, 224.

15. Walter Winchell, *NYM*, 5 November 1951, MCNY, SC 15.

16. Frank Ferguson, letter to Fox, 11 June 1952, UCLA: 20th Century–Fox Legal Records, box 564.

17. "Biography of Sol Siegel," AMPAS: Sol Siegel file.

18. Unidentified article, ca. December 1952/January 1953, MCNY, SC 16.

19. Fox had procured Alton, like O'Connor, from MGM, the studio more renowned for its musicals than Fox. Alton's work on *Madam* exceeded the ten weeks for which he was initially contracted (at twenty-five hundred dollars per), but this was typical, especially for productions of this scale. Details of Alton's contract reveal the growing importance of choreographers to musicals on both coasts—as well as Alton's growing stature and prestige. Fox gave the choreographer permission to shoot his own numbers and to choose his own assistants at salaries commensurate with the wealthier MGM. Alton fought for the credit "Dances directed by," Fox insisted on "Dances staged by," and they compromised with "Dances and musical numbers staged by," based on precedent set at MGM (UCLA: 20th Century–Fox Legal Records, box 1032, Robert Alton folder). Alton would give the film version several additional dance scenes, primarily to showcase the talents of O'Connor and Vera Ellen and to help develop their courtship. The Ocarina folk festival features "The Ocarina" as its song, and Ethel appears in an added ball sequence, in which she sings "The International Rag."

20. EM, quoted in Edwin Schallert, "Hi-Test Opportunity Knocking for Ethel," *LAT,* 7 September 1952, MCNY, SC 16.

21. EM to unidentified interviewer, clipping, MCNY, SC 16.

22. Louella Parsons, unidentified clipping, MCNY, SC 16.

23. Hosted by Edwin W. and Bobbe Pauley for their fifteenth anniversary.

24. Sidney Skolsky, "Hollywood Is My Beat," *Hollywood Citizen News,* 6 August 1952, MCNY, SC 16.

25. "20th Muffles 'Madam' Mikes for Merman," *Variety,* 14 August 1952, MCNY, SC 16.

26. EM, quoted in Schallert, "Hi-Test Opportunity Knocking for Ethel."

27. Louella Parsons, *Miami Herald,* 14 December [1953], MCNY, SC 16.

28. Donald O'Connor, interview with PM, transcript, 5–6, USC, HMC: Pete Martin Collection.

29. Sidney Skolsky, "Hollywood Is My Beat," *Hollywood Citizen News,* 11 September 1952, MCNY, SC 16.

30. David Bongard, "A Producer Is No Mere Joy Boy—He Must Also Know His Job," *Los Angeles Daily News,* 2 March, 1953, AMPAS: Sol Siegel file.

31. Shriners benefit program, October 1952, in MCNY, SC 16.

32. "20th to Roll 9 Pix during September; New Studio Record," *Variety,* 20 August 1952, MCNY, SC 16.

33. Over four months he had prepared not only *Call Me Madam* but also *Gentlemen Prefer Blondes* and *There's No Business Like Show Business.*

34. "Sol Siegel Ducks 20th-Fox Musical Unit, Not Wishing to Type Himself," *Variety,* 13 September 1952, MCNY, SC 16.

35. Writer's working script, 25 March 1952, UCLA: 20th Century–Fox Legal Records, file 2523.2.

36. Conference with Zanuck, 2 April 1952, UCLA: 20th Century–Fox Legal Records, file 2523.3.

37. Ibid.

38. Ibid.

39. There is even a line that seems to announce Merman's new residence-to-be. On the phone asking "Harry" about his daughter's piano career, she asks, "Denver? How did it go? Hmm [pause]. Even in Denver. Well, the critics don't know everything."

40. Charles LeMaire, confidential letter to Lew Schrieber, 4 June 1952, UCLA: 20th Century–Fox Legal Records, box 564.

41. Sidney Skolsky, "Hollywood Is My Beat," *NYP,* 2 September 1952, MCNY, SC 16.

42. Unidentified "Publicity Man from Fox on Lou Irwin," interview with PM, transcript, 14, USC, HMC: Pete Martin Collection.

43. Dorothy Kilgallen, "Voice of Broadway," *NYJA,* 10 October 1952, MCNY, SC 16.

44. Joseph Breen, letter to Col. Jason Joy, 26 November 1951, AMPAS: Production Code Collection, *Call Me Madam.*

45. Joseph Breen, note to Col. Jason Joy, 30 April 1952, AMPAS: Production Code Collection, *Call Me Madam.*

46. Conference with Zanuck, 2 April 1952.

47. Breen, note to Joy, 30 April 1952.

48. Mike Connolly, "Rambling Reporter," *Hollywood Reporter,* 13 November 1952, MCNY, SC 16.

49. *NYJA,* 6 December 1952, MCNY, SC 16.

50. Danton Walker, "Broadway," unidentified clipping, MCNY, SC 16.

51. "Ethel Merman Likely to Pursue Films," *LAT,* 29 August 1952, MCNY, SC 16.

52. Hy Gardner, *NYHT,* 29 September 1952, MCNY, SC 16.

53. Radie Harris, "Broadway Ballyhoo," *Hollywood Reporter,* 16 December 1952, MCNY, SC 16.

54. White Company advertisement, MCNY, SC 16.

55. Lydia Lane, "Hollywood Beauty: Gals Need Individuality," *Long Island Sunday Press,* 14 December 1952, MCNY, SC 16.

56. Ibid.

57. "Solid Talent Lineup for Ike's Inaugural Show—but sans Ike," *Variety*, 24 December 1952, MCNY, SC 16.

58. Earl Wilson, "Nobody Was Happy after the Ball," *NYP*, 21 January 1953, MCNY, SC 16.

59. James O'Neill Jr., "Ethel Could Have Even Made the Democrats Happy," *Washington Daily News*, 20 January 1953, MCNY, SC 16.

60. Inez Robb, "To the Ladies / Ethel Merman Is an Auction Addict," *NYJA*, 2 March 1953, MCNY, SC 16.

61. Leonard Lyons, "Lyons Den," *NYP*, 29 January 1953, MCNY, SC 16.

62. *NYJA*, 3 March 1953, MCNY, SC 16.

63. Unidentified clipping, *Los Angeles Examiner*, 5 March 1953, MCNY, SC 17.

64. *Daily Variety*, 13 March 1953, MCNY, SC 16.

65. Ed Sullivan, "Little Old New York," *New York News*, 4 March 1953, MCNY, SC 16.

66. Groucho Marx, telegram to EM, 3 March 1953, MCNY, SC 16.

67. *Variety*, 4 March 1953, MCNY, SC 16.

68. Hy Gardner, "Review of *Call Me Madam*," *NYHT*, 4 March 1953, MCNY, SC 16.

69. "Review of *Call Me Madam*," *Time*, 23 March 1953, MCNY, SC 17.

70. Marie Torre, "Just Call Her Ma," *World Telegram*, 7 March 1953, MCNY, SC 16.

71. UCLA: 20th Century–Fox Legal Records, box 564.

CHAPTER 11: LIFE WITH SIX

1. A1, 224.

2. A2, 182.

3. EM repeated this sentiment in various sources.

4. JS, interview with PM, transcript, 28, USC, HMC: Pete Martin Collection.

5. A1, 225.

6. "Paging the New," radio broadcast transcript, 7, WABC, 2 August 1955, MCNY, SC 19.

7. Robert Serling, *Maverick: The Story of Robert Six and Continental Airlines* (New York: Doubleday, 1974), 104.

8. RL, letter to author, 27 February 2007.

9. A2, 187.

10. Serling, *Maverick*, 105.

11. "I can cook eggs, but not a whole meal." A1, 226.

12. RL, interview with author, July 2004.

13. RL, letter to author, 27 February 2007.

14. RL, letter to author, 9 February 2005.

15. Ibid.

16. RL, letter to author, 27 February 2007.

17. Ibid.

18. RL, letter to author, 21 April 2005.

19. Ibid.

20. RL, interview with author, July 2004.

21. Bob Krauss, "In One Ear," *Honolulu Advertiser,* 16 February 1954, MCNY, SC 17.

22. RL, letter to author, 27 February 2007.

23. Hope Johnson, *NYWT,* 20 June 1957, MCNY, SC 20.

24. A1, 197.

25. *Hollywood Reporter,* 6 August 1953, MCNY, SC 18.

26. A1, 44, 34, 10.

27. Robert Molyneux, "Brash, Brassy, Breezy," *Pittsburgh Press,* 3 July 1955, MCNY, SC 19.

28. Betsy Stinson, unidentified clipping, [1955], MCNY, SC 19.

29. PM, transcripts, USC, HMC: Pete Martin Collection.

30. E. L. Holland Jr., "Ethel Merman Story Like Ethel," *Birmingham News,* 3 July 1955, MCNY, SC 19.

31. A1, 51.

32. A1, 33.

33. USC, HMC: Pete Martin Collection, folder 3.

34. Danton Walker, "Broadway," *NYDN,* 28 June 1955, MCNY, SC 18.

35. This correction appears with a 11 July 1955 piece of correspondence from Kate Steichen, assistant to Doubleday publisher Ken McCormick, who had written a nice letter to Merman about the book. That letter was stapled to the promotion copy on which Merman had penciled her correction. MCNY, SC 19.

36. Beth Judson, "La Merman May Sing Loud but She Whispers to God," *Miami Herald,* 30 July 1955 (syndicated), MCNY, SC 19.

37. Serling, *Maverick,* 104.

38. DF, interview with PM, transcript, 1 and 30, USC, HMC: Pete Martin Collection.

39. Serling, *Maverick,* 124.

40. RL, interview with author, July 2004.

41. Ibid.

42. RL, letter to author, 27 February 2007.

43. Ibid.

44. RL, letter to author, 21 April 2005.

45. RL, interview with author, July 2004.

46. TC, conversation with author, August 2006.

1. Robert Six, letter to George Rosenberg, 30 June 1953, UCLA: 20th Century–Fox Legal Records, box 1374.

2. Eddie Cantor, "Entertainers Hit Millionaire Class," *Long Island Star-Journal,* 8 December 1954, MCNY, SC 18.

3. EM, letter to 20th Century–Fox, UCLA: 20th Century–Fox Legal Records, box 1374.

4. Sol Siegel, letter to Daryl Zanuck, 3 January 1953, UCLA: Arts Special Collection, box 580, "There's No Business Like Show Business."

5. Frank Ferguson, letter to Harold Collins, 22 June 1953, UCLA: 20th Century–Fox Legal Records, box 1374.

6. Laurence Bergreen, *As Thousands Cheer: The Life of Irving Berlin* (New York: Viking, 1990), 518.

7. As conveyed by Jason Joy to Fox Legal Department, "Brief Sketch," 18 March 1952, USC: Fox Scripts "There's No Business Like Show Business."

8. Lamar Trotti, Writer's Working Script for *There's No Business Like Show Business,* 12 January 1952, USC: Fox Scripts "There's No Business Like Show Business," file 595.3, 1.

9. Ibid., 10.

10. It is unclear if Zanuck is referring to "Heat Wave," "A Pretty Girl Is Like a Melody," or "Alexander's Ragtime Band."

11. Darryl Zanuck, memo to IB, 13, 17 December 1952, UCLA: 20th Century–Fox Scripts Collection, box 580, file 258.6.

12. Production notes, "20th Century Fox/Wolfson on Sol Siegel and *There's No Business Like Show Business,"* Paramount press sheets, 1 August 1935–31 July 1936, AMPAS.

13. Darryl Zanuck, memo to IB, 3, 17 December 1952, UCLA.

14. Jason Joy to Fox Legal Department, 18 March 1952, UCLA: 20th Century–Fox Scripts Collection 10.

15. Darryl Zanuck, memo to IB, 13, 17 December 1952, UCLA.

16. Sol Siegel, note to Darryl Zanuck, 3 January 1953, UCLA.

17. Sol Siegel, "Reaction to Step Sheet," 28 February 1953, UCLA: 20th Century–Fox Scripts Collection, file 2556.11.

18. Darryl Zanuck, memo to IB, 13, 17 December 1952, UCLA.

19. This is according to preliminary memos sent from Lew Schrieber to George Wasson, 28 February 1952, UCLA: 20th Century–Fox Legal Records, box 887, *There's No Business Like Show Business* file.

20. Darryl Zanuck, memo to IB, 17 December 1952, UCLA.

21. Siegel, "Reaction to Step Sheet."

22. Sol Siegel, letter to EM, 3 March 1954, MCNY, SC 4.

23. Other versions include Francesca Mitzi Marlene de Czarayicon Gerber or

Mitzi DeCzanyi Von Gerber. Her father was a Hungarian cellist, and her mother was a dancer of Austrian descent. AMPAS: Mitzi Gaynor files.

24. Oscar Levant (unidentified source), AMPAS: Mitzi Gaynor files.

25. Walter Lang, letter to EM, 12 November 1953, MCNY, SC 4.

26. Phoebe and Henry Ephron, step sheet for *There's No Business Like Show Business,* 28 February 1953, 3, UCLA, 20th Century–Fox Scripts Collection, file 2556.11.

27. George F. Custen, *Twentieth Century's Fox: Darryl F. Zanuck and the Culture of Hollywood* (New York: Basic Books, 1997), 350–51.

28. Lilly Sawyer is retained in a small role, as a heavy-drinking older woman whom Tim dates before getting involved with Vicky.

29. Darryl Zanuck, conference note to Sol Siegel, 26 January 1953, USC: Fox Scripts "There's No Business Like Show Business," box 580.

30. A1, 236. Pete Martin took these words from an interview he conducted with an unidentified publicity representative from Fox. After noting Lang's "wonderful way with people," the publicist said, "In most of Walter Lang's pictures *[With a Song in My Heart, On the Riviera, Call Me Madam]*—there aren't any heavies. They're happy pictures and . . . you're surrounded by people who are nice." Publicity man for Lou Irwin, interview with PM, transcript, 14, USC, HMC: Pete Martin Collection.

31. Unidentified newspaper article, 6 July 1954, MCNY, SC 18.

32. Earl Wilson, "Happy Honeymooner," *NYP,* 19 December 1954, MCNY, SC 4; italics added.

33. Quoted in Bob Thomas, *I've Got Rhythm! The Ethel Merman Story* (New York: Putnam, 1985), 132–33.

34. Unidentified newspaper column, MCNY, SC 4.

35. Joseph Breen, letter to Frank McCarthy, 24 May 1954, AMPAS: MPAA Production Code Administration files.

36. Letter from Joseph Breen to Col. Joseph Joy, 20 October 1937, in AMPAS: MPAA Production Code Administration files, *There's No Business Like Show Business* file.

37. When Steve announces his decision to enter the ministry, he says, "The way I see it, Dad, some people are meant to be one thing, some another."

38. Communications between Joseph Breen and Frank McCarthy, 24 and 26 May 1954, AMPAS: MPAA Production Code Administration files, *There's No Business Like Show Business* file.

39. Joseph Breen, letter to Frank McCarthy, 20 April 1954, AMPAS: MPAA Production Code Administration files, *There's No Business Like Show Business* file.

40. Personal correspondence from fan (Michelle L.) to author, 2004.

41. John M. Clum, *Something for the Boys: Musical Theater and Gay Culture* (New York: St. Martin's Press, 1999), 146, 147.

42. RE, interview with PM, transcript, 18, USC, HMC: Pete Martin Collection.

43. A1, 230.

44. RL, interview with author, July 2004.

45. Letter of complaint in box 887, UCLA: 20th Century–Fox Legal Records.

46. Siegel, "Reaction to Step Sheet," 28 February 1953, UCLA: 20th Century–Fox Scripts Collection 10, file 2556.11.

47. Final draft of *There's No Business Like Show Business,* 17 December 1953, 48, UCLA: 20th Century–Fox Scripts Collection 10, box 581, file 2595.13a.

48. A1, 235–36.

49. Hedda Hopper, "Hollywood," *NYDN,* 15 June 1954, MCNY, SC 18.

50. Otis L. Guernsey Jr., "Review of *There's No Business Like Show Business,*" *NYHT,* 17 December 1954, MCNY, SC 18.

51. Final draft of *There's No Business Like Show Business,* 60, 17 December 1953, UCLA.

52. *Biography* episode: "Ethel Merman: There's No Business Like Show Business," A&E, 1999 broadcast.

53. Earl Wilson, "Happy Honeymooner," *NYP,* 19 December 1954, MCNY, SC 4.

54. *Biography* episode: "Ethel Merman: There's No Business Like Show Business."

55. A1, 234.

56. PM, draft notes for A1, USC, HMC: Pete Martin Collection.

57. Lew Schreiber, confidential memo to Frank Ferguson, 20 March 1953, UCLA: 20th Century–Fox Legal Records, box 1374.

58. Ibid.

59. Lew Schreiber, letter to Frank Ferguson, 21 May 1953, UCLA: 20th Century–Fox Legal Records, box 1374.

60. Rose Pelswick, "New Film at Roxy Box Office Natural," *NYJA,* 17 December 1954, MCNY, SC 4.

61. C. A. LeJeune, "At the Films," *London Sunday Observer,* 6 February 1955, MCNY, box 15.

62. Mitzi Gaynor, telegram to EM, MCNY: "Ethel Merman: 1954–5" folder.

63. Alton Cook, "Musical Miscasts Merman," *NYWT,* 17 December 1954 MCNY, SC 18.

64. Sol Siegel, conference note to Darryl Zanuck on *There's No Business Like Show Business,* 18 October 1952, USC: Fox Scripts "There's No Business Like Show Business," file 2595.

65. Jack Moffitt, "Review of *There's No Business Like Show Business,*" *Hollywood Reporter,* [December 1954], MCNY, SC 4.

66. Custen, *Twentieth Century's Fox,* 351.

CHAPTER 13: FROM MRS. SIX TO MAMA ROSE

1. Walter Winchell, *New York Daily Mirror,* 21 March 1956, MCNY, SC 19.

2. Steven H. Scheuer, "Ethel Set for One More Show," *Long Island Press,* 28 March 1956, MCNY, SC 19.

3. Alex Murphree, "Ethel Merman Packing—Back to Broadway," *Denver Post,* 5 August 1956, MCNY, SC 19.

4. *NYJA,* 19 May 1956, MCNY, SC 19.

5. William McCullam, "Ethel Merman Returns Shouting, 'I Love Broadway,'" *NYJA,* 5 September 1956, MCNY, SC 20.

6. A2, 198.

7. Howard Lindsay and Russel Crouse, *Happy Hunting* (New York: Random House, 1957), 114.

8. Ibid., 45.

9. Ibid., 159.

10. "Merman and Spouse Form Own Film Company," *Variety,* 13 February 1957, MCNY, SC 20.

11. Robert Downing, "This Is the Story of Two Majestics—One in Cedar Rapids, One in New York," *Cedar Rapids Gazette,* 27 January 1957, NYPL, Billy Rose Theatre Collection: *Happy Hunting* file.

12. Lamas was also a follower of the Church of Religious Science, which maintains that adversity can be cured through prayer. He explained its influence: "As soon as a depressing thought comes into my mind, I substitute another." Lamas in Frances Herridge, "Curtain Cues," *NYP,* 24 September 1956, MCNY, SC 20.

13. Sheila Graham, "Hollywood" (syndicated), 19 September 1956, MCNY, SC 20.

14. *Rocky Mountain News,* 3 April 1956, MCNY, SC 19.

15. Howard Crouse and Buck Lindsay, letter to EM, 6 August 1956, MCNY, SC 20.

16. Various sources in NYPL, Billy Rose Theatre Collection: *Happy Hunting* file.

17. Lindsay and Crouse, *Happy Hunting,* 105.

18. Bob Thomas, *I've Got Rhythm! The Ethel Merman Story* (New York: Putnam, 1985), 138.

19. A2, 199.

20. "Ethel Merman Protests to Equity," *NYHT,* 22 August 57, NYPL, Billy Rose Theatre Collection: *Happy Hunting* file.

21. Quoted in Thomas, *I've Got Rhythm!* 141.

22. Marie Torre, "Taking Stock of Things, Merman Style," *NYHT,* 22 August 1957, NYPL, Billy Rose Theatre Collection: *Happy Hunting* file.

23. Dorothy Kilgallen, "Voice of Broadway: Merman Wins Another Round," *NYJA,* 4 September 1957, NYPL, Billy Rose Theatre Collection: *Happy Hunting* file.

24. Ed Sullivan, "Little Old New York," *NYDN,* 23 August 1957, MCNY, SC 21. His response to her thank-you is dated 27 August, also in SC 21.

25. Leonard Lyons, "The Lyons Den," *NYP,* 20 November 1957, NYPL, Billy Rose Theatre Collection: *Happy Hunting* file.

26. Bill Fields, letter to EM, 25 August 1957, MCNY, SC 21.

27. "The Theatre: New Musical in Manhattan," *Time,* 17 December 1956, NYPL, Billy Rose Theatre Collection: *Happy Hunting* file.

28. Hobe Morrison, "Shows on Broadway," *Variety,* 12 December 1956, MCNY, SC 21. Also quoted in Sherri R. Dienstfrey, "Ethel Merman: Queen of Musical Comedy," PhD dissertation, Kent State University, 1986, 135.

29. Dienstfrey, "Ethel Merman," 134–35.

30. A2, 197.

31. Cecil Smith and Glen Litton, *Musical Comedy in America: From the Black Crook through Sweeney Todd* (New York: Routledge, 1978), 214–15.

32. TC, interview with author, 11 September 2004.

33. Dienstfrey, "Ethel Merman," 131.

34. Lindsay and Crouse, *Happy Hunting,* 23.

35. Ibid.

36. The local *Rocky Mountain News* of 4 February 1957 awarded her once again the title "Best Tressed."

37. Quoted in Marie Torre, "TV/Radio Today," *NYHT,* 20 September 1957, MCNY, SC 20.

38. Armstrong had recently criticized President Eisenhower for the incident at Little Rock, a reference to the September 1957 "Little Rock Crisis," in which Arkansas governor Orval Faubus ordered in the National Guard to prevent nine African-American children from entering an unintegrated school. Eisenhower responded by deploying military troops. Armstrong's criticism inflamed certain factions enough to call on him to cancel his appearance on the show. The pro–civil rights trumpeter stayed on, along with Diahann Carroll, Mahalia Jackson, and Dinah Washington, in an integrated cast.

39. George Rosen, "It's No Longer a Case of Money," *Variety,* 25 September 1957, MCNY, SC 20.

40. A2, 201.

41. Lee Morimer, "New York Confidential," *NYDM,* 9 July 1957, MCNY, SC 20.

42. Alan Brian, "No One Ever Calls Him 'Mr. Merman,'" unidentified clipping, [1957], MCNY, SC 20.

43. Margaret McManus, "Not Tied Down by TV—Ethel Merman," *Paterson Evening News* (NJ), 14 August 1957, MCNY, SC 20.

44. A2, 196.

45. RL, letter to author, 20 August 2004.

46. RL, letter to author, 28 February 2007.

47. Ibid. Hearst's birthday was in late April; Levitt's suicide was at the end of January.

48. TC, interview with author, 11 September 2004.

49. Robert Serling, *Maverick: The Story of Robert Six and Continental Airlines* (New York: Doubleday, 1974), 125.

50. TC, interview with author, 6 July 2006.

1. See Ethan Mordden, *Coming Up Roses: The Broadway Musical of the 1950s* (New York: Oxford University Press, 1998), 251.

2. Keith Garebian, *The Making of Gypsy* (New York: Mosaic Press, 1998), 12.

3. This is the original title as it appeared in the program. It has since been reproduced on *Gypsy* cast recordings as "Let Me Entertain You," which is taken from the lyrics used when Louise performs the song in the second act.

4. This title, too, has known several different incarnations, such as "If Momma Were Married," with "Momma" spelled a variety of ways. Tony Cointreau reports that this is the version lyricist Stephen Sondheim understands to be correct (conversation with author, August 2006).

5. Arthur Laurents, *Original Story by Arthur Laurents: A Memoir of Broadway and Hollywood* (New York: Applause Books, 2001), 375.

6. Phyllis Pattelle, " 'Gypsy' in Merman's Soul," *NYJA*, 1 June 1959, 13, NYPL, Billy Rose Theatre Collection: *Gypsy* file, MWEZ, nc 26, 491.

7. Emily Coleman, "The Dance Man Leaps to the Top," *NYTM*, 19 April 1959, MCNY, SC 23.

8. Robbins was tormented about his decision for the rest of his life. See Greg Lawrence, *Dance with Demons: The Life of Jerome Robbins* (New York: Putnam, 2001).

9. JS, quoted in Craig Zadan, *Sondheim & Co.* (New York: Harper and Row, 1977), 38 and 41.

10. Meryle Secrest, *Stephen Sondheim: A Life* (New York: Knopf, 1998), 132.

11. Ibid., 134.

12. Ibid., 140.

13. Quoted in Laurents, *Original Story by Arthur Laurents,* 379.

14. Dorothy Kilgallen, "Voice of Broadway," *NYJA,* 30 March 1959, MCNY, SC 23.

15. Garebian, *The Making of Gypsy,* 35.

16. Paine Knickerbocker, "How Leland Hayward Would Save the Theater," *San Francisco Chronicle,* 6 July 1961, MCNY, SC 27.

17. Laurents, *Original Story by Arthur Laurents,* 378.

18. Ibid.

19. Barbara L. Wilson, "Gypsy Conquered Reluctant Writer," *Philadelphia Inquirer,* 3 May 1959, MCNY, SC 27.

20. RL, letter to author, 9 April 2005.

21. Thanks to Al F. Koenig Jr.

22. Radie Harris, *Reporter,* [12] February 1959, MCNY, SC 21.

23. Laurents, *Original Story by Arthur Laurents,* 391.

24. Unidentified clipping, *NYT,* 21 September 1974, 15, NYPL, Billy Rose Theatre Collection: Ethel Merman, 1970s folder. Merman repeated this on countless talk shows throughout the 1960s and '70s.

25. Laurents, *Original Story by Arthur Laurents*, 381.

26. Quoted in Zadan, *Sondheim & Co.*, 46.

27. Quoted in Secrest, *Stephen Sondheim*, 136.

28. Laurents, *Original Story by Arthur Laurents*, 394.

29. Quoted in Secrest, *Stephen Sondheim*, 139.

30. Laurents, *Original Story by Arthur Laurents*, 395.

31. Secrest, *Stephen Sondheim*, 139.

32. Jeanette Lovetri, interview with author, 7 November 2003.

33. From Al F. Koenig Jr.

34. Quoted in Zadan, *Sondheim & Co.*, 50.

35. Ibid.

36. Laurents, *Original Story by Arthur Laurents*, 385.

37. Quoted in Zadan, *Sondheim & Co.*, 45.

38. KB, interview with author, 5 October 2004.

39. Quoted in Secrest, *Stephen Sondheim*, 136; also recounted in Laurents, *Original Story by Arthur Laurents*, 382.

40. Unidentified clipping MCNY, *Gypsy* scrapbooks.

41. Ernie Schier, "*Gypsy* Brings Merman to Shuberts' Stage," *Evening Bulletin* (Philadelphia), 14 April 1959, MCNY, *Gypsy* scrapbooks.

42. Dorothy Kilgallen, "Voice of Broadway: Merman-Robbins at Odds on '*Gypsy*,'" *NYJA*, 29 April 1959, MCNY, *Gypsy* scrapbooks.

43. RL, interview with author, July 2004.

44. Laurents, *Original Story by Arthur Laurents*, 397.

45. "*Gypsy* Could Do $81,000 a Week," *Variety*, 15 April 1959, MCNY, *Gypsy* scrapbooks. The article says that *Gypsy* had a potential weekly gross of about $80,000 to $81,000 at $8.60 top weeknights and $9.40 weekend nights.

46. Louis Sobol, *NYJA*, 23 May 1959, MCNY, SC 23.

47. Laurents, *Original Story by Arthur Laurents*, 348.

48. Ibid., 399.

49. Robert Serling, *Maverick: The Story of Robert Six and Continental Airlines* (New York: Doubleday, 1974), 125.

50. Walter Kerr, "First Night Report," *NYHT*, 22 May 1959, NYPL, Billy Rose Theatre Collection: *Gypsy* file.

51. Kenneth Tynan, *New Yorker*, 30 May 1959, MCNY, *Gypsy* scrapbooks.

52. Walter Winchell, "The Broadway Hits," *NYDM* [25 May] 1959, MCNY, *Gypsy* scrapbooks.

53. Mark Steyn, *Broadway Babies Say Goodnight: Musicals Then and Now* (New York: Routledge, 1999), 101.

54. Mordden, *Coming Up Roses*, 253.

55. Tom Donnelly, "A Ten-Strike for Ethel and All Hands" (date unidentified), *Washington Daily News* (Washington, DC), MCNY, *Gypsy* scrapbooks.

56. *Newsweek*, 1 June 1959, MCNY, *Gypsy* scrapbooks.

57. Douglas Watt, "Record Review," *New York News,* 21 June 1959, MCNY, *Gypsy* scrapbooks.

58. Glenne Currie, "Ethel Merman: Still a Show-Stopper," *New York Graphic,* 1 September 1978, 9, NYPL, Billy Rose Theatre Collection: Ethel Merman, 1970s folder.

59. John Chapman, "A Critic in Favor Says Aye," *New York News,* 1 May 1960, MCNY, SC 24.

60. Radie Harris, "Broadway Ballyhoo," *Hollywood Reporter,* 28 April 1960, MCNY, SC 24.

61. Stacy Wolf, *A Problem Like Maria: Gender and Sexuality in the American Musical* (Ann Arbor: University of Michigan, 2002), 106.

62. Quoted in Zadan, *Sondheim & Co.,* 51–52.

63. Quoted in ibid., 52.

64. Quoted in ibid.

65. *Miami Herald,* 20 March 1961, MCNY, SC 25.

66. Radie Harris, "Broadway Ballyhoo," *Hollywood Reporter,* 2 December 1960, MCNY, SC 25.

67. Rosalind Russell, letter to EM, 4 June 1960, MCNY SC 23.

68. Frank Morriss, "No Roses Blooming for *Gypsy,*" *Toronto Globe and Mail,* 2 February 1963, MCNY, SC 27.

69. Stanley Eichelbaum, "Ethel Merman Deserts Broadway," *San Francisco Examiner,* 28 March 1962, MCNY, SC 28.

70. Dorothy Kilgallen, "Voice of Broadway," *NYJA,* 1 November 1962, MCNY, SC 26.

71. Mordden, *Coming Up Roses,* 251.

72. "Broadway Wilts; Only Four Sellouts," *Variety,* 26 August 1959, MCNY, *Gypsy* scrapbooks.

73. Mary Martin, note to EM, 21 August 1959, MCNY, *Gypsy* scrapbooks.

74. TC, interview with author, 11 September 2004.

75. JS, note to EM, MCNY, *Gypsy* scrapbooks.

76. CP, telegram to EM, 25 November 1959, MCNY, SC 24.

77. Dorothy Kilgallen, "Voice of Broadway: Ethel's Disenchantment No Surprise," *NYJA,* 28 December 1960, MCNY, SC 24.

78. Bill Fields, letter to EM, 21 December 1959, with mock-up of unpublished newspaper article attached, MCNY, SC 25.

79. MCNY, SC 25.

80. *Variety,* 18 May 1960, MCNY, SC 25.

81. Menu in MCNY, SC 24.

82. MCNY, SC 24.

83. Miscellaneous clippings, ca. December 1960, MCNY, SC 25.

84. Conversation with author, New York City, October/November 2003.

85. From acetate collection of Al F. Koenig Jr.

86. Leonard Lyons, "The Lyons Den," *NYP,* 3 January 1961, MCNY, SC 25.

87. Thanks to Al F. Koenig Jr. for his recollections.

88. Hal Boyle, "Producer Devoted to Sea Epic," *Denver Post,* 3 August 1958, MCNY, *Gypsy* scrapbooks.

89. In the film, Norman Bates's psychosis is blamed on his overly close relationship with his overbearing mother. So close is that identification that he dresses as his mother when he kills his victim in the famous shower scene.

90. It's important to add that in the '50s, moms of both film and stage tended to avoid the bland, domesticated clichés common to television during the same time, such as in *Leave It to Beaver, Father Knows Best,* and other programs. Stage and screen venues were subject to less censorship than TV, and so these venues presented postwar American families that were typically more dysfunctional and less idealized.

91. Laurents, *Original Story by Arthur Laurents,* 377.

92. Garebian, *The Making of Gypsy,* 12.

93. Archer Winsten, "Reviewing Stand," *NYP,* 19 November 1959, MCNY SC 29; italics added.

94. Barbara Bladen, *San Mateo Times,* 12 August 1961, MCNY, SC 27.

95. Don Ross, "Mother—It's Murder / Stage Holds Up Mirror to a Tarnished Image," *NYHT,* 8 May 1959, MCNY, SC 24.

96. Mordden, *Coming Up Roses,* 245.

97. TC, interview with author, 11 September 2004.

98. Laurents, *Original Story by Arthur Laurents,* 378.

99. TC, interview with author, 6 July 2004.

100. RL, interview with author, July 2004.

101. Paine Knickerbocker, "How Leland Hayward Would Save the Theater," *San Francisco Chronicle,* 6 July 1961, MCNY, SC 27.

102. Sheri Giles, "La Merman Sings Chicago's Praises," *Chicago American,* 31 July 1961, MCNY, SC 27.

103. Quoted in Donnelly, "A Ten-Strike for Ethel and All Hands."

104. *Gypsy Rose Lee and Friends,* broadcast in 1965.

105. Kevin Kelly, "The Magic of Merman Loud and Irresistible," *Boston Globe,* 11 June 1963, MCNY, SC 28.

106. Laurents, *Original Story by Arthur Laurents,* 378.

107. TC, interview with author, 11 September 2004.

108. Ibid.

109. Gerald Bordman, *American Musical Theater: A Chronicle* (New York: Oxford University Press, 1978), 667.

110. Kaye Ballard, conversation with author, 28 June 2004.

111. Jerry Lewis, letter to EM, 9 August 1961, MCNY SC 23.

112. Anonymous fan, conversation with author, fall of 2003.

113. Anonymous fan, conversation with author, spring of 2004.

114. Miles Krueger, conversation with author, spring of 2004.

115. Josef Mossman, "It's Not True What They Say about Ethel," *Detroit News,* 5 April 1961, MCNY, SC 27.

116. Harlowe Hoyt, "New Ethel Merman Is a Delight," *Cleveland Plain Dealer,* 18 April 1961, MCNY, SC 27.

117. *Variety,* 10 May 1961, MCNY, SC 26.

118. Nathan Cohen, "Glum 'Gypsy,'" *Toronto Daily Star,* 19 May 1961, MCNY, SC 27.

119. Sheri Giles, "La Merman Sings Chicago's Praises," *Chicago American,* 3 July 1961, MCNY, SC 27.

120. Quoted in ibid.

121. Both quotations from *Chicago Daily Tribune,* 22 June 1961, MCNY, SC 27.

122. Radie Harris, "Broadway Ballyhoo," *Hollywood Reporter,* 1 June 1961, MCNY, SC 27.

123. Radie Harris, "Broadway Ballyhoo," *Hollywood Reporter,* 11 August 1961, MCNY, SC 25. Harris goes on to relay Merv Griffin's greetings to Ethel. "When I relayed this message, I kiddingly added, 'I didn't want to tell you this, Ethel, but he wants you to dub the singing for Roz Russell!' Ethel howled, as she vehemently spiked the rumor of any animosity."

124. *San Francisco Chronicle,* 24 July 1961, MCNY, SC 27.

125. Herb Caen, *San Francisco Chronicle,* 21 August 1961; postcard to EM; newspaper clipping; all in MCNY, SC 27.

126. Maggie Daly, "Daly Diary," *Chicago American,* 1 August 1961, MCNY, SC 27.

127. Pat Rob, "Hackett's Busy Making Movies," *San Francisco New Call Bulletin,* 2 September 1961, MCNY, SC 27.

128. A2, 217.

129. Sidney Skolsky, "All about Ethel Merman in 'Gypsy,'" *LA Citizen News,* 4 October 1961, MCNY, SC 27.

130. JS, telegram to EM, MCNY, SC 27.

131. Cary Grant, telegram to EM, 2 October 1961, MCNY, SC 27.

132. Letter to EM, 25 September 1961, MCNY, SC 27.

133. Letter to EM, MCNY, SC 27.

134. Wolf, *A Problem Like Maria,* 107–8.

135. D. A. Miller, *Place for Us: Essay on the Broadway Musical* (Cambridge, MA: Harvard University Press, 2000), 73.

136. See John Kenrick's wonderful essay on this on his Web site www.musicals101 .com, spring 2005.

137. Most influential among these critics has been Wayne Koestenbaum, *The Queen's Throat: Opera, Homosexuality, and the Mystery of Desire* (New York: Poseidon Press, 1993).

138. Laurents, *Original Story by Arthur Laurents,* 376.

139. Wolf, *A Problem Like Maria,* 90.

140. Ibid., 91.

141. Barbara Seaman, *Lovely Me: The Life of Jacqueline Susann* (New York: Seven Stories Press, 1996), 246.

142. Ibid., 245.

143. Ibid., 248.

144. Ibid., 247.

145. Ibid., 245–46.

146. TC, interview with author, 11 September 2004.

147. Quoted in Dennis McGovern and Deborah Grace Winer, *Sing Out Louise! 150 Stars of the Musical Theatre Remember 50 Years on Broadway* (New York: Schirmer Books, 1993), 155.

148. Bob Thomas, *I Got Rhythm: The Ethel Merman Story* (New York: Putnam, 1985), 188.

CHAPTER 15: IT'S A MAD, MAD SCHEDULE

1. Paul Speegle, "Ethel Not Mad, Mad at World," *San Francisco News Call Bulletin,* 4 April 1963, MCNY, SC 28.

2. Whitney Williams, "Cinerama's Single-Lens Projection Not Only Cuts Those Lines, It Cuts Costs," *Variety,* 7 June 1963, MCNY, SC 28.

3. Mike Connolly, *Hollywood Reporter,* 29 June 1962, MCNY, SC 26.

4. Quote from *Variety,* 5 November 1963, MCNY, SC 29. Only two other women were featured players, Edie Adams and Dorothy Provine.

5. Ethel Merman, "Another First for Me," *Hollywood Reporter,* 20 November 1962, MCNY, SC 28.

6. "Global Press June to H'wood," *Hollywood Reporter,* 12 April 1963, MCNY, SC 28.

7. MCNY, SC 26.

8. Merman, "Another First for Me."

9. *Variety,* 5 November 1963, MCNY, SC 29.

10. Paine Knickerbocker, "Ethel Merman's New Movie Career," *San Francisco Chronicle,* 29 March 1963, MCNY, SC 28.

11. Quote regarding Merman's character is from Vernon Scott, "Ethel Merman Songless," *Los Angeles Herald Examiner,* 27 June 1962, MCNY, SC 26.

12. The New York premiere was November 17.

13. MCNY, SC 26.

14. Stanley Kramer, letter to EM, MCNY, SC 26.

15. Stanley Kramer and Thomas M. Coffey, *A Mad, Mad Mad Mad World: A Life in Hollywood* (New York: Harcourt Brace, 1997), 194.

16. Press release, August 1963, MCNY, SC 28.

17. *Scotsman* (Edinburgh), "Anthea Takes a Look at the Festival," 23 August 1963, MCNY, SC 28.

18. Donald McMillan, letter to EM, MCNY, SC 28.

19. Mamie Chrichton, "The Star Who Is Happy in the Wings," *Daily Express* (Edinburgh), 20 August 1963, MCNY, SC 28.

20. John Sandilands, "She's Mad, Mad, Mad, Mad about the Show" *Daily Sketch* (Edinburgh), 20 August 1963, MCNY, SC 28.

21. *Variety,* 5 November 1963, MCNY, SC 29.

22. "Bad, Bad, Bad, Bad: Review of *It's a Mad, Mad, Mad, Mad World,*" *Newsweek,* November 1963, MCNY, SC 29.

23. Sandilands, "She's Mad, Mad, Mad, Mad about the Show."

24. Judy Garland, card to EM, [25 October 1963], MCNY, SC 26.

25. "SUNdial," *Las Vegas Sun,* 28 October 1963, MCNY, SC 26.

26. Sheila Graham, "Hollywood," *New York Mirror,* 1 December 1962, MCNY, SC 28.

27. "Hayward Produces Anita Colby's Show," *Los Angeles Times,* 5 December 1963, MCNY, SC 28.

28. Ralph Pearl, "Vegas Daze and Nites," *Las Vegas Sun,* 27 October 1963, MCNY, SC 26.

29. Credits indicate that the script was based on an idea by Cy Howard and Arthur Julian.

30. Ethel kept the original soundtrack acetates, titled *Trader Brown.*

31. Hank Grant, *Hollywood Reporter,* 20 September 1963, MCNY, SC 28.

32. Bob Williams, "On the Air," *NYP,* 27 January 1966, NYPL, Billy Rose Theatre Collection: MWEZ, nc 26, 491, Ethel Merman, 1960–69.

33. TC, interview with author, 11 September 2004.

34. Various sources in MCNY, SC 26.

35. A2, 11.

36. MCNY, SC 28.

37. Typed lyrics in MCNY, SC 26.

38. Van Johnson, telegram to EM, 11 April 1963, MCNY, SC 28.

39. Miles White, postcard to EM, MCNY, SC 28.

40. Elliot Norton, "Ethel Merman Starred in Summer Tent Show," *Boston Herald-Examiner,* 11 June 1963, MCNY, SC 28.

41. Leo Sullivan, "The Merm Belts 'Em at the Bowl," *Washington Post,* 19 June 1963, MCNY, SC 28.

CHAPTER 16: THE SIXTIES AND THE ART OF LOVE

1. Bob Lardine, "More Movies on the Way to TV," *New York Sunday News,* 22 April 1963, MCNY, SC 26.

2. A2, 225.

3. " 'Villainous' Merman," *Philadelphia Inquirer,* 22 December 1963, MCNY, SC 29.

4. A2, 225.

5. RL, interview with author, July 2004.

6. Marilyn Baker, interview with author, June 2004.

7. James Bacon, "Must Be Love: Ethel and Ernie Unfamiliar with Each Other's Work," *Newark Evening News,* 5 April 1964, NYPL, Billy Rose Theatre Collection: MWEZ, nc 26, 491, Ethel Merman, 1960–69.

8. At the time, *Marty* was the only picture whose Oscar promotion budget ($400,000) had exceeded its production costs ($343,000). Damien Bona, "75 Years of Bribes, Lies, and Overkill," *NYT,* 9 March 1964, 13.

9. Harrison Carroll, "Lana Turner Taking Vacation; Denies Rift," *Los Angeles Herald Examiner,* 12 June 1962, MCNY, SC 26.

10. Ernest Borgnine, interview with Hedda Hopper, 16 May 1962, AMPAS: Hedda Hopper files, Ernest Borgnine folder, file 229.

11. Sheila Graham, *NYJA,* 3 January 1964, MCNY, SC 29.

12. TC, personal communication with author, 6 April 2006.

13. BG, interview with author, July 2004.

14. Sheila Graham, *NYJA,* 2 January 1964, MCNY, SC 29.

15. May Okon, "'The Merm' Marries 'Marty,'" *New York Sunday News,* 19 July 1964, NYPL, Billy Rose Theatre Collection: MWEZ, nc 26, 491, Ethel Merman, 1960–69.

16. Louella Parsons, *Los Angeles Herald Examiner,* 4 August 1964, AMPAS.

17. Various sources in NYPL, Billy Rose Theatre Collection.

18. It is possible that sections were removed, since some signatures of the scrapbooks have been lost or have shown up in other collections such as the NYPL, Los Angeles Film Archives.

19. TC, interview with author, 11 September 2004.

20. *VH-1 All Access* episode "Shortest Celebrity Marriages," VH1, 2005 broadcast.

21. Radie Harris, "Broadway Ballyhoo," *Hollywood Reporter,* 1 October 1964, SC 29.

22. A2, 231.

23. TC, interview with author, 6 April 2006.

24. Jack O'Brian, "Voice of Broadway," *Star-Ledger,* 20 February 1984; and Paul Good, "The Belter!" *New York Sunday News Magazine,* 9 May 1982, 6, NYPL, Billy Rose Theatre Collection.

25. RL, interview with author, July 2004.

26. A2, 235.

27. "Art of Love Synopsis," 3, AMPAS.

28. Louella Parsons, unidentified clipping, 29 September 1965, MCNY, SC 26.

29. Elke Sommer, interview with author, 13 February 2005.

30. "Showman's Manual, University City Studios," 4, AMPAS.

31. Censors had been sure to deprive the women of any "bumps and grinds or other motions of a 'strip routine.'" Letter from Shurlock to Kathryn McTaggart, AMPAS: Universal Production Code Files for *Art of Love,* 26 June 1962.

32. "It was agreed that the mechanics and details of prostitution would be completely eliminated in the . . . script." Letter from Shurlock to Kathryn McTaggart,

AMPAS: Universal Production Code Files for *Art of Love,* memo from (EGD) *[sic],* 15 May 1962. Censor letters condemned terms such as *virgin, son of a sonora, stimulating,* and excessive *damns, hells,* and *oh my Gods.* Had Mae West been available for the part that Merman played, there probably would have been even more complaints.

33. Phyllis Battelle, "Broadway? Not for Ethel," *[NYJA],* 22 January 1965, MCNY, SC 29.

34. Louis Sobol, *New York Cavalcade,* 1 July 1965, MCNY, SC 29.

35. William Peper, "All-New Merman Back in Town," *NYWTS,* 28 May 1965, MCNY, SC 29.

36. John Wilson, "Familiar Voice amid a New Setting," *NYT,* 12 November 1963, NYPL, Billy Rose Theatre Collection: MWEZ, nc 26, 491, Ethel Merman, 1960–69.

37. "Britons Get a Kick out of Merman," unidentified clipping, 20 February 1964, NYPL, Billy Rose Theatre Collection: MWEZ, nc 26, 491, Ethel Merman, 1960–69.

38. Unidentified clipping, *Newsweek,* 22 July 1963, NYPL, Billy Rose Theatre Collection.

39. Press release, 7 March 1966, NYPL, Billy Rose Theatre Collection: MWEZ, nc 26, 491, Ethel Merman, 1960–69.

40. The show was later performed at New York City's Fashion Institute, on 27th Street.

41. Henry Beckett, "Broadway Stages a Memorial for Gentle, Witty Crouse," *NYP,* 27 May 1966, MCNY, SC 30.

42. Howard Lindsay, note card to EM, 27 May 1966, MCNY, SC 29.

43. Al F. Koenig Jr., "The Television Acetates," *Joslin's Jazz Journal* (1998), 2.

44. Reports circulated that Jerome Robbins had also approached Merman to play Bertolt Brecht's Mother Courage, Mama Rose's German counterpart. (Other accounts say Robbins had Anne Bancroft in mind all along.) It is likely that Robbins mentioned the role to Ethel in casual conversation; Merman, for her part, told the press that it was "a little too heavy for an opener," that is, for her return to the stage (unidentified interview, *NYT,* 29 May 1966, [section unknown], 3, NYPL, Billy Rose Theatre Collection: MWEZ, nc 26, 491, Ethel Merman, 1960–69).

45. Ethel Merman, "Ethel Won't Let Long Run Shows Pin Her Down," *Long Island Press,* 12 June 1966, NYPL, Billy Rose Theatre Collection: MWEZ, nc 26, 491, Ethel Merman, 1960–69.

46. Leonard Harris, "Merman Is 'Annie' Again and Her Heart Sings," *NYWTS,* 5 April 1966, NYPL, Billy Rose Theatre Collection: MWEZ, nc 26, 491, Ethel Merman, 1960–69.

47. Shirley Eder, "The Merman You've Never Met," *Detroit Free Press Sunday Magazine,* 10 July 1966, 18, MCNY, SC 30.

48. RL, telegram to EM; and Shirley Eder, letter to EM, 4 August 1966; both in MCNY, SC 30.

49. Shirley Eder, *Detroit Free Press,* 25 July 1966, MCNY, SC 30.

50. *NYT,* 23 June 1966, NYPL, Billy Rose Theatre Collection: MWEZ, nc 26, 491, Ethel Merman, 1960–69.

51. Harris, "Merman Is 'Annie' Again and Her Heart Sings."

52. Ibid.

53. Edith Efron, "Doin' What Comes Natur'lly," *TV Guide,* 18 March 1967, 10–14 (quotes from 11, 12–13), NYPL, Billy Rose Theatre Collection: MWEZ, nc 26, 491, Ethel Merman, 1960–69.

54. Ibid., 14.

55. Ethel Geary, card to EM, MCNY, SC 26.

56. *NYP,* 2 March 1961, MCNY, SC 26.

57. BG, interview with author, July 2004.

58. Ibid.

59. RL, interview with author, July 2004.

60. BG, letter to author, April 2006.

61. BG, interview with author, July 2004.

62. Ethel Merman, "How to Be a Hit," *NYHT This Week Magazine,* 6 March 1960, 8, MCNY, SC 24.

63. BG, interview with author, July 2004.

64. RL, interview with author, July 2004.

65. Carol Friesen, interview with author, December 2003.

66. Ibid. "Our honeymoon was sort of cursed," she and her husband, Jerry, say today. "On the first day up, the brakes of our car broke; then this happened two days later, on our last day. The story made the hometown paper before we even got back." Fortunately, the bad luck has not dogged the Friesen's marriage, and their willingness to help others is as strong as ever. Carol and Jerry Friesen have raised nearly twenty foster children together in their small Mennonite town. My gratitude to the Friesens and to Louise Koehn for putting me in contact with them.

67. TC, interview with author, 11 September 2004.

68. A2, 243; RL, correspondence to author, April 2007.

69. BG, letter to author, summer of 2005.

70. BG, interview with author, July 2004.

71. A2, 244.

72. TC, interview with author, 11 September 2004.

73. "Suicide Report Was Incorrect," *Miami Herald,* 30 March 1968, MCNY, SC 31.

74. Carol Channing claims that Ethel tearfully confided this to her in a limo on the way to shoot *The Love Boat.* Carol Channing, *Just Lucky I Guess: A Memoir of Sorts* (New York: Simon and Schuster, 2002), 41, 234.

75. BG, interview with author, July 2004.

76. RL, interview with author, July 2004.

77. BG, interview with author, July 2004.

78. This musical was later renamed *Look to the Lillies,* with Shirley Booth. Radie Harris, *Hollywood Reporter,* 10 June 1967, MCNY, SC 30.

79. Bob Freund, "Ethel Merman Reflects: 'I'm Lucky with Composers,'" *Ft. Lauderdale News and Sun-Sentinel,* 24 March 1968, MCNY, SC 30.

80. RL, interview with author, July 2004.

81. Bob Freund, "Ethel Merman Reflects."

82. Stephanie Fuller, "Still 'Klass with a Capital K,'" *Chicago Tribune,* 10 March 1968, MCNY, SC 31.

83. Ibid.

84. Mary Kimbrough, "Miss Merman of the Muny [Municipal]: The Quiet World of Broadway's Loudest Star," *Globe Democrat,* 22 July 1968, 1, MCNY, SC 31.

85. Virginia Kay, *Chicago Daily News,* 10 March 1968, MCNY, SC 30.

86. Fuller, "Still 'Klass with a Capital K.'"

87. BG, interview with author, July 2004.

88. Kimbrough, "Miss Merman of the Muny"; and Leonard Lyons, "Lyons Den," *NYP,* 9 July 1968, MCNY, SC 31.

89. BG, interview with author, July 2004.

90. Freund, "Ethel Merman Reflects." Levitt says he never had a house in Sausalito (letter to author, April 2007).

91. RL, letter to author, 17 May 2007.

92. Telegram to EM, December 1967, MCNY SC 31.

93. RL, interview with author, July 2004.

CHAPTER 17: AFTER THE BIG STEM—THE SEVENTIES

1. Fynsworth Alley, Jerry Herman interview, 13 November 2002, http://fynsworthalley.com/sd, accessed fall 2006.

2. Howard Kissel, *David Merrick: Abominable Showman* (New York: Applause Books, 2000), 295.

3. Quoted in Bob Thomas, *I've Got Rhythm! The Ethel Merman Story* (New York: Putnam, 1985), 188.

4. Tom Mackin, "Merman Takes Role," *Christian Science Monitor,* 30 March 1970, NYPL, Billy Rose Theatre Collection: MWEZ, nc 26, 491, Ethel Merman, 1960–69.

5. Richard Coe, *Washington Post* (unidentified date), NYPL, Billy Rose Theatre Collection: Ethel Merman, 1970–79 folder.

6. Walter Kerr, "Merman: A Kid Who Wins All the Marbles," *NYT,* 12 April 1970.

7. Kissel, *David Merrick,* 297.

8. Thanks to David Lugowski for his observations.

9. *Hello, Dolly!* press release, Associated Press Newsfeatures, 17 May [1970], NYPL, Billy Rose Theatre Collection: MWEZ, nc 26, 491, Ethel Merman, 1960–69.

10. Kissel, *David Merrick,* 380.

11. Unidentified clipping, *Newsweek,* 21 September 1970, microfilm, AMPAS.

12. Al F. Koenig Jr., "Merman—Solid New York," *Joslin's Jazz Journal* (1998).

13. "Too Many Smaller Stars Could Take Lessons from Her," *Home Furnishings Daily,* 10 March 1967, MCNY, SC 30.

14. A2, 251.

15. Bob Hope, telegram to EM, MCNY, SC 31.

16. TC, interview with author, 11 September 2004.

17. RL, interview with author, July 2004.

18. RL, letter to author, 16 January 2004.

19. Ibid.

20. Stephen Mo Hanen, letter to author, 20 February 2004.

21. RL, interview with author, July 2004.

22. TC, interview with author, 11 September 2004.

23. RL, interview with author, July 2004.

24. BG, interview with author, July 2004.

25. RL, interview with author, July 2004.

26. TC, interview with author, 11 September 2004.

27. RL, letter to author, 15 May 2007.

28. RL, letter to author, 18 May 2007.

29. TC, interview with author, 11 September 2004.

30. RL, letter to author, 15 May 2007.

31. Kaye Ballard, interview with author, June 2004.

32. A2, 251.

33. Al F. Koenig Jr., letter to author, 2004.

34. Ibid., 252.

35. Al F. Koenig Jr., letter to author, February 2006.

36. A2, 16.

37. RL, interview with author, July 2004.

38. A2, 17.

39. Ruth Munson, conversation with author, fall of 2003.

40. A2, 260.

41. Al F. Koenig Jr., "A Beginning," unpublished essay.

42. A2, 260.

43. Koenig Jr., "A Beginning," 1.

44. Kaye Ballard, interview with author, June 2004.

45. A2, 258–59.

46. Ibid., 263.

47. Ibid.

48. Al F. Koenig Jr., letter to author, 14 February 2005.

49. TC, interview with author, 11 September 2004.

50. The *New York Post* reported cattily that sales of the book were flat. "Barnes

and Noble, for instance, has sold only five copies." The reason? The *Post* surmised it was because she refused to spill the beans on her marriage to Ernest Borgnine. *NYP,* 1 August 1978, NYPL, Billy Rose Theatre Collection: Ethel Merman, 1970–79 folder.

51. A2, 143.

52. Frances Swaebly, "La Merman's Baffled [by] 'New Show Biz,'" *Miami Herald,* 7 April 1968, MCNY, SC 31.

53. TC, interview with author, 11 September 2004.

54. Lewis Segal, "Merman Sings at Hollywood Bowl," *Los Angeles Times,* 8 August 1977, NYPL, Billy Rose Theatre Collection: 1970s folder.

55. Unidentified clipping, ca. February 1968, MCNY, SC 31.

56. TC, interview with author, 11 September 2004.

57. Carol Channing, *Just Lucky I Guess: A Memoir of Sorts* (New York: Simon and Schuster, 2002), 41.

CHAPTER 18: TWILIGHT AND TRANSFORMATION

1. Fred Bernstein, "Don't Worry about the Size of Ethel Merman's Belt," *People,* 24 September 1979, NYPL, Billy Rose Theatre Collection: 1970s folder.

2. Quoted in Peter Brown, "Ethel Merman Making Debut as Diva of Disco," *Los Angeles Times Calendar,* 29 July 1979, 5, AMPAS.

3. *NYT,* 24 August 1979, 11, AMPAS.

4. Dave Hirshey, "Crowd Pleasers," *New York Sunday News,* 23 September 1979.

5. TC, interview with author, 11 September 2004.

6. Bernstein, "Don't Worry about the Size of Ethel Merman's Belt."

7. RL, interview with author, July 2004; TC, interview with author, 11 September 2004.

8. Thanks to Al F. Koenig Jr.

9. Arthur Bells, "Bell Tells," *Village Voice,* 27 August 1979, NYPL, Billy Rose Theatre Collection: 1970s folder.

10. TC, interview with author, 11 September 2004.

11. Howard Kissel, *David Merrick: Abominable Showman* (New York: Applause Books, 2000), 16.

12. RL, letter to author, April 2007.

13. RL, letter to author, 16 February 2005.

14. Quoted in Bob Thomas, *I've Got Rhythm! The Ethel Merman Story* (New York: Putnam, 1985), 203.

15. Personal communication with author, 2003.

16. TC, interview with author, 11 September 2004.

17. Thanks to Al F. Koenig Jr. for program notes and recollections.

18. Clive Barnes, "La Merman at Carnegie Hall: Still and Simply the Very Best!" *NYP,* 11 May 1982, NYPL, Billy Rose Theatre Collection: Ethel Merman, Music Clippings file.

19. The show had begun in 1977, with Hugh Downs as host.

20. Thomas, *I've Got Rhythm!* 213.

21. Fans have speculated that Martin's close friendship with Gaynor was actually a lesbian relationship, a liaison that exists passionately in the minds of many but not in historical reality.

22. RL, letter to author, 28 January 2007.

23. TC, interview with author, 11 September 2004.

24. RL, interview with author, July 2004.

25. Thomas, *I've Got Rhythm!* 205–6.

26. Ibid., 210.

27. TC, interview with author, 11 September 2004.

28. Courtesy Al F. Koenig Jr.

29. Considering the aftermath, it is hard to imagine how the letter got to Marchesani. Was Ethel able to send it off? Did someone else?

30. Copy of the note to Marchesani and the story of Ona Hill provided by Al F. Koenig Jr.

31. Thanks to Tony Cointreau for his account. TC, intreview with author, 6 April 2006.

32. Ibid.

33. RL, interview with author, July 2004.

34. Ibid.

35. TC quoted in *Biography* episode: "Ethel Merman: There's No Business Like Show Business," A&E, 1999 broadcast.

36. RL, letter to author, 28 January 2007.

37. Murray Schumach, "Ethel Merman, Queen of Musicals, Dies at 76," *NYT,* 16 February 1984, NYPL, Billy Rose Theatre Collection: Ethel Merman, Music Collection.

38. BG, interview with author, July 2004.

39. Radie Harris, "Broadway Ballyhoo: Lack of Sentiment," *Hollywood Reporter,* 15 October 1984, MCNY, box 1.

40. RL, letter to author, 28 January 2007.

CHAPTER 19: AFTERLIFE

The epigraph is from JS, interview with PM, transcript, 27, USC, HMC: Pete Martin Collection.

1. A2, 249.

2. Some say it was the Imperial.

3. Christopher Edwards, *Daily Mail,* reprinted in the *London Theatre Record* 5, no. 13 (19 June–2 July 1985): 611–12.

4. Clive Hirshorn, *Sunday Express,* reprinted in *London Theatre Record* 5, no. 13 (19 June–2 July 1985): 611–12.

5. Dennis McGovern and Deborah Grace Winer, *Sing Out, Louise! 150 Stars of the Musical Theatre Remember 50 Years on Broadway* (New York: Schirmer Books, 1993), 150.

6. Nellie McKay, "Change the World," *Get Away from Me,* compact disc, Columbia–Sony Music Entertainment, 2004.

7. BG, interview with author, July 2004.

8. RL, letter to author, 16 January 2004.

9. A pun on the Book of Mormon (Blackhurst was raised in Utah).

10. KB, interview with author, 5 October 2004.

11. Margo Jefferson, "An Echo of Merman: Nothing to Hit but the Heights," *NYT,* 19 April 2001.

12. KB, interview with author, October 2004.

13. Ibid.

14. John M. Clum, *Something for the Boys: Musical Theater and Gay Culture* (New York: St. Martin's Press, 1999), 147.

15. Ibid., 149.

16. Interview with author, April 2006.

17. RL, letters to author, 9 April 2005 and revised 15 May 2007.

18. TC, interview with author, 11 September 2004.

19. Bob Fosse quoted in John Kenrick's "Our Love Is Here to Stay: Gays and Musicals" at www.musicals101.com, accessed fall 2004; Clum, *Something for the Boys,* 146; Stacy Wolf, *A Problem Like Maria: Gender and Sexuality in the American Musical* (Ann Arbor: University of Michigan, 2002), ch. 2.

20. E-mail to author, fall 2003.

21. Podcast of 23 December 2004.

22. Lillian Libman, *And Music at the Close: Stravinsky's Last Years, a Personal Memoir* (New York: W. W. Norton, 1972). Thanks to Richard McQuillan.

23. A1, 36–37.

24. Earl Wilson column, *NYP,* 17 December 1968, MCNY, SC 31.

25. Donald O'Connor, quoted in *Biography* episode: "Ethel Merman: There's No Business Like Show Business," A&E, 1999 broadcast.

26. Henry Pleasants, *The Great American Popular Singers* (New York: Simon and Schuster, 1985), 336.

27. Bob Thomas, *I've Got Rhythm! The Ethel Merman Story* (New York: Putnam, 1985), 14.

28. RL, interview with author, July 2004.

29. George B. Bryan, *Ethel Merman: A Bio-Bibliography* (New York: Greenwood Press, 1992); Geoffrey Mark, *Ethel Merman: The Biggest Star on Broadway* (Fort Lee, NJ: Barricade Books, 2005).

30. TC, interview with author, 11 September 2004.

A WORD ON THE SCRAPBOOKS

1. MCNY, box 1.

STAGE WORK

1. Historically, show directors were rarely credited as such until the postwar era. Before then, credits were usually given as "staged by." Stage Work uses the "directed by" credit throughout, even on shows whose *Playbill* doesn't reflect that language.

INDEX

Text:	11/13.5 Adobe Garamond
Display:	Adobe Garamond, Perpetua
Compositor:	Binghamton Valley Composition
Printer and binder:	Maple-Vail Book Manufacturing Group

Freda Lightfoot was born and brought up in the mill towns of Lancashire. She has been a teacher, bookseller and smallholder but began her writing career by publishing over forty short stories and articles and five historical romances. She has a flat in the Lake District and a house in a small mountain village in Spain. To find out more information, visit Freda's web site on www.fredalightfoot.co.uk.

Praise for Freda Lightfoot:

'Charming and exciting . . . A lovely story by an author with extraordinary feeling in her writing.'
Bangor Chronicle

'Freda Lightfoot's talent for creating believable characters makes this a page-turning read.'
Newcastle Evening Chronicle

'The kind of character-driven saga that delights the Catherine Cookson and Josephine Cox audience.'
Peterborough Evening Telegraph

Daisy's Secret

FREDA LIGHTFOOT

CORONET BOOKS
Hodder & Stoughton

First published in Great Britain in 2003 by Hodder & Stoughton
A division of Hodder Headline
First published in paperback in 2003 by Hodder & Stoughton
A Coronet paperback

A CIP catalogue record for this title is available from the British Library

ISBN 0 340 82005 5

Typeset in Plantin Light by Phoenix Typesetting, Burley-in-Wharfedale, West Yorkshire

Printed and bound in Great Britain by
Clays Ltd, St Ives PLC

Hodder & Stoughton
A division of Hodder Headline
338 Euston Road
London NW1 3BH

To Mim, number one fan, who loves to read my
books when not watching Manchester United.

Prologue

Laura

'I thought I might stay on for a bit.'

'Stay on, in heavens' name what for?'

Laura glanced about the empty room, the last few people having said their farewells and departed, their faces sad, their condolences genuine and heartfelt. They'd made the customary offers of support, shaken her hand with polite formality, told her how proud Daisy would have been that she'd coped so well with the day. Laura had thanked them for coming and now they were alone, she and Felix, still with decisions to make, at least so far as she was concerned.

'Aren't there always things to attend to, after funerals?'

'Don't be childish. Do you imagine the family solicitor is going to turn up and read the will or something? They don't perform such silly melodramas nowadays, Laura, and we really should be getting back. What is so important that can't wait till we come and clear the house ready for the sale?'

She couldn't, offhand, think of a single thing, not one sensible enough to convince Felix. Her husband was always the one to deal with important financial affairs, keeping the wheels of their busy life oiled and endlessly turning. Yet she knew that she didn't want to leave and whatever he said, whatever arguments he put in her way, Laura resolved that she had no intention of doing so. On this occasion she meant to stand firm. She'd always felt stubborn and strong willed inside, but perhaps it was a side to her character she'd neglected to reveal often enough.

She stood at the window and watched the cars trundle out

of the farmyard as loyal neighbours hurried homewards, their minds already turning to the next chore to be done, cows to be milked, sheep checked, meals to be made. This was a busy time of year for them with lambing about to start. It was amazing that so many people had turned out for one old woman, though she had lived in their midst for years and must have known them all well.

Laura felt suddenly chilled and out of place in her smart black town suit and high-heeled shoes, knowing she was the stranger here, not them. She could see a faint outline of herself mirrored in the glass against the deepening dusk of the sky, superimposed upon the scene beyond like a double exposure. Anyone could see that she didn't belong. She didn't have their healthy, country robustness; was too thin, too serious, too plain and unhappy for a woman in her early thirties, supposedly in the prime of life, an image not entirely the result of a long, rather stressful day. Even her long, dark hair lacked its usual lustre, scraped up tight about her head with barely more than a few wispy curls to soften the stark hairline.

It was wet and blustery out, typical weather for a funeral. Laura remembered many such days here as a child, with rain beating on the windows and the wind roaring in from the east over Blencathra with nothing to stop it in this barren landscape but the stone walls of the farmhouse itself. She used to lie in her bed high in an attic room, all tucked up cosy and warm and listen as it howled and whined with the ferocity of a wild beast, flustering the hens in the old outhouse, tossing wheelbarrows, harrows and other farming implements about the yard like corks, and hammering on the tightly fastened shutters as if somehow determined to gain entrance. But as so often happened in this mountainous region with its fickle weather systems, the following morning she would wake to a day that was blithe and bonny, the sun beaming benignly upon them all, the greens and golds and russets of the land luminous in the glow of early morning, like a freshly washed face.

How Laura had loved spending time here, helping to feed the hens and lambs, being spoiled by the guests who came to stay at Lane End Farm to enjoy Daisy's ham and egg breakfasts. And then for some reason she had never quite fathomed, the visits had stopped. There were no more long summer holidays in the Lake District, no more picnics to look forward to on Catbells, no more sailing on Bassenthwaite or long, breathtaking hikes over Helvellyn, and nobody would tell her why.

She turned to Felix now with a preoccupied smile, half her mind still clinging to this mystery and to recalling memories of a happy childhood, the rest attempting to find a way to exploit the situation to her advantage. The prospect of not returning with him to Cheadle Hulme was intoxicating, exciting. Would Daisy mind? Somehow she didn't think so. She tried to explain but he hardly seemed to be listening as he paced restlessly about the room, clearly anxious to depart himself.

'Daisy used to tell of this house being used as a refuge by so many people during the war. She likened it to a fortress, a bastion of strength against the man-made evils of the world. Isn't that a lovely thought?'

'Where's my cell phone? Did you borrow it, Laura, or put it somewhere?'

'She made the house available for those who sought shelter within its thick stone walls. A sanctuary. Don't you think that was a generous thing to do?' Yet there wasn't a war on now, except one conducted in bittersweet undertones between herself and Felix.

Felix stopped looking for his phone long enough to scowl furiously at her. 'Don't try my patience any further with this, Laura. We need to leave in the next half-hour to have any chance of getting home by eight. You know I still have the accounts to do and there will no doubt be a long tailback on the M6 as usual, so can we please get a move on?'

Laura began poking down the sides of the sofa, ostensibly looking for the phone, yet her mind still focused on the need for escape, the idea of barricading herself away from all the frustrations of her life. From the moment she'd been told that Daisy had left her the house, she hadn't been able to get the idea out of her head. It was so tantalising.

'People – lodgers, evacuees, friends and family all came to stay here; all hanging together to get through the hostilities; all dreaming and hoping for a future when the war finally ended and they could start new lives. I once called it the House of Dreams but Gran had laughed and said more like a House of Secrets. I always wondered what she meant by that. Though I know of one secret she was forced to keep, it sounded as if there were more. Perhaps . . .'

'For God's sake Laura, you haven't even packed my bag.' Snatching up the empty suitcase he strode upstairs, the echo of his footsteps resounding in the empty house.

Laura looked up in surprise, as if she'd half forgotten he was there, then fell into a fit of stifled giggles. That must be a first. Packing his own suitcase. But the moment he came back downstairs, bag in hand, she went to him and kissed his cheek. 'I've definitely decided to stay on for a bit. You can manage without me for a little while, can't you, darling? There's so much to attend to here. Gran's things to go through for one, her clothes, books and other belongings, all the usual stuff. Someone has to do it.'

'You can surely leave all of that to the auctioneers.'

'No! She's my own grandmother, for heaven's sake. I'm not having strangers go through her personal things till I've at least checked them first. It wouldn't be right. That's why I wanted to come in *my* car, in case I decided to stay.' As she talked, she went to the phone and rang for a taxi, having no wish to take him herself to the station and prolong the lecture still further; then began to collect up dirty cups and saucers, empty glasses and used napkins. 'I'll also need to see old Mr Capstick, the family solicitor; deal with any papers, deeds and suchlike, for the take-over of the house.'

'You can safely leave me to do that by phone,' Felix told her, sounding irritated as he tossed cushions aside and flung open cupboards and drawers, still looking for his phone. 'And next week is going to be a particularly stressful time for me, getting everything organised before the Gift Fair.'

'I know darling. I was rather thinking I'd give it a miss this year. I'm sure you don't really need me. It's not as if you ever take any notice of my opinions, now is it? Ah, there it is.' Laughing, she picked up the mobile and tucked it safely away in a pocket of his briefcase, then giving a quick frown, returned to the issue which so occupied her. 'Do you think I should let Dad have the farm after all, despite it being left to me?'

Felix gave her a startled look and his tone became clipped and sharp, punctuating his words as if he were speaking to a five-year-old child. 'Don't talk ridiculous! Sometimes, Laura, I wonder what you use for a brain.'

'It's just that it seems such a waste to sell it. I mean, we don't really need the money and he . . .'

'For God's sake, people always need more money, and this isn't the time or place for philosophical discussions about your father and his numerous problems. Look, I have to go. Make sure you see that solicitor. Do something useful with your time here besides wallowing in nostalgia, and tell the dithering old fool to get a move on. Property prices are buoyant right now but who knows what might happen to the market in the next few months.'

'But what if I decide not to sell?'

Felix let out a heavy sigh. 'We've been through all of that and the decision has been made. We cannot afford sentiment, for God's sake.'

'No Felix. *You* have made a decision. *I* haven't. I said I needed time to think about it. So, I shall stay here for a little while longer and sort through Gran's things and do whatever is necessary while I give the matter some thought. Anyway, the rest will do me good. This peace is utter bliss.'

'Peace? Huh, deathly quiet more like. Your problem, Laura, is that you are a hopeless romantic.'

'Isn't that why you fell in love with me?'

'Damnation, that's my taxi, where's my bag?' He flung her a kiss a good half-inch from her cheek before charging off through the door. Laura ran after him with his overnight bag, quickly stowing it in the boot of the taxi, she gave a cheery wave as the taxi driver slammed all the doors and revved up the engine, just catching his final words, 'I shall expect you home by the end of the week, darling,' as it roared off at a cracking pace, no doubt under Felix's specific instructions.

Laura stood in the farmyard long after the taxi had disappeared, relieved that he'd allowed her no time to respond to this latest instruction. She wondered if Daisy had felt this explosive burst of happiness when she'd finally broken free of her restrictive home life? But then Daisy's situation had been so different from Laura's. Only once had she spoken of the tragedy of her loss, the 'shameful secret' her strict parents had forced her to keep. How on earth had she endured it?

Daisy

1939

1

'Don't think for a minute that you can carry on as if nothing has happened. Not after behaving so shamefully. We're done with you now, Daisy Atkins. You're no longer any daughter of mine. As for your father, he's made it abundantly clear that he'll not have you set foot in the house. Not ever again. We might be poor with not much to call us own, but we have us standards. Make no mistake about that.'

Daisy looked into her mother's set face and saw by the pursing of her narrow lips and the twin spots of colour on each hollow cheek, that she meant every hard and unforgiving word. 'Then what am I to do? Where am I supposed to go?'

'You should've thought of that before you – well – before you did what you oughtn't to have done.' Rita Atkins sniffed loud disapproval and folded her arms belligerently across her narrow chest. Daisy noticed that she was wearing her best black coat and hat for the visit, the one that she wore for chapel and for all funerals and weddings in the family. It bore a faint sheen of green and smelt strongly of mothballs. 'I'll not have it. I won't. It's just like your Aunt Florrie all over again.'

Daisy let out a heavy sigh, feeling a prickle of resentment by the comparison which had been flung at her more times than she cared to remember in these last, agonising weeks.

Aunt Florrie had brought disgrace to her family by running off with a man almost twice her age to live in the wilds of the Lake District. Daisy had no real memory of her, beyond the odd Christmas card but she'd always rather envied this adventurous, long-lost aunt who had escaped the boring inevitability of life in Marigold Court, Salford. She'd run away from broken windows, strings of washing and the reek of boiled fish and cabbage. And who could blame her? Certainly not Daisy. Whenever she'd ventured to say as much, she'd been slapped down by her mother, which Daisy didn't understand at all. She thought it would be the most glorious thing in the world to breathe clean, fresh country air and live where the grass stayed green and wasn't always covered in soot. Hadn't she long dreamed of just such an escape?

She'd thought she could achieve it by marrying her sweetheart Percy, who kept a market stall out at Warrington. He'd certainly seemed smitten by her, proclaiming how much he adored her halo of golden brown, corkscrew curls, which Daisy privately loathed, longing as she did for more sophisticated, smooth bangs like Veronica Lake. He'd told her frequently how her soft, brown eyes just made him melt inside, how he adored each sun-kissed freckle and he'd certainly been more than happy to kiss the fragile prettiness of her small, pink mouth.

He'd talked endlessly about his own hopes and ambitions for the future: how he aimed to have a string of market stalls one day, or better still, a whole row of shops, selling meat and fish as well as vegetables. She would listen to this extravagant fantasy, head tilted attentively to one side, eyes intent on his face, not wishing to miss a word.

'And will I be able to help you in these shops?' she'd enquire coyly . 'Or will it be some other girl?'

'Course it'll be you, Daisy,' he'd say, pulling her close. 'You're my girl. Always will be. You can serve behind the counter.'

'Happen I don't want to be your girl and work on a market

...g her baby away but whenever she tried to object, Rita ...relate horrific tales of girls driven to having a back-...abortion, or to taking their own lives rather than shame ...families. She would listen to all of this with deepening ...may and no amount of argument would deflect her mother ...n her purpose.

...ercy went off to join the navy, kissing her goodbye and promising to write every day. Since then she'd had only a couple of letters, telling her how busy he was and how exciting his new life was going to be; how he hoped she could sort out her 'little problem'. *Little problem!* Daisy felt deserted by everyone, as if there was no one at all to love her.

When the baby was born, a boy, who had slipped easily into the world and exercised his lungs almost instantly on a bellow of rage, Daisy cried with delight, not even noticing the pain. But within seconds, he was taken from her. The stern-faced sister who officiated at the birth wouldn't even allow her to hold him.

'He's not your child, Daisy. He belongs to another woman now. Best you don't even see him,' and nor did she, not properly. She glimpsed a tuft of red-brown hair, just like Percy's own, before he was swaddled in a blanket and whisked from the room. She could hear his cries fading in the distance as the nurse marched him away down the corridor. It felt as if they had ripped her heart from her body.

At first, she hadn't even cried, quite unable to take in the full impact of what was happening to her. She'd sat up in the bed all day long in stunned disbelief, her ears tuned for the slightest cry she might recognise. Once, she sneaked out and prowled the corridors, hoping to snatch him up from the nursery and run off with him, but she'd been apprehended by a young nurse, duly scolded and marched back to bed.

It was then that the tears had come and once having started, Daisy felt they might never stop.

stall or behind the counter of a fruit and veg shop. Mebbe I want a big house in the country.'

'Then you shall have one, Daisy girl. I'll build you the biggest house you ever did see, with a fine garage for the car, and stables for horses. 'Ere, I could run 'em in t'Grand National, eh? Come on, chuck, don't be mean, give us another kiss,' and Daisy would sigh with pleasure at the joy of being in love.

Sadly, these dreams had been dashed by discovering that the one and only occasion she'd foolishly allowed him to go 'all the way', she'd got caught. At first, in her innocence, Daisy had felt excited at the prospect of motherhood. They'd intended to get married anyway, she told herself, so it meant only that she could leave home even sooner and escape the claustrophobic restrictions her mother imposed upon her. She would marry Percy and they'd find a pretty cottage in the country and while she minded the children, she'd also keep hens and grow flowers and vegetables which he could sell on his market stall. Oh, life would be just perfect!

All such foolish daydreams had been swiftly shattered.

Percy had been struck speechless with shock when she'd announced proudly that he was about to become a father. 'Nay, Daisy lass, that's bit of a shaker. I'm not old enough to be a dad, any more than you're old enough to be anyone's ma. Tha's only sixteen and I'm nobbut a couple of years older, fer God's sake.'

'Don't you love me?'

'Course I do. I'll allus love thee, but how would we manage? I've hardly any money coming in, nor will have for some long while yet. Can't we wait for a bit longer?'

'How can we wait? The baby's coming now.'

'Nay, I can't see how we'd manage. It's too soon.'

She'd argued against this point of view, naturally, attempting to explain how much they would love the baby, once it was born, and carefully outlining her plans for their future. Far from reassuring him, his horror had increased, and he started making all manner of excuses about why this couldn't possibly work. He couldn't live anywhere but Salford, he said. He only knew how to sell fruit and veg, not grow them, and he really wasn't ready yet to start his own business, particularly in a strange place where he wasn't known. Again and again he kept repeating that he still loved her but that it was too soon, the timing was all wrong, as if the baby were an unwanted gift that could be sent back. And then one day he'd come to her triumphant.

'There's going to be a war, Daisy, so that settles it. I've volunteered to join the Navy. Tha'll have to get rid of it, or do as thee mam says and have it adopted. Best thing all round I'd say. There's plenty of time for us to start having babies, later, when the war's over.'

Daisy was filled with fear. She knew nothing about war. She'd been far too caught up with being in love, and the youthful exuberance of simply enjoying herself to even care, let alone understand what was going on in the wider world. If she'd noticed any rumblings on the wireless, or overheard worried comments from her parents, Daisy had ignored them, imagining that such things didn't concern her and certainly would not affect her life in any way. How wrong could she be? The war was taking her sweetheart away from her.

As if that wasn't bad enough, there had been one almighty row when she'd happily told her parents the news. Her father, as always, had simply looked mournful and said little, leaving it to her mother to rant and rave at her, though that was after she'd almost fainted with shock and needed the application of sal volatile to recover.

Daisy was their only child and Rita Atkins had never really accepted that her daughter had grown up. She believed in keeping her safe at home and never allowing her to have many friends beyond those she met each Sunday at chapel. Percy

had been kept a secret as Daisy fear approved of, his family not being quit order as themselves since they were all they lived only a few doors down. D instinctively that although her mother might have an notion of her own worth and take on airs, this was sim way of hanging on to her pride, a way of proving she quite in the gutter for all the lowly status of her husband' As a humble rag-and-bone man, Joe Atkins owned not more than the horse and cart which he drove around streets of Salford, handing out donkey stones for rubb doorsteps in exchange for other folk's cast-offs.

Rita told Daisy she'd never fit in with that stuck-up lot, an that she was far too young to wed. She scoffed when Daisy explained how she was in love, and that she'd intended to marry Percy anyway, saying that at sixteen she'd really no idea what love was all about. She was a strong-willed woman, and, in her opinion, there was only one way to do things: her way. She made it abundantly clear that Daisy had let her down by such loose behaviour.

Discussions on what should be done about 'the problem' had gone on interminably and neither parent, it seemed, was prepared to listen to a word Daisy said, or cared a jot about what she wanted. It was made clear to her, in no uncertain terms, that she must give up her precious baby the moment it was born.

She'd cried for weeks in the Mother and Baby Home but no sympathy had been forthcoming. Her mother maintained she was fortunate to have family willing to help her; that they'd chosen a good Christian place and not a home for wayward girls, which was most certainly what she deserved. Though how they'd managed to afford to pay for it, Daisy didn't quite understand, since to her knowledge her parents had never had two halfpennies to rub together. Daisy endured countless sleepless nights agonising over the prospect

The next day her mother lectured her on how she must put this mess behind her and forget all about it.

'Forget? How can I forget? He's my baby. My child!'

'No he's not. He belongs to someone else now, like Sister said.'

'Who?'

'That's none of your business. He's being adopted. You've no say over the matter at all.'

'But I haven't even given him a name,' Daisy wailed.

'Nor must you. The very idea. It's not your place. His new parents will do that. All you have to do is sign the paper and it's all done and dusted.'

'But Mam . . .'

'No buts. You're lucky it's turned out as well as it has. A fine healthy boy is always easiest to place. It'll all be done privately, very hush-hush. But you must never mention a word of this business to anyone, do you understand, Daisy? Not a single word,' and she wagged a finger in her daughter's face, to emphasise the point.

Daisy stared at her mother, wide-eyed with shock. 'Never mention him? Whyever not?'

'Because it'll make you look cheap, that's why. This business could ruin your reputation. No chap would have you as a wife if this ever got out. Men don't like used goods.'

For once in her life Daisy was struck speechless. Such a prospect had not occurred to her. She'd never, in fact, thought beyond the moment of the birth itself, worrying about how she would feel when the baby was taken away from her. She'd given no thought to how her life might change thereafter.

Rita gave her a little shake, urging her to pay attention. 'This has to be our little secret. Do you understand, Daisy? It must never be mentioned, not to anyone. *Ever!* Is that clear?'

Eyes glistening with fresh tears, Daisy could do nothing but nod.

Perhaps she'd assumed, if she'd thought about it at all, that once the baby had been safely delivered to its new parents she might be able to visit it from time to time, and when she was old enough, get him back and take care of him herself.

But Daisy saw now how very naïve that dream had been, both in allowing herself to trust in Percy's love in the first place, and in imagining she could in any way keep the baby. She'd behaved very foolishly and her only excuse was that she'd been young and innocent, had felt desperate for some breath of freedom away from Rita's stifling control.

Even after she'd signed the adoption papers, as demanded of her, Daisy wasn't about to be forgiven for her transgression. Nor would her father ever be allowed to speak to her again. Though why should she care? When had he ever cared about her? If he wasn't out on his cart, he'd be in the pub or with his mates. He'd never had much time for a daughter. A son would have been much more use.

Yet it seemed awful that she wasn't even going back home. How could she be sure of ever seeing Percy again if she was to be sent even further away. Daisy didn't care to imagine where she might end up. Tears spilled over and slid down her already wet cheeks as a lump of fear lodged painfully in her chest. The future looked bleak, more uncertain than ever, her dreams all crumbled to dust.

'Why can't I go home?' she begged one more time, desperation in her voice as her longing for Percy, for someone to love and care for her, almost overwhelmed her. She imagined him marching in, saying he'd changed his mind and they could get married after all. Then he'd carry her off to the pretty cottage in the country, baby and all.

'Because you can't. Anyroad, the exodus has already begun.'

'Exodus?'

'The Great Trek, the evacuation, what d'you think I'm talking about? Stop arguing, girl. My nerves are in ribbons already, what with the war and everything, let alone worrying about you. Like I say, you're nowt but trouble, just like Florrie.'

'I'm not a bit like Aunt Florrie,' Daisy protested hotly. 'I haven't run off and got wed, more's the pity. I did as you asked, even though it's not *my* choice to have the baby adopted. I want to keep it. And why shouldn't I? I've nobody else to love. No one gives a tinker's cuss about me.'

Rita Atkins flicked out a hand and smacked her daughter smartly across her cheek, leaving an imprint of four red lashes where her fingers had made contact. 'Don't you *dare* use such language with me! I'll have none of your lip, madam. I've had as much as I can take. Now then, get your coat and hat on. It's time to go. I'll not be responsible for you a minute longer, not with a war starting. The bus leaves at twelve sharp.'

'Bus, what bus? Where *am* I going?' Tears stood proud in Daisy's eyes but she refused to let them fall, holding on to her defiance for as long as she could.

'Stop asking so many fool questions. I've told you already, I've no idea. You're fortunate they'll take you, great girl like you. Anyroad, I've fetched a few things from home what I thought you might need, and your gas mask,' indicating a cardboard box and the small brown suitcase standing by the bed which Daisy had taken to mean that she was going home, until she'd learned different. Now she was being banished to goodness knows where, perhaps for ever. 'Don't sit there like a lump of lead, pack your night things and get yerself ready.'

Having issued this instruction, Rita herself began to fold Daisy's night-dress, then opening the bedside cabinet began to draw out the few personal items she'd brought with her to the home. Soap bag and flannel, brush and comb and a small satchel of handkerchiefs which she'd painstakingly stitched for herself, fussy madam. She followed this with a book and magazine Daisy had been reading, snapped shut the suitcase and hooked the strap tight.

'Right then. That's you ready for off.'

'But off *where*?' Daisy once more appealed, naked misery in her tone.

'How many times do I have to say it? *Evacuated.* Off to these pastures new you've always pined for. Well, now you'll get your chance to live in the country, though it's more than you deserve in the circumstances. You should thank your lucky stars you've got off so lightly. And remember, not a word about this business to anyone. Not ever!'

At the bus stop, Rita handed the case to Daisy, together with a bus ticket and instructions over what time she needed to be at London Road Station where she would be joining dozens of other evacuees, mostly children younger than herself. 'When no doubt all your questions will be answered and somebody in charge will tell you where it is you're to be sent.'

The bus arrived seconds later, the wheels churning through a puddle that splashed Daisy's clean stockings, coat and skirt, speckling them with spots of mud.

Rita clicked her tongue in dismay, spat on her hanky and began to rub frantically at the offending marks. 'Nay, why didn't you step back, you gormless lump? Why have you never any sense? It's time you took your head out of the clouds girl, and started to think about what you were doing. You can't go on being Daisy Daydream, you really can't.'

The bus conductor, watching this display of motherly fussing for some seconds with wry amusement, finally remarked, 'Do you do short back and sides an' all?'

Rita Atkins gave her daughter a little push, to urge her on her way. 'Get off with you. They won't wait all day,' just as if it had been Daisy holding up the bus, and not her mother at all. But now Daisy did hesitate, hopeful perhaps of a goodbye kiss, a fond hug, good wishes for the future, or even an assurance that her mother would write.

But Rita was busy tucking away her now grubby handkerchief in the big black handbag she always carried on her arm. Then with hands clasped tight at her waist, mouth compressed in its usual firm line of censure she took a step back, clearly mindful of a possible repeat of the unfortunate incident.

Reluctantly, Daisy climbed on board but even then stood clinging to the rail on the conductor's platform before finding a seat. 'I'll write, Mam, when I get to wherever it is I'm going.'

The engine chose that very moment to rev up and roar as the bus jerked forward, and Daisy was never afterwards entirely sure whether she had heard her mother correctly, but it sounded very like, 'Don't bother. I'll not be answering no letters from you, madam. Your father neither. Not if I've any say in the matter.'

Daisy felt stunned by the speed of events, overwhelmed by the crush of children on the platform, many of them crying, others excitedly enjoying the novelty of a train journey into the unknown. All of them clutched tight to a suitcase, brown paper parcel or kitbag, a doll or teddy and of course their gasmask box strung across their chest where was carefully pinned a large label stating their name and age, just as if they might forget it in the trauma of events.

'Don't play with the doors. Take your seats quickly, there's a good girl.' A woman in a green hat skewered to her iron-grey hair with a long hat pin, issued these orders in a loud, crisp voice, anxious to make herself heard above the din of a platform packed with children; a false, cheery smile fixed on her face.

Tens of thousands would be leaving Manchester over the next few days, as well as London, Birmingham, Liverpool and cities right across the land. London Road Station seemed to be filled with people giving orders: police and railway officials, local borough councillors who'd come along to offer support plus dozens of teachers, nurses, members of the Friends' War Victims Relief Committee, and WVS ladies, all of whom had evidently responded to government posters to help with the evacuation process.

Now, at last, all the plans were coming to fruition and they were off, and everyone seemed excited by the prospect. Everyone except Daisy.

Daisy felt affronted at being evacuated with a host of

children. She'd noticed a carriage full of pregnant young mums further along the train who'd been provided with their own midwife, just in case one of them should go into labour during the journey, she supposed. Daisy felt a burst of enyy for them. They would all be allowed to keep their babies, of course, because they were married to husbands who loved them.

The woman with the green hat and loud voice permitted herself one censorious glance at Daisy before ushering her into a carriage and slamming shut the door on her protest, almost as if she knew her dreadful secret and had decided she deserved no better consideration than to be left with a bunch of noisy ten-year-olds. It made Daisy feel confused. What was she then, child or woman?

Perversely now, she'd no wish to leave home for the idyllic bliss of the countryside, or to abandon her beloved Manchester which was suddenly under threat of war. In any case, she'd miss all the excitement and really she should be doing something useful, not being spirited away as part of this 'Great Trek' or whatever they called it, to some unknown safe haven, however well meaning these bossy people might be.

'Don't cry, Trish. You know what to do, remember? Just like we practised at school. Stick tight to teddy and we'll be all right.'

'I feel sick.' The piping voice at her elbow brought Daisy from her self-pitying reverie to find two small girls at her side. The face of one, little more than four or five, was wet with tears and a river of mucus from each nostril. The other, older by a year or so, was attempting to comfort her and mop her up.

'Where's me mam? I want me mam?' wailed the smaller one.

'She's waving from the platform. See, there she is,' and the older girl attempted to hoist her sister up so that she could see out of the carriage window to view some unidentified mother amongst the crush of women waving and bearing brave smiles as they sent their children off into the care of strangers.

Daisy sprang into action. 'Here, let me hold her for you,' and she grabbed the child to hold her high at the half open carriage window where she waved frantically, her small face a heartrending mix of joy at the sight of her mother, and pain at their parting. The other, older girl, hung out of the window long after the train had drawn out of the station, still waving when all sight of the crowd of sorrowful women had disappeared in a cloud of steam. 'Come on, love. Let me pull it up with the strap, or you'll get grit and soot in your eyes.'

The two little girls sat huddled in the corner of the seat opposite to Daisy, skinny arms wrapped tight about each other. They were dressed in navy blue gabardines far too long for them, yet with several inches of skirt trailing below the hem, presumably to leave ample room for growth. Each of their small, round heads was covered with a large beret, revealing only a few tufts of brown hair which stuck out around the edges. Daisy almost suggested they remove them, and then thought better of it. Who knew what lurked beneath? Their faces were drawn and anxious, the skin a familiar pallor that Daisy knew well, but then there wasn't much sunshine to be had in the back streets of Manchester. They looked so thoroughly miserable that she attempted to jolly them into conversation by asking them their names.

'I'm Megan,' the older girl solemnly responded. 'And this is Patricia, although we call her Trish for short.'

'Mine's Daisy,' said Daisy. 'And I'm happy to make your acquaintance.' They both exchanged weak smiles. 'Do you, by any chance, know where we're going on this train?'

Megan shook her head. 'I expect the King does.'

'Oh, I expect he does,' Daisy agreed. She glanced again at Trish who was still suffering from hiccuping sobs and seemed far from reassured by this news. When the tears finally subsided she curled up into a tiny ball, cuddled against her sister, popped her thumb into her mouth and went to sleep. The only time she perked up was some hours later when Megan drew out a packet of sandwiches, one for each of them.

Feeling a pang of hunger herself, Daisy reached down her case from the luggage rack and searched through it for a similar thoughtful gesture by her own mother. She found nothing. Embarrassed by this lack of attention, she quickly snapped it shut and returned it to the rack.

'Didn't you bring no food? We were told to fetch enough for one day.'

'It's all right. I'm not hungry.'

Unconvinced by the lie, Megan held out her packet. 'It's only fish paste, but you're welcome to have one. Mam allus makes plenty.'

'Thanks.' The fish paste sandwich went down a treat, followed by a second offered by Trish who even managed a shy smile, and thus their friendship was born.

'Weren't you given a list of what to bring? We were.'

'I don't know. It was all a bit sudden and – er – unexpected.'

'Mam had a bit of a job finding some of the stuff. We had to have a toothbrush, one *each*, spare socks and plimsolls, and a warm jersey. We've never had owt spare before, have you?'

'And a macktosh,' put in Trish, now bright-eyed and filled with vim and vigour after her sandwich.

'Mack*in*tosh,' Megan corrected. 'Did you have to buy a new one, Daisy? We did. Well, new to *us* that is. We got them on the flat iron market. Look, aren't they grand?' she said, smoothing down the lapel with pride.

'And I've got a face cloth. A blue one,' Trish added with some importance.

Daisy admitted that she'd no idea what was in her suitcase since her mother had packed it, and the pair looked at her askance, evidently having taken great interest in the treasures their mother had collected for them.

'D'you think we'll see the sea? Mam said we might.'

'I don't know.' Daisy shook her head and tried to smile in response to Trish's bright gaze. The little girl was rallying, seeing it all now as the adventure her mother had promised. If only she could view it in the same light. Oh Percy, where are you? If only you hadn't let me down. If only there hadn't been a war. If only I hadn't been so foolish as to get pregnant, or if only they'd let me keep the baby, then everything would have been so different. So many if onlys. If none of it had happened, she'd have been happy to go on this train today and steam away into the unknown. It would've been a new beginning. Instead, she'd been ordered to shut all that 'shameful' part of her life away, just as if it had never happened and her baby boy had never been born. Daisy turned her face to the window so the children couldn't see her tears.

It had seemed, while they had waited interminably in London Road Station, as if the journey would never start, now they thought it might go on for ever. The train would chug along for a while, and then stop, back up into a siding and wait for seemingly hours until some express or passenger train had thundered by, before edging slowly forward again. Dusk fell and at each station after that the carriage lights would go out just as the train drew into a station which made it difficult to read the signs on the equally dark platform, and then twenty or thirty children would get off and troop out to the buses usually lined up on the street nearby. The 'exodus' seemed to be very well organised and just a little alarming. Daisy had realised they were heading north, which cheered her and made her think of Aunt Florrie again, though they could end up in Scotland, which would be no help at all. When finally it was their turn, they were released, late in the evening, on to a small, unknown, country platform seemingly in the middle of nowhere. She felt stiff and nervous, certain they must have been travelling for days, though it was probably a little over seven hours.

'You're a very lucky girl to be here at all,' was the frosty response when she dared to ask the woman in the green hat why it had taken so long. 'Evacuee trains can't be given priority over the normal service. People still have to get to and from work, you know. Now, more than ever.'

This all seemed rather odd to Daisy. Why evacuate them at all if it wasn't an emergency? And if it was an emergency, then why not give the trainload of children priority? As things stood, it not being a corridor train, desperate little boys had been peeing out of the window, and little girls quietly weeping over the state of their knickers. Poor little Trish had been in floods of tears since this was apparently the first time she'd ever worn knickers in her life and they were brand new. It had been a great relief to escape the stink of the stuffy carriage.

Green Hat was speaking again, in an even louder voice this time as hundreds of confused, tired children milled about the rapidly darkening platform. She clapped her hands smartly together, to bring them to attention. 'Since we've arrived much later than expected, the dispersal officer isn't here. Probably gone back home, assuming we'll arrive tomorrow instead. However,' she continued with forced brightness, 'our spirits are undimmed, are they not? We shall sleep tonight in the station waiting rooms. Boys in the gents. Girls in the ladies. Now stand in line and make your way in an orderly fashion. No pushing and shoving.'

They were given a hot drink of Bovril made on the station waiting-room fire and bread and butter, by the ladies in smart uniforms, and afterwards, blankets were handed out. Daisy, Megan and Trish huddled up together for warmth beneath one but the September night was cold, the waiting-room floor hard and Trish kept sniffling and sneezing while Megan got a fit of coughing, which worried Daisy. Eventually they slept fitfully, woken with a jerk in the early hours by a cry of alarm that quickly spread, creating panic when the word 'gas' was heard.

The ladies in charge acted quickly. Whipping off all the children's blankets, they fled to the lavatory where they soaked them in water and then hung them at all the doors and windows for protection. The night was even colder after that and the three new friends gave up all hope of sleep though they were grateful at least for Megan and Trish's 'mack-toshes', their only protection against the blast of cold air that roared under the waiting-room door every time a train went through.

As the children stood about in a ragged group in the cold light of early morning, a trickle of local women began to appear. Green Hat told them that the women came not only from the local villages, but also from nearby Penrith, a town in the northern Lakes and Daisy felt a burst of hope. Wasn't it somewhere round here that Aunt Florrie had come to live? Desperately she tried to remember her married surname but for the life of her couldn't bring it to mind. All that had ever been written on the infrequent Christmas or birthday cards was '*Yours, as always, Florrie*'.

Bullied by the dispersal officer, who had finally arrived, the village women made their selection, and all Daisy could do was search their faces to see if any one of them resembled her own mother. None did.

'I'll have this one.'

'I'll take her.'

'I'll have that little lad over there.'

One woman put a hand on Trish's collar and was about to haul her away when Megan made a grab for her, loudly protesting. 'No! Our Trish stops with me. Me mam said we had to stay together. Daisy too,' she added for good measure, casting a quick glance in her new friend's direction. Daisy did not protest. The decision seemed to have been made without the need for words during the long, cold, miserable night. No matter what, they meant to stay together.

Unfortunately, this proved to be asking rather much of the good ladies of the Lakes. Many were glad to help the evacuees, some did so out of a sense of patriotism or duty, while others took the attitude that having to take one child was bad enough, two was an imposition, and three quite impossible. It became alarming, and then frightening to see the other children marched off one by one, and still be left hanging about on the cold platform with a diminishing number of possible hosts, or 'foster parents' as they were optimistically described.

'Does nobody want us, Daisy?' Megan asked, a slight wobble to her voice.

Trish tugged at Daisy's skirt. 'I feel sick.'

'Don't think about it, then you won't be.'

'Shall I be sick in me beret, only me mam told me not to take it off.'

'No, no, your mam's right. Leave it on, love. You won't be sick, I promise.' And, by a miracle, she wasn't.

In the end, there were only the three of them left, and Green Hat came over to inspect them. 'Really, this determination of yours to stick together isn't very helpful. How would it be if everyone adopted such stringent rules?'

The three stared up at her, uncomprehending. At last Daisy felt obliged to respond, since she was the eldest. 'They're only young, four and seven, and Trish is just getting over a bad dose of flu, so they need special care. I've promised to help since their mother had to stay and look after elderly relatives.' Daisy had heard the whole sorry story during the long night, about the entire family going down with the flu, grandpa dying and their grandmother still poorly with pneumonia. The two children, Trish in particular, were feeling homesick already.

Eyebrows arched quizzically. 'Oh, so you are not related then?'

'They are. To each other, I mean. I'm not, but . . .'

'Ah well, that changes everything. You should have said,' the woman responded briskly. 'In that case, you shall go with that old gentleman over there, and the two little ones with Miss Pratt. There, that's settled you all nicely. A good job well done.'

Daisy and Megan exchanged glances of dismay while Trish let out a great wail of protest and flung her arms about Daisy's leg, as if she might never let go. But there was no hope of escape. Abruptly disengaged from her hold, the weeping child was smartly handed over to a tall, thin, elderly woman with whiskers on her chin who was regarding the two little girls as if she'd never set eyes on such creatures in her life before.

'Can't I go with them? Please?' Daisy gasped, as the pair were dragged away.

'No indeed. You will go to the billet selected for you. Mr Witherspoon? She's all yours.' Within seconds there was no sign of a WVS uniform or large hat of any colour or description left on the platform. Daisy swivelled about in panic, took one glance at the haggard, unsmiling face of the old man beside her, then turned tail and ran after the wailing children.

'Miss Pratt,' she yelled. 'Miss Pratt, please wait a moment.' She caught up with the woman out on the station forecourt, quite out of breath and keenly aware of Mr Witherspoon bearing down upon them, like the devil incarnate. 'I'll do anything, clean your house, do the washing, anything. I'll make myself really useful and promise faithfully to keep these children out of mischief and off your hands. You need me, you really do. Young children are a great deal of work, and I don't eat much, I swear.' This last was quite untrue, but she thought perhaps the elderly woman might be worrying about feeding them all. She was certainly looking preoccupied.

'That is not a consideration at this juncture. I have a large garden and produce much of my own food, and naturally I have someone come in to do for me, though I do wonder if Gladys said she might be going to her sister's in Edinburgh.' Her eyes took on a vague, troubled look. 'But perhaps you may have a point with regard to the children. I have other commitments after all, and certainly could not tolerate any bad behaviour.'

Daisy held her breath. So far, in her own short life, she'd made a frightening number of mistakes, managing to ruin her entire life at just sixteen. Now, some half-formed idea in her head was telling Daisy that perhaps by helping these two children through their own troubles it might compensate in some way for the baby she'd lost, and that the pain in her own heart might somehow reduce.

After a moment, Miss Pratt swung around and called across the forecourt to Mr Witherspoon, still shambling towards them, his breathing laboured. 'I've decided to take the older girl as well, Mr Witherspoon. If it doesn't work out, I'll let you know.'

He paused, lifted one hand and waved to her by way of conceding defeat. It was difficult to tell if he was relieved or not, as only his flowing beard was visible beneath a wide-brimmed hat that completely obliterated the rest of his grim face.

To Daisy it seemed like a reprieve.

Her relief was short lived. Almost at once Daisy began to experience grave doubts. Miss Pratt's house, only a short walk from the station, was a gaunt, rather forbidding grey-stone property with tall, ornamental chimneys, mullioned windows, and a date – 1644 – carved over the lintel. It stood in a large walled garden overlooking the street, the kind of house once occupied by a notable packhorse owner, a carrier of merchandise between the North and London, York,

Kendal and Edinburgh. Not that Daisy would have recognised it as such, nor be able to imagine for one moment what it must feel like to own such a place.

Despite the evidence of new measures put into place for the sake of the war, splashes of white paint on kerbs, walls and railings so that people could find their way in the blackout, a poster stuck to a nearby lamp post urging women to offer their services to the local council for evacuation work, and stacks of sandbags everywhere, the tiny village seemed to be an embodiment of all her dreams. Its neat, grey-stone cottages with their bright gardens surrounding a wide expanse of village green was like something out of a picture book. The setting of the house was stunning. The panoply of blue-grey mountains that enfolded it, gleaming benignly in the early morning sunshine, quite took Daisy's breath away. Never had she seen such a glorious place, such splendour, so much space! There were sheep grazing on the village green by an old, grey-stone church that must have stood there for centuries. It was a beautiful, magical scene.

Oh, but she was tired, a dragging ache low down in her belly serving as a nagging reminder that she'd only recently given birth, hardly slept the night before and her knees felt all wobbly, as if they might buckle under her at any minute. How she longed to lie down in a bed and just sleep and sleep. The two bedraggled children beside her were, however, wide awake, mouths agape, hardly able to believe their good fortune. 'Is this where we're going to live?' Megan asked in awed wonder. 'In this big house?'

'Where's the sea?' Trish wanted to know. 'Is there some sands an' all?'

Miss Pratt was opening the front door with a large key she'd taken from the pocket of her tweed suit but paused to consider the child, as if her words had indicated some sort of criticism. 'No, we are nowhere near the sea, and have no sands for you to play on.'

Trish looked crestfallen. 'Me mam said we'd be able to buy a bucket 'n' spade.'

'My family has lived here for centuries and never felt deprived by the lack of a beach.'

Daisy intervened swiftly. 'Oh, she wasn't complaining. They're just a bit stunned by their good fortune, that's all. We all are. We – we're not used to anything so – so grand.'

Miss Pratt let out a bark that might have been laughter and marched off down a central lobby. 'Grand? Stuff and nonsense. This house isn't in the least bit grand. Needs a few repairs here and there but nothing I can't fix, given time. It's a big, draughty barn of a place, and I can only hope that you won't be bothered by damp, nor the odd ghost or boggart. Part of its country character, don't you know? Certainly doesn't bother me. You'll just have to cope without any fuss. No patience with fusspots.'

'Oh, we'll be fine,' Daisy assured her. 'Don't worry about us. Not at all.' Living with damp she fully understood. There'd been plenty of that in the tenements of Salford, and however much in need of repair this place might be, it certainly couldn't be in as bad a state as the two miserable rooms she and her parents had occupied in Marigold Court off Liverpool Street.

'What's a boggart?' Megan enquired tentatively, still hesitating to cross the threshold, Trish still clinging on tight to the belt of her sister's mackintosh.

Miss Pratt marched smartly back and with an impatient flap of her hand, urged both children to hurry up since she didn't have all day. 'It's a naughty imp or elf that is always up to mischief. I hope you two aren't going to be naughty?'

The pair gazed up at the old woman from beneath the rim of their large berets, eyes wide with fear and, wordlessly, shook their heads.

Again Daisy rushed to intervene, gathering them in her

arms and drawing them along the lobby. 'They're very good children, really.'

The woman looked doubtful and began to mutter to herself as she cast a critical eye over them. 'Glad to hear it. Still, brainwave of yours to come along. Know nothing about bairns. Never married, d'you see? More into dogs myself. Had to make the offer though to take a couple of vacees. Got to do my bit, no choice really. They'd have billeted some on me whether I liked it or not.'

Is that what they were? 'Vacees'! Some sort of disease to be foisted upon people? This wasn't at all how she'd imagined it would be, Daisy thought. Oh dear. How complicated life was. And how would she ever find Aunt Florrie now?

Laura

3

Laura had been awake for hours, had watched the sun come up through the narrow window of her lofty bedroom, seen the first rays light the yellow flowering broom into a glorious blaze of gold, and on the distant horizon a dazzling glint of snow crusting the summit of Helvellyn. By seven she found it impossible to stay in bed a moment longer, pulled on a pair of clean jeans and sweater and, padding to the kitchen in her woolly socks, made herself toast and coffee which she ate standing on the doorstep, marvelling at the view and revelling in the sensation of clean, fresh air that tingled on her face and sparkled like champagne in her lungs.

The night before, once everyone had gone, she'd trawled the house like a lost soul and then, like a homing pigeon, found herself up in the attic, the room she had always slept in as a child. The blue and white gingham curtains still hung at the window, though they were now somewhat faded from the sun; the patchwork bed cover that Daisy herself had stitched out of scraps of old curtains, still covered the bed. On impulse, Laura had run back downstairs for her wash bag and night-shirt, slipping with a sigh between sheets that smelled slightly musty, of a different age and old lavender, yet dry and soft against her skin. She knew it was sentimental of her, but she'd always felt safe there, cosy and strangely secure, and quite blissfully alone. With a pair of socks warming her cold toes and her night-shirt tucked firmly around her knees she'd soon thawed out, for all the wind was howling and rattling at the windows and the rain still hammering on the panes of glass.

It must have played out its temper during the night for the morning brought one of those rare, unexpectedly sunny days of spring, perhaps heralding a good summer to come. It was far too wonderful to waste by eating inside. Up on the higher slopes she could see the sturdy, dark Herdwicks, heavy with lamb. Perhaps the weather had lifted their spirits too for they seemed almost frisky as they browsed for new young grass shoots. And who could blame them, having carried their progeny through the long, grim months of an endless Lakeland winter, with freedom from their labours almost in sight.

Some said the Herdwicks had come to Lakeland with the Armada, others that it was the Vikings who had brought these small, sturdy sheep to these shores, darkly beautiful with their hoar-frosted faces. Or then again, it might have been the Celts who'd first appreciated their hardiness, unless of course Daisy's theory had been correct, that they'd always been here, walking these barren passes long before even man attempted to tame this landscape.

Finishing her toast, Laura brushed the crumbs from her hands, tugged on a warm jacket and boots, for the breeze would be cold higher up, and set off up the smooth slope of Blease Fell. It was a long and tedious climb but fresh air and exercise, she decided, were the perfect antidote to stress. By the time she reached Knowe Crags her heart was pounding but there was the view as recompense for her effort. She sat on the slope to catch her breath and look back upon a chain of mountains, only a few of which she could name: Wetherlam and Black Sails, Helvellyn of course, Crinkle Crags and Scafell Pike. The glint of Derwentwater to her right and the grey huddle of houses that was Keswick. And further away still, in the far distance, the hills of Scotland and the Solway Firth.

The grandeur of the scene had a marvellous effect upon her, seeming to fill Laura with a joy as heady as wine. There was much still to explore on the mountain itself, which would have to wait for another day. Daisy had always called Blencathra a proud mountain, a benevolent giant who kept watch on the cluster of white walled cottages that formed the village of Threlkeld in the valley below. Its shape, being that of twin summits linked by a curved depression, had tempted the Victorians to give it a new name: Saddleback. Daisy hated this pet name. If it had originally been named Blencathra, then Blencathra it must remain. Strong, indomitable, lofty, rather like herself in a way. She'd loved living here, claiming that the Lake District, and in particular this mountain, had captured her heart from the first moment she'd set eyes upon it, and Laura could only agree.

Daisy had stayed for the rest of her life but how long could she stay? Was it pure fantasy to even consider such a prospect? Living under the harsh conditions that were common in these climes, wasn't something to take on lightly. In the upper reaches of Lakeland, summer and autumn could be magical but winters were long, and spring more often than not little more than wishful thinking. Could she cope?

As she sat there, a lone walker passed by several feet below her, acknowledging her presence with a cheery wave. Perhaps he was staying at the Blencathra Centre further down, the restored Victorian buildings that had once housed the Sanatorium and was now a Field Study Centre. The mountain was certainly busier than in Daisy's day, with its procession of walkers heading for the summit via various ascents, Wainwright in hand; but still lonely, still empty for much of the year.

How much easier it would be for her to decide, if Daisy herself were here to talk to and share her troubles. Laura's eyes filled with a rush of tears. Yet she could guess what she might say. 'Do what you must, girl, but remember men are delicate creatures. Tread softly. Make your point, aye, but don't go at it like a bull at a gate.'

And Laura could only agree. Felix was not one to let go easily.

'Don't argue with me all the time, Laura, it's an irritating fault of yours,' he would say whenever she attempted to put forward her own opinion on a subject. Or, if she expressed a desire to go somewhere: 'You're far too attractive to allow out of my sight for a moment. One sideways glance from those soft brown eyes of yours and any man would be putty in your hands. I certainly am.'

It wasn't true of course. She had never been the one to look outside the marriage for her pleasures. Besides, in Laura's estimation she could only pass for pretty after a great deal of effort and expense, not to mention hours in the bathroom, titivating. She saw herself as entirely unprepossessing with long, dark brown hair which showed an infuriating tendency to curl, pale skin and a far too slender, non-voluptuous, figure. Even her legs were long and gawky, and her feet too big. It never ceased to amaze her that Felix had chosen her, above all the other girls desperate for a date with him. Was it any wonder if he strayed from time to time with such an unexciting wife to come home to?

Yet, besotted by his charm, his good looks and ambitious, go-ahead style, as well as being anxious to be a good wife to him in the new house he'd bought for them in a fashionable part of Cheshire, Laura had dutifully gone along with all his high-flown plans and done everything she could to make him happy.

Chin in her hands she recalled how, as a new bride, she'd so looked forward to spending their days working together, building a business to be proud of. But then the rules of the game had been made properly clear to her and excitement, and hope, had slowly faded.

Laura was not, after all, to be allowed to actually work at Felix's Fine Arts Gallery. It dealt only in specialist material, he'd explained, needing a particular expertise, so he'd hired a young, attractive graduate called Miranda, for the task. When Laura had readily volunteered to attend classes in modern art or interior design, do whatever was necessary to enable her to be a useful member of the team and perhaps, ultimately, a partner in the business, he'd appeared highly amused.

'Stick to answering the telephone and making appointments for me, darling. You can't do much damage there. As well as making those delicious lemon cheesecakes, of course. There isn't anyone who could resist doing business with me, having tasted one tiny sliver of your delicious desserts.'

'But it seems so little, just to cook and entertain for you. So unimportant.'

'It is not in the least unimportant, my darling. Food, next to sex, is a vital ingredient of a happy marriage.'

And certainly the sex they'd enjoyed together had been good, at least in those early days, for when he was not actually working, they'd spent the time largely in bed. She'd been captivated, at first, by this evidence of his need for her, and of how he appreciated all she did to create a lovely home. And if, as the years slid by, he spent more and more time at the gallery and less with her, wasn't that only to be expected when he was so successful? She learned not to complain about the eighteen-hour working days, the times when he rang to say he couldn't make it home as he had to dash off to the outer reaches of Yorkshire or Derbyshire at a moment's notice to view a Lowry or whatever. He never recognised evidence of his own neglect, because he considered that she had sufficient to occupy her, looking after him.

Laura had endured his bossiness and tolerated his need for control largely in silence over the years; even been amused and flattered by his unwarranted and foolishly obsessive jealousies. On the whole, she'd shown exemplary courage and patience above and beyond the calls of wifely duty. But she'd discovered there were limits, even to her patience.

Nurtured by a stubborn determination to rescue herself from miserable oblivion, somewhere, at the back of her head, an idea was taking shape. Laura wasn't sure when it had nestled there, but it seemed to be settling in nicely, fighting off all attempts to brush it away. And where was the harm in giving this crazy notion an airing? Wasn't that why she'd wanted to stay, to give herself time to think, to dream.

All she had to discover was whether she could find the strength to carry it out, whether she could match the kind of fortitude Daisy had shown during her own troubles.

The house at Lane End Farm was large and rambling and old, probably built some time during the seventeenth century with slate walls nearly four feet thick, a storm porch at the front to keep out the worst of the Lakeland weather, and a confusing array of circular chimneys. Its most historic feature was a priest hole off one of the upper rooms that Laura remembered Daisy saying had once been used as the family chapel, as well as some rather nice linen-fold panelling in the dining room.

The sound of her footsteps sounded hollow on the uncarpeted stairs and upper landing, throwing open doors as she went along. The silent, empty bedrooms, of which there were six, not including the attic, were furnished in a somewhat outmoded, nineteen-fifties style. It was like entering a different world. There must have been eight at one time but two of the smaller rooms had been turned into bathrooms. Nevertheless, Daisy had done well here in her day, particularly taking into account that she'd started with absolutely nothing, and most of her youth had been blighted by war.

But it was the atmosphere of the house which moved Laura the most. It wore a sad air of abandonment. Wheelbarrows, harrows and a myriad of other farm tools rusted quietly away in the huddle of broken-down outbuildings, from which issued no happy squawking or other farmyard sounds. The house itself seemed to weep and mourn, wearing a shroud of sorrow for the woman who had loved it and lived within its four walls for more than half a century, generously sharing her home with all who wished to find sanctuary here; a place to nurse wounds, dream dreams and mend broken hearts.

Today, it was Daisy's own granddaughter in dire need of such care and it seemed to be opening its arms to her, offering her peace, almost like a warm embrace as a solution to all her troubles.

Wouldn't it be good to repay that generosity by bringing the house back to life?

Wouldn't it be fun to open up the guesthouse again, Laura thought. To do up the faded rooms and welcome a new generation of walkers and lovers of the Lakes. She certainly had no fears about producing good food for them. Even Felix had nothing but praise for her dinner parties, and she did love to cook.

Of course it would be hard work. There would be beds to make, bathrooms to clean, and very little privacy with guests coming and going all the time. She'd need help of some sort, and money to get started. She would have to advertise, yet it was a popular route for walkers and those stressed out by their jobs in need of peace and fresh air, as well as folk who didn't care for air travel or beach holidays. Many people loved to escape to a place like this, so was it such a crazy idea? Could she make it work?

Laura went back to the kitchen and made herself a mug of coffee. Cradling it in her hand, she sat at the kitchen table and thought about this plan with mounting excitement. She could surely refurbish and update the place without spending a fortune, though she'd need to make one or two of the larger bedrooms en-suite by installing shower rooms. And the entire house would need redecorating, of course. After a while she abandoned the coffee half drunk to continue with her exploration, moving restlessly about the house, picking things up, putting them down again and going on to the next room. And all the time turning the idea over in her head, examining it from every angle, weighing up likely costs and finally admitting that if she went for it, she would effectively be declaring her marriage to be over. She would have to leave Felix.

Was she ready for that?

The thought doused her enthusiasm and brought back the depression, as if a cloud had passed over, blotting out the sun. She had loved him so much. Why had it all gone so badly wrong? And would he even notice she was gone? For all his claims to jealousy and constant declarations that he needed her to be there for him, he was rarely at home. He spent almost every waking hour working either at the gallery, meeting clients, making contacts, or travelling.

Laura flopped on to a sofa. Perhaps it might have been different if they'd had children, but Felix had made it clear quite early on that they were not to be a part of the picture. Laura's wishes on the subject were, apparently, to be ignored.

Felix had one daughter already: Chrissy, the child of his first marriage who had brought nothing but worry and anxiety into his life, so he'd no wish to repeat the experience. Chrissy was fourteen and lived with her mother, Julia, who claimed to be a diligent and caring parent while generally seeming to be in a perpetual state of dissension with her rebellious child. Reminding Felix if Chrissy had a birthday coming up, or of a school function he must attend, was one of Laura's chief functions in life, although there were occasions when she was required to stand in for him. In theory, Felix was expected to take most of the flak when things went badly wrong; in practice whenever he was summoned to unscheduled meetings with the girl's despairing teachers, he was more often than not mysteriously occupied elsewhere and so the task would fall upon Laura's shoulders.

But then Laura's main roll in life was to smooth the way for

Felix: to remove unnecessary obstacles of stress which seemed in danger of wasting his valuable time, or causing undue annoyance. To say she resented this fact was putting it mildly, but then she'd come to privately resent a good many aspects of her life.

If the gallery was ever overloaded with work because of an upcoming exhibition, Laura would be permitted to deal with simple correspondence and any non-specialist matters considered too trivial for Miranda's expertise. She would be the one expected to ring the press and marshal interest; the one who kept fretting artists at bay when they rang constantly to see why their work wasn't selling quite as well as they'd hoped. And when everything proceeded smoothly as a result of her efforts, it was generally the lovely Miranda who took the credit.

'She's such a marvel, that girl. How would I manage without her?' Felix would say.

Laura knew, instinctively, that he was unfaithful. She tried to be adult about it, modern and forward thinking, but it hurt her deeply. She'd given Felix her all, every scrap of her being, her love and loyalty, and yet whenever she'd confronted him with her suspicions he'd simply laughed them off, accusing her of being over-emotional, as if she were unstable in some way, which usually resulted in Laura apologising for not trusting him, as though she were the guilty one.

But then he never took her 'little rebellions' seriously.

Now, at the back of her mind was the worry that perhaps he'd given in to her whim to stay on at the farm rather too easily. Placating or ignoring her was what he excelled at, and no doubt he did indeed expect her to come crawling home by the end of the week.

So what would happen if she didn't?

She really mustn't allow it to matter what Felix did, what Felix thought, or what he planned. She couldn't build a future on a sense of misplaced loyalty. It was time to give more thought to herself. All that was important now was what *she* wanted, what *she* decided to do with her life.

By leaving her the house, it was as if Daisy had offered her a glimpse of the freedom she so longed for and needed, and it was irresistible. Laura knew that if she didn't grab this opportunity, she might never get another.

Daisy had been an ideal grandmother, of whom she'd been inordinately fond. Bright and fun, unfussy and surprisingly go-ahead, full of energy and with a wry sense of humour. Laura could see her now, her wildly curling hair like an aureole of white about her head as she busied herself about the house and yard, always seeming to be in a tearing hurry, setting off on some new scheme or other, never still for a moment. She felt an increasing curiosity to discover more about her. What had happened to her as an evacuee? How, exactly, had she come to Lane End Farm? And how had a girl from the slums of Salford come to own such a fine house?

What had caused her to deprive Laura's father of his heritage? A situation which filled her with guilt, though she'd no wish to hand it back. Losing the house was the last thing Laura wanted, for hadn't she always loved it, even as a child?

It was tragic really, that Gran and Dad never properly made up their quarrel, whatever had caused it in the first place. Both too stubborn and hot-tempered, she supposed, and determined always to be right. He never even spoke of his own father who had died when he was about seventeen, the year after Robert had left home to join the navy, so it would appear that memories of him were painful too. How very sad!

What was at the root of it all? she wondered. Following the enforced estrangement, Laura had begun visiting her grandmother again during her years at university, the moment she was free of the restrictions placed upon her by Robert. Sadly, they'd lapsed again during her marriage to Felix. She felt guilty about that too. Yet despite the enforced absences between visits, she and Daisy had remained close.

Which was more than could be said about Laura's relationship with Robert. That had always been difficult, particularly since the death of her mother. Twelve was a difficult age for a girl to lose a mother and they'd spent much of her teenage years at odds. Even the question of her education had been a source of conflict between them. Her father had actively prevented her from attending a *cordon bleu* course in Paris by telling her that there were no places left, when, in fact, he'd never made any attempt to book her in. He'd secured her a job in the bank instead and, naïvely, Laura had believed his story. It had been Felix who had laughingly told her the truth, years later. The only thing she had ever done which her father had approved of was to marry Felix, whom he'd considered to be quite a catch.

She glared at the phone, willing it to ring. Why did he never call her? There were times when Laura believed that if she didn't take the trouble to ring, she might never hear from him again. Why didn't he ring to apologise for missing the funeral, or at least ask how it went, how she'd coped with it? Right now, she could do with some support. Every time she rang him, she hoped that he'd break a lifetime's habit and offer some.

With a sigh, Laura picked up the phone. Nothing would be gained by allowing pride to stand in the way, as had happened between Robert and Daisy. She certainly had no intention of treating her father with the same kind of cavalier neglect that he had used upon his own parent. That wouldn't improve matters one bit. 'Hi Dad, it's me. Laura.'

'Of course it must be you, Laura, who else would call me by that infernal name?'

Her heart sank. Clearly in one of his moods again. She felt her hand tighten on the receiver, even as she tried to put a smile into her voice. She'd discovered long since that reacting to his black humour only made matters worse, yet conversation between them was always difficult at the best of times. 'I just thought I'd ring to see how you were.'

'How do you think I am? I'm not quite senile yet, you know.'

Oh, definitely on good form. 'So, you're quite well. Good.'

'Last time I looked I was still alive. Hale and hearty in fact.'

'Excellent. I began to worry you might be ill.'

'If this is a criticism about my not turning up to that dratted funeral, you can save your breath. I'd never any intention of going and Daisy would not have expected me to be there. A hypocrite I will not be.'

'She was your mother, and she's dead.'

'Well, I rather assumed that, since they were burying her.'

Laura stifled a sigh. 'Whatever happened between you two, is over now.'

'You have a sad talent for stating the obvious, Laura. Look, if you've only rung to castigate me for my lack of filial duty, you could have saved yourself the bother. It was my prerogative to decide, not yours. No doubt you're ringing from some airport or other, on that damned fancy mobile of yours. Where is it you're gadding off to this time?'

'No, no, I'm still at the farm. Anyway, I'm not the one always gadding about, that's Felix. I'm the little pig who stays at home, remember? The one who keeps the home fires burning, except that I'm not any more.'

'Stop talking in stupid riddles, Laura. If you've anything to say, say it in plain English.'

She took a deep breath. 'OK, what do *you* say to my starting up Daisy's guesthouse again? Wouldn't that be fun?' The sound of breathing echoed loudly down the wire like the rattle of gunfire. 'Dad, are you still there?'

'I think there must be something wrong with this line, I thought you said you were going to start up Daisy's guesthouse again.'

'That's right, that's exactly what I'm going to do. What do you think?'

Again a short silence, followed by a sound very like a suppressed explosion of rage. 'Does Felix know about this?'

'Not yet, but I mean to tell him.' Just as soon as she'd plucked up the courage, or got matters so far advanced there was nothing he could do to prevent it.

'Ah, well he'll soon put a stop to such nonsense. Really, Laura, what a child you are. Fancy ringing me up in the middle of my post-prandial nap to prattle on about some stupid fantasy you're having.'

'It's not a fantasy. I mean to do it. I intend to find out as much as I can about Daisy, then follow in her footsteps.'

'I'm coming over.'

'What?'

'You've clearly taken leave of your senses. I'm coming up. Not to that dratted farm. I'll take a taxi from the station and you can meet me at the Golden Lion. I'll buy you lunch.' He named a date and time and before Laura had time to say whether or not this was convenient, she found herself talking to the dialling tone.

Daisy

4

The room allocated to them was next to the kitchen, which itself was a surprisingly dark, cold room with tiny windows set high in thick stone walls and a huge pine table taking up much of the available space. When Miss Pratt had flung open the door, Daisy had tried not to show her surprise. It smelled strongly of dogs, though there wasn't one in sight. A cat rubbed itself against her legs, either by way of greeting or hopeful of some dinner. Along one wall was stacked a pile of wooden boxes in which were a variety of plant pots, string netting, bamboo canes, old pairs of boots and other gardening items. It seemed odd to store such things in a bedroom and Daisy guessed that that was its real purpose – for storing *things*, not children. There were no curtains at the narrow windows, no rug on the stone floor, simply a tatty piece of straw matting. There were only two beds in the room, for which Miss Pratt did not apologise, merely commented that she'd prepared for two vacees, not three.

'Oh, we can manage, thank you.' Daisy had expected to be taken upstairs where there must surely be half a dozen bedrooms, though perhaps this was how the old lady lived, all on one floor, even in a big house like this. Miss Pratt's next words explained everything.

'It's not much but I dare say it's better than you're used to, so you won't notice. Can't have you sleeping in my best beds, dear, though I accept it's not your fault if these children are verminous and semi-literate. So would anyone be, coming from the slums.'

The remark brought a flush of annoyance to Daisy's cheeks, and for some reason recalled her mother's comment, 'We might be poor but we have us standards.' She cast down her eyes, willing herself not to reveal these thoughts. The old lady was opening up her home to complete strangers, after all.

'There aren't *really* any ghosts are there?' Megan enquired timorously, a slight frown puckering her brow. The two children were hovering at the kitchen door, unwilling to venture in any further, remove their coats and berets, or even set down a single bag until these concerns had been dealt with. Trish's mouth had taken on the shape of an upside-down U as if she might burst into tears at any minute.

Allowing no time for Miss Pratt to open these floodgates with horrific tales of headless horsemen or clanking chains, which would surely give the children nightmares, Daisy barged in with, 'Course there aren't. You'll be nice as ninepence here, won't they Miss, once they've settled in?'

'I've certainly come to no harm living in this house, child. No harm at all. And if you hear any odd noises in the night, pay no attention.'

Megan said, 'What sort of noises?' and Trish gave a little whimper but this was apparently as much sympathy as they were going to get.

Daisy had half expected some dragon of a housekeeper to emerge, such as those who occupied the pages of the penny novelettes she devoured from Boot's Library. Or Gladys, the woman who 'did', if she hadn't gone to her sister's house in Edinburgh. No such person had appeared and Daisy's longing for a mug of hot, sweet tea was becoming over-whelming. She ached to put up her feet and rest, feeling bone weary after the sleepless night and the long walk from the station. She could feel a sticky residue of blood between her legs and thought even more longingly of a hot bath and clean underwear. Not that she dare mention any of this, of course, but at least they'd arrived at last and soon these needs and longings would be attended to.

Trish gave her sleeve a little tug, pulling Daisy down to her level so she could issue a fearful whisper in her ear. 'You won't ever leave us on us own here, Daisy, will you?'

Daisy squeezed her hand, as much to reassure herself as the child, and exchanged a cheery smile with Megan. Both little girls looked nervous but at least they were moving about more freely now, as if they couldn't quite make up their minds whether to be excited by this unexpected turn of events, or turn tail and run home to their mam. Deep inside, Daisy felt much the same way.

That first day had been a nightmare. They stowed their personal belongings in a wooden trunk with a heavy lid that stood between the two beds. It was not ideal since it smelled of mildew, but there was nowhere else.

'What now?' Megan asked in fearful tones, voicing all their thoughts.

'Oh, I'm sure Miss Pratt has done her best to make us comfortable, and we must be grateful and make the best of it. She just didn't expect quite so many of us,' Daisy remarked brightly, wishing she felt as confident as she sounded.

There came a chorus of excited barking from the back garden and all three clambered up to peep out of the window to see what was going on. They couldn't, unfortunately, see anything beyond a tangle of weeds and shrubs but they could hear Miss Pratt's strident voice clearly enough. She was talking to the dogs, calling them to her and then after a few minutes all went quiet.

'She's happen giving them some dinner,' Megan whispered.

'Can I have mine now?' Trish piped up. 'I'm hungry.'

Moments later they heard the old woman pass by the kitchen door, muttering to herself as she strode back along the lobby, followed by the slam of the front door.

'P'raps she's gone shopping.'

As they sat huddled together for warmth on one of the beds, waiting for her to return with food for their dinner, it slowly began to dawn upon Daisy as the minutes and then an hour, and then two hours ticked by, that she might not return at all, or if she had, she'd entered through a different door and they hadn't heard her come in. Either way, she seemed to have forgotten all about them.

'Come on,' Daisy said at last, her voice sounding strained and over-bright as she rallied the drooping children. 'She's made me responsible for you both, so that's what I'll be. Responsible!' Surely, she thought, with a quaking sensation in the pit of her stomach, she hasn't taken me at my word and left me to cope with these children on me own? 'Let's raid the kitchen cupboards and see what we can find.'

They could find disappointingly little. A large bag of flour, one of oatmeal and a smaller one of salt. Further explorations revealed a larder with slate shelves upon which Daisy located a tray of eggs and boxes of potatoes, onions, leeks and other vegetables. 'Oh, look at these. Treasure indeed!'

She quickly set about gathering the ingredients for an omelette, but was then confronted by the next challenge. How to cook it. Faced with a stove that might well have been put in at the same time the house was built in 1644, judging by its rusty appearance, it proved, as Daisy suspected it would, depressingly difficult to light. By the time they'd finally got it going, driven more by their intense hunger rather than any notion of the correct procedure, not only had the morning passed by but much of the afternoon as well. By which time Megan was almost in tears, Trish was curled up on a piece of sacking with her thumb in her mouth and Daisy could easily have eaten the eggs raw.

At last, however, grit and determination paid off and some small measure of heat began to filter through. Daisy found a frying pan, a knob of beef dripping and soon an appetising aroma of frying onions was filling the kitchen, making young mouths water and eyes shine with anticipation. Then she beat up six eggs in a jug and tipped those over the onions into the hot fat, smiling in delight as the mixture bubbled and frothed. They all felt much better after the meal, washed down by a pint of tea each. There was even a little bit of milk left over for the cat. But then came the realisation that the autumn day was drawing to a close and dusk was falling with no offer, thus far, of the much longed-for hot baths.

In the circumstances, this was unfortunate in the extreme. It had soon dawned upon Daisy that although she herself came from one of the worst parts of Salford, her mother's puritan strictness had ensured stringent cleanliness, even if she rarely bestowed upon her daughter the smallest scrap of love. Young Trish and Megan, though more blessed in that department and assured of their own mother's love and concern for them, could not, by anyone's estimation, be considered clean. Each child bore the telltale, sweet-sour smell of stale urine and, once the berets were finally removed, hair crawling with head lice was all too plainly revealed. They were, as Miss Pratt had rightly predicted, verminous. There were also ominous looking scabs and cracked skin between their fingers which looked in sore need of attention.

Using some of the warm water from the kettle she'd boiled, Daisy washed the children's hands and faces with a large bar of carbolic soap she found in the pantry. The necessary attention to their hair would have to wait till tomorrow, she decided, as they were far too tired tonight. Besides, something stronger than carbolic would be required to solve that particular problem. Daisy made a mental note to find Miss Pratt first thing in the morning and ask if she would get them something from the chemist, or perhaps from the dispersal officer.

That would also provide a good opportunity to mention one or two other matters which were troubling her. There were only a few eggs left in the tray, and the Bovril jar was empty so there was nothing for supper. If she was to be responsible for these children, Daisy needed to know who would do the shopping. Daisy was outraged at being so ignored. There should have been postcards for the children to write and send home to their mother, to let her know where they were. And apart from the very essential matters of food and general care and cleanliness, there was also the question of school for the two girls, and work for herself.

She tucked them up together in one of the beds and sang them a lullaby, and it came to Daisy in that moment that she should have been singing to her own child this night. Tears sprang to her eyes as she wondered in whose arms her little son was cuddled at this precise moment. The image brought a stab of pain to her heart and she struggled to block it out. Dwelling on her loss wouldn't help one bit, and she'd been assured that he was safe and well, that he'd been found a good home with parents who would love him as their own. In the circumstances, it was the best she could hope for.

When tired eyelids began to droop with sleep, Daisy crept from the room, poured fresh warm water into the bowl and began to wash herself. The soap and water felt good against her skin. After that, she scrubbed all their stained underwear as best she could, and left them to soak in salt water as her mother had taught her, before crawling into the other bed. Just before she slipped into a deep sleep, she told herself that at least they were safe from Mr Hitler's bombs, and there was surely nothing wrong with their billet that couldn't be put right in the morning.

Daisy used the last of the eggs to boil for breakfast, since there was little else in the larder, and tried not to think about what they would do for dinner. She felt thankful that she'd at least thought to bank up the stove with coke so that it had stayed in overnight but she'd also need to investigate later where the rest of the coal store was, and if there was a better way of getting hot water other than by boiling kettles? These, and various other important matters were in dire need of attention.

Since early morning she'd heard stairs creaking, doors banging, dogs barking, Miss Pratt muttering to herself as she moved about the place, and had every hope that soon she would come to see how they were after their first night. Daisy had initially meant to ask for a more comfortable bedroom than the one they'd been allotted but now that the stove was warming it up a little, and supposing she could find extra supplies of coke to refill the big coal scuttle, she was having second thoughts about that. It might be even colder elsewhere in the house.

Yet no one could consider the arrangements satisfactory and Daisy worried that Trish might start up with flu again, or Megan's cough get worse. Like herself, they were more used to an overcrowded, sheltered, city life, where the close proximity of other people at least helped to keep you warm. Here, there seemed to be nothing but draughts, wide open spaces and bitter cold. Surely the dispersal officer would call eventually, to check they were all right?

It proved easy enough, in the event, to find the coal cellar and, together, the two children and Daisy shovelled sufficient coke into the huge coal scuttles to last them throughout the day. It was less easy to carry them back up the stairs into the kitchen, but with a great deal of gasping and heaving, puffing and blowing, they finally managed it between them.

'I still need to talk to her though,' Daisy said.

'Perhaps she'll be in the garden, giving the dogs their breakfast,' Megan suggested.

To their dismay, they found the kitchen door locked. Megan went pale with fright. 'We can't get out, Daisy! Will we have to stay locked in here for ever?'

'What, till we die?' Trish wailed.

'Not if I can help it.' Daisy was so appalled she could feel herself actually start to shake with fury. How dare the woman lock them in? Heaven help us, no one should treat children in such a manner. Making a game of it, she urged the children to search for an alternative way out but the only exit, in the end, proved to be through a pantry window.

'Ooh, what fun. Go on, Trish, you first. I'll give you a boost up.'

It felt good to be out in the autumn sunshine but Miss Pratt was not, after all, in the garden. Nor were the dogs. 'Looks like she's taken them out for their morning walk. Let's have a scout around and see what else we can find.'

They found the hens and on seeing how frantic they went at the sight of the three of them, all running about and flapping their wings, getting very excited, Daisy concluded that their hostess must have forgotten to feed them as well. A search in a nearby outhouse supplied the necessary mash, and she put some in their metal hopper while Trish filled up the water dish and Megan carefully collected three fresh, warm eggs.

'Well, we won't starve, that's for sure. Though we may end up clucking a bit,' Daisy joked.

There was little else to see. The garden was wild and neglected with nothing but an old crab apple tree, practically bare of fruit and even that was sour, judging by the one Daisy risked trying, not realising they weren't meant for eating straight off the tree. Beyond the dry-stone wall at the bottom lay a wide expanse of ploughed field that looked as if it was growing something, though what it might be, Daisy couldn't guess, knowing nothing of such matters. It started to rain so, mindful of Megan's cough, she hurried the children back inside and boiled the kettle for yet more tea, though sadly without milk.

'Mam used to make soda bread sometimes,' Megan said, looking at the big bag of flour. 'Perhaps we should try,' but since none of them had the first idea how to begin, that idea quickly foundered.

The three girls patiently waited throughout all of that day and the next, for Miss Pratt to call in and check on them. They somehow weren't surprised when she didn't. Daisy did her best to keep the children amused by telling them stories, or teaching them little songs and nursery rhymes. There were no books, nor even pencil and paper in the kitchen so it was hard to devise games beyond I-Spy, and they quickly tired of that one. The house had become strangely silent and they preferred being out in the sunshine. Playing in the garden helped to fill the empty hours and they made sure the hens were well taken care of. They lived on eggs, mashed potato and fried onions. But the children were badly missing their mother and Daisy was growing increasingly uneasy. This wasn't the way to look after children, vacees or not. She felt overwhelmed by the responsibility, quite out of her depth. If she hadn't been considered capable of looking after one tiny baby, how could she possibly care for two little girls?

The third night they were disturbed by the dogs howling. The sound was so alarming, they all ended up cuddled together in one bed.

'Was that a boggart d'you think, Daisy?'

'Or a ghost?'

'No, it's just the dogs, disturbed by the wind I expect. Go to sleep.' Easier said than done. It was a fine night, with not a breath of wind and Daisy lay wide-eyed throughout, her ears pricked for the slightest sound.

By eleven o'clock the next morning with still no sign of their host, and with not even any eggs left for breakfast, Daisy felt they'd been patient long enough. She instructed the two little girls to stay put in the kitchen, while she went to search further afield.

'No, no, don't go Daisy,' Trish begged, wide-eyed with fear.

Megan added her own plea. 'What if the boggarts come again, Daisy?'

'Don't be silly, they weren't boggarts, only the dogs and they're quiet now.' That was another odd thing. They hadn't seen hide nor hair of a dog in days. 'I must find Miss Pratt and if I can't find her, then I shall look for the lady in the green hat, or some other official. There must be *somebody* responsible for us 'vacees'. I mean to find out who.'

But she had reckoned without Trish who refused, absolutely, to let her go.

Mouth downturned into the familiar curve, cheeks awash with tears, it would have taken a harder heart than Daisy's to prise the child's fingers from their fierce grip upon her skirt and simply walk away.

'All right then, we'll all go. But wrap up well.'

The navy gabardines and berets were put back on, scarves tied into place, and the inseparable trio set off together. 'Just like the three Musketeers,' Daisy joked. 'We'll soon find Miss Pratt and get this all sorted out.'

They walked the length of the village street knocking at every door, but an hour later, were no closer to finding her. Many of the neighbours expressed their concern, urging Daisy to call again if they didn't find her.

'She has got a bit odd lately,' one woman admitted. 'Taken to walking them dogs for hour upon hour on the hills. But she loves her garden and her hens. She'll be back soon, I'm sure.'

Eventually, one kindly shopkeeper took pity on them and suggested they take the bus into Penrith and try the town hall 'T'isn't right, you children wandering about the place with nobody to look after you,' she said, quite outraged at the very idea. Daisy could only agree with her.

'How much is a bottle of milk?' she enquired politely,

counting out the few pennies her mother had given her for the journey.

'Oh lord, don't tell me you haven't even any milk? I allus knew Miss Pratt were a bit eccentric like, and she's been going more and more peculiar lately, but by heck, this takes the biscuit. Ah, that's a thought. Biscuits. Now, I've some nice garibaldis somewhere.' The kindly woman began to rummage on her shelves and soon handed over a packet of biscuits, together with the milk, waving away the six pennies Daisy had managed to get together. 'I'll put it on her bill. Anything else you need? Bit of bacon? Slab of cheese? Dab of butter?'

All further searches for their missing hostess were postponed as the three gleefully watched the shopkeeper fill a brown paper bag with these goodies and gathering up their prize, scampered back to the kitchen. Afterwards, stomachs stuffed with food, they lay down on their beds and fell into a sweet, dreamless sleep.

Laura

5

Lunch with her father was every bit as disastrous as Laura had expected. Over the soup he castigated her over her obstinacy in staying on at the farm after the funeral, instead of going home to her husband like a good little wife, presumably. During the fish course he reminded her how her own amateur efforts at cooking couldn't be compared with this sort of professional cuisine. And finally, when the cheese was served (her father didn't eat dessert and made the assumption that his daughter wouldn't require one either), he warned her of the perils of defying her husband's wishes to sell.

'Lane End Farm will fetch a good price, and Felix is so much more skilled than you in such matters. You must be guided by him.'

'Why must I? The house was left to me, not Felix.' As soon as the words were out of her mouth, Laura regretted them, since they sounded so arrogant, almost as if she were bragging. 'I didn't mean that quite as it sounds. It should be yours, of course, and . . .'

'Don't twist yourself into knots over this, Laura. I don't want the damned farm. Never have. Wouldn't touch anything of Daisy's with the proverbial bargepole.'

'Oh, for heaven's sake, what was it with you two? Why didn't you get on? You've never properly explained it to me.'

'I don't see that it's any of your business.'

'Well, I think it is. She was my grandmother, after all. I mean, why did she leave the house to me, and not to you?'

'Because she knew I wouldn't accept it and she wanted it to stay in the family.'

'So tell me, what was the problem? Something silly, I'll be bound.'

'We didn't agree on what was important in life, that's all. We had a completely different set of values. I believe in honour and openness, Daisy the complete opposite. No doubt as a result of being dragged up out of the gutters of Salford.'

'That's rather an unfair attitude, not to say a most provocative remark, and completely untrue from what I've learned about her, even in this short time. Her neighbours and friends here seem to think she was lovely. A charming, cheerful soul always ready to help others. They say she was generous to a fault.'

'Oh, she was that all right, in more ways than one.' He dug the cheese knife into the Camembert and cut himself a large portion.

'What is that supposed to mean?'

He placed a portion with painstaking care upon a cracker and, noting how entirely focused he was upon eating it, refusing, absolutely, to respond, Laura gave up and ordered coffee. They took it in the lounge, in a strained, uncomfortable silence and it wasn't until after the bill had been paid when he was shrugging into his overcoat, that he again referred to her plan to reopen the house to guests.

'I hope you'll put an end to this nonsense forthwith, opening guesthouses and the like. Utter tosh! In any case, how could you afford to?'

'I shall use the money Mother left me. It might just stretch to a few renovations.'

Robert snorted his disapproval and changed tack. 'Neither will I have you prying into Daisy's life. Sell the dratted farm and have done with it.'

'I don't think I can do that.'

He glared at her, the expression in his grey eyes hard as flint. 'Are you deliberately defying me, Laura?'

She shook her head, desperately trying to curb her impatience. 'I'm simply trying to understand the woman who left me a house she loved, presumably because she thought I would love it too. And I'm not sure I deserve such generosity, since I feel I neglected her shamefully. My own grandmother!'

'For which you blame me, I suppose.'

Laura sighed. 'I'm sorry you found it necessary to cut me off from her as a child but I wouldn't dream of blaming you. How can I, since I don't have a proper explanation of what went wrong between you? If anything, I blame myself.' She kept her eyes downcast as she began to button up her own coat, deliberately avoiding the chill of his gaze. 'I should have stood up to you more as I got older, and to Felix. I intend to do so now.'

'Damnation, Laura, is there some man involved?' he roared, making heads turn in the lobby and bringing a flush of embarrassed crimson to her cheeks. Snatching her arm he drew her into a corner where he could snarl at her in comparative privacy. 'Is that what this is all about? Some sort of silly revenge against Felix's indiscretions? Because if so, it won't do, Laura. It won't do at all. Dammit, I won't have you shame me, or Felix.'

Laura stared at him in disbelief. 'For God's sake, what are you implying?' She might have laughed, had not the notion that it was perfectly acceptable for Felix to have affairs but not herself, filled her with cold rage. Was she of such little consequence that she had no rights at all? Or was he suggesting that no man would be interested in her? It might also be worth starting an affair, she thought, just to prove she was equal to the challenge.

'You want to know exactly what grievance I had against my mother? She was a *whore*! Nothing less. There, now you know, and if you cheat on Felix then you will deserve exactly the same contempt that I gave her.'

Laura was stunned. 'What a terrible thing to say. What on earth are you suggesting? In what way was my grandmother a whore? Surely you're not saying that Daisy had an affair? Oh – because she had a baby before she married, is that it?' Her frown cleared. 'Oh, for goodness' sake, Dad, don't be so old-fashioned. No one bothers about such things these days.'

His face turned a dark red and for a moment Laura feared for his health. The last thing she wanted was to induce a stroke. She hastily began a halting apology, hand raised in supplication but his roar blotted out every pacifying word.

'I am *telling you*, nay – *ordering you* to stop all this prying into Daisy's life. It's over and done with. Past history. *Leave it alone!* There's absolutely nothing to be gained by digging up old hurts and miseries. So be a good girl, go home to your husband and stop being so damned interfering.'

As she drove back to the farm, Laura railed over why she'd never thought to ask questions when Daisy was alive, or paid more attention to what little her grandmother had told her. Why had she allowed herself to remain happily ignorant of the facts until now, when suddenly it seemed vitally important that she discover them. Laura no more believed that Daisy had cheated on her husband than she herself would cheat on Felix, despite being given plenty of provocation. Daisy simply wasn't the type.

And why should she give up her quest to find out more about her?

She found herself drawn like a magnet to Daisy's bureau but the little desk produced nothing more exciting than a drawer stuffed with bills, most of them fortunately paid, as well as old accounts from when the farm was fully functional during the war. She was bitterly disappointed. She'd been banking on some sort of diary, however small, to reveal more about the woman who had occupied this house before her.

Even so, she spent the next two days going through the bureau with meticulous care, obstinately refusing to give up. There were several smaller drawers tucked beneath the roll top, and a number of pigeon holes, all filled with a detritus of paperwork: auction details, programmes for the County Show, orders for hen pellets. Laura felt a burst of excitement as her hands closed over a bundle of letters. Tucked right at the back they were tied up neatly with pink string, the kind farmers call binder twine. She smiled at this practical touch, so typical of Daisy but which also seemed to indicate that the letters had been read recently, since such material surely hadn't been available during the war. Perhaps Gran had put her affairs into some sort of order before her death.

Laura pulled out the first one. It was short, but clearly a love letter, and was addressed to a mother and baby home. It was the one from Percy and had clearly been read many times for it was coming apart at the folds and the paper had gone brown with age. Laura slipped it carefully back inside its envelope.

Tucked behind, interleaved between this envelope and the next were two or three sheets of blue lined paper pinned together at one corner with a rusty pin, each filled with closely written handwriting which Laura recognised as Daisy's own.

The first was headed with the somewhat outmoded phrase: '*To whom it may concern – The way things were!!!*' Laura was enchanted, particularly by the exclamation marks but, as her eyes swiftly scanned the contents, saw that it was not the diary she'd hoped for, more a chronology of events with short explanations and comments of their effect: the date the first bomb was dropped in Manchester; of folk watching dog fights in the skies during the days of Blitzkrieg; the collapse of France. The list went on to include details such as when rationing had been introduced, together with a droll comment that she'd like to see the government survive on such a meagre meat ration. There were instructions on how to turn a pair of flannel trousers into hot water bottle covers and some fairly pithy remarks outlining her despair over how they would manage to get any eggs at all, now the hens could only be given household scraps. 'What scraps!' she had written, and Laura could almost sense her indignation. More pragmatically, it was followed by a recipe for using dried eggs.

Laura smiled to herself and put the pages to one side with the rest of the letters, to read more fully later.

She glanced quickly through a book which listed purchases and sales of livestock, no doubt in order to keep a record of their movement and progress. The latest recorded date appeared to be 1958. Were records no longer needed by then? Or was that when it ceased to be a farm and the land was then let off? If the latter, what had occurred to cause this change?

There was also a visitors' book from when the house had operated as a guesthouse, starting with the first lodgers during the war and the later pages going on well into the fifties and sixties. Laura sat on the floor to glance through it, her back propped comfortably against the bureau.

'Miss Geraldine Copthorne,' Laura read out loud. 'I wonder who she was? Sounds rather grand. And what was her reason for being here during the war?' She'd written a few lines by her name in a carefully curving script. '*Home from Home. I shall never forget you Dear Daisy and how you made me part of your family.*' Laura read some of the others: Ned Pickles - '*Not much cop in the Home Guard, untidy guest, but a lifelong friend for you Daisy.*' Tommy Fawcett - '*Best day of my life when I landed up here. Shall never hear* Lady Be Good *without thinking of you all.*' There were any number of others. So many names. Pages and pages of them: couples, families, maiden ladies with their companions, lone walkers coming to explore the mountains, all saying what a wonderful time they'd had, how they'd loved the Lakes, the walks, the view of Helvellyn, Daisy's cooking. Would it be possible to trace any of them, after all this time? Probably not. Laura smiled to think she might have acquired her own culinary skills from her grandmother. Most of all she felt a fresh kindling of excitement. Perhaps that's why Daisy had left her the house, so that she could carry on where she had left off. The rooms were still here, after all. Intriguingly, inside the front cover of the book was a short dedication written by Daisy herself:

To Florrie, who allowed me to take over her kitchen and carry out my crazy ideas, often against her better judgement. To Clem, for being the father I'd always wanted, counsellor and best friend. And most of all to my dear husband, for always letting me have my own way, even when it would have been wiser not to.

'I should think he had no option,' Laura said out loud, chuckling softly. 'You were ever one with a mind of your own, Grandmother dear.'

'I'd say that was a true assessment of Daisy's character, bless her heart.'

Laura dropped the book with a clatter, so startled was she by the interruption. She'd thought herself quite alone in the house, as well as in the void of empty countryside around, and it came as a huge shock to look up into a grinning face, one eyebrow raised in quizzical amusement as a perfect stranger picked up the book and handed it back to her. She felt thoroughly unnerved by the encounter, and quite unprepared to be challenged by an unknown male in what was now her own home, let alone one so flagrantly pleased with himself.

'I didn't hear the front doorbell?'

He threw back his head and roared with laughter. 'I announced myself with a shout from the back door. That's the usual method here in the country. You must have been too absorbed to hear me.'

For several long moments each considered the other. He

with curiosity, she with open animosity. Laura noticed at once that he was exceptionally good-looking, which rather seemed to undermine her confidence all the more and she found herself rubbing her dusty hands over her jeans, now rather grubby themselves after days of scrabbling about in attics and old cupboards. She even found herself tidying away a few straying wisps of hair. He was about her own age, in his mid-thirties, and with an unruly thatch of black curls that flopped over a wide brow. Beneath this were winged eyebrows that were still quirking most irritatingly upwards as if amused by some private joke, and long curling lashes over wickedly teasing, light blue eyes. The whole set in a face that bore the kind of chiselled features usually seen on male models, if sufficiently weather-beaten to indicate a life spent largely outdoors that in no way detracted from his charms.

Laura felt herself becoming slightly flustered by the impact of this blue-eyed scrutiny and levered herself quickly to her feet, setting the visitors' book carefully among the bundle of letters on the bureau as she did so.

'Interesting is it, reading other people's love letters?' Before she had gathered her thoughts sufficiently to answer that one, he went on: 'Perhaps you like your own way too, to be prying so swiftly into her affairs. You won't find any hidden share certificates or premium bonds, I'm afraid. I don't think Daisy believed in saving for a rainy day. Always claimed she'd had plenty of practice dealing with those in the past. I think she gave away more money than she ever spent on herself.' When still she didn't reply, he frowned and asked more politely, 'I take it you are the granddaughter?'

Laura stared blankly at the hand thrust out before her, making no move to take it as she struggled to damp down the hot curl of anger spiralling up inside her. Eventually he slid it back into his pocket with a shrug. He was wearing jeans and a blue checked cotton shirt open at the neck over a white

T-shirt, despite the cold wind that had sprung up again outside and was now blasting its way through every crack and cranny. It crossed her mind, inconsequentially, that if the house didn't have some sort of heating system, it would cost a fortune to put in. But was that a good enough reason to return to the home fires of Cheadle Hulme?

'Hello? Anyone at home?' He interrupted her thoughts with a quizzical smile. 'Would you like me to go out and come in again? I seem to have lost your undivided attention.'

'I don't think you ever had it. Who the hell are you, anyway?' Laura switched to attack because she knew, instinctively, that her cheeks had gone quite pink, though really she'd no reason to be embarrassed as she'd every right to be going through Daisy's papers. 'I'm trying to deal with my grandmother's affairs. And I still haven't caught your name, which is?' Asked in her frostiest tones.

'Sorry. Remiss of me.' Again he thrust out the hand. 'David Hornsby, your nearest neighbour, and lessee of the land.' The smile might have been considered encouraging, or simply vague, for his gaze had moved back to the bundle of letters which Laura had left propped on the drop-down lid of the bureau. 'Never seems quite right to me, to pry into a person's life just because they are dead.'

Laura took a moment before answering, quietly drawing in a calming breath. 'My grandmother was seventy-nine, old enough to have decided long ago which material she wished to keep and which should be consigned to the fire. I feel safe in assuming that any letters or other papers she has left, she is quite happy for me to read.'

'OK, good point. Hadn't thought of it that way.' A slight pause and then he added. 'Anything interesting?'

It was on the tip of her tongue to say she wouldn't tell him if there were when he picked up the guest book she'd just been reading and flipped it open. 'Ah yes, I remember her showing e this once, telling me about some of these people.'

'She talked to you about them?' Despite her initial antipathy to the guy, Laura couldn't disguise her surprise. She was instantly intrigued, wanting to know more.

He glanced up, recognising the interest in her voice. 'Sure, why not? We were near neighbours for almost ten years, and she was on her own, so enjoyed a bit of a gossip. I was very fond of Daisy.'

'I didn't see you at her funeral.'

He gave a sad little chuckle. 'She gave me firm instructions not to come. Said she hated the things, had been to more in her lifetime than anyone ever should and too many folk either wept and mourned with little sincerity, or started sharing out the household silver before the incumbent was reclining in her grave.'

They both laughed and Laura admitted there was some truth in the comment.

'Genuine grief, Daisy said, should be carried out in private, and I was to drink a toast to her instead, and get on with my life. Her philosophy was to live for today, and let tomorrow take care of itself.'

'There are some who might consider that to be a dangerous policy.'

'Not Daisy.'

'I wish I'd known her better,' Laura burst out, suddenly envious of this man's inside knowledge of her grandmother.

'If you want to hear more, I'd be happy to tell you. Why don't you come for supper tonight and I'll tell you everything I know, as much as I can remember anyway.'

Despite her curiosity, Laura instinctively backed off from the speculative light she recognised in his eyes. She really didn't need any further complications in her life right now. Not until she'd finally made up her mind what to do about Felix. She shook her head. 'Thanks, maybe another time.'

He looked disappointed. 'Oh, I thought you were genuinely interested in Daisy, and not just in whatever it is she left you

Again Laura's cheeks started to burn, and the tone of her reply was stringent. 'I am.'

'Well then, come to supper. You have to eat after all, and it is a Friday, which is as good a reason as any.' He glanced at the book and stabbed a blunt fingertip on a name. 'I could tell you how she met Harry Driscoll for instance, the love of her life.'

'Harry? But that wasn't my grandfather's name. At least – I don't think it was.'

'Was it, or wasn't it?'

For the life of her, she couldn't remember. Had she ever been told his Christian name, or simply not paid attention? He'd died before she was even born. She knew a great deal about her maternal grandparents, who were sweet and supportive and had recently retired to Torquay. But of her father's family she knew less than nothing, which wasn't at all surprising. What she did know was that her father's surname, her own maiden name wasn't Driscoll. 'Where did she meet this Harry Driscoll, and if he was the love of her life, why didn't she marry him? Was he killed in the war?'

'Oh dear, you really don't know anything at all, do you?' Laughing, he shrugged his wide shoulders and swung away from her, back towards the door. 'But, if you're not hungry, either for food or information right now, I'll leave you in peace. Give me a call if you change your mind.' And to her utter fury and frustration, he strolled calmly away.

After he'd gone Laura headed for the shower, hoping to take the steam out of her temper. Almost at once she began to regret that she hadn't accepted his invitation. I mean, what else did she have to do but wash her hair and eat a limp salad? Maybe that's what she needed in her life, a little more impulsiveness. A touch of recklessness. And he was rather gorgeous. She'd really lost touch with how to handle such delicate matters, though perhaps it was just as well. She was still a married woman after all. Laura groaned and stepped under the jet of hot water, letting it do its work.

Later, wrapped in a huge towelling robe, she forsook the salad and sat on the sofa eating crackers and cheese, kicking herself for the missed opportunity. He was probably her best contact to find out more about Daisy, and she'd blown it. Accepting the simple offer of supper, off the cuff as it were, would have meant she could have gone in her jeans, cobwebs and all, with easy informality, just to be neighbourly. Now, although she was burning to hear what he had to tell her, nothing would induce Laura to ring and ask if she could come over. It would seem too contrived, too artificial, almost like asking him for a date. He'd think her a control freak who must do everything her own way, in her own time.

She switched on the TV, then turned it off again. The sound of it was too startling in the empty room, seeming to emphasise a loneliness she hadn't previously noticed, but then the ensuing silence folded disconcertingly in upon her, which was worse. They'd had quite a set-to, she supposed. She certainly hadn't been very polite to him, or welcoming. Laura couldn't help but compare the sparks that had flown between them, two perfect strangers, to the conversations she'd had recently with her husband. Felix always shied away from confrontations, rode over tender feelings and sensitivities that he had no wish to acknowledge, just as if they weren't there. Laura had learned early on the fruitlessness of revealing her softer side, for he only trampled on it.

Nothing mattered to Felix except cutting the deal; making the big bucks. He'd even found time on the day of the funeral to read through some papers he'd brought with him, sneaking off into some quiet corner while Laura handed round the sherry and accepted everyone's commiserations. She'd made no comment but, deep down, had been hurt by such insensitivity.

Surely he hadn't always been that way. He'd once been so

full of enthusiasm, so animated about his plans. 'This is just the start, Laura,' he'd say. 'The first of a chain of smart little galleries all over the country. Once we're established we can franchise the idea and make a small fortune.' Laura had listened, spellbound by his passion, at first perfectly in tune with his ambition to make something of his life. Being the son of an unemployed miner had left him with the need to prove that he was as good as everyone else. She'd admired that in him, at least until that need had grown into a huge chip on his shoulder.

Nowadays their relationship was too tired, too predictable to bring any excitement into their lives. And Felix was very much his own master. No one could make him do anything he had no wish to do. She was fortunate, Laura supposed, that he'd agreed to come to her grandmother's funeral at all, which probably had more to do with wanting to assess the value of her inheritance than to pay any last respects.

Why was she so harassed by infuriating men? No wonder Robert approved of Felix, they were alike in so many ways, both obstinately determined to have their own way and be in control.

Her father's parting words following that dreadful lunch came back to her with haunting clarity. 'Be a good girl and go home to your husband.' It told her so much about herself.

Perhaps the fault was entirely hers in a way, because she'd allowed him to control her. Is that why she'd never asked questions, never liked to pry into her father's life or emotions? Because she'd wanted him to love her, for him to see her as a good girl? He'd certainly done his level best to govern every last detail of her life, even to keeping her from her own grandmother. The result had been that it had left her a prime candidate for marriage to an equally controlling husband. Laura had never properly appreciated that fact until now. If this were true, then it was long past time she decided what she meant to do about it, because it was what *she* wanted from life that was important now. She'd been a good girl long enough.

Having stirred up her sense of injustice to a suitably high pitch, she picked up the phone and called her new neighbour to accept his invitation to supper. Though of course, only because she wanted to hear more about Harry.

Daisy

6

Daisy and the children slept the clock round, waking late the next morning. It being a Saturday, still with no sign of their host, and facing the prospect of an empty larder for the entire weekend ahead, Daisy made the decision to go into Penrith. She and the children joined the queue at the bus stop with every intention of finding the town hall and making a complaint, or at least a polite enquiry. This was not at all what they had expected by being evacuated. It didn't seem right that someone, beyond Daisy, wasn't available to look after these children. Fond as she was of them, the responsibility worried her. There was a war starting, after all. What if something happened to her parents, and she had to dash home for some reason? Who would look after the two children then?

Her more immediate concern, of course, was what on earth had become of Miss Pratt. The old lady had indeed seemed odd, and quite unused to children. Even so, it was most peculiar just to go off with the dogs and leave them, not even think to call in from time to time to see how they were.

So engrossed was she in her own troubles, and adjusting the children's berets and scarves when it started to rain, that it was only when the bus drew up some minutes later, that Daisy paid proper attention to the queue ahead of them and realised it comprised entirely airmen and soldiers. When it was their turn to get on, the conductress put out her hand to prevent them climbing aboard. 'Sorry, this is a special services bus, no civvies allowed.'

'Oh, isn't it going into town?'

'Aye, but like I say, it's for services personnel only. You can allus walk, young, fit girl like yourself.'

'But how far is it? I don't know the way.'

'Stranger to these parts, eh? Thought so.'

'How long before the next bus?' Daisy asked.

'There'll no doubt be one along in the next hour or so.'

'*An hour or so?*'

'Aye, well, there aren't so many buses these days. Short of drivers, d'you see. There is a war on, tha knows.'

'But it's so cold and wet, and the children haven't been well.'

'Nowt to do wi' me. Not my place to mollycoddle children,' and she reached up to ring the bell but her hand didn't quite make it. Her wrist was caught and held, a grip so uncompromising it prevented the conductress from moving an inch.

He was tall, almost six foot, in RAF uniform like all the rest, square-jawed and with a wide, smiling mouth, his forage cap tilted at just the right angle over neatly clipped brown hair. His face was more what you'd call homely than handsome but to Daisy it was the most cheerful, the most friendly face she'd encountered in a long while.

Harry Driscoll had been watching this little exchange with interest, and had decided to put in his four pennorth. He hated bullies, particularly female ones. Besides, the young girl was quite pretty. 'She's with me.'

'I beg your pardon?' The conductress was furiously attempting to pull her arm free, blotches of scarlet gathering high on her cheekbones. 'If you don't take your flippin' hand off me this minute, I'll call the driver and have you all thrown off.'

He released her with a small bow. 'Nevertheless, she's with me. This coffee and bun fight we were all treated to at the village hall, she helped organise it, so you can let her on. Can' you see them nippers are soaking wet through already. Have a heart, love.'

'I don't get paid to tek civvies on this bus.'

'We'll have a whip round. Either you let them on, or we all get off. Then we'll be late back and our CO will want to know why. Ain't that right lads?' A rousing cheer echoed from behind him, most of the men not having the first idea what the dispute was about but ready enough to support a mate. Seeing herself defeated, the conductress's stance crumbled and, moments later, Daisy and the children were being found a seat in the depth of the warm bus and being chatted up by at least a dozen servicemen.

'Thank you,' Daisy said, having eyes only for her rescuer who stood grinning down at her. 'That's the first good deed anyone has done for us in an age, though that was a fib you told. I didn't have anything to do with the bun fight at the village hall.'

He shrugged. 'So what? Good deeds are all in a day's work for us hero types.' He held out a hand. 'Harry's the name. Harry Driscoll.'

'Daisy Atkins.' She put her hand into his and felt the warm strength of a firm grip. He made no effort to release it as he looked straight into her eyes, his gaze steady and direct and both of them fell silent, each shyly considering the other. His eyes were a greeny-grey, quite the nicest eyes Daisy had ever seen. The next instant Harry became aware of being studied by two other pairs of eyes, both blue, and laughingly released her hand. Daisy felt bereft, wanting to hold on to him.

'They're surely not yours?' He jerked a chin at Trish on her knee, and the older girl leaning against it. Was that a shade of anxiety in his voice as he asked the question? Daisy smiled and shook her head. 'Do I look old enough to have kids like these?'

But she did have a child. She did! She did! A shameful secret ▸ must never tell. Daisy pushed the thought away.

'You don't look old enough to be out on your own, let alone be getting a free ride with a bus full of service personnel.'

'We're evacuees, from Manchester,' she offered, by way of explanation. 'Are you a pilot?'

This innocent remark was met by a roar of laughter. 'They wouldn't let him loose in a plane. He gets lost with no road signs to help him, let alone no roads.'

'Anyway, his hair's too long. It'd get in his eyes when he was flying.'

'And his mam don't like him being out at night.'

Daisy laughed along with them, enjoying the banter. They seemed a cheerful bunch, and at least it was warm on the bus. They were certainly eager to chat, telling her how they were undergoing training at the RAF base in Longtown. Also on the bus were men from the tank corps stationed at Lowther, though what exactly they were up to, they were not at liberty to say, they explained. All very hush-hush! Several offered to take her out, give her a conducted tour of the area or fill her in with more details of their life history, strictly in private of course. Nor did they forget the children, who were presented with a variety of sweets, and even a cough drop for Megan. It was all so good-hearted and fun, Daisy was soon wiping tears of laughter from her eyes, which made a change from the other sort.

She would like to have stayed on the bus for hours but in no time, it seemed, the conductress was calling out her stop and she was getting to her feet and ushering the children off. As a way was made for them along the aisle, Harry grabbed her hand again.

'Where are you billeted?'

She told him, but quickly added. 'It's not very good. I'm hoping they might relocate us.'

'Move along the bus please, we don't have all day,' the conductress shouted, determined to maintain some contro over this obstreperous crew.

'Aw, stop moaning, woman. Give 'em a minute, fer God's sake.'

Galvanised into action by the conductress's ill temper, Harry began to desperately search his pockets. 'I need a pen. Somebody find me a pen.' There was a flurry of activity, more laughter and joking as the entire busload searched pockets until a pen was finally found and Harry began to write his address on the back of her hand. Once more he looked deep into her eyes. 'You can't lose that. Write to me.'

Daisy glanced down at the scribbled words, a mere blur through the stars in her eyes.

'Are you getting off or not? I've a few more runs to make today, if you please,' the conductress snapped.

As Daisy struggled through the crush of servicemen, she strived to keep her gaze upon him, couldn't bear to tear it away. There were plenty more offers of addresses but the children were being helped down from the platform, the conductress was dinging her bell with grim determination this time, and if Daisy didn't hurry the bus would leave and she'd still be on it. As it was, she jumped off just in time before it jerked forward.

'Don't forget! See that you write. A letter to that address will find me, wherever I am,' he yelled.

As she gathered the children about her, Daisy plucked up the courage to call back: 'I will write. I won't forget. I promise.'

She wasn't even sure if he'd heard. As she walked away, heart pounding, keeping a lookout for anything likely to be the town hall, Daisy wondered what right she had to make such a promise? None at all, not with her shameful secret.

The visit to the town hall turned into a quagmire of questions and bureaucracy, of being passed from pillar to post, nobody being quite prepared to accept responsibility until, at last, they were taken to an entirely different office, in a separate part of the building where they finally met the billeting officer, a large woman with a sour face. She looked down her nose at the trio as if they really had no right to be there and even after listening to Daisy's story, denied that any such thing could happen on her patch.

'Our billeting hosts are most carefully chosen, *most* carefully, and Amelia Pratt is a dear friend of mine.'

'Then perhaps you can find her. We're at our wits' end. In the meantime, these children need breakfast, but just make sure it isn't eggs.'

Some long hours later, investigation proved that the poor woman had not, in fact, abandoned them. She'd died quietly in her sleep, her dogs gathered protectively all around her.

Daisy was shocked. 'Oh, poor Miss Pratt. No wonder they were howling. How dreadful!'

Megan tugged at her hand. 'Does that mean there weren't any ghosts after all?'

'Yes love, that's what it means.'

'But if the lady has died, isn't she now a ghost?'

Daisy stifled a smile at the innocent question, since this wasn't the moment for explanations. 'It doesn't quite work that way.'

'Why doesn't it?' Megan was annoyed that Daisy should think her stupid. Everyone knew ghosts were dead people, and Miss Pratt was now dead, wasn't she?

'Hush now, I'll explain it to you later. Meanwhile, I think we need a new billet, and some medical attention for these two children.'

To Megan's complete horror, quick as a flash, the billeting officer took a bottle from her desk drawer, whipped off the girls' berets and poured an evil smelling liquid over both their heads. Trish started to sob and Megan was hard put to it not to give the woman a smack in the eye.

Megan had no wish to be 'vacee'. She'd had enough. It wasn't at all the adventure she'd been promised. It was boring and alarming and frightening. She wanted to go home to her mam. Whenever Mr Hitler dropped his bombs, she'd run away as fast as her legs could carry her and miss them all. If her mam and gran could stop at home when they didn't run half so fast as her, then where was the problem?

'Can't I go home? I want to go home?' she wailed, but Daisy only made a shushing sound, and the woman ignored her completely. Megan didn't like being ignored, so tried again, 'How will Mam know where we've gone?'

'Don't worry, you'll get a postcard this time so you can write and tell her.'

They were handed over to a middle-aged couple who already had two children of their own. The boy was a year older than Megan and the moment they were left alone 'to make friends' he pinched her hard and called her awful names like 'Smelly' and 'Pee-wee'. Megan thumped him hard and he started to yell. His sister was younger and she kicked Trish in the shin, which made her tune up in unison.

Megan could tell this was going to be a disaster and she was absolutely right. Even though the couple had agreed to take Daisy as well, and Mrs Hobson claimed to be the motherly type, she was furious when Megan accidentally smeared blackberries all over her white sheets. Megan didn't see what all the fuss was about. Serve her right for putting sheets on the bed in the first place. They always used blankets at home, although she knew that her mam did keep one sheet in a cupboard, in case someone should die and need covering up before they were buried in the ground. It had been used for an old aunt once, and Megan had kept careful watch, just in case the old lady wasn't really dead at all, and might rise up beneath it.

Anyroad, she'd been hungry, and had gone out into the garden at first light to pick a handful of the blackberries she'd spotted earlier, which she'd eaten under cover of the sheets so that no one would know. It wasn't her fault if she'd happened to drop a few without noticing and then fallen asleep on top of them, squashing them flat.

Megan thought it equally unfair that she was blamed for breaking the best sugar basin at breakfast, when it was the nasty son who'd handed it to her and then let go before Megan had quite taken hold. It'd just rolled off the table and smashed to the floor, scattering precious sugar everywhere. An hour later they were back before the billeting officer.

Their next billet was with a vicar and his wife, who were very kind but a bit vague. The first thing they did was to offer them a bath. Megan was horrified and point blank refused to get into it. It stood like an enormous white pot basin on six legs and a witless fool could see by all the water inside it, that she'd drown. Then when the stupid woman lifted Trish into it, despite her screams and Megan's pleading, she very nearly did drown. Megan was appalled to see her little sister go right under the water as she went completely stiff in some sort of hysterical fit.

Worse, Megan and Trish's room contained a night commode and after waking one night to find the vicar enthroned upon it, she decided that enough was enough.

The next day the vicar's wife sent her on an errand to the corner shop. Megan insisted on taking Trish with her, explaining how they must never be separated. But instead of buying bread they got on a bus and used some of the money to buy two tickets to Preston. Here they changed buses to one bound for Manchester. It was pretty full, but the other passengers made room for them and one lady even gave them a few sweets. Hours later, while everyone was no doubt still frantically searching every corner of the village for them, Megan and Trish walked into their house in Irlam, telling their startled mother that they were back.

It upset Megan that instead of giving them big hugs and kisses, Mam was cross. She shouted at her, calling her terrible names like selfish and naughty and irresponsible.

'You've risked your life, and that of your little sister, in the most dangerous way. What were you thinking of to do such a daft thing?'

Tears sprang to her eyes. 'But there's been no bombs dropped yet. Daisy says so.'

'Who's Daisy?'

'Her what looks after us.'

'Well you should have stayed with Daisy.' Then Mam softened slightly, seeing the tears, Trish's stricken face and the wobble to her lower lip. 'I can't keep you here, love, much as I'd like to. I love the bones of you both but it's dangerous here. There's a war on and I have to work. I've got a job in the munitions factory.'

'Who'll look after Gran if you go to work?'

To her dismay, Megan was informed that her grandmother too had died, of the pneumonia, and life suddenly seemed desperately fragile, what with everyone dropping down dead all the time. Mam wouldn't even let them share her bed, as she'd used to do. There was a sailor in it now, called Jack, and he wasn't moving out for no one, he said, certainly not two little whippersnappers who should learn to do as they were told.

Worse than all of this, the very next day Mam begged a day off work and took them straight back to the Lakes.

A new place was found for the two little girls, this time with a Mr and Mrs Marshall, who were a policeman and his wife. They had no children but Daisy took to them on sight. Megan and Trish, however, were understandably nervous.

'Will she make us take a bath and have a commode in our room?' Megan asked, feeling it best to know how things stood from the start.

'Not if you don't want to, though I think baths can be quite good fun if you don't have too much water in them,' Daisy explained, deciding to make no mention of their more usual benefits.

'Will the lady lock us up and leave us on us own?' Trish wanted to know.

'No love, she won't ever lock you up.'

'But what if she dies too?'

'She won't die. She's quite young and healthy.'

'Has she any boggarts?'

'Or ghosts?'

Daisy gathered them close. 'Listen. This is a nice lady. She has no ghosts, no boggarts, not even any peevish little boys to pinch you. What she does have is a warm bed for you both, plenty of food in the larder and she's promised faithfully not to leave you alone for a minute. The only thing . . .' Daisy hesitated, feeling emotion block her throat as she came to the difficult part. 'She can't take me as well.' As the protests started, tears spurted and Trish's mouth did its upside-down act again, Daisy did her best to mollify them, kissing their cheeks and trying to mop them dry all at the same time. 'No, no, don't worry. It's all right. I shall be close by in a neighbour's house, at least until I'm sure you two are all right.'

'Will we see you every day then?'

'Every single day.'

'Promise?'

'Cross my heart and hope to die. Oh no, sorry, I didn't mean that.' But even Megan managed a crooked smile at her mistake. 'Oh, and Mrs Marshall says she has a dog, a little cocker spaniel which you can take for walks, if you like.'

They glanced at each other, still uncertain but their little faces had brightened. The idea of walking the dog was winning them over.

Megan took a deep breath. 'All right then. We've decided we'll go, haven't we, Trish?' And Trish nodded her agreement.

The elderly couple with whom Daisy was staying just next door, were kind enough, if set in their ways and unused to having a young person about the place. She could tell this by the way Mr Chapman stared at her sometimes, as if he was trying to dig under her skin and find out what she was thinking. But then he was so old, in Daisy's estimation at least, being well into his fifties, that he'd probably forgotten what it was like to be young.

He was a solicitor and very generously found a job for Daisy in his office, opening letters and addressing envelopes, the post boy having volunteered for the navy. Within a week Daisy envied him his escape, dangerous though the seas were at this time, for this was the most boring job imaginable, working all alone in a dusty corner of the mail room. Mr Chapman did his best to make things easy for her though, by popping in to see her at frequent intervals to explain anything she didn't quite understand, such as the way he liked the stamp book kept, or the deeds tied up. He would pat her kindly on the shoulder, see that she took regular tea breaks, and once brought her a cushion when she complained of the hardness of the chair she had to sit on all day, tucking in her skirts for her as she settled it in place. He really was most kind and attentive. Her own parents had never shown such care and she thanked him for his thoughtfulness.

'We simply want you to be happy with us, Daisy. If you ever feel lonely, you must say so. You're so very young to be sent away from home, and such a pretty girl, not at all the usual sort of evacuee that we get here who hail from the dregs of society. You are special, my dear, I can tell, and we feel privileged to have you. Consequently we must make an extra special effort to see that you are well taken care of.'

Daisy rather enjoyed the notion of being considered special and pretty, but then he was only trying to make her feel at home, which was nice of him. She'd heard enough horror stories from some of the other evacuees to feel grateful for her good fortune and if her life seemed rather dull with a sameness about it, at least she was warm and well fed. She thanked him warmly, thinking what a charming old fusspot he was.

Mrs Chapman stayed home to keep house and make the meals, and although there was always plenty to eat, they too were sadly predictable. You could guess what day of the week it was from the food put before you on the table. Bacon and mashed potatoes on Mondays, which was wash day with no time for cooking. Welsh Rarebit on Tuesdays. Cottage pie on Wednesdays. On Thursdays it was invariably liver and onions though sometimes they might have heart, which Daisy loathed. And on Fridays – a nice bit of fish. Daisy looked forward all week to the home-made pie that Mrs Chapman baked on a Saturday, and the roast on Sundays which they ate in silent splendour in the front parlour to celebrate the sober importance of the day.

Daisy had a room to herself in the attic. It contained one narrow bed and a chest of drawers, a bentwood chair and a cupboard built under the eaves into which she hung her few clothes. The only view from the tiny window was of a chimney pot but at least nobody told her what time she must go to bed, though early rising was essential.

The couple's motives for taking Daisy in soon became all too apparent. Mrs Chapman suffered ill health, in truth she revelled in it. Each morning, before leaving for the office, it had apparently been Mr Chapman's task to take breakfast in to his wife on a tray while she reclined in bed; a duty he quickly delegated to Daisy. Likewise in the evening, she was expected to wash up the dinner things, and give the kitchen a wipe over before doing any bits of ironing Mrs Chapman had not felt well enough to tackle during the day.

'You don't mind helping with the odd chore, my dear, do you?' Mrs Chapman would enquire in her timorous voice. She was a fragile, birdlike creature with grey hair fashioned into tight little waves all about her head. She always wore a plain grey skirt with a twin set, also in grey or a serviceable blue, and a single strand of pearls.

Daisy assured her that she did not mind in the least. 'I'm only too happy to help, since you're offering me a safe billet.'

'We thought that would be the case. Counting one's blessings is so important, I always think. And of course you must be so grateful to be out of Salford and off the streets,' making it sound as if living in the slums automatically branded her a prostitute.

Daisy could do nothing but nod in mute agreement before running to her room to laugh herself sick.

Daisy soon discovered that there were more chores to be counted than blessings, an increasing number each week in fact. She would be asked to prepare the vegetables each evening ready for the following day, to clean Mr Chapman's shoes, the fire grate each morning and the household silver once a fortnight. Cushions had to be kept nicely plumped, newspapers folded away into the rack and beds promptly made. And if she fell short of Mrs Chapman's high standards, that good lady would gently point out her deficiencies.

'I realise you don't know any better dear, but I do prefer the napkins to be folded into triangles. A square is so common, don't you think?'

And although Daisy had no objection to doing her share of household tasks, she had not come to them as a housemaid but as an evacuee, and she was fully aware that the Chapmans were being paid to accommodate her, partly by the government, and partly by a contribution from her own parents. The Chapmans were legally obliged to open their home to someone, and it really wasn't Daisy's fault that there was a war on, so constant proof of her gratitude shouldn't be expected of her.

But Daisy said nothing, uncomplainingly bearing the burden of more and more chores each evening, despite having spent a long day addressing envelopes for the various secretaries and clerks Mr Chapman employed, while Mrs Chapman sat in her comfy chair and read *Woman*. She told herself that she didn't mind the extra work, as it gave her something to do and kept her mind fully occupied.

It was the quiet moments alone in her room that were the worst. Those were the times when she thought of what might have been, of how things could have been so different if Percy had not let her down, if she hadn't had her lovely baby taken from her. But where was the good in self-pity? It only ever ended in Daisy sobbing into her pillow, which left her red-eyed and exhausted the next day and did her no good at all.

Yet it was hard not to feel abandoned. Despite all her valiant efforts to keep cheerful and to cope, Daisy was lonely.

Sometimes she even found herself thinking fondly of Marigold Court with its back entry cluttered with dustbins, groups of gossiping women pegging out threadbare washing and men hanging around street corners smoking dimps, hoping their each-way bet on the dogs would come up. Daisy hated to admit it but, like Megan and Trish, she was home-sick for the familiar streets and markets, for her ineffectual, ever-silent, hen-pecked father who'd never stood up to his domineering wife in his entire life, not even when his own daughter had been shown the door.

To her shame she didn't miss her mother one bit, but, one evening alone in her room, Daisy wrote a letter to her parents, giving her current address and telling of her adventures to date. She cried as she wrote it, for all it made her feel better afterwards when she'd popped it into the postbox. Perhaps, one day, her father at least might send a reply. It would be something to look forward to.

In the weeks following, she watched every morning for the postman but no letter came for her and Daisy strove to accustom herself to her new life, pondering on how easily promises were made – and broken. Percy's promise to love her for always had certainly meant nothing. He'd been a mistake, a bad one, and she would take much more care in future over where she bestowed her love.

The image of a pair of steady grey-green eyes sprang

instantly to mind. Harry Driscoll, the young airman she'd met on the bus.

She'd once considered writing to him. Daisy had carefully copied out the address he'd written on her hand because, after all, if it hadn't been for him she might never have got into town that day and they'd have been forced to spend another night in that awful house with poor Miss Pratt dead upstairs. Unfortunately, she'd never quite plucked up the courage to actually put pen to paper, which made her feel a bit guilty about breaking her promise.

But where was the point, she asked herself? He would no doubt be sent out on ops soon, or whatever they called them, and she might well be moved again herself. Daisy still dreamed of finding her aunt. If only she knew where to look, and under what name. You'd think her mother would be prepared to help her there, but no, not a word.

Her own parents' obligation of love and care had failed her too, just when she needed them most. Daisy was quite certain, deep in her heart, that she would never have made that dreadful mistake and fallen pregnant, if her mother had properly explained to her the facts of life. It had been her own ignorance, in comparison to Percy's obviously superior experience, which had been her downfall.

Even poor Miss Pratt, who'd promised to 'do her bit' and look after them, had broken her word through no fault of her own. But then that was the problem, wasn't it? How did anyone know what was going to happen next? You could cross your heart, spit on your hand as they'd used to do in the school playground, write a promise in your own blood and nail it to a tree but lightning could strike the tree, or someone in higher authority could simply pick you up and move you, just as if you were an insect to be plucked from one place and dropped somewhere entirely different. It was really most alarming how very little control Daisy had over her own life.

And those two little ones, homesick for their mam, must

feel even worse. She was glad that at least she'd been able to do something to help them.

In the event the two children settled in remarkably well. Mrs Marshall was a kind-hearted woman and although at first she was alarmed and distressed by the state of them, in no time at all she persuaded Megan into the bath with the lure of a rubber sailing boat, and soon had the pair of them shining clean, their hair cut and glowing like a pair of polished chestnuts. Each day as they walked the dog Trish would describe, in painstaking detail, every scrap of food they had eaten and Daisy would ask Megan about school. She still wasn't the most forthcoming child, but she was getting better and sometimes could be quite entertaining.

'The other children say we talk funny, so I said they did too. At least we don't ask someone, "Are you gaily?"' and she did a fair imitation of the Westmorland accent.

'So how would you ask someone how they were?'

She thought about this for a minute and then said, in her broadest Lancashire. 'Hey up? Howarta?' and then collapsed into a fit of giggles. Trish put her hand to her mouth and giggled too, though she wasn't entirely sure why or what she was laughing at.

Daisy joined in with the hilarity, mainly because it was good to see the children happy for once, and tried to think of more silly words. 'What about lish for lively? Or thrang for busy? They say that too round here.'

'Mrs Marshall calls her bread knife a gully. I thought that was the same as what we would call an alley,' Megan said. 'And porridge she calls poddish. That's the silliest word I ever heard.'

'I know a sillier one. How about powfagged?' Daisy said, wiping tears of laughter from her eyes. 'My grandma complained of being that all her life.'

'What does it mean?' Trish asked.

'Weary, which is what I am now after this long walk. Come on, let's see if Mrs Marshall can supply some lemonade.' And she hugged them both, feeling a huge relief and sense of satisfaction that all was going well with them at last.

Megan thought the war was overrated. There were no aeroplanes dropping bombs on them and flattening their houses, no tanks thundering through the village streets. They never had to run for their lives to an air-raid shelter, only creep down into a dark, damp cellar where there were spiders and goodness knows what else. Not even any enemy soldiers invading to take them prisoner or shoot at them, as she'd been led to expect. War was boring.

Everyone was calling it the phoney war and Mr Marshall said that more people were being injured falling over in the black-out than by enemy action. 'The common bicycle is turning into a lethal weapon,' he mourned, as he went out every morning on duty.

Each night they all had to listen to the news on the wireless and a man had talked about an aircraft carrier being torpedoed by a U-boat. It was called *Courageous* which Mrs Marshall said was a most appropriate name.

Megan had asked if this meant that the war would end soon, and Mr Marshall assured her that hostilities would all be over by Christmas.

Megan was glad to hear it. Perhaps then she could go home and stay at home. Many of the evacuees in her class at school had started to go back already because they were missing their family too much. Megan was annoyed that she wasn't allowed to go too, for not only did she think the war boring but so was living in this village with nothing more exciting to look forward to than collecting newspapers for the Armed Forces, though how the soldiers would find time to read them with all that fighting and shooting they had to do, Megan couldn't imagine.

Soon, they were going to have something called a Weapons Week. Megan had got quite excited about this at first, thinking that at last she might get to see some real guns, or even have a go at shooting with one. But then Mrs Marshall had explained that it meant they were to hold a rummage sale and coffee morning, and do other things like pay to guess the weight of a pig in order to raise money for the war effort. Megan had lost interest at once.

For months she'd been moved about from pillar to post, with nobody really wanting either her or Trish, calling them 'little nuisances' or dropping dead on them. And then they'd landed up here, stuck in the dullest place on earth.

On that first morning they'd stood together, she and Trish, in the school hall along with a load of other vacees from Tyneside while they'd been allocated classrooms and given instructions about not trespassing into the next-door farmer's field, and to remember always to bring their gas mask to school. One day Megan forgot and Mrs Crumpton, their teacher, made her walk all the way home again to fetch it. It felt like miles! What a waste of time, as if the Germans might suddenly decide to land on that particular morning. Megan hated her gas mask. It smelled funny and made her feel sick every time she had to put it on during gas mask drill. It was red and looked like Mickey Mouse but Megan wasn't fooled. She knew perfectly well that if she wore it for too long, she'd stop breathing all together.

The week before Christmas something exciting did happen. Megan had been looking out of the window when she suddenly gave a yelp of joy. 'That's Mam. Look, it's our mam. She's in the street outside.'

Trish instantly burst into tears and Mrs Marshall didn't know whether to pick her up and cuddle her, or dash outside to bring the poor woman in, since she seemed reluctant even to approach the door. Megan solved her dilemma by flinging open the front door and careered across the street to be swept straight up into her arms.

When all the hugs and kisses had been exchanged and Trish was safe and warm on her mother's knee, a cup of tea before her on the kitchen table, the tale of her nightmare journey began. 'The train were that full of soldiers, airmen and civvy workers, I had to stand up most of the way, squashed up in a corner of the corridor. We stopped at every set of signals, broke down near Preston when we all had to get off and go on to another train. Then we were rerouted to Wigan for no reason I could see. Eeh, I thought I'd never get here. Still, it were worth it to see my little lambs again.'

All of this was related later to Daisy, together with how Mrs Marshall had brought out her best biscuits as well as a Dundee cake, and then had left them quietly on their own so they could talk. To her shame, Daisy felt a burst of envy at their good fortune. 'Mam stayed nearly two whole hours,' Megan told her, breathless with excitement. 'It were wonderful.'

'And she give us Christmas presents,' Trish added.

'Which we mustn't open until Christmas Day,' Megan warned her sternly. 'I saw you trying to peep, our Trish, so I gave them to Mrs Marshall. She'll make sure you don't, so think on, you behave. Right?'

Trish nodded slowly, looking suitably chastened.

'And how did you feel when she had to go back home?' Daisy enquired gently.

Both little girls exchanged a glum look before, eyes cast down, Megan gave a little shrug of her thin shoulders and admitted quietly. 'I cried, and our Trish was sick. But I'm glad she come, Daisy. I am that. I'm right glad she come to see us. We know she's all fine and dandy now, don't we, and she's given that sailor his marching orders she says, because he was a mucky bugger.'

'Don't say that Megan. It's not a nice word.'

'And me mam's promised she won't die, hasn't she our Trish?'

Trish nodded solemnly.

'Of course she won't die,' Daisy said, shocked by the very idea. 'Whatever made you think such a thing?'

'Well, that other lady died, and me gran did, though she were old, and Kevin Lupton, a boy in my class said that when the Germans start dropping their bombs, we might all die.'

'What a very silly boy he must be.'

Trish was nodding again but her little mouth was turning down all the same and Daisy judged that it was time to change the subject, the conversation having taken a somewhat morbid turn. 'Well then, we'd better give this little rascal his walk. He must have felt a bit neglected today, what with the Christmas preparations, and all these tea parties going on.'

The two little girls ran for the dog lead, eager to cast their worries aside. And, because they were children, that's exactly what they were able to do. Daisy could only envy them their innocence.

Christmas came and the two children had a marvellous time with presents from Mr and Mrs Marshall in addition to the small gifts their mother had brought. Neither of Daisy's parents came near, nor even sent her a present. She received a card, of course, with the simple, unsentimental message, *Hope this finds you well, as are we,* in her father's best handwriting but nothing more. Mrs Chapman gave her a pair of knitting needles and some wool so she could knit balaclavas for the soldiers.

'How very kind,' Daisy said, thinking quite the opposite.

Daisy helped Mrs Chapman cook a small goose for their Christmas dinner, which they ate in reverent silence in the parlour with properly folded napkins, and crackers to mark the importance of the day. Afterwards, Mr Chapman insisted they play a few hands of canasta, which he seemed anxious to teach Daisy, helping her to play the right card and hold them correctly in her hand. After that, Mrs Chapman made a pot of tea and cut them each a thin slice of Christmas cake.

'Who knows when we may get another, what with rationing threatened in the New Year. Dear me, this war is getting most unpleasant.'

'War usually is, my dear,' Mr Chapman murmured, giving Daisy a huge wink, just as if only the two of them could properly understand what was going on.

Daisy escaped as soon as politeness allowed, slipping next door to spend the remainder of the evening with the Marshalls, Megan and Trish. Trish had got thoroughly overexcited and even Megan couldn't stop talking about the wonders of the day, her blue eyes shining with happiness. They'd stuffed themselves with so much good food it was perfectly clear they'd never had a Christmas like it.

It was on Boxing Day that they experienced the biggest thrill of all. It was a bright, sunny afternoon, if rather crisp and cold and Daisy was out with the children walking the dog as usual when the sky suddenly seemed to darken. Glancing up she saw it was filled with parachutes.

'Crikey, we're being invaded!' Daisy stood rooted to the spot with shock. Everyone else seemed to be reacting in just the same way. There had been no air-raid siren, so perhaps even the authorities had been taken by surprise. Daisy felt overwhelmed, terrified by what might be about to happen. The sky seemed to be filled with dozens, if not hundreds of men. Is this how the war will end, she wondered in alarm, with us being murdered by Germans dropping out of the sky?

Moments later men were hitting the ground, rolling over the wide expanse of grass and, finally coming to her senses, Daisy grabbed the children's hands and began to run. She wouldn't give in without a fight, oh dear me no!

'Why are we running?' Megan gasped.

'Will they dead us?' Trish asked in sheer terror, her small legs pumping like pistons as she desperately tried to keep up.

'Not if I can help it.'

And then, miraculously, out of the blue, she heard her name being called. '*Daisy!* Daisy for God's sake stop running and slow down, I can't keep up with you, not with all this gear on.'

Slithering to a halt she turned to find an apparition in leather helmet and flying suit rushing towards them, a silken parachute dragging behind him. Trish gave a frightened scream, yelling something incomprehensible about ghosts and hid behind her skirts, which Daisy didn't really wonder at. This was the nearest to a ghost she'd ever encountered herself. Only Megan seemed to have her wits about her.

'It's that nice man from the bus,' and pulling herself free of Daisy's hand, ran towards him. 'Harry, Harry! Are you in a tangle?'

He laughed. 'You could say that, sweetheart.'

Daisy could feel her cheeks flush with pleasure. She'd found him again, or rather, he had found her.

The next minute he was standing before her, that famous grin splitting his face from ear to ear. 'Well, this is a fine how-do-you-do. I don't usually have to put on a parachute and jump out of a plane in order to get to see a girl but if that's what it takes, who am I to object?'

Daisy, at a complete loss for words, was having trouble even catching her breath. She hadn't expected to ever see Harry again, let alone in this startling way. Hadn't she only recently repeated her vow to have nothing more to do with fellas? Seeming to recognise her confusion, Harry took charge and started chattering away, happy to answer a string of questions from Megan about whether he had hurt himself and how he'd come to be falling out of the sky, and if he'd be doing it again.

'I expect so on another day and yes, I'm fine, thanks. This is nothing to worry about kids, just a training exercise. Christmas or no, our CO likes to keep us busy. And he thought it might give you good folk of the Lakes a feeling of comfort to know how swiftly help could be summoned, if needed. However, since it is Christmas, what about a hot potato as a treat, eh? Nothing better, I've always thought, on a cold day. Or perhaps a lollipop? If I can get my hand in my pocket – I'm sure I must have a few pennies here somewhere.'

Within seconds, or so it seemed, the two little girls had helped him delve into his flying-suit pockets, extracted the pennies and run off in the direction of the cart with the big black stove and tall chimney at the edge of the green, where the hot potato man had optimistically set up business for the day.

The moment they'd gone, Harry grabbed both of Daisy's hands, holding them tight and warm in his own. 'I've got maybe five minutes at best, probably less. Where are you living now Daisy? Are you all right? Are the children OK? Is there any chance that I could see you again?'

She felt dazed, utterly stunned by events. One minute she'd been reflecting, yet again, on her lonely state, the next, happiness had literally dropped out of the sky, bringing an unexpected sudden ray of sunshine into her life.

He seemed to be watching the thoughts spinning in her head. 'Please don't keep me in suspense. Say you will.' He glanced anxiously back over his shoulder and for the first time Daisy noticed that his comrades were swiftly gathering up their parachutes and hurrying over to a truck standing not far off. People were hindering their departure by thumping them on their backs, pumping their hands in vigorous handshakes, as if anxious to thank them for the risks they were about to take. 'I'll have to go in a minute. Please, Daisy, say yes. I've got an evening off next Thursday, how would that be? There's a dance. I could pick you up. God knows how long we'll be at Longtown. We could get our new posting at any time.'

She looked at him properly then, her eyes focusing upon the eagerness in his young face, the anxiety in his grey-green eyes and she thought, why not? Perhaps she was too young to give up men for life, after all. They couldn't all be as heartless as Percy, surely? And he seemed harmless enough. A nice young man, honest, cheerful, but not as handsome, nor so full of his own self-importance as Percy had been. A girl could surely feel safe with Harry Driscoll. Besides, he wasn't at all the sort of chap she could ever go crazy about, or fall head over heels in love with. 'All right,' she said. 'Why not?'

He gave a whoop of delight, picked her up and swung her round so fast and furious, the pair of them got hopelessly tangled in the cords of the parachute and tumbled to the ground together, all trussed up like a chicken. Daisy could barely speak for laughing as they both struggled to release themselves from the muddle. Eventually, she found both breath and voice. 'You're quite mad, Harry Driscoll. Do you know that? Stark, staring crazy.'

'You're absolutely right, Daisy, I am. Crazy over you. I love your bright, brown eyes, and the adorable way you tilt your head to one side whenever anyone speaks to you. I love every freckle, I adore . . .'

'Shut up, you clown, and get me out of here.' She might have managed to untangle herself if she hadn't been so fully occupied wiping tears of laughter from her eyes.

'Oh, I don't know. I've really no objection at all to lying on this grass with you, cold and damp though it undoubtedly is. I can't think of anyone I'd rather be tied up with, and would happily stay here all day, if it weren't for the fact that I'd probably get court-martialled.'

'Well, I *do* object. Stop acting the fool and behave yourself,' but there was no disapproval in her voice. She was still helpless with laughter, her sides aching with it. He really was a card, was Harry Driscoll. Going out with him would certainly be fun, if nothing else.

Finally, and with great reluctance, he helped her back on to her feet, but even then didn't quite let her go. He gathered her small face between his two large hands and said, 'Happy Christmas, Daisy. You've made my day.' Then he kissed her. It was a light, friendly, unromantic sort of kiss but yet filled with tenderness, and strangely moving. The sort of kiss that kept Daisy awake half the night remembering it.

Laura

8

Laura was entranced by the tale, soaking up every word and the meal had been good too. A simple pasta dish, but delicious. They'd enjoyed a surprisingly companionable evening, just the two of them and talked for hours afterwards over an excellent Chardonnay, curled up on old comfy sofas before a blazing log fire.

'It's all so sad. Daisy couldn't have married Harry in the end, since he was called Driscoll, and Daisy's married name was Thompson.'

David shrugged. 'She could easily have married twice.'

Laura's eyes widened. 'I hadn't thought of that. Damn, I was so occupied fending off my father's anger, I never did ask him the first name of my grandfather. Did Daisy ever mention it to you?'

He shook his head. 'Not that I recall. She only ever talked about Harry. Harry, Harry, Harry. As I said, he was undoubtedly the love of her life.'

'Do you think they married and then something terrible happened to him in the war? Was that it? He surely wouldn't leave her once he learned of her secret child, or get a divorce, would he? Oh, I want to know so much more. What happened at the dance, for instance? When did Daisy realise she loved him? Did she ever tell him about the baby? Oh, it's so frustrating. I want to know everything about her. I hate my father for cutting me off like that.'

'Did you tell him that? Is that why he was angry with you, or shouldn't I ask?'

Laura screwed up her nose, not quite sure how to respond. 'He took me out to lunch to give me one of his little lectures on how I should organise my life. He's stubborn and dogmatic and uncommunicative. No wonder he and Daisy fell out.'

'So this search into her past is some sort of guilt trip, is it?' David tossed another log on to the fire and a shower of sparks flew up the wide, inglenook chimney. Outside, for once, all seemed to be quiet, the wind having died away.

Laura gave a rueful smile. 'In a way, but there's more to it than that.' She felt totally relaxed here, replete with good food and wine, thoroughly mellow so didn't take exception to the question. Besides, she'd discovered that she quite liked this man. He'd been perfectly frank about his own life, the difficulties of running a farm in today's economic climate, yet how determined he was to hang on. His uncle had left it to him about ten years ago because, like David himself, he'd remained a bachelor and had no children of his own. Beckwith Hall Farm had consumed him all of his life, as it now possessed David, leaving him little opportunity to socialise or look for a wife. If he didn't make a fortune working it, then so be it. His needs were small, he explained, with only himself to think about.

Laura said, 'I find Daisy fascinating and genuinely want to understand her. But there was some silly quarrel between her and my dad, so I didn't see as much of her when I was growing up as I would have liked. And he's furious with me for "interfering", as he calls it, for trying to find out more about her.'

'How old were you when this quarrel took place?'

Laura frowned. 'Maybe about seven or eight.'

'Well, I can understand you being under your father's control for some years after that. But you've been a big girl for a long time. Time enough to make your own decisions about who you see or don't see.'

Again she felt herself flushing, feeling the need to justify herself without divulging all the complicated intricacies of her marriage. 'True, but . . . there were other reasons why I didn't get in touch as often as I should, even after I left home.'

Felix had seen little point in wasting valuable time visiting relatives. He'd once driven Laura up to the Lakes to see Daisy and complained bitterly about the mud which had splattered on to the underside of his brand new Mercedes. He'd refused, absolutely, to take a walk, claiming it would likewise ruin his highly polished shoes, nor would he borrow a pair of old boots, probably because they would look odd with his smart new suit. He'd also objected to country smells, messy animals and Daisy's plumbing, as well as her lack of fitted carpets and central heating. He'd never come again. Not until the funeral.

But how could she properly explain any of this, without making him sound a complete prig? Nor had she any wish to go into the fact that he'd objected to Laura coming on her own. She'd fought a battle every time she wanted to visit her grandmother so, in the end, had opted for the easy course and stayed away, thinking there'd be time to try again later when Felix was less tied up with the business and had got over his silly mood. Only there never had been enough time.

Explaining none of this, she confined her comments to, 'My husband doesn't much care for the country.'

'Ah, I see. It takes some people that way. All this fresh air and space. Is that why he's not here with you now?'

'He's a busy man, with a business to run.' If David Hornsby wished to read more into that, let him.

'Of course.'

Laura felt certain that he noted how she was avoiding his shrewd gaze. She could sense him considering her more intently, as if he'd like to ask her another question but apparently changed his mind at the last moment and offered her more coffee instead, which she refused politely. He gave a little deprecating shrug. 'OK, so I'm nosy. Living here, one grabs one's gossip where one can.' He grinned at her and made to top up her wine glass but she quickly put her hand over it.

'No, no, it's late. Heavens, yes, it's nearly midnight.' Laura stood up. 'I really must go.'

He didn't press her to stay longer or make any silly jokes about her changing into a pumpkin on the stroke of midnight. He simply collected her coat and offered to walk her back up the fields. Laura shook her head. 'I have my torch, and I came properly shod.' Slipping off the indoor shoes she'd brought with her, she pushed her feet into a sturdy pair of boots. They looked rather clumsy against her long blue evening skirt but would keep her feet dry, and what did glamour matter out in a field in the middle of the night? 'Thanks for a lovely evening. Most enlightening.'

'Glad you came?'

She glanced up at him, at the relaxed way he stood before her, hands in pockets, his smile warm and friendly. 'Yes,' she said, finding to her surprise that she meant it. 'I am. You must come to me next time. I cook pretty good too.'

'There is going to be a next time then?'

A small pause. 'I expect so. We'll have to see, shan't we?'

'I shall look forward to it.'

It was as he opened the door on to a still and cloudless night that he asked her the question that had clearly been on his mind all evening. 'What about your husband then. Doesn't he object to you having dinner with strange men?'

Laura busied herself fastening buttons and tying on her scarf so that he couldn't see the troubled expression in her eyes. 'Oh, probably, but he isn't here, is he?' and stepped over the threshold into the yard before he could pursue that particular line of conversation any further. 'Look at all these stars. Aren't they magnificent? We can rarely see them in town these days. Too much light pollution, I suppose. It's good to know they're still there, keeping watch over us.'

'Perhaps Daisy is one of them now, keeping an eye on us all.'

Laura turned to him with a lopsided smile, 'What a lovely thought. Thanks again for the delicious meal. Perhaps we can talk again some time, about Daisy.'

'Of course. There's lots more I could tell you, I'm sure.'

She let out a regretful sigh. 'If only she'd left a journal, as the Victorians used to do. It would make things so much easier.'

'I suppose it would, but sometimes a little effort can be so much more rewarding, don't you think? Goodnight, Laura.'

Laura's morning walks became a regular routine, a wonderful way to allow the fresh air to cleanse her troubled mind, sort out her confused thoughts, and ensure that she fell asleep like a baby the minute her head touched the pillow.

She was used to spending time alone, hours and hours of it in the big empty house in Cheadle Hulme, but this was different. This was a special kind of solitude: invigorating and refreshing which brought with it a sense of enormous peace and well-being. She delighted in the bloom of purple heather, the sight of a lone curlew circling in an infinite sky polished to a brilliant lapis lazuli blue, the sound of a rushing beck and she could never grow bored with the ever-changing dance of the clouds on the mountains beyond. Laura felt as if she were rediscovering the world, rediscovering herself.

As she strode out along the path she would list her assets, ticking them off one by one in her mind. She was strong, stronger than Felix gave her credit for, and self-willed. She was intelligent with many skills at her fingertips, and also capable of learning new ones. She wasn't afraid of hard work. She was still young enough at thirty-four to make a fresh start. Most of all, she was perfectly capable of coping without him. It had felt marvellous simply to refuse to go home, and although nothing had been finalised between them he rang daily to remind her that he still expected her to return soon. Laura knew that he could manage perfectly well without her, for all he may claim otherwise. No doubt the miraculous Miranda would move in and cook for him, if she hadn't already.

Laura giggled at the thought, no longer troubling to feel jealous as she speculated on whether the poor girl would be quite so keen when she realised all that was involved in being Felix's wife, rather than his mistress.

As always after one of these self-therapy sessions, she returned from her walk feeling cleansed and light-hearted, as if she had scoured off a mask of troubles, looked the devil in the face and survived. A fanciful notion but could she survive here through the aching cold of a long winter without the undoubted comforts of life that her husband could provide? Could she build a business and make enough money out of it to provide for herself?

Back in the kitchen she toed off her boots, made herself a coffee and carried it into the living room. There were surprisingly few chores to be done. Daisy had spent her last weeks in hospital during which time the house must have been standing empty but someone had stripped the old woman's bed, washed and ironed the sheets, left her bedroom all spick and span. She rather thought it might have been David and had tackled him on the subject when she'd encountered him once in the lane.

He'd shrugged her thanks aside. 'Someone had to do it. It was no big deal.'

In the days following the funeral, Laura folded and packed up clothes which most obviously needed to be disposed of. At first it had felt like an intrusion but she shook aside any sense of shyness since at least she cared about Daisy, and wasn't some unknown auctioneer simply listing her belongings in a dispassionate way. She opened every cupboard and drawer, all of which appeared to be stuffed with linen and clothes which must have lain neatly stored there for years, reeking of mothballs or old lavender. Some of the linen was so beautifully embroidered, or made from such deliciously soft Lancashire cotton, that Laura couldn't imagine ever disposing of them.

But then she didn't have to. They would come in very handy if and when she opened the house for guests. She spent a couple of days making a full inventory, counting every cup, saucer, plate and table napkin, anything which might be useful in her new business. After that she gave the kitchen a thorough clean and threw away packets and tins which had passed their sell-by date. Now, there was nothing more to be done than sit down and relax: to do a little thinking and perhaps doodle a few notes about her plans.

She ate only when hungry, and then something simple like an omelette or a cheese sandwich. Nobody called and she felt quite alone in the world, free to stay in bed all morning if she so wished, or get up at dawn and walk over the mountain, or down through the lanes and fields for miles. On her return, Laura would feel so soporific that she would frequently fall asleep over whatever book she happened to be reading from Daisy's collection. Free of Felix's endless demands for the first time in years, she was at last able to think properly with blissfully few interruptions. And apart from his regular telephone call each evening, the phone didn't even ring.

As the time for his call approached, she would pour herself a glass of wine, ready to brace herself before picking it up. 'Hello darling,' she would say, as brightly as she could.

Felix, as always, would come straight to the point. 'How much longer are you going to be away?'

'I thought perhaps you might come up here on Friday evening. If you brought some more of my clothes, we could make a weekend of it. I can't recall when we last spent some free time together, must be a couple of years now. And the weather is glorious, you'd love it.' She could then choose her moment to reveal her plans and talk through their problems in a civilised fashion.

'I'd hate that Laura and you know it. Besides, I have to pop over to Toledo for a couple of days. Something about a picture which might be a Greco.' Felix was always dreaming of finding some undiscovered work of art which would make him a fortune. Laura paid no attention to this.

'Well, don't expect me home quite yet. I'm having a lovely time being lazy and spoiling myself rotten. Don't you think I deserve to once in a while?'

She heard his exasperated sigh hiss down the phone line. 'It sounds inordinately selfish to me. Stop wallowing in nostalgia and come home where you belong. The sheets need changing, there's nothing in the fridge, and the house is like a morgue. I can hardly bear to be in it.'

'But you rarely are in it anyway, darling, even when I'm there.'

'Are you trying to be deliberately provocative, Laura? If so, I'm not amused. I work only for your benefit you know, to provide you with a lovely house, clothes, etc., etc.'

'So you keep saying, and I keep asking you to allow me to work with you so that I wouldn't be so bored and you so over-stretched, but somehow I don't believe you're listening.'

'I don't intend to turn this call into another marital argument. I shall be catching an early flight home on Monday morning. I shall expect you to be at the airport to pick me up.'

Laura took a deep breath. 'Sorry, darling, no can do. I – I have an appointment to see the solicitor on that day.' The appointment was for Tuesday but the last thing she wanted was to rush home, spend the weekend cleaning up the house, restocking the fridge and then dashing to the airport to pick up Felix at the crack of dawn on Monday morning. Nevertheless, Laura could feel herself flushing at the deliberate lie and put her hand to her cheek, almost as if she were afraid he could see her guilt over the phone.

'Tell him you need to bring it forward. Or better still cancel it and I'll deal with the blithering old idiot by phone.'

'I could always come with you to Toledo. How about that? I wouldn't mind a romantic weekend somewhere warm and sexy. Then we could both fly back together on Monday morning and I'd nip back up here to see the solicitor.'

'I'm going to be busy all weekend. You'd be thoroughly bored. Stop arguing and do as you're told for once, Laura.'

'I always do as I'm told. Perhaps I'm growing tired of it. Anyway, there'd be the evenings, and the nights together. Is Miranda going to be there?'

'Monday morning, Laura. My plane lands at six-thirty. Don't be late.' There was a click and he was gone, subject closed, as abrupt and imperative as ever. She noticed that he'd not answered her question about Miranda. Laura stuck out her tongue at the now silent instrument and, finding the wine bottle empty, went to pour herself a drop of port from a bottle she'd found in a cupboard. Sly old Daisy had clearly enjoyed a tipple herself now and then.

On Saturday morning, when she knew that Felix would be away, Laura drove down to Cheadle Hulme, let herself into the empty house and packed a couple of suitcases with clothes and a few personal items she needed. The fridge was indeed empty with nothing more than a bottle of sour milk and a lettuce that was running to liquid in the chill tray. Closing the door again, she made no move to clean or restock it.

She checked through the mail lying on the mat but left it there unopened. She rarely received either letters or bills and could see nothing beyond a bit of junk mail. She did risk taking a few of her favourite CDs from the rack, guessing that Felix would be no more likely to notice they were missing than he would think to check her wardrobe. By the time he did both, it would no longer matter. She would have made up her mind and come to a firm decision about her future, one way or the other.

She paused to linger for a moment and gaze at their wedding photo on the dresser, recalling with painful nostalgia the hope she had felt on that day. It was a close-up of the happy couple, cheek to cheek, with their arms about each other, Laura looking young and desperately in love. Felix was wearing his embarrassed, 'I'll be glad when this pantomime is all over' expression. Had he ever loved her? she wondered. If not, then why had he married her? Because she'd suited the image he had in mind for a wife? She was reasonably attractive, good in bed, and could cook. An excellent CV for matrimony. And was apparently willing to fit in entirely with his wishes and do exactly as he told her to.

Not any more.

Laura carefully locked up the house again and drove back to the Lakes. It really had proved to be incredibly simple to break free. By the time she was past the Blackpool turnoff and the motorway traffic eased, she felt quite light-hearted for the first time in months, as if she had rid herself of a great weight.

On Tuesday morning, Laura set off bright and early to drive to Keswick. She took Daisy's clothes to a local charity shop, then explored its miscellany of shops and narrow streets, hidden courts and yards, past the Moot Hall and market place, pausing only to eat lunch in a tiny café and buy food to take back with her to Lane End Farm. She considered taking in a play at the new Theatre By The Lake but decided against it and settled instead for a visit to the museum and art gallery in Fitz Park where she studied the original manuscripts of Southey, Ruskin and Walpole, among others.

At three-thirty prompt, she kept her appointment with the family solicitor, not old Mr Capstick but his son Nicholas, who turned out to be surprisingly young and smart, his office filled with a battery of computers. Even Felix would have been impressed.

He told her to call him Nick, said how pleased he was to meet Daisy's granddaughter at last, then expressed his regrets on hearing she was planning to sell. 'It's not a good time to sell. Farms aren't fetching high prices right now and Lane End is little more than a smallholding now.' He chewed on his lower lip for a bit. 'Trouble is, because it's so remote, it will only attract a particular sort of buyer. It's unique. A fine house in many ways and you would sell it eventually, but it could take a year or two.'

'A year or two? Heavens, I think Felix was thinking in terms of a couple of months.'

Nick gave a hollow laugh. 'No chance. Not the way things work with this type of property. If I were you, and it's really none of my business, but unless you're strapped for cash I'd hang on for a bit. View it as an excellent investment for the future.'

Laura sat back with a satisfied little sigh. He couldn't have said anything guaranteed to please her more. Now she had some real ammunition with which to fight Felix. 'Thank you for your advice. I'll tell my husband what you suggest.'

He nodded, punched some keys on his computer and, after a moment, said, 'Apart from that, everything is progressing nicely so far as the probate is concerned. The land doesn't come with the house, you do understand that?'

'Oh yes, that was made clear.'

He nodded. 'You're the only beneficiary so there shouldn't be any complications. Not that there's much actual cash. The house was her main, well – her only remaining asset.'

'That's fine. The house is wonderful.' Laura got up to go. 'Oh, my grandmother didn't leave any papers with you, did she? Letters perhaps, or a diary?'

He frowned slightly while he considered this. 'Not that I know of. I believe we only have her will. She kept all her papers, such as there were, in her bureau at home, including the deeds of the house. We offered to store those for her too but Daisy enjoyed browsing through them from time to time, because it was the story of Lane End Farm. She said everything had a life story, the house, the mountain, even the stones in the road.' He smiled fondly. 'Old folk get that way, a little fanciful in their declining years. But she loved that house, and why not? She didn't have much of a start in life, I believe, so deserved her bit of good luck.'

Laura had sat down again. 'You'd have thought then, if she believed a house had a story to tell, that she'd be happy to tell her own.'

'In my experience people very often say one thing and mean another. Hard to fathom at times. Have you spoken to David? David Hornsby, your nearest neighbour. They were great friends and I'm almost sure he encouraged her to do something of that nature.'

Laura was flabbergasted. 'He never said. I had supper with him the other night but he denied all knowledge of a diary.'

'Oh, I could be entirely wrong. Don't quote me. And Daisy was far too active to sit still for more than five minutes, let alone keep a diary. That much I did learn about her in the few years I knew her. If she wasn't mending walls, she was reroofing the barn or whatever. She felt an enormous pride in keeping the house up to scratch, and a great sense of responsibility, though it got too much for her in the end. Clem had been determined that the property be left to her and not to Florrie, his wife. She would be Daisy's aunt, if you remember, who'd lived at the farm since they married. A bit before my time but they were an odd couple apparently.'

'In what way, odd?'

'Oh, something to do with him being a good bit older than her for a start, Florrie being one for a good time and Blencathra not really having its fair share of night spots. I think she found it rather lonely up there. And then there was the loss of their child, which didn't help.'

'Oh, how dreadful. What happened?'

He shook his head. 'Bit of a mystery and a long time ago, of course. The pair blamed each other, I believe. Did their relationship no good at all.' The telephone rang and he picked up the receiver with an apologetic smile. Seconds later he put it down again. 'My next appointment, I'm afraid. Well, it's been good talking to you, Mrs Rampton.'

'Laura, please.'

He smiled. 'I hope you come to enjoy living in the house as much as Daisy did. You may even change your mind and decide not to sell after all.'

'You never know. I'm certainly curious to learn more about her life, and anyone else who occupied the house before me.'

He led her to the door. 'You should talk to my father, retired and taking life easier now but he would have been around when Daisy was here, even if not when Clem was making his will. He may know something about it. Memories live long in these parts. Certainly my dad is sharp enough for anything that happened forty or fifty years ago; ask him what he had for his lunch yesterday and that's another matter.'

'Thank you,' Laura said with a smile. 'You've been most helpful.'

On her drive back from town the sky grew heavy with snow, grey and threatening, the surrounding mountains seeming to retreat gradually and vanish in the gloom. A late snowfall would play havoc with the lambing and no doubt with her own plans. She took the precaution of stopping off at a super-market for further supplies, mindful of the warnings of blocked lanes. The idea of being snowed in was not un-pleasant, an excuse to postpone the inevitable confrontation with Felix but she'd no wish to be marooned without suf-ficient sustenance. Not that Felix could be ignored indefinitely. If she was going to turn Lane End Farm back into a guesthouse, she should tell him of her decision sooner, rather than later. She must face it at some point, and delay would only make his temper worse.

She bought meat, chicken, flour, herbs and spices, unsalted butter and other delicious ingredients together with a new cookbook she'd been promising herself for ages. She meant to take advantage of the respite by trying out some of the recipes. Laura also purchased a large notepad, in which she meant to start making lists and outline her plans for the house. She enjoyed making lists, was never happier than with a pencil in her hand organising something, that's when she wasn't up to her elbows in flour of course. She would restock the freezer and invite David Hornsby round to act as guinea pig for some new dish or other. It would give her the opportunity to ask him again about a diary, and whether he had, in fact, succeeded in persuading Daisy to keep one, had perhaps been holding out on admitting as much and making her work for it.

She also bought such items as paint, brushes, turps, nails, screws, sandpaper and other unexciting but essential items. She meant to get started with the refurbishments just as soon as she'd spoken to Felix.

With the solicitor's advice to back her up, she felt a surge of new confidence, a tiny nub of excitement burning in the pit of her stomach.

The snow didn't look like it would stick, fortunately, but David Hornsby happily accepted her invitation when she came across him late that afternoon in the lane. She challenged him about the diary but to her disappointment, he repeated his belief that Daisy hadn't kept one. 'It's true that I did try to persuade her but, as I told you before, failed utterly.'

They leaned on the dry-stone wall looking out over towards Skiddaw Forest, chatting amicably: Laura explaining how she intended to try out a new recipe and David speaking of his concern for his ewes whenever the weather took a turn for the worse. 'The sky still looks heavy with snow. The last thing we need are blizzards to coincide with lambing. January and February are bad enough in these parts. But then you'll probably be gone by next winter.'

He cast her a sideways, speculative glance and Laura hesitated only momentarily before launching into an explanation of her plans to turn Lane End Farm back into a guesthouse. 'I've never done anything of the sort in my life before, and could easily make a complete mess of it.'

His face became alert with interest. 'I'm delighted to hear that you might be staying on, though I can't imagine your making a mess of anything, not for a moment. Daisy too was practical, a capable, no-nonsense, non-fussy type, and I'm quite sure you must be the same.' An odd sort of compliment which nonetheless brought a schoolgirl flush to her cheeks, more from the look in his eyes than the words themselves. Then he was continuing with his story of Daisy and Harry, and as Laura became totally absorbed by it, as always, everything else vanished from her mind. She forgot all about her cooking, and about ringing Felix to tell him what the solicitor had said about the house.

Daisy

9

When Thursday came round, Daisy was in a dither of indecision. What should she wear for her first date with Harry? She had very few clothes and no money to buy any new ones. Yet for some reason she felt torn in two, anxious to look her best, wanting him to like her while at the same time being unwilling to give the impression that she'd made any special effort. Mindful of the disaster that her first love affair had led her into, Daisy was afraid of making a mistake, and reluctant to take any similar risks, or encourage him in the slightest way.

In the event, in the hours before he was due to arrive Daisy was kept so fully occupied she didn't have a moment to think, let alone study the contents of her meagre wardrobe. To start with she was late home from work, then the moment she came through the door, Mrs Chapman sent her straight out again to join a queue she'd heard was forming at the butchers, though she hadn't the first idea what it was for. Daisy stood impatiently stamping her feet against the winter cold, fretting and worrying about how long this ritual might take and when, an hour later, she returned bearing the prize of half a dozen pork sausages, Mrs Chapman tartly remarked that it had hardly been worth the effort.

'If only you hadn't been late, and had joined the queue earlier, then you might have been more successful.'

Daisy gritted her teeth against the desire to defend herself by saying that Mr Chapman was the one to blame for her being late, by asking her to tidy the stationery cupboard quite late in the day. He'd then hindered the process by keep popping in to interrupt and check on how she was getting along. She knew he only meant to be kind but there'd been one moment, when he'd squeezed into the cupboard with her, that Daisy had felt quite claustrophobic, trapped by his bulk in the confined space. He was a large, stocky man and when he'd reached up, quite unnecessarily, to bring down a box for her to sort through, the smell of sweat from under his armpits had made her feel quite nauseous.

'You don't have to stay,' she'd told him. 'I can get a stool and manage very well on my own, thanks.' She didn't like to say that there wasn't room enough for the two of them in the narrow space.

'No, no, I'm happy to help. I'll hold you up, shall I?' To Daisy's alarm, he'd grasped her by the waist and lifted her off her feet so that she could reach the next box. She could feel his plump fingers digging into her ribs just below her breasts and went quite hot with embarrassment.

She'd been saved by the arrival of one of his clerks who came to tell him a client had arrived for their appointment. He appeared not in the least nonplussed to find his employer lurking in the stationery cupboard with the post girl, nor did he seem to notice how flustered Daisy was. But it was this small incident which caused her to experience her first doubts about Mr Chapman and his veneer of kind generosity.

As if this wasn't enough, she was further delayed by Megan and Trish who were waiting for her at the garden gate full of excitement over some news they were bursting to tell her.

'What d'you think Daisy, Mrs Marshall is going to have a baby.'

Daisy was startled. She hadn't realised ladies as old as Mrs Marshall could still have babies. She must be very nearly forty, if not that already. 'Really, how do you know?'

'We heard her telling the cleaning lady. She said how they'd been trying for years and had given up all hope. Isn't that good, Daisy? Trish and me like babies. P'raps they found the right place what sells them.'

'Yes, perhaps they did,' Daisy agreed, but even as she nodded and smiled, promising to meet up with them later for their usual early evening doggy walk, there was a smidgen of worry at the back of her mind. Would Mr and Mrs Marshall still be prepared to keep the two little evacuees once they had a baby of their own?

But all of these concerns melted away as anticipation of the evening ahead tightened in the pit of her stomach, making her feel very slightly sick. She couldn't get the image of Harry's cheerful face out of her mind as she set about her nightly chores with extra vigour, eager to get them done quickly then she could be on her way.

Daisy cleaned the kitchen, polished Mr Chapman's shoes and sharpened a batch of pencils for the holder on his desk, not forgetting the promised walk with the children and the dog, which left her just enough time to quickly wash her face, drag a comb through the tangled corkscrew curls and pull on the first clean blouse and skirt that came to hand. So much for studying her wardrobe.

Even though she flew down the stairs the moment the doorbell rang, pausing only to grab her coat, by the time she reached it Mr Chapman was already standing in the hall, holding the door wide open. 'There appears to be someone here for you, Daisy.'

'Yes,' she agreed, slightly breathless from her headlong dash and from the blast of cold wind that roared up the lobby. 'Hello, Harry.'

Looking exceptionally smart in his blue uniform, he saluted her deftly. 'Evening.'

'Aren't you going to introduce me to your young man, Daisy?'

She did so, hearing her own voice sounding all stilted and embarrassed, stumbling over the words, although why it should affect her in that way, Daisy couldn't imagine. It was really no business of Mr Chapman who she went out with, and, strictly speaking, Harry couldn't be called her 'young man' at all, only a friend who happened to be male. But Mr Chapman was frowning at Harry in a curiously critical way and she was anxious, suddenly, to be off.

'I won't be late,' she called, grabbing Harry's arm and pushing him out on to the step, in readiness for a quick exit.

'Indeed I should hope not. That wouldn't be right, not on such a short acquaintance. It would be most unseemly of your young man to return you home much beyond nine.'

'Nine?' Daisy was appalled. That barely gave them more than a couple of hours together.

Harry remarked bravely, 'We're going to a dance, sir. I could have her back by ten.'

Mr Chapman appeared to consider. 'Very well then, ten o'clock. Not a moment later. We are responsible for you to your parents, after all, Daisy. What would they think if I absconded on my duty?'

Daisy made no response to this as she hurried Harry quickly down the garden path and along the street, though she could feel him bristling with anger. 'Who does he think he is to lecture me about what's right or wrong? Does he imagine I'd do something to hurt you? Silly old cove. Anyway, how does he know how long I've known you, or what your parents would think of me?'

Daisy knew for certain that her mother would jump quickly to the conclusion that Harry wanted to have his wicked way with her, as Percy had done. If she'd been here, Rita would have warned her to make no mention of her dreadful secret, not if she wanted to keep her reputation intact, nor be taken advantage of. Not that Daisy had any intention of ever telling anyone about the precious, nameless baby who'd been taken from her, though for a very different reason. It was a subject far too painful to discuss with anyone, let alone a new acquaintance. Giving no indication of these troubled thoughts, she smiled brightly up at him. 'Take no notice, Harry. Like he says, he is responsible for me, in a way, since I'm an evacuee. And I am only seventeen.' She was properly grown up now that she'd had another birthday.

'And I'm only twenty-two. Too young to be fighting in a bloody war. But if I'm old enough to die for my country, I'm old enough to take out any girl I fancy.'

Daisy cast him a sidelong glance from beneath the sweep of her lashes, her mouth pursing upwards into a teasing smile. 'So you do fancy me then, eh?'

'I fancy you rotten, and don't pretend you don't know that already.'

The dance was being held at the village hall, put on specially for the 'boys in blue' by grateful locals who feared for what these young men might soon be facing, wanting their last memories of this small Cumberland village to be happy ones. Outside, the helm wind might blow across the tops with its usual fervour, guns might be sounding in far distant places, but here, within these four walls, all was merry and light-hearted. The music was loud, the room packed with air crew and starry-eyed village girls; a substantial supper of pork pies, sandwiches and home-made cakes to satisfy healthy young appetites during the interval. No one spoke of the war, or where they might be tomorrow, or the day after that. Here, for one night at least, everyone could feel safe and warm, happy and free to simply enjoy themselves.

Daisy was having the time of her life. She danced every number with Harry, even the square tango and the Boston Two Step at which they were both so hopeless they fell over each other's feet and very nearly ended up in another tangle on the dance floor.

'Oh lord, me mam allus did call me a clumsy oaf,' Daisy mourned and, for the sake of the other couples still dancing, suggested that perhaps they should sit the next one out. 'Otherwise we might get ourselves arrested for causing an obstruction.'

They sat on a couple of the hard, wooden chairs set around the perimeter of the room, Daisy sipping a lemonade while Harry quaffed a welcome beer. She could feel the heat of his body pressing against hers and this somehow seemed strangely intimate. Smitten with a burst of shyness, she couldn't think of a thing to say throughout the length of two more dances. The long silence was nevertheless a contented one and it was Harry who broke it by saying it was getting late and perhaps they ought to be starting the long walk home. 'In any case, I don't know about you, but I could do with a breath of fresh air.'

The January night was crisp and frosty, with a horned moon riding high amongst the stars in a clear, bright sky. All around were the undulating folds of the Northern fells, filling the horizon, deceptively benign, their smooth faces blanked out by the darkness, it was here that the RAF aimed their dummy bombs. Daisy had watched them practise day after day, flying in low, searching for the wooden arrows on the ground which marked their target. Some time soon their target would be a real one, and not quite so passive. Tonight though, all was silent, save for the crack and splinter of ice underfoot as the young couple walked along the rough track. Harry tucked up the collar of Daisy's coat. 'Are you warm enough?'

'Yes, thanks.'

He put an arm about her and hugged her close to his side, just to make sure, he explained. Daisy didn't object. She liked the feel of him beside her, warm and strong, solid and comforting, and the pressure of his hand moving up and down her arm was bringing small shivers of excitement deep in her belly. The more time she spent with Harry, the more she liked him.

They walked for a long time in silence, and then he said, 'Back home, in Manchester or Salford, wherever it is that you live, is there anyone special?'

'Special in what way?' Daisy asked, knowing full well what he meant, but needing time to consider her answer.

'You know in what way.'

'Well – there was once.' She knew she sounded hesitant and unsure, unwilling to speak of it.

'But not now?'

For one mad moment she almost told him. She could simply say: I was young and foolish and got myself into trouble because I thought we were in love. Except that instead of marrying me, as I'd hoped and longed for, he joined up and left me to deal with the consequences on my own. Yet how could she? She was scarcely much older even now. A wave of sickness hit her, and she was back in that Mother and Baby Home, arguing with Mam, pleading with her to let her keep the baby, crying for Percy to come for her.

Daisy realised that in a way, perhaps her mother had been right. She had indeed been far too young to care for a baby at sixteen. How could she even consider herself a responsible person when here she was, a matter of months after losing both Percy and her precious child, falling in love with someone new. Didn't that prove how fickle she was? How she was 'no better than she should be', as her mother was so fond of accusing her. How terrible to have to admit such a thing, or to confess that she'd recklessly lain with a boy without giving any thought to the consequences. What would Harry think of her then? Daisy couldn't bear to explore these thoughts any further and pushed them firmly to one side, saying only, 'No, not now. There's no one special at all.'

'I'm glad.' He stopped walking and drew her into his arms. 'If it weren't for the war, Daisy, I'd come happily courting you for weeks, take you out and about, see you whenever I could, letting us slowly get to know each other. But who knows how long I'll be at Longtown. Not much longer, I dare say. We could be given our new postings at any time, any day now. The training must soon be over and God knows where I'll end up. We might not see each other again for weeks, months even.'

Her heart was thumping like a mad thing as she thought about this, about not being sure of when she might see Harry again, of knowing that he could be somewhere high in the sky shooting at enemy aircraft, and worse, being shot at, maybe even killed. Fear coursed through her at the unknown horrors ahead of them both, waiting to snatch all hope of happiness at the very moment they had found each other.

When he kissed her this time, Daisy put her arms about his neck and held him close, pushing her fingers up into his hair, pressing herself against him, wanting the kiss never to end. His cheeks were cold against hers but freshly shaved and smooth, smelling beguilingly of soap and clean, frosty air. His mouth was warm and demanding, searching and exploring her own with an intensity that frightened her even as it burst open that tight bud of excitement within. She sensed his vulnerability coupled with the fire of his need, and felt an answering need in herself. She wanted him, no doubt about it but whether that meant she was in love with him, or Harry with her, was another question entirely.

This thought somehow brought her to her senses and Daisy broke free from his embrace. What was she thinking of to let him kiss her with such abandonment? Delicious though it was, and despite longing for it to go on and on, she pushed him away gently. It was far too soon. Hadn't she suffered burnt fingers already for loving too easily? 'I really think we should be getting home. Mr Chapman will be waiting up.'

Harry was gazing at her, his eyes dazed with emotion yet with a hint of puzzlement in them, not quite understanding her reaction. 'Yes, of course, you're right. Oh, Daisy, I've never met anyone quite like you. I'd really love it if you'd say that you'd be my girl, if you'd write to me – when I'm posted. Will you do that?'

How could she refuse, when he was going off to war and might never come back, when even now, despite all the sensible thoughts in her head, she just longed to kiss him again? Her throat had gone all dry, choked with emotion. Daisy told herself that it would be unkind not to write, that whatever reservations she might feel inside he deserved that at least. And it didn't mean that she was committing herself to him, not in any way. If he did survive to return to her in one piece, and God help him that he did, there would be time enough to reveal her dreadful secret but not now, when the poor boy had enough on his plate. So Daisy nodded, her heart a vortex of hope and fear and need. 'Oh I will, Harry. Every day.'

'Aw, that's great!' He was still holding her in his arms, smoothing the curls from her cheek, kissing her pert nose. 'So what about next week? We could go to the pictures. I'll see what's on. Not that it matters what's on, I just want to be with you, Daisy, and to hold you. You must know by now how I feel about you. I believe some people are meant for each other, don't you?'

Daisy sighed with delight, little tremors of passion running through her as he again kissed her on the mouth, a mere butterfly kiss this time but so tender she could have wept. 'Oh, I'd like to think so, Harry, I really would. It would explain everything.' She meant that it might all have been worth it, having Percy reject her, even losing the baby if Harry could love her for ever, as she so longed to be loved.

'I felt that way the minute I saw you standing at that bus stop, looking so lost and forlorn in the pouring rain. When this blasted war is over . . .'

She stopped whatever he might be about to say with a gentle touch of her fingertips. 'Let's take it a bit more slowly, shall we? As you say yourself, who knows what tomorrow might bring?' Suddenly Daisy felt afraid, realising what she risked by falling in love again. If she lost Harry, she didn't think she'd recover half so well as she had from the other tragedy in her life.

He walked her home, pausing only briefly on the doorstep of the Chapmans' house to give her one last lingering kiss to which Daisy did not respond with quite her former enthusiasm, being acutely aware of twitching curtains in the front parlour.

They said their goodbyes and she waved to him as he walked away, her heart aching for him, yet how could that be? she asked herself, a sudden rush of tears blocking her vision so that she fumbled for her key in the dark. Hadn't she lost all faith in love? Hadn't she sworn never to trust a man again, and it was certainly true that the coming of war, with its impetus to make and seal friendships all in a rush before the loved one was snatched away, made it even more difficult to judge which love was fleeting and which would last the test of time. Oh, why did it all have to be so confusing?

As Daisy finally found the keyhole and was about to push in her key, the door was flung open, flooding the path and street beyond with light. She barely had the words out of her mouth to remind Mr Chapman about the black-out, before he grabbed hold of her wrist and pulled her quickly into the hall.

'What do you think you're doing, showing us all up by kissing your young man in full view of the street? Have you no shame?'

Daisy gasped. 'We weren't doing nothing wrong. Anyroad, who was there to see us in this black-out? Nobody, at least not until you put the searchlight on to us. Harry got me back by ten o'clock, like you told him to, didn't he? It's only a quarter to, in point of fact, so I'll be off to me bed now, if you'll excuse me.'

She marched away from him but at the foot of the stairs he caught her again by the elbow. Daisy could hear how his breathing was strangely laboured, coming in jerky, shallow bursts, as if there was something wrong with his lungs and they weren't quite working properly. He'd taken off the jacket he wore to the office and replaced it with a cardigan, but he'd not removed the formal black tie from beneath the stiff white collar, firmly pinned in place with a gold tie pin. Daisy fixed her gaze upon it, hoping he would release her arm soon, for she hated him to come too near. He still smelled oddly, of stale sweat and old wool, and she longed to go up to bed and relive every moment of this lovely evening.

'You mustn't mind me, Daisy. I was worried about you, that's all.'

'Well, there's no need to be,' she remarked huffily.

His grip slackened and he gave a little sigh, as if alarmed by her tone. 'You aren't angry with me, are you? I'd hate you to be cross with me. You know I want only what's best for you, Daisy. I want you to be safe. It's quite a responsibility looking after a young girl, particularly one as pretty as yourself.'

She glanced into his face and saw how stricken he was, and her anger melted away instantly. He was, without doubt, an old fuddy-duddy but harmless enough. There'd been no creeping about at night, no fiddling with her bedroom door knob or attempts to touch her in an inappropriate way apart from that time in the stationery cupboard, which had no doubt been entirely accidental, she was sure of it. He was, as Harry rightly said, a silly old cove who enjoyed her youthful prettiness.

Perhaps seeing her go out with her young man this evening had upset him, made him realise that his own days for courting pretty young girls were long gone. But that was his problem, a fact of life that he must come to accept whether he liked it or not. 'Don't worry, Mr Chapman,' she said, pushing him gently but firmly away. 'I can take care of myself, thanks all the same,' and so saying, marched up the stairs.

Oh, but was it true? Could she indeed take care of herself? Daisy reflected ruefully. She certainly hadn't succeeded in doing so thus far.

Daisy saw plenty of Harry in the weeks following and life was sweet but then the bombshell dropped. Not a physical one, although it seemed equally devastating to Daisy. She was walking home from the Saturday market when Mrs Marshall called her in for a quick cup of tea and regretfully informed her that due to her delicate state of health and the need to take extra precautions and lots of rest, having lost two babies previously, she'd been forced to ask the billeting officer for Megan and Trish to be moved.

'We've written to their mother, of course, and although the poor woman has expressed her sadness that the girls have to move yet again, she understands perfectly.'

Daisy was filled with concern for her young friends. They'd been through so much together it was as if she alone, and not their mother, were responsible for them. 'But where will they go? They'll want to stop near me.'

'I'm sure they will, dear, and I'm equally sure that the billeting officer will do his best to ensure it. I did mention their fondness for you and he promised to do his utmost to keep them in the area.'

Knowing the difficulties of finding a good billet, Daisy was less convinced and made a private vow to call in at the office and put in a word on her own account. Perhaps Green Hat could help, though how could she ask for her, if she didn't even know the woman's real name? Serve her right for not paying proper attention. 'Do they know yet?'

Mrs Marshall shook her head. 'We thought it best to wait until we'd found a new home for them. Make it easier.'

Daisy could only agree with this assessment, though how she would manage to keep the devastating news quiet, she really didn't know. They'd already been in enough different billets, and had settled in here so happily. It broke her heart to think of them being moved, yet again. She understood the Marshalls' reasons, but was nonetheless concerned. All Daisy could hope to do was ensure that they went to a good place, near enough for her to visit them regularly.

She might have visited the billeting officer that very day, had it not been a Saturday, and for what happened next. Daisy had no sooner gone next door and put away the Saturday shopping when she was called into Mr Chapman's study.

'I've taken the liberty of contacting your father. I hope you don't object, Daisy, but I was concerned for your moral welfare.'

'Moral welfare?' Daisy stared at him dumbfounded, hardly able to believe her ears. This was too much. The foundations of her world seemed suddenly to be shaking to pieces yet again. 'What are you talking about?'

'I'm talking about what you get up to with this young man of yours. I've been watching you these last weeks, kissing and canoodling at every opportunity.'

Daisy felt mortified at being spied upon in this way, and her Salford accent was very much to the fore in the tone of her reply. 'We don't get up to owt, not anything we shouldn't anyroad.' Not that it's any business of yours, you dirty-minded old bugger, she longed to add but managed not to. Instead she retreated into her usual bitterness where her parents were concerned. 'What would Dad care anyroad? He gave up on me years ago. He's never been particularly inter-ested in what I do. He's always left my "moral welfare", as you call it, to Mam, so why should he start to take an interest now?'

'I thought he should come and talk to you, that you were in need of some parental help and advice.'

Daisy made a little tush sound deep in her throat, scoffing

at the very idea. 'He'd not take the trouble to walk to the bottom of our back yard to help me, let alone catch a bus or train to come up here.'

'Well, that's where you're wrong, Daisy. He did come. He's sitting in the parlour at this very moment, even as we speak, very much looking forward to seeing you.,

It was some seconds before Daisy could find her voice. 'Dad? In the front parlour?'

'Yes Daisy, so run along and talk to him, there's a good girl. I'll give you half an hour, then I'll have Mrs Chapman bring in tea and sandwiches. He'll be peckish after his journey, I dare say.'

'Aye, happen he will. Tell her to put arsenic in them.'

Joe Atkins was a quiet, self-effacing man, though some might describe him as weak and ineffectual. Never one to push himself forward, or offer his opinion on anything, he preferred to take the easy route and leave all the major decisions in life to his wife, which included the rearing of their only child.

He spent his days collecting folk's cast-offs in his cart and selling them on to other dealers for a bob or two. Scrap metal was on the up and up at the moment. He'd happen do all right out of this war if he played his cards right. The work required more instinct than skill, which suited him perfectly. In the evenings he would eat the supper Rita had prepared for him, keeping his head down while she ranted on over something or other, then he'd escape to the pub, or a race meeting. If he'd had a bad week and he'd no money, Joe was happier standing on a street corner talking to his mates than stopping in with his family. He avoided trouble and his wife, with equal dedication, and, as Daisy grew into a young woman and began to rebel against the strictures set by her mother, his only response was to stay out even more.

Joe was well aware that he'd neglected his only daughter, that being out of the house so much had left him with not the first idea how to talk to her. If she'd been a lad, happy to come fishing with him, or stand him a pint, it might have been different. He would've liked a son but, after Daisy's birth, Rita had made it abundantly plain that there would be no more babies. Most men would have stood up to Rita's bossiness, maybe even clocked her one now and then to bring her into line, but that wasn't Joe's style. He'd opted for a different course. Not once, in all the years of their marriage, had he ever contradicted her in anything. Some might judge this as weakness on his part, but then they hadn't seen the way she treated her own sister, or her dying mother for that matter. No, Joe didn't see his behaviour as weakness, he looked upon it as his best means of survival.

Now she'd sent him to do her dirty work, as was her wont. Not that he'd had owt to do with that other business, refusing to take any part in it. He'd been disappointed, angry too in a way that Daisy, a child of his, should behave so wantonly but he'd said nowt to anyone about the matter. Only once had he come close to expressing an opinion to Rita on the subject.

'I'm not happy about this business,' he'd remarked mildly.

'You're not, eh?'

He'd seen the challenge in her eyes. 'Not that it's owt to do wi' me. If'n you want to give away our Daisy's babby, then you find it a home. Don't ask me to do it. That's women's work.'

'Aye, and we know what men's work is,' she'd told him, her mouth twisted in that nasty way she adopted whenever she spoke to him. 'To take their pleasure and leave us holding the babby. Oh, I'll find it a home right enough, in fact I reckon I've found one already. So you keep yer trap shut. No prattling to yer mates if I tell you whose it is.'

'No, don't tell me. I don't want to know.' And he'd walked out of the house to avoid hearing the details.

After the child had been born, and it was a boy, a part of him wished he'd let Daisy bring the kid home. It might've been nice to have a babby about the place again, the boy he'd always longed for. But then, it would never have worked. Rita would have made all their lives a misery from dawn to dusk. So happen things had worked out for the best after all.

He glanced up at Daisy now as she came into the room and

was filled with a rush of pity for her. He'd forgotten how pretty she was with all that mass of bright golden brown curls. No wonder the chaps all fell for her but she wasn't a bad lass, only a bit daft and dizzy, as many were at her age. She'd grow out of it, as they all did. She looked better, in fact, than he'd seen her look in a long while: lost that pastiness about her skin and was positively blooming. Happen it suited her, living here in this Cumberland village.

Daisy stood awkwardly at the door, reluctant to enter, fingers grasping tightly to the brass knob; the very shadows of this rarely used room seeming to reflect the sombreness of her mood. She expected to be faced with the inevitable questions, the silent expression of disappointment for ever evident in her father's face. Yet all her life she had only ever longed for him to love her.

When Daisy entered, he'd been sitting on the edge of Mr Chapman's armchair, straight-backed and awkward, probably wishing he'd never agreed to come or that Rita hadn't made him. As she approached he leaped to his feet and came to her with hands outstretched. 'Eeh, our Daisy, tha's lookin' reet well, all pink-cheeked and blooming.'

From his words, anyone would think he was pleased to see her, yet the truth was revealed in the way he dropped his hands before he reached her, attempted to put them in his pockets, then remembering he was in his best suit letting them hang loose at his sides, not quite sure what to do with them. It was a relief to Daisy that he made no attempt to kiss her, merely stood a few feet off, considering her, as if she were an unknown exhibit in a museum. They'd never been close. In many ways he was like a stranger to her and, in Daisy's opinion, it was far too late to change things now.

'This is a surprise,' she said, for want of something to say.

'Aye well, when we got Mr Chapman's letter, Mother thought I should come and, er – um, have a bit of a chat like.'

'Why didn't she come herself?' Now that would have been

no surprise at all. One whiff of scandal and Rita Atkins was usually on the trail like a bloodhound.

'She's not been too well lately, to tell you the truth. Not at all herself. In fact, I were glad of the excuse to come. That's why I'm here really. The fact is, Daisy, Mother wants you back home.'

'She what?' This was the last thing Daisy had expected to hear.

'She wants you to come home. Most of the evacuees are back by now, since nowt seems to be happening in the war like, so it wouldn't look odd, and that other business – well, nobody knows nowt about that, save for them involved. It were all quietly and privately arranged. Least said, soonest mended, eh? Like I say, Mother's not been so good lately and she wants you back so, in the circumstances, happen it'd be fer t'best.' It was a long speech for Joe, and left him breathless.

'In the circumstances?'

He shifted his feet, looking trapped. 'Well, we don't want any more – haccidents, now do we?' He pronounced the word with an aitch in it, as he always did when wanting to emphasise a word. 'Nay, I'm sure you've learnt from your mistakes in the past, and wouldn't dream of repeating them. I told Mother as much, but she said it's better to be safe than sorry.'

'What's that supposed to mean?' Daisy could feel the usual sense of injustice fuelling her anger inside and she obstinately refused to show any sign of understanding her father's words. Why did her mother always think the worst of her? If he'd something to say, let him come right out and say it, instead of all this nonsense about Mam not being well.

Joe again shuffled his feet, glowering down at the polished toes of his Sunday best boots. He thrust his hands in his trouser-pockets and pulled them as quickly out again. Nay, but this was a bad business. Why did women have to be so blasted difficult? If she'd been a lad, he could've come straight out with it, given him a leathering, and that would've been the end of the matter. A girl was more canny, good at saying one thing and thinking another, and this lass of his was as slippy as a wet herring, more like her mother than she cared to admit. 'You know very well what she means. This young chap what you're seeing. Best you put a stop to all that nonsense, afore it all gets out of hand like. Anyroad, what with the way she's feeling right now, like I say – she needs you back home.'

'Are you saying she wants me to look after her?'

'Aye, that's about the way of it. She's done her back in, d'you see, summat to do with a slipped disc, and she can barely move an inch. Nay, she's in a proper pickle, lass, having to stop in bed all day, and sleep on a board. She needs you to look after the house, mek the meals, do the washing and so on. So here I am, to fetch you back home,' and he beamed at her, just as if he were doing her a favour.

He'd stretched the truth of course, as had Rita when she'd told him what to say. She'd strained a muscle, lifting something she shouldn't, but every disc in her spine, as with every cell in her cunning brain, was fit and strong and working well.

Truth or lie, he could see the tale wasn't working. Daisy was looking at him as if he were out of his head. 'You think I'd come back after you told me never to darken your doors again? After you threw me out and gave away my baby? You think I'd even want to stay in the same house as you? Don't make me laugh. Things haven't been easy since I left home, but life is a darned sight better than it was before and I'm certainly not leaving here now, not when I'm just settling in.'

Not when she'd just met Harry.

His face became, if possible, even more sombre and his voice adopted a doleful, censuring note, for the idea of returning to Salford without Daisy, as instructed, didn't bear thinking of. Rita would never let him hear the end of it. 'Don't let us down again, girl. I told Mother you wouldn't. Don't prove me wrong.'

Daisy's eyes filled with a rush of tears, though whether with temper or anguish she couldn't rightly have said. She blinked them away angrily. 'Oh, for goodness' sake, why can't either of you trust me? Why can't you show some faith in my common sense?'

'Because you haven't got any, Daisy. You're a dreamer. Daisy Daydream that's what you are, what you've always been.'

'That's not true. You know it isn't.'

'Oh aye, it is, Daisy. You act straight from the heart without even stopping to think, that's what you do. Always did.'

'Well there are times when showing a little affection and care is no bad thing. I'd certainly have benefited from a bit more of that from you two. Mam calling me a daydream is her way of avoiding her share of the blame. How could I know about babies and suchlike if she didn't tell me? And what I did learn from my friends was mainly old wives' tales and not to be relied upon. I was an innocent, just waiting to be taken advantage of, and she knows it. All right, so I made a mistake, a bad one as it turns out but for heaven's sake, I've paid a high price for it. And how many times do I have to apologise, eh? Why don't you both just leave me in peace?'

Daisy thought he might see how upset she was and put his arms about her to comfort her. But in the awkward silence that followed this impassioned little speech, Joe Atkins stood, cap in hand, awkwardly wishing he'd gone and played dominoes with his mates and not got himself mixed up with women's business after all. He certainly wouldn't again.

Mrs Chapman, listening at the door for an appropriate moment to make her entrance, chose this moment of obvious silence to come sailing in, without a knock and quite unannounced. Daisy turned away quickly to stare out of the window, her vision of the street outside blurred by unshed tears. 'Ah, there you are dear. I do hope you are having a lovely visit with your father. I've made tea and sandwiches for him. Go and fetch the tray from the kitchen, Daisy, there's a good girl.'

The pair of them stood in the street as Daisy explained with a calm and measured firmness, why she wouldn't be returning with him to Salford. The last hour had passed with painful slowness with Mrs Chapman performing her social role of hostess with an increasing desperation, doing her utmost to maintain a flow of polite conversation while Joe responded in awkward monosyllables and Daisy had simply wished the floor would open and swallow them all up.

Daisy was saying how it was far too late to play happy families. 'You both had your chance and you let me down, every bit as badly as you seem to think I failed you. Let's be honest, neither you nor Mam ever had much time for me, and were probably glad to see the back of me. Let's just leave things as they are, shall we?'

Joe looked disconcerted by such plain speaking and, as usual when confronted with an unpalatable truth, avoided responsibility by placing any blame firmly in Rita's lap. 'It weren't my idea to give t'child away and you know how there's no stopping your mother, once she's getten an idea in her head.'

'Don't I know it.'

'But she wants you home now, to keep an eye on you properly like. If I go back without you, she'll say that it's not your place to decide what's best, that you're still under age and should do as we tell thee. Mother has only ever wanted to do what's right for you.'

'What's right for her, you mean.'

'That's an unkind thing to say Daisy, and unworthy of you.'

Daisy looked upon this self-righteous stranger who was her father and felt a deep sadness inside. Why wouldn't he face up to the truth and take some share of the responsibility for the mess they were in? Rita had never given consideration to anyone but herself, and Joe had never stayed in the house long enough to challenge her word of law.

'All Mam really cares about is what the neighbours would think, what people might say. That has been her yardstick all along, not my welfare, nor the child I gave birth to.'

The familiar choking sensation blocked Daisy's throat as again she ached to know where her son might be at this precise moment. Whose arms were holding him, who was kissing his soft baby cheek, changing his nappy, giving him his feed? Consequently, her tone acquired a hard edge in her parting words. 'Tell Mam I'm sorry she's not well, if that's really true, but I don't need anyone to keep an eye on me. I can look after meself these days, ta very much, and I've no intention of making me life any worse than it already is by giving in any more to her whims and fancies. I've broken free of her domineering ways and mean to remain so. Tell her that!'

Joe looked shocked. 'Nay, lass. She'll not like that. She'll not like that one bit.'

'Just tell her, that's all.'

'Eeh, well, I'll do me best,' he said, the mournful note back in his voice. 'I'll do what I can for thee, lass, but don't bank on her agreeing to leave you here. Don't bank on it at all.' If Joe knew anything about his wife, she'd never stop her scheming ways, not till they were hammering the coffin nails in.

He swung about and began to walk away, shoulders hunched, hands sliding thankfully into his pockets, as if his duty had been done and he could be himself again, at last.

It was as he turned the corner of the street that the thought came to Daisy, and she ran after him to catch him up. 'Aunt Florrie – remember? Doesn't she live here in the Lakes somewhere?'

'Aye.'

'Do you know where?'

'Near Keswick, so far as I can recall. I've no idea of the address.'

'And what's her name, her married name?'

'Pringle. She's called Florrie Pringle.'

'Thanks.' She'd never called him Dad, and she didn't now. The moment had been missed long ago.

Silence descended once again as father and daughter stood awkwardly facing each other, each wondering how to end the misery of this meeting. Joe settled the matter by jerking the neb of his cap in a gesture of farewell, muttered something about not wanting to miss his bus, then sidled away, his pace quickening with each step, as if he couldn't escape quickly enough. 'Ta ra then. We'll see you soon, happen.'

'Happen,' Daisy agreed, both somehow aware that this might be the last she ever saw of either of her parents.

Daisy didn't linger to watch him go but turned on her heels and hurried inside. She flew upstairs to her room, closed the door and leaned back against it with a sigh of relief before promptly bursting into tears.

Daisy's natural inclination was to turn to Harry for comfort, but how could she? That would involve explaining why Joe was so concerned, how he expected her to misbehave because she'd already done so once before, which would never do at all. She'd no wish to take any risks over losing Harry. She needed him too much. Finally Daisy acknowledged, to herself at least, that she was in love, but, instead of being ashamed of getting over Percy so quickly, as she should be, she felt positively brimming with excitement. Just being with Harry filled her with joy and happiness and with each passing day he became more and more important to her, the dread of separation growing ever greater for them both.

So why would she risk spoiling that by telling him stuff that would only upset him?

He was being trained to fly Tiger Moths, but even that couldn't last for ever. Some day soon, he'd be off, and then what? Daisy worried about this as she lay in her bed every night. Whenever he could wangle a day off to take her out, she'd feel sick with anticipation beforehand in case this was the day he would say goodbye. She loved him so much but sometimes she'd wonder where it was all going to lead? Would they ever get together? Would the war ever end? He loved her too, she was certain of it. Well, almost certain. But how would he feel if he knew the truth about her? What would his reaction be then?

Hadn't her mother made it clear that a man wasn't interested in second-hand goods and that he'd discover any lies she'd told him, on her wedding night. Daisy believed all of this as a matter of course, that in this respect at least, Rita must be right. It filled her with fear that Harry might find out about her murky past and decide she wasn't the girl for him. Men got funny ideas in their heads yet she didn't believe it was possible, or right, for her to keep her secret for ever.

Often, on the days they were together, happy and loving, she would scold herself for only looking on the black side, for not trusting him and only expecting the worst. After all, he'd never asked for more than she was prepared to give him. A kiss and a cuddle seemed to be enough whenever they walked out in the countryside, or when they sat in the back row at the pictures together, even when he walked her home afterwards in the black-out. This seemed to prove that he respected her, and Daisy loved him for that too.

If only she could keep that respect, even after she'd fully confided in him. Then she would know that he truly loved her. And surely he would appreciate how very young and naïve she'd been at the time? All she had to do was to work out the best way to tell him.

'Have you ever had any other girlfriends, before me?' she asked him one day. 'Serious ones, I mean, where you – you know. Did *it*!' Her cheeks flushed bright crimson, yet Daisy didn't regret asking the question. This might be the very opening she needed to confess her own terrible secret.

He glanced at her, then quickly away again, shrugging his shoulders, trying to look casual and manly, but when he caught the querying look of hope and anticipation in her eye he misjudged it completely and gathered her close in his arms. 'Aw, don't look like that, love. I know chaps are supposed to have loads of experience before they settle down but, to be honest, I haven't had much at all. I've never done it with anyone, any more than you have, eh?'

The smile in his eyes as he looked down into hers was almost more painful than she could bear, for he clearly expected a negative response, and that's what he got.

'Course I haven't. What kind of girl d'you think I am? It was only that, like you say, chaps are supposed to spread their charms and get in a bit of practice first.'

'Well, not this one. I was saving myself for the right girl. Aren't I soppy?'

'Oh no, I think that's lovely.'

'And after meeting you, Daisy, I'm that glad I did.'

And her heart just melted inside at the thought that he'd saved himself specially for her. Harry couldn't understand why she burst into tears.

Daisy couldn't remember a winter as cold as this one. Rivers froze over, pipes burst, roads became blocked by snow and utterly impassable, and the dreaded rationing started in earnest, cutting down on supplies of bacon, sugar, butter and other fats. It didn't lessen her own happiness one bit but Mr and Mrs Chapman rarely stopped complaining about how bad things were. Finland fell in March, Denmark was occupied in April, the blame for which Mr Chapman put squarely upon Neville Chamberlain's lap rather than Hitler's, as they'd got everything wrong from the start, in his opinion. He would explain this to them at great length each evening, as they sat with the black-out curtains drawn, listening to the wireless.

'If they'd shown more sense, we wouldn't be in the mess we're in now.'

'Yes, dear,' said Mrs Chapman, barely pausing in her knitting of balaclavas, save to correct Daisy in the mistakes she was making with her own effort, or pick up yet another stitch that she'd dropped.

It was in April too that Harry finally got his posting, to Silloth, just along the coast. He wasn't expected to be there long but it was the best news they could have hoped for, as it meant they could still see each from time to time, if not perhaps as regularly as before.

'You won't forget to write, Daisy? I'll be watching for your letters.'

'Every day, like I promised. And you'll write to me too.'

'Aye, but if you find your Aunt Florrie, you'll let me have the address of where you move to, won't you?'

'Oh, Harry, course I will. You'll always be the first to be told everything about me.' Well, she thought with a gentle sigh, almost everything. She'd been so much in love, so engrossed with the excitement of looking forward to her next meeting with Harry, that she'd forgotten all about her earlier determination to find Aunt Florrie. It no longer seemed quite so important. Seeing Harry, that was all that really mattered.

Mr Chapman expressed himself highly relieved when, in May, a coalition with Winston Churchill was formed, and not a moment too soon as it was swiftly followed by the fall of Holland and Belgium. A call sent out via word of mouth for whatever small craft could be made available, conveyed the frightening message that British troops were very possibly trapped with the sea in front of them and the Germans behind. Later, when pictures of the Dunkirk rescue emerged, together with stories of wounded and war weary soldiers being dramatically plucked from the beaches, it seemed that the war wasn't phoney any more. And far from boring. Defeat now seemed a terrifying possibility, making even Megan determined to do her bit.

'I've told Mrs Marshall that if she'll let us stop on a bit longer, I'll not be naughty no more. And our Trish says she won't cry in the bath never again, even when she has her hair washed.'

'That's good, Megan. That's very good indeed, and what did Mrs Marshall say?'

'She said she'd ask Mr Marshall.'

So all their lives were still hanging in the balance, even the children's although Daisy hoped and prayed she could keep them safe. So far, she'd managed to stave off the proposed move by persuading Mrs Marshall to keep them on the promise that she herself would go in every evening, after work, to help put them to bed. And, being equally concerned for Mrs Marshall's health, she offered to do some heavy chores for her, in addition to the ones she did for Mrs Chapman.

Mrs Marshall protested that Daisy had enough work to do already, not being unaware of the situation in the Chapman household.

'I don't mind, really I don't. They love being here with you, and I get to see them every day.'

'But only if you have the time, Daisy.'

'I'll come whenever I possibly can, I promise. So you put your feet up and look after yourself. Just try to hang on a little bit longer. Please! You never know, they might be a real boon when the baby comes, another pair of hands you know.' And because Mrs Marshall loved children so much, and had grown quite fond of these two imps, as she called them, she'd agreed to let them stay a few more weeks. But the time for her confinement was drawing near.

'When I must finally decide what's to be done.'

It was the best Daisy could hope for.

Mrs Chapman expressed an opinion that her neighbour was misguided and Daisy a saint. 'You're wasting your time trying to save those children, my dear. Such creatures are beyond redemption, nothing but a trial, having already polluted dear Mrs Marshall's carpets and mattresses. Their mother seems to be quite unable to raise them properly, devoid of any sense, and bone idle to boot. Oh, do put the kettle on dear, I'm gasping for a cup of tea. We would certainly not have taken on anyone younger than yourself, dear Daisy, however much the authorities may have insisted.'

Daisy said nothing. Obligingly, she put on the kettle, made tea and brought it to her landlady, together with the biscuit tin. Mrs Chapman always enjoyed a wafer biscuit late in the afternoon, so long as Daisy was there to fetch it for her.

'And for what, I ask myself? For eight shillings and sixpence a week? Why, we couldn't feed a kitchen maid on that, should we be fortunate to have one,' she remarked tartly.

Daisy thought that she really had no need of a kitchen maid, not while she had her. But then Mrs Chapman invited her to sit down, help herself to a biscuit and tell her all about her day, and Daisy remembered why she liked her. She was lonely and tired, that was all. Who knew what old age would bring for any of us, Daisy concluded generously, and went to fetch herself a cup.

Laura

11

Lane End Farm kitchen had a flagged floor, now sealed but which in the old days would need to be scrubbed on a daily basis; an old fashioned range with a rocking chair beside it and a clippy rug in front of the hearth. A hinged bar still swung out over the fire from which would once hang a kettle or pan to heat water. The baking would have been done in the side oven and Laura could imagine her grandmother baking scones and pastry first when the heat was at its most intense, followed by the lighter baking and then the bread, and last of all when the oven was 'falling', the favourite tatie pot or casserole for supper. In later years, Daisy had been professional enough to install an electric cooker and it was this that Laura used for her own cooking.

Laura made a new version of chocolate mousse, the traditional sticky toffee pudding and some sourdough bread. She also tried her hand at oatcakes, or haverbread, as it was more properly called. With a little flour added for greater elasticity, it would have been eaten with every meal at one time, rolled up with hot bacon, or dipped in stews or gravy, filling hungry stomachs and supplementing meagre rations. Laura wasn't sure whether her own was quite crisp enough, and decided to roll it out thinner next time.

Tired, but satisfied with her first efforts at traditional Cumbrian fare, she headed straight for the shower. The water was blissfully hot and refreshing, soothing frayed nerves as well as tired muscles. Afterwards, she lay down on the bed and must have fallen asleep because when she woke it was quite dark, and she hadn't the faintest idea what time it was. It took a moment before Laura realised someone was banging about downstairs. An intruder, and there was something about the sounds coming up the stairs which made his identity plain. At one time her husband might have woken her with a kiss and some passionate love-making. Now, he apparently achieved the same effect by bashing pans together in her kitchen.

'Felix, this is a surprise.' She'd brushed her dark hair loose over her shoulders, quickly applied eye make-up and lipstick and slipped into a long skirt and silk shirt. Though Laura would have loved to simply slop about in jogging trousers and T-shirt after her long tiring day, Felix hated to see her anything less than smart and her current rebellion didn't stretch to annoying him any further, not until she'd achieved her object. 'How did your trip go? Get what you wanted?' She kept her tone light deliberately.

He was bashing the ice tray against the sink, hence the noise, had clearly downed one whisky already and was about to pour another. She took the tray from him and ran it under the tap, fixed the drink just how he liked it and handed it to him with a smile.

He took a large swallow. 'The trip was a total waste of time and money. Complete fake. And I really don't have time for all this nonsense, Laura.' His voice sounded as brittle and cold as the ice that chinked against his glass.

'All what nonsense?' Laura leaned back against the sink, considering him, something she hadn't done properly in ages. He'd put on weight, was beginning to look positively paunchy and flabby about the face, almost florid. He'd never been the most patient of men but now his temper seemed to be growing increasingly irascible, his movements jerky and abrupt as if he was having trouble keeping control. 'I'm afraid I don't quite understand what you're talking about. The trip, or something entirely different?'

'You know damn well what I'm talking about. All this dashing back and forth up the motorway to the damn Lakes. And you said the weather was glorious. Look at it, freezing cold and starting to snow. It's a miracle I arrived in one piece.'

'Don't exaggerate Felix. The roads are all perfectly clear, I've driven out myself most days. You haven't dashed back and forth, and this is only your first visit since the funeral more than two weeks ago.'

'And my last. Get your bags packed. We're going home right now.' He shot back the whisky in one, slamming the glass down on the sink with far more force than necessary. When Laura gave no indication of moving, he continued in tight, clipped tones, 'Would you like me to do it for you?'

'At any other time in our marriage, help with the packing would have been welcomed. But not now, Felix. It's far too late. I'm not leaving, you see. I'm staying. Not just for a week, or for a month, but for as long as I feel like it.' This wasn't the way she'd intended to tell him but he'd driven her to it.

'I beg your pardon?' His face was not florid now, but puce, darkening to a deep crimson even before her eyes. 'Is this some kind of joke?'

'No joke. But it is certainly going to be better fun than my life has been for the last several years, with you. I've done quite a lot of thinking this last week or two, and I've made up my mind. I intend, by early summer, to reopen Lane End Farm as a guesthouse, to take over where Daisy left off when she retired all those years ago. I've thought it all through. I'll need to refurbish of course, bring the rooms up to date, have the necessary inspections done, register with the tourist board and so on, and hopefully be ready to open by early June.'

'Have you gone quite mad?'

'I don't think so. It seems an eminently sensible plan to me. I'll admit I haven't settled the finer details yet, found plumbers or whatever, but intend to do so over the next few weeks.'

His face seemed to have set like stone, rigid with temper. 'I've already made it perfectly clear to you, Laura. We are selling this house.'

Even now, when she'd finally made her decision to end her marriage, it still hurt that he didn't express any regret over the fact that she was leaving him, that his first – perhaps his only thought was for the money he would lose by not selling. She blinked and turned away, took a packet of minced beef from the fridge and started to heat some olive oil in a pan. 'I don't think so, Felix. Selling wouldn't be a good idea right now.'

'So you mean to bankrupt me, do you?'

'Oh for goodness' sake, your sense of drama is magnificent. Any hole you are currently in is, I am sure, temporary. You've wriggled out of every other. Besides, I spoke to the solicitor and agricultural property isn't selling well right now, so putting it on the market wouldn't be an answer. It could take years. It would be a far better investment, he told me, to hang on to it for as long as we can.'

'What the hell does an old fuddy-duddy solicitor in some backwater know about the property market?' The sarcasm had gone and he was shouting, reaching again for the whisky bottle as if needing to refuel his anger.

Calmly Laura dropped the meat in the hot oil and began to sear it, turning it gently. 'A great deal actually. And he isn't an old fuddy-duddy but quite young and with it.'

'Ah, fancy yourself with a toy boy, eh?'

'Now who's being ridiculous?'

'I told you to leave everything to me. Didn't I say it would be a mistake your staying here? Now, on the word of some tin-pot local brief, you've decided against selling and got some foolish fantasy into your head about going into business. You imagine opening a guesthouse is the answer to your mid-life crisis, do you? And what about me? I'm supposed to just smile and say fine, yes dear, do as you like dear?'

'I don't really think it is any concern of yours what I do.

Not any more.' Laura selected a knife from the rack and began to chop onions.

Felix pushed his face to within inches of her own, not lowering his voice one decibel as he raged at her like a mad thing. 'Your head is *empty*, Laura, except for the cotton wool that comprises your brain. Don't overtax it. Stick to your cooking.' He was jabbing a finger hard at her skull.

Despite how her head was jerked by each stabbing motion, Laura studiously ignored it, continuing to chop onions until finally he ran out of breath and stopped. Calmly, she set the meat to one side in an earthenware casserole, and tossed the onions into the pan.

'Are you *listening* to me?'

She was finding it hard to breathe although her voice, when she finally found it, sounded remarkably calm. 'I rather thought that a guesthouse would be a good idea, and I'd enjoy the company. I get rather lonely stuck at home, all on my own the whole time.'

'Is that meant as some sort of criticism? Are you implying that I neglect you?'

'Heaven forbid! Felix, our marriage hasn't worked in years, for many reasons. It might have helped if I'd been allowed to work at the gallery. I would have loved that.' She scattered two or three mild chilli peppers on to the meat, her hand shaking slightly, hoping he wouldn't notice. She wanted him to simply accept what she had to say, and go.

'And *you* know how hopeless you would have been, far too gawky and clumsy. You'd have dropped a priceless vase, broken a valuable picture frame or some such.'

'You sound just like my father.'

'Perhaps because he and I show sense, and you don't.'

Laura could feel the tension tightening inside her, a coiled spring of emotion that threatened to break free and let fly. She knew he was deliberately attempting to provoke her. So often, in their rows, she was the one in a rage of tearful frustration who wanted to throw something, and Felix cold and manipulative.

Now, the tables had been turned and she was the cool one, outwardly at least, calm and composed about her decision, and supremely rational. She'd no intention of dissolving into tears so that he could mop them dry and tell her this was what happened when she started dreaming foolish dreams and expecting the impossible; reminding her how well he looked after her and kept her safe from harm. Of course he did. Locked up in luxurious but rigid seclusion while he got on with living his life, Laura thought. No, no, she couldn't go on any longer. Not any more. Imagining him with Miranda or some other young girl he currently fancied while she waited by the phone for him to say when, or if, he was coming home. Where was *her* life? *Her* needs? *Her* desires? Not to mention her pride and sense of self-worth.

She drew in a deep, calming breath. 'I believe what I'm trying to say is that I'm leaving you. It wasn't an easy decision to make and it's come as something of a surprise to me too, that I've actually found the courage at last. Perhaps being left this house has helped.'

'Don't talk stupid!' Flecks of spittle from his fury spattered across her face. 'Absolutely no question of you doing anything of the sort! You can't stay here, and you certainly aren't leaving me. I won't allow it.'

Laura laughed, though there was little humour in the sound. 'And how do you propose to prevent me? You don't keep a wife by issuing an order, or sending her a fax to that effect. You do it with love and care and attention, all those things you've tended to ignore over the years. As for the house, it may have slipped your notice Felix, but it's mine. Not yours. So the decision of what to do with it is mine, and for the moment at least, I've decided to keep it.'

Laura thought, for a brief moment, that he was going to hit her and experienced a jolt of unexpected fear. Perhaps she'd finally driven him to the limits too. She moved quickly away across the kitchen, ostensibly to fetch a tin of kidney beans from the cupboard but wanting to put some distance between them, fervently wishing that she hadn't chosen this precise moment to reveal her plans. What with the threat of snow and him heading once more for the whisky bottle, it would mean he couldn't drive, so he'd be forced to stay overnight, a situation she did not relish. He might well continue in this fashion, ranting and raving at her until, finally exhausted and desperate for peace, she'd repent and back down from her stand.

Exactly as her father had done, he claimed to have misheard her. 'I'm not sure I quite got that, Laura.'

She mustn't let him bully her. Hadn't she stood up to Robert firmly enough, and could do the same against Felix if she held her nerve. Laura knew it was the only way to survive. Going back to life as she had known it at Cheadle Hulme, after catching a glimpse of what it could be here at Lane End Farm, was quite out of the question. 'Oh, I think you did. Daisy left the house to me. *Me!* I don't want to sell it. Which is my choice to make.'

He was spluttering with fury, pacing the kitchen like a caged lion, pausing occasionally to fling some fresh insult at her, about how stupid she was, how ineffectual, how she could never cope without him, how she depended upon him entirely. 'Hell's teeth, I'll not let you get away with this. You'll ruin my reputation, my *business* for God's sake, with your childish act of rebellion. You think you can go over my head as if this house has nothing at all to do with me, when we've been married all these years?'

'You know that I'm always interested in your opinion, Felix, but my decision is made.' Laura put on her brightest, hostess smile. 'Now, to more practical concerns. Have you eaten? Would you like some dinner? Oh, and if you were thinking of staying the night, due to the whisky and the worsening weather, I could make up a bed in one of the spare bedrooms. Otherwise, you might care to call a taxi, while the roads are still reasonably clear.'

'You're selfish, do you know that?' he roared. 'Always were. It's *me, me, me*. That's all you care about. You haven't the first idea what you've done, have you, Laura?'

'Oh yes, I know exactly what I've done, and what I'm going to do next.' Laura was reaching for a jar of basmati rice but managed to withhold the quip that she'd just made some chilli con carne and now intended to make the rice. This wasn't the moment for silly jokes.

Perhaps he guessed her thoughts from the light-hearted tone of her voice for he snatched the jar from her hand and threw it with all his might. It hit the kitchen dresser which stood against the opposite wall, where it smashed into a dozen pieces, scattering shards of pottery all over the flagged floor, taking with it several broken cups, saucers, plates and other items.

'Dear God!' Laura put her hand to her mouth, heart racing with real fear this time.

Swinging round on his heel, he grabbed her by the arm and shook her violently, like a dog. For an instant she thought that he was about to fling her in the same direction when a voice from the door paralysed them both.

'I think it's time you left, don't you? Don't worry about the mess. I'll clear it up.'

Laura could hardly believe her eyes but she'd never been more pleased to see anyone in all her life. David Hornsby stood in the open door, looking perfectly relaxed, and as if he had every right to be there. His sheepskin coat was covered with a light scattering of snow which now he began to unbutton casually. He tugged the woollen hat from his head and unwound the loose scarf knotted about his neck but the benign smile on his face was entirely at odds with the light of grim determination in the blue eyes.

She whispered his name in a mixture of wonder and relief, at exactly the same moment as Felix yelled: 'Who the hell are you?'

David merely smiled and dumped his wet clothing into the utility room opposite, giving the impression he'd been doing that for years, which he probably had, Laura thought, whenever he came to see Daisy. Ignoring Felix completely, he walked calmly over to Laura and remarked amiably, 'Hm, something smells good. I did come on the right night, didn't I? Only, with seeing the car outside, I did wonder.'

Laura somehow managed to swallow the bolt of hysterical laughter that had come into her throat. He was telling her that he'd seen the car, been concerned, and, as before, had walked in bold as brass, just to check she was OK. In any other circumstances she'd have called that arrogant. 'Yes, yes, of course. Dinner won't be long. This is my husband, Felix. He's rightly anxious about the threat of snow which looks as if it's started already. Is it bad?' Felix still held her wrist in a punishing grip but, shaking herself free of his hold, she moved back to the cooker to check on the chilli.

'Quite a covering up on the high fells but the main roads are still clear, for now. I certainly face a cold night ahead, checking on my stock.'

It was all so civilised it was almost laughable, were it not for Felix seething quietly beside her it might well have seemed like the start of a pleasant dinner party. Laura turned to him with a smile, determined to maintain the charade. 'I assume you'll want to be on your way then, Felix, before it gets too bad. You won't want to risk not being able to get to the gallery in the morning. Oh, sorry, I was forgetting. This is my neighbour, David Hornsby. He rents, or owns, much of the land around here and has promised to help me find out more about Daisy.'

David acknowledged the introduction with a brisk nod but did not offer to shake hands. Laura could tell by the narrowness of his gaze that Felix had been weighing up his options, toying with the notion of planting a fist on David's jaw but had begun to reconsider. Bullying a wife was easily within his grasp, tackling a fit, well-muscled male would not, perhaps, be quite so wise.

Ignoring the introduction, he strode to the door. 'Stay on for a while longer then, if that's what you want, and see where it gets you. A few months in this freezing hell-hole with only the company of peasants and you'll be begging to come back to me and civilisation. You'll come to your senses Laura, I know it.' He slammed out of the house, gunned up the engine and roared off down the lane at cracking speed. Laura had to sit down, she was shaking so badly.

'Feeling better? Or do you need more of this?' Dinner was over, although Laura had found her appetite quite gone and eaten very little. They'd demolished one bottle of wine already and David was holding up another, a quirk of one eyebrow asking her consent to open it.

'Why not? Drowning my sorrows sounds like quite a good idea.'

'I'll allow you another glass only if you eat up your dinner like a good girl.'

'Don't call me that.'

'I'm sorry.' He looked startled by the snappy response to his joke, as well he might. It was so unlike her.

Laura stared gloomily down at her plate. 'I'm sorry too. It's not you that I'm angry with, so I've no right to take out my bad temper on you.'

He set the bottle to one side and sat down beside her. 'You're not in a temper. I couldn't imagine you ever being, but you are upset and have a right to be so. Any man who treats his wife in that fashion doesn't deserve to have one.'

'Nor will he have for much longer. That's what made Felix so angry. I told him about my decision to stay, which of course will mean divorce.'

'So be it! You deserve better.'

She turned and looked into his eyes. They were the palest shade of blue outlined with a rim of darker blue around the iris, looking at her with such an intensity that Laura found it impossible to break away. Even when he did so, it was only to allow his gaze to move over her face, her hair, seeming to take in every detail of her appearance, as if forming a picture he never wanted to forget, finally fastening on her mouth. 'I can't think of anything to say except something truly naff and clichéd like: did anyone ever tell you how lovely you are?'

'Why don't you say it then? Maybe I like those sort of clichés.'

Did she? Did she want this? Was she ready for it? Despite the undeniable attraction between them, was she prepared to break her marriage vows just because she'd finally decided on a divorce? Mind whirling and emotions spinning out of control, in that moment Laura couldn't have answered her own questions. She knew only that for the first time in years, she truly wanted a man other than her husband, to kiss her.

Yet to even start along that path would lead to disaster. It was far too soon. Turning away abruptly, she couldn't prevent a small sigh of regret escaping the tightness of her chest.

Perhaps he heard, or was sensitive to her feelings for he smiled, 'Maybe I should be on my way before I run the risk of taking advantage of the situation.'

'What situation?' Eyes suspiciously bright, she found the courage to face him.

'Your delicate emotional state, and increasing inebriation on an empty stomach.'

He got up to go and for the space of a second she very nearly cried out in protest but thankfully managed not to. What on earth was happening to her, behaving like a schoolgirl? Laura followed him to the door, the warm feeling inside growing and spreading like a fever as he buttoned the sheepskin jacket, turned up his collar and hooked the scarf she handed to him, loosely about his neck. Despite her best efforts, her eyes were betraying her, revealing how very much she wanted him to stay; how she longed to forget the weather, the sheep, Felix, everything but this unexpected and indefinable need.

There was no sign of a smile now as he gathered her face gently between his hands and kissed her, a soft sweet kiss with the barest hint of passion in it. In that moment she ached to respond, to reach her arms up around his neck, may well have done so but the next moment he was stepping away from her with a small shake of his head.

'If, or when, we do get together, you and I, and I certainly hope that it is the latter, I want it to be when you've had time to give proper consideration to the implications. Goodnight, lovely Laura. Lock the door after me, and take extra-special care of yourself.'

12

Britain responded to the deepening crisis by taking down signposts, painting out names on railway stations and other hoardings, and issuing a list of instructions and new regulations.

Daisy was particularly alarmed by the one which said that 'All persons could be required to place themselves, their services, and their property at the disposal of the government.' Did that mean she too might be moved, whether she liked it or not? She wasn't concerned about leaving the Chapmans particularly, but desperately needed to stay in the area to be close to Megan and Trish, as well as not wanting to move too far away from Harry.

Not that she'd have minded in the least if the government had decided to move her to a different job. She hated working in Mr Chapman's office. He still insisted on coming in to see her in the post room at frequent intervals, fetching her a warming mug of tea or leaning close over her shoulder, breathing down her neck while he checked that she was addressing the envelopes correctly. Often he would ask her to stay on to help him with what he termed 'a few end-of-the-day tasks', on the premise that she could be taken home in style, in his Morris car, afterwards.

There was something about the prospect of being confined with Mr Chapman in a motor car which did not appeal and Daisy always refused, saying she had to hurry home to do her chores for Mrs Chapman, so that she could then go and help look after the children next door.

'You've taken on far too much, Daisy dear. You'll wear yourself out.'

'No, no, I enjoy it. I like working about the house. I wouldn't do it otherwise.'

But one day, finally beaten down by his persistent persuasion, she agreed to stay behind. She was helping everyone else, why not Mr Chapman? Daisy spent an extra hour or more at the end of her normal work shift, cleaning out his desk and tidying his filing cabinet, which wasn't easy with him still using them. If she opened a drawer he would suddenly appear at her elbow, pressing up close as he reached in the cabinet for a file. She only had to move an inch in the wrong direction and he would choose the exact same moment to move too and they'd collide, which was unnerving, or she'd trip over a pile of files and scatter them everywhere and he'd then have to help her tidy them all up.

His size seemed to grow alarmingly in the small, cluttered office, and the smell of his sweat became overpowering.

'You're a good girl,' he told her. 'But I believe you're tired. Let's go home and you can finish this job tomorrow.'

The thought of another late session in his office was depressing but it was with a vast sense of relief that Daisy watched while he locked the office door and they finally headed homeward. Except that the car wasn't waiting for him outside the office, as it should have been. After several telephone calls, Mr Chapman was hugely affronted to discover that it had been driven away by the police, all because he'd left it parked on the street all day without locking the doors, also leaving the key in the ignition.

'I have been leaving it there for years,' he shouted at the young constable who had the misfortune to inform him of this fact. 'No one would dare to steal *my* car.'

'Well, happen a German soldier might, Mr Chapman, him not knowing how important you are,' the young constable commented tactfully.

They then had to go down to the police station and Mr Chapman had to fill in a great many forms, produce several documents to prove ownership of the car, and listen to a long lecture by the desk sergeant. By the time they finally did arrive home it was to find Mrs Chapman in a fine paddy, and neither one of them dared to complain about the fact that their dinner was cold.

Laura spent most of the following morning again searching the house for any sign of a marriage or birth certificate, or diary of some sort. She found a bundle of deeds for the house which kept her happily occupied for a good hour or more struggling to decipher the old handwriting, none of which added anything further to her stock of knowledge on Daisy. Could Daisy have deposited some of her private papers with a bank? It seemed hardly likely. Laura wondered if her father had any in his possession because, if so, there was little hope of persuading him to let her see them. He had most firmly put the past behind him, determined to blot Daisy out of his life, and out of Laura's too.

The implication that she'd been generous with her favours sat oddly with everything else she'd learned about her grandmother. Daisy didn't at all seem to be the sort to have an affair.

Laura sat back on her heels and closed her eyes. There was a time when she might have said the same thing about herself, and yet last night . . . She put her fingers to her lips, recalling the tender moments of David's kiss. The snow had melted with the morning sun, almost as if it were part of some magical fantasy, a strange mix of dream and nightmare. Felix storming about her kitchen while she calmly made chilli and then David doing his knight-in-shining-armour bit. It had taken on a surreal quality. The meal together after Felix had roared off had been delightful and exciting. Laura had indeed wanted them to be snowed in so that he would stay and the good feeling could go on and on.

There was no denying that she'd ached for him to make love to her. Was that what she wanted? And would it have led to an affair? Or simply a one-night stand? Either way, it might well have made it more difficult for her to gain a divorce, so she really ought to take care and show more sense. She was staying on here to build herself a new life, create a new independence and for that she needed income, which meant getting the guesthouse going. Soon. It would certainly not be conducive for clear thinking to fall into bed with the first good-looking male who happened along.

Perhaps Daisy had fallen for someone in just the same way. Perhaps Daisy and Harry had married too quickly, because of the war, and discovered they weren't suited quite so well as they'd imagined? Or he'd never come back at all.

'Oh, but that would be so sad.' Laura found that she'd spoken the words out loud. She wanted Daisy to marry her sweetheart and live happily ever after, have some time together at least.

Perhaps she'd fallen for Clem, as well as his house. Was that why he'd left it to her? No, no, far too mercenary. Yet if something had happened to Aunt Florrie, it might have left Daisy and Clem living dangerously intimate lives alone at Lane End Farm. But none of this seemed at all likely and so, in Laura's opinion, her father's condemnatory attitude towards his mother must be because of a foolish, youthful mistake, which anyone could make. What was it about men that drove them to cast the blame entirely on the woman when it quite plainly took two people to get into that sort of mess?

Laura still wondered if Daisy had some other dark secret, and, if so, how it could be discovered. If only walls really did have ears, and could speak as well, what a tale they would have to tell.

Looking in despair at the jumble of papers spread all over

the rug, she tidied them away hastily and reached for the phone. Time to see old Mr Capstick. The best person to tell her about Daisy's documents was Daisy's old solicitor.

It was half past nine by the time Daisy went next door and rattled Mrs Marshall's letterbox. The door was opened by her husband.

'Oh, hello Mr Marshall, I'm so sorry to disturb you but I just popped round to say that I'm sorry I wasn't able to come and help tonight but I . . .' Her explanation was stopped in mid-sentence as Mr Marshall cut in with the blunt words that his wife had been taken off to hospital.

Daisy paled. 'Oh no, she isn't losing the baby, is she?'

'They're hopeful that the problem is nothing worse than simple exhaustion. There's no bleeding this time, thank God, but she has some pains in her back so just in case, they've taken her in to keep her under observation overnight. I called the billeting officer and the children have been taken away.'

'Taken away?' Daisy was mortified.

'I packed their things myself. My wife is far more important to me than two waifs from Salford.'

'But . . .' Lost for words she took a deep breath and started again. 'Couldn't you at least have waited till I got home, Mr Marshall?'

'I'm sorry, Daisy, I know you're fond of them but as you said yourself, you weren't here and I didn't know whether you were coming later or not. Had you been, I might well have spoken to you about it, though it wouldn't have made the slightest difference. Generous as you are with your time, you can't be with them every minute, can you? You have your own work to do, after all. I'm not an unfeeling man but those two little live wires are more than Mabel can cope with right now, for all she's done her best.'

'Oh, I know she has. I know.'

'The little one, Trish, screamed the house down when I tried to explain to her that if we didn't send my dear wife away for a rest, the baby might die.'

'Oh dear, she probably thought that it was all her fault,' Daisy said. 'She's very sensitive about death, having already lost her gran, and Miss Pratt.'

'I can't help that. I must put my wife and my own child first. Megan thought at first I was saying there'd be no more room for them here, after the baby came, so she offered to sleep under the table. And when I said nobody will sleep under the table in my house, she said that it didn't bother her because she was used to it. That's where she'd slept at home when her mam had got a sailor in her bed. Really Daisy, I can't have such children around, not with a young, vulnerable baby to care for.'

'No, no, I do understand, and I'm not blaming you at all, Mr Marshall. It's just that . . . Did the billeting officer say where he was taking them?'

Mr Marshall shook his head. 'He said he'd find somewhere.'

Daisy felt too sick at heart to be able to respond to this without dissolving into tears. Since she'd lost her own little son, she seemed to have turned into a proper cry baby but she'd so hoped to keep the little girls close by her, where they felt secure and happy, and she could keep an eye on them. 'I'll go to the town hall tomorrow and ask where they are so that I can at least visit.'

Daisy felt sorry for Mr Marshall. The poor man was only trying to do his best for his wife, after all. The last thing they all wanted was for her to lose the baby. And Daisy was so concerned for Mrs Marshall, as well as being worried about Megan and Trish going to yet another unknown billet, that she felt quite unable to sit in the living room and listen to the wireless as she usually did at the end of the day, let alone sit and knit balaclavas and listen to Mrs Chapman's aimless chatter. She made the excuse of a headache, saying she wanted to go straight up to bed.

'Do you want a Beecham's powder, dear? Help yourself, you know where they are.'

'I'll be all right, thanks, nice as ninepence after a good night's sleep.' No, she wouldn't, Daisy thought. She felt devastated by the loss of her two little friends, and desperate to think of some way to help them. She lay awake for hours, shedding quite a few tears into her pillow, struggling to find a solution until exhaustion finally claimed her.

Laura found old Mr Capstick living in sheltered accommodation, not at all the doddering old man she'd expected but lively and alert or, as he said himself, 'still bright-eyed and bushy-tailed'. He claimed to be one of the useless males of his generation who couldn't cope once his wife had died. At a guess he was well into his eighties so she told him he deserved a little tender care and attention after a lifetime of hard work.

'It's certainly a treat to be visited by an attractive young woman. I'm sure there must be more to it than my ageing charms. What can I do for you, my dear?'

Laughing, Laura explained who she was and how interested she'd become in finding out more about Daisy. 'Admittedly all due, in the first place, to an enormous sense of guilt. I neglected her rather, for various reasons. Now I'm absolutely gripped, keen to learn anything I can about her. I was talking to your son, Nick, and he told me that it was through trying to locate Aunt Florrie that she came to Lane End in the first place. And apparently it's Uncle Clem we should thank for the house, since he insisted on leaving it to her and not to Florrie.'

'Oh yes indeed, that is very true. Clem wouldn't have it any other way. I'm afraid he and his wife didn't get on.'

This seemed to fit in uncomfortably well with her theory that Clem might have been Daisy's lover, and Laura wondered how to phrase her next question but, blushing slightly, decided to risk it. 'He wasn't a blood uncle though, was he? You don't think there was – well, anything between them, and that's why he chose Daisy in place of his wife?'

Old Mr Capstick put back his head and let out a great belly laugh. The chuckle rumbled from deep inside his plump stomach and soon Laura was laughing too. It was hard not to, as she'd clearly said something highly amusing. He took off his spectacles to wipe tears of laughter from his eyes, gave them a good rub with his handkerchief before continuing, 'Sorry to disappoint you, my dear, but nothing quite so melodramatic. Anyway, I doubt Clem would have had it in him. No, no, Florrie was a miserable old bugger and they didn't have a particularly easy marriage. Nothing suited her and she moaned from dawn to dusk about absolutely everything. As we say in these parts, she was never happy unless she had something to complain about. Daisy, bless her generous heart, was the only one who could deal with the woman.'

Laura was intrigued and yet disappointed all the same. She'd thought perhaps that this might be the answer, the secret that Daisy had kept to herself all these years. She was quite convinced that there must be another, besides the illegitimate child she bore, otherwise why call it a house of secrets? Plural! Why would her own son hate her with such a vehemence? Laura wasn't convinced this was simply because of the baby. 'Was that because of the child they lost? Nick mentioned something about it. That was perhaps why Daisy got on so well with her, because she too had lost a child.'

Old Mr Capstick glanced at her quizzically, eyes narrowing into a little frown. 'You know about that then, do you? About the child?'

'I know she had one and that he – I don't know all the details but I seem to remember when once she briefly told me the story, Daisy letting slip that it'd been a boy – and that he was given up for adoption against her will. Evidently her parents insisted that she keep the matter a secret, just as if it were something to be ashamed of.'

'That was certainly the way of it in those days, my dear. I'm afraid I can tell you nothing about the child, or about Daisy's personal life. It wouldn't be right. I acted for her in a legal capacity from time to time and maintained her confidentiality in life. Therefore, it is not for me to break it now that she is dead, not unless she had left strict instructions to the contrary. She was a very private person, living in seclusion up there on the side of the mountain. Though I can tell you that yes, you're right, it was a boy.'

'Thank you for that anyway.'

At that moment, a woman with a bright smile bustled in carrying a tray. 'What's this, Doris, ah tea? A gin and tonic would be more welcome.'

'Get away with you, it's only four o'clock. Not past the yard arm yet, or whatever you call it. You'll have to make do with tea and a bun for now.' Then she gave him a wink and promised him a shot of whisky later.

'I shall look forward to it, dearest Doris. Prompt at six.' The sparring had brought a fresh twinkle to his faded grey eyes and he seemed to soften slightly as Laura poured out the tea and handed him a slice of cake. 'Daisy was lovely,' he continued, a fond smile on his wrinkled old face. 'I was very fond of her. Always ready to help others with their problems, even when she had more than enough to deal with on her own account as well as running that boarding house which kept her on the go from morning till night, I can tell you that much.'

And he did, singing Daisy's praises at great length, chattering on for some time about how she helped do the place up and took folk in, at first as if they were strays in need of care, and then for more businesslike purposes; what a wonderful cook she was and how she still found time to help on the farm, selling her eggs on Keswick market.

'She confessed to me that once she'd come close to walking out, even to packing her bags and standing them in the hall. I think this was when the place was packed full with lodgers, every bed occupied and all with their own worries and troubles about the war, and so on. "Frightened them all to death, I did" were her exact words. Can't remember what had driven her to such a course of action but she threatened to up and leave.' He laughed. 'Very determined woman, our Daisy, for all her sweet nature. Not that she ever would abandon them, too soft-hearted, and they probably knew it. But she wouldn't hesitate to give them a good telling off from time to time if she thought them in need of one; sharpen their ideas up a bit.'

Laura chuckled, 'And would they behave any better afterwards?'

He smiled fondly. 'I should think so, for a little while at any rate, until their innate selfishness shone through again. But Daisy would forgive them. She was a saint that woman. No, that's not true. Everyone thought she was a saint, which isn't quite the same thing, and actually a greater responsibility.'

Frowning, Laura asked politely what he meant by that.

He blinked a little, drained his cup and set it down with care. Laura felt quite convinced that he was about to explain, but then said something quite different instead. 'In reality, I think Daisy had rather a sad life, certainly a hard one, but you would never have guessed it. Not for a moment would she allow anything to get her down. She was good at making the best of things, of doing what suited her and living for the moment. So long as she felt it to be right, it didn't matter to her whether others agreed or not. She was even prepared to put up with the gossip, for all she hated it with a venom. Daisy would simply shut her ears to it and draw more and more into herself, into her little kingdom up there.'

'What sort of gossip?'

'There's always gossip in a small community.'

'I suppose so.' Laura was intrigued. 'My father and Daisy fell out, quite badly, when I was about seven or eight. Do you know anything about that?'

'I really couldn't say.' He frowned in thought for a moment. 'You won't remember old Clem. Died in the mid-sixties I seem to recall, probably before you were born. He reached a good age, eighty-two or three.' The old man smiled, 'But there was no hanky-panky between him and Daisy, sorry to disappoint you. He looked upon her more as a daughter.'

'I confess I would've been surprised and more disappointed, if there had been. From my own memories of my grandmother, I believe her to be an honest, upfront sort of person, except that love can have the strangest effect on people, make them do wild, unpredictable things. Anyway, whatever went wrong between her and my father perhaps makes him try to justify himself by blaming Daisy entirely.'

'Very possibly.'

'I mean, he's not an easy person for *me* to get along with, for heaven's sake. The other day he even accused *me* of having a man tucked away somewhere, as if that were the reason I was staying on.'

'When really you want to find out about Daisy?'

'Yes.' Laura thought for a moment. 'What happened about the baby? Did she ever tell Harry about him? I've been trying to find Daisy's marriage certificate, or the baby's birth certificate, so far without success. I know you say you can't talk about her personal life but I wondered if there was any other place she might have stored her papers, besides the bureau? Or if there is anything more, anything at all, you can tell me about her.'

The silence went on for so long this time that, for a moment, Laura thought he might have dropped off to sleep. Then the old solicitor sat up and, perhaps refuelled by the little nod-off or the tea and several cakes he'd consumed, suddenly he seemed to brighten. 'I could tell you about

Florrie. Miserable old goat that she was and a bit of a gadfly by all accounts. Utterly selfish.'

Laura agreed that would be most interesting. Unfortunately, they were interrupted in their cosy chat by Doris bringing his whisky which he routinely enjoyed before his dinner at six-thirty. Laura hadn't realised it was so late and got up to go. 'May I come again?' If hearing about the dreadful Florrie was the only way to discover more about Daisy, then why not? It might all add to the picture.

The old man looked pleased and gratified by her interest, clearly not averse to her calling again. He probably didn't get many visitors and still missed the company of his wife, so he enjoyed a bit of a gossip about the old days. They arranged a date for early the following week and Laura took her leave.

She drove home thinking of all she still needed to ask. Names, dates, whys and wherefores. Friendly as old Mr Capstick was, he had his boundaries beyond which he was not prepared to go. Evidently he was of the old school of solicitors who considered client confidentiality as tantamount to an oath of honour; one this old gentleman would never dream of breaking. Therefore, Laura needed facts, and if she couldn't get them from him, and she certainly had no wish to again ring her father, she could always contact the Public Record Office for copies of Daisy's marriage certificate. Perhaps she should have done that in the first place but it had seemed an unnecessary expense when someone probably had the simple information she needed, or it was lying about the house somewhere, perhaps in a drawer.

She drove past Beckwith Hall Farm, her gaze scanning the darkened windows for any sign of occupation, then sweeping over the empty fields for sight of him but David was nowhere to be seen and Laura felt vaguely foolish, like a schoolgirl peering over into the boy's playground for a glimpse of some fourth former she'd got a crush on.

The telephone was ringing as she walked through the door. It was Felix. 'Feeling better?'

'I beg your pardon?'

'After your little tantrum the other night.'

'*My* tantrum?' Only Felix could create mayhem and lay the blame squarely on her. Laura took a careful swallow. Losing it now wouldn't help at all. 'I'm very well, thank you. Never better.'

'Ah, lover boy came up with the goods, did he?'

'Don't be vulgar Felix. It wasn't at all that sort of dinner. I invited him out of politeness in order to be sociable and, as I've explained, because he knew Daisy.'

Having successfully ruffled her feathers, he blithely changed the subject. 'Some clients of mine are interested in the house. They're coming over to view it next Friday afternoon. We've agreed a price, assuming they like it, which will save us any estate agency fees.'

'*What?*'

'I'm sure you can arrange to be in. You've little else to do up there.' At which point the line went dead and Laura was left swearing at the dialling tone.

After a hot shower and a soothing bowl of home-made soup, Laura gathered up the bundle of letters and took them to bed to read. She'd glanced through some already, now she meant to read more. Anything to keep her mind off what she would like to do to Felix. She certainly had no intention of allowing him to bully her into selling the house.

Most were from Harry to Daisy but a few of Daisy's letters were there too. Not in any particular order, they were generally filled with plans for a future they dreamed of having together after the war. In almost every case a letter would contain some evidence of concern for others.

'*I'm worried about the girls. I haven't heard from them in ages. I'm afraid they might be unhappy again.*' They must be the two little evacuees Daisy had taken under her wing. *'I wish I could have them here with me. Should I ask Clem, do you think?'*

Many were little more than short notes arranging a meeting, declaring that she still loved him, that she'd see him soon. Laura read slowly, savouring the sweet missives. Others were from Harry begging her not to get too friendly with the men who came to the farm. Would they be guests, Laura wondered, or hired workers? *'What would I do if you fell for someone else?'* was the heart-rending plea and despite her brave words to David Hornsby, Laura did feel it intrusive that she should be reading these intimate exchanges.

She could hardly wait for her next visit to old Mr Capstick and indeed he was eagerly waiting for her when she appeared at his door at the appointed hour, tea and cakes at the ready.

Carefully Laura led him back over old ground, relating what she had discovered herself from the letters, and from David Hornsby, and then reminded him gently of his promise to tell her about Aunt Florrie.

'Ah yes, indeed. The most irritating thing about the woman was that she could have helped Daisy, her own niece, right from the start, had she been so inclined and saved her a deal of misery, perhaps even further tragedy.'

'What sort of tragedy?'

'The tragedy which led to Daisy finally finding Lane End Farm.'

'Oh, do tell me more.'

Something must have woken her. It was still pitch dark and although Daisy felt sick with exhaustion and lack of sleep, she was wide awake and could almost swear there was someone else in the room. But how could there be, unless Mrs Chapman had popped in to see how her headache was? Wasn't that the sound of someone breathing, quite close by? And then she smelled the unmistakable scent of stale sweat and wool.

Daisy froze. Even before the covers were lifted and a heavy body slid into bed beside her, she knew who it was. She tried to move but an arm clamped itself tight around her, fat fingers starting to stroke her throat, moving slowly down to her breasts. 'Don't fret, little Daisy. I saw you were upset and I've come to give you a cuddle. Nothing like a cuddle to make a person feel better. You can cry on my shoulder, if you like.'

Daisy lay petrified, not knowing whether to scream and risk upsetting Mrs Chapman, hit out at him which could result in him turning violent and hitting her back, or suffer the soft pawing of his groping hand in silence. She opted for the latter in the hope an opportunity might present itself for her to make an escape. She wasn't optimistic. The weight of his overwarm body against hers was suffocating. Daisy could feel the pounding of her heart in her ears and her skin start to crawl as his hand lifted the hem of her nightgown, the stubby, ink-stained fingers now walking up her leg as he chanted a little nursery rhyme in her ear.

'Incy-wincy spider climbed the spout one day.'

She shot out of bed faster than a bullet and flew to the door, fumbling with the handle in her frantic anxiety to get out, until finally she wrested it open and almost fell out of the room, a jabbering Mr Chapman hard on her tail. 'It's all right Daisy. It was only a *little* cuddle. Be a good girl, there's a love, and don't make a fuss. Mrs Chapman wouldn't understand.'

'Nor do I, you dirty old bugger!'

'Daisy, please. Let me just explain . . .'

What it was he might have said, they were never to discover. As Mr Chapman came blundering out on to the landing, Mrs Chapman appeared suddenly at the top of the stairs in her long nightgown. Perhaps she'd come to check on Daisy's headache, or else to see what all the noise was about. It was quite by accident, in the heat and rush of the moment, that the pair collided but, for the rest of her life, Daisy would never forget the expression of total surprise on Mrs Chapman's face as she tipped backwards down the stairs, arms and legs flailing like a rag doll, her last image on this earth that of her husband prancing about stark naked on the landing in front of her evacuee.

Florrie Pringle took the letter from behind the clock where she'd tucked it more than a year ago and reread it with close attention, even though she knew the words off by heart already. She'd recognised the handwriting the moment the letter had arrived, even after all this time, and had guessed that it would carry no loving message. She'd been right, of course. Not a word of forgiveness, not even an apology for the years of silence, let alone for the bitter, cruel words that had driven her from home in the first place.

Ever since their mother had died and Dad had walked out on the arm of another woman, Florrie had spent her adolescence being bossed by her elder sister, furiously resenting the authority she insisted on exercising as of right. To be fair, Rita had probably found it hard to deal with a young girl who thought herself a bit of a flapper and liked to dance, listen to jazz and flirt with every young man in sight, and most shocking of all, smoke.

Florrie now considered where that piece of rebellion had got her. Out of stinking Marigold Court and the tenements of Salford certainly, far away from the harping criticism of her elder sister, but what had she gained in its place? A life of misery and back-breaking toil. Not at all what she'd had in mind when she'd kicked up her heels recklessly and run off with Clement Pringle, seventeen years her senior and owner, or so he'd boasted, of a large historic house in Cumberland that had been in his family for four centuries, together with nigh on seventy acres of land, not to mention grazing rights on several hundred acres more.

Florrie had imagined a Georgian mansion with a deer park, formal gardens, a wine cellar, and perhaps a housekeeper or a servant or two to answer her every need. It wasn't that Clem had actually promised her these things, nor lied to her in any way. It was more a case of leaving the finer details unexplained. She'd made the mistake of not asking specific questions, had been so desperate to escape that Florrie had never thought to take off her rose-coloured spectacles long enough to question his bragging more closely.

At thirty-seven, he'd been quite handsome in his way, funny and attentive, kind and supportive, his robust, stocky figure giving the illusion of stature and power, an instant allure to an adventure-seeking nineteen-year-old. She'd been utterly captivated. And it's not as if there were a great many suitors to choose from. Many of the young men she'd grown up with had been killed during the First War so was it any wonder that she'd snatched at the chance he offered, without pause for thought?

She still carried a clear memory of the day she'd arrived. Florrie could see herself standing in the middle of the kitchen in her high heels and the smart little frock and coat she'd bought for going away in; the entire modish ensemble completed with the very latest cloche hat in a matching periwinkle blue. Her hair had been cut in a stylish bob, her scarlet lipstick thickly applied, but instead of sitting down to a delicious dinner cooked and served by a fawning housekeeper, she was faced with a cobweb-strewn, damp wreck of a house with a leaky roof and smoky chimneys.

'Good God, when did you last take a duster to this place?' she'd asked, her horrified gaze taking in the stack of dirty dishes left mouldering in the stone sink, the filthy towels hanging on the rack above the inglenook, and the clippy rugs all moth-eaten and caked with mud. The only tidy bit of the room amongst the clutter, was a row of filthy boots, not at all the kind of image she'd had in mind.

Clem had scratched his head and thought for a moment. 'Not since Mam were alive, I reckon.'

Through tightly clenched teeth she'd politely asked when that had been, thinking he'd say twenty years, or at least ten. It would surely take all of that time to create such mayhem. He'd thought for a bit before responding with, 'Three months last Tuesday. Mind you, she hadn't been herself for months.'

If it hadn't been so dreadful, Florrie might have laughed. Instead, she replied, 'Well, she could've washed up before she left.'

He'd been hurt, of course, by the caustic comment, had done his best to hide the wound, the first of many he would be forced to endure in the years ahead. Right then he'd tactfully explained that, as his wife, it would naturally be her task to look after him, and do all the housework. 'Isn't it like that in Salford?'

'Course it is. Don't talk so daft. I just thought . . . I mean I rather expected . . .' But it was no good. Putting her dreams into words would only make her sound foolish and naïve, so Florrie had set them aside, along with the fancy hat and the scarlet lipstick, donned a pinny, rolled up her sleeves and set to work. It was almost like being back at home and, to her utter dismay, Florrie found herself wishing she was.

The silence of the fells weighed heavily upon her. She couldn't bear the emptiness of the landscape. Their nearest neighbours were a couple of miles down the lane in the little village of Threlkeld. No one had been foolish enough to build above them, which was presumably why the house had been named Lane End Farm. Save for Blencathra Sanatorium, a bleak Victorian monstrosity for all those poor sick folk with TB forced to sleep in freezing bedrooms with the windows wide open in all weathers. They did not encourage visitors, not that Florrie would ever go near, it gave her the shivers, seeming to embody her hatred of this place

She found the presence of the brooding mountain, rearing up behind the farm buildings overpowering and unsettling. Florrie would wander from room to room, gazing out over the empty fields below in the hope of seeing someone pass by, perhaps a local exercising their dog, then she would rush out and beg them to come in for a cup of tea and a chat. But this was too rare an occurrence to rely upon; Blencathra's austere beauty was seldom challenged save by a few crazy hikers in high summer. And Florrie would feel a desperate longing for a rain-sodden Manchester street, for the sound of children happily playing with skipping ropes and swinging round a lamp post, as she had used to do as a child, the women gossiping on their doorsteps. There was no chance of such social chit-chat here.

If she'd thought Rita to be a cold, unfeeling woman, that was before she'd tried living with the silent, frugal Clem, who had turned out to be the most taciturn and grumpy of men, stuck in a routine which had remained unchanged for centuries, and in a house that should long since have been razed to the ground.

Florrie stared again at the letter in her hand. It amazed her that her sister had even troubled to write, let alone ask for her help. Astonishing! Rita firmly believed God had given her the right to stand in judgement over others, dealing particularly harshly with members of her own family who had, in her puritanical opinion, in some way transgressed. So it had been with Florrie in her day, and now, apparently, with her own daughter. Perhaps, Florrie thought, that was why she'd kept the letter, out of pity for the poor girl, understanding exactly what she was going through.

She tugged the sleeve of her cardigan over her hand and used it to rub a smear of dust from the oval mirror set in the mahogany mantle. The face which looked back at her was that of a stranger. It certainly showed no sign of the young woman who had once flouted convention. Florrie trailed a finger over the bruised circles beneath blue-grey eyes that had long since lost any glimmer of hope; smoothed a hand over pale, sallow skin which no longer glowed with youth, and tracked a contour of lines that pulled down a discontented mouth which did not flaunt the scarlet lips men had found to be utterly irresistible.

'You always said I'd come to a bad end, Rita. Mebbe you were right. Though I'll make damn sure you never find out just how much of a mess I have made of me life.'

No, no, best she continue to do nothing about the letter, nothing at all. What other option did she have? She'd no wish to bring her tyrant of a sister back into her life, let alone drag young Daisy into the midst of this silent war zone.

Resisting the urge to tear it to shreds, she folded the letter carefully, slid it back inside its envelope and returned it to the dark recesses of the dusty mantelshelf, well hidden amongst a wad of bills that Clem never touched.

Now that had been another disappointment. The lack of money. Florrie had assumed, from the way he'd so zealously courted her, taking her out to dinner and buying her little trinkets that he was quite well placed and comfortably off. Sadly that had not been the case. It'd been all show. He'd needed a wife to help him on the farm and with no hope of finding one in this remote spot, he'd saved hard for months, then headed for the city determined to 'buy' himself a bride. Florrie had fallen for it all, hook, line and sinker.

She drew in a deep calming breath as she glanced at the clock, listening to the echo of its tick in the empty room and wondered if Clem had met with problems which made him so late home from the weekly auction mart, or whether he'd stopped off for a drink with his cronies. Not that it mattered to her one way or the other, Clem was far too careful with his money to ever have more than half a pint. His dinner was keeping warm in the oven, and she'd be off to bed soon, the warmest place to be on such a cold, blustery night. However glorious the rest of the country, this little corner of Lakeland always managed to have a weather system all its own.

As if echoing her thoughts, she heard the kitchen door crash back against the wall, caught by the vicious wind no doubt. She made no move to go to him. Nor did he call out to her, or announce his arrival in any way. Why should he? No one else would be mad enough to be out on a night like this, so who else could it be but him? She could almost hear the wind chuckle with devilish delight at having gained entry at last, and a final whoosh of disappointment as Clem slammed shut the door, forcing it back outside where it belonged. She put a match to the fire she'd laid ready for his arrival and walked briskly into the kitchen.

'I'll fetch your supper.' Florrie had no intention of asking him about his day, though there were times when for no reason she could fathom, he'd readily tell her. This was apparently one of them.

'Them yows fotched good prices at the mart,' he said.

Florrie didn't trouble to reply. They either did fetch good prices, or they didn't. It was all the same to her.

She noted how he carefully put his cap to keep warm on the hook over the old kitchen range, how his boots had been placed on a piece of newspaper by the back door; odd little touches for such an unfussy man. She took the plate from the oven and placed it on the table before him. Clem picked up his knife and fork without comment and began to eat an over-cooked steak and kidney pie.

Tucking lank strings of bleached blonde hair behind her ears, her one remaining vanity, Florrie stood and watched him for a moment, staring at his grey head bent to the task of eating, noting how his once handsome face was now crazed with lines, like a dried-up river bed; his proud shoulders hunched and stooped. Whatever had made him the man he was had died along with their darling Emma, and Florrie could find no pity in her heart to spare for him; she needed it all for herself.

This was the other, more poignant reason, why she hadn't written back agreeing to Rita's request. Because she'd no wish to have a baby around the place. That wouldn't do at all. An unknown child sleeping in Emma's cot? Florrie felt a shudder run through her at the very thought, knowing she could never bear it.

Don't think about Emma, she told herself. Not today. Not just now.

It was fortunate really that the modern young flapper inside her had died too. Otherwise, she'd have gone quite mad, as would Daisy, if she came here. This was no place for a lively young girl.

Then as if to make sure that she didn't weaken, Florrie snatched the letter from its hiding place and tossed it into the fire. When every last scrap had been consumed by the flames, she turned and went upstairs to bed, leaving her husband to his own company, as she did every night.

Laura began the redecorating with the smallest bedroom, in case her first attempt wasn't too good. It took a full day simply to strip the paper from the walls and give the whole room a thorough scrubbing, then a further two to paint and paper it. Nevertheless, she was pleased with the result when it was finished.

'Not so useless after all, Laura old girl,' she told herself, admiring her handiwork with justified pride. 'Right, only five more to go. On to bedroom two.'

The prospective buyers came to the house prompt at two o'clock on Friday afternoon. Laura was waiting for them, not that she'd made any special preparations, as advocated by television programmes on 'how to sell your house'. She'd stripped the wallpaper and coated the old plaster of the second bedroom with size, preparatory to repapering. It gave off a pungent aroma. As she heard the car draw up outside, she calmly set down the brush on the edge of the can and only when the front doorbell sounded, did she wipe her hands on a cloth and go to let them in.

They were a middle-aged couple in their late forties, the woman with a thin, sallow complexion, not a hair out of place and lips painted a bright cerise pink. She was smartly dressed in a navy trouser suit and boots that had walked on nothing more taxing than tarmac. The man wore tweeds and brogues, as if he thought this to be appropriate gear for a day in the country. Laura smiled brightly at them. 'Mr and Mrs Carr? Ah, do come in. I was expecting you.'

The moment they stepped over the threshold the woman wrinkled up her nose, hard. 'Is that paint I smell?'

'Indeed it is, I must confess. And size, for the wallpaper you know. It's a never-ending job isn't it? Particularly in a place as old as this.' She gave a trilling little laugh as she led them to a small room at the back. Once used as an office, clearly it hadn't been touched in years: wallpaper peeling off the walls, a torn green paper blind hung at the window and paintwork dingy and thick with grime.

The couple looked upon the room in open horror. 'Is that fungi on the ceiling Mrs Rampton?'

'I believe it must be, Mr Carr. As you will appreciate, this is an historic house in a cold area. You don't mind the cold I assume, Mrs Carr? I'm afraid it does necessitate a good deal of attention, because of damp you see. And no matter how many times I paint it, it still shows through in no time, all black and horrid, and then I have to start all over again.'

She put her hands together in mild supplication. 'Oh dear, you don't mind my describing the house, warts and all as it were, do you? I mean, I'd hate you to think I was being anything but entirely honest.'

'No, no, please proceed, Mrs Rampton. We appreciate your candour.'

Laura continued with the tour. The front parlour, once inhabited by the guests, was a little better if with a slightly musty smell to it. She'd made no effort to do any cooking today and had let the range go out so the kitchen was not only cheerless but freezing cold. Laura smiled apologetically. 'One has such problems with these old ranges, doesn't one? Still, you could always throw it out and put in central heating.'

She could see from their shocked expressions they had not budgeted for such a vast expense, and were far from impressed. They'd clearly had the cosy warmth of a modern Aga in mind.

'We were led to believe that this was a fully restored property. Completely habitable.'

'Habitable, oh indeed it is, yes, if you don't mind roughing it a bit. But to be absolutely honest with you, Mr Carr, I've just inherited this property from my grandmother and it has been sadly neglected over the years. However, as I say, with a lick of paint and a few refurbishments such as a bathroom here and there, once you've eradicated any possible dry rot and woodworm, that is, and you'll have a bargain on your hands. An absolute bargain.'

She caught the expression of panic exchanged between them as she moved them briskly along the passage. 'Now, here is the utility room, or wash house as my dear eccentric grandmother probably dubbed it. Pay no attention to the old boiler, it doesn't work, and it was only the wind which broke the panes of glass. I shall get it fixed directly, meanwhile it's securely boarded up.'

'Wind?'

'Indeed, we get positive howling gales up here, being situated on the side of the mountain, as we are. Oh dear, I wouldn't recommend you trying the taps Mrs Carr, the drain is blocked, unfortunately, at present. There seems to be some problem with the plumbing but I'm sure it's nothing that can't be remedied. Perhaps it is vermin stuck in the pipes. You know, a field mouse or rat, or . . .' She frowned. 'Or it may be the septic tank, I suppose, assuming there is one and not just a soakaway.'

'Soakaway, Mrs Rampton?' whimpered Mr Carr.

'Mice? Rats?' wailed Mrs Carr.

'I'm sure it's nothing at all to worry about, nothing a good plumber couldn't fix.'

'At a price,' mumbled Mr Carr as they lumbered back into the hall.

'Now, shall we go upstairs, or would you prefer to view the outbuildings, and the privy out the back?' Laura smiled upon them both beatifically.

'*Privy?*' The man barked. 'Damp? Dry rot! Woodworm! Vermin! I believe we have seen enough, Mrs Rampton. Thank you so much for your time.'

It was ludicrously satisfying to see how very quickly they escaped to their car. Laura had to sit down she was laughing so much. 'Oh dear, forgive me Daisy for maligning your memory but I hope you understand it was necessary, in the circumstances.' Wiping the tears of laughter from her eyes, she picked up her brush and went on with the painting.

'I shall finish this wall, then I'll relight the stove and cook myself a large steak for dinner. And I might open

a bottle of wine. Why not?' She deserved it. No doubt
Felix would ring later, and it wasn't going to be a pleasant
experience.

Laura was absolutely correct in her supposition. Felix
demanded a full briefing on the prospective buyers, refusing
to accept her bland comments that they seemed slightly put
off by the isolation and maintenance required with such an
old property.

'You put them off deliberately didn't you?'

'Felix, what a thing to say.'

'What did you tell them?' He was shouting down the phone
so loud, Laura had to hold it some distance from her ear.
'That it had rampant dry rot, I suppose?'

'How did you guess?' she said sweetly. 'Don't send anyone
else, Felix. Remember what I said: the house is not for sale.
And if you are so foolish as to try, I'll see them all off in exactly
the same way.'

'Are you threatening me?'

'Of course not, darling. Simply being entirely honest, open
and frank, as I was with the Carrs. Believe me I find it tiresome to have to keep repeating myself, but until you start
listening, I must continue to do so. The house is not—'

'I'm not done yet, Laura. Don't think you'll beat me,
because you won't. I'm not giving up on our marriage and
unless you intend to ruin me, neither am I giving up on selling
that damned house.'

After he rang off, Laura wondered why she didn't feel
pleased that he wasn't giving up on their marriage, only
deeply uneasy.

On Sunday, David took her out for a pub lunch. They drove
to Borrowdale along the eastern shore of Derwentwater,
taking a detour to visit Watendlath by way of Ashness Bridge,
made famous by Hugh Walpole as the home of Judith Paris,

then passing the Lodore Falls and on to Rosthwaite, marvelling at the graceful beauty of the silver birches, the glimpses of sparkling lake and green mountain, fresh charms revealed at every twist and turn in the road.

'From Borrowdale comes the wad to make the lead pencils for which Keswick is most famous,' David told her. '*Crayon d'anglais*. Provided riches equal to a diamond mine in its day. The area was rife with illegal digs and smuggling on secret paths and trods across the fells. I shall take you to see the pencil museum another time.'

They exchanged smiling glances, each reading more into the simple suggestion than the history of the humble pencil could possibly justify.

They took lunch at the Royal Oak at Rosthwaite, opting for spicy Cumberland sausage which David claimed was his favourite local fare. Laura told him about the Carrs and he laughed so much he got the hiccups and she had to pat him on the back.

'I must be mad to play such dangerous games. Felix isn't the sort who likes to lose. He's bound to fight back.'

'Let him. You have your rights, and it is your house.'

'Trouble is, he doesn't always play by the rules.'

He looked at her questioningly for a moment, then took her hand between both of his. 'You know where I am. Should you need a friend.'

'Thank you.' Acutely aware of her hand being warmly enclosed by the strength of his grip, Laura felt as tongue-tied as a young girl, and then recalling his earlier words, began to giggle. 'I thought you said I was the practical, capable, no-nonsense and non-fussy type, so surely with such attributes I should be able to cope on my own?'

'Why do I get the feeling the compliment has not come across quite as I intended?'

Laura widened her eyes in pretended innocence. 'Is that what it was?'

'I did add beautiful, charming and deliciously sexy, didn't I?'

Laura shook her head slowly. 'You were comparing me to Daisy, I seem to recall, who was almost eighty when she died, I believe.'

He hung his head. 'No, it clearly didn't come across at all as I intended.' He glanced up at her and gave his lazy smile. 'What about dessert by way of recompense for my clumsiness?' He insisted she try hot gingerbread with rum butter. 'It's a traditional dish of the Lakes so I won't take no for an answer.'

'Might as well be hung for a sheep as a lamb,' Laura laughed. 'It feels sinful enough to be out with a man other than my husband.'

'We're only having lunch. There's surely nothing very wicked about eating lunch, is there?'

Still holding her hand, he dipped his lips to her fingertips and kissed them, the glint of mischief in his eyes making her heart turn right over. 'Not that I'm aware of, no.'

'You don't sound too convinced.'

'Then don't look at me like that.' She pulled her hand free and self-consciously tidied her hair. He helped her, tucking a strand tenderly behind one ear. 'Don't. Let's stay in neutral, shall we?'

'What a spoilsport you are. I was just beginning to enjoy myself. All right, I'll engage neutral. So, what was it you were telling me about the Carrs? Ah yes, I dare say they thought they'd walked straight into a nightmare.'

'Absolutely.' Laura took a sip of her lager, steadying the race of her heart. 'You should have seen their faces when I mentioned rats blocking the drains,' and they both set off laughing all over again.

Daisy

14

Daisy fortified herself for the day ahead with a cup of tea and a scone in Storms Lunch & Tea Rooms, then stood in the tiny market place at a loss to know what to do next. Despite it not being market day, the place was bustling with people, all dashing about and plainly with some specific purpose in mind. It made her feel quite alone in the world. Stuck on the windows of a tall building proclaiming itself to be the Moot Hall, there were advertisements for a War Weapons Week that had taken place in May, and one on the dedication of a new assembly hall at Keswick School to be held in June. A badly torn poster urged the residents of Keswick to come to see *Twelfth Night*, performed by the Old Vic Players. And yet another announced that there would be dancing every Tuesday night at the Park Hotel.

Daisy felt a lump come into her throat as she thought of the dances she'd attended with Harry. It had become a regular event for them after that first date, at least until he was posted to Silloth. Despite her better judgement, she'd fallen head over heels in love, and worrying about him was now a part of her life. Loving Harry was the last thought in her mind as she slipped into sleep each night, and the first when she woke every morning. But she didn't regret loving him. Oh dear me, no. Daisy had resolved to live for the moment. It seemed the only way to cope. So long as she got his regular letters, telling her that he was fit and well, that he still loved her, what else need concern her? The war couldn't go on for ever, and then they would be together at last. Oh, and didn't she love the bones of him? He made her head positively spin whenever he kissed her, which made it difficult not to let matters run out of control. She could remember all too clearly the last time that they very nearly had; replay every blissful moment in her head.

'Harry, I must be careful,' she'd whispered, as they'd lain together in some dappled patch of woodland, all flushed and hot and rumpled from their loving. He'd lifted her blouse to fondle her breast, and she'd made no attempt to stop him. Didn't she long for him to love her properly? In no time, lost in a riot of emotion, he'd been lifting her skirt, smoothing his hand along her thighs, over her flat belly, and still she didn't protest. But Daisy hadn't wanted him to think her cheap. 'What would my mother say if she saw us like this?' Oh, but didn't she just know what Rita would say?

'You can trust me, Daisy. I love you too much to risk hurting you.' But he'd sat up and lit a cigarette, drawing deeply upon it and remaining silent for a long time as if he couldn't quite trust himself, before talking about the war and how uncertain life was. 'The worst of it is, how can I bear to be away from you, knowing some other chap might snap you up while I'm gone.'

Daisy giggled as she smoothed down her skirt. 'Nobody's going to snap anything on me, take my word for it. No one shoves Daisy Atkins around, not without my say so.' Not any more, said a small voice at the back of her head.

He'd turned to her, eyes burning with an intensity she'd never seen in them before. 'If anything did happen – between us – I wouldn't mind too much. I love you, Daisy, every hair of your head, the sound of your voice, your lovely smile, every last freckle. I love everything about you that makes you who you are, so if we were to make a child, so be it. I'd love him too.'

There was a great swell of happiness in her breast. It was all going to be all right, after all. Perhaps she should tell him now, about the baby she already had? 'Oh, Harry, and I love you too. We'll make everything good between us, war or no war, I know we will. It'll be all fine. The thing is . . .'

He kissed her then like he never had before, with a hunger that made her ache with renewed longing. When they broke away his eyes were dark with need. 'I'm not sure how much longer I can be satisfied with just a few kisses. I need you Daisy girl, all of you.'

'And I need you,' Daisy said on a sudden burst of shyness. 'We could always . . .' But she stopped the words with the flat of her hand.

'Don't say it. Don't ask anything of me, not just yet, eh? We've only been going out together for a short while and it's too soon. Where's the fire, eh? Give us a kiss and be happy with that, for now, eh?'

And he'd groaned, tossed away the butt of his half-smoked cigarette and pushing her back down into the sweet-smelling grass, proceeded to kiss her with such a passion that it made her head spin.

Daisy couldn't bear to think that a dirty old man had attempted to touch her as Harry had. Not that she had any intention of telling Harry about Mr Chapman's fall from grace. Yet another secret to carry with her through life. It would only upset him, remembering how he'd called him a silly old cove and taken exception to his lack of trust when Harry had taken her to that very first dance.

But she could cope well enough. At least she hoped so.

But then she'd naïvely imagined that she could cope with Mr Chapman's wandering hands though really she'd got off lightly, considering what might have happened. She didn't dare let herself think about poor Mrs Chapman. That was too dreadful to contemplate. Poor woman. Daisy rather thought the guilt of that moment would live with her for ever She'd gone over and over in her head how she might have prevented the accident. Perhaps if she'd not dashed so recklessly out of the room, or if she'd tried to talk rationally to him. Yet Daisy knew that would have been hopeless. Mr Chapman had not been in a rational frame of mind. He'd had his hand up her night-dress, and God knows what he might have been about to do next.

The incident was accepted locally as a tragic accident. Daisy certainly had no intention of becoming embroiled in any difficult questions to the contrary. She would never forget her employer's grey pallor on the day she'd left, for all she'd kept her mouth shut and said nothing to anyone. His face bore the look of a broken man: the confident, self-important and slightly pompous person he'd once been had gone for ever. He'd allowed the dark side of his nature to overtake him, and now he could never get back to the sunny side.

She hadn't waited for the funeral. She'd taken the money he offered, packed her bag and walked out. It had seemed the right moment to find Aunt Florrie. Catching the bus to Keswick had been simple enough; finding where her aunt lived was proving to be more problematic.

'I've a tongue in me head. All I have to do is ask,' she'd told herself when she'd first arrived but the morning was almost over and she was no nearer to fulfilling her quest to find her aunt. With increasing desperation Daisy had discovered that no one had heard of Florrie Pringle, let alone have any idea where she might live.

But she wasn't for giving up. Oh dear me, no. The last thing she wanted was to look for a fresh billet with yet more strangers, or worse, be forced to return to Salford and her mother. Nothing would induce her to do such a thing. Florrie was family, after all, and she must be around here some place. All she had to do was find her, then she could write and give Harry her new address. There must be no question of losing touch with Harry. She adored him far too much to contemplate such a dreadful prospect happening. Daisy had written to tell him that she'd moved and that her new address would follow shortly.

But if she didn't find Florrie soon, she faced a night in the open, although Daisy didn't feel particularly concerned about this. She'd decided there were worse places to sleep than under the stars. It was a warm day in August so it needn't be unpleasant, even quite exciting. There was still all the afternoon ahead of her, plenty of time in which to find her aunt.

She stopped and asked several more people but then, quite worn out with trekking around the streets, headed for the quiet of Derwentwater where she got out the sandwiches she'd brought with her.

It proved to be so pleasant sitting in the sun watching the rowing boats setting out from the landings that Daisy could almost imagine herself on holiday, and not a homeless evacuee at all. A mother with her two children was paddling about in the shallows; with skirts tucked up and fishing nets in hand they made a perfect picture of family fun, and Daisy felt a surge of envy. But then, how could you tell whether the mother wasn't grieving for a husband, or at least anxiously awaiting news. Somehow Daisy didn't think they had much hope of catching even a minnow with all the giggling going on, so perhaps all was well for them after all. Daisy sighed, as if she'd been relieved of a genuine cause for concern.

Soft white clouds bounced lightly from mountain top to mountain top and she gazed upon them with awe, ignorant of their names but marvelling at their beauty; at the way the dappled sun chased the cloud shadows across their smooth, sleek slopes, the green so brilliant it almost hurt her eyes to look upon them. There was grace in every fold; pride, majesty, and an odd sort of security. Their timeless beauty seemed to cleanse her soul of the grubby fingermarks left by a dirty old man and bring peace to a sore and fearful heart.

She felt young and strong, bursting with energy and optimism, free of all restrictions. Ever since she'd left Salford, Daisy had discovered that she'd become quite adept at standing on her own two feet, as well as solving whatever problems the war, or other people, threw at her.

Look at how she'd cared for Megan and Trish: how she'd found food for them when poor Miss Pratt had unexpectedly died without them knowing, stood by them as they were moved from pillar to post. Thinking of her two friends, Daisy modified her boast ruefully because, sadly, she'd failed to help them this time. She'd believed she could persuade Mrs Marshall to let them stay but, in the end, the poor woman's ill health had changed everything. The children had been taken to yet another strange home where they were at least safe and well cared for.

Daisy felt cast adrift, as if they'd all been buffeted about like tiny ships on the open sea, caught up in a storm not of their making and left with no one but each other to depend upon. She could only hope that they weren't too unhappy, or missing her too much. She certainly missed them. Before leaving the village, Daisy had gone into Penrith and talked to the billeting officer who'd given her the address where they'd been sent.

They'd both burst into tears at the sight of her. Megan had at once begged, 'Have you come to tek us home, Daisy?' It had near broken her heart to have to say no.

'You are all right here, aren't you?'

Silent nods had indicated that they were, Trish's mouth turned upside-down in the familiar U-shape, and Megan was clearly doing her best to be brave. 'But we miss you, Daisy.'

'And we miss the dog,' Trish added.

Daisy had given them both a hug and a kiss, smiling to herself that at least she'd been put before the dog. 'Soon as I find Aunt Florrie, I'll write. I'll keep in touch, I promise. I'll let you have my new address so that if ever there's anything wrong, you can let me know.' She didn't make any other promises; that maybe she could persuade Florrie to allow them to join her, which was what she hoped to achieve. That was far too risky.

'You'll come and see us again?' Megan wanted to know, hanging on tight to Daisy's hand while Trish wrapped her arms about Daisy's waist as if she might never let her go.

'Course I will. We're bosom pals, right? The three musketeers.' And then they'd all wept, for how could they not when parting was so painful?

Life, Daisy had discovered, at the ripe age of seventeen, was desperately uncertain and insecure and you never knew what might be waiting for you around the next corner. She was forced to admit that really she'd had very little control over what had happened to her thus far, only in the decisions she made to deal with it.

Now she was in a strange town she didn't know, looking for a woman nobody had ever heard of. Daisy had knocked on the door of every fine house which seemed a likely candidate, remembering how her mother had never stopped complaining over how her sister had got above herself, living in grand style in Keswick.

'Too posh to talk to us now. Thinks she is someone. Always did give herself airs, that one.' Just as if Rita would never dream of doing such a thing.

Several of the imposing terraced houses with their dark slate walls and bright windows looking out over the fells, had turned out to be boarding houses with landladies grumbling about the war ruining the holiday trade. Daisy had even rung the bell at the Keswick Hotel, mistaking it for a private house which looked fine enough for an aunt who had gone up in the world. Instead, she learned that some posh school called Roedean had been evacuated into it. Several other equally grand houses and hotels nearby had suffered the same fate. She didn't envy these girls in their smart uniforms, all cooped up together like chickens. Daisy valued her freedom too much.

She'd called at the station to make enquiries there, and found herself in the middle of a geography lesson in the waiting room. Daisy had begun to feel like Alice-in-Wonderland in a world gone mad, where everything was topsy-turvy and not at all what it should be. Even those houses which had not turned into something entirely different, whose doors were opened by smiling maids or the lady of the house, knew no one of the name of Florrie Pringle.

Daisy tossed the last few crumbs to the ducks swimming about on the water's edge. The sun was hot on her neck now, making her feel quite sleepy but she couldn't allow herself to succumb to a desperate need for rest. She must do her utmost to find her aunt. Focusing her mind on the problem, Daisy recalled that the last time she'd wanted help and information, on that occasion over Miss Pratt, she'd gone to a corner shop. So that's what she'd do now. Aunt Florrie must do her shopping somewhere. She'd visit every shop in town till she found the one she patronised.

A few miles outside of Keswick, living on the side of a mountain and chaffing over a life which didn't suit her, Florrie pegged out her washing thinking how she longed for a bag of fish and chips and a dish of mushy peas soaked in vinegar, followed by an afternoon at the flicks with her friends. How she would love to put on her glad rags, doll herself up and go to Benson's Dance Hall. This year she would turn forty, surely young enough to still hope to find a bit of fun and romance, in place of this living death up here in the middle of nowhere?

She'd soon been disabused of any hopes for a lively social life amongst the country set. No hunt balls or harvest suppers for Florrie. A church coffee morning or rummage sale, and occasional visits to the Alhambra Cinema in Keswick with her nearest neighbour, Jess Jenkins, were the limits of her delights, and then only in the early days of her marriage. Florrie couldn't remember the last time she'd been out with Clem, probably when they were courting and he'd still been trying to win her. He never had time for such treats nowadays, couldn't bear to tear himself away from his precious farm.

The second shock had come when she'd learned that she was expected to help with the animals on the farm, feed the hens and calves, make milk and butter, and when a pig was killed, do all kinds of dreadful things with the bits that came out of it. She'd been thoroughly alarmed. 'What, me?'

'Aye, why not? Mam did.'

'I dare say your mam was born to it. But I'm a city girl, Clem, a townie. I haven't the first idea where to start. Oh heck, why did you choose me for a wife?'

And his eyes had darkened as they'd rested upon her. 'You know why.' And he'd taken her upstairs.

Oh aye, there'd been compensations at first, at least within the confines of the bedroom. But then in those halcyon days the expression in his dark eyes whenever he'd looked upon her had made her heart beat faster, filled as they were with intense interest and admiration, and a frank, raw need.

Life in the farmyard, however, was another matter. The kind of tasks that any country housewife would take for granted, were quite beyond her. Frequently she forgot to feed the hens, or to put some of the eggs in isinglass as she'd been told to, so they'd have none to eat when the hens went off laying. Once, she'd left the pop hole open and a fox finished off the lot. Then when they got new hens to replace them, she forgot to clip their wings and they all flew away. She just seemed to get everything wrong.

'They might fly back, don't you think?' she'd asked.

'I reckon Mr Todd has had them for his supper by now,' Clem had drily remarked.

'Well, why can't you see to them? The farm is your responsibility, after all.'

'Looking after poultry is allus the job of the farmer's wife,' Clem explained carefully, and would patiently go through the tasks expected of her all over again.

Florrie did her best but would get confused over when to plant the potatoes, leeks or other vegetables in the little plot behind the house, or she'd plant them in the wrong place and they wouldn't thrive and Clem would be forced to buy some from the market, which he said was a waste of money when they could easily grow their own. She was happy enough to feed the pet lambs he brought to her kitchen, while they were still small, but getting up at three-hourly intervals during the night and walking out on to the freezing cold fell to feed them as they grew a bit older, was another matter entirely. She refused point-blank to do it.

'If I look after the hens, it's surely your job to look after the sheep.'

'Not the pet lambs, love. They're your responsibility. It's not as if you have to go far, they're kept close to the house, after all.' So she'd wrap herself in several layers against the raw cold, pull on a pair of Clem's old boots and go out into the freezing darkness, tripping over her night-dress and hating every minute, wishing she'd never set eyes on Clem Pringle.

Now there was a war to trap her even more firmly, spending her days in an endless litany of dull chores. Today she'd fed and cleaned out the hens, churned the butter, dug some potatoes and earthed up the rest. Florrie had mended the roof on the outhouse, since she was tired of asking Clem to do it. She'd fetched the peat and chopped several logs, winter being just around the corner. She'd scrubbed and cleaned, mended and fixed, heaved and shifted, and the worst of it was that tomorrow, much of it would all have to be done over again, in addition to whatever tasks she generally did on that particular day of the week. The drudgery seemed endless.

'And our Rita thinks she's got it hard.'

Silence had become a way of life, conversation non-existent, save for Clem's stock phrases. Florrie served him his supper on this particular evening as on every other, which he ate without a word, without even lifting his head. Except that at the first mouthful he said, 'It's warm, bless it.' And as he lay down his knife and fork at the completion of the meal he'd commented, 'That were reet tasty,' just as he did every night.

In fact Florrie felt certain she could mark the progress of each day with these remarks. The moment he set foot out of the door each morning he'd tug on his cap, lift his face to the mountain as if sniffing the air and out would come another, 'We'll get a wetting afore nightfall,' or, 'We might escape it today,' depending on the direction of wind and density of cloud, but he always liked to prove that he knew better than the man on the wireless what the weather was going to do.

And when he returned, after a long day out on the hills, dog at his heels he'd say, 'It's cowd enough up theer to freeze a brass monkey.'

He never failed to go to chapel on a Sunday. Afterwards he would read his bible and, as the clock chimed ten, climb into bed in his long nightshirt, pull the covers up to his chin and remark quietly, 'A Sunday well spent brings a week of content.'

Sometimes Florrie felt she might scream as she waited for the next predictable response. She hated the dull repetition of her life, the grinding routine, the habitual treadmill of the farming year, and the knowledge that if something didn't happen soon, she'd go quite mad.

His favourite remark was to look at her, shake his head and say in his droll way, 'Nay Florrie lass, it's seeing you so cheerful what keeps me going.'

It was almost as if he enjoyed her misery.

She told herself that it didn't matter any more what she did, nor that she often saw no one from one week's end to the next. Florrie had no desire to walk into Threlkeld and seek out friends, not any more. She knew she should be grateful for small mercies: a roof over her head, food in her belly. What else need concern her? Anyone she did meet at chapel or market, would see only the superficial picture of a couple disappointed by life but giving every appearance of getting along in a contented marriage. They went through the motions of living together, doing chores, eating meals, sharing a bed even, although more out of habit than for any other reason. Clem didn't bully her, hit her or order her about, rarely in fact acknowledged her presence. He asked only that she put food on his table as and when required, keep his clothes and home in reasonable, though fortunately not pristine good order, and work every daylight hour as he did himself.

Florrie understood that this was the only way he knew how to cope. It was simply not an answer so far as she was concerned.

Rarely a civil word had been exchanged between them in years, not since that terrible day. The promise of their early love affair had withered and died, killed by grief, she supposed, and she had neither the will nor the facility to resurrect it. But she mustn't think of little Emma just now, not so late in the day. She'd never sleep.

Florrie took a moment to bring her emotions back under control before plunging her hands into the soapy washing-up water. Wallowing in self-pity did no good at all, it simply leaked away the last remnants of her strength, and she needed every ounce of that, oh indeed she did.

'It's ten o'clock. I'm off to bed, Florrie.'

Lips pressed together tightly, she didn't trouble to nod or acknowledge his words in any way. Hadn't she heard them a hundred, nay a thousand times. She'd once used to ask him if he'd locked up, barred the back door, but against who or what? There was no one fool enough to come up this mountain at dark of night.

Left to herself, Florrie gave a small sigh of relief then stirred the ashes of the fire, pulling the few remnants of unburnt logs together to kindle a flame. Over a comforting mug of hot, sweet tea, she pulled out an old Christmas card she'd kept, safely tucked into her knitting bag. It was from Daisy. The childlike, cursive handwriting informed Florrie that she'd recently been evacuated to the Lakes, was being forced to change billets but had failed to find her aunt, not knowing where she lived or even her married name and could she please let her have the address. The girl had sent the card via Salford, and Rita, for reasons best known to herself, had forwarded it on. She'd added a postscript, as dry and cutting as ever.

'*I'm sending you this from our Daisy, though I don't suppose you're interested in your family now that you've got so high and mighty.*'

But it was the last sentence which cut to the heart of her: '*Don't worry, we got rid of the encumbrance.*'

Such a heartless remark, and so typical of Rita. This presumably meant that she'd given up the child for adoption whether Daisy agreed or not. Florrie thought of Daisy, of how she must have felt at only sixteen to give birth to, and lose, a child. Devastated! Florrie, more than most, could well understand what the poor girl must have gone through. The weight of such pain and sadness bowed her own shoulders each and every day, and kept her awake night after night till she felt crippled by it. She too was not to be allowed anyone of her own to love which proved that her marriage had been a terrible mistake; the whole enterprise cursed from start to finish. But Florrie had always believed that to go back home would be an admission of failure. She'd rather die than see her sister gloating over her misery. Heart of stone, had Rita. She certainly would not understand a fraction of what her poor lass was suffering now.

Perhaps, Florrie thought, she should have agreed to help, after all. Would it have been so impossible? Guilt gnawed at her. She could at least have let Daisy spend the months of waiting here, safe from Rita's machinations. Wasn't there enough anguish and pain in the world, what with the war and all, without creating their own?

As Florrie sat watching the fire flicker and die and the last of the wood turn to ash, she came to a decision. Reaching for pen and paper, she began to write a letter. It was to Daisy, and she meant to send it to her via Rita but halfway down the first page she screwed up the paper and tossed it in the fire. She pulled out another sheet and started again. After four more sheets of paper had been woefully wasted in this way, Florrie stopped writing. This wouldn't do at all. Paper was a precious commodity. Weren't they supposed to be conserving resources, not tossing them away in the fire? There must be another way.

The next morning Clem milked their two shorthorns, did his few chores about the yard and ate a substantial breakfast of bacon and eggs, as always. Then he stood at the kitchen door tugging on his boots and cap. 'We're in for a bit of a wetting afore nightfall, I reckon. Them clouds don't look good.' So saying, he called up his dog and went on his way, shoulders slumped, head thrust forward and knees slightly bent in the characteristic gait of a man used to walking on hills.

Florrie watched him go till he was no more than a speck on the mountainside, then she buttoned on her coat, picked up the overnight bag she'd packed while he was out of the house doing his morning chores, closed the door and walked away. In her mind she could already smell the smoke and tar of Salford Quays. For the first time in years, she felt something akin to excitement. War or no war, she was going home. Daisy had given her the very excuse she needed.

Having spent the night huddled on a bench by the lake, and a second day knocking on doors, finally Daisy discovered that Florrie in fact lived at Lane End Farm by enquiring at a small grocer's shop on the edge of town. She managed to hitch a lift out in a milk lorry heading back to the village of Threlkeld, and now it was almost eight o'clock, the day's warmth fading as Daisy toiled up the seemingly endless lane to the farm. She was half dragging her suitcase, a stitch in her side and dripping with sweat from the exertion. She doubted she'd have had the strength to climb this mountain in the full heat of the day after her long, exhausting search.

When she reached the gate, and saw a dirty, chipped board bearing the name Lane End, she stopped to catch her breath. The house was certainly old, a typical Lakeland farmhouse so far as Daisy could tell with its lime-washed stone walls, thick enough to keep out the worst of the mountain weather and dark, narrow windows peeping out from beneath a heavy, slate roof. Behind was a cluster of outbuildings in varying stages of decay, and some short distance from the house, half hidden in a copse of tall trees, stood what appeared to be a small stone barn, the roof partly crumbled away. A line of washing hung across a green sward of grass, beneath which hens pecked about, their soft cackling making a surprisingly comforting sound.

She set down her suitcase in the porch and hammered on the front door. 'Hello! Anyone in?'

When no one answered and the door remained firmly

closed, she walked round to the back and tried again there, with the same result. It would be just her luck if Florrie had gone down into town shopping. Or perhaps she was out in the fields, tending to the sheep, or whatever farmer's wives did. Daisy didn't know what she'd expected but not this. Somehow she must have got it all wrong. It was perfectly clear that her aunt had not gone up in the world, as they had all imagined. No wonder no one had heard of Florrie in Keswick. She wasn't a fine lady living in a grand mansion. By the looks of it she was nothing more exciting than a humble farmer's wife.

And yet where was the harm in that? None at all. Daisy marvelled at Florrie's good fortune at being able to spend her life in such a wonderful place. It seemed an incredible place to live. With the mountain at its back, the farm looked out across the most magnificent countryside Daisy had ever seen. A wide valley, to the right of which could be seen the grey cluster of houses which was Keswick, and the glint of the lake where she'd sat and had her sandwiches just behind the town. Following the railway line from there led her gaze to a scar in the land which looked like a quarry, and ranged behind and beyond this seemingly endless common, were the mountains. Daisy knew none of their names, save that the highest was Helvellyn, but the scene took her breath away and she made a vow, there and then, to learn them all.

The pity of it was that Florrie had never told them about this enchanting place, never given them her address, or allowed them the opportunity to visit. Why hadn't she? Why had she lied?

Daisy fell in love with Blencathra on sight. The mountain seemed to hold out its arms to her, its softly rounded folds like an embrace and, tired though she was, she could barely restrain the urge to climb it there and then, to explore its buttresses, crags and water courses, to reach its lofty summit and look out across the whole of Lakeland. Wouldn't that be a sight?

'Noo then lass, were thoo wanting our Florrie?'

The voice broke into her thoughts, making her jump and Daisy turned to find herself gazing into a face as round, red and wrinkled as an old, well polished apple. It possessed a hawk nose and a firm, square jaw, but this was no gentleman farmer in his flat cap, made from checked woollen cloth and tugged well down over his brow. The fustian trousers had seen better days and the waistcoat, worn over a blue and white striped, collarless shirt, gaped open with not a button in sight. He wasn't smiling but he seemed to Daisy more shy than solemn, reserved in his manner rather than deliberately unfriendly, and studiously polite to this stranger who had appeared on his doorstep. If this was Aunt Florrie's husband, yet again he was not at all what she'd expected. She swallowed her surprise as best she could and held out a hand in friendly greeting.

'You must be Uncle Clem.' Daisy patiently waited while he seemed to consider the outstretched limb, wiped his own hands on the backs of his trousers then thought better of it, all the while continuing to study her with a keen, sharp-eyed gaze. When still he said nothing, she continued, 'I'm Daisy, if you remember? Florrie's niece.' She struggled to recall if she'd ever met him before when she was a child, and gave up.

Clem walked past her to push open the door. 'I know 'oo you are. Thoo'd best cum in. By leuk of you, thoo's in need o' summat to wet thi whistle.'

Why would anyone choose to build a farm on the lip of this awesome giant of a mountain? Daisy wondered as she gratefully drank the glass of cold milk and ate the cheese sandwich he provided. And how had Clem himself come to live in this remote, magical place?

'Did your family build this farm?' she asked.

'Aye.'

'Why here particularly?' Daisy waited patiently, hoping he might add something more but he continued to placidly chew on his sandwich. The room in which they sat evidently served as both kitchen and living room and had developed a warm fug, not simply from the lingering heat of the day, but also from the smoky fire. They were seated by the great inglenook which incorporated an ancient bread oven, well blackened by age and usage. Despite it having been one of the hottest days of the year, it was necessary to have a peat fire burning in order to boil the kettle that swung from a crane over the fire, its own blackened surface revealing it had served this purpose for many years. On the scrubbed flags before the hearth lay a pegged rug and against one wall stood a large deal table and a cupboard with four doors, all of which stood open wide, just as if Clem might need to reach for something at a moment's notice.

He'd removed his cap carefully, she noticed, and set his boots with a line of others by the door. In their place he'd put on a pair of carpet slippers. Daisy found it hard to believe that this quiet little man had so captured her aunt's heart that she'd up and left her family and the home she loved. Perhaps she now loved the fells more.

'How is she then, Aunt Florrie?'

'She's gaily weel.'

'Has she popped out to do a bit of shopping?'

'She's away just noo, aye.'

Again they fell silent and Daisy was beginning to find the conversation hard going. She'd already run the gamut of the weather, his health and her being evacuated to the Lake District, tactfully making no mention of her need for a new billet. It seemed somehow premature to venture into those sort of details. She felt nervous of explaining more fully how and why she needed a bed for the night, for several nights in fact. Where was Aunt Florrie? If only she'd come, then they could sort everything out, woman to woman. The old man seemed lost in thought and Daisy didn't like to interrupt.

She was wilting in the over-warm room, half asleep in the chair when finally he spoke again, 'Because it always was here, and always will be.'

Daisy blinked, struggling to concentrate and recollect what they'd been talking about. 'What was?'

'The mountain.'

'Oh.' She'd forgotten that she'd asked him about how he came to be here. She rubbed the sleep from her eyes and sat up, ready to listen. 'Was the farm left to you by your father then?'

'Aye.' Clem didn't say that he loved it, or stayed here because it was beautiful, nor did he wax lyrical about its serenity or its grandeur, yet all of that seemed implicit in the simple explanation which followed, and in the pride and contentment in his faded, grey gaze. 'It's a challenge, d'you see, living here? It takes sturdy stock wi' some Norse blood in thee veins to cope wi' life on these harsh fells. The first men o' my family to farm here decided the low lying pastures was guddish ground, but they'd build a bit higher up, so's they could see who were cummin like. Them were troubled times, and no one can approach this farm without us being aware of it.'

'I can see that. It must have been hard work, building right in the teeth of the wind? It will get very windy this high up, I suppose? Won't it blow the house to bits in the end?'

Clem seemed unconcerned by such a possibility. 'Whatever thoo does the house'll be gone in the end. Four – five hundred years is but the blink of an eye when you set it against the life of a mountain. One day the slate will be wiped clean like, by nature, though Blencathra will remain.'

Daisy couldn't help thinking that it was perhaps this philo-sophical approach to house maintenance which explained the poor state of the property. She'd noticed dry-stone walls falling down, several outbuildings in dire need of repair and a number of slates missing on the house. Even inside it looked in a sorry state with one of the hinges on the front door missing and several window panes cracked. And the chimney must be in dire need of sweeping, judging from the cloud of smoke that hung low in the room. The whole place gave the appearance of being about to fall apart.

The old man, seemingly oblivious to all of this, was well into his stride, speaking of a subject dear to his heart. 'There's a stone circle not far off at Castlerigg. Put there hundreds, if not thousands of years ago by the first men who ever come to these hills. There's no sign of the mud huts they must hev lived in once, and the stones themselves are toppling over. Man has done his best to tame this mountain, fed his flocks on it, drained the marshes at its foot, mined deep within its belly robbing it of its secret wealth, and building cottages on its face to live in while they did so. But none of that lasts. Nothing does, save for Blencathra himself. You can't fight him, d'you see, great giant that he is. Love him or hate him, thoo has to learn to live with him because he'll outlive us all.'

Daisy had not, for one moment, expected to hear the old farmer speak so movingly, or so fully, about his home. But she understood precisely what he was trying to say. He was telling her that the mountain gave him a sense of belonging, a permanence, made him feel one with the soil, a part of the fabric of his environment. And Daisy rather thought she could easily come to share that view.

Having said his piece, suddenly he stood up, lit a tilly lamp and with a jerk of his head urged her to follow him. 'Thoo can sleep up in t'loft. Theer's only the swallows and house martins to disturb you up theer. But I'll show you wheer t'petty is fost.'

He led her outside into a clear moonlit night, almost but not quite dark, along a stony path which trailed back as far as the wooded copse, Daisy following the circle of light from his lamp. 'Here it is. Allus tek a light with thoo to t'petty, so's we know it's occupied. It shows through th'hole like.'

Cut into the front of the door, at eye level, was a small diamond shaped hole. As well as serving the current incumbent to make his presence known, it also gave the next visitor the opportunity to peep in and check for a vacancy. Taking a lamp inside sounded like an excellent idea though. 'What happens in daytime, when you don't need the tilly lamp?'

'Can you whistle?'

'No.'

'Then sing. Watch out fer t'nettles on yer way back.' He handed her the lamp without another word and left her to make her acquaintance with the ramshackle building. Daisy sat on the wooden seat laughing till the tears ran down her cheeks. Why couldn't the silly old man fit a bolt on the inside? She could always try fixing one herself. In the meantime, she'd best learn how to whistle. It couldn't be any worse than her singing.

Back in the house, he was waiting for her at the foot of the stairs. Daisy dutifully picked up her bag and clattered up after him. They were surprisingly fine and wide with a carved banister rail and panelling on the walls, all sadly scratched and pitted with dirt, but beautifully crafted. She felt a knot of excitement somewhere deep inside. Something good was going to come out of finding Lane End Farm, she could sense it.

Daisy said. 'What time do you get up?'

'Early.'

'Will you wake me?'

'If you like.'

'Yes please. I'd like to help. I don't know anything about farming, but I feel sure I could learn. I want to pay me way. If you'll let me stop on for a bit, that is.'

He'd paused at a turn in the stairs to listen to this breathless little speech, lamp held high so that he could consider her with his keen-eyed gaze. She thought he might be about to say that he didn't want her to, or ask how long she intended staying, but whatever he saw in her face must have satisfied him for he simply nodded and continued to climb. Clearly a man of few words.

The loft bedroom was tiny, containing a narrow bed, a chest of drawers and nothing else. But from its tiny window under the eaves came again that breathtaking scene, fold upon fold of mountain in a landscape that seemed to stretch into infinity.

'That's Skiddaw over there,' Clem pointed out. 'And over theer, beyond Mungrisdale Common and Coombe Height you can see the Scottish Hills and the Solway Firth, in daylight that is. The light's fading fast right now.'

Daisy felt quite certain that she'd chanced upon heaven, and who knew what tomorrow might bring? She washed her face, scrubbed her teeth in the bowl that sat upon the chest, then quickly undressed, pulled on her nightgown and stretched out between the clean sheets, toes curling with excitement.

Tomorrow she'd explore further, take a peep in all the other rooms and outhouses, perhaps climb to the top of Blencathra, this friendly giant, just to see what it felt like to stand on top of the world. Daisy knew she wouldn't sleep a wink. It was all far too wonderful and thrilling. But with two long days' exercise behind her, the fresh air and a soft feather bed to sink her tired body into, her eyelids were drooping in no time. Her last conscious thought was that she hoped Aunt Florrie would be back tomorrow, from wherever it was she'd gone.

And deep in her heart Daisy knew that whatever happened, she'd be all right here at Lane End Farm. She was quite certain of it. It almost felt like coming home.

*

Florrie walked up Liverpool Street with hope in her heart, revelling in the familiar smells of smoke and tar, dust and grime, the crowds of people bustling about, grim-faced and unsmiling admittedly but that was the fault of the war, not Salford. She looked with pleasure upon the rows of back to back houses, the lines of washing blowing in the breeze, and the tall chimney stacks. She heard the shunt of trains, the sound of children's laughter, the clatter of clogs on the setts. She was home.

It was only as she neared the entry leading to Marigold Court that her pace slackened and doubt crept in. What reason would she give for choosing this moment to come? Why had she only now, after nearly a year, concerned herself with Daisy?

And what sort of a welcome could she expect from Rita after the years of silence?

And then on a rush of pain came the memory of the last occasion she'd visited her home city. Oh dear God, why had she done that? What had possessed her to abandon her child, even for only two days, just so she could have a bit of fun?

She stopped walking to lean back against a wall, gasping for breath and found, to her horror, that tears were rolling down her cheeks as the memories rushed in, forcing her to confront them. Convinced she'd made a terrible mistake and still deeply homesick when she had discovered she was pregnant, Florrie had cried throughout the entire nine months. Looking back now it filled her with shame and remorse how she'd longed to be free of the *encumbrance* of a baby, so that she could escape the chains of a bad marriage and life on the harsh, unforgiving fells. She'd felt that way until her beloved child had been born. Her darling, sweet, adorable Emma. The months following had been the happiest of her life, filled with joy and happiness. She'd even managed to cope better with her chores, and Clem, besotted by his new daughter, had been happy to relieve her of as many of them as he could.

But then one sunny day in April, all that happiness had crumbled to dust. Every single day of her life since, she'd longed to turn back the clock, to unwind her life like a piece of bad knitting so that she could change the pattern of it and stay at the farm. Had she done so, then surely her child would have been alive today?

Clem had made no objection when she'd asked to spend a couple of days with her family. On the contrary, he'd been pleased. 'Aye, it's long past time you went to see them, and they'll be glad to see our Emma, I'm sure. Just take care, love.'

Florrie knew he was telling her not to go out dancing or anything foolish of that sort, to be sure and come back safely to him, but she was still suffering deeply from homesickness, the quietness of the fells. She felt desperate for some fun, a bit of life and laughter. Her intention was to visit some of her old haunts, have a drink or two with friends. If she took baby Emma then Rita would be on at her the whole time not to go out, insisting she should stop in and mind her, as well as criticising everything she did for the child. Where would be the fun in that? What harm would it do to give herself a day or two away? 'I feel in need of a break, Clem. Couldn't you manage her on yer own, just fer once?'

He'd looked a bit nonplussed but had rallied quickly. 'Aye, course I can love. The rest will do you good,' he assured her, beaming proudly as he glanced over at his sleeping child in the pram standing out in the sunshine, 'and we can't both go away together, now can we, what with the lambing well under way?'

So Florrie had put on her glad rags as Clem called them, and set off with a light heart for a much-longed-for taste of city life. Her family had been surprised to see her, had chided her for not writing to warn them to expect her, and for not bringing the child. But Florrie had successfully kept up the fiction of being comfortably off. In her best frock and with the smart new coat Clem had bought her to wear at chapel, she'd certainly looked the part. They'd all been most impressed.

She'd had a good time showing off in front of her best friend, Doris Mitchell, too; performing a tango with her husband Frank and flirting outrageously with him.

It'd all been taken in good part, everyone just having a laugh but in the end Doris had butted in, told her to stick to the husband she'd got and leave hers alone, thank you very much. Florrie's was rich and Frank had nowt, only her, and she meant to keep it that way. Amused by his wife's jealousy, Frank had climbed up on to the bar counter, dragging Doris with him and done the tango with her there, tiptoeing between the glasses and sending several flying in their merry state.

It had all seemed so different from life on Blencathra, Florrie had been reluctant to leave and return home, save for her eagerness to see her child.

She'd returned to find Clem waiting for her at the station, standing forlornly by his farm truck, the expression on his face saying everything. Florrie had stopped short some twenty yards away, her heart in her mouth as fear crept through her like a black tide.

'What is it? What's happened?'

He told her then that their precious daughter was dead. On his way to the milking he'd taken a peep in at her and his shepherd's instinct had told him something was wrong.

'She didn't look right Florrie, so I went to pick her up. But it were too late.' Florrie felt as if she'd turned to stone, as if the world had stopped turning, as if everything inside her had been emptied out and destroyed. She stood listening but his words meant nothing, failing to penetrate her profound sense of disbelief. 'Theer were nowt I could do. I've brought any number of lambs back from the dead, but I could do nowt for me own lass.'

She saw the sobs well up in him, spill over, even in this public place and he an intensely private man. His whole body was shaking with the effort to control them but Florrie could do nothing to ease his distress.

She railed at him, beat him with her fists, fought him tooth and nail, screaming that he should have looked after her properly, while he struggled calmly to hold her, tears running silently down his cheeks. Florrie accused him of handling her roughly; demanded to know if he'd left her to choke on her bottle, or carelessly smothered her with a blanket? How could her precious child simply fall asleep and not wake up? Deep in her heart she knew that that was what had happened. It was nothing more than a terrible misfortune, the kind of thing that occurred all the time with babies, but why to them, why to their child? Didn't she deserve one piece of happiness in her life?

How he had got her home in that state she couldn't afterwards remember. The days following were a blur, but against all reason her anger needed someone to blame and Clem was the most likely candidate.

Florrie instructed her sister not to come to the funeral and Rita wrote back tartly informing her that God had taken the child away as punishment for her own wickedness, for her immoral behaviour in the past. Deep down Florrie believed this to be true. Hadn't she once considered her own child an *encumbrance*? It took all of her will-power not to scream at the undertakers when they'd carried away the tiny coffin. She would never get over her child's death. Never.

From that day on, everything changed. Florrie knew Clem must blame her too for he'd barely looked her in the eye since, nor had she ever let him touch her again. Never. She didn't dare take the risk, in case the same thing happened to another child.

She never went out, rarely stirred from her chair. If she did, she would forget what she had gone for and end up trailing from street to street as if searching for something, someone. Florrie became convinced that Emma was only just out of reach and if she searched hard enough, she would find her. She had only to glimpse a pram to be drawn to it like a magnet. She would stand and gaze upon the child within, drinking in the sight of a soft cheek, fluffy fair hair and tiny star-like fingers, seeing not an unknown child but her own precious Emma. She knew, in her heart, that it was not Emma, yet her longing was such that Florrie attempted by sheer will-power to conjure her own child in its place.

On one terrifying occasion, the baby was crying and needed a cuddle, and some part of her brain lost track of reality and she'd lifted the child from the pram. The mother came running from out of a nearby shop and shouted at Florrie. Bemused, she'd handed the baby over without a word and walked blindly away.

The pain had been so bad following that occasion, that Florrie rarely ventured far from the farm again. There were times when she chided herself for not making more of an effort to at least visit her nearest neighbours in the huddle of houses in the valley below, but Florrie shied away from the pity she saw in her friends' eyes, the sound of it in the special tone of voice they adopted whenever they spoke to her. Her loss was hard enough to bear. She'd no wish to be constantly reminded of it. Besides, she didn't trust herself. What if one of them had a baby, or her feet took her searching again? She couldn't take the risk.

Jess had clung on longer than most, trying to persuade her to continue with their Thursday afternoon outings into town, a bit of shopping, trip to the pictures followed by tea and cakes. They tried it once or twice but somehow Florrie had lost the ability to take part in small talk or chit-chat so that, in the end, Jess too had stopped coming. Florrie hadn't seen her in years.

Now she wondered what had brought her back to this

place. Why put herself through all of that pain again? Hope, and dreams, Florrie had discovered, were things of the past. Her child was dead and each and every morning when she woke, she too longed for that same state of oblivion. Which must surely be a sin too. Why had she come here? She didn't belong. Not in Salford, not in the Lakes. She had no real home, no family, no one at all to love her.

Perhaps things would have been easier over these last years if she'd been honest with Rita and Joe from the beginning about her situation; if she hadn't tried to hide the truth of her disappointment in Clem, or the situation she'd faced as a young bride in a strange setting. But then she'd hoped to make a go of her marriage, despite everything. She sometimes fooled herself into believing that she might well have succeeded, had Emma lived. But there was no proof of that.

She wiped away the tears, drew a lipstick from her handbag and applied it carefully. She would put on a brave face at least.

He woke her early, as he had promised, and again Daisy wondered where Florrie had gone but didn't like to ask, despite her curiosity. Clem would no doubt tell her when he was good and ready.

At breakfast, which he ate largely in silence while nodding sagely at Daisy's endless chatter about her adventures and worries over Megan and Trish, there'd been no mention of a missing wife. The nearest he came to referring to Florrie's absence was when he got up from the table, paused a moment, looking slightly perplexed then quietly remarked: 'Florrie generally sees to all this.'

Daisy glanced at the already full sink and hastily offered to wash up.

Clem nodded. 'She usually fills that girt box wi' peat morning and neet, an' all. The coup cart is in t'shed.'

'Right, I'll do that too, and should I stoke up the fire to keep it going?'

'Aye, pack it wi' peats and scatter a bit o' coal on top, only a tidy bit mind. That'll see it reet fer today. I dun't know what else she does in the house. Washing and such like. I know she meks bread on a Friday, gingercake and apple pasties usually; allus thrang she is on that day. Other than that, I can't say fer sure. I could show you the yard.'

It was almost as if, Daisy worried, he wasn't expecting Florrie back. But why would that be? Where could she have gone?

His pride was evident as he showed her around the farm,

not seeming to notice the way an outbuilding leaned peril-ously as if about to tumble over, loose guttering hung from a roof, or the way an unhinged door banged to and fro in the wind. He was too busy explaining how the calves needed feeding morning and night, on something called oilcake poddish, and the pigs mainly on household scraps. 'We likes 'em fat.' Then he told her how he used to 'butch' a bit at one time. 'After the war that were, the last one that is. Ah've gin it up now, save fer us own use.'

He instructed her on how to care for the hens, showing her the correct quantities of mash and corn. 'Awk'ard things, they are. More trouble than theer worth but we need the eggs. They 'as to be kept clean, d'you see, or you'll get problems. It's stinky in theer now. Leuks like they happen could do with a muck out. Florrie's bin a bit tekken up wi' other things lately like. Anyroad, it's not her favourite job to tackle.'

'I'll see to it.' Daisy said, eyeing them with nervous ap-prehension. The closest she'd ever come to a hen before was at Miss Pratt's. She supposed she could manage but would her aunt object? 'Aunt Florrie won't mind if I do a bit of tidying up, will she?'

'Nay, she'll niver notice,' and he walked away to indicate the subject was closed.

Was something wrong between them? Daisy wondered. Surely not. This set up wasn't at all the kind of life she'd been led to believe her aunt was living in the Lake District. No fancy house. No servants. Yet why would she lie? Why be ashamed of this? It surely couldn't be the fault of this harm-less little man who clearly still adored her, despite his main passion undoubtedly being his precious farm, and the moun-tain, of course.

Could that be it? Daisy wondered shrewdly. Did Florrie hate the farm? Did she not feel that she fitted in, or was she jealous of her husband's love for it? Only time would answer that puzzle, and she certainly didn't have any to spare to stand about pondering the problem. If she finished her chores by early afternoon, she could take a walk on Blencathra and see it for herself, and then write a postcard to Harry.

Rita was standing at the wash tub in the back kitchen, elbow deep in soap suds when Florrie walked in, and in that moment it was as if she'd never been away. She could smell the familiar, eye-watering odour of washing soda, feel the warm dampness cling to her hair in the steamy kitchen. Rita stopped rubbing the collar of a shirt against the rubbing board to stare at Florrie open-mouthed.

'By heck, which ill wind blew you in?'

Florrie walked over to the stove. 'I'll put t'kettle on, shall I? I'm fair parched with thirst and I dare say you need a cup of hot sweet tea for the shock.'

The tea was drunk largely in silence, Florrie having decided not to give any explanation about why she was there. She asked about Daisy but Rita only shrugged her shoulders.

'Don't ask me, I'm only her mother. We've no idea where she is. She's left her billet. Gone off in a sulk somewhere, I shouldn't wonder. Allus was independent to a fault. Cut off her nose to spite her face, that one. We offered her the chance to come home but she refused. Getten hersel' another chap up there in the Lakes, so she's running true to form, no better than she should be and we know where she gets that from, don't we?'

Florrie didn't rise to the jibe. 'Have you been to see her recently then?'

'Me? No, why should I? I sent our Joe.'

'But it's been near a year.'

'She doesn't deserve no namby-pambying from me.' And then the whole sorry tale was told from start to finish, Rita savouring every word as if to justify her actions. Florrie listened in silence. What was there to say? 'Poor girl,' was all she managed in the end.

'Poor girl?' Rita looked affronted. 'What about us, her mam and dad? What about the shame, the immorality of it all? We're the ones who have to live here, amongst all the sly looks and behind-hands gossip. Poor girl my foot. She doesn't deserve one jot of sympathy, nor will she get one, not from me.'

'I shouldn't imagine she expects to,' Florrie remarked drily. Draining her cup, she set it down for Rita to refill it. A small silence followed as each sister took refuge in their own thoughts by way of defence, as if wary of confrontation. It was Rita who, itching to know what was going on, gave in first. 'So, to what do we owe this unexpected pleasure? How come you've landed up here, doing a bit o'slumming?'

'I can come and see me own family, I hope, without needing to say why?'

'I don't know about that, not after – what is it now – near twenty year? Tha's a niece tha's never seen for one thing.'

'That's not true, I have seen her. I saw Daisy when she were little, that time I paid you a visit before – before we lost our Emma.'

'Oh aye, I forgot about that. You acting daft as a brush wi' Frank Mitchell. You didn't have another then?'

'No.'

'Thought not. Too busy living the life of Riley I suppose, to want it spoiled with kids.' Rita's tone didn't soften in the slightest, not even noticing as Florrie flinched at her words. She poured some of the hot tea into her saucer, blew on it, then slurped it up from there. Florrie watched the perform-ance in silence but the disgust must have shown in her face for Rita said, 'Don't look like that. We don't all have your chances to learn how things are done proper. We do what we wants to here. Anyroad, it's still a fair while since you come, so, what's fetched you now? Has he run off and left you?'

'Don't be daft. I found that letter of Daisy's and I was wondering how she was, that's all, sorry I didn't offer to help when perhaps I should've done. What happened to the baby?'

'What d'you think? It's getten a good home, and nobody can pin it on us. What else matters?'

'Daisy's feelings perhaps. I'd like to see her. Where was she evacuated to, and why is she moving billets? Don't you know?'

'Nay, I've no idea. She fell out wi' her dad and took herself off, happen wi' this new fella of hers.' Rita started to laugh. 'It's a bit of a turn-up, you being here when she's somewhere in your neck of the woods. Up in the Lakes.'

'Yes, I saw that she was from that Christmas card you sent on to me. I meant to write to ask exactly where but – but I've been so busy I – I forgot, and then I bethought mesel to come and see you all instead.'

'Tha should have let us know fost. I'd've put out the flags.'

Another silence, time enough for Florrie to reflect that her coming back home had been a complete waste of time. It was far too late to help Daisy, even if she could be found. But now that she was here . . . Florrie cleared her throat. 'I was wondering about stopping on for a bit. You'd have no objection, would you?'

Rita's eyes flew wide and Florrie could see that her head was buzzing with questions, that she was itching to know what on earth had happened to make her sister walk out on her fancy life and rich husband. 'Well, strike me down with a wet kipper, what's getten into thee? We've no maidservants nor butlers here, that's for sure.'

'If you're just going to be rude to me, p'rhaps it were a mistake me coming.' Florrie got up as if to go, but Rita wafted a hand at her to sit down again.

'Allus jumping on yer high horse. I niver said tha couldn't stay, I were just making the point that I'll not wait on you hand, foot and finger. Tha's still family so I reckon there's no reason why you shouldn't stop on fer a bit, but you looks after yersen and thee hands over your ration book.'

Florrie slapped it on the table. 'Can I go and have a wash now? Or does hot water come extra?'

After a wash and a bite to eat, Florrie took a chair and went to sit at the front door, as she had used to do years ago. From here she could see people going about their business. Women carrying their shopping baskets in search of 'a bit o' summat fer tea', or 'camping' in doorways, having a 'sup o' tea' afore their men get home from the mills.

She wondered how often these conversations had concerned herself and Clem, speculating on this grand life she was supposedly living in the Lake District, or Daisy and her sudden disappearance. What a family they were, although Florrie doubted they were any more unfortunate, or less moral than any other. These were hard times, always had been to Florrie's way of thinking.

She saw her old friend Doris Mitchell go by, arm in arm with Milly Crawshaw. Florrie called out a greeting but when Doris glanced in her direction, she didn't wave or come galloping over for a gossip, she looked quickly away again, chin high, as if she didn't want to know and the pair strode on up the street, faces set in a mirror image of contempt.

'And to think she was once me best friend. We went everywhere together,' Florrie complained.

Rita, coming to join her on the doorstep at that moment, gave a loud sniff. 'If you act all toffee-nosed wi' folk, why should they bother about you? Anyroad, she doesn't trust you with her husband.'

Florrie made no reply, more hurt than she cared to admit by the rebuff. This wasn't at all what she'd hoped for. She hadn't expected it to be easy to pick up her old life where she'd left off but she'd hoped that her friends, at least, would welcome her back. Apparently she was wrong.

The muffin man came along next, calling out his wares. 'Muffins and pikelets. Buy 'em while they're fresh.'

Tempted by the prospect of hot crumpets with a dab of marg running through the holes, and needing something to cheer her, Florrie ran to fetch her purse and bought a couple for each of them. Rita didn't thank her. 'Think I can't afford to buy me own food now, do you?'

'Don't be daft! Course I don't. I just reckoned they'd be a treat.' She stowed them away in the bread jar to keep fresh till supper and went back to sit in the chair. But all the happiness she had felt when she'd decided, on impulse, to come at last to Salford, had quite evaporated. It had been a mistake. First, it had reminded her of that last visit and her subsequent loss. Secondly, Rita clearly wasn't going to make things easy for her, and last, but by no means least, she didn't seem to have any friends here either.

Florrie wondered what Clem's reaction would be when he found her note. Happy to have a bit of peace for a while, or glad to be shut of her? How long did she mean to stay, and where else could she go? Where did she belong? She'd give it a couple of weeks or so, and make up her mind then.

Daisy came to like Clem more and more with each day, each week that passed, recognising his dry wit and warming to it, his solid strength and unflappable personality. She knew he wasn't yet sixty, though he looked older, and that her aunt was considerably younger than him but she couldn't help wondering what had driven Florrie from her home? Why had she chosen to leave, and where had she gone? According to the wireless, September had been a terrible month with raids in many major cities, so that even the King had gone to see how the people were faring. Where was Florrie, and was she safe?

The year was passing quickly and Daisy knew that here in the Lakes, the back end, as they called it, was actually the start of the farming year, war or no war in a few weeks' time the

tups would be put to the ewes. Would Florrie be back by
then? At length, curiosity got the better of her and Daisy
resolved to find the answer.

She found Clem in the barn one morning, mixing a dose
for his sheep. It smelled dreadful but, determined not to be
put off, she held to her purpose and asked her question. 'I was
wondering about Aunt Florrie. How she was and that. Will
she be back soon, d'you reckon? And where was it, exactly,
that she went? I'm curious to know.' She felt all fluttery and
nervous inside, fearful of hearing bad news. 'I'm so looking
forward to meeting her. We've never had a chance to get to
know one another proper.'

'Tha's only a li'le lass, tha wouldn't understand about
married foalk.'

'How will I know, if you don't tell me?'

He stood stock still to consider her, then he took off his cap
and scratched his head while he gave the matter more
thought. 'If anybody had telt me as being wed were so difficult, a feather would a felt me. Once I'd see'd her, I thowt I'd
be in clover but she's not easy i'n't Florrie. Not an easy
woman at all. 'Afe the time she leuks like she's swallowed a
shilling and f'un' a penny.' A shaft of sunlight coming
through the door glinted on his silver-grey hair and Daisy got
the feeling that he wasn't usually so forthcoming, that in some
way he was opening his heart to her. But what could she
possibly say in response to this mild criticism of the absent
Florrie? And if she really was an old misery-boots, as he
seemed to be implying, perhaps she had good reason.

Daisy sat down on a bale of hay and waited, vowing that
if she had to wait all day, she'd get to the bottom of it. She
couldn't go on living in another woman's house, or start
making changes to it unless she knew how she stood. It took
no more than twenty seconds before he carefully replaced
his cap and sat down beside her. Then he stunned her by
saying that odd as it may seem, while Daisy was here in

Lakeland looking for her aunt, Florrie was in Salford looking for Daisy.

Daisy's mouth dropped open in shock. 'Why didn't you tell me that in the first place?' And then she saw why, reflected in the sadness of his faded grey eyes. 'You thought I'd go after her, if you told me, didn't you? And you didn't want me to go. You wanted me to stay.'

'It gets a mite lonely up here. I like the quiet but . . .'

'You can have too much of a good thing, eh?'

'Florrie allus says I talk more t'yows than I do to her. I used to say it's because they don't moan all the time.' He gave a shamefaced smile. 'Happen she's right.'

Daisy pressed her lips firmly together to stifle a giggle at this entrancing picture of Florrie talking to Clem and getting no answer, while Clem talked to his precious sheep because they didn't nag him or moan. But then his next words wiped the smile from her face. 'It might've been different, if 'n we hadn't lost the bairn.'

'What bairn?' Daisy edged closer, all ears, and then it was as if a plug had been drawn and Clem, once having started talking couldn't seem to stop. He told her all about the joy he'd felt when Florrie had given him a daughter, her trip to Salford to see family and friends and how he'd been left in charge of the infant, only to wake and find her dead in her cot. 'It fair shattered us both, I don't mind telling you.'

'I can imagine.'

'And she didn't have any more children?'

'Florrie weren't keen.' Clem looked away and Daisy realised she'd accidentally trodden on tricky territory.

'I see. The pain would have been terrible, of course. I can see why she would be afraid of it happening again.'

'Can you? It's not generally summat folk can understand, unless they've experienced it fer themselves.'

'I had a baby,' Daisy said, surprising herself as much as him by the sudden need to reveal her secret. He turned to stare at her wide-eyed, bushy brows raised in open curiosity. 'Didn't you know? I thought Mam wrote to Aunt Florrie.'

He shook his head. 'Nay, I wouldn't know about that. Women's stuff. Nowt to do wi' me.'

Daisy told him anyway. He'd been honest with her and she was equally so with him. He didn't judge her, or tell her she was a bad lass but by the time the tale was told, Daisy knew they were going to be firm friends.

'Leuks like we've both been in t'wars then,' and they smiled shyly at each other in perfect understanding and acknowledgement of the other's pain. Somehow or other it seemed in that moment as if they had forged a special relationship, an empathy that Daisy had never experienced with anyone else, certainly not with her own father.

'You won't tell, will you? I'm supposed to keep quiet about it. It's meant to be a secret. Mam says I've to say nothing to anyone, because of the shame.'

'And how do you feel about that?'

'I don't know.' Daisy frowned. 'I have a fella, Harry.'

'And you haven't towd him like?'

'No, I haven't told him. Not yet. Do you think I should?'

'Nay, it's not fer me to advise.'

'He's asked me to marry him.'

'Then happen, when thoo's ready to wed him, tha'll be ready to tell him about the bairn. Do you know where it is?'

Daisy shook her head. 'Mam said he's gone to a good home.'

'It were a boy then?'

Daisy nodded, quite unable in that moment, to speak, as they both considered the implications. Daisy knew instinctively that he was wishing he'd known sooner, that he would willingly have given her baby a good home and loved it with all his heart, yet for reasons best known to herself, Florrie evidently hadn't felt the same way. Daisy couldn't bear to think about how grand it would have been to have come here to have her baby, to see it brought up within her own family. And yet, if she couldn't have him all to herself, perhaps that would have caused jealousy between herself and Florrie. Perhaps Mam was right, and it was better not knowing where he'd gone, or whose arms held him.

'How about a cuppa?' Daisy offered, fiercely blinking the unshed tears away. 'Usually I have a brew about this time, do you?'

'Aye, if I get chance.'

Later, he said: 'You'll have to forgive Florrie for not offering to help. Happen Rita didn't write after all. I'm sure she would have done, had she known.'

'I'm sure she would,' Daisy agreed, and didn't tell him that Rita most definitely had written to her sister, months ago, and cursed her when she'd got no reply.

It had taken only a matter of weeks in Salford to convince Florrie that this couldn't be considered a permanent arrangement. Rita was constantly dropping hints that she'd like to see the back of her with such comments as, 'You can't feed three as cheaply as two, tha knows,' and 'There's some what can just sit on their backside and let others get on with all the work and worry.'

Florrie considered both charges to be unfair and uncalled for and would valiantly defend herself. 'I've not been well.'

'You and the rest of the flamin' army,' would be Rita's stinging response. 'You need to give yoursel' a good shake, you. Start by doing more around th'house.'

'I can't lift anything heavy. I've a bad back.'

'Don't try that one with me. You're as healthy as they come and I've told thee, there's no flippin' servants to fetch and carry for thee here.'

No one could win an argument with Rita.

Certainly Joe never attempted such a thing. Florrie had at first felt some contempt for the mild mannered little man, and then a reluctant sort of affection. Joe would sit with his head buried behind the *Daily Herald*, saying nothing throughout his wife's rantings, then he'd quietly put on his cap and go off to the pub. He claimed to be full of ideas for his rag and bone business, going from strength to strength he said, with the price of scrap metal being what it was, which would help him to stash away enough savings to get them out of Marigold Court once hostilities were over. Yet he never seemed to get round to putting these plans into effect. The money went out as fast as it came in. Each evening he'd go off to place a bet, or for a pint or two with his mates. Then he'd stagger home the worse for wear and from the upstairs back bedroom, Florrie would lie listening to the row coming from down below. She'd hear the crash as something was knocked over as he slumped into his chair, or if Rita flung his supper at him. She'd pull the covers over her ears to avoid listening to the furious argument which followed between husband and wife. When he was in drink, was the only time Joe had the courage to answer her back.

In a way, he reminded her of Clem and yet there was a difference. Clem might have little to say but even Florrie recognised his strength. Clem was a worker. He put everything he had into his farm and there was rarely a penny left over to squander on betting or going down to the pub despite his enjoying a half-pint now and then after an auction. Joe, on the other hand, would readily take a morning off if he was suffering from a hangover. Florrie decided that unlike Clem, who had time only for stark reality, Joe was a man of dreams, but he'd never fulfil those dreams, not in a million years. Joe was weak. He was too henpecked by a carping wife and too hell-bent on self-preservation and escape, as a result.

Yet he alone offered Florrie some sort of a welcome. 'Just think of it as yer own home, lass,' he told her.

'Nay, we're not half grand enough for that,' Rita

commented drily. 'How long are we to be honoured with your ladyship's presence then?'

'I haven't decided yet.'

'Ooh, hoity-toity!'

'Nay, leave t'lass alone,' he remarked bravely. 'How can she go anywhere when t'bloody Germans are bashing our boys to bits in the skies every night. Have you noticed, Rita, that there's a war going on outside your front door? It says in the *Daily Herald* here that the East End is taking a licking, and Liverpool was bombed for four nights on the trot at the end of August. Manchester won't escape. Mark my words.'

'Never!' Rita snorted, as if even the Germans wouldn't dare to cross her, or bomb her city. 'The worst we've had is when that policeman were hit on the head by that bundle of propaganda leaflets.'

'Well, just in case, I'd best mek sure that Anderson shelter is sound and waterproof.' And off he ambled, any excuse to make his escape, as usual.

Joe was soon proved right. Large-scale bombing was taking place in every major city from London to Liverpool, from Bristol to Coventry. 'Britain can take it,' rang out from everybody's lips. Nobody was ready for giving up, not yet, not ever. Hadn't Winston Churchill himself urged them 'to dare and to endure' in his speech at the Free Trade Hall only last January? Words which were to prove prophetic, for Manchester suffered its first air raid at the end of December 1940.

Rita paid not the slightest attention to the siren when it went off on the evening of the twenty-second. She was too busy moaning about how she was going to manage to feed an extra mouth all over Christmas, and berating her sister over something and nothing, as usual.

Rita was notoriously mean when it came to food, and thoroughly self-righteous. She'd ladle a pitifully small quantity of meat on to Florrie's plate together with a pile of cabbage and happily tell her that green vegetables were better for her anyway. She could make a two-ounce weekly ration of tea go further than anyone Florrie knew, mainly by scalding the leaves over and over till there was no flavour left in them. She'd once saved up her sugar coupons for weeks in the hope of having enough to make jam, but then the grocer had told her that if she could manage a month without her regular supply, she could go on doing without it. Florrie had been so pleased to see Rita put in her place, she'd laughed like a drain.

That's what the argument was about now. A spoonful of sugar.

Florrie was badly missing her own kitchen, a place where she could put on the kettle without feeling as if someone was standing over her counting how many spoonfuls she used, or whether or not she'd spilled any precious grains, which is what she'd accidentally done on this occasion. 'I need lots of sugar, to keep my strength up,' she'd defended herself when Rita had flown at her with fury-filled eyes. 'I'm so tired all the time.'

'Hard luck! Thee can have saccharine, like the rest of us.'

'Damn you Rita Atkins. Can't you think of anything but food, of anyone but yourself, anyone else's needs but your own? You're that flamin' selfish you turned your own daughter out because of *your* shame, not *hers*. And God knows where she is now, poor lass.'

Somewhere, not too far off there came a loud explosion and the small house shook, scattering powdered plaster dust over both women. Neither seemed to notice, or moved an inch as they stood, almost nose to nose, hands on hips roaring and shouting at each other above the din.

'Don't you preach to me, Florrie Pringle! You could have helped our Daisy but you were too high and flamin' mighty to even write back.'

Because this was dangerously close to the truth, if an unfair distortion of it, Florrie turned her back and swung away, feeling sick to the heart at her own callousness, knowing it was too late now to do anything. The baby had been adopted and there was an end of the matter. And it was all her fault. 'I wish you'd just sent her to me, instead of writing.'

'What difference would that have made, if I had?'

'I don't know. Everything, perhaps. You know how afraid I am of getting too fond of children in case . . . but if I'd been faced with it, I might've managed to get over that. You never know.'

'Oh, put away the violins.'

Florrie flushed. 'Why do you have to be so heartless?

You're her mother, for God's sake. You should have done more.'

'What? What could I have done? Don't you put the blame on me. Why would I send my daughter to a sister who never visits, never writes and can't even be bothered answer a cry for help. Well? What do you say to that? What's wrong wi' us that we don't warrant more than a Christmas card?'

Once more Florrie attempted to leave, oblivious to the dust and mayhem outside, the fires that had started up and down the street and were even now being fanned by a stiff breeze. But before she reached the door, Rita made a grab for her sister's hair and yanked her back, making her scream out in agony. 'Don't you *dare* walk away from me, not when I'm talking to you. There's summat tha's not telling us and I want to know what it is. What fetched thee here in the first place? Why asta left your precious husband, all your riches, your posh house and servants. What is it you're after?'

Within seconds the pair were rolling on the floor, scratching and tearing at each other while countless incendiaries and high explosive bombs dropped on the city all around them. The two sisters simply raised their voices and screamed and yelled all the louder as the argument raged on, so that it looked as if one might surely murder the other before ever the war settled the matter for them. Nobody, certainly not Mr Hitler, was going to interfere with this, Rita's most important mission in life.

When Joe stuck his head round the door minutes later, looking frantic, he took in the scene at a glance. 'Flamin' Nora, what's got into the pair of you? This is no time for a fisticuffs, the world's coming to an end out here,' and he bundled the pair of them under the stairs, Rita protesting loudly that she didn't want to be anywhere near her dratted sister.

'Well put your mind to it, or you'll be sharing a coffin instead.'

The following night when the siren sounded, Rita was the first to head for the shelter, Florrie and Joe hot foot behind. The three of them ran through the rushing crowds of people, some shouting for loved ones, others shrieking in fear, children crying and explosions going off everywhere. They sat huddled together in silent misery until the 'all-clear' sounded some twelve long hours later. When they finally emerged, bleary eyed, black-faced and badly shaken, it was to discover that bombs had fallen on the bus and tram depot on the corner of Eccles New Road and even a tram had been hit, killing all the passengers inside.

'We're lucky to be alive,' Florrie said, appalled by the destruction that met her eyes.

'Aye,' Joe said. 'So I'll have no more squabbling from you two. Think on, let's have peace between our own four walls for Christmas, at least.'

Back home, they moved blankets and pillows under the stairs, and since all the glass had been blown out of the windows, Joe nailed black roofing felt to the frames. 'And no more locking the doors,' he warned them. 'Just in case we need to be rescued.'

'We could be murdered in our beds,' Rita complained hotly.

'Save Hitler a job then.'

It was a grim thought. And so they spent a cold and miserable Christmas, with neither electricity, gas nor water, only a meagre fire for comfort, and cold corned beef sandwiches to eat since they couldn't cook. Nor did they take any pleasure in each other's company by way of consolation. But even Rita was too frightened to object loudly.

When Laura had taken the booking for a single room from a Mr Beazley, she'd thought nothing of it, assuming him to be a walker. Strictly speaking she wasn't open for business until next week as she still had one or two tasks to finish off but she'd decided it would be good practice before the rush started, so had gladly accepted it. Now Felix was standing on her doorstep smiling his devilish smile and admitting that Mr Beazley was none other than himself, that he'd made the booking in an imitation Scots accent and looking thoroughly pleased with himself for having taken her in.

'Well you can't possibly stay. That's trickery.'

'I don't see why not. Even if you hadn't just let me a room, I'm still your husband, so stop being hysterical, Laura, and let me in. We have things to discuss.'

This was certainly true. 'You stay in the room that you booked, then. No prowling about making a nuisance of yourself, imagining you can turn back the clock.'

'Of course not,' he commented mildly, as if the thought had never crossed his mind.

To say they enjoyed a pleasant evening together would have been stretching the truth somewhat. She'd explained her plans to him in a civilised fashion at last, outlined recent conversations with her solicitor and warned him to expect papers to sign soon regarding the divorce. He'd taken all this in without argument, in fact they hadn't disagreed about a single thing. Had Laura not been quite so thankful that the evening had passed tolerably well, and that he was leaving first thing in the morning, this might have troubled her more. As it was, she carefully locked her bedroom and went straight to sleep.

She was woken at six by the sound of an engine throbbing loudly right outside her window, and the hiss of air brakes. Climbing sleepily out of bed she went to the window to investigate. What was going on? A removal van stood at her front door. She could quite clearly see the top of it but because of her bedroom window being so high up in the loft, she could see nothing more. She could, however, hear Felix's voice issuing instructions, the words unclear at this distance.

Laura splashed her face with cold water and dressed as

quickly as she could, desperate to know what was happening downstairs. By the time she got there, three men were already struggling to get the carved oak court cupboard out of the front door.

'What the hell are you doing?' Flushed with fury, she stood rooted to the spot in shock. Felix turned and gave her a lopsided smile.

'Just taking my cut, darling. My share from the inheritance. There are one or two choice items of furniture here which will fetch a good price at auction and since you were too busy to deal with the matter, I organised it myself. It will partly compensate me for your intransigence over the matter of the sale. Of course, should you change your mind about that then I'll call a halt, since antique furniture of this quality left *in situ* would hike up the property value quite a bit.'

'Property value? Auction? What is this? Some sort of blackmail? You think you can bully me into agreeing to sell by pinching my furniture? *Put that down this minute!*' She stormed up to the three removal men. 'That cupboard is mine, left to me by my grandmother, and it's going nowhere.'

Looking troubled and having no wish to become embroiled in a marital dispute, one, clearly the leader of the little trio, ordered his men to put the piece down. 'We'll leave you two to talk things through while we go and have breakfast in the van. Let us know when you've sorted it all out.' Whereupon they began to shuffle off.

'Oh no you don't,' Felix said, blocking their exit. 'I hired you to do a job and you'll do it. My wife is simply being difficult but will come around to reality any moment.'

'Oh, no she won't.' Laura informed him briskly.

'Indeed you will, darling.'

'Aye, well when she does, *if* she does, you let us know mister. We'll be in the van.' And they scuttled out before he had the chance to stop them.

'Now look what you've done by your stupid obstinacy. I've

paid a fortune to get them here.' Felix was spitting his fury at her. 'I could always send in the bailiffs if you prefer.'

Laura was already on the phone, ringing Capstick who told her, in no uncertain terms, that the furniture belonged to her, not her husband, and that he could not remove it without risk of being sued. She handed the phone to him. 'Nick would like to talk to you. Be polite, we're fortunate he's the diligent sort of solicitor who believes in an early start to the day. I believe he wishes to explain the law of theft to you and how he'd have you arrested before you reached the end of the lane.'

While Felix argued and railed at the young solicitor, issuing dire threats which didn't seem to get him anywhere, Laura made a cup of tea for the removal men. It wasn't their fault after all, and they'd come all the way from Cheshire, making an exceptionally early start, and would return empty handed. Obligingly, they returned the court cupboard to its proper place, even putting back the precious pieces of china they'd taken out before moving it. 'I'm sure my husband will compensate you with a hefty tip for your inconvenience.'

'Damned if I will,' roared Felix. 'Don't think you've beaten me, Laura. This is but the first skirmish.'

'Would you like your bill, Mr Beazley, since you're checking out?' she enquired sweetly, and he said something very rude to her, climbed into his Mercedes and drove away in a flurry of gravel.

'Don't worry love,' said the removal man. 'We got our money up front.'

With breakfast over, having expelled her excess of temper by beating rugs, bashing pillows and scrubbing baths, Laura had got her heart rate back down to normal and thankfully made herself a welcome cup of coffee. If this was a skirmish, she didn't care to think what the next assault might be. Felix really was the most objectionable man. It made her wonder what she had ever seen in him. Couldn't he understand that the more he bullied her, the more stubbornly she clung to her rights? She would not be driven into selling this place, no matter what tricks he tried.

Laura reached for Daisy's letters as she often did when she needed to feel close to her grandmother. Sometimes her presence was very strong, almost as if she were here beside her, which was somehow a comfort in the grieving process.

She handled the precious love letters with care, some quite hard to decipher in tiny, crabbed writing as if to save paper, others she'd read several times and almost knew by heart.

Laura glanced at one which was simply a diary of events finishing with, '*Yet another boring day in the post room, you will come on Thursday as usual, won't you?*' Had that been when she was working for Mr Chapman? she wondered. And then one marked with a later date said: '*I love it here at the farm, not that I'm much good at anything yet. I cleaned out the hen house this morning and tried to put mite powder under all their wings. Only caught about three of them but you should have heard the racket! I've probably put them off laying for weeks. Oh, and our day out in Silloth was smashing. I can't wait for the next.*'

She must have written to Harry several times a week for one bundle contained a flurry of letters all dated within quite a short period of time, full of amusing snippets of all that had been involved in getting the boarding house ready.

Another said: '*Florrie was cross with me today because I've made some changes she doesn't approve of. It can't be easy for her with the way things are at present. It's her kitchen, after all. She insists that my boarding house idea is doomed to failure. Clem said to her, "Thanks for your vote of confidence, Florrie. We knew you'd be keen." He has such a droll wit at times he makes me laugh, but Florrie can never see the funny side of anything which makes him worse. What a pair they are. You will get some leave soon, I hope.*' This one was dated September 1941. So they must have got the boarding house going by then or at least had some lodgers. But life was not entirely without problems for them either by the sound of it, and poor Florrie being her usual, pessimistic self.

Laura picked up another and read it with painstaking care, the writing even more crabbed and scribbled than usual, as if dashed off in a great hurry. She could feel the anguish in every word, like a cry from the heart. '*Oh, when do you think you'll get some leave? There's something awful happened. I need to explain and it can't be done by letter. Mother is here and she's being very difficult but I daren't say anything as we can't get married without her permission.*'

The letter closed, '*Oh, do say you're coming soon Harry. I'm having such problems.*' What could have happened? What kind of problems was her mother causing now? Laura rifled quickly through the next few letters but could find no further references to Rita, no more letters to Harry after that date, only a mundane catalogue of events or everyday gossip. It was then that she chanced upon one short letter from Harry. Almost in shreds, it had been singed brown, as if someone had tried to burn it and then changed their mind at the last moment just before it burst into flames, which had made it largely unreadable. A few clear words which had escaped destruction almost broke Laura's heart: '*How could you do this to me Daisy, after all we've meant to each other? I think I might die.*'

She sat with the letter on her lap and shared his anguish. What had Daisy done that had hurt him so badly? It could only be that she'd cheated on her lovely Harry, after all.

'Oh, Daisy, how could you? And after your romantic day out in Silloth. What on earth had gone wrong?'

Daisy walked arm in arm with Harry on the West Beach at Silloth all the way along to the pier. They would like to have explored the docks as far as the lifeboat station and watch the fishermen bringing in their freshly caught flounders but Harry said that area was closed to unauthorised personnel, which reminded Daisy about the war and made her feel a bit sick and uncomfortable inside. A few families or other couples, servicemen and their sweethearts like themselves, sat huddled together, warming each other against a cool spring breeze. Once a favourite destination for holidaymakers, there were few around today and not simply because it was too early in the season. Holidays seemed to be a thing of the past, taken at a time when the sound of German bombers didn't fill the air every night, when the sky over Barrow and Liverpool didn't glow ominously red.

Evacuation was again under way and Daisy would often think of her two little friends, Megan and Trish. She wrote to them regularly and wished they were here with her now, enjoying the sunshine though the paddling pool was almost empty and the donkeys were nowhere in sight. Daisy had lost a few pennies on the slot machines in the amusement arcade but had soon grown bored. She didn't have enough in her pocket to risk losing and where was the fun in watching other people win?

But having no money was of no consequence to Daisy. She felt perfectly content. All that truly mattered was that she and Harry were together again after many long weeks apart. This had been partly because of her change of billet, but also Harry had been involved in some op with the Coastal Command.

'It's seemed like years,' she said, hugging his arm close and rubbing her cheek against his shoulder. The fabric of his uniform felt rough against her skin but it smelled of sunshine and hair cream, of warmth and love and his gentle strength, of whatever made him uniquely Harry. It was an intensely masculine, erotic scent, enough to kindle a nub of excitement within.

'How about we buy an ice cream each and go and find those sand dunes? We can shelter from the wind and maybe find a bit of privacy for an hour.'

told her that he wanted somewhere private so that
kiss her again, and Daisy was more than willing.
ttle of pop?'

He grinned. 'What sort do you like?'

'Tizer.'

They sat enjoying their treat in silence, too full of emotion
to find the words to express them. Then they lay together
in the curve of a dune, protected from the wind and the eyes
of the world, and Harry told her over and over how much he
loved her as he kissed and caressed her. He promised faithfully that he'd always come home to her safe and well, no
matter what, war or no war. Daisy held him tight and offered
him all her love in return, fighting back the tears, desperately
striving to be brave. 'I wouldn't mind,' she said, 'if you
wanted to – you know.'

'*I* would mind, very much.' He sounded faintly shocked.
'What sort of a chap d'you think I am? If there weren't a war
on . . . No, I won't say anything, not yet. I can't.'

'Say what?' Heart in her mouth, Daisy had believed for a
moment that he was about to propose, but that was foolish.
They'd hardly known each other five minutes.

Harry looked down at her, his loving gaze moving over her
face as if memorising every feature, but he said nothing, only
shook his head, giving a sad sort of smile.

Daisy frowned. 'What's wrong? You're quiet today. What
is it?' Then she put her hands to her mouth, her face going
all white as the blood drained away. 'Oh, no! You've been
posted, haven't you? Why didn't you tell me right away?'

'I didn't want to spoil our day.'

'Oh Harry!'

He put both his arms about her then and let her weep into
the solid warmth of his tunic. 'You see, that's why I didn't tell
you. I didn't want you upset.'

'I'd have been upset anyway.' After a moment or two,
Daisy dashed the tears away with a determined smile. 'But

you're right, there's nothing we can do about it, so we mus[t] enjoy today. Every minute of it. I want you to think of m[e] smiling, not blubbering all over you.'

He kissed her mouth, a soft, sweet, lingering kiss that held a promise of so much more. 'That's why I love you.'

'Why?'

'Because you're so strong, so full of life and joy, so – so thoroughly nice.'

Daisy giggled. 'If you like nice girls, you picked a wrong un here.'

'I don't believe that. I picked the best.'

Daisy swallowed. 'Oh Harry. You say such lovely things.'

They each had difficulty resisting the emotions that were running high between them as they kissed and cuddled, but it was Harry who pulled away first, his face filled with guilt and pain. 'We leave the day after tomorrow. Don't ask me where to, because I don't know, but you can be certain, Daisy love, that I'll write to you at the first opportunity I get.'

And she had to be satisfied with that. She had to send him on his way with love and hope in her heart, after which she got back on the train and cried all the way home.

A winter of bombing gave way to yet more fears of invasion and finding themselves in more danger in their billets on the coast, many evacuees returned to their home towns. Megan and Trish were allowed no such luxury. Their new guardians, a Mr and Mrs Carter, were at pains to point out how very fortunate they were to be billeted with them, and what a mistake it would be for them to go back to their mother and their drab city lives.

They burned all the clothes the children had been given by the Marshalls. 'Just in case,' Mrs Carter told them, barely touching them with the tips of her dainty fingernails. Megan wasn't sure what she meant by this exactly but when their mam came on her next visit and all three of them were expected to sit in the garden and not come into the house, she said it again. 'You all stay out there. Just in case.' The fact that it was bitterly cold and starting to rain didn't seem to strike her as a problem.

Megan suggested it might be because a bomb could drop on the house while they were sitting having tea, but her mam said they didn't get bombs in Penrith, which was why she felt safe to leave them there, so the mystery remained. Not that it greatly mattered. The children were too thrilled to see their mother to care one way or the other where they sat, or whether or not it was raining. Daisy had visited them once or twice but it was a long way for her to come now she was in Keswick and without their best friend they were desperately homesick. Trish had been sick twice recently, just from crying too much, and Megan hated her new school with a fierce loathing. They tried once more to persuade their mother to let them come home but, sadly, she was having none of it, telling them horrifying tales of the blitz, and what lucky girls they were to be missing it.

'Don't I love the bones of you both? What would I do if owt happened to you two? I'd be fit fer nowt. I'd die of a broken heart, I would. No, no, you stop here, warm and snug, till it's all over.'

But the mystery deepened when, on discovering new scabs between Trish's fingers, Mrs Carter moved them out to what she called the summer house, little more than a large shed at the bottom of the long garden. 'There,' she said, 'won't this be exciting, sleeping here in your own little house? Think of it as your very own air-raid shelter.'

'Why, is Penrith going to be bombed after all?'

'No, no, of course it isn't. Now be good little girls and don't ask quite so many questions.' She appeared flustered as she began to fetch blankets and pillows. No sheets, Megan noticed with some relief. They weren't expected to die out here then.

Trish spotted a spider and began to cry. 'I don't like it. I want Daisy.'

Megan said, 'Have we to stop in this shed all the time?'

'It's a summer house, dear.'

'Whatever it is, it's a bit draughty,' giving a little shiver to prove her point.

'Nonsense! Good, healthy temperature. If necessary I could always send Trish to a hostel for problem children. That might be for the best. Just in case.' So there it was again, those same words.

'In case what?' Trish asked in a panic, when camp beds had been made up for them and Mrs Carter had vanished indoors, leaving a trail of Attar of Roses in her wake. 'What are problem children, and why have I to go to hospital?'

'A hostel,' Megan corrected her, cold fear gathering about her heart.

'I'm not going nowhere without you, our Megan.'

'No, course you aren't. I don't expect either of us is going anywhere. We'll stop here in this nice shed – er, summer house.'

Tears gathered in Trish's eyes as she glanced anxiously about her, on the lookout for more spiders. 'Why can't we go indoors then? Why does she want to send me away? What have I done wrong, Megan? I haven't been naughty, have I?'

'No, love, course you haven't,' and Megan hugged her little sister tight. The whole thing was a puzzle beyond her comprehension, but her small mouth was a tight curl of anger and misery. She'd quite lost patience with the war, with do-gooders who took in vacees when they really didn't want them. With Mr Churchill who kept prattling on about everyone needing to be brave and strong and pull together, and with Mr Hitler who had started all this mess in the first place. When adults fell out, they caused a whole lot of bother for everyone, in her opinion. And she'd take a guess neither of them was living in a garden shed.

The new year brought no let-up. Eighteen-years-olds were now liable for call-up and also, for the first time, women between twenty and thirty years old. They were obliged either to register for war work, or join the women's forces. Daisy's occupation at the farm was accepted as 'doing her bit', however, since that day on the beach at Silloth, an idea had been growing in her head. One that refused to be dislodged all winter.

It came to the fore again one wet day in late January when a Miss Geraldine Copthorne came to the door. She was a tall, ungainly woman in her mid-forties, not in the least out of breath from the long walk up the hill, to politely enquire if they had rooms to let.

Daisy was flabbergasted. 'Well, that didn't take long for the local jungle drums to start beating. I only mentioned in passing to the fishmonger the other day that I'd have no objection to taking in a lodger.'

'It's enough,' Clem remarked drily, eyeing the newcomer with wary rumination.

'I need to be close to the children.'

Miss Copthorne informed Daisy that she was unmarried because of a tragedy to her fiancé during the First World War, and had no intention of ever being so. She had devoted herself to teaching, and was in the area in charge of a group of children from her home city of Newcastle. 'It really is most unsettling and often distressing to see some of these youngsters missing their homes and families so dreadfully. They're coming and going all the time, and don't always fit in well with the village children. One does what one can, of course, but it never seems enough.'

Over a cup of tea and a scone, Daisy told Miss Copthorne all about Megan and Trish. 'I tried recently to contact them in their new billet but was put off going to see them. The woman seems a very pleasant, no-nonsense sort but she explained in her letter how they've been a bit homesick and it would only upset them more if I went. I haven't had a letter in ages and I suspect they may be wanting to go back home. They did run away once, as many evacuees have. But their mother sent them back again.'

'Poor things, they sound as if they've had a remarkably tough time. I could always try and find out something about their situation, if you like. I do know the right people to ask.'

'Oh, that would be lovely. How very kind.'

Miss Copthorne went on to explain her dissatisfaction with her current lodgings, since the landlady had taken to denying her the right to sit in the front parlour, or to have a fire if she did. 'Would that be allowed here?' she enquired.

Daisy assured her that it would. It was not a room that they

used, except on rare occasions, so it would be for the exclusive use of their guests. 'Coal is extra, mind,' she was
careful to explain.

'Of course.'

In view of their getting along so well, Daisy had not the
slightest hesitation in offering her the room and it was agreed
she would move in the following Sunday, her day off.

'Are you asking for references?' Clem wanted to know later
as they sat discussing the matter over supper.

'No, why should I? She didn't ask for references from me.
We'll either suit each other or we won't. We'd better spruce
the place up a bit, don't you think?'

'Happen,' Clem admitted, looking glum.

By February, Daisy had turned the house upside down.
Miss Copthorne was warned of the impending chaos but
didn't seem in the least perturbed. 'Don't fret, Daisy. I'm
sure we'll get by. What right do I have to complain when
there are so many far more inconvenienced.' She was a
remarkably placid and unflustered sort of woman. Probably
this was necessary if you were in charge of children. 'And
I'm still making enquiries about your young friends. I
haven't forgotten.'

The spring cleaning proved to be a mammoth task but at
least served to keep Daisy's mind from worrying too much
about the two children, and about Harry. Just remembering
that lovely day they'd enjoyed together by the seaside was
enough, for now at least. Each night, cuddled up in bed in her
loft bedroom, she would replay every moment of that magical
day.

She was doing it even now as she scrubbed and cleaned and
tidied.

'This place will be like a new pin when I'm done,' she said.
Clem was backing out the door, anxious to be off up the fells
before she found him a job to do. She'd really got the bit

between her teeth. Wanting to please her, he told her that he'd never seen his kitchen look so clean.

'Of course it isn't clean. It only looks better because there are no dirty dishes in the sink. There's a deal of work to be done yet.'

The kitchen cupboards filled one entire wall and it took half the morning to simply empty them. By the time Clem returned for his midday meal, Daisy was standing in the middle of the floor surrounded by every pot and pan, ladle and colander, every dusty utensil and item of crockery.

'By heck, we could feed an army here, if we had to. Thoo's enjoying this, eh?' Clem challenged her, and Daisy giggled.

'I suppose I am in a funny sort of way. I've never lived in a place like this before. It's marvellous to have so much space to live in, as well as all this light and fresh air.' She handed him a plate piled high with sandwiches. 'Only cold today, I'm afraid.'

'Leuks gradely.' There wasn't an inch of table free so they ate their meal perched on stools, munching companionably. After a while, Clem said: 'Florrie didn't take to country life quite so well as you seem to be doing.'

Daisy didn't know what to say to this but confined herself to platitudes about how the long holiday with her sister would probably help Florrie to see things in a different light. 'Anyone spending several months with my mother would be bound to view anything as an improvement,' and they both laughed.

'Happen we should let them know that you're here like, safe and sound,' Clem said, giving her a sidelong look.

It was some long moments before Daisy acknowledged the remark with a half shrug of agreement, reluctant to do anything which might bring the forces of Rita bearing down upon her. 'There's no rush is there?'

'Happen not.'

Clem again considered the array of crockery and cooking utensils stacked on the kitchen table. 'Much of that stuff must be my mother's. Haven't set eyes on it in years.'

Daisy stared at it too. 'It was right what you said earlier. We could feed an army here, at least, not literally an army but several other people besides ourselves and Miss Copthorne. If we wanted to, that is. And she's been no trouble, has she?'

'Out with it. What are you getting at?'

'Nothing, only . . .' Daisy took a deep breath. 'I was thinking mebbe we could take in more lodgers. We've plenty of room, what with all those unused bedrooms.'

Clem looked dumbstruck by the suggestion, which Daisy didn't wonder at.

'What sort of lodgers?' he asked, ever cautious.

'Oh, I don't know. Evacuees maybe.' She cast him a side-long glance, wondering if she dare risk making her request to have Megan and Trish with her, but thought better of it. It was too soon. She didn't want to rush him. But she could perhaps plant the start of the idea in his head. 'Aren't you supposed to take one for every spare bedroom you have? It's something we might have to consider later.

'As for guests, well, I know this isn't Windermere or Silloth, and there's a war on so the holiday trade is pretty slack, but there are so many people looking for accommodation and we have it here in plenty.' She began to get excited as the ideas tumbled out of her head. 'Those who've been bombed out of their homes, young married women who are coming to visit their sweethearts, or sons, stationed nearby. Folk who don't want to risk living in the city. Oh, there must be loads of people. And we have – er, you still have plenty of empty bedrooms, which seems such a waste. I know folk would have to go out the back for the privy but I'm sure they wouldn't mind. It doesn't trouble Miss Copthorne, does it? And in time we could perhaps put in a proper toilet and bathroom in that little boxroom on the first landing. Oh, and it would be fun, don't you think?' Daisy finally stuttered to a halt in order to draw breath.

Clem was chuckling, entranced by her enthusiasm. 'Thoo's getten it all worked out, eh?'

'I've been thinking about nothing else for ages, and then when I started counting plates it all came pouring out.' Daisy giggled. 'Oh, do say we can. Mebbe it would do Aunt Florrie good to have a bit of company around the place.'

'It'd mean a lot of work.'

'But I must do something to earn my keep.'

'Thoo's no need to worry on that score,' he said, his face closing into that all too familiar tightness. 'Thoo may only be my niece by marriage, but so far as I'm concerned thoo's family, and I'll not have you feel beholden. I'm sure I can afford to feed one li'le lass.'

Daisy, regretting her tactlessness, hastened to soothe his hurt pride. 'I didn't mean it that way. I'm used to working, and we're all expected to do our bit, we women, what with the war and all. And if I don't pull my weight here, I'll have to join up as soon as I turn twenty. Which would you prefer?'

'Nay, heaven help us. We've come to a pretty pass when we has to get women to fight us battles fer us. Do as you wish, lass. I won't stand in yer way. But if we're going to tek in lodgers, I reckon we should clean t'chimley afore you wash all them pots. It's fair thick wi' smoke in here.'

This seemed like a wise precaution to which Daisy swiftly agreed. 'Ooh, you're right Uncle Clem. Best get on with it then.'

'What, now?' In a voice high pitched with astonishment.

'Why not now? No time like the present, as they say.'

It might well be true, but for Clem this was a revelation. Work on the farm moved at the measured pace of the changing seasons. Being rushed into a job went against the grain, particularly one which would be of no benefit to his animals. But already he had learned to recognise the light of determination in Daisy's eye. Besides, he was quite taken by the idea of taking in lodgers. He'd no objection to Miss Copthorne, a quiet sort of body who wouldn't say boo to a goose, and he found he quite enjoyed a bit of company about the place. So with a resigned sigh, he went to fetch the necessary equipment.

Chimney sweeping was a complicated task which involved Clem climbing up on top of the house via the outbuildings and dropping a rope, weighted by a stone, down the chimney. Daisy waited at the bottom to tie on a sack filled with an old pillow to plump it out. Once it was secure, she gave a couple of tugs to indicate that all was in place and Clem pulled the sack up the chimney. The result was predictable. Daisy had forgotten to properly block off the chimney opening and as Clem tugged the sack up and down, a great whoosh of soot and dust came roaring out into the kitchen, covering not only the unwashed pots and pans but also Daisy from head to foot. By the time he arrived back in the kitchen, it was to find huge swathes of the stuff billowing over every item of furniture, and Daisy equally black with it.

'Well, we might have a clean chimney and have come up with a brilliant idea,' she said, wiping a smear of soot from her face along with the tears of laughter. 'But I reckon we've put hours more work on to the spring cleaning.'

Intermittent but regular air raids continued throughout January, February and March of 1941. The Docks, Ship Canal and Trafford Park were obvious targets and naturally suffered the worst of the bombing, which made local housing vulnerable. Several shelters were available close to Marigold Court, including one behind Ariel Street, another on a piece of spare land near Guide Street and a third on the corner of Weaste Road provided by Winterbottom's Book Clo Company, which was the one Joe preferred as it was lar than the others, with more trenches to sit in. All had re-inforced concrete slabs by way of a roof with earth piled on top, walls that were at least fourteen inches thick well protected by sandbags, and designed to hold forty or fifty people. In Joe's opinion it was little enough protection against a German bomb, but better than nothing. Better than cowering in their back entry under a makeshift shelter but, proud as the city fathers might be of these facilities, Rita was scathing.

'I'll die in me own bed thank you very much.'

'That's all right. You do that love, if you must. Just don't expect me to be with you.' Joe was taking no chances. Just inspecting the damage wrought upon his beloved city was terrifying. The marketplace had turned into a heap of rubble, though he was pleased to note that the Wellington Inn was still largely intact, which proved to Joe there was some justice left in the world. The Victoria Buildings and the Bull's Head, among others, had vanished off the face of the earth. Even the Royal Exchange had been hit. The smell of cordite was in the air, and fear was in his heart.

'Why don't we all go back wi' our Florrie to the Lakes? We'd be a lot safer there,' he said one morning as he viewed pictures of the damaged Cathedral in his morning paper.

'No,' Florrie said, quick as a flash. 'I've had enough of that place. We'll be all right here, if we keep us heads down.'

Rita rolled her eyes heavenwards, as if saying, didn't I tell you how impossible she was. 'Well I've certainly no wish to intrude where I'm not wanted. Not while I have a home of me own, humble though it may be, thanks very much,' she remarked tartly, determined not to appear needy.

Joe said, 'The pair of you want yer heads looking at,' and stumped off to check on the Anderson shelter as he did every morning, for all he held even less faith in it than in the muni-pal ones.

Joe was no hero and carefully followed all the rules, those

that benefited him anyway, and obeyed all the posters, 'Your country needs scrap for shells.' Keen to do his bit he collected all the scrap iron he could, and some of it he even let the government have for free. 'Rats and pilferers, both steal rations' said one poster on Salford Quays. Joe wouldn't dream of stealing but he was not averse to getting a few bob for the odd ration book which happened to come his way. He was particularly fond of one asking if his journey was really necessary, which generally persuaded him to stop at home and not go to work after all, even though he never travelled by train or bus anyway.

And as for 'Be like Dad and keep Mum', he was an expert on that one.

Florrie felt occasional bouts of guilt over evading her responsibility at the farm, yet not enough to make her go back. Not yet. She needed Clem to understand why she'd left, how badly he had neglected her. A part of her hoped that he might come to Salford looking for her, to urge her to come home, declaring that he missed her far too much to live without her. But these were simply fanciful romantic dreams. Clem had too much on his plate to have time for romance these days, even had he been given cause to believe that such a gesture would be welcomed. But the longer Florrie put off returning, the harder it became. Perhaps the opposite might happen and Clem find that he was quite happy living without her. Florrie couldn't quite make up her mind whether this would be a relief or not. It was all too confusing.

Throughout that long, cold and dangerous winter, she'd continued to feel like a stranger, a spare part about the place. Salford might have been her home once but it didn't feel like that now. She wasn't settling. Perhaps she'd stayed away too long, or it was asking too much for the two sisters to live comfortably together in one house but Rita was driving her barmy. She'd seek any way she could to create an argument.

'Shape thissen,' she'd say in bitter tones, the minute Florrie put up her feet for two minutes together. 'Tha's done nowt since thi come here.'

'That's only because I needed the rest.'

'What would you need rest for when you don't work?'

'Yes I certainly do work. I'll have you know . . .'

'What? What will you have me know? You told us that thee lives the life of Riley.'

Realising she was about to make a bad mistake by revealing more than she should about her life, Florrie desperately tried to retrieve it, putting on her posh voice. 'Clem might be well off but he doesn't believe in wasting money. He doesn't mean to be hard on me but I'm not nearly so cosseted as you seem to imagine. He doesn't really understand how fragile I am. In fact, it's been quite a hard life,' and pulling out her handkerchief, she manufactured a tear in the hope of winning sympathy.

Rita's expression was one of dubious disbelief and she pumped Florrie all the more with questions about this fancy life she supposedly led in the Lakes, about which she'd kept so quiet. 'How many maids have you got then? I bet you get breakfast in bed every morning. I've told thee not to expect owt o' that sort here. And when's your Clem going to come and see us? Or is he too grand for the likes of us now?'

Fervently wishing she'd never embarked on this conversation, Florrie made all manner of excuses to fend off Rita's persistent questioning as best she could, finally blurting out some nonsense about Clem holding a vitally important job, all very hush-hush and high-up; the implication being that it had something to do with the war effort and was very well paid.

Even Rita was impressed. Utterly stunned, she asked, 'What, he works for the government? By heck, which department? What does he do?'

Irritated by her own foolishness, Florrie's tone was harsh.

'Didn't I just tell you, it's all hush-hush. Much too secret. He doesn't even talk about it much to me, and I'm his wife.' The trouble with telling lies was that one always seemed to lead on to another, and another one after that. It was all very worrying. Florrie would really like to be rid of the whole mess, wishing she'd never got herself into such a tangle and simply told the truth from the beginning. She seemed to have achieved very little by coming back to Salford. She hadn't even succeeded in helping Daisy. Desperate to evade any further questions, she made a dash for her coat, claiming she had a hair appointment. 'I'll get us a nice bit of mackerel for our tea while I'm out, shall I? And I'll cook for once. Give you a little break.'

'Ta very much, I'm sure. Dusta want me to bow and scrape wi' gratitude?'

Florrie fled. At least one good thing about being back in the city was that she could console herself by spending. Florrie treated herself to some of the new utility clothes which she found to be really quite smart, certainly a pleasant change from the dull old working skirt and blouse she wore day after day on the farm. She'd had her hair cut and waved more stylishly and bought several new hats to show it off to advantage. She could eat fish and chips whenever she'd a mind to, or go to the flicks, just as she'd longed to do when up on the fells. But despite all of these much longed-for pleasures, she was still lonely. Her old friends were conspicuous by their absence and although Rita had agreed to accompany her on the odd occasion, more often than not she made an excuse not to.

'It's safer stoppin' at home. Thee can come a reet cropper walking about in t'black-out.'

'We'll go to a matinée then,' Florrie would suggest.

'Dusta think I'm med o' brass?' Rita never failed to get in a dig at her sister's supposed wealth.

Florrie realised she was running low on money herself,

having used up all the savings she'd been secretly stowing away over the years, and was forced to write and tell Clem exactly where she was staying so that he could send her some more. To her surprise he replied within a week, enclosing a postal order for her to cash and a short note expressing his hope that she was enjoying her stay with her sister, and that he would soon see her back at the farm, when she was ready to come home.

The door was still open then. But was she ready to walk through it?

For Daisy, preparations were going well. She scoured the house from attics to cellars, turning out every cupboard, beating every rug, scrubbing every inch of wainscot and window frame with scalding hot water and washing soda, and Clem found himself rolling up his sleeves and working alongside her. He would never have believed himself capable of getting involved in what he considered to be women's work, but there was something about this li'le lass which had captured his heart. Every pan had been scoured, every cup, saucer and plate, knife, fork and spoon in the house had been given a thorough dunking in washing soda. And when she ran out of dry tea cloths, Clem boiled kettles and washed them for her, drying them on the rack over the fire.

The house seemed to be in a continual state of siege, filled with steam and the smell of bleach, but he didn't care. More than anything he wanted desperately for her plan to work. And so he put the kettle on and, for the first time in his life, Clem brewed a pot of tea without being asked and presented a weak, milky cup to Daisy that tasted as if it had never been near a tea leaf and was indeed the washing-up water he'd used for the tea towels.

'Here, let me do it.' She refilled the two mugs with a good strong brew, and set one down in front of the old man on the now scrubbed and shining kitchen table.

When they were happy with the kitchen they started on the bedrooms.

'It's not that they're dirty,' Daisy hastily informed him, not wanting him to feel ~~mother or his absent wife, 'but a good~~ then does no harm at all. Mind you, I feel in a flatspin ~~the~~ that much to be done before we open properly. But it'll work out grand, I know it will.'

'I'm banking on it,' Clem told her. In his heart he knew that he never wanted this cheerful lass to leave and he suddenly had an inkling of what Florrie might have experienced when she'd first come to the fells: the empty bleakness of it all, the feeling of being overwhelmed by loneliness. All hill farmers were aware of the threat, and the resulting depression that could creep up upon them unnoticed, particularly during hard times, it was not something Clem had ever suffered from. Yet now he knew that if Daisy left, he too would feel alone, as never before.

'I've a bit of money saved up,' Daisy told him. 'It's for when Harry comes home, but that won't be for ages yet. How would you feel about getting the odd washbasin installed, and happen some new lino?' She made the suggestion with diffidence, wary of causing offence, and Clem seemed to consider the idea with a worried frown.

'Eeh, I wish Florrie were here. She'd know what to do fer t'best.'

'But she isn't here, is she?' Daisy reminded him quietly.

Clem was silent for a moment and she could see by the bleak expression in his faded eyes that he was remembering her, perhaps thinking of the early days of their marriage when everything had seemed so hopeful, so good between them. She prodded him gently back to the present.

'Don't worry, there's plenty of time for me to save up some more. I don't reckon we've seen the end of this war, not by a long chalk. But we have to get through it as best we can. So, what do you say?'

She saw how he made a visible effort to brighten. 'I'd say you were off your head, but it's your money, lass.'

'Right, that's settled then,' and they grinned at each other, well pleased with the decision, and with their burgeoning friendship.

Clem contacted a plumber friend who said he could get some second-hand basins dirt cheap from derelict bomb sites. It seemed a bit mercenary to benefit from other people's tragedies but money too was in short supply.

'Needs must when the devil drives,' was Clem's droll comment.

Daisy said, 'Think of the good that'll come of it.'

'I reckon we could afford three between us,' Clem said, determined to do his best to hold on to her.

Daisy was so tired she could hardly sip from the cup but progress was being made, so she had not one word of complaint to make, except in a good-humoured way. 'I'm fair powfagged,' she laughed, resting her head on her aching arms, and suddenly found her eyes filling with tears as she remembered joking with Megan and Trish about silly words.

'What's up lass? Not fretting about your chap, are you? Go and see him, if you want. Ask him over, I don't mind.'

Daisy wiped away the tears. 'I'm fine, a bit tired that's all. But I wouldn't mind asking Harry to come over, if that's all right. I'll drop him a line.'

'That's the ticket. Life's too short for tears.' He beamed at her, well pleased with his suggestion and, seconds later, jumped to his feet and began rummaging in the pantry under the stairs to reappear carrying a number of rather battered tin trays. 'These might cum in useful. What d'you reckon? I suddenly bethought mesel that they were there.'

Daisy couldn't help but laugh. 'Clem, you're a treasure. You've put new life into me. We'll be ready by Easter, I swear it.'

Clem had begun to wonder if they ever would be ready. When he came in each night after a long day on the fells, he'd be presented with the sight of Daisy in a flowered apron, her hair tied up in a turban, and 'leftovers' for his tea. She rarely had time for cooking these days so it was hard to know what these were left over from. No doubt she made a bit more of an effort for Miss Copthorne. Clem considered himself fortunate if he got a plate of fried spam and tomatoes, a chip buttie, or a cold cheese sandwich. Yet he made no complaint. Perhaps because she would so often pop a kiss on his forehead and promise him wonderful meals every day, once they got under way. Nor did the ever-patient Miss Copthorne object to the mess and disruption but was full of praise for the improvements, and delighted that her own room was also one to be fitted with a washbasin.

'We're not done yet,' Daisy warned her.

A shortage of sheets proved to be a problem, so a trip to Preston market was planned to buy good Lancashire cotton to make more. Daisy watched, open mouthed in amazement, as Clem ushered a sheep into the back seat of his little Ford car.

'Why is that ewe coming with us? We aren't stopping off at the auction mart, are we?'

'Nay, but we can't get no petrol coupons if we don't prove we're on farm business.'

Giggling uncontrollably, Daisy cuddled up on the back seat with the sheep, just to keep an eye on her and see she didn't fall over on the bends, and off they went. 'I hope she's a good traveller.'

On their return Daisy got down to the task of cutting up and hand sewing several yards of unbleached cotton into sheets. She washed out the size which was put in during the process of manufacture, dipped them in dolly-blue to whiten them, and finally dried them in the sun till they were fresh and soft enough to sleep on.

Wandering Winnie, as the ewe came to be affectionately known, was getting on in years and surprisingly tame. She accompanied them thereafter on many such expeditions to sales and auctions for bits and bobs that they needed. Daisy became convinced that she actually enjoyed these little outings. One trip was to Kendal in order to buy offcuts of lino, since the original had to be ripped up for new pipes being laid for the washbasins. The friendly salesman at the warehouse took one look at Daisy and offered to deliver, even to help lay it.

Clem accepted readily, explaining how they'd no room in the old car. 'I'm delivering this yow,' he said, studiously not explaining where to, or why anyone would want such an ancient creature. Daisy stifled a fit of the giggles.

Last, but by no means least, he rooted out a variety of old curtains from the attics. 'Mam allus liked thick wool curtains for t'winter and chintz for summer, so we've plenty.'

'Oh, they're wonderful.' Some were badly moth-eaten, but whichever ones appeared sound Daisy washed, ironed, and hung up on poles at the windows. At least they made the black-out blinds look less formidable and brought warmth to the rooms. The bits left over she fashioned into make-do-and-mend bedspreads in a patchwork of colours. It took weeks of work but Miss Copthorne gladly helped and, in the end, Daisy felt it had all been worthwhile.

At last the day came when there was nothing left to clean or wash, nothing to cut, sew, mend or repair. 'That's it, work finished, all done and dusted.'

Clem said, 'It'd be more accurate to say that this is only the first peck of work. Thoo's now ready to actually start. So until we get us first customers, tek t'chance to get some well-earned rest. Where is thoo going to find them, by the by?'

'Who?'

'Our first customers?'

Daisy's face was a picture of dismay. 'Lord, I hadn't even given that a thought. Where *will* we get them from? This isn't Blackpool, is it? They aren't going to come wandering along the prom looking for somewhere to stay for a few nights, or book through the town tourist office. Oh, hecky thump. And there is a war on.'

'You'll have to advertise.'

Eyes alight again, Daisy rushed to find paper and pencil. 'You're right. We'll put an advertisement in the *Westmoreland Gazette*, that'll bring 'em rolling in.' But the wording had to be just right, she decided. They didn't want riff-raff, nor to make it sound expensive or beyond ordinary folk's means. A task which proved surprisingly difficult but, tired as she was, Daisy sat up for hours writing and rewriting until finally she fell asleep with the pad on her knee and pencil still in hand.

The effort paid off as the advertisement worked. She got not one, but two letters of enquiry.

'Oh bliss! We're in business.'

'Chrissy?' Laura stared in stunned surprise at the dejected figure standing in a dripping puddle on her doorstep. 'You're the last person I expected to see.' At least she was an improvement on the last visitor.

'Thought I'd pay you a visit. Got a problem with that?'

'No, no, of course not. Come in. You look soaked to the skin. Sorry about the rain. One of those Lakes days, as we call them round here.' Laura led her into the warmth of the kitchen and put on the kettle, privately thinking that the girl would have withstood the weather better had she been dressed more appropriately. In her baggy cotton trousers and skimpy T-shirt, revealing a sparkly navel stud, the only sensible item of clothing she possessed were her boots, which looked as if they'd done service in at least one world war. Certainly they would come into their own on this terrain although, strangely, they didn't even show a speck of mud, and if she carried a waterproof in the rucksack slung over one shoulder she hadn't bothered to use it. But the most startling thing about the fourteen-year-old was her hair. Not only did it hang in damp rats' tails about her neck, but was also a bright purple streaked with yellow.

Knowing better than to comment upon this radical change from her usual mouse brown, Laura handed her stepdaughter a towel to dry it, then turned her attention to making coffee. 'Does Felix know where you are?'

'I'm not a child.'

This was a line of argument along which Laura never ventured. 'He needs to know, so that he won't worry.'

'Huh! When has Dad ever worried about me?'

Laura handed her a mug. 'Have you two quarrelled?'

Chrissy pouted. 'He doesn't like my hair. Neither does Mum, just because I was sent down from school.'

'You haven't been expelled?' Not again, she almost added, but managed not to.

Chrissy shook the offending locks, which were really quite pretty, in an alarming sort of way. 'No, I've been told to dye it back to its normal colour, and I refused.'

'I see.' Laura considered this as they drank their coffee. 'Were you expecting me to put in a word on your behalf? I mean, is the school likely to be persuaded to change their mind?'

For a brief moment an image of the vulnerable child she truly was, appeared in the hazel eyes, but only for an instant. 'They're so *old-fashioned*. Over the hill, you know? It's just a little colour, after all,' she wailed, sounding rather like a TV commercial. Laura tried not to smile. In Chrissy's opinion, the world was not yet ready for her, she being way ahead of her time.

'Why don't I ring and tell your mum where you are, then we can relax and think about what we want for supper.'

Chrissy brightened. 'Can we have garlic bread? Mum never lets me have it. She says I'm fat enough already.'

'It's only puppy fat. It'll go. I'll make you some garlic bread if you promise to speak to her and apologise for frightening her. She must be out of her mind worrying about where you've got to.'

'What, thinking I've been abducted or something?' Chrissy mocked.

'Something of the sort, yes.'

She mulled this over for a moment, then gave a sulky nod of agreement.

Julia was not best pleased by her only daughter absconding but tempers were finally soothed, tears mopped, bridges built and an agreement reached whereby Chrissy would stay for a short holiday at Lane End Farm, in view of her having no school to go to at present and it being almost the end of term in any case. Meanwhile Julia would negotiate terms with the headmistress. Perhaps a slight toning down of colour could be agreed upon.

'It won't be much of a holiday in the accepted sense of the word,' Laura warned as she put down the phone. 'There's too much to do. You can help put the finishing touches to the decorating, and generally getting organised.'

Chrissy wrinkled her nose and groaned, physical labour not being high on her agenda of fun things to do. 'Why should I? That's why I did the hair thing, because I was sick of doing nothing but work, work, work. I need to chill out.'

'Well, you've come to the wrong place for that. I'm planning to open up as a guesthouse again.'

Chrissy looked slightly taken aback. 'Cool! That'll make you independent of Dad, which won't please him one bit.'

Laura solemnly considered her stepdaughter. 'You're really quite shrewd underneath, aren't you? I did hope to open by the Spring Bank Holiday but kept getting sidetracked by other issues. Now it's the middle of June and I already have bookings for this weekend. So, an extra pair of hands would be most useful.'

They spent the afternoon doing nothing more taxing than

putting wrapped miniature bars of soap together with sachets of shampoo and shower gel in all the new shower rooms, then counting out tea bags and making up hospitality trays. The telephone rang several times and Laura answered various enquiries from the local tourist office, fended off attempts to persuade her to reduce her rates on the grounds of the magnificent views she could offer from all her guest rooms, and took a satisfactory number of bookings.

'How are you with computers?'

'I'm a whizz.'

'Great. You can help me design and produce a brochure. I can't afford to pay for one to be properly printed, not until I get some regular money coming in.'

'Lead me to your software.'

They spent a happy couple of hours scanning photographs and cutting and pasting, as well as falling about in laughter over flowery phrases intended to advertise the merits of the premises, most of which sounded too hilarious and off-putting to risk using.

'Maybe we've done enough for today,' Laura said, wiping tears of laughter from her eyes. 'Tomorrow, you can help me finish painting the skirting boards and doors in room five. Then all we have to do is clean the adjoining bathroom, make up all the beds, set the tables in the dining room and we're done.'

'Sounds a snip,' Chrissy remarked drily.

Laura considered her more carefully. 'How would you feel about waiting on, and perhaps working here for the summer as a chambermaid, assuming your mum agrees of course?'

'Does that involve having to clean bathrooms and make beds and stuff?'

'That sort of thing, yes. But I'd pay you well, and with your pretty face, not to mention the Technicolor hair, you might also attract quite a few tips.'

'OK, I'll give it a whirl.'

'Excellent. Let's hope your headmistress doesn't want you back till next term,' and the pair grinned happily at each other, as if sharing a private rebellion.

Chrissy's eyes were surprisingly anxious as Laura put down the phone. 'Did he go ballistic, threaten to disinherit me and cut me off without a penny?'

'Not quite, but he wasn't best pleased. Ranted and railed for a bit but I managed to calm him down. Says he sent you here to bring me home, not have me persuade you to stay.' Laura folded her arms and considered her stepdaughter with a quizzical frown. 'You forgot to mention that Felix actually drove you most of the way from Cheshire, *and* paid for a taxi up the lane.'

Chrissy pouted. 'I walked the last half-mile or so. I needed to get wet so you wouldn't be suspicious, you see.'

'Yes, I do see.'

'Sent me as ambassador.' And when Laura looked sceptical, added more truthfully. 'All right, wanted me to use my unique skills to disrupt your life, and persuade you to give up. Dad's worried about you, apparently,' she confided, licking her fingers clean of garlic butter.

'Whatever for?'

'Thinks you're having it off with someone.'

'What nonsense! Where does he get these fantasies from? I suppose it means that at least *he* doesn't think I'm over the hill.'

Chrissy shrugged. 'He's pretty old himself, so that's no recommendation.'

'No, I suppose not.'

'He says you want a divorce, and he's no intention of giving you one.'

'Does he indeed?'

'Wanted me to apply pressure, you know, all the guilt stuff of abandoning me, making me a child from a broken home.

Two broken homes actually, since I've already been through one messy divorce,' said Chrissy with a hint of drama in her tone. 'Hey, that'd be one up on my friend Lucy.'

'Oh well, that's all right then,' Laura commented drily, 'if you can be one up on Lucy.' And then more seriously. 'Look, I'm sorry about all of this. I've no wish to mess up your life too.'

'He's the one messing things up.' Chrissy considered her, out of old-young eyes. 'He's having it off with that Miranda, isn't he?'

Laura winced, as much at the bluntness of the girl's language as the images the words presented. 'You must ask him that, not me.'

'He's a head-case. How will that solve anything, or help him get things back on track?'

'Sorry, am I missing something here?'

Chrissy leaned forward, dropping her tone to a whisper as if she were relaying a secret, or exchanging a confidence. 'Dad says the business is on the skids and you're being obstinate and cruel in refusing to sell this half-derelict house, since you helped him to spend the money in the first place.'

'I did not! He's the one spending money as if it were going out of fashion, dashing all over the Continent, and wining and dining night after night, not me.' She almost added – and attempting to steal what is rightfully mine – but decided against it. Laura slapped a chocolate mousse down on the table and Chrissy's eyes lit up. 'Anyway, it isn't half-derelict. A bit run-down perhaps, but with great potential. Is that what he instructed you to do, imply he was about to go bankrupt? What else is there? Why don't you get it all out into the open, while you're at it?'

Looking decidedly sheepish, Chrissy shook her head, making the purple strands glimmer like silk in the light from the lamp, then gave a little giggle. 'Actually, he didn't tell me any of that stuff about the business, only about his not wanting a divorce. I was ear-wigging. He and Gramps were having a right old barny, trying to think of a way to make you sell. Maybe Dad really does have problems this time, I don't know.' Picking up her spoon, she tucked into the dessert as if she'd been starved for weeks.

'Gramps? Are you saying my father and Felix were having a row? What about?'

'You, mainly,' Chrissy mumbled through a mouthful of chocolate mousse. 'About whether or not you should be forced to sell the house and what Gramps should do about the land. Dad suggested Gramps might like to sell that instead, and come into the business as a sleeping partner but Gramps wasn't up for it. Said he wanted to have nothing at all to do with it, though whether he meant the land or the business, I'm not quite sure. It all got a bit muddled at that point because they were shouting over each other's words. Anyway, something about it being a huge bind, and that he'd done his bit by trying to persuade you to see sense and go home. What happened next was not his concern.'

Laura sat looking bemused. 'I think I've lost the plot. What land are we talking about here?'

Chrissy was busy scraping the last of the mousse from the glass dish. 'Oh, you know – land. The kind you use for growing things, like that stuff cows and sheep eat.'

'This is no joke, Chrissy, this is serious stuff. I didn't even know that my father owned any land. How? Where? What land?'

Chrissy dragged her attention away from the dessert dish, surprised by this revelation, eyes narrowing speculatively. She always did love a mystery. 'Why, here of course. Where else? You might own the house, but your dad owns all of this farmland. So, are you going to sell it or not? The house I mean. Don't let Dad bully you into it, if you don't want to.'

'Don't worry, I won't.' Laura's reply was vague. She was still trying to come to terms with her father owning the *land*.

Not that she'd paid any attention thus far as to who owned it. But her own *father*? Why hadn't he said?

'Is there any more?'

'What?'

'Chocolate mousse.'

'No, you've had quite enough already. Drink your apple juice and go to bed like a good girl.'

Chrissy pulled a face. 'Don't you start. I've enough with those two on my back the whole time. The best thing about having you as a reserve mum, as it were, is that you never go in for the nagging bit. If you and Dad – you know – split up, can I still come round? Even after these summer hols, I mean.'

Laura began to clear away the dishes, longing suddenly to be alone, to have ten minutes' peace and quiet to think things through properly. 'Of course you can. You're my step-daughter and always will be. Look, why don't you go and watch television while I wash up?' The kitchen was as good a place as any for some private thinking, not being one of Chrissy's favourite places.

'Won't you be lonely living up on this mountain all on your own?'

'I shall be too busy to even think about it.'

'Isn't there any talent around?'

'Not that I know of, no. None at all.'

'Pity. Anyone would be better than Dad.'

20

It was one morning in early April that the letter came. With a little jump of her heart, Florrie recognised the handwriting instantly as being Clem's, but unfortunately it wasn't addressed to her, it was for Rita and there was nothing she could do about vetting it before it was opened.

Clem had very kindly written to say that Daisy had spent the winter safely at Lane End Farm, that she was perfectly well and they were not to worry. '*I thought it best that I inform you of her safety.*' He apologised for not having written sooner but had kept expecting Florrie back any day, he explained, and then the weather had been bad so he hadn't been able to get out for several weeks. He made no mention of the fact that Daisy had been reluctant to contact her mother, or that he'd no real proof of where his wife was staying until she'd written asking for money. '*Not that Florrie need hurry home on my account, if she's enjoying her stay with you. We're busy doing a thorough spring clean.*' He closed by saying that Daisy was proving to be quite handy about the farm.

Rita's jaw dropped open in stunned amazement. 'Farm, what farm? You told us you lived in Keswick, in a big fancy house by the lake.'

Florrie gave a false little laugh. 'Whatever gave you that idea? What does he say about Daisy? My word, fancy her persuading him to do a spring clean. Clem hates jobs of that nature,' she said, hoping that changing the subject would put Rita off the scent.

'Aye, that's our Daisy, never happier than when she's getten her nose stuck in other folk's business.'

'Oh, I'm sure she's not like that at all.'

'So, what's a top government official doing working on a farm?' Rita asked the question with open contempt in her tone.

'Part of his cover,' Florrie said and scuttled away, anxious to avoid any more awkward questions.

But Rita was not one to let go quite so easily. It didn't surprise Florrie in the least when she followed her out into the back yard and waved the letter under her nose.

'Are you going to explain this, or what?'

'I really don't know what you mean. Anyway, I would have thought you'd be delighted to hear that your daughter was safe. Haven't you been worrying all winter about which billet she's moved to?' Knowing that Rita had not been in the least concerned about her daughter, nor mentioned Daisy in months.

'Don't talk lah-di-dah to me, it won't wash. I'm the one what saw you with a mucky face and a snotty nose when you were little, remember? Anyroad, our Daisy can look after herself. I want to know about this 'ere farm. Is that where you've been living all these years? Is that why I'm still waiting for an invitation to visit this so-called posh house of yours?'

'It is a big house. Biggish, anyway. And life is very busy. We work seven days a week,' Florrie said, floundering for an excuse.

'Oh aye, but not for the government eh? Not a fine house by the lake, no grand estate neither but a flamin' farm. Is that the way of it?'

Florrie clenched her fists in silent fury. For years she'd managed to keep her secret, the pretence of being well-placed. Now, thanks to Clem's excessive thoughtfulness to inform Daisy's mother that she was safe, or *thoughtlessness*, depending on how you viewed it, the truth was out at last. She could spit, she could really! Why couldn't the stupid man have kept quiet? It didn't seem to occur to her that she could have evaded the issue by returning home, that perhaps he'd been allowing her time to do so. Or even that she might have precipitated the letter by begging for money to allow her to stay away even longer.

Rita, on the other hand, was beginning to see the funny side.

'So you're not Lady Muck, after all. Only Mrs Muck, the cowman's wife.' She began to chuckle. 'Nay, and you've led us nicely up the garden path all these years. Letting us believe that you were someone important. Madame Nose-in-the-air. You made out that your precious Clem were a gentleman wi' a deal of brass in his pocket and all the time he's nowt but gas and hot air? Is that the truth of it? This grand love affair turned out to be a pig in a poke, did it? Literally!' And she burst out laughing.

'It's not funny.'

'It is from where I'm standing. Aw, come on, I'm yer flippin' sister. It's time you got it all off yer chest and told us the truth. Be honest for once in yer life, lass.'

Feeling cornered, and thoroughly vexed, Florrie buckled under the pressure. 'Oh all right, yes it's true. He's just a farmer and not a rich one at that, so go on, have a good laugh at my expense, why don't you? I've had a miserable time from start to finish if you want to know the truth, which will no doubt amuse you even more.'

By the time Laura's first guests arrived, Lane End Farm Guesthouse was as ready as she could make it. Every room had been completely redecorated and refurbished. Fresh new curtains hung at the windows, new mattresses on the old iron frame beds, the solid wood furniture polished to perfection and new lamps, cushions and pictures placed wherever it seemed appropriate to put them. Laura and Chrissy had taken great pleasure in choosing these, entering into lively debates when their tastes clashed, which was fairly frequently. Laura preferred flowers or landscapes while Chrissy leaned more towards abstracts in bold, primary colours. A compromise was reached by opting for the quieter style for bedrooms and bolder colours to brighten the hall and dining room.

The advertisements she'd placed in various regional newspapers and holiday guides seemed to be working and she and Chrissy spent a lot of time posting off brochures all over the country.

Felix still rang regularly if not quite as often as he had used to, and mainly to speak to Chrissy. He would be dismissive when Laura answered, as if punishing her for being uncooperative. Not that it troubled her in the least, for whenever he did take the time to talk to her it was only to issue another lecture.

'It won't work, this nonsensical idea you have of becoming a landlady.'

'Don't be sniffy, Felix. They call them proprietors these days. And I rather think it will work. I'm fully booked for most weekends to the end of June and through July already. This is a popular area for walkers with not a great deal of accommodation in the locality.'

'And what about us?'

'There hasn't been an *us* for some time. As soon as I get a free afternoon, I mean to pop back into Keswick and see Nick, my solicitor, and get things moving on the divorce. No point in letting it drag on.'

'Don't you ever listen to a damn thing I say, Laura? *There isn't going to be any divorce.*' Quietly Laura put down the phone.

Chrissy, who had been unashamedly listening in to the conversation, said: 'You know how Dad hates to lose. Since he hasn't managed to change your mind on this over the phone, failed to make you be nice to prospective buyers, and sending me here hasn't worked either, he'll only hatch up some other plot. Be on your guard Laura. He isn't done yet.'

'There's nothing he can do to me now,' Laura assured her, wishing she felt half so confident as she sounded. Felix's attitude troubled her deeply, but not for a moment would she allow him to know that. If he imagined that clinging on to a dead marriage would help him to get his hands on her inheritance, he couldn't be more wrong.

The first breakfast was something of a nightmare. Chrissy kept forgetting to ask if they would like coffee or tea and mixed up several orders, handing scrambled eggs to one lady who had asked for bacon and tomato, and giving a half-frozen croissant to another who'd requested a full English breakfast. Laura dropped a poached egg on the floor just as she was slipping it on to the plate, and had to start all over again to cook another one. The kitchen was steaming hot and over all hung the unappetising aroma of burnt toast since Chrissy kept jamming them too hard into the ancient toaster which prevented it from popping up properly.

'I'll buy a new one. This very afternoon.'

It seemed a miracle to them both that the half-dozen guests sitting patiently in the dining room didn't walk out long before the painful ritual was over. Somehow or other, they did all get fed and went happily on their way to explore the area. Laura breathed a sigh of relief, put the kettle on and began to stack the dishwasher. 'It can only get better.'

'Or worse,' Chrissy remarked gloomily. 'Seven weeks of this? I'll go bonkers. Did you see that chap's face when I forgot to warn him how hot the plate was. I thought he was about to burst a blood vessel. Anyway, your breakfasts went down a treat, saved the day. I think the guy in number four would marry you just for your black puddings.'

'He must be seventy if he's a day.'

'Perfect.'

'Right miss, all we have to do now is clean bathrooms, tidy

bedrooms, polish and vacuum upstairs and down, scrub pans and re-lay the tables for tomorrow.'

'Simple, if you say it quickly. No evening meals then?'

'Not till I feel strong enough to cope with them.'

'Which if I have any say,' said Chrissy, 'will not be for a long, long time.'

It was Laura's misfortune that a couple of nights later, David called, just on the off-chance that she might feel like popping out for a drink down at the Salutation Inn in Threlkeld. Worse, he walked straight in without even bothering to knock, it being so wet, he explained, and not wanting her to get drenched by coming to the door. All explanations stopped short when he spotted Chrissy sitting in front of the TV set, staring at him wide-eyed with disbelief.

'And Laura said there was no talent round here.'

'Sorry? Ah, you have company, I didn't realise.'

'I would have said, if you'd knocked,' Laura remarked drily. 'Still, now you're here, allow me to introduce to you my stepdaughter.'

'I'm the wild child,' Chrissy said, with some degree of pride in her voice. 'I expect she's told you all about me already.'

'Not really. Why are you wild? Were you brought up by wolves or something?'

To Laura's utter amazement, she saw Chrissy flush and give an entrancing giggle. Obviously, David's charm transcended age and, since he made her blush too, perhaps she wasn't quite over the hill after all.

It took something of a tussle but Laura finally shooed Chrissy off to bed and over a bottle of wine told David about the startling revelation that her father actually owned the land he leased. She demanded to know why he'd never mentioned it and, to her surprise, he replied calmly that he hadn't known either. Apparently rent payments were made through his solicitor to a Trust, the name of which gave no indication of ownership.

They both considered this for a moment before David murmured his thoughts out loud. 'He must have owned it for quite a while. I've been dealing with the Trust ever since I took the place on. I mean, it's fairly common practice, to leave the house to one person and the land to another but I wonder why he never told you? Why be so secretive about it?'

'Because he doesn't wish to appear beholden to Daisy, the mother he hated. What else could it be? I'm assuming that she was the one who gave it to him, perhaps years ago. Which means she didn't disinherit him after all, and he let me think that she did, the silly old man. Was that so I'd feel sorry for him, or perhaps not nag him to come to her funeral? If only there were some way I could find out more about her. If she'd kept a diary . . .'

David cast his eyes heavenwards, his face inscrutable. Laura watched him for a moment, thinking that perhaps he had something more to say, perhaps even some quip about Daisy having better things to do with her time than scribble in a diary but he said nothing and it finally dawned on her that his silence was telling. A burst of excitement exploded within her.

'She did keep a diary, didn't she? Where is it? Tell me. Oh, I would so love to see it.'

'Sorry, no, that wasn't her style. But I was just thinking, Daisy was a member of the Local Oral History Society.'

'Oh!' All the excitement drained out of her. Although Laura appreciated that these sort of tapes were a valued method by which an older generation could pass on information on how they'd lived their lives in the days before television and computers and technology changed employment and lifestyles for ever, yet she was disappointed. 'I wanted more than snippets about how the war was won, or when rationing was brought in. I long to discover more personal, intimate details, to know and understand the woman herself; to get inside her head.'

'Suit yourself Laura, but you might find them worth a visit. I don't think you'd be disappointed. I have the telephone number of the secretary somewhere. I'll drop it in tomorrow if you like.'

The secretary, a plump, bustling lady with spectacles hanging on a chain around her neck, led Laura with a cheery smile to an impressive filing system. 'If your grandmother recorded anything, anything at all, it will be listed here. What was the name again? Daisy Thompson.' An agonising wait while she riffled through countless cards. 'No, sorry, nothing under that name.'

'Oh well, it was just a thought.' Laura turned to go.

Chrissy, who had insisted on coming with her on this quest, said, 'Perhaps your gran was a modern woman and used her own name for personal matters. What was it?'

'Atkins. Daisy Atkins.'

The secretary tried again. 'Ah yes, well done, dear. Daisy Atkins. Not just one tape, in fact, but several. You'll need to provide references, fill in a form, become a member of the library and so on, if you wish to borrow them.'

'No problem,' Laura said. She felt as if she'd struck gold.

Daisy's own voice came over strong and clear. '*My name, for the sake of the tape, is Daisy Atkins, although I am known locally as Thompson, my married name.*'

'Lord, she sounds as if she's giving evidence in a police station,' Chrissy said.

'Hush, I can't hear.' Laura rewound the tape to listen again to the bit she missed. They were all three, Laura, David and Chrissy, sitting in the kitchen at Lane End Farm, anxious to hear whatever the tapes could tell them.

'*This is my story, a part of it anyway, for those of my family who wish to hear it. An oral diary, and because of the personal nature of what I am about to disclose I hope listeners will bear in mind that I did always what I thought was for the best.*'

David said, 'This sounds pretty private. Would you like me to go?'

'No, I want you to stay. You've heard so much of Daisy's story already, and she was your friend. You might as well know the rest. There are too many tapes to hear it all at one go, so we'll start with this one – intriguingly labelled "Robert's, Inheritance".'

'*Twice I have lost a son and in neither case through death, though it might just as well have been for the pain it caused. I don't blame Robert for leaving. He was upset and cross. I hope and pray that he will not prove stubborn about accepting his due inheritance which I give to him now, as a gift, before I die. I've put it in trust for him so that he can't do anything silly in a temper, like selling it. With that in mind, I tell my story. Perhaps, in time, he will forgive me, or at least understand.*'

They came to the part where she'd finally found the farm, and how Daisy had taken at once to Clem. '*Florrie was not settling back in Salford. She got caught up in the blitz, and that's when everything changed.*'

For once in her life, Rita sat quietly and listened to the tale without interrupting, so avid was she for every mouth-watering detail. She learned all about Florrie's many disappointments over the state of the farmhouse, the hard work she had to do, the loneliness of the place, even the foulness of the weather. Her sister's bitterness at the way things had turned out was all too evident.

'Oh, Rita. You can't imagine what I've gone through,' Florrie moaned, dabbing at her eyes with a fresh white handkerchief. 'I've been so lonely up there, on that mountain. And you wouldn't believe the wind and the rain we get.

My nerves are in ruins.' But if she'd hoped for a glimmer of pity, or a softening of Rita's stance, she was soon to be disenchanted.

Rita folded her arms across her skinny bosom and gave a smirk of satisfaction. 'Serves you right, you daft happorth. You should've had more sense than to run off wi' him in t'first place: a man old enough to be your father, and a perfect stranger you knew nowt about. I warned you not to marry him and see how right I was.'

'I thought I was in love.'

Rita made a pooh-poohing sound. 'You fancied yer chances at lording it over the rest of us. But it hasn't worked, has it?'

Florrie glared moodily at her sister. Sometimes Rita had an unhappy knack of putting her finger right on the pulse. Of course she'd hoped that marrying Clem would take her up in the world, out of Salford and into a fine house smoothly run by a housekeeper and a bevy of servants so that she wouldn't have to lift a finger. Why else would she choose to marry such an unexciting man as Clem Pringle, fond though she'd been of him at the time? Instead, all she'd got was a lifetime of toil and misery.

'Sometimes Rita, I don't think you have a heart. I've really suffered, can't you see? Have you no pity?'

'Not when it comes to no-good little madams like you were when you were young, and like our Daisy is now. You've got your just deserts, no doubt about it. And if our Daisy isn't careful, she'll get hers an' all.' Rita was positively glowing with moral rectitude. She'd waited years for this moment. 'Ever since you walked through my front door months ago, we've heard nowt but how hard done to you are: how tired and lonely, how Clem doesn't understand you. Now you tell us your husband isn't rich, you don't live in a posh house, you've no servants and tha's overworked. You and the rest of the flippin' universe. Hard cheese. You aren't the only one to be suffering, so stop feeling sorry for yourself and get on with life.'

If there was an iota of common sense in her sister's advice, Florrie certainly wasn't in the mood to take it. Twin spots of fire burned on flat pale cheeks as she furiously sought self-justification. 'What about losing my child? You don't seem to appreciate how that has affected my life.'

'You could've tried again but no doubt a child would have got in the way, taken Clem's attention away from you.'

'That's not true. I would've loved another only I was too afraid the same thing might happen again. Anyway, you're wrong. Clem isn't the attentive sort. He doesn't like a fuss, and he's far too busy on the farm.'

'Ah, that's the way of it, is it? You were wallowing in self-pity and he wasn't fussing over you enough. So you turned into this moaning Minnie where nothing were ever right.'

'How can you be so cruel?'

'I speaks me mind, take it or leave it. There's others have lost childer, them what grew up and were loved for years. Nay, not me, thank God, but plenty in this street, and there'll be more afore this war is done. They don't wallow in self-pity. They pull themselves up by their boot straps and carry on.'

'Drat you, our Rita.' Florrie's tears were all too real now, though more from anger and frustration than genuine distress. She was utterly convinced that throughout her married life she'd suffered terrible deprivation and anguish and nobody cared; not her husband, not even her own sister. 'You never did like me and I'll not stop where I'm not wanted.'

'Nobody's asking you to. You don't belong here, Florrie Pringle. So stop thee moaning, pack thee bags and go on home to your husband, even if he isn't flippin' rich. Or else batter somebody else's ears with your troubles. I can't say we care one way nor t'other where tha goes or what tha does, but we've had enough of your whining here.'

'I'll not stop where I'm not welcome.'

'And you're certainly not that.'

Florrie marched upstairs, stuffed her new clothes into her bag and stormed out of the house, making sure she banged the door shut behind her. Determined to have the last word, Rita whipped it open again to stand screaming from the doorstep as her sister strode away through the entry. 'See if I care, you useless baggage!'

When Joe came home later, he gazed with suspicion upon his wife standing quietly at the sink and asked where Florrie was.

Rita prevaricated, concentrating on peeling potatoes with short, furious stabs of the knife. 'How should I know? I'm not her flippin' keeper.'

'Why have you got that frosty look on yer face? Nay, you two haven't had another falling out? Not in the middle of all this.'

'She started it. Miss High-and-Flippin'-Mighty. Does she think she's the only one with problems? I told her: you can go and jump, you. Go and lord it over someone else fer a change.'

Joe shook his head, looking exasperated. 'Nay lass, you're a nasty piece of work at times. What else did you say?'

'I told her to go to her husband. Happen she'll listen this time.'

'It's not your place to tell her what to do. For once in your life, woman, don't interfere. Haven't you done enough damage to our Daisy? Leave well alone, why don't you?'

Rita turned on him in a fury. 'What's come over you all of a sudden, sounding off? I've done nowt to our Daisy save what was best for her.'

'What's best for *you*, you mean.'

'You agreed. You did nowt to stop me.'

'I'd need to call out the Manchester Brigade and the Auxiliary Fire Service to stop you, once you've getten an idea in yer head. And what else happened? Go on, tell me the worst.' Joe was determined to get to the bottom of this matter because he could see by the triumphant expression on his wife's face, there was more to it than she was telling.

Rita smirked. 'I were right all along, she's been lying to us all these years. There is no fancy big house, only a flamin' farm.'

'Nay lass,' Joe said, his tone weary, 'I knew that already. Didn't you ever guess? It were fairly obvious when she never wrote to show off her new-found wealth, or invite us over to view this grand house she supposedly lived in. Why you bother to be jealous of her, I've never been able to work out. She's got nowt to write home about at all, none of her dreams have come true. No big house, no rich husband, no wonderful love-match, and she'd give her eye-teeth to have a daughter like our Daisy.'

His words seemed to inflame her rage still further. 'She's welcome to her, wittering on about that flippin' child she lost, as if she were the only one. What about me? Haven't I suffered most with our Daisy behaving like a loose woman? I told our Florrie to go home to her husband, and good riddance.'

Joe grabbed his wife by the arm, an unheard of action in this house, and gave her a little shake. 'Damn you, Rita, you can be a venomous old cow when you put your mind to it. You know she's depressed. Has been for years, ever since she lost the babby. She can't help it, poor lass, that's the way she is.'

'Well, she doesn't have to weep all over me. I've enough troubles of me own.'

'She's yer bloody sister, fer God's sake,' Joe shouted and turned to the door, his face a mask of concern and anger. 'I'll go after her. It's not safe out there. Bombs dropping all over the damned show. Didn't you hear the siren? We're in for another battering. Who knows when the next one will drop.'

Rita was untying her pinny, reaching for her coat and scarf.

'Don't you try to play the hero, or stick up for that little madam, it doesn't suit you. Get down the shelter. I'll fetch her back. The silly woman can't have got far.' Rita slapped the potato peeler into his hand. 'And finish them spuds afore you go. We need us tea, German bombs or no German bombs.'

Rita caught up with Florrie at the corner of Weaste Street where she was arguing with an ARP warden. He was ordering her into a nearby shelter and Florrie was resisting furiously. 'I have to catch my train. I'm going down no shelter. Anyway, I suffer from claustrophobia.'

'You'll suffer from much worse, Missis, if you don't get off this street right this minute.'

'I'll take me chances. I'm going home, I tell you.' Florrie made to set off but the warden grabbed her arm and dragged her back to the entrance of the shelter.

'Don't be so flamin' stubborn. It's my job to see you're safe.'

A mother and two children appeared on the scene and joined in the argument. 'Nay, leave her be. She's not the only one who doesn't like bleedin' shelters. I've left a pan simmering on the hob, Bill, so I'll just nip back to tek it off afore I go down.'

Rita said, 'We've a shelter of us own in t'back yard. We'll go there, thank you very much, if we need to,' and she made a grab for Florrie, capturing her in an arm lock so she couldn't run off again.

'There's no time for a flippin' mothers' meeting here, fer God's sake!' The ARP Warden looked about him in desperation, as if he might whip off his tin helmet and tear his hair out if the irate trio didn't behave. 'Women! Do as tha's told for pity's sake. Tek them childer in that shelter this minute.' Then he pushed the young woman and her two childre down the steps into the crush of people already hurryi below ground for protection. As he turned to do the same with Florrie and Rita, the world exploded all around them. It came with a surprisingly dull clunk but they felt the pavement shake and open beneath their feet, smelled the acrid scent of smoke and raw fear, saw the sky itself blaze with fire as they were lifted, arms wrapped tight around each other, and thrown backwards on a blast of hot air.

21

The next guest to follow in Miss Copthorne's intrepid footsteps during Daisy's first week of business was a commercial
traveller in agricultural foodstuffs by the name of Tommy
Fawcett. He wouldn't be permanent, he explained, but
definitely a regular as staying on farms was generally his preference; so much more convenient in his type of trade.

It was arranged that whenever he was going to be in the
area, he would write and let her know his dates well in
advance. 'You'll soon get used to my routine, it doesn't vary
much,' he explained, tipping his brown felt hat over one eye,
'not like my dance routine which is even more imaginative
than Fred Astaire's.'

Daisy laughed. 'Nobody can dance as well as Fred Astaire.
I won't have folk who tell fibs in my boarding house. We
might as well start as we mean to go on.'

He pulled a sad face. 'I can't resist trying to impress a pretty
young girl. Mind you, my mother always told me my bragging would get me in trouble one day. If I were as good as him
I'd be in the films too.' He pronounced it filums. 'All right,
mebbe he has the edge, but I *am* involved in amateur
dramatics. Back home in Blackburn, I'm famous for my
twinkle-toes,' and he did a few steps, there and then on the
lino, making such a lovely clicking noise that it brought Miss
Copthorne and Clem to see what the noise was all about. In
no time they were all laughing as he jumped up on to a chair,
then tap danced across the kitchen table and down on to the
next chair. Oh yes, he was a real card, was Tommy.

Next came a widower by the name of Ned Pickles. He was a small, wiry man in his late fifties, as stiff and starched in his manner as the high collar about his long skinny neck. One glance at his tired, gloomy face, the dusty spectacles, thread-bare suit and well polished, if down-at-heel shoes, and Daisy decided he needed looking after. Clearly he was missing his late-lamented wife, which would mean he'd have something in common with Clem, who was still pining for the absent Florrie. Daisy hoped the two of them might get along famously. She pushed her carefully devised list of rules back into her apron pocket unread and put him in the back bedroom; the one with the blue eiderdown and a book-case since he claimed to be fond of reading and had brought a stack of books with him when he moved in the very next day.

She informed him that breakfast was served sharp at eight, evening meal at six, and left him to it.

Sometimes, Daisy wondered at her own temerity in embarking on such a scheme. Here she was in the midst of getting a lodging house started just as rationing was going from bad to worse. The value of the meat ration had been dropped from 1s 6d to 1s 2d, a state of affairs she complained about loud and long to anyone prepared to listen, quite certain that those in power would not be struggling on such meagre rations. Jams and marmalades were also now on ration and Daisy made a mental note to dig out Aunt Florrie's recipe books and have a go at making her own; assuming she could get the sugar, of course.

But she meant to do things properly. People were already sick and tired of 'Lord Woolton Pie', 'Boston Bake', mock cream, mock marzipan, mock beef soup and mock every-thing else. Daisy knew that she must feed her guests well if she was to keep them. Living on a farm and being able to produce better food than was generally available in the town shops was her one advantage, the most sound reason for her lodgers to put up with the long trek up the lane every day.

They were so lucky, having this lovely place to live in.

Florrie was the first to recover. Finding herself unexpectedly clasping her sister to her breast, she pushed her away quickly and gave her shoulder a little shake. 'Are you all right, our Rita? By, that was a close one.'

Rita struggled to sit up, looking dazed as she began to pick bits of plaster out of her hair. 'Am I all in one piece? Eeh, thank God!' She began to cough, her throat thick with lime dust.

'I reckon we must have cushioned each other as we fell.'

'What, saved each other's life d'you mean, while I was hell-bent on wringing your neck? There's a turn-up for the book.'

What amazed them most was the calm. People were gathering up their belongings and walking away quietly, some to wait for their bus or tram as if nothing amiss had taken place. The world appeared to be falling apart in mayhem and chaos, yet they were concerned only with whether or not they caught the 54 bus on time. A woman appeared out of a haze of dust, a tray of tea mugs in her hand.

Rita gazed at her open-mouthed. 'How long have we been out cold, or was she boiling that kettle even as the bomb dropped?'

Yet another woman appeared out of nowhere, insisting that she sit still to have her head examined.

'Nay, me head has needed examining for years. Happen the bomb will have knocked a bit of sense into it.'

They might have laughed had it not been so awful. What remained of the shelter was a flattened pile of rubble and as Florrie and Rita sat in stunned silence contemplating the horror of it, they each realised that being thrown backwards into the street together was indeed what had saved them. The mother and her two children, along with the rest of the occu-ants who had dived below for safety had been less fortunate.

The ARP warden was even now scrabbling at a hole he'd found in the heap of smoking bricks, desperately trying to find some sign of life within.

'Don't just sit there ladies. Give us a flamin' hand.'

With one accord they struggled to their feet, heads still spinning yet they hurried to help. All hope seemed lost and then a baby's cry was heard and they dug all the harder to retrieve it. Black with smoke and dust yet it proved to be alive and well, unharmed in any way. 'You're one of the lucky ones, chuck,' said Rita, plonking it in an upturned barrel while she got on with the digging.

'That's no way to treat a bairn.' Florrie hurried over and picked up the baby in her arms. The child rewarded her with a beaming smile but then began to splutter and cough, a dribble of sooty saliva running from its mouth as it finally let out a howl of distress. 'Oh there, there, don't take on now.' With practised ease Florrie put the child against her shoulder and began to rub its back, rocking gently. 'Poor lamb. It needs to see a doctor.'

'Oh dear God, I've found a leg here.'

Quickly, Florrie sat the baby carefully back in the half barrel and ran to help her sister while Rita vomited her breakfast into the gutter.

They dug for hours and neither felt able to stop, even though far more experienced people than them came along to help. They pulled bodies out of the rubble one after the other, many with bricks and shrapnel buried in their chest or back, limbs broken or missing. Some suffered dreadful gaping wounds, others had their clothes and skin burned off by the blast or were so covered in blood it was impossible to identify where the injury might be, if they were alive or dead. A whole group of factory girls on their way to work were found to be still clutching each other, bus tickets in hand, a pink ribbon from one fluttering merrily in the breeze as she was dragged from the smouldering ruin that had been th shelter. Of the hundred or more people who had gone in, less than a dozen survived, though whether these could be called lucky, or would ever be the same again, was another matter.

Finally, driven by exhaustion and an increasing sense of futility, the two sisters turned wearily for home, only their numbed silence and the horror imprinted in their eyes revealing what they had gone through.

Without thinking, Florrie had picked up the crying baby, an infant of eighteen months or so, and carried it on her hip. The two women still held on tightly to each other for the length of that terrible journey, not simply for much needed support but in order to find the strength to face the stark devastation that had come to their city. They stumbled over broken glass and smoking ruins, by-passed fires, turning their agonised glances away from the fallen bodies which lay like rags in the rubble. As they made their way along Eccles New Road, they could see a wall of fire on the other side of the Ship Canal.

'Some poor soul's lost the battle there, right enough,' Rita murmured, her voice sounding shaky and weak.

Whole streets had been gutted, some houses still ablaze as fire fighters did battle. Liverpool Street was thick with smoke and a never-ending line of people carrying a pathetic few remnants of what remained of their life; awesomely silent and resigned as they walked they knew not where, thankful at least to be alive for all they were homeless and leaving behind everything they owned, in some cases their loved ones as well. It seemed strange that the sun still shone, filtering through the dust and smoke like a benedict of hope for the future. Buses still ran, taking long detours to carry people to some sort of safety out of the city. There was no panic, no hysteria, only a strange, eerie silence broken now and then by a shout as someone was found buried alive under the fallen masonry, or quiet sobbing of a mother over a child who was not.

they reached their own entry they quickened their pace,

so that as they turned the corner, Rita was actually running. Florrie didn't recall ever having seen her sister so distressed but she understood why. Where once there had been Marigold Court, a row of back-to-back tenement houses, smoke blackened and old maybe but nonetheless solid and the place they had always called home, now there was nothing beyond a burning heap of rubble. A line of nappies flapped bizarrely in the breeze; a still smoking fireplace spilling its contents into a black hole that had once held a parlour; upper floors broken open to the elements, a bed hung precariously on the edge as if any second it might plunge into the morass of destruction below. Water poured from broken pipes and over everything was an all-pervading stink of gas.

Rita stood stock-still and stared, hollow-eyed, at the scene before her. 'Dear Lord, I hope that for once in his life, Joe didn't do as I told him and stopped to peel that bloody potato.'

It was the first time Florrie had heard her sister swear.

The next few weeks proved to be the happiest in Daisy's life. She wouldn't have been without any of them, even poor, sad Mr Pickles with his constantly long face and dusty appearance, for all he claimed to be so much happier here on the farm than alone in his old home. He would explain, at length, to Daisy how he'd felt quite unable to continue in the empty house they had once occupied together. He did have a daughter but had no wish to be a burden to her, so had come to Lane End. 'At least here I am not alone, and you have made me so comfortable. I appreciate that, Miss Atkins.'

'Ooh, call me Daisy for heaven's sake, or you'll make me feel as old as Miss – I mean older than I really am, and she hastily assured him how glad she was that he felt at home.

That first night she'd presented her guests with lamb cutlets, new potatoes, and carrots and turnips mashed together with a dab of margarine. Even this had brought the ghost of a smile to Ned Pickles' lugubrious expression despite him declaring that the meal was delicious. Tommy Twinkletoes, on the other hand, had been effusive in his praise. On the second night she gave them fish, with oxtail soup and spam fritters on the third, all served up by Clem who moved about with surprising alacrity, carrying plates and cups with the speed of a greyhound just released from the starting gate.

'Give 'em time to enjoy their meal before you whip their plates away,' Daisy warned. Poor man. He didn't seem to know what had hit him. One minute he'd been leading a quiet life, unchanging save for the seasons, now he was the proprietor of a boarding house. Well, at least it would keep his mind off worrying over Florrie.

He returned to the kitchen with plates mopped clean of the last speck of gravy. 'The dog couldn't leave these any cleaner but what's up wi' that Pickles character? Face as long as a wet fortneet. Has his wife run off with a sailor? Mind, any woman'd run off with t'next door's cat if she had to wake up to that miserable face every morning. He makes me want to cut me own throat I feel that depressed after talking to him for just five minutes. He's as miserable as a yow on a rainy day. I towd him once: a smile costs nowt.'

Daisy had to ask, 'And what did he say to that?'

Clem sighed. '"Life is a vale of tears." Eeh, I could've wept blood.'

Stifling the inappropriate giggles, Daisy explained about poor Mr Pickles' recent loss and later noticed Clem serve him with an especially large helping of bread and butter pudding.

Ned's reaction to such generosity was to take every opportunity to enlighten Clem with his opinions about the state of the nation or his view of current military tactics, acquired by attending regular lectures, talks and lantern slide shows put on at the school hall in Keswick which he visited regularly on his bicycle. He was more than ready to share his passion for political propaganda by encouraging his fellow residents, in particular Daisy herself, to accompany him. She would politely decline on the grounds she had far too much work to do caring for her guests. Instead, she did her best to try to persuade Clem to join him. Clem always looked anxious to get away, fidgeting as if there were a million and one jobs he'd much rather be doing, like shovelling muck in the cowshed.

'Why would I want to go?' he grumbled. 'I see enough of the miserable old bugger about the house all day.

'But he's lonely.' She didn't say that Clem too was lonely but managed, after a week or two of persuasion, to get him to go along. The pair set off together one evening in a silent fug of resentment. Ned preferring to have escorted Daisy, and Clem wishing he could stop at home with his carpet slippers.

She watched them go with a fond smile on her face. If only Florrie would come home. Maybe she'd find Clem changed, ready to talk about his grief now. Sometimes you could almost accuse him of being chatty. She chuckled softly, gazing up at the bright stars and wondering where Harry was at this moment. Was that what they called a bomber's moon? Would he be flying tonight? She shivered and rubbed her hands up and down her arms, as if a goose had stepped over her grave. Best she didn't know when he was flying, or where. He rarely spoke of it but she knew he wasn't the pilot, only the gunner at the back. Surely he'd be safer there? Or would he?

Deliberately she turned her mind back to more practical, safer issues, such as what Florrie would say to having her house turned upside down by a bunch of strangers. Daisy quailed at the thought. She'd certainly have some explaining to do when her aunt finally did come home. So long as she didn't bring Rita with her, she'd cope somehow. Thinking of her mother reminded Daisy of her father, and the awkwardness of their last meeting. She really shouldn't be too hard on him. After all, he must be a saint to have lived with Rita all these years.

After a moment, she closed the door on the chill of the evening, and pulling a chair up to the kitchen fire set about writing him a letter. You only had one father after all. And keeping in touch with family was important.

By the end of the first couple of weeks, Laura and Chrissy counted themselves as experts. 'Look at that.' Chrissy held out a five-pound note given to her by one of the guests. 'This is a great job. And everyone likes my hair. Didn't I say it was only that stuffy headmistress?'

Wisely Laura made no comment.

It was as she was heading through the hall en route to the dining room that the doorbell rang and she hurried to answer it, guessing it must be the new guest for room three, a Mrs Crabtree.

A man with a clipboard stood in the yard with that special smile on his face which marked him as a salesman of some sort.

'No double glazing today, thank you,' Laura began but he interrupted her.

'We haven't met but I've spoken to your husband. It is Mrs Rampton, isn't it? Mrs Miranda Rampton?'

Laura had very nearly closed the door when these last words gave her pause. 'What did you call me? My name is Rampton, yes. Laura Rampton.'

He looked confused. 'Oh dear, I must have got the name wrong. It's in connection with the loan.'

'What loan?' She was standing before him now, arms folded. 'I know nothing about any loan.'

'The second mortgage. Your husband did say he would deal with the matter, have you sign the necessary papers. However, it's our normal practice to visit the property in question.'

'I think you'd better come in.'

Once Laura had fully appraised him of the situation, he

readily informed her that Felix had given Miranda as his wife's name, his new address as Cheadle Hulme, and named Lane End Farm as a country retreat.

By the end of a most lively and enlightening half hour's chat, washed down with some of her excellent coffee, Laura and the man with the clipboard were bosom pals. He'd shared with her horror stories from his own divorce and Laura had expressed her appreciation for his diligence in the matter. Had he not called upon her, in direct opposition to Felix's wishes, she might well have simply have been presented with a wad of forms to sign.

'And, if he'd bullied or confused you sufficiently, you might well have signed them. Is he a bully, your husband, Mrs Rampton?' The young man asked with touching sympathy in his voice.

'Indeed he can be.'

'Well, no harm has been done. We, as a Society, are always most particular about ensuring all parties and property are thoroughly checked out. I shall write and refuse him the mortgage, and see that these forms are destroyed forthwith. Good day to you, and good luck with your new project.' She led him to the door and saw him on his way with one of her brochures tucked in his inside pocket.

Some time later, Laura showed Mrs Crabtree, the new guest, up to her room, helped with her bags and gave out the necessary information about breakfast times and whether she would like a morning paper. She was a woman in her mid to late sixties, full of smiles, looking interestedly about her as Laura turned to go, her mind already moving on to the tables she must lay and the pile of bed linen waiting to be ironed. Mrs Crabtree said, 'I must say you've done the house up lovely.'

'Thank you.'

She gave a self-conscious little laugh. 'When I saw y

advertisement in the *Manchester Guardian*, I couldn't resist ringing up and booking for a short break. It was a chance too good to miss. This is a trip down memory lane for me.'

Laura was at once all ears. The incident over the second mortgage had shaken her badly but she was determined not to give up on her dream, not only of establishing a good business, but of finding out more about Daisy. 'Why, have you stayed here before when my grandmother ran it?'

The woman's face was a picture of shock and delight. 'Daisy was your grandmother? Oh my, I assumed you'd simply bought the house. Then your father must be . . . Tell me dear, his name wouldn't be Robbie, by any chance, would it?'

Laura couldn't help but smile even as her mind whirled with questions, never having heard the diminutive used in connection with her father before. It didn't seem to suit him at all. 'Robert actually. Do you know him?'

'Only as a child. I was brought here as an evacuee. Daisy was my great friend, and I adored your father when he was a baby, absolutely adored him. My name is Megan, by the by. I don't suppose Daisy ever mentioned me, did she?'

Laura was staring at the woman, stunned. 'Megan? Of course. You and your sister Trish travelled with her to the Lakes on the train.'

The woman beamed with remembered pleasure then burst out laughing. 'That's us, in our overlong trailing mackintoshes and dreadful berets. Trish emigrated to Canada after she married but I used to come here quite a lot. Became quite a regular until well into the sixties, till I started a family and life got too hectic, you know how it is. Daisy and I would reminisce about old times. Quite a pair of old gossips we were.'

Laura's eyes were shining. 'I certainly have heard all about ɔu. How wonderful to meet you in person. Perhaps, when ʋ've settled in, you'd come and have a gossip with me. I'm ‿ys happy to learn more about Daisy.'

'Be glad to. I can tell you how she came to open this place, and how she found your father?'

'Found?'

'Didn't you know that Daisy had a son who was given away for adoption? Didn't your father ever tell you?'

'Heaven help me, what are you saying? You mean Daisy *found* him again? Could that be possible? That my father was actually her lost son?'

'Of course it could. Whyever not? How old is he?'

'Excuse me?'

'When was he born?'

Laura considered. 'I'm not sure. He's sixty-three, born during the war, no, just before it.'

'There you are then. Daisy's lost son. The age fits.'

A moment's silence while Laura absorbed the implications. 'How can you be sure? I've practically taken the place apart and found no sign of any birth or marriage certificates, no documentary evidence of any kind.'

'Well you wouldn't, would you? What with the adoption and the war and everything.'

'But I don't understand any of this. How did it all come about? How did she find him?'

'You could always ask him that.'

'You don't know my father. Having warned me off poking and prying into Daisy's life, he'd simply blow his top again. No, no there has to be some other way.'

'Shall I tell you what I know? It might help. I could tell you how we found Daisy again.'

'Oh, please do. Perhaps we could get together this evening, over supper? What happened after the bomb? And tell me more about how you came to know my father.'

'So what d'you think you're going to do with it then? You can't keep it. It's not yours.'

Florrie looked at the baby and began to cry. The pair w

sitting on a pile of broken bricks and splintered window frames, all that remained of their home. From the harshness of her tone a stranger might be fooled into thinking that Rita didn't care that her husband was probably buried somewhere beneath it all. Florrie knew different. Rita was always at her nastiest when she was most upset. Besides, her eyes were red, her nose was running and she could barely get the words out through the tightness of the pain constricting her throat. 'How should I know what we ought to do with it, but right now it needs feeding. God almighty – and changing.' She lifted the baby, wrinkled her nose and shook her head in despair. 'Aw, poor little love.'

'Never mind the baby being a poor little love, what about us? We're homeless. Bombed out. Or haven't you noticed?'

Florrie looked with pity on her sister. And you're a widow, but didn't have the courage to say as much in so many words. Between first finding the ruins of their home, not to mention all of the other houses in Marigold Court, to them arriving back here and seating themselves upon its smoking remains, the two women had trailed from one air-raid shelter to another in their search for Joe, not missing a single opportunity to ask if anyone had seen him, or check out a place where he might have taken cover.

'He's a goner,' Rita had finally admitted, not a tear in sight. 'I bet he stayed put, peeling that bloody potato. Never did know what was best for him, the silly old fool. Now what are we supposed to do? No home, no husband, no job, no money. What now?' She rooted in her pocket for a bit of grubby rag that passed for a hanky and blew her nose upon it, loud and hard.

'And we've the bairn to think about, don't forget.'

Rita shot a venomous glare at Florrie. 'Aren't you listening to a single word I've said? We've bigger problems to consider than a lost child. Anyroad, there's some nappies, over ere. I reckon they'll be dry by now.' Rita's black humour seemed stronger than ever as she gazed upon the ruins of her world.

Florrie stared in horror at the washing line with its row of terry napkins. Who had washed them, and where was the child? Had it, or the mother, survived? Even if they had, she could surely spare one nappy in the circumstances. Propping the baby on her hip, Florrie picked her way over the heap of loose chunks of plaster and burning debris to unpeg the cleanest one from the line, deciding to take a second as well, just to be safe. Milk for the baby was another matter.

Back beside her sister, Florrie pointed out this problem as she cleaned up the baby as best she could and pinned on the clean nappy. 'He must be weaned by now, mustn't he, but a bairn still needs milk.'

'Never mind milk for the babby, what are we going to eat? Dirt, I suppose.'

A woman who happened to be passing by as Rita asked the question, answered it for her. 'We're to go down to t'council school. There's soup on offer from the WVS, and summat fer t'child an' all, I reckon.'

Rita didn't thank her but simply nodded, by way of a greeting when she saw whom she addressed. 'That's what I've got coming to me now, is it? A blanket and a bit of hard floor in an old schoolroom, and handouts from a soup kitchen. It'll be the flamin' workhouse next.'

'Reckon we've all come down in t'world today. Some of us with a bump.'

'How's your Percy?'

'Fair to middling.'

'It's a boy, a fine one at that,' Florrie said, quite inconsequentially, paying no attention to the conversation between the two neighbours as she buried the dirty nappy amongst the rubbish around her.

The woman stared at the baby with bleak eyes. 'At least yo_ can be thankful he's too young to fight. Unlike my lad. G near shot to pieces, he did. You'd think he'd be safe on a big ship like that, wouldn't you?'

'What about your Annie and the nippers?' Rita asked, but the woman only jerked her head in the direction of the destruction behind them, and even the hard-hearted Rita seemed moved by the gesture. 'Joe an' all,' she said, acknowledging their mutual loss. Both women looked away, embarrassed by their own vulnerability and not yet able to cope with pity.

'I'd best be going.' Without pausing to linger, she went on her way, dragging her feet as if the effort even of walking were too much for her, face pinched and drawn with suffering.

Reality finally began to penetrate. An entire area, all the entries and yards and courts with their fanciful names and long history of gloom and poverty had been destroyed this day. No loss, some might say, save for the number of mothers and children, old folk and loved ones who'd been lost along with them. Every one an innocent victim of war. Rita expelled her anger by blaming not only the German planes who'd dropped the bombs but the local authorities for their inadequate means of protection, the government, and even the ARP Warden who, in her opinion, had very nearly been the death of them.

Florrie was still preoccupied with the baby. 'Who does he belong to? Did you see anyone who might have been his mam? We should take him back to the ARP Warden, get him checked out by a doctor. There, there, don't cry little chap. Hush now, hush.' She sat him on her lap and began to rock him to and fro, crooning gently as she gave him a finger to suck to ease his hunger. Rita was saying nothing, only sat staring at her in an odd sort of way.

22

Daisy was enjoying herself hugely and finding them all to be excellent guests. They paid their rent on time, were perfectly amenable and pleasant to live with. And if she made mistakes with her cooking, they were most forgiving, this being a new enterprise for her and she so young. They didn't mind in the least the blackened toast, the soggy vegetables, the somewhat leathery Yorkshire puddings because they were so enchanted by her cheerful smile, her lovely face, and by her willingness to be helpful.

And she made a point of listening to their problems. It soon became clear why Miss Geraldine Copthorne had been barred from the parlour at her previous lodgings. Nothing at all to do with the price of coal. The woman was a bore. Well-meaning, stoic, hard working, but nonetheless a crashing bore. She barely stopped talking long enough to take a breath, and certainly never seemed to expect a reply.

As April gave way to May and the blossom on the cherry trees supplied a stark contrast to the dark horror that continued to fall from above, lighting the skies over the coast where Harry was stationed to a dull red, Daisy kept her mind occupied by taking great care of her guests. She worried so much about him that she was glad of the distraction. She worried too about Megan and Trish, having had no reply to her last two letters.

In addition to her regulars, there would often be a young soldier with his sweetheart sneaking off for a weekend. She would make sure they were comfortable but allow them plenty of privacy, not appearing to even notice if they didn't come down to breakfast. She might envy their joy in each other a little, but didn't begrudge them their need to escape from hostilities. One of these was a pilot by the name of Charlie Potter. Charlie and his girl became regulars during those first months, often popping in just for one of Daisy's high teas, even if they didn't stay overnight.

'There's no one like you Daisy,' he'd say. 'Most landladies are dragons. Not our Daisy.'

Another was a Mr Enderby who came to visit his elderly mother but swore he couldn't live in the same house as her or there'd be murder done. He would put his shoes outside the bedroom door to be cleaned, just as if he were staying at the Savoy. Daisy would always clean them, and place them neatly back there the following morning.

'You're too soft for your own good, girl,' Clem would warn, but Daisy only grinned.

Daisy found herself sitting for hours with the spinster teacher in the parlour, hearing about her work, and her intention to take night-school classes in French once the war was over, which might gain her a much improved teaching post, perhaps in a girls' private school. She would offer to hold the wool if Miss Copthorne wanted to wind it. Knitting and sewing were her favourite forms of relaxation, next to talking, that is, and as she knitted socks, wound wool or hemmed handkerchiefs she would drone on and on, going over and over the same conversation night after night. Daisy felt duty-bound to listen; in truth there was little chance of escape once she'd got going. She learned more about education than she really felt the need to know; the woman's one topic of conversation being her precious charges and how difficult it was to keep up the necessary standards.

'We must still do our arithmetic, our algebra and get our school certificate,' she would declare sternly, followed by the oft-heard cry, 'war or no war.'

Miss Copthorne would discuss the relative merits of chain stitch as opposed to feather and why it was essential for each girl to learn plain sewing while the boys concentrate their efforts on running the school allotment. 'Even the children must play their part, dear Daisy, and dig for victory. However, education cannot be neglected. Oh, dear me no! War or no war.'

She was so thrifty that she would cut exercise books in half.

Daisy laughed, and said that she was just as bad with soap. 'I always think it will go twice as far if I give people half as much.'

'Ah, but is it thrift or the terrible sin of hoarding, dear Daisy, if a frugal housewife saves bars of soap, for instance, against a possible future shortage? Is it patriotic to be thrifty or are you a liability to your compatriots? A moot point don't you think?'

'I wouldn't know the answer to that one,' Daisy said, 'but I do know that anything we need to do here on the farm seems to require six sheets of foolscap to deal with it.'

'Oh indeed, I know all about forms, believe me. And you can be fined for throwing away your bus ticket in the street.'

Daisy enjoyed these lively exchanges but soon they'd be back on the same old treadmill of discussion on education and examinations, upon which Daisy could make less of a contribution. She did become familiar with the words of *The Young Lochinvar*, and *The Forsaken Merman* which Miss Copthorne was fond of reciting by heart.

Miss Copthorne was also concerned about the evacuee children who had returned to Newcastle, about whether her old school would open again to admit them despite the seemingly endless bombing, and how they would cope without her if they did.

'I certainly dare not leave these precious mites here all on their own.'

'Of course not,' and Daisy would helplessly wonder if the

poor woman bored the children at their lessons in exactly the same way, by endlessly dull repetition, drumming facts into their tiny heads until they were heartily sick of it. Or perhaps her little charges brought out the best in her.

In the secret depths of her heart Daisy too worried about the evacuee children, two in particular. She still held on to her dream of having Megan and Trish come to live with her at Lane End Farm. Again she'd written and got no response and if Miss Copthorne's enquiries revealed that they were in any sort of difficulties, or the slightest bit miserable, she would take her courage in both hands and beg Clem to take them in. There was plenty of room, after all, and at least then she would know they were safe.

And then one morning there came a knock at the door. Daisy hurried to answer it, curious as to who it might be since they didn't get many visitors living so high up on the mountainside.

It was Harry, brown hair cut shorter than ever, polished boots caked in mud from the long walk up the lane, and an ear to ear grin wreathing his face. Daisy leapt into his arms on a shriek of delight. 'Have you got some leave?'

'Two days.'

'Oh bliss!' She hadn't seen him for weeks, not since he was posted, and this was the first time that he'd come to the farm. It felt wonderful to have his arms around her again, to breathe in the scent of him and lose herself in the glorious power of his kisses. But he wasn't alone.

'Look what I've got here,' he said, when they stopped hugging and kissing long enough to stand apart a little, smiling shyly into each other's eyes. And from behind his back he drew out two small figures.

'Megan! Trish! I don't believe it.' Tears of joy sprang to her eyes as Daisy gathered her two small friends to her in a fierce hug. They were bounding with exuberance, like a pair of puppies wriggling and yelping with glee so that they knocked Daisy over in their excitement and all three were soon rolling about on the grass while Harry stood by, laughing in delight.

Wouldn't he do anything for his Daisy? And bringing the children to her had seemed to him the perfect way to prove that. He couldn't quite get over his good fortune at attracting her attention in the first place, him being such a homely sort of bloke and she a real looker.

'I decided it was time you three musketeers got together again,' he explained as they sat in the kitchen and Daisy fussed about heating soup and buttering bread, saying how she wished she'd known they were coming then she would have baked something special for the children. 'When you said in your last letter that you hadn't heard from them in ages, I took it into my head to call and see how they were.' He was frowning slightly as he said this, and something in his face told Daisy not to ask any more questions just then, so instead she went to him and kissed him.

'I'm so glad you did.'

Megan said. 'He just walked up the garden path bold as you please.'

'Right into the shed, picked us up out of our camp beds and carried us away in his arms. Mrs Carter said she'd never seen such cheek in her life,' Trish added, slapping her hand over her mouth to hold back her giggles.

Daisy listened to this in astonishment. She longed to ask what on earth the children were doing sleeping on camp beds in a garden shed, but mindful of the warning in Harry's eyes and of Megan's small mouth pursed into mutinous angry silence, she managed to hold her tongue.

Trish, realising she'd revealed more than she should, cast her sister an anxious, sidelong glance before adding in hushed and horrified tones, 'She were going to send me away. To an 'ospital. On me *own*.'

'Hostel, for problem children,' Megan corrected her quietly in a tight little voice.

Later, as Daisy sat cuddled beside Harry while the children played ball, he told her the full story and she was appalled to hear how they'd been treated. How could anyone put two such lovely children in a garden shed, just because they might have scabies, or some other problem which was not of their making?

Harry too had been more shocked than he could say when he'd found them like that, all huddled up together like a pair of frightened mice. He knew from his own experience, coming from a large, close-knit family, the value of a happy childhood. Didn't he go back to Halifax to visit them whenever he could? His own mother had taken in two evacuees, despite having a full house already, and treated them as members of the family.

'I know I've created a problem, broken some rules maybe, but I couldn't just walk away and leave them like that.'

'Course you couldn't. The very idea.'

'Unthinkable. I like children too much.'

'Do you?' Daisy gazed up at him starry-eyed. Perhaps she should tell him now, about her own baby? But then Trish fell down and started yelling and the opportunity was missed.

Once she'd been put back on her feet, bruised knees wiped and kissed better, Daisy looked on with concern as they played. Trish seemed even more jumpy and excitable, constantly crying out for attention while Megan was quieter, more withdrawn. The smiles and joy at having found each other again had quickly vanished and she'd withdrawn into some sort of shell, which Daisy didn't wonder at. These two had spent the entire war being shifted about from pillar to post with no one prepared to take responsibility for them. It was utterly inhuman, and settled the matter once and for all so far as she was concerned. 'They're staying here with me now, come what may.'

'I guessed you might say that,' Harry grinned. 'That's why I brought their stuff.'

'Oh Harry, did you really?' Her eyes were round with surprise and delight.

'I left their bags round the back, in the barn.'

'Harry Driscoll, you old softy.' Daisy leaned into his strong shoulder, curling an arm about his neck as she smiled up into his green-grey eyes and knew a moment of such all encompassing love, she felt choked with emotion.

'I am, where you are concerned, Daisy.'

'So that's how she found you again?' Laura said.

'Yes, through Harry. He was the kindest man I know. And the most patient. He adored Daisy, would do anything for her. And that was the most wonderful summer I can ever remember.' Megan Crabtree got up from the table. 'But I'm an old woman now and must away to my bed. That was a lovely meal, thank you. Perhaps tomorrow, I can tell you a little more.'

Laura said goodnight, had a slight tussle of wills with Chrissy but finally got her off to bed too. Which left her alone with David since she hadn't been able to resist inviting him along to hear more of the tale, and he couldn't resist coming. Now she turned to him with smiling eyes.

'I'm so glad Daisy was happy with her Harry. Happiness is so important, don't you think?'

'You have gorgeous eyes, do you know that? So alive.'

'I beg your pardon?'

David's mouth twisted into that irrepressible grin. 'Your eyes. Did anyone ever tell you how lovely they were? All dark and mysterious. A soft, velvet brown. Most inviting.'

'David, for goodness' sake. We're discussing important issues here, important to me anyway.'

'Your eyes are pretty important to me too, as a matter of fact. Hey, don't scowl at me, it spoils the effect. OK, I find Daisy fascinating too, but . . .'

'You're bored.'

He pulled her very gently into his arms. 'I was only thinking that perhaps we've discussed family history long enough, and maybe it was time to move on to more personal concerns.'

'So what subject would you like to discuss?' She found she was having difficulty holding on to her scowl, it kept slipping into a smile. Could that be because of the nearness of him, the solid strength of his arms, or the mesmerising motion of his hand smoothing up and down her back?

He was kissing her nose, her throat, moving round to her ear. 'I didn't actually have talking in mind.'

Laura could feel herself starting to melt, rapidly losing control as a pleasurable sensation began to grow deep in the hollow pit inside her, a place more accustomed to despair and misery in recent months. His arms had tightened about her, his breathing shortened and there was an increasing intensity to his kisses. Laura slid her arms about his neck and gave herself up to them. Sensation rocked her, throwing her completely off balance. How long had it been since she'd properly loved a man? She and Felix had become distant strangers. Felix, oh heavens! What was she thinking of? She pushed David away, knowing her eyes were glazed with wanting, her face as flushed as a newly awakened girl.

'Look, you're a nice guy but . . .'

'I know, you're still married. You need time and space. This is all going too fast for you.' His voice was soft, a caress in itself.

'So you read minds too?' She couldn't take her eyes off his. They were asking a question she couldn't answer. Demanding. Compelling. Challenging her to give in to the inevitable, and filled with a quiet certainty that in the end, she would. Yet there was also in the depths of his gaze a rare understanding, a reassurance that he would tread delicately through this minefield of her emotions. Together, these produced a intoxicating combination that left her weak with need. Lau cleared her throat. 'The fact is, I'm a bit out of my depth here, and out of practice.'

'I could help you rehearse and get back into step.'

She giggled. 'I'm sure you could.'

'Perhaps I should call every day to take you through your paces. Lesson one, relax.' He pushed her back gently on to the cushions of the sofa, smoothing his hands over her bare arms, lifting them above her head while he kissed her softly, increasing the pressure on her mouth as she made no move to resist; taking his time over the kiss, savouring it, making it last as long as possible. He slid one hand beneath the silk blouse to smooth it lightly over her breast, making her groan softly. He pulled away to look unsmiling into her eyes and it was she who pulled him back to her, begging him to kiss her some more for it was much too late to protest now. One minute her fingers were wandering of their own accord through his hair, the next tugging at the buttons of his shirt.

He slid her silk blouse from her shoulders, dropping it to the floor with barely a whisper, making no comment about how her body trembled as he lay her upon the rug with reverent care. 'Are you sure about this?' was all he said as she struggled with the buckle of his jeans.

Her mind in turmoil, unable to think of anything but the touch of his fingers on her over-sensitised skin, Laura had never been less sure of anything in her life. She'd set the wheels in motion for the divorce but there was months to go before she would be a free woman, and was afraid of something going wrong in the meantime. With Felix, it felt a bit like lighting the touchpaper and standing back to wait for the explosion. There seemed to be plenty of explosions going on inside of her right now. 'I'm quite certain that if you don't take me soon, I might ravish you instead.'

'I've no objection to a bit of ravishing.'

'The only thing is,' she murmured breathlessly through several more kisses. 'You can't stay *too* much longer. I have to be up early tomorrow to cook breakfast, and there's still the washing-up to do.'

He let out a heavy sigh of resignation and finally, reluctantly, released her, albeit with a smile. 'OK, lead me to the dishwasher.'

'Do you think having a love affair was any easier in World War Two?'

'You mean everything to me, Daisy. I don't ever want us to be apart.' Even as he said these glorious words, Harry was kissing her face, her throat, her lips with such tenderness, Daisy felt she might weep she wanted him so much. Then he pulled away and smiled very tenderly into her eyes. 'But I mean us to do everything proper like. I mean us to wed, if you'll have me.' He was fumbling in his pocket, pulling out a box, and Daisy could hardly believe her eyes as he opened it to reveal a tiny, solitaire diamond on a twist of gold, glittering in the sunshine. 'I know I should ask your parents first, you being under age, but until I get the chance, we could at least get unofficially engaged. If that's all right with you?'

'Oh Harry. It's lovely.'

'I take it that's a yes? I couldn't bear it if it wasn't.'

She gave a soft little chuckle and kissed his nose. 'Silly boy, don't you know by now how much I love you?'

'And I love you, Daisy. Don't ever forget that.'

'As if I could.'

'You and me for ever girl, right?'

'For ever and ever.'

Being together for a whole afternoon was magical, over much too soon and Daisy felt all wobbly inside at having become engaged to the most wonderful young man in the world. But she didn't dare to wear the ring, not yet, not till everything had been made official between them and she wasn't yet ready to confront her mother. Carefully she wrapped it in a handkerchief and hid it in her undies drawer

Perhaps she wouldn't ever need to, if Harry was prepared to wait a year or two till she was twenty-one. It would be sensible not to rush anyway, what with the war and everything. And it would give them time to save up. Daisy gave a happy little sigh and fell asleep dreaming of wedding bells and white frocks, the scent of apple blossom in the air.

Following the intriguing information that she'd learned thus far, partly from Megan Crabtree and partly from the tapes, Laura rang her father and asked if he'd like to come and stay for a few days.

'Why would I want to?' he barked down the phone.

'Lane End used to be your old home. Wouldn't you like to see what I've done to it? See if you approve.'

'You know my opinion on the matter, Laura. I certainly would not approve. If you choose to ignore my advice, on your own head be it. You'll lose Felix, run out of money and come to regret this madness of yours in the end.'

'I hope not. It's hard work but I'm rather enjoying it. Guess who is here? Megan Crabtree. Do you remember her? She remembers you with great affection as a baby, so you must have been adorable once.' Laura chuckled. 'Sends her fond regards and hopes to meet up with you again one day. Actually, that's partly why I rang. I was wondering – well, it crossed my mind that you might like to pop up now, she's here for the week, and the pair of you could catch up on old times. What do you say?'

For the first time in her life Laura appeared to have left her father speechless. The silence lasted for so long that she had to ask if he was still there.

'Of course I'm still here.'

'Have you forgotten Megan? She seems to remember you well enough: a sturdy little chap, she called you. Claims she spent a good deal of time picking up your toys.'

'I remember Megan perfectly well. She used to read

me endless Beatrix Potter stories. And Trish. They were evacuees. Went home eventually, after the war, then came back again.'

'Really? She never mentioned that. Well, what do you think? A reunion might be fun?' Laura fully expected him to refuse. Robert could not be called the most gregarious of people at the best of times. However, she was wrong. He mumbled something about having to look up train times, and which days weren't suitable because of golf or bridge commitments but, in the end, a day was agreed upon. Laura told Megan Crabtree, who was thrilled with the promise of meeting up with 'little Robbie' again so soon. 'I can't wait,' she said.

Neither can I, thought Laura.

It was the most touching sight she could ever have imagined. Laura parked her Peugeot on the gravel forecourt and by the time she'd climbed out, Megan was at the front door, waiting anxiously. She took one look at her 'little Robbie', now a sixty-something grey-haired man with a paunch, and held wide her arms. To Laura's utter amazement, her father beamed and happily succumbed to being thoroughly hugged and kissed. In fact, he seemed to be doing quite a bit of that sort of thing on his own account.

Laura was stunned. Even Chrissy, standing equally slack-jawed beside her, whispered, 'Would you believe it? Soppy old Gramps.'

The pair rarely stopped talking for the entire afternoon, most of it incomprehensible to Laura, all about school friends, nature rambles and concerts, not to mention numerous teachers, a Miss Copthorne being the only name she recognised. Megan held a particularly fond memory of herself and Trish dressing up as Gert and Daisy.

'Don't remember that,' Robert said. 'I was probably too young at the time.'

'It was perhaps during that first wonderful summer. Oh, but it was great fun. Trish was always a great mimic, had them off to perfection. Do you remember the Christmas carol concerts and the time Trish was the Virgin Mary and dropped the baby doll?' Roaring with laughter they were off into other reminiscences.

Chrissy slipped away halfway through the afternoon, saying she was going to meet a friend down in Threlkeld. Laura was pleased that she'd found one and made no objection, knowing it must be rather dull for her to spend all her time with boring adults. It briefly crossed her mind to ask who it was but then the telephone rang and by the time she'd taken another booking, Chrissy had gone. Laura went to put on the kettle, to freshen up the tea.

It wasn't until her father was about to leave that Laura plucked up the courage to mention the subject of the land. She knew it would be a delicate issue, with deep connotations. Helping him on with his coat she tried, and failed, to persuade him to stay overnight.

'No, no, I don't want to be any trouble. Besides, I've things planned for tomorrow.'

'Wouldn't it be nice for you to stay in your childhood home for one night? You could have your old room. Which was it?'

'Unlike you, Laura, I have no wish to revisit the past.'

'You just have, with Megan, for an entire afternoon. You mean Daisy's past I suppose, since you, personally, have scarcely mentioned her name, for all it has cropped up countless times out of Megan's mouth. For goodness' sake, why? I should perhaps warn you that I've found out about the land, about you owning it, I mean. Did you think I wouldn't? I'm not sure why you kept it from me though I'll admit it really is no concern of mine who owns it.'

He looked shocked for a moment, his usually florid face paling slightly and the mouth tightening to a grim line. 'I have nothing to do with it. Nothing at all. Never touch the rent from it, it stays in the Trust.'

Laura's mouth dropped open. 'You mean you've never used the money, and you so often crying poverty? Where's the point in deliberately depriving yourself of a decent standard of living? That's not what Daisy wanted.'

'I've not touched a penny of it. Never will. What about the way she behaved with Harry? She cheated on my father with him. Betrayed him. He deserved better. Hadn't he suffered enough as a casualty of war?'

'We don't know that for sure. We don't yet know what happened between the three of them. And there was a war on; circumstances were difficult.'

'I agree there may be some things we never discover, or fully understand. But I'll not touch her damned money. It's nothing at all to do with me.'

'But she was your *mother*!'

His gaze was filled with fury now as he turned on her. 'No, Laura. She was *not* my mother. God knows who I was, but I didn't belong to Daisy. Haven't you understood anything you've heard from Megan and from these damned tapes you've been telling us about. I wasn't Daisy's child at all. I was stolen. Florrie told me so just before she died. That's why we quarrelled. That's why Daisy never loved me.'

Her father was so upset after this declaration that he stormed off into the night, slamming the door in Laura's startled face. For a whole thirty seconds she stood rooted to the spot before being galvanised into action by the sight of his fleeing figure. Grabbing her car keys and coat, she jumped in the car and went in pursuit of him down the lane.

They were sitting outside the railway station, talking quietly now. Robert had calmed down but his eyes still looked suspiciously bright. Very gently, Laura asked him why he believed that Daisy hadn't loved him.

'She lied. She told me I was her lost boy returned to her, the one she'd thought never to see again. Then Florrie told me I wasn't at all, that she herself had picked me up out of the rubble during the blitz and they hadn't the first idea who I belonged to. All that tale about Percy's sister and brother-in-law adopting me was a complete fabrication.'

Laura listened in silence as the hurt came pouring out. So this was the reason for that terrible quarrel, the family feud. 'I can see that it must have been painful to learn such a thing, but it doesn't prove that Daisy didn't care for you. Perhaps she believed Rita's story; had been taken in by her own mother's lies. And if she had ever discovered otherwise, perhaps she kept up the pretence because she wanted you to feel secure. That's what mothers do. In any case, even if she knew all along that you might not be her son, perhaps she wanted, needed, to believe that you were.'

He stared at her, saying nothing. 'Why would she choose to do that?'

'Because she loved you, why else? She didn't want to lose you. She says on the tape how she lost her son twice and hoped you would forgive her for the hurt you suffered.'

'I was either a foundling or illegitimate,' he snarled. 'I don't know which. Not much of a start in life, is it? If the former, as Florrie insisted was the case, then Daisy only kept me out of pity, because she felt sorry for me as she did for Megan and Trish. Just another evacuee. We were her compensation for the baby she lost, not a genuine, heartfelt love. That's what has haunted me all my life. '

'Oh no, I can't believe she'd ever simply do things out of pity. She adored Megan and Trish, I can tell that from the tone of her voice let alone all the other evidence I've heard. As for you, you were special. You were her son. Whatever the truth, whether you were her own natural child or adopted, she wanted to keep you out of love for you, not pity. None of it was your fault, nor Daisy's, and nothing at all to be ashamed of. I expect she was angry with Florrie for telling you, for putting that doubt into your mind but Florrie was an old and bitter woman. You'll have to forgive her too.'

He looked at her then, his eyes beseeching her to convince him.

'Dad,' Laura said. 'I love you too,' and she put her arms around him and hugged him.

'And I love you,' he mumbled into her collar.

23

Clem had no objection to the two little girls staying on, not if it meant that Daisy would stay with them, and personally went to see the billeting officer to make it all right. 'Just what we need, to have a couple of young 'uns about the place.'

'They can help with the cleaning,' Daisy said, laughing when they both pulled mock faces of dismay, for their shining eyes were telling quite a different story.

They quickly came to love the old man and readily obeyed his every word, trailing behind him wherever he went. 'Like Mary and her flippin' lamb,' he would say with a great chortle of mirth, secretly delighted to have such adulation.

Clem showed them how to collect eggs from the hens, still warm from the nests, without getting pecked by the bad-tempered cockerel. He taught them how to cut peat and trundle it back to the shed in an old wooden coup cart. They were allowed to help him fill the paraffin lamps each evening, and to wash and carefully dry the lamp glasses, so long as they were careful, but were never permitted to use matches. The ceremony of lighting the lamps was strictly in Clem's domain.

He was quite strict with them in other ways too, making it clear they must never come anywhere near his plough, harrow or other sharp implements which he kept in the barn. 'These aren't playthings and this in't toytown, so think on, leave well alone. We don't want no chopped off fingers messing up the works, now do we?'

Trish gave a delicious squeal of horror while Megan shook her head solemnly.

But it wasn't all work. He tied a piece of wood to a length of rope and hung it from the big old ash tree behind the house. The pair of them would happily swing on it for hours. Sometimes, he let them take jam sandwiches and a bottle of tea down to the beck and they'd tuck up their skirts and paddle, Daisy along with them, something they'd never had the opportunity to do in their lives before. And he bought them a tin hat each for sixpence at the church jumble sale, just like the one William wore in the Richmal Crompton books. They were rarely seen without them after that.

'Well, at least them two nippers is ready for the invasion, even if we aren't,' he quipped.

Their favourite task was to feed the calves and Dolly the old shorthorn cow. Megan loved their big brown eyes and long lashes, and Trish loved anything that made Megan happy. They'd fill a bucket with water down at the beck, and another of feedstuffs mixed to Clem's secret recipe and stand quietly by, watching while they dipped in their noses and munched away. When the bucket was completely empty the calves would lick their hands instead, their rough tongues making the children shriek with laughter.

Miss Copthorne found them a place in the village school and marched them there every morning at breakneck speed. 'Perhaps we might purchase a bicycle each,' she suggested one day, when she saw Trish having difficulty in keeping up.

Megan said gloomily, 'It would be fine riding down in the morning, but cycling back up the lane every afternoon wouldn't be much fun.' Anyway, she loved to dawdle, nibbling 'bread and cheese' from the hedgerows, as the local children called the hawthorn leaves that grew along each side of the lane.

The evacuee class used the schoolroom in the mornings, while the village children had it in the afternoon. When the children couldn't work inside, they put on their coats and were taken for long rambles to study flowers and trees, draw pictures, do bark rubbings and potato prints, or do some digging and weeding on the school allotment. And then they held a school concert and Megan and Trish pretended to be the famous music hall act, Gert and Daisy. They had the whole school in tucks of laughter, even Miss Copthorne.

It felt a bit odd to be with Miss Copthorne all day as their teacher, and then to walk home with her after school and have her turn into one of Daisy's lodgers. They tried not to speak to her much in the evenings, anyway, she was generally busy with marking homework, or filling in forms, about which she complained a good deal on their long trek homeward.

'I have to fill them in for everything: milk, clothing, national savings, not to mention dozens from the clinic and several more from the canteen. Anyone would think I had nothing else to do all day but collect information to put on these pestiferous forms.'

Megan would maintain a shrewd silence but Trish's eyes would grow round. She always loved it when her teacher used rude words.

It was an unforgettable summer, and in September while Russian pilots flying Hurricanes and Spitfires desperately defended Leningrad, Clem looped a piece of string through a National Dried Milk tin and the pair went happily off blackberry picking, without a care in the world.

All in all, everything was going well for Daisy too. September was by tradition a month for shows. Clem had reminisced for days over how it used to be before the war, the serious discussions that would take place over whether the animal was well ribbed up, if its ears were pricked at just the right angle. And how he generally won a prize or two for the carefully bred tups and ewes he showed. Most had been cancelled, because of the war but the one Clem was attending today was going ahead, war or no war. It would be a mere shadow of its former self, of course, more of a shepherds' meet for the purpose of buying and selling prize stock, borrowing tups and returning strayed ewes; a time to have a bit of a crack and a chance to share problems. He'd wanted Daisy and the children to go with him but she'd said no, there was too much to do.

'Anyway, you don't need me getting under your feet. You have a good day with your chums.' And she'd packed him a substantial lunch box of home-made pies and home-cured ham butties.

The children returned from their expedition, faces black with juice. Daisy was up to her elbows in flour from making bread and pastry for the pies, her two small assistants helping or hindering, depending upon your perspective when the door flew open and Daisy finally came face to face with the kitchen's owner.

'Florrie?'

But it wasn't her aunt who held her sole attention. Nor even Rita standing beside her, a look of malicious triumph on her face, as if to say: I've found you at last.

It was the sight of the child held in Florrie's arms who captured her utterly, heart and soul. Daisy walked over and gazed at him with open longing in her eyes. She took in the red-brown hair, the bright blue eyes and her heart turned slowly over inside her, just as if she were on a big dipper. No matter how hard she tried to push it to the back of her mind, deep inside the hurt had never gone away. She wanted her baby back as badly as ever, so much that it was a physical pain clamped tight around her heart. 'Who is this? Clem didn't say anything about a baby. Is he yours, Aunt Florrie?'

It was Rita who answered. 'Nay lass. Don't you recognise him? He's your son. Yours and Percy's. He's come home to his mam at last.'

Daisy heard the fear in the children's voices as she slid to the floor.

★

It seemed too good to be true. When Daisy came round after her faint, she half expected to find it had all been a dream but no, there he still was, sitting on Florrie's knee, happily kicking his chubby little legs while her mother stood guard over the teapot and Megan and Trish knelt anxiously beside her, their little faces as white as the streaks of flour down their pinnies.

'Are you all right, Daisy?' Trish stroked away a tear from her cheek, then patted it kindly.

'I thought you'd dropped dead too,' said Megan, in a worryingly matter-of-fact tone.

Daisy sat up quickly and pushed her hair from her eyes. A rush of blood to her head made it spin dizzily but she smiled nonetheless. 'No, no, I'm right as rain. Just had a bit of a turn, that's all. Must be the heat of this kitchen after all our cooking.'

Rita made no move to assist her daughter as she struggled to her feet, merely remarked, 'I reckoned you'd come round some time.' Just as if Daisy had deliberately allowed herself to faint and deserved to be left lying on the cold kitchen floor.

Assisted by her two small friends, Daisy dragged out a chair and heaved herself into it. 'What would I do without you two?' she said, smiling and hugging them close, and even as she offered further reassurances that she was perfectly well, her eyes were glued to the baby. Was he truly her child? He was about the right age, coming up to two years old. Heavens, was it so long? It felt like only yesterday. He had Percy's hair, brown with a hint of red if not quite so dark. Perhaps she'd got it all wrong, had indeed dreamed it in a way: wishing so hard that he could be hers that she'd misheard what her mother had actually said. She cleared her throat, feeling suddenly nervous.

'He's a fine baby, Florrie. You must be proud of him.' Best to play safe and assume he belonged to her aunt. She seemed so vulnerable with her deeply sunken eyes, purple shadows beneath, stringy bleached blonde hair in need of a wash, and yet on her feet a pair of red slingback shoes, boldly making a declaration of the woman she had once been. Oh, how Daisy wished Clem was here, but he'd warned her to expect him to be late home from his meet. Florrie looked up, a mixture of surprise and anxiety on her tired face as she flicked her gaze to Daisy and then quickly over to Rita.

Rita said, 'I told you, lass. He isn't our Florrie's. He's yours. Yours and Percy's. Don't you recognise him? He's the spitting image of his dad.'

There seemed to be a roaring sound in her head. She couldn't quite take it in. This was the second time Rita had announced this fact but Daisy was still finding it hard to believe the evidence of her own eyes and ears. Could it be true? Why would her mother lie? But wasn't she the one who wanted rid of the child? Wasn't he supposed to be a secret? Yet here he was, her own flesh and blood, or was he?

'Don't you want to hold him?' Rita asked, again with that odd little smirk on her face, thoroughly pleased with herself.

Daisy shook her head, panic washing over her. She daren't go anywhere near him. If she picked up the baby she might never let him go. She had to be sure, absolutely certain in her heart of hearts that he was hers, before she ever took the risk.

A small hand gently shook her shoulder. Megan was again offering her a mug of strong, sweet tea and Daisy smiled her gratitude at the child and took a few sips. She began to feel stronger almost at once. Something was wrong. She couldn't quite put her finger on what it was, but something wasn't right about all of this. She needed to find out exactly what was going on. Daisy turned to the two little girls. 'Why don't you go and play out on the swing for a bit.'

'What about our blackberry pie?' Megan asked, her mouth in a sulk.

'I'll give you a shout when I'm ready to put it in the oven.'

Trish went over to the baby and stroked his silky brown hair. 'Can he come and play too?'

'Tomorrow perhaps. He'll be tired just now, after all his travelling. Aunt Florrie will be putting him to bed for his nap soon, I expect.'

Florrie shot to her feet, as if a signal had been given for her to escape. 'I'll take him now. He'll need changing anyway,' and she flew up the stairs.

When the children too had gone and they were alone at last, Daisy turned to face her mother. 'I don't understand. You gave him up for adoption. Said he was to be for ever a secret. What changed? Where has he been all this time, and how come he's with you now?'

All questions Rita had been prepared for, along with several others. 'Nay lass, take a breath, will you. Give me a chance.' She settled herself comfortably at the table, poured a fresh mug of tea which she sweetened generously, with no regard to shortages, and then launched into her carefully rehearsed tale.

Rita had realised, the moment she'd clapped eyes on the remains of her home that she was done for, that there was no way her daughter would take her in off the streets. Not willingly anyroad, not after the way she'd been treated. There was too much bad feeling between them. It was a sad fact, in Rita's opinion, that today's generation didn't have the morals of her own. She'd done her best to bring up Daisy clean and decent, but the girl had let her down badly. So if she refused to be dragged down into the mire with her, where was the fault in that? But in the circumstances, it had left her in a pretty pickle.

It was finding the baby which had put the idea into her head. He could well be the key to Daisy's heart.

She'd dismissed it at first, on the grounds that it was too risky. Daisy wasn't stupid. But throughout the long weeks of trekking around vainly seeking accommodation, and with Florrie time and time again refusing to even consider returning to the Lake District or ask Clem to offer Rita a home, she'd begun to have second thoughts on the matter. She'd taken her time, letting the seed grow in her head, thinking it through from every angle till it blossomed into a fully fledged plan. Rita felt sure that she'd now examined all possible difficulties. The delay in putting it into effect had been no bad thing, as it turned out. As well as overcoming one or two minor problems, Florrie had been allowed sufficient time to grow fond of the child, even to give him a name. Robbie. So when Rita had finally put forward her plan, she'd very cleverly been able to put the stopper on further objections without any difficulty whatsoever.

'I don't really think you are in any position to argue, do you?'

'But you can't possibly let Daisy think this child is her own, when we know for certain that he isn't.'

'But we don't know that, do we? Not for certain,' Rita had remarked blithely, thin lips curling into a humourless smile. 'Since we've no idea who the lad is, he could very well be Daisy's babby.'

'It's not very likely though, is it? That would be too much of a coincidence. We found him in the shelter.'

'Who's to know where we found him, if we don't tell them? We need a roof over our heads before winter comes, and you can be absolutely certain that our Daisy won't offer one unless we make her.' Rita had given a careless shrug. 'Course, it's your house by rights, not our Daisy's, so you could happen exercise some power over that husband of yours.'

Florrie had paled visibly at the suggestion. 'Clem wouldn't listen to me. Not now. He happen won't have me in the house, let alone you. Not after walking out on him. Anyroad, I've told you already Rita, I'm not going back.'

'Oh yes you are, girl. You're coming with me. You'll do exactly as I say or else you might find yourself up for baby-snatching. Then where would you be?'

'Baby-snatching?' Florrie's voice cracked with fear. 'But I didn't snatch him, I picked him up – to nurse him, to look after him because I thought his mam had been killed, or hurt or something.'

Triumph gleamed from Rita's boot button eyes. 'So why have you done nowt about handing him back? How will you explain keeping him all this while, eh? And you know what they'll say, the polis. Didn't you lose a baby of your own once, Mrs Pringle? Sent you a bit wrong in the head, has it? Happen you'd best go into an asylum then. It'd be for the best, don't you think? Can't have you going around pinching other folk's babbies.'

Florrie had sobbed for days but, in the end, had complied with the plan, as Rita had known that she would. Simply because she had no choice. Nevertheless, it would be politic to keep a close watch on her, tighten the screws from time to time, just to make sure that she didn't defect.

None of this was revealed to her daughter as Rita calmly explained how the child she'd given birth to had been taken, not by strangers as she'd supposed at the time, but by Percy's own family. Rita had fabricated this tale as the only one Daisy would be likely to find credible; that Percy's sister and brother-in-law had agreed to take the child, because loving children as much as they did, one more was neither here nor there. 'And they wanted to help Percy. You remember Annie, lovely girl she was. The poor lass was taken, along with all her children, in the same blast what got your dad. It's a miracle this little one escaped.' Which of course meant there was no one to dispute her story, beyond the girl's mother who was unlikely to hear of it, and Percy himself of course. Not that he cared one way or the other. Like most young men, he was more interested in himself and had found no difficulty in accepting the yarn Rita had spun him too.

She was the only one who knew the truth, the only one ever likely to know.

Daisy's whole body jerked as if she'd been struck, one fact alone standing out among all the jumble. 'Dad? Dad's been killed? For God's sake why didn't you tell me?'

'I'm telling you now.'

She was on her feet, leaning over the table and banging upon it with her fist. 'You let me sit here, supping tea, and me dad's *dead*? What kind of mother are you? Have you no heart?'

'Close to him were you?' Rita asked, a challenge in the glitter of her hard eyes, and Daisy sank back on to her seat with a sad sort of sigh. 'Thought not. There's a war on, if you haven't noticed. Don't suppose you have, living here in paradise. But while you live up on t'top o' world, some of us down in the gutter have had it hard and lost everything. My home is nowt more than a heap of muck and rubble. Everything gone. Most of our neighbours in Marigold Court copped it.' She stabbed a thumb against her own skinny chest. 'And me and Florrie would have bought it too, if we hadn't been having a barney with an ARP Warden at the time. With nowt but the clothes we stand up in, we've been like two gypsies all summer, striving to put a roof over us head. We've slept in schoolrooms and church halls, air-raid shelters, bus shelters for heaven's sake, at times.'

'I don't believe you,' Daisy interrupted, unable to keep quiet any longer. 'I know how you always love to dramatise.'

Rita leaned across the table and spat her bitter disappointment of life into her daughter's face. 'I'm telling you the truth. Would I lie about your dad? Useless lump that he was, and he left me nowt.'

'No, not even a sore heart, because you have none.'

Rita sat back in her seat on a long-drawn-out sigh of resignation. 'Well, that's a nice way to talk to your mam, I must
say. Florrie and me have filled in hundreds of flamin' forms,
sat for hours in council offices trying to persuade some po-
faced official that we should be given priority for proper
accommodation, what with the baby an' all. We might as well
have cried for the moon. In the end we gave up, and here we
are. It's still your aunt's home remember, madam, so far as
I'm aware.'

Daisy stared at her mother in horror. 'I know it is, but don't
think *you* can stop here as well. It's not on.'

'Why isn't it on? Florrie has led me to understand there's
plenty of room, any number of bedrooms in fact. I only
need one. And it's surely on her say-so, not yours.' Having
delivered her speech, Rita levered herself out of the chair,
rested her hands on her hips and gazed about her in a propri-
etorial way. The gesture brought a chill to Daisy's heart.

'You can't do this. I've turned it into a boarding house. At
least, Clem and me have opened it up to a few lodgers. Most
rooms are taken.'

'Most? Then there's some still empty by the sound of it.
Like I say, I only need one.'

The instinct to dispute any plans Rita made was still too
strong in her for Daisy to let go of the argument; even when,
strictly speaking, she really had no right to say who lived here
and who didn't. That was up to Clem. But knowing how soft-
hearted he was, she didn't want to put him in the position of
having to decide. It wouldn't be fair. He'd feel obliged to say
yes, simply because Rita was her mother. But the prospect of
living under the same roof as Rita was too appalling, far too
dreadful to even contemplate. It would be a living hell. 'No,
no, we need those bedrooms too, all of them, for occasional
visitors, for Charlie and his girl, and for Mr Enderby, and
those who come to see relatives, forces sweethearts and the
like. There are plenty of regulars who come and stay.'

'Well, they'll be unlucky in future.'

Daisy could feel herself starting to panic. She could not, would not, allow her mother to destroy this little piece of heaven she'd found, or the business she was building with such love and care. 'No, I'm sorry. We've no room.'

Two spots of feverish crimson appeared on Rita's flat cheeks as her face tightened with fury. *'No room?* So you'd turn me out into the cold, would you? Your own mother, a homeless widow.'

Daisy was struck silent by this awful truth. Put like that, her attitude did indeed sound heartless and cruel. Yet Rita had always been the cruel one, the one with a heart of stone. *She'd given away her own grandchild, for God's sake!* 'I swear to God, Mother, I could never be as heartless as you.'

'I only did what I thought was for the best. If I was wrong, I'm sorry. Truly sorry.'

'Are you?'

'Didn't I just say so? What more d'you want, for me to prostrate meself on t'floor? What about this babby then? Doesn't he deserve a mam? You'd find room for him, no doubt?'

'You know I would,' Daisy said, in a voice barely above a whisper. 'If I could truly believe he was mine.'

'Well, then. Why don't you ask his father?'

'I beg your pardon?'

'Why don't you ask Percy hissel. He's coming over on Sunday, to say hello. Did you know he'd been invalided out of the navy? Got shot up, apparently.'

'No, I didn't know. I'm sorry to hear that.' This was all happening far too fast. She couldn't think, or quite take it in. 'Why would he be coming here?'

'He wants to see you.'

'After all this time?'

'He's worried about the babby. Now his sister and her family are gone, God rest their souls, he wants to be sure little

Robbie is taken proper care of. I reckoned you'd be pleased to see him, in the circumstances.'

Daisy's heart was thumping like a mad thing. Dear lord, how would she feel about seeing Percy again, after all this time, after all that had happened as a result of their foolishness? There was no love between them now, no feelings of any sort, not now that she'd found Harry. But he wasn't coming for her sake, but for the baby's, and it was good of him to be so considerate, particularly when Daisy recalled how uninterested he'd been in his son when he'd been born. Perhaps fighting in the war had matured him, made him grow up a bit as he needed to, as they both had needed to do. For the first time, a kernel of hope sprang up inside. Could it really be true? Could this be the answer to her dream? 'I am pleased. It'll be nice to see him again.'

'Course it will. You was always fond of young Percy. So, I reckon I deserve a bit of consideration, don't you, for arranging it all? It would be a pity if you missed this opportunity to be reunited with your own son.'

Daisy became very still, her gaze narrowing as she watched her mother pace about the room, picking up a jar here, a plate there, as if inspecting it for any sign of careless dusting. 'What are you saying? Are you suggesting that I can't have my son back unless I agree to take you in as well?'

Rita's smile was triumphant. 'I'd say that was fair, since I found him, wouldn't you?'

24

Daisy was so brimming with fury she had to keep her mind firmly on preparing the evening meal for her guests, that way she might manage not to take a knife to her mother's throat. The whole argument had been so distressing her only refuge seemed to be in anger, otherwise she might start crying and never stop. She wanted desperately to believe that the baby truly was hers, and that she could trust her mother. Yet how could she, after all that had happened?

And if it were true, wouldn't that only present her with a fresh load of problems? What would her guests think to discover that their landlady had a child, an illegitimate child since she wasn't even married.

And then there was the question of Harry. Oh, darling Harry, why didn't I tell you ages ago when I had the chance? Daisy thought. Now it'll be a thousand times more difficult. It's all going to seem so contrived, as if I planned it all along; as if I just waited for him to properly propose before presenting him with the fact that I already have a child. He'll hate me now. Any man would. Oh, what should I do?

The blackberry pie had been baked, the two children packed off to bed but Daisy steadfastly refused to go any-where near the baby, leaving him entirely to Florrie. Florrie had offered to hand him over, had cast anguished glances over in her direction while she bathed, changed and fed him.

'Are you sure you don't want to put him to bed yourself?'

'No thanks. You do it. I'm busy.' Still simmering from the confrontation with Rita and worrying over the complexities of her problem, Daisy was in no mood to take issue over who should care for the baby, not right then. It was all too sudden, too confusing.

Rita, content that everything seemed to be going perfectly to plan even if she had stirred up trouble, headed for the front parlour to meet her fellow lodgers. Not that she considered herself to be one of them, she being family while they were paying guests. Nor would she be eating in the dining room. She would take her meal in the warm kitchen later, with her daughter and sister, naturally.

Daisy was chopping vegetables ferociously, tossing them with such abandon into the pan that Florrie, who had offered to help once she'd put the baby down, kept a safe distance away and quietly got on with laying the tables. It was vital, she decided, that she said not a word, that she didn't get involved. Just hold your tongue, Rita had hissed at her as she'd slipped by. And indeed, Florrie was an expert in that skill. Hadn't she had long years of practice?'

When the meal was ready, Daisy felt calmer. Cooking was proving to be a good therapy, homely fare but always well received by her guests. She'd made a big pan of stew, to be followed by the blackberry pie and custard.

'We shan't ever want to leave here,' Miss Copthorne told her, as Daisy took round the pie dish for second helpings. 'You look after us far too well.'

'I certainly shan't,' agreed Ned Pickles, managing a small smile by way of reward for Daisy's culinary efforts, while holding out his plate for more. Daisy had grown used to his lugubrious air. She thought him a dear man if rather sad, so determined not to be a burden to his only daughter that he'd settled here as a permanent lodger. It was clear he still missed his wife, not least because she must have tidied up after him all the time as Daisy constantly found herself falling over piles of books he'd left on the stairs. She'd discover his scarf or hat tucked down the back of the settee or under his bed, or he'd leave heaps of lecture notes drifting all over the dining table which she had to move in order to lay it. Why he needed to collect so many, she really couldn't imagine. In the end she had taken him to task over the matter, pointing out the book-case she had provided him with, the wardrobe cupboard, the row of hooks behind his bedroom door, and was there perhaps something more that he needed in order to keep his belongings under control? Sheepishly he'd declared himself more than content with the arrangements and thereafter made a valiant attempt to be more organised.

'Your cooking has come on a treat these last weeks, Daisy love,' he told her now. 'An absolute treat.'

'You have too, Ned. You're a new man, now that I'm around to keep an eye on you. Even your spectacles are polished,' and he grinned at her, not in the least taking offence.

'S'matter of fact, Daisy, I was thinking of signing up for the Home Guard,' he confided in a hushed whisper. 'Now that I'm feeling more settled.'

'Good idea. Do your bit, eh? Here y'are love, have the last slice,' and she slid it on to his plate

'Hey, what about me?' said Tommy Fawcett.

'You've had two already, cheeky tyke.'

'That's true. It's your wonderful cooking, Daisy. Can't resist it,' and he jumped up and tap-danced all around the dining room, just to prove how much new energy she had given him, making them all laugh.

Flushed with pride and satisfaction in her work, Daisy went back into the kitchen still chuckling, her good humour restored. 'We have a house full of satisfied customers.' Seated by the hearth opposite his wife, sat Clem.

'I heard,' Florrie said, without a vestige of pleasure in her voice.

Daisy made herself scarce.

*

The first thing Daisy did was to write to Harry. She needed him to come on another visit, and quickly. She needed to talk to him, to see him, to explain, just the minute he could get some leave. The last letter she'd had from him was post-marked Ipswich, so it would all depend on transport as much as anything. It was a difficult letter to write as she'd no wish to throw him into a panic and it was desperately important that he come as soon as possible.

> *There's something awful happened. I need to explain and it can't be done by letter. Mother is here and she's being very diffi-cult but I daren't say anything as we can't get married without her permission. Though you may change your mind about wanting to marry me when you hear what I have to say. Oh, do say you're coming soon Harry. I'm having such problems.*

Yet a secret part of her was overjoyed by this turn of events. That first evening, as she'd gone up to bed leaving Clem and Florrie to talk out their differences in private, she'd crept into the children's room. Megan and Trish were fast asleep, all curled up together in their usual fashion, like a pair of spoons, cheeks flushed in sleep. Daisy smiled, happy to see them at last thriving and content. Harry had done the right thing by bringing them to her. If only she'd done the right thing by tell-ing him, from the start, about her own child. Oh, Harry, what a pretty kettle of fish this is. What a mess!

On this thought, she moved over to the cot which Florrie had set up in the corner. This must have been baby Emma's cot. Daisy wondered how much it had cost her to bring it out and use it for a child other than her own. The baby lay on his back, arms flung up above his head, snuffling quietly, but as she gazed upon him, enthralled, fascinated by the blue veins on his eyelids, the curl of his red-brown hair, the sturdiness of him, his eyes suddenly flickered open and he gazed up at her very solemnly, just as if he could read every thought in her head.

'Hello, little Robbie. I'm so very pleased to see you again.' She stopped, alarmed by the implication of what she'd just said, almost fearful of the baby understanding. Nothing had been proved yet. No decisions made. 'What I mean is, none of this muddle is your fault, and I'm not sure how it's all going to work out but – but I *am* glad you're here, truly I am. I don't want you to feel unwanted. I hate the thought of you being abandoned because Annie has been – because she's no longer able to take care of you. Lot's of people here at Lane End Farm are in the same boat, so you're very welcome, you really are. And somehow, we'll find the answer.'

She was rewarded with a huge smile and Daisy was able to see, quite clearly, that he had eight teeth, four along the top and another four along the bottom. He was a fine baby. Annie had looked after him well. Unable to resist, she smiled back which lit up his small face still further and he gave a gurgle of delight. And then he spoke: 'Mama,' he said.

Daisy's vision was suddenly blinded by tears, and she turned and rushed out, back to her own attic room right at the top of the house where she sobbed her heart out. She felt drained afterwards, and still with no idea how she was going to set about finding any answers.

Laura switched off the tape and rubbed her eyes. She'd been listening to it far too long and her grandmother's voice had broken with emotion at times, so painful was it to relate. She was longing to hear Harry's reaction to this news when he next came to visit, and what Percy would have to say, but it was past midnight and she had to be up by seven to begin preparations for breakfast. Laura switched off the bedside lamp and settled down to sleep.

Megan had reluctantly taken her leave the previous day, having stayed far longer than she intended but promising to come again soon, and Laura realised how much she would miss the older woman. Even in the short time she'd been here they'd become great friends and she would miss their cheerful chats. And somehow, miraculously, the visit had cauterised the wound in Robert's heart and all the pain he'd stored against Daisy had come pouring out like pus from a festering sore.

Perhaps now they're own relationship might also start to heal.

Nothing else was going according to plan. It had all started so well but now Chrissy was in a sulk and being difficult. She claimed to be vastly overworked, which was true, and although Laura did her best to keep bedroom changes down to a minimum by not taking single night bookings over a weekend for instance, demand had compelled her to provide evening meals. In a way this was her favourite part of the day. The trouble was, she already felt overstretched.

Her first effort had been only this last week when she was faced with cooking dinner for three couples, requiring her to juggle a variety of starters and two different main courses. Chrissy had gone out with a friend, a more regular occurrence these days.

'I need some *fun*,' she'd declared when Laura had asked if she could change her plans for the evening. But she really couldn't expect the girl to act as kitchen skivvy as well as do her chambermaid job.

Laura was beginning to wonder if perhaps giving her step-daughter the job had been a mistake. She was so young and should be having fun, not feeling tied to housework all the time. And she was beginning to cut corners, be far less accommodating than at the start. On two occasions recently, Laura had discovered she'd forgotten to put out fresh towels in the bathrooms. The difficulty was that staff were so incredibly hard to find. Anyone with any go about them was soon snapped up by the larger hotels in and around Keswick. Laura had put notices in the windows of various local businesses as well as on the library noticeboard. She'd even put advertisements in the newspaper, all to no avail. A few people had rung, two women had come along for an interview, and one had gone so far as to promise to start first thing the following Monday, but had never turned up. So she'd been surprised and thankful when Megan had offered to help with the meal.

'Can't cook to save my life but I could prepare vegetables, wait on tables and wash up. How would that be? And don't say I'm here as a guest. I like to be busy and I'd be doing it for Daisy as much as you. I owe her a great deal.'

Laura said, 'I'm filled with guilt that you should offer, but I'll accept with gratitude on the basis I take it off your bill.'

They'd prepared melon in a raspberry coulis, tuna salad and home-made soup for starters, followed by a choice of grilled haddock with a creamy sauce or lamb cutlets baked in rosemary. For dessert there was fruit salad, cheese, or a traditional Rum Nicky pudding. The pair worked seamlessly together, Megan proving adept with a knife and chopping board and smilingly winning over the guests, keeping them happily chatting while Laura frantically grilled, baked, boiled, tossed and generally tried her best not to panic in the kitchen.

'If you ever feel like moving to the Lakes, let me know,' Laura said as they'd sat flushed and happy at the end of the evening, enjoying a well earned glass of wine together. 'There's always a job for you here.'

Megan had smilingly made no comment, and a day or two later she'd gone back to Manchester and Laura was forced to cope on her own.

As if this weren't bad enough, they were due an inspection from the Tourist Board at any time. She'd been warned by the local office, situated in the Moot Hall, that the booking would come in the form of a single room, usually with the requirement of an evening meal.

In her blackest moments at the end of yet another long tiring day, Laura began to question her own wisdom at embarking upon this venture. She hadn't underestimated the amount of work involved, but perhaps she had overestimated her ability to carry it out on her own. And yet she loved the work, she enjoyed meeting people, chatting to them and doing her best to make them comfortable and give them a good holiday. True, there were difficult customers at times but most people simply wanted a pleasant room and good food put before them. All of which Laura took great pleasure in providing.

But she possessed only one pair of hands and there was no doubt that she needed more. How on earth had Daisy coped?

Over the next few days Daisy could hardly concentrate on what she was supposed to be doing. From not wanting to touch the baby, she'd gone to not being able to get enough of him. He was a complete and utter distraction. She would put on the soup and then start to read him a story and forget to take it off again. She'd go outside, meaning to feed the hens, and then rush back in to make sure he was still safely playing in his playpen where she'd left him, forgetting all about what she was supposed to be doing.

Wherever she went in the big old farmhouse, she felt compelled to take him with her, all the time aware of Florrie's watchful eyes upon her, silently envious of her prior claim upon him. Sometimes Daisy would abandon her work altogether, so she could take him outside to play on the grass, laughing delightedly when he went charging after the poor beleaguered hens on plump, sturdy legs only to topple over through going too fast.

'Slow down, you're not a steam train,' and she'd run to pick him up, concerned he might have hurt himself but the two-year-old would simply offer up his toothy grin and be off again, determined to explore every corner of this exciting new world.

Megan and Trish adored him too and became slaves to his every whim, constantly picking him up and carrying him about, teasing and tickling him, fetching his toys every time he dropped them out of his pram for all he was supposed to be having an afternoon nap in the autumn sunshine. He'd wait quietly till they'd put the toy back in and crept away before giving a deliciously wicked gurgle of laughter and tossing it out again.

'He's a little monkey,' Trish would say, rushing to repeat the trick all over again.

'He's lovely though, isn't he?' Megan would quietly remark, her gaze softening whenever she looked at him. Megan loved to help feed him, teaching him to use his spoon and pusher with tender care so that Daisy could only look on with pride and love. The little girl would build up his bricks into a high tower and laugh when he knocked them all down again. Daisy could see that having the baby around was relaxing her, bringing her out of her shell and giving her a sense of security and belonging.

'And you're good for me too, little Robbie. I love you to bits already, do you know that?'

'Mama!'

'Oh yes, I can see you could wheedle your way into any woman's heart, you little rascal.'

All the same, despite a growing sense of happiness and belief in the fact that he was indeed her child, miraculously returned to her, tension was mounting within. There were so many problems to be resolved. Daisy was waiting for Harry to write and say when he might be able to get leave; waiting for Sunday when Percy would arrive. What would he have to say to her? Daisy had carefully worked out what she must say to him. She would offer her condolences over his loss, of course, then thank him for persuading his sister Annie to look after little Robbie, which she had clearly done very well. Had they paid for her to go into the mother and baby home? Daisy wondered. And most of all she would promise faithfully to keep him safe and love him with all her heart. Only then

would she explain about Harry. She would say how she held
no resentment against Percy for leaving her in the lurch in the
way that he had, because she'd been given a second chance
at love, and was hoping against hope that Harry would understand and forgive.

All in all, it would be good to see him again, and there was
absolutely no reason why they shouldn't discuss the situation
in a perfectly reasonable manner. What had happened
between them was all in the past, over and done with now and
they'd both made a fresh start, a new life for themselves.

But when Sunday came and Percy stood before her, some
instinct told her that this wasn't going to be nearly as easy as
she had hoped.

There was the roar of a motorbike and the spit of flying gravel
as it crunched to a halt, followed by the loud blast of a horn.
Chrissy tossed aside the tea towel and reached for her jacket.
'Got to fly. See you.'

'Hold on,' Laura said. 'Fly where? Who's the knight on the
white charger?' From the kitchen window she could just catch
a glimpse of a helmeted, leather-clad figure on a bike, impatiently revving up the engine as he waited.

'It's a quad,' Chrissy informed her with mocking sarcasm
as she half backed out the door.

'What on earth is a quad?'

'Oh for goodness' sake, a sort of bike. Look, I've got to go,
Gary doesn't like to be kept waiting.'

'And who is Gary?' Laura was following Chrissy out of the
kitchen, through the hall to the front door, wiping her hands
on a towel as she went. 'Do I know him? Is he local? Why
doesn't he come in and be properly introduced?'

'Oh get real. This isn't the nineteenth century.' Chrissy's
tone held all the contempt of her superior youth. But even as
she reached for the door handle, Laura moved with the speed
of experience.

'Not so fast. I'm quite keen to meet Gary myself, then we'll decide if you can go out with him. Have you spoken to your mum, or Felix about him? Do they allow to have boyfriends?'

The horn blasted again and a look of anxiety flashed across Chrissy's face. 'Stop hassling me, will you. I've got to go.'

'Chrissy, you have to realise that while you're living here, you are my responsibility and I can't just let you go off with a complete stranger.'

Chrissy rolled her eyes heavenwards. 'He's not a complete stranger. I know him quite well, actually.' The smirk on her insolent face was not reassuring.

Laura held on to her patience. 'I need to check him out first, make sure your parents agree.'

'Ask your precious David to check him out then, if you want to be priggish about it, but not now, right? I'm in a hurry.' And as the horn blasted a third time she thrust Laura aside, flung open the door and stalked off. Laura reached the bike just as the machine roared away down the lane, Chrissy barely having climbed astride. At least she'd protected the purple locks with a helmet. It was Laura's only consolation.

'Oh God, what do I do now?' The last thing she needed was to have to call Felix. He'd be sure to put the blame on her, accuse her of being slipshod and irresponsible with his daughter's well-being. She went and called David instead. No answer. Of course, he'd be out with the sheep. This was a busy time with the dipping and shearing under way. The summer months were hectic for farmers.

Laura spent the entire day fretting and worrying, one eye constantly on the clock, or checking her watch. Why hadn't she insisted on knowing where the girl was going? Why hadn't she instituted a curfew, or better still, arranged to go and collect her at an appropriate time from wherever it was. Who knew what might happen to her? How old was this boy? Would he behave properly with her, and appreciate how very young Chrissy was? They might crash into a ditch at the very least.

She wasn't even her true parent, so why would Chrissy listen even if she did issue a set of rules? What had possessed her to let the girl stay? She must have been mad. How could she ever be free of Felix and start a new life for herself while she was still burdened by his daughter. Because she'd never viewed her in that way. Despite her show of rebellion, Laura was fond of Chrissy, always had been, and felt rather sorry for her being stuck with two parents as useless and selfish as Julia and Felix. She'd always done her best to remain neutral, not to take sides, and to be affectionate and reliable. Now she'd made a bad mistake. Being a stepmother suddenly seemed to be fraught with problems.

At seven on the dot, Felix rang. 'Laura, how are things?' The coldness of his tone always chilled her, even though they rarely had anything to say to each other these days and more often than not it was Chrissy he chatted to.

'Felix, um, you can't speak to Chrissy right now, she's in the shower,' Laura lied, crossing her fingers. 'She shouldn't be more than ten minutes, of course if she decides to wash her hair that may be rather an optimistic estimate. Perhaps you'd like to try later?' The brightness in her tone sounded false even to her own ears.

'It's not Chrissy I wanted to speak to, it's you.'

'Oh? Well, I'm not sure I want to speak to you,' she tried to make a joke of it but her voice cracked with nerves.

'You sound rather odd.'

'Do I?'

'Is something wrong?'

'Of course not. What could be wrong?'

Felix made a harumph sound in his throat. 'Exhaustion, I'd say. Impending bankruptcy because of your stubbornness. Robert says you're vastly overworked. Are you ready yet to call it a day?'

'Not at all, I'm loving it.' Felix had always been far too cosy with her father. Dealing with each of their idiosyncrasies was bad enough. When they ganged up together it became well nigh impossible. 'Whatever it is you have to say to me, Felix, can you make it snappy, I have meals to prepare for my guests this evening. Oh, and if you were thinking of consulting another building society about a mortgage on this place, let me tell you that you'd be wasting your time. I'm wise to that trick now.'

'That was a mistake,' he mumbled. 'Miranda's idea.'

'Oh yes?' Laura said, in a tone of disbelief. 'I heard you were rather cosy.'

'That was a temporary arrangement only. She's moved back into her own flat now.'

Laura began to giggle. 'Not quite working out then, after all?'

'Look, what I've rung about is that I've been speaking to the estate agent again and he's found someone else who may be interested in Lane End. As you said yourself, people prepared to live so far out in the sticks are thin on the ground, so don't screw this one up, Laura. We need the money. I'll tell him to send them along, shall I?'

'Absolutely not! Felix, what do I have to do to convince you that this is my house and I'm staying. I live in it. I've done up the place. I'm earning a living here. Of sorts,' she added more cautiously. 'What's more, I've spoken to my lawyers and you should by now have received the divorce papers.'

It was as if she hadn't spoken. 'They're from Surrey and will arrive first thing on Saturday morning. If we get a good price I can pay off the bank loan and the mortgage, then we could buy a little place in France, take more time out from the business to smell the roses. We could have a fresh start, a second honeymoon.'

There was Florrie wanting a second chance at her marriage, and Laura being offered one and wanting only to escape. 'But you don't even like gardening,' she quipped, making a point of not taking him seriously.

'It's a metaphor, Laura. I need to get my head above water to make life easier all round. Stop being so damned difficult. You can't escape reality by hiding away in the Lake District. If you don't bloody co-operate over the house, then you can deal with the debts.'

'What debts? Now who's being melodramatic? Stop exaggerating. I've got to go Felix. I have guests to see to. But if there really is a problem we should talk about it seriously, through our solicitors if necessary, but not now. OK?'

'Is Chrissy not out of that damned shower yet? I'll hang on and have a word. Might as well.'

'Oh, there's someone at the door. Sorry, try again later,' and she put down the phone hurriedly before he could say anything more.

25

Daisy abandoned her idea of a friendly chat over a pot of tea and suggested a walk instead, assuming Percy felt up to it. The question needed to be asked, as the robust young man she remembered had quite gone. In his place was a tortured soul whose eyes reflected untold pain, who walked with an awkward stiffness for all he did his best to disguise a slight limp. Even the once glorious red-brown hair seemed dull, prematurely streaked by a few strands of grey. He'd said little since he'd arrived, revealing none of the cheerful warmth Daisy remembered so fondly, and his cheeky bounce and arrogant confidence had quite disappeared. It was as if his body was still alive and functioning, but his spirit was dead.

Nonetheless he declared himself agreeable to a short trek and they set out to walk on Blencathra, the wind in their faces. The September day was undoubtedly cold but the mountain itself, barren and treeless, somehow seemed unusually forbidding this morning. The dramatic majesty of the giant's naked shoulder reared up before them, filling Daisy with an unusual sense of awe, as if it were turning its back on her and sulking, refusing to smile upon her. It was not a place that offered comfort and Daisy had to speak firmly to herself to shake off the giddiness, the brooding sense of unease.

She felt at a loss to know how to begin. They'd gone through the usual pleasantries and all that was left now was the purpose of his visit. Daisy took a deep breath and launched into her prepared explanation. Percy, unfortunately, chose exactly the same moment to launch into his.

'Sorry, you first.'

'Nay, Daisy, I like listening to you.'

'I allus did talk too much, remember?' and they both laughed. Sadly, it in no way relaxed the tension.

When he said nothing more, Daisy cast him a sidelong glance. He was frowning as if trying to work out what to say, or why he was here. She tried to think of a way to bring a smile to soften his sternness, since one of them must make an attempt to lighten the atmosphere and get to the heart of the matter.

'Heavens, what a sombre mood everyone's in this morning. The mountain, you, even little Robbie had a fit of the sulks and wasn't interested in his usual porridge,' and having finally spoken his name, nothing would stop her now. The words just poured out, her sorrow over the bomb having killed so many of Percy's family on that terrible day during the blitz, her gratitude for the way Robbie had been cared for, and how thrilled she was to have him back. Percy heard her out in silence. When he said nothing, she blundered on.

'And I bear you absolutely no ill will over the way things turned out between us. These matters have a way of coming out right in the end, don't they? I mean, we were far too young to be sensible. Mind you, we had some fun, eh?' She smiled at him fondly, wanting him to smile back and share the happy memories with her. He simply glowered. Daisy pressed on. 'Now that I've met Harry, I can see how very naïve and foolish we were, and it's probably just as well we didn't do anything rash, you know, like get married or something.'

Percy cleared his throat, the sound seeming to come from deep inside him and took a long time in the execution of it. Finally, he asked in a soft, mildly enquiring voice, 'Who's Harry?'

'He's my boyfriend, well fiancé I suppose, since we're engaged. Unofficially you understand, until I'm of age.' Daisy could feel herself blushing.

'Everything's worked out nice as ninepence for you then, Daisy. I'm glad. Some of us haven't been so lucky.'

Despite his kind words, there was bitterness in his tone and Daisy felt mortified by her own insensitivity. What was she thinking of, to go on about her own good fortune in this selfish way? Hadn't Percy been on board a destroyer when it was sunk with most of the hands lost and he himself injured to the extent that his navy career was at an end? 'I heard about your experience. It must have been terrible to see so many of your comrades die, and to think you might die yourself. I can't even begin to imagine how you must have felt. Your nerves must be all in pieces.'

He didn't respond, making Daisy feel that she'd strayed on to forbidden territory and shouldn't have mentioned the tragedy at all. His next words only confirmed that feeling.

Without pausing in his somewhat shambling stride, he said, 'Rita told me she was fetching you the babby. I thought that were good, because you're his mam. But tha knows, I'm his dad.'

'Of course I remember, only – well – I rather thought you were the one who didn't want to get tied up in all of that responsibility. Not that I blame you for feeling that way. Like I say, we were both far too young.'

'I'm still his dad though.'

Daisy felt puzzled by this childish persistence, wondering why he felt the necessity to repeat it, and then a thought occurred to her. 'Oh, you mean even when Harry and I marry? Well, yes of course, that's true. You would still be his dad. But I don't honestly see that as a problem, do you? I mean, it's up to the three of us to make the rules, don't you think? If you want to see little Robbie at any time, there's no reason why you shouldn't. We can tell him the true facts, once he's old enough to understand. Not that I've explained any of this to Harry yet, but I will, and I'm sure it'll be all right. I'm quite certain he loves me enough to understand.' She didn't add – and forgive, though the words echoed in her head, unspoken.

A pair of steady blue eyes considered her in open disbelief. 'Dun't he know about the baby?'

Now the flush on her cheeks deepened to crimson. 'It never quite seemed the right moment, but I will tell him, I will. In fact, I've written to ask him to come over. I mean to get it all off me chest. Aw, Percy, it hasn't been easy. I missed my lovely baby so much, and I missed you too at first. Then there was Mam, bullying me as usual. I felt so miserable, all alone in the world. And after I was evacuated I made myself responsible for Megan and Trish, to compensate in a way for losing – anyway, we've had no end of troubles in our billets. This is the first time since this whole sorry saga started that we've felt any sort of security. And I owe all of that to Clem. Him and me get on really well. He's a great chap, like a father to me. A better father than me own, in point of fact, and I know I shouldn't say that when he's dead and gone, but it's true.' She was talking too much but didn't seem able to stop.

Percy nodded slowly. 'Aye, he seems reet champion. A good sort of bloke.'

'Oh, he is, he is. He's made me so welcome, let me have Megan and Trish come and stay, encouraged me to take in a few lodgers to keep meself out of mischief and earn a bit towards the housekeeping and, oh, just been a friend when I needed one.'

'He says I can stay on, an' all.'

'Oh – I hadn't thought about that. I assumed you'd be going straight back home tonight. But of course you can stay. We've still a room vacant, if you can call it that. Once was a priest hole, would you believe, and little bigger than a cupboard but you're welcome to it.'

'Not just for t'night.'

'Pardon?'

'Clem says I can stop on as long as I like. Theer's no place else fer me to go. I've not so much as a cupboard to call me own, now t'house and family is gone.'

Daisy stopped walking to stare at him, dumbfounded. Not for a moment had she considered this as a possibility. Yet why hadn't she? He was right. He had no one, no home, nothing. He was bombed out. Dispossessed. 'Oh, but . . . you wouldn't want to stay too long, would you? Not as one of our paying guests. You'd be bored out of your mind, just like Florrie. No, you'll be wanting to find yourself a job, a new home, a girl. Life goes on, as they say,' she finished on a falsely bright note.

He too stopped walking, to turn and face her. The wind was whipping Daisy's already unruly curls into a frantic halo all about her head, but she paid it not the slightest notice. Her attention was focused entirely upon Percy's face, taking in, for the first time, the tragic, almost self-pitying droop to his shoulders, the sulky downturn to his mouth, like Trish when she was in one of her moods, and an odd sort of blankness about the eyes. He wasn't simply injured but also deeply depressed, as if he was carrying the whole world on his shoulders; and confused, which she didn't wonder at after being shelled. There were many such coming out of this war, so battle-scarred they would never be the same again. She could feel herself grow quite still, a premonition of what he might be about to say creeping down her spine like ice water.

'Why don't you tell me exactly what it is you want, Percy? What you came for.'

'I don't know which way to turn, Daisy. I know what you mean when you say you felt lost and lonely. That's how I feel now. No home, me sister and her kiddies all dead. Did Rita tell you? I don't know what I would've done without your mam.' He looked bewildered and her heart went out to him.

'Yes Percy. She did tell me. I'm so sorry.'

'And Mam's vanished off the face of the earth. Folk tell me she was spared the blast but I can't find her nowhere. I reckon she's wandered off some place and got lost. Mebbe doesn't know who she is any more. I've no home, nowhere to go, Daisy. Except here with you. And since we were sweethearts, fond of each other like, and now we have a child I've come to you. It's the answer, eh?'

She hardly dared ask the question. 'What is?'

'We can get wed now, can't we? Like we were going to once before. Then he'll have a mam and dad. Won't that be grand? Isn't that the right thing to do?'

'You can't be serious?'

'Why can't I?' The mouth set in a stubborn line. 'What else am I supposed to do? I've lost me job in the navy, the proper use of me legs and with a hole in me back that won't properly heal. We can start again Daisy. A second chance for us both, eh? You and me together, with our little Robbie.'

She gave a half laugh of disbelief, unwilling even now to accept his suggestion as genuine. There was something naïve about the assumption that she would allow him to stay, something pitiable, and also deeply worrying, for Daisy saw that he was completely serious. Obstinately so, in fact. 'But we don't love each other, not any more. What we had was a juvenile thing, all in the past. I have Harry now, and you . . .'

'I have Robbie. Rita says he were with my sister but she's gone now.'

'Yes, Annie's gone.'

'Well then, I must look after him. He's my, what d'you call it – responsibility. Rita says it's the law, 'cause I'm Annie's next of kin.'

'Does she?'

'Aye,' he looked pleased with himself for remembering this important fact. 'So if you want him back Daisy, you'll have to take me on too. That's fair, isn't it?' And he laughed, but for once Daisy didn't join in.

Daisy felt as if she were living through a nightmare. Rita followed her up to her room, walking straight in without knocking, just as if she owned the place. 'Well, is it all sorted? Have you and Percy made it up?'

'Made what up? We never fell out. He was simply over-whelmed by what happened, as I was. But no, if you must know. Nothing is sorted out. If anything, it's got a hell of a sight worse.'

Rita sat down on the edge of the bed, making herself comfortable. 'So go on, tell me why. What's the problem? Nothing that can't be put right, I'll be bound. You always were a drama queen, our Daisy.'

'*Me*, a drama queen?' Daisy swallowed her natural inclin-ation to do battle with her mother for she needed to get on her right side, so that she'd give permission for her to marry, assuming Harry still wanted her. Oh, what a mess! It was no good waiting for Harry to turn up and do things properly by the book in the prescribed manner. They were way beyond that now. Very quietly, and with excessive care, Daisy said, 'I want you to be honest with me. I want you to tell me if it's true. Is the baby really mine?'

She needed an answer desperately. If this was all one of Rita's cruel games, she couldn't stand it, she really couldn't. She'd pack her bags and leave first thing in the morning, and she and Megan and Trish would take their chances elsewhere. Nothing could be more important to her than her son: not Lane End Farm, not the disapproval of their lodgers, not even Clem of whom she'd grown so fond. There was only one person's opinion who really counted, and she'd have to face him when the moment came. But how could she even begin to deal with Percy and his sudden decision to lay down rules and provisos, unless she knew the facts. The long silence made her impatient for a response. 'Well?'

'Are you accusing me of being a liar or summat, your own mother?'

'I'm not accusing you of anything but I never know where I am with you. I'm only saying, are you sure there hasn't been some sort of mistake? Where did you find him? Was he with Percy at the time? What exactly happened that day, you've never said.'

'I don't like to talk about it. It were awful. Dreadful. Explosions going off all over shop. Me and your Aunt Florrie near blown to bits in an air-raid shelter. Then we got back to find us home smashed to smithereens and me husband dead. You'll have to excuse me if things seem a bit confusing after that, if I were a bit shocked like. And you'll have to take my word for it about the babby. Anyroad, why would I say he's yours, if he weren't?'

'I don't know, perhaps to get your feet under my table?'

'It's not your table, or at least it wasn't last time I looked. It's our Florrie's.'

Daisy flushed with embarrassment. This was a fact she yet had to deal with. Would Florrie be as keen for her to stay as Clem?

'Anyroad, tha's talkin' soft. He's a grand little chap. Most women would be pleased to have their child returned to them, not interrogate their mother in this ungrateful way. So, what about you and Percy? Have you mended your differences, whatever they were?'

'It's not quite so easy as that. There's something I need to show you.' Daisy sank on to the bed next to Rita, then pulling the folded handkerchief from the drawer in the chest by the bed, unwrapped it and slid the diamond ring on to her finger.

'Well, I'll go to the bottom of our stairs, has Percy given you a ring already? By heck, the sly . . .'

'No, he hasn't,' Daisy interrupted quickly. 'This is from Harry. We got engaged, unofficially, just a few weeks ago. I love him, and he loves me, so I've no intention of marrying Percy, not now, not ever. Sorry, but there it is.'

Rita's mouth tightened into a slit of angry disapproval. 'Is this the chap your dad warned off that time he came to visit?'

'He didn't warn anyone off. He told me to stop seeing

Harry, that I'd to come home and look after you because you had a bad back, and I refused. Just as well I did, there doesn't look to be much wrong with you that I can see.'

'It mended, no thanks to you madam,' Rita said tartly.

Daisy got up from the bed and walked to the window, putting some distance between herself and her mother. Perversely, Blencathra looked benign now as a westerly sun dropped lower in the sky, lighting it to gold. 'It's good that you can manage so well without me, because I'm not coming back to Salford, even after the war. Clem has made it clear that I'm welcome to make my home here, at Lane End Farm, if I want to.' She turned to Rita, her face expressionless. 'What do you plan to do, Mother? Ask the council to find you a new place, I expect. I don't reckon it would work for you to stop on here. Not that there would be room, with all the visitors we get. You must see that.'

Rita was on her feet now, glaring at her daughter and spitting her fury into her face. 'So this is the gratitude I get, is it, for reuniting you with your son? You won't make the smallest sacrifice, or give a thought for anyone but yourself. You'd throw Percy, and me, back on the slag heap, just so's you can marry your precious Harry and swank over this nice little set-up you've got going for yourself here. You'd cut us off, just as Florrie did.'

'Mother, for goodness' sake, I don't swank, I just want . . .'

'Have me out of the way. Oh, I've got the message.' Rita stormed to the door, her face a mask of seething anger. 'Well don't you forget for one minute madam, that you're under age. I'll never give my permission for you to marry your beloved Harry. Percy's a good lad. Happen I made a few mistakes about him in the past, but all he needs is a bit of tender loving care after all he's been through. And if you want to keep little Robbie, I'd give his offer serious consideration if I were you.'

Even as Daisy struggled to find a suitable answer to this

attack, something in Rita's face changed, a perceptible alteration of her mood. As she moved thoughtfully back into the room to where Daisy was standing by the window, she was almost smiling. 'You have told him?'

'I – I beg your pardon?'

'You heard. Have you told this Harry about your little indiscretion?'

'Mother, for God's sake, what words you choose.'

'Well, have you? Come on, don't mess me about. Does he know you had an illegitimate child or doesn't he?'

Daisy would have given anything in that moment to have had the satisfaction of saying that yes, he certainly did know and didn't care a jot. Instead, she bit her lip so that Rita wouldn't see it tremble and said nothing at all. Triumph blazed in the boot-button eyes.

'I thought not. Kept your little secret a bit too well, eh?'

'That was your fault, you told me . . .'

'I know what I told you. And now I'm telling you that when your too trusting sweetheart hears the truth about you, he'll drop you like a red-hot brick. So show a bit of sense and settle for what you've got. Percy. He has the benefit of being steady, unlikely to stray with those injuries, and you get to keep your son. As for where I'll be living from now on, well, we'll see how things pan out, shall we? See what our Florrie makes of having her kitchen taken over by a mere slip of a lass.'

It was half past eleven when Laura heard the sound of a bike in the yard. She made no move to meet her at the door, deciding it was too late to start an argument tonight. Besides, she was far too relieved simply to have Chrissy safely home.

The next morning, the moment breakfast had been served and the pair were clearing away, Chrissy began chattering about a disco Gary was taking her the following weekend.

'I don't think so, Chrissy. You're gated. Grounded. Confined to barracks.'

'*What?*'

Laura explained to her quietly that because of the lateness of the hour when she'd finally returned the previous night, in addition to her general unruly behaviour, she wouldn't be going to the disco or anywhere else for that matter. 'Not without your father's permission.'

'If I don't get to go, then I'm not doing any more work for you,' she responded peevishly, tossing aside the tea towel.

'Oh yes, you will. We have an agreement. You've three changeovers this morning, so you can leave the kitchen to me now and get on with it. We'll discuss this later.'

Should she ring Felix, or shouldn't she? He wouldn't be pleased. He'd lecture her mercilessly about the purple hairdo, and as for our friend on the motorbike who may be quite a nice young man for all she knew, Felix was perfectly capable of taking him apart, limb from limb. Laura started scrubbing the grill pan and decided against it. On balance, it seemed best to give the girl a chance to come round, which she surely would do. Chrissy certainly wouldn't thank her for calling in the heavy guns at this sensitive stage. She was a young girl struggling to find who she was, and her place in the scheme of things. Didn't she have problems enough right now with the divorce and everything? She'd keep a better eye on her and cope, somehow.

An hour later David popped in. 'I always find you at the kitchen sink. I think it's time I took you away from all of this and whisked you off somewhere romantic.'

'Don't you start. I've enough with Felix nagging me to stop working. I like what I do, OK?'

David's smile vanished. 'What's happened? Something wrong?' Laura apologised profusely for her shortness of temper, then confessed to being worried over Chrissy. She told him about the motorbike, about the mysterious Gary, and the late night out.

David grimaced. 'Teenage angst. I'd forgotten how awful

it was. All those hormones jumping. And it must be especially hard dealing with it as a stepmother. Maybe you should try it for real next time.'

Laura turned to look at him and was shocked to find herself blushing at the impish light of meaning in his eyes. 'I don't think this is quite the moment to discuss it.'

'Perhaps not. I beg leave to return to it on a more suitable occasion. Gary Slatterly isn't a bad lad, though none too bright and he has got his wilder side. His father tends to use him as punchbag from time to time which does him no good at all. I'll have a word with him, if you like. Don't fret about the bike. It can get up a fair speed but it's not exactly a Harley-Davidson. I wouldn't worry, if I were you.'

'Yes but you're not me, and you don't have Felix breathing down your neck.'

He pulled her into his arms and kissed her long and slow. 'Oh yes, I do, otherwise I'd be allowed much more than this.' They spent a contented half-hour chatting together over coffee before David went back to his shearing and Laura to her shopping and ironing, at least feeling more relaxed and happy as a result of his visit. David was good for her. Wherever this relationship was leading, and it looked as if it might be going a long way, she wasn't in any hurry to stop it. Laura found that she liked having him around. They'd agreed to get together on Friday evening for a drink and, as soon as the clipping was over, he'd take her out for that romantic meal. It couldn't come soon enough for her. She was ready and willing for some romance in her life.

26

Winter was approaching, Daisy's second at Lane End Farm and she was doing her utmost to make her lodgers comfortable but it was far from easy. She put a small green baize card table in the parlour so that they could play cards or dominoes, and a chenille cloth over the best mahogany one so that Tommy could use it to write out his orders or Miss Copthorne for filling in her countless forms, without causing any damage to its polished surface. She found an old wind-up gramophone in the attic and put that in the parlour too so that when Tommy Fawcett, or Twinkletoes, as he was more fondly known, wasn't working he could entertain them with his toe tapping. Or they could all have a bit of a dance, if they'd a mind. And Daisy always made sure there was a bright fire burning in the grate, flowers in the vase and nicely plumped cushions on the comfy chairs. She fed her guests well, despite the restrictions, and continued to take the time and trouble to be interested in their lives and their own personal problems.

Not that anyone asked after her own problems. They accepted the presence of a baby in the house, and Percy too, by politely showing no curiosity at all. What they said to each other in private over this puzzling state of affairs, Daisy didn't care to consider.

However, her aunt was a different matter. Florrie was not at all taking to having another woman in her kitchen. Whatever Daisy did, Florrie seemed to take exception to it and deliberately undermine her efforts. She folded up the card table and took it away, saying it made the small room too crowded. She complained loudly about the amount of fuel being consumed, and put an ugly oilcloth over her best chenille tablecloth, to protect it from spills of ink. As for the two little girls, she banned drawing and painting because it was too messy, as well as dominoes and tiddlywinks which she complained went all over the carpet and, more often than not, rushed them off to bed far too early because she said they were making too much noise and giving her a headache. Finally, she put away the gramophone, along with every magazine, newspaper, book, comic and jigsaw and left the parlour looking sterile and cheerless. Rather like herself.

'They weren't doing any harm,' Daisy protested, aghast at these changes.

'We shouldn't encourage them. This isn't their home and there's no point in them thinking that it is.'

Daisy felt utterly flabbergasted, at a loss to know how best to deal with this attitude. It was as if she were treading on eggshells the whole time, on the one hand with her mother and Percy, and on the other with Florrie, desperately trying not to offend her now that she was back home and taking up the reins again. Even decisions over where to site the flour bin, hang the pans or which drawer to put the wire sieve proved to be a political minefield. And yet, low on patience because of the tension still building inside her, Daisy refused to buckle under. Now she spoke her mind rather forcefully. 'I can't agree, Florrie. This is the nearest these people will come to having a home until this war is over. You surely don't begrudge them a bit of fun?'

'Why should they have fun, at my expense?'

'I suppose you mean because you aren't having any. Well, that isn't their fault, Florrie, it's yours. I'm sorry for your troubles but really it's time to put them behind you and make a fresh start. I seem to remember hearing how you were fond of a bit of fun yourself, once upon a time. Anyroad, it's not at your expense. These people are paying good money – hard-earned money, to stay here. They deserve a bit of home-from-home comfort. As for the children . . .'

But Florrie had walked out of the kitchen and slammed shut the door long before she reached the end of the sentence.

Two women in one kitchen was bad enough, three women in one house was impossible. Rita would follow Daisy about from room to room criticising whatever she was doing. She'd complain that the floor needed sweeping, or the tablecloth in the dining room was grubby, even when it had been freshly laundered, and when Daisy gave her a job to do to get her out of the way Rita would robustly declare that she certainly wasn't going to act as skivvy for her own daughter, and that setting tables was not her line of work at all.

'What is, Mother?' Daisy would ask in near despair. 'What is?'

Rita seemed to take pleasure in being difficult with the other guests too, generally insulting them even to ridiculing poor Ned when he demonstrated his new Home Guard uniform and the fact they only had one rifle between three men. 'Why would you need more? You wouldn't know what to do with an invading German if you fell over one. Run a mile, I dare say.'

Ned glanced across at Daisy and gave her a half-smile, silently telling her he wasn't in the least offended, and urging her not to be anxious.

Adopting all the airs and graces she could muster, Rita made it plain at every opportunity that she was not one of them, availing herself of the best chair in the parlour nearest to the fire; often insisting on something different for her evening meal to whatever it was they were having. Daisy would grind her teeth with frustration but was determined not to cross her too much, not until she'd had the opportunity to talk to Harry. Oh, if only he'd hurry up and come.

Rita's self-appointed task appeared to be to issue orders and point out errors and faults when things weren't quite to her liking. She gave the distinct impression that she was the one actually in charge and running the establishment, and not Daisy at all.

'I don't know how she would've coped if I hadn't turned up when I did.'

'She seemed to be managing well enough,' Miss Copthorne mildly remarked, resenting this slur on Daisy's character.

'Ah, but she was leaning heavily on Clem, and he has enough on his plate, poor man, running this place. And certainly my sister Florrie is no help at all. She suffers from depression, don't you know.'

Miss Copthorne didn't wonder at it, with a sister like Rita finding fault from dawn till dusk. 'Still, everything seems to be in order, wouldn't you say? Daisy has made us most comfortable.'

'Ah yes, but you've never kept house, have you, you being a spinster, so how can you judge?'

Miss Copthorne flushed, taken aback by such bluntness. 'I'll have you know I kept house for years, for my dear parents.'

Rita sniffed. 'Not the same thing though, is it?' and sailed away, nose in the air, before the lack of logic in her statement could be questioned.

Daisy picked up Robbie and went in search of some fresh air.

The September sky was a glinting blue, illuminating the patches of purple heather and making the horizon shimmer with light. The day held that autumn stillness, as if the land was revelling in the last of the summer's heat before it cooled. Somewhere above, clear as bell, she could hear Clem's voice echoing through the silence: 'Ga way,' he shouted. 'Ga way by,' as he worked his dogs on the higher fells.

She set little Robbie down and the child gave a shout of pure joy and began to run in his ungainly way towards the sound of this familiar voice, making her laugh out loud. Daisy ran with her son, matching her pace to his, waving to Clem as they drew nearer. He was driving the dogs forward, to have them mark the sheep who were bunching together for protection against this opposing force. Daisy reached for little Robbie and swung him up in her arms. 'Oh no, little man, we can't have you startling either dogs or sheep.'

Clem eased them into the pen, patiently waiting whenever they hesitated and then urging them forward again at exactly the right moment. Daisy watched, holding the child in her arms, marvelling at the skill required. A ewe broke away and a dog quickly cut off her escape, nose down, belly low to the ground, directing her quietly back on course till all were safely in the fold and Clem was able to close the gap with a hurdle. He turned and grinned at her, then with a quiet whistle called up his dogs and walked down the hill towards her.

'I've brought you some tea,' she held out the blue tin can with its screw lid. 'And a bacon buttie.'

'Eeh grand, I could do with a break, let's have a bit of a crack.' They sat with their backs to a dry-stone wall, enjoying the sunshine, and a moment's respite from the day's routine. Daisy gave a rusk to little Robbie and he went and sat with the dogs to happily share it with them.

Clem said, 'She dun't change much, your mam, does she? She's exactly as I remember her.' And Daisy giggled, knowing it was not meant as a compliment.

'You don't have to put up with her bitchiness. It's your house. You could ask her to leave.'

'Nay, not with the war on, and everything up in the air like. There'll be time enough to mek changes when we've put all of this kerfuffle behind us. Theer's talk of the Yanks coming in with us. That's what we need, a bit of new muscle to help our tired and aching ones.'

'Let's hope so.' Daisy wrapped her arms about her knees and was thoughtful for a moment. 'What about you and Aunt Florrie, or shouldn't I ask?'

Clem pulled a wry face. 'We're like a couple of banty cocks, circling each other and tekkin a savage peck ivery noo and then. Neet afore last we had a reet ding-dong.'

'Does that mean you're talking now?'

Clem frowned. 'Nay, I joost says we'll happen get a wetting afore tomorrer, and she storms out in a reet paddy. I were asleep afore she coom back to bed. I reckon she thinks me a bit of a bore. Happen I am. But we has to mek a show of getting on.' A shadow crossed his face and some of his bravado deserted him. 'Happen I should try harder to be more entertaining like. I just want to mek her happy, that's all.'

Daisy realised that she couldn't add to his troubles by telling him of her own problems with Florrie; or spill out all her fears about losing Robbie if she married Harry, or losing Harry if she married Percy in order to keep her baby. Harry might not want her in any case, once he'd heard the whole sorry tale. He'd probably be ashamed of her, as her own mother was. No, this was her problem, and Clem had enough of his own. She watched with sadness in her eyes as he shambled away in that familiar loping walk, back up the fell with the dogs at his heels.

As if recognising her gloomy mood, Robbie came and put his chubby arms about his mother's neck to kiss her cheek. Heart full of love, Daisy gave him a hug. 'What a muddle! What a mess we make of our lives.'

Maybe the only way was to face it, head on. She could start with Florrie, for their differences had nothing at all to do with card tables or comics. Perhaps it was time to see if bridges could be built.

From the moment the idea of taking in lodgers had occurred to her, Daisy had been nervous of her aunt's reaction. Florrie

There are so many lonely people around, so many in need these days. Oh, I know we can only take in a few, but these folk were all alone in the world before they came here.

'Miss Copthorne lost her fiancé in the First World War and has spent her entire life since nursing elderly parents, missing out on a chance to find a new man herself; only coming to teaching late in life, after their death. All right, she rattles on a bit but she means well, and you can't fault her on the way she looks after her charges. Poor Ned Pickles, well, he's still grieving for his wife but he and Clem are becoming fast friends, against all the odds, mind, for they're like chalk and cheese.' She smiled at Florrie's bewildered expression. As for Tommy Fawcett, you'd never think so to listen to him but he was the loneliest of the lot. His entire family was killed in an air raid, a fact he spilled out to me one night, and the dancing is only his way of coping, of putting on a front so that he can bear to get up each morning and live through the day.

'But you're right about Megan and Trish, in one respect at least. I did want a stable home for them. And why not? We all deserve a happy childhood and them two little 'uns have had a raw deal so far. But *I'm* the one responsible for them, no one else, for all Clem loves them to bits. I can tell that by the way he never stops talking about them.'

'Talk? You've got Clem *talking*?'

'Never stops. All I have to do is listen.'

'Perhaps that's a skill I should cultivate.' Florrie gave a weak smile as she shook her head in disbelief. 'You've achieved so much Daisy, know so much about them all. I can see that you really care, that you're not at all the sort to get depressed; to give up and sit about feeling sorry for yourself, as I was. Still do, I suppose. You're far more capable than me.' She fell silent again, her quiet gaze still on Daisy, measuring her up, considering the situation.

In Florrie's opinion, Daisy was not in the least bit as she had expected, or rather as Rita had led her to believe. She wasn't flighty or silly, nor beautiful in the conventional sense of the word. Not at all the sort of drop-dead beauty you'd expect men to go for. She didn't flirt or flash her eyes, or behave in the giddy way young girls often do. Her hair was soft and well washed, a lovely brown; her smooth young skin lightly tanned and freckled from a summer spent largely outdoors. She was no Betty Grable, that was for sure, so, if Clem had taken a shine to her, there must be some other reason, some inner beauty that had appealed to him. And perhaps this was it, her generosity of spirit. The love that shone out of her for her fellow human beings. Perhaps he saw her as a daughter, replacing the one he had lost.

After a moment Florrie said, 'And what about the bairn? What about this little chap? Have you decided what to do about him? We mustn't forget that he needs a mother.'

Softly, Daisy said, 'Maybe he's got two, one in me, and one in you. I know about Emma. Clem told me. I'm so sorry.' There was a long, drawn-out silence which seemed to go on for ever. Daisy didn't dare breathe as she waited for Florrie's response. At length it came, spoken in the softest of voices.

'Jealousy is a terrible thing. Like loneliness, it eats into the heart of you, robs you of your soul. Seeing you with little Robbie was like losing Emma all over again. I know it's not the same, it's just . . . it reminded me . . . brought back all those feelings . . . all that pain.'

'I can understand that. But more than one person can love a child.'

The two women looked at each other, the hope in Florrie's eyes meeting with compassion in Daisy's. 'I don't know whether I can bear it or not Daisy, but I'll give it a go. That bairn needs a young mum, not an old one. I'll settle for being his favourite aunt.' She smiled, a genuine smile this time which warmed them both. 'You deserve him, Daisy Atkins, if only for making Clem a happy man again.'

'So you and he are . . .'

Florrie blushed to the roots of her bleached blonde hair. 'No, no, I wasn't meaning owt o'sort. Me and Clem have a long road to climb yet, I reckon. And happen he isn't even interested in trying.'

'Are you?'

There was anguish in Florrie's gaze as she turned to look out the window on to the empty fells beyond. 'I reckon it's too late for us to make a fresh start. I've blown me chances. I very much doubt he cares enough about me now to give me another.'

That very evening, as if to make up for her sulks and misery, and to stop herself brooding over the state of her marriage, Florrie flung herself into helping Daisy with renewed energy. She laid the dining table willingly without needing to be asked, and offered to serve while Daisy dished up.

'Many hands make light work.'

'Florrie, you're a treasure.'

Daisy smiled to herself at the sound of her aunt's red sling-back shoes clattering back and forth up and down the passage. In the background she could hear the strains of music coming from the front parlour. A Fred Astaire number, what else? At least Florrie didn't have time to be lonely now. If only she and Clem could talk things through properly, she'd have some chance of shaking herself free of this depression, but the distance between husband and wife seemed to be going worse, not better.

Florrie had spread the big table which the guests shared in the dining room with a bright blue check tablecloth, set out all the knives, forks and spoons and was on her way back for the cruet, which she'd forgotten, when she cannoned into Tommy Fawcett. To her utter surprise and astonishment, he pulled her into his arms and swept the blushing Florrie into a two-step to the tune of 'Lady Be Good', right along the passage and back into the kitchen just as if he really were Fred

Astaire. He didn't let her go until the record had finished, by which time he'd twice circled the kitchen table, making Daisy jump out of the way to avoid his flying feet and spun Florrie around in a dizzying pirouette to finish the number. Megan and Trish, both sitting at the table eating boiled eggs, watched the entire performance goggle-eyed. Little Robbie, chortling with glee, banged his spoon on his high chair very nearly in time to the music.

'What a star she is. Did you see that step and slide? A professional couldn't have done better.'

Florrie, one hand leaning on the table while she nursed a stitch in her side with the other, burst out laughing, her cheeks flushed to an even brighter pink. Tommy doffed his brown trilby which had miraculously stayed glued to the back of his head throughout, winked outrageously, then declared himself mortified at not being in a position to take her to a proper dance that very evening but he'd promised to accompany Ned Pickles to another dull lecture on the need for new health reform. 'You could always come with us?' he suggested hopefully but Florrie hastily shook her head, before finally regaining sufficient breath to actually speak.

'Some other time perhaps,' she puffed, patting her hair back into place and glancing flirtatiously up at him through her lashes. Hadn't she known all along that being over forty didn't mean she was past it; that she was still young enough to attract a man? Yet even in her wildest dreams she'd never imagined being actually asked out on a date. 'You can always ask me another evening if you like. I used to be quite good on the dance floor once over. So I might even say yes.'

'I shall hold you to that,' Tommy said, clowning a cheery salute, then with a click of his heels he looped an arm about her waist and hung her backwards over his arm in a fair imitation of a tango, or the *paso doble*, making Florrie screech with delight and the children cheer and applaud loudly.

It was at this precise moment that Clem walked in. He

stood at the door in his blue work overalls, mouth sagging open in surprise to find his wife thus engaged.

All of a fluster, Florrie pushed Tommy away and pretended to scold him, though not very convincingly. 'What a card you are Tommy Fawcett. Behave yourself, do. We're just having a laugh,' she said, seeing the grim expression on her husband's face.

'So I see.' It was very plain that he didn't see at all.

Tommy stepped forward hastily, whipped off the brown trilby and bowed low. 'It was all my doing, Mr er . . . um . . . Dingle . . . er Tingle,' he joked, just as if he didn't already know his name. 'Dear me, I've quite lost my senses over your charming wife,' and Florrie stifled a giggle while Daisy quietly groaned as she saw Clem's face darken.

'The name is Pringle, Clement Pringle,' Clem informed him stiffly, with not a trace of his usual good humour. 'As I am sure you are aware. And Florrie is my wife. Happen that'll help you remember in future,' and he lifted one clenched fist and popped it on Tommy Fawcett's nose, sending him sprawling backwards on to the floor, a surprised expression on his face and blood spurting everywhere.

As Florrie rushed to help him to his feet, Clem spoke to her in his frostiest tones. 'When thoo's finished flirting or dancing or whatever it is you were having a laugh aboot, I wouldn't mind a bit of supper. Nor, I am sure, would our guests.'

'It's almost ready,' Daisy hastily intervened, dashing to the stove. 'I'm about to dish up,' but Clem had gone and she was talking to the kitchen door.

'Sorry about that love,' mumbled Tommy, dabbing at the blood with his handkerchief. 'Must've got a bit carried away,' and hastily made his own exit.

Florrie met Daisy's eye and now they were both smiling. 'Seems you've nothing to worry about at all, Florrie. The green-eyed monster might be working in your favour for once.'

27

Harry came one damp autumn day in early October. He arrived while Daisy was still serving breakfast, taking them all by surprise. With only a twenty-four-hour pass, he'd managed to get an overnight train and had hitched a lift from the station. Just the sight of him standing there before her, beads of rain on his uniform greatcoat, his forage cap tilted provocatively at just the right angle, brought an ache to her heart. She'd longed for him to come for so long and now here he was; the moment of truth had arrived.

Daisy left Florrie to dish up the kippers and dragged him away from the house, and from prying eyes, as fast as she could. Blencathra was covered with a thick layer of mist that morning, so this wasn't too difficult a task. She took him behind the barn, certain no one would venture out on such a morning.

It was only after they'd satisfied the first flush of kisses and Daisy was cuddled within the unbuttoned greatcoat, held close against the solid warmth of his chest that Harry asked the question, 'What's all this about then? What difficulty is your mother causing?'

Daisy wished the sun was shining and they could lie in the sweet-smelling green grass together, or they were in Silloth on the sand dunes. She felt a desperate need to have everything appear wonderful and perfect when she told him her news, so that it wouldn't seem quite so terrible. A wet mountain swathed in mist seemed entirely inappropriate, the least romantic place in the world, and she ached for all the missed chances, all the times she could have opened her heart to him and hadn't done so.

She glanced up at him from under her lashes, trying to judge the right approach, having gone over it a thousand times in her head. 'There's something I need to tell you. Something I couldn't say in a letter.'

Harry grinned. 'Obviously, that's why I'm here.' And when still she said nothing, he took her cold face between his two warm hands and held it in a loving caress. 'Whatever it is, remember that I love you. So come on, tell me. It can't be so terrible.'

Daisy's eyes filled with tears. Grasping his hands she held them tightly in her own for a moment before taking a step away to give herself space to think. 'I'm going to say it quickly, to get it over with, right?'

The smile faded and his expression became solemn. 'You're frightening me now, Daisy. What is it? If you're trying to say that you no longer love me . . .'

'No, no, it isn't that.'

'Well, thank God for that, then nothing else . . .'

'I have a child.'

'What?'

'He's turned two years old. I had him at the start of the war when I was just sixteen.' She didn't look at Harry while she announced these blunt facts, then shot him a quick glance, noting the stunned expression in his eyes, the way his jaw had tightened but when he made no response she hurried on, explaining all about Percy not wanting to know about the baby, him joining the navy and her mother packing her off to a mother and baby home and forcing her to give him up for adoption. Finally running out of both breath and words, she fell silent.

Harry hadn't moved a muscle. He stood looking down at her for some long moments before he said, 'Well, that's a shaker. The last thing I expected.'

'I know. And I would understand if it was too much for you to accept, if it means that you no longer want to marry me, I . . .' She was forced to pause. There was a lump in her throat the size of a golf ball. 'I realise it's asking a lot, only I'd just say in my own defence that I was too young and ignorant to properly understand what I was doing. My mother wasn't the sort to fill me in on essential details which might have helped me avoid such an accident, if you take my meaning. Not that I'm trying to put all the blame on to her, or wriggle out of it. I was stupid, there's no denying it, all I'm saying is that I didn't make a habit of it, I'm not a loose woman. It was only the one time and . . .'

'Daisy, stop it. Don't torture yourself. I don't want to know the sordid details. And I don't, for one minute, see you as a loose woman.'

Now they both fell silent, Harry trying to digest what she'd told him, Daisy unsure how to proceed. But she'd only told him the half of it so far, and proceed she must. 'There's more,' she said at last, in the smallest of voices.

'Dear God, what else can there be?' His face had become rigid, etched with pain.

'He's here.'

'Who is here?'

She drew in a deep, shaky breath and launched into the rest of her tale: of Rita and Florrie being involved in the bomb blast, of how they'd found Percy, the only survivor from his own family, and little Robbie who'd been returned to her after being looked after by Percy's sister all this time and not sent to strangers after all. None of it could have taken more than a few minutes to relate. It felt like an hour.

'So little Robbie's here. And Percy too, as a matter of fact.'

Harry's eyes looked like dark coals burning in the death-white ash of his face. 'Where is all of this leading, Daisy?'

'Well . . .' she began, giving a slight shrug of her shoulders, quite sure he must be able to hear the frantic beat of her heart, 'he still wants to marry me. Because of the baby. He thinks we owe it to little Robbie to marry and give him a proper mam and dad. Course, I said no, not on your life. It's you I love, Harry, not Percy, and I'm sure there must be some way round this.'

'You mean some way you can keep both your child, this – little Robbie – and me?'

Fear clutched at her heart as she noted the brittle hardness in his tone. 'Yes, I dare say that is what I mean.'

'I think I need to think this through.' Then he turned on his heels and strode away from her, up the mountain side, hands thrust deep in his pockets, shoulders hunched. He didn't invite her to go with him, and Daisy knew better than to try.

Laura spent the evening going through her accounts to see what she could afford in the way of extra staff. 'I'm going to have to try another advert. This isn't working,' she informed Chrissy, who was lying sprawled on the sofa watching a *Star Trek* movie on television with her eyes half closed. Laura wondered whether she should say anything further about the other night and, if so, what. Chrissy had barely spoken to her in days.

'Right,' Chrissy mumbled.

Laura sighed. Where was the sparkling wit, the sharp rejoinder for which her stepdaughter was well known? She chewed on her lower lip, thinking frantically. Money was tight, tighter than she'd expected and July had been surprisingly quiet. Everyone warned her not to get too alarmed about this. August, September and October were the busiest months in the Lakes. There was time yet to make her fortune, or at least a decent income for the season. Yet the prospect of entering the busiest period of the season with no one but a recalcitrant teenager to assist her, was too dreadful to contemplate.

'Look, I'm sorry about your missing the disco, but there

have to be some rules. I can't have you running wild all over the countryside with young men I don't even know. Sorry, but that's how it is. If you don't like it, Chrissy, then perhaps you'd best go back to your mum for the rest of the summer. I'm not sure I feel able to accept the responsibility of having you here, unless you are prepared to co-operate.'

Laura held her breath. Was this the right approach: firm but fair? She hadn't the faintest idea. She'd tended to leave the discipline side of things to Julia, and to Felix who would weigh in every now and then with a tirade of instructions. Right now, she had enough on her plate without having to learn the tricks of good parenting.

Chrissy didn't take her eyes off the television. Was she genuinely tired or simply sulking? Perhaps that was the problem. They were both in dire need of a break.

Laura put aside her files and papers. 'Look, what we need is a day out, an afternoon at least, to cheer us up. Where would you like to go? Perhaps for a sail on Derwentwater, or to the theatre and a slap-up dinner afterwards, perhaps pony trekking or water skiing?' Laura was trying desperately to think of ways to amuse a grumpy adolescent. 'Could I fix up some climbing instruction for you, or canoeing? This is the Lake District after all, or even a long ramble over the fells. Whatever you like. What do you think? Is there something you fancy doing? My treat.'

'Forgot to mention,' Chrissy murmured, completely ignoring the lengthy list. 'Dad rang.'

'Oh? He caught you this time then. Good. Did he have anything interesting to say?' Laura kept her smile in place, controlling the urge to comment tartly on his obstinate refusal to respond to the divorce papers which had been sent for him to sign three weeks ago. She preferred not to make snide remarks about Felix in front of his daughter, or involve her in their arguments, but it wasn't easy. His long silence was beginning to grate on Laura's nerves.

'He's coming tomorrow to take me out, so you don't need to bother. Thanks all the same.'

It was one of those put-downs that only Chrissy, in her crass, adolescent ignorance, could employ. A blunt reminder to Laura that she was only a reserve parent, not a real one. No matter how fond she was of Chrissy, and despite the time she devoted to her well-being, the PTA meetings she'd attended on her behalf, the wheedling she'd done over the years with irate teachers, and even this overpaid job she'd given her, she would never be anything *but* a reserve. It was a sobering thought and, at thirty-four, Laura wondered fleetingly, and painfully, whether she ever would have children of her own; if she hadn't missed that particular boat and it was all far too late. She had hoped they could at least be friends.

'Fine. It'll be good for you to see your dad.'

'Yep.' Chrissy pulled the cushion to a more comfortable position beneath her head.

The feeling of resentment was palpable. 'If you're so tired after your late night, wouldn't you be better in bed?'

'Nope. It's not nine o'clock yet, and I don't have a telly in my room, unlike your privileged guests.'

Laura thought longingly of her own bed, soft and inviting, of the small cassette recorder beside it upon which she could listen to Daisy's tapes whenever she'd a mind. She'd taken the first three back to the library, borrowed the final two, and really couldn't wait to get to them. Daisy was a good story-teller and could certainly talk. Laura felt she knew the farm, and also understood her grandmother so much better as a result. She'd also loved having the opportunity to meet and talk with Megan. The older woman's memory had remained sharp and filled with affection and joy, perhaps because she'd been a child at the time. But she'd promised to come again, having thoroughly enjoyed her visit, particularly seeing 'little Robbie' again and the pair had vowed to keep in touch.

Laura stretched and yawned. 'Well, I think this over-the-hill decrepit would be much better off in bed. I'm going to have an early night. See you in the morning, bright and early.'

'Yep,' murmured Chrissy, idly flicking between channels during the commercials. And Laura crept off to bed, leaving her to it.

Having fallen asleep listening to another of Daisy's tapes, Laura jerked awake to discover it was half past ten and the house was very quiet. She decided to check that the house was secure and locked up safe for the night, the guests each having their own key, and that Chrissy had remembered to switch off the TV. She could make herself a cup of chocolate at the same time. She'd make Chrissy one too. Perhaps they could make friends again over a conciliatory mug of hot chocolate.

Chrissy's room was empty. She wasn't watching TV either, or anywhere in the house. What's more, her jacket had gone from the stand in the hall, and on her dressing-table was evidence of a heavy make-up session with bottles and tubes and lipsticks left scattered about. It came to Laura in that chilling moment that the girl had disobeyed her and gone to the disco after all.

She tore down the lane in her Peugeot far too fast, concern and anger warring for supremacy. Long before she reached the Village Hall she could hear the pound of music. Without pausing to think, she abandoned rather than parked the car and went straight over. The room was packed with young people, steaming hot and with ear-splittingly loud music seeming to vibrate the entire building. Any hope of easily finding Chrissy faded instantly. Nor did Laura pass unnoticed in the smoky atmosphere. As she made her way between the sticky, gyrating bodies, she was made to feel very much out of place in comparison with the thirteen-, fourteen- and fifteen-year-olds around her. She was seen as being thoroughly ancient and the subject of much ribald humour and laughter.

'Lost your zimmer frame, love?'

'Looking for the bingo? It's on Thursdays.'

Eventually, when she'd trawled every corner of the room, peered curiously into every face to see if she recognised anyone, which wasn't easy in the dim light, Laura gave up. Chrissy wasn't here, not that she could see.

Back outside again, she walked dejectedly to the car. Now what? Felix was coming tomorrow and she'd have to explain all of this, explain why she had allowed his daughter to break a curfew and go off with a young man Laura hadn't even met, let alone checked out.

And then she heard the giggle. Unmistakable. Laura stopped in her tracks to peer through the semi-darkness, narrow eyed. Surely the sound wasn't coming from behind the bike sheds? They were, in fact, behind a hedge and the pair were so wound about each other it was difficult to tell which leg or arm belonged to whom. They could have been any one of a dozen youngsters in similar gear, of either sex, so identical was their appearance. But the purple hair was a dead give-away. Laura marched over and grasping Chrissy's shoulder, gave it a shake. 'Right, I think you'd best come with me. You and I have some talking to do.'

'Laura!' Chrissy looked up horrified, the dark red lipstick clownishly smudged, the childlike eyes heavily black ringed with pencil liner. What had she done to herself?

'Come on. It's a fair cop as they say. You'd best come quietly.'

Gary was on his feet in seconds, the tension in his body like a tightly coiled spring. 'Who the hell are you? Leave her alone. We've done nowt wrong.' He was older than Chrissy, perhaps nineteen or twenty. Far too old for a fourteen-year-old, in Laura's opinion.

'This is between Chrissy and me, thanks very much. She knows what she's done wrong.'

'You're not my parent,' Chrissy protested loudly. 'You've no right to tell me what to do.'

'I do when you're living and working with me. Come on.'

'Leave off,' Gary shouted and as Laura reached out to take hold of Chrissy's arm he lashed out a fist and punched her in the stomach. Laura doubled up, gasping for breath, as much with shock as anything. 'I said leave off, will you,' and before she had time to recover, he kicked her in the shin.

Chrissy started to scream. 'Don't do that. *Stop it! Stop it, Gary!*' But Gary wasn't listening. Perhaps he'd had enough of folk telling him what to do, or being the one on the receiving end but he kept on kicking and punching Laura, long after she'd stopped resisting and lay unconscious on the ground.

Florrie had finished the washing-up and cleared the tables in the dining room by the time Daisy got back. Rita, apparently, hadn't yet risen, for which she felt truly grateful. The two girls had eaten and gone off to school with Miss Copthorne and little Robbie was happily splattering porridge all over his face as he got to grips with mastering his spoon. A perfectly normal morning.

Florrie took one look at Daisy's face and put the kettle on.

'I don't want to talk about it,' Daisy said defensively. 'Not just yet.' She took the spoon from the baby's hand and cleaned his face with it, then lifted him out of the high chair on to her lap to finish the job off with his bib. 'Did everything go all right? Did you manage breakfast on your own?'

'Just about. Mind you, Tommy Twinkletoes took his time this morning. It was near half past nine before I managed to get rid of him.' Her cheeks were flushed as she said this and Daisy couldn't help but smile. She could only hope Florrie didn't push Clem's evident jealousy too far. They'd already been given strong evidence of it and, apart from anything else,

Tommy Fawcett was a good customer. Not one it would be wise to lose. She had noticed a slight thawing in relations between husband and wife. Some mornings it was almost humorous to see Clem standing on the doorstep, preparatory to making his usual departure, desperately trying to think of something witty and original say, and Florrie patiently waiting, a pained smile of alert attention on her face.

Percy walked in as Daisy was jiggling Robbie on her knee. She was singing 'Ride-a-Cock-Horse', which he loved, as much to cheer herself up as the baby. Putting two and two together, Florrie decided to make herself scarce and hurried away to make a start on the bedrooms.

'I'll be along to help when I've drunk me tea,' Daisy called after her. '*To see a fine lady upon a white horse.*'

'No rush.'

'Was that him? Lover boy?'

Daisy glanced up with a frown. 'Don't call him that.' Percy's hair had grown quite long since he'd left the navy and looked tousled and unkempt, there were holes in his sleeveless pullover and his shirt had been buttoned up wrong. A rush of pity came to her, even as she sat waiting and fretting for Harry to decide upon whether or not they had a future together. Percy was a sad imitation of his former self, nervous and constantly restless, always fretting or demanding long explanations over something or other. He was like a fractious child. He would ask why he must wear a coat when he went out. Why did he have to go out at all if he didn't feel like it? And why couldn't he tear pieces about the war out of the newspaper if he wanted to, even if no one else had read it yet.

If he wanted to sleep all day, or eat all night, or walk about barefoot if it made his leg feel better; who was she to stop him?

Always, when Daisy was on the point of tearing out her hair in frustration, or ready to scold him for some grumpiness or tantrum, he would put his arms about her, kiss her gently on the cheek and tell her how much he adored her. 'I love you, Daisy. You're my very special friend, right?'

'Of course.'

'Am I being naughty? Is Daisy cross?'

'No, of course not.'

'No bombs here. Safe with Daisy.'

'Yes,' she would assure him kindly. 'You're safe here with me.'

Somewhere in his innermost being must still be the person she'd once fancied herself in love with, though now badly damaged, broken by the war. Thinking of all this her frown faded and she smiled up at him. 'There's tea in the pot. Help yourself.'

'I will, I don't need waiting on.' He still sounded to be in an irritable mood.

Daisy sighed. 'I should think not indeed. You'll not get it here. Not in this kitchen.'

'Have you told your friend Harry that you're going to marry me now?'

Daisy looked away, avoiding his probing gaze, deliberately striving to keep herself relaxed for the sake of the child. 'I've told him about Robbie. Have you thought better of what you said the other day?'

'What I said?'

'*Rings on her fingers and bells on her toes.*' She kissed the baby's bare toes, making him squeal with laughter. 'About you not being prepared to give up little Robbie unless I agree to marry you. Because if not . . .' She paused for a moment, wanting to make matters abundantly clear. 'If not . . . you need to understand, Percy, that I no longer love you. I'm sorry, but there it is.'

He looked nonplussed, the hurt caused by her words clearly evident in his eyes. 'But I need you Daisy. How could I make a go of things without you? You don't really mean it. You *do* love me, I know you do.'

Daisy was desperately trying to let him down gently. Surely he would see that it was all over between them. How could he not see? All she needed was for Harry to forgive her, to not mind about the baby and then everything would be right between them again, and they could go on as before. 'Perhaps I never did love you, not in a proper, grown-up sort of way. We were barely more than kids, after all. And I certainly can't agree to ruin my entire life by sacrificing the man I do love.'

He flinched, and Daisy wondered if he understood a half of what she was trying to say. Perhaps her words had been a touch too blunt, too cruel, yet she was fearful now of retracting them. Percy had to get it into his head that there was no hope. It had to be made clear because the longer she let it go on, the worse it would get. 'I was fond of you, Percy, still am, but I don't feel for you what I now feel for Harry. So you see, I could never give him up.'

'Not even for Robbie and me?' He sounded like a spoilt child being deprived of a treat, and Daisy felt a surge of annoyance. Why wouldn't he understand? Why did he persist with this nonsense?

She turned away, to smile into her son's laughing eyes. '*She shall have music wherever she goes.* I don't believe you'd be so cruel as to deprive me of my lovely child, just because I can't agree to marry you.'

'Of course you and me must marry, Daisy. What would I have to live for if you didn't?'

'Don't be silly, you have lots to live for.'

'No I don't. My ship got hit tha knows, and the navy sent me home and told me not to come back. It's all over for me. I only have you.'

'Don't be silly, Percy. Your *war* is over, not your life. You're still young. You'll find someone else to love one day, you'll see.'

'But I don't want someone else, I want *you*.' He was getting agitated, as he seemed to do when crossed or if he was denied something. Daisy patted his hand, trying to calm him.

'I'm sorry, love, I know it's hard but there it is. You can't have me. It wouldn't be right. I'm promised to Harry.'

Percy stood unmoving for a moment, fists clenched like a child about to throw a tantrum, and then he sat down at the table, put his head in his hands and began to cry, terrible wretched sobs that dragged up from the very core of his being. Daisy was astounded. She'd never seen a grown man cry before and didn't know what to do, what to say or how to react. The poor man was evidently on the verge of a breakdown. 'Don't,' she said, reaching out to him again. 'Please don't upset yourself. I never meant to hurt you, Percy.'

He shook her off and jumped to his feet. '*Leave me alone!*' he shouted. 'You don't understand. You're just like everyone else. You only care about Harry. Nobody loves me.' Then he ran from the room, tears streaming down his face.

Daisy was aghast. This was the last thing she'd wanted, to see Percy so upset. Hadn't he suffered enough? Oh, what on earth should she do? Go to him, or leave him to calm down on his own? Unable to decide what was for the best, she held her baby close and did nothing. Things seemed to be going from bad to worse, spiralling completely out of control.

28

It was almost dinner time when Harry got back from his walk. Daisy had not seen hide nor hair of Percy since his outburst and presumed he was sulking in his room. Florrie was finishing off upstairs and little Robbie had been given his lunch and put down for an early nap. So she was alone when Harry walked into the kitchen. He came straight over but stopped a few feet away from her. She wanted him to gather her into his arms but he made no move to do so.

Daisy knew before ever he opened his mouth that she'd lost. His face looked pinched and drawn, a white line of anger above his upper lip and he seemed distanced from her in some way, a cold chill in his voice. She heard a roaring in her ears, felt a giddiness in her head, as if all the blood were rushing from it. Finding that her legs would no longer support her, she collapsed into a chair, shaking. She could see his lips moving, knew he was talking to her, explaining, apologising, but she couldn't make out the words. She forced herself to listen, to concentrate on what he had to say.

'So there it is. I'm sorry, but that's how I feel. I know it's stupid in a way, that I should be big enough to overlook your – your indiscretion, but I can't. You were *my* girl, not anyone else's. I can't bear the thought of . . . what you might have . . . I can't bear it, that's all.

'Besides, how could I risk being the one to come between you and your child. If Percy insists that he wants you *and* little Robbie, how could I begin to compete? It wouldn't be fair to expect me to.'

'But it's *you* that I love, not Percy.'

'And you love Robbie, your son.'

'Yes, of course I do.'

'Are you saying you'd give up your son for me?'

There was a long and terrible silence in which Daisy frantically sought an answer, a way to salvage this one great love of her life that she was surely about to lose. In the end all she could think of was, 'That's a silly question.'

'A very pertinent one, apparently, in the circumstances.'

'Then no, of course I couldn't give him up, not for anyone.' She leaned earnestly towards him, desperation in her voice. 'But I'm sure it won't come to that. Percy will see that it simply isn't on to expect me to.'

'And if he doesn't? I'm sorry Daisy, but I'm not getting involved in this sort of blackmail. I love you, but I can't marry you. Everything has changed.'

Tears were blocking her throat, filling her eyes, her nose, and only by sheer force of will-power did she prevent them from falling. 'Won't you think about it some more? *Please!* You might feel differently tomorrow.'

'I don't expect I will.'

'But I can't bear to lose you.'

'Nor I you. I believed in you, Daisy, and you lied to me. Can't you see how that hurts? Maybe you never loved me, simply wanted a father for your child.'

'Oh, Harry, that's a terrible thing to say, and quite untrue.'

'Is it any more terrible than what you have done to me? You had ample opportunity to confide in me but you didn't, not until after I'd proposed. What am I supposed to read into that? How can I trust anything you ever told me?'

She felt stricken, at a loss to know how to convince him of her sincerity, to express her regret and sorrow at not having told him sooner. Nonetheless she tried, recognising by the closed look on his face that she was getting nowhere. After a moment or two he sank on to the old settle, elbows on his knees and head in hands, not interrupting, not saying anything, just letting her pour it all out. But in the end, she too ran out of words and fell silent.

How long they sat there, saying nothing, simply nursing the hurt of their loss, she couldn't rightly have said, but neither of them heard Daisy's name being called from some distant part of the house. Not until the door flew open and Florrie burst in, panting for breath, her face a mask of fear.

'Thank God, there you are, Daisy. I've been calling and calling. Daisy, you must come. Right away.'

'Why, what is it? What's happened?'

'It's little Robbie. I just looked in on him and he's not in his cot. He's gone. And so is Percy.'

They searched everywhere, every room in the house, the barns and outbuildings, right along the lane to the cottages in Threlkeld at the bottom and as far up the high fell as seemed feasible. They found no sign of either man or baby anywhere. Once alerted, Clem volunteered to continue searching the summit, crags and gullies while they explored further in the villages beyond.

Even Rita joined in, shamed into doing so by her own part in this sad affair. 'Where can the daft cluck have gone? What possessed him to do such a thing? Oh, don't tek on so, Daisy. He thinks the world of that child. Percy wouldn't harm little Robbie.'

'Course he wouldn't,' Harry agreed, though privately he feared they'd no real idea whether the bloke would or not. Plenty like him had gone off their heads in this blasted war.

Florrie kept wailing, 'If only I'd popped into Robbie's room sooner. If only I hadn't taken so long over the bedrooms. Oh, why did this have to happen? Not again. Not again. Why would he take the baby?'

'God knows!' Rita said.

'To punish me,' said Daisy, breaking her silence at last with an ominous resonance. 'And it's working.'

'Don't let it. We'll find him, I swear we will,' Harry assured her and Daisy shot him a look of intense gratitude. Despite their differences, he wasn't deserting her, not yet anyway. 'We need to look further afield. He's not anywhere round here. Do you know anyone with a vehicle? He can't have got far with a child, not without transport.'

The rest of that day seemed unreal, reaching nightmare proportions. How could this be happening? How could one young man and a baby vanish quite so quickly in so many acres of empty space? Bill the Postie gladly offered the use of his van, driving it himself up and down countless lanes, all to no avail. When there was still no sign of the runaways after three hours of searching, they were forced to call on the local bobby, who wasted no time in ringing the station to alert mountain rescue.

'Best to take no chances. It's dangerous up there. I wish you'd called me sooner, lass.'

'I felt sure we'd find them hiding in one of the cottages or barns.' Daisy stared into the deepening hue of dusk, cold fear griping her heart. 'I'm beginning to believe that he might well have taken the child out on to the high fells. In this weather, he must be out of his mind.'

Harry said, 'I hate having to leave in the middle of all this, Daisy. I want to go with them and help but my commanding officer would eat me alive if I didn't show up on time. I'd be listed as AWOL, court-martialled for sure. It's time for me to go.'

She turned to him and knew in her heart that this was goodbye. The way he didn't quite meet her gaze told Daisy that there was to be no eleventh-hour retraction. This was the end. It was all over between them. 'Don't you fret. I'll be fine,' she said, shaping her mouth into a brave smile. How she was managing to hold back the tears she couldn't rightly have said.

Her whole body ached for him to put his arms about her one more time, to kiss her as he had done earlier today, when he had still loved her, before she'd told him her terrible secret. 'The police will find them, I know they will. Thanks for helping, for your – support. Whatever happens, Harry, those lovely times we've spent together will live for ever in my heart.'

Daisy thought, for a moment, that she detected a slight tremor about his mouth but then it tightened and he nodded, quite brusquely. 'You'll let me know if – if things turn out all right – with Robbie. You'll write.'

'I will Harry. I'll write and let you know.'

'And if anything happens to – to change things.'

She nodded blindly, unable to speak another word.

'Tha'll have to hurry,' Bill the Postie interrupted gently, 'if you don't want to miss that train.' Then Harry turned from her, climbed back into the van and away it roared, spitting and belching out clouds of smoke in its effort to pick up speed. Daisy stayed where she was, the unshed tears burning the backs of her eyes till the van had vanished from sight, then she turned on her heel and walked back up the lane to the farm.

It was the longest night in Daisy's entire life. She sat with Florrie and her mother in the big farm kitchen, quite unable to speak, not even allowing herself to think. Somehow the guests had been fed: cold spam salad which they'd eaten without complaint. She'd been thankful for the activity, taking twice as long as usual over the simplest of tasks. The entire household was subdued, Megan and Trish in tears at the loss of their chum. Daisy had struggled for hours to settle them both, up and down the stairs with cups of water and soothing words but, in the end, had given up and brought the children down to sit in the kitchen with the grown-ups. There was nothing left to do now, but wait.

Around midnight, Clem returned exhausted and hollow-eyed, sent back by the rescue service to get some rest while they took over. He looked at his wife's stricken face, at the tears rolling down her cheeks and went and put his arms about her.

'Nay, Florrie love, dun't tek on. It's not your fault. None of it was your fault, not the loss of this little chap, any more than with our Emma. It were just one of those things.'

'All these years I've kept telling meself that,' Florrie said. 'But I thought you blamed me.'

'And I thought you blamed me.'

'I did, at first. It got so's I couldn't get it out of me head, couldn't do anything but think of our Emma and long to turn back the clock. By the time I realised I'd lost you, I didn't know how to get you back. Oh, I've been that lonely and miserable.'

'Nay, I'm not lost, thoo's still got me. Allus will have, so far as I'm concerned. And they'll find this little un. He's not lost to us yet, not by a long chalk.' And he sat down beside her on the settle and took a firm grasp of her hand.

Having listened to all of this, Rita turned to Daisy and said, 'And I suppose you blame me for all of this mess?'

Daisy smothered a sigh. 'I don't blame you for anything, Mother.'

'Aye you do. You blamed me for taking the babby away from you in the first place, an act of mercy for your own good. And now you blame me for losing him again, 'cause I fetched poor sick Percy back into your life when you wanted to run off and wed meladdo.'

'This isn't the time for an inquisition. Leave it, Mother. I've had enough of your manoeuvring and manipulation.' Daisy didn't know how it was she could sit here, so outwardly calm, when inside she was falling apart, the pain in her heart tearing her to pieces.

'There you are then, didn't I say that you blamed me?'

looking from one to the other of Florrie and Clem as if for support. Neither paid her the slightest attention, having eyes only for each other as they chatted away, nineteen to the dozen, at last catching up on years of brooding silence.

Daisy too was still talking, taking this moment's lull to get a few things off her chest. 'I'll make my own decisions in future, thanks very much, without any help or interference from you. Whatever I decide to do, it's my choice, my life. And once this war is over, you'll pack your bags and go on your way. So bear in mind that your stay here is temporary. There'd be blue murder done if we had to suffer each other's company for too long.'

'Hear, hear,' Rita said with feeling. 'You'll not catch me stopping on, anyroad I see what our Florrie means. I reckon nowt to this wild, open country. I were thinking of going and staying with cousin Billy. He's got a place out at Irlam, and he could probably do with the company, and somebody to look after him like.'

Poor cousin Billy, Daisy thought. 'Fine. Well, there's no hurry. So long as we understand each other.'

'Oh we do, madam. We understand each other very well.' As always, Rita must have the last word.

A pale dawn was creeping into the sky before they heard the welcome sound of a police van in the yard. Daisy was the first to rush out the door, Clem and the two women close behind. Megan and Trish were curled up together on the rug fast asleep, and slept through it all.

'Your runaways didn't get far,' said the police constable. Sat the night out in a shepherds' bothy. Bit cold, but the baby has been checked over by a doctor and passed fit and well.'

Daisy gathered little Robbie into her arms, breathing in the sweet scent of him as she held him against her heart. 'Oh thank you, officer, thank you. I can't tell you how grateful I am.' The tears were coming now, fast and furious as they rained down her cheeks and she slapped them away with a hiccuping laugh. 'What about Percy? He won't be charged, will he?'

'The young man is a different kettle of fish. Seems he had it in mind to top himself.'

'*What?*'

The constable looked sorrowful and dropped his voice to a whisper so that the child didn't hear, for all he couldn't possibly understand. 'We found a rope, d'you see, hanging from the rafters of the bothy. But because of the night being so cold, we think he was too worried about the child getting hypothermia to get round to doing anything. We found the pair cuddled up together, safe and well. How long they'd've lasted like that if we hadn't found them so soon, I couldn't rightly say. But no, there'll be no charges. It's been put down to battle fatigue. Pretty common problem these days, I'm afraid.' And then in his normal, official sounding voice. 'The hospital is keeping him in for a few days' observation. They need to know he's in no danger, to himself or to others.'

'I see.' Daisy was trembling, could hardly take in what she was hearing. Had she driven Percy to this? Was it because she had rejected him that he'd stolen Robbie and run off, threatening to take his own life?

Percy came home a week later, with not quite such a clean bill of health but, as the doctor carefully explained to Daisy, 'What he needs most of all, lass, is some tender loving care from a good woman such as yourself. Your husband will settle in time, though I can't promise he'll be as he was before. Few are, who've lived through this damned war and suffered what he's suffered. He needs to believe in life again and the possibility of a future, to know that he's safe, and feel secure. He'll heal eventually, with love and care. Just give him time.'

She began to explain that she wasn't Percy's wife, that she wasn't the one to give him tender loving care, but one glance at the sheepish guilt in Percy's anguished face, the needy appeal in his eyes, stopped her in her tracks. Someone had to be responsible for him, and who else did he have? Where else could he go? And who else did *she* have, now that she and Harry were finished? Weren't the pair of them both in the same boat?

But she had her son, safe and warm in her arms.

That night, Daisy sat in her room and wrote her last letter to Harry. She'd moved the baby's cot beside her own bed, knowing she could never risk losing him again, or taking her eye off him for a moment. Harry had made his decision and she had made hers. In the letter, she told how she bore him no ill will, how she would always love him.

'*You will ever be the love of my life, Harry, but I can see that I've hurt you and spoiled things between us. I never meant to, any more than I set out to lie to you, I just kept putting it off till it was suddenly too late. I shall do my duty and probably marry Percy. I hope you can find another girl one day to make you happy, so's you can start again. I shall love you always. Yours ever, Daisy.*' Her face was wet with tears, her vision blinded long before she'd finished it.

Harry's reply was swift in coming, and heartbreaking in its brevity. '*I can't believe that you lied to me. How could you do this to me Daisy, after all we've meant to each other? I think I might die.*'

Daisy believed she might die too, or go mad at least. She kept reading his words over and over till her head spun. The letter upset her so much she screwed it up and threw it in the waste-paper basket, then put a match to it to burn it before suddenly realising what she was doing: destroying Harry's last words of love to her. Frantic now, she doused the flame which had only caught at one corner although the paper had gone brown and scorched all over. Daisy put it carefully away in a drawer with the rest. It was over. They had both made their choices. Harry was too hurt to forgive her. If marrying Percy and giving him the care he needed won her peace of mind as well as the return of her son, then she must somehow learn to be content with that. Perhaps she'd been expecting too much to ask for love as well. She prayed that one day Harry would forgive her and be happy again. She could only hope so.

Laura

29

'Didn't I say you were quite mad? Completely off your head. It would seem I've been proved right. Not only are you quite incapable of running your own life sensibly, you can't even be responsible for a child.'

Laura looked up wearily at Felix and wanted to protest that Chrissy wasn't a child but a stubborn, rebellious teenager whom anyone would find difficult to deal with, except that she hurt too much to risk moving her head even an inch, let alone attempt to speak. Someone was beating an iron bar against her skull and lying prone in a hospital bed swathed in heaven alone knew how many bandages, wasn't the ideal place to start an argument. Her eyes swivelled to the door, willing it to open and admit David. What she wouldn't give right now to see his smiling face, and for his solid support. No doubt he was still shearing sheep and blissfully unaware of the fracas she'd caused.

'This settles the matter once and for all. You're not staying here a moment longer. This is an unsafe place both for Chrissy, and for you. The doctor says you've got off lightly. No broken bones, though with enough bruising to make you look as if you'd gone three rounds with Mike Tyson. You're coming home with me and don't try to argue. I won't take no for an answer.'

'No.' Until the word popped out, Laura wasn't certain she'd ever speak again. Her throat felt dry and sore, and the pounding in her head was making her feel all hot and funny again. 'Water.'

Felix thrust the glass into her face, then when it dawned on him that she wasn't able to move quite yet, lifted her head and reluctantly helped her to take a sip. Laura closed her eyes in blissful gratitude.

'I intend to tell your clients to pack their bags and leave. I'm going to close the house this very day.'

'You – are – not!' Three words. She was improving.

'Enough, Laura. No more of this wilfulness. My patience has quite run out. It's a wonder Chrissy wasn't raped or murdered. What were you thinking of to let her go out with that maniac, and so late?'

'I didn't . . .'

'Don't deny it. Why else would she be there with him in the middle of nowhere in the dark? I simply can't believe even you would be so *stupid* as to allow it.' He was striding back and forth in the hospital room, a private one Laura noticed, wondering who would pay for it if Felix truly was on the verge of bankruptcy. She sincerely hoped it wasn't going to be her. His fury was such that his face very nearly matched the colour of Chrissy's hair.

'How – is – Chrissy. Is she OK?'

'Fine. No thanks to you. Dear God, Laura, what were you thinking of? You really are the most obstinate woman I ever met. Was this your idea of revenge for that little fling I had with Miranda, allowing my daughter to be ravished by a lout?'

'That's a despicable thing to say. And she wasn't being ravished.' The rekindling of the anger she always felt when Felix started ranting at her, was bringing strength soaring back into her veins like new blood.

'Doing drugs then.'

'They were talking, and kissing. Nothing worse than that, so far as I know.'

'How would you know anything, you stupid woman?'

'I've done my utmost to be the parent you've failed to be. You *and* Julia. Someone has to give Chrissy the time she needs, and neither of you ever have any to spare for anyone but yourselves.'

'Don't start on the injured wife routine again, please.' He rolled his eyes in a fair imitation of Chrissy when she was playing her exasperated-with-adults routine.

Laura drew in a deep, calming breath. 'If you dislike me so much, why do you want me back? Why not settle for the miraculous Miranda? Or has she too grown tired of your foul moods and endlessly cooking wonderful dinners for you. If so, then find somebody else to take her place. Why does it have to be me?'

'Because you are my *wife*!' he roared, inches from her face.

'And you still love me? I don't think so. Could it possibly be because I'm the one with property to sell by any chance? Because I can't think of any other reason why you would want this mockery of a marriage to continue.' Oh, she was firing on all cylinders now. 'We're getting a divorce, remember?'

'Dammit, *I'll* decide if and when we divorce, not you.'

'Which will be after my house has been sold, presumably, and you've robbed me of my inheritance. Sorry, Felix, but I wasn't born yesterday. Well, aren't I right? Isn't that the truth of the matter?'

'Yes, if you want to know. I've a right to a share in anything and everything you own, as your husband. If you want to know the truth I've been offered a golden opportunity to buy into a business, one of the best art dealers in the country. They've offered me a partnership but I need to invest some capital.'

'So that's why you're so desperate for me to sell Lane End. Nothing to do with debts after all, only a desire for a bigger slice of the pie.'

'It's a very juicy pie, and you're being damned difficult, and unco-operative as usual. I intend to take this partnership, Laura, with or without you.'

'Oh, well if I have a choice, which I most certainly do, then

I'd prefer you did it on your own, without me, thanks all the same. This isn't the nineteenth century and I'm a free woman, or at least intend to be pretty soon. I'm sorry about Chrissy. All I can say is that looking after a teenager isn't easy for anyone, let alone a stepparent, and I did my best. It wasn't good enough, I can see that and I'm too fond of her not to feel some guilt on the issue. But you and I are a different matter entirely. It's time we went our separate ways. I want a divorce and intend to get one while I'm still young enough to start again, whether or not *you* agree. I believe I have sufficient grounds.'

Felix growled, 'Give me my half-share of the house and you can have one without a battle. Gladly. Otherwise, I'll fight you every inch of the way.' Then he turned on his heel and walked out the door.

Laura sank back on the pillow and closed her eyes on a sigh of resignation. If it cost her to be rid of him, maybe it would come cheap at the price. But surely not half the value of the house, he must owe her something for all the years she'd had to put up with him as his long-suffering wife? She'd speak to her friendly solicitor on the matter. Let him sort out Felix. She'd had enough.

She'd almost drifted off to sleep again when the soft touch of a hand on hers brought her eyes flying open again. 'Laura, are you OK?'

'Chrissy. Oh love, never mind about me. How are you? He didn't hurt you too, did he?'

Chrissy's eyes filled with tears as she shook her head. The hair framing the pale face glowed a warm nut brown in the stark hospital light. It had been professionally trimmed too and looked enchanting. 'I was so frightened. I've been such a fool, and you were so kind to me. Can you ever forgive me? And don't worry about the guesthouse. I rang Megan and she came right over. She moved into one of the attic bedrooms and has taken charge, with my help. We're coping fine. So can we still be friends? Please.'

Laura smiled. 'I'm thrilled to hear Megan is back. I shall offer her a job forthwith and make sure she stays. But if all this is a presage to a hug, can you make it a gentle one?' And they both burst into a fit of giggles yet somehow managed it without too many cries of agony from Laura.

'There's someone waiting patiently outside longing to hug you too. Shall I call him in?'

'I think that's an excellent idea. Oh, but how do I look? Is my hair a dreadful mess? Felix says I look like I've gone three rounds with Mike Tyson.'

Chrissy studied her with a mock seriousness for a moment. 'For one who's well past her sell-by date and with a jaw well on the way to matching my previous tint, you look pretty good actually. I doubt he'll care, anyway, what you look like.'

And, surprisingly, she was right.

Daisy

30

January 1947

The severe cold had an iron hard grip upon the land. Temperatures were well below zero with every hollow, boulder and hummock covered by a thick layer of snow. Where once had been a hedgerow or dry-stone wall, now lay a smooth ripple of drifting snow, dipping only slightly in the lane buried deep beneath it. A fox picked his way gingerly through the dusting of ice and snow in the farmyard, keeping a wary eye open as it looked from right to left. Clem spotted it through the window of the farmhouse and reached for his gun. 'That's gaan for my hens, the bugger.'

Percy, watching him load, said, 'I want to see the fox. I'll come with you.'

'Nay lad. You stop here, in t'warm. I'll fettle it.'

Percy got up and put his hand on Clem's arm. 'Don't. Don't shoot it, Uncle Clem. It's hungry, that's all. I don't like guns. Call in the dogs. Send for the hunt.'

Daisy looked up from the sock she was darning. 'It's all right, Percy. Don't fret.'

'Thoo knows well enough we don't have no hounds in these parts lad, nor fancy horses galloping about a country where they'd be sure to break their necks. And how can the hunt get through in this weather? It's best I tek a pot at it mesel'. Don't worry, I'm a fair shot and he's an old rogue, a bandit, nowt else. Reynard i'n't getting his jaws on my chickens.'

Percy became agitated as he watched Clem stride away, so

that Daisy got up and came to put her arms about him to soothe and calm him down. It was ever the way of it when something unpleasant occurred. 'It's all right. Don't worry. The fox will be long gone before Clem gets anywhere near, frightened off by the sight of him, believe me,' and such proved to be the case. Clem stalked him as quietly as he could, but the fox dodged capture with wily skill, his sense of smell and acute hearing allowing him to live to fight another day.

Clem returned to the house later, thoroughly cross and very cold. He stamped the snow off his boots, unloaded the gun and stowed it safely away in the case, double locking it carefully afterwards. Percy watched the procedure with great interest. It troubled Daisy that much as he hated the loud bangs made when Clem went to pop off a fox or a rat, yet the guns in the case never ceased to fascinate him. Once, Daisy had found him standing by the case fiddling with the lock.

'What are you doing? You know you mustn't touch Uncle Clem's guns.' She'd taken hold of him, tried to move him away but he'd resisted her.

'Don't like guns. Want to move them. Shouldn't be in the house. Might blow up.'

'No, no Percy. They won't blow up. It's all right. They have no bullets in them, in any case. Clem takes care of that.' But the next day, he was back again, picking at the lock with a bit of bent wire. That's when Daisy made Clem put on a padlock as well, just to be safe.

Fearful of a repeat of the incident when he'd suffered a breakdown and attempted to take his own life, they all of them kept a close watch on him.

Daisy didn't believe he was any real danger either to himself or to anyone else, quite certain that her care and control had done its job. All the same, they remained vigilant: Clem, Florrie and Daisy, even seven-year-old Robbie who followed his father about everywhere. The pair were inseparable and Daisy knew her child was safe, that Percy adored his son too much to harm him.

'I like foxes,' Percy said now.

'You would, you daft bugger,' but Clem was smiling.

Daisy smiled too, relieved Percy was again settling back in the armchair with his *Hotspur* comic. She never failed to appreciate the old man's endless patience with him. Percy was not the same man he once was, had grown ever more simple-minded over these last years, as if he couldn't face being a part of the adult world any more. He'd settled in nicely at the farm and loved the quiet of the high fells so much that he rarely left them, not even when she drove the old Ford van into Keswick for fresh supplies. Nor did she encourage him to do so, knowing that he felt secure here, and safe. The very quiet of the place kept him calm and happy.

The war had broken him, leaving him quite incapable of looking after himself. The ulcerous sores on his back and legs had never properly healed, and he was very nearly stone deaf. Because of these disabilities, he could easily become disoriented and panic if he strayed too far from the farm. If his routine deviated in the slightest, he would become agitated and nervous. Daisy recognised the signs and knew how to calm him, as did Robbie. Caring for him was very like minding a child, and a stubborn one at times.

Her consolation and joy was found in her beloved Robbie. She had Florrie and Clem for company, and the boarding house kept her fully occupied throughout the day as it continued to prosper, although their original guests were long gone.

Miss Copthorne was back in the North-East, presumably still teaching. Ned Pickles had gone to live with his daughter, who had decided at last to take responsibility for her elderly parent. Tommy Twinkletoes was no longer selling agricultural foodstuffs but running a grocery store in Preston. He called to see them from time to time and bore Clem no grudge at all over the thump on his nose, though Clem remained fairly cool and distant towards him.

The worst moment had come with Daisy's mother. Following the recovery of Robbie, Rita had proudly showed off her grandson to all the guests as if she personally had rescued him from the jaws of death. 'Isn't he a little marvel? And his poor dad couldn't help it, losing his senses 'cause he were such a hero blown up in that destroyer. Poor man,' she warned, tapping the side her head.

Miss Copthorne had jiggled the baby's hand, then turning to Daisy said, 'So Percy is your husband, is he? I hadn't realised.'

Daisy would never forget the intensity of the silence which followed. It probably only lasted a matter of seconds but to her it seemed like an hour: her tongue all tied in a knot so that before she'd got it sorted out, Rita had shoved her oar in, as was her wont.

'Oh indeed, yes he is. They were married years ago, before the war. All right and proper. Fine young chap he was then. Daisy doesn't like to talk about it because it upsets her too much, remembering how he used to be. But he's done his bit for his country, so no one can ask for more than that, now can they? And we'll all stand by her in her hour of need, will we not? Ours not to question why, only to do or die.' She spouted many more clichés but Daisy was too dazed to listen.

'Oh dear me yes, of course we will,' agreed Miss Copthorne. 'The poor man has given his life, in a way,' and she cast Daisy a look half of surprise, that she should have felt the need to keep her marriage to such a hero quiet, and half one of pure pity, for who knows how one might react in similar circumstances? Daisy snatched the baby from her mother's arms and ran upstairs. She could stand no more.

She'd packed a bag, put on her coat and hat, dressed Robbie in his coat and leggings and gone back downstairs.

Guessing something was wrong, all the guests had gathered at the bottom of the stairs.

Daisy began with Rita. 'You've been organising me for as long as I can remember. All my life, in fact, since I first drew breath. But I've already made it clear that I'll not stand for it any longer. This is the final straw. I'm off. You can look after Percy. I've got my baby. I'm certainly not prepared to live a lie, not any longer. I've lost the only man I truly love because you made me keep my baby a secret, so I reckon it's time I faced up to the truth.'

And then addressing the assembled guests: Ned Pickles, Tommy Fawcett, Miss Copthorne, Mr Enderby and one or two others who happened to be staying, quietly announced, 'I'm not married to Percy but it's true that he is Robbie's dad. My baby is illegitimate, so you can put that in your pipe and smoke it. Mam gave him away for adoption, and I never thought I'd see him again. Now that I've got him back, I don't care what anybody thinks of me, or whatever the gossips say. I think he's smashing and he's mine. I've packed me bags, so you won't be soiled any further by my immoral behaviour.' So saying, she picked up her bags and set off for the door, balancing the baby on her hip.

Ned Pickles was the first to be galvanised into action. He dashed after her and grasped her arm gently. 'Don't go, Daisy. We'd be lost without you. We all love you, and we don't care what Robbie's status is, whether you're married or you're not. There's been a war and everything is topsy-turvy, nothing as it should be. What we do know is that you've seen us all through it. We wouldn't have managed half so well without you and we need you here. You've made a big difference to our lives. Don't leave on our account.'

'Hear-hear!' A rousing cheer went up. Tommy Fawcett was relieving her of her bag, Mr Enderby was offering her a spanking clean handkerchief and Miss Copthorne was lifting Robbie from her arms because Daisy looked in dire danger of dropping him, she was shaking so much. And Ned Pickles was holding her while she sobbed.

Rita had been the one to leave, not Daisy, if not without playing her mischief right to the end. She told Percy that, as Daisy's husband, he was the most important person in the household.

'Did we get wed then?' he asked, frowning as he struggled to remember the wedding ceremony.

'Course you did, love. Don't you recall having a drop too much bevy at the reception?'

'Aye, I usually do,' Percy agreed, eyes shining.

And somehow, the idea that they were married, once planted in his head, couldn't be shifted. He kept calling her his wife, looking pleased as punch, calling her Mrs Thompson. And somehow that stuck too. The regulars, fully understanding the situation accepted it as a game of pretence, rather like playing a game with a child. Daisy went along with it too because it kept Percy calm and content and in any case, she was quite sure it would all blow over as jokes usually did in the end.

And if anyone asked she would say no, straight out. Percy and she weren't married at all but he liked to think that they were. It was the war, did something to his brain. That way, she wasn't telling any lies. Just playing along to keep Percy happy and well.

Only the game didn't go away. By the time the regulars had all left, gone their separate ways to get on with their post-war lives as best they could, the entire neighbourhood had quite forgotten how the fiction had all begun, had become quite convinced that Daisy and Percy were indeed man and wife. In fact, there were times when Daisy herself believed it, calling him her dear husband, and then remembering and feeling guilty, as if she'd been caught out in a lie after all. But though the union didn't have the blessing of any church, in truth she cared for him like a wife, in every way but one. It was a marriage in name only, literally. And there was no law against calling yourself whatever you liked. She'd checked that out with Mr Capstick, the family solicitor.

Daisy was happy enough. She'd fallen in love with Lane End Farm at first sight and hadn't regretted staying. Clem and Florrie would never have a perfect marriage either but were thankfully over the worst of their difficulties and got along tolerably well these days. Her aunt could even be heard singing as she went about her work. Having a regular supply of visitors to the farm for bed and breakfast after the war was proving to be good for her too and she was able to spoil Robbie dreadfully, of course, which helped to counter some of the bitterness she would for ever carry in her heart for the child she lost.

On her days off, Daisy would leave Percy in Clem's capable hands, set a pie on the dresser for them to warm in the oven later while she and Florrie went off to the Alhambra or the Pavilion Theatre to see a show. There were no evacuees now in Keswick, they too had all gone home. Even Megan and Trish had finally made a tearful and reluctant farewell, promising faithfully to keep in touch. Daisy wasn't sure which of them cried the most, it felt awful to say goodbye.

'I don't know how we'll manage without you, Daisy.'

'You must come every summer for a holiday.'

'Oh we will. We will.'

They wrote every single week, without fail, always looking forward to their summer break at Lane End Farm which sometimes stretched to months at a time when their mother wasn't coping too well. She'd married her sailor and produced several more children, so often welcomed a break from the two eldest.

And if, deep down, Daisy was lonely and longed for what-might-have-been, she gave no indication of it. She didn't blame Harry for the decision he'd made, knowing she'd hurt him badly but the longing for him was a living ache in her heart.

He came with the thaw in late spring of that year. The ice and snow had melted save from the highest peaks, and the Herdwicks were keeping the fresh new grass close cropped as a bowling green. The leaves in the hedgerows on the lane up to the farm were unfurling all pink and new and soft, the woods behind the barn an azure lake of breathtaking blue. Daisy saw the figure in the distance and knew at once it was him. Every instinct alerted her senses and long before she could see his face she was running, galloping, jumping over nettles, racing to reach him. She flung herself into his arms on a breathless cry of exultation, and he swung her round, laughing and hugging her.

She didn't take him immediately to the farm but walked him up Blease Fell, out on to the ridge of the saddle to Foule Crag looking down over Sharp Edge to Scales Tarn below; a place where they could be alone on the top of the world with a view not only over all of Lakeland but to Silloth where they had spent their courting days, to Barrow where the bombing had been at its worst and many young airmen, colleagues of Harry, had lost their lives. But also further afield, to Scotland, Ireland, the Isle of Man and beyond. It was almost like being given a vision of their past and future all in one, for both knew in their hearts that having now found each other, they could never again bear to part.

'Are you married?' he asked at last, when their first passion had been sated and he could bear for a moment to release her.

Daisy shook her head. 'Percy thinks that we are. He's not quite right in his head. Being blown up on the ship messed it all up. His needs are simple and don't include anything . . . anything physical. But he has to be carefully watched and he needs me, Harry. Apart from anything else he adores Robbie, lives for him. The pair are inseparable. I can't leave him.'

'And I can't leave you.'

'I won't allow you to.'

'I was wrong. I shouldn't have judged you so harshly. You were merely a girl, little more than a child. I'm sorry, Daisy. Can you forgive me?'

'You're here. The war's over. That's all that matters.'

They sat and talked, and loved for hours. They lay cradled in a fold of the mountain and it was here, in Blencathra's embrace, that Daisy gave herself to the man she had always loved, and would ever love. Much, much later, she took him home.

'See who's come to visit us, Percy,' Daisy said, leading Harry into the kitchen by the hand

Percy turned trusting, excited eyes in the direction of the newcomer. 'Who is it Daisy? Who have you fetched for me?'

'This is Harry. An old friend of mine I'd like you to know.'

'Are you stopping with us, Harry?'

'I am,' Harry said. 'if you'll have me.'

'Oh aye,' Percy said. 'We welcome friends here, don't we Daisy? We love 'em all, i'n't that right?'

'It is, Percy. Everyone is welcome at Lane End Farm, especially old friends. Now eat up your tea then you can listen to *Henry Hall's Music Night*. You always enjoy that, don't you? And Harry and I will sit here and talk for a bit.'

The strength of Daisy's personality came across forcefully on the tape, her clear tones bridging the years with her memories. *'And so Harry was returned to me, just as Robbie was. I have been a most fortunate woman. Percy lived with us quite happily till he died in 1956 of pneumonia. Harry and I meant to marry after that, could have done so, I suppose. At first we didn't for fear of upsetting Robbie and then as the years slipped by there didn't seem any point. It became almost a feeling between us that we might spoil our good fortune if we did. Then Harry became ill and died in June 1969, aged fifty-one leaving me a widow in my heart at least. If the gossips sometimes suspected the truth about our* ménage à trois, *I turned a deaf ear. We kept our own counsel and did what was best, for Percy, for Robbie, for each other. People must judge us as they think fit, bearing in mind the cards we'd been dealt.*

'*I deeply regret that the facts were revealed to Robert in such a cold, unfeeling way. Poor Florrie, managing to cling on to the remnants of her misery to the end. And even more sorry that it forged such a wedge between us he couldn't bear to listen to my version of the truth. It's a terrible thing to accuse your own mother of being a liar but Rita was. We don't know, we shall none of us ever know for certain, if Robert was the child I gave birth to. Nevertheless, so far as I am concerned he is my dearly beloved son, and always will be. I have no regrets and no more secrets. They are all told.*'

Laura was quite alone, resting in her room on her first evening home, as she listened to the fifth and final tape. Afterwards, she smiled as she wiped the tears from her eyes. 'So your secrets are now all told, Daisy. Thank you for sharing them with me. Robert understands now, I think, that you loved him. And I hope *you* know that in his heart he is reconciled with you at last. Perhaps you will forgive us both now for our shameful neglect. I'd like to think my quest has achieved that at least, in thanks for all you have given me.'